The Fifth Fighter Command in World War 2
Vol. 1

The Fifth Fighter Command in World War II

Volume I: Pearl Harbor to the Reduction of Rabaul

William Wolf

Schiffer Military History
Atglen, PA

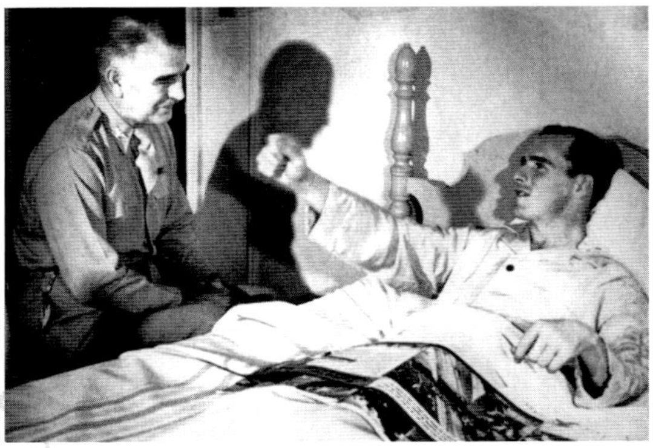

Dedication

To the brave, unheralded men of the Fifth Fighter Command who gave up their youth and often their lives to win the relentless air war over New Guinea and the Philippines.

Book Design by Ian Robertson and Stephanie Daugherty.

Library of Congress Control Number: 2011937278

Printed in China.
ISBN: 978-0-7643-3955-4

Published by Schiffer Publishing Ltd.
4880 Lower Valley Road
Atglen, PA 19310
Phone: (610) 593-1777
FAX: (610) 593-2002
E-mail: Info@schifferbooks.com.
Visit our web site at: www.schifferbooks.com
Please write for a free catalog.
This book may be purchased from the publisher.
Please include $5.00 postage.
Try your bookstore first.

In Europe, Schiffer books are distributed by:
Bushwood Books
6 Marksbury Avenue
Kew Gardens
Surrey TW9 4JF, England
Phone: 44 (0) 20 8392-8585
FAX: 44 (0) 20 8392-9876
E-mail: Info@bushwoodbooks.co.uk.
Visit our website at: www.bushwoodbooks.co.uk
Try your bookstore first.

Contents

Preface

While authoring 12 WWII aviation books, I have come to admire Roger Freeman's gargantuan efforts in memorializing the "Mighty Eighth" Air Force in several definitive volumes. Over the years the Pacific air war has been largely overlooked as compared to the extensive number of works on the European air war. The Fifth Fighter and Bomber Command was as instrumental in winning the war in the Pacific skies, as was the Eighth Fighter and Bomber Command over Europe; perhaps more so. After the defeats in the Philippines, the East Indies, and New Guinea in early to mid-1942 due the lack of air superiority, MacArthur and Kenney realized that gaining air superiority, while not eliminating the use of ground troops to win the victory, was the key to winning the war in the SWPA. MacArthur's infantry, without the exposure to enemy air intervention, were able to secure advanced airbases from which Kenney's fighters and bombers could extend the bomb line to attack distant enemy airbases and destroy enemy aircraft in the air, and more importantly on the ground. The westward leapfrogging infantry operations along the northern New Guinea coast and on to the Philippines were predicated on gaining air superiority, and would not have been possible without it. I have previously written a comprehensive account of the 13th Fighter Command in the Pacific (*13th Fighter Command in World War II: Air Combat over Guadalcanal and the Solomons, Schiffer, 2004*), and now after 65 years of neglect I have had the time, inclination, and resources to offer the first comprehensive and definitive account of the Fifth Fighter Command and its predecessors and successors from 8 December 1941 until VJ-Day.

The collection of the research material and photos for this work has involved 40 years, while the writing of the text required over two and half years of time and great effort. I offer these three volumes as the first definite work on the Fifth Fighter Command, which has been long overdue and may never be done on this scale again.

Author in his 20,000 book library.

Acknowledgments

My lifelong hobby has been WWII aerial combat, and over the past 40 years I have collected over 20,000 books and magazines, along with hundreds of reels of microfilm on the subject. I probably have nearly every book written on WWII aviation and complete collections of every combat aviation magazine published since 1939. Also included in my collection are hundreds of aviation unit histories; intelligence reports; pilot, crew, flight, and training manuals; and technical, structural, and maintenance manuals for aircraft ordnance, armament, engines and equipment. My microfilm collection includes vintage intelligence reports; hundreds of USAF, USN and USMC group and squadron histories, After Combat Reports (ACRs), Narrative Combat Reports (NCRs), and Individual Combat Reports (ICRs); complete Japanese Monograph series; and complete U.S. Strategic Bombing Surveys, as well as complete USAF Historical Studies. The author wishes to thank the hundreds of persons, museums, and libraries that contributed photos and materials to my collection during the past 40 years.

Thanks go to cover and profile illustrator, Steve Ferguson, who has done the outstanding covers and profiles for my other books and continues his superb artistry on these volumes. Steve has become a friend over the years, and has been a pleasure to work with and to spend time talking about our passion of WWII aircraft and pilots. My appreciation to Ian Robertson, who is responsible for the layout and integration of the 100s of photos, drawings, and maps into the rather lengthy texts of my 12 books published by Schiffer. I would also like to thank meticulous researcher Dr. Frank Olynyk for compiling his invaluable *USAF (Pacific Theater) Credits for the Destruction of Enemy Aircraft in Air-to-Air Combat*, which I kept at my fingertips to check names, ranks, and dates.

Again, my thanks go to my persevering wife, Nancy, who allows me to spend many hours researching and writing, and patiently (mostly) waits while I browse bookstores and visit air museums in search of new material and photos. Also, I thank her because her car sits out in the hot Arizona sun as my library luxuriates in the remodeled, air-conditioned three-car garage.

Foreword

22 year old 1Lt. Ralph Wandrey, World War 2 Ace.

The Fifth Fighter Command is the story of U.S. Army Air Corps pilots in the South Pacific Area who pushed the Japanese out of New Guinea, the Philippines, and attacked Japan itself. The story of the Fifth Fighter Command is not a glamorous tale glorifying the air war there. Air and ground forces fought a war not only against a fanatical enemy, but also against the tropical jungle, weather, disease, insects, and at times boredom. They were the tail end of all supply lines, receiving only what was left after all other fronts had been supplied.

Early on the men fought with what was available: inferior aircraft and few pilots to fly them, badly outnumbered and pushed out of the Philippines, Java, and New Guinea back to Australia to await everything that was needed not only to defend themselves, but to begin an offensive. Their only weapons to defend themselves were Curtiss P-40 Warhawks and almost obsolete Bell P-39 Airacobras. Their courageous resistance slowed and finally stopped the Japanese advance for the first time in the Pacific, allowing the fighter pilots of the 13th Army Air Force and their fellow Marine Corps and Navy pilots to begin the advance north and west from Guadalcanal in August 1942. In the Southwest Pacific Area the 5th Fighter Command made hard won moves up the coast of New Guinea to places like Port Moresby, Dobodura, Nadzab, Gusap and Biak.

In March 1943, when I arrived in New Guinea, I was sent to Dobodura, where the 9th Fighter Squadron flew. I was in charge of 12 other P-38 pilots, the first men trained in P-38s to reach the 9th, which had just been assigned Lockheed P-38s, leaving the 7th and 8th squadrons still flying and fighting with P-40s. We did not fly an offensive mission against the Japanese for two months, as we could only defend our field from enemy bomb and strafing attacks. We had to be supplied entirely by air from Port Moresby, on the South Coast of New Guinea, and a thirteen thousand foot mountain range stood between us, as we were on the north shore by the Buna Plantation, which was still controlled by the Japanese. Their front lines were just north of our airfield at Dobodura. Behind us was 40 miles of swamp land. During the March typhoon season rain prevented the C-47 transports from bringing us supplies, and we were short of fuel, ammunition, and at times food. The Japanese army pilots opposing us had been fighting since 1938 in Manchuria, China, the Philippines, and were stationed at Lae, Wewak and Rabaul, which was also a big naval base. Until my first combat I had never fired my guns at an aerial target. By October 1943 we were strong enough to attack the Japanese bases at Wewak and Rabaul. We destroyed many of their planes on the ground and eventually neutralized both bases and bypassed them. Our P-38s were taken from us and given to the 13th Air Force, and we had to fly P-47 Thunderbolt single engine planes for 61 missions before we got our P-38s back and prepared to move into the Philippines.

I was often Wingman to Richard I. Bong, who became America's top ace with 40 confirmed victories. My Squadron and later Group Commander was Gerald R. Johnson, a good tactician who had 22 victories confirmed. I also led the squadron with Charles A. Lindberg on my wing teaching us how to fly further and save gas. I flew over 200 missions before ending my combat tour in August 1944. My last mission was leading a raid to the Halmahera Islands; it was six hours and 15 minutes long. I had confirmation for six victories and I had six probables when I came home.

Fifth Fighter and Bomber Commands were instrumental in winning the war in the South Pacific over great distances where our ground troops depended on us to neutralize the Japanese Air Forces, airfields, and shipping before they could advance. Unlike the Eighth Air Force in Europe, we never received credit for our efforts under much worse conditions. I hope Dr. Wolf's books will correct this oversight.

86 year old Ralph Wandrey and Author.

Introduction

During my research for the history of the Fifth Fighter Command I used the usual bibliographic sources (books and magazines), but also utilized several singular sources that were invaluable and will be described to give the reader an appreciation as to the scope of my research.

RAAF Attack Report
Prior to early 1943, when record keeping was not a requisite as compared to survival, the Pursuit Groups of the Army Air Corps used the Royal Australian Air Force (RAAF) Attack Report: Form C.F. (A.108 B). Form C.F. was a printed two page form (instructions on the front and the report on the back) that was completed by initially hand, and then by typewriter by the end of 1942. The front INSTRUCTIONS page consisted of six paragraphs (see sample), and the paper was so thin that the printing on the other side bled through. Because the pilot's report (Form C.F.) was on one page, the answers were necessarily (very) short and therefore made it difficult to piece together that particular day's air combat. These RAAF Attack Reports were included the National Archive Individual Combat Report (ICR) microfilms, and the format and an example are included next.

RAAF Attack Report: Form C.F. (A.108 B)

General
Pilot: Rank/Name/Serial Number
Observer: Rank/Name/Serial Number
Squadron
Place
Date
Time
Height
Description of Attack
Target and Position (Type and Location)
Nature of Target
Method of Attack (e.g. High Level, High Diving, etc.)
Weight, fuse setting, type and number of bombs dropped, and type of sight used
Number of torpedoes released, type of warhead, range of release, height, and method of sighting.
Estimated number of rounds fired against vessels, ground targets including personnel). Rounds fired in air combat are NOT to be included.
Observed effects/Estimated number of hits and damage inflicted.
Enemy AA Defense encountered
Location
Type
Strength
Enemy Air Activity
Position of Patrols
Type and number of aircraft
Did engagement result?
Estimated number of hits
Damage inflicted
Reconnaissance Report (if any)
Casualties to own aircraft and personnel (NOT through air combat)
Special Comments

See a sample of Form C.F. format below, which includes Page 1: Instructions and Page 2: 2Lt. Richard Bong's first and second career victories on 27 December 1942 recorded on Form C.F. (Because the C.F.s were to be completed in triplicate they can be difficult to read depending on the copy microfilmed.)

Individual Combat Report (ICR)
From early 1943, Army Air Force participants in air combat were required to complete an Individual Combat Report (ICR) describing their involvement as per a standardized format (see format below).

Individual Combat Report (ICR)

General
Aircraft type and number; own position in formation; take off time.
Mission assigned by order of Controller; course followed; rendezvous time and place; arrival time at target.
Approach
Own height when enemy first sighted; height of enemy; time; position of enemy relative to own; height at which combat began; number and positions of own fighter aircraft (and bombers, if present).
Number, type, and formation of enemy aircraft seen or engaged (Give time, course, and altitude)
Combat Tactics
Orders by Control, formation leader, etc.
Type of attack made.
Action taken by our formation: tactics, evasive action, use of cloud cover, etc.
Action taken by enemy aircraft attacked and by enemy aircraft not attacked.

INSTRUCTIONS.

1. FORM C.F. is to be completed in triplicate by Intelligence Officers for the recording of combat particulars from the interrogation of aircrews (F. and G.P. aircraft).

2. FORM BLUE, Combat (Fighter) is to be completed, with abbreviated details, from FORM C.F. for immediate despatch to A.C.H.

3. In the case of interception by day, Section 10 is to include the following information, on a separate sheet if necessary:—

(a) TECHNICAL.

Type of sight used, range and span setting, deflection allowed, details of range and/or length of bursts, signs of hitting on enemy E/A, rounds fired per gun, R/T communication defects, if any.

(b) INTELLIGENCE.

Camouflage and markings on E/A, position of guns on E/A, amount and type of E/A return fire.

4. In the case of interception by night, Section 10 is to include:—

(a) TACTICAL.

Method of control used, if any, how enemy was contacted, weather, light and visibility conditions.

(b) INTELLIGENCE.

Use of lights or other special methods by E/A.

5. In the case of E/A operating as part of a wing, Section 16 is to include reference to tactics adopted and effectiveness of co-operation between squadrons.

6. A copy of any Personal Contact Report rendered by a pilot at his own option is to be attached to this report.

FORM C.F — R.A.A.F. Form A.108(A).

COMBAT (FIGHTER) REPORT

Unit: 35th Fighter Group

Report No.

Pilot: 2nd Lt. R. I. Bong 0433784 — Squadron: 39th

Aircraft No. 15

Duty: Interception — Place: Buna

Date 27/12/42

Time: 1210 hrs.

(1) Number, type and formation of our own aircraft taking part in attack: 12 P-38's in flights of 4

(2) Height when first sighting enemy: 21,000 ft.

(3) Position of enemy (relative to own aircraft) when first sighted: Below our A/C D/B's low, Vals at 4,000 ft. Zekes above Vals 2-3000 feet.

(4) Type of enemy aircraft: Vals Zekes

(5) Number and formation of enemy aircraft: 7 or 8 Vals and 7 or 8 Zekes

(6) Was own approach observed or unobserved: Observed

(7) Type of attack delivered on enemy: Dived on Zekes.

(8) Action taken by enemy: Zekes followed on tail.

(9) Result of engagement, including own and enemy casualties: Sat P-38 No. 26 on transport strip, Dobodura, on nose. Fired at range of 350 yrds at Val which blew up & crashed into water. Fired short burst at Zeke which passed in front of me. Zeke crashed in water. (2 enemy A/C down)

(10) Special comments: (See Instructions paras. 3 and 4.) Nil

IN THE CASE OF ESCORTED ENEMY FORMATIONS, THE FOLLOWING ADDITIONAL INFORMATION:—

(11) Number, type and formation of escorting aircraft: Saw 7-8 Zekes

(12) Position of escort relative to main force: Zekes above D/B's

(13) Was attack directed against escort or main force: Escort and main force.

(14) Action taken by escort: Counter-attacked.

(15) Action taken by main force: Not observed.

(16) Special comments: (See Instructions para. 5.)

Signature .... R.I. [illegible]

A.M.M.—11/41—[illegible]

RAAF Attack Report: Form C.F.
Instructions. (Left side), Pilot's Report. (Right side)

Range at which fire opened; deflection shots, and duration of our fire in each attack (approximate length of bursts).
Number and types of each enemy aircraft destroyed and probably destroyed, with details and witnesses.
Estimation of own and enemy tactics.
Miscellaneous
Observation of other friendly aircraft.
Amount and type of enemy anti-aircraft fire.
Positions of guns on enemy aircraft (caliber and type etc.) and effectiveness.
Enemy camouflage and markings.
Comments on ground control.
Defects of own equipment.
Weather, sightings (air, land, and sea).
Damage to own plane.
Time combat ended, route home, time of landing.
Criticisms and recommendations.

The Modern Military Field Branch of the National Archives microfilmed the Individual Combat Reports (ICRs) and the RAAF Action Reports of the Fifth Fighter Command about 40 years ago on nine microfilm reels, each having between 900 and 1,000 pages of ICRs. The microfilm reels can be purchased @$65 each but require a reel-to-reel microfilm reader, on which many of the individual frames are difficult to read, plus the reels require extensive and frustrating rolling back-and-forth to find the Groups, Squadrons, pilots, and dates (see sample frames on these pages). The microfilmed ICR frames vary greatly in quality depending if it were an original or a second or third carbon copy, and often had to be read using a large magnifying glass while looking at the microfilm reader screen.

A much easier method to read the ICRs is to purchase them on nine CDs @$125 per CD, as each frame is shown on a computer screen and can be magnified to show two or three sentences, which makes distinguishing e's and c's that look like o's, etc., and also saves the reader's eyesight. In addition all 900 to 1,000 pages per CD can be quickly scrolled by using an index (see Bibliography at the end of Volume 2 for this index).

Three actual ICRs shown below illustrate the difficulty in reconstructing an air battle flown by 10 pilots (most battles involved from two to 20 pilots). Three well known aces each describe their version of a combat on 26 July 1943 when 1Lt. Gerald Johnson scored his first two of 22 victories, 1Lt. Richard Bong scored four victories to give him 15, and Capt. James Watkins got four victories to make him an ace on his way to 11 victories.

Note Bong's usual brief and impassive account of his combat. The squadron historian added the following comment on one of Bong's modest

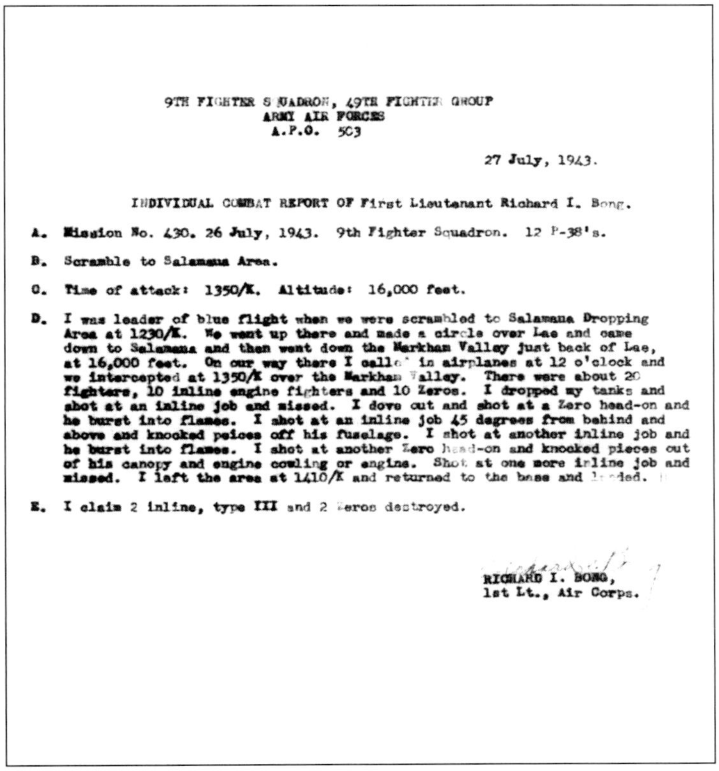

9TH FIGHTER SQUADRON, 49TH FIGHTER GROUP
ARMY AIR FORCES
A.P.O. 503

27 July, 1943.

INDIVIDUAL COMBAT REPORT OF First Lieutenant Richard I. Bong.

A. Mission No. 430. 26 July, 1943. 9th Fighter Squadron. 12 P-38's.

B. Scramble to Salamaua Area.

C. Time of attack: 1350/K. Altitude: 16,000 feet.

D. I was leader of blue flight when we were scrambled to Salamaua Dropping Area at 1230/K. We went up there and made a circle over Lae and came down to Salamaua and then went down the Markham Valley just back of Lae, at 16,000 feet. On our way there I called in airplanes at 12 o'clock and we intercepted at 1350/K over the Markham Valley. There were about 20 fighters, 10 inline engine fighters and 10 Zeros. I dropped my tanks and shot at an inline job and missed. I dove out and shot at a Zero head-on and he burst into flames. I shot at an inline job 45 degrees from behind and above and knocked peices off his fuselage. I shot at another inline job and he burst into flames. I shot at another Zero head-on and knocked pieces out of his canopy and engine cowling or engine. Shot at one more inline job and missed. I left the area at 1410/K and returned to the base and landed.

E. I claim 2 inline, type III and 2 Zeros destroyed.

RICHARD I. BONG,
1st Lt., Air Corps.

Bong ICR

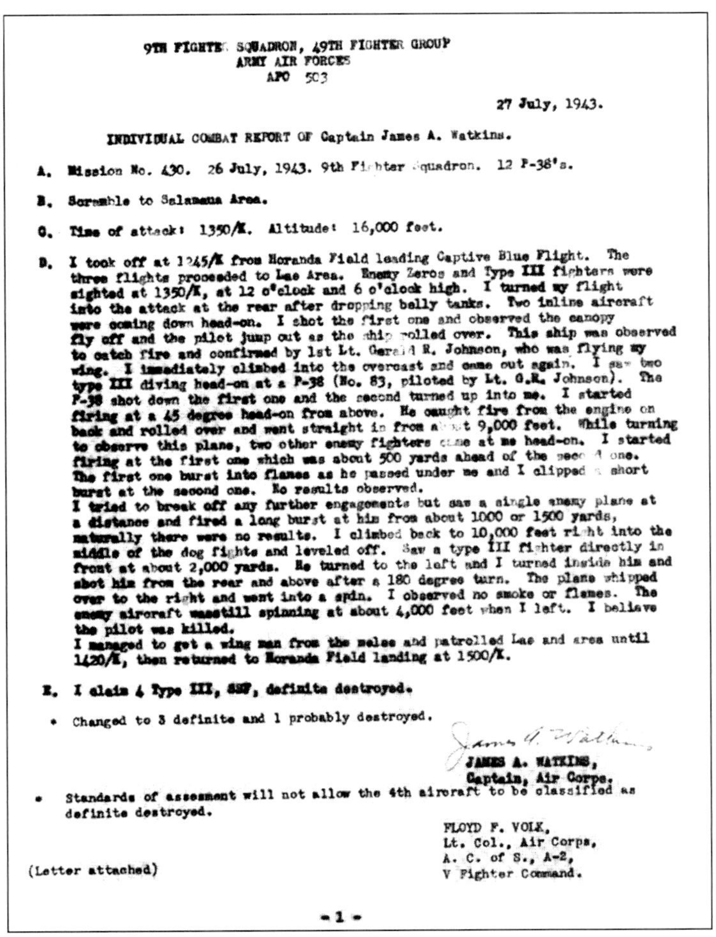

9TH FIGHTER SQUADRON, 49TH FIGHTER GROUP
ARMY AIR FORCES
APO 503

27 July, 1943.

INDIVIDUAL COMBAT REPORT OF Captain James A. Watkins.

A. Mission No. 430. 26 July, 1943. 9th Fighter Squadron. 12 P-38's.

B. Scramble to Salamaua Area.

C. Time of attack: 1350/K. Altitude: 16,000 feet.

D. I took off at 1245/K from Horanda Field leading Captive Blue Flight. The three flights proceeded to Lae Area. Enemy Zeros and Type III fighters were sighted at 1350/K, at 12 o'clock and 6 o'clock high. I turned my flight into the attack at the rear after dropping belly tanks. Two inline aircraft were coming down head-on. I shot the first one and observed the canopy fly off and the pilot jump out as the ship rolled over. This ship was observed to catch fire and confirmed by 1st Lt. Gerald R. Johnson, who was flying my wing. I immediately climbed into the overcast and came out again. I saw two type III diving head-on at a P-38 (No. 83, piloted by Lt. G.R. Johnson). The P-38 shot down the first one and the second turned up into me. I started firing at a 45 degree head-on from above. He caught fire from the engine on back and rolled over and went straight in from about 9,000 feet. While turning to observe this plane, two other enemy fighters came at me head-on. I started firing at the first one which was about 500 yards ahead of the second one. The first one burst into flames as he passed under me and I clipped a short burst at the second one. No results observed.
I tried to break off any further engagements but saw a single enemy plane at a distance and fired a long burst at him from about 1000 or 1500 yards, naturally there were no results. I climbed back to 10,000 feet right into the middle of the dog fights and leveled off. Saw a type III fighter directly in front at about 2,000 yards. He turned to the left and I turned inside him and shot him from the rear and above after a 180 degree turn. The plane whipped over to the right and went into a spin. I observed no smoke or flames. The enemy aircraft wasstill spinning at about 4,000 feet when I left. I believe the pilot was killed.
I managed to get a wing man from the melee and patrolled Lae and area until 1420/K, then returned to Horanda Field landing at 1500/K.

E. I claim 4 Type III, SSF, definite destroyed.

- Changed to 3 definite and 1 probably destroyed.

JAMES A. WATKINS,
Captain, Air Corps.

- Standards of assesment will not allow the 4th aircraft to be classified as definite destroyed.

FLOYD F. VOLK,
Lt. Col., Air Corps,
A. C. of S., A-2,
V Fighter Command.

(Letter attached)

-1-

Watkins ICR

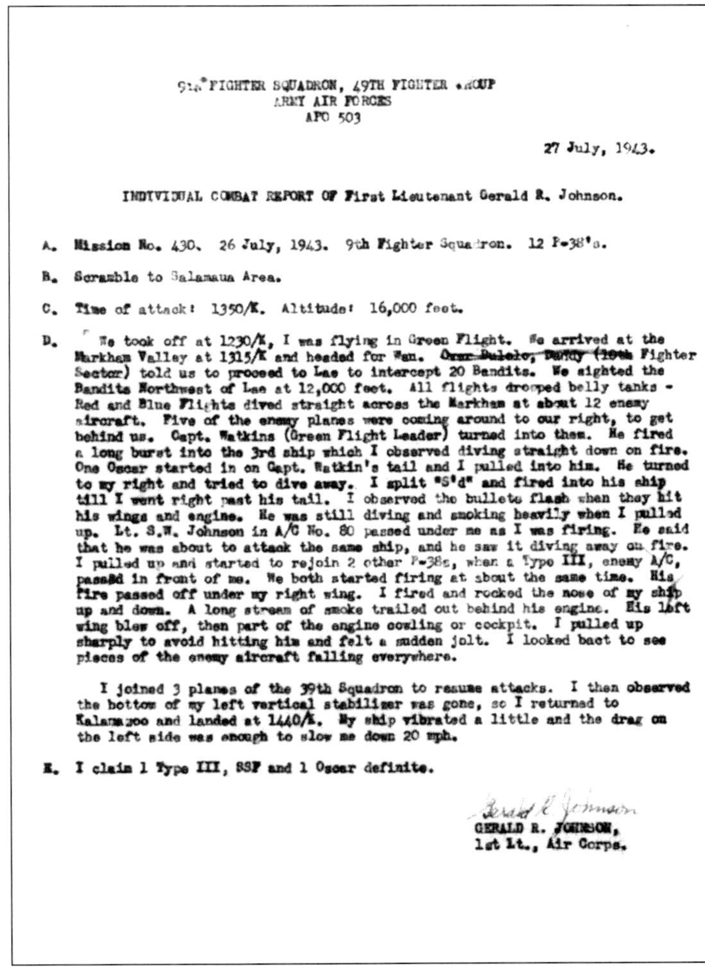

9TH FIGHTER SQUADRON, 49TH FIGHTER GROUP
ARMY AIR FORCES
APO 503

27 July, 1943.

INDIVIDUAL COMBAT REPORT OF First Lieutenant Gerald R. Johnson.

A. Mission No. 430. 26 July, 1943. 9th Fighter Squadron. 12 P-38's.

B. Scramble to Salamaua Area.

C. Time of attack: 1350/K. Altitude: 16,000 feet.

D. We took off at 1230/K, I was flying in Green Flight. We arrived at the Markham Valley at 1315/K and headed for Wau. ~~Oscar Duleko, Dandy (10th~~ Fighter Sector) told us to proceed to Lae to intercept 20 Bandits. We sighted the Bandits Northwest of Lae at 12,000 feet. All flights dropped belly tanks - Red and Blue Flights dived straight across the Markham at about 12 enemy aircraft. Five of the enemy planes were coming around to our right, to get behind us. Capt. Watkins (Green Flight Leader) turned into them. He fired a long burst into the 3rd ship which I observed diving straight down on fire. One Oscar started in on Capt. Watkin's tail and I pulled into him. He turned to my right and tried to dive away. I split "S'd" and fired into his ship till I went right past his tail. I observed the bullets flash when they hit his wings and engine. He was still diving and smoking heavily when I pulled up. Lt. S.W. Johnson in A/C No. 80 passed under me as I was firing. He said that he was about to attack the same ship, and he saw it diving away on fire. I pulled up and started to rejoin 2 other P-38s, when a Type III, enemy A/C, passed in front of me. We both started firing at about the same time. His fire passed off under my right wing. I fired and rocked the nose of my ship up and down. A long stream of smoke trailed out behind his engine. His left wing blew off, then part of the engine cowling or cockpit. I pulled up sharply to avoid hitting him and felt a sudden jolt. I looked bact to see pieces of the enemy aircraft falling everywhere.

I joined 3 planes of the 39th Squadron to resume attacks. I then observed the bottom of my left vertical stabilizer was gone, so I returned to Kalamazoo and landed at 1440/K. My ship vibrated a little and the drag on the left side was enough to slow me down 20 mph.

E. I claim 1 Type III, SSF and 1 Oscar definite.

GERALD R. JOHNSON,
1st Lt., Air Corps.

Johnson ICR

brief reports on his destruction of four enemy fighters: "He would describe a major engagement in the same amount of space another man would take to tell of drinking three beers."

Below is my sample composite description of the 26 July 1943 combat taken from Bong's, Johnson's, and Watkins' IRCs, as well as seven other ICRs. There were 10 viewpoints which needed to be correlated regarding the entire Squadron, then those of the lead element and second element pilots of each flight. (Note: Red Flight was usually the lead flight, typically followed by Blue and/or White and then Yellow and/or Green.) After separating the 10 pilots into flights and elements the combat had to be broken down to individual descriptions and then interrelated into the context and chronology of the entire battle. The pilots who didn't score described their contact with the enemy, and their interaction with their squadron mates and their ICRs frequently were given to confirm victories. I found that it was often confusing to correlate each of the two to 20 ICRs in each combat because air warfare is confused and each pilot saw the battle from a different viewpoint, and often joined other flights and shot enemy fighters off the tails of pilots from not only from his flight, but from other flights and even other squadrons.

26 July 1943: 49FG/9FS
"On the 26th, Capt. Lawrence Smith's three Flights of the 9FS were investigating a plot from the Air Controller and were sent up the Markham Valley for an interception. After the 1230 take off from Horanda Strip, two pilots aborted with engine problems and only 10 Flying Knights reached the Markham River Delta but did not find the enemy. Smith and Wingman

2Lt. Ralph Hays, second Element Leader, 1Lt. Normand Hyland, and Wingman, James Harris searched due north further inland for 20 miles over the Markham River Valley at 14,000 feet. Mission Leader Smith turned them back toward the Markham Delta as clouds began to close in and Blue Flight Leader Watkins went into a shallow descent, trying to keep Smith in sight.

"The area just beyond Lae airdrome was surrounded by thick clouds but in a clear area the Knights met Oscars and Type III fighters (Tonys) flying down the Markham Valley at 12,000 feet. Smith ordered the Lightnings to drop their tanks but Smith's and Hyland's tanks hung up and Smith led Red Flight through the nearest clouds where Smith and Hyland were unable to shake their tanks loose and orbited the area while Hays and Harris returned to the combat. Hays peeled off after an Oscar that flew through Hays' fire and the Oscar "wavered and then continued his flight losing altitude." Hays did not follow as the enemy fighter flew under him for a probable. Hays was able to find Smith and the two returned to base individually. Meanwhile, Harris dove on a Type III enemy aircraft 2,000 feet below climbing toward him. Harris half rolled and fired a three second burst and saw pieces coming off the enemy fighter which fell off on its wing and passed under Harris. A Zero got on Harris' tail and when the American climbed toward another P-38 the Zero turned away. Harris claimed the Tony as destroyed on his ICR but was given official credit for a probable.

"Trailing a short distance behind on the left flank was the Blue Flight led by Deputy CO, Capt. James "Duckbutt" Watkins, who was accompanied by Wingman, 1Lt. Richard Bong, with second Element Leader, 2Lt. Robert Wood, and Wingman 2Lt. John McLean at 16,000 feet. (Note: In his ICR Bong claims to be Blue Flight Leader but it appears that Watkins being the Deputy CO and a Captain was Blue Leader and Bong was the Element Leader and Wood was Watkin's Wingman). Flying further off on the right flank was 1Lt. Gerald Johnson's Green Flight of Wingman 2Lt. Stanley Johnson and Element Leader Capt. Ross Blachly, who decided to tag along on the mission with Wingman, 2Lt. Glade Hill. Since Smith was unable to drop his belly tank Watkins' Blue Flight became the Lead Flight.

"Veteran James Watkins was near the end his tour and had not scored a victory since his P-40 victory on 26 December 1942 over Dobodura and was determined to score at least one more victory. Watkins would have his chance to score when his Blue Flight was confronted by Tonys turning head on in front and by other Tonys approaching Blue Flight's rear quarter. Watkins turned into two Tonys coming down head on and hit the canopy of one forcing its pilot to bail out. Watkins then climbed into the overcast and when he exited he saw five Tonys diving to get behind Gerald Johnson. A Tony turned into Watkins who fired from 45 degrees head on above and its engine caught fire and it rolled over straight in from 9,000 feet. But while Watkins was watching it go down two enemy fighters came at him from behind and Watkins turned and fired at the first one which burst into flames as it passed under him. The second got on Watkin's tail and Johnson pulled into it as the enemy pilot turned to the right and tried to get away. Johnson Split-S'd and fired until he flew past its tail, getting hits in its wings and engine and it was confirmed by 2Lt. SW Johnson who was about to attack as it diving away on fire.

"As he tried to break away Watkins saw a single fighter ahead and fired a burst from to long range at 1,000 to 1,500 yards and "naturally" without result. Watkins climbed back to 10,000 feet into the middle of a dogfight and saw a Tony about 2,000 yards ahead. The enemy pilot turned left and Watkins turned 180 degrees into him and fired from the rear and above. The Tony "whipped over" to the right and went into a spin without smoking and was last seen still spinning when Watkins left. Watkins claimed four definitely destroyed but soon "the standards of assessment will not allow the fourth aircraft to be classified as a definite destroyed (Lt.Col. Floyd Volk, A-2 5th FC)." But it seems despite this reassessment this fourth victory continued to be credited and Watkins became an ace.

"After Johnson shot down his Tony he joined two other P-38s and when an Oscar passed in front of him he and another Lightning began to fire. But it was Johnson who "rocked his ship's nose up and down" to maximize his long burst of fire that blew off its port wing and pieces of its engine cowling and cockpit. Johnson pulled up sharply just as the Oscar exploded violently. When he looked around to access any damage Johnson saw that his port vertical stabilizer was blown off from the boom and headed to Horanda with his first two victories of 22 of the war.

"1Lt. Richard Bong fired a quick burst at a Tony, missed, dove out to regain speed, and came upon a Zeke head on. Bong fired quickly and the enemy burst into flames. Bong then positioned himself above and behind a Tony and gave it a quick burst which knocked pieces off the fuselage. Coming around in a port turn from the rear quarter Bong saw another Tony and his long burst set it on fire. Immediately, a Zeke came head on and Bong fired a long burst which knocked off the Zeke's canopy and struck its engine. The four victories for the day made Bong a triple ace with 15 victories. Bong's Wingman, Blue #4 2Lt. John McLean, dove too fast and had to use his trim tabs to bring his fighter out of its dive and then found three Zeros on his tail and had to dive away. Once free he was alone and returned to base.

"Meanwhile, in Green Flight Element Leader, Capt. Ross Blachly and Wingman 2Lt. Glade Hill became separated from Green Flight Leader Johnson and had to climb out of the combat and joined the 39FS top cover. After Johnson's Wingman, 2Lt. Stanley Johnson, dropped his tanks and accelerated he blew out his starboard supercharger and was able to stay with Johnson through his first pass on the Oscars but could not re-engage."

At the same time that day the 39th Fighter Squadron of the 35th Fighter Group scored three victories, two probables, and four damaged over Lae, and this air battle is also described in the same detail.

Narrative Combat Report

After each mission and debriefing, the Narrative Combat Report (NCR) would be drafted to be submitted to Squadron, Group, and Fighter Command HQ, and was used to tie the description of the air combat together. These NCRs were collected from the Air Force Historical Research Center's microfilm series on histories of 5FC Fighter Groups (see Bibliography). The format of the NCRs was prescribed as follows:

Narrative Combat Report

Mission #

Date

Squadron Group Base (Home not staging)

Number of Aircraft Type

Mission (Specify interception, patrol, fighter sweep, attack or bombing, escort of bombers or transports)

Place (Specify area of patrol, destination of escorted aircraft, area of interception, target or targets location)

Place and Time of Combat (To also include place and time combat terminated)

Times and Routes (Take off time; landing and take off time to staging area, if any, time over target area; and time last aircraft landed. Routes were assumed to be direct or nearly direct unless; otherwise stated.)

Weather (Enroute, over target, and return. To include visibility and cloud cover)

Number of aircraft not reaching target (No reasons were to be stated)

Ammunition Expended (Quantities and caliber)

Bombs on Target (Insert only when applicable: number and type, account for bombs not dropped in target area)

Own Losses:
Aircraft (Number lost, destroyed, or damaged sufficiently to be removed from Squadron roles.)
Personnel (State number known to be missing, killed or wounded. No names were to be stated except for pilot or ground personnel)
Enemy Losses (Number and type of definites or probables)
Opposition Encountered (NOT air combat. AA fire, barrage balloons, searchlights. Any evidence of radar for warning or directing AA fire was to be mentioned)
Air Combat
Enemy Aircraft (Total number and types seen)
Altitude and Position of Enemy Aircraft (Give number of feet above or below "our" aircraft and clock position when first sighted)
Own Altitude (In feet)
Own Formation (If all on one level, so state; otherwise state horizontal or vertical deployment)
Relation to Escorted Aircraft (If applicable then state horizontal and vertical relationship to escorted aircraft)
Initial Observation (State whether own or enemy aircraft made first observation)
Initial Attack (If our formation made first attack, so state, giving information if all or part of the formation attacked and manner of attack, e.g. diving, head on, out of the sun etc. If enemy formation attacked first then give same information as own formation)
Initial Reaction (How enemy reacted to attack or vice versa)
Enemy Objective (Interception or evasion of escorts? Attack bombers or transports. Tactics)
Own Objective (Did escorts defend bombers or transports or did they attack enemy? State tactical development of assigned mission or its modification due to circumstances)
Enemy Tactics (State specifically the tactics enemy used to hinder our mission or to accomplish their own. Include evasive tactics)
Own Tactics (Supply additional information; giving spatial limits of the combat i.e. altitude, etc. and modes of individual attacks)
End of Engagement (Who broke off? Why and How?)
Evaluation of Enemy (Summarize pilot's judgment of enemy skill, airmanship, tactics, and material. Emphasize any new developments)
Evaluation of Own Forces (Summarize pilot's assessment, especially the leaders, of own skill, tactics, and materials. Mention errors, improvements, skills, name errors of flight and radio discipline. Give specific suggestions for future operations.)
Bombing and Strafing Results (Omit unless pertinent. State definite results as observed; whether bombs fell within or without of target area. With shipping; how near the misses.
Sightings (Use JUST for shipping of military importance. Location, course, and speed)
Malfunctioning Equipment (Specific failures and result)
Miscellaneous (Anything needing greater elucidation than is possible on subjects above, especially in reference to tactics. Difficulties surmounted or not should be described in some detail. Acts of great resourcefulness should be described, but without names or personalities and similarly with outstanding failures.

USAAF Historical Studies
The USAAF Historical Studies Microfilm numbers 9, 13, 16, 17, and 43 (see Bibliography) gave in depth descriptions and appraisals of the Pacific air war from summer 1942 through March 1944, and were written during the late war (without modern day revisionist bias).

Author with part of his autograph/photo collection numbering over 75 albums and 10,000 pages/12,000 photos.

Photos
Over the years I have been fortunate to meet many fighter aces, other pilots, and fellow aviation buffs who have shared stories, material, and photographs with me (I have over 5,000 photos of fighter aces alone). Over the years, before digital cameras and *PhotoShop*, I made many multi-day expeditions to various military libraries, museums, and photo depositories with my copy machine, film camera and copy stand, accumulating literally reams of information and 1,000s of photographs. The photos credited to the American Fighter Aces Association (AFAA) were mostly collected during 1985-88 when I researched WWII aces as a co-editor of the American Fighter Aces Association Album (which was finally published in 1996). During this time I was fortunate to be able to meet with or corresponded with 100s of aces and copied 1,000s of photos from their personal albums and those in the extensive AFAA archives. At one time I had a photo darkroom where I developed 1,000s of rare photos from microfilm negatives. Also, many photos were copied from contemporary magazines and publications, and because of their age many were deteriorating and discolored and have been scanned to improve their quality. Many photos were taken from wartime group photos to obtain an individual pilot photo and were grainy, but were the only ones available of the individual pilot mentioned in the text. Over the years the origin of many of the 1,000s of photos I have been lent to copy or have copied and collected personally have become obscured. Most are from military and government sources, but many are from private individuals, and I apologize in advance, as most are uncredited and should be considered as part of the author's collection.

Japanese Aircraft Code Designations
In order for the reader to differentiate the numerous Japanese aircraft encountered in the text I have included a table of the Allied code names for Japanese aircraft in service with the Japanese Navy (JNAF: Japanese Naval Air Force) or the Army (JAAF: Japanese Army Air Force), manufacturer, Japanese designation, and a brief description.

In summer 1942, Australian Air Commodore J.E. Hewitt, Allied Director or Air Intelligence (SWPA), assigned U.S. Army officer Capt. Frank McCoy of the Technical Air Intelligence Unit (TAIU) to devise a system of nomenclature to help identify the expanding number of Japanese aircraft for intelligence and communication purposes (question: was A6M2 or Ki-32 any more difficult than Me 109 or FW 190?). The basic guideline for naming was:

1) Fighters and reconnaissance seaplanes were given men's Christian names or first names (Zeke, Tony)
2) Bombers, dive bombers, torpedo bombers, flying boats, and reconnaissance aircraft other than seaplanes received women's Christian names or first names (Betty, Kate)
3) Transport aircraft were given girls' names beginning with T. (Tess, Tabby)
4) The names of trees were used for trainers (Willow, Oak)
5) Gliders were named after birds. (Gander, Buzzard)

Since McCoy was from Tennessee and had a hillbilly name, so his first selections were names like Zeke, Nate, Rufe and Jake. Once hillbilly names were expended, TAIU personnel used the names of wives and family. McCoy's wife, Louise, and daughter, June, were used etc., etc. McCoy used his first name, Frank, and then those of his two assistants, Francis (T.Sgt. Williams) and Joe (Corp. Gratten).

Capt. Frank McCoy

The Betty bomber, with its large gun blisters, was named after a voluptuous Pennsylvania woman. The Sally was named after the wife of McCoy's earlier CO, Gen. Fay Upthegrove. The Val was one of the first Japanese aircraft to be code named, and was named after an Australian friend of McCoy's Supervisor who made the specific request.

The Zero was named because it was the Mitsubishi Navy Type 0, but was replaced by the name Zeke; however, Zero remains the most well known today. The Model 32 Zeke was originally named the Hap after Air Force Chief Gen. Henry "Hap" Arnold. But during a headquarters intelligence briefing Arnold heard of all the Haps being destroyed in the Pacific and became furious, and very soon the Hap was redesignated as the Hamp. The Tojo first appeared in the CBI, and was given that name there after Japanese Prime Minister Tojo. When it appeared in the SWPA it was named John, but this name was soon dropped for Tojo. When the K-61 single engine fighter appeared in the SWPA it was thought to closely resemble the Italian Macchi MC 202 and was given the Italian type name Tony. But since it also looked like the Messerschmitt Bf 109 from a distance a number of early ICRs reported Bf 109s appearing in combat. The George was named by Flt./Sgt. George Remington of the RAAF, who was attached to the TAIU.

Allied Code Name	Service	Manufacturer	Designation Type	Description
Ann	Army	Mitsubishi	Ki-30 Type 97	2 place SE light bomber
Betty	Navy	Mitsubishi	G4M	7 place TE bomber
Claude	Navy	Mitsubishi	A5M Type 96	1 place SE carrier fighter
Dinah	Army	Mitsubishi	Ki-46	2 place TE night/recon fighter
Emily	Navy	Kawanishi	H8K	9 place TE recon flying boat
Frances	Navy	Kugisho	P1Y	2-3 place TE bomber/night
Frank	Army	Nakajima	Ki-84 Type 4	1 place SE fighter/FB
George	Navy	Kawanishi	N1K2-J	1 place SE fighter
Grace	Navy	Aichi	B7A	2 place carrier torpedo/DB
Helen	Army	Nakajima	Ki-49	8 place TE heavy bomber
Irving	Navy	Nakajima	J1N1	2-3 place SE recon/night
Jack	Navy	Mitsubishi	J2M3	1 place SE fighter (land)
Jake	Navy	Aichi	E13A	2 place SE float recon
Jill	Navy	Nakajima	B6N	2 place SE carrier bomber
Kate	Navy	Nakajima	B5N	3 place SE carrier bomber
Lily	Army	Kawasaki	Ki-48 Type 99	4 place TE light bomber
Nate	Army	Nakajima	Ki-27 Type 97	1 place SE fighter/FB
Nell	Navy	Mitsubishi	G3M	5 place TE bomber
Nick	Army	Kawasaki	Ki-45 Type 2	2 place TE FB/night fighter
Oscar	Army	Nakajima	Ki-43 Type 2	1 place SE fighter
Peggy	Both	Mitsubishi	Ki-67 Type 4	6-8 place TE bomber
Pete	Army	Kawasaki	Ki-10 Type 95	2 place SE observation
Rufe	Navy	Nakajima	A6M2-N Type 2	2 place SE float fighter
Sally *	Army	Mitsubishi	Ki-21 Type 97	5 place TE bomber
Sonia	Army	Mitsubishi	Ki-51 Type 97	2 place SE light bomber
Tabby	Navy	Showa	L2D	3-5 place TE transport
Tess	Army	Douglas	DC-2	3-5 place TE transport
Tojo	Army	Nakajima	Ki-44 Type 2	1 place SE fighter
Tony	Army	Kawasaki	Ki-61 Type 3	1 place SE fighter
Val	Navy	Aichi	D3A Type 99	2 place SE carrier DB
** Zero	Navy	Mitsubishi	A6M Type 0	1 place SE carrier fighter

*also Jane ** also Zeke, Hap, Hamp
SE=Single Engine and TE=Twin Engine

Abbreviations

To decrease the large number of entries and make reading and perusing the text easier, the complete names of individual units have been abbreviated. For example, the Fifth Fighter Command has been reduced to 5FC; the Forty Ninth (or 49th) Fighter Group to 49FG; the Ninth (or 9th) Fighter Squadron to 9FS, etc. Also ranks have been abbreviated: Lt. Colonel, Captain, First Lieutenant, etc. to Lt.Col., Capt., 1Lt. etc.

Part One
Philippines

PHILIPPINE ISLANDS
STATUTE MILES
0 10 50 100 200
BATAN ISLANDS
Aparri
Vigan
Tuguegarao
Lingayen Gulf
San Fernando
Baguio
Rosales
Tarlac
Cabanatuan
LUZON
Iba
Fort Stotsenburg
Clark Field
S. Fernando
Olongapo
BATAAN
Manila
CORREGIDOR
Lamon Bay
San Miguel Bay
Legaspi
MINDORO
San Jose
CULION
MASBATE
SAMAR
PANAY
Iloilo
NEGROS
CEBU
Cebu
LEYTE
Tacloban
BOHOL
Surigao
PALAWAN
SULU SEA
Cagayan
Del Monte
Malaybalay
MINDANAO
Lake Lanao
Cotabato
Davao
Zamboanga
JOLO
BORNEO
CELEBES SEA
CHINA SEA
PACIFIC OCEAN

Between the Wars: Preparedness vs. Readiness

Between the two World Wars, America considered three possible strategies to determine its military policy pertaining to the Philippines and the Far East. The first was to withdraw entirely; or it could attempt to maintain the status quo with the available forces stationed there; or third, it could build up sufficient forces to ensure the enforcement of its policies and to protect its interests in the Far East. Although the latter policy was preferred, circumstances prevented its implementation, as public opinion and the political atmosphere prevailing during the late twenties and the thirties favored disarmament. During this time Congress, pressed for domestic defensive military funding, chose not to provide personnel and equipment for remote Pacific outposts. Even if the Army were able to establish a formidable presence in the distant Philippines, the Navy would be unable to provide adequate offensive and logistical support in case of war, so the War Department had no choice but to pursue a policy of attempting to maintain existing strength.

Late 1930s

In the late 1930s, as Japan expanded in Asia, America attempted to build up air strength in the Philippines. In September 1939 Lt.Col. Carl Spaatz, Chief of the Plans Division, sent a memorandum to Maj.Gen. H.H. Arnold, newly appointed AAC Chief, which outlined possibilities for a strategic offensive in the Far East; concluding that a force based in Luzon be formed and be capable of sustained air operations. Spaatz recommended that this force consist of two groups of heavy bombardment, two squadrons of long range reconnaissance, three groups of medium bombardment, three squadrons of medium range reconnaissance, and two interceptor pursuit groups. This force was not to be posted to Luzon until "the entire force was organized, equipped, and trained," and base facilities were adequate for its operations.

However, the United States was unable implement this plan, as during the previous month, August 1939, the Plans Division had proposed the organization of a Composite Wing consisting of two medium Bombardment Groups, one Pursuit Group, two Reconnaissance Squadrons, and two Observation Squadrons. The only method of implementing the Philippine's Plan would be to either increase this new Plans Division program for enlarging the Air Corps or to decrease the number of units assigned to other commands, such as Hawaii or the GHQ, Air Force.

1940

The Philippines Plan remained in plan from until April 1940 when Col. H.C. Richards, Air Officer attached to the Philippine Department, requested "a few modern airplanes" (three each P-35s, P-36s, and B-18s and a few B-17s) to accommodate recent Training Center graduates, as the Philippine Department had only a few obsolete aircraft, such as P-26s, O-46s, and B-10s. The request could not be fulfilled and the Philippine Department's 28 P-26 pursuits "would have to suffice until late in the year 1941, at the earliest."

On 6 May 1940 the one medium bombardment squadron, the one observation squadron, and the three pursuit squadrons (3rd, 21st, and 34th) which represented the Air Corps' total strength in the Philippines had been organized into the Philippine Department Air Force. In the same month the pursuit squadrons began to receive P-35s as replacements for their obsolete Boeing P-26s, and during the summer and fall a limited number of P-40Bs and P-400s arrived. On 16 September these pursuit squadrons were organized into the 24th Pursuit Group and placed under the command of Maj. Orrin Grover.

In November 1940 48 P-35s were diverted from a Swedish export order to the Philippines which dictated additional personnel, and the 17th and 20th Pursuit Squadrons received orders to proceed to San Francisco with 40 officers and 314 enlisted men to sail on or about 4 November 1940.

Maj.Gen. Henry H. **Arnold**, AAC Chief. (left), and Lt.Col. Carl **Spaatz**, Chief of the Plans Division. (right). (AFHRC)

Seversky **P-35**. (AAF)

Boeing **P-26** "Peashooter". (AAF)

Maj. Orrin **Grover**, CO of the 24th Pursuit Group. (AAF)

In early November 1940 the 4th Composite Group (bombers and fighters), based at Nichols Field under Col. L.S. Churchill, was reinforced by the 17th Pursuit Squadron of the 1st Pursuit Group, commanded by Maj. K.J. Gregg, and the 20th Pursuit Squadron of the 24th Pursuit Group, commanded by Capt. Orrin Grover. Headquarters and HQ Squadron, the 3rd Pursuit Squadron, the 17th Pursuit Squadron, and the 20th Pursuit Squadron were all equipped with the obsolete Boeing P-26. In May Col. Churchill assumed command of Nichols Field and Maj. Gregg became the CO of the 4th Composite Group, which would receive the Swedish P-35s.

Early 1941: Situation

In February 1941, the Air Corps in the Philippines was intended to be a token force and never had been envisaged as capable of meeting "serious contingencies." Using a study by Col. Spaatz, Maj.Gen. George Brett, the acting Chief of the Air Corps, determined that "the minimum air garrison for an effective defense should comprise not less than, one long range Bombardment Wing of three or more Groups and one Pursuit Wing of three or more Groups, together with such additional ground and air components as may be required to constitute a balanced force". However, at the time it was impossible to provide either the necessary personnel or the aircraft for Brett's recommendations. Nevertheless, during the spring and summer of 1941 there was some piecemeal reinforcement. On 19 April, the merchant ship *American Manufacturer* sailed from the U.S. carrying 31 modern P-40Bs to the Philippines.

With new aircraft and the prospect of receiving others, Brett decided to create a more modern Air Corps organization in the Philippines. The 4th Composite Group had been organized from previously undermanned Department units and was based at Nichols Field, outside Manila, and once the 17th and 20th Pursuit Squadrons had arrived in late November 1940 they were incorporated into that Group. In addition to these newly-arrived squadrons, the 4th Group consisted of a Headquarters and Headquarters Squadron and the 3rd Pursuit Squadron based at Nichols Field. The first of a series of important steps in reorganization occurred on 6 May 1941, when the units composing the 4th Composite Group together with the 20th Air Base Group and miscellaneous supporting units were incorporated into the Philippine Department Air Force. The War Department transferred Brig. Gen. Henry Clagett, the CO of Selfridge Field, MI, to command this newly constituted organization.

Maj.Gen. George **Brett**, Acting Chief of the Air Corps, in a photo during the 1931 National Air Races.

Brig.Gen. Henry **Clagett**, CO of Selfridge Field, MI, was transferred to the Philippines to command the Philippine Department Air Force. (AAF)

Lt.Gen. **MacArthur**. (front) with. (behind: left to right) Lt.Col. Richard **Sutherland**, Col. Harold **George**, and aides Lt.Col. William **Marquart** and Maj. LaGrande **Diller**. (AFHRC)

Once Clagett assumed command he found he had insufficient enlisted men and trainees; too few authorized units; inadequate airdrome facilities; and that he needed cooperation from civilians and officials of the Philippine government, which would probably require bribery of some type. On 27 July 1941, the Department became more aware of the growing importance of the Far Eastern Theater when Gen. Douglas MacArthur, who had been serving as military adviser to the Philippine government, was named as the Commanding General of the United States Army Forces in the Far East (USAFFE). This appointment allowed for a further reorganization of American air units. On 30 June, the War Department received a request from the Philippine Department for a more flexible air command and suggested the establishment of an Air Force Headquarters with a Composite Group and a Pursuit Group composed of the Pursuit squadrons then in the Philippines. Spaatz, now a Brigadier General and Chief of the Air Staff, vigorously agreed with the suggestion, realizing it was capable of easy control and expansion. Shortly after the creation of the USAFFE, Clagett's command was reorganized. On 4 August, the Philippine Department Air Force was redesignated as the Air Force, United States Army Forces in the Far East, which was to operate directly under MacArthur, except for routine administration and supply, which would still operate under Headquarters, Philippine Department.

November 1941

On 20 November 1941, the USAT *Winfield S. Scott*, the heavy cruiser USS *Louisville*, and the USS *Coolidge* sailed into Manila Bay. Aboard the *Coolidge* were 15 pilots of the 21st Pursuit Squadron and 16 pilots of the 34th Pursuit Squadron who were attached to the 24th Group until the arrival of their own organizations. These pilots would be the last fighter pilots to reinforce the Philippines before Pearl Harbor. They expected that they would be flying new Curtiss P-40s at Nichols Field, but found that they were consigned to the well-worn Seversky P-35s diverted from the Swedish order of a year earlier and had been flown by the 3rd, 17th, and 20th Pursuit Squadrons until they received P-40s during the summer of 1941. These three squadrons had divided up the newly arrived P-40s and supplemented them with their obsolete P-35s, and were then equipped with 53 P-35s, 28 P-40Bs, and 25 P-40Es. After they received their P-40s they underwent rigorous gunnery training at Iba Field, located about 90 miles northwest of Manila on the west coast of Luzon.

Order of Battle
The U.S. Far East Air Force (Maj.Gen. Lewis Brereton)
V Interceptor Command (Brig.Gen. Henry Clagett)
24th Pursuit Group (Maj. Orrin Grover)

3rd Pursuit Squadron, equipped with 18 P-40Es under the command of 1Lt. Henry Thorne at Iba.
17th Pursuit Squadron, equipped with 18 P-40Es under the command of 1Lt. Boyd Wagner at Nichols.
20th Pursuit Squadron, equipped with 18 P-40Bs under the command of 1Lt. J. H. Moore at Clark.

35th Pursuit Group Detachment
(attached to the 24th Pursuit Group):

21st Pursuit Squadron, equipped with 18 P-40Es under the command of 1Lt. William Dyess at Nichols.
34th Pursuit Squadron, equipped with 18 P-35As under the command of 1Lt. Samuel Marett at Del Carmen.

The 35th Pursuit Group was activated on 2 December 1939 and was composed of the 18th, 21st, and 34th Squadrons, which were activated on 1 February 1940. The Group trained at Moffett and Hamilton Fields in California before its 21st and 34th Squadrons were deployed to the Philippines in early November 1941. The Group's HQ remained in the U.S., and the two Squadrons were attached to the 24PG until the HQ was scheduled to leave the U.S. on 5 December 1941 (it never left due to Pearl Harbor).

The 2nd Observation Squadron, equipped with 0-46 and 0-52 aircraft plus several obsolete Douglas B-18 bombers and training-type aircraft, made up the remainder of the Far East Air Force. The newly formed Philippine Air Force supplemented the FEAF, flying a few obsolete Boeing P-26A fighters and Martin B-10 bombers.

This new organization continued to be no more than a token force with only the 31 P-40Bs which had arrived in May regarded as modern aircraft, while the 21 P-26s, 56 P-35s, 10 0-46s, 10 A-9s, 9 A-27s, 14 B-10s and 18 B-18s were considered obsolete. The number of trained pilots was gradually increasing and airfield facilities were being improved. However, only Clark Field could handle heavy bombers, but the runways at Nichols Field were to be completed 1 October. Pursuit aircraft could use six fields within 60 miles of Manila, but these lacked all fuel and repair facilities, and six additional fields scattered throughout the Archipelago were principally useful only for dispersal. In July 100 new pilots arrived from training schools in the States, and it became necessary for the 4th Composite Group to train these pilots and a pursuit training unit was established at Clark Field.

P-35A flown by 1Lt. Boyd Wagner of the 17PS at Nichols Field. (AAF)

P-40B flown by Lt. Charles Sneed of the 20PS at Clark Field. (AAF)

P-26 of the 17PS at Iba Field in early summer 1941. (AAF)

Seversky **P-35s** were diverted from the Swedish order of a year earlier and flown by the 3rd, 17th, and 20th Pursuit Squadrons until they received P-40s during the summer of 1941. (AAF)

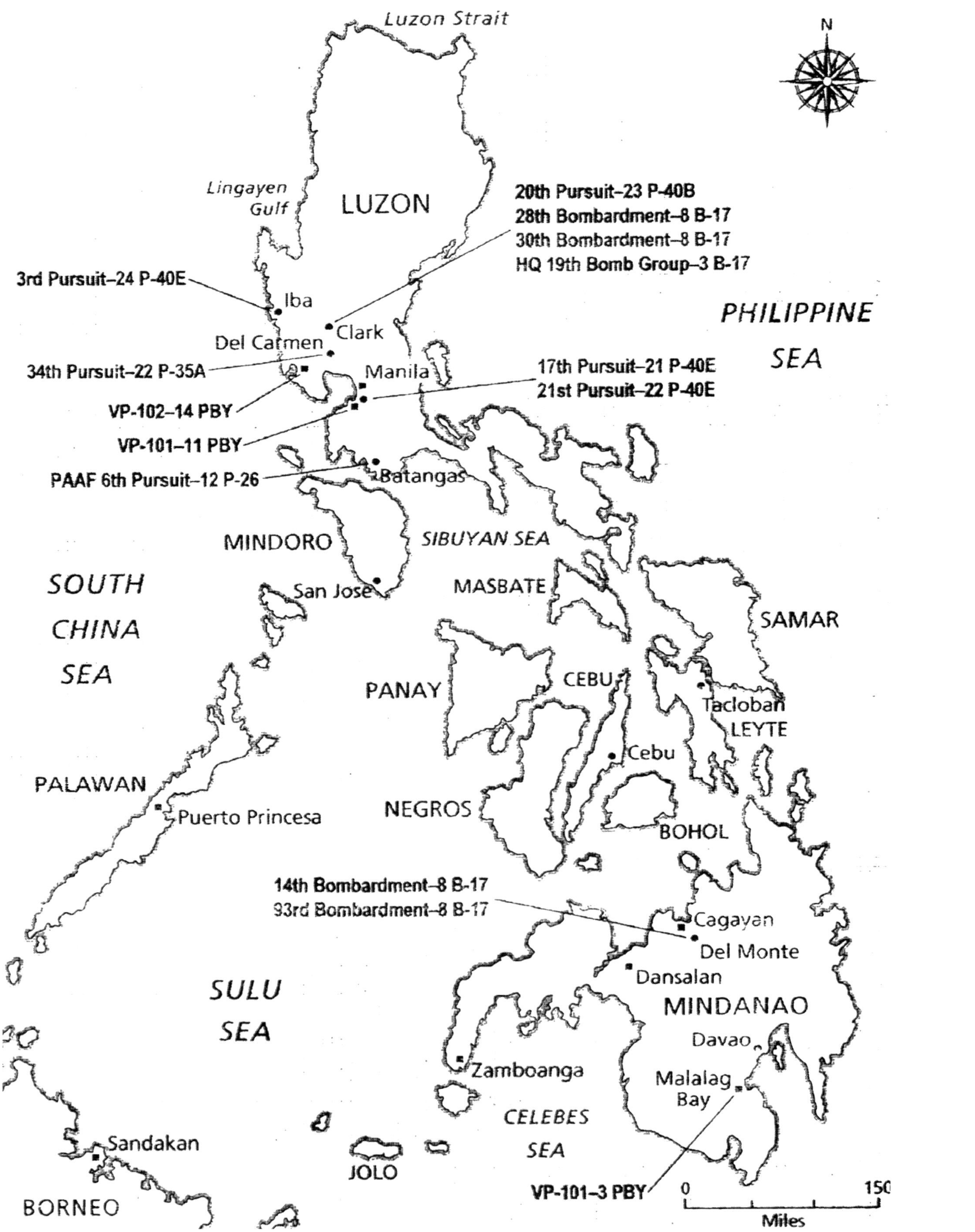
Luzon Strait
N
Lingayen Gulf
LUZON
20th Pursuit–23 P-40B
28th Bombardment–8 B-17
30th Bombardment–8 B-17
HQ 19th Bomb Group–3 B-17
3rd Pursuit–24 P-40E
Iba
Clark
PHILIPPINE SEA
Del Carmen
34th Pursuit–22 P-35A
Manila
17th Pursuit–21 P-40E
21st Pursuit–22 P-40E
VP-102–14 PBY
VP-101–11 PBY
PAAF 6th Pursuit–12 P-26
Batangas
MINDORO
SIBUYAN SEA
SOUTH CHINA SEA
San Jose
MASBATE
SAMAR
PANAY
CEBU
Tacloban
LEYTE
Cebu
PALAWAN
Puerto Princesa
NEGROS
BOHOL
14th Bombardment–8 B-17
93rd Bombardment–8 B-17
Cagayan
Del Monte
Dansalan
SULU SEA
MINDANAO
Davao
Zamboanga
Malalag Bay
CELEBES SEA
Sandakan
JOLO
VP-101–3 PBY
BORNEO
0
150
Miles

Clark Field during summer 1941. (AAF)

In fall 1941 the U.S. increased diplomatic pressure on Japan; therefore, the Joint Army-Navy Board considered "a substantial increase of our forces in the Far East" to be vital and gave primary consideration to the creation of a "moderately strong air force" in that theater. They believed that four heavy bombardment groups, consisting of 272 aircraft and 68 in reserve, along with two pursuit groups of 130 planes each would be required to maintain "a strategic defensive in Asia and for the protection of American interests in the Philippines." Their proposal included the military strengthening of the Philippines to protect present and future air bases, and the disposition of these "required" two pursuit groups to provide protection for the Manila area and for bombardment bases in northern Luzon, and the movement of these "required" four heavy bombardment groups to the Philippines as soon as possible. Funds were to be allotted for air warning equipment and airfield improvement to accommodate the new aircraft.

General Spaatz began arrangements for 50 P-40s to be sent directly from Curtiss factories and for 28 P-40Bs to be transferred from operating units, which were to be crated and shipped in September. However, the major effort was focused on supplying MacArthur with heavy bombers, and the 19th Bombardment Group was reinforced and began to arrive in the Philippines in September. On 2 October 31 P-40 and 19 P-35 pursuits had reached Manila on the *President Pierce*, the *President Coolidge*, and the *American Press*. At the time MacArthur was informed of a proposal by Gen. George Marshall to increase the number of his pursuit squadrons from three to five, and two weeks later a plan was being considered to transfer two pursuit squadrons from Hawaii by 1 January 1942. Marshall's promise of additional pursuit aircraft was rather vague and was secondary to the transfer of bombardment units.

Developments prior to November, such as the creation of the USAFFE under MacArthur, the reorganization of air units under Clagett, the appropriations for airfield facilities, and the plans for reinforcement of pursuit and bombardment units had laid a foundation for further expansion of both ground and air forces. MacArthur believed, however, that a new organization was necessary for a more effective employment of his air units, and early in the fall had requested that Maj.Gen. Lewis Brereton be sent to the Philippines. Following Brereton's arrival, the air force was completely reorganized as per the changes determined during the Washington conferences, which became effective on 16 November 1941 as the Far East Air Force (FEAF).

The newly-activated Far East Air Force included the 5th Bomber Command under Lt.Col. Eugene Eubank, who also remained the Commanding Officer of the 19th Bomb Group; the Far East Air Service Command under Col. L.S. Churchill, former commander of the 4th Composite Group; and the V Interceptor Command under Gen. Clagett, who had expected to be named as CO instead of Brereton with a promotion. Clagett's V Interceptor Command consisted of the 24th Pursuit Group, composed of the 3rd, 17th, and 20th Squadrons; and the 35th Pursuit Group, composed of the 21st and 34th Squadrons. The pilots of these units had received considerable training in pursuit tactics in a special training unit at Clark Field and in gunnery at Iba Field, 75 miles northwest of Manila. Clagett applied for a transfer

LEFT: Maj.Gen. Lewis **Brereton** reorganized the Philippines Air Force. (AAF)
RIGHT: Lt.Col. Eugene **Eubank,** CO of the 5th Bomber Command. (AAF)

back to the U.S. that was granted on 13 December but not implemented due to the increased Japanese Asian threat.

December 1941
The Opposing Air Forces

FEAF

When war came to the Philippines, the recently designated Far East Air Force under Maj.Gen. Lewis Brereton, headquartered at Nielson Field, just south of Manila, had been built into the largest of the American overseas air forces with 8,000 officers and men and more than 300 aircraft, concentrated largely on the island of Luzon. However, less than half of these aircraft were contemporary, much essential equipment was pending shipment from the United States, and even with all the recent preparations the FEAF was still grossly inadequate. Of the projected 240 modern pursuit aircraft only 107 P-40s had arrived, and of a projected 165 modern bombardment aircraft only 35 B-17Cs and Ds were available. The 5th Bomber Command, commanded by Col. Eugene Eubank, was composed of the 19th and 27th Bombardment Groups. The ground echelon of the 27th Bombardment Group had arrived, but its air echelon, equipped with Douglas A-24 dive bombers, had not arrived, and upon the outbreak of war would be diverted to Australia. Two squadrons of the 19th Bombardment Group with 16 B-17s had been deployed to Del Monte Airfield on Mindanao, while the two remaining squadrons, composed of 19 B-17s, remained at Clark Field near Manila.

The 24PG was more adequately equipped than the 5BC. The 21st Squadron, led by Lt. William Dyess, flew the old P-35s from Nichols Field until 4 December, when they received new P-40Es from the air depot. Their obsolete aircraft were then passed along to the 34th Squadron under Lt. Samuel Marett at Del Carmen, which was the only squadron not flying P-40s. The 34th was in the process of receiving their Warhawks, but would not have an opportunity to test all its new aircraft, as it did not receive its last P-40 from the depot until the evening of 7 December. The 20th at Clark Field, commanded by Lt. Joseph Moore, still had old P-40Bs, but the 3rd at Iba, under Lt. Henry Thorne, and the 17th under Lt. Boyd Wagner were equipped with P-40Es. These American squadrons were supplemented by the 6th Squadron of the Philippine Army based at Batangas, commanded by Capt. Jesus Villemor, which was equipped with the old P-26s.

One year prior to the outbreak of the war the Philippines had only three major military airfields: Clark Field, about 60 miles north of Manila; and Nichols and Nielson fields on the outskirts of Manila. Of these, only Clark was suitable for use by heavy bombers. On Mindanao Island, in the southern Philippines, construction was soon begun on Del Monte Field, which was to be large enough to accommodate heavy bombers. By early December 1941, three additional fields on Luzon were being used by pursuit aircraft, four more (O'Donnell, San Fernando, Rosales, and Ternate) fields were nearing completion, and construction had been started on a number of others.

The Philippines air warning system was deficient, having one radar set in operation at Iba and another set in the process of being installed 60 miles west of Aparri, while a third set was being sent to Legaspi for installation. The air warning system was primarily dependent on Filipino spotters on the ground using a very inefficient telephone system. The time delay between the spotting, reporting, and reception at V Interceptor Headquarters at Manila varied from five to 25 minutes.

Beginning 15 November Brereton placed all pursuit aircraft on constant 24 hour alert, fully loaded, armed, and with pilots on 30 minute call. On 27 November, MacArthur was notified by Gen. George C. Marshall, US Army Chief of Staff, that negotiations with the Japanese seemed to be at a dead end. MacArthur was authorized to begin reconnaissance flights and take other measures necessary for the defense of the Philippines. But Marshall also cautioned MacArthur not to take any overt hostile action; if there was to be a war the Japanese were to be the instigators. Between 30 November and 6 December all squadrons were undergoing intensive interception and gunnery training. The pursuit squadrons trained in conjunction with bombers in day and night interception in coordination with AA batteries. The gunnery training unit at Iba experienced a high level of gun malfunctions due to incorrect adjustment and installation (all gun installations would require modification). It seemed as though war was imminent.

Japanese Air Forces

The Japanese had built up their forces on Formosa and Indo-China since early 1941. By December the Japanese Navy had amassed 115 Mitsubishi A6M2 Zero-sen and 12 Mitsubishi A5M Type 96 fighters, 192 land-based attack bombers, 24 flying boats, and 18 reconnaissance aircraft. The Zero had been introduced in combat in China, where it created its initial illusion of invincibility and would gain its reputation as one of the war's greatest fighters with its astonishing agility and climbing ability, great range, and the heaviest armament of any Japanese fighter of that time. The A5M (later "Claude") was used for defensive duties.

The Japanese Army Air Force added 265 first-line fighters, including 197 Ki-27s and 59 Ki-43s, and 234 bombers, as well as 185 reconnaissance aircraft. The most numerous JAAF fighter was the Nakajima Ki-27 (later "Nate"), which was a fixed gear and lightly armed fighter, but could more than hold its own due to its maneuverability in the hands of a veteran pilot. The fame of the Zero eclipsed the JAAF's newly introduced Nakajima Ki-43 (later "Oscar"), whose performance was equal to the Zero, and it achieved excellent results over Malaya, Singapore, and the Netherlands East Indies despite being outnumbered by nearly twice as many Zeros. In addition, the

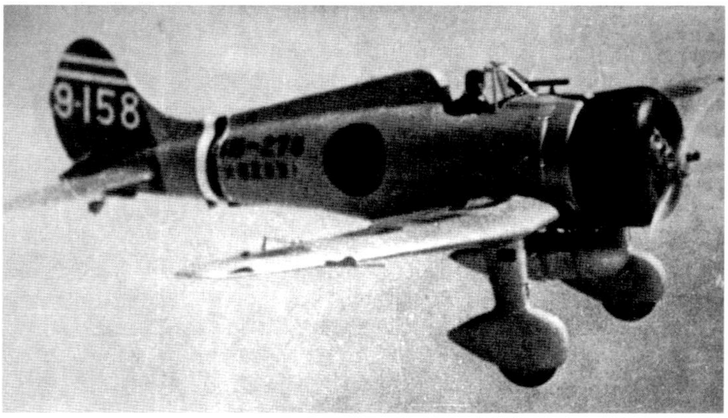

A5M Claude Japanese Navy Air Force. (AFHRC)

A6M2 Zero Japanese Navy Air Force. (AFHRC)

Ki-27 Nate Japanese Army Air Force. (AFHRC)

Ki-43 Oscar Japanese Army Air Force. (AFHRC)

JAAF introduced nine pre-production Ki-44 (later "Tojo") fighters, which would later achieve results as fast, heavily armed interceptors.

The Japanese Navy Air Force had originally planned to strike the Philippines early in the morning on 8 December. Their primary targets were to be Iba and Clark Field, while the Army Air Force was assigned the targets at Aparri and Baguio. Heavy ground fog had prevented the Navy aircraft from becoming airborne, while the Army fields were clear. This resulted in the early morning raids on the targets at Aparri and Baguio with no strikes being made on the primary Luzon airfield targets.

2-6 December 1941

From 2 to 6 December, for four successive nights an enemy aircraft was sighted over Clark Field at about 0530. After the first sighting, orders were given to force the enemy to land or to destroy it. On the next three nights it was impossible to make an interception due to the moonless darkness or the enemy aircraft not entering the searchlight area. On the fifth night all aircraft were kept on the ground and the AA batteries alerted, but no enemy aircraft were located.

8 December 1941

Simultaneous with the 7 December attack on Pearl Harbor, at 0330 in the Philippines on 8 December 1941 (due to the International Date Line), the lone radar set installed at Iba Field detected a formation of aircraft about 75 miles offshore heading towards Corregidor. The Interceptor Command immediately sent up 3rd Pursuit Squadron P-40Es under 1Lt. Henry Thorne to intercept the uniden-

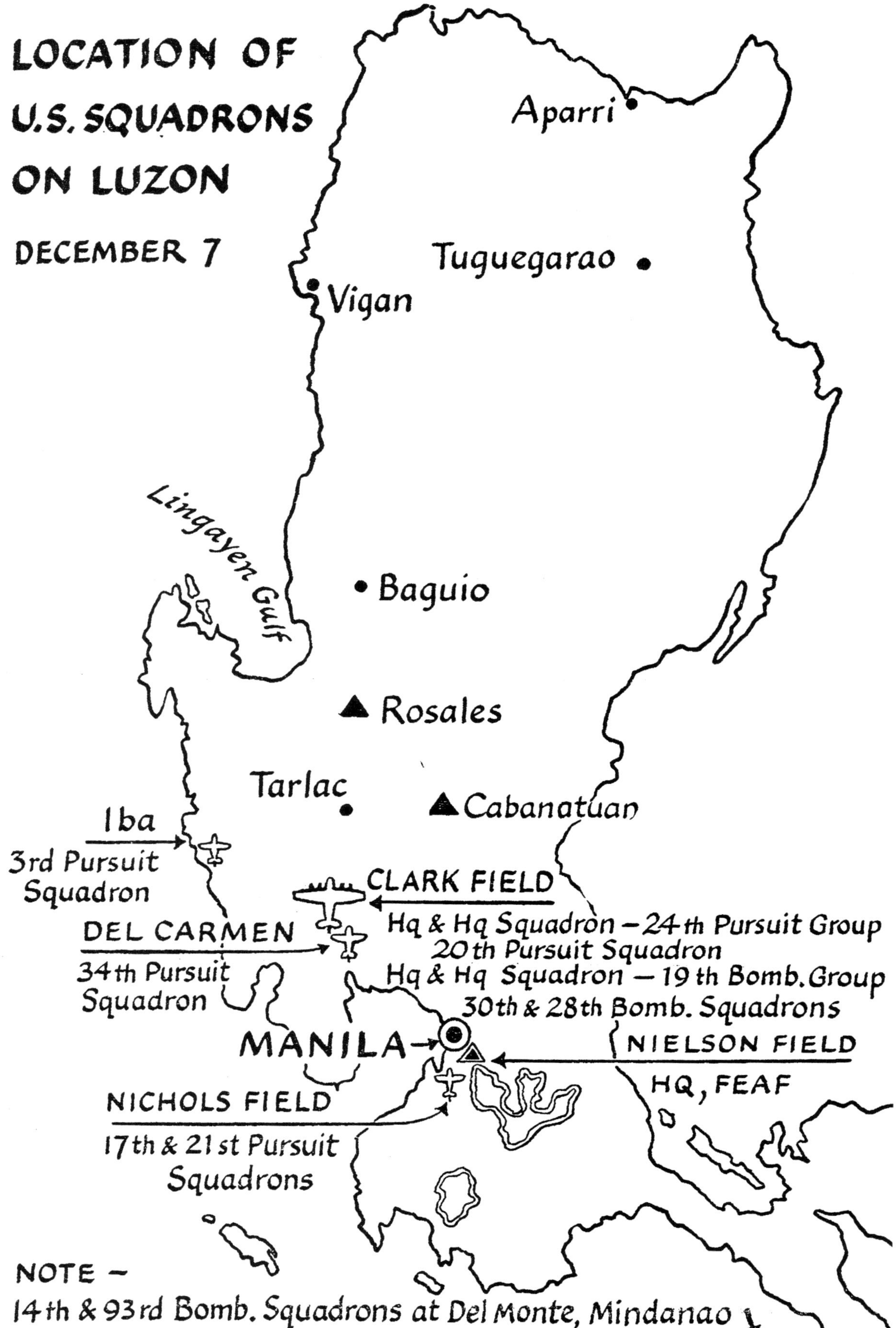
LOCATION OF U.S. SQUADRONS ON LUZON
DECEMBER 7
Aparri
Tuguegarao
Vigan
Lingayen Gulf
Baguio
Rosales
Tarlac
Cabanatuan
Iba
3rd Pursuit Squadron
CLARK FIELD
Hq & Hq Squadron – 24th Pursuit Group
20th Pursuit Squadron
Hq & Hq Squadron – 19th Bomb. Group
30th & 28th Bomb. Squadrons
DEL CARMEN
34th Pursuit Squadron
MANILA
NIELSON FIELD
HQ, FEAF
NICHOLS FIELD
17th & 21st Pursuit Squadrons
NOTE –
14th & 93rd Bomb. Squadrons at Del Monte, Mindanao

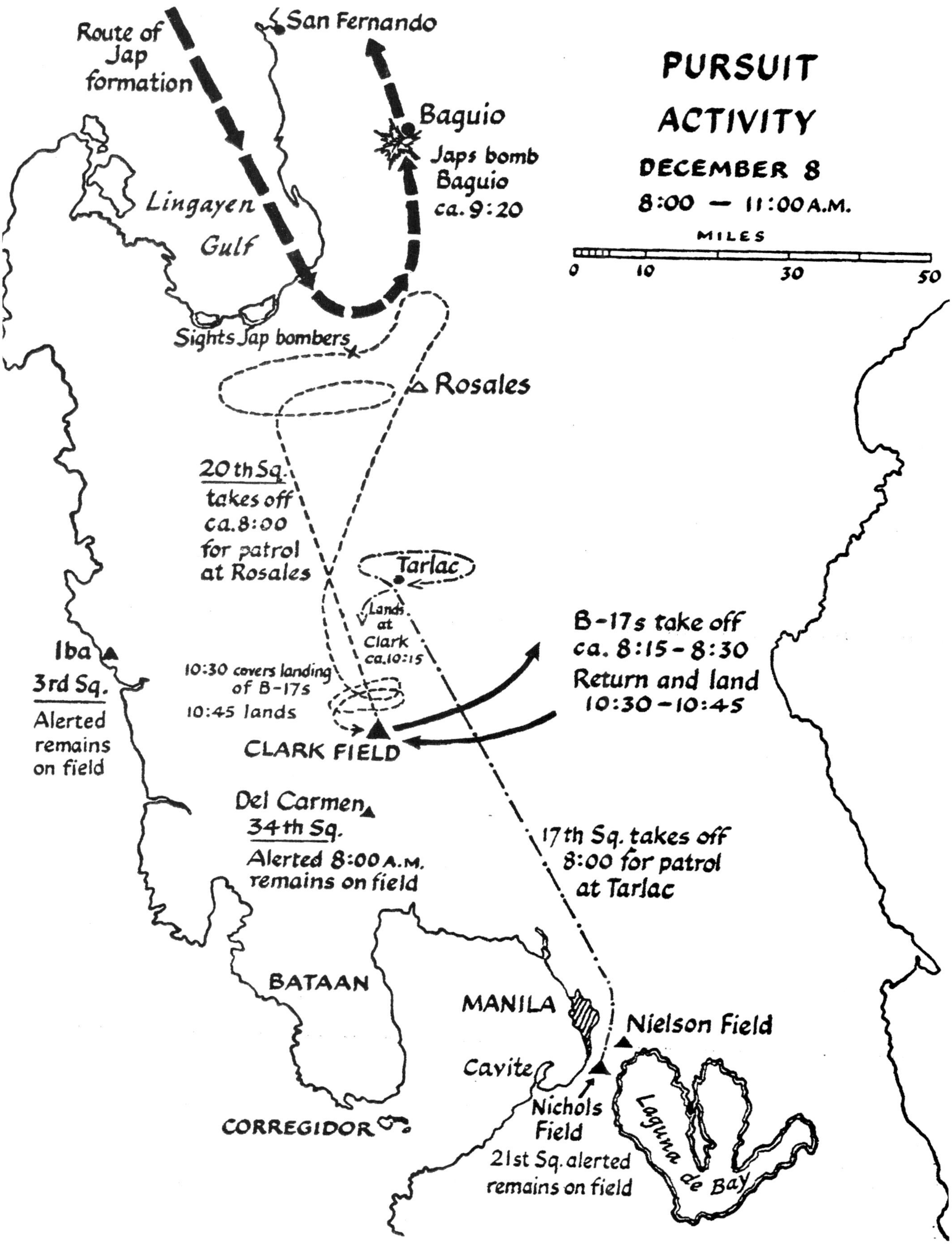
PURSUIT
ACTIVITY
DECEMBER 8
8:00 — 11:00 A.M.
MILES
0
10
30
50
Route of
Jap
formation
San Fernando
Baguio
Japs bomb
Baguio
ca. 9:20
Lingayen
Gulf
Sights Jap bombers
Rosales
20th Sq.
takes off
ca. 8:00
for patrol
at Rosales
Tarlac
Lands
at
Clark
ca. 10:15
B-17s take off
ca. 8:15-8:30
Return and land
10:30-10:45
Iba
3rd Sq.
Alerted
remains
on field
10:30 covers landing
of B-17s
10:45 lands
CLARK FIELD
Del Carmen
34th Sq.
Alerted 8:00 A.M.
remains on field
17th Sq. takes off
8:00 for patrol
at Tarlac
BATAAN
MANILA
Nielson Field
Cavite
Nichols
Field
21st Sq. alerted
remains on field
CORREGIDOR
Laguna
de Bay

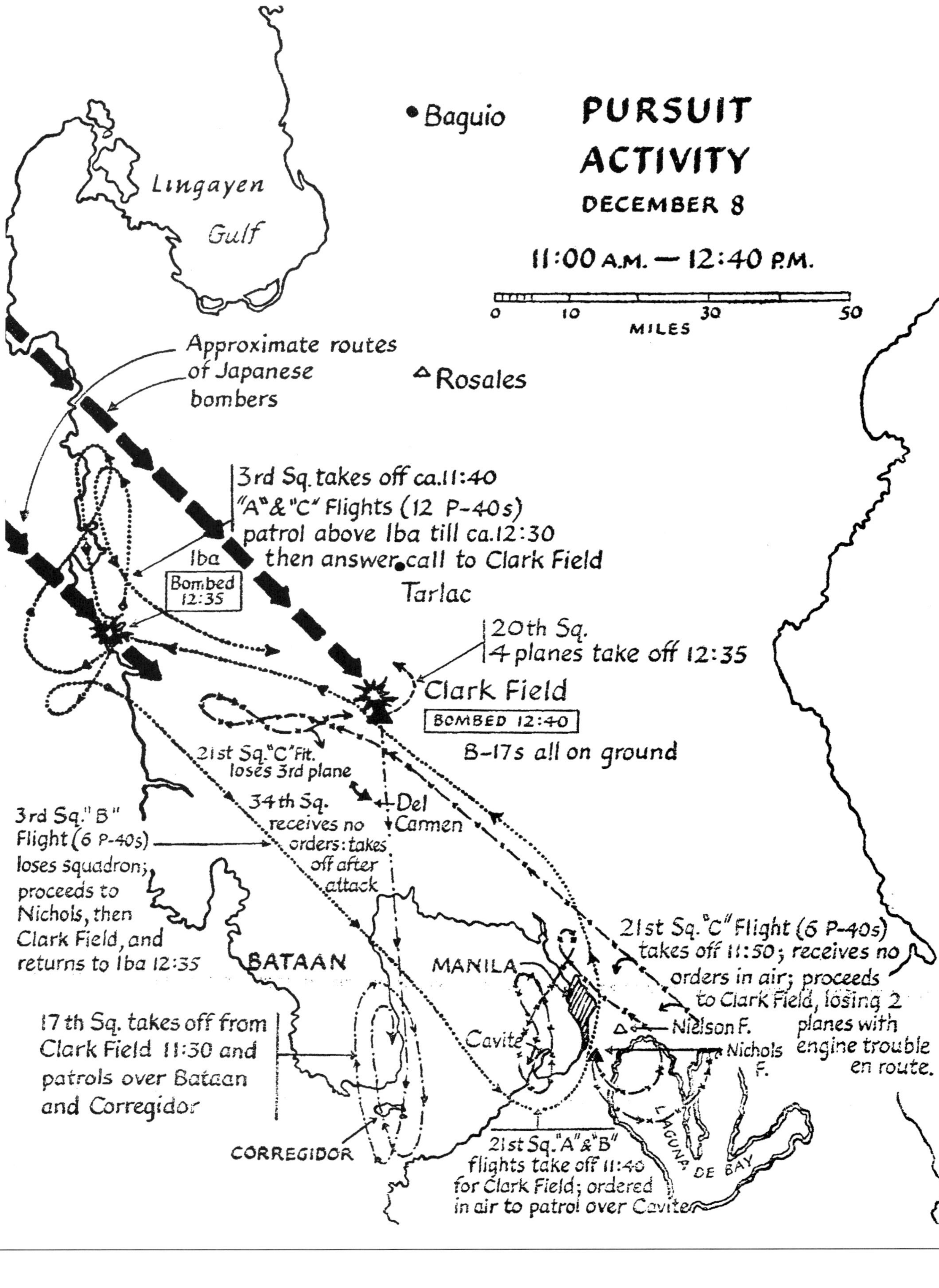
PURSUIT ACTIVITY
DECEMBER 8
11:00 A.M. — 12:40 P.M.
0 10 30 50
MILES
Baguio
Lingayen
Gulf
Rosales
Approximate routes of Japanese bombers
3rd Sq. takes off ca. 11:40 "A" & "C" Flights (12 P-40s) patrol above Iba till ca. 12:30 then answer call to Clark Field
Iba
Bombed 12:35
Tarlac
20th Sq. 4 planes take off 12:35
Clark Field
BOMBED 12:40
B-17s all on ground
21st Sq. "C" Flt. loses 3rd plane
34th Sq. receives no orders: takes off after attack
Del Carmen
3rd Sq. "B" Flight (6 P-40s) loses squadron; proceeds to Nichols, then Clark Field, and returns to Iba 12:35
21st Sq. "C" Flight (6 P-40s) takes off 11:50; receives no orders in air; proceeds to Clark Field, losing 2 planes with engine trouble en route.
BATAAN
MANILA
Nielson F.
Nichols F.
Cavite
17th Sq. takes off from Clark Field 11:30 and patrols over Bataan and Corregidor
CORREGIDOR
21st Sq. "A" & "B" flights take off 11:40 for Clark Field; ordered in air to patrol over Cavite
LAGUNA DE BAY

tified raiders. The radar operator gave the fighter pilots a course bearing but could not give them an altitude for interception. The P-40s continued to climb into the darkness until they reached their altitude maximum of 15,000 feet, which was set by the lack of oxygen equipment on the P-40. The Americans continued flying below the higher enemy formation without making contact, but for unknown reasons the Japanese turned back to Formosa without dropping their bombs and the 3PS returned to Iba to go back to bed and prepare for a 0630 patrol.

Official confirmation of the attack on Pearl Harbor was given by MacArthur's headquarters at 0445. In the early morning JAAF bombers from Formosa bombed northern Luzon without interception, while to the south Navy fighters from the small carrier *Ryujo* attacked the naval base at Davao. These enemy raids caused the Americans to scramble the 20PS at Clark, which was sent to intercept an approaching enemy formation, while at Nichols Field the 17PS under 1Lt. Boyd Wagner was ordered to fly air cover Clark Field. However, the approaching enemy bombers avoided the American interceptors by veering to the northeast and bombing Baguio, the summer Philippine capital, and Tagagarau. Meanwhile, at 0930 the B-17s at Clark Field were ordered into the air to avoid being caught on the ground, but were called back to Clark Field when the Japanese did not appear. The 20PS, which had spent two hours patrolling, was also ordered to return to Clark, but was first to cover the landing of the B-17s on the way in.

At 1130 almost all American aircraft were on the ground. The B-17s were being prepared for an attack on Formosa that had been ordered for that evening. The 20PS at Clark and the 17PS at Nichols were being refueled, while the 3PS at Iba, the 34PS at Nichols, and the 21PS at Del Carmen were placed on standby, awaiting orders. At 1145 the radar installation at Iba picked up another enemy formation south over Lingayen Gulf, but MacArthur's air warning system was disrupted. Radio reception was overwhelmed by static caused by systematic Japanese jamming of the American frequencies, preventing the message from getting through. At about the same time, the Interceptor Command took precautions to protect the approaches to Manila, with the 17th Squadron ordered to cover the Bataan Peninsula, the 3rd Squadron sent out over the China Sea where an enemy formation had been reported, the 34th to patrol the Manila area, and the 21st to cover Clark Field, where the fighters based there were being refueled and the bombers were made ready for a mission against the Japanese bases on Formosa.

1Lt. Boyd **Wagner** (on right) was the CO of the 17PS. (AAF)

When the 54 Betty bombers of the Japanese Navy Air Force (JNAF) and 34 Zero fighters of the Tainan Air Corps headed for Clark Field, they felt certain that any chance of surprise was gone and that all available American fighters would be in the air to intercept them. As the two Japanese V formations crossed the mountains at 18,000 feet, their crews looked down and saw the nucleus of American air power in the Philippines lined wing tip to wing tip on the airfields below. The Betty bombers approached the target, and the first formation was almost to their release line before the alarm was given at Clark Field.

20PS

A thick dust haze over Del Carmen Field delayed the take off of the 21st Squadron, which was to cover Clark, and left it with no air cover, so at 1215 the 20PS, whose P-40s had not completed refueling, were hurriedly ordered to cover its own base. But a large V-formation of 27 Japanese bombers began dropping small fragmentation and 100 pound bombs and was followed by another similar sized formation. The bombers attacked with great accuracy for 15 minutes before their escorting fighters began swarming over Clark. A Flight's 2Lt. Max Louk was killed sitting in his fighter, while 2Lt. Daniel Blass' fighter was badly damaged but Blass was unhurt. B Flight's P-40s were trying to take off when the bombs started falling and suffered grievous losses. 2Lts. Jesse Luker and Tod Mulcahy were killed, and 2Lts. Guy Iverson, Max Halvorson, and Frederick Armstrong were badly burned in their aircraft, while bombs badly damaged the aircraft of 2Lt. Carl Gies and James Fosse. Four P-40s got off the ground led by Squadron Commander 1Lt. Joseph Moore. As soon as he got off the ground 2Lt. James Drake was shot down and killed, but Moore and 2Lts. Randall Keator and Edwin Gilmore climbed to 21,000 feet and pursued the retreating bombers without success. The Flight then encountered a number of Zeros and became separated. Keator attacked a flight of three enemy fighters and shot down two to become the first American to shoot down a Japanese aircraft in the Philippines. 2Lt. Edwin Gilmore also shot down a Zero over Clark Field, and in a series of dogfights Moore destroyed two other Zeros over Nichols Field. After the initial bombing attack on Clark Field, the Japanese fighters carried out low level strafing attacks on the grounded American aircraft for over an hour. Of the 23 20PS Warhawks, 20 had been destroyed or seriously damaged. But the most serious loss was 12 of 14 operational B-17s destroyed and two being repaired were set on fire and destroyed. In addition, about 25 "miscellaneous" aircraft (A-27s, B-10s, and B-18s) were destroyed.

3PS

In the resulting confusion, the 3rd Squadron did not find the enemy formation incoming from the China Sea and its B Flight, under 2Lt. Edward Woolery, became separated from the rest of the squadron. So B Flight headed for Manila, where they expected to receive additional orders from 24PG headquarters at Nichols Field. When the Flight arrived over Manila everything seemed normal, and when a radio call was received that sounded like "bandits over Clark," Woolery's P-40s raced northward, where everything there also appeared normal. By this time the Flight was running critically low on fuel and headed back to Iba to refuel. As they

LEFT TO RIGHT: 2Lt. Randall **Keator** shot down two enemy fighters to become the first American to shoot down a Japanese aircraft in the Philippines. (AAF)

1Lt. Joseph **Moore** destroyed two Zeros over Nichols Field for his only two victories of the war. (AAF)

2Lt. Edwin **Gilmore** shot down a Zero over Clark Field for his first of three victories. (AAF)

approached Iba they circled the field in their landing approach, and as Woolery's aircraft touched down first the airfield was hit by explosions. Woolery's Warhawk was destroyed by bombs as it touched down, blowing him out of the cockpit unhurt into a shell hole. Woolery raced over to another P-40 and flew it out of danger to Rosales. The Zeros fired at 1Lt. Frank Neri and 2Lt. Vernon Ireland as they were landing, but Neri was able to escape to Rosales with cannon holes in his wing; Ireland was shot down and killed. 2Lt. F.C. Roberts ran out of fuel and ditched off shore, then waded to shore and safety. 2Lt. Andrew Krieger, who was bringing up the rear of the flight and circling to cover the landings, put his P-40 into full throttle and climbed, trying to spot the enemy aircraft. Krieger leveled off at 10,000 feet and circled back over the field, where he sighted what he thought was a squadron of P-35s in a Lufbery circle getting ready to land. However, as he closed Krieger saw that these aircraft were Japanese, and he radioed for help and dove to attack. He got on the tail of a Zero but immediately got three of the nimble enemy fighters on his tail. He fired off a short burst and broke away in a quick maneuver which luckily lost his pursuers, landing at Rosales just before he ran out of fuel. Six P-40s from 3PS' C Flight approached Clark, where Zeros were strafing, and although they were very low on fuel, they pressed the attack. 1Lts. Herbert Ellis and Grant Mahony shot down a single and two Zeros, respectively. (Note: Ellis' victory was credited in Squadron records but not in post war official records.) Ellis was pursued by three Zeros that set his tail surfaces on fire, and Ellis headed into a cloud and was forced to make a high speed bail out at low altitude; he made it to the ground safely. 2Lt. George Ellstrom ran out of gas during the combat and bailed out, but was strafed in his parachute and killed.

21PS and 17PS

Both the 17th and 21st Squadrons were very low on fuel and had made no contact with the Japanese, except for one 21PS Flight led by 1Lt. Samuel Grashio. The Flight began with six P-40s, but three dropped out with engine problems, leaving Grashio with 2Lts. I.B. "Jack" Donalson and Augustus Williams. When Grashio sighted several enemy aircraft below he led them into the attack. 2Lt. Donalson shot down two Zeros over Clark Field and then shot down another over Nichols a few minutes later. Grashio became separated during the fight and was pursued by two Zeros on his tail; a cannon shell hit his port wing but he was able to dive away to safety.

2Lt. Max **Louk** was KIA during the battle. (AAF)

Clockwise from Top Left: **1).** 1Lt. Grant **Mahony** shot down a Zero to finally become an ace on 17 April 1944. (AAF); **2).** 2Lt. Herbert **Ellis**' victory was credited in Squadron records but not in post war official records. During the combat Ellis was forced to make a high speed bail out at low altitude, but made it to the ground safely. (AAF) **3.** 2Lt. I.B. "Jack" **Donalson** shot down two Zeros over Clark Field, then shot down another over Nichols a few minutes later to become the first AAC pilot in the Philippines to score a triple. (AAF) **4).** 1Lt. Samuel **Grashio**. (AAF)

2Lt. Ben **Brown** shot down a Zero for his first of three victories. (AAF)

34PS

The 34th Squadron pilots waiting at Del Carmen saw the smoke rising from Clark Field and took off in their P-35s without orders. Before reaching Clark, two Zeros were encountered in a cloud base at 6,000 feet and were driven off. 1Lt. Samuel Marett's guns failed to operate and he returned to base, leaving 2Lt. Ben Brown to lead the squadron. Brown proceeded to Clark at about 8,000 feet and was attacked by four aggressive Zero pilots. Brown got a shot in at 90 degree deflection and downed a Zero, but the other inexperienced P-35 pilots were unable to score any more victories. There are reports that 2Lt. Stewart Robb was also credited with a victory. Robb's P-40 suffered heavy damaged and he made a successful dead stick landing at Del Carmen.

8 December 1941: Accounting

Despite losing 10 Zeros, the first Japanese attack in the Philippines was a notable success, with Clark Field suffering particularly heavy damage. The Japanese bombers destroyed hangars, shops, supply buildings, and the crucial communications center that cut off Clark and prevented any attempt to direct the pursuits from the ground. Bombing had not been particularly effective against the dispersed B-17s, but enemy fighters systematically chose a target and concentrated their machine gun fire, destroying 18 B-17s. At Iba, eight aircraft were destroyed on the ground and its important radar installation was temporarily inoperable. American air power had been reduced by half, with 18 of 35 B-17s destroyed, 55 of 105 P-40s lost either in combat or on the ground, and of the remaining P-35s no more than 15 were operational. The aged B-18s, B-10s, and other obsolete aircraft also were victims of the devastating Japanese bombing and strafing. The American losses on the ground appear to be 47 to 49 aircraft, while the Japanese claimed that 15 AAC aircraft were destroyed in air combat with nine probables and one crash landing. Ground personnel casualties were 100 dead and 250 wounded.

The heavy pursuit fighter losses required a reallocation of the remaining aircraft and pilots. The 3PS at Iba had taken the heaviest losses, and its air echelon and remaining aircraft were absorbed into 1Lt. Wagner's 17th Squadron, which was relocated to Clark, and into the 21st Squadron, which remained at Nichols. The 20PS was down to three P-40s, but two more were later salvaged. The ground echelon of the 3rd was transferred to Nichols Field to bring the 34th Squadron up to strength. During the evening of 8/9 December the ground crews at Clark Field cannibalized aircraft which had been badly damaged to repair less damaged aircraft to get them airworthy.

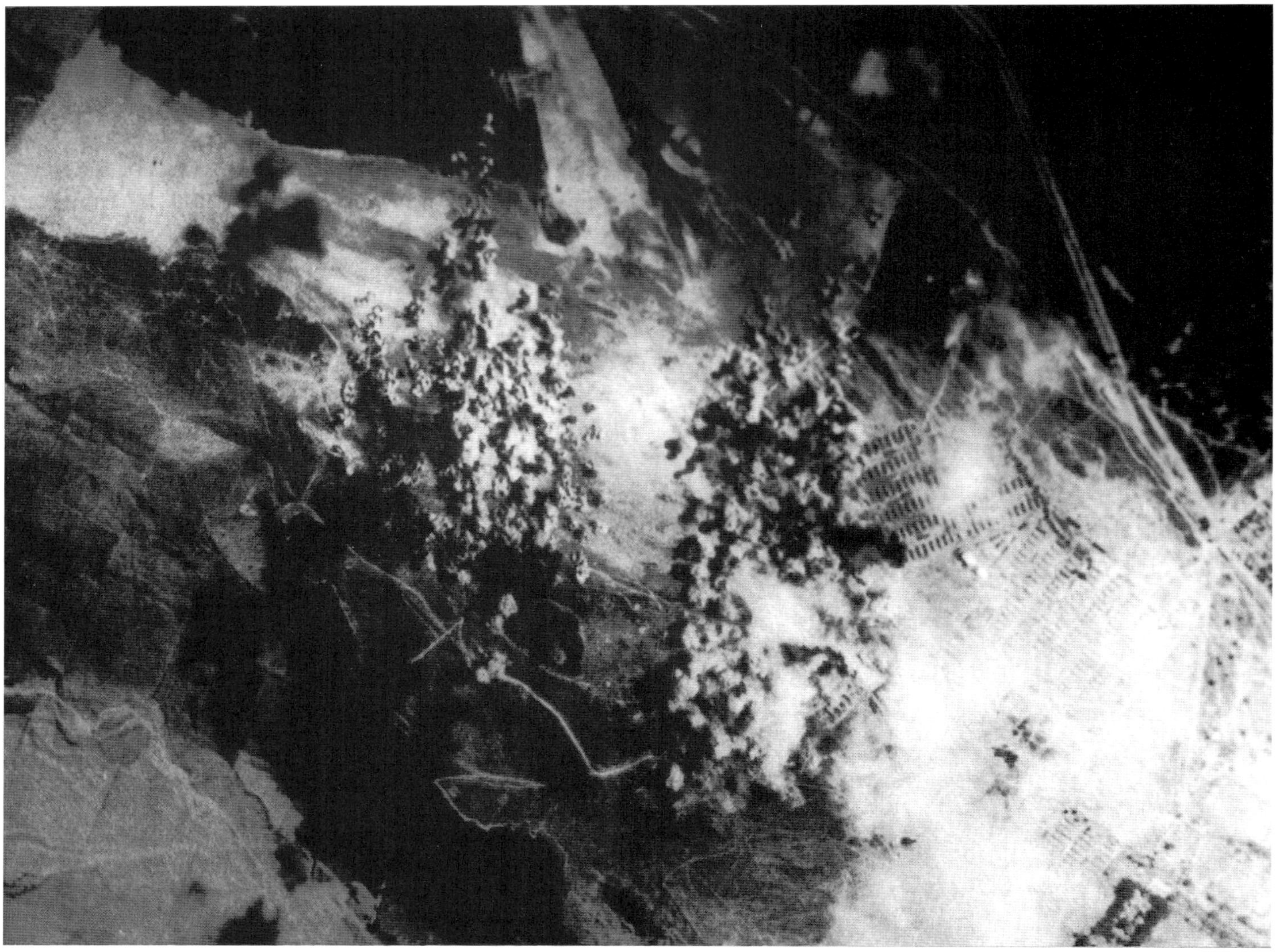

25

CAN WE KEEP IT UP?

9 December 1941

At 0300 the Japanese sent nine Bettys to bomb Nichols Field and Fort Stanley, and three officers and enlisted men were killed and 15 wounded, one hangar was destroyed by fire, and two B-18s were damaged. Before their transfer to Clark, one flight of six P-40s of the 17PS led by 1Lt. William Feallock was sent up to intercept these Bettys, and the darkness and dust on the field again hindered the take off and caused 2Lt. Lawrence Lodin to become disoriented and crash into a parked aircraft. The other P-40s were unable to make the interception in the dark.

Although the remainder of the day was relatively quiet, the first scramble of the morning resulted in two 21PS P-40s colliding at Clark Field. 2Lt. Robert Clark's fighter then went out of control and crashed into one of the damaged but repairable B-17s, and Clark was killed and his P-40 and the B-17 were destroyed.

1Lt. George **Kiser** shot down two of the escorting Zeros. (AAF)

10 December 1941

During the night of 9/10 December USAFFE headquarters received reports of large Japanese invasion convoys carrying Lt.Gen. Masaharu Homma's infantry divisions approaching the northern coast of Luzon, causing plans for bombing attacks on Formosa to be canceled. B-17s of the 19th Bombardment Group, plus the 17th and 34th Pursuit Squadrons, made preparations to attack the convoys during the morning of 10 December. These Flying Fortresses had been transferred from Mindanao to replace those lost on 8 December. Shortly after dawn a patrolling PatWing 10 PBY and 1Lt. Grant Mahony of the 3PS on a lone recon both located the Japanese convoy off Vigan and returned with critical information concerning their number, size, and course of the ships.

17PS

PatWing 10 sent out five Catalinas armed with 500 pound bombs and five B-17s loaded with 100 pound demolition bombs took off from Clark to attack the Japanese Invasion Fleet. This air attack force was to be joined by 17th Squadron P-40Es at the target area. After the 17th and 20th Squadrons' aircraft were combined, 17PS CO Boyd Wagner and 20PS CO Joseph Moore flipped a coin to determine which squadron would fly the first mission under the new agreement for squadrons to alternate missions. After winning the toss Wagner selected John Brownewell and Allison Strauss to lead the two flights of six P-40s in a strafing attack. After takeoff, Brownewell found that his guns would not test fire and Jack Dale moved up to lead his flight. The flights became separated on their way to Vigan, as they entered thick overcast soon after take off. They reached the invasion shipping at 0715 and began strafing the destroyers and a cruiser in the area. The .50 caliber machine gun bullets did little damage and several of the pilots experienced malfunctioning guns. Dale and Strauss led their flights back to Clark in the face of increasing enemy AA fire.

William Sheppard had been left behind when the 17th left for Vigan, but at 0900 he took off in his newly repaired P-40 to join the squadron at Vigan. As he approached Vigan, Sheppard was unexpectedly joined by another P-40 and three miles inland from the Luzon coast near Vigan, Sheppard and the other pilot saw three twin-engined Japanese bombers at about their altitude of 15,000 feet. In his first pass on the unsuspecting Japanese, Sheppard saw that only two of his six guns were firing. He turned into the bombers for a second and then a third pass, knocking pieces off the bombers, but receiving return fire from the bomber's gunners. Soon his coolant warning light flashed and Sheppard realized that he would have to bail out or land. He tried to leave the area of the Japanese beachhead at Vigan to avoid possible capture and carefully flew the stricken P-40 up the river valley toward Bangued. A few minutes later the P-40's Allison engine burst into flames, forcing Sheppard to bail out. After landing safely he joined some Filipinos who took him to the town of Bangued, where he met the Mayor and another American pilot, Edward Houseman, who had also bailed out during the 34PS' mission over Vigan. The two pilots returned to their unit a week later and Sheppard reported that the unit had engaged Ki-48 Lilys that were supporting their troops in the Vigan area. Sheppard downed two, while 1Lt. George Kiser of Moore's flight shot down two of the escorting Zeros and 2Lt. Allison Strauss had another.

Left: 1Lt. William **Sheppard** shot down two Lily bombers, but had to bail out safely on the way home due to engine failure. (AAF) Right: 1Lt. Joseph **Moore** led his flight to strafe the ships, landing barges, and shore installations. (AAF)

34PS

In the meantime, 16 P-35As of the 34PS had flown up from Del Carmen to stage through Clark to attack the convoy. Two flights of eight P-35s led by 1Lt. Samuel Marett took off, but eight pilots had to soon return due to mechanical problems experienced by their aging fighters. One more reached the target area, but its pilot had to bail out due to engine failure. Marett had miscalculated the time required for the slow P-35s to reach Vigan and finally arrived just as the P-40s and B-17s

Opposite (Clockwise from Top):
Clark Field under Japanese attack on 8 December. (AAF); US Propaganda photo of a destroyed P-35A of the 34PS after the attack on Nichols Field. (AAF); Another P-35A of the 34PS destroyed at Nichols Field. (AAF)

completed two bombing runs on the transports, which were unloading troops and supplies. The P-35 pilots, with no armor protection or self-sealing tanks, repeatedly strafed the invasion shipping with only two .30 caliber and two .50 caliber machine guns. Despite intense antiaircraft fire, Marett made repeated passes on a minesweeper that finally exploded. The violent explosion (the magazine?) tore the wing off his fighter, sending it and Marett tumbling into the sea. The B-17s and pursuits hit a number of vessels, but apparently only one transport was sunk, and regardless of the sacrifices of the strafers, the initial Japanese landings were successful, not only at Vigan, but in the Aparri area, on the northern tip of the island of Luzon. When the six 34PS survivors landed at Del Carmen they taxied into line with the eight P-35s that had been forced to abort the mission. Despite cloud cover at Del Carmen 12 Japanese Zeros swept over the field strafing, destroying 12 P-35s and damaging six others which were in various stages of repair or disrepair. Fuel storage and bowsers were destroyed, putting Del Carmen temporarily out of service.

20PS

After their return to Clark Field from their attack on Vigan at 0845, the 17PS' 12 P-40s were being refueled and rearmed. Joseph Moore was assigning pilots from his 20PS to fly the second Vigan mission as per the rotation he and Wagner had agreed on. Many of Moore's pilots had little or no time in the P-40E and had spent the previous night with flashlights examining the cockpit and different control arrangement! At an early morning briefing Moore explained the different characteristics of the heavier E Model as compared to their B Model. Moore and his Wingman, Randall Keator, threw up dust as they took off. Edwin Gilmore didn't see a bomb crater in front of him, and as his fighter tipped into the hole his prop hit the ground. The other pilots in the flight had problems with the dust and then became separated in the overcast and carried out the mission as individuals. When Keator arrived over the target area he dove on a transport and began firing, but only two guns functioned and then the other quit as he reached the transport. After he cleared the ship he remained low over the water to avoid the AA fire bursting just above him. Once out of AA range Keator began to pull up and spotted several enemy fighters diving on him from about 8,000 feet. Keator throttled forward, trying to outrun the Japanese, and soon left them behind. On his return to base, 2Lt. Morgan McCowan, unused to landing the P-40E, went out of control and was killed, as was 1Lt. Glen Alder on the ground.

3PS/17PS/20PS/21PS

A Japanese formation was reported to be approaching Clark and orders were given for all aircraft to take off, so the pilots of the 17th, 20th, and 21st Squadrons engaged in an unruly scramble to get airborne in the P-40s that had not been adequately refueled or rearmed. 2Lt. Robert Newman, detached to the 21PS, became disoriented in the dust stirred up by the P-40s taking off ahead of him and collided with the wing of a B-17, destroying the bomber, but he walked away from the accident. 21PS CO Edward Dyess took off without his goggles, helmet, and parachute, and was dazzled when he broke out of the overcast and almost hit Wagner's P-40. Edwin Gilmore of the 20PS and Allison Strauss of the 17PS joined ranks, and when they approached Del Carmen, they noticed Zeros above the overcast, preparing for a strafing run on the base. Gilmore dove from 2,000 feet and fired, but after only one burst his guns stopped. He unsuccessfully tried the hydraulic gun charger but was unfamiliar with the E model, and did not know the chargers had been disconnected. He looked back at the Zero, which was trailing some smoke, and although he left without seeing it go down he was given credit for a victory.

2Lt. Clark **Gies** shot down two Zeros for his only victories, but his fighter was so badly damaged during the combat that it had to be written off after landing. (AAF)

Jack Dale also had problems with his guns but before reaching Del Carmen, and got four of the six to fire at that time, but when he closed to 150 yards of a Zero strafer all his guns failed and he had to break away for Nichols Field to have the guns cleared manually. When Parker Gies and Henry Rancke arrived over Del Carmen with the 20PS they dove through the overcast and Gies opened fire into an enemy strafer and sent it smoking into the ground. When Gies rejoined Rancke, they immediately were attacked by three Zeros and Gies turned into them and set one aflame, causing the other two to break away. Gies' fighter was badly damaged, but he was able to fly it back to Clark. This combat marked the end of the 34PS flying together as a squadron. Of the 15 P-35As that were on the field at the time of the Japanese attack, seven were destroyed by the strafers and three were badly damaged, leaving only five, which were all out of commission. Fortunately, the squadron lost no personnel. Later that afternoon Ben Brown, who became the 34th's CO after Marett's death, ordered the 34th personnel to evacuate the field.

During the 1230 scramble from Clark, 24th Group Headquarters at Clark reported that the Japanese bombers had flown over Clark without attacking and were apparently heading toward Manila instead. The airborne pilots were ordered to intercept the enemy bombers over Manila. 2Lt. John Posten was halfway to Manila when he encountered Zeros and, in his inexperience, entered into a dogfight with one of them. Soon his fuel tank, both wings, and the tail had been peppered by the Japanese pilot and Posten decided to break off combat by diving steeply away from 15,000 feet. Dyess saw the bombers dropping their bombs on the dock area, and before climbing to attack he decided to test his guns and nothing happened. He tried them again for a third time without result and dejectedly returned to base.

Two 20PS pilots had close calls during the mission. 2Lt. Milton Woodside had taken off in a P-40 that had not been rearmed and was attacked by Zeros and had to bail out. 2Lt.Varian White was surprised by Zeros that started his engine on fire and he, too, bailed out safely.

1Lt. William Feallock's Ill-fated Flight

After covering Nichols Field, 1Lt. William Feallock of the 17PS was beginning to lead a flight of pilots from mixed squadrons down for a landing when the radio reported that Cavite naval base was being attacked by low-flying aircraft. With only enough gas for 10 minutes of combat and already in the landing pattern, Feallock radioed Nichols for order but was told to use his discretion. Feallock and his flight chose to attack a string of three Zeros at low altitude, five miles over Zablan, on the outskirts of Manila. Feallock retracted his landing gear and hoped that his guns, which had frozen previously at 20,000 feet on this mission, would fire. Feallock closed on one of the Zeros and when he fired nothing happened, and the Zero pilot quickly got on Feallock's tail. Feallock decided that his only chance was to lead his pursuer into friendly AA guns around Nichols Field. On his way at tree top level Feallock's aircraft was hit and began to burn. He pulled his stricken ship up to 200 feet, rolled back the canopy, and jumped, spraining both ankles as he landed only feet away from his burning fighter that was cooking off the ammunition that he was unable to fire. 2Lt. Andrew Krieger (3PS) was about to fire on a Zero when his engine quit and the Zeros got on his tail and fired, putting his fighter into a spin. Somehow, Krieger was able to recover from the deadly spin with his engine cutting in and out. Meanwhile, the Zeros continued to follow while Krieger used the last of his fuel to fly low through ravines, around hills, and just over the trees. Finally, his engine stopped and he bailed out with the Japanese strafing him. He landed safely and returned to base. 1Lt. Ray Gehrig (3PS) of Feallock's flight was attacked by three diving Zeros and was unable to turn into them as his guns, too, were not firing. A cannon shell exploded and blew out his canopy and most of his instruments. Gehrig went into a tight turn and entered some clouds to escape. Bleeding and without instruments, he approached Del Carmen and saw Zeros strafing there and headed east to a small civilian field at Plaridel, 25 miles southeast of Del Carmen. As he neared the field and was lowering the gear by hand his engine stopped, and his fighter floated down into the trees and crashed. Gehrig suffered a broken cheekbone and upper jaw when his face hit the gunsight. A fourth pilot in Feallock's luckless flight was 2Lt. William Rowe (17PS), who was jumped by Zeros but was unable to shake them by diving away. He headed back as fast as he could toward Del Carmen, but Rowe found that the field was being strafed. He headed toward Clark with the Zeros close behind. Rowe went into a half roll and dove straight down at top speed, and when he pulled out he had lost his pursuers. The upset and anxious Rowe cut off a B-17 as it was landing at Clark but landed safely. 1Lt. Edward Erickson (17PS) was too low to bail out of his crippled fighter and crash landed on the field and careened into a fuel truck which exploded, but Erickson was somehow blown clear and was not injured. 2Lt. Augustus Williams of the 21PS was also patrolling over Nichols, and as he was about to run out of fuel he approached Nichols to land but was warned that fighters were strafing the field. He was out of gas in his landing approach and saw no strafers, so he decided to land. As he touched down he saw planes strafing hangars and aircraft at the far end of the field. He rolled down the runway and hurriedly parked his fighter and took refuge. 2Lt. John Burns was flying with Williams and also was nearly out of fuel, so he decided to head for a Philippine Army Air Force base 60 miles due north of Manila. On approaching the field he saw it was covered with oil drum obstacles and buzzed it so the Filipinos would remove them. The anxious Burns landed before the field was cleared and crash landed through the drums unhurt, but his P-40E was destroyed.

17PS

At 1235 Grant Mahony's seven ship flight had just taken off from Nichols and were at about 2,000 feet when they were bounced by the Zeros that minutes earlier had attacked Feallock's flight. The totally surprised Americans broke away in all directions. When the combat was over, of the seven fighters that took off only Mahony and 2Lts. Donald Steele, Robert Hanson, and A.W. Balfanz had managed to get their P-40s back to base safely. 2Lt. Wilson Glover's instrument panel was hit by a 20-mm shell and soon his electrical system was out and his engine overheated. Glover headed for Clark Field, but he was forced to bail out safely over San Fernando. 2Lt. James Phillips was chasing two Zeros that had been attacking two PBY Catalina flying boats when a Zero got on his tail. Phillips headed for the safety of US Marine antiaircraft at the Cavite base, but when the Marines fired on the Zero they hit Phillips' P-40 instead, and he had to bail out over Manila Bay, where he was picked up by the Navy. Shortly after his takeoff, 2Lt. Forrest Hobrecht was flying low over Nichols Field during the enemy strafing raid and a Zero got on his tail and set his P-40 on fire. While bailing out he hit the stabilizer and fell to the ground with his chute unopened.

Capt. Jesus **Villamor** led the small Philippines Air Force in the P-26 Peashooter and scored a Zero victory. (AAF)

Philippines Air Force

The small Philippine Air Force had made a valiant effort to intercept the Japanese on 10 December when Capt. Jesus Villamor led three P-26s against the bombers raiding Zablan. Lt. Jose Gozar attacked one of the bombers, and when his guns jammed he attempted to ram the aircraft. The enemy bomber broke and ran, and the little Peashooter pursuit plane was unable to overtake it. Two days later, Villamor led six P-26s against Japanese bombers and he awarded each of his pilots 1/6th victory for downing an enemy aircraft. Villamor was also successful in downing one of them before Zeros came on the scene and aircraft scattered everywhere. The P-26 was no match for the Zero, and the Philippine pilots were fortunate to lose only two aircraft and one pilot, thus ending combat for the Philippine Air Force.

Accounting for 10 December

The Americans shot down just seven Japanese aircraft in the combat. Of the 51 P-40s available for operations at the start of the day, only 28, including six requiring repairs, were available, for a loss of 23. Also, 10 P-35As had been destroyed or heavily damaged and only five remained (not including one or two P-26s). The 10 December loss of 33 fighters nearly matched the 35 lost on the 8th. Although incredibly only Hobrecht was KIA, eight others had to crash land or bail out; though in some cases this was due to lack of fuel, their fighters were nonetheless out of action.

Japanese records indicated an overly optimistic 30 destroyed and three probables in the air and 34 on the ground. The Japanese bombers had attacked at altitudes out of reach of the P-40s and dropped their bombs very effectively on the Manila docks. Without opposition they continued on toward Nichols Field and the Navy base at Cavite. Nichols was heavily bombed and for all practical purposes was put out of the war. The entire shipyards, warehouses, and quarters at Cavite were destroyed by the heavy bombardment.

Mainly, the pilots learned that their P-40s were no match for the agile Zeros and suffered from having a maximum altitude disadvantage. The pilots reported an inordinate number of gun failures. The guns jammed because of either ammunition feeding problems or the residue of cold hardened Cosmoline left around the breech block. The pilots could not remedy the situation in the air and the guns had to be cleared and recharged on the ground. In addition, the pilots regularly found themselves having to take off to intercept with only a few minutes warning of an incoming attack because of the absence of any functioning air warning system.

With over 70% of its aircraft destroyed after only three days of the campaign, the 24th Pursuit Group now had a large surplus of pilots in relation to aircraft, and a decision was made to reserve the remaining aircraft for the most senior and experienced pilots of the group. The others were assigned to non-flying duties in communications, transportation, and other ground support activities of the USAFFE.

The USN still had 24 PBYs in service for recon, but this figure would soon change. Gen. Brereton ordered that there would be no further interception missions for the pursuits except on specific orders. Those that remained were to be used for observation and reconnaissance duties in place of the 2nd Observation Squadron, which had been decimated during the first two days of the war. So, after 10 December, instead of carrying out actual combat missions, American pursuit aircraft in the Philippines were assigned areas for reconnaissance patrols: the 21st and 34th Squadrons combined to cover southern Luzon, while the 17th and 20th were assigned the northern part of the island.

11 December 1941: Situation

The decision to reserve pursuit aircraft for reconnaissance missions meant that American bases on Luzon would be even more vulnerable to enemy air attack, and the Japanese were free to bomb targets in the Philippines at will. The prospect of enemy land-based planes within 250 miles of Manila made it necessary for American heavy bombers to abandon Luzon bases. Consequently, before the completion of the missions of 10 December, it had been decided to dispatch the remaining B-17s to Del Monte. The distance of Del Monte from the principal enemy forces now on Luzon decreased the striking potential of the Far East Air Force and the enemy landings were continuing almost unopposed.

The Japanese now had unchallenged air supremacy over the Philippines, and the only support the FEAF could provide during the withdrawal of the Army to Bataan was reconnaissance missions flown by pursuit aircraft. The AAC American heavy bombers had already been forced to move their base 600 miles south of Clark Field to Del Monte, and then the threat of Japanese air attack and lack of maintenance facilities there forced a 1,600 mile move to Darwin, Australia. Despite the decision to transfer all heavy bombers to Australia, there was no intention of permanently abandoning the defense of the Philippines, as both MacArthur and Brereton believed that the Philippines could be reinforced. To do this Brereton emphasized that time was critical, as available reinforcement routes could soon be closed by the Japanese advance, and on 14 December he stated that 10 squadrons of pursuit aircraft were an immediate requirement. According to Brereton, this meant that, in addition to the 52 A-24s and 10 pursuit aircraft which were expected to arrive in Australia before the end of the month, it would be "advantageous" to have 200 pursuit and 60 dive bombers delivered by aircraft carrier. Also, 65 heavy bombers were authorized to be ferried via the South Atlantic and India route. He believed that airfields for these planes could be defended and maintained satisfactorily, and that airfield construction following the outbreak of war had been accelerated. Brereton decided to test the effectiveness of bombardment missions conducted from Australian bases, which were almost 2,000 miles from the Philippines front lines, by using Del Monte as an advanced base for refueling. However, Del Monte was being bombed regularly, and the few bombardment missions had little effect in halting the Japanese advance. So during this period AAC pursuit aircraft were flying more frequently than AAC bombers, with the pursuits flying reconnaissance and observation missions; usually in pairs, but many times a lone aircraft was sent out against great odds.

11 December 1941

Poor weather would give the Americans a respite. Because of the loss of aircraft there were more pilots than aircraft available, and only experienced pilots were assigned to missions. Precious fighters were allocated for reconnaissance and were ordered to engage in combat only in "self defense." At Clark, 2Lt. Robert Newman's P-40 crashed into a B-17, and while there were no casualties, both aircraft were destroyed.

12 December 1941

On the morning of 12 December, 1Lt. Boyd Wagner (17PS) took off from Clark Field on a reconnaissance patrol of the Japanese invasion shipping at Aparri, in northern Luzon. He had to rely on his compass and dead reckoning to fly through the overcast to Aparri. At approximately 200 miles he descended through the overcast and found himself just over two enemy destroyers that opened AA fire on him. He "turned nose down and dove within a few feet of the water to avoid the heavy barrage." He then flew inland "directly into the morning sun" and saw tracers flying by his canopy. He looked back and saw two enemy fighters on his tail and three more above. Wagner reported that he "pulled nose up, directly into the sun at full throttle…The two Nippos lost me and I went into a half barrel roll onto their tails….They were in close formation and both burst into flames almost simultaneously." However Walter Edmonds, in his book *They Fought with What They Had*, contradicts Wagner's narrative, describing his combat as occurring just north of Aparri Airfield when he was bounced by four Ki-27 Nates and, using previous combat experience, he dove his heavier P-40 to the deck trying to outrun the enemy fighters. Only two Nates were able to follow, but these pilots stayed on Wagner's tail until Wagner "suddenly throttled back and let the astonished enemy flash past," putting Wagner's P-40 on their tails. Before the enemy pilots were able to take evasive action, Wagner quickly fired and sent them both down in flames. Wagner approached Aparri Airfield and surprised 12 enemy aircraft parked in a row and made two firing passes, and "saw five of them burst into flames. As he pulled up from his second pass three more Nates attacked Wagner: "I dropped my empty belly tanks...and dived close to the ground, then gave it the needle and easily outdistanced them." Wagner goes on to say that he saw "two columns of black smoke, but "My gas was running low so I returned home." Reliable source Frank Olynyk gives Wagner credit for the first two Nates using a 29 December 1941 *Life Magazine* article by Walter Edmonds ("Boyd Wagner's Story: America's First Ace Tells How He Shot Down First Two Planes"). He uses the Official 24th Fighter Group History as the source for the second two, but adds may be "folklore." According to Chris Shores, Brian Cull, and

1Lt. Boyd **Wagner** claimed four victories, but there is some doubt as to the veracity of his claims. (AAF)

Yashuo Izawa in their book *Bloody Shambles*, there is no confirmation in the incomplete Japanese records of Ki-27s lost on the 12th except for one destroyed in a strafing attack. However, enemy records do show that 18 Nates were lost to all causes between 8 and 15 December.

That afternoon 1Lt. Robert Hanson of the 3PS flew cover for Grant Mahony, whose P-40 was armed with bombs to attack the railway in the Legaspi landing area. After Mahony dropped his bombs Hanson came down and strafed the Legaspi Airstrip through heavy AA fire, and then strafed the transports and landing barges. As he turned to make another strafing run he saw a flying boat (or cruiser floatplane?) and shot it down.

14 December 1941: 17PS

In the early evening 1Lt. Grant Mahony took off on a lone recon over Legaspi Airfield and damaged two Zeros and five Bettys during his strafing attack.

16 December 1941: 17PS

During the early morning 2Lt. Russell Church had flown a recon mission to Vigan and found that the enemy had flown in 25 more fighters, and several more troopships had arrived. Lore has it that Wagner and 3PS CO Capt. Joseph Moore had volunteered to lead an unauthorized mission to Vigan and flipped a coin. Wagner won, and Wagner and Church were to attack the area with three 30 pound (or six 20 pound?) fragmentation bombs, while 2Lt. Allison Strauss was to fly top cover for the duo. They took off at 0600 from Iba and reached the target area at sunrise. Wagner assigned Strauss to top cover while he and Church descended to 2,500 feet into heavy enemy AA fire from the shipping below. Wagner led the attack with Church only a few hundred feet behind and dropped his bombs safely, getting some apparent hits. As he went into a dive Church's P-40 received a direct hit from AA fire from the alerted enemy forces, setting his aircraft on fire, but he continued to head for Aparri Airfield, where he released his bombs on parked enemy fighters in a "perfectly executed attack," stated Wagner. Wagner goes on: "For seconds it seemed that Russell would be able to regain control but the plane suddenly rocked wildly and plunged sideways to earth." After Church went down Wagner was joined by Strauss and made five vengeful strafing attacks on the enemy field. The enemy pilots were cut down as they raced for their fighters, but on his final pass Wagner spotted a lone Nate taking off on the far end of the field and rolled over and shot it down. The two Americans reported 17 enemy aircraft destroyed or burning, and numerous enemy personnel dead or wounded were left on the field. The mission was the most devastating suffered by the Japanese to date and would make Wagner America's first ace and win him the DFC, but HQ was not particularly happy with the unauthorized success.

1Lt. Grant **Mahony** took off on a lone recon over Legaspi Airfield and strafed and damaged five enemy aircraft on the ground. (AAF)

1Lt. Boyd **Wagner**. (L) and 2Lt. Russell **Church** strafed Vigan airfield, and Church was hit and went down. Wagner would become an ace when he shot down a Nate. (AAF)

18-19 December 1941: Clagett and Brereton Leave Australia

On the 19th the Japanese finally discovered Del Monte Airfield and its B-17s and proceeded to dispatch a strafing attack. This attack prompted both Generals Clagett and Brereton to leave the Philippines for Batchelor Field, Australia, to establish a new headquarters. Clagett left via the last B-17 and Brereton and members of his staff in two PBYs on the 24th.

Upon his arrival in Australia Clagett was relegated to be the Commanding General of the US Army supply base at Townsville, Australia, from 1942-1943, and then Commanding General of Sheppard Field, TX, until he retired in 1944 due to a "disability in line of duty." However, an underlying reason for Clagett's demotion was that he was said to be a notorious alcoholic. During an official banquet in China in 1941, Clagett and aide Lester Maitland became so ingloriously drunk that the State Department wanted them recalled and MacArthur did nothing to defend them, but they remained in their postings. So it appears "disability in line of duty" was a euphemism for alcoholism (?).

18-21 December 1941: 27PS

During this period the 27th Group, located in the Manila area, also became involved in the confusion of the retreat. On 18 December the Group's CO, Maj. John Davies, and a dozen other officers left Luzon for Australia to pick up and return with the overdue A-24 dive bombers. Consequently, on 21 December the Squadron had been ordered to prepare new fields at Lipa, 40 miles south of Manila, to handle the A-24s. Three days later, however, just after these bases had been completed and occupied, another order directed all squadrons to evacuate their bases and to proceed to Manila and evacuate to Bataan.

22 December 1941: Further Japanese Landings

On 22 December the Japanese made two further landings in the Lingayen Gulf area, employing 76 transports carrying 80,000 troops and covered by two cruisers and 20 destroyers, as well as Ki-27s from the 4th Flying Battalion. The American and Philippine infantry were totally outnumbered and overwhelmed, and were only able to fight a delaying action. The Interceptor Command decided to use all its remaining serviceable aircraft against the landings at San Miguel Bay, but the FEAF's P-40s ineffectively opposed the landings.

17PS

The 17PS had six P-40s available with four armed with underwing bombs. Wagner chose 2Lts. Steven Crosby, William Hennon, George Kiser, William Sheppard, and Walter Wilcox to fly the 0545 mission to attack the Japanese invasion force at Lingayen Gulf. Four P-40Es carried six 30 pound fragmentation bombs under their wings. Immediately after takeoff, the P-40s entered a solid overcast extending up to 10,000 feet and Wagner and his Wingman Hennon kept circling the field, trying to form up with the rest of the flight, but could not find the others. Finally, after about an hour circling fruitlessly they headed to Lingayen, arriving at about 0715. They spotted "80 to 90" transports laying in a four or five mile line, with half of the transports about a half mile offshore and the other half in a parallel line three miles offshore. There were also numerous small boats and barges close to shore. Wagner and Hennon dove on the small landing boats offshore and troops on the beach. The two then strafed the troops on the beach, who fired back on them with their small arms. Wagner and Hennon became separated. Hennon was attacked by seven Nates and climbed into a cloud to evade them. When he exited the cloud he found even more above him at about 6,000 feet. Hennon ignored them to make one more strafing pass on the troops and quickly headed into the mountains chased by the Nates. Hennon escaped under the clouds and headed down a valley to central Luzon and Clark. Meanwhile, Wagner encountered very heavy AA fire while strafing a cruiser and a minesweeper. Wagner was bounced by a number of bogeys that hit Wagner's cowling and shattered his windshield. A bullet hit his left shoulder and glass splinters and pieces of metal cut his face and both eyes. Kiser and Wilcox had finally arrived and guided their half-blinded CO back to base. Except for Wagner and Hennon, the other 17PS pilots had all arrived individually over Lingayen and strafed the barges and troops until they expended all their ammunition. Crosby had been impressed by the sight of a huge fleet of transports and warships below as Sheppard set a transport afire, but had a Nate close on his tail and evaded it with steep dives and high G-turns into the overcast. Sheppard spotted a destroyer (?) and expended his ammunition on it into heavy antiaircraft fire. Sheppard's plane was hit by the AA fire on the mission, and on his approach to Clark his engine quit, and he made a dead stick landing. After landing his ground crew counted over 200 holes in his fighter, which was written off. After landing safely Wagner had the glass removed from his eyes but had to be evacuated to Australia.

20PS

Six 20PS also left to attack the Lingayen invasion, but only 1Lt. Joseph Moore and 2Lts. Carl Gies and Varian White arrived at Lingayen. They strafed the shipping and troops through heavy AA fire and all returned safely but shaken by the experience.

At the end of the day only 12 P-40s (17PS) and six P-35s (34PS) of the 24th Group were serviceable. Thus far heavy casualties had been sustained by trained personnel, including 17 killed and 16 wounded, one of which was the newly made hero, 1Lt. Boyd Wagner.

On 22 December, the Japanese made two further invasion landings in the Lingayen Gulf area employing 76 transports carrying 80,000 troops and covered by two cruisers and 20 destroyers, as well as Ki-27s from the 4th Flying Battalion. (AFHRC)

Nine of the 14 B-17s based at Batchelor (Australia) were flown into Del Monte the previous evening to attack the Japanese convoy and then refuel at San Marcelino for the return flight to Batchelor. Because they had to be fitted with auxiliary bomb bay fuel tanks these bombers were only able to carry half their normal bomb load (four 500 pound bombs). Shortly after take off only four B-17s remained to attack the convoy. They were attacked by 14 enemy fighters and the B-17s were separated; only one arrived over the target and dropped its bombs without result.

24 December 1941: 20PS/17PS

The Japanese had made a new landing at Lamon Bay, only 60 miles southwest of Manila, and the V Interceptor Command decided to oppose it with four P-35As of the 20PS and four P-40s of the 17PS from Clark Field.

20PS

In the late morning Joseph Moore asked for four 20PS volunteers, and 1Lt. Marshall Anderson volunteered to lead the flight of P-35As in the first attack, which included Hugh Marble, William Carter, and LaMar Gillett (17PS). The four P-35As had been hidden under trees and were in well-worn condition. They arrived over the target area about noon and descended below the overcast to strafe the Japanese shipping and the troops on the shore. Suddenly, several Zeros broke through the overcast and attacked the P-35As. At this point records are muddled, with Anderson and Gillette each claiming to have shot down a Zero, but Japanese records show that only one Zero was lost that day. Anderson's P-35A was badly damaged and he crash landed safely at Nichols.

17PS

The 17PS moved to Pilar airstrip on Bataan, while the remaining aircraft (12 patched P-40s and six P-35s) flew up to attack the 40 transports in the Bay. Four P35s arrived over Lamon Bay and dropped fragmentation bombs and made many strafing runs, causing minor damage, but two of the P-35s were so badly damaged that they crashed before reaching their base. One of these P-35s was flown by 2Lt. James Rowland, who crashed into Laguna de Bay and was rescued by a fisherman. Japanese records show that one Zero had been shot down, but there are no claims made by either the 17PS or the Filipino 6PS, which flew its last mission of the war.

24 December 1941: Evacuation

After the mission the pilots were notified that all AAC units were to evacuate their Luzon bases as part of the general withdrawal to Bataan. By noon on Christmas Eve the Japanese advance from the north threatened Clark Field. The evacuation began on 24 December, and the pursuits were to be based first on three newly constructed fields at the head of Bataan Peninsula. If the Japanese continued to close in, these bases were to be evacuated and the pursuits were to evacuate to three fields nearer the sea: Miraveles, Cabcaben, and Bataan. The aircraft were to be flown by pilots chosen from the 24PG, and the remainder of the Group personnel, except for sufficient enlisted men for maintenance, were to be posted as infantry reserves of the 2nd Infantry Regiment (Provisional) and assigned it to the 71st Division.

Theoretically, the intent of all operations in Australia was the reinforcement and maintenance of the Philippines. But Brereton found that the situation in Australia did not justify any hope that reinforcements and supplies could reach MacArthur's beleaguered forces. A large convoy loaded with troops and supplies badly needed by MacArthur reached the Brisbane area on 22 December, where it was to be unloaded and transported overland to Darwin, on the north coast, for shipment to the Philippines. Numerous logistical problems, including the lack of necessary equipment, personnel, transportation, and communications facilities, plagued the shipment of these supplies to Darwin in time to help MacArthur's forces in the Philippines.

29-31 December 1941

On 29 December, 650 officers and enlisted men of the 19th Bomb Group had been transferred to Del Monte; thus, the only AAC personnel remaining on Bataan were men of the Interceptor Command, now under the capable Col. Harold George, who had arrived in the Philippines with Gen. Clagett over eight months before. George had only a skeleton staff, which in theory was to be expanded as personnel, supplies, and equipment began to arrive from the build up in Australia. On 31 December the first contingent of pursuit pilots had been evacuated from the Philippines in Philippine Air Lines Beechcrafts, and two days later a second contingent was flown out. The Beechcrafts were in poor condition, and the route south was under constant surveillance by enemy aircraft, but both flights managed to arrive in Darwin safely. From Darwin the pilots were flown to Brisbane.

The Interceptor Command at Bataan was now under the capable Col. Harold **George**. (AAF)

January 1942

Situation in the Philippines

Gen. Brett arrived in Darwin on 28 December 1941 as a newly promoted Lt. General, and was appointed Deputy Supreme Commander of the American-British-Dutch-Australian Command (ABDA), under Gen. Archibald Wavell, on 1 January 1942. Soon the Philippines were relegated to a secondary role in future Allied plans. On 2 January, Brett radioed General Marshall that he could only conduct minimal tactical operations until "a stable establishment" existed in Australia, and that this would involve the construction of a large air base at Darwin and a "major repair, maintenance, and supply base at Townsville." By this time the War Department also had, for all practical purposes, abandoned the large scale reinforcement of the Philippines, as it was evident that a large supply of equipment and personnel could not be built up in Australia before all facilities for transferring them to the Philippines was cut off by the enemy. There was no hope of ferrying short range aircraft to the Philippines or of breaking the Japanese sea blockade with naval escort.

Newly promoted Lt.Gen. George **Brett** arrives in Darwin to take over command of the ABDA in Java. (AAF)

FORMOSA
SOUTH
CHINA
SEA
PACIFIC
OCEAN
LUZON
Bataan
MANILA
Corregidor
MINDORO
SAMAR
PANAY
LEYTE
NEGROS
PALAWAN
Del Monte
MINDANAO
MALABANG
Davao
Gulf of
Davao
TARAKAN
BORNEO
HALMAHERA
SAMARINDA
CELEBES
BOEROE
CERAM
AMBOINA
NEW
GUINEA
MAKASSAR
TIMOR
KOEPANG
Darwin
Proposed Ferry Route
For Pursuit Planes
AUSTRALIA
FANITA
LANIER
1947

So by January 1942, the Philippines were no longer considered of primary importance to American Pacific strategy, except by MacArthur. The Japanese had forced the AAC to abandon its forward bases and had isolated the Philippines, and were pushing back the Allied line of resistance to the Netherlands East Indies. The fate of the Philippines was sealed. It had been decided in Washington that Germany was the Allies' primary enemy now that the United States had also declared war against Germany and Italy, and the majority of men and equipment would be sent to Europe. The personnel who remained in the Philippines would fight a holding action until they were overwhelmed by the Japanese and what few of them who could be evacuated would get out.

After Brereton's departure on 24 December the Interceptor Command had become, for all practical purposes, the entire Air Force in the Philippines. Col. Harold George became the V Interceptor Commander and was promoted to Brigadier General on 30 January 1942; he had, in fact, become the Commander of all Air Force personnel. By this time, the relationship of the Air Force in the Philippines to that in the East Indies was obviously vague, since each was carrying on its operations according to the exigencies of the moment. On paper, the situation became even more confused following a recommendation by Gen. Brett in January that the Far East Air Force should be redesignated as the Fifth Air Force. By 2 February Gen. Arnold had concurred with this recommendation, and three days later the Adjutant General officially authorized such a change. This did not affect air units in Java, however, as the Adjutant General's authorization had stated that the re-designation did not change the present assignment of units. At that time, the Far East was still officially assigned to the Philippines and the re-designation apparently did not apply to the units in Java or to those in Australia. Furthermore, high ranked personnel in the Philippines either did not know about the change or did not give official attention to it. The new organization, therefore, existed only on paper until 3 September 1942, when the Fifth Air Force was actually constituted and Maj.Gen. George Kenney put in command.

Meanwhile, the absence of US naval forces gave the Japanese complete freedom of movement around the Philippines and enabled them to land their forces anywhere unopposed. Two weeks after the war began the Japanese landed large forces on Luzon and were operating pursuit aircraft from fields at Aparri, Vigan, and Legaspi. With the Japanese capturing airfields and gaining air superiority, the defenders of Luzon suffered frequent and heavy air attacks. The Japanese had concentrated 80,000 to 100,000 troops along the Aringay-Agee-San Fabian line, which were opposed by approximately 40,000 Allied troops in partially equipped units. Except for surrender to these numerically superior forces, MacArthur's only logical course of action was to fight a delaying action on successive defensive lines in central Luzon with a final defensive position in Bataan, north of the island fortress of Corregidor. By 1 January MacArthur ordered the retreat to Bataan.

So long as Macarthur could hold Corregidor and the Manila Bay defenses, Manila's harbor and naval base would be of no value to the Japanese when they inevitably captured the Philippine capitol. On 24 December, in order to spare the civilian population, MacArthur removed the Philippine government from Manila to Corregidor, withdrew his forces toward Bataan, and then declared it an open city. The Japanese ignored the proclamation and continued to mercilessly bomb the defenseless city until its occupation on 2 January.

The tactical situation determined the employment of the Far East Air Force during the remainder of the Philippine Campaign. Because of overwhelming enemy air superiority and lack of suitable bases, the American heavy bombers had been withdrawn to Australia. The withdrawal of Army troops to Bataan meant that the few remaining pursuit aircraft had to move to bases on the Peninsula, which was accompanied by the move of Far East Air Force headquarters to Australia. On Christmas Day, when MacArthur's forces were withdrawn from Manila, Brereton and a small staff of officers had left Luzon in two PBY Catalinas for the south. Their mission was to establish the necessary bases and facilities for operations from Australia, staging through Mindanao against the Japanese on Luzon. One of the PBYs flew directly to Darwin, where Lt.Col. Charles Caldwell, the senior officer, established a temporary headquarters. Brereton, having been authorized to cooperate with forces of the Netherlands East Indies, as well as with Australian forces, stopped at Soerabaja and Batavia long enough to make preliminary arrangements for the use of air bases in that area. Upon arriving at Darwin, Brereton continued negotiations for the use of certain facilities in Australia. Prior to the outbreak of war MacArthur had been given the responsibility for developing the eastern end of the South Pacific ferry route, along with establishing a ferry route for pursuit aircraft from Australia to the Philippines via Koepang, Kendari, Sandakan, Balikpapan, Tarakan, Del Monte, and Santa Barbara (on Panay). As Commander of the Far East Air Force, Brereton held conferences with Australian and NEI representatives regarding the project. Plans for staff coordination and for the use of Australian facilities were formulated, and this groundwork was to be useful when the course of events forced the FEAF to require bases outside the Philippines.

Throughout the heroic defense of Bataan, pursuit aircraft of the 24PG served as all-purpose aircraft, acting as an entire air force. They bombed enemy landings on Bataan, strafed and bombed enemy aircraft at Nichols and Nielson Fields, attacked shipping in Subic Bay, intercepted numerous air attacks on Corregidor, photographed enemy artillery positions at Cavite, performed reconnaissance missions as far north as Lingayen, ferried medical supplies from Mindanao to Bataan, and transported personnel from Bataan and Corregidor to Mindanao.

Comparatively few Air Corps officers and enlisted men in the Philippines had an opportunity to perform the duties for which they had been trained. In the withdrawal, what probably concerned the AAC personnel most was whether they would be assigned to infantry units or retained by the Interceptor Command to fly the dozen or more remaining P-40s. From the middle of January, elements of all squadrons would participate in ground fighting, as pilot officers led ground crews against enemy beach positions or spearheaded an infantry advance. Except for a handful of pilots and maintenance men, the bulk of air personnel in Luzon were used as infantry and shared the fate of the other defenders of Bataan.

January 1942: Air Operations

After the wounded Wagner and 16 other pilots were ferried to Australia on 31 December and 1 January, the dwindling number of P-40s would be active, as they were constantly in the air conducting reconnaissance missions, occasionally patrolling the forward areas, strafing Japanese transport and communications centers and landing barges. Due to the confused situation and poor communications records of that time are incomplete and sketchy.

3 January 1942: 17PS

2nd Lts. Earl Stone and A.W. Balfanz were on a reconnaissance mission from Pilar Field and spotted Japanese aircraft on the field at Cabanatuan. Stone dove with Balfanz covering him and went into a strafing run across the strip newly occupied by the Japanese and set a bomber on fire. As he pulled up he came upon a Ki-36 Ida, a single-engine JAAF observation aircraft, approaching Cabanatuan Field to land. The enemy pilot tried to outmaneuver the Warhawk in his agile aircraft but Stone sent it on fire.

That day the Bataan air echelon sent up 18 P-40s against enemy bombers approaching Corregidor. With no radar or air warning in service HQ sent out the Warhawks using the knowledge they had gained about the previous enemy attack schedules and routes. At 1200 one flight of nine P-40s under 2Lt. Edward Woolery was sent over Corregidor, while another flight under 1Lt. William Dyess was sent to cover the approaches to Corregidor north of

Mariveles. The enemy bombers evaded Dyess' flight, but were intercepted by Woolery over Corregidor without reported results.

16 January 1942: 17PS

Lt.Gen. George had been instructed to limit his missions to recon missions and to shoot down pesky enemy observation aircraft. The II Corps had complained to MacArthur of their harassment by enemy observation aircraft that directed their bombers, fighters and artillery on their attacks on II Corps frontline troops.

The pilots and aircraft at Bataan had become known as the Bataan Field Flying Detachment, and pilots Marshall Anderson, Jack Hall, John Posten, William Rowe, and Lloyd Stinson took off at 0700. They flew north up the coast of Bataan to fly cover over the front lines in the Abucay area to defend against Japanese air attack. Rowe spotted an enemy observation aircraft near Orani and made a firing pass from below astern but missed, and the Japanese pilot escaped into the cloud cover. Posten flew protection behind his flight and became separated from them when they went into the overcast. Posten saw a lone enemy aircraft about 2,000 feet below and made a diving attack but missed. Posten maneuvered into firing position again but his guns malfunctioned. As the flight returned to base they observed a convoy of six to eight trucks below on the Hermosa-Orani Road and strafed the trucks. They encountered enemy AA fire and then strafed the antiaircraft positions to the ovation of II Corps troops below, boosting their morale with the sight of some friendly aircraft. At noon, in retaliation, the Japanese sent Ann bombers to dive bomb and strafe Bataan Field, killing one and wounding another. At sunrise the next day nine Nate fighters made a surprise strafing attack just as the American pilots were heading for breakfast.

17 January 1942: 17PS

At 1030, 2Lts. Marshall Anderson, Jack Hall, and Lloyd Stinson taxied their P-40s out of their camouflaged revetments to intercept Japanese observation planes over the front lines. As they took off into heavy overcast Stinson blew a tire and had to abort the mission. Soon after take off, Anderson and Hall spotted a Japanese observation aircraft about five miles east of Cabcaben on the east coast. They chased after it, with Anderson's machine guns causing it to crash Manila Bay within sight of men on the ground at Bataan Field. Flying over the front lines, they circled the area waiting for more enemy aircraft. A formation of nine light bombers approached and the Americans immediately turned after them. The enemy pilots spotted the closing P-40s and jettisoned their bombs, scurrying back to their base. The P-40 pilots broke off their attack for fear of meeting a larger force and losing more precious fighters. Continuing further north behind enemy lines, Anderson and Hall saw a convoy of from 12 to 15 trucks on the Samat-Orani Road and strafed it for about a quarter hour. They broke off their attack when two observation planes approached Hermosa to the northwest. Hall attacked and shot one down but the other escaped. Low on ammunition, the two returned to Bataan Field at 1125 with two victories. MacArthur was informed of the successful mission and ordered Anderson and Hall to be awarded the Distinguished Service Cross. At 1615 the Japanese retaliated when nine dive bombers bombed Bataan Airfield and scored hits on the runway and drove the pilots and ground crews into foxholes. The runway was so damaged that a 1630 recon mission had to be canceled.

18 January 1942: 17PS

When it was informed that the previous afternoon recon mission had been cancelled, AFFE Headquarters ordered a mission to be flown the next morning, as the rear echelon of the 31st Infantry Regiment was repositioning and required air cover. At 0645, 2Lts. Charles Sneed and William Rowe took off from Bataan Field, but 2Lt. Kiefer White was unable to taxi his fighter out of its revetment. The two flew to the area of the Pilar-Bagac Road, which crossed east-west across Bataan. Once over the front lines, they patrolled over and under a layer of clouds at 6,000 feet. Rowe soon saw two JAAF Ki-30 two place Ann light bombers approaching from the east, above the clouds. Rowe flew under the overcast to a point where he thought the Anns would be directly above him. Rowe chandelled through the cloud cover and exited directly behind them and fired tracers into both enemy bombers until the enemy rear gunners stopped firing. Rowe finished off the defenseless bombers and both fell, smoking, into the clouds. Rowe then flew back into the clouds and pulled up and discovered a Nate that had been flying cover for the dive bombers. Rowe closed on a head on quarter attack and fired and the Nate pulled up in a stall, then spun down through the clouds with its engine smoking. Meanwhile, Sneed had descended below the clouds to patrol and had missed the combat; he had not seen Rowe's three apparent victories and he would receive no credit. Sneed rejoined Rowe to patrol for a while, and then both headed for Bataan Field, but as they were about to land they were informed that Japanese aircraft were in the vicinity. They climbed to intercept but made no contact, and landed safely at 0810.

At 1545 2Lts. Wilson Glover and John Posten took off on a recon mission over the Subic Bay area. As they approached south of Silanguin Island, they saw a large vessel resembling a cruiser heading east with a catapult plane circling. When the enemy aircraft saw the P-40s, it dropped its two bombs into the sea and tried to escape. Both Americans fired on the ill fated floatplane, and it descended steeply, smoking heavily, with Posten getting the victory credit. Continuing on their recon mission, Glover and Posten flew east to the mouth of Subic Bay, where they saw two vessels, identified as a troopship and a destroyer, but passed on an attack when they saw a two-seat observation plane east of Binangan. Posten attacked, but the more maneuverable small plane escaped and both pilots landed at Bataan Field at 1645.

19 January 1942: 20PS

At 0700 2Lts. Marshall Anderson, Kiefer White, Lloyd Stinson, and William Baker took off from Bataan Field to cover the arrival of the four P-40s expected from Del Monte. Anderson and his Wingman Stinson began climbing to 15,000 feet west across the Bataan Peninsula and continued west, circling the eastern shore of Subic Bay, then flew east, heading toward the Bataan front lines. Stinson saw eight enemy dive bombers below, which appeared daily over Bataan. Stinson and Anderson climbed in their direction and went into a wingover toward the enemy. But as they approached the Japanese aircraft the Americans discovered that they were not the expected dive bombers but enemy fighters. A Zero (actually a Ki-27 Nate, as there were no Zeros in the theater at that time) quickly made a head-on firing pass at Stinson, who climbed away but went into a stall and had to roll into a dive to gain airspeed. When he pulled up out of his dive Stinson saw another Zero and fired a long burst and rolled down off that Zero and climbed back up again. Stinson then saw a Zero chasing a P-40 and fired a good long burst and rolled away when his guns malfunctioned. He climbed and tried to recharge his guns, but the starboard guns did not charge and the port guns continued to jam; finally all his guns shut down. The disgruntled Stinson descended to the deck and headed back to Bataan Field. Once the Flight completed the 30 minute mission and landed back at Bataan they discovered that Anderson had not returned. Stinson assumed that Anderson's P-40 was the one he saw being attacked. Later, 17PS ground and US Navy observers reported that two enemy aircraft had been seen to crash. Stinson reported that he had shot both down, but later Anderson was credited with one of the victories. Anderson had been seen bailing out near Bagac, but was then was strafed in his chute by two of the Japanese planes and he fell the final 1,000 feet to his death. After Stinson landed, inspection showed his Warhawk had several holes in the right wing and fuselage, with one shell passing through the fuselage fuel tank directly behind him. The hits in the wing had severed the wiring to his three .50 caliber guns and caused them to be inoperative.

21 January 1942: No New P-40s

On 21 January the 24PG included nine operational P-40s, seven P-40Es, two P-40Bs, and 11 pilots. Lt.Gen. George remained optimistic in securing reinforcements from Australia. He had contacted MacArthur's Deputy Chief of Staff and asked for even a few P-40s at Cabcaben Airfield, five miles to the south of operational Bataan Field, which would soon be operational after the completion of its 3,900 foot runway. The field at Mariveles, on the southern tip of Bataan, was being built using an existing road as part of its runway.

Maj.Gen. Brereton, CG of the Far East Air Force now based in Australia, had flown into Darwin during the afternoon of 18 January after returning to Australia after meetings with ABDACOM leaders for nine days. The next morning Brereton met with 17 pilots of the 17th Pursuit Squadron (Provisional), which had been organized five days earlier under the command of Maj. Charles Sprague, previously George's Operations Officer of V Interceptor Command in the Philippines. Sprague, Blanton, Coss, Dale, Gies, Gilmore, Hennon, Irvin, Kiser, Kruzel, Neri, and Rowland had been evacuated from the Philippines on 31 December and 1 January, and were in Darwin waiting to receive orders to fly their newly assembled P-40Es to the Philippines via Timor in the Dutch East Indies. However, the staging sites in the Dutch East Indies along the ferry route to the Philippines were currently either seized by the Japanese or about to be so. The 17PS was to continue to Java instead to delay the Japanese offensive toward Australia. So, unknown to George, all hope of securing any P-40s disappeared. However, George did have the consolation of being promoted to Brig. General on 25 January.

26 January 1942: 17PS

2Lt. Charles Sneed and Wingman 2Lt. Samuel Grashio and 2Lt. John Posten and Wingman 2Lt. Earl Stone took off at 0920 on a reconnaissance mission over the front lines on Bataan and Subic Bay, with Posten and Stone carrying six underwing 30 pound bombs. As they approached Subic Bay they saw two vessels being towed by two other vessels heading south. Posten and Stone dove in a bombing and strafing attack and damaged all four. As the Flight headed down Bataan's west coast the two elements became separated. At 1015 Posten saw three Japanese dive bombers about 4,000 to 5,000 feet below over Luzon Point flying up the coast, just south of Agloloma Bay. Posten and Stone dove through a cloud on the unaware enemy Ann bombers, with Posten immediately flaming one. The other two bombers jettisoned their bombs and then desperately maneuvered to escape. Stone got hits on another that flew away, and then the two P-40s continued to fire on and damage the third, expending their ammunition as it too flew away. The next day the II Corps reported that the two Anns were seen to crash near the front lines to confirm the second and third victory. Both P-40s had been hit by fire from the enemy rear gunners, who holed Posten's hydraulic line and Stone's damaged oil line and crankcase.

Grashio had also spotted the dive bombers below and radioed Sneed, who continued flying on course. Grashio thought Sneed was deciding when to dive on the enemy, but Sneed did nothing as the dive bombers flew on. Grashio again radioed Sneed, and again Sneed continued to fly without taking any action. During several previous missions Sneed had aborted under questionable circumstances, and Grashio decided to inform Brig.Gen. George of Sneed's failure to attack. However, although the incident quickly made the rounds among the Bataan pilots, George did nothing.

26/27 January 1942: 17PS

On the 25th George had been informed that Japanese aircraft were on Nichols and Nielson fields, near Manila, and obtained permission from USAFFE HQ on Corregidor to carry out a surprise attack. The night of the 26th promised to have a full moon, which would give good visibility for a night mission. The six P-40s were towed out of their revetments on the blacked out field, and the first three fighters lined up and were ready for take off, each armed with six underwing 30 pound fragmentation bombs. 2Lts. Jack Hall and William Baker took off, but as 2Lt. Robert Ibold taxied into take off position he became blinded by the dust churned up by Hall and Baker. On this, his first mission from Bataan Field, Ibold misjudged the strip's width and his right wheel went off into the rutted outside edge of the runway. Then his right wing dipped and hit a large boulder, and the three fragmentation bombs on this wing exploded violently. The ground crew ran to the burning wreck, expecting to find Ibold dead, but incredibly he was alive but badly burned and in shock. Following Ibold's accident, George canceled the second three plane flight scheduled for the mission.

Although 1Lt. David **Obert** made no aerial combat claims over the Philippines, he took part in many missions. (AAF)

Meanwhile, after circling over Corregidor waiting for Ibold, Hall and Baker continued on to Nielson Field. Shortly after arriving over the field, they were amazed when the Japanese turned on their landing and field lights, apparently thinking that the two P-40s were their own fighters. Hall and Baker descended and dropped their bombs on the well lit target and then strafed the field, meeting AA fire only at the end of their attack. When Hall and Baker returned to Bataan they reported the results of their attack to George, who decided to organize another attack at 2300. This mission would include the six P-40s originally planned. 1Lt. Edward Woolery would lead 2Lts. Lloyd Stinson and Samuel Grashio on Nielson, while 2Lt. David Obert would lead 2Lts. William Baker and Earl Stone on Nichols.

Woolery thought he knew the Manila area well from flying in the area since late 1939, but on his arrival over the blacked out city he flew over the area for a considerable period before Stinson spotted the field below. Stinson and Woolery descended to attack while Grashio remained above to fly top cover. The two attacked the field from west to east strafing and then dropped their bombs over the parked aircraft, but because of the darkness they were unable to determine the results of their attack.

Obert and his wingmen had no trouble in locating Nichols Field, but as soon as the three P-40s flew within range of Nichols' AA defenses they met heavy fire. Obert chose the area on the field where earlier recon flights reported enemy aircraft were parked and started his dive. At 2,000 feet he released his six fragmentation bombs and pulled out, and as he looked into the darkness he saw a plane zoom past, missing him by only a few feet. In his dive Obert had lost his two wingmen, and now all were flying blind in the darkness; he decided to leave before there was a midair collision. The enemy AA fire continued unabated, but the Japanese were evidently shooting at the sound of the P-40s, as the tracers were always behind Obert. As he left the Manila area, Obert headed northwest across Manila Bay, where he hoped that he might find a target behind Bataan's front lines and strafe it with his full load of .50 caliber ammunition. At 0010 he arrived over the north tip of the Bay and saw what appeared to be a grass fire in the distance. But as he closed he saw a large Japanese convoy of about 50 trucks, driving along the highway with all its lights on. Obert circled to get in front of the column and then dove on it from about 1,500 feet, firing all six machine guns. Obert systematically attacked from front to rear, strafing the entire convoy before the drivers thought to turn off their lights. While concentrating on keeping his sights on the trucks, Obert almost flew into the ground and had to pull back on his stick to climb away. He then headed for the front lines and saw lights behind the lines; he made a firing pass, but after only a few bursts his guns stopped, as he had expended his ammunition. Obert turned back south for Bataan Field, and as he crossed over the lines he encountered AA fire from the American and Filipino positions and had to head out of their range by flying over Manila Bay, and then was the last of the six P-40s of the mission to land.

30 January 1942: 20PS

On 29 January, the Intelligence Section at San Jose, Mindoro, 160 miles south of Bataan Field, advised Gen. George that 12 Japanese bombers had arrived at Waterous Field, which was five miles from San Jose. George decided to launch a bombing and strafing attack on Waterous at sunrise the following day, with each of the P-40s carrying a 30 pound fragmentation bomb under each wing. Edward Woolery was to lead the mission with Jack Hall as his Wingman, and David Obert would lead the second element with Earl Stone as his Wingman.

The Flight left before dawn, but Stone was late taking off and was unable to find Woolery, Hall, and Obert, who continued to Mindoro without him. The three arrived over Waterous just at sunrise, and Woolery started into a dive on the field and leveled out at about 100 feet, but did not drop his bombs. Obert immediately followed Woolery down and released his bombs at that altitude, and its explosion almost forced his P-40 into the ground, but he managed to right his fighter and then circled to check on the results of the attack. Obert saw that the bombers he had bombed were in fact a few shrubs! The three American pilots decided to land at nearby San Jose, where they had breakfast and then took off carrying a 100 pound bag of scarce sugar to Bataan. Woolery and Hall were still carrying their bombs, and it was decided that they would attack the Japanese front lines before returning to Bataan Field. Since Obert had no bombs, he would fly top cover for Woolery and Hall while they looked for a satisfactory target to dive bomb.

The three P-40s took off from San Jose at about 0900 and arrived 30 minutes later over northern Bataan, with Woolery and Hall at about 7,000 feet and Obert weaving over them at about 8,000 feet and to their rear. Obert watched as Woolery and Hall saw two low flying Japanese dive bombers about a half mile off shore over the northwest corner of Manila Bay. He saw both go into a dive, with Hall following about 300 yards behind Woolery. Obert quickly checked for enemy aircraft in the area, and when he looked back for Woolery and Hall they had disappeared! Suddenly, he saw a large midair explosion far below and then saw a parachute and fragments of a plane falling into the water. As Obert started down to investigate, he briefly saw another aircraft burst into flames near the surface of the water and crash. Obert thought that these planes were the dive bombers that Woolery and Hall had dove on and shot down. For about a half hour before heading back to base Obert looked for Woolery and Hall and for any other Japanese dive bombers to attack. Obert found nothing and, assuming that Hall and Woolery must have already returned to base, Obert headed back for Bataan.

Once he landed Obert found that Woolery and Hall had not returned. The two aircraft that crashed below Obert must have been Woolery and Hall, but Obert had not noticed any Japanese AA fire in the area. It seems that the only reasonable explanation could be that Woolery's bombs had detonated prematurely, and not only destroyed his lead plane, but also Hall's fighter following directly behind. Possibly Woolery had armed the bombs during the dive, which triggered the notoriously unreliable fragmentation bomb mechanism. Ibold's crash was caused when the frags on his fighter exploded but should not have under the circumstances. Of the four pilots who had flown in from Del Monte 10 days earlier (Woolery, Ibold, Benson, and Obert) only Obert was left to continue on.

February/March/April 1942

9 February 1942: 17PS

FEAF fighter missions were ordered to be restricted to reconnaissance and supply drops to guerrilla bands. As the number of fighter aircraft declined to eight serviceable P-40s, pilots continued to fly important reconnaissance missions from the strip on Bataan. On 9 February MacArthur ordered the photographing of well-hidden large caliber artillery emplacements near Cavite, which were shelling Corregidor Island from ten miles across Manila Bay. The location of these guns was needed for the Corregidor guns to return fire.

The Philippines Army Air Corps was to supply a two-seat Stearman 76D3 biplane trainer flown from Bataan Field by Capt. Jesus Villamor, the hero of the early days of the war who volunteered as the pilot, while M/Sgt. Juan Abanes was to be photographer. Five of the six remaining P-40s were to fly escort on the mission. Lloyd Stinson was to take off from Cabcaben Field to fly top cover at 23,000 feet; David Obert, taking off from Cabcaben, and Wingman John Posten, taking off from Bataan Field, were to rendezvous and fly at 19,000 feet. Flight Leader Ben Brown and Wingman Earl Stone would fly from Bataan Field and cover Villamor from 17,000 feet, as he was at 15,000 feet.

The mission arrived safely over the Cavite area, which was only 16 miles from Bataan Field, but Stinson had become separated from the Flight. Villamor began his photo run without interference from the enemy or the weather, and a few minutes later he finished his photo assignment and headed toward Bataan Field escorted by the four Warhawks. But the Americans had been alerted that six enemy fighters were headed toward them. Villamor's Stearman had no radio and continued back over the Bataan Field area at 4,000 feet, unaware of the threat. The four P-40s circled protectively as the Stearman started its landing descent. Meanwhile, Stinson was about to land at nearby Cabcaben Field and saw Villamor and the four P-40s approaching Bataan Field and remained over the area.

At Bataan Field, Obert saw a plane closing behind the P-40s and at first thought it was Stinson, but then realized that it was a Japanese aircraft. Soon Ben Brown and the other two P-40 pilots saw the six diving Japanese fighters. Villamor was into his landing pattern when the Japanese closed, and Villamor quickly put the old biplane into a steep dive and pulled out at 1,000 feet with no Japanese on his tail. The four P-40s had no time to gain altitude as the Japanese Nate fighters closed. Brown, Posten, Stone, and Obert turned up and into them, firing short head on bursts and then turning sharply to port as the enemy planes passed over them. Partially through his turn Obert saw a Nate on the tail of a P-40 and fired a short burst before his guns jammed. The agile enemy fighters then closed and fired on Obert, who went into a turning dive toward Corregidor. While Stone chased a Nate, Flight Leader Brown fired at one to his starboard and then fired head on at another as it passed him. Brown saw another Nate somewhat below and at 90 degrees and tried to fire and turn with the highly maneuverable enemy when he spun out. Finding himself between Corregidor and the southern tip of Bataan, Brown dove out of the combat.

As Villamor touched down, enemy machine gun fire hit the runway and holed the Stearman's wings as he taxied hurriedly down the field and toward a revetment. Villamor and Abanes, gripping the camera, jumped out of the aircraft and headed for cover. Obert was able to clear his guns while circling just above the water near Corregidor and climbed for altitude. After he leveled off Obert saw a Nate 500 feet below over Corregidor and fired a long burst before his guns jammed again. He headed back for Corregidor and cleared his guns again, then headed north. Brown had climbed back up in the Corregidor-Mariveles area, but found no enemy and headed for Bataan Field. He was the first to land at 1730, followed by Obert, who landed at Cabcaben. Posten's P-40 had sustained damage during his dogfight with a Nate, and he landed safely at San Jose at sunset. Stone had not arrived at Bataan after sundown, but one of the ground crew at Mariveles reported

1Lt. John **Posten** shot down a Zero to give him his last victory (3½) over the Philippines. He would later join the 49FG/7FS. (AAF)

Cpl. Satoshi **Anabuki**. (Lansdale)

seeing a P-40 being chased by a Nate and the two went into a cloud over Mt. Mariveles; seconds later they heard an explosion.

Although none of the P-40s claimed a victory, USAFFE Headquarters credited them with six victories and announced the score over the "Voice of Freedom" radio that night. Some sources (Olynyk) give Posten a victory credit. A damaged Japanese fighter made an emergency landing on Pilar Field, but was set on fire by a USAFFE artillery battery the next day. The recon photos were rushed to Corregidor, where counter-battery fire from Corregidor made a number of direct hits on the concealed Japanese emplacements. However, the Japanese responded and moved their guns to new positions and resumed shelling. (Note: During this combat Cpl. Satoshi Anabuki scored his first two victories of the 51 which would make him the top scoring JAAF fighter ace of the war.)

March 1942: 21PS and 34PS

As fewer serviceable aircraft were available, the remaining pilots and their ground crews joined several hundred other Air Corps personnel and served as provisional infantry. By February most members of the 21PS and 34PS were being used as infantry. The Japanese blockade was growing tighter, and only small fast boats could slip in supplies through it, so gradually malnutrition, dysentery, and malaria wore down the troops and became more of an issue than enemy attacks.

March-April 1942: New FEAF Airfields

In the first week in January, MacArthur continued to believe that a strong American force could be established in Mindanao, that supplies could be delivered by ship through the Japanese blockade, and that bombardment missions from the south could eliminate enemy air strength in Mindanao. So in early January MacArthur ordered the building of airfields throughout the entire unoccupied Philippine Archipelago as quickly as possible as the first step in retaking the northern Philippines from the Japanese. Maj. Fernando of the Philippine Army and Maj. Raymond Elsmore of the Air Base Group supervised an emergency program to build these bases using air base personnel and local native labor. By 1 March there were at least seven all-weather landing fields suitable for all types of aircraft on Mindanao, three on Cebu, one on Panay, one on Bohol, and four on Negros. At the same time there were nine fields on Mindanao, two on Negros, one on Panay, and one on Leyte suitable for pursuit aircraft only, and numerous others which were recommended for use only in dry weather, or in case of emergency. Probably the most extensive construction was accomplished on Mindanao, and Maj. Elsmore subsequently listed 42 fields as having been completed between the opening of hostilities and 1 April 1942. Connected with Del Monte alone there were eight fields, one of which had its operations headquarters in a tunnel bored 65 feet into an adjacent mountain side. Another Del Monte field had a 3,000 foot runway leading directly into a tunnel approximately 40 feet wide and 100 feet deep, in which five P-40s could be parked. Auxiliary bases commanded by air officers also were constructed at strategic points on the island.

2 March 1942: 17PS Last Offensive Air Action in the Philippines

John Posten was assigned to be the first to attack enemy shipping in Subic Bay, and at 1300 climbed from Bataan Field and headed along Bataan's west coast toward the Bay carrying three 30 pound fragmentation bombs under each wing. Meanwhile, 20PS pilots Varian White and Wingman Erwin Crellin took off from Mariveles Field, also carrying three 30 pound fragmentation bombs under each wing, and climbed to 10,000 feet and turned toward Subic Bay.

Once over Subic Bay, Posten saw an enemy tanker at the Bay entrance north of Grande Island and dove, releasing his bombs. He did not see the outcome of his attack and landed safely at Cabcaben Field at 1415. When White and Crellin arrived over Subic Bay they saw four large vessels north of Grande Island, but they also saw a warship near the Olongapo docks at the eastern end of the Bay and decided that it was a more valuable target. White dove first, followed by Crellin, and they dropped their bombs in the face of AA fire. When White pulled out of his attack he looked for Crellin, who had disappeared, and then headed back to Mariveles alone, fearing that Crellin had been shot down by the warship's AA fire.

Meanwhile, at 1350, before Posten and White returned, Edward Dyess' P-40 struggled off Bataan Field burdened with a 500 pound bomb that been fitted with a makeshift bomb release mechanism fabricated from Chevrolet valve springs by WO Jack Bay. At Cabcaben Field Donald Crosland had also taken off at 1350 to fly cover for Dyess. The two rendezvoused south of Cabcaben and climbed to 12,000 feet, heading northwest for Subic Bay. Over the target area, Dyess begin his descent with the sun at his back, and at 10,000 feet saw that the reported concentration of enemy ships was not located at Olongapo, but was unloading on the north side of Grande Island. As he closed he saw two cruisers, two destroyers, and two other transports inside the harbor and other ships outside it. Dyess chose a medium-sized transport that was surrounded by three smaller vessels and a destroyer escort just entering Subic Bay, between Grande Island and the western shore. Dyess rolled into a dive from 10,000 feet, and at 2,000 feet released his 500 pound bomb. As he pulled away he saw that he had missed the transport by 40 to 50 feet. Because there was minimal AA fire from the shipping and shore Dyess turned a 180 and went into a shallow dive over the transport and made three strafing passes, directing his fire on its bridge. Crosland joined Dyess, and the two began separate strafing runs at targets of opportunity. Dyess fired on four small warehouses on the shore near two transports that were unloading. Dyess and Crosland then spent their ammunition while strafing a wooden boat and headed back to base as the boat was sinking.

At 1415 Sam Grashio took off in the P-40 that Posten had used in his first mission and had rearmed with three 30 pound fragmentation bombs under each wing. Grashio observed three transports and one cruiser north of Grande Island, but continued north over toward a single transport. Grashio maneuvered into position for his attack and dropped his bombs, but saw no explosions or splashes and started back for Cabcaben Field. As he approached the Field he was given the "Do Not Land" signal from the tower, which radioed him that his bombs were still attached. It was necessary to land, as his engine and oil temperatures were high, and he had to choose between having a bomb drop off and explode on landing or to bail out over the jungle of Manila Bay. He decided to land on Marivele's longer runway and landed safely at 1530.

Meanwhile, Edward Dyess had landed at Bataan Field at 1415 and Crosland had landed at Cabcaben at 1450. At 1505 Crosland received a phone call from Dyess, asking if he would fly another mission with him? Dyess had his Warhawk rearmed with another 500 pounder, and at 1700 Dyess took off of Bataan Field and Crosland from Cabcaben Field, and the two met again over southern Bataan for another attack against enemy shipping in Subic Bay. Dyess chose the two freighters still unloading at Grande Island as his targets and went into a dive from 10,000 feet, releasing his bomb from 2,000 feet. The bomb overshot one of the freighters and exploded amid a nearby concentration of barges and lighters that were transporting cargo from the larger ships. The bomb caused heavy damage to the barges and lighters and nearby personnel on the docks. Crosland joined Dyess, and the two strafed the personnel, warehouses, and two motor vessels until they depleted their ammunition. At 1740 Crosland landed at Cabcaben and Dyess returned to Bataan at 1745.

On landing, the ground crew found several AA holes in Dyess' fighter, including one large hole near the cockpit. The holes were patched and Dyess' P-40 rearmed with ammunition and another 500 pound bomb for a third sortie in the waning daylight. John Burns of the 21PS was to fly cover for Dyess in Crosland's P-40. At 1840 Dyess took off from Bataan while Burns took off from Cabcaben. At 1845, Lloyd Stinson and James Fossey of the 20PS, who had been on alert all afternoon at Mariveles Field, took off in two P-40s, one of which was Grashio's that had landed three hours earlier. Over Subic Bay again, Dyess saw that the two freighters had left the Grande Island dock and he targeted the large supply dumps at the northern end of the Island. He dove from 10,000 feet and released his bomb at 1,800 feet, scoring a direct hit that immediately started large fires. As the sun set and through heavy AA fire, Burns joined Dyess for a strafing attack on the Island dock area, causing more fires. While returning to Bataan, Dyess and Burns received a radio message from V Interceptor Command HQ that a heavily loaded vessel was leaving Subic Bay, along with another large ship preparing to follow it. The two pilots turned back for Subic Bay, again joined by Stinson and Fossey, who were returning to their fields. Flying north across Subic Bay, Dyess saw the first ship towing barges, silhouetted in the sunset; Dyess strafed it from amidships to the stern, followed by a strafing pass over the bow and into the bridge. Burns also strafed the ship and fires broke out over the deck. As Dyess was making another attack at only 1,800 feet the ship exploded, sending debris high into the sky. Dyess pulled back on the stick to avoid flying through the debris and blacked out momentarily. Dyess turned south to return to base with Burns but saw another, even larger silhouetted ship. As he closed on the ship it fired up more AA fire than the average tanker or transport, but Dyess made another strafing attack nonetheless. Dyess' .50s started fires at both ends of the ship on his first two runs, and during a third pass Dyess fired his remaining ammunition into the ship, which was enveloped in flames and heading toward shore. To reach the American-held area Dyess carelessly crossed over the Japanese-held western Bataan shoreline, instead of flying low over the water, and was subjected to heavy AA fire and had to climb quickly away to safety.

Meanwhile, Stinson and Fossey reached Subic Bay, but found no shipping until they were about a mile south of the western part of the Bay, where they saw a large 100 ton motor cruiser or launch. Stinson led the diving strafing attack from 4,000 feet and started fires, and after continual strafing passes the small vessel suddenly exploded.

Dyess landed heavily at Bataan due to a strong tail wind, but when Burns landed at Cabcaben the tail wind caused his fighter to land too fast and bounce. Every time his fighter bounced the wing guns fired, as Burns unknowingly had his finger on the trigger. Then, as he headed toward the end of the runway he hit some tree stumps, veered, and toppled over on a wing, destroying the landing gear and damaging the wing and the propeller of Joseph Moore's old P-40, the last survivor of the original 31 Warhawks that the 20PS had received when they arrived in the Philippines.

Stinson and Fossey were about to land at Mariveles in the strong winds. As Stinson tried to land his fighter kept floating over the runway and skidded off the end. His port wing hit a water truck and the starboard wing destroyed a small building, but Stinson was unhurt. Fossey landed and rode his brakes until he, too, overran the runway and his wingtip hit a tree, also demolishing his valuable fighter. Later, observers reported that an 8,000 ton freighter had exploded, an 18,000 and 12,000 ton ship had been beached and both were burning, and there were many fires on Grande Island. However, three of the remaining five P-40s were lost and one damaged, and Crellin was KIA. Only Dyess' P-40 remained operational. The next day MacArthur sent a radiogram from Corregidor to Washington which stated:

> We made a surprise attack on olongapo and subic bay destroying the following vessels colon one of twelve thousand tons one of ten thousand tons one of eight thousand tons and two motor launches stop inflicted much damage on smaller craft stop large fires were started at shore installations on grande island and olongapo.

Characteristically, MacArthur's communiqué had not mentioned General George, nor the Pursuit pilot's role in the attack, and led the reader to believe "We," meaning he, had a primary roll in planning the surprise attack.

1Lt. Edward **Dyess** led a courageous strafing and bombing attack on the enemy shipping in Subic Bay. (AAF)

11 March 1942: Gen. George Leaves the Philippines

Gen. Harold George was ordered to leave Mariveles by PT Boat that night, which would take him to Corregidor and on to Australia. Lt.Col. Kirtley Gregg was to command the Bataan Air Force after George left, but Col. Lawrence Churchill, the CO of the Far East Service Command, did not recognize Gregg's position. A power struggle ensued, in which the higher-ranking Churchill prevailed, but Churchill elected not involve himself with tactical command of flying operations and the recently promoted Lt.Col. Orrin Grover assumed these duties.

12 March 1942: 34PS Last Victory over the Philippines

The 5th Fighter Command History credits 2Lt. Ben Brown with two Zero victories over Cavite in his DFC citation, but no other information is available on this combat. These victories would give him three total for the war.

2Lt. Ben **Brown** scored two Zero victories for the last victories of the 34PS. (AAF)

Late March 1942: Air Operations

The remaining few aircraft in the Philippines were valuable for transport purposes. The P-40s performed an occasional mission carrying medical supplies between Mindanao and Bataan, dropping them to isolated units. Two Navy PBYs also performed similar missions, but most of the inter-island transportation was carried out by what was referred to as the "Bamboo Fleet," which was a diverse collection of unarmed aircraft, consisting of three civil aircraft together with two Beechcraft, a Waco, and two dilapidated P-35s. The last flight to Corregidor was made by a Bellanca carrying quinine. Other aircraft carried personnel and records from Bataan to Mindanao.

April 1942: Air Operations

During March 1942, Lt.Gen. Jonathan Wainwright, the Commander of US Forces in the Philippines, had asked that a squadron of bombers be sent to the Philippines to help break the Japanese blockade and allow supplies to be moved from Cebu to Corregidor. On 27 March information was received that US Navy ships were to run the enemy blockade, supported by an AAC bombardment unit. To support this action, on 3 April there were only four P-40s and two P-35s on Bataan, plus four P-40s on Mindanao, which were reinforced by three more P-40s from Australia. On 5 April these aircraft carried out reconnaissance between Mindanao and Luzon.

Gen. Ralph **Royce** led a Squadron of B-17s and B-25s to Del Monte. (AAF)

Ten B-25s and three B-17s took off from Darwin on 11 April and flew 1,500 miles to Del Monte Airfield on Mindanao, personally led by Lt.Gen. Ralph Royce. All the planes arrived safely, and over the next three days the B-17s flew two sorties and the B-25s over 20, carrying out a series of small air strikes against shipping and harbor facilities at Cebu, the harbor and airstrips at Davao, and Nichols Field on Luzon. After the Japanese destroyed one B-17 and damaged the other two Royce returned with the squadron safely to Australia. However, the blockade would not be broken, as the ships were destroyed by the Japanese at Cebu before they could head for Corregidor. Meanwhile, the American pursuits carried out recon and strafed Davao, destroying several enemy aircraft on the ground, but lost a valuable fighter and pilot during a take off.

10 April 1942: 24PG Last Victory over the Philippines

During the afternoon of 9 April, 1Lt. Walter Putnam of the 24FG was returning to Panay after a long recon mission to Palawan when he heard a report of the Japanese naval force moving toward Cebu. Putnam called Lt.Col. Grover at Del Monte for permission to attack the Japanese but was ordered to remain on patrol.

The next morning Putnam approached the Tanon Straits, separating Negros from Cebu, and saw the main Japanese convoy cruising slowly north up the Bohol Straits on the opposite side of narrow Cebu Island. Putnam continued and saw a large ship on the east coast of the island docked at Argao, 35 miles from Cebu City. He descended to investigate, and as he circled he saw the ship was an enemy troop transport with a dozen landing barges surrounding it. Putnam dove in to strafe it with a long burst from his six .50 caliber machine guns. As he was about to make his second run, he saw a motor launch leaving the shore headed for the transport and directed his guns on it, heavily damaging it with a two second burst. On his next runs he fired on the surrounding landing barges, hitting them and the engine room of the troopship. After his fourth run he was fired on by the AA fire of the escorting cruisers (destroyers?) moving down the Strait to Argao, and later he counted 73 holes in his Warhawk. With his ammunition exhausted and fuel running low, Putnam returned to Santa Barbara Field on Panay to refuel and rearm.

Putnam took off again just after noon to attack the Japanese landing force. On his first attack Putnam chose a large troopship, the last in the line of four. Putnam dove out of the sun and decimated the ill-fated Japanese troops packed on the deck. As he passed over the troop ships his fighter was hit by small arms fire from the four transports and the AA fire from two approaching cruisers. Just as he was climbing away from his fourth pass Putnam surprised two floatplanes that climbed away. Putnam chased after them, but found that his engine had been hit by AA, slowing him down. The two enemy aircraft turned into him and Putnam fixed on one and fired a short burst with his two functioning guns. While watching pieces fly off his victim as it was heading into the sea in flames, Putnam had to turn sharply to starboard to avoid the fire of the second floatplane. This floatplane broke away and descended toward the protection of the cruiser's guns. Putnam dove after it and closed on the Japanese from the rear only 50 feet over the water, firing and sending it flaming into the sea. Putnam pulled up to escape the AA fire from the two cruisers and then headed back to attack the transport again. But neither of his two remaining previously functional guns would fire and he headed back to Santa Barbara in his damaged, laboring fighter. After landing the ground crew repaired Putnam's P-40 using parts cannibalized from Dyess' wrecked P-40 that had crashed on Manduriao Field during the evening of 8/9 April. However, the fighter's guns could not be repaired and the electrical system still was not functioning. That night, Grover informed Putnam by that he had sunk two transports, a motor launch, and a number of landing barges, plus destroying the two floatplanes. But Grover also instructed him not to disobey orders, as all aircraft were to be used for reconnaissance only.

12 April 1942: 17PS Last Victory over the Philippines

2Lt. Harold Cocanougher, flying a P-35 from Del Monte at 0520, immediately encountered two JAAF Pete Ki-10 two place observation floatplanes below him that were about to attack the base. Cocanougher went into a dive, firing his .50 caliber wing guns until they jammed. He then went into a dogfight, unsuccessfully exchanging .30-caliber fire with the floatplanes.

Shortly after Cocanougher had become airborne, 1Lt. John Brownewell in a P-40E and 2Lt. Gus Williams in a P-40B of the 17PS taxied out on the Dalirig Strip for a reconnaissance and strafing mission over Davao. As they reached the far end of the Strip to turn around, Williams saw the two Cocanougher Pete floatplanes overhead and was anxious to take off before the Japanese saw them. Shortly after take off, Brownewell also saw the Japanese, and both P-40s started a steep climb to get above them. However, Williams' older P-40B fell further and further behind Brownewell's newer P-40E. The floatplanes separated, and at about 11,000 feet one of them turned and made a head on attack on Brownewell. The two began firing at each other as they closed, and Brownewell scored hits on the Pete's engine or pilot and the frail floatplane immediately went into a spiral dive and crashed a few miles south of Del Monte. As the stricken Pete spiraled past Williams about 2,000 feet below Brownewell, Williams started circling to watch for the pilot to bail out. While in the fairly tight turn, Williams' fighter suddenly snapped to the outside, losing the canopy and heaving Williams partway out of the cockpit without goggles and helmet. The aircraft was at full throttle, spinning wildly, preventing Williams from getting back into the cockpit and reaching for the throttle. Finally the engine quit and Williams was able to get back into the cockpit and recover from the spin at about 1,500 feet over the Dalirig strip. As he was about to land with a dead engine, Williams lowered his landing gear and just above the ground the engine started up at high RPMs and increased airspeed, and Williams aborted the landing attempt and went around for another landing at reduced airspeed and came in without a problem. Meanwhile, Brownewell continued down to Davao, where he was credited with strafing four aircraft.

End in the Philippines

MacArthur's messages to the War Department showed that his optimism waxed and waned on the prospect of continuing to hold the Philippines. On 13 January, encouraged by the effect of accurate American artillery fire, he stated that "there is every indication that for the present I have drawn the fangs of the enemy attack." Ten days later, however, he was discouraged over heavy losses, which had amounted to approximately 35% of his entire force, and radioed: "I wish to take this opportunity while the army still exists and I am in command to pay my tribute to the magnificent service it has rendered. The troops have ever done so much with so little. I bequeath to you the charge that their fame and glory be clearly recorded by their countrymen. In case of my death I recommend that my chief of staff Gen. Sutherland be designated as my successor." Then, a month later, he believed that the enemy had been "badly mauled on Bataan," and he radioed: "I may have gained the respite I so desperately need."

MacArthur's intention to build up sufficient forces for a counterattack could not succeed, as he was apparently unaware of the weakness of American air and naval forces in the Pacific. He had requested two or three pursuit squadrons from Gen. Wavell late in January and was surprised to learn that at the time there were only 16 P-40s available in the theater. By the first week of February he still had some hopes of bringing aircraft close to the Philippines via an aircraft carrier, but if it were impossible to provide a carrier, he suggested that either A-24s equipped with auxiliary fuel tanks or two or three squadrons of longer range P-39s and A-20s should be flown in from Australia.

MacArthur's evacuation to Australia marked that a new phase of the war in the Far East had begun. His instructions from the War Department contained the familiar platitudes of "checking the enemy's advances along the Malay Barrier and of maintaining the American position in the Philippines." But with each passing day it was becoming evident that these were goals to be accomplished in the rather

MacArthur (L) and **Sutherland** in Malinta Tunnel, USAFFE HQ, on Corregidor. (AFHRC)

Japanese **Betty** bombers attacking Corregidor. (AFHRC)

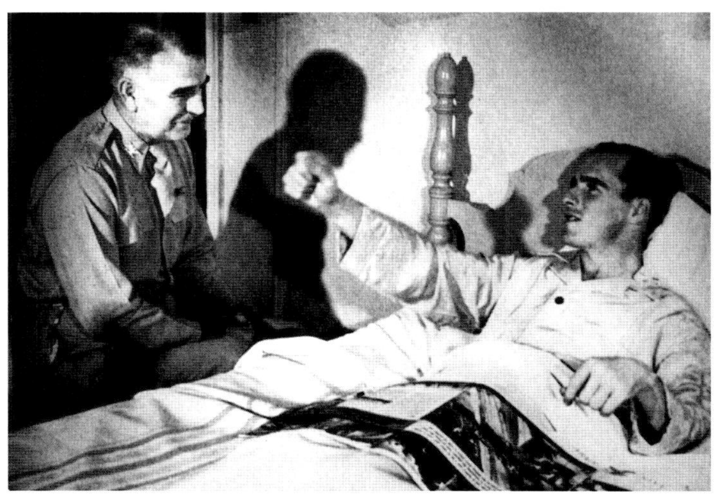

Dyess recuperating in a US hospital after surviving the Bataan Death March, captivity, and an escape and submarine rescue in July 1943. Returning to flight status in December 1943, he was killed in a flying training accident. (AFHRC)

Idealized drawing of 1Lt. I.B. Jack **Donalson** fighting as an infantry soldier due to the lack of available fighter aircraft. (AFAA)

distant future. The immediate aims were to hold Australia and to protect the sea and air lines of communication to the Southwest Pacific.

The 24th Pursuit Group had suffered heavy losses during the Philippines Campaign. Of the 93 tactical aircraft available on 8 December, all had been destroyed except for three that ran the blockade. Of the 220 officer personnel, 26 had been killed in action, and 51 were transferred to Australia and a few to Java, while the remaining 143 were listed as missing in action, wounded, or many became prisoners of war. The fate of the enlisted men is unknown, but probably was the same as the officer corps. The 44 pilots of the 24PG shot down 103 enemy aircraft (although this figure in subject to conjecture) and damaged or destroyed numerous ships and installations.

Once the 21PS was decimated, Squadron CO William Dyess gave his fighter to I.B. Jack Donalson, who flew to Australia. Dyess then transitioned to serve as an infantry officer and, along with other pursuit squadron and USN PATWING men, fought the Japanese valiantly during the Battle of the Points. After the fall of Bataan, Dyess was captured and survived the subsequent Bataan Death March. After a year in captivity he escaped with Sam Grashio, and after three months of fighting with the Filipino Guerillas he was evacuated from the Philippines by the USN submarine *Trout* in July 1943 and returned to the US. During his hospital stay Dyess related his story of the brutality of the Bataan Death March and his time as a POW. The US Government, however, refused to release his book, *The Dyess Story*, for publication, fearing that it would incense the Japanese and risk the cancellation of the delivery of Red Cross relief supplies to American POWs in Japanese captivity. However, there has been conjecture that *The Dyess Story* was, in fact, suppressed by both the Pentagon and White House, which were concerned that an incensed American public would demand a greater exertion of the Pacific War when the US and its Allies had settled on the "Europe First" strategic policy. After recuperating, Dyess was promoted to Lieutenant Colonel and assigned to fly P-38s in preparation for his return to combat. On 22 December 1943, his Lightning caught fire while on a training mission over the highly populated area of Burbank, CA. Despite sufficient opportunity to bail out he remained with his burning aircraft and guided it to a vacant lot, saving numerous civilians on the ground.

Boyd Wagner, 17PS CO, had been evacuated from the Philippines after suffering injuries when his windshield was shattered on 22 December and arrived in Australia in January 1942, where he would help reform the 17PS but would not lead it to Java. He was assigned to the 5FC, where he would lead two P-39 Squadrons of the 8PG. 2Lt. Maurice Hugette was assigned as Wagner's replacement, and on 22 December was replaced by 1Lt. David Obert when he was injured after crashing into runway barricades while landing in the dark. On 9 January Obert was replaced by 1Lt. Raymond Sloan, who was the most senior 17PS officer on Bataan. Sloan was wounded on 8 February during a Japanese infantry attack and died of his wounds a few days later. Sloan was replaced by 1Lt. Hugh Marble, who escaped to Corregidor and was evacuated by PBY.

Henry **Thorne**, 3PS CO. (AAF)

Joseph **Moore**, 20PS CO. (AAF)

When Gen. Royce's nine B-25s arrived at Del Monte at dusk after their final mission over the Philippines they were fitted with long range fuel tanks for their long trip to Australia, but the tanks limited the number of evacuees to three on each bomber. Gen. George was instructed to send all Pursuit Squadron COs to Australia, but only Joseph Moore, CO of the 20PS, and 3PS CO Henry Thorne could be found to be evacuated (Marble was still on Corregidor, while Dyess of the 21PS and Robert Wray of the 34PS had been captured by the Japanese).

After his evacuation from the Philippines Thorne attended the Army Command and General Staff Schools and went on to command newly formed fighter units in the US. Near the end of the war he rose to staff positions with the 7th Fighter Command and Chief of Operations with the 5FC in 1946, then as General became the CO of the 8FC in Japan. He continued in the USAF in various command positions until his retirement, including CO of the 4th Fighter Bomber Interceptor Group in Korea.

After his evacuation Moore remained in Australia before returning to the States in August 1942, where he held several posts before being transferred to the ETO in November 1943, where he participated in D-Day and the invasion of Germany. Following the war, Moore transitioned to command-level assignments in both Europe and the US, commanding Fighter Bomber Wings and then as Chief of Staff of the Ninth Air Force. In 1959 B.Gen. Moore commanded the 4th Tactical Fighter Wing, where he received the Bendix Trophy for flying a Republic F-105 for a world speed record of 1,216mph on 11 December. He was the CO of the Second Air Division in Vietnam and Lt.Gen. Moore retired as the Inspector General of the Air Force in August 1967.

Part Two

Java and the Netherlands East Indies

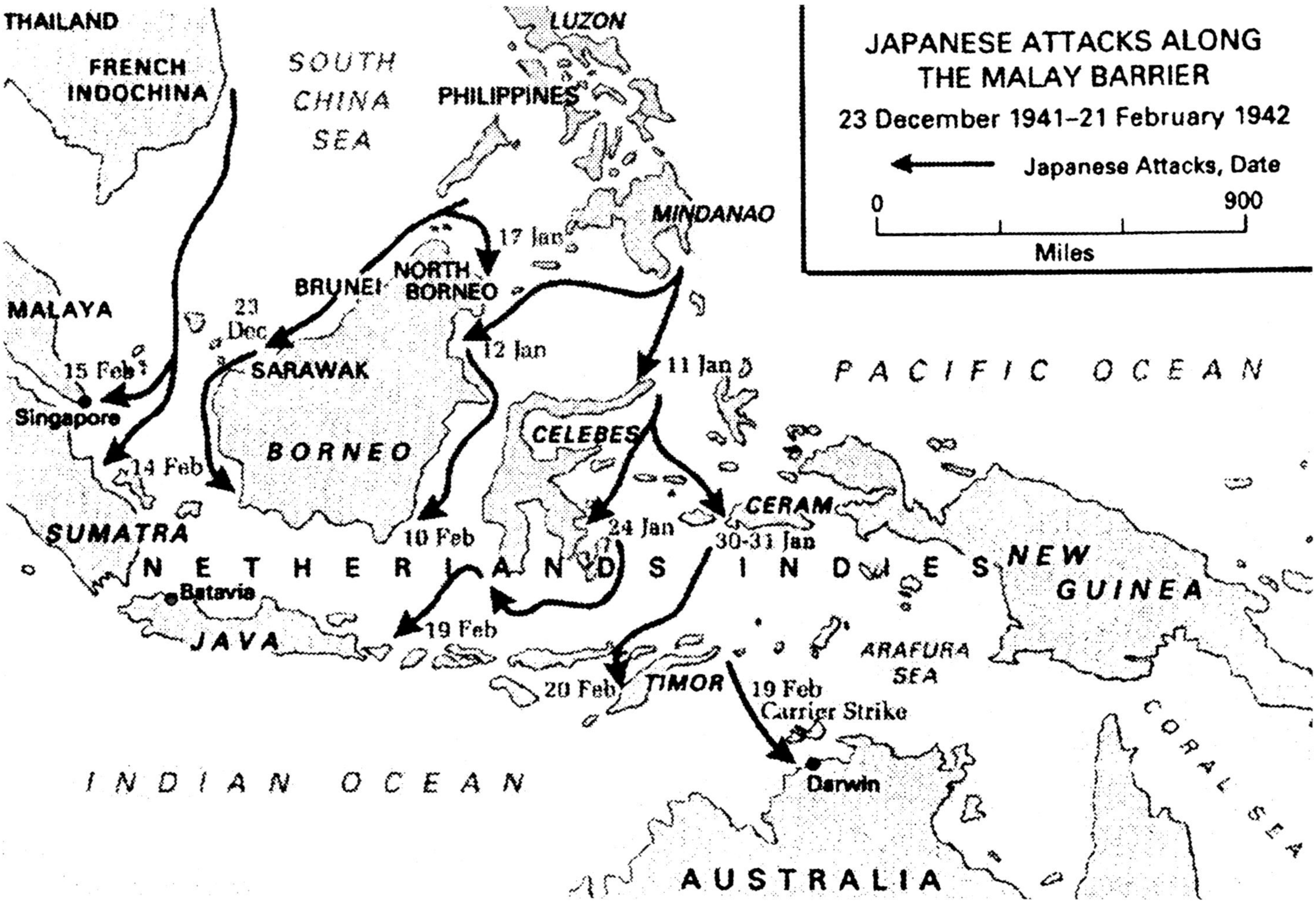

The conquest of the Philippines was not the ultimate objective of the Japanese; it was only one phase of a plan of aggression in widespread areas throughout the Far East and the Pacific. While vast numbers of enemy troops were pouring into the Philippines during December, others were attacking Hong Kong, Thailand, and Borneo. The British garrison at Hong Kong capitulated on 25 December under concentrated land and air attacks. Japanese incursion of Thailand met with only token resistance, and a pact signed between the two governments on 11 December paved the way for a further breach into Malaya. The landings on the northern coast of Borneo on 11 December, apart from an encircling movement around the Philippines, marked the initial encroachment in the Netherlands East Indies (NEI).

With its thousands of islands providing convenient stepping stones from southeastern Asia to Australia, the Netherlands East Indies occupied a strategic position of primary importance. Also, the NEI archipelago was unusually rich in natural resources. Large oil fields and abundant supplies of rubber, tin, spices, sugar, and other tropical products would add much to the resources available to the Japanese, while their loss would be a serious blow to the Allied economy. For these reasons the defense of the Netherlands East Indies against Japanese aggression assumed major importance and induced the maximum efforts of the American, British, Dutch, and Australian Allies.

After the evacuation of the Philippines, the Allies established a new defensive line called the "Malay Barrier" that ran roughly from the Malay Peninsula in the west, then east to Sumatra and Java, and was anchored by Darwin on the North Australian coast. The Malay Peninsula, with its bastion at Singapore, was to be held by the British, while the Netherlands, which had been well-aware of the danger from Japan's ambitions in the Far East, had not neglected its defense of the East Indies, where it had stationed 40,000 men supplemented by perhaps 100,000 native troops. The Dutch Air Forces and those of any Allies would fly principally from military and commercial airfields in Java. Batavia, Java's capital and heart, had both commercial and military airfields, along with a well-camouflaged large military airfield outside the city. As the Dutch were unable to defend all the islands in their empire they posted small garrisons at strategic locations and concentrated their main force on Java. Their plan was to defend Java, the key to the Malay Barrier, with ground troops and attack Japanese convoys with naval and air forces.

By the end of December 1941, the Japanese advance was progressing so well in the Philippines that their forces began to strike deeper into the South Pacific and Far East. The Second and Third Japanese fleets, free of their duties in the Philippines, were making preparations for the move south. Japanese plans called a task force to move to the east with invasion of Manado, Kendari, and Makassar in the Celebes, while another task force moved against Tarakan, Balikpapan, and Bandjermasin on the eastern coast of Borneo. Another force was poised to move to occupy the strategic Australian outpost of Rabaul in New Britain. In the Far East, Hong Kong had fallen ahead of schedule and the Japanese began to assemble their forces for the drive south through Burma to conquer Rangoon and Singapore. The battle for Malaya and the Netherlands East Indies had begun.

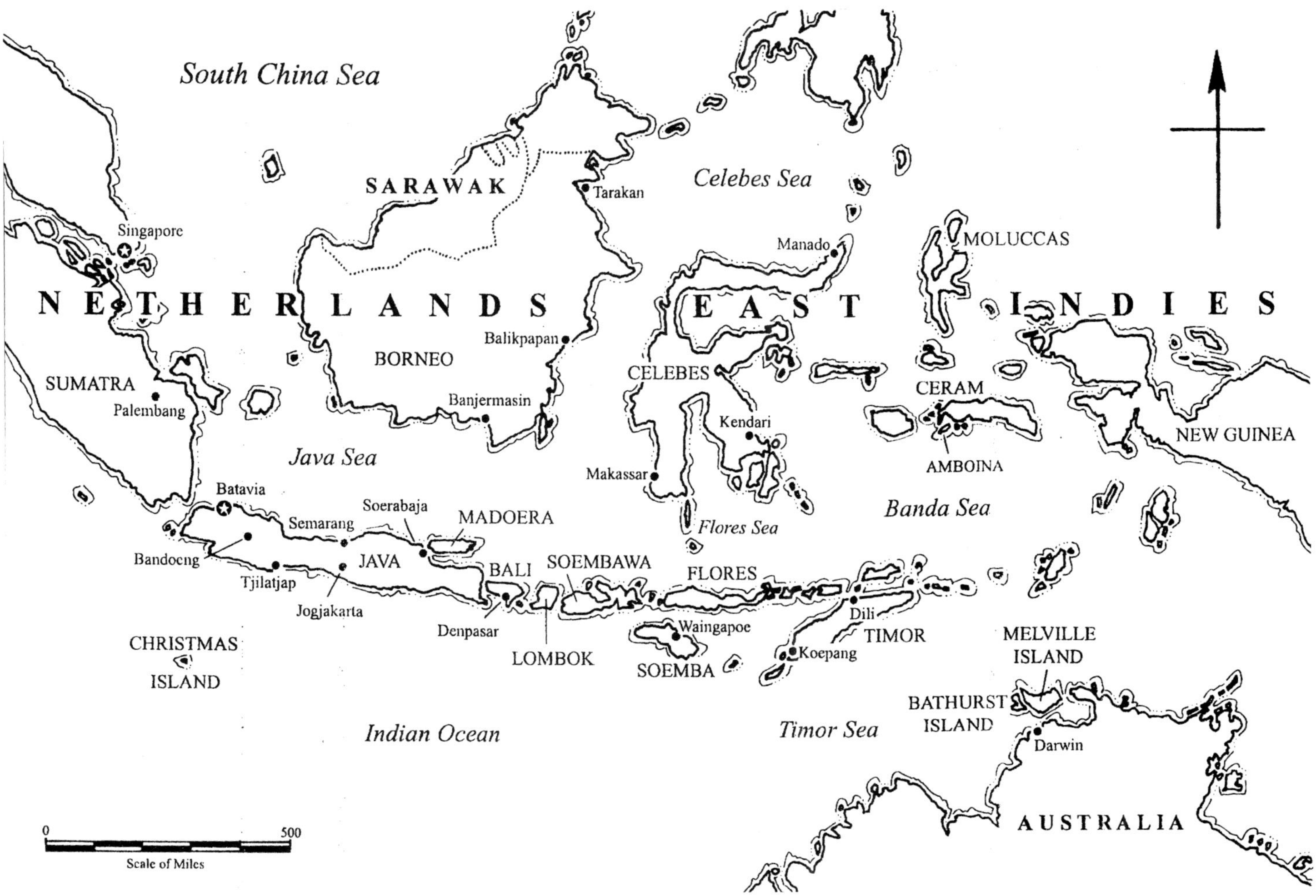

ABDACOM

The transitory combined command, the American-British-Dutch-Australian Command (ABDACOM), was established on 22 January 1942. The ABDA was formed to defend the participating Allied countries' possessions in the Southwest Pacific. These participating countries primarily operated under their own command to defend their areas, but there were some combined operations conducted with naval and air forces placed under other nations' command. Within the ABDA area were the Netherlands East Indies, the Philippines, and a few British possessions, and it extended all the way to Formosa, bordered on China's south coast, and ran north to Japan's Ryukyu Islands. Burma and the Malay States were included in the ABDA area, as were Thailand and Indochina, which were already occupied by the Japanese. ABDACOM would be dissolved on 22 April 1942, when most of the area was conquered by the Japanese, and was succeeded by the Southwest Pacific Area (SWPA).

In the meantime, at the first of the year the FEAF had no pursuit aircraft in commission, no steady supply of fuel, and its ground crews had inadequate spare parts or maintenance equipment. For the first time in the war, an American air unit was to be enlisted in the active defense of foreign soil and to operate, theoretically at least, under the supreme command of an officer of another nationality. The ABDA powers (American, British, Dutch, and Australian) found that they required a unified command for their air, land, and sea forces. By 1 January, Gen. Sir Archibald Wavell had been named the Supreme Commander of British and Commonwealth forces in the Philippines, NEI, Malaya, Burma, and Northern Australia. After Wavell had failed to relieve Tobruk in the undermanned North African Campaign, Churchill replaced him with Gen. Claude Auchinleck, who was Commander-in-Chief in India. So, in effect, Wavell exchanged positions with Auchinleck. Soon Wavell once again had the misfortune of being placed in command of a short-handed theatre when the Japanese declared war in December 1941.

Gen. Sir Archibald **Wavell**, the Supreme Commander of British and Commonwealth forces in the Philippines, NEI, Malaya, Burma, and Northern Australia. (AFHRC)

THE ABDACOM AREA
January–February 1942
ABDACOM Area
Sub-Command
0
1200
Miles at the Equator
KOREA
JAPAN
BHUTAN
INDIA
CHINA
Iwo Jima
FORMOSA
Hong Kong
BURMA
NORGROUP
FRENCH INDOCHINA
THAILAND
LUZON
Manila
PHILIPPINES
MARIANA ISLANDS
Guam
SOUTH CHINA SEA
PHILIPPINE SEA
ANDAMAN ISLANDS
MINDANAO
NORTH BORNEO
BRUNEI
MALAYA
SARAWAK
SUMATRA
Singapore
WESGROUP
BORNEO
CELEBES
NETHERLANDS INDIES
CENGROUP
Batavia
EASGROUP
DARWIN
NEW GUINEA
JAVA
TIMOR
Darwin
INDIAN OCEAN
AUSTRALIA
100
120
140
20
0
20

Hein ter Poorten, the commander of the Royal Netherlands Indies Army (KNIL), was named the commander of Allied land forces during early 1942. Upon Lt.Gen. Gerardus Berenschot's death in a flying accident near Batavia on 13 October 1941, Lt.Gen. Ter Poorten was promoted to Commander in Chief of the KNIL, and in January 1942 Ter Poorten was appointed Commander of land forces in the ABDACOM. By March, Ter Poorten became the de facto head of all Allied forces on Java, and following rapid Japanese advances and the disintegration of ABDACOM he unconditionally surrendered Java to the Japanese. He spent the remainder of the war in POW camps until being repatriated to the Netherlands in 1945.

Gen. Hein ter **Poorten**, Commander of the Royal Netherlands Indies Army (KNIL), and also Allied land forces Commander during early 1942. (AFHRC)

Lt.Gen. George Brett arrived in Australia in late December 1941 to assume command of all US Army forces there, while Maj.Gen. Lewis Brereton remained in command of the remnants of the Far East Air Force. Wavell chose Maj.Gen. Sir Henry Pownall as his Chief of Staff. Previously Pownall held a series of Command and Senior Staff positions. He had been appointed Chief of General Staff for the British Expeditionary Force (BEF) until the fall of France in May 1940. He then assumed the position of Inspector General for the recently formed Home Guard and was Commander of British Troops in Northern Ireland, before being appointed the Vice Chief of the Imperial General Staff in the War Office in 1941. He subsequently became Commander-in-Chief of the British Far East Command in South East Asia until 1942, when it was succeeded by ABDACOM, where he became Chief of Staff to Wavell. However Pownall outranked Brett, and to head off any friction between the two Brett was also promoted to Major General. On 17 January the War Department designated Brereton as Commanding General of the American tactical forces in the ABDA area and Brig.Gen. Julian Barnes as Commander of Base Facilities in Australia. Brett had dual responsibilities as Wavell's Deputy Commander and as Intendant General. On 20 January, as Wavell's Deputy Brett was authorized to command all air activities in Java, and as the Intendant General he was to be responsible for coordinating all administrative, supply, and maintenance functions for all ground and air forces. Despite this apparent definition of responsibilities there continued to be a lack of coordination between Wavell and his American subordinates that threatened the unity of command. On 15 January 1942 Gen. Marshall stepped in and dictated to Brereton, Brett, and Barnes that Wavell was the Supreme Commander of the ABDACOM, whose orders were to be carried out with "all available forces."

Brereton's replacement as ABDAIR (codename of the Supreme Allied HQ, SWPA) Commander, AVM Sir Richard Peirse, was the son of Admiral Sir Richard Peirse, and rose in RAF ranks so that by 1933 he was an Air Commodore and by 1936 he was an Air Vice-Marshal. On 30 April 1940, as an acting Air Marshal he was appointed Vice Chief of the Air Staff. In 1940 Peirse was made Air Officer Commander-in-Chief Bomber Command. During early 1942, he was overall commander of Allied air forces in the ABDA, supreme command for all Allied forces in South East Asia.

Maj.Gen. Sir Henry **Pownall** was Wavell's Chief of Staff. (AFHRC)

AVM Sir Richard **Peirse** was Brereton's replacement as ABDAIR Commander. (AFHRC)

The ABDA Naval Command included Adm. Thomas Hart and V.Adm. Karel Doorman. Hart was assigned the temporary rank of Admiral Commander-in-Chief, Asiatic Fleet on 25 July 1939. For the next two years, as unease increased in the western Pacific, Hart prepared the small Asiatic Fleet for war with Japan. He reduced the presence of his fleet in China and concentrated it in the Philippines in anticipation of the impending Japanese attack. After Pearl Harbor Hart was assigned command of ABDA naval forces, and would direct the naval defense of Java until mid-February 1942, when he returned to the US and retired in July. In early 1942 Doorman took command of the Combined Striking Force ABDACOM. Doorman was killed in action when his ship HNLMS *De Ruyter* was sunk in the Battle of the Java Sea. Doorman, following the naval tradition, chose to go down with his ship.

Adm. Thomas **Hart** (L) with Lt.Gen. George Brett and Maj.Gen. Lewis Brereton. After Pearl Harbor Hart was assigned command of ABDA naval forces and would direct the naval defense of Java until mid-February 1942. (AFHRC)

V.Adm. Karel **Doorman** took command of the Combined Striking Force ABDACOM in early 1942. (AFHRC)

January 1942: Allied Air Situation

While the Dutch constructed excellent airbases in the Indies, the Dutch Air Force consisted of 160 aircraft, most of which were virtually obsolete, such as the Curtiss P-36 and Model 21, Brewster F2A pursuits, and Martin B-10 bombers.

Neither the Australian Air Force nor RAF could spare any aircraft due to their defense of Singapore, so the burden of the air defense of Java fell to the American Far East Air Force.

At the beginning of 1942 the Americans had amassed a force of 18 P-40s and 52 Douglas A-24s at Brisbane. The ground echelon of the 7th Bombardment Group had arrived at Brisbane from the US, and these men were pressed into duty assembling the crated P-40s that were being rushed into the theater. Moving south to join them were 14 B-17s of the 19th Bombardment Group which had been evacuated from Del Monte in the Philippines. In order to strike at the Japanese moving into new bases in the southern islands of the Philippines and Borneo, Gen. Brereton ordered the 19BG north to Java in early January. Col. Eugene Eubank quickly sent his small force into combat. These courageous B-17 crews were based on grass fields at Singosari, Java, and attacked Japanese Philippines targets at Davao and the island of Jolo by using intermediary shuttle bases at Kendori (Celebes), Palembang (Sumatra), and Samarinda (Borneo). These missions were beset with problems caused by the weather, which not only interfered with reaching and bombing the target, but also with utilizing the grass fields at the home and shuttle bases. On 15 January these bombers were joined by the first reinforcements from the 7th Bombardment Group, which arrived at Malang. These six B-17s and 4 LB-30s (an export version of the Consolidated B-24 that had been built for the RAF) were the first new heavy bombers to enter the combat zone since the beginning of the war. A few of the aircraft of the 7th Group would be ferried from the US to Australia via Hawaii, but most of the unit's aircraft flew the longer route: South America, Africa, the Middle East, and India to Java. These bombing missions achieved little in preventing the Japanese expansion in Borneo and the Celebes. With each successful invasion the Japanese moved within escorted bombing range of the American shuttle bases, and then their home bases on Java. The Javanese bases lacked adequate anti-aircraft defense and there was a need for an Interceptor Command. The obsolete Dutch pursuits were no match for the Japanese, and the 160 FEAF P-40s delivered to Australia were still based near Brisbane.

The Dutch Indies Air Force consisted of 160 aircraft, most of which were virtually obsolete, such as the **Model 21 Brewster F2A**.

After the fall of the Philippines Brereton's available aircraft and personnel were greatly diminished, so the War Department decided to reinforce the FEAF with two heavy bombardment groups, two medium bombardment groups, one light bombardment group, and two pursuit groups. However, these units would not be available until March or April, and aircraft, not

Curtiss P-36 Hawks of the Dutch Indies Air Force

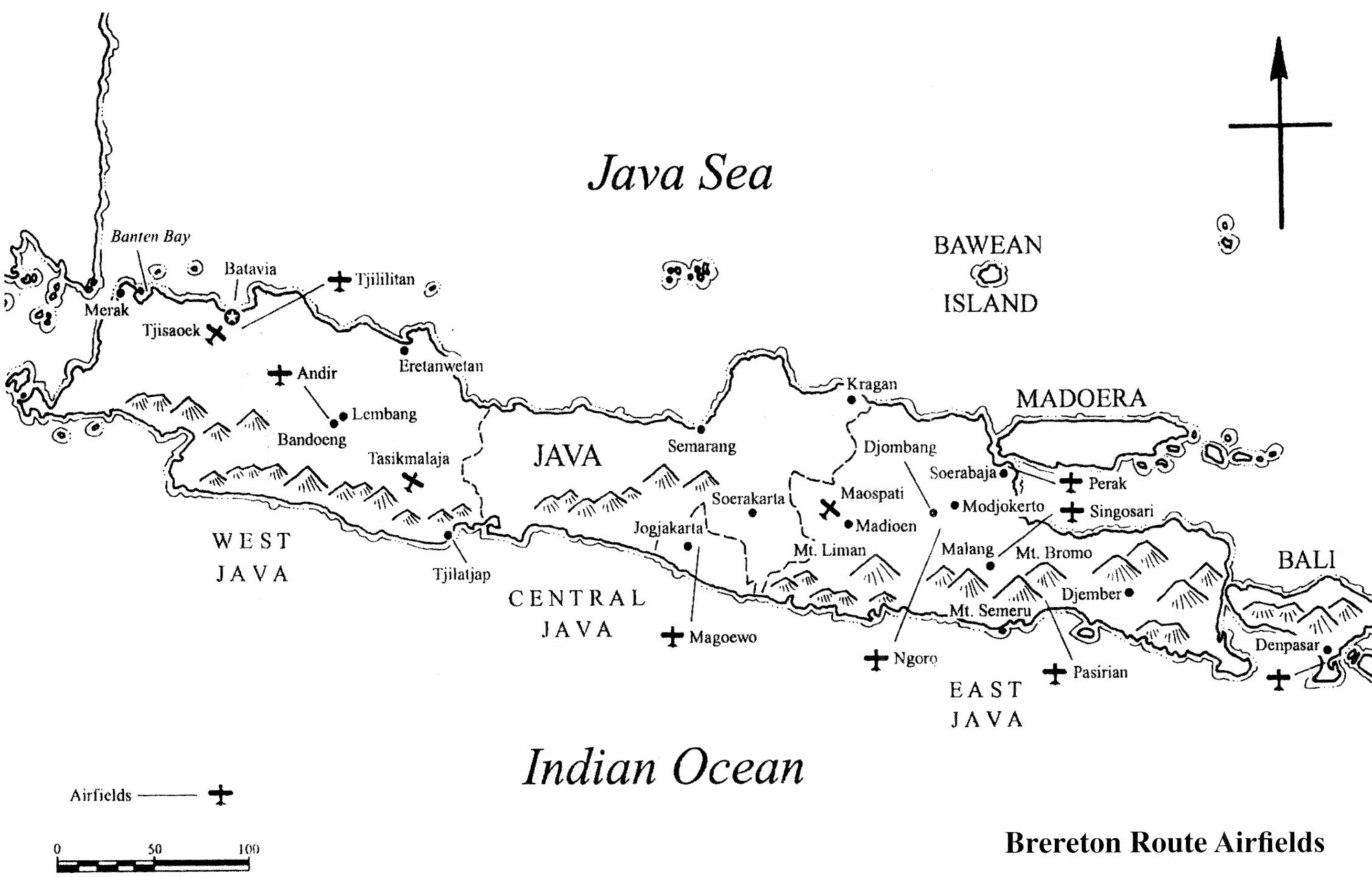

Brereton Route Airfields

organized units, were the requirement to meet the immediate Japanese threat. By the first week in January the *SS Polk* and the *SS Mormack Sun* were underway loaded with 112 P-40s, while the *SS Mariposa* and the *SS Coolidge* with 50 additional pursuits were almost ready to leave the US. The urgent need for heavy bombers was to be fulfilled by the release of 160 B-17s and LB-30s as soon as they left the production line.

"Brereton Route"

As early as the summer of 1941, MacArthur sent his new FEAF CO, Gen. Lewis Brereton, to Australia to choose a southern supply route across Australia that would supply the Philippines forces in case of an invasion. By the end of November a network of air strips and supply bases were selected that crossed the expanse of what would be known as the "Brereton Route."

When Gen. Brett, the new USAFIA Commander, arrived in December he was to ensure the Brereton Route was "a priority operation," but found that the fields along the Route were only dirt strips cleared in the 1930s for bush pilots and flying doctors. These strips could only operate fighters and light bombers, and the RAAF did not have the engineering units available to improve them. After an 1,100 mile flight between Townsville on the Australian east coast and Darwin on the northwest coast there were only three hard packed runways at Katherine Field 100 miles south of Darwin, Batchelor Field 50 miles south of Darwin, or RAAF Field at Darwin that were capable of supporting heavy bombers.

Initially, fighters and light bombers arriving from America were intended to be assembled at the airfields in the Philippines, but by late December 1941 that was no longer possible. In January all pilots and crews from the US were diverted to ports in eastern Australia, mainly to Brisbane and Townsville, where air bases and assembly facilities were operational. The aircraft were assembled by American and Australian mechanics, often with the help of the pilots, and were then flown across Australia. From Brisbane, they flew 400 miles due west to Charleville to be refueled before they took off northwest, following ranch trails and the telegraph line for 550 miles to Cloncurry, a sheep station in Queensland. The ferry flights from Townsville flew directly to Cloncurry, which was due west 400 miles along the railroad line. The next leg was the most perilous, as the pilots would fly northwest 500 miles across the desolate Red Outback to the desolate station at Daly Waters, Northern Territory. Beyond Daly Waters, the Route traversed 200 miles over the stations of Katherine and Adelaide River, beyond which were the grasslands of the Northern Territory which merged into the "Bush," the lush eucalyptus forest, which eventually met the swampy tidal flats of the north coast and the port town of Darwin, "Base One" on Beagle Gulf, the last secure harbor in the Southwest Pacific. From Darwin it was 2,000 miles to the Java battlefront. The Brereton Route was nearly 3,600 miles long, extending from Brisbane to Java, and was possible if the rarely available navigation aircraft could lead the fighters. (The airbases near Darwin are discussed later.)

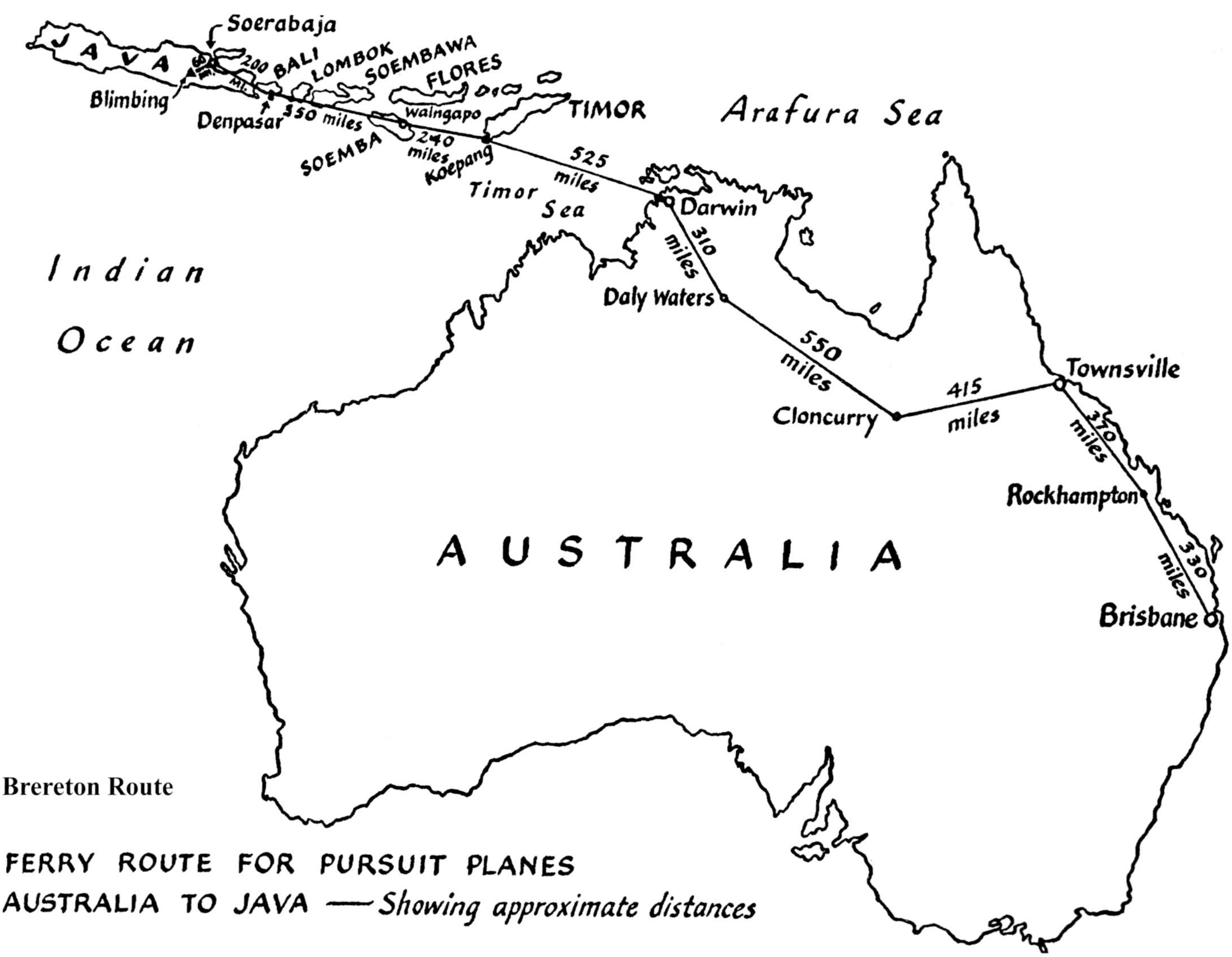

Brereton Route

Capt. Paul "Pappy" **Gunn** navigated the 17PS P-40s to Java flying an old twin-engine Beechcraft. (AFAA)

Cloncurry Airdrome. (AAF)

17th Pursuit Squadron (Provisional) Organized

The majority of the veteran fighter pilots evacuated from the Philippines to Australia on 31 December and 1 January 1942 were to organize new squadrons for duty in Java. As the campaign in the Netherlands East Indies progressed, five Provisional Pursuit Squadrons were formed utilizing the pilots with combat experience as leaders of the newcomers, many of whom had arrived as part of the 35th Pursuit Group. All but one of the Provisional Squadrons would bear the designation of the old fighter squadrons of the 24th Pursuit Group, which had ceased to exist in the Philippines. In the order they were formed these Provisional Squadrons were the 17th, 20th, 3rd, 33rd, and 13th.

The 17th Pursuit Squadron (Provisional) came into being on 14 January 1942 at Brisbane, Australia. Only 17 P-40Es were available from a shipment that had arrived from the United States on 22 December, but there was sufficient Prestone to make only three operational. Maj. Charles Sprague was given command of the unit after he and Boyd Wagner flipped a coin for the position. Wagner lost and remained in Australia to train pilots who had arrived on the Polk two days earlier. Allison Strauss and Grant Mahony both remained unassigned, as they were slated to lead other newly formed squadrons. The squadron's nucleus was composed of 13 veterans of the Philippines, while four more were new arrivals to fly the 13 fighters available to the Squadron. The Philippine veterans included: Nathaniel Blanton, Walter Coss, Jack Dale, George Kiser, John Kruzel, William Hennon, Robert McCallum, William Sheppard, and James Rowland of the 17PS; Carl Geis and Edwin Gilmore of the 20PS; Ben Irvin of the 21PS; and Ben Neri of the 3PS. Four new men (Bryan Brown, William Stauter, Raymond Thompson, and Chester Trout) arrived from Hamilton Field, CA.

Between 16-18 January 1942 the 17PS left on the 3,600 mile flight from Brisbane to Java over desolate Australian terrain with few landmarks and poor communications, and it would prove to be a trail blazing flight for the 17th. The combat echelon of the squadron split into two flights and departed on the first leg of its journey on 16 January. The first nine aircraft, led by Sprague and followed by Geis, Gilmore, Hennon, Kiser, Neri, Rowland, Stauter, and Trout, were navigated by former Philippines airline Captain and now AAC Capt. Paul "Pappy" Gunn flying an old twin-engine Beechcraft that had flown them out of the Philippines. The second flight of eight P-40s, led by 1Lt. Walter Coss and followed by Blanton, Brown, Dale, Irvin, Kruzel, McCallum, and Thompson, departed a half hour later with two RAAF Fairey Battles to lead them. Blanton lost his left brake and could not take off. The first leg was to Rockhampton, 330 miles north of Brisbane, where the first P-40 was lost when Geis' P-40 experienced electrical failure. He was forced to come in without flaps or brakes; he tried to ground loop to stop but overshot the field and crashed into a fence, but was not injured. Both flights then proceeded to Townsville's Garbutt Field, where Brown collapsed his landing gear when turning off to the taxiway and Kiser lost a wingtip when he hit a small building. One of the Battles was sent back to Rockhampton to pick up a replacement wingtip for Geis' plane. When the Squadron arrived at Rockhampton they found Blanton, who had arrived earlier after having his brakes repaired and then self-navigated from Townsville. The following day the Squadron flew its longest and most challenging leg, the 420 mile flight to Cloncurry, over the desolate Outback, where they remained to have lunch and refuel to fly 540 miles to Daly Waters. However, Neri and Gilmore were unable to take off and remained behind. Although the flight to Daly Waters was particularly tiring, Sprague decided to refuel and continue on to the RAAF Field at Darwin, where they landed just at sunset after seven and a half hours of flying with two stops. Since the refueling at Cloncurry was a slow one-at-a-time process, Coss' second flight remained behind overnight and took off and arrived at Darwin the next day. Due to the illness of Trout, the Squadron was down to 14 aircraft. The Squadron's enlisted men arrived in C-39s to service the P-40s before their flight to Java.

26 January 1942: New P-40s Arrive in Java

The first P-40s would not arrive in Java until 26 January, and no more than 40 would ever arrive. There were a number of reasons for their delay. The P-40s arrived in Australia in crates and were reassembled there by the 7th Heavy Bombardment Group maintenance ground crews. Despite their inexperience, the 7BG assembled 138 Warhawks between 22 December and 1 February. The first P-40s assembled were grounded (except three) due to the chronic lack of Prestone in Australia, and it was not until February that sufficient supplies of Prestone arrived to supply several squadrons. Further delays were caused by the lack of trained pilots. In December and January the training school at Amberley trained pilots who had averaged less than eight hours flying in a combat aircraft, and many had never fired guns. Three experienced pilots back from the Philippines Campaign, 1Lts. Boyd Wagner, Grant Mahony, and Allison Strauss, were added to the school's staff, and they estimated that it would require three months and 15 aircraft to be written off to train 70 pilots for combat. During this training period 2Lt. James Hamilton came in for a landing and his fighter unexpectedly nosed over, and as veteran, James Morehead, landed directly behind, his prop cut into Hamilton's cockpit, gruesomely killing him. Morehead became so depressed that he needed to be hospitalized. Investigation determined the cause of Hamilton's death and other non-fatal accidents to be the faulty assembly of the P-40s in Australia.

Experienced pilots back from the Philippines Campaign, 1Lts. Boyd **Wagner** (L), Grant **Mahony** (R), and Allison Strauss (not shown), were added to the training school's staff at Amberley. (AAF)

23 January 1942: 17PS Arrives in Java

After arriving at Darwin, Sprague's pilots waited restlessly for orders to proceed to their permanent base, known as Ngoro, at Blimbing. The two 4,000 foot grass runways and taxiways at Ngoro were under construction in the jungle. During the morning of 23 January, Sprague led 13 pilots in two flights of seven fighters on their first leg to Java, a nonstop 540 mile over-water flight to Koepang. Sprague's flights were again led by Pappy Gunn's old Beechcraft, which also carried three Crew Chiefs. The Warhawks were carrying an external fuel tank, but it had no capacity gauge, and timing was used to determine approximately when these tanks would run dry. When they landed safely at Penfoi Airfield at Koepang, Ben Irving of Coss' Flight reported that he was not feeling well (Dengue Fever), and Sprague ordered Coss' Flight to remain behind while his Flight and Gunn continued on the short 240 mile hop over the Savu Sea to Waingapoe, on Soemba Island. Upon landing there Edwin Gilmore reported that he, too, was sick with Dengue Fever. The next morning Gilmore reported that he was feeling somewhat better, but during take off his fighter blew a tire and he remained behind. Sprague led his Flight on the final 540 mile leg to Perak Field, Soerabaja.

Gunn returned to Penfoi to guide Coss' Flight to Soerabaja. Gunn had radioed to Darwin to have a new tire sent and later flew back to Koepang for the tire, and the tire was put on Gilmore's P-40. Despite feeling poorly, Gilmore did not wish to stay at Waingapoe and flew safely to Perak with Coss' Flight. On 26 January, after being held up by bad weather for two days at Darwin, two RAAF C-47s arrived at Perak Field carrying 22 crew chiefs and armorers.

Once at Soerabaja, Sprague named Walter Coss as his Executive Officer, who was to concentrate on operational duties. Coss would allow Sprague to focus on his Command and liaison responsibilities, not only with FEAF Chief Emmett O'Donnell, but also with 5th Bomber Command Col. Eugene Eubank and with the Dutch, as well as to monitor their construction progress at Ngoro. The Americans spent the next few days in interception practices and test flights in conjunction with the ADC. During this time, as the Japanese juggernaut moved closer their air raids increased and the Dutch air warning system proved to be inadequate to American Pursuit Squadrons, who were unfamiliar with the Dutch procedure. Twenty to 30 minutes before a raid the American pilots were given warning that enemy bombers were approaching Soerabaja, but by the time the P-40 pilots climbed to reach the Japanese flying at 21,000 feet the bombers would have bombed their target and left.

27 January 1942: 3PS Formed

Capt. Grant Mahony had been directed to form the 3rd Pursuit Squadron for service in Java. For the nucleus of his Squadron Mahony chose Philippine veterans Ben Irving, Allison Strauss, and Parker Geis. Mahony had hoped to obtain veteran pilots from the 27th Bomb Group but was refused, so the other 21 pilots were to be transferred from the neophyte pilots in the training program. The first 12 trainee pilots, many of whom had not flown a P-40 since leaving the US, joined the 3PS on 29 January. Seven pilots were chosen from Class 41E and five were chosen from Class 41F. Mahony had taken all the available 41Es and Fs and had to take 13 more trainees from Class 41G that had just arrived from the US by boat. The next day the new pilots were assigned their newly assembled P-40Es, some of which had not been checked out. On 5 February Mahony was ordered to proceed to Darwin.

Capt. Grant **Mahony** had been directed to form the 3rd Pursuit Squadron for service in Java. (AFAA)

Late January 1942: Ngoro Airfield

Sprague asked Walter Coss to fly down to Ngoro to inspect the progress of the Dutch construction. Coss flew in his P-40 that was led by a bright red civilian Dutch DeHavilland Tiger Moth biplane. As they approached the Ngoro area Coss could not make out anything that looked like an airfield, but the biplane pilot landed and taxied to one side. As Coss approached he only saw low bushes, but trustingly continued in to land safely on top of the bushes, which gave in and then snapped back up in place; the perfect camouflage. The Dutch had built two, 2,000 foot runways in a T-shape on a former cane field. The excellently camouflaged airfield looked like rice paddies with a road running through them and three native villages close

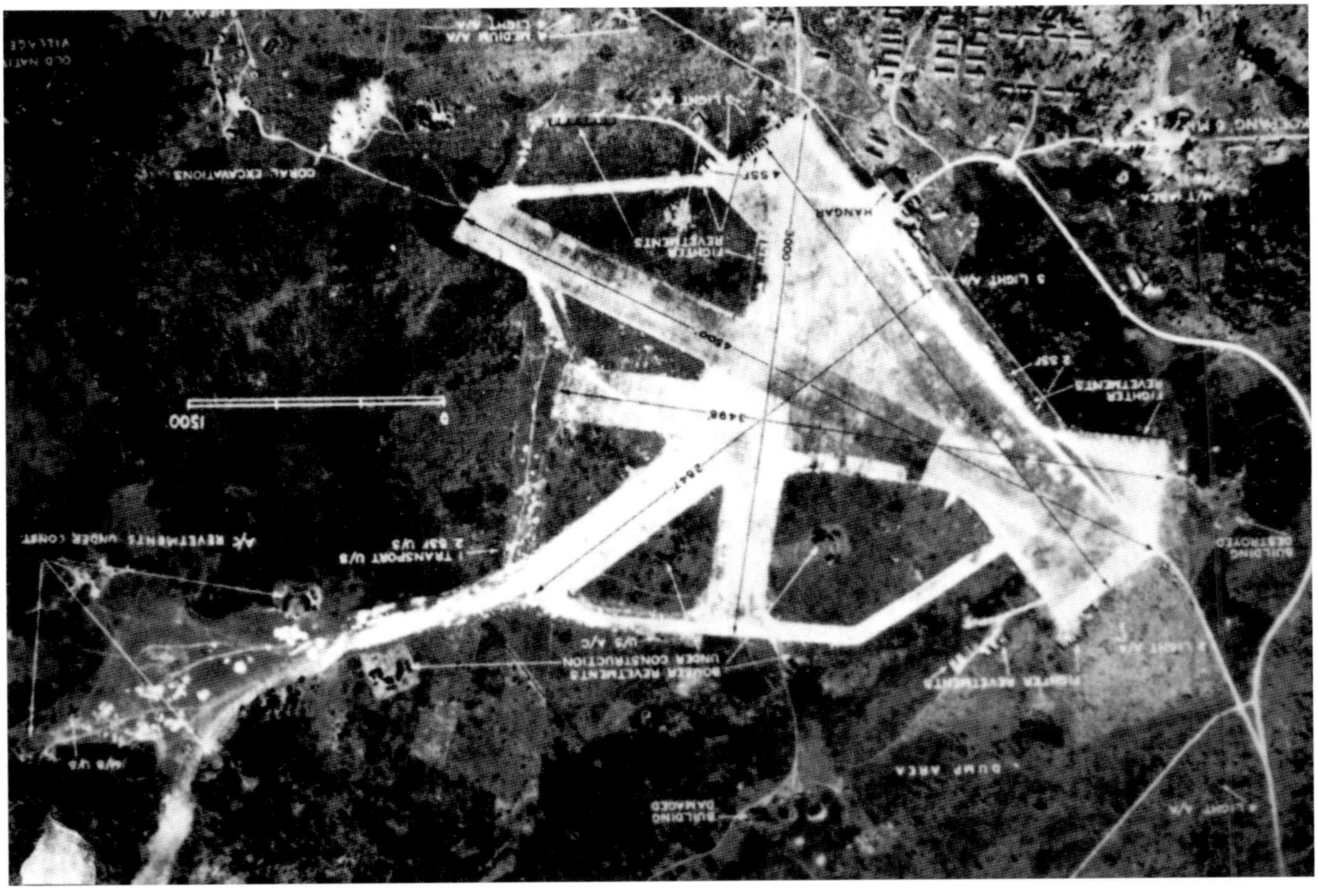

Penfoi Airfield, Koepang. (AAF)

Perak Field, Soerabaja. (AAF)

by. There were three revetments for bombers and 12 for fighters. To maintain the camouflage no large buildings would be built there, and the pilots and ground crew would be billeted at the village of Blimbing a few miles away. The pilots' billeting was to be the houses left empty by evacuated Dutch sugar mill employees.

28 January 1942: 17PS

A Dutch submarine crippled by enemy depth charges was moving into port protected by Dutch PBYs. Maj. Sprague was assigned to lead a flight of P-40s to protect the submarine from air attack, but the weather proved to be very bad and the flight was recalled. Fortunately, the poor weather also protected the submarine, which arrived in port safely.

29 January 1942: 17PS

The next day Sprague led another mission to investigate unidentified aircraft, but the Philippines veteran turned too tightly in the base leg of his landing and lost speed and stalled, hitting the end of the runway and striking his head on the gunsight. He suffered cuts to his face and head, but also had his ear sliced off. The 17th was now down to 12 of its original 17 Warhawks.

February 1942

Early February Situation

On 1 February, four troop ships that had left San Francisco on 12 January arrived in Australia, bringing Air Corps troops comprising the main strength of the 45th and 51st Air Base Groups, the 35th Pursuit Group (less three squadrons), the 49th and 51st Pursuit Groups, with their attached medical, chaplain, ordnance, and quartermaster services, the 4th Air Depot Group, and the 808th Engineers Battalion (Aviation). From this shipment, and from some of the AAC troops already in Australia, another convoy was formed in late February for the reinforcement of Java. After discussing the situation with Wavell, Brett decided that there were a sufficient number of Air Corps troops in Java already to operate all the aircraft which they had or were likely to have, and the newly arrived troops from the convoy were to be reloaded at Fremantle, Australia, and sent to India. Accordingly, on 22 February the convoy sailed to India, and included in this shipment was the 51st Pursuit Group, Headquarters and Headquarters Squadron and the Interceptor Control Squadron of the 35th Pursuit Group.

The ABDA Combined Fleet was too small to tangle with the Japanese Fleet without adequate air cover. On 4 February, Dutch Rear Admiral Karel Doorman's Combined Fleet tried to stop the Japanese invasion force sailing for Makassar. Japanese bombers attacked and the USN cruisers *Marblehead* and *Houston* were badly damaged. The Allied situation on the ground was no better. Wavell was facing five separate lines of attack, each supported by heavy air forces. The impending loss of Singapore meant that any promise of reinforcements was nil.

Meanwhile, Brereton's replacement as ABDAIR Commander, AVM Sir Richard Peirse, inherited a particularly "precarious" situation. On 3 February, the Japanese dispatched a large force of fighters and bombers from Balikpapan and Kendari which devastated Soerabaja, Singosari, and Madioen, and then two days later sent a fighter force that eliminated Dutch fighter forces on Java. A flight of 20PS lost a large number of fighters at Bali on its way to Ngoro to Australia. Peirse's bomber command at Singosari had suffered losses of B-17s in the air, on the ground, and to bad weather. The Australian government was becoming more concerned about the enemy threat to Darwin and potential ABDA reinforcements were diverted to northern Australia. On 1 February, Brig.Gen. Julian Barnes, USAFIA Commander in Melbourne, sent the USAAC 49th Fighter Group to Darwin to serve under the RAAF there (which will be discussed later).

3 February 1942: 17PS

The 17th Squadron moved to its new base at Ngoro on 1 February and spent the next two days engaged in training flights and aircraft maintenance. At 1045 on 3 February, Japanese bombers attacked Java for the first time, and the Squadron got insufficient warning (20 to 25 minutes) of two formations of 19 and 17 bombers approaching at 21,000 feet. The standby flight of six P-40s pilots was without their leader, Maj. Charles Sprague, who was at ABDA HQ discussing his unit's lack of equipment. Walter Coss, the senior leader in Sprague's absence, took off first with Edwin Gilmore and James Rowland, and they were followed by a flight consisting of George Kiser, William Stauter, Jack Dale, and William Hennon. Gerald McCallum, Nathaniel Blanton, and Raymond Thompson were to stay behind to protect the returning P-40s.

Coss' Flight finally climbed to 17,000 feet, where they spotted 19 Nell bombers about 80 miles south of Soerabaja, heading north from Malang at 8,000 feet, but still 4,000 to 5,000 feet above and ahead of them. As they climbed after the Nells they soon saw six Zeros directly above with an altitude advantage of 4,000. The Zeros split into two Vs of three and dove on the Americans, with one V turning head on into Coss and Rowland, while the other V positioned themselves to attack the lagging Gilmore from the rear. Coss and Rowland turned into the Zeros and fired quick bursts and dove away, while Gilmore, who saw tracers whizzing by his tail, went into a tight diving port spiral. After escaping their pursuers, Coss and Rowland leveled off and climbed, as did Gilmore some distance away. Gilmore

Lt. William **Hennon** shot down a bomber for his first of seven victories. (AAF)

reached 20,000 feet but did not see any enemy fighters, but when Coss and Rowland reached 16,000 feet they saw six more Zeros above them in the sun. Two Zeros dove on them, and Coss climbed into them and hit one, which began to trail heavy smoke as it passed by. Coss fired a burst at another Zero diving out of the sun without effect. In the combat Rowland became separated from Coss, and as Coss broke off his combat he saw Rowland's P-40 trailing smoke and being followed by a Zero. Meanwhile, a Zero got on Coss' tail, forcing him to dive into a cloud and then return to Ngoro low on fuel. While heading back at 10,000 feet at 1130 he saw six "Seversky-type" fighters below heading toward Soerabaja. He dove on them from out of the sun and fired on the last fighter in the formation, exploding it. Coss overran the enemy formation, which placed him in position to be attacked by the lead Zero, but he was able to dive away safely.

Meanwhile, by the time Kiser, Stauter, Hennon, and Dale reached 4,000 feet the Japanese Betty bombers, flying in a V of nine and a V of eight, had dropped their bombs on the Soerabaja naval base and Perak Airfield. They managed to chase the bombers, which were unescorted, about 85 miles out to sea to Baween Island at 17,000 feet. When they finally caught the Bettys, they were flying in a formation that was able to put up fearsome 7.7mm and 20mm defensive fire against the Americans. Kiser and Stauter had to return early, as they were low on fuel. Dale made one unsuccessful pass, while Hennon was able to make a single pass, shooting down the rear Nell, which burst into flames and crashed into the sea. The enemy escorts did not interfere, as they were bring engaged by Dutch fighters.

The day in air combat was a disaster for the Allies, as they lost 16 American, RAAF, and Dutch fighters shot down or crash landed, along with three flying boats and two B-17s. They also lost 10 to 12 anchored seaplanes and flying boats and four parked B-17s. Rowland was never seen again and listed as KIA.

Early February 1942: 20PS on the Way to Java

By early February, ABDA prospects in the NEI were bleak, as over 50% of the Dutch Air Force had been destroyed, only 11 FEAF P-40s were operational, and the Japanese were close to cutting off the ferry route for receiving additional aircraft from Australia. The Australians were pressing to have American P-40s diverted to Port Moresby, New Guinea, which the Japanese were threatening, and 25 P-40s of the recently organized 20PS (Provisional) were ordered there in late January. These aircraft and personnel had arrived at Darwin as part of the 35PG in January under Capt. William Lane. However, the order to divert to Port Moresby was rescinded at the last minute on 29 January, and the 24 P-40s of the unit left Brisbane and arrived at Darwin in the evening of 31 January. The next day the 20PS was scheduled for its first long range ferry flight north to the Dutch-held field at Koepang, led by an escorting navigation B-24. However, the next day the weather was very bad and Capt. Paul Davis did not get his 24 P-40s off until 1700. After only 30 minutes of flying, violent storms caused Davis, in the lead B-24, to decide to turn back. The very heavy rains continued, and on 4 February Davis had his Warhawks taxi out through heavy mud; during the afternoon 14 P-40s took off to try a second ferry flight to reach Koepang. It would not be until 1700 that all the P-40s rendezvoused with Davis' B-24, who led the inexperienced pilots around weather fronts. Low on fuel, all landed successfully at Koepang at 1915, just as it was getting dark.

5 February 1942: 20PS

At 0600 14 Warhawks (ferry leader Capt. William Lane, Cornelius Reagan, Jesse Hague, Lawrence Landry, James Morehead, Gene Bound, William Gallienne, Dwight Muckley, Robert McWherter, William Turner, Paul Gambonini, Thomas Hayes, Marion Fuchs, and George Haynes) left Koepang, navigated again by Davis' B-24 and headed for their stopover at Den Pasar Airfield on Bali for refueling on their way to Soerabaja, Java. Engine trouble prevented McWherter's P-40 from taking off, but the other 13 formed up behind the B-24. As they were approaching Den Pasar low on fuel, unidentified aircraft were reported in the area, so Capt. Lane ordered his pilots to land on the grass field and quickly refuel from 55 gallon drums, but there was only one hand pump available, so each Warhawk had to taxi up to the drums and refuel singly, and then immediately take off and patrol in case the enemy attacked the vulnerable P-40s refueling below. Lane refueled and took off first, followed by Bound, Gallienne, and Hague. During the slow refueling process the first patrolling P-40s were using precious fuel needed for the flight to Soerabaja. Muckley, Turner, Landry, and Reagan were next to finish refueling. As Lane and Bound climbed to 5,000 feet they were bounced by three Zeros, and all eight P-40s in the air scattered; Gambonini saw the Zeros as his fighter was being refueled and decided to cut his refueling short to join the combat above. One of the Zeros dove between Lane and Bound and gave Bound a good shot, but he did not see it crash. Bound had lost Lane, so he looked around and saw two P-40s below, but as he joined them he saw that the trailing fighter was actually a Zero and closed behind it and fired a short burst that tore off pieces, and it headed nose first into the sea. As Bound flew on he saw flames coming out of his engine and looked around and saw a Zero firing on his fighter. He was rapidly losing speed, and Bound realized that his fighter was doomed, so he ducked into a cloud in preparation to bail out. He delayed bailing out until about 1,000 feet, fearing that the Japanese would strafe him in his parachute. As his chute opened the harness jerked and badly dislocated his shoulder, breaking a bone. When he crashed into the tree canopy it held him 20 feet off the ground for 45 minutes until natives came by and cut him down. Jesse Hague was number four in line and had two Zeros attack him from directly above. Hague dove away through enemy tracers and lost his pursuers, only to have another Zero get on his tail as he climbed out of his dive. It was at this point that Hague realized that he had not dropped his tank and released it, but forgot to switch to his main tank and dove again with his engine sputtering until fed by its new fuel supply. Hague was about to join another P-40 when he was bounced by a Zero and headed inland and maneuvered to escape, but every time he looked back he saw the Zero firing on his tail. Hague twisted and turned through every valley and around every hill, but the Zero pilot continued after him; he finally gave up the chase when he either ran out of ammunition or ran low on fuel. Fortunately, Hague was able to find his way back to Soerabaja after the chase by identifying a landmark volcano near the base.

Dwight Muckley and Wingman William Turner had taken off after Hague and saw a P-40 (Bound?) being attacked by several Zeros; they dove on the enemy and the two became separated. When Muckley came out of his dive he saw Turner being attacked by eight Zeros from above, but before he could help his Wingman three Zeros dove on him. Muckley went into a steep full throttle dive and slowly pulled away over the jungle canopy, and finally the enemy pilots broke off. Turner also dove away, but his fighter suffered several hits; he managed to land safely back at Den Pasar with a flat tire. Lawrence Landry and Wingman Cornelius Reagan were the next element to take off, but soon Regan came under attack and Landry turned to the rescue. As Landry fired into one of Ragan's attackers he was attacked by two Zeros from astern. Landry's aircraft was severely hit, and he crashed into the sea with his fighter. Reagan's P-40 had its rudder damaged, engine sputtering, and hydraulic system shot out, but he was able to make a wheels up landing at Den Pasar, saving himself; his fighter was written off. At the same time that Reagan landed he was followed by Turner, who came in for a crash landing after scoring a victory. Paul Gambonini then landed his damaged fighter, which was out of fuel after his earlier partial refill. As the last of the Squadron fighters landed, 27 Japanese bombers approached Den Pasar at 18,000 to 20,000 feet, and the pilots and Hayes, Fuchs, and Morehead, who had not refueled, headed toward shelter in a nearby coconut grove. After surviving some near misses during the bombing they returned to the field to survey the damage to their aircraft. After salvaging and cannibalizing they were able to get two P-40s into flying condition. Meanwhile, the natives were filling enough craters to make the runway wide enough for the P-40s to take off.

After Capt. Lane shot down an enemy aircraft he went into a steep dive to evade other enemy aircraft and landed at Singosari and was joined by Blanton at 1500, and the two navigated around and through thunderstorms on their way to Ngoro. Gallienne had flown, fought, and escaped during the entire combat with his external tank still attached. Muckley's Warhawk was "shot all to hell," but he landed safely with many holes in both wings, and with the rudder, elevators, and ailerons non-functioning, radio out, and two flat tires. The C-53 carrying the 20PS' 26 enlisted men also landed safely at Soerabaja. Sprague was at Ngoro Field when he was informed of the whereabouts of his dispersed Squadron. By 5 February there were 20 American fighters on the new airfield at Ngoro, which was located between Djombang and Soerabaja, about 10 miles from Blimbing. The new field was not discovered by the Japanese until the day before the invasion of Java. However, the remaining 10 20PS Warhawks were on their way, led by a Beech 18 piloted by Capt. Louis Connelly that landed at Penfoi Field, Koepang, just before dark. Among the pilots were Flight Leader Hubert Egenes, David Coleman, Al Dutton, Wallace Hoskyn, Elwin Jackson, Les Johnson, Robert McWherter, B.J. Oliver, James Ryan, and Roger Williams.

6 February 1942: 20PS

At sunrise the remaining 10 20PS P-40s took off on the 600 mile trip to Den Pasar navigated by a Beechcraft 18. At 0630, while flying over the Savu Sea at 12,000 feet, a JAAF twin engine G3M Nell (misidentified as a Me-110) attacked the Beechcraft. Connelly dove his unarmed Beech toward the sea while Hubert Egenes led his flight of five on the enemy bomber. Robert McWherter attacked first, and although only two of his guns were working started a fire in its port engine. Andrew Reynolds then dove to attack next and started a fire in its starboard engine. Egenes fired and "sawed off" a wing. David Coleman and Albert Dutton were about to follow up, but the enemy bomber was going down in flames with 1/3 victory credited to each pilot. After the combat, the Beech and Egenes had disappeared. Coleman and Dutton had correctly dropped their tanks before entering combat, but McWherter and Reynolds had not. After the combat, and without the navigating Beech, McWherter and Reynolds disagreed on their location and decided to separate. Reynolds and Coleman flew south, while McWherter and Dutton headed north in their search for a landing field; but Reynolds and Coleman soon decided to turn north to rejoin. Coleman and Dutton, who had dropped their tanks, began to run low on fuel and would not have enough to reach Den Pasar. They scouted an area on Lombok Island to make a crash landing and both were successful, with Coleman injuring a hip. When Reynolds and McWherter landed at Den Pasar on the last of their fuel they were greeted by Connelly and the other six P-40 pilots who had landed on the cratered runway at 0945. The seven 20PS pilots of the first group had landed at Den Pasar the day before, and Turner's and Hynes' damaged P-40s were almost repaired, but Fuchs, Gambonini, Hayes, and Reagan were without aircraft. Morehead was the only pilot with a serviceable fighter and volunteered to fly top cover for the Beech (which had arrived at Den Pasar) when it left with the eight second echelon fighters the next morning. Gambonini and Fuchs would fly as passengers in the Beech, while Hayes and Reagan would remain behind. After dodging the craters on the runway all aircraft continued uneventfully to Soerabaja, where they were met by Sprague, who had flown in from Ngoro and would lead them to the secret field. While the Japanese had been testing the Americans at Soerabaja, more new P-40 reinforcements arrived at the new airfield prepared for the Americans at Ngoro. This field was located between Djombang and Soerabaja, about 10 miles from Blimbing, and would not be discovered by the Japanese until the day before the invasion of Java. Meanwhile, Dutton and Coleman were met by natives who were local Dutch police conscripts, and they took the pilots to the Dutch Governor. After a bath, a change of clothes, and dinner the two boarded a sailboat and were taken to Den Pasar.

6 February 1942: 17PS

Eventually, 17 of the 24 fighters that landed at Darwin made it on to Java, but only 12 were fit for combat; all were incorporated into the ranks of the 17th Pursuit Squadron. Another P-40 was lost when Capt. Willard Reed, a Marine Corps pilot familiar with Java operations on temporary duty to the 17PS, had his Warhawk's engine cut out as he was testing the fighter. He crashed inverted into a flooded rice paddy and was unable to free himself and drowned.

9 February 1942: 17PS

During the next few days the Japanese tested the American fighter defense of Java by being intentionally detected by the air warning system, causing a flight of American fighters to be scrambled; the Japanese then quickly withdrew before combat was engaged. The Japanese discovered that if they sent intruders in from many different directions the air warning system was confused and ineffective.

During the late morning, four flights of 16 P-40s were on standby to intercept the usual Japanese attacks on Java. Each of the four flights was headed by a Philippines veteran, as were the Elements, but the other eight wingmen were rookie pilots. Gerald McCallum headed A flight; Walter Coss led B flight; Jack Dale led C flight; and George Kiser headed D flight. At 1035 the Air Defense Command (ADC) in Soerabaja reported a formation of Japanese bombers heading for Malang, near the 19BG's base at Singosari. However, the Japanese bombers would have dropped their bombs before the P-40s arrived, and the ADC directed them to intercept them north of Soerabaja on their return flight.

At 1050 the four flights left the two strips to climb slowly to their assigned altitude of 23,000 feet to search for the bombers. However, when they reached that altitude they were unwieldy and their P-40s flew sluggishly at that altitude. Two formations of eight and nine Betty bombers were 50 miles south of this patrol flying at 15,000 feet. At 1107 Joseph Kruzel's Wingman, Roger Williams, in Dale's C flight, spotted the bombers. When the excited Williams radioed his sighting it was not understood. Jesse Hague had sighted the bombers but was alone, as his Element Leader, Edward Gilmore, returned to Ngoro Field when he found his guns were not working. Hague also radioed a warning that was not heard, and he followed them just out of range of their gunfire. Finally, he decided to attack the escaping Bettys alone, and in his excitement in his first combat fired short. Collecting himself, he attacked again, and could see he was getting some hits before his guns malfunctioned and he had break off and headed back to Ngoro.

B flight leader Walter Coss, and his Wingman, Robert McWherter, continued climbing after losing Gilmore and Hague of their second element and spotted twin-engined bombers and single-engined fighters in the distance. As Coss and McWherter came closer, they identified 17 Betty bombers and nine escorting Zero fighters, heading towards Malang. Moments later, the Zeros went into a high-speed dive towards them and Coss and McWherter went into a steep evasive dive and escaped their pursuers and became separated. McWherter climbed and leveled, and after a few minutes encountered nine enemy bombers returning from bombing Malang. McWherter began climbing toward the nine Bettys speeding away at 25,000 feet. It took McWherter's P-40 15 minutes to catch them. Finally, at about 25,000 feet he closed from the rear on the bomber on the extreme left side of the V formation and began firing, causing smoke from its port engine. But to his great surprise he had noticed "twinkling fire" from the tail guns of all nine bombers. On his second and third passes McWherter fired at the rear of all nine bombers in order to extinguish the fire from their tail gunners. McWherter expended all his ammunition and returned to Ngoro after watching the Betty with the smoking engine head down. Later Dutch spotters saw a bomber go down northeast of Soerabaja, which was credited to McWherter.

Williams and Elwin Jackson, in Dale's C flight, fired on and hit the Japanese but made no claims. McCallum's A Flight and Kiser's D Flight patrolled for 1:45 northeast and southwest of Soerabaja but saw no enemy aircraft.

9 February 1942: 3PS

The next day, nine surviving P-40s of the 3rd Pursuit Squadron (Provisional), led by Lt. Allison Strauss, and three A-24 dive bombers of the 27BG/91BS left Darwin for Koepang led by a LB-30. Seven of the P-40s had already been lost while flying north from Brisbane to Darwin. One P-40 developed engine problems and was forced to return to Darwin, and soon the A-24s fell behind, leaving the LB-30 guiding the eight P-40s. Upon reaching Java, tropical storms forced the LB-30 to return to Darwin, leaving the P-40s on their own. By the time the aircraft reached Koepang, the fighters and the lagging dive bombers were nearly out of fuel, and one by one they went down into the storm searching for the airfield. Some pilots made crash landings and some bailed out, and all eight P-40s were lost, along with one pilot. The three A-24s managed to get into the field at Koepang, although they were mistaken for enemy aircraft and two of them were hit by friendly AA fire.

10-11 February 1942: 3PS

Capt. Grant Mahony left Darwin with the second flight of 11 P-40s in the morning and all arrived over Pasirian, a field in the southeast of Java, the next day. However, one of the fighters nosed over on landing and another came in wheels up when the gear refused to come down, and both were out of service. After refueling, the remaining seven took off and landed at Ngoro. The surviving P-40s of the 3rd Squadron were merged into the 17th Squadron under Maj. Charles Sprague, with Capt. Lane as his XO. The reinforcements brought the strength of the 17th up to 47 officers and 81 enlisted men, and the ground crews brought the Squadron's strength to its greatest during the Java campaign. The dedicated efforts of the ground crews brought the operational strength of the Squadron to 24 P-40s with one under repair, while five had been written off for spares and the two at Pasirian were under repair.

15 February 1942: Japanese Advances

The situation was becoming even bleaker for the ABDA, as on 15 February Singapore surrendered, the Japanese fleet was on its way to support the paratroop landing at Palembang, Sumatra, and a second enemy naval force was gathering off the Celebes in preparation for an attack on Java. Following these warships were the transports that would bring about the full scale invasion of the Netherlands East Indies. The Japanese needed to establish themselves on the newly captured airfields on Sumatra, and this would give the Allies a few days of respite before the Japanese renewed their attacks.

15 -16 February 1942: 17PS

Meanwhile, the FEAF fought on with what they had. At 0800 Maj. Charles Sprague and eight of his most senior pilots (Capts. Walter Coss and Grant Mahony, and 1Lts. Gerald McCallum, George Kiser, Joseph Kruzel, William Hennon, Hubert Egenes, Edwin Gilmore, and Dwight Muckley) took off from Ngoro on a short hop to Madioen to have bombs installed on their wing racks before continuing on to Batavia. This was to be the first time the 17PS' Warhawks were to be used as fighter bombers. However, there were problems attaching the bombs, which were too large for the racks, and those bombs which could be attached would then not release. Each bomb had to be modified to fit each rack, and during the process a Japanese air raid was called and the P-40s had to scramble so as not to be caught on the field. The enemy attack never materialized, but delayed the adapting of the four bombs to each P-40 until mid-afternoon. The Squadron took off minus Gilmore, whose fighter experienced problems, and proceeded to Tjililitan Airfield, south of Batavia. On their arrival the Squadron encountered near darkness and rain showers, but all landed safely except Muckley, who badly damaged his fighter but was unhurt. The tired pilots were put up at a local hotel for the night. Meanwhile, Sprague had been ordered to FEAF HQ, where he learned that the Japanese had landed at Palembang, Sumatra, about 250 miles northwest, and the Squadron's mission was to bomb and strafe the landing barges in the Moesi River, the oil refinery, and two airfields. A-24s, B-17s, and LB-30s were also to be part of the attack plan. The next morning the weather was rainy at Batavia and Sprague had not returned to Tjililitan, so the mission was postponed.

17 February 1942: 17PS

The next morning the weather was marginal but the ceiling was higher, and Sprague decided to take off at 0900 with each Warhawk (except Sprague's) armed with two 45 pound (20kg) bombs and carrying a belly tank. For most of the 250 mile direct flight to Palembang to the northwest, the 17th encountered light rain and low ceiling, but as the American fighters arrived over the Java Sea the weather cleared somewhat. At 1020 the Squadron saw eight fixed landing gear enemy fighters identified as Nakajima 97 Nates, which were considered rather innocuous radial engined aircraft. Sprague's Flight (Capt. Walter Coss and 1Lts. Gerald McCallum and George Kruzel) immediately salvoed their bombs and belly tanks to meet the enemy attack. The Nates were found to be surprisingly agile, with a very short turning radius, but Sprague shot one down immediately. Coss made three firing passes, but each pass was frustrated by an aerobatic maneuver and Coss stalled on the third pass and lost the Nate. However, 1Lts. McCallum and Kruzel quickly got on the tails of their targets and easily shot them down. Two pilots of Capt. Grant Mahony's flight, 1Lt. George Kiser and 2Lt. Hubert Egenes, didn't jettison their bombs and made their bombing run on ships and barges along the Moesi River bank. After dropping his bombs Kiser attacked three Type 97s and shot "one to pieces" before dropping his bombs. Egenes shot down a "Zero," while Mahony claimed a probable and then strafed the enemy. Hennon did not jettison his bombs and went after the Nates instead. He fired at one but his guns jammed, so dove away to clear his guns. After he got his guns working, Hennon dropped his bombs on some barges in the Moesi River and then strafed the swimming survivors. He then flew over the Palembang Airfield and shot down a Nate that was in the landing pattern. Hennon returned to the Moesi area and continued to strafe before returning to Tjililitan. As he was returning, his Warhawk developed a bad oil leak and he ran his fuel tanks dry in case he had to crash land, but his late arrival at Tjililitan, while causing consternation among his squadron mates, was successful. Coss also had an anxious moment upon landing, as his landing gear

1Lt. Joseph **Kruzel** scored his first of three victories in the Pacific. (AFAA)

and flaps would not extend, but he was able to extend them manually and land safely. Coss was to remain at Tjililitan to have his fighter repaired. After spending the night at Tjililitan, Sprague led the Squadron to Bandoeng, minus Hennon. The Dutch mechanics were unable to repair Coss' fighter by the next morning, so Coss "stuffed the loose wires into his cockpit" and took off with the Squadron. The Suadron landed safely for fueling, repairs, and a victory party thrown for them by Gen. Emmett "Rosie" O'Donnell at FEAF HQ. After spending the night at Bandoeng, Sprague and the five others (now minus Coss) took off for the four hour flight back to Ngoro. At Tjililitan that morning Hennon finally had his fighter repaired after using a line from Muckley's wreck, and he took off alone for the nonstop flight all the way to Ngoro Field, 420 miles to the east.

17 February 1942: Ngoro

The weather was still bad at Ngoro on 17 February, but patrol flights were sent up in the afternoon. Paul Gambonini led his C flight on a two hour patrol over Soerabaja at 1400, flying at 23,000-27,000 feet. At 1500, D flight took off for its patrol and Harold Lund got separated in the bad weather conditions and did not return with the fight. Two aircraft were sent out to search for him but without success. At 1900 Lund finally called saying that he had run out of gas and made a wheels up landing in a rice field near Madioen. He reported that he was uninjured and that his fighter only suffered damage to the radiator and had a bent propeller.

18 February 1942: 17PS

At this time the Japanese stepped up their air activity in anticipation of their invasion of Java. The Japanese established a fighter base at Bandjermasin/Martapura Airfield, on the southeast end of Borneo, and at Makassar/Maros, in the southern Celebes. While the Japanese advance toward Java now put worthwhile targets within the range of FEAF pursuits, dive bombers, and heavy bombers, it also made the American airfields vulnerable to attack. On this day the Japanese were to conduct concerted bombing and strafing sweeps over Java. That morning the Japanese sent out 21 Bettys from Kendari escorted by eight Zeros on a bombing raid to Soerabaja. One formation of nine bombers missed their rendezvous with the Zeros and proceeded to Soerabaja unescorted.

At 0900, as Sprague and his pilots were returning to base from Palembang, Hague and Morehead requested and received permission from 1Lt. William Lane, who was in command in Sprague's absence, to have belly tanks attached to their fighters in anticipation of another mission to Palembang. At 1045, the 17PS P-40s standing on alert from early that morning were given sufficient warning and were able to have an advantage in their attack on the unescorted bombers reported heading towards Soerabaja. The P-40s were ordered to scramble to intercept three separate enemy bomber formations. With Sprague and all the other senior 17PS pilots away, 1Lt. Cyril Blanton had been designated to lead the Squadron, composed of four flights, in the interception. There were two other P-40s available on the field and Hague and Morehead headed toward them, but were outraced by Mahony and Gilmore, who took off in them. Hague and Morehead then ran back to Lane and asked if they could remove the belly tanks from their fighters to join the others, and it took 45 minutes for these two to take off.

The Zero escorts were late to escort their bombers, and Blanton led the Warhawks from out of the sun, at about 45 degrees into the line of flight of the Bettys. Blanton was diving too fast, which would decrease the time for the first firing pass. Blanton concentrated his fire on the lead Betty and hit its starboard engine, then turned his fire onto the cockpit when the engine started smoking. As he finished his very short firing run, he dove past the Japanese formation and saw the Betty heading down. He pulled up out of his dive and turned back to come up underneath the rear end of the formation and made a firing pass at a Zero which had just arrived.

1Lt. Ben **Irvin** shot down a bomber for his first of two victories. (AAF)

LEFT: After two victories with the 20PS in the Philippines, 1Lt. Edwin **Gilmore** got his third and last victory of the war. (AAF) RIGHT: 2Lt. Andrew **Reynolds** scored his victory, and would later become an ace with the 49FG/9FS. (AFAA)

Blanton was followed by 1Lts. Edwin Gilmore, Marion Fuchs, Ben Irvin, Roger Williams, and Capt. Grant Mahony, who each shot down a bomber (Mahony also heavily damaged another for a probable claim). The Zeros finally arrived and attacked as the remnants of the Japanese bomber formation scuttled away. Blanton and 2Lt. Andrew Reynolds shot down one Zero each. A second flight of bombers arrived over Soerabaja, but this time they were escorted by about a dozen Zero fighters. In the turning dogfight 2Lt. Frank Adkins got one of the Zeros and 2Lt. Morris Caldwell shot down two bombers. The enemy bombers were flying in a step down formation in line, which permitted the tail gunner of each bomber to protect the belly of the bomber above. Caldwell attacked the top bomber in the formation first and sent it down in flames. He then descended and climbed under the bottom bomber in the formation and shot it down. The massed fire from the bomber tail gunners hit Caldwell's fighter and his first effort to bail out against the slipstream was without success, but a second adrenalin-fueled push got him out and he parachuted safely. Because of the confusion and poor record keeping of the time some sources (Olynyck) do not credit either pilot with these claims.

Caldwell landed safely and traveled slowly north toward Ngoro from village to village, having to stop and "have tea" in each along the way. Atkins, on his first mission, had not returned, and had become separated while being chased by Zeros after a diving attack on the Bettys. He eluded his pursuers but became lost and spotted a B-17 below with its gear down, apparently heading in for a landing at a big field, which he thought to be Singosari. Adkins decided to follow the B-17 and lowered his gear, landed, and taxied to a hangar and was greeted by 19BG personnel.

14-18 February 1942: 33PS

The Allies in Java were desperate for supplies and reinforcements, and in a last ditch effort troops were loaded on two Australian and two American transports escorted by several warships at Darwin. On 12 February, a last minute order was given to have a P-40 squadron report to Darwin to escort the convoy to Koepang on the 14th. The 33rd Pursuit Squadron (Provisional), the only American fighter unit available, had just arrived at Port Pirie, on the southern coast of central Australia, when orders were sent to its CO, Maj. Floyd Pell, to fly to Darwin at once. The Squadron had an entire continent to cross to meet the deadline and arrived at the RAAF field at Darwin late on the 15th after the convoy had departed.

During its three days at Darwin the 33rd Squadron got its aircraft combat ready, and on 18 February Maj. Pell was informed that the Squadron was to fly to Java to reinforce the 17th Squadron and was to depart the next morning. After an initial delay, Maj. Pell took off with 10 P-40s at 0915, following a B-17E that had been assigned to navigate them to Java. Twenty minutes after take off Pell was informed by radio that the weather was bad at Koepang and becoming worse. Since most of his pilots were relatively inexperienced flying the P-40, Maj. Pell decided to return to Darwin.

Maj. Floyd **Pell**, CO of the 33rd Pursuit Squadron. (Provisional). (AAF)

19 February 1942: 33PS and Darwin: Australia's Pearl Harbor

After their conquest of Sumatra, the Japanese were now ready to isolate Java by invading Bali and occupying Timor. The capture of Timor was crucial to the Japanese, as it was a vital Allied "stepping stone" in its air reinforcement route from Australia. Its loss would mean that no more short range aircraft could be delivered to the East Indies by air. After Ambon and the Celebes were in Japanese hands, it was obvious to the Allies that Timor would soon be invaded and they would have to counter this threat. So on 15 February three US Army transports, *Meigs*, *Mauna Loa*, and *Port Mar*, and the Australian coaster *Tulagi* were loaded with 1,800 Australian and US troops and equipment, and left Port Darwin to reinforce Timor. The convoy was escorted by the USN cruiser *Houston* and destroyer *Peary*, as well as two RAN sloops (*Swan* and *Warrego*). As soon as the convoy was underway it was spotted by an enemy H6K Mavis flying boat, which proceeded to shadow the vessels and report on their position. The anxious Captain of the *Houston*, Albert Rooks, desperately called Darwin for fighter protection, which was answered by a lone P-40 flown by Lt. Robert Buel of the 21PS; the fighter was one of only two available. Initially Buel was unable to locate the flying boat despite the *Houston* firing her guns in the intruder's direction. Buel finally spotted and pursued the flying boat and closed in. He fired and hit its fuselage forward of the fuel tanks, killing the W/T operator and starting a fire. However, Buel's fighter was also badly hit and dove into the sea in flames. The pilot of the badly damaged and rapidly burning flying boat managed to skillfully ditch it, and its crew was able to escape. They eventually reached Melville Island, where they were taken prisoner.

This reinforcement convoy to Timor caused the Japanese High Command to designate the convoy a priority target. At 1100 on 16 February, the Japanese sent out 35 Betty and 10 Mavis bombers to attack the convoy, but expert maneuvering and heavy AA fire warded off any direct hits on the convoy. Nonetheless, all four transports began to leak as a result of concussions from near misses, but the heavy enemy attack on the convoy had the desired effect, as all the ships were forced to turn back towards Darwin, leaving Timor defenseless. Following the attacks on Rabaul and New Guinea, the four Japanese carriers of the 1st Carrier Fleet, the *Akagi*, *Kaga*, *Shokaku*, and *Zuikaku*, had returned to Truk at the end of the month. An attack on the Marshall Islands, the first USN carrier strike of the war and carried out by aircraft from the USS *Enterprise*, had sent the enemy carriers dashing northwards in an unsuccessful attempt to intercept. *Shokaku* and *Zuikaku* then headed for Japan to counter any possible attack on the Home Islands, while *Akagi* and *Kaga* headed back southwards to Palau to join *Hiryu* and *Soryu*, which had just supported the Ambon landings. On 15 February all four carriers, escorted by cruisers and destroyers, left Palau under V.Adm.Choichi Nagumo and arrived near the Ceram Islands three days later. They waited near Amboina to launch their attack against Darwin at dawn on the 19th.

Darwin was the main Allied supply base from which reinforcements and equipment could be delivered to the East Indies and to the forces still resisting in the Philippines. Thus, Darwin was the greatest threat to the Japanese at this time; not only to their invasion of Timor, but also to their important base at Rabaul. The 1st Carrier Division and the land-based bombers of the 21st and 23rd Air Flotillas were assigned to launch a full scale attack on Darwin. On the 19th, Port Darwin Harbor held 47 vessels at anchor, including 11 merchant ships and the four returned transports of the aborted Timor convoy; the USN destroyer *Peary* and the small seaplane tender *William B. Preston*, the latter a converted destroyer which had escaped from the Philippines. There were two tankers and a hospital ship and 32 mainly auxiliary and boom defense vessels. There were also a number of military and civil flying boats present. At RAAF Darwin Airfield were nine Hudsons of 2 and 13 RAAF Squadrons (Daly Waters based eight more Hudsons), USAAF P-40Es of the newly arrived 33PS, and also the sole remaining P-40

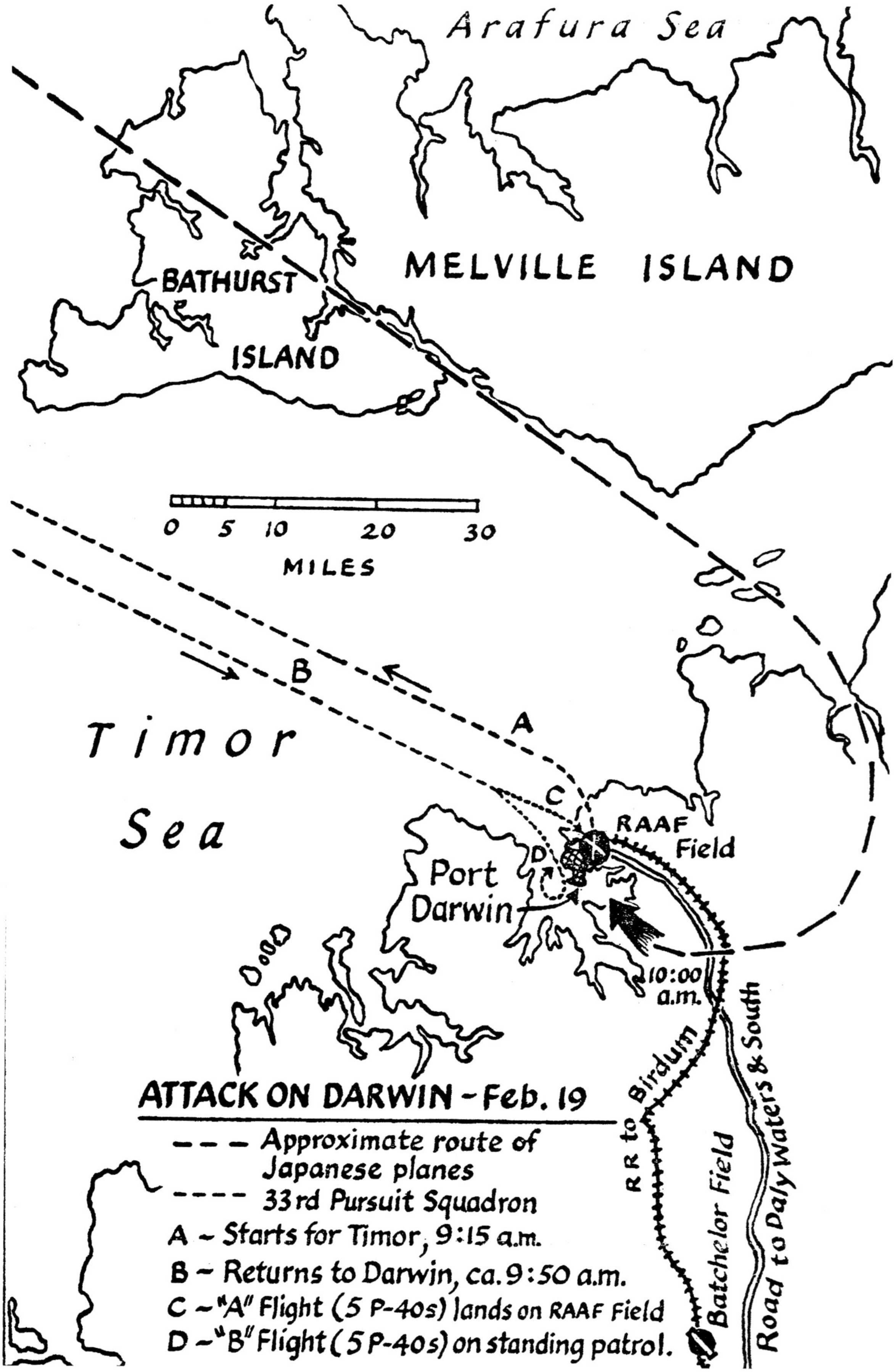

Arafura Sea
MELVILLE ISLAND
BATHURST
ISLAND
0 5 10 20 30
MILES
B
A
Timor
Sea
C
D
RAAF
Field
Port
Darwin
10:00
a.m.
RR to Birdum
Batchelor Field
Road to Daly Waters & South
ATTACK ON DARWIN - Feb. 19
--- Approximate route of Japanese planes
---- 33rd Pursuit Squadron
A - Starts for Timor, 9:15 a.m.
B - Returns to Darwin, ca. 9:50 a.m.
C - "A" Flight (5 P-40s) lands on RAAF Field
D - "B" Flight (5 P-40s) on standing patrol.

of the 3PS. This aircraft and its pilot, Lt. Robert Oestreicher, now joined the 33PS, which was about to begin the flight up to Java.

First off from the carriers were B5N Kate bombers: 18 from *Akagi* leading the way, led by the strike force commander, Cdr. Mitsuo Fuchida; followed by 18 more from *Soryu*, led by Lt. Heijiro Abe; 18 from *Hiryu*, led by Lt.Cdr. Tadashi Kusumi; and 27 from *Kaga*, led by Lt.Cdr. Takashi Hashiguchi. After the Kates took off they were followed by 18 Zeros: nine from the *Soryu*, led by Lt. Iyozo Fujita; and nine from *Hiryu*, led by Lt. Sumio Nono. The initial launching was to head for Melville Island, some 90 minutes away, where it would rendezvous with the faster dive bombers, which would follow with their own escort. Half an hour after the first Kates had taken off, the D3A Val dive bombers began to follow: 17 from *Hiryu* (Lt. Michio Kobayashi), and 18 each from Akagi (Lt. Takehiko Chihaya), *Soryu* (Lt.Cdr. Takashige Egusa), and *Kaga* (Lt. Shoichi Ogawa). Escort was provided by nine Zeros from Kaga (Lt. Yasushi Nikaido) and nine from *Akagi* (Lt.Cdr. Shigeru Itaya). Other fighters from *Soryu* were launched three at a time during the morning to fly defensive combat air patrols. Meanwhile, from Celebes and Ambon 54 Bettys, 27 each from the Kanoya (Lt.Cdr. Toshiie Irisa) and 1st Kokutais (Lt.Cdr. Takeo Ozaki) took off for the same target.

At 0915, 10 P-40Es took off from RAAF Darwin and joined a B-17 which was to navigate them to Koepang Airfield on Timor, on the first leg of their journey to Java. Soon after take off bad weather was reported ahead and they were ordered to return to base. As Darwin was in a state of high alert, Air Control ordered half of the returning fighters to patrol overhead while the others landed and refueled. However, a radio call from a coast watcher on the northern tip of Melville Island was received at RAAF HQ, reporting a "large number of aircraft," which was construed as to refer to the P-40 formation, even though Melville Island was north of the proposed route! Another radio message received at RAAF HQ which reported "an unusually large air formation bearing down on us from the north-west" was not acted upon. Consequently, no advance warning was given at Darwin of the impending attack. On his arrival at Darwin RAAF base Pell took his flight of five in to land and instructed Oestreicher, who had joined the

AAC P-40 destroyed at RAAF Darwin. (AAF)

Darwin docks on fire after the attack of 19 February 1942. (AAF)

The **RAAF** base at **Darwin** was bombed on 19 February 1942. (AAF)

33rd, to hold his flight on patrol for a few hours orbiting at 15,000 feet, and were notified of a Japanese formation approaching Darwin 50 miles out. The Japanese formation of 70 dive and medium bombers, escorted by 18 pursuits thoroughly bombed the crowded port and was immediately followed by 54 more enemy bombers.

As the Japanese dive bomber formation approached its rendezvous area, a USN PBY was patrolling over the USN supply vessel *Florence D*; and one of the *Kaga* Zeros escorting the formation broke away to attack the PBY and forced it down. After the Zero pilot completed his attack on the PBY he became separated from his formation and continued on alone. When he reached the Darwin area he saw the five patrolling P-40s and bravely dove to attack. Surprised Patrol Leader 2Lt. Robert Oestreicher spotted the Zero and, unaware that this was a single aircraft, Oestreicher jettisoned his tank and dove, but the Zero was already upon the others in his flight.

At 0945, shortly after B Flight began circling over the field to provide top cover for A Flight's landing, the pilots heard an unidentified voice (not Pell's voice, but Oestreicher's) ordering all the P-40s overhead to return to the field. John Peres, leading the first element, decided on his own to head back to the field to get a clarification, and apparently without informing the others he left his Wingman, Elton Perry, to lead the element, with Oestreicher as the flight's weaver. Peres was shot down immediately. (Note: Peres' body was found the next September, when Aborigines discovered his burnt out P-40 in the sea along the coast only 20 miles south of Darwin. The reason it took seven months to find Peres reveals the hostile and barren desert located on the edge of the sea in which Darwin is situated.) About 15 minutes later, Oestreicher began weaving above Max Wiecks and his Wingman, William Walker, and suddenly rolled to the right and went into a steep dive. Walker thought Oestreicher was in trouble and watched him in his sudden dive, then saw him drop his belly tank about 500 feet into the dive. Moments later, Walker heard Oestreicher shout "Zeros" over the radio. Walker thought that Oestreicher was mistakenly diving on an A-24, and watched as Oestreicher dove to about 2,000 feet and pulled out, then headed quickly south. The inattentive Walker then spotted nine radial engine fighters diving on him and Wiecks. Walker pulled around into the Japanese and started firing, but didn't score any hits because of their diving turn. Walker tried to turn tighter, but bullets tore through his cockpit and ripped a large chunk out of his left shoulder muscle, and Walker dove toward the field.

After Oestreicher dove away from his flight, he flew through scattered clouds for about half an hour when he spotted two single engine aircraft with their landing gear down. Initially, he thought they were P-40s with their gear down heading towards Batchelor Field for a landing. As he closed he saw their "meatball" insignia and identified them as enemy fixed landing gear dive bombers flying at about 1,500 feet. As soon as Oestreicher began firing the two Japanese broke away, one to the right and the other to the left. Oestreicher fired on the right bomber and saw it "burst into flames and go down." He then closed on the other, but lost it when it entered clouds trailing some smoke, either from gunfire or perhaps from the enemy pilot firewalling his aircraft. Oestreicher flew in and out of the clouds trying to find landmarks to guide him to base, and about a quarter hour later found the railroad tracks below and followed them to Darwin and the RAAF airdrome there. As he arrived over the field at about 1140 he showed his Stars & Bars to the Australian AA gunners and then came in for a landing. After rolling down three quarters of the runway he stopped, worrying about ground looping, which turned out to be a good idea, as his left wheel and tire were damaged. His P-40 was later destroyed on the ground by the second wave of Japanese attackers.

Meanwhile, Wiecks was fiddling with his malfunctioning radio, and when he looked up to check his position he spotted a Zero just below that was firing at Elton Perry's lead P-40, which was heading down in flames. Wiecks chopped his throttle and tried to get behind the Japanese, but during his turn found himself being fired on from behind. Suddenly his Warhawk went into an out of control dive, and as he tried to pull out he couldn't get any response from the controls. As he reached 4,000 feet he decided to bail out, but after opening the canopy and releasing his seat harness he found he was unable to get out because of the forces of the diving P-40 and the bulky RAF-type back pack parachute. Finally he was pulled out of the fighter by the slip stream and just managed to get his chute open at a very low altitude. As he hit the water one of the parachute straps caught on his canteen, causing him to be dragged through the water. Wiecks had the presence of mind to rip off his web belt to collapse the chute. As he inflated his Mae West a Zero passed just overhead, but the pilot apparently didn't see him and Wiecks floated, waiting to be rescued.

2Lt. Robert **Oestreicher** destroyed a dive bomber for his only victory. (AAF)

Pell's flights had just landed when enemy aircraft appeared over the field. Pell and McMahon still had their drop tanks attached and detached them onto the ground, and they were cleared by the ground crews as the P-40s began to move out to the runway. Rice and Glover were racing down the runway, and as Glover was retracting his landing gear, the right one hit one of the empty barrels the Australians had placed around the field as obstacles to deter enemy landings, but Glover managed the take off.

McMahon applied maximum power for take off and headed down the runway, and just before becoming airborne he lifted his left wing to avoid hitting the rudder of a P-40 on the runway (William Walker). Automatically checking his rear, McMahon saw three radial engine aircraft about 500 feet above him and slightly to the left rear in a line abreast formation in the landing pattern. At first he thought they were A-24 dive bombers until he saw the "meatballs" on their wings. McMahon cleared the field and tried to sneak past the attacking Zeros, and after passing under the last Zero in the formation he sped northeast. But the Zero leader saw him and pulled off in a shallow, highspeed diving turn after him. To prevent the Zero from getting on his tail McMahon rolled back to port in a maximum G turn and pulled up into a head on firing pass, hitting the Zero, which had pulled up. Immediately, the enemy Wingman closed to 600 yards head on and the two opened fire, with McMahon tearing a piece off its engine as it passed. A third Zero approached and McMahon pulled up to meet him, but his airspeed was almost to stalling and McMahon dropped his nose to gain speed and started a turn to the right. As he looked down he spotted a P-40 being chased by two Zeros racing across the edge of the RAAF field. Before he could dive McMahon heard loud noises and then felt his P-40 shake. McMahon chopped his throttle and looked over his right shoulder to see a Zero coming up on his right and firing at him. Suddenly, his fighter decelerated, caused by the dropping of his gear, as his hydraulic lines had apparently been hit. As McMahon skidded under his attacker, a second Zero dove at him from 8 o'clock and bullets hit his left wingtip. McMahon skidded and then reversed the skid in an attempt to look like his aircraft was falling out of control. He purposely flew erratically, descending eastward, looking as though he had been badly damaged. The Japanese apparently believed he was about to crash and none followed him. At 400 feet McMahon leveled out and raced away, but the Japanese saw McMahon, and two quickly caught up to him and dove on his flanks, while a third headed for his tail. With his gear down McMahon could not outrun the Zeros, and he headed off to where he thought Rice and Glover could come to his aid. When the Zero on his tail began firing, McMahon pulled his P-40 up and around in a snap roll and then began a turn to take him north to Darwin Harbor, where he hoped friendly AA would cause the Japanese to turn away. McMahon adeptly "jockeyed" his way west, parallel to the coastline, avoiding the fire of the three Zeros. McMahon's fighter was losing coolant, and he knew that his engine would soon freeze. He opened the engine's coolant flap to wide open and headed down to cool the engine with rushing air. As McMahon looked around he spotted another flight of at least six Zeros diving from a high angle to aid his original pursuers. McMahon almost collided with one in the wild fray as he continued west for the protection of Darwin's AA guns. As he neared Darwin he saw a large formation of single engine aircraft at about 8,000, apparently heading for the ships in the harbor. Suddenly he saw a P-40 heading towards him, but it began firing at him and he dove and barely cleared the cliffs and trees surrounding Fannie Bay. He was surprised to see tracers hitting in front of him, but found that in his excitement he had pressed own his gun switch. As he passed over the smoke and fires of Darwin, McMahon tried to evaluate the damage to his fighter and saw smoke and fire coming from the engine's exhaust stacks and prepared to bail out soon. As he looked around he found that the Zeros were closing, and also saw two large oil tanks belching heavy black smoke and dove into the smoke to elude his pursuers. Upon exiting he found himself flying just over the Darwin roof tops, but still with a Zero on his tail. McMahon broke left and down in the opposite direction, flying parallel to the Darwin Harbor anchorages, where a destroyer was firing at enemy attackers. But when he approached it he also came under its fire, as with his landing gear down he looked like a Japanese dive bomber. McMahon rolled right, exposing his US Stars & Bars at the destroyer, and the AA fire stopped, but when he banked back left and flew a parallel course at just off the water, the destroyer opened fire on him again. At least all this fire caused his pursuers to break off and head away. McMahon climbed to about 2,000 feet and headed for the northern side of Darwin Harbor to look for a place to bail out. He saw PBY flying boats at anchor near a seaplane and prepared to bail out near them. As he approached, he was shocked to see one of the Catalinas erupt into a ball of flames and then saw that the escaping crew were being strafed by three Zeros. McMahon dove straight down and fired on a Zero and the strafers left. The smoke from his engine's exhaust had subsided, and McMahon climbed to 1,000 feet to be able to bail out safely. As he climbed he spotted two more Zeros closing on him and he chopped his throttle; one Zero filled his sights as it passed by, but as he squeezed the trigger nothing happened and the enemy passed safely by him. McMahon decided to bail out, and on his way down he heard machine gun fire, which he thought was from the strafers after the PBYs again. He looked back and was stunned to see that Zeros were firing on him, and McMahon collapsed his chute and curled up into a small target as the Zeros' tracers cut through his chute. Just as he was about to hit the trees he opened his chute to slow his fall, and he landed uninjured, except for a lower leg wound from a bullet during the air combat. Hanging from the trees, McMahon freed himself from the chute and dropped to the ground. Soon he spotted a small boat heading in his direction and he began yelling and jumped into the water, swinging his life jacket, and was picked up.

After having their long range auxiliary fuel tanks hurriedly removed while on the ground, Maj. Floyd Pell and his four inexperienced pilots tried to take off, but all came under immediate attack from Zeros just as they got airborne. After evading three Zeros on take off Pell headed north, and as he flew over Lee Point and turned right, still at treetop level, and about 10 miles northeast of the RAAF field, a Zero suddenly dove on him. The Japanese pilot fired continuously into the P-40's tail and Pell opened his canopy and bailed out at 100 feet, but his chute did not open before he struck the ground.

Charles Hughes took off immediately after Pell and just barely cleared the field; he was heading north when he was bounced just above treetop level by a Zero. He escaped the Zero's first pass, but the Japanese pilot did a 360 loop and got behind Hughes again, raking the American's P-40. Hughes crashed into the brush a few miles from the north end of the runway and was killed.

In the third position on take off was Burt Rice, who also just missed the obstacles on the field and cleared the field heading northeast. But at about 1,500 feet he was attacked by the three Zeros and went into a shallow dive at maximum speed and was able to stay out of range as he went into a slow climb. But soon the Zeros were gaining on him and turned inside of him, getting into firing range. As Rice headed back to the southeast he felt and heard his fighter being hit and tried to evade them in a shallow dive, when he suddenly realized he had no elevator control. Rice decided to bail out, and when he jumped his face hit the tail, knocking him momentarily unconscious. When he regained consciousness he was floating down in his chute, with Zeros making passes and firing at him. He landed in large mangrove trees in a swamp about 10 miles east of the RAAF field. He was uninjured, except for a severe eye wound from hitting the tail of his P-40 while bailing out.

John Glover took off after Rice and also cleared the field, despite hitting a barrel on the runway, but was not attacked by the three Zeros that attacked Rice shortly after his take off. Glover flew to the northeast and climbed to about 3,000 feet at maximum RPM, then turned east in a high speed shallow climb. As he climbed he noticed a parachute and three radial engine fighters circling it about 500 feet below him. As one of the Japanese was leveling out and firing on the pilot in the chute the angry Glover closed on the Zero from behind at 20 degrees and relentlessly fired and exploded the Zero. When the other two Japanese broke away, Glover recognized the parachutist as Rice, who seemed to be dead. Meanwhile, the other two Zeros had climbed to the 8 o'clock high position and Glover decided to lead them back to the field and into Australian AA machine gun fire. Using maximum military power, Glover went into a shallow dive from 2,800 feet, but when he looked back it appeared that the Zeros were gone. He slowed down at tree top height, but when he looked back he was shaken to find the two Zeros he thought he had eluded closing and firing at him. Automatically he shoved the throttle to the firewall with his attention fixed on the closing Zeros. Glover was now over the northeast edge of the field, which was bordered by tall eucalyptus trees, and when he turned to look forward he found himself flying directly into the trees. On impact, his propeller tore off branches that ripped into his fuselage. A tree trunk ripped off his right wing and his trashed fighter bounced off the ground in an open area on the airfield before stopping near another stand of trees. In shock and bleeding profusely from a deep wound extending from his forehead down to his chest, Glover crawled out of his cockpit and sat down on his parachute while a Zero descended to strafe him. Glover had crashed near one of the Australian AA machine gun nests surrounding the field. Two of the Australian gunners ran out and dragged the helpless American pilot to safety.

The Japanese attack on Darwin has been called "Australia's Pearl Harbor." Eleven of Darwin's P-40s were destroyed that day, in addition to six Hudsons, a LB-30, and three PBYs that were on the ground. Darwin's port facilities were almost completely destroyed, and most of the ships in the harbor were either sunk or severely damaged, along with 262 persons killed and 311 injured. During the air battle Rice, Glover, McMahon, Wiecks, and Walker (strafed on the ground) had been shot down and wounded, while Pell, Perry, Peres, and Hughes were shot down and killed.

19 February 1942: 17PS

At the secret Ngoro Airfield, 2Lts. Joseph Kruzel, Nate Blanton, and Jesse Hague were about to take off on a recon mission to check on reports of a Japanese landing in the Bali area. Before they left the Bali landing, reports were confirmed and the mission plan was changed; the 17PS was to escort A-24 dive bombers of the 91BS to attack the enemy ships off the Bali coast. From the very early morning, small numbers of B-17s and LB-30s from Singosari and Madioen had already unsuccessfully bombed the enemy transports and escorting warships. The seven 91BS' A-24s, on their first mission, landed at Singosari at 0705 for refueling and bomb loading, but the armorers had problems adapting the one 500 pound and two 100 pound bombs to the racks of the A-24s. When the P-40 escort was delayed it was decided to call off the mission.

However, at 1130 Maj. William Fisher at the ADC in Soerabaja ordered the 17PS to intercept an incoming Japanese bomber and fighter force. The 16 P-40s on alert took off immediately from Ngoro in four flights led by Capt. Grant Mahony. As the P-40s approached the Soerabaja area, 18 Betty bombers were spotted heading in over the Flores Sea,

Lt. Joseph **Kruzel** claimed his second victory. (AFAA)

Lt. Jesse **Hague** scored his only victory of the war. (AAF)

and Mahony detached two of his flights to intercept them. The bombers, perhaps having been discovered, dropped their loads on innocuous Bawean Island, which was due north of Soerabaja, and turned away. Although the bombers aborted their attack on Java, the 18 escorting Zeros continued on toward Soerabaja. When the other two P-40 flights, one headed by Capt. Mahony and the other by 1Lt. Walter Coss, arrived in the Soerabaja area, they spotted nine Zeros already there and with altitude advantage. Four P-40s climbed into the Zero formation, and several Zeros got on Jesse Hague's tail; he immediately dove for a layer of clouds. After he leveled out, Hague spent the next few minutes coming to the rescue of P-40s with Zeros on the tails. Hague fired at one at long range, forcing the enemy pilot to break away without causing any damage. Hague next slow rolled down on a second Zero, firing at closer range, and saw the Japanese go into a cloud, smoking. He dove on a third Zero and got hits, but the normally incendiary Zero did not catch fire. Hague turned 90 degrees to close on the resilient Zero again, but its pilot surprised Hague by going into a 360 degree turn to get on his tail. The Zero pilot chased the wildly maneuvering Hague all the way to the south side of Java before he broke off.

In the cover flight, Nate Blanton and his Wingman, American Indian 2Lt. Quanah "Chief" Fields, were at about 16,000-18,000 feet when their flight was attacked by the nine Zeros that Hague had first seen. The Flight turned into the Zeros head on, expecting the Japanese to pull up sharply as they usually did and give the Americans a belly shot. Blanton and the Zero pilot exchanged fire as they approached each other and then both pulled up. Just as the Japanese started his roll to check on Blanton, he momentarily became a textbook target and Blanton fired, exploding the Zero in a huge fire ball. As Blanton flew through the debris, he discovered heavy smoke pouring out of his engine and that he had no throttle control, so decided to bail out of his doomed fighter. As he pulled his canopy back and was about to jump he saw two Zeros diving on him. He sunk back down into his cockpit and rolled his fighter over and dove straight down. When he leveled out at about 2,000 feet he had lost his pursuers, but the engine was making noises and losing power and he had no controls. He then decided a belly landing in water off the coast of north Java was better than a ground landing inland. He went into a 90 degree turn and braced himself in his seat as his fighter began to stall almost parallel with the shoreline. Just as his P-40 hit the water, he was thrown around in the cockpit because he had forgotten to refasten his safety belt. The P-40 immediately slowed to a stop in shallow water, and as Blanton stood up in his cockpit he saw two Zeros heading towards him. In pain, he climbed out of the cockpit and laid down on one of the wings, getting ready to roll over into the water. The two Zeros passed over without firing and left. Blanton began wading to shore and to a nearby native settlement. As he approached he found it was uninhabited, but soon he spotted a man standing on the rice paddy dike ahead of him. Blanton yelled the native words meaning "friendly army" and was taken to a Dutch outpost, where he found an English-speaking Dutch officer and explained his situation. Blanton soon arrived back in Soerabaja and then was transported to Ngoro.

Although the other two flights scored no victories, they arrived in time to turn the bombers back before they reached the target. Meanwhile, the four flights returned to Ngoro and found three members missing. Mission leader Mahony's Wingman, Edward Gilmore, was seen to be shot down and bail out with his P-40 on fire, while Blanton made a water landing off the Java coast. Quanah Fields was believed to be KIA after he bailed out of his badly damaged fighter and was strafed in his parachute. He would be the first Native American to die in action. Of the returning pilots, Capts. William Lane and Grant Mahony, 1Lts. Joseph Kruzel and Jesse Hague, and 2Lt. Andrew Reynolds claimed a Zero each. It was not known if Gilmore or Fields had any victories before being shot down. After bailing out, the badly burned Gilmore was rescued and treated by Dutch doctors. The squadron was now down to 24 P-40s with 18 serviceable.

Lt. Andrew **Reynolds** scored his second victory. (AFAA)

Lt. Quanah **Fields** was the first American Indian flier to be lost in the war. (AAF)

20 February 1942: 17PS

By the morning of 20 February, the Australian lifeline to Java had been cut, as Darwin's Harbor was in ruins and no more fighter reinforcements would fly to Java, since the Japanese now occupied the surrounding airfields on Southern Sumatra, Bali, Borneo, and Celebes. Following an Allied cruiser and destroyer naval attack against Japanese naval units on the night of 19/20 February, the AAC continued with its bombing attack on the enemy naval forces supporting the invasion of Bali.

At 0640 three LB-30 (B-24) heavy bombers of the 19th Bomb Group, B-17s of the 7BG, and 91st Squadron A-24 dive bombers were to be escorted by 16 P-40s led by newly promoted Lt.Col. Charles Sprague, with 1Lts. Grant Mahony, Walter Coss, and Joseph Kruzel leading the other three flights to their targets around the newly landed enemy Bali beachhead on the Straits of Lombok. It was critical that the rendezvous with the bombers be made on time, but on take off Coss' P-40 would not start. He quickly abandoned it and ran to a spare and got it started with only minimal time lost. They headed toward Bali at 12,000 to 14,000 feet, and the P-40s formed up with each flight positioning themselves at each corner of the bomber formation: Sprague at the left front, Coss at the right front, Mahony at the left rear, and Kruzel at the right rear. At 0800, as they approached Sanur Harbor they saw at least six vessels in Lombok Strait, with numerous barges heading back and forth to shore. 2Lt. Paul Gambonini had aborted the mission and headed back fifteen minutes before the Squadron reached Bali. Gambonini had landed on the bomber field at Singosari and returned to Ngoro the next morning.

2Lt. Edwin Gilmore called out Zeros attacking above and behind Coss' Flight and made a hard starboard dive. After diving away from the Zeros in their initial pass, 2Lt. Walter Coss was alone at 8,000 feet over the airfield at Den Paser, which had been occupied by the Japanese. Coss positioned himself for a strafing attack with the sun at his back and went into a dive on the airfield. As he approached he saw that the field was empty except for a lone Zero parked outside the main hangar, and he strafed it with a long burst from 50 feet. As Coss turned toward Ngoro at 1,000 feet, William Stauter pulled along side and indicated that he was worried that he would not have enough fuel to return to Ngoro. As they reached landfall on the eastern end of Java, Stauter headed north, up the Java coast, where he ran out of fuel and landed on a beach. He borrowed a bicycle from a Javanese and rode back to base. Coss managed to land safely on reserve fuel despite a wrecked Warhawk on the end of the field. 2Lt. Thomas Hayes had enemy 20mm shells hit his fuselage and tail, tearing off an elevator. Hayes struggled back toward Ngoro, hoping his fuel would hold out and knowing he would have to crash land, as his canopy was jammed by enemy fire. Not on flying

After his tour in the Pacific, Lt.Col. Joseph **Kruzel** transferred to the ETO, serving as the CO of the 361FG (shown), where he scored an additional 3½ victories from February to June 1944 flying the P-47 (1½ v.) and P-51 (2 v.). (AFAA)

LEFT TO RIGHT:
2Lt. Paul **Gambonini** was another pilot who was in the thick of combat but never made an aerial claim. (AAF)

2Lt. Thomas **Hayes**. (AFAA)

1Lt. Jack **Dale**. (AAF)

The photo shows **Hayes** in his 357FG Mustang with two Japanese victory markings. Hayes scored two strafing victories with the 35FG in New Guinea which were not recognized in that theater. However, the 8AF did recognize strafing victories, and Hayes had them shown on his fighter. (AFAA)

duty that day, 2Lt. Jesse Hague witnessed a horrific crash landing and ran to the crash site expecting the worst. The canopy was closed, with blood covering the Plexiglas. Hague tried unsuccessfully to open the damaged canopy, but managed to use the emergency release and helped Hayes out of the cockpit, virtually uninjured. Ironically, Hague found that the fighter that Hayes had been flying that day was his personal fighter *Colleen*. After Hayes recovered from his wounds he transferred to the 35FG HQ Squadron on 21 May 1942 and scored two ground strafing victories. He returned to the US in October 1942 and transferred to the 357FG, stationed in England, and scored his first of eight and a half victories on 24 February 1944 flying a P-51.

After shooting down a Zero, Capt. Grant Mahony also made a strafing attack on Den Paser when a Zero got on his tail. Mahony tried every trick to shake the tenacious Zero pilot, finally diving to the deck and heading north over Bali at full throttle, but the enemy pilot stayed with him. Upon approaching a cliff at treetop level, Mahony dove down over the cliff, made a sharp turn, and the enemy pilot missed Mahony's turn, allowing him to escape. 1Lt. Jack Dale was also credited with shooting down a Zero that morning.

Kruzel led his flight in a dive away from the Zeros and saw a lone Zero under attack by three P-40s. As the enemy pilot climbed in a steep turn to evade his attackers he flew directly in front of Kruzel, who fired a long burst that sent the Zero into the sea for his third and last victory in the Pacific. After his tour in the Pacific Kruzel transferred to the ETO, serving as the CO of the 361FG, where Kruzel scored an additional 3½ victories from February to June 1944 flying the P-47 (1½ v.) and P-51 (2 v.)

2Lt. Bernard Oliver was circling over the dive bombers when he spotted two P-40s being pursued by a lone Zero. Oliver had an altitude advantage of several thousand feet and slowly followed down after the intent Zero. As Oliver closed, the Japanese pilot suddenly pulled up in a steep climb and momentarily hung in his gunsight, allowing Oliver to fire a medium burst that surprisingly did no apparent damage, and he headed back to base without a claim. 2Lt. William Hennon and Wingman 2Lt. Robert Johnson were also circling the A-24s when Johnson spotted a lone Zero above him. Hennon took after the Zero and shot it down, but Johnson found that he was suddenly surrounded by several Zeros; in the brief combat his Warhawk was badly damaged. Johnson did not want to bail out in the midst of the recently landed Japanese troops and decided to head west towards Java, hoping to make it back to the base. That morning the schooner, USS *Lanikai*, was anchored in Rajeg Wesi Bay, on the southeast coast of Java, and saw a P-40 descend to masthead level and run parallel to the shoreline, wheels up, then belly land on the sand beach at the north shore of the Bay. The USN ship's Captain anchored the *Lanikai* about two hundred yards off the beach and took the schooner's dinghy to the beach, where they saw the pilot climb out of his plane, apparently unhurt, and walking around waving his arms. As the Navy reached the beach the pilot introduced himself as Lt. Robert Johnson, and he had decided he would walk back to Ngoro. However, when he was informed that Ngoro was 120 miles away he then allowed the *Lanikai* to transport him to Ngoro, where he arrived on the 23rd.

After evading Zeros, 2Lt. George Kiser and his Wingman, 2Lt. Winfred (Bill) Gallienne, were returning to Java from Bali when Kiser heard cannon fire and saw Gallienne's P-40 descending in flames. Gallienne had forgotten to jettison his drop tank upon entering combat, and an enemy pilot hit it with a 20mm shell, exploding the nearly empty but vapor-filled tank. Gallienne's face was badly burned, but he was able to bail out and landed in shallow water. There was no further news, however, until it was learned he had been captured, and he spent the rest of the war as a POW.

The 17PS lost their CO, Maj. Charles **Sprague**, on 20 February. (AAF)

The A-24 dive bombers attacked first and were reported to have fared admirably by scoring at least 10 hits on four ships (an over claim) in the landing force, while the LB-30s that followed only got a few hits. However, the P-40s were unable to keep the Zeros away from the bombers, as reported American bomber losses were two A-24s and five B-17s. The 17PS had lost five P-40s in exchange for three Zeros: Kruzel, Hennon, and Mahony. The Squadron was down to 13 serviceable fighters, but of all the major NEI islands only Java remained in Allied hands, but for how long?

The squadron's major loss was their CO, Maj. Charles Sprague, whose fate was unknown, but the USN submarine *Seawolf* reported seeing a parachute over Nusa Besar and a Japanese radio report indicated that an American Major had been captured, but nothing further was heard about Sprague's fate. Later, a Dutch seaman who had swam to shore after his destroyer had been sunk reported finding and burying a body that had a knife inscribed "C.A. Sprague."

20 February 1942

Some of the American pilots had already departed by rail to pick up new P-40s at other points in Java. A convoy of five ships left Fremantle, Australia, including the British ship *Seawitch* with 27 P-40s in crates; the old carrier USS *Langley*, which had 32 assembled P-40Es on her deck, plus 30 pilots and 12 crewmen on board; and three other ships with 10 crated P-40s between them. The three other ships were ordered to Burma, while the *Langley* and *Seawitch* were sent to Java. As they left the harbor they separated.

21 February 1942: 17PS

At 0930 12 Zeros based on Bali escorted 21 bombers to attack shipping at Soerabaja at 20,000 feet. Four 17PS flights were led by: A Flight, led by Capt. Grant Mahony (2Lts. George Hynes, William Hennon, and Marion Fuchs); B Flight, led by 1Lt. Jack Dale (2Lts. William Turner, Herbert Egenes and Lester Johnson); C Flight, led by 1Lt. Walter Coss (2Lts. Bernard Oliver, Gene Wahl, and Wallace Hoskyn); and D Flight, led by 1Lt. George Kiser (2Lts. Jesse Hague, William Turner, and Frank Adkins). A and B Flights took off first, followed by C and D Flights. Once A and B Flights were over Soerabaja they began to patrol at 21,000 feet, and they saw two formations of Betty bombers flying about 50 miles out to sea and were unable to make an interception. As they were about to turn back to base they were bounced by six Zeros and were forced to dive away. Lt. Hynes was shot down, and was seen to crash land on a beach. While the Zeros were busy with the first two flights, the Coss and Kiser flights got through to the bombers. Coss' Flight chased after a lone Betty headed out over the Java Sea, and after a quarter hour the Betty pilot put his plane into a shallow dive, trying to escape. Oliver got out front and took an ineffective 20 degree deflection shot, and as he turned to make another pass Zeros attacked him. Wahl and Hoskyn, flying behind and above, were attacked by Zeros and a dogfight ensued. Hoskyn shot down two Zeros while being pursued by Zeros that finally shot him down. Hoskyn radioed that he was going to try to make it to the Java coast, and his Warhawk was seen to make a wheels up landing on a beach. Dale and Adkins destroyed Zeros, while Mahony had scored his fourth victory to go with three probables and was awarded the DFC.

After landing back at Ngoro at 1130, four 17PS P-40s took off a half hour later on a B-17 escort to Bali. Day after day the pilots of the 17th were taking their toll of the Japanese, but they also were losing fighters, not only in combat, but also to ground attacks and wear and tear, and there would be no replacements, as the Japanese were closing in on Java.

1Lt. Jack **Dale** shot down a Zero for his second and last victory of the war. (AAF)

Capt. Grant **Mahony** scored his fourth victory to go with three probables and was awarded the DFC. He would later become an ace in the CBI flying a P-51A. (AAF)

23 February 1942: 17PS

The Japanese sent up bombers escorted by Zeros to Soerabaja and Malang, and at 0930 three flights made up of the 12 serviceable P-40s of the 17PS rose to 22,000 feet to intercept the attacking Japanese over Soerabaja. As the Americans approached Malang they saw nine Betty bombers 2,000 feet below escorted by nine Zeros flying higher and behind the Bettys, all heading for the 19BG base at Singosari. 1Lt. Gerald McCallum, leading A Flight with 2Lts. Bernard Oliver and Raymond Thompson, dove on the Bettys before the Zeros could intervene. They passed through the Bettys without seeing any results, and as Thompson pulled up he shot down a Zero. 1Lt. George Kiser, leading B Flight with 2Lts. Harold Lund, William Hennon, and James Morehead, dove on the Bettys, but were also immediately driven off by the Zeros, with Kiser and Morehead making claims. 1Lt. Nathaniel "Cy" Blanton and his C Flight got in position to hit the nine bombers and made a quick pass, but also encountered the Zeros escorting them. All three American flights only had time to make a single quick diving pass and break away before the horde of Zeros could overtake them. Only Morehead leaves a description of his combat in his biography, *In My Sights*. At the tail end of Kiser's B Flight, Morehead had trailed behind and below, as he was flying one of the older Warhawks. As he approached the Bettys he was not attacked by the Zeros, who were chasing the rest of his flight. So as not to enter the field of 20mm fire from the Betty's tail gunners, Morehead raced to the front of the enemy bomber formation. Once there he turned into them and made a 45 degree frontal attack at the lead Betty of the second V, but attacked out of range and missed badly. He pulled up his fighter's nose, fired, and hit the Betty, and continued firing as he closed and finally had to pull abruptly up to avoid ramming it. As he positioned himself to fire at the lead Betty a Zero headed directly toward him. Morehead feinted, diving away, but Split-S'd away instead. Morehead then pulled up in a loop to get under the enemy bomber formation and fired at the lead bomber in another V and shot it down. Realizing that he now would be the target of the Zeros, he went into a steep, jinking dive. As he broke out of his dive Morehead's windshield was fogged, but he found that he had lost the Zeros. He was running low on fuel and saw a large airfield directly below; he landed and was refueled. Morehead back to Ngoro, where he made two forbidden victory rolls, but CO Sprague was no longer around to protest.

1Lt. James **Morehead** shot down two bombers for the first of his seven victories. (AFAA)

23 February 1942: Mahony, New 17PS CO

Capt. Grant Mahony was given command of the 17th Squadron to replace the MIA Sprague, but his tenure would be very brief, as two days later he was ordered to accompany Gen. Brereton on an inspection trip to India, where he would remain with the new Tenth Air Force. He would then serve with the 51FG without seeing any combat. He was transferred to the CBI as the CO of the 76FS/23FG as a Major, and then was rotated to the US in June 1943. He went back to the CBI as CO of the First Air Commando Group flying the P-51 in Burma, where the Lt. Colonel shot down an Oscar to become an ace on 17 April 1944. 1Lt. Gerald McCallum took over as 17PS CO.

19-25 February 1942: The End in the Netherlands East Indies

The disastrous 19 February Japanese raid on Darwin and a looming Japanese invasion of Australia caused the Allies to consider the evacuation of the air bases laboriously built in the NEI and order the withdrawal of all American air echelons before they were cut off. Wavell wanted the continued defense of Java for as long as possible with the concurrent build up in Northern Australia and Burma, which would take some of the pressure off Java. Brett also favored the continued, but doomed defense of Java and a buildup in Burma. However, the Japanese success in Burma in February led the Joint Chiefs of Staff to approve the establishment of an American Air Force in India rather than Burma, with aircraft drawn from those originally allocated to Australia. Included in the Indian allocation were at least 80 pursuit aircraft from Australia and 80 more en route to Australia or directly from the US. The American Far East policy was now devoted to India to the exclusion of Australia.

On 19 February Gen. Lewis Brereton, with Gen. George Brett's backing, decided to withdraw all American Air Forces from Java and wired Gen. Marshall, Chief of Staff, for instructions. Meanwhile, Gen. Archibald Wavell requested that Brereton wait 48 hours so he could get instructions from the Combined Chiefs of Staff as to the exact date for the dissolution of the ABDACOM. Nonetheless, Wavell felt that "effective air resistance" could be maintained for at least two weeks longer, and that "even this delay to the Jap's advance would be worth the sacrifice." The next day Brereton wired the War Department, saying that it was "against the best interests of the United States to maintain the American Air Forces on Java or to attempt any further air operations." Wavell agreed only if Brereton would keep his air forces in Java to cover the evacuation of combat units, which Brereton insisted should begin immediately.

It was not until the 22nd that Brereton received Marshall's reply, which left it up to Brereton to decide in what manner and at what time to withdraw, but that a "timely withdrawal is important." Marshall stated that "all fighting units for whom there were arms must continue to fight without thought of evacuation but that air forces which can more usefully operate in battle from outside Java and all air personnel for whom there are no aircraft.... should be withdrawn."

Brereton had had chronic differences with Peirse since arriving on Java on 18 January, and had unsuccessfully requested relief from command on 8 February and was impatient to leave Java. He wrote Wavell the following:

> "I felt it necessary to request General Wavell to relieve me of my duties. The morale of my own air force was low and my presence was required with it. I was criticized by General Wavell and General Brett for what appeared to them to be a somewhat unwarranted and pessimistic attitude.
>
> "I was also having some honest differences with Peirse (Air Marshal Sir Richard Peirse, Commander of the Allied Air Forces in ABDA) concerning the employment of American bombers. It was evident that Peirse was being subjected to the strongest pressure to employ them piecemeal and concentrate them on the Malay Peninsula, whereas in my judgment the whole bomber effort had to be directed against the Japs in the Makassar Straits. In view of our differences, I did not want to embarrass Peirse by continuing to act as his deputy."

Brett finally ordered Brereton to India on 22 February after allocating "the mass of all troops" and 160 pursuit aircraft there two days earlier. After the fall of Singapore, the British transferred Burma from the ABDA Command to the Indian Ocean (India-Burma) Theater, with the Americans to control a vaguely defined Pacific Ocean Theater. The establishment of the new India-Burma Theater would mean another theater in which American command would be subordinated, which Brett was not going to allow in view of the "previous and present difficulties" in the ABDA and "American control must be insisted on from the beginning." On the 24th Brett left for India via Australia before orders from Arnold to organize an air force in Australia could reach him. On 5 March 1942, Brereton took command of and began to organize the new Tenth Air Force in New Delhi. In addition to setting up the new air force, Brereton was also ordered to prepare an air route for the resupply of China.

On the 23rd, the Governor General of the NEI announced that ABDACOM would be officially dissolved at noon on 25 February, and the defense of the NEI would be assumed by the Dutch. Meanwhile, Wavell received orders from London to set up headquarters elsewhere. Gen. Brett arrived in Melbourne on 24 February and temporarily assumed command of all US Army personnel in Australia. Once in Australia, Brett continued with plans for reinforcement of Allied troops remaining in Java. The transfer of heavy bombers to Java was suspended, but efforts were made to get a large number of P-40s into Java. Some of the American pilots had already left by rail to pick up new P-40s at other points in Java and from the *Langley* and the *Seawitch*, still at sea.

Wavell dissolved ABDACOM with control of the battle to be in Dutch hands with the assurance that American land, sea, and air forces would continue their support. Despite Brett's desire to move on to India, he had been assigned to command all US forces in Australia. The Japanese threat to Australia led the War Department to give priority to protection of the sea lanes leading there by garrisoning New Caledonia, but US air operations would be determined by "circumstances." Wavell left for India, and Brett and Brereton left, providing for the evacuation

Brett sent **Brereton** to India on 22 February, and on 5 March Brereton took command of and began to organize the new Tenth Air Force in New Delhi. (AAF)

The command of the AAC in Java was left to Col. Eugene **Eubank** to carry out the last air attacks on the advancing Japanese. (AAF)

On 24 February **Brereton** left for India via Australia on this B-17 seen in transit at Archer Field. (AAF)

of US troops from Java. The command of the AAC in Java was left to Col. Eugene Eubank to carry out the last air attacks on the advancing Japanese. Eubank was given the following instructions by Brereton before leaving:

1) To operate the American air units in Java as long as an effective operational force existed. The decision for the termination of operations was to be made by Eubank, and Dutch Headquarters was to be notified.
2) To evacuate personnel not needed for the tactical operations of equipment available to Australia.
3) As aircraft became unsuitable for tactical operations, to remove personnel so released from the combat zone.
4) To include in each evacuation a proportionate share of personnel with combat experience. These were to be used for reconstituting units.

24 February 1942

The Japanese sent out their biggest raid yet on Soerabaja, including 54 bombers, and it was met by Grant Mahony leading A Flight, George Kiser headed B Flight, Jack Dale C Flight, and Joseph Kruzel D flight. At 0915 Japanese bombers were reported flying west, with Soerabaja the supposed target. At 1000 the 16 P-40s of the 17PS approached the Soerabaja area at 27,000 feet and saw 24 Betty bombers in two formations in the distance. The Japanese had already bombed Soerabaja harbor and were heading home. The P-40s tried to catch the Bettys but struggled at this high altitude, and only Kiser's Flight was able to catch up to them. Kiser and Robert Dockstader scored hits on the Bettys in one of the formations. However, Zeros surprised the P-40s and hit several of them. At noon, all P-40s landed at Ngoro Field, with Kiser and Dockstader claiming Bettys. After the mission six P-40s were declared too badly damaged to fly without repairs.

1Lt. George **Kiser** shot down a bomber to become an ace (he had two victories over the Philippines). He would score four more victories with the 49FG/9FS. (AAF)

After only two days as CO of the 17PS, FEAF headquarters in Bandoeng had ordered Capt. Grant Mahony to assume a position directly under Maj.Gen. Brereton in India. That morning Maj. William Fisher in Soerabaja ordered Mahony to choose two more Squadron pilots plus 25 enlisted men to accompany him. Mahony chose William Hennon, who refused to leave, and then chose Gene Wahl and Raymond Thompson as the two to leave. Later in the afternoon Mahony left with Wahl, Thompson, and the enlisted men for Soerabaja, where they were to board a train for Jogjakarta. Mahony's 40-A flying school classmate, Bo McCallum, was left in charge, as McCallum had been promoted to captain five days earlier.

25 February 1942: 17PS

With the departure of Grant Mahony, command of the 17PS passed on to 1Lt. Robert McCallum, the most senior officer remaining. He was left with 18 aircraft, but only 10 were combat ready (three more would be ready the next day due to great effort by the ground crews). On the morning of the 25th McCallum led his squadron for the first and final time. Three flights led by McCallum (A Flight) and Element Leader Irvin, Dale (B Flight) and Element Leader Gambonini, and Kiser (C Flight) and Element Leader Hennon took off at 0930 after the ADC issued an interception order. As they approached Soerabaja at 26,000 feet the Americans spotted 20 Bettys in several formations stacked up at altitudes from 27,000 to 30,000 feet. At about 30,000 feet were nine Zero escorts waiting for the P-40s. There was no way the worn P-40s could reach that altitude and C Flight dropped out, but A and B Flights continued to climb after the bombers; they were attacked from above by six of the Zeros and immediately went into a dive to escape. McCallum broke into the Zeros in a futile attempt to break up their attack. He was quickly outnumbered by the enemy and his P-40 took hits in the engine and caught fire, but McCallum was able to bail out of his burning fighter. Dale was almost shot down when he pulled out of his dive at tree top level and he was bounced by two Zero pilots that missed on their firing runs. Kiser's C Flight, waiting below, found themselves in position to intercept the unsuspecting diving Zeros, and 2Lts. Andrew Reynolds and William Hennon each downed a Zero. It was Reynolds' 3.33 victory so far, while Hennon became an ace. Less than a minute later, 1Lt. Ben

2Lt. Robert **Dockstader** scored his only victory of the war. (AAF)

2Lt. Andrew **Reynolds** claimed his third and last victory with the 1PS, but would later score six more with the 49FG/9FS. (AFAA)

Irvin also downed a Zero for his second and last victory of the war. That afternoon Kiser and Hennon flew a reconnaissance flight, superficially to locate the Japanese invasion fleet approaching Java and to search for McCallum, but found neither it nor McCallum. Later McCallum's body was found machine gunned in his parachute. Capt. George Kiser took over the command of the 17th.

26 February 1942: 17PS

Only 12 pilots, including the three Dutch in the Brewster Buffalo F2As, were on alert at Ngoro in the early morning. After the loss of McCallum the day before, the 17PS was down to 17 P-40s, but only 14 were in service. Capt. George Kiser was now acting as Squadron CO, with 1Lts. Jack Dale and Joseph Kruzel as the other two flight leaders. At 0930 an alert was called when a large Japanese force was heading toward Soerabaja. Kiser led the formation on their approach on Soerabaja in overcast skies at 26,000 feet, where they found 26 Betty bombers flying at between 27,000 and 30,000 feet. Again, neither the worn out 17th Warhawks nor the Dutch in their Brewsters were able to climb above 26,000 to attack the enemy bombers. However, the heavy cloud cover caused the Bettys to drop their bombs ineffectively from high altitude, with none hitting any of the warships of the Combined Striking Force in Soerabaja Harbor. Unexpectedly, the Allied pilots were attacked by eight escorting Zeros flying at 27,000 feet, but were able to dive away without any losses. As the Zeros began returning to their base at Den Paser, Hennon spotted two of them flying east at 15,000 feet and closed on them unseen from the rear. Hennon closed to 100 feet, and when he squeezed the trigger only several guns fired, but the fragile Zero took some hits and went down for the 17PS' last victory of 44 victories over Java. The victory made Hennon an ace (he would score two more victories with the 7FS/49FG).

During afternoon the ever-dwindling group of American pilots was joined by six Brewster Buffaloes and six Hawker Hurricanes, all flown by Dutch pilots, to patrol against possible Japanese air raids. These fighters were the remnants of the British fighter squadrons in Southeast Asia and had been handed over to the Dutch on their departure. The Dutch Air Defense Command (ADC) refused to allow the mediocre Buffalos to fly the bomber escort requested by the Allied Bomber Command at Malang. The Hurricanes were unable to fly until 1 March because of lack of hydraulic fluid and ammunition. The Dutch pilots only had two or three hours time in their fighters, but they would fly them bravely until the end.

26 February 1942: Naval Battle

Following the attacks on Darwin on 19 February, V.Adm. Chuichi Nagumo's 1st Carrier Fleet had sailed to Kendari, in the Celebes, where its two battleships, four carriers, two heavy cruisers, and destroyer flotilla were joined by two more battleships, three heavy cruisers, and three destroyers under the command of V.Adm. Nobutake Kondo. On 25 February, this formidable force sailed for the Indian Ocean, to cut off the Allied escape route from Java. If the Allies were going to delay or interrupt these Japanese naval plans, they had to strike while the remaining strength of their navies was still intact. During the day V.Adm. C.E.L. Helfrich ordered all available Allied warships in the west to join R.Adm. Karel Doorman's Eastern Striking Force at Soerabaja.

On 26 February, Helfrich ordered a determined naval attack by a combined force consisting of two heavy cruisers (USN *Houston* and RN *Exeter*), three light cruisers (Dutch *Java* and *De Ruyter* and RAN *Perth*), and ten destroyers. The Allied force was to attack the Japanese force, consisting of 39 to 45 transports protected by two battleships (heavy cruisers?), four to seven cruisers, and 13 destroyers. The ensuing battle occurred over 24 hours, and two or three Japanese cruisers and two or three destroyers were hit and several probably sunk. But the battle was a crushing defeat for the Allies, with the *Java* and *De Ruyter* and three destroyers sunk without reaching the transports. All the remaining ships were damaged, several seriously.

1Lt. William **Hennon** shot down one (some reports credit two) to make him an ace. He would score two more victories with the 49FG/9FS. (AAF)

Helfrich sent out his remaining ships over the next several days, and only four USN destroyers were able to escape from Java, while the other ships were sunk in undocumented battles.

27 February 1942

The battered B-17s in Java were departing for Australia while the Japanese invasion fleet was approaching, and only the small fighter force of 10 P-40s led by 1Lts. George Kiser and Jack Dale escorting three A-24 dive bombers of the 27BG remained to challenge the Japanese. The P-40s escorted the A-24s during the afternoon, and oddly no enemy fighters were covering the convoy, which was 90 miles off the Java coast. Despite heavy AA fire, the dive bombers sunk a 14,000 ton transport.

27-28 February 1942: *Langley* Sunk and the *Seawitch* Arrives too Late

The beleaguered Dutch requested that the Interceptor Command be reinforced, and at first Brett was going to use some of the Warhawks allocated to India. However, a convoy with the tender *Langley*, with 32 assembled P-40s on its deck, and the *Seawitch* with 27 crated P-40s in its hold, were headed for Fremantle, Australia, on 22 February. The *Langley* was diverted to Tjilatjab, Java, with the assurance of "suitable and proper" protection. The *Seawitch* received similar orders but left much later. On the morning of the 27th the *Langley*, escorted by two destroyers, was attacked at 1200 by nine twin engine bombers and sunk by five bomb hits and three near misses only 74 miles from its destination. Only six personnel were killed and five missing, while the remainder were picked up by the escorting destroyers and transferred to the tanker *Pecos*. The *Pecos*, carrying 670 men, then headed for Fremantle, but was attacked in the mid-afternoon and sunk, taking 450 personnel with it. The *Seawitch* arrived safely at Tjilatjab, but before they could be assembled the Japanese approached with a convoy of 80 ships and the fighters were abandoned. Two flights of three B-17s bombed the convoy off the coast of Java without result. This attack was followed by three 91st Squadron A-24s escorted by two flights of P-40s. The dive bombers sunk one transport and no enemy aircraft interfered with the attack. Thus, of the 140 P-40s intended for the Java Campaign only 32 reached their units of the Brereton Defense Force.

There were 33 pilots (25 from the 13PS and eight from the 33PS) and 12 enlisted men aboard the *Langley*. Two pilots were saved by the *Pecos* and returned to Fremantle by the destroyer *Whipple*. Several pilots and enlisted men were picked up by the destroyer *Edsall*, which was sunk in 1 March. Japanese records indicate that the few *Edsall* survivors were picked up and held as POWs at Kendari and probably executed.

28 February 1942

On the last day of February 1942, three flights of P-40s and four Dutch Buffalos tried to intercept the Japanese bombers, but their worn engines were unable to reach the high flying enemy to engage and they returned to base. Later that day 10 P-40s and the four Buffalos were dispatched to intercept 12 bombers and nine Zeros, and again could not reach their altitude. One Buffalo pilot had engine problems that caused its pilot to bail out. The P-40's engines had over 150 hours of flying time and were in need of overhaul, instead of the rudimentary maintenance that was attempted in the brief periods that the fighters were standing down from all day alerts.

March 1942

1 March 1942: 17PS: Last Significant Mission from Java

The Japanese had landed their main force at Rembang 70 miles west of Soerabaja that night, but were continuing to land supplies and troops in barges and small vessels from about 30 transports anchored in parallel to the coast. The transports and barges that were in line, seven or eight deep, were tempting targets, but were protected by heavy AA fire from ships and shore batteries. Anti-aircraft guns had been set up on the beach to place the attackers under heavy AA fire as soon as they began their strafing run.

The last significant mission from Java took place at 0530, when nine P-40s took off along with the six Hawker Hurricanes and four of

Seawitch. (USN)

Langley. (USN)

Japanese landings at Merak, Java. (AFHRC)

the Brewster Buffaloes. 1Lt. George Kiser led 1Lt. Frank Adkins and 2Lt. Lester Johnson; 1Lt. Jack Dale led Lts. Morris Caldwell and Robert McWherter; and 1Lt. Joseph Kruzel led Lts. Cornelius Reagan and Marion Fuchs, while the Dutch followed in two strings behind them. As the Allied fighters came in over the rice paddy fields outside Rembang they met heavy AA fire from guns that had been set up on the beach, as well as from the shipping off shore, which put them into a vicious crossfire as soon as they began their strafing run.

Caldwell was hit immediately and crashed into the Java Sea. Reagan's plane was hit and caught fire. McWherter, who was flying Reagan's wing, motioned for him to head for the beach and bail out. Reagan acknowledged him, but then McWherter relayed a story that probably is a myth. McWherter saw Reagan, who was perhaps severely wounded or perhaps had his parachute holed, not head for the beach, but take a cigarette from his pocket, roll back the canopy, lean forward to light the cigarette on the burning engine and, with the cigarette in his mouth, fly and crash land his P-40 in a rice paddy near the north Java shore. Reagan hid in the jungle by day and traveled by night. As he was trying to commandeer a boat he was caught by a Javanese enemy sympathizer and turned over to the Japanese. Reagan claimed to be an Irish war correspondent and thus was from a neutral nation, which the enemy interrogator somehow believed. Reagan would spend the war in a less harsh Japanese political prison.

Adkins bounced his fighter off the water when he came in too low on his first strafing run, but made two more strafing runs before being hit by AA fire and bailing out, landing about 300 yards from the Japanese positions. Legend has it that Adkins stole the bicycle of a Javanese who was peddling down the beach. He then peddled away in a hail of bullets and returned to base just before the squadron evacuated Java. (Alternative story: Adkins jumped on the handlebars of the bicycle and he and the Javanese left the area at top speed, and Adkins arrived at base in time to be evacuated.)

Meanwhile, the Allied fighters sunk several small boats and barges filled with troops and knocked out several AA positions. Johnson got back to Blimbing, but his aircraft had taken hits in its oil tank and oil line. Of the six surviving P-40s that landed at Blimbing, all had been hit and were being rearmed and refueled when four Zeros that had been shadowing them back to base came in to strafe the base and destroyed them and the surviving Dutch planes.

Early March 1942: Evacuation from Java

Meanwhile, the FEAF had made plans to evacuate, as five officers were sent to Broome to set up evacuation facilities there to accommodate Dutch, American, and Australian military and civilian refugees. All American ground equipment was turned over to the Dutch, and the Squadron personnel proceeded to Jogjakarta, which was the last remaining Allied base in Java, where they were transported at 1730 by B-17s to Broome, Australia. The B-17 pilots determined that 23 passengers was the safe limit for the war-weary B-17s to carry the 1,100 miles to Broome. The pursuit pilots were also in competition for passenger space with the 7th and 19th Bomb Group evacuees. Col. Eubanks was always considered to be "hostile" toward the pursuit pilots, and was said to prefer enlisted men to officers. 17PS CO Capt. William Fisher was chosen, but former 20PS CO 1Lt. William Lane was left behind to supervise the evacuation. Acting 17PS CO George Kiser, Joseph Kruzel, Ben Irvin, James Morehead, Andrew Reynolds, William Hennon, Robert Dockstader and Jack Dale were selected, but Edwin Gilmore was left behind to make room for all nine 17PS enlisted ground crew Eubank selected. Once selections were made, two thirds of the 17PS had to wait to be evacuated. However, five B-17s and two LB-30s landed on 6 March and all the other 17th pilots boarded (Franklin Adkins, Marion Fuchs, Paul Gambonini, Edwin Gilmore, Spence Johnson, Harold Lund, Robert, McWherter, and Roger Williams), as did the rest of the enlisted ground crew.

The Java Campaign ended six hours later. Equipped with new aircraft, the men of the 17PS would take the war to the Japanese once more as leaders in the 35th and 49th Fighter Groups. By 3 March the evacuation was nearly completed, after B-17s and LB-30s evacuated the last personnel

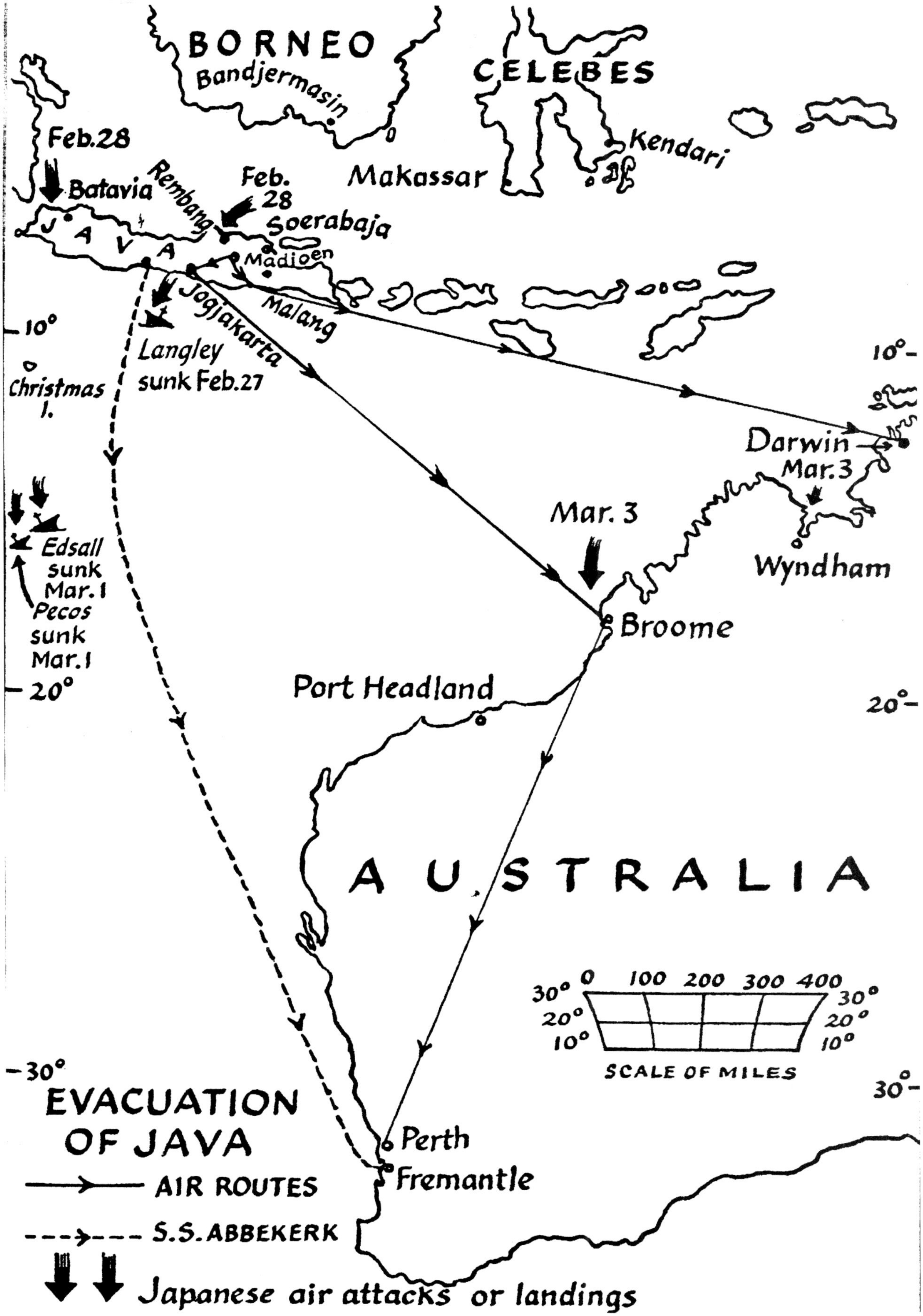
BORNEO
Bandjermasin
CELEBES
Kendari
Makassar
Feb.28
Batavia
Rembang
Feb. 28
Soerabaja
JAVA
Madioen
Malang
Jogjakarta
10°
Langley sunk Feb.27
Christmas I.
Darwin
Mar.3
Mar. 3
Wyndham
Edsall sunk Mar.1
Pecos sunk Mar.1
Broome
20°
Port Headland
AUSTRALIA
0 100 200 300 400
30° 20° 10°
SCALE OF MILES
30°
EVACUATION OF JAVA
Perth
Fremantle
AIR ROUTES
S.S. ABBEKERK
Japanese air attacks or landings

with the Japanese only 18 miles away. During the evacuation the Japanese had destroyed 12 flying boats, two B-17s, two B-24s, and two Hudsons, and they killed 45 Dutch civilians and 20 American airmen.

End in Java

The evacuation of American forces from the NEI and MacArthur's evacuation to Australia from the Philippines on 17 March made the immediate American objective to defend Australia and protect the sea and air lines of communication to the Southwest Pacific. After Brereton left Java for India Brett was the highest ranking US Army staff officer in Australia. He resumed command of the USAFIA with Gen. Julian Barnes as his deputy on 24 February. The Allied Command withdrew to Melbourne, and neither they nor the Australian Chiefs of Staff could determine the location or date, or what countermeasures remained to thwart the projected enemy invasion. So as the Allies left Java on 6 March, the Australian people and the Allied Command stiffened their resolve as the enemy juggernaut paused off Java for their attack somewhere along the northern Australian coast.

Wavell was sent back to India as Commander-in-Chief and was charged with the defense of Burma, where British troops had recently suffered serious setbacks. He initiated the Arakan Offensive in September 1942, but by March 1943 the Arakan situation had become untenable, and in June newly promoted Field Marshall Wavell was replaced as military commander by Auchinleck, but became a Viscount and Vice Roy of India. In this post he dealt with fractured Indian politics and future Indian Independence, but was not supported either by Churchill nor his successor, Clement Attlee, and was replaced as Viceroy by Lord Mountbatten. In March 1942, ABDAIR Commander Richard Peirse was appointed commander of British Air Forces in India, and on 16 November 1943 he was made Commander in Chief, Allied Air Command South-East Asia. However, his career came to an abrupt halt in 1944 when he eloped with the wife of Gen. Sir Claude Auchinleck.

The USAAC suffered a lack of depot facilities and spare parts which resulted in a rapid deterioration of combat aircraft. There were a small number of maintenance personnel who worked from 16 to 20 hours at a time, but even then the most elementary servicing was difficult. Airfields, though numerous and satisfactory for dry weather use, were generally grass and dangerous after heavy rains. Furthermore, the fields were almost completely undefended. Modern aircraft warning equipment and AA guns were lacking and only a few machine guns defended American bases. Because of this lack of suitable air warning facilities and ground defenses, the Interceptor Command was placed under great pressure, with much of Java prone to enemy bombing attack. The 17PS, with inadequate manpower and insufficient aircraft and supplies, was able to engage the Japanese from Palembang, Sumatra, to Koepang, Timor. To perform this mission, rarely were there more than 20 P-40s in service, and of at least 120 pursuit aircraft sent to Australia during January and February, no more than 40 reached Java. Those that arrived always fought against heavy odds; nevertheless, they shot down at least 33 enemy planes while losing 14 aircraft and nine pilots.

Six pilots were listed as KIA (Roland, Fields, Hoskyn, Hynes, McCallum, and Caldwell), three as MIA (Sprague, Gallienne, and Reagan), and no enlisted men were lost. The losses during the ferry flights from Darwin to Java and in combat were caused mainly by the numerical superiority of the enemy forces which they faced, but a contributing factor was the inexperience of many of the American pilots. The short period of training given after their arrival in Australia from the United States in many cases proved insufficient, particularly for those who had never been in a pursuit plane before leaving the United States. In addition to the nine 17PS pilots lost, 61 other pilots had been assigned to the 33PS and 13PS (Provisional) and were sent to Java but never arrived. Of the 10 pilots of the 33PS who arrived at Darwin on 15 February, nine fought in the 19 February air battle over Darwin. All were shot down and four were KIA (Pell, Peres, Perry, and Hughes). Robert Buel of the 3PS, attached to the 33PS, had been shot down and killed four days earlier after shooting down a Mavis flying boat over the Timor Sea. Also, adding the 31 pilots of the 33PS and 13PS who perished in the sinking of the *Langley*, the final total of pilots of the five provisional pursuit squadrons assigned to Java who were subsequently killed was 50 of the 124 pilots assigned to the five squadrons.

The total number of P-40s lost during combat or in accidents was 110 aircraft of the 129 assigned to the five squadrons: all 68 assigned to the 17PS, 20PS, and 3PS (including the seven destroyed at Ngoro by the 17PS during the evacuation on March 1). Combat losses were 31, which included 20 shot down over the Dutch East Indies, one over the Timor Sea, and nine over Darwin, plus one on the ground at Darwin. Accurate figures for aircraft losses due to accidents are not available, as many P-40s wrecked during training at Amberley Field were not repaired. Many aircraft were lost on the ferry route to Darwin. Of the 25 3PS P-40s, only seven arrived on the trip from Amberley to Darwin. In early February, Amberley Instructors Grant Mahony, Boyd Wagner, and Allison Strauss estimated that it would require three months and 15 crashed aircraft to train 70 pilots for combat, as the large majority of the pilots arriving from the US had less than 10 to 15 hours of flying a P-40 and almost no gunnery training. However, many accidents were thought to be caused by faulty assembly of the crated P-40s by (bomber) mechanics with no previous experience in assembling pursuit aircraft and no technical manuals to direct them. Also, the difficult conditions of flying the long route to Darwin over the featureless Australian outback tested even experienced pilots.

By the end of February, 86 of the 102 pilots assigned to the new 49PG had no pursuit time, while in the 35PG 27 of the 29 pilots had no pursuit training. However, the evacuation and arrival of the combat-experienced Java veterans would give these Groups the leaders that would weld them into effective units. The 49PG was to fly P-40Es in the defense of Darwin, and would benefit from the most experienced of the Philippines and Java veterans: Nate Blanton, Walter Coss, Jack Dale, William Hennon, Ben Irvin, George Kiser, Joseph Kruzel, and Allison Strauss. Joining them were Java veterans Robert Dockstader, Lester Johnsen, Ray Melikian, James Morehead, Robert Oestreicher, Andrew Reynolds, and Robert Vaught. The 35PG was to fly the P-39 and P-400 into combat over New Guinea, and would receive 35 Java (and Darwin) veterans, including Frank Adkins, Hubert Egenes, Paul Gambonini, Jesse Hague, Thomas Hayes, Robert Johnson, Robert McMahon, B.J. Oliver, George Parker, William Stauter, Raymond Thompson, and Robert McWherter. Gerald Dix, James Naylor, and Max Wiecks of the 33PS were allocated to the newly arrived 8PG, which would fly P-39s and P-400s to New Guinea at the end of April. Java veterans Bryan Brown, Pete Childress, Thomas Christian, David Coleman, Al Dutton, Bruce Erwin, Vernon Head, Robert Kaiser, Robert Kerstetter, and John Lewis were deployed to the 67PS on New Caledonia, and would fly P-39s and P-400s for 347FG over Guadalcanal. Five veterans did not receive combat assignments: Parker Gies, Edwin Gilmore, Ken Glassburn, and Dwight Muckley were assigned to aircraft assembly or test flying at Amberley.

In January, to provide for the defense of New Guinea, New Britain, and the whole of Australia except Darwin (which was considered in the ABDA area), the RAAF had a total of only 43 operational aircraft, including 29 Hudsons, 14 Catalinas, and no fighter aircraft. With heavy losses being sustained daily in the New Guinea area, this small force was rapidly depleted by the end of January.

Part Three
Preparation and Combat

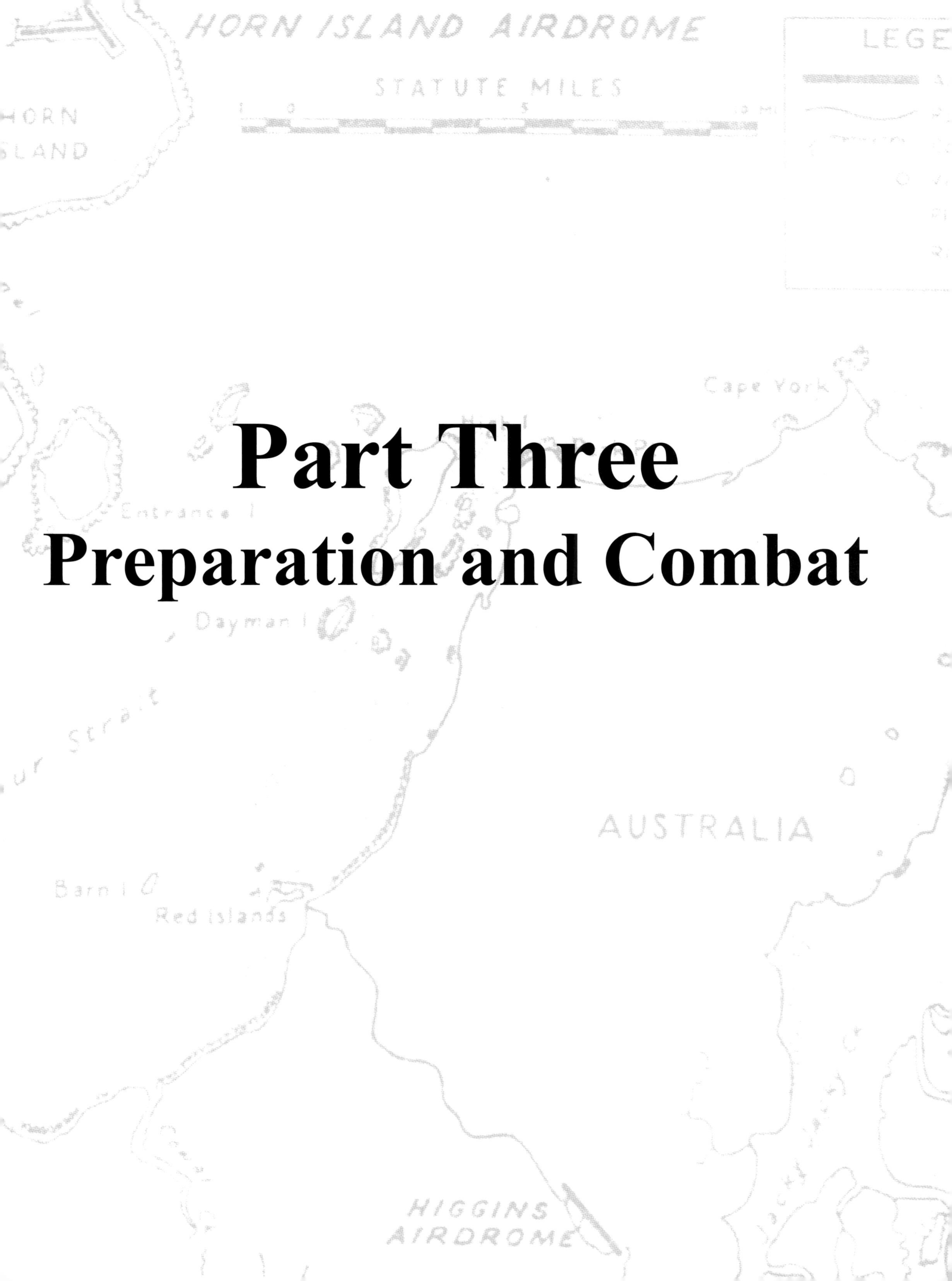

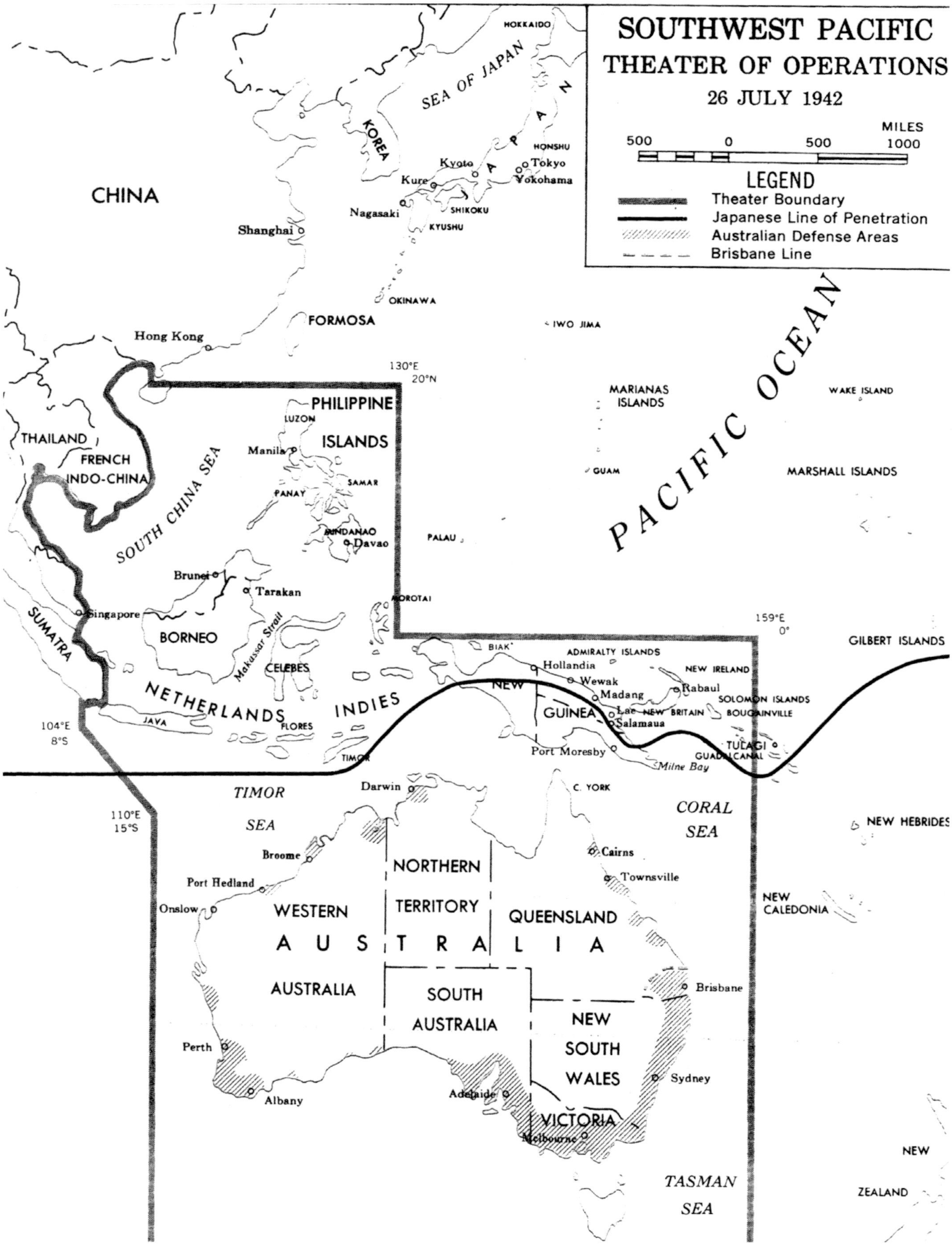
SOUTHWEST PACIFIC
THEATER OF OPERATIONS
26 JULY 1942
MILES
500 0 500 1000
LEGEND
Theater Boundary
Japanese Line of Penetration
Australian Defense Areas
Brisbane Line
CHINA
HOKKAIDO
SEA OF JAPAN
JAPAN
KOREA
HONSHU
Kyoto
Tokyo
Yokohama
Kure
Nagasaki
SHIKOKU
KYUSHU
Shanghai
OKINAWA
FORMOSA
IWO JIMA
Hong Kong
PACIFIC OCEAN
130°E
20°N
PHILIPPINE ISLANDS
LUZON
Manila
SAMAR
PANAY
MINDANAO
Davao
MARIANAS ISLANDS
WAKE ISLAND
GUAM
MARSHALL ISLANDS
THAILAND
FRENCH INDO-CHINA
SOUTH CHINA SEA
PALAU
Brunei
Tarakan
MOROTAI
SUMATRA
Singapore
BORNEO
Makassar Strait
CELEBES
159°E
0°
GILBERT ISLANDS
BIAK
ADMIRALTY ISLANDS
Hollandia
NEW IRELAND
Wewak
Rabaul
Madang
SOLOMON ISLANDS
NEW GUINEA
Lae
NEW BRITAIN
BOUGAINVILLE
Salamaua
NETHERLANDS INDIES
JAVA
FLORES
104°E
8°S
TULAGI
GUADALCANAL
Port Moresby
Milne Bay
TIMOR
Darwin
C. YORK
TIMOR SEA
CORAL SEA
110°E
15°S
NEW HEBRIDES
Cairns
Broome
NORTHERN TERRITORY
Townsville
Port Hedland
NEW CALEDONIA
Onslow
WESTERN AUSTRALIA
QUEENSLAND
AUSTRALIA
Brisbane
SOUTH AUSTRALIA
NEW SOUTH WALES
Perth
Sydney
Albany
Adelaide
VICTORIA
Melbourne
NEW ZEALAND
TASMAN SEA

Early 1942: Situation in Australia

In January 1942, the impending Japanese conquest of the Netherlands East Indies, concurrent with their occupation of Rabaul in New Britain, threatened northern Australia. From their new bases in the East Indies the Japanese could easily bomb Darwin, and from Rabaul their bombers began to attack the northern coast of eastern New Guinea.

Meanwhile, units of the Far East Air Force retreated to Australia, and other AAC units, on their way to the Philippines when the war started, were diverted to Australia to stem the Japanese advance in the Southwest Pacific towards Australia. The exhausted remnants of squadrons arriving in Australia from the NEI and new units from the United States found that operating an air force thousands of miles from the source of production and supply could cause continual problems in establishing air strength in Australia. In addition to the obvious logistics problems involved in moving the hundreds of personnel necessary to maintain ground services and all the bombs, ammunition, fuel, repair machinery, and spare parts necessary for the operation of aircraft, there were even greater problems involved in moving aircraft to the Southwest Pacific. The only practical means of delivering large numbers of bombers was to first establish air routes to Australia, via both the Pacific and the South Atlantic, and then to fly them to their destination. In the meantime, however, medium bombers and fighters could be dismantled and shipped by sea and reassembled. The South Pacific ferry route, even though tenuous and unreliable at first, was to be developed as the lifeline for the AAC in Australia, and without it there would have been no rush delivery of desperately needed supplies and personnel and no long range heavy bomber replacements to bomb the Japanese occupied territories in the SWPA.

During the first three months of war in the Pacific, AAC units in Australia were hindered by a lack of organization and labored to train combat crews to assemble aircraft, and generally to assist in reinforcing the Allies, who were trying to stop the Japanese advances through the Philippines and the Netherlands East Indies. This was a time when changes of command had to be made before officers were able to acquire a full understanding of their missions, when Allied plans had to be revised almost before they could be put into operation, and when Air Corps units had to be transferred to new locations before they were settled in their former ones, all because of the rapid Japanese advances.

At the end of November 1941 a large convoy left Hawaii carrying 4,600 troops (including 2,600 AAC personnel and 48 pilots), 3.5 million rounds of ammunition, 600 tons of bombs, 6,000 drums of aviation oil, 3,000 drums of aviation gasoline, and crated P-40s and A-24s. The convoy arrived at Brisbane on 23 December, but several factors slowed their quick redeployment to the Philippines. In the US, the convoy had been loaded on a peacetime basis, with no effort made to store equipment on the same vessel with its intended unit. Consequently, the entire cargo had to be unloaded, sorted, and reloaded before any ships could be sent to the Philippines; a task requiring six days. However, four days after their arrival in Australian waters their destination was changed to Darwin because of the rapidly deteriorating situation in the Philippines. The 48 pilots who had debarked at Brisbane, some being aviation cadets and most of the others never flying a combat aircraft, required additional training before they could be permitted to take aircraft into combat. But before any training could be started the crated P-40s had to be assembled.

Southwest Pacific Area (SWPA)

The Southwest Pacific Area succeeded the short lived ABDA Command and was under the command of Gen. Douglas MacArthur's US Far East Force, but Australian forces played a major role in this theater. The large SWPA included Australia, New Guinea, the Bismarck Archipelago, the Netherlands East Indies, and the Philippines, where its boundary turned back to the west, south of Formosa, and to the north end of Hainan Island in the Gulf of Tonkin, off the south coast of China. It then turned to the northeast coast of French Indochina, following the coastline south along Thailand, and then the Malay States, edging the east end of Sumatra (within the CBI) and to the west end of Java. On 1 August 1942, this boundary was shifted 1° west to facilitate South Pacific Area operations in the Solomons.

Establishing AAC Command in Australia

Upon his arrival in Australia on 1 January 1942, Gen. George Brett immediately began to organize his command and named his staff. After designating Gen. Julian Barnes as his Chief of Staff and Gen. Henry Clagett to command the port at Townsville, Brett began a hasty survey of the facilities and units in his command. With four pursuit groups, one light, two medium, and two heavy bombardment groups scheduled for his command, he planned to use the Darwin area as a jumping off point for tactical air units and as a secondary base for first and second echelon maintenance; the Townsville area for a major repair, maintenance, and supply base; and the Brisbane area as a larger maintenance and trans shipment point for Townsville and Darwin.

Before he had time to make more than these preliminary arrangements, Brett was appointed Deputy Supreme Commander of the newly formed ABDA Command. Brett represented the US Army interests at ABDA headquarters in Bandoeng, Java, but had no direct responsibilities for the control and operation of the American forces. On 12 January 1942, US Army forces in Australia and other areas of the Southwest Pacific (excluding the Philippines, which continued to be under MacArthur's command) were placed under the command of Lt.Gen. Brereton, who was also acting as Deputy Chief of the Air Staff in the ABDA Command.

Throughout January the AAC command situation was in a state of flux. Although Brereton was relocating to Melbourne to assume his duties

Lt.Gen. George **Brett**. (L) was appointed Deputy Supreme Commander of the newly formed ABDA, while Maj.Gen. Lewis **Brereton** was acting as Deputy Chief of the Air Staff in the ABDA Command. (AAF)

as directed, four days after his appointment he voiced his dissatisfaction with his existing status to General Marshall. To simplify Brereton's assignment, Col. Francis Brady was assigned temporary command of the Far East Air Force and also to act as a member of the ABDA Air Staff. Gen. Julian Barnes was placed in command of all AAC forces in Australia, although by the end of January he remained somewhat in doubt as to his relationship with the ABDA Command and with Brett.

Developing Australia as a Base

The AAC personnel who survived the Philippines and Java Campaigns gradually were evacuated to southeast Australia as an unorganized force without aircraft and supplies. In the first week of March it seemed impossible that these remnants of units could, along with the units already in Australia, become a new air force any time soon.

Three months of reversals since Pearl Harbor caused a change in Allied strategy, and the Air Corps units in Australia faced an uncertain future. Australia was threatened not only from the northwest, but also from the northeast, and it was apparent that Australia now was to become the main base for operations against Japan in the Southwest Pacific and was no longer just the supply base for forward units. In order to defend and then use the Australian Continent as an offensive base, Australia presented difficult logistical problems which were caused by its geography, terrain, inadequate transportation and communications facilities, and governmental policies. With a land area about the size of the contiguous United States and with over 12,000 miles of coastline, Australia could not be easily defended. Because it was the world's largest island, the Continent was dependent upon sea power and the control of particular sea lanes for its survival, and their loss would devastate Australian military and naval power. Australia's sparse population, which in 1941 was less than a twentieth of that of America, was largely concentrated in the coastal cities and towns of Sydney, Melbourne, Adelaide, Brisbane, Hobart, Fremantle, Townsville, and Darwin (its Central Great Desert region was virtually uninhabited). These centers of population, all of which were important seaports, were the strategically vital areas of Australia. The southeast coast was the most important, with Sydney, as the country's population, industrial, and agricultural center, being the object of a potential Japanese invasion.

Australia's inadequate communication and transportation systems made the organization and operation of Air Corps units difficult. The country's radio, telephone, and telegraph systems, already handling heavy traffic in peacetime, became overloaded with wartime traffic. With all these communications systems under the control of the Australian Army, the Americans were forced to depend upon the Australians until they could set up their own systems, which was finally accomplished in mid-summer 1942.

Probably the major difficulty to the rapid development and organization of the AAC in Australia was the large distances between strategic areas and in the inadequate methods of traversing those distances. Australia's railway

Australia and New Guinea

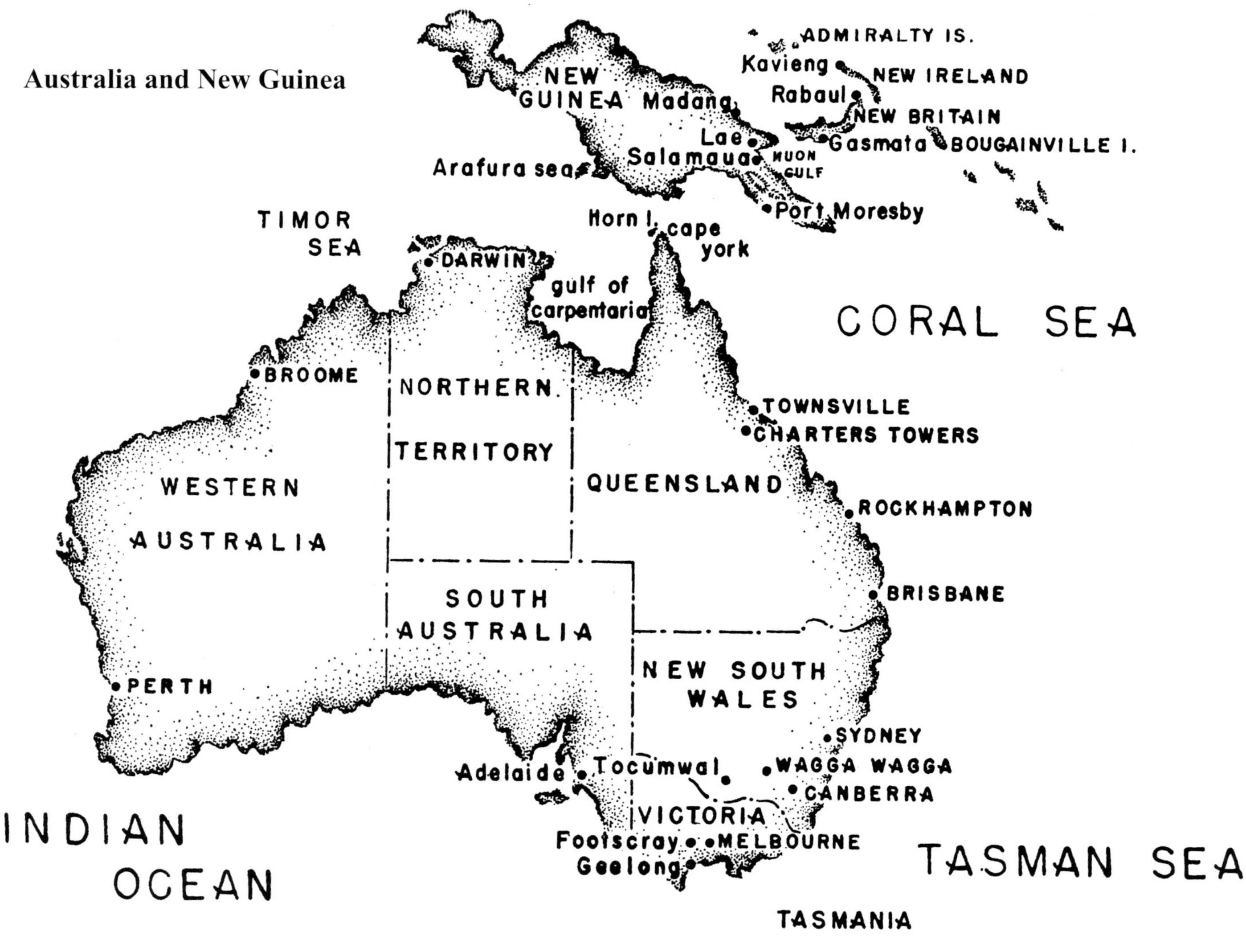

South Pacific Island Ferry Route

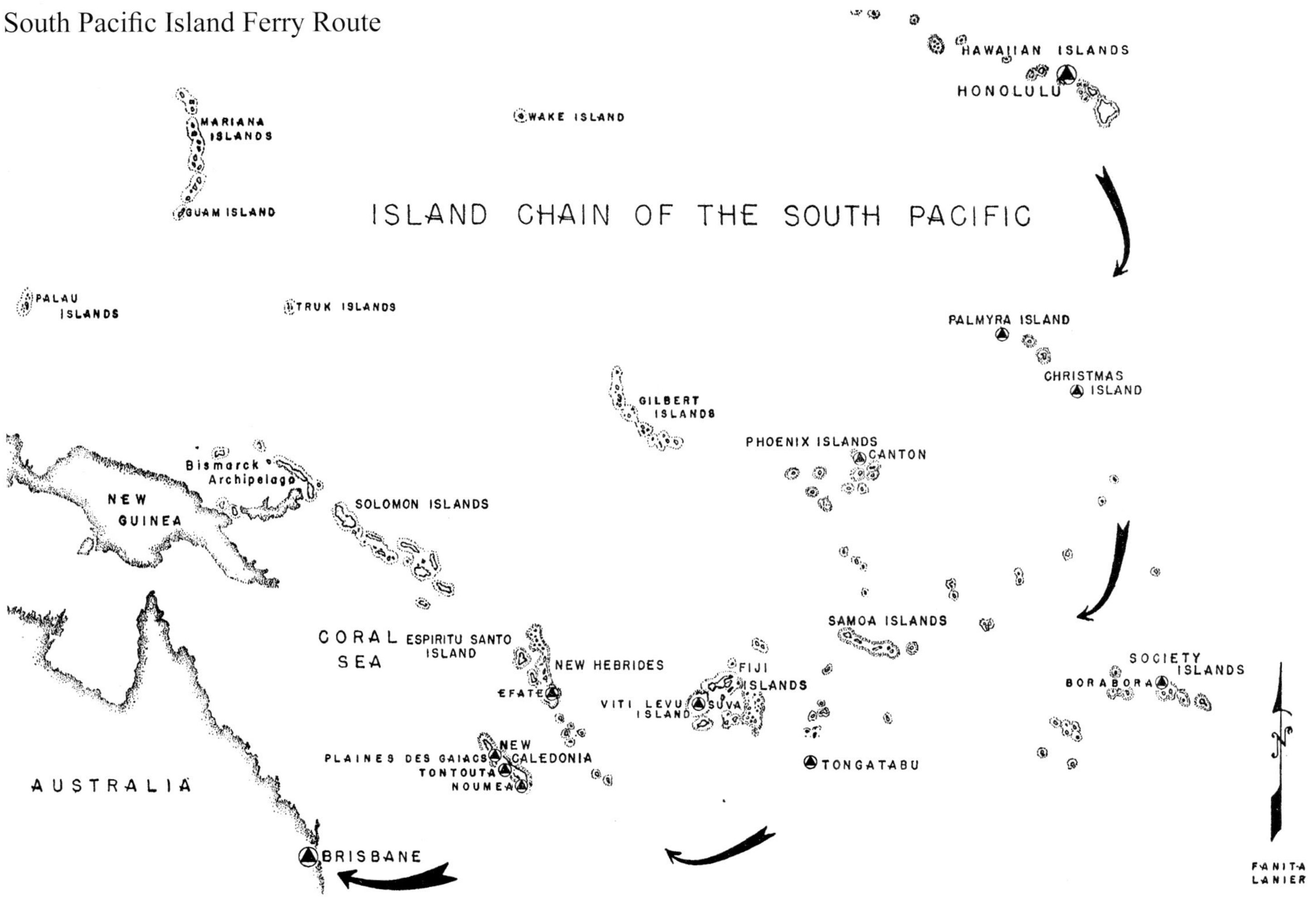

system in miles per 1,000 square miles ranked among the bottom three in the world, and to complicate matters, the system was composed of five different gauges and antiquated rolling stock. The road system was also insufficient, with very few surfaced roads, with about half being graded and covered with gravel or crushed rock and mostly impassable during rainy weather. The other half of the roadway mileage consisted of ungraded and unsurfaced tracks with narrow bridges that limited load carrying capacity. When large shipments of materiel and personnel were to be moved over large distances, the AAC had to depend to a large extent upon maritime transportation from one major port to another. However, this movement was subject to submarine attack and was slow, and the need for widespread air transport was imperative from the first day that American air units arrived in Australia. The need continued to grow as the tactical air units became dispersed, and as the forces expanded in size and increased their operations. Although air transport had been used extensively by the Australians before the war, the Americans did not find a large number of well-constructed airdromes and airfields which were ready for combat operations. With the few exceptions of airdromes near the large cities, the airfields were not well situated from a tactical standpoint, nor were they large enough to accommodate heavy military aircraft. Minor landing fields could be constructed easily and at low cost because of the flat terrain on most of the Continent, but along the east coast and in the extreme north the rocky terrain and dense forests greatly hindered the construction of military fields. The AAC developed a rapid, efficient method for building operational strips for heavy bomber and transport aircraft operation. These strips were 6,000x300 feet, but had only the middle of the strip constructed of hard surface, which caused a considerable dust problem.

Establishing and Protecting Bases on the Pacific Ferry/Supply Route

In the spring of 1942, the reinforcement of New Zealand, New Caledonia, the New Hebrides, and the Fiji Islands, as well as Australia, was part of the Allied strategy of preparing bases to open a strong offensive against the Japanese. The Japanese realized that it was imperative for them to prevent this by cutting the lines of communication and supply between the United States and Australia by occupying the islands to the northeast and east of Australia.

With the southward advance of the Japanese, it became increasingly apparent that the newly established boundary between the South and Southwest Pacific areas provided a tactical disadvantage for the Allied commanders. Since the line of enemy advance was not in the South Pacific or SWPA, the situation demanded a high degree of coordination between the two Allied commanders, Gen. MacArthur in the Southwest Pacific and Adm. Ghormley in the South Pacific. However, even before the formal establishment of these two areas, the American forces in Australia had cooperated in the transshipment of the task force sent from the United States to New Caledonia in February. Small numbers of troops under Gen. MacArthur's command, including specific air force units, were to be sent to several island garrisons to the east of Australia. New Caledonia was located on the right flank of any defense against an enemy advance toward southeast Australia, and Gen. Marshall requested that MacArthur take immediate steps to provide air support for the Army force on New Caledonia, which was under the command of Brig.Gen. Alexander Patch. One squadron of the 36th Bombardment Group (M), then in Australia, was designated for transfer to Patch's command, but the flying echelon of the squadron was still in training in the United States and was not expected to

Coral Sea Area

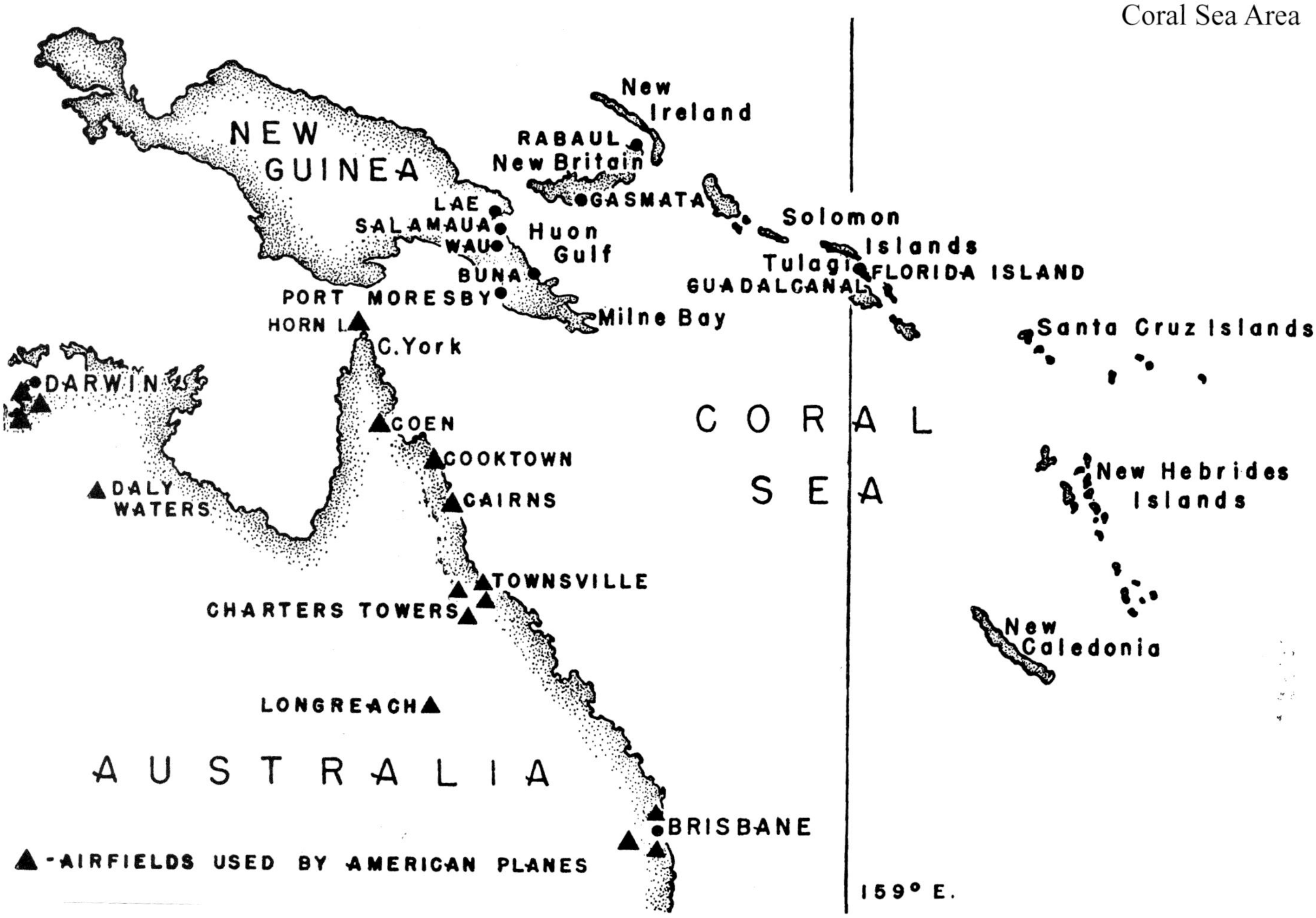

be sent to the South Pacific until the first of June, or until its training was completed and its full equipment was supplied.

In the meantime, aerial protection for the forces on New Caledonia had to be limited to whatever assistance the Allied Air Forces, concentrated on the east coast of Australia, could provide. Considering the enemy concentrations to the north, Gen. MacArthur felt it was too late, as well as too dangerous, to attempt any direct reinforcement from Australia. Fiji was being used as an aircraft staging area and as a naval anchorage. New Zealand had accepted responsibility for the defense of Fiji soon after the beginning of the war in Europe, and by May 1942 had stationed approximately 10,000 troops at Vitta Levu. At this time the total US Army force there consisted of 25 pursuit planes and 600 men, including personnel for operation and maintenance of airdromes at Nandi. Because of the importance of Fiji and New Caledonia as links between Australia and the United States, these islands were subjected to enemy raids. On 13 May, to provide for the relief of the New Zealand forces and to insure the continued holding of the strategic island of Fiji, the US assumed responsibility for their defense and immediately initiated action to send strong reinforcements to the islands. With the gradual establishment of strong American forces in New Caledonia, the New Hebrides, and the Fiji Islands, the lines of communication between Australia and the United States were more firmly established, assuring the continued use of the South Pacific ferry and shipping route.

While the Americans were strengthening their lines of communication to the SWPA, the Japanese were escalating their efforts throughout the area by massing more reinforcements into specific positions in the Netherlands East Indies, the New Guinea northeastern coast, New Britain, and in the northern Solomons. Japanese aircraft were constantly patrolling the Broome and Darwin area, and were observed as far inland as Alice Springs. Japanese submarine and air patrols were also reported off Sydney, Melbourne, Tasmania, Adelaide, and Perth.

Darwin

Darwin's harbor facilities were located on a main square-shaped peninsula which had a second smaller, narrower peninsula named East Point projecting from it. Larrakeyah Beach was the western shore of the main peninsula, on which new anti-aircraft batteries were sited. To the north of Larrakeyah was Dripstone Cliffs, where an early warning radar unit was positioned directly on the path between the RAAF airdrome and distant Timor Island. While the set was operational at the time of the disastrous 19 February raid, it was not manned, but by the end of March it was operated 24/7 by the RAAF as a main component of Darwin's early warning system. To the south and inland, Darwin Harbor extended into a very irregular flood plain with a convoluted shore line. To the east were the East Point headlands and the town and the docks. The Harbor was the delta of the Elizabeth River, whose mouth extended into the desert to the southeast known as the East Arm. Directly to the west was the natural land jetty called Middle Point, which was used as the main landmark for the flight path to the harbor area. The inlet on Middle Point's west side was the delta of the Blackmore River, a crocodile infested tangle of mangrove known as the Middle Arm. West of the Middle Arm mangroves was the headland of the Cox Peninsula, whose northeastern horn was called West Point and whose northwestern horn was called Point Charles, where the lighthouse was located. The forested eastern shore of the Cox Peninsula was the Swires Bluff, a stony mound laying three miles across the harbor from the Darwin docks.

Fifty miles due north from Darwin across Beagle Gulf were Melville and Bathurst Islands, which were separated by a narrow strait. Bathurst, the smaller island laying to the west of the strait, was colonized by European missionaries and an aboriginal population. The islanders volunteered to be part of the network of coast watchers for the defense's Northern Territory.

The first airfield constructed in the Northern Territory was built in 1938 near Darwin to serve as the municipal airfield for the town (which it does today). RAAF Station Darwin was established on 1 June 1940 from elements of No. 12 and No. 13 Squadrons of the RAAF. This previously remote airfield became an important airbase after war broke out, and after Allied units retreated to Australia in early 1942, it became a target for Japanese air attacks. After the large 19 February 1942 Japanese raid, the Northern Territory and parts of Western Australia's north were bombed 62 more times between 4 March 1942 and 12 November 1943. RAAF Darwin was continually repaired and expanded during WWII, and about 75 units from the RAAF, AAF, and RAF operated there during the war.

Before December 1941, Batchelor Field was a primitive prewar RAAF training base. When the Philippines were evacuated it was used as a receiving base for aircraft, and then was used to regroup these aircraft. The four B-17s that evacuated MacArthur and his family and senior staff landed here on 10 March 1942. In late December 1941 squadrons of the 19BG and 7BG staged through Batchelor to Singosari Airdrome, on the northern coast of eastern Java. Once a pursuit pilot left Batchelor for a patrol over Darwin he headed north and followed the Track Highway and its parallel railroad line to the Elizabeth River Crossing, where he turned WNW along the river bed, flying directly out over Middle Point, then crossed Darwin Harbor at 10,000 feet to pass over the docks to climb to the patrol altitude of 20,000 feet or more above Beagle Gulf. It was not too long before Batchelor became overcrowded and 34 Mile Strip was constructed (later called Livingstone).

Livingstone Field, located off the main road 34 miles south of Darwin, was built by the 808th Engineer Aviation Battalion from 16 March to 13 April 1942. The field consisted of a 5,000x100 foot runway paved with four inches of clay bound gravel and a coat of diesel oil. There also was 2,000x30 feet of taxiway. The field was named after Lt. Livingstone, who was the first pilot killed in action at the airfield on 4 April 1942. The initial tent camp at the airfield was built by 9PS of the 49PG in the bush next to the runway near a cattle farm called Humpty Doo. The 9PS commandeered beds from their hotel in Darwin for their tents. An Officer's Mess was a hut with a concrete floor and a tin roof, but was open on all sides for ventilation. The 9PS pilots also commandeered the mess table, some benches, and easy chairs looted from the Hotel.

As described previously, on 19 February the large naval base at Darwin was heavily bombed by two waves of Japanese carrier-based aircraft, resulting in serious naval and aircraft losses to the Australians and Americans. Aircraft losses for the Allies totaled nine P-40s shot down and six Hudsons, two P-40s, and one LB-30 destroyed on the ground, while the Japanese lost five to ten aircraft. The main result of the raid was the loss of the use of port facilities at Darwin, which were being used extensively in transshipping reinforcements and supplies to the forces in the Netherlands East Indies. Also, the success of the raid was a portent of the enemy's capability and intention of bringing the war to the Australian Continent. However strategically, the Japanese attack on Darwin actually prevented the Allies from sending valuable men, equipment, and supplies to Java, which would have soon fallen into enemy hands. Following the Darwin attack, the proximity of Japan's recent advances in the Netherlands East Indies to the northwestern coast of Australia was thought to make military installations there vulnerable. Therefore, the Australians ordered the demolition of airdromes within several hundred miles and the evacuation of civilians to the interior. (Note: Darwin's experience in World War II was highlighted in the 2009 Hugh Jackman/Nicole Kidman movie *Australia*.)

RAAF Darwin. (AAF)

Livingston Field. (AAF)

Batchelor Field. (AAF)

Darwin Area Airfields

The 19 February attack on Darwin made it apparent to Brett that the Allied resistance in the NEI could not be maintained much longer, and he began to make plans for the evacuation of American forces from Java, with the majority of the troops being scheduled for shipment to India, since a sufficient number of troops had been allotted to Australia. By 20 February, all aircraft which were not in combat operations were being employed in the evacuation of non-essential personnel. On 3 March, unopposed Japanese air attacks on Broome and Wyndham, on the northwest coast of Australia, took 65 lives and 17 aircraft, most of which were being used to evacuate civilians.

March 1942

March 1942: Disposition of AAC Fighter Units in Australia and Port Moresby

By mid-March 1942 the AAC in Australia had 33 P-39s, 52 P-400s, and 92 P-40s in service; apportioned to the 8th, the 35th, and the 49th Fighter Groups.* The original pilots of the 35th had been sent to the NEI campaign and were currently were engaged in much needed rest and recuperation. The 8th Group had just arrived at Brisbane on 10 March, which meant that

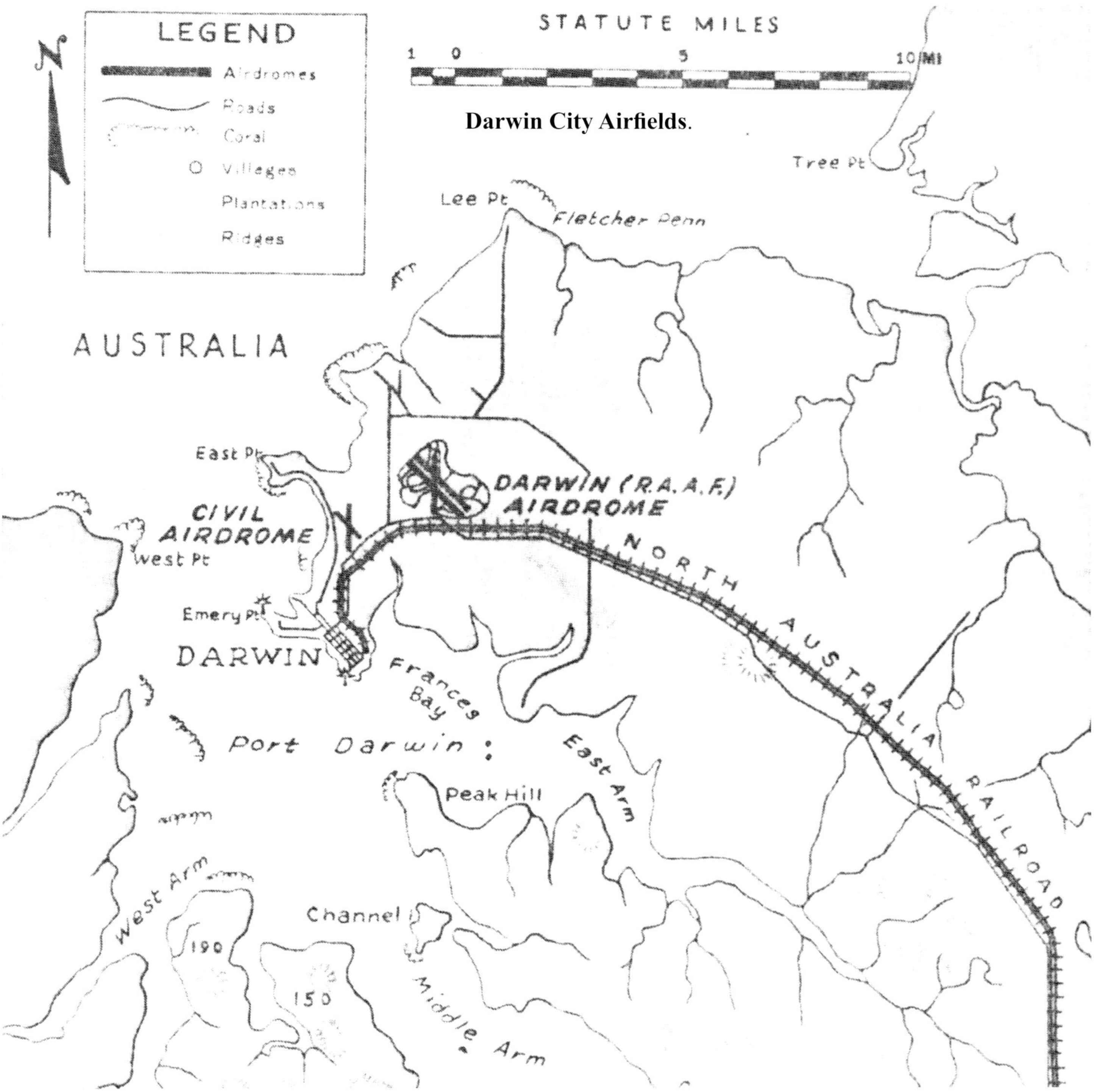

Darwin City Airfields.

(RAAF)

the 49th Group would be designated first to enter combat. (*Note: The Army Air Corps (AAC) was designated as the Army Air Force (AAF) on 20 June 1942, and although it did not officially redesignate all pursuit and interceptor units as "fighter" until 15 May 1942, most were designated as such in the early spring of 1942.)

The fighter squadrons in the Port Moresby area were the 35th Squadron of the 8th Fighter Group (less two flights), based at 12 Mile Airdrome (12 miles from Port Moresby), and the 36th Squadron of the same group, with two flights of the 35th Squadron, based at 7 Mile Airdrome. Attached to each squadron was one flight of P-400s and pilots from the 39th and 40th Squadrons of the 35th Fighter Group. Many of these pilots had been flying three to six hours a day on operational missions for over a week without relief. Each squadron had only 26 pilots (although the T/O called for a minimum of 35), and by the end of May were able to maintain only 18 to 20 aircraft in service. Most squadrons were controlled by "Visual from a ground alert status," and on every alert all available aircraft were put into the air, since it was considered too risky to leave aircraft on the ground to be destroyed during enemy raids. While this preventative action may have conserved

Brig.Gen. Martin **Scanlon** was in command of all air units. (AAF)

aircraft, pilots were under great stress, and sickness and fatigue reduced pilot numbers to the point that every available pilot was on alert 12 hours every day. (Note: The airdromes around Port Moresby will discussed in detail in Part 4.)

There was no tactical headquarters to coordinate the operations of the two squadrons, and while Brig.Gen. Martin Scanlon was in command of all air units in the area, he had no fighter operational staff, and the lack of such a staff resulted in uncoordinated action by the squadrons. The squadron commanders resorted to mutual agreement on operations, which was a poor substitute for the proper coordination that could be provided by a higher headquarters. Briefing before missions was often haphazard, and was frequently passed on from one squadron to another. A supply officer was especially needed to oversee the unloading, storing, and distributing of supplies, responsibilities which were being carried out by the already overworked ground crews. The result of this lack of organization and shortage of needed personnel was the lowering of efficiency and morale.

49th Pursuit Group

The 49th Pursuit Group (PG) was formed at Selfridge Field, MI, on 20 November 1940, and was comprised of the 7th, 8th, and 9th Pursuit Squadrons, with 130 non-commissioned personnel and nine pilots. Maj. Glen Davasher initially commanded the 49th, but ill health caused him to resign that post, and he was succeeded by Maj. John Egan in February 1941.

In May 1941 the 49th was ordered to Morrison Field, in West Palm Beach, FL, with 19 officers and 280 enlisted men. Now under the command of Maj. George McCoy, the squadron COs were Lt. Allen Bennett (the 7th), 1Lt. Robert Van Auken (8th), and Capt. Victor Pixey (9th). Pilot and ground crew training continued during the summer, but was hindered by the lack of modern equipment. Squadron pilot air training was limited to single Stearman PT-17 and Ryan PT-13 trainers, three obsolete Seversky P-35 pursuit fighters, and one weary Curtiss P-40 fighter per unit.

Once America entered the war at Pearl Harbor, the training intensified and flying hours increased. Maj. Paul Wurtsmith was given command of the 49th, while the 7th PS, "the Screamin' Demons," was led by 1Lt. Robert Morrissey and the 9th, the "Flying Knights," by 1Lt. James Selman, while 1Lt. Van Auken continued in command of the 8th PS, "the Eightballs."

On 4 January 1942 the 49th crossed the country on a four day train journey to San Francisco, where they were bivouacked in the County Livestock Pavilion with thousands of other AAC personnel en route to the Pacific. After the Group had received 75 new pilots and over 500 enlisted men, it was the first AAC fighter group in the war to be posted overseas from the US. On 12 January, most of the 49th personnel embarked on the USAT *Mariposa*, with the remainder boarding the SS *Coolidge*.

Both vessels arrived at Melbourne, Australia, on 1 February. On their arrival, the Group's pilots were scheduled for urgently needed training, since of the complement of 102 pilots in his group, only Wurtsmith, with 4,800 hours of pursuit time, and his executive officer, Maj. Donald Hutchinson, with 2,600 hours, were veteran pilots. Five others had more than 600 hours and nine had about 15 hours, while the remaining 89 pilots had no pursuit time at all. The 49th's three squadrons were assigned to different fields for combat training: the 7th to Bankstown, outside Sydney; the 8th to a Royal Australian Air Force (RAAF) airfield east of Canberra; and the 9th to Williamtown, near Newcastle, north of Sydney. The Group's P-40Es had been transported with the Group (19 aboard the *Mariposa*, 32 on the *Coolidge*, and seven as deck cargo aboard the SS *Monroe*). The Warhawks needed to be assembled ASAP before they were flown to the various training bases, as the Squadron's pilots were given only two weeks to be prepared for combat. Each unit received 25 P-40s, which were scrupulously tested. Wurtsmith received welcomed assistance from combat veteran Capt. Boyd "Buzz" Wagner, the AAC's first ace from the Philippines, to create the training syllabus. The pilots had difficulties with the P-40's engine torque on take off and numerous ground loops occurred, with 30 accidents being recorded in the first two weeks of training.

During this time the 49th received welcomed veteran reinforcements from the Philippine and Java Campaigns. Besides Wagner, Capt. Walter Coss was assigned to the 49th's Headquarters' Squadron, while 1Lts. Nathaniel Blanton, Jack Dale, William Hennon, and Lester Johnson were sent to the 7th PS and 1Lts. Robert Dockstader, George Kiser, and James Morehead joined the 8thPS. 1Lts. Joseph Kruzel, Ben Irvin, and Andrew Reynolds went to the 9th PS, which was already stationed in Darwin.

8th Pursuit Group

On 5 October 1930, the Adjutant General informed the Commanding General of the 3rd Corps Area that the 8th Pursuit Group was activated (The official activation date is commonly recorded as 1 April 1931 at Langley Field, VA: Maurer). Its first assigned squadron was the 36th Pursuit Squadron, which had been activated only three days before at Selfridge Field on 2 October 1930. On 7 June 1932, the 3rd Corps Area activated the 33rd and 35th Pursuit Squadrons at Langley Field. The following day, the 36th left Selfridge to join the 8PG and completed the initial cadre of the group. On 25 June 1932, the 8PG was formally activated at Langley Field with an initial strength of 42 officers and 559 enlisted men, with Maj. Bryon Jones as its first CO. Shortly after its activation on 1 September 1933 the 37th Attack Squadron, flying A-8s and A-17s, was assigned to the 8PG to test the principles of fighter and bomber coordination.

The early history of the Group is muddled or missing from the records. During the early to mid-1930s the Group was equipped with Curtiss P-6s and Boeing P-12s, and took part in a number of exercises and maneuvers. In February 1934 Congress determined that several airlines were receiving favored treatment in the granting of profitable air mail contracts. President Roosevelt took the contracts away from the airlines and assigned them to the Air Corps, after Air Corps Chief Gen. Benjamin Foulois assured him of the viability of the military flying air mail. The decision turned out to be a debacle, as 14 Army pilots were killed in administrative or training flights, but only one was killed on an operational mail flight. The small, open cockpit, fabric covered P-12s that the 8PG flew were wholly unsuited for flying the mail in the snow and cold of the Eastern Zone. The only pilot to die on a scheduled mail run was the 8PG's Lt. Durwood Lowry on 22 February, but with nine other deaths over the next three weeks the Army suspended flying for a week so that flyers could receive proper orientation. Operations resumed on 19 March, and the results remained acceptable until 7 May 1934, when the Army's airmail responsibility was terminated. Maj. Jones was relieved of command of the group during the air mail operation and was succeeded by Capt. Albert Guidera.

After its airmail phase, the 8PG continued its participation in maneuvers throughout the mid and late 1930s, which would later prove invaluable training, as these men would be veterans by the time the war began and passed on their valuable experience to rookie pilots. During March 1935 the 8th Pursuit Group became the 8th Pursuit Group, General Headquarters Air Force under a reorganization that stationed three Wings at Langley, VA,

Lt.Col. Frederick **Smith** had been 8PG CO since January 1941. (AAF)

Barksdale Field, LA, and March Field, CA. Lt.Col. Adlai Gilkeson assumed Group command from Capt. Albert Guidera in May 1935. In September 1936, the 58th Service Squadron was combined with the 8th Group Headquarters to form the Headquarters and Headquarters Squadron, 8th Pursuit Group. This organization proved to be cumbersome, but would continue until the Group had been in combat and was finally reorganized in September 1942. Over the next several years the Group overcame limited budgets and indecisive AAC policy, all the while gaining valuable experience in flying and maintaining its aircraft. Gilkeson turned the command of the Group over to Lt.Col. William Kepner on 7 July 1938. After the extended exercises at Fort Bragg, NC, in October 1938, the Group was reequipped with new Curtiss P-36 fighters at Langley, and by January 1939 the squadrons were fully complemented when 80 P-36s arrived. The P-36 was phased out with the introduction of the P-40 in 1940.

On 1 February 1940, Col. Kepner was promoted to an AAC headquarters position and Lt.Col. Edward Morris assumed Group command. Because the AAC was expanding exponentially, selected personnel and equipment of the Group were transferred to form the nucleus of the new 36th Pursuit Group, as the AAC would use these veterans to pass on their experience to these newer units and bring them quickly up to operational standards. The Group made up these personnel losses with the influx of new recruits and took part in maneuvers and demonstrations. In October 1940 their P-40s made the first take off of Army fighters from an aircraft carrier cruising off Norfolk, VA. On 11 November 1940 the Group received orders to move from Langley to Mitchel Field, where they remained to complete their training and make their final preparations for combat. Col. Frederick Smith took command of the group on 17 January 1941 and would continue with the Group to New Guinea, eventually taking command of 5th Fighter Command near the end of the war. In mid-1941 the P-39 Airacobra replaced the Group's Warhawks, so training in this new fighter became the imperative for the rest of 1941. The Group participated in exercises at Barksdale Field, LA, then moved to Fort Bragg, NC, in September.

During the first half of 1941 the 33rd Squadron was detached from the 8PS and assigned to the Iceland Base Command in August. The 33rd received P-39s and became part of the 342nd Composite Group on Iceland for most of the war. On 14 August 1942 the squadron was involved in the first confirmed U.S. Army aerial victory when 2Lt. Joseph Shaffer was credited with 1/3 shared victory over a Focke-Wulf FW 200 which was shot down near the Icelandic coast for the first American air-to-air victory over a German aircraft.

The day after Pearl Harbor, 19 officers and 51 enlisted men of the 35PS under Capt. William Wise left for Providence, RI, for patrol duty in the new war. After several weeks of patrolling the coast around Rhode Island and New Jersey in their P-39s, the 35PS and the rest of the 8PG returned to Mitchel Field on 10 January 1942. At this time Maj. Wise was transferred to Group Headquarters, and 1Lt. George Greene would become the 35PS' first combat commander. Also on this day the Group received its third combat squadron; the 80th Pursuit Squadron (Interceptor), which had been activated on 6 January and was to receive staff and equipment from the other three squadrons and from the recruit center at Mitchel Field. 1Lt. Philip Greasley was the squadron's first Commander, and Lieutenants Joseph McNay, George Austin, and William Greenfield were named Flight Leaders. Due to the crisis in the South Pacific, a number of the group's pilots and enlisted men were detached and rushed overseas, where they saw service in the Darwin area; they were returned to the 8th by the time it was assigned to New Guinea.

On 26 January, the 8PG Group boarded a troop train for a four day trip to San Francisco, and when they arrived they almost immediately boarded the old Matson Line Hawaiian passenger ship *Maui* headed for "*Destination X*." However, two days later they had to disembark, as the *Maui* required repairs, and they were temporarily quartered at Fort McDowell, near San Francisco. After spending the next few days on leave in the city, on 9 February the *Maui* was ready for boarding again for the voyage across the Pacific. Afterward the *Maui* anchored in San Francisco Bay until 12 February and then passed under the Golden Gate Bridge and headed south toward the Equator. It crossed the Equator on 21 February, and those men who had never been to the southern hemisphere were initiated in the traditional King Neptune ceremony. On 5 March, the 21st day of the voyage, the *Maui* finally dropped anchor off Brisbane. The ship docked the next morning, and the men boarded trucks which transported them to an Australian Army camp at Ascot Racetrack. On 12 March the 35PS moved to Eagle Farms, near Brisbane, which had a landing strip for their Airacobras. The next day the 36PS moved to Lowood, about 70 miles from Brisbane, where the skeletal 80PS was also based. It was finally decided to leave the 80th behind as a replacement unit for the 35th and 36th Squadrons when they moved north to New Guinea. 1Lt. Philip Greasley was the Commander of the 80th, with George Austin as Operations Officer and Lieutenants Harley Brown, Todd Dabney, William Frank, William Greenfield, David Hunter, Gentry Plunkett, and Daniel Roberts the assigned pilots (75 additional pilots would be sent from Brisbane to reinforce the 35PS when they were training at Townsville). Plunkett was sent to the 35PS as a replacement pilot during its initial combat in New Guinea. Roberts was thought to be too mild mannered for combat and was put in charge of a Doodnadatta, a bleak base in the middle of the Australian desert. Fortunately the future ace and combat leader was given a reprieve by a prominent General who heard his plea to see combat, and he was reassigned to the 80th in mid-July.

Training was rushed through early spring 1942 at bases near Townsville, Rockhampton, and Woodstock, as Allied air power was effectively nonexistent to defend either Port Moresby or Milne Bay. On 11 April, new pilot 2Lt. Bernard Gillingham of the 35PS was the first 8PG fatality of the war when his P-39 suffered a mechanical failure during a take off from Woodstock during a familiarization flight. His fighter caught fire and he elected to land and was successful, but he was unable to get out of the burning aircraft and perished. By May 1942 Lt.Col. Frederick Smith, who had been 8PG CO since January 1941, felt strongly that many of his pilots were not adequately prepared for combat and asked for further training. He was ordered to have all pilots ready to be sent to Port Moresby or he would be replaced. Lt.Col. William Wise replaced Smith on 22 May, and although he agreed with Smith, he knew if he disagreed he, too, would be replaced, almost assuring the selection of a commander from outside the 8PG. Wise had no choice but to abide by the order and, as he and Smith had predicted, the weather and geography around northern Australia and Port Moresby would require more training, which was now denied.

Reorganizing the AAC in Australia March 1942

During the two months following the end of the Java campaign, while the AAC units in Australia were getting some additional training and awaiting the arrival of much of their equipment, the veteran remnants of squadrons which were withdrawn from Java were incorporated into new units and a foundation was laid for the reorganization of the Allied Air Forces in Australia.

The Japanese were threatening Australia from the northwest, but from the first week in March 1942 they also presented a new threat from the northeast. By this time the Japanese were established in strategic positions throughout the Bismarck Archipelago: at Rabaul and Gasmata, New Britain; at Kavieng, New Ireland; and on Mussau Island, northwest of New Hanover. They had also occupied positions on Buka Island (southernmost of the Solomons), and reportedly were occupying Kieta in the Salmons and Rossel Island in the Louisiades. Repeated air attacks on the lower Solomons and on the New Guinea port towns of Lae, Salamaua, Buna, and Port Moresby signified the Japanese intention of expanding to the south toward Australia. On 7 March, following air raids on Lae and Salamaua and shelling of the two ports by warships, the Japanese landed and quickly captured both areas in *Operation SR*. The small Australian garrison in the area withdrew as the Japanese landed and did not contest the invasion. The Japanese invaded and occupied the area to construct an airfield and establish a base to cover and support the advance of Japanese forces into the eastern New Guinea and Coral Sea areas.

The Japanese assault on New Guinea caused a change in plans for certain forces in the Australia-New Zealand area. Arrangements had been made for naval Task Force ANZAC to provide protection for the movement of American forces from Australia to New Caledonia. These American troops had arrived at Melbourne on 26 February for transshipment to New Caledonia by the Task Force. On the night of 6 March Task Force ANZAC left for its destination, supported by naval Task Force ANZAC. Allied plans for the protection of this troop movement included carrier-based attacks on enemy ships and installations in the Bismarck-Solomons area. The plan was changed when intelligence was received on 7 March that a Japanese convoy, consisting of transports, a cruiser, and several destroyers, was moving toward New Guinea, and when further information was received the following day that 11 additional enemy ships had begun to shell Lae and Salamaua. The Allies scheduled an assault on these newest enemy attacks for 10 March.

After terrain and weather data had been obtained from Townsville and Port Moresby, USN Task Force 17, including the carriers *Yorktown* and *Lexington*, operated in a coordinated carrier attack for the first time in US naval history. They sailed into the Gulf of Papua and launched over 104 planes across the New Guinea Owen Stanley Mountains to attack enemy naval forces at Lae and Salamaua. After the carrier attack, eight B-17s of the 435BS of the 19BG from Garbutt Field, Townsville, and a number of No. 32 Squadron RAAF Hudsons from Port Moresby also took part in the attack, concentrating mainly on additional ships which were sighted 25 miles off the coast. With a loss of only one scout bomber, which was shot down by shore-based antiaircraft fire off Lae, the Navy and AAC sank a reported total of five merchant ships, two heavy cruisers, one light cruiser, and one destroyer probably sunk, with six other vessels seriously damaged. This report was exaggerated, as the raid actually sank three transports and damaged another, and damaged a light cruiser, two destroyers, and several other ships. Although these losses greatly hampered their efforts, the Japanese continued with the occupation of Lae and Salamaua and began the construction of a base and airfield. Air units based at the airfield later supported an air superiority campaign against Allied forces at Port Moresby. The Japanese invasion was viewed by Gen. Brett as preliminary to the first phase of operations against the northeast coast of Australia, or possibly New Caledonia and the Solomons. The Allies expected that, with the consolidation of their gains in the Netherlands East Indies, the Japanese would send at least two divisions and one or more aircraft carriers to be used for a joint task force operation against the northwest coast

Horn Island Airfield was an isolated airstrip located at the northern tip of Cape York, but was only 75 miles south of Japanese-held New Guinea. (AAF)

7PS CO Capt. Robert **Morrissey** and 49FG CO Lt.Col. Paul **Wurtsmith**. (AAF)

of Australia. Enemy attacks were also expected on shipping in the Indian Ocean and on Fremantle.

Actually, any location on the Australian continent was vulnerable to air attack because of the flexibility of enemy carrier based operations. In order to counter this threat, Brett found that air units would have to be stationed in each of seven widely separated areas: Darwin (Base Section No. 1); Townsville (Base Section No. 2); Brisbane (Base Section No. 3); Melbourne (Base Section No. 4); Adelaide (Base Section No. 5); Perth (Base Section No. 6); and Sydney (later to become Base Section No. 7). To provide the defensive and offensive air strength in Australia, Brett estimated that the following units would be required: three heavy bombardment groups of four squadrons each, three medium bombardment groups, three light bombardment groups, six pursuit groups, three transport groups, two air depot groups, two engineer battalions (aviation), and the necessary air support organizations. However, at this time the situation throughout the AAC was that the demand for combat units far exceeded supply. The attitude of the Chief of Air Staff, Plans at Headquarters, AAF, was that Brett's strategy should be revised, and only the more critical areas defended if he found his allotted three pursuit groups and one light, two medium, and two heavy bombardment groups insufficient for the defense of the seven critical areas.

However, in contrast with this scheduled air strength, at the and of February there were only 16 bombers, 29 dive bombers, and 110 pursuit planes reported available for combat. Brett had no pursuit squadrons in place to use these 110 aircraft. On 8 March, Brett estimated that he should have an AAC fighter squadron to be equipped with 25 P-40s ready for combat within 10 days, and that an additional squadron could be made ready within a month. The 15 A-24s of the 3rd Bombardment Group (L), which had arrived at Brisbane on 25 February, were being assembled. Of the 52 A-24s which had arrived on 23 December in the convoy scheduled for the Philippines, only 29 remained in Australia.

During the first week of March, the depleted squadrons from the Java area were evacuated to the west coast of Australia. On the opposite coast of the Australian continent other groups, some newly arrived, were assigned various duties. On 9 March the 3rd Bombardment Group and the 35th Air Base Group were at Charters Towers, engaged in training and maintenance. The 49th Pursuit Group was in the Sydney area, engaged in operational training; the 35th Pursuit Group and the 46th Air Base Group were at Mt. Gambier, engaged in training and maintenance; while the 8th Pursuit and 22nd Air Base Groups were disembarking at Brisbane.

By the mid-March, the three Pursuit Groups had absorbed the remnants of the 3rd, 17th, and 20th Pursuit Squadrons (Provisional). They were equipped with aircraft and were moved into tactical position in three of the critical areas of Australia. First of the three groups to get into operations was the 49th, commanded by Lt.Col. Paul Wurtsmith and equipped with P-40s.

On 4 March Wurtsmith asked 7PS CO 1Lt. Morrissey if he had enough combat-qualified pilots to send a detachment to Horn Island, which was an isolated airstrip located hundreds of miles distant in the far northeast at the tip of Cape York, Queensland. The airfield was located on a two mile wide spit that jutted out into the Coral Sea only 75 miles south of Japanese-held New Guinea. Twelve pilots and P-40s were available, and had to use maritime maps for navigation over the long, barren route to Horn Island. Of the 12 P-40s sent out, only nine arrived at Horn Island.

The urgency of the times caused a snafu, in that no transportation had been arranged for 49th ground crew, and the pilots would have to service their own aircraft, so for the time being they moved to the RAAF airdrome in the Darwin area. After training, Capt. Robert Van Auken led 25 pilots and planes of the 8th Pursuit Squadron to Melbourne to provide combat air patrol over the city. The 8th Pursuit Group, equipped with P-39s, was preparing to take up its position in the Brisbane area, while the 35th Group, equipped with P-400s, was moving into position in the Sydney area. Gen. Brett's urgent request for three additional pursuit groups could not he granted, in view of the critical shortage of pursuit aircraft throughout the AAF.

Air Operations: March 1942

14 March 1942: 49FG/7FS: First Combat and First Victory

A flight of 7th Squadron pilots from the 49th Group had been temporarily deployed to the RAAF station at Horn Island, which was an advanced operational base off the northern tip of Cape York. On 14 March 1942 the Squadron, under the command of Capt. Robert Morrissey, claimed their first victories when they intercepted a formation of enemy bombers escorted by fighters during an attack on the RAAF air base on Horn Island.

Coast watchers on New Guinea alerted Horn Island of a large formation of enemy bombers escorted by fighters heading toward Australia. At 1130, nine P-40s of the 7th PS divided into two flights took off just before noon. A Flight consisted of 7PS CO Maj. Robert Morrissey and 2Lts. A.T. House, Claude Burtnette, and Clarence Sanford, while B Flight was flown by Flight Leader 2Lt. William Reddington and 2Lts. Charles Johnson, Wilson Chapman, Harold Martin, and Stephen Andrews. The P-40s took off at 1145 in 15 second intervals and assembled at 10,000 feet over their base. Morrissey ordered his pilots to test their guns, and Morrissey found that he had only one functioning gun and immediately returned to the airstrip to clear the jams, leaving the formation to be led by Reddington. After 45 minutes Morrissey rejoined his flights, which were strung out south of Horn Island while the Japanese had bombed that RAAF base. Reddington found that his guns had also jammed and returned to base, leaving the B Flight under 2Lt. Johnson. With Sanford and Martin nowhere in the area Morrissey decided to attack the Japanese bombers with his five remaining aircraft.

Meanwhile, Harold Martin had been climbing toward the enemy bombers, which were descending to gain speed to head home and had managed to sneak through the fighter escorts. He fired at the maximum range at the rear three bombers and picked one out at optimum range and fired his remaining ammunition, claiming the first 49th Group victory. As he rolled away Martin's fighter was hit by the bomber's gunners, but he returned to base safely.

After Morrissey spotted eight descending enemy bombers with a lone trailing escort (actually Martin) he saw six Zeros closing on his right. The bomber's high fighter escort was concentrating on Martin, and Morrissey, followed closely by his Wingman, 2Lt. A.T. House, went into their attack, but the second element hesitated momentarily because they had not received their attack signal clearly. Morrissey shot down the rear most Zero, but the remaining five Zeros turned into the P-40s and got on Morrissey's tail. House followed Morrissey, and from minimum firing range he hit one of the Zeros, which began to descend trailing smoke. House then flew directly across another Zero chasing Morrissey, but his tight turn at high Gs caused his guns to jam. Another Zero then turned into Morrissey and, despite his malfunctioning guns, House closed on the Zero and intentionally drove his wingtip onto the Zero's cockpit, killing the pilot and causing it to crash. With three feet of his right wingtip missing House's rugged P-40 went into a cartwheel, but he managed to get his fighter under control and watched the Zero spiraling toward the sea. House returned to Horn Island, but needed three attempts to land at a safe speed; nonetheless, his fighter was written off. Morrissey flew on alone and shot down a Zero in the first element, but was forced to dive away without attacking another because he was being attacked from behind.

LEFT: Capt. Robert **Morrissey** shot down his first of three enemy aircraft. (AAF) RIGHT: After his guns jammed, 2Lt. A.T. **House** saved Morrissey by dipping a wingtip into an attacking Zero's cockpit for his second victory of the day. (AAF)

The other P-40s surprised the Zeros over Torres Strait, but their advantage quickly ended when the veteran Japanese pilots flying their nimble Zeros riddled 2Lts. Burtdette and Andrews' P-40s and forced them to retreat to base. Meanwhile, Johnson and Chapmen attacked a Zero, with Johnson being given credit for the victory in a post-mission discussion and decision. Both P-40s were attacked by a Zero, and Johnson had a bullet hit and ricochet around his cockpit and hit his foot. An exploding cannon shell hit Chapman's armor plate on his seat and cut his shoulder. The two Americans dove away from the battle and landed safely, but their wounds grounded them temporarily from operations.

2Lt. Charles **Johnson** was given a victory after being wounded in combat. (AAF)

2Lt. Clarence Sanford was last reported as being attacked by Zeros, with his P-40 badly damaged and retreating out to sea. Disoriented in the haze above Torres Strait, he ran out of fuel and bailed out over Cape Arnhem and nearly drowned as he swam to a small island. He was rescued by natives and eventually evacuated to Darwin and was sent home.

During the celebration that followed these first victories, Wurtsmith brought out a magnum of brandy and announced that he would open it when the 49th scored its 500th victory in the air. The Group would carry the bottle around "like it was a household God.... It had become a symbol of a goal that they were shooting for and they were certain that they would reach ahead of any other group." After their five victories the 7PS had only seven fighters and six pilots available for combat. To preserve its integrity, the 7th Squadron was ordered to Iron Mountain and then to Darwin at the end of the month.

16 March 1942:49FG/9PS

On 16 March, the air echelon of 25 P-40s making up the 49th Group's 9th Squadron, led by Capt. James Selman, took off for the long 2,000 mile flight from New South Wales to Darwin, and was followed by their ground echelon traveling by train. Weather and maintenance problems along the way delayed the remaining 21 pilots from reaching Darwin until the end of the month. At this time the RAAF base at Darwin had become a regular target for Japanese bombers, who were virtually unopposed by the decimated RAAF defending it. The base had been so badly damaged in Japanese air raids, particularly the devastating air attack on 19 February, that it became virtually inoperable, and the Squadron was assigned to Batchelor Field, about 50 miles south.

22 March 1942: 49FG/9PS: The First Action over Darwin

During March the Japanese Navy had transferred its reconnaissance squadron and fighter units to the deserted former Allied air strip at Koepang, Java. On 22 March they dispatched a Ki-15 reconnaissance bomber to investigate the Darwin defenses before sending large formations of Betty bombers. Coast watchers on Bathurst Island reported the recon aircraft, and their sighting was confirmed by the RAAF radar at Dripstone Cliffs and immediately relayed to a 9PS patrol of four P-40s flying just south of Melville Island.

The four 9PS P-40s that had recently arrived at Batchelor Field were on patrol at 1000 at 20,000 feet, and had separated into two flights to search to the west. At 1310 hours, 2Lts. Clyde Harvey and Stephen Poleschuk climbed toward the lone enemy recon aircraft and surprised it, as its pilot never tried to evade when Poleschuk made 30 degree beam attack and fired from only 200 feet, hitting the bomber. After having his aircraft hit, the Japanese pilot went into a 180 degree diving turn and then a shallow climb to the right as Harvey fired on the flaming bomber. The stricken bomber then descended toward the ocean just west of Bathurst Island, with one of its crew parachuting before the crash. At base there was a coin toss, and the kill was awarded to Poleschuk. More flights were sent north to patrol until dark, but no other contact was made, even though that afternoon Japanese bombers probed 100 miles inland unmolested to Katherine Field in search of the Allied bomber forces.

2Lt. Stephen **Poleschuk** scored his only victory of the war. (AAF)

March 1942: 49FG/9PS

During the last week of March 1942, 9th Pursuit CO Capt. James Selman received reinforcements of aircraft, pilots, and ground crew directly from the assembly base at Brisbane's Amberley field, or from the 9PS training reserve base at Williamstown Field. Some were sent to RAAF Darwin, and a larger contingent to the RAAF airdrome at Batchelor Field. Selman assigned four plane patrols to fly north from Batchelor Field, trying to have eight fighters constantly airborne and four P-40s in standby.

There was friction between Selman and the RAAF warning system. Selman felt the coast watchers and RAAF radar system did not consider the P-40s' performance, as they could not warn his squadron in

Capt. James **Selman** 9PS CO. (AAF)

sufficient time to allow the slow-climbing P-40s enough time to intercept the enemy formations approaching the coast at 20,000 feet or more. Selman immediately devised a more efficient system for interception by organizing the Squadron's four flights into Alert Units. One flight was to be kept on constant alert status by remaining in their cockpits or nearby, ready to scramble. The second flight was on "five minute" alert; ready to take off five minutes after the first scramble order. The third flight was on 15 minute standby alert, while the fourth flight was off flight status that day. Selman's flights rotated through that schedule, which worked well, especially because each flight was given a rest every fourth day to prevent fatigue.

On the other hand, the RAAF was disappointed that the American interceptors could not stop Japanese bombers coming in from Timor Island.

16-23 March 1942: Japanese Attacks

The Japanese sent a small raid against Darwin on 16 March, the day before Selman's P-40s arrived. On the 19th and 23rd, the Japanese bombed Darwin and cratered the runway, again without Allied fighter interception. On the 22nd, Japanese bombers probed 100 miles inland to Katherine Field in search of the Allied bomber forces and only had a reconnaissance plane intercepted. Fortunately, the damage done by these raids was negligible.

28 March 1942: 49FG/9PS

The Japanese decided, since their recent raids had met no opposition, they could safely send an unescorted bomber mission to Darwin on the 28th, and Selman's new patrol alert scheme would be put to the test. When the early warning signal was received, Selman already had one flight up over Beagle Gulf: 1Lt. Robert Vaught led 2Lt. Mitch Zawisza's four ship flight consisting of Wingman 1Lt. William Sells and 2Lts. Clyde Harvey and Steven Poleschuk to the interception. The AAC fighters descended over the harbor and turned to pursue the enemy bombers, which had already reached the RAAF strip and dropped bombs that caused minimal damage to the runway. When the enemy bombers descended to 18,000 feet over the Darwin dock area just before noon Zawisza's flight attacked in line, firing at the starboard flank of their V formation. They then continued with second and third attacks, scattering the formation and with Sells scoring a victory.

Vaught made a climbing attack and fired a fatal burst into another Betty's belly. Harvey chased a fleeing bomber seven miles out over the ocean before he was able to make a diving attack through the rear gunner's fire, and then climbed back to fire a fatal burst into the bomber's belly. Poleschuk chased a fleeing bomber from the dwindling formation to about 100 miles out to sea and fired a burst at long range and was credited with a probable.

31 March 1942: 49FG/9PS

Now aware of the P-40 reinforcements at Darwin, the Japanese bombers returned three days later and were escorted by Zero fighters. The 9PS was patrolling over Beagle Bay with 2Lt. Andrew Reynolds, a Java veteran with 3.33 victories, leading the flight. At 1300, his flight of five P-40s was vectored back toward the mainland to intercept the Japanese attack on the RAAF base. Although outnumbered, Reynolds was able to down a Zero in a wild melee over the Cox Peninsula, but two P-40s were shot down. 2Lt. James Porter managed to crash land back at Batchelor, but his fighter was written off. 2Lt. Robert McComsy bailed out of his P-40 and descended into an impenetrable tidal marshland only three miles from Darwin. He was not rescued until early the next morning after spending the night fighting the rising tide, voracious insects, and a "curious" crocodile.

March 1942: 49FG: "Johnny Zero"

Canadian born 2Lt. John MacIsaac flew P-39s and P-40s with the 9FS in the defense of Darwin in January and February 1942. In March, MacIsaac joined the 80FS at Archer Field, Brisbane, and continued in combat until late April 1942, when an aircraft he was ferrying caught fire and crashed at Lowood, Queensland. He was severely burned and, after being hospitalized for several months, was assigned as a transport pilot at 5AF HQ. After his tour he participated in a war bond tour in the US. During this time numerous newspaper articles credited MacIsaac with shooting down two Zeros and a probable and two destroyed on the ground with the 49th or 80th Squadrons, and he was given the nickname "Johnny Zero." However, neither *USAF Historical Study 85* nor Frank Olynyck's *Pacific Theater Destruction of Enemy Aircraft in Air-to-Air Combat* give MacIssac credit for any claims.

1Lt. William **Sells** (under prop hub with 1Lt. Joseph Kruzel (left) and 2Lt. Thomas Andrew Reynolds) scored his first of two victories. (AAF)

1Lt. Robert **Vaught** claimed his first of five victories. (AFAA)

2Lt. Clyde **Harvey** claimed his first of three victories. (AAF)

2Lt. Andrew **Reynolds**, a veteran of the Java air war with the 17th Pursuit Squadron with 3.33 victories, scored his first victory with the 9PS. (AAF)

April 1942
AAC Buildup in Australia

In the seven weeks following the fall of Java, the tactical and organizational situation had changed for the AAC in Australia. The rapid advances made by the Japanese increased the need for additional American air units. By April there were 1,650 officers and 17,115 enlisted men in the AAC, but these personnel were awaiting the arrival of their equipment, the building of their bases, and the establishment of operational plans before they could enter combat. Until sufficient infantry troops, equipment, supplies, and the naval support to conduct amphibious operations were on hand, it was obvious that the first phase of operations in the SWPA would be from the air. The War Department had not issued any directives to Brett, who thus had difficulty in formulating plans for air operations in the Southwest Pacific Area.

During March 1942, the Allied command in Melbourne was undergoing a radical transformation. After MacArthur's evacuation from the Philippines on 17 March he looked to appropriate power in Australia, and only three days later he was officially appointed Supreme Allied Commander of all Allied forces west of the Solomons and in the Southwest Pacific Area. MacArthur was determined to begin a counter offensive on New Guinea before the winter monsoon season in June and July. MacArthur also believed that the Japanese would attempt to capture Port Moresby in May before the winter monsoon floods, and was supported by Allied Intelligence, which had deciphered coded Japanese radio communiqués.

In Brisbane, MacArthur and his staff worked on the defense of Port Moresby. Facing the apparently invincible Japanese juggernaut, the Australians promoted the air defense for both Queensland and Northern Territory until Australian and American ground forces and the combined RAAF-AAC Air Force could re-equip in Queensland, where rail and air services had already been established. MacArthur would then reinforce New Guinea for an August counter attack.

During a meeting, Generals R.B. Sutherland, MacArthur's Chief of Staff, and Staff Advisor Robert Richardson cautioned MacArthur about the rising American opposition to RAAF demands and recommended replacing George Brett, USAFIA Commander. MacArthur concurred with the Brett removal recommendation, but there was no immediate, plausible replacement for him. Gen. Harold "Pursuit" George, Staff Air Commander, was present at the meeting, but was not considered as a Brett replacement, since he was essential in the organization of fighter units for the defense of northern Australia. Meanwhile, Brett was kept on, as he was the only high ranking officer who was knowledgeable about logistics in Australia and could continue the administration of the USAFIA facilities in Melbourne until a replacement could be found. To preserve fighter unit autonomy, MacArthur authorized George the power to override any RAAF order and requisition any personnel or equipment to bolster AAC defenses at both Port Moresby and Darwin.

2Lt. John **MacIsaac** was known as "Johnny Zero." (AAF)

Gen. George designated two 8th Pursuit Group squadrons to be based as soon as possible at the recently constructed air strips on the south coast of New Guinea. George found he only had two ranking officers in New South Wales who were capable of commanding a neophyte fighter squadron against veteran Japanese Navy pilots: Lt.Col. Paul "Squeeze" Wurtsmith, CO of the 49th Pursuit Group; and Maj. Boyd "Buzz" Wagner, his XO. George assigned Wagner to lead the 8PG squadrons to Port Moresby by the end of April, while Wurtsmith was to continue with the 49PG. Wurtsmith was aware that the Darwin warning system required improvement, and chose Capt. Robert Van Auken as Wagner's replacement due to his extensive expertise in radio communication and knowledge of the RAAF interceptor air control

LEFT TO RIGHT:
Gen. Harold "Pursuit" **George**, Staff Air Commander. (AAF)

Lt.Col. Paul "Squeeze" **Wurtsmith**, CO of the 49th Pursuit Group. (AAF)

Ace Maj. Boyd "Buzz" **Wagner**, 49PG XO. (AFAA)

systems. Van Auken modified the RAF warning system used during the 1940 Luftwaffe attacks on London. A grid system was devised for ten square mile sectors over the landing strips along the Track, the Darwin Harbor area, and Beagle Gulf. The RAAF HQ interceptor team positioned the courses of P-40 patrols on a large map table surrounded by radio operators, who directed the appropriate P-40s into their assigned sectors. The P-40 patrols were color coded, instead of by letter, for easier identification on the table.

On the evening of 18 April 1942, the same day Doolittle's Raiders had bombed Japan and 32 days after MacArthur had arrived in Australia, an announcement was made that MacArthur had been named the Supreme Commander by all Allied nations. Two days later MacArthur announced that he had named Gen. Sir Thomas Blamey Commander of all Allied Land Forces (and second in command in the SWPA); Lt.Gen. George Brett as Commander of Allied Air Forces; and V.Adm. Herbert Leary as Commander of Allied Naval Forces (after a dispute with MacArthur Leary would be relieved as MacArthur's naval commander by R.Adm. Arthur Carpender in September 1942.)

As Supreme Commander in the Southwest Pacific Area, MacArthur was not entitled to directly command any national force; and, in accordance with the directive to him, the operations in this area would be designed to accomplish the following:

1) Check the enemy advance toward Australia and its essential lines of communication by the destruction of enemy warships, troop ships, and supply ships; aircraft; and bases in Eastern Malaysia and the New Guinea-Bismarck-Solomon Islands region.
2) Exert economic pressure on the enemy by destroying vessels transporting raw materials from the recently conquered territories to Japan.
3) Support the operations of Allied forces in the Pacific and Indian Ocean Areas.
4) Maintain the Allied position in the Philippine Islands.
5) Route shipping in the Southwest Pacific Area.
6) Prepare to take the offensive.

MacArthur was authorized to issue "all communiqués concerning the forces under his command and to direct and coordinate the creation and development of administrative facilities and the broad allocation of war materials." However, he was not responsible for the internal administration of the various forces under his command, nor was he responsible for grand strategy. Control over grand strategy policy and related aspects were to be implemented by the Combined Chiefs of Staff, while jurisdiction over all matters pertaining to operational strategy was to be exercised by the US Joint Chiefs of Staff.

Lt.Gen. George **Brett**, Commander of Allied Air Forces. (AAF)

Gen. Sir Thomas **Blamey**, Commander of all Allied Land Forces (and second in command in the SWPA after MacArthur). (AFHRC)

V.Adm. Herbert **Leary**, Commander of Allied Naval Forces. (AFHRC)

The Combined Chiefs of Staff (Australia, New Zealand, the United Kingdom, the Netherlands, and the United States) designated the entire Pacific Theater as an area of American strategic responsibility. The Pacific Theater was divided into three large areas: the Southwest Pacific, the Southeast Pacific, and the Pacific Ocean; the latter was further divided into the North, the Central, and the South Pacific Areas. Closely related to the Southwest Pacific Areas, the South Pacific Area (which included New Zealand and New Caledonia) was set up as a naval command under the Commander in Chief of the Pacific Ocean Area.

Early in April, the Combined Chiefs of Staff made the decision to "rid Australia and New Zealand of the menace of Japanese invasion," and to strengthen the tenuous supply lines to those areas. For the next four months, however, this objective had to be limited to "paper strategy," awaiting the Navy's ongoing recovery from its losses at Pearl Harbor and awaiting the consolidation and organization of Allied forces in the Southwest Pacific. It was apparent that no offensive campaign could be launched from the Southwest Pacific Area at this early phase of organization and consolidation. So with the limited naval, ground, and air forces available to him, MacArthur could only consider the tasks assigned to him by the Combined Chiefs of Staff basically as a blueprint for future development.

The air forces under MacArthur's command were even less prepared for the offensive than the ground forces. The development of the RAAF would require many months, after which it would be required for the defense of the far-reaching Australian coastlines. The strength of the AAC in Australia comprised only two heavy bombardment groups, two medium bombardment, one light bombardment group, and three pursuit groups, which were scheduled to be totally equipped with operating aircraft with a 50% reserve and with no specific number being assigned for wastage. The organizational and training situation was far below the required criterion, and it was estimated that at least four months of intensive effort would be required to attain a satisfactory condition.

Even before the official organization of the Allied Air Forces, however, Brett could report that they were destroying six Japanese planes for every Allied plane lost. At the same time he reported that the Allied Air Forces were being organized "with the best man getting the importance without regard to nationality."

Brett officially assumed command of the Allied Air Forces on 20 April with the following assignments to his command:

1) All AAC tactical units and associated service elements of the U. S. Army then in Australia,
2) Operational control of all service squadrons (not including training units) of the RAAF, and
3) Operational control of all service squadrons of the Royal Netherlands East Indies Army Air Force.

On 2 May Brett announced his Staff Officer appointments, which were evenly divided between the Australians and Americans:

Air Vice Marshal William Bostock, RAAF Chief of Staff
Col. Edwin Perrin, Deputy Chief of Staff
Brig.Gen. Ralph Royce, Senior Air Staff Officer
Col. Eugene Eubank, Director of Plans
Col. Ross Hoyt, Director of Operations
Air Commodore Joseph Hewitt, RAAF, Director of Intelligence
Group Capt. Frederick Scherger, RAAF, Director of Defense
Group Capt. Carl Wiggins, RAAF, Director of Communications
Wing Cdr. Valston Hancock, RAAF, Assistant Director of Plans
Wing Cdr. Allan Walters, RAAF, Assistant Director of Operations
Lt.Col. Reginald Vance, Assistant Director of Intelligence
1Lt. Warner Croxton, Assistant Director of Communications

Air Vice Marshal William **Bostock**, RCAF Chief of Staff. (AFHRC)

Despite this seemingly equal representation between the two air forces, Brett did not have complete control of the RAAF (except for operations), as it was taken from him mainly due to "Australian political interference and sabotage." In fact, AAC air units were controlled largely by the Australians due to the general concept of the Australian military system in 1942. Australia was divided into five military districts: the Northwestern, Northeastern, Western, Eastern, and Southern areas. Each district was under the command of an Australian officer, who in turn was commanded by a General of the Australian ground forces. Since all military organizations in the respective areas were controlled by the area commander, the American air units were, in effect, were not commanded by their own officers. This situation was not limited only to the highest echelon, but extended to American air units that were stationed at airfields under Australian control. AAC officers were not assigned to some of the command positions because there were not enough American officers who were qualified by experience to take over these positions. Brett had the same problem in the ABDA Command during the Java campaign, when the War Department failed to or were unable to provide air officers of suitable rank and experience, and the AAC officers on hand were forced to occupy subordinate positions under British and Australian officers.

General Brett fervently believed that it was contrary to War Department policy for AAC units to be commanded by RAAF officers. Yet, in February it was becoming increasingly apparent that this situation would again arise if suitable Air Corps commanders were not furnished by the War Department to the Australian area. A sufficient number of qualified officers did not arrive from the United States and, as a result, when pursuit squadrons were being moved into the Northeastern and Northwestern areas in early April, there was not a single station in the entire area commanded by an American officer. The existence of this situation was verified on a tour of inspection by General Brett, who again urgently requested the War Department to send qualified personnel for relieving the situation, which was having a definite effect upon the morale of the American airmen. No relief was sent, and as late as midsummer 1942 no qualified personnel arrived and no improvement was made in the situation. However, even if the AAC and RAAF in Australia could have retained their integrity through separate commands, the Americans would still have been dependent upon the Australians for their facilities and communications, and under the circumstances no other arrangement was possible.

Despite the problems caused by the combined operation of the two air forces, the new Allied organization was an improvement over the former, which had no coordination or centralized control of operations. The new organization required divergence from the typical air force organization, as group organization was not well suited for the type of warfare anticipated in the Southwest Pacific, largely due to its lack of flexibility. The integrity of the groups was to be maintained by assigning their respective squadrons in the same area. For example, the 43rd and 30th Bombardment Groups (less two squadrons) were placed in the Northwestern Area and the 19th, 22nd, and 3rd Bombardment Groups were placed in the Northeastern Area. Likewise, each pursuit group, after receiving its equipment, was put into operation as a unit. All groups were to have their attached organizations, such as ordnance platoons and medical detachments, assigned to them.

Soon, tactical conditions forced Area Headquarters to transfer the squadrons of the various groups from place to place, so that they were unable to remain together. A lower echelon of the Area Headquarters command was the Fighter Sector Control Unit, which controlled all the pursuit units in combat. When the tactical situation at Port Moresby demanded more aerial reinforcements, two squadrons of the 3rd Bombardment Group moved to Port Moresby and rotated approximately every two weeks with the remaining two squadrons at Charters Towers. Similarly, after the RAAF pursuit units at Port Moresby were diminished in combat operations, they were replaced in April by two AAC squadrons from Townsville. Also at Townsville were two additional pursuit squadrons of the RAAF and two more American squadrons transferred there to replace them when they moved to Port Moresby. These moves resulted in the following situation: at Port Moresby there was a RAAF sector control unit with two American squadrons; at Townsville there was a RAAF sector control unit with two American squadrons and two RAAF squadrons; at Sydney there was an American group less two squadrons; and at Brisbane, there was an American group less two squadrons. Since the American groups each had their own interceptor control equipment and organization, the RAAF control units were later withdrawn.

Even though the American units continued to maintain their group headquarters, these organizations were virtually useless, as the tactical situation in the SWPA demanded a high degree of mobility among air units. Since the groups could not maintain their integrity with the expected forward movement of the squadrons, there was need of some kind for an air force command which would remain in an area as long as combat units were there, and then would be able to leapfrog with the advancing units. Therefore, AAC commanders in Australia were unable to act in terms of the group, as the basic unit for tactical deployment and a further revision in the traditional organization of an air force was required. To meet this demand Brett created Air Command No. 1 under Brig.Gen. Albert Sneed at Darwin and Air Command No. 2 under Brig.Gen. Martin Scanlon at Townsville. Created as flexible units, these Air Commands were capable of taking over a sector headquarters or a bombing (or pursuit) unit or both, as the situation required.

In the beginning of April 1942, the shortage of qualified AAC personnel to fill positions in the Allied Air Forces' staff and higher echelons also reached down to the smallest unit. The lack of experienced officers and enlisted men had a direct effect upon the operational efficiency of combat units. Generally, the personnel shortages were due to two main causes: one organizational and the other operational. Organizationally, some operational units were sent from the US without being brought up to full strength, while operationally shortages of personnel occurred as a result of casualties, flying fatigue, and disease, particularly Malaria and Dengue Fever. AAC Headquarters stated that the experience level of air officers assigned to the SWPA was in "excess of the authorized allotment," and that "no further action would be taken on sending additional experienced officers from the United States to Australia." The increase of forces in this theater was to begin only when it would not be detrimental to forces in other theaters and to the training programs in the United States.

Thus, during the early months of war the AAC was to be handicapped by an unusual tactical situation and insufficient personnel, which were the principal determining influences in the organization of the Allied Air Forces in Australia, and more particularly in the position occupied by the American forces. Only when those factors were ultimately changed did the Allied Air Forces undergo any major change, and until then, its organization existed substantially as it was set up.

Air Operations: April 1942

April 1942: 49FG Deployment

During April, Capt. Robert Morrissey's 7PS moved from Bankstown, New South Wales, to Batchelor Field to replace Capt. James Selman's 9PS, which moved to Livingstone Field. Capt. Allison Strauss' 8PS arrived from Canberra at the Adelaide River base. The Squadron's ground echelons were flown in by a varied assortment of transport-type aircraft, with the last arriving on 19 April.

4 April 1942: 49FG/9PS

Just after noon, the Dripstone radar station detected an enemy formation of six Betty bombers escorted by six Zeros. 9th Squadron CO Capt. James Selman dispatched two flights of P-40s: six P-40s of B Flight led by 2Lt. Andrew Reynolds from Darwin RAAF Field and four P-40s of C Flight led by 2Lt. Grover Gardner from Batchelor Field. Gardener's P-40s were flying at 26,000 feet over Darwin and spotted the enemy formation seven miles south of Darwin, with six of the bombers in an extended V formation and three Zeros in two "Vs" above and behind as high escorts. Gardener led his men in a line formation, completely surprising the bombers, which attempted to climb when alerted. Gardner shot down a Betty and swung away, and his flight ran directly into the trailing Zeros. 2Lt. John Sauber and his Wingman, 2Lt. John Kelting, each claimed a Zero and joined their squadron mates in a circling dogfight that was interrupted by the arrival of Reynolds' flight. Reynolds shot down a Zero, and the Japanese pilots dove away from the now uneven battle. Gardner and his Wingman, 2Lt. John

LEFT:
2Lt. Andrew **Reynolds** scored two victories to become an ace with six. (AFAA)

RIGHT:
2Lt. John **Landers** scored his first two of six he would be credited with in the SWPA. (AFAA)

Livingstone, proceeded after the bombers, which were now bombing Darwin Airdrome, and each downed a Betty apiece. The two pilots then crossed the shoreline when RAAF AA gunners opened fire. Gardener's P-40 was hit, and he bailed out when his engine caught fire. Livingstone's fighter was hit and he was wounded. He tried to return to Livingston (34 Mile) Drome. He attempted to land, but was too high on his first attempt and circled around for a second approach, during which his fighter slammed into the trees and burst into flames, making him the 49th's first KIA.* Meanwhile, Sauber and Reynolds had become separated from their flights and joined up and closed on the remaining three bombers over the Cox Peninsula at 11,000 feet. Both pilots expended their last ammunition to shoot down a bomber each; Reynolds' victory made him America's second ace of the war. 2Lt. John Landers had engine problems on the way and lagged behind. When he reached the battle area he spotted the two other Japanese bombers, which were straggling behind, and shot them down to begin an illustrious career that would see him become an ace in both the Pacific and European Theaters. (*2Lt. Frank Stiertz of the 7PS was the first 49PG pilot to be killed when his P-40 crashed on 14 March while practicing touch-and-go landings at Bankstown).

2Lt. James **Morehead** shot down three bombers to become an ace. (AFAA)

25 April 1942: 49FG/7PS/8PS

With all three 49FG Squadrons in the Darwin area, Van Auken prepared his defensive posture and strategy. However, the Japanese suspended their assault on Darwin after the 4 April attack, as they sent their air forces in the Celebes to support their campaign in northern New Guinea. By the last week of April, the Japanese had captured a succession of new bases running west to east: Babo, Hollandia, Wewak, Finschhafen, and Lae, to establish an essential supply route from the Philippines to support their attack on Port Moresby. After this route was opened, the Japanese Air Force returned to Java and renewed their armed reconnaissance over northern Australia, where they detected the new bases south of Darwin.

In the mid-morning of the 25th the Japanese sortied 24 Betty bombers with 13 Zero escorts from Koepang, Java, but all 13 Zeros lost contact with their bombers in the clouds near Timor. Once over Darwin the Zeros attempted to rendezvous with the bombers, but were spread over a wide area. The Allied warning system's alert came only after the Bettys had dropped their bombs and, despite Wurtsmith having placed his three squadrons to full alert status for the last week of April, they were only able to catch the Japanese heading over the sea back to their base.

2Lt. Edward **Miller** scored his only two victories of the war. (AAF)

2Lt. James **Martin** got his only victory of the war. (AAF)

2Lt. Richard **Dennis** got his first two of three career victories. (AAF)

Yellow Flight Leader 2Lt. James Morehead scrambled his novice flight, consisting of his Wingman, 2Lt. Edward Miller, Element Leader 2Lt. Richard Dennis, and Wingman 2Lt. Montie Eisenberg from Adelaide River at 1330 hours, and set off to the north in a climbing pursuit of the raider that had already bombed Darwin's RAAF field. Blue Flight Leader 1Lt. Mitchell Sims followed five minutes later with Wingman 2Lts. Clyde Barnett, Element Leader 2Lt. Donald Morse, and Wingman 2Lt. Harvey Martin.

At 1430, after flying for 30 minutes past Darwin, Morehead spotted the retreating Bettys above the clouds at about 1,000 feet higher. Morehead's Yellow Flight climbed and crossed behind the bombers, flying in a triple chevron V formation to position the Flight at 18,000 feet, up sun, on the enemy's right flank. Yellow Flight dove into the attack, followed seconds later by Blue Flight. Morehead and Wingman Miller found themselves in the middle of the chevron formation in a line assault on the right hand elements in the second V. Yellow Element Leader Dennis (minus Eisenberg, who returned to base earlier) followed a similar course just to their left and through heavy fire from enemy bomber turrets. Morehead fearlessly closed on a beam approach, throttling fully back, and fired a long fatal burst on the enemy bomber, while Miller downed the following Betty. Dennis also downed a bomber on the left flank. Morehead searched the sky for escorting Zeros and, seeing none, rolled his fighter back toward the bombers with Miller tight in the wing position for a second pass. Dennis and Miller stayed close to veteran Morehead as they closed on the lead bombers, but as Morehead and Miller broke off to the right, Dennis turned to the left. Morehead then went into a steep turn to the right to come up under the right hand echelon of the enemy formation to get on the rear of two bombers and fired a burst to destroy the most rearward bomber. Miller followed Morehead and got his second Betty. Morehead then found he had a Zero on his tail and immediately dove and then pulled up steeply, sighting another coming Zero head on. He fired a quick burst, but soon found that he had another Zero on his tail and broke off the attack, again using the combat-proven diving escape. The solitary Dennis had been momentarily turned away during his second pass by the Zeros and dove away for safety, but then turned back toward the bombers and was joined by Sims' Blue Flight.

Before they reached the descending bombers, Sims' Blue Flight had encountered Zeros that had slipped behind them. Barnett spotted the Zeros and turned toward them to cut them off to protect Blue Flight Leader Sims. Barnett fired a high deflection shot that missed but scared off the Zero. Two more Zeros appeared, and Blue Element Leader Morse fired across the path of a Zero which went down in flames. In the swirling dogfight the wingmen began to separate, and soon dove away to safety, as the combat broke off. Sims and Barnett pursued the last V of five Bettys in loose formation, just southwest of Bathurst Island. Simultaneously, Morehead and Miller met Dennis and Yellow Flight joined Sims and Barnett of Blue Flight to close in on the fleeing bombers, which separated to escape, as their protecting Zero escorts had disappeared. The Warhawk pilots chased them toward Java, and Morehead, Dennis, Sims, Martin, and Barnett each destroyed one. The 8PS pilots were no longer together, and when the Zeros made a much belated reappearance the American pilots broke off and turned south at full throttle to navigate toward Adelaide River.

The useless Zero escorts tried to reform far out over the Gulf, where they were intercepted by a flight of 7PS Warhawks scrambled from Batchelor Field. Flight Leader and Java ace 2Lt. William Hennon closed unnoticed to within 200 yards dead astern of a Zero that was still carrying its drop fuel tank. Hennon's accurate fire detonated the tank into a ball of fire for Hennon's sixth kill.

The combat had scattered the 8PS pilots far out to sea and, low on fuel, several had to land at alternative bases. Sims put his fighter safely down on an island beach, but was able to fly it off to Adelaide the next day. Edward Miller ran low on fuel and totaled his fighter during a landing on a dirt field that was too short. Morehead arrived safely over Adelaide and performed three perfect victory rolls, followed by a perfect landing approach which abruptly ended when his P-40 tipped over on its prop. Morehead was unaware that his wing had been hit, destroying his landing gear and ultimately damaging his ego. Nonetheless, the first combat for the 8PS was a rousing success with 11 victories.

2Lt. Earl **Kingsley** claimed his first of three victories. (AAF)

Capt. George **Kiser** shot down two bombers and a Zero escort to give him eight victories. (AFAA)

27 April 1942: 49FG: 7PS/8PS/9PS

During the morning of 27 April, the Japanese attacked with 18 bombers accompanied by a strong escort of 18 Zeros, which were met by the P-40s of the 9th and the newly arrived 7th and 8th Fighter Squadrons. The Japanese escorts stayed together on this mission and met about an equal number of American interceptors, which was only about half of those which left their bases, as the remainder failed to reach the combat area.

8PS

The 8th Squadron scrambled four flights of P-40s from Adelaide River Field, with Squadron Leader Capt. Allison Strauss' Green Flight (one abort), consisting of 2Lts. Earl Kingsley and Pierre Alford, the first to encounter the large enemy formation just beyond the tip of Middle Point. Strauss led his flight on a firing run through the bombers, but the aggressive enemy escorts forced the flight into an unwanted dogfight, in which the three Americans became separated. Strauss' P-40 was hit repeatedly and abruptly broke vertically, stalled, rolled over and plummeted into Darwin Harbor. Kingsley had turned into a Zero as he lost Strauss, but then continued and hit and destroyed another escort. The more numerous Zeros regained the advantage, and Alford and Kingsley fled for Adelaide, where they reported the loss of Capt. Strauss. The other 8PS Flights arrived and entered combat. Blue Flight, led by Capt. George Kiser, caught the bombers just before they crossed the shore west of Darwin Harbor. To reduce the weight of his fighter to better maneuver with the agile Zeros, the veteran Kiser had removed his Warhawk's two outboard guns and reduced the ammunition loading for his remaining four guns. Kiser and his Wingman, 2Lt. Harvey Martin, zoomed through the enemy formation on several passes, and Kiser would claim two Bettys and a Zero to make him America's leading ace with eight victories. In the combat, the rookie Martin lost Kiser in the clouds above Cox Peninsula and was shot down by an enemy fighter. Martin was able to crash land on the shore just south of the Cape Charles Light House, where he would spend the night. In other 8PS' combat, 2Lt. Clyde Barnett claimed a Betty and 2Lt. Donald Morse claimed a Zero. Flight Leader 2Lt. Charles Johnson's Wingman, 2Lt. Owen Fish, was shot down by the Zeros during their first pass. Capt. William Hennon's Yellow Flight attacked the bomber formation, but was cut off by the enemy escorts. Hennon and 1Lt. Mitchell Sims escaped, but 2Lts. Chester Namola and Richard Werner were both slightly wounded when their fighters were hit but safely returned to Adelaide.

9PS

The 9PS met the Zeros over Darwin Harbor, and 2Lt. Mitchell Zawisza shot down a Zero and his Wingman, 2Lt. Richard Taylor, was credited with a Zero as probably destroyed.

7PS

2Lt. Steven Andrews of the 7PS was credited with a Zero destroyed and a Betty damaged but was shot down. Andrews bailed out and swam to shore, where he was found by an Australian patrol and joined Harvey Martin at the Cape Charles Light the next morning; the two downed pilots would be returned to their Squadrons.

After Strauss' death, a new airfield to be named 27 Mile Airfield (as it was 27 miles down the Track from Darwin) was renamed Strauss Field in his honor. The extremely competent Maj. Robert Van Auken was divested of the command of the 8PS but remained as 49th Group XO, while Capt. Mitchell Sims was assigned as the CO of the 8PS.

29 April 1942: The Death of Gen. Harold George

Late in April, MacArthur had sent his Staff Air Commander, Lt.Gen. Harold George, on an inspection tour of bases in the Northern Territory using a Lockheed C-40 transport. In the late afternoon the Lockheed pilot was unable to find the well-camouflaged Livingstone Field and returned to Batchelor Field, landing at twilight. Just as the C-40 taxied to a stop at the end of the runway, 1Lt. Jack Dale and 2Lt. Robert Hazard taxied their P-40s for a practice tandem take off. George and his entourage exited the C-40 to meet the jeeps that were to transport them to 49th Group HQ. As they waited for the P-40s to take off, Hazard's fighter blew out a tire on the take off run and the Warhawk swerved across the runway and crashed into the waiting group, killing a war correspondent and the jeep driver instantly. George was hit in the chest and head by flying debris and was critically wounded. He was transported to the Batchelor Field dispensary and then airlifted to Coomalie Creek Hospital, where he died the next morning. The death of the competent George would later have implications once Gen. Brett's command deficiencies had been exposed and MacArthur would need a replacement.

Capt. Allison **Strauss**:
After Strauss' death a new airfield which was to be named 27 Mile Airfield was renamed Strauss Field in his honor. (AAF)

Lt.Gen. Harold **George** was killed in a flying accident on 29 April 1942. (AAF)

May 1942
Lull in the Air Combat over Darwin

After 27 April, the air raids against Darwin declined dramatically for the entire month of May, and it would not be until the middle of June that the Japanese would again increase their attacks on Darwin. During this lull the 49FG continued to conduct routine daily patrols and training. The Flying Knights of the 9PS under Capt. Jack Selman operated out of Livingstone Field; the Eightballs of the 8PS under Capt. Mitchell Sims operated out of the newly renamed Strauss Field; and the Screamin' Demons of the 7PS, commanded by Capt. Robert Morrissey, were based at Batchelor Field.

However, while Darwin received a reprieve, the Japanese were accelerating their operations over New Guinea. After the Japanese landings on New Guinea, Port Moresby, the key Australian outpost on the island came under heavy and repeated Japanese air attack. To counter these attacks the RAAF established and sent No. 75 Squadron equipped with American-built Curtiss P-40 "Kittyhawk" fighters to Moresby. The Australian pilots were under continual assault, defending Port Moresby from 21 March until the end of April, at which time their strength was reduced to only three serviceable fighters.

8PS Eightball ground crew under Capt. Mitchell Sims work on P-40E out of **Strauss Field.** (AAF)

Veteran Flying Knight pilots of the **9PS** under Capt. Jack Selman operated out of Livingstone Field: (L to R) 1Lts. James **Morehead**, George **Kiser**, Andrew **Reynolds**, unknown, and William **Hennon**. (AAF)

More veteran **9PS** pilots: (L to R): Capt. Richard **Taylor**, 1Lt. Steven **Poleshuk**, Capt. Clayton **Peterson**, 1Lt. John **Landers** meet with a ground officer. (AAF)

June 1942

Air Combat Resumes over Darwin

By early June 1942, the Japanese had failed to shut down the vital sea supply routes in the Central Pacific from the US to the SWPA, which opened the Solomons and New Guinea to Allied attack. The tactical setback at the Battle of the Coral Sea in early May and the momentous loss at the Battle of Midway caused the Japanese High Command to reassess its strategy against MacArthur's air forces. Using their immense supply base at Rabaul, the Japanese planned a rigorous air offensive against Allied air bases at Guadalcanal in the east, Port Moresby in the center, and Darwin in the west.

After Midway, Allied Intelligence expected Japanese retaliation raids against northern Australia, particularly Darwin, which was substantiated by increased Japanese reconnaissance flights during the second week of June. The Japanese reconnaissance had been unable to accurately determine the extent of Darwin's port and logistic facilities or the strength of the military presence there, and Darwin's possible effect on the Port Moresby/Guadalcanal Campaign. During May 1942 there was little aerial action, except for the Japanese reconnaissance flights, but the Japanese increased the tempo when they attacked Darwin on four consecutive days, beginning 13 June. The 7FS and 9FS of the 49FG were assigned to Darwin's defense.

13 June 1942: The First Raid on Darwin

At 1120 on 13 June, after six weeks of relative tranquility, the radar station at Dripstone Cliffs received the reflection of a formation of aircraft flying very high approaching from the northwest near Melville Island. The Japanese bomber units changed their tactics and would fly at over 20,000 feet with substantial fighter escort to circumvent the intercepting AAC P-40s.

Maj. Robert Van Auken, Group Operations Officer, and 2Lt. Ben Brown were already at 5,000 feet above Darwin Harbor participating in a training exercise with the RAAF coastal anti-aircraft batteries. Van Auken broke off the exercise to check on a coast watcher's report of unidentified aircraft approaching from the north. When Van Auken received the report from Dripstone radar he and Brown climbed to the west at full throttle, heading toward the approaching enemy formation of 27 heavy bombers flying high overhead, accompanied by a huge fighter escort of 45 Zeros that had just turned into their bomb run on Darwin's docks and RAAF Station strip. After climbing for 20 minutes Brown's engine began having problems and he turned back to base. Van Auken chased the bombers alone as they made their routine descent near Bathurst Island. He closed at 16,000 feet, but was attacked by the Zeros and desperately dove; as he turned his aircraft was hit and caught fire, and the badly burned Van Auken bailed out at 800 feet. On his descent he was fired on by the Zeros but was not hit and landed on Melville Island. A native medicine man treated his burns and he was transported by canoe to the mainland.

The standing 8PS patrol of eight P-40s led by 2Lt. Earl Kingsley contacted the enemy bombers as they were on their bombing run over the RAAF airfield. The Eightball Warhawks were immediately bounced by the Zeros, and 2Lt. Pierre Alford was the victim of their first pass. Alford bailed out of his stricken fighter at 3,000 feet over Gunn Point and was attacked by two Japanese fighters as he descended. Alford maneuvered his chute violently to escape, and as he did Kingsley closed from behind one of Alford's preoccupied attackers and shot it down, then drove off the other. Alford landed safely on Shoal Bay beach, where a RAAF de Havilland Tiger Moth picked him up the next day.

The aggressive Zero escorts turned on the utterly outnumbered 8PS fighters, which broke off their attack after three were heavily damaged and limped back to Strauss Field. 1Lt. Richard Dennis managed to safely land his perforated P-40, but 2Lt. Monty Eisenberg ground looped and ended up inverted in the middle of the runway, but was only slightly injured. 1Lt. Charles Johnson was wounded by a 20mm shell that exploded in his cockpit, but he made a safe belly landing.

14 June 1942: The Second Raid on Darwin

The next day the Japanese changed their tactics by sending 27 Zeros, which approached via Bathurst Island, while nine Bettys flew directly west over Cox Peninsula to bomb Darwin's harbor and docks. This move thwarted an effective interception by the 28 49th FG P-40s. The three 49er Squadrons scrambled flights but none could find the enemy bombers, and the 7PS and 9PS ran into the escorts over Middle Arm Inlet while the 8th did not see the enemy fighters.

Veteran Capt. Nate Blanton, who had scored three victories over Java and joined the 7PS during May, was on a standing patrol at 20,000 feet over Cox Peninsula. As the enemy formation approached Blanton led his flight in a shallow dive into the fighters and quickly shot down two Zeros to become an ace. However, his flight did not fare as well against the veteran Japanese fighter pilots. Novice pilot 2Lt. Keith Brown was shot down by enemy cannon fire and just managed to bail out from his plummeting fighter south of Darwin RAAF strip. The burned pilot landed in a tree and broke his left leg on impact but survived the ordeal.

Of the 12 Warhawks scrambled by the 9th Squadron from Livingstone Field, only Blue Flight made enemy contact. Flight Leader 2Lt. Andrew Reynolds took off with 2Lts. John Sauber, John Landers, and Jack Donal-

2Lt. I.B. **Donalson** shot down a Zero for his fourth victory. (AFAA)

2Lt. Andrew **Reynolds**. (L) with 1Lt. James Morehead scored his seventh victory. (AFAA)

son to reach the air combat at the same time as the 7PS left the battle. Donalson, Landers and Reynolds each shot down a Zero during the 30 minute battle.

15 June 1942: The Third Raid on Darwin

The next day the Japanese duplicated their tactics of the previous day when they sent out 21 Zeros preceded by 27 higher flying bombers. The 49th sent up 28 Warhawks, but again, the 8th Squadron was unable to break through the shield of escorts and did not hit the bombers in the initial contact over Beagle Gulf. The 7th and 9th Squadrons again were in the thick of the fighting.

The 9PS was on their routine patrol above Darwin town, with 2Lt. George Manning leading a flight comprised of 2Lts. Thomas Fowler, Clay Peterson, and Robert McComsey, who had only recently returned to flight status from his bailout on 31 March. In the air battle Manning, Fowler, and McComsey shot down a Zero each, but the enemy bombers reached Darwin's downtown and the docks and dropped their bombs, then headed west toward home.

As the bombers turned west and began to accelerate in a descent over Cox Peninsula toward home, they were met by two flights of the 7th Squadron flying at 24,000 feet. The P-40s were at this high altitude to ensure they would intercept the bomber formation, which had been missed at their higher altitudes in the two previous raids. Blue Flight was led by

2Lt. John **Landers** got his third victory. (AFAA)

2Lt. Robert **McComsey** scored his only victory of the war. (AAF)

Ops Exec Capt. William Hennon and Red Flight by Squadron Deputy CO Capt. George Prentice. The two flights dove to a left rear quarter attack on the Bettys, but only Hennon and Wingman 2Lt. Charles Johnson were able to get within firing range before the Zeros arrived. Hennon damaged a Betty and then shot down a Zero for his seventh and last victory of the war. After hitting a bomber Johnson's Allison engine lost power momentarily, and a Zero quickly separated him from his flight. The Zeros riddled his fighter, which caught fire, and Johnson bailed out at 18,000 feet over Cox Peninsula.

Meanwhile, Prentice and Wingman 2Lt. Claude Burnotte of Blue Flight had downed a Zero escort each, while 2Lt. Gilbert Portmore of the second Red element downed a third Zero with a high deflection shot. The Squadron was quickly inundated by Zeros and its pilots became separated. After damaging a Betty and evading a Zero, Burtnette was alone and was attacked again near the Bay's west shore by a Zero whose 20mm cannon fire ripped off the top of the starboard wing ammunition bay panel. Burnotte bailed out and landed in the water near Indian Island and floated in his Mae West while Hennon circled until the Zeros left. It took Burnotte over two hours to paddle to Quail Island, where he was spotted by a RAAF Wirraway patrol aircraft that recorded his position and an Australian lugger rescued him early the following morning.

After Hennon scored his last victory he would return to the US and join the 326FG, but then be transferred shortly afterward to the 352FG, where he served as its CO until his death in a flying accident. Hennon disappeared while flying a BT-14 from Trumbull Field, LI, on 31 March 1943.

16 June 1942: The Fourth Raid on Darwin

On the last June raid on Darwin, the Japanese sent down the usual large formation of 27 bombers escorted by an equal number of Zeros using the same successful high altitude formations and were able to hit two of the valuable oil tanks on Darwin's docks.

The Java veteran 1Lt. Joseph Kruzel led 9th Squadron's Yellow Flight on a mission to draw off the Zero escorts so that 2Lt. Thomas Reynold's Blue Flight could attack the bombers. Yellow Flight was partially successful in drawing off some of the escorts, as 2Lt. Tom Fowler downed a Zero. Only 2Lt. Robert McComsey's P-40 from Yellow Flight had been hit, but he crash landed on the artillery range west of the Track while trying to reach Adelaide River Field. 2Lt. Andrew Reynolds was leading Blue Flight, consisting of "shooters" Sauber, Landers, and Donalson from Livingstone Field and climbed to 26,000 feet. After Kruzel's P-40s broke off for Livingstone Blue Flight inter-

2Lt. Claude **Burtnotte** got his only claims of the war; a Zero victory and a damaged bomber but was shot down and rescued. (AAF)

Capt. William **Hennon** became an ace with his 7th and last victory. (AFAA)

Capt. George **Prentice** scored his first of three victories; one each with a different units. (7FS, 39FS, and 475FG). (AAF)

cepted the bombers and Zeros 30 miles west of Darwin on their escape descent over the Cox Peninsula at approximately 21,000 feet. Reynolds took his flight down in a line attack against the last V of nine Bettys. He dove on the bombers, setting one on fire on his first attack run and later set fire to a No. 3 man in the enemy formation, and would be credited with a probable victory. However, Reynold's engine was hit by a turret gunner, damaging the oil and Prestone coolers, and Reynolds had to shut down the engine and make a successful dead-stick belly landing in a small field on the Cox Peninsula. During the attack approach Landers lost the flight and returned to base. Donalson and Sauber were able to keep their wing element together and successfully offset the escorts by twisting through them while firing during a hard diving turn, in which they shot down a Zero each.

The 8PS flight, led by Capt. George Kiser, scrambled from Strauss Field and made contact with the Zero escorts, then were outnumbered and outflown. 2Lt. Bruce Harris was forced to dive away in his first contact, but set off after the bombers in a climbing pursuit due west over Cox Peninsula. After about 75 miles he caught up with the bombers, and as he closed in and began firing his guns they jammed, and the frustrated pilot broke off combat for the long flight back to Strauss Field. Harris soon realized that he didn't have sufficient fuel to reach Strauss and tried to land on the west coast of Cox Peninsula. The RAAF had designated the Cox Peninsula, Bathurst, and Melville as suitable emergency landing sites, but Cox's mud flats were rugged and tidal. Upon touching down his gear collapsed on the rough mud flats and then his fuselage fuel tank ignited. Harris hurriedly excited the inferno and waited at the burnt wreckage until the tide rose. He decided to leave for the sandy beaches to the north, but his trip was cut short by a river mouth infested with crocodiles. Luckily he was spotted by a scout plane which returned to drop him rations and a .45 caliber pistol to fend off the crocodiles. During the morning of the third day Harris was rescued and returned to Strauss Field. 2Lt. Harvey Martin of the 8PS was also separated from his flight by the escorts on the first pass at 22,000 feet, and as he dove away his Allison engine overheated. Martin made a perfect flaps down belly landing in the surf off the south shore of Melville Island. It was not until the morning of the third day that he was rescued. 2Lt. Chester Namola was shot down by a Zero escort in his first pass and was last seen spiraling down toward the harbor, but he was not found after several days of extensive searching.

So for four consecutive days the 49th was able to cause the Japanese enough losses to make them realize that, while they could still get through to Darwin, they would have to be prepared to lose a number of aircraft each time. The 49er pilots were flying their P-40s at the extreme limit of the fighter's altitude capability against the superior Zero piloted by experienced Navy pilots. For the beleaguered American pilots, it was time for the introduction of the P-38 or P-47s coming off American production lines but destined for the European Theater.

2Lt. John **Sauber** was awarded his third and last victory before he was killed in a mid-air collision with George Preddy on 12 July. (AAF)

2Lt. Thomas **Reynolds** claimed his eighth victory and a probable. (AFAA)

July 1942
The 49th Fighter Group During the July Lull

After the assessment of the combat losses in June, the July sojourn from combat gave the 49th Fighter Squadrons a chance to significantly engage in much needed additional training. As inexperienced pilots continued to muster into the squadrons, the veterans who would lead them commenced a regimen of demanding training flights to simulate combat as realistically as possible. During one of these flights the 49th would lose one of its veteran pilots and the AAF nearly lost one of its future top aces.

12 July 1942: 49FG: 9FS: George Preddy Injured

During the afternoon of 12 July 1942, Capt. Ben Irvin was leading a scheduled 9FS training flight consisting of Lts. Paul Blakely, Leon Howk, George Preddy, John Sauber, and Richard Taylor, during which Preddy, Taylor, and Blakely were to play the role of enemy bombers, while Irvin would lead the attackers, Howk and Sauber, who were joined late by Andrew Reynolds. Reynolds made the first attack, followed by Sauber, who chose Preddy's P-40 as his faux target. Sauber dove on Preddy but appeared to become disoriented, misjudged his speed and distance and attempted to evade, but his P-40 went into a violent snap roll and hit the tail of Preddy's P-40. Both fighters dove out of control, and the flight saw only one parachute open and both P-40s crash. Once he landed, Irvin commandeered an ambulance and he and Lucien Hubbard and William Irving headed toward the downed pilot in the approaching darkness, aided by Lt. Clay Tice, who spotted his position from his P-40. Preddy had crashed through a gum tree that shredded his parachute and dropped him through the branches onto the ground below. When the rescuers arrived they found Preddy bleeding badly, laying on his parachute with a broken leg, and deep, bleeding wounds in his hip and shoulder. Sauber's burnt out fighter was found the next morning with its pilot still in the cockpit.

Preddy and Sauber had been two of the original 49FG pilots who arrived from the States in January 1942. Sauber had claimed three victories, two on 4 April and one on 16 June, while Preddy had claimed several bombers as damaged and had survived a crash landing in a P-40. After a protracted hospital stay Preddy eventually recovered sufficiently to return to the States. After he recuperated he flew two tours in the ETO assigned to the 352nd Fighter Group of the 8AF flying P-51D Mustangs. Preddy became the third-ranking American ace in the ETO with 26.83 victories before he was shot down by friendly AA fire on Christmas Day 1944 near Leige, Belgium. Preddy had been pursuing a pair of FW 190s on the deck when a mobile AA unit fired on all three aircraft. The FW 190s escaped, but Preddy's Mustang *Cripes A' Mighty* was hit; he made a belly landing. However, Preddy had been hit by two .50 caliber rounds and had been killed.

2Lt. George **Preddy**. (AFAA)

Preddy become the third-ranking American ace in the ETO with 26.83 victories before he was shot down by friendly AA fire. (AFAA)

25-29 July 1942: Japanese Night Attacks

During the last week of July the Japanese renewed night bombing attacks, which differed from earlier night attacks, as they were directed farther south on the Track. From 25 to 29 July the Japanese sent two sorties per night along the Track. While not a direct threat to the 49FG Squadrons at Strauss, Livingstone, or Batchelor Fields, the crews there were continually wakened from their sleep in the middle of the night to take refuge in air raid shelters. On the fifth night, 8th Squadron veteran James Morehead had had enough, and after midnight he got in his P-40 and took off. Morehead kept his canopy open to give him better night vision, but it was not long before he discovered that the exhausts of the Allison engine blinded his forward vision and made his mission impossible. As he turned to find Strauss Field he became totally lost and radioed ground control to have a truck shine its lights down the runway. Because the air raid alert was still in effect his request was denied, so he turned toward Batchelor Field, which was equipped with emergency landing lights, but the alert was in effect there also. The RAAF controller there directed him to circle until the alert was canceled, and Morehead was finally cleared for landing at Batchelor just at sunrise. He quickly refueled and immediately took off for Strauss Field, where he was met by CO Mitchell Sims, who praised him for his initiative and then grounded him for a week. The disciplinary action would put the ace out of action when the Japanese returned over Darwin on the 30th.

30 July 1942: 49FG/7FS/8FS/9FS
The Japanese Air Force Returns to Darwin

The Japanese did not attack Darwin in numbers until 30 July, when nine Vs of three Betty bombers appeared with escorts at about 1400. This time an early warning gave the 49ers time to scramble 46 P-40s of all three squadrons, of which 36 made contact. The Eightballs were first to attack, and although they would not claim any victories, they had no losses, and disrupted both the enemy fighters and bombers as they flew over Darwin. The P-40s of the 7th and 9th Squadrons had an altitude advantage, and they attacked out of the sun and achieved surprise with very good results, as six Zeros and three bombers were confirmed as destroyed with two claimed as probables for the loss of one P-40.

7FS

The 7th Squadron Screamin' Demons were represented by 1Lt. Raymond Melikian, who led wingmen 2Lts. Gene Drake, Donald Lee, and John Fisher of X Flight, while Capt. Nate Blanton led 2Lts. John Yancey, Gilbert Portmore, and Oliver Vodrey of White Flight. A third improvised flight led by Capt.

Robert Morrissey consisted of 2Lts. John Posten and Edward Steere, and was designated Sterling White Flight. Melikian's X Flight was at 25,000 feet and Blanton's White Flight was at 27,000 feet when they dove in single file to attack the lead bomber V. The confident escort pilots cut them off in mid-dive and dispersed White Flight, with Portmore and Yancey being wounded, and joined Blanton and Vodrey in diving away at high speed without firing.

From the start of the combat, X Flight had only a slight altitude advantage above the bombers, whose trailing elements were stacked in a downward angle to the port. The enemy gunners put up a screen of machine gun fire as X Flight closed in from head on. Melikian shot down a Betty before retreating from the enemy gunners. There would be no chance for a second pass, as nine Zeros quickly got behind Lee and Fisher, who dove under the bombers tenaciously holding their formation as they dropped their bombs on Darwin's Harbor. 2Lt. Drake had trailed behind his three companions, but he nevertheless chose to attack the second V to his right at this lower altitude. Drake hit a Betty with a long fatal burst and sped through past the Zeros, who got on his tail. With the Zeros on his tail Drake climbed in a chandelle and fired at the third bomber V but missed. As he broke away his fighter was hit by gunfire from two Zeros and burning engine fumes filled his cockpit. Drake bailed out at 12,000 feet and landed safely in the surf off the tip of West Point on Cox Peninsula.

Despite continual harassment from a much larger force of Zero escorts, Posten's Sterling White Flight was the most successful 7FS flight in the day's combat. The three White Flight pilots dove from 25,000 feet out of the sun just as the escorts regrouped over the bomber echelons off Cox Peninsula. Posten and Steere were in an ideal firing position against the escorts which dove too late to escape, as both Posten and Steere scored fatal

2Lt. John **Landers** scored his fourth victory. (AFAA)

2Lt. Andrew **Reynolds** scored his ninth and last victory. (AFAA)

Philippine veteran 2Lt. I.B. **Donalson** became an ace. (AFAA)

9PS Scorers 30 July. (L-R): 2Lt. I.B. **Donalson**. (5th to become an ace), 2Lt. John **Landers**. (4th), 2Lt. Andrew **Reynolds** . (9th), and 2Lt. John **Sauber**. (none had 3). (AAF)

2Lt. John **Posten** shot down a Zero and was awarded a Zero probable which left him short of becoming an ace with 4½ victories for the war. (AAF)

1Lt. Clay **Tice** scored his first of two victories. (AAF)

bursts on their Zero targets from head on. Posten continued after the Zeros and got good hits on a second but did not see it go down for a probable. His last victory of the war gave Posten 4½, and the probable claim kept him from becoming an ace. Capt. Morrissey followed the two but was unable to get off a shot and led Posten and Steere back to Batchelor Field.

9FS

Simultaneously, 1Lt. Andrew Reynolds' 9FS Blue Flight attacked the right flank of the escorts as the 7th Squadron's Sterling White Flight attacked the left flank. This hit-and-run attack was executed so perfectly that the surprised Japanese were unable to counter-attack. Single victories were claimed by Reynolds (for his last and 9.333 victory of the war), 1Lt. Jack Donalson (for his fifth victory to make him an ace), 1Lt. Clay Tice, and 2Lt. John Landers. Blue Flight's attack diverted the Zero escorts and simultaneously permitted the Flying Knights' Yellow Flight to strike the bombers. Yellow Flight Leader 2Lt. Clyde Harvey closed in for a head on pass, during which he riddled a Betty that trailed smoke as it plunged toward the sea. Harvey then maneuvered through the escorts to get hits on another bomber which was credited as a probable. After this brief attack all of the Knights pilots escaped safely back to Livingstone Field. After this raid the Japanese returned to night operations against 49er bases but had no success in finding them to bomb.

After becoming an ace and ending his SWPA tour, Donalson was promoted to Captain and Major in the US and served briefly as CO of the 328FS/352FG, and then served with the 487FS and retired from the Air Force (May 1968) as a Colonel. Reynolds also remained in the Air Force, retiring as a Colonel in August 1969.

August 1942

23 August 1942/7FS/8FS: The Last 49th Fighter Group Defense of Darwin

Japanese reconnaissance aircraft had finally discovered Strauss and Livingstone Fields, and the RAAF Hughes medium bomber field. The Japanese sent a formation of nine Vs of three Bettys each, escorted by an equal number of Zeros flying high cover. The enemy formation was to fly southwest of the harbor and proceed directly over the 8th and 9th Squadron bases. Allied radar discovered the enemy formation while it was still far out over the ocean and, aided by radio communication stations that had been added along the north shore of Cox Peninsula, the 49er fighters intercepted the bombers 25 miles off the Cox Peninsula at 25,000 feet. The 8th Squadron made the first contact.

8FS

Capt. George Kiser led 2Lts. Marlin Smith and Donald Morse on a head on run against the lead V of three approaching bomber chevrons. The three Eightballers shot down three Bettys and broke away before the escorts could dive from their high cover position. It was Kiser's ninth and last victory of the war. With fortunate timing, the 7th Squadron began their attack as the 8FS Flight dove away.

Another 8th Squadron Flight led by 1Lt. Charles Johnson was the next 49er Squadron to arrive, and met the enemy bombers just as the formation crossed the western shore of the Cox Peninsula. Johnson attacked an approaching Zero while Wingmen 2Lts. Rufus Jordan and William Day closed in on a burning bomber on the starboard flank of the lead V. Both the bomber and escort were plunging toward the sea as the victorious pilots dove away.

The Eightballers' dogfighting the escorts overhead were led by veteran 1Lt. James Morehead, with Wingmen 2Lts. Earl Kingsley and Monty Eisenberg. The three chased the Japanese to the shores of Bathurst Island before the combat ended with three victories: two Zeros for Morehead for his seventh and last victories of the war and a bomber for Kingsley.

7FS

This Screamin' Demon flight was led by 1Lt. Raymond Melikian, and consisted of 2Lts. Donald Lee, Gene Drake, and Wilson Chapman. While still over the Timor Sea their P-40s dove for a head on attack with a 1,000 foot height advantage over the extended bomber formation. The Americans sped past the lead enemy element and chandelled up to engage the diving Zeros, which had failed to intercept the previous very quick 8FS attack. 2Lt. Lee separated from his element momentarily in the ensuing dogfight, but the other three 7FS pilots remained in formation and each shot down a Zero before rolling out of the area.

Meanwhile, 2Lt. Donald Lee of the 7FS had regained altitude after he became separated from Capt. Melikian's flight. Lee assumed that the enemy bombers were headed inland toward his base and continued his pursuit through the concealing clouds over the peninsula. Using the cloud cover Lee was able to surprise a Zero, and he was able to destroy the solo Zero with a burst from dead astern. Shortly thereafter, 2Lts. John Posten and Oliver Vodrey arrived as the bombers turned north over the Track and began their bombing runs. Lee, Posten, and Vodrey harassed the escorts as far as Middle Arm Inlet before they were forced to break off after expending their ammunition and running low on fuel. In the pursuit, Lee shot down a Zero and Vodrey damaged a Zero and then moved in to shoot down a bomber.

2Lt. Donald **Lee** got his first of four victories. (AAF)

A third Screamin' Demon Flight was scrambled from Batchelor Field and climbed to 22,000 feet, observing the bombers as they accelerated in a shallow dive to pick up speed as they headed back to the northwest above the harbor. Flight Leader and Java veteran 1Lt. Lester Johnsen, with 2Lts. Edward Steere and Frederick O'Riley, attacked the trailing V elements of the retreating bombers. O'Riley fired from dead astern on one while Johnsen and Steere fired on four others. They were able to sustain their attacks on the now undefended bombers, as 8th Squadron P-40s were engaging the escorts directly above. O'Riley was credited with a bomber, while Johnsen and Steere were credited with probables.

This final bombing of Darwin was a success for the 49er P-40 pilots, as the Japanese lost eight Zeros and seven bombers. The Japanese had little to show for the mission. The runway at Strauss Field was hit by a single bomb, while Livingstone Field was hit by a string of bombs that did minimal damage. Only the 7th Squadron's Frederick O'Riley was a casualty of the battle, as he became disoriented in the cloud formations over the sea and ran out of fuel. He safely landed his gasping fighter down on the beach of Finke Bay and was rescued the next day.

Morehead returned to the US in September 1942 and was promoted to Major (August 1943), then transferred to the 71FS/1FG (March 1944). He was promoted to Lt. Colonel (September 1944) and left active duty in July 1947, then resigned from the Air Force in June 1955 as a full Colonel.

An Assessment of the 49th Fighter Group's Australian Air Campaign

A few days later, the 49th FG was informed that they were being withdrawn from Darwin for a new assignment. While the fighter units had to operate under unfavorable conditions, they nevertheless achieved notable results against the superior Japanese enemy in the Darwin area. From 7 April until 23 August, the group downed 64 enemy aircraft with a loss of only 16 P-40s. It was felt that credit should be given the 49th Group for twice this number, for many more Japanese aircraft were undoubtedly lost in the 500 mile over water flight back to their base as a result of mechanical failures, lack of fuel, and/or damage sustained in combat.

The functioning of armament had been a problem in the Philippines, and also was a problem in dry, dusty northern Australia and the damp tropical areas of New Guinea, but part of the Group's success was certainly due to careful maintenance. Every third night the armorers removed all guns and completely stripped, oiled, and polished them, reducing gun failure to a minimum. Furthermore, all belted ammunition was unbelted each night and each round was oiled, polished, and rebelted. Also, all gun openings were carefully sealed as a protection against dust and sand.

The tactics developed by the Group were mainly determined by the characteristics of the P-40. Because of its slow rate of climb and inability

2Lts Earl **Kingsley** scored his third and last victory. (AAF)

2Lt. Donald **Morse** got his third of three victories. (AAF)

1Lt. James **Morehead** claimed two Zeros for his seventh and last victory of the war. (AFAA)

to operate at high altitudes, the P-40 had to use hit and run tactics against enemy fighters. On all encounters with enemy bombers the P-40s were climbing to meet the enemy, and were therefore in a poor position to attack the bombers. In many interceptions the fighters found Japanese bombers at 30,000 feet, which was 5,000 feet above their maximum operational altitude.

The No. 75 Fighter Squadron (RAAF) had a similar experience with the P-40 while operating out of Port Moresby. By 11 May that squadron had destroyed approximately 50 enemy aircraft for a loss of 15 P-40s and four pilots. All P-40 squadrons in this theater, including those provisional squadrons operating during the Java Campaign, had maintained an average of three to four enemy aircraft downed for every P-40 lost, but the pilots were always operating against superior odds and in a fighter aircraft which could not always reach the altitudes flown by the enemy. At medium altitudes (10,000 to 18,000 feet) the P-40 was estimated to be 40 to 50 miles faster than the Zero fighter and was considered an excellent fighter to intercept bombers; above 18,000 feet, however, the Warhawk's performance was sluggish. The P-40's rate of climb, moreover, was considered too slow at all altitudes, and its wing loading was too high to allow maneuvering with enemy fighters. Similar difficulties were encountered with the P-39, although this fighter got into combat slightly later than the P-40. Two American fighter squadrons moved into Port Moresby in late April to relieve the RAAF units that had been literally decimated in combat.

Organization of the Fifth Air Force

Another cause for concern for the Americans was Australia's control over the AAF. As American air power increased in size and efficiency it was less reliant upon the Australians for many basic services, and they came to resent Australian control. On his tour of the Southwest Pacific in June and July, Deputy Chief of Staff Gen. Robert Richardson heard complaints about Australian control at every station he visited, and found that the system of organization which placed Americans directly under the command of the Australians was deeply resented by officers of all ranks. He found that there was no dislike of the Australian personnel but merely of the system of control, and that the Americans had the "highest admiration and praise for the courage and fighting capabilities of the RAAF."

Obviously, there was a need for a change in the organization which would allow both American and Australian forces to retain their integrity while at the same time coordinating their action. The 5th Air Force, a designation which had been given to the Far East Air Force in February, existed only on paper. After some air units in the Philippines had been returned (on paper) to the United States, the designation "5th Air Force" was to be given to the American components of the Allied Air Forces, under a reorganization in the late summer and fall of 1942. Until this time, however, the Allied Air Forces continued to operate under substantially the same organization which had been established in the spring of 1942.

Despite criticisms, much of which were based on Brett's personality rather than performance, he had credibly commanded the air forces in Australia until he was relieved by Maj.Gen. George Kenney on 4 August 1942. As Commander of the USAFIA, Brett had guided the Allied Air Forces through a labored but necessary period preliminary to conducting extensive operations. Organizing the Allied Air Forces certainly had not been an easy undertaking, and it was to Brett's credit that the air forces operated as smoothly as they did. This organization had served its purpose, and the eventual changes were no reflection upon the early commanders, but the natural result of the growth of the American forces in Australia. The newly formed Fighter and Bomber Commands would be the major components of the expansion and reorganization of the air units in the SWPA.

Obviously, the operation of the American units as a separate air force during the spring and early summer of 1942 had not been practicable or possible, but during the summer of 1942, not only the organizational status, but the tactical situation were rapidly changing. During July, plans were being completed for the beginning of the first offensive to be launched in the South Pacific Area. Adm. Ghormley flew to Australia on 7 July for a two day meeting with MacArthur, where plans were made for the joint use of their respective forces. D-Day was set for 7 August, with landings in the Solomons and aerial and naval operations throughout the general area. So finally the Allies would redeploy from a solely defensive phase of the war, and their forces in the South and Southwest Pacific would go on the offensive, which would result in a high degree of coordination between the land, air, and sea forces to realize an unbroken series of hard won victories.

Meanwhile, on 21 and 22 July the Japanese landed large forces near Buna, on the northern coast of New Guinea, and by the end of the month they had penetrated approximately 50 miles inland and were in contact with Allied patrols. At the same time, Allied forces in Australia and the Japanese were converging upon the pivotal area of Port Moresby.

As more widespread combat operations developed over New Guinea to the north, Allied headquarters also moved north from Melbourne to Brisbane on 20 July. The squadrons of the 8th Fighter Group based in the Brisbane area were preparing to move to the Townsville area, while the remaining squadrons of the 35th Fighter Group were to join the units of that group already at Port Moresby. Furthermore, as the tempo of operations increased, the entire 8th Air Base Group was preparing to move to Port Moresby. The Allied Air Forces were thus entering into a new phase of operations as well, as an organization in New Guinea.

The Air Force Prepares for the Battle for New Guinea

In early May, the Battle of the Coral Sea would prevent a major enemy attempt to land invasion forces on the southern coast of New Guinea, and would emphasize the Allies' need for greater aerial strength in the SWPA. The enemy obviously was determined to take Port Moresby, which was the key to Allied defense of northern Australia and the stepping stone for future Allied offensive operations throughout the Bismarck Archipelago. The tempo of aerial operations centered on this critical area was rapidly increasing, for on eight of the 12 days proceeding the 7 May start of the battle the Japanese heavily bombed Port Moresby. During the same 12 days the Allies carried out 12 raids on Japanese installations along the northern coast of New Guinea, centering on the airfields at Lae and Salamaua. The Japanese bastion at Rabaul, with several airdromes and a large concentration of shipping in Simpson Harbor, was also heavily bombed. From the first American raid on 23 February, this enemy stronghold had been one of the most regularly bombed targets in the Southwest Pacific. These bombing operations were hampered somewhat by unfavorable weather, by the great distances that had to be flown (necessitating the use of bomb bay fuel tanks, which lessened the bomb load), and by the lack of fighter protection for the bombers, which were vulnerable to enemy interceptors and forced to bomb at very high altitudes with much less accurate results.

By this time in the Philippines, after 28 days of fierce siege on Corregidor, the outnumbered, starving, and exhausted troops under Lt.Gen. Jonathan Wainwright surrendered to the Japanese. Thus, for the Allies to retake the Philippines became an even more remote possibility, and the priority was to halt the Japanese advance through New Guinea, New Britain, and the Solomons, and the holding of Australia as a base for future offensive operations.

The three American fighter groups, along with No. 76 Group of the RAAF, were engaged in defensive operations, protective cover, and attack missions. A study of the operational experience, requirements, and losses of these groups made in early May provides some revealing statistics on the condition of these units and on the effects of their operations. By this time the groups, as a whole, were equipped with their allotted number of aircraft, including a reserve of 50%. More specifically, the 8th Fighter Group had 89 P-39s; the 35th Group had 70 P-39s and P-400s; the 49th Group had

70 P-40s; and the 76 Group (RAAF) had 81 P-40s, making a total of 310 fighter aircraft. This number, with the 130 aircraft in storage, assembly, or en route, made a total of 440, the exact number required for 100% operational status and 50% in reserve for the four groups.

Operational losses were unusually high, as during the four months prior to 8 May there was a loss of 399 fighter aircraft, or an average of 100 per month. Certain qualifying factors should be taken into consideration, however. First, 30% of these losses were sustained in the ferrying of planes and can be attributed to the inexperience of the pilots. Secondly, the period included the Java campaign, when abnormally high losses were suffered because of the lack of bases and also supply, repair, and maintenance facilities. On the basis of British air experience in the war, the four fighter groups in the SWPA would require a total monthly replacement of 84 aircraft to maintain operational strength.

After MacArthur arrived in Australia from the Philippines in May, the defensive strategy to protect Sydney and Melbourne was changed. The Allies decided on a new offensive policy in which Allied bombers would fly from Australian bases and stage into Port Moresby, refuel and remain overnight, and attack Japanese positions at Madang, Buna, Wewak, or Rabaul. They would then return to Moresby and leave for their Australian bases the next day. In this plan fighters would be needed to protect Port Moresby and Northern Australia. Lt.Col. Frederic Smith decided that a definite plan was needed to rotate the six fighter squadrons that were available for combat. He recommended that the 39th and 40th Squadrons of the 35th Fighter Group based at Townsville relieve the 35th and 36th Squadrons, which in turn would relieve the 80th Squadron of the 8th Group at Brisbane and the 41st Squadron of the 35th Group at Sydney. The 80th and 41st Squadrons would then move by rail to Townsville, arriving in time to replace the 39th and 40th Squadrons on the day of their move to Port Moresby. Not all these recommendations were fulfilled, but the 35th and 36th Squadrons were eventually relieved from Port Moresby, and by early July were stationed in the Townsville area. The 39th and 40th Squadrons, moreover, were at Port Moresby; the 80th and 41st Squadrons were both in the Brisbane area, the latter having moved from Sydney.

While the three American groups were up to their authorized strength in aircraft, they were below strength in officer and enlisted personnel, and there was a total shortage of 104 pilots and 454 enlisted men. In addition, three fighter sector headquarters, then undergoing reorganization, would require 25 more officers qualified in fighter control and intercept plotting, creating a total shortage of 129 pilots. The casualty rate called for an average monthly replacement of four pilots per squadron, or a total of 44 pilots. The actual casualty rate was 57, rather than 18, but because of the Java Campaign this figure was felt to be slightly higher than it would otherwise have been. The fighter units then in combat areas were suffering a monthly casualty rate of 63 enlisted men per squadron, including both fatalities and wounded. It was found that approximately 25% of this number would be returned to duty within 30 days, thus leaving a monthly replacement figure of 45 enlisted men per squadron, or an estimated total of 180 enlisted replacements for each fighter group in a combat area.

In addition to the tangible numbers required to bring the fighter units up to authorized strength, there were the intangibles of the necessity of reducing losses and maintaining high morale, training, and combat efficiency. Many of the losses resulted from the employment of inexperienced personnel, which was caused when the squadrons arrived in the theater at only cadre strength, filled with inexperienced personnel, and because of the rapid Japanese advances they were not given sufficient training for combat. Consequently, it was considered essential that all personnel be thoroughly trained before joining the fighter units. Another recommended requisite was pilots be given R&R, since it was "definitely proven that a pilot left in the combat area for any length of time is a casualty." Ideally, an entire unit would be relieved from the combat zone after 30 days of arduous action. Actually, the limited number of fighter units which were ready for operations in the spring of 1942 did not allow for the immediate establishment of a rotation system. A final recommendation was that experienced pilots be provided for ferrying aircraft from the assembly point in Australia to the combat zone.

While these organizational problems were being resolved, requests were persistently being made from the SWPA for the allocation of fighter aircraft which could equal the climbing performance and operational altitudes of Japanese fighters that had taken advantage of the Allies' P-39s and P-40s. At the end of May Col. Boyd Wagner reported that:

"There has seldom been an even fight between Japanese Zero type fighters and our own. Only by the virtue of armor plate protection, leak proof fuel tanks, and ruggedness of construction of our fighters has there not been a great many more of our pilots killed and airplanes destroyed. Our fighter pilots have proven their courage and ability to fight continuously against superior odds and still sustain a very high morale. This high morale, however, has been with fighter pilots a forced one, with the knowledge that Japanese fighters would be just as high above tomorrow as they were today, and that the first enemy combat would be an attack from above out of the sun."

At this time the P-38 and P-47 were the only American aircraft in production which incorporated the required characteristics for fighter aircraft in the SWPA. However, prior commitments for these fighters to Europe did not permit their allocation to this theater. The Director of Air Defense urgently recommended that a minimum of one group of P-38s be provided in Australia, but without increasing the total number of groups assigned to that area. He suggested that the P-38s be sent as replacements, at the rate of 65 per month. Once 120 P-38s had been assigned, approximately one third of the 65 required each month for attrition could be P-38s. The Director of Air Defense believed that the assignment of P-38s to Australia was of sufficient importance to justify the assignment of P-39s, rather than P-38s, to one of the groups in the Western Defense Command.

However, there were to be no immediate fighter aircraft reinforcements available for the Fighter Command in Australia. In June, the contemplated deployment of six P-38 groups to the Eighth Air Force, in conjunction with photo-reconnaissance aircraft requirements, left no surplus P-38s for use in Australia in the immediate future. A faint hope was held out in the conditional statement that P-38s might be available for use in Australia early in 1943 if 100% of the production estimates were realized, and if the conversion of the British Model 322 was effective. Finally, a commitment was made for a small allotment of P-38s to Australia, beginning with 25 sent in July, with the same number to arrive monthly for August and September. Although the 25 was significantly below the recommendation by the Director of Air Defense, it was, nevertheless, an indication of the commitments which eventually would be increased as production and availability permitted.

With the gradual arrival of the P-38s, the morale of fighter pilots would improve, as these fighters could perform at the altitude of the Zeros, and their twin-engine design gave the pilots added security, as with one engine shot out the other engine could bring them back to base. Another factor that affected the morale of the pilots was that many had been in combat since the beginning of the war with no definite

Brisbane Dock Gallery

Carrying airtcraft on the open decks of Escort Carriers exposed them to the corrosive action of salt spray. (AAF)

To carry more aircraft on the decks the outer wing sections were removed as can be seen on the P-38 lifted by the crane. (AAF)

Protective tape and later anti-corrosive spray were used to protect fighters in transit. (AAF)

stated policy on their relief; the reason being that there were no personnel available to provide their relief. Fatigue, Dengue Fever, and Malaria reduced the number of crews to a minimum and resulted in grounded aircraft. In early spring AAF Headquarters suggested the exchange of some of the experienced crews for inexperienced ones, but American commanders in Australia felt that no exchange could be made because of the lack of training facilities in Australia and because of the critical need for experienced personnel in that theater.

By late July, arrangements were being made to permit the interchange of combat personnel between Australia, the South Pacific, and Hawaii, allowing personnel from the more active combat areas to have a tour of duty in a quieter area and, on the other hand, giving less experienced crews a chance to get into combat. The specific control of personnel in the various theaters was considered a matter for the commanders concerned, but AAF Headquarters was optimistic that Maj.Gen. Millard Harmon, new Commander of Army Forces in the South Pacific, and Maj.Gen. George Kenney, who was soon to replace Gen. Brett, would be able to overcome the objections previously raised by Gen. MacArthur to this exchange of Air Force personnel.

AAF personnel were also disheartened by slow promotions, as many of the officer personnel who had been pilots, navigators, or bombardiers for more than six months were still second lieutenants. Meanwhile, men stationed in America in units "defending" against U-Boats and the possible Japanese invasion were being promoted at a much faster rate. For instance, 2Lt. Jack Donalson, who had shot down three Zeros in the Philippines with the 21PS on 8 December 1941 and then added two more Japanese aircraft over Darwin with the 9FS to become an ace, was not promoted to 1Lt. until late June 1942.

The Australian Ferry Route

Melbourne, in the southeastern state of Victoria, was Australia's second largest city, and was one of the principal ports for the delivery of combat aircraft from America. The aircraft were unloaded and sent to the Commonwealth Aircraft Company plant located at Fisherman's Bend Airfield, where they were assembled and readied for the flight north.

Sydney, Australia's largest city with about 20% of the Continent's population, is located about 500 miles north of Melbourne along the east coast. It has a large and beautiful port and

Brisbane Airfields Gallery

P-40 assembly. (AAF)

Amberley. (AAF)

Amberley. (AAF)

P-39 assembly. (AAF)

Eagle Farms. (AAF)

Eagle Farms. (AAF)

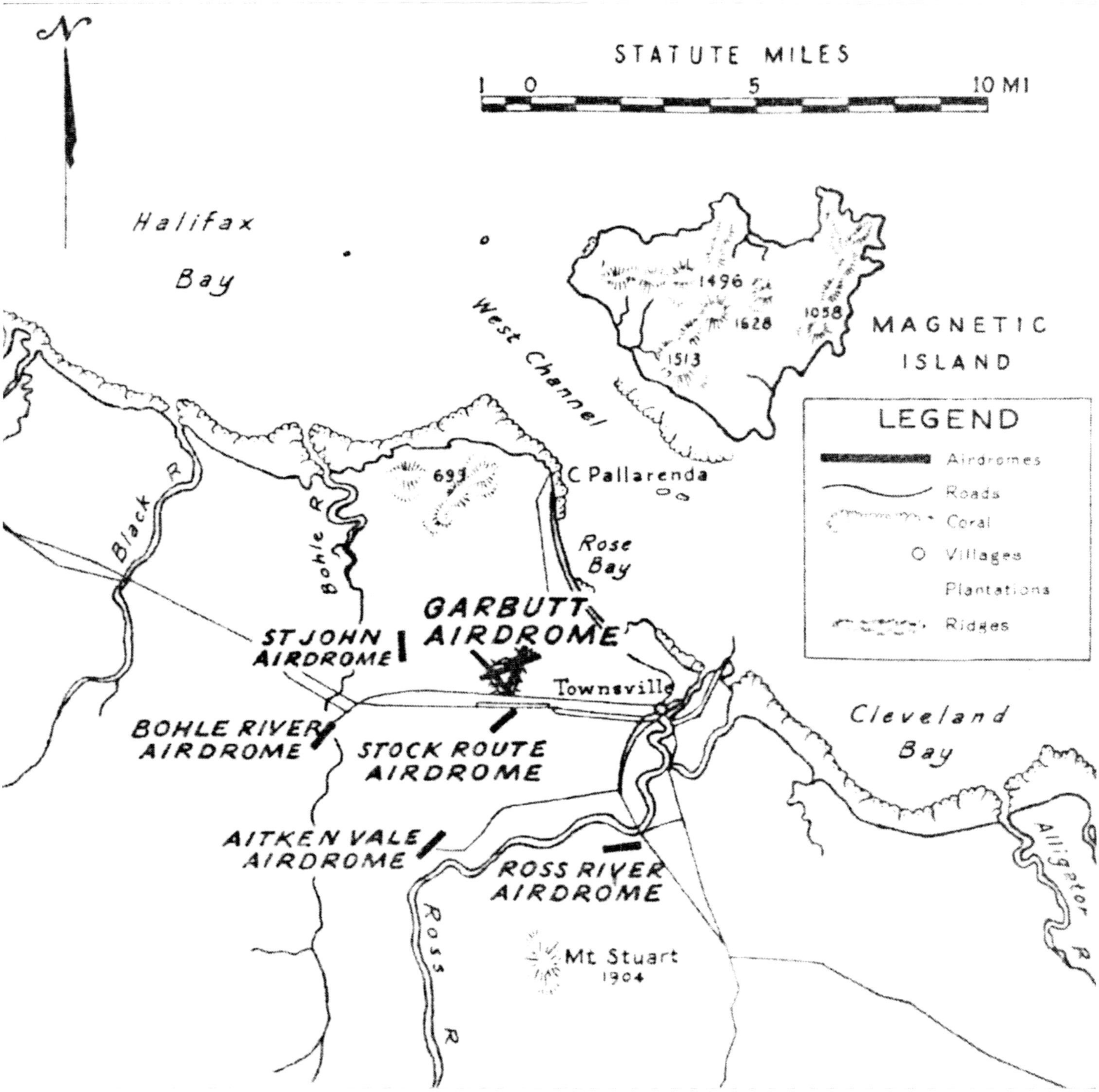

sizeable airport named after the Australian air pioneer Sir Kingsford-Smith. This airport was commonly referred to by the pilots as "Mascot," as it was located in the Mascot area of Sydney. The US Army also established an interim camp at Warwick Farms, which was a former horse race course.

Brisbane was another 500 miles to the north, and was the primary unloading port for combat aircraft. Once aircraft were unloaded from their ships they were transported on trucks through the city's streets and assembled at Eagle Farm Airfield. There were a number of airfields in the area: Archer Field (west of the city), Amberley Field (about 20 miles west at Ispwich), and the Royal Australian Air Force (RAAF) base, which was also heavily used by the 5AF. Two former horse race courses, Ascot (the largest) and Doomben, were acquired by the US Army for use as camps. At this time Brisbane served as Gen. MacArthur's Headquarters.

After their arrival in Australia, some of the deck loaded pursuit aircraft were in no condition to be flown. Even though the seams where aluminum sheets met on the fuselage were taped the aircraft were still damaged by the corrosive action of salt spray. Gen. Brett suggested that deck loaded equipment be sprayed to prevent corrosion, and the Air Service Command immediately issued instructions that every possible precaution should be taken to protect such equipment. Some of the pursuit aircraft were found to have further damage after they were

Garbutt Airfield, Townsville. (AAF)

Horn Island. (AAF)

Refurbish Battle-worn P-39

unloaded due to being taken directly from maneuvers and hurriedly prepared for shipping without depot inspection before crating.

Rockhampton was a small town about halfway between Brisbane and Townsville that had a large RAAF air base that acted as an intermediate stopping point for some fighter aircraft on the ferry route to the north.

Townsville was another 600 air miles north along the coast from Brisbane. Garbutt Drome was a large airfield that provided a jumping off point for most aircraft operations across the Coral Sea to Port Moresby in New Guinea. Air crews often alluded to this base as "Ant Hill Plains," because of the huge ant hills on the surrounding plain. Townsville also

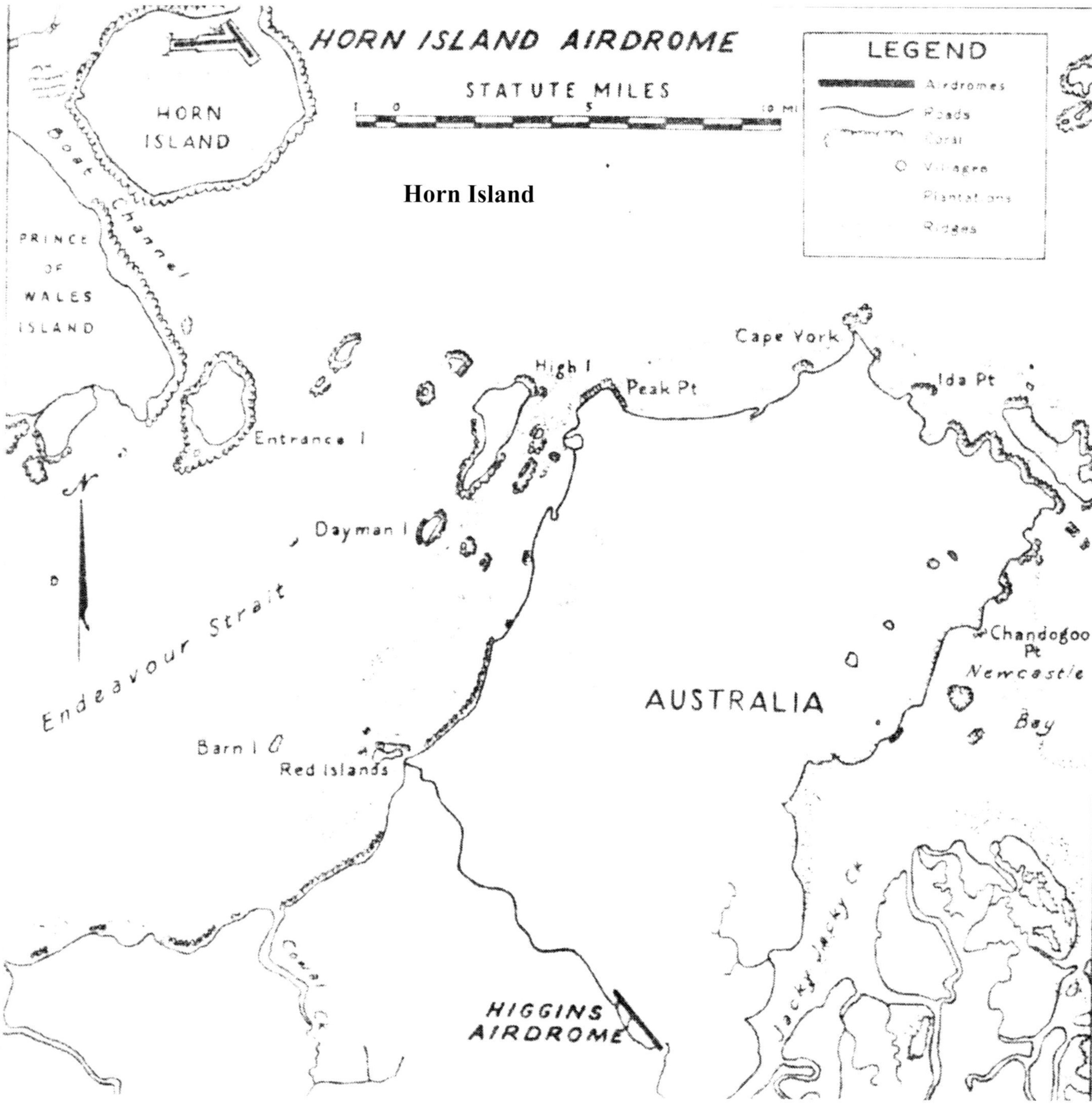

Horn Island

had a protected anchorage which served as an assembly point for naval vessels and transports and small convoys that would move north into the war zone. The facilities at Townsville were to refurbish war-weary aircraft flown in from the north. The most northern tip of the Continent was another 600 miles north of Townsville.

About 175 miles from Townsville was the very small town of Cairns, with its small port and airfield. From Cairns north along the Cape York Peninsula the terrain was jungle and virtually uninhabited until Horn Island, a very small island located just off the extreme end of the Peninsula. Here the RAAF maintained the last air base before flying to New Guinea. All fighter aircraft that were ferried to New Guinea were staged through Horn Island because their range prevented a direct flight across the Coral Sea from Townsville to Port Moresby.

The other end of the ferry route was Darwin, the largest city in the Northern Territory, laying 700 miles west of Horn Island; it had several airfields nearby. The town was built on a low bluff overlooking Darwin Harbour, flanked by Frances Bay to the east and Cullen Bay to the west–all part of the Timor Sea–while the remainder of the city is flat with low laying, coastal areas. There were a number of airfields near Darwin which were discussed in Part 2.

Part Four

Papuan Campaign

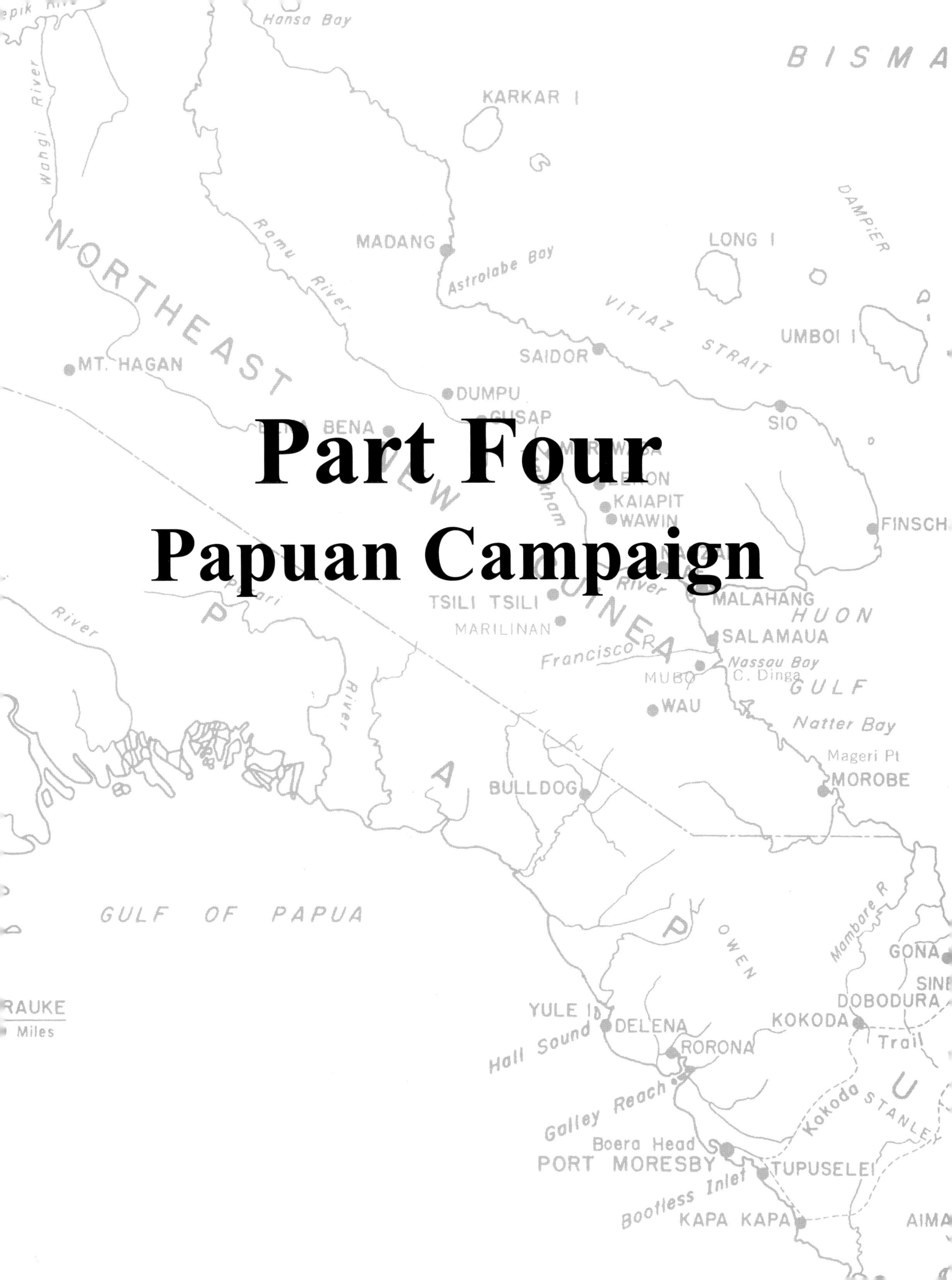

1

New Guinea Description

After Greenland, New Guinea is the second largest island in the world, being about 500 miles wide, north to south, and 1,500 miles long from southeast to northwest; combined with many off shore islands, the land mass actually stretches to about 1,800 miles. New Guinea, sometimes referred to as Melanesia (the dark islands) or Papua, is located directly south of the Equator. The length of the island is dominated by a tangled maze of jagged and steep-sided, multiple mountain ranges traversing spine-like to the end of the Papuan Peninsula. Four of these mountain ranges equal or exceed the heights of mountains in the United States: the Owen Stanleys, the Finistere, the Bismarcks, and the Nassau Ranges, all of which have peaks ranging from 13,000 to 16,000 feet. Every mountain and ridge side is rutted with steep ravines, draws, and gorges. The mountains are covered with dense rain forests, with open areas being very infrequent, and are often shrouded in clouds at the higher elevations. Much of the forest is congested with vines and thick canopy that blocks out sunlight.

Several large rivers cut into the island, the most important being the Sepik (sometimes Sepic), the Fly, the Ramu, and the Markham. These rivers meander over large areas and are broken by large areas of lakes and freshwater swamps. A broad swampy valley is found in the western portion of North East New Guinea, through which the twisting 600 mile Sepik River flows from the west, originating in the Owen Stanleys near the Dutch New Guinea border, and is navigable for almost 300 miles. The Sepik is the largest river in North West New Guinea and flows generally parallel with the north coast, bounded by the Owen Stanleys on the south and the coastal Victor Emanuel Mountains on the north, and then bends gradually to the northeast to flow into the sea. Many smaller rivers and streams flow out of the mountains and hills, often turning sluggish as they approach the north coast. The narrow coastal plain is forested with interspersed open areas that may be covered by marshes of four to seven foot high kunai grass. Many of the forested areas cover swamps, but dry forested areas have dense underbrush. Much of the north coast is bordered by mangrove swamps. Sand beaches are narrow with coral outcroppings and peripheral reefs. There are numerous bays and inlets that do provide landing sites, the most notable being Milne Bay on the end of the Papuan Peninsula, Goodenough Bay, Collingwood Bay, and Huon Gulf at the Peninsula's northwest base.

The south side of the mountains, the area occupied mainly by Papua, is significantly different from the north. Irregular, sharp, steep ridges drop out of the mountains, abruptly terminating at the coast. The number of streams rushing out of the mountains increases westward. At the Gulf of Papua on the south coast, the shoreline turns south away from the foothills of the Owen Stanleys. The land levels out into a broad undulating and hilly, forest-covered plain which is cut by the 650 mile Fly River, navigable for 500 miles. Its source is high in the Owen Stanley Mountains near the Dutch New Guinea border. Rushing southwest out of the mountains, the longest river on Papua curves sharply to the southeast, with its elbow jutting into Dutch New Guinea comprising a portion of the border. The Fly then flows across the plains and coastal lowlands into the Gulf of Papua,

The rugged, inhospitable **Owen Stanley Mountains** ran along the New Guinea spine and had peaks ranging from 13,000 to 16,000 feet. (AAF)

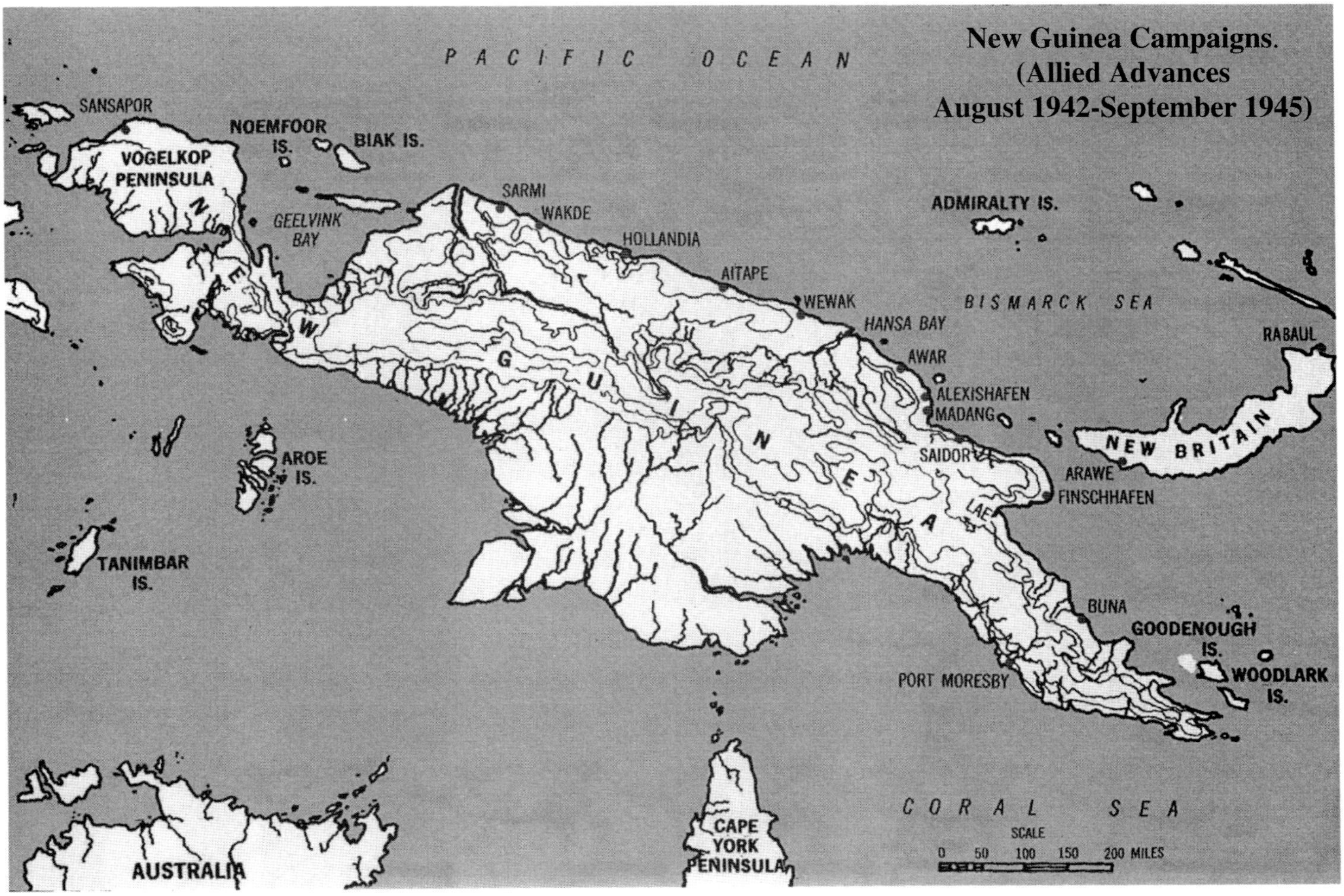

New Guinea Campaigns. (Allied Advances August 1942-September 1945)

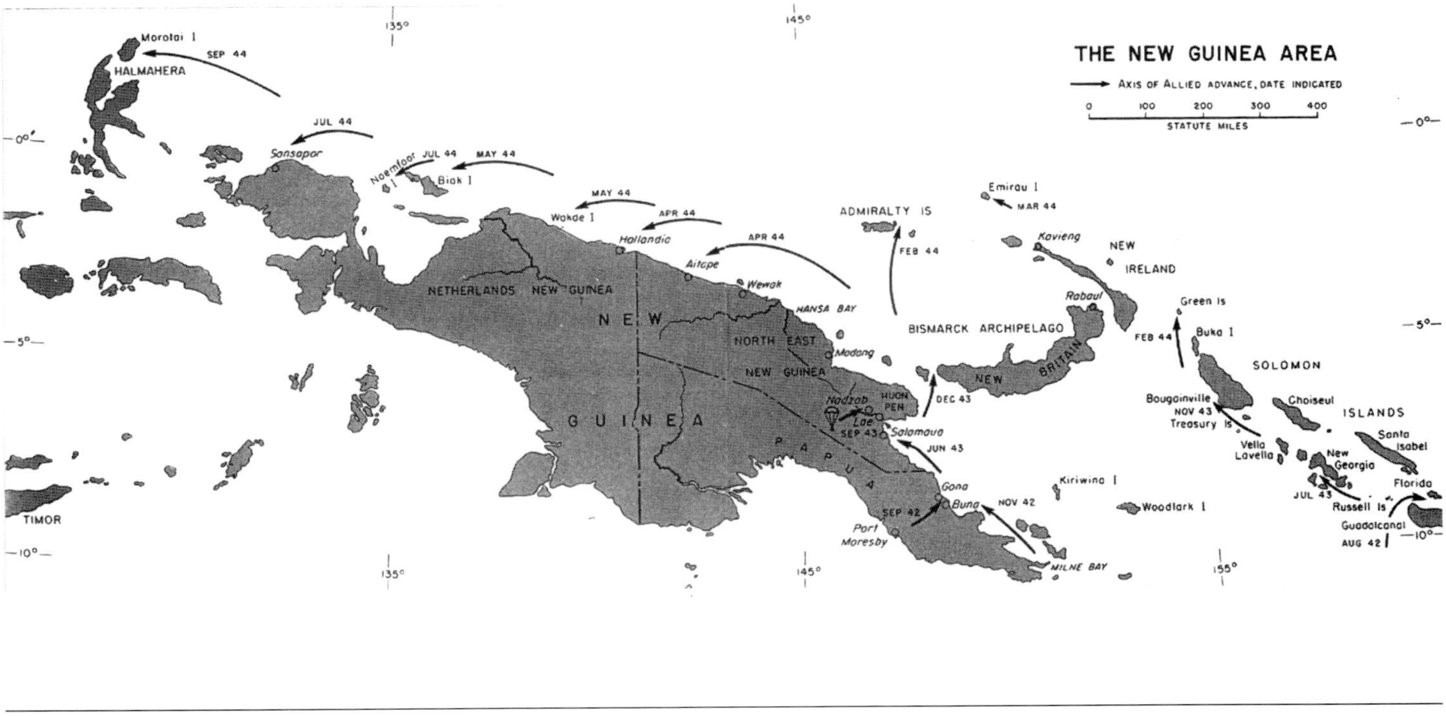

THE NEW GUINEA AREA

with its mouth forming a large delta. The lowlands between the river are inundated by one of the world's largest swamps. Recent studies indicate that enough fresh water drains into the Fly River daily to supply the needs of the entire population of the world.

Some of the most severe tropical weather in the world occurs in New Guinea. Torrential rains vary from 150 to 300 inches a year depending on the area. During the rainy season, called the "Northwest Monsoon," it can rain up to 10 inches a day. There are two seasons, the Northwest Monsoon, occurring from October to April with heavy rains, heat, high clouds; and the Southeast Monsoon, occurring from April to September, which is somewhat milder and drier. However, while rain is encountered throughout the year, periodic droughts also occur. The temperature varies little during the year, remaining hot and humid along the coasts to quite cold in the mountains, even during the day. Generally, further east on to the Papuan Peninsula it is comparatively milder, while the western areas, especially along the coasts, the Papuan Gulf, and the Fly River Delta areas the climate is particularly severe and unhealthy.

Prior to World War II, the principal resource had been the gold fields discovered up the Markham River Valley north of the village of Lae. During 1931 to 1934, Lae's airport was the busiest freight airport in the world, as it was supporting the gold fields to which land transportation was impossible. Amelia Earhart began her last flight from this airport toward Howland Island. In 1940, the population of all New Guinea was estimated at approximately one million, of which only approximately 10,000 were foreigners (Europeans, Asians, etc.). Most indigenous peoples were still living in a Stone Age type civilization, with some tribes living in the Nassau Range still practicing headhunting and cannibalism. New Guinea was governed in three sections. The western half of the island was a colony in the Netherlands East Indies and governed by the Dutch, called Dutch New Guinea or New Guinea. The eastern half of the island was governed by the English and the Australians. Papua (pronounced "Pap-yoo"), the southern half of the eastern portion, was under the administration of England and Australia. The northern half, a former German colony (hence the many German names), had been taken over during World War I and had since been administered by the English and the Australians. Today the eastern half of New Guinea, New Britain, New Ireland, and the Solomons have all been consolidated in a self-governing country now known as Papua New Guinea, while the western portion contains the Indonesian provinces of West Papua and Papua.

The flight east across the Coral Sea from Horn Island to Port Moresby was about 370 air miles. Port Moresby had only a very few small businesses, but was the major town and port in the area. In the Port Moresby area, the Allies had constructed five major air bases. (Wartime New Guinea air bases normally consisted of one main runway with taxiways and dispersal areas.) Initially, the airdromes were named by the approximate distance from the small town of Port Moresby to the airfields (i.e. 5 Mile and 7 Mile Dromes), and later took the names of pilots who were KIA (i.e. 5 Mile was renamed Wards, while 7 Mile was renamed Jackson).

About 100 air miles east of Port Moresby, on the north coast of New Guinea, was the major Allied base at Buna, which had been taken from the Japanese early in 1943 in a long and bloody battle. The airfield complex at Buna was normally referred to as Dobodura, named for what had been a small native village in the vicinity. Port Moresby and Buna were separated by the treacherous Owen Stanley mountain range rising to almost 14,000

When war came **Port Moresby** had only a very few small businesses but was the major town and port in the area and the Allies would constructed five major air bases in the Port Moresby area. (AAF)

feet. Mount Victoria, the highest peak at 13,363 feet, was 53 miles west of the Dobodura airfields.

Later bases would be constructed on Goodenough and Kiriwina Islands. Goodenough was located 175 miles east of Dobodura and would be developed into a major staging base for US Army and Air Force assault forces that were to operate northwestward toward the Philippines. An air base would also be developed on Kiriwina, east of Goodenough, and occupied and defended by RAAF units. Kiriwina provided a staging and emergency landing area for 5AF units that had been attacking the major Japanese base at Rabaul on the island of New Britain. Further to the east, at 400 to 500 miles, were the Solomon Islands. This area was the responsibility of the US Navy and the 13AF and formed the South Pacific Command (SOPAC).

Rabaul, the major Japanese base in the South Pacific area, was located on the northeastern tip of the island of New Britain, and was about 410 miles northeast of Dobodura, which could be compared to the distance between London and Berlin. Rabaul was protected by five major airfields, four of which had concrete runways. Two other fields were in the construction stage at this time. These fields provided revetments for 166 bombers and 265 fighters, besides extensive unprotected dispersals. Rabaul's expansive Simpson Harbor had seven wharves, and these were supplemented by newly constructed piers and floating cranes. The Japanese 8th Supply Depot of the Southeastern Fleet maintained a six month inventory at Rabaul of all supplies intended for their Army and Navy in the Bismarcks, Solomons, and eastern New Guinea. In addition to fleet units always present in the harbor, there were 367 antiaircraft weapons, 192 operated by the Army and 175 by the Navy. An extensive and efficient early warning radar system was in place throughout the area. The Rabaul or its airfields would never be captured, but would be neutralized by continued heavy bombing.

The Japanese built a large military and naval base at Kavieng, on New Ireland Island, which lay west of Rabaul and was about 450 miles north-northwest of Dobodura. The Admiralty Islands, with two airfields and an extensive harbor, were west of Kavieng and about 475 miles north of Dobodura. These last two locations provided the needed steps from the Japanese base at Truk to the forces in the entire south and southwest Pacific Ocean areas.

Northwestward, along the New Guinea coast, the Japanese had constructed major air bases at Madang, Alexishafen, Hansa Bay, Wewak, Tadji, and Hollandia. These bases ranged from 300 miles from Dobodura to Madang to 500 miles from Dobodura to Wewak. Nine Japanese airfields provided for Japanese operations from Madang to Wewak. The initial Allied strategy for the battle for New Guinea was to use bases at Port Moresby to gain air superiority to bomb and then capture Japanese positions on the Huon Peninsula (Lae, Finschhafen, and Salamaua); successively repairing captured enemy airfields there or building new ones. From these new fields Kenney and MacArthur could extend their bomb line and establish forward air superiority to repeat the process, driving the Japanese west along the northern New Guinea coast. Between Dobodura and the Japanese on New Guinea would be new Allied air bases centering on Nadzab, in the Markham River Valley, 200 miles away; then 100 miles west of Nadzab, in the Ramu River Valley, would be the most advanced Allied base, at Gusap. Then 100 miles east of Nadzab, on the Vitiaz Strait, would be a base at Finschhafen. Because of their importance to Allied strategy, these air bases will be described in detail throughout the war.

Port Moresby Dromes

On 31 March 1942, MacArthur sent his Chief Engineer, Brig.Gen. Hugh Casey, and his Air Officer, Brig.Gen. Harold George on a reconnaissance of the Port Moresby area to find new airdrome facilities, as there were only two airdromes in operation in the area at the time. One of these was the 7 Mile (later named Jackson) Drome, located seven miles from Port Moresby, which had been developed by the Royal Australian Air Force (RAAF) and consisted of a single runway which was being used principally as an advanced refueling point for Australian based aircraft. The other airdrome was a civil field which was located at Kila, three miles from Port Moresby. Work had already been started on two other airdromes: at Laloki (later named Schwimmer) Drome, and at a small field, located west of Seven Mile Drome, for use as a dummy and emergency landing field (it was later expanded and named Wards Drome).

Generals Casey and George found there was a critical shortage of engineer troops and equipment in the area to develop Port Moresby into an adequate and effectual base for air operations. There was only a company of Royal Australian Engineers that were spread throughout the area, and follow-

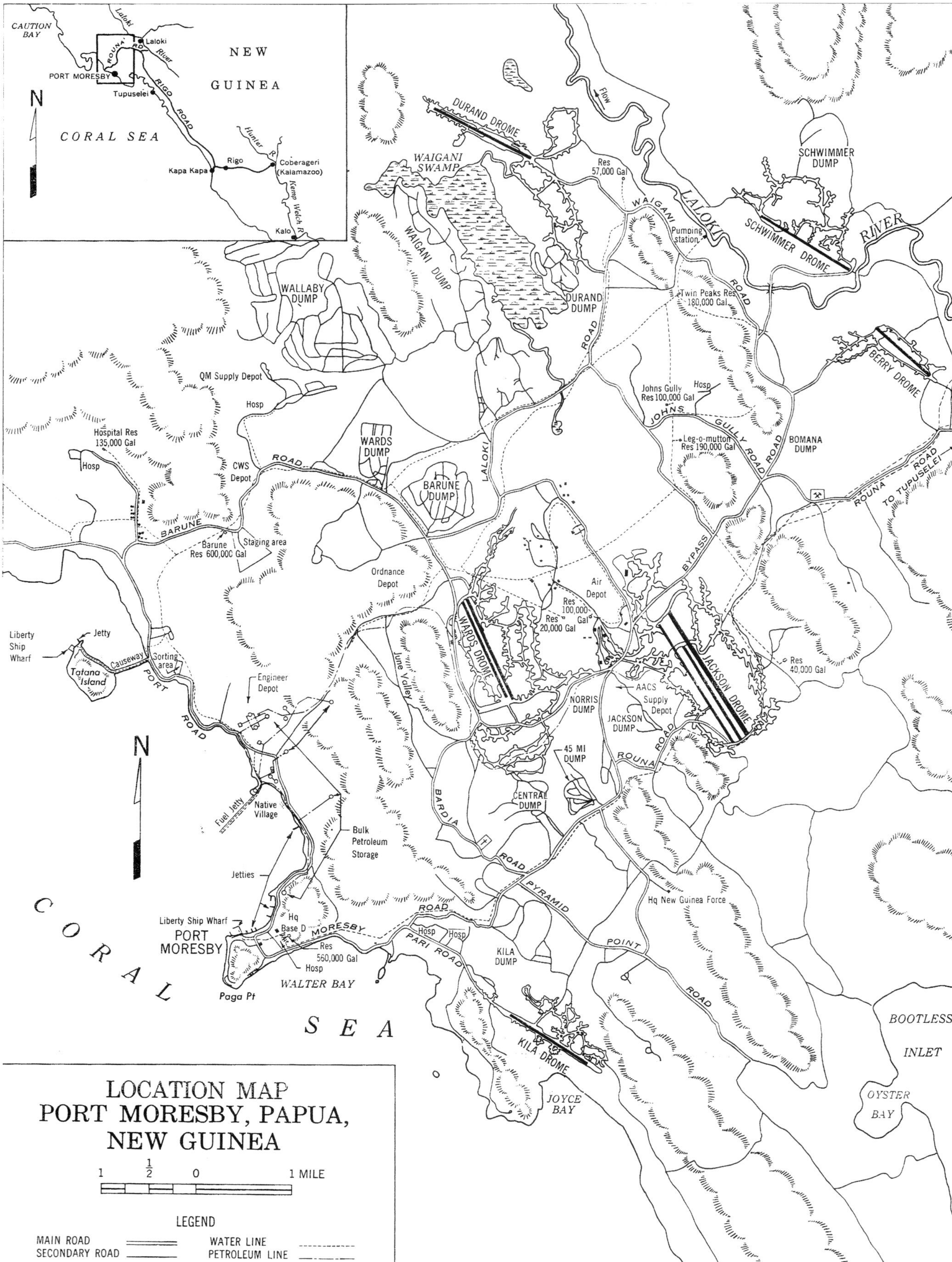

LOCATION MAP
PORT MORESBY, PAPUA,
NEW GUINEA

Brig.Gen. **Hugh Casey** was MacArthur's Chief Engineer. (AAF)

Philippine's veteran, Col. **Harold George**, was promoted to Brig. General to become MacArthur's Air Officer. (AAF)

ing the reconnaissance the 96th Engineer Battalion was immediately ordered to Port Moresby as soon as it arrived in Brisbane on 6 April 1942. When the first elements of the Battalion arrived it was without its mobile equipment, which was left behind upon its departure from the United States. It was then equipped with borrowed Australian farm equipment until the equipment and entire Battalion arrived in June 1942.

Kila or Kila Kila Drome (3 Mile Drome)

Initially, the existing commercial airfield at Kila had been considered to be too poorly located to convert into a military airdrome. Kila Drome was named due to its proximity to Kila Kila Village and 5 Mile Drome, as it was located three miles from Port Moresby. Situated as it was, with a high ridge about 2,000 yards beyond one end of the runway and only a narrow, low saddle immediately off the other end, the take-off of aircraft was limited to one direction only. Although hazardous for air operations, it had, nevertheless, proved a vital field, because it seldom was fogged in and could accept air traffic when all other airdromes in the area were closed by bad weather. Also, by the middle of 1942 Port Moresby, which was only three miles northwest, was being threatened by Japanese infantry attacks via the Kokoda Track. Therefore, Kila Drome, despite its dangerous air approach, became a strategic airfield, especially since there were few adequate airdrome sites in the neighboring mountainous terrain that could be developed by the limited engineer construction forces available. The original plans for Kila were immediately reconsidered, and plans were prepared to expand the existing runway to 5,000 by 100 feet for Allied aerial operations. The 96th Engineers performed most of the preliminary earth moving before the project was assigned to the 808th Engineers, who extended and coated the runway by the middle of November 1942. However, before the final seal coat could be applied and the necessary drainage completed, the 808th was diverted to another project. Before the 96th could arrive to finish the remaining work, rain delayed the laying of the Marsden steel mat (PSP) until late November and work continued 24/7 until completed. Concurrently with runway construction, work had proceeded on dispersal areas. Initial plans had contemplated utilizing the airdrome for fighter operations only, but as more aircraft arrived in the area and other fields became crowded, plans for Kila Drome were expanded to include parking areas not only for more fighter aircraft, but for medium bombers and transports as well. These hardstands were revetted using coconut tree logs, dirt filled gasoline drums, and earth fill. It soon became apparent that the logs would not stop bomb fragments and the drums rusted rapidly and disintegrated. However, at first it had not been possible to construct the more effective 12 to 14 foot high earth-filled revetments for all hardstands because there was not enough earth-moving equipment available for their construction. Japanese air raids did not especially disrupt construction at Kila Drome.

Kila Drome. (3 Mile Drome). (AAF)

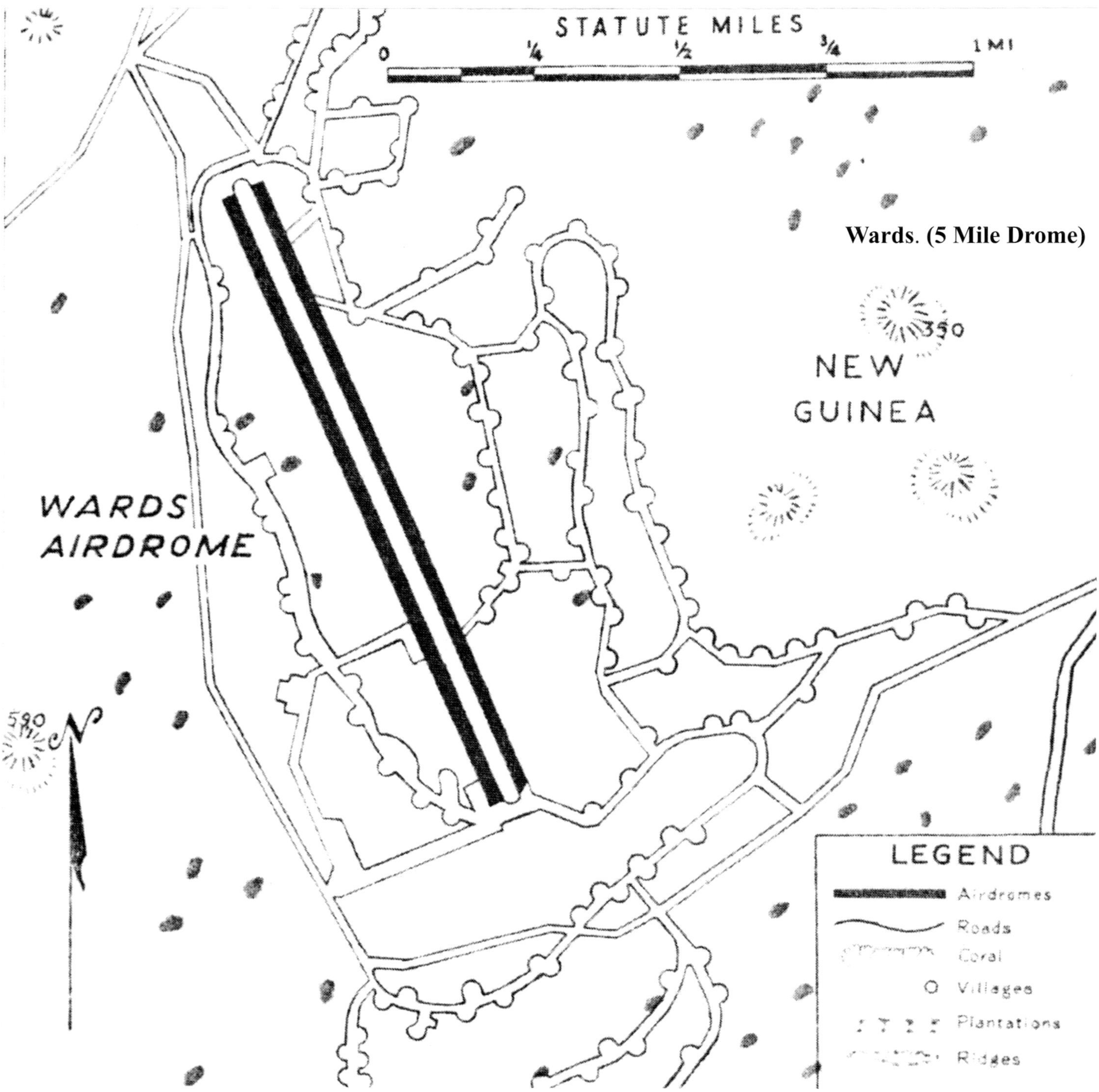

Wards. (5 Mile Drome)

USAAF Units based at Kila

3BG/8BS	(A-24s, A-20)	Charters Towers early April 1942
3BG/89BS	(A-20)	Charters Towers
49FG/8FS	(P-40)	
8FG/80FS	(P-39)	to Milne Bay April - October 1943
8FG/35FS	(P-40)	
347FG/67FS	(P-39)	New Caledonia 30 May 1943 to 28 June 1943 Milne Bay

Wards Drome (5 Mile Drome)

To provide for the staging of heavy bomber missions from the Port Moresby area, construction of two additional airdromes had been directed by General Headquarters, Southwest Pacific Area (GHQ, SWPA). One, referred to as Ward Drome, was at the site of the dummy and emergency field near Jackson Drome, and the other (later designated as Durand Drome) was at Waigani, located northwest of Schwimmer Drome. Wards was built by the Australians in middle 1942 and surfaced by American engineers. The construction was led by Australian 53rd Construction Battalion CO Lt.Col. H.K. Ward, who was KIA on 27 August 1942 during fighting along the Kokoda Trail. At Wards Drome, construction of two parallel runways, 200 feet apart, each measuring 6,000x100 feet, was assigned to the RAAF mobile works squadrons, while a battalion of the 46th Engineer Regiment was responsible for construction of the dispersal system providing revetted dispersal for heavy and medium bombers. Upon completion of an initial dry-weather strip and many dispersal areas for immediate aerial operations, construction immediately began on the parallel strip to permit operation of heavy bombers during the rainy season. At the same time, construction on access roads had to be rushed because supplying the drome with fuel and bombs was dependent upon completion of the roads prior to the beginning of the rainy season. As soon as the all-weather runway was completed, the original dry weather strip was renovated into all-weather standards.

USAAF Units based at Wards:

374TCG/22TCS	(C-47) Garbutt 24 January 1943 and 29 August 1944 to Finschhafen
90BG/320BS	(B-24) Iron Range 10 February to 1 December 1943 to Dobodura
90BG/321BS	(B-24) Iron Range 10 February to 1 December 1943 to Dobodura

RAAF Units Based at Wards:

9 Group/22 Squadron (A-20)
9 Group, 30 Squadron (Beaufighter) 12 September 1942 to ??
Fifth Fighter Command Units: None

Jackson Drome (7 Mile Drome)
The single 5,100x75 foot runway at Jackson Drome was in existence when Casey and George did their reconnaissance, but the surface of this airstrip was mediocre, as an excess of bitumen had been applied when sealing the runway against the prevailing tropical heat and the wheels of parked aircraft would sink into the surfacing. The drainage facilities were also found to be inadequate. A makeshift Engineer Battalion began work at Jackson Drome in three phases: patching the runway so it could be used after daily enemy bombings; extending the runways between air raids; and clearing and grading a crash strip alongside the originally paved runway. The frequent Japanese bombings left many craters which, after backfilling and patching, required steady maintenance. They also built additional hardstands along the improvised taxiways and attempted to provide a degree of blast-proofing with dirt filled gasoline drums. Their non-engineering tasks included the refueling of aircraft and loading them with bombs, the unloading of shipping in the port, and other miscellaneous service-type functions. The field was named "Jackson" on 10 November 1942 in honor of RAAF pilot John Jackson, who was shot down and killed in action 28 April 28 1942 while flying a P-40. When the fully equipped 808th Engineers arrived, the complete reconstruction and rehabilitation of the drome was undertaken, commencing with provision of adequate taxiways and blast proof hardstands. The 96th's crash strip was regraded and surfaced, and additional taxiways and blast proof hardstands were built. Then the deteriorating original runway was removed, regraded, and paved, and after approximately eight months Jackson Drome was considered completed. By May 1943 Jackson Drome included both a sealed bomber runway, 7,500 feet by 150 feet, and a fighter runway, 5,250 feet by 100 feet, as well as extensive taxiways, hardstands, and revetments. A network of taxiways between Jackson (7 Mile) and Wards (5 Mile) made it possible to taxi between the two airfields. Subsequently, construction of a concrete runway for B-29 bombers was considered, but shortages of personnel, equipment, construction material, and shipping to supply the latter delayed the start of this project until many of the advanced airdromes of higher priority on the northeastern coast of New Guinea had been built, and then changes in the tactical situation made this construction unnecessary; instead, an additional runway, 8,000 by 100 feet, was constructed and surfaced with steel mat. Work was begun in early September 1943, and the runway was largely completed in February 1944. Later, both bomber runways were expanded to 9,000 feet while the fighter runway was downgraded to emergency landing field status.

Wards. (5 Mile Drome). (AAF)

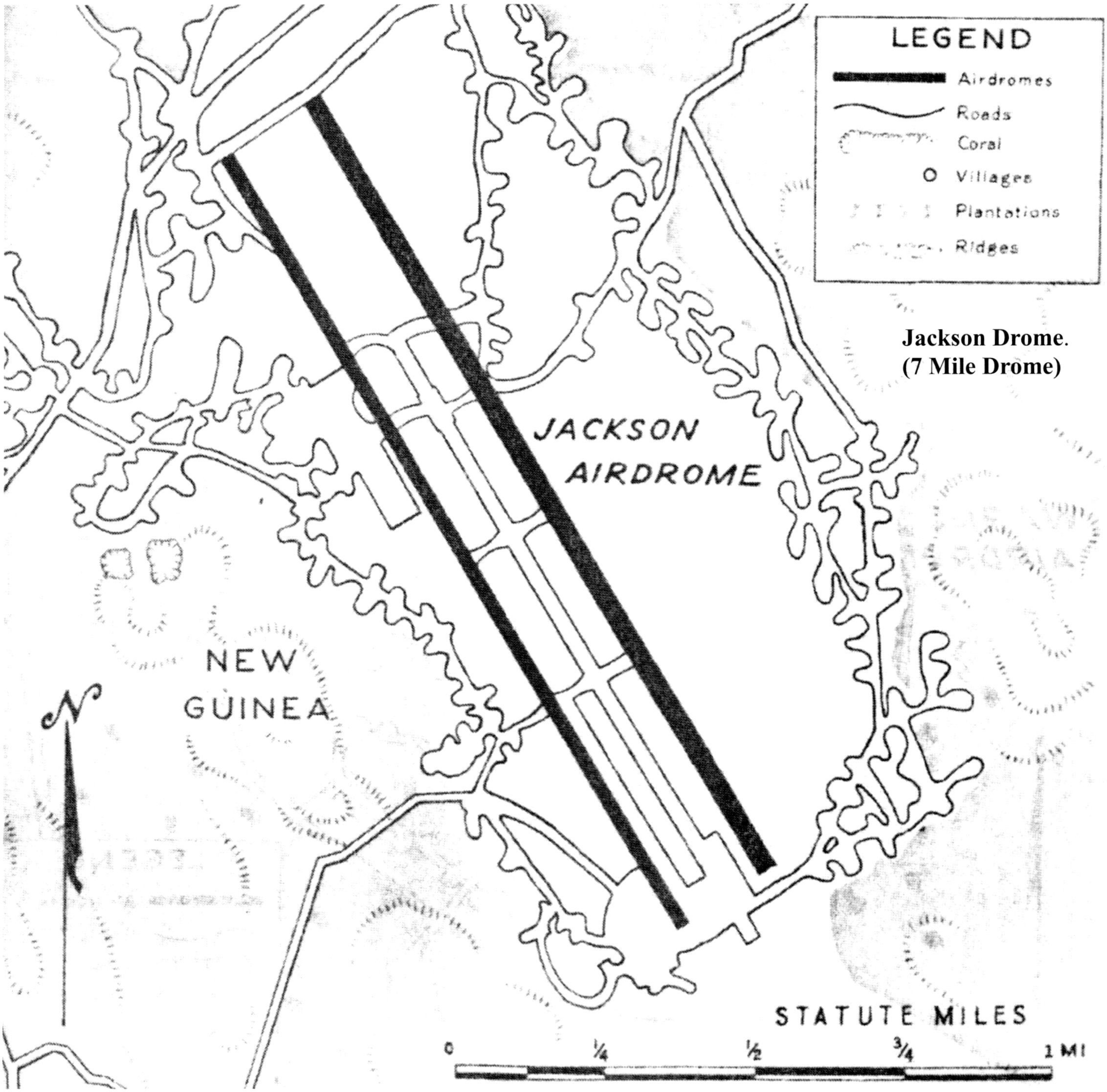

Jackson Drome.
(7 Mile Drome)

RAAF Units Based at Jackson

75 Squadron	(P-40s) 21 March to May 1942 USAAF Units Based at Jackson
43BG/HQ	Mareeba January 1943 and 10 December 1943 to Dobodura
43BG/63BS	(B-17) Mareeba 20 January 1943 and 29 October 1943 to Dobodura
43BG/64BS	(B-17) Mareeba 20 January 1943 and 29 October 1943 to Dobodura
43BG/65BS	(B-17) Mareeba 20 January 1943 and 11 December 1943 to Dobodura
43BG/403BS	(B-24) Mareeba 11 May 1943 and 13 December 1943 to Dobodura

Fifth Fighter Command Units:

35FG/40FS	(P-39/P-400) Antil Plains 1 June 1942 to end July Antil Plains
35FG/41FS	(P-39/P-400) Bankstown 20 July to 16 August 1943 Tsili Tsili

Berry Drome (12 Mile Drome)

Bomana Drome, the 12 Mile Drome, was officially renamed "Berry Drome" in honor of P-39 pilot Maj. Jack Berry on 10 November 1942. Berry was located on the high ground to the southeast of Schwimmer Drome, and was also among the first priority airfield sites indicated for rapid development in New Guinea following the Casey and George reconnaissance. The

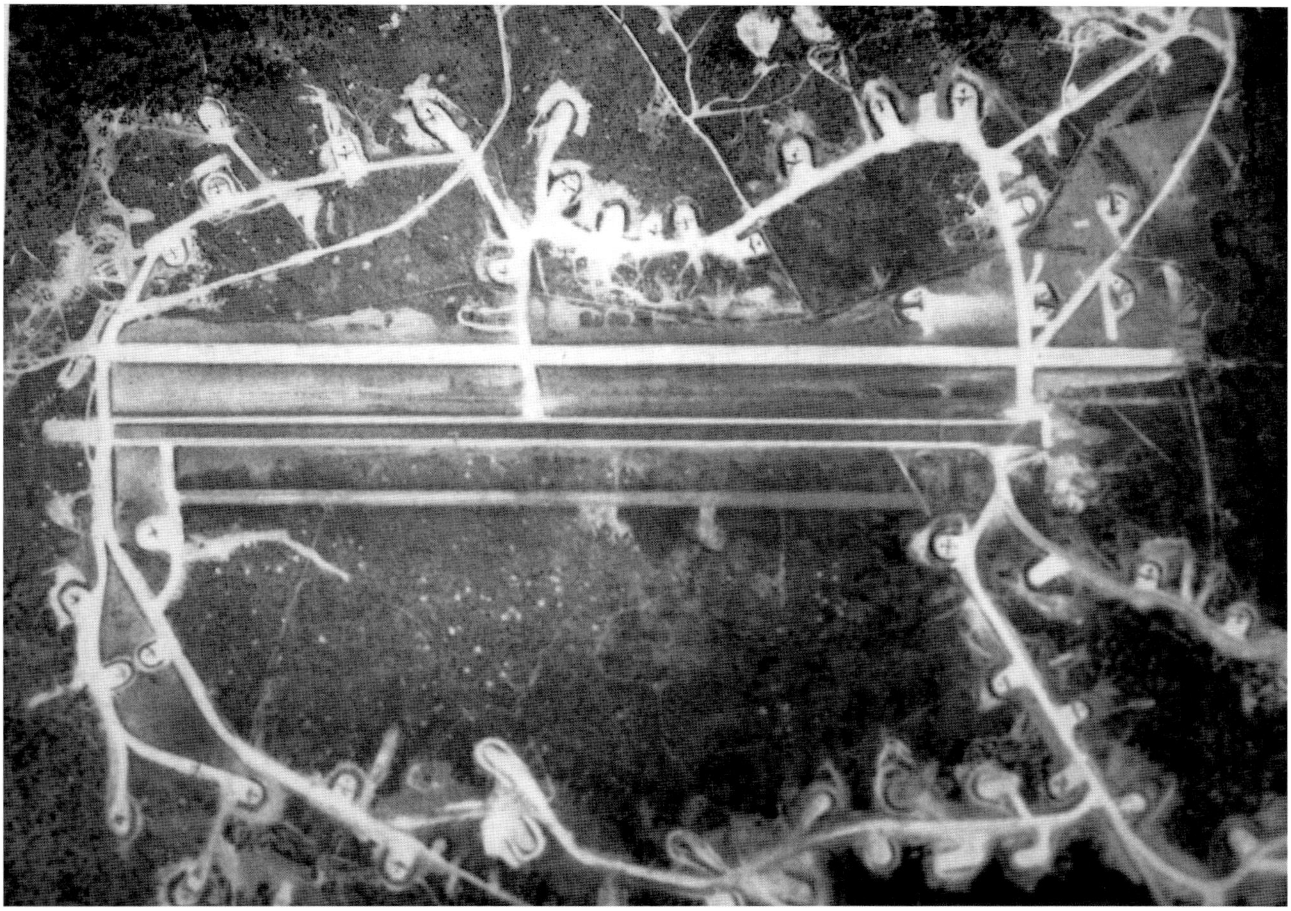

Jackson Drome. (7 Mile Drome). (AAF)

Wards Drome. (center) and Jackson Drome. (upper left). (AAF)

Berry Drome. (12 Mile Drome).(AAF)

96th Engineers began construction during late 1942, when the existing dry weather earth strip was cleared and extended to 4,500x150 feet. Further extension of the runway in either direction was impossible without extensive earth-moving, and this short runway length limited its tactical use primarily to fighter and transport aircraft. To maintain continuous air operations while the airdrome was under construction, grading was carried out gradually by dividing the runway into two 75 foot widths and working on each width alternately. By 15 May 1943, through synchronization of engineer effort with simultaneous air operations, the entire strip was surfaced with crushed rock and pit gravel for about an eight inch thickness. Subsequent improvements to the drome included four miles of dispersal roads accommodating 40 dispersal bays and four alert areas, each of sufficient size for 15 fighter aircraft.

RAAF Units based at Berry

RAAF 75 Squadron (P-40) 25 April 1942 and ?? transfer

Fifth Fighter Command Units based at Berry

8FG/80FS (P-39) 20 July 1942 to 8 November 1942 to Turnbull
35FG/40FS (P-39) to 7 Mile June 42
35FG/41FS (P-39) Antil Plains late November to early December 1942 to 14 August 1943 to Tsili Tsili

Schwimmer Drome (14 Mile Drome)

Laloki Drome, or 14 Mile Drome, was officially renamed "Schwimmer Drome" on 10 November 1942, in honor of Charles Schwimmer, lost in his P-39 while intercepting Japanese aircraft over Port Moresby. At Schwimmer, the former heavy timber and jungle growth were bulldozed away and a 4,600 foot by 100 foot runway, covered with steel mat, was completed by early August 1942. The Drome was situated on a low, flat plain only a few feet above the normal water level of the Laloki River, and so the runway was prone to periodic flooding. The base material for the runway was alluvial mud over alluvial sand and gravel, making the runway unsuitable for satisfactory all-weather operations. A second, parallel all-weather runway was constructed of Laloki River gravel which had been excavated with drag lines. The gravel, still wet, was spread and rolled, and dried to form a hard and durable base. Most of the steel mat surfacing was removed from the original runway and used to cover 5,500x100 feet of the new all-weather 6,000x100 foot runway, which was completed in mid-November 1942. Subsequently, taxiways and hardstands were constructed at Schwimmer Drome.

USAAF Units Based at Schwimmer

3BG/13BS (B-25s)

Fifth Fighter Command Units Based at Schwimmer

49FG/9FS (P-40) Darwin 10 October 1942 and 6 March 1943 to Dobodura
35FG/39FS (P-39, P-38) Townsville 19 October 1942 and 15 December 1943 to Nadzab
6PRG/8PRS (F-4s) Townsville 9 September 1942 and ?? to Dobodura

Durand Drome (17 Mile Drome)

On 10 November 1942, 17 Mile Drome was officially renamed "Durand" to honor P-39 pilot Edward Durand, missing on a mission against Lae. The Durand location was hurriedly selected under wartime urgency. There were dangerous obstructions within a mile of the planned airfield that could jeopardize heavy bombers carrying a full bomb load, but the immediate operation of B-17s from this site was essential. Before Kila and Wards Dromes were started or Jackson Drome enlarged, the 808th Engineers were quickly assigned to the urgent assignment of constructing Durand. Despite limitations in personnel and equipment, in three weeks these engineers cleared a 6,000x100-foot runway, surfaced it with four inches of clay-bound shale, and sealed it with tar and chips. However, the heavy bomber usage soon mandated that the runway be covered with steel mat.

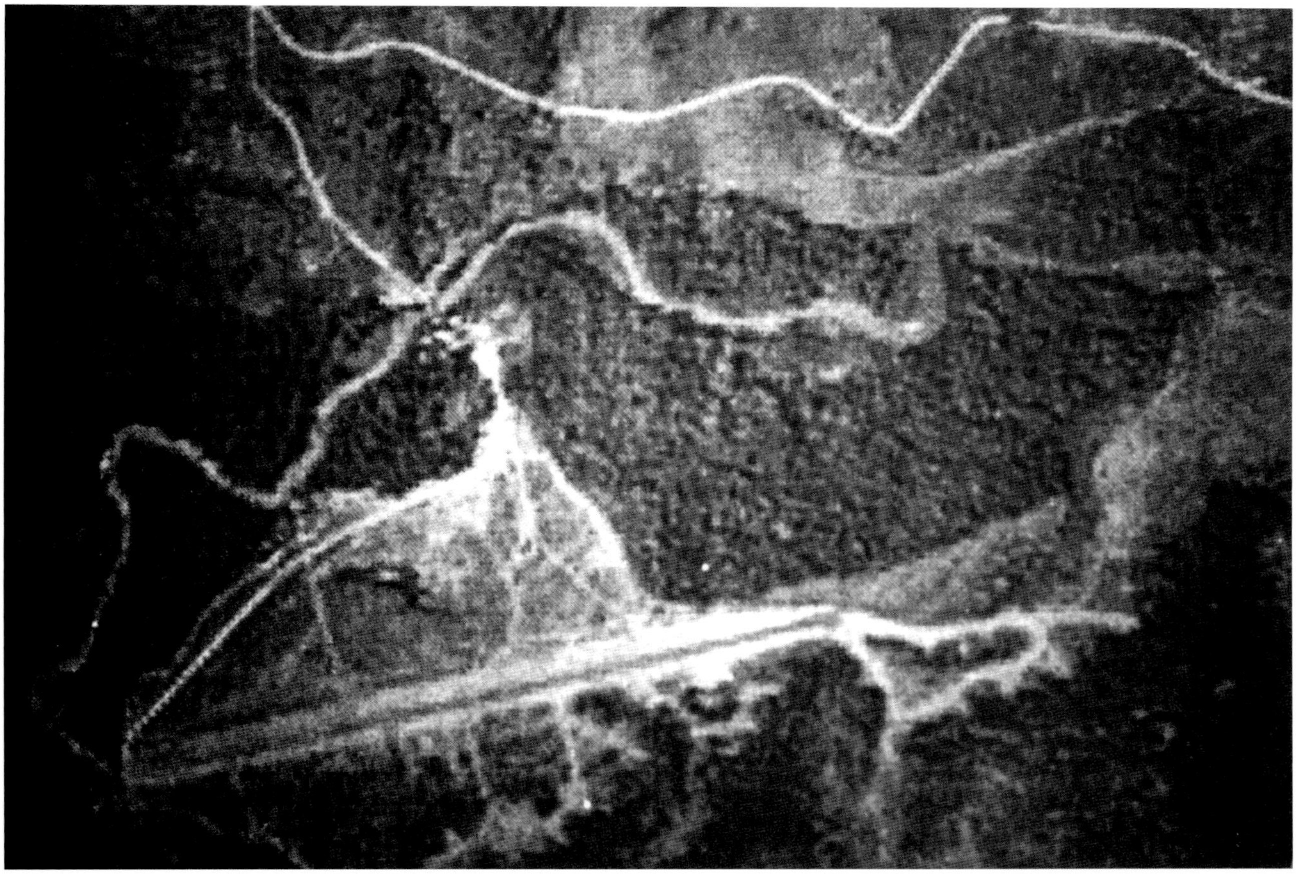

Schwimmer Drome. (14 Mile Drome). (AAF)

39FS P-38s taking off from **Schwimmer** Drome. (AAF)

Durand Drome. (17 Mile Drome). (AAF)

Rogers Drome. (30 Mile Drome). (AAF)

USAAF Units Based at Durand	
3BG/13BS	(B-25) 7 October 1942 and ?? to ??
3BG/90BS	(B-25)
38BG/71BS	(B-25) Breddan 1 October 1942 and 5 March 1944 to Nadzab
38BG/405BS	(B-25) 25 October 1942 and 6 March 1944 to Nadzab
345BG/499BS	(B-25) ? and 15 January 1944 to Dobodura
Fifth Fighter Command Units based at Durand	
49FG/7FS	(P-40) ?? and ? to Dobodura

Rogers (Rorona Drome/30 Mile Drome)

On 15 November 1942, Rorona Drome (30 Mile Drome) was renamed in honor of Maj. Floyd "Buck" Rogers, CO of 3BG/8BS, who was KIA flying an A-24. Construction of the airdrome located at Rorona, on Galley Reach, was assigned to the 43rd Engineers, immediately upon their arrival at Port Moresby. Galley Reach is an inlet about 30 miles northwest of Port Moresby, and can only be accessed by water transportation through a long, narrow, and tortuous channel across a wide coral reef. The problems for transporting equipment into the area made the employment of large numbers of Papuan natives necessary to hand load river gravel into trucks to construct a dry weather fighter strip ASAP. This dry weather strip was completed by 20 June 1942 by paving the runway with unbound but rolled gravel. However, to facilitate supply, an essential prerequisite before the final completion of the drome was the early completion of two docks on Galley Reach and approximately 10 miles of road from these docks to the airdrome site. The forced early withdrawal from the drome was a possibility, as Japanese forces on the Kokoda Trail were approaching Port Moresby and Japanese patrols were reported operating only a few miles from Rorona. The newly installed air warning facilities were dismantled and removed, and construction during the remainder of the month was halted. After the enemy threat subsided, the improvement of the runway to all-weather standards was delayed by a low priority for steel mat. Without the PSP it was impossible to develop the runway sufficiently for all-weather use by heavy bombers prior to the rainy season with the equipment and engineers available. Finally, by late November 1942, the 43rd, through resolute and strenuous effort, extended the runway to 6,000x100 feet and had covered a 1,865x80 foot section at each end with steel mat. By the beginning of 1943, further work on Rogers Drome was suspended and the 43rd Engineers were moved to Milne Bay. While changes in the tactical situation had outdated Rogers Drome for operational purposes before it was completed, this air facility did prove of use less than nine months later as an advantageously situated rehearsal area for a projected offensive operation.

Units based at 30 Mile Drome (Rogers, Rorona) 5FC	
49FG/7FS	(P-40) September 1942 and 6 March 1943 to Dobodura
35FG/40FS	(P-39, P-400) ? 1943
35FG/41FS	(P-39, P-400) ? - 1943

Daugo Island Emergency Airfield

The Australians built an emergency field off shore Port Moresby in early 1944 on Daugo Island (also called Fisherman's Island).

Moresby Dromes into 1943

With the exception of Rogers Drome, work continued on all airdromes in the Port Moresby area throughout 1943. These airdromes were brought to permanent operational standards with hard-surfaced access roads, taxiways, hardstands, and revetments. Aviation gasoline storage tanks with pipe lines connected to tanker piers for bulk fuel handling were installed. Headquarters buildings for both the Army Airways Communications System and the Air Transport Command were also constructed at Jackson Drome. In March 1943, construction was started on a site between Jackson and Wards Drome for a large advance air depot to provide facilities for repair, maintenance, and salvage of aircraft in this area.

By the end of 1943, the Allied advance had reduced the significance of Port Moresby as a major base, and the US Engineer Construction Units were moved to forward areas. Gradually the airdromes around Moresby were returned to the Australians or deactivated and dismantled. The steel mat was salvaged from all airdromes except Jackson and Wards. It was put through a straightening machine and packed and shipped to forward areas. Bulk petroleum tanks were dismantled, cleaned, and shipped to forward areas. Prefabricated buildings were dismantled and shipped forward, along with salvaged lumber, water pipe, electric wire, and fixtures. After the elimination of any immediate threat to Port Moresby itself, the overall base facilities provided in the Port Moresby area made possible the continuation of the vital logistical support to numerous other early Allied offensive operations which followed.

Airdrome Construction

Gen. Hugh Casey in New Guinea

All discussion of wartime American construction in the Pacific requires that Gen. Hugh Casey's life and contribution be included. Hugh John Casey was born in Brooklyn, New York, on 7 June 1898 and educated at Manual Training High School from 1910 to 1914, graduating at 15. He won a New York State scholarship and entered Brooklyn Polytechnic Institute, where he studied civil engineering. After a year there, he took a competitive examination for West Point and ranked first out of 62 applicants for the appointment, but to enter Casey had to be older, and used his brother's birth date. Casey entered West Point in 1915, where his best friend and roommate was Lucius Clay, who would become the architect of the post war Berlin Airlift.

Due to America's entry into World War I, Casey's class graduated early on 12 June 1918. Casey was ranked third in the class and was commissioned as a Captain in the US Army Corps of Engineers. Casey spent the War in the US, first as an instructor, and then from September 1918 as a company commander with the 219th Engineers. After the War he served with the US Occupation forces in the Rhineland from June 1920 to May 1922. While there he married Dorothy Ruth Miller, the daughter of Col. R.B. Miller, the chief surgeon of the American forces there. From 1922 to 1926, Casey was the officer in charge of the Engineer Unit of the Reserve Officers Training Corps (ROTC) at the University of Kansas. In 1927, Casey received his first civil works assignment, as assistant District Engineer at the Pittsburgh District, where he prepared a voluminous report on flood control that was considered "over engineered for a flood that would never happen" and was shelved until 1936, when the flood did happen. From 1927 to 1933 Casey held waterway and harbor posts, after which he was awarded a fellowship from the American Society of Mechanical Engineers to study hydraulics and civil engineering in Germany. For the next two years he attended the Technische Hochschule in Berlin, earning a Doctorate in Engineering. Returning to the United States in June 1935, Casey was posted to various water power and dam projects, and was promoted to Major 1 February 1940.

Gen. Hugh Casey. (AAF)

Casey returned to Washington, D.C. in October 1940 to become Chief of the Design and Engineering Section in the Construction Division of the Office of the Quartermaster General, under Brig.Gen. Brehon Somervell. At this time a vast construction program was in progress to meet the demands of the impending war, and Casey was part of a staff that was assigned to revise standard building and barracks designs. Casey was promoted to Lieutenant Colonel on 8 April 1941. On 17 July 1941, Somervell appointed Casey and George Bergstrom, a former president of the American Institute of Architects, to design a colossal office complex to house the War Department's 40,000 personnel in one building. Over that weekend, Casey and his staff roughed out the design for a five story, five sided structure, which would ultimately become the Pentagon, the largest office building in the world.

In September 1941, Gen. Douglas MacArthur requisitioned Casey as his Chief Engineer, and he arrived in Manila in October 1941 shortly before the outbreak of the war. Casey supervised demolitions as MacArthur's troops retreated to Bataan. Unlike the rest of MacArthur's headquarters, Casey did not relocate to Corregidor, but remained on Bataan with a small staff of five officers. Casey was promoted to Colonel on 19 December 1941 and Brig.General on 25 January 1942. Casey then joined MacArthur and 16 other members of his staff in their escape from Corregidor by PT boat in March 1942.

In Australia, Casey became Chief Engineer at MacArthur's GHQ, Southwest Pacific Area (SWPA), where he would encounter enormous engineering problems. Most of New Guinea consisted of mountains and jungle, with very few airstrips, ports or roads; all of which had to be developed to support combat operations. To provide his expertise in construction, Casey requested that Leif Sverdrup be assigned to his staff as Chief of the Construction Section, with the rank of Colonel. In the SWPA there were few US Army engineers, and Casey worked closely with Maj.Gen. Clive Steele, his Australian Army counterpart at General Sir Thomas Blarney's Allied Land Forces Headquarters. A major undertaking Casey faced was to coordinate the activities of the various military and civilian agencies. Among Casey's problems were having to avert attempts by the US Army Air Forces to gain control of his Aviation Engineer Battalions and to direct RAAF airbase construction squadrons to do his bidding. Casey also had to deal with Australian civilians of the Allied Works Council who were involved with construction. Casey's initial requirement was for engineer units to begin a daunting construction program with inadequate engineering supplies and equipment. Engineer units arrived without their equipment, or had it stowed on different ships, which often arrived at a different port in a theater where ports were hundreds or thousands of miles apart. In the absence of a suitable stock control system, an overall coordinating agency, and an adequate number of engineer depot units, the allocation and distribution of the inadequate supplies on hand was a difficult task. Critical shortages of tractors, graders, concrete mixers, and welding equipment occurred, but the worst problem was spare parts for this equipment, which was operated 24/7 under severe conditions and soon wore out or broke down. Requisitions sent to the US took months to arrive, and so the limited sources of supply in Australia had to be relied upon. In New Guinea, logistics and construction activities were coordinated by task force engineer staffs, but these were often hastily assembled and had not always been able to meet the demands imposed by base development in such a demanding theater of operations.

Strategy and Logistics

The importance of airfields in the SWPA can not be overemphasized and will be discussed in detail. The Southwest Pacific was always a theater in which logistic plans had to be quickly changed to meet the new requirements imposed by the fluctuating conditions of the battlefront. These great variations in both the Allied and Japanese combat situations forced significant modifications to the planning and construction of airfields and bases. Areas of once great importance suddenly became insignificant, and key installations built to meet anticipated needs would become unnecessary as the strategic situation changed.

Despite these strategic adjustments, there were several conditions that were general to most Southwest Pacific operations:

1) The enormous distances involved for both combat and supply operations;
2) The especially unfavorable rugged terrain, primal jungle, and torrential rainfall;
3) The nonexistence of existing facilities that could be adapted to the military requirements of a theater;
4) The primary tactical importance of the air force;
5) The primary logistical importance of seaborne transportation;
6) The primary dependence of both the Navy and Air Forces on construction to provide operating facilities;
7) The continual critical shortages of construction personnel and materiel;
8) The continuing necessity to improvise;
9) The single pattern of tactical operations which was "the stepping stone advance."

These stepping stone advances, which had their beginning in early 1943 after the defeat of the Japanese at Buna, consisted of movement forward or to either flank under air cover and the development of the captured area, first as an air base, then as a port and supply base for support of the next offensive step. Often, forward movement was made possible by a flanking action which cut or disrupted every line of air and sea communication to an intended forward objective and, subsequently, with the objective in Allied hands, provided protection to that area's flank. For example, the Allied base at Saidor, in addition to being a stepping stone in the Allied advance, flanked the Admiralty Islands and protected that important area from enemy attacks launched from Hollandia during the Allied invasion, and then during the ensuing consolidation and base construction in those islands. Correspondingly, later the Admiralties protected Allied held Hollandia from invasion by enemy naval forces from the east and northeast. As the Allies' advance moved forward the rear most stepping stones became of less and less use and were eventually abandoned. This was especially true of the many major installations in southern and southeastern Australia that were planned and constructed in the early operations in the SWPA which were abandoned shortly after completion. The rapid Allied advance, along with the long distances involved, made it necessary to construct new and larger facilities forward for use.

Airbase construction in the SWPA during World War II experienced changes which necessitated the development of engineering design and construction procedures and methods to meet unusual circumstances, many of which had not been encountered before. Throughout operations in the SWPA, the engineer construction corps suffered through extreme shortages in manpower, materials, and equipment. The success of Allied tactical operations relied mainly on quick completion of bases for air, ground, and naval forces, and to surmount these deficiencies engineers were forced to improvise and adapt but remain true to the fundamental engineer doctrines of military construction:

"1) Rigid adherence to first things first;
2) Concentration of effort on the vital task or portion of that task;
3) Completion of the vital portion of each task to usable condition at the earliest moment, then concentration on the next controlling item;
4) Stringent economy of effort and material;
5) Utmost simplicity of design."

In the Southwest Pacific, the construction policy was "a natural and common sense outgrowth of the existing situation." Directives were issued to define the role of construction in the theater, and all of these directives emphasized keeping construction to the minimum and established priorities of construction in the forward areas to be:

First Priority (various items to be executed concurrently):
1) Initial beach landing and docking facilities,
2) Initial road access from docks to supply areas;
3) Initial airdrome facilities to provide, in order:
a) Landing strip for transport aircraft;
b) Landing strip for fighter aircraft with alert and dispersal facilities;
4) Water availability;
5) Minimum storage;
6) Defense installations

Second Priority (various items could be executed concurrently but with priority of effort given in relative order):
1) Hospital facilities;
2) Complete wharves and docks;
3) Complete water supply installations;
4) Complete necessary runways and dispersal areas for fighter and heavy bomber aircraft, and necessary operations buildings;
5) Complete roads;
6) Complete warehousing;
7) Bulk petroleum storage and distribution facilities;
8) Revetments in dispersal areas for the protection of aircraft.

Third Priority: construction of minimum administrative and service installations, and of utilities, other than those included above, which were considered essential.

For estimating purposes, and for comparisons of types of construction, a battalion-month yardstick was used. A battalion-month was defined as the total construction effort of an experienced and properly equipped engineer aviation battalion during one month of continued operations. It was assumed that 35% of such a unit was absorbed in overhead and losses, leaving a working force of approximately 500 men, and that each man worked eight hours per day, six days a week, and that nearly all items of equipment were employed three shifts a day.

Airfield Construction

World War II was the first war where widespread use was made of air power. In addition, the SWPA was the first theater in which the USAAF had to operate from facilities provided for them in a combat zone, constructed and operated under enemy action, in remote locations on undeveloped and primitive terrain, and the aviation engineers had to adapt and adjust to meet conditions without precedent. Since the air forces were the primary tactical weapon in the SWPA, the construction of airfields and related facilities was the most important single objective of construction. From Australia to Okinawa, more than 200 runways and innumerable supporting facilities were constructed between 15 February 1942 and 15 August 1945.

The primary mission confronting construction engineers assigned to a new project was to determine the basic purpose of the new air facility and the absolute minimum work necessary to meet that purpose. Basically, they defined an airfield as:

"....a runway suitable for aircraft landings and take offs, with facilities for commanding, parking, supplying, and servicing aircraft and the aerial units which flew and maintained them. In forward areas, protection of the installation from hostile aircraft, provision for crash landings, and provision for repair of bomb damages were additional elements."

Prior to 1942, design standards for military airfields included cleared areas of at least 1,000 feet wide with paved runways 300 to 400 feet wide along the center line. Airdrome standards were for three intersecting runways in the directions of the three prevailing winds. Runway lengths were determined by the type of aircraft to be operated from the runway, and the following standard lengths were established: 3,000 feet for fighters, 4,000 feet for medium bombers, and for heavy bombers, at least one 5,000 foot runway. All runway surfaces were to be designed to resist landing stresses of the entire weight of the aircraft concentrated on one wheel, plus an additional 50% for impact.

Construction Specifications

A number of construction specifications had to be immediately modified in SWPA to meet the conditions there:

Type of Airfield: Early in the war it was found impossible to designate any particular airfield exclusively for use of one type of aircraft. In the first nine months of 1942 the tactical situation was very changeable, and so a field started for use by fighter aircraft might be used almost immediately by medium or heavy bombers. Consequently, every airfield had to be designed to withstand the heaviest loads, and this practice continued throughout the Allies' stepping stone type of advance.

Length of Runway: There were several factors that determined the change in the specified length of runways. B-26 medium bombers assigned to SWPA actually needed longer landing and take off runs than did the B-17 and B-24 heavy bombers. In addition, all US aircraft in SWPA were flying to targets at such extreme ranges that fuel overloading was indispensable. Because of the increased fuel weight, long runways and long approach areas beyond the ends of the runways were required. Another important factor in determining increased runway length was to accommodate damaged aircraft returning from combat flown by exhausted or wounded pilots.

Width of Runway: Soon it was recognized that a 7,000 feet long by 100 feet wide runway had several advantages over one 3,500 feet long by 200 feet wide. It was easier for the pilot to align his landing on a narrower but longer runway and then have enough length to come to a stop. In addition, the narrower width of the runway and shoulders eliminated much grading which would have otherwise been necessary. Graders and paving equipment normally traveled down the long axis of a runway and would not lose time in turning and backing up on the narrower runways as they did on the wider runways. This concentration on runway length rather than width resulted in much more actual working time for the equipment and the completion of many more airdromes than would have otherwise been possible with the few men and machines available.

Runway Layout: Both in the United Kingdom and in the United States, crossing runways in the direction of the three prevailing winds was a standard specification. In the SWPA, however, winds were found to be generally gentle–seldom more than 15 miles per hour–and generally in the same direction as the theater, except very close to the Equator, which was in an area of prevailing trade winds. These mild winds blew from completely opposite directions during two particular seasons, and between the two seasons they were very mild winds of variable direction. For instance, in southern New Guinea, during June through September, winds were almost entirely from the southeast, whereas from November through April they were almost always from the northwest. Thus, it was possible to orient one runway northwest-southeast and eliminate cross winds of any strength. Occasionally, due to the terrain, the runways had to be located between hills, regardless of wind direction, but it was found that cross winds had only a minor effect on landings and take offs at the high speeds of modern combat aircraft. These aircraft did not stall in to a 3-point landing, but flew in until two wheels touched the runway. Hence, although where practicable the runways were oriented into the diametrically opposite prevailing wind directions, such orientation was not entirely essential, and it was possible to use other orientations to meet criteria of terrain and availability of engineer manpower and equipment. There were two reasons that the building of crossing runways was abandoned. First, an enemy bomb dropped at the point of intersection would put both runways out of action; and second, by not crossing the runways, each could be located in such a way as to make optimum use of the space available, regardless of the grade of a possible intersection. Increased construction and then operational efficiency were obtained with parallel runways. The first runway to be built was prepared for immediate use by fighter aircraft, but did not receive its final surface treatment at that particular time. With increased operational demands a second runway, paralleling the first, was built 200 feet or more away and completely drained and paved; then the first runway was drained and paved. It was generally necessary to provide a smooth and compacted but unpaved emergency crash strip somewhere in an airdrome area.

Special Situations: Over 40 months of construction by a battalion were saved in the first nine months of 1942 by eliminating major drainage and, in some instances, paving from specifications in airdromes constructed in Australia and a few in New Guinea. This construction was started at the beginning of the Australian nine month dry season, so no major drainage was needed or authorized on airdromes until shortly before the wet season would begin. As the occupancy and use of these installations was not certain, the expenditure of time, materials, and effort to drain them was not justified in order to provide more airfields earlier in view of the inadequate engineer personnel and equipment available. Likewise, the paving of many of these runways was not specified, which proved to be a correct decision, as some of these airfields weren't occupied for tactical operations, whereas the important forward operational airfields were paved.

Design of Pavement: The original runway surfacing design criterion, which assumed that the entire weight of the aircraft plus 50% for impact would be concentrated on one wheel at the instant of landing, was found to be erroneous. At the instant of landing, it was found that the aircraft was still airborne and its weight was carried by the wings, and that the trauma to the pavement at the instant of touchdown was almost entirely due to the unsprung weight of the landing gear alone. This supposition was confirmed by the air pressure carried in the tires and by the examination of the many landing tire marks. The most severe stresses on the runway surface actually occurred near the end of a landing run, when the aircraft was no longer running fast enough to have much weight carried on its wings, such as on taxiways, in warm-up areas, in hardstand or dispersal areas, and at the apron before take-off.

Plans and Drawings: There were no early attempts to classify airfield construction in the SWPA, but once advances occurred along the north coast of New Guinea the GHQ, SWPA issued standard diagrammatic plans for airfields to be used by different types of aircraft. The standard airfields were:

Type A: Initial Transport Strip;
Type B: Normal Transport Strip;
Type C: Fighter;
Type D: Fighter-Medium Bomber; and
Type E: Fighter-Heavy Bomber.

These plans were intended so that an airfield built initially for transports could be developed in turn for use by fighters, medium bombers, and finally heavy bombers with a minimum of engineer effort, and without wasting the previous construction. In addition, standard plans were issued for dispersals and taxiways. The constructing agency in the field was authorized to adapt these standard plans to meet operational requirements.

Site Selection and Construction: In July and August 1942, GHQ, SWPA formalized and standardized specifications governing site selection and construction of airfields. During the New Guinea Campaign, airdrome sites were chosen, supposedly by Task Force Commanders, and, after approval by a local representative of Allied Air Forces, construction was started. But sites were actually selected by the Task Force Engineer and then approved by a Fifth Air Force representative, or were made by them jointly. Fifth Air Force decisions regarding such items as airdrome layouts and locations of hardstands were final and binding, despite any discrepancy between views of Fifth Air Force and Allied Air Forces on these subjects. Shortly before the Philippines Campaign, Allied Air Forces insisted that the GHQ, SWPA give them responsibility for selection of airdrome sites, which they obtained. Thus, responsibility to determine airdrome sites was given to an organization which did not have adequate reconnaissance and

Two prevailing terrain features in New Guinea were found to be the most adaptable for the location of airfields. These were the low, sloping lands near the sea and the higher benchlands between these lowlands and the inland mountains. (AAF)

Clearing. (mowing) of thick kunai grass. (AAF)

Rough clearing after tree removal. (AAF)

survey parties under its control to gather information during the earliest phase of a landing as a basis for its decisions on airdrome sites. On 15 October 1944, only a few days prior to the start of the Leyte Campaign, the responsibility for selection of airdrome sites was returned to the Task Force Commanders.

Two prevailing terrain features in New Guinea were found to be the most adaptable for the location of airfields. These were the low, sloping lands near the sea and the higher bench lands between these lowlands and the inland mountains. In the lowlands, the best sites were usually found in existing coconut groves. On the benches, the choice locations for airfield development were in areas where kunai grass was the most prevalent vegetation. In these areas it was often possible to land transport aircraft after the grass had been cut and any holes were filled and tamped down. These early transport fields were often selected as the basis for subsequent construction of complete operational airdromes. When all-weather landing fields were required, engineer units and local native labor were assigned to improve runways, as at Nadzab and Gusap, located northwest of Lae.

When a site was considered suitable for the development of air facilities, one or more Engineer Aviation Battalions or General Service Regiments were assigned to the construction of the project. Usually, initial construction of minimum facilities for fighter aircraft was undertaken, after which these facilities were developed gradually to accommodate medium bombers, then heavy bombers, and finally depot and repair units. Hypothetically, development of air facilities followed an outline as follows:

1). The chosen area was cleared and leveled as a grass runway for transport aircraft;
2). This runway was lengthened and surfaced as an advanced fighter airfield;
3). Dispersal facilities were enlarged and the runway further lengthened for use by medium bombers; and
4). As a last step, if required, the runway was still further extended to 7,000 feet for use by heavy bombers.

In actuality, 7,000 foot runways were seldom built, as B-17s and B-24s normally operated satisfactorily from runways 5,000 to 6,000 feet in length. When each successive type of aircraft was moved in, the preceding type moved forward to another, more advanced site where the same development was taking place. Typical of this development by phases was the situation in April 1944, when heavy bombers operated from Dobodura, medium bombers from Nadzab, fighters from Finschhafen, Saidor, and Cape Gloucester, and transport aircraft moved supplies onto the newly captured runway on Los Negros, in the Admiralty Islands.

Clearing: Clearing of airfield sites in the Southwest Pacific ranged from the relatively easy mowing of thick kunai grass to the removal of thick and extensive rain forests. The extent of necessary clearing depended upon a number of factors, including the height of surrounding trees and local conditions, such as natural obstructions like hills, cross winds, and direction of runway in regard to prevailing winds.

In Australia's Northern Territory, clearing operations were relatively simple. A one inch cable was stretched across the proposed runway and attached at each end to a D-6, D-7, or D-8 tractor. As the two tractors moved forward across the runway

D-7 Dozer. (US Army)

Carryall. (US Army)

area, nearly all the trees–which averaged 12 inches in diameter, with a very few exceeding 18 inches–were completely uprooted, and it was then necessary to remove only the sawed off stumps. Occasionally, a 5,000x100 foot area was cleared in 10 hours by a crew of 10 men. However, when the dry season was well under way the ground became so hard in some areas that many trees broke off near the base instead of being uprooted.

Clearing coconut palm groves sometimes became extremely difficult because of their massive root system. After trying a number of removal methods, it was found that using the scoop on a D-8 bulldozer to give a low lifting scoop on the falling side to loosen the root ball and then follow with a deep dig under the root ball on the opposite side with a heavy pushing lift would remove the tree and root ball quickly and effectively. However, this method also loosened the coconuts in the palm tops, which endangered the dozer operators, who donned combat helmets until the dozer cabs were equipped with a suitable protection over the cab.

It was quickly discovered that the clearing of the extremely dense New Guinea rain forest would require a great expenditure of both man- and equipment-hours. Initially, some engineer units mistakenly assumed that clearing the rain forests would be similar to lumbering and cut down the trees. When they attempted to pull stumps they found it was more advantageous to use the weight of the tree itself to pull the stump. A short trench was dug by hand alongside the tree and then blown out by explosives or gouged out by heavy equipment. To remove the larger trees, a bulldozer was used to build an earth platform on the other side of the tree from the trench. The D-8 bulldozer was then driven up the platform to push as high up on the trunk as possible; assisted in difficult situations by a cable fastened high on the opposite side of the tree and pulled by a heavy truck or tractor. At Cape Sansapor, it was found that approximately three trees per acre were of such large size that they had to be blown down by explosives, cut into several pieces, and then removed by bulldozers working in pairs.

Drainage: As dry Australia was left behind and Allied advances proceeded into areas of intense rainfall, the necessity for adequate drainage facilities and for continuous drainage maintenance was repeatedly stressed by the Chief Engineer, GHQ, SWPA. In early operations in the SWPA there was no specific criterion for drainage, and it was mostly learned from field experience. The need for, the extent, and the methods of providing adequate drainage for surface water at airfield facilities were designed in the field to fit local conditions. Of course, wherever possible, airfields were located where it would not be necessary to divert large quantities of water. However often, after clearing a promising no-drainage site, graders, ditching machines, bulldozers, carryalls, or draglines had to be brought in to dig drainage ditches parallel to the runways in order to drain the water from the surface and subgrade. In well-selected airfield sites, it was possible to cut ditches to the required depth and size with a grader. When major streams had to be diverted, large cross section ditches were usually excavated with carryalls. Some very satisfactory ditches of considerable magnitude were excavated with a very large tow grader pulled by two and sometimes three D-8 tractors. In a few instances where soil conditions were such that neither graders nor tractors could operate efficiently, draglines were used to excavate these main ditches.

A high water table and saturation of the subgrade often caused problems during airfield construction in New Guinea, especially at Embi, Merauke, Hollandia, and Cape Sansapor, where it was necessary to dig large ditches by dragline in order to drain the area under construction. At Jackson Drome at Port Moresby, underground springs in the runway area developed at the start of the rainy season, and it was necessary to install an elaborate system of drains.

In the development of airfields on new sites in forward areas, the initial consideration was to build an operational runway and limited aircraft dispersal facilities as quickly as possible using a minimum expenditure of time, labor, and materials. The runway and dispersal areas, which often covered 2,000 acres of dense jungle, were cleared without paying any attention to the minor topographical variations that were the determining factors in the correct design of area drainage. So, without the benefit of a topographic survey of the entire area and the lack of rainfall records, the construction of the immediately needed runway proceeded with only limited attention to proper drainage. Then, as the airfield was further developed, the required drainage structures were built and improved at the expense of increased total man hours of work to complete the airfield. This two-stage method of development satisfied the initial tactical requirements in a minimum of time, and also satisfied the engineer policy of obtaining the earliest completion of a facility to a usable condition with the later addition of improvements or modifications.

In a memorandum on 7 June 1944, Maj.Gen. Hugh Casey summed up the basics of drainage:

> "Every effort must be made in the earliest stages of construction to find the best potential drainage channels and to initiate as first priority effort the opening up and cleaning out of such drainage channels, side ditches, etc., to permit easy runoff and maximum possible draining of sub-base....

> "In almost every case, it is far easier to pull the water surface and ground water table down by a foot or more by adequate drainage than it is to haul in and place thousands to hundreds of thousands of cubic yards of selected materials to build up the roads, airdromes and hardstand areas on a soft and unstable foundation above the water table. Relatively little effort spent on such drainage relief will effect major savings not only in the overall initial construction, but also in subsequent maintenance.... The need for continuing drainage maintenance cannot be over stressed."

Runway Base Course: In the construction of airfields in the rain forests and coconut groves of New Guinea and nearby islands, it was usually necessary to strip off the one to two foot layer of humus which overlaid the relatively firm subsoil. After removal of the humus, the base courses for runways, taxiways, and hardstands were constructed of local materials, usually mixtures of sand, clay, and gravel. In those locations where relatively soft coral was available, it was used in preference to any other material. Where coral or suitable bank gravel was not available, it was often necessary to mix gravel from stream beds or beaches with sandy clay from bank sources. Beach and stream gravels were usually poorly graded, and consisted principally of large stones and sand without sufficient binder material. Therefore, rock crushers were used extensively to break down the large stones to form suitable gravel.

Runway Surfacing (Wearing Course): In the course of airfield development in forward areas, a runway could have a successive number of different types of surface. If the runway was located in a kunai grass area, the initial surface was usually sod, which was suitable for early use by transport aircraft. When improved for fighter use, the runway normally received a surface of locally procured coral or mixtures of sand, clay, and gravel. If surfacing materials were not available locally, the runway was covered with pierced steel plank landing mat. Later airfields were seldom improved beyond requirements for fighter aircraft, but when bomber operations were planned, a bitumen seal coat was normally added to runways surfaced with local materials.

In providing all-weather runways for the early operation in New Guinea, a base course of four to five inches of compacted decomposed shale, granite, or even clay-sand-gravel was first constructed. However, since the depth of the base course had to be varied according to the type of soil and bearing capacity of the subgrade, there were many cases where a much thicker base course was necessary. On the more developed type fields, this base course was primed with a 50% tar and 50% mixture of diesel oil and gasoline. On top of the priming came the following, in order: a thin layer of hot asphalt, a layer of 3/4 inch stone chips, another layer of hot asphalt, a layer of 5/8 inch stone chips, another layer of asphalt and, if available, screenings and dust. (On some runways two layers of asphalt were placed instead of three; one coarse layer and one fine layer.) Sometimes, this thin surface layer was picked up under the wheels of a heavy aircraft or from a propeller blast at take off, but these small damaged areas were easily repaired with patches. In this way, a great number of man-hours were saved in quarry and rock crusher work and in runway construction itself. Runways with this type of base course and surface, as at the Port Moresby dromes, Dobodura, and Nadzab, were in maximum operation under heaviest load and tropical rainfall conditions for more than 18 months without requiring excessive maintenance.

Marston Mat or Pierced Steel Planking (PSP) was used on many runways in the SWPA with outstanding results. PSP was invented by Gerald Greulich of the Pittsburgh Steel Co. for the AAC in 1941. Its name, Marston, was derived from the location of its first field test during maneuvers in November 1941 at Marston, NC. Each piece was 10 feet long, either 15 or 18 inches wide, and a quarter inch thick. Each plank was pierced with holes to save weight. The steel plank section weighed 66.2 pounds, but the later aluminum plank weighed 32.5 pounds, and each was transported in compact bundles. When 60,000 were locked together they created an all-weather runway 5,000 feet long and 150 feet wide, and equaled the bearing weight of four inches of concrete (60,000 pounds). The planks were joined by sliding interlocking projections on one panel which fit into slots on the next. Simple, small pins locked the mats together and kept them in place. After damage by enemy bombs or heavy use the planks could be replaced with relative ease, and when an airfield was no longer needed the planks could be removed and transported to cover a runway elsewhere. PSP was manufactured by 29 plants across the US which produced 180,000,000 square feet weighing 477,000 tons; enough to build 240 runways measuring 5,000 by 150 feet. PSP was best laid over stabilized subgrade, thus eliminating the need to transport and lay thousands of tons of base materials and then more tons of sand, concrete or asphalt. A 5,000 by 150 foot runway could be finished in 175 hours by 100 unskilled laborers. After the surface was prepared, a crew of 75 laborers could lay and secure PSP at one foot per minute, laying four planks across the 150 foot wide future runway in five minutes. PSP continued in use during the Korean and Vietnam Wars, and pieces of PSP can still be found in use in the Pacific by the locals for fences, foot bridges, etc.

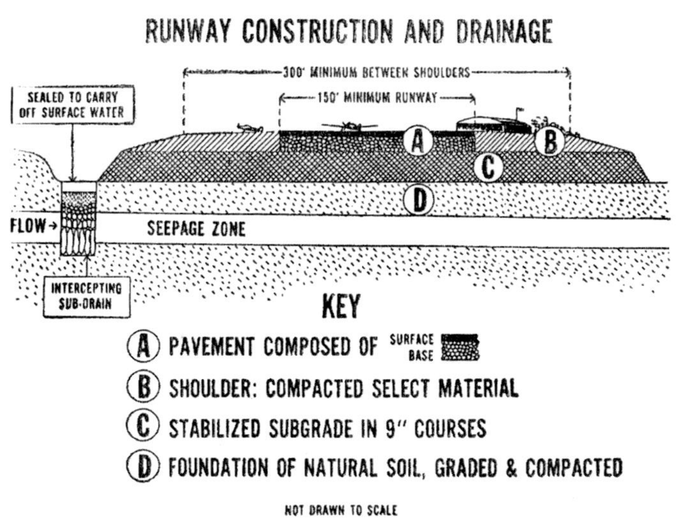

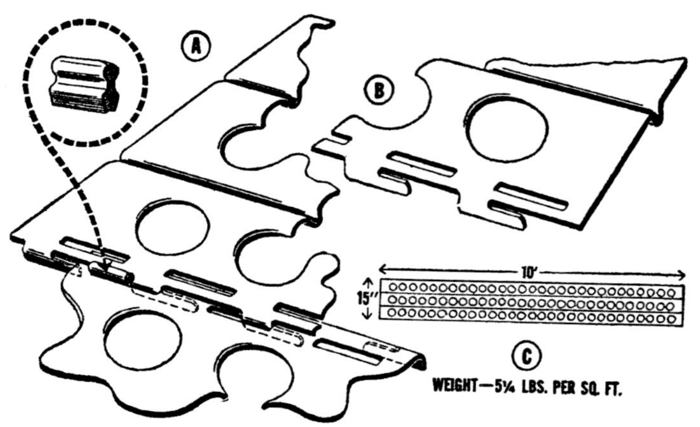

PIERCED PLANK LANDING MAT SHOWING:—A—MANNER OF JOINING WITH LOCKING SPRING CLIP;—B—DETAIL OF BAYONET HOOK JOINT;—C—COMPLETE PLANK

Straightening **PSP** for reuse. (AAF)

It was necessary to have a well-compacted subgrade, and usually a layer of some sort of surfacing material under the mat. Mat could be used over creek sand-gravel surfacing material which, because of lack of a binder, would not otherwise furnish a satisfactory surface. Landing mat was also placed on beach sand subgrades under which were only two inches of coral or other similar material. At Lingayen Drome, on the shores of Lingayen Gulf, PSP was placed on a compacted beach sand subgrade with only palm leaf thatch or woven bamboo mats between the landing mat and the subgrade. This surfacing performed very satisfactorily for approximately two months of the critical operational period under continuous operation by fighter and medium bomber aircraft. The surfacing material placed under the mat and the palm leaf thatch and bamboo served mainly to prevent an incohesive subgrade from working up through the holes in the mat and to prevent excessive dust. At Gurney Drome, Milne Bay, when imminent Japanese landings created an urgent tactical need for maximum speed in runway construction, the mat was placed directly on a subgrade that was not thoroughly consolidated and drained. After heavy rains mud oozed through holes in the mat and, due to the slippery condition, several aircraft skidded on landing and were slightly damaged. In an attempt to correct this condition, the mat was rolled back and the base treated with bitumen.

Repairing damaged **PSP** on #4 Strip at Hollandia. (AAF)

Gen. Hugh **Casey** supervising the laying of PSP

PSP was not only used for runways but also for taxiways as seen here at Tadji. (AAF)

PSP was relatively easy to install and was held in place by pins. (AAF)

As the Allies advanced along the coast of Netherlands New Guinea, coral deposits became more available and were easily quarried. The coral placed on the runway was rolled, sprinkled, scraped, and then rolled through several cycles until a dense hard concrete-like surface was achieved. However, on Cape Sansapor and Morotai Island the coral deposits were too hard, and much time was lost in search of usable deposits or in locating substitutes. At Tacloban Drome, Leyte, the hydraulic pipeline dredge was employed to pump sand from the adjacent bay in order to supplement the inadequate quantity of coral quarried ashore.

The runway surfaces generally withstood traffic with only occasional minor failures. There were two main causes for these failures: the poor choice of fill or surfacing materials and improper drainage, along with the inadequate repair of bomb craters. When construction work was started at Port Moresby in 1942 and the airfields there were under daily Japanese air attack, the bomb craters were filled by bulldozing the displaced material into the crater and compacting the filled crater with sheepsfoot rollers. Craters refilled by this method were found to settle under traffic, and it became necessary to clear and square up each crater, to backfill it with rock, tamping and compacting as the backfilling process went along, and then to resurface it.

Taxiways, Dispersals, Hardstands, and Revetments: The construction of taxiways and dispersed hardstands at airfields in forward areas required far more construction work than that required in the preparation of the runways. Usually a separate dispersal area was provided for each aircraft to be based at an airfield with the initial requirements satisfied on the basis of one heavy bomber, two medium bombers, or three fighter aircraft for each dispersal area. It was necessary that all dispersals be connected to runways by a system of all-weather taxiways. In order to reduce the engineer effort required on such construction, the width of taxiways to fighter and medium bomber dispersals was reduced from 50 feet to 40 feet, while the normal 50 foot width was used only where heavy bombers were to be dispersed.

Dispersals were located along the taxiways in such a way that the centers were spaced a minimum of 300 feet apart. In addition, these centers were placed 110 feet from the center line of the taxiway for use by fighters and 120 feet for bombers. During early New Guinea operations, circular dispersals were constructed with a diameter of 60 feet for fighters, 80 feet for medium bombers, and 100 feet for heavy bombers. In early 1944, plans were issued by GHQ, SWPA, for standard dispersals: Types 1 and 2. The Type 1 Dispersal, with the diameter increased to 80 feet, accommodated a fighter or medium bomber, while a Type 2 heavy bomber dispersal diameter remained at 100 feet, but the minimum distance between centers was increased to 450 feet.

Construction of taxiways and dispersed hardstands was similar to that of runways. During the war hardstands were often referred to as "hardstandings." Humus, if present, was stripped off, and a base of locally obtained material was prepared. Surfacing was the minimum required to eliminate dust and reduce maintenance. It usually consisted of a thin layer of crushed rock or gravel bound by asphalt emulsion or cutback.

The word "revetment" is used to denote any form of sheltering wall or bank, either above or partially below ground. Such protection was employed in Australia and New Guinea during early operations and prior to the development of air superiority to safeguard dispersed aircraft against enemy bomb blasts and splinters. They were usually constructed of earth and timber, but occasionally of sandbags, coconut logs, and earth-filled oil drums. The standard earth-fill revetment was semicircular, and its size varied with the type of aircraft it was intended to protect. For fighters, the fill was eight feet high and the inside bottom edge was 45 feet from the center point of the dispersed hardstand. For bombers the earth fill was 14 feet high, while the distance from the center point of the hardstand to the

As the Allies advanced along the coast of Netherlands New Guinea, **coral deposits** became more available and were easily quarried. The harder coral was dynamited while softer coral could be bulldozed and then crushed for use. (AAF)

P-39D. (41FS) sitting in a 14 foot high **bomber revetment**. (AAF)

P-47 protected by a standard 8 foot high **fighter revetment**. (AAF)

Hangers were also built for aircraft repair and maintenance and storage of weather vulnerable supplies. (AAF)

inside bottom edge was 50 feet for medium bombers and 75 feet for heavy bombers. Earth revetments never received more than an intermediate priority on early airfield construction projects. By July 1943 their construction was given a low priority on a revised priority list, and after October 1943, due to the large construction program and the improved situation in the air war (i.e. fewer enemy bombing attacks), revetments were omitted as a "calculated risk." Hangars were constructed for aircraft maintenance and supply storage.

Soil Stabilization and Dust Control: The gravel and dust swirled into the air by propellers damaged aircraft structure and engines, and to minimize the damaging effect consideration was given to soil stabilization during early SWPA construction. Soil stabilization also improved the load bearing properties of a soil by mixing another material that reduced the water holding capacity of the soil and increased its plasticity. Among the admixtures tried were molasses, bitumen, and a mixture of cement and soil known as soil-cement, but the best treatment for dust control was the use of a light shot, which was approximately 0.2 gallon per square yard of cutback asphalt. This mixture was used in some cases on coral runways, which had a tendency to become dusty during dry weather. It was also used prior to laying pierced steel mat and on top of or through the mat. It served as an excellent dust palliative for the duration of the combat use of the facility.

Maintenance: Wherever bituminous surface courses were used, frequent daily maintenance was necessary, especially near the ends of the runways, where aircraft touched down, and at points on the taxiway where aircraft did considerable turning. These surface abrasions required immediate attention, since deeper wear required removal of the surface course and replacement with premixed bituminous patching material of preheated asphalt mixed with coral. In order to make these repairs efficiently, a centrally located premixed asphalt plant was built. Before making the patch, edges of the surface were trimmed vertically after the faulty portion of the surface was removed. The outline of the area to be patched was cut in straight lines parallel and perpendicular to the paved center line. Before placing the hot mix, vertical sides of the cut were painted with asphalt to promote bond between the old and new materials. The patching material was then evenly spread and leveled, and a fine, dry coral was sprinkled over the patched area. Immediately the surface patches were compacted to grade by rolling with a five to eight ton roller in a longitudinal direction, beginning at the outer edge of each patch and working toward the center, with each pass of the roller overlapping the previous one by one-half the width of the roller.

Air Base Sanitation and Medical Conditions

Each airbase camp had separate kitchens and mess halls for officers and enlisted men. Each kitchen was covered and screened, and had a cement floor and piped-in water. The food was supplied in sufficient quantity, but the quality and variety left much to be desired.

Dry garbage was burned in incinerators, and after incineration it was buried in deep pits, while cans were crushed and buried. Liquid waste was disposed of through grease traps and soakage pits.

Bitumen undersurface being applied at Gusap Airdrome. Bundles of PSP ready to be laid can be seen on left. (AAF)

Airfield Construction Gallery.

Removal of top soil when needed. (AAF)

Leveling and filling of runway area. (AAF)

Preparation of subsurface. (AAF)

Addition of gravel/ coral surface. (AAF)

Compacting for laying of PSP for aircraft use. (AAF)

The water supply was pumped in through a pipe system to a storage area where the water was precipitated and filtered. Drinking water was chlorinated, and was usually checked every one to two weeks by the Hygiene Section; cultures were done upon request by a mobile laboratory. The water system located on the Laloki River had a capacity of 25,000 gallons per hour. All showers were equipped with shower heads, cement floors, and duck boards. At times of excessive water use the showers were inoperable.

The wooden box type latrine was most commonly used, and the area around the holes was scrubbed daily with soap or a weak creosol solution. Sometimes gasoline drums were used and were frequently burned out daily.

Most of the medical problems were influenced by the climate and topography. The climate affected the efficiency of the personnel as shown by loss of weight and lack of energy and initiative, especially in the men who had been there for a year or more. Diarrhea was common, and the most annoying of the minor medical troubles, but various skin diseases afflicted about three quarters of the men at some time during their tour: dermatitis (skin rash, the most common), epidermophytosis (fungal skin infection), heat rash, fungus, furuncles (boils), and urticaria (hives). Lacerations and abrasions were common among mechanics and other ground crewmen, and could become infected if not treated properly.

Tropical Diseases

The frequent tropical rains and the surrounding jungle made Malaria the worst medical problem, followed by Dengue Fever and Scrub Typhus. Lectures on disease control were given at intervals, and each unit had an anti-Malaria/Dengue/Typhus control detail. All drainage ditches were treated with an oil solution once or twice weekly for mosquito control, and the high grass around the camps was cut frequently.

Malaria

Malaria is an infectious disease caused by the Plasmodium parasite, which infects the red blood cells and is characterized by cycles of chills, fever, pain, and sweating. Of the four species of Malaria, the most serious type is Plasmodium falciparum Malaria, which can be life-threatening. Malaria occurs in about 100 countries; approximately 40% of the world population is at risk for contracting Malaria. The life cycle of the Malaria parasite is complicated, and involves two hosts, humans and Anopheles Mosquitoes. The disease is transmitted to humans when an infected Anopheles Mosquito bites a person and injects the Malaria parasites (sporozoites) into the blood. The period between the mosquito bite and the onset of the Malarial illness is usually seven to 21 days. The symptoms characteristic of Malaria include flu-like illness with fever, chills, muscle aches, and headache. Some patients develop nausea, vomiting, cough, and diarrhea. Cycles of chills, fever, and sweating that repeat every one, two, or three days are typical. There can sometimes be vomiting, diarrhea, coughing, and yellowing (jaundice) of the skin and whites of the eyes due to destruction of red blood cells and liver cells.

For hundreds of years quinine was used in the prevention and treatment of Malaria. Quinine is found in the root, bark, and branches of cinchonas and other trees native to the Andes Mountains in South America.

In 1932 the chemists at the large German chemical company, I.G. Farben, synthesized quinine from coal tar, which they marketed under the name Atabrine. In the early 1930s Atabrine was introduced in the United States as a Winthrop Drug Co. product, but it was manufactured by Farben. Just before the bombing of Pearl Harbor, Winthrop severed its ties to the German company and increased production, then licensed the production process to other manufacturers without taking royalty fees. As a result, the US wartime production of Atabrine in 1944 reached 3.5 billion tablets. Atabrine was bitter and some of its side effects were headaches, nausea, and vomiting. There was a rumor that Atabrine was given to decrease the men's sex drive and could even make them sterile. Yet Atabrine was effective, but only if the troops could be made to take it. In an effort to ensure that the Atabrine was actually swallowed by the soldiers, medics or NCOs from the combat units stood at the head of mess lines to carefully watch the soldiers take their little yellow tablets.

Malaria reached epidemic proportions among American troops fighting the Japanese in the South Pacific and early in the war a campaign in the prevention of Malaria was initiated. To solve this problem quickly, concentrated anti-Malaria and mosquito research and operational control programs were developed and implemented. So along with the development of effective anti-Malaria drugs to replace quinine; new insecticides and more effective systems for delivering these insecticides were developed. German chemistry student, Othmer Zeidler, synthesized DDT in 1874 but the insecticidal property of DDT was not discovered until 1939 by Paul Muller in Switzerland (he would be awarded the Nobel Prize for Medicine in 1948). The company sent samples of the compound to the Orlando laboratories of the Department of Agriculture's Bureau of Entomology in October 1942 where it was demonstrated to be superior to other insecticides, especially as a larvicide for anopheline Malarial mosquitoes. Within a year it was being distributed in quantity to the services and the War Production Board launched a program to increase the supplies of DDT in December 1943, by granting A-1 priorities to four companies to expand their manufacturing facilities. Production, which had totaled only 153,000 pounds in 1943, increased to 10,000,000 pounds by the end of 1944, and by the end of the war had reached 36,000,000 pounds a year. The day before the Sansapor landings on 30 July 1944, DDT was sprayed to a depth of a mile inland. Kenney described the occasion, "The miracle insecticide had just recently arrived in the theater and we wanted to give it a real service test, for if it worked we had a requirement equal to that of any place in the world." On 15 September the DDT spraying procedure started at Sansapor was repeated at Sansapor while the landing operation was going on.

Dengue Fever

Dengue (pronounced DENG-gay) Fever is a disease caused by a family of viruses that are transmitted by mosquitoes. Dengue is prevalent throughout the tropics and subtropics being widespread in the South Pacific, Southeast Asia, the West Indies, India, and the Middle East. Nearly 40% of the world's population lives in an area endemic with dengue.

The virus is contracted from the bite of a striped Aedes Aegypti Mosquito that has previously bitten an infected person. The mosquito, that also carries Yellow Fever, thrives during rainy seasons but can breed in very small water-filled areas (i.e. discarded tires, ditches, etc.) year-round. One mosquito bite can cause the disease, particularly in people with low immunity levels. The virus is not contagious and cannot be spread directly from person to person as there must be a person-to-mosquito-to-another-person pathway.

After being bitten by a mosquito carrying the virus, the incubation period usually ranges from five to eight days before the signs and symptoms of Dengue appear. The presence of the "Dengue Triad" of fever, rash, and headache (and other pains) is particularly diagnostic of Dengue. The disease begins with a painful aching in the legs and joints, with chills, headache, and low backache. The victim's temperature quickly rises to as high as 104° F. The eyes become reddened and painful upon moving. A flushing or pale pink rash appears over the face and then disappears. Fever and other signs of Dengue last for two to four days, followed by rapid drop in temperature with profuse sweating. A period with normal temperature and a sense of well-being then occurs that lasts about a day followed by a second rapid rise in temperature. A characteristic rash appears along with the fever and spreads from the extremities to cover the entire body except the face and the palms and soles may be bright red and swollen.

Because Dengue is caused by a virus, there is no specific medicine or antibiotic to treat it. For typical Dengue, the treatment is purely concerned with relief of the symptoms. Typical dengue does not result in death and is fatal in less than 1% of cases. The acute phase of the illness with fever and muscle aches lasts about one to two weeks. Convalescence is accompanied by a feeling of weakness and full recovery often takes several weeks.

Scrub Typhus

Scrub typhus is transmitted by the bites of some infected species of mites ("chiggers") which are found in areas of heavy scrub vegetation. Scrub typhus is endemic to a part of the world known as the "tsutsugamushi triangle", which extends from northern Japan and far-eastern Russia in the north, to northern Australia in the south, and to Pakistan and Afghanistan in the west.

Scrub typhus is an infectious disease that is transmitted to humans from field mice and rats through the bite of mites that live on these animals. Humans acquire the disease when an infected mite bites them while feeding and the mite larvae attach themselves to the skin. The bite is often painless and unnoticed. The mite inoculates the parasite under the skin, and after an incubation period averaging 8 to 10 days the bacteria multiply at the inoculation site and form a small painless lesion/bump rising from the skin. At this time there is an abrupt onset of high fever (104-105°F), headache, malaise, transient skin rash, and muscle pain. The bite gradually enlarges and becomes a dark and crusted ulcer.

Without treatment, the fatality rate was as high as 40% but with the use of antibiotics, fatalities decreased to less than 2%. A solution was formulated which could impregnate clothing and act as a mite repellent and by burning off the grass the scrub typhus problem was greatly alleviated.

In November 1943, the airdrome at Dobodura was established near Embi Lake which was a beautiful clear lake and seen as an ideal campsite. However, the local natives would not go near the area saying it was taboo. At first the airmen thought that the lake was infested with crocodiles but after dynamiting the lake they found no reptiles. The taboo was determined ten days later when an epidemic of scrub typhus broke. Scrub typhus was also encountered around Nadzab, up the Markham Valley, and on Owi Island. During World War II, 18,000 cases were observed in Allied troops.

Dysentery

Throughout the ages armies have been plagued with dysentery and besides Malaria, dysentery in all its forms, was the most insidious disease dealt with in the SWPA. Since many newly arrived airmen seemed to be more vulnerable to dysentery, it was supposed, even by medical personnel, that that the change in diet and climate was responsible and not poor sanitation. The worst type of dysentery was Amoebic dysentery caused by a parasite called Entamoeba histolytica. The disease was spread when the cysts (eggs) from E histolytica contaminated surfaces, food, or water and were then brought into the mouth and ingested. The result was an intestinal illness associated with stomach pain and cramps, bloody, loose stools, nausea, fever, and weight loss. After awhile the men learned to live with the consequences of dysentery as part of the wartime experience.

2

Papuan Campaign Initial Operations

Papuan Campaign: Background

This campaign, referred to as the Papuan Campaign in AAF histories, was the culmination of the Japanese advance in the Pacific, and along with the decisive Guadalcanal Campaign, abruptly ended the previously unrelenting Japanese drive through the South and Southwest Pacific. After the Japanese landed at Buna on 21 July 1942, the Allied Air Forces repeatedly attacked enemy shipping and bases, successfully defended their own bases, transported troops, equipment, and supplies, provided direct support for ground troops, and finally established air superiority over Papua, which was a significant factor in achieving victory in January 1943. The campaign was conducted with limited resources and in an unfamiliar territory, causing Gen. MacArthur to remark on 24 January 1943 that: "The outstanding military lesson of this campaign was the continuous calculated application of air power, inherent in the potentialities or every component of the air forces, employed in the meet intimate tactical and logistical union with ground troops."

Because of the complexity of previous events, a brief reveiw is needed to clarify and set the stage for the Papuan Campaign. The Japanese advance through the South and Southwest Pacific was overshadowed by their initial successes in the Central Pacific with the occupation of Tarawa and Makin, in the Gilbert Islands, on 9 December 1941. The Japanese then overran the Bismarck Archipelago and Rabaul, New Britain, on 23 January 1942 with 17,000 to 20,000 troops supported by an estimated 140 bombers and fighters. Rabaul possessed two airfields and Simpson Harbor, which was large enough to provide anchorage for a substantial naval force. The capture of New Ireland and New Britain gave the Japanese bases to commence a two-pronged attack into the Solomon Islands and against New Guinea. By 4 April Buka, Bougainville, Sohana, and Faisi in the Solomons had been captured. A month later Allied Air Forces were attempting to stop a Japanese fleet headed for Tulagi, in the Solomons, which was captured during the first week of May. This southeastward enemy advance threatened to cut the shipping and air supply lines between Australia and America, and also threatened the northeastern coast of Australia. Meanwhile, the capture of New Britain placed the Japanese within easy bombing distance of New Guinea. Lae and Salamaua, located on the Huon Gulf of the northeastern New Guinea coast, had undergone air raids as early as mid-January. The small Australian garrisons at Lae and Salamaua were overrun on 8 March, and Finschhafen fell two days later. By May 1942, the Japanese advance brought them to within 200 air miles of Port Moresby, which was the major Allied port in New Guinea and whose possession was crucial to both combatants.

A turning point came on 4-8 May 1942, during the Battle of the Coral Sea, when a Japanese naval attack to land troops on New Guinea was repulsed. During the summer it became obvious that New Guinea would become the focus of the quickly developing Pacific war, and that the Allied strategy would be to secure the narrow overland Kokoda Track leading northward from Port Moresby to capture Buna, the site of potential airstrips at the end of the Track.

In order to mount an offensive in New Guinea, the Allies faced many topographical deterrents to military operations. Dominating the whole of southeastern New Guinea were the Owen Stanley Mountains and their connecting and radiating foothills and steep ridges that ran down the central spine of the island. The area was cut by many rivers and creeks which drained the upper areas into the swampy coastal lowlands. The coastal forests were verdant and often impassable foliage extending inland, and were often broken up by tropical grasslands made up of broad-bladed kunai and the shorter kangaroo grasses. The lower slopes of the Owen Stanleys and their connecting ridges consisted of tropical rain forest rising to about 5,000 feet forming canopies of vegetation covered with thorny vines, while above 5,000 feet heavy rainfall produced dense bamboo and pine mountain forests.

These topographical obstacles prevented rapid movement in an area where transportation facilities were generally lacking. There were no railroads or roads connecting the main towns and administrative centers, and where possible transportation was by boat. Any overland movement from Port Moresby to Buna was dependent upon a network of native tracks which usually became little more than muddy ruts after frequent rainstorms. Thus, military movement in New Guinea would be chiefly dependent upon seaborne or airborne transport. Important towns and government stations at Kokoda and Buna, and at Lae, Salamaua, and Wau possessed all-weather airstrips, while patches of kunai grasslands could be easily converted into temporary landing strips.

In summer 1942, the tropical Australian military outpost of Port Moresby became the focus of both the Allies and Japanese. The town was situated on a narrow coastal plain, and was protected from most seaward approaches by dangerous coral reefs. It possessed the only harbor in eastern New Guinea large enough to shelter a sizable naval fleet. While Port Moresby was not located in jungle, the roads leading from the town ran only a few miles along the coast before they were interrupted by mangrove and swamps. The barren hills immediately north of the town soon became dense rain forest that led into the Owen Stanley Range, over which several tracks led to other regions of New Guinea. Engineers and soldiers improved the roads leading to nearby airfields that were either under construction or were being improved, and by November seven airfields were regularly used by the Allied bombers, fighters, and transports.

On 18 April 1942, Gen. Douglas MacArthur assumed the Allied command in the Southwest Pacific Theater. His command consisted of the Allied Land Forces commanded by Gen. Sir Thomas Blamey; the Allied Naval Forces under USN V.Adm. Herbert Leary; the US Army Forces in Australia under Brig.Gen. Richard Marshall; and the Allied Air Forces under Lt.Gen. George Brett. Though these forces were small, plans had been made for the recapture of Buna and were coordinated with a larger plan for the future capture of Rabaul. The complicated structure of the Allied command made planning and execution of operations difficult, as the war in the Pacific had been acknowledged as the primary responsibility of the United States. The original directive regarding SWPA gave the Joint Chiefs of Staff "jurisdiction over all matters pertaining to operational strategy" as distinguished from strategic policy, which was the province of Combined Chiefs of Staff. The Pacific War Council was to consider the requests of Australia, New Zealand, and the Combined Chiefs of Staff. While the chain of command appeared to be well and clearly established, there were several problems. MacArthur's command included the Australian Army, Navy, and Air Force, so he had to contend with the Australian War Cabinet, and had to consider the effect of his policies on Australian politics. The organization of the Allied Air Forces also was a problem. The most experienced American air units in Australia had been transferred from the remnants of the earlier Far East Air Force in the Philippines, and although this organization had been redesignated the Fifth Air Force on 5 February 1942, it is important to point out that this redesignation did not authorize a change of assignment. Through the spring and summer of 1942, the Fifth Air Force per se existed only on paper, and technically it had not been moved from the Philippine Islands. It would not be until September 1942 that American air units in Australia were organized into a separate air force. Meanwhile, from 18 April to 4 August, until Maj.Gen. George Kenney assumed command, these units continued as a part of the Allied Air Forces, commanded by Gen. Brett.

When the original organization of air units in the Southwest Pacific was contemplated, the Australians were able to supply the communications and headquarters personnel which the Americans could not, so an Allied Air Force incorporating both American and Australian units had seemed to be the plausible solution. Consequently, the Australians continued to have the principal control over air organization and operations until fall 1942. In the spring and early summer, control of air operations had been the responsibility of two of the five Australian defense area commands. Air Commodore G.C. Bladen of the Northwestern Area and Air Commodore Frank Lucas, with headquarters at Townsville and advanced headquarters at Port Moresby, directed the operations in these two major areas. Americans subordinate to these Australians were Brig.Gen.Albert Sneed at Darwin and Brig.Gen. Martin Scanlon at Townsville, controlling Air Commands Number 1 and Number 2, respectively. These Air Commands had been established by Brett to further control operations in two widely separated areas. This system gave rise to conflicting areas of authority, and when questions arose they were complicated by uncertainty as to who had the final decision. Contradictory orders were often issued, and squadron commanders necessarily used wide discretion in their operational decisions.

The resolution of these command problems depended partially on a final decision regarding the composition of the Allied Air Forces; whether it was to be comprised primarily of American or Australian units. The Americans considered the SWPA as secondary to their commitment to the "Europe First" priority. The Australians, faced with the threat of invasion, began an ambitious program to provide for at least 30 squadrons by 24 August; as many as 45 squadrons by the end of 1942; and then more than 70 at some unstipulated later date. However, this plan existed mainly on paper, and by August only three Australian squadrons were equipped with P-40s, and the majority of the RAAF pilots still were equipped with Hudsons, Wirraways, Walruses, PBYs, and an assortment of aging transports. Both the replacement of these obsolete aircraft and the implementation of the expansion program depended largely upon the aid of the United States.

On 31 June 1942 American air units in Australia consisted of 1,602 officers and 18,116 enlisted men. On paper there were two heavy, two medium, and one light bombardment groups, three fighter groups, two transport squadrons, and one photo squadron. On 1 May three fighter groups were reported to be 100% complete with a 50% reserve, and by July two squadrons of the 35th Group, equipped with P-39s and P-400s, were moved north to Port Moresby. The 8th Group had withdrawn its P-39s to Australia, while the P-40s of the 49th continued to be mainly active in the defense of Darwin.

Preparations for the Guadalcanal Campaign acutely curtailed the delivery of men and aircraft to Australia and New Guinea. The Japanese stepped up their New Guinea offensive in the summer of 1942 in the direction of Port Moresby against a desperate holding action by Australian infantry and Allied air power that was restricted by shortages of personnel and equipment. The goal of American fighter units was to defend Port Moresby as best as possible in the situation, and to take part in limited escort and ground support missions. But as the Guadalcanal Campaign progressed, the role of the Allied ground forces and air units became more and more important, for the approaches to Australia had to be held or the costly campaign in the Solomons would have been lost.

Once the Papuan Campaign began, the existing balance between American and Australian air units was to be maintained, as American production lines could supply aircraft to no more than the number of American units already in Australia plus to 27 RAAF squadrons. If the RAAF wanted aircraft for more than 27 squadrons then American units would be transferred to another theater and leave their equipment to supply the RAAF. The Combined Chiefs of Staff were to make this decision, but they asked MacArthur to make this choice, and he supported the decision to equip only 27 RAAF squadrons, with three more to be equipped with British Spitfires by 1 April 1943.

Combat losses, widespread sickness, and battle fatigue became serious problems in veteran units that had served in the Philippines and Java, and the question of replacements arose. There also was the need in the United States to return experienced combat pilots for training purposes, or to form the nucleus for new units. However, the impasse of the AAF High Command in 1942 was to balance the urgent need for pilots in combat theaters with the requirement that those to be sent to these theaters were adequately trained.

In one group of 29 US fighter pilot replacements arriving in August, only four had flown P-35s or P-36s, and the remaining 25 had not progressed beyond flying the AT-6 trainer. To train them in the combat aircraft available in Australia and give them additional gunnery training was estimated to require two months. Also, there was the requisite of learning the idiosyncrasies of the climate and topography of northern Australia and the Australian system of communications.

Maintenance was an overwhelming problem for the US Army Air Services under Maj.Gen. Rush Lincoln, as the SWPA was over 7,000 miles from its major source of supply in the United States. The Pacific supply line was threatened by enemy attack and shipping space was limited, as transports were prioritized for the Atlantic supply run to England, and so were destroyer escorts for convoys. Often aircraft which left the States fully equipped arrived without navigation and other equipment which were "borrowed" at bases along the ferry route. Once the aircraft arrived in Australia, a shortage of spare parts and trained mechanics, poor landing fields, the inadequate Australian transportation system, unreliable weather, long distances, and interminable combat made it difficult to keep even as many as 50% of available aircraft in service. A wastage factor of 20% had been established but was soon found to be conservative, mainly due to the lack of trained maintenance units. In July 1942 there were six air base and two air depot groups to maintain the widely scattered AAF units. This wide dispersion of combat units required a larger number of maintenance organizations, and on 15 July three additional air base groups and three additional air depot groups were requested. At this time, the demands of other theaters was too great and the requests for these additional service units were refused.

Until summer 1942, adequate tool and repair shops were mostly unavailable in Australia, and private companies did much of the work until military facilities for maintenance and repair improved by fall 1942. However, the lack of spare parts continued to be a problem. For example, the lack of bearings for Allison engines grounded many American fighters. While the bearings were requisitioned in August, none were available for shipment until 11 October, at which time all 14 main bearings needed changing in five out of six Allison engines in Australia, and nearly 200 engines were waiting for overhaul.

April 1942

25 April 1942: 8FG/35PS: To Port Moresby

The arrival of the 8FG at Port Moresby in late April signaled the beginning of the air portion of the Papuan Campaign, which was to end on 23 January 1943. The naval portion of this Campaign would begin and virtually end with the Battle of the Coral Sea (4-8 May), while the land portion would begin with the Japanese effort to capture Port Moresby when enemy troops landed at Buna, Gona, and Sananananda in July 1942. Initially, the Allies were able to offer only meager air and ground opposition to the enemy forces that pressed southward through Papua, but the Allies were building their strength in Australia.

After their arrival in Australia, the 8PG began a rigorous combat training program which was cut short on 25 April when the young pilots of the two squadrons were dispatched from Townsville to defend Port Moresby. After first AAC Ace and hero Lt.Col. Boyd "Buzz" Wagner was named as the new American Fighter Director in Australia, he wanted to get AAC units into combat ASAP and rushed the 8FG's P-39s to New Guinea, since the Australian 75th Squadron was decimated at Moresby.

On 25 April 1942, 15 pilots of the 35PS took off from Woodstock for the Cairns stopover to Port Moresby, while three officers and 72 men were flown there by flying boat. The 15 pilots flying to Cairns, led by Capt. George Greene and including Lieutenants Casey, Campbell, Chivers, Egan, Erickson, Hall, Hooker, Jacobs, Long, McGovern, Morris, Nowlin, Quandt, and Ward, landed at 0930 in clear weather. It had rained about half an hour earlier and the runway was very muddy, but all pilots landed safely. For the next leg from Cairns to Horn Island, Greene separated his pilots into two flights. He led "A" Flight first with James Egan, Norman Morris, and Gerald Quandt as Element Leaders, followed by Charles Campbell leading "B" Flight, with Irving Erickson and Jefford Hooker as Element Leaders. The weather between Cairns and Horn Island was reported as good, with broken and scattered clouds and light rain showers trending towards clearing. In the vicinity of Cape Grenville, the two flights ran into a solid storm front and tried to find a way through. After a while the pilots were running low on fuel and were still 125 miles from Horn Island and 270 miles to a turn around destination at Cooktown, which was out of range. Greene decided to try for Horn Island, and as he approached Cape York the visibility became somewhat better. After he passed over the Cape the rain stopped and the clouds were scattered and broken. Finally, over Horn Island it was clear and Greene and his Wingman, John Casey, landed safely, but the remainder of the flight was not seen. The other members of the flight turned back and made successful landings, including Lieutenants Nowlin, Morris, and Quandt, while John Jacobs made a wheels up landing. Jack Hall and John Long were missing and later declared KIFA. Hooker and Erickson led their other "B" Flight pilots down safely as they turned back toward Cooktown.

Of the 41 P-39s that left Brisbane, only 26 fighters, 13 from each squadron, landed at 7 Mile Airdrome outside of Port Moresby from Woodstock; the others were lost in crashes in route. Among the pilots of the 35PS who arrived at 7 Mile with Wagner were Lts. Arthur Andres, David Campbell, John Casey, Edward Durand, Irving Erickson, Frederick Featherstone, David Greene, John Jacobs, Jefford Hooker, Thomas Jennison, Leonard Marks, David McGovern, and Robert Wilde. Among the pilots arriving from the 36PS were Lts. Patrick Armstrong, John Barley, William Bennett, James Bevlock, Paul Brown, Charles Chapman, Elmer Ghram, Robert Harringer, Joseph Lovett, John Mainwaring, Donald McGee, Louis Meng, and Charles Schwimmer.

28 April 1942: 8PG

At 1100, the 8PG experienced their first enemy attack on 7 Mile Drome when eight bombers and nine fighters dropped 22 bombs. One bomb landed on the end of the runway, but relatively little damage was done. Seven Australian 75 Squadron P-40s intercepted and one Australian pilot was missing with another wounded after the raid. During a break in the weather, 35PS pilots Lieutenants Arthur Andres, Edward Durand, Fred Featherstone, and Thomas Jemison landed at 7 Mile Drome from Woodstock, along with several other unnamed pilots of the 35th and 36th Squadrons to reinforce 7 Mile Drome.

29 April 1942: 8PG

At 1130 Japanese bombers flew over 7 Mile Drome, but during the 45 minute attack they only succeeded in dropping most of their bombs onto the nearby hills; however, the personnel on the ground were kept in their slit trenches with several anti-personnel bombs and strafing. No interceptors were sent up, and an Australian Hudson bomber and P-40 were damaged on the ground.

30 April 1942: 8PG/35PS: First Air Battle over New Guinea

During the morning Col. Boyd Wagner led 26 more P-39s to Port Moresby to conduct a mission over Salamaua. With so many P-39s packed on the 7 Mile Drome, any enemy air reconnaissance would not only predict Wagner's upcoming operations, but presented enemy bombers and fighters a valuable and vulnerable target. The American camp had been located far from the flight line because of the probability of being strafed and bombed at any time by Japanese fighters that would roar down John's Gully on the deck. There was a rumor that Wagner was preparing the first offensive P-39 raid without orders from Gen. George Brett, who had assumed command of all Allied Air Forces in the theater on 20 April and still was not organized to coordinate a mission.

Emmett "Dusty" Rhoades, Commander of the Advance Echelon of the 8PG in New Guinea, met Wagner on the field as he landed. The impatient Wagner wanted to get off on the mission as soon as possible, but the P-39s needed to be serviced and refueled and have drop tanks installed. Wagner was to lead the entire force of 14 P-39s with Capt. George Greene of the 35PS as Deputy Mission Leader. Other 35PS pilots included Lieutenants Andres, Campbell, Casey, Erickson, Featherstone, and Durand, while the 36PS pilots included Lieutenants Schwimmer, Brown, Bevlock, Meng, Ghram, and Bennett. To suppress Japanese air power that day, a mixed force of Australian and 20 AAC B-17s, B-25s, B-26s, and Hudsons attacked enemy airdromes in the Lae area.

The squadrons, equipped with drop tanks, took off at 1330, but one P-39 never got off the ground and Casey and Featherstone of the 35PS were forced to turn back with engine trouble, leaving 11 P-39s to attack Lae at 1437 in three (three plane) elements, plus two with each element in echelon right. The P-39s climbed to 20,000 feet to cross the Owen Stanley Mountains and then flew a 50 mile approach out over the Huon Gulf at a height of approximately 100 feet to avoid detection. At about 20 miles out, four Airacobras were sent ahead to engage any enemy aircraft patrolling over their airdrome. The enemy patrol was drawn off to the east and the other P-39s approached the field unopposed at 1437. They strafed two lines of 10 enemy bombers and fighters each, and then strafed buildings and supplies and ignited fuel dumps while encountering inaccurate ground and AA fire during the attack. The mission plan was then to proceed to Salamaua and repeat the process. The P-39s zoomed out over Lae Harbor and strafed three floatplanes anchored near the shore.

The Lae attack had been a complete surprise without any air interception or AA fire, and Wagner then led the P-39s over Salamaua, strafing installations, exploding a fuel dump, burning a supply dump, and strafing three camouflaged aircraft. At 1507, the P-39 formation began to pull away from the Salamaua area when a number of Zeros from Lae attacked the last four P-39s in formation. In the meantime more Zeros appeared, and it was estimated that there were 12 to 13 altogether. The four P-39s were hopelessly outnumbered, so the remaining seven P-39s turned back and a furious and now equal dogfight ensued. This fight continued down the coast for about 30 miles and back again.

Capt. George Greene saw a Zero on the tail of another P-39 and dove to the rescue. As the Zero went into a stall climb Greene fired two good bursts as his Airacobra went into a stall. 1Lt. David Campbell got some shots at two Zeros and damaged one, while 1Lt. Paul Brown of the 36PS heavily damaged a Zero for a probable. 1Lt. Irving Erickson also got a good passing shot at one for a probable. Wagner's score for the combat is somewhat ambiguous in the existing records. Officially (and by claims expert Fran Olynyk) he is credited with three Zeros, which would be his last to give him eight total for the war, although some records cite from one to three confirmed air victories. Louis Meng led James Bevlock into a diving starboard turn when Zeros broke into them and they continued their dive to evade the Japanese fighters. As they were headed north out to sea Meng and Bevlock made a climbing turn over the mountains into the clouds but the Zeros caught them. The two Airacobras were then engaged in a running fight, dodging in and out of the clouds, desperately trying to reach home. Meng lost Bevlock, but outran the Zeros and made it back to Port Moresby with virtually empty fuel tanks. The cost of the mission was heavy, as four P-39s were either shot down or crash landed on the way back to Port Moresby. Bevlock, Paul Brown, Arthur Andres, and Edwin Durand were missing when the rest of the squadron landed back at 7 Mile. Bevlock ran out of gas and crash landed on a beach, while Brown crash landed safely because of coolant loss. Both returned safely with the help of area natives; Bevlock returned on 2 May and Brown came back a few days later. When Brown arrived he had a Japanese pilot as his prisoner that the Australians had captured near where Brown force landed; they handed him to the American to take back to 7 Mile. Andres returned on 27 May after his P-39 had been damaged by AA fire and he force landed safely about 18 miles south of Buna. Durand was observed to land safely 20 miles south of Salamaua, but intelligence reported that he had been captured by the Japanese and executed. Later 17 Mile Drome was renamed in his honor.

May 1942

1 May 1942: 8PG/35PS/36PS

On 1 May, Airacobras of the 35FS and 36FS encountered their first interception over Port Moresby when seven Zeros strafed aircraft parked on 7 Mile Drome. As the Zeros climbed away they were intercepted by a mixed flight of five Airacobras from the two Squadrons.

1Lt. John Mainwaring and 2Lt. Patrick Armstrong took off just after 0600 to fly airfield cover over 7 Mile Drome in the lead element of the 36PS, followed by 2Lt. Donald McGee and his Wingman, who would have mechanical trouble and remained on the ground. The flight orbited the field for two hours and began to run low on fuel, then headed back to base. The field was partially covered with fog, and when Mainwaring attempted to land he destroyed his fighter's landing gear and blocked the runway. McGee had descended to 3,500 feet when the Controller radioed that Zeros were attacking the field. He saw a Zero making a strafing run across the revetment area, but McGee's fuel gauge showed only about 20 gallons remaining, which gave him barely 10 minutes flying time. Although low on fuel and having the double combat disadvantage of low speed and low altitude, McGee turned to attack the enemy pilot, who had not yet seen the P-39. As McGee went after the Zero he was joined by 1Lt. David Campbell of the 36PS, who followed him. McGee cut back on power to conserve fuel but could not catch the enemy fighter, which was now closing behind another P-39 taking off from the field. McGee fired off an aiming burst that missed to the right and then fired a second burst that passed under the still unsuspecting Zero pilot. The American's next burst hit the Zero's fuselage, and it rolled over to the left and exploded into the jungle as McGee passed overhead at 150 feet with Zeros firing on his tail and hitting his Airacobra. One round came through his canopy and shattered his sunglasses without harming him. McGee evaded, skidding over the treetops before the Japanese turned toward home, apparently also low on fuel. Campbell shot down a Zero and Armstrong damaged a Zero, as did two 36PS pilots: 1Lt. Irving Erickson, who damaged three, and a Lt. ?? Hooker, who claimed one damaged. As

Col. Boyd **Wagner** shot down three Zeros to give him eight total for his career. (AAF)

1Lt. Irving **Erickson** had problems finishing off attacking enemy fighters as he was credited with three damaged Zeros. (AAF)

McGee landed and taxied he ran out of gas, and as he got out of his fighter he inspected his damaged aircraft. He saw that it had been hit by two 20mm cannon shells in its tail, multiple machine gun bullets in its wings, and then the frightening hole in the canopy just behind his head. McGee's victory, the first for the 36PS, was easily confirmed, as the wreckage was found only about a mile from the strip. McGee's P-39 was badly damaged, and it and Mainwaring's Cobra, which had crash landed in the fog, were cannibalized and transformed into one operable fighter.

2 May 1942: 8PG/36FS/35FS

Early in the morning, seven P-39s of the 36PS intercepted a formation of nine bombers escorted by Zeros after they had dropped their bombs on 7 Mile Airdrome. 2Lts. Donald McGee and Charles Schwimmer hit two Zeros, which escaped as probables. Later these Zeros were reported to have crashed at Mount Victoria, but continued on the official tallies as probables.

Later in the morning, the Japanese sent another air raid over Moresby that was intercepted first by P-40s of the Australian 75th Squadron, which lost a Warhawk. Capt. Lewis Meng of the 36FS was leading a patrol of 12 Airacobras flying in one flight of seven and another of five fighters over Port Moresby when Controller, *Golden Voice*, called in a flight of Zeros approaching low over the northwest end of the runway. Meng dove into the area of the Japanese strafers and engaged them at 0750. One of the Zeros seemed to be breaking away from the fight, and Meng slid in from behind and below and fired one burst that caused the Zero to explode in flames as Meng passed over it. When Meng looked around to confirm his victory he saw 20mm shells passing over his port wing and made an immediate hard break to the left; he saw that he had lost his Wingman, who had his windshield covered with oil and had left early in the combat. Despite Zeros swarming everywhere Meng lost his pursuers in a dive and returned to 7 Mile without serious damage. Capt. John Mainwaring and 2Lt. Joseph Lovett of the 36PS both attacked Zeros head on. Mainwaring's prey fell away pouring black smoke, while Lovett's Zero dived steeply away toward the sea. Their two P-39s sustained moderate damage, one with cannon damage to its wings, and the other with its engine compartment hit by machine gun fire. Also for the 36PS, 2Lt. Charles Schwimmer sent a long burst into a Zero and 2Lt. William Bennett fired tracers behind the cockpit of another for victories. 1Lt. David McGovern claimed a Zero destroyed in a head on attack for the 35th Squadron's only victory of the day.

3 May 1942: 8PG/35PS/36PS

On 3 May, 12 bombers escorted by eight Zeros attacked 7 Mile Drome again, and 10 P-39s had enough warning to climb to 23,000 feet to attack the bombers before the Zeros could intervene. Three of the P-39s attacked the lead bomber of the formation, and 1Lt. David Campbell got there first and shot it down. 2Lts. William Bennett and John Barley of the 36PS attacked the #3 bomber on the lead bomber's port wing head on, and it fell from the formation with an engine on fire and Barley was credited with the victory. 2Lts. Charles Schwimmer and C.H. Chapman of the 36PS closely followed the first attack and fired on the #2 bomber on the leader's starboard wing, with Schwimmer getting the victory credit. Chapman attacked and destroyed another bomber. 1Lt. David Campbell of the 35PS had to evade the Zero escort to hit the lead bomber, which fell away with its engine burning. Schwimmer got on the tail of a Zero and claimed to have shot it down, but there was no eyewitness confirmation. None of the Zeros were shot down, but a number of bombers were streaming smoke as they left the area and undoubtedly didn't arrive back at their base. 2Lt. Joseph Lovett did not return to base, and when a search party was sent out to the crash site they only found one leg still in the boot. However, the Group received some good news when it was informed that Arthur Andres, who did not return from the Lae mission, was alive and returning to base.

1-4 May 1942:
8th Fighter Group Victors.

1Lt. David **Campbell** scored his first victory. (Zero) of four on 1 May and then added a bomber two days later. (AAF)

2Lt. Donald **McGee**. (36FS) got his first victory of five on the 1 May and then added a probable the next day. (AFAA)

4 May 1942: 8PG/35PS/36PS

The Japanese flew a bombing raid at 0925, when nine bombers escorted by Zeros were intercepted by seven P-39s that were orbiting on base patrol, instead of trying to scramble to climb and meet them. For once the Airacobras had the altitude and sun advantage when attacking. 2Lt. Robert Wilde (35PS) hit a Betty bomber, but had to dive away to shake two Zeros from his tail; later it was reported to have crashed at Mount Victoria and Wilde was variously reported with a victory or a probable in Squadron records. 2Lt. Harold Chivers was MIA, and 2Lt. Frederick Featherstone's engine failed and he was critically injured in the crash landing. These casualties were only the first mishaps in a day of combat that was to be the most costly of the war so far.

Twelve Airacobras of the 35th and 36th Squadrons took off in the fog and mist that hung over 7 Mile Drome during the early morning to strafe the airfield at Lae. The fighters climbed steadily to attempt to get out of the weather, but it deteriorated into torrential rains as they continued toward their target. Soon Capt. Robert Mainwaring and Lts. Donald McGee, Thomas Jemison, and ?? Toubuan returned early for the 36PS, but Lts. Donald Campbell, Irving Erickson, Victor Talbot, Andres, Jefford Hooker, Patrick Armstrong, and Charles Schwimmer continued on through the weather. Four P-39s penetrated the weather and reached the target, strafing the field, destroying a bomber, and damaging four others. After the mission Talbot, Hooker, Armstrong, and Schwimmer did not return; whether they became lost in the bad weather or over the target was never determined. 17 Mile Drome was named in Schwimmer's honor. At the end of this cheerless day a funeral service was held by the 36PS for Joseph Lovett, and the squadron was reminded that war was truly Hell when only his leg was available for burial.

May 1942: Wagner's Report on the P-39 in Combat

After these first two combats, Wagner forwarded a report to the Commanding General of the Allied Air Forces. The report not only recounted the details of the two enemy encounters, but also was the consensus of his pilots' reactions to their first combat and their conclusions regarding their aircraft and those of the Japanese. The report, entitled "Report on first action against Japanese by P-39 type airplane," dated 1 May 1942, to the Commanding General, USAFIA, Melbourne, Lt.Col. Boyd Wagner, listed the following conclusions formulated after the 30 April combat:

"1) Lack of armor plate rear protection for the engine and the resultant high vulnerability are the greatest disadvantages of the P-39 type airplane. All P-39s shot down were hit in the engine and the coolant system.

2) P-39F Hydraulic propellers throw oil making visibility forward very poor due to oily windshield. Attempts have been made to stop this oil leakage by installation of new type gaskets, but complete success has not resulted.

3) Armament.

a) All guns should have hydraulic gun chargers. Charging forces are too great except for .50 caliber fuselage guns for average pilot.

b) .50 caliber gun solenoids are too weak and frequently fail indicating either inferior equipment or faulty installation design.

4) Main landing gear tires are too small causing the plane to bog down very easily in soft ground or spongy runway. P-40 size tires have proved quite satisfactory,

5) Nose gear is too delicate to withstand normal operations on the type landing strips now in use. Many have been broken even while taxiing.

6) Radio installation is out of date. A single transmitter and receiver has been found to be insufficient in close up .operations where our frequencies are frequently and easily jammed. Radio installation in the Curtiss P-40E-1 is the most desirable. This installation provides for two transmitters and three receivers.

7) Only one belly tank is provided for each P-39 airplane. For missions over 100 miles from home airdrome, belly tanks should be used, be dropped in case of combat. It is estimated that at least five belly tanks should be provided with each airplane.

8) P-39 gives very poor performance above 18,000 feet. The hand wobble pump or emergency electric fuel pump must be used to maintain sufficient fuel pressure for good engine operation.

Generally speaking, the P-39 is an excellent anti-bombardment fighter at altitudes up to 18,000 feet. Above 18,000 feet performance is sluggish

The pre-war designed **P-39** was inferior to the P-40 and the Japanese Zero but was a rugged aircraft and could withstand a lot of punishment. (AAF)

and rate of climb very low. The 37mm cannon is an extremely desirable weapon but "bugs" are still being eliminated. Stoppages in the air are frequent and it is difficult to reload and recharge during combat because of the high loading and charging forces. Its effect against enemy aircraft in the two previously described missions was excellent.

Comparatively speaking in performance the P-39 airplane is believed to be about ten percent better in every respect than the P-40 airplane, except in maneuverability in which case the P-40 is slightly better.

Above statements are the consensuses of opinion of pilots participating in the above described combat missions.

Signed,

B.D. WAGNER Lt Col., Air Corps."

May 1942: 8FG: Change in Tactics

Although they could rarely put more than 20 aircraft into the air at one time, the Americans were making progress in gaining air superiority over Port Moresby. By this time Brig.Gen. Martin Scanlon, CO of Air Command No. 2, had moved to Port Moresby and modified the tactics of his fighter aircraft. Due to excessive losses experienced during early attacks, the P-39 strafing raids on Lae and Salamaua airdromes were canceled; considering the distance and the fighter's inadequate fuel capacity, bomber escort missions to these targets were also abandoned. Scanlon limited AAF fighter operations to patrols and interception of enemy attacks in the vicinity of Port Moresby. These combats reasserted that the P-39 definitely was not an interceptor, and a dogfight with a Zero was a losing proposition. Air warning usually was received too late for the slow climbing Airacobras to intercept enemy bombers before they had dropped their bombs, and if Zeros were escorting the American pilots had further problems. When confronted by the enemy escorts, all the American pilots could do was to turn into them and then quickly dive for the deck. So, the pilots of the 35th and 36th Fighter Squadrons bravely fought on with what they had.

4-8 May 1942: Battle of the Coral Sea - SWPA Implications

Meanwhile, on 4-8 May 1942 the Battle of the Coral Sea was fought in the waters to the southwest of the Solomon Islands and east of New Guinea, in what was to be the first of the Pacific War's sea battles fought by opposing aircraft carrier forces. The battle was the first naval engagement in history in which the participating ships never sighted or fired directly at each other. Instead, manned aircraft acted as the offensive artillery for the ships involved. The battle resulted from an intended Japanese amphibious operation to capture Port Moresby, located on New Guinea's southeastern coast. A Japanese air base there would have threatened northeastern Australia and supported their plans for further expansion into the South Pacific. Preliminary operations on 3-6 May and two days of active carrier combat on 7-8 May cost the US Navy one aircraft carrier (*Lexington*), a destroyer, and one very valuable fleet oiler, plus damage to the second carrier (*Yorktown*). Though the Japanese could claim a tactical victory in terms of ships sunk, it was an operational and strategic defeat for them and their first major setback on the great offensive they had begun five months earlier at Pearl Harbor. In the fighting, they lost the light carrier *Shoho*, a destroyer, and several smaller ships. The carrier *Shokaku* received serious bomb damage, and the carrier *Zuikaku's* air group was badly depleted. Most importantly, these two carriers were eliminated from the upcoming war-changing Midway Battle, where their presence may have been pivotal, as was the diversion of Japanese shipping to the Coral Sea.

Initially, the Allied Command in Australia was disappointed with the outcome of the Battle of the Coral Sea, fearing that the thwarted Japanese invasion was the precursor to a larger invasion of the Australian mainland and this setback to Japan was only temporary. The Japanese were forced to cancel their invasion of Port Moresby, whose garrison would most likely have been overwhelmed by the Japanese troops. The results of the battle also had a substantial effect on the strategic planning of both sides. Without a base in New Guinea the subsequent Allied advance, difficult though it was, would have been much more demanding. For the Japanese High Command, which focused on the tactical results, the battle was seen as only a temporary setback. The results of the battle confirmed the low opinion the Japanese held of America's fighting capability and supported their belief that future carrier operations against the US were assured of success.

Later in June, because of their disastrous carrier losses at Midway, the Japanese were unable to support another attempt to invade Port Moresby from the sea, forcing them to attempt to take Port Moresby by land. Japan began its land offensive towards Port Moresby along the Kokoda Track on 21 July from Buna and Gona. By then the Allies had reinforced New Guinea with additional troops, primarily Australian. These additional forces slowed, then eventually halted the Japanese advance towards Port Moresby by September 1942, and overcame an attempt by the Japanese to overpower an Allied base at Milne Bay.

In the meantime, the Allies sought to take advantage of their victories at Coral Sea and later Midway by seizing the strategic initiative from Japan. The Allies chose Tulagi and nearby Guadalcanal as the target of their first offensive. The failure of the Japanese to take Port Moresby and their defeat at Midway had the effect of exposing their base at Tulagi without effective protection from other Japanese bases (Tulagi was four hours flying time from Rabaul, the nearest large Japanese base).

5-6 May 1942: 8PS

For the next few days (5-6 May), the weather and the Battle of the Coral Sea gave all combatants a brief but welcome break for recuperation and reorganization. By the end of 4 May the 8th Pursuit Group, soon to be re-designated as the 8th Fighter Group, had experienced eight air raids in nine days. Nine pilots had been killed in action, and at least 14 P-39s were shot down in exchange for 13 Japanese aircraft. While the Battle of the Coral Sea ended in a tactical stalemate, it gave the Allies new hope and the Japanese temporarily lost momentum, which caused them to suspend their assault on Port Moresby. During these two days the 8FG ground crews were able to refurbish five additional fighters for combat.

May 1942: 8PG: Ground Crews

Day after day, the men of the 35th and 36th Squadrons provided combat air patrol over their bases and Port Moresby against an enemy that attacked in ever-increasing numbers. The pilots and ground crews of these units were plagued not only with inferior aircraft, but by primitive living conditions, poor food, and Malaria and Dengue Fever. Maintenance was performed under the most difficult conditions, with mechanics and armorers under the constant threat from strafing and bombing attacks. Spare parts were almost nonexistent, and badly damaged aircraft were cannibalized to keep the other Airacobras in service. That the ground crews were able to keep as many of the fighters operational as they did was indicative of their skill, ingenuity, and devotion to duty.

7 May 1942: 8PS/35PS

At 1000, about a dozen Zeros strafed 7 Mile Drome, destroying two B-25s waiting on the runway and killing and wounding their crews. Ten P-39s of the 35FS scrambled amid the gunfire and engaged a flight of four Zeros. 2Lt. James Egan followed a Zero in a vertical stall climb, and through skill or luck he was able to draw enough lead in the stall to fire a burst into the enemy fighter's belly and watched it crash into the jungle. No AAF losses were reported in the air combat, but 2Lt. Richard Nowlin, who had survived the 25 April bad weather debacle, was killed during a non-operational flight in a crash on a beach near Murdock Point, Australia.

8 May 1942: 8PG/35PS/36PS

The 35th and 36th Squadrons remained on alert throughout the morning, and 13 mixed Squadron P-39s (five from the 35FS; Captain George Greene and Lieutenants Egan, Erickson, Marks, and Jacobs, and others from the 36FS including Falletta, Yundt and Brown) intercepted about eight Zeros that were coming over 7 Mile Drome at about 1430.

35PS

Captain George Greene claimed one Zero for the 35th when he got on the tail of a Zero before it could climb away and shot off its entire empennage with his cannon. 2Lt. John Jacobs got on the tail of a Zero and got hits, but as he was concentrating on the kill his canopy was shattered by shells from a Zero that had slipped in on his tail. He skidded and then rolled sharply away from his pursuer, and although his engine and controls still functioned he was wounded and becoming woozy. His choices were either bail out of his fighter and treat his wounds on the ground and hope to be rescued or fly back to safety after the combat over 7 Mile Drome ended, possibly passing out from loss of blood and crashing. Jacobs chose the latter and flew 50 miles out to sea, waiting until the combat ended and he felt it was safe to land. After landing successfully, Jacobs had to be lifted out of his cockpit and carried to an ambulance. He was awarded the Purple Heart and later received the first Silver Star awarded to his squadron for risking his life to save his valuable fighter.

36PS

1Lt. Robert Yundt of the 36PS fired at a Zero that had made a shallow dive on his P-39 from the rear and overshot. His burst hit the fuselage of the enemy fighter before it disappeared into a cloud for a damaged claim. 1Lt. Charles Falletta dove from 20,000 feet onto the left rear of two Zeros at 6,000 feet. He disintegrated the tail of one unsuspecting fighter with one burst of cannon fire, but in the heat of battle Falletta's victory was not confirmed. The now alerted second Zero pilot dove away while Falletta turned on two more Zeros which evaded. 2Lt. Paul Brown was chasing a Zero when another dove on him from out of the sun. Brown quickly turned into the attack and fired damaging shots, but lost the Japanese fighter after the two fighters passed each other for a probable claim.

2Lt. James **Egan** shot down his first enemy aircraft of the war. (AAF)

9 May 1942: 8PG/36FS

The Japanese raids on Moresby's airdromes continued, and the outnumbered and outclassed Airacobras climbed to intercept, but due to late or non-existent air warning, their interception was often made after the enemy bombers dropped their bombs or not at all, as the bombers were out of range. The Americans continued to down a few enemy bombers and Zero escorts during each interception and managed to keep their own losses manageable.

At 0730, the Japanese sent a surprise attack by 16 Zeros on 7 Mile just after the base patrol landed. 1Lt. Grover Gholson was halfway down the runway

On 7 May 1942 about a dozen Zeros strafed 7 Mile Drome destroying two B-25s waiting on the runway; killing and wounding their crews but were intercepted by 10 P-39s of the 35FS. (AAF)

when the strafing Zeros hit his P-39. He jumped out of the cockpit and hid under a wing until his fighter began to burn. Two B-25s were also destroyed in the attack. While the 8FG suffered no casualties, a Crew Chief was killed and four other enlisted men injured from other units. Six 36FS P-39s did take off in time to engage the attacking Zeros, and Capt. Robert Harriger and 2Lt. William Bennett each claimed a Zero destroyed. Bennett's nose wheel collapsed when he landed at 3 Mile Drome. 2Lt. Donald McGee was shot at by his own AA over 7 Mile and was forced to crash land on Fisherman Island.

10 May 1942: 8PG/35PS

At 0730, five P-39s of the 35PS intercepted about 10 Zeros. 2Lt. John Casey made three ineffective passes at the Zeros, and 1Lt. Irving Erickson had similar results from a head on attack on another Zero. 1Lt. Leonard Marks had to make three passes at a Zero before its engine began to smoke heavily and the Zero fell off into a spin into the water. 1Lt. David McGovern got the other confirmed victory when the Zero he attacked was observed to go into an uncontrollable spin. 1Lt. Norman Morris' Flight was on patrol when he saw Zeros below his formation. He sent one element down to the right while he and his Wingman would take the two Zeros on his left. The two P-39s dove on the two Zeros, but the enemy pilots saw their attackers and separated. Morris immediately ordered his Wingman to attack the one on the right while he went after the one on the left. Morris built up diving speed, and just as he was about to fire the Zero pilot turned sharply to port and then went into a vertical climb. In his first combat, Morris tried to follow the nimble Zero in the beginning of a loop, but soon approached a stall while the Zero continued to climb and then turned to get on the P-39's tail. Morris had no choice but to try to outrun the Zero and dropped his fighter's nose to gain as much speed as possible. The Airacobra slowly increased its airspeed, but the Zero continued to come around into firing position. Morris skidded to the left and right to disrupt the enemy pilot's aim, but enemy tracers passed close by his cockpit. Morris needed to keep the Japanese pilot from hitting him until the better diving momentum of his heavy fighter propelled him out of range. Morris continued his skidding dive until he neared the water and was forced to pull up, which would expose him to the Zero's guns. Just as he reached the water, Morris looked back to see the Japanese pilot turning away, perhaps out of ammunition or afraid to hit the water!

1Lt. Leonard **Marks** was credited with the first of his two victories. (AAF)

11 May 1942: 8PG

The Japanese made another surprise attack on 7 Mile when 18-20 Japanese bombers attacked the strip around noon. Six 36PS P-39s suffered damage of varying degrees. Sgt. Russell Hutchins of the 36PS was working on his P-39 when he became the first enlisted man in the 8PG to be lost when he was killed instantly by a fragmentation bomb.

12 May 1942: 8PG/35PS

At 0745, the 35PS put up five P-39s that took off from 12 Mile just as about a dozen Zeros attacked. (The P-39s of the 35PS had transferred to the new 12 Mile Strip to ease the crowding on 7 Mile.) 2Lt Robert Wilde managed to shoot down a confirmed Zero and then shot down another which was not confirmed. But the Japanese soon got the upper hand in the air battle, as Wilde's fighter was last seen trailing heavy black smoke and plummeting into the jungle. He was listed as MIA until his body was recovered two months later. 2Lt. Alva Hawkins' fighter was also badly damaged, and he crash landed at Vari Island, northwest of Port Moresby, but he returned uninjured two days later. 1Lt. Charlie Falletta of the 36PS, who it seems took off with the four 35PS pilots, claimed another Zero. During the Japanese attack, Corp. John Lang noticed two Airacobras landing while the runways were being strafed and decided that the pilots would be killed. He quickly got into an ambulance and raced out to the flightline and picked up the two pilots to drive them to safety and was awarded the Silver Star for his bravery.

13 May 1942: 8PG/35FS/36PS

Six 35PS P-39s intercepted the same number of Zeros over Seven Mile just after noon, and were joined by two P-39s from the 36PS. Capt. Paul Brown and 2Lt. Elmer Ghram each were credited with an enemy fighter. 2Lt. Hervey Carpenter's was damaged, and he crash landed at Redscar Bay, northwest of Port Moresby, and returned to 12 Mile the next day.

2Lt. Elmer **Ghram** got his only victory of the war. (AAF)

14 May 1942: 8PG/36PS

The Japanese conducted a series of raids on Moresby from about 0745 until well into the afternoon. During the first attack, 11 P-39s of the 36PS met 15 Zeros that had just begun their run on 7 Mile when 1Lt. Paul Brown led five other P-39s on eight Zeros. Brown attacked the last Zero in the formation with a single burst and had to pull up sharply to avoid a collision. However, his fighter glanced off the Zero, severing part of its right elevator and vertical fin, and the enemy fighter fell off into the jungle. 36PS' 1Lt. James Bevlock's flight, including Harvey, Yundt, and Cook, with Falletta, Gholson, and Oxley of the 35PS joining in, made a quick diving attack that scattered a formation of Zeros, but their first attacks were ineffective. 1Lt. Harlock Harvey took shots at three different Zeros which climbed away from his P-39 to escape. Bevlock, Oxley, Cook and Falletta all hit Zeros with uncertain results and no credits. The two confirmed victories for this formation went to 1Lts. Grover Gholson and Robert Yundt. Gholson had fired at two Zeros, and the first went down with a smoking engine. Yundt attacked and shot down another Zero over the Drome which was witnessed by the ground crews.

1Lt. Grover **Gholson** got his first victory of five. (AFAA)

Mid-May 1942: P-400 Replacements

By mid-May the fighter units at Port Moresby began to receive not only replacement pilots, but replacement aircraft from Australia. The replacement fighters were Bell P-400s, which were basically P-39s originally built for England, but were taken over by the AAF after the United States entered the war. The primary difference between the two was that instead of mounting a 37mm cannon in the nose, the P-400 mounted a 20mm cannon.

17 May 1942: 8PG/36PS

A three day pause in the combat took place after 14 May, but on 17 May 8PG P-39s flew a reconnaissance and strafing raid running from Zaka to Buden Bay in the Salamaua area.

However, the cloud ceiling was down to 50 feet, preventing strafing and any beneficial observation. Later that day, nine Zeros tried to strafe 7 Mile but were intercepted by a formation of 36PS fighters led by Capt. Paul Brown. No Zeros were claimed, although 2Lt. Bland damaged a Zero; he was hit and forced to ditch in shallow water at Bootless Inlet.

17 May 1942: 35PG/40PS

1Lt. Harvey Scandrett of the 40PS scored the 35th Pursuit Group's first victory on 17 May when he downed a Zero over Seven Mile Airdrome.

18 May 1942: 8PG/35FS/36FS

The Japanese increased the intensity of their attacks, and the Moresby defenders claimed more Japanese attackers in their combat reports. During the early morning of 18 May, the Japanese mounted their largest bombing mission to date against Port Moresby when two formations of 18 and 16 bombers escorted by 15 Zeros crossed the Owen Stanley Range. One formation of bombers headed for 7 Mile Airdrome, while the other's target was 12 Mile Airdrome. Fortunately, the air warning system gave the Airacobras time to get into the air and climb to intercept the bombers before they began their bombing run.

36FS

Three pilots of the 36th Squadron made the first attack on the enemy formation from above, at 20,000 feet. 1Lt. Paul Brown attacked the second and third bombers of the first formation and hit the first target numerous times, causing it to burst into flames, trailing a long stream of smoke as it dove toward the ground. 1Lt. James Bevlock (36PS) downed a Zero, and several other pilots hit their targets which were not seen to go down. The P-39s managed to break up the attack against 7 Mile Airdrome and the bombs fell to the north of the target. The Zeros then bounced the P-39s, and the Americans were forced away from the bombers. During this battle, 2Lt. Charles Chapman was last seen diving down to attack the bomber formation and other pilots reported a midair collision, as it was thought that Chapman had crashed into one of the Japanese bombers. The Japanese bombers attacking 12 Mile Airdrome were able to drop their bombs and two aircraft and its runway were damaged, along with some fuel supplies set on fire. A P-39 with one of its doors missing landed on 7 Mile, and when the ground crews reached the fighter they saw the cockpit was covered with blood and 2Lt. ?? Beeson, who was attached to the group from the 40PS, was pulled out with his entire right arm muscle shot away from the shoulder. The 35PS had to return to 7 Mile Drome because of the damage at their home base.

1Lt. Harvey **Scandrett** scored the 35th Pursuit Group's first victory and his only victory of the war. (AAF)

1Lt. Paul **Brown** ended his scoring with his third victory and two probables. (AAF)

1Lt. James **Bevlock** claimed his only victory of the war. (AAF)

35FS

1Lt. Thomas Dabney of the 35th Squadron was credited with one of the bombers.

20 May 1942: 35PG/39PS (Attached to 8PG)

During this time the first contingent of pilots from the 39PS of the 35PG began operations attached to the 35PS of the 8PG. Eleven P-39s encountered an equal number of Zeros at 0900 over Waigani. 1Lts. Thomas Lynch, Frank Adkins, and ?? Carey of the attached 39PS joined eight pilots of the 35PS; they had the altitude advantage and dove out of the sun for only one good pass. Lynch quickly shot down two and then wisely left the dangerous area. Because Lynch had to leave the area without actually seeing the

1Lts. Thomas **Lynch** was credited with the first two of his 20 victories. (AAF)

Zeros crash he claimed only two probables. The Zeros recovered and shot down Carey, who was able to bail out and was rescued, but was too badly injured to resume combat missions. Several days later a patrol found the wreckage of two Zeros near the area, and Lynch was officially credited with the first two of 20 victories over his illustrious career.

23 May 1942: 8PG/35PS

Wau Village was in a strategic position only about 10 minutes flying time from Salamaua to the northeast. It had a small, but important airstrip that was defended in a tight perimeter by a small Australian force that depended on air drops for supply. On the 23rd, the 35PS was sent on two missions to escort transports to Wau, but poor weather prevented the transports from getting through with their cargo.

26 May 1942: 8PG/35PS/36PS/39PS

On the 26th, seven 35PS P-39s, the four attached 39FS pilots, and several others from the 36th took off at 1000 to escort five C-47 transports carrying supplies and men to Wau. When the formation approached Mt. Lawson at 1115 they were attacked by 16 Zeros. 1Lt. Thomas Lynch of the 39PS turned into a head on attack on two of the Zeros and shot one down in flames, then went on to damage the other Zero, but it was not seen to crash. 39th Squadron mates 1Lts. Eugene Wahl and Frank Adkins each shot down a Zero. The Zero would be Adkins' third and last victory in the Pacific after previously scoring two Zero victories with the 17PS over Java (18 and 21 February). He contracted Dengue Fever and was evacuated to the US, eventually becoming the CO of the 313FS of the 50FG in the ETO. Lt.Col. Adkins shot down two Me-109s on 26 August 1944 to become an ace. He was killed in a flying accident in Texas on 23 February 1945. 2Lt. Clifton Troxell of the 35PS dove after another Zero and got hits on its tail, and it dove into the ground. After ferrying a P-39 to Moresby, 2Lt. Arthur Schultz of the 80PS was assigned to temporary duty to the 35PS, and while there took part in this fateful mission and was listed as MIA. The Americans claimed four Japanese fighters for the loss of one P-39 and the transports completed their mission without interference.

2Lt. Clifton **Troxell** got his first of five victories. (AFAA)

1Lt. Eugene **Wahl** got his only victory. (AAF)

27 May 1942: 8PG/35PS/36PS

Relief was on the way but the war weary pilots of the 35th and 36th Squadrons were in combat until the very end of their combat tour in New Guinea, as the enemy continued to attack Port Moresby day after day. During the mid-morning two formations of Zeros, one flight of nine and another of six, were called in by the Controller with enough warning to scramble 20 P-39s of the 35PS and 36PS off 7 Mile Drome. Capt. John Pitchford of 8PG Headquarters was on base and joined 35PS pilots Hervey Carpenter, Leonard Marks, Thomas Jemison, Alva Hawkins, and Clifton Troxell. Pitchford, Carpenter, and Jemison all fired at Zeros without result. Troxell hit a Zero that got away for a probable. Marks hit a Zero and claimed a probable that was later upgraded to a victory when the wreckage was discovered. 2Lt. Hawkins was MIA south of Rigo after the mission. Capt. Charlie Falletta, leading a small 36PS flight, claimed a victory, while 1Lt. John Barley damaged a Zero. Capt. ?? Hornsby of the 36PS made a crash landing on a beach and was rescued unhurt.

1Lt. Leonard **Marks** claimed his second of two victories. (AAF)

Capt. Charlie **Falletta** got his second of two victories to go with two probables and a damaged claim. (AAF)

28 May 1942: 8PG/35PS/36PS

At 0750, 20 Zeros were reported heading toward 7 Mile, and the 35PS sent up six P-39s, while the 36PS was able to scramble 12 P-39s and a single P-40. The six 36PS P-39s intercepted the Zeros over the field and dived to the attack. 2Lt. James Egan's guns tore off large pieces of a Zero's tail and the fighter fell off in a dive into the ground northwest of Port Moresby. 1Lt. Irving Erickson fired on a Zero that took a number of hits and rolled over toward the ground trailing thick smoke. He looked around and saw another Zero closing on his tail and pushed the stick forward and went into a life-saving dive. 1Lt. Leonard Marks dove on Zeros, but when he looked back to clear his tail before he fired, he saw several Zeros and had to dive away at full power. 35PS Lieutenants Miller, Selzer, and Connell fired at Zeros, but were driven off by other Japanese fighters before they could press their attacks. The other 35PS formation was bounced by Zeros and Arthur Andres' fighter was hit; when he tried to bail out his parachute caught on

LEFT:
2Lt. James **Egan** got his second and last victory. (AAF)

RIGHT:
1Lt. Irving **Erickson** got his only victory after damaging three Zeros on 1 May. (AAF)

a jagged edge and opened too soon, dragging him out of the cockpit and injuring his leg, but he landed safely and returned to base the same day for the second time after being shot down.

The 36PS encountered a formation of Zeros and 2Lt. Donald McGee chased after them, descending over a mile from 21,000 feet, where he fired on one that was on the tail of another P-39. He then dropped to 4,000 feet, where he saw another Zero circling a gravely damaged Airacobra that was in a flat glide on the way to the ground. His bullets hit the wing of the circling Zero, which dove away. The pilot of the crippled P-39 was Capt. ?? Exum, who safely bailed out of his smoking fighter at 500 feet.

29 May 1942: 8PG/35PS/36PS

Eighteen veteran Zero pilots approached 7 Mile on a fighter sweep during the morning, intent on engaging American fighters. The alarm was given at 0930, and four P-39s of the 35PS that were already on patrol headed toward the sea when they met a formation of Zeros. 2Lt. Clifton Troxell sent a Zero spiraling into a low overcast and then fired at a second fighter that escaped after sustaining some damage. 1Lt. David Campbell also shot down a Zero for the 35PS before the enemy formation flew off.

Eleven P-39s and two P-400s of the 36PS scrambled to intercept Zeros reported heading north, which may have been the same Zeros intercepted previously by the 35PS. The Airacobras climbed south toward Rigo to gain an altitude advantage before returning over 7 Mile Drome to patrol at around 23,000 feet. When no enemy aircraft were sighted eight 36PS Airacobras turned back south, where they found two dogfights underway. 2Lt. Donald McGee dove steeply from about 24,000 feet to 18,000 feet to attack a Zero's Wingman from below and behind. The Zero saw him and began to pull up, but McGee's speed was so high that he was able to close directly behind his target for a no deflection volley that caused the Zero to roll over and start to burn. McGee had to make a quick turn to starboard to avoid a collision and was soon dead astern the lead Zero; he fired at about 75 yards, also sending it rolling down trailing flames. Later, McGee saw a B-17 flying along the coast with a Zero on its tail. He closed for a firing pass on the Zero, but decided that the enemy was too close to the bomber and he might it the Flying Fort with his fire, so he turned away. Surprisingly, the Zero also turned away from the bomber and went after McGee, who had trouble evading this veteran Japanese pilot and was only saved by diving into heavy clouds. When McGee finally emerged from the clouds he saw that he was heading directly toward the jungle at high speed and had to struggle to level out.

2Lt. Clifton **Troxell** got his second victory in three days. (AFAA)

1Lt. David **Campbell** shot down his first of four Japanese aircraft. (AAF)

2Lt. Donald **McGee** claimed victories #2 and #3. (AFAA)

1Lt. Grover Gholson was flying as a Wingman and heard his leader call out Zeros below to port. At the time, the two were about 2,000 feet above the other 36PS fighters being attacked, and dropped their belly tanks and rolled over to the combat below. Gholson followed his leader in an attack on two Zeros hovering above the combat. One Zero saw them and went into a fast climb as Gholson put a heavy burst of fire into its wing. Gholson pulled the stick back, trying to keep up with the Zero's climbing turn. Finally, at 25,000 feet Gholson's P-39 ran out of power and began shaking into a stall, then started spinning downward out of control among numerous Zeros. As Gholson regained control he saw tracers fly by his cockpit, with some piercing his wings and fuselage. Soon smoke and flames entered his cockpit, and he went out of the Airacobra's car door head first. Unfortunately the door latch caught his shirt, causing a severe cut under his right arm. Gholson was at 15,000 feet when he bailed out, and he delayed opening his parachute so that the Zeros would not shoot him in his parachute. After falling through the cloud layer he pulled the rip cord and landed on a grassy hill in the mountains about 20 miles from the coast. Once on the ground he treated his burned arms and deep cut by cutting bandages from his parachute. After walking for three hours he met natives who took him to their primitive village. For the next two days and nights the natives led Gholson 50 miles to a rubber plantation owned by an Australian, who tended the now very ill downed American pilot. It was not until 23 June that Gholson was well enough to take a boat to Port Moresby and return to his squadron.

June 1942

1 June 1942: 8PG/35PS/36PS

No alerts were sounded on 30-31 May, but 12 Mile Drome was drenched by rain, and its runways were so muddy that fighters were unable to take off. On the 31st, all serviceable aircraft took off from 12 Mile and were stationed on the overcrowded 7 Mile Drome to be scrambled in case of an attack. Fortunately, the next alert was sounded on 1 June, when 18 Betty bombers escorted by nine Zeros were sighted at 1100 on their way to bomb the Port Moresby docks. The Zeros were piloted by very experienced pilots who would become some of the top Japanese aces: Hiroyoshi Nishizawa, the top Japanese ace on the war with 86+ victories; and Saburo Sakai, the top Japanese ace to survive the war with 60+ victories. The 35th and 36th Squadrons finished their combat tours by sending up 24 P-39s and P-400s to engage 18 enemy bombers escorted by 12 Zeros.

36PS

More than 30 P-39s and P-400s intercepted the Japanese force at 1150, with the 36PS making the first contact. Many of its pilots reported damaged or destroyed enemy aircraft, but after the claims were analyzed only 1Lt. William Bennett received a confirmed Betty bomber victory. Bennett was the first into the battle, attacking a bomber in a steep, diving turn, and pumping cannon shots into the center of the bomber, killing or wounding the crew. A second cannon burst set the bomber's port engine on fire, and the bomber rolled over on its back and dove earthward. Capt. Charlie Falletta was credited with two smoking Bettys as probables; 1Lt. James Bevlock a Betty probable; and 2Lts. Merle Else and Carl Taylor a bomber probable each. 2Lt. Thomas Rooney was KIA, and was most likely shot down by one of the Japanese aces.

4-2-22<cap>Bennett

35PS

The 35PS attacked the enemy bombers next. 2Lt. John Casey was the only 35PS pilot granted a claim when his cannon hits caused a bomber to fly away smoking. Casey was turned away from his attack by the bomber's defensive fire and did not see the bomber crash, and so was awarded a probable. 1Lt. Irving Erickson also made a diving beam attack on a bomber and damaged its fuselage. Lieutenants Gibson, Egan, Quandt, and Wiecks reported firing at enemy bombers with varying but unconfirmed results. Two 35PS pilots were listed as MIA: Lts. William Hosford and Gentry Plunkett. Plunkett became separated from his flight at 15,000 and three Zeros got on his tail and shot him down. Plunkett pulled his rip cord at once, and he fell unconscious from the opening shock. When he came to he was sitting on the ground uninjured with his parachute hanging in the trees. He began to walk through the jungle toward Port Moresby. After two days he came upon a river that would lead him to the coast quicker. While he was swimming in one of the streams he felt a sharp pain in his shoulder and saw a huge crocodile. He quickly dived to escape, but the jaws snapped on his shoulder again. The panic stricken pilot struggled to take his knife from its sheath and stabbed the crocodile until it decided it had had enough. Bleeding profusely, the exhausted Plunkett struggled to shore, where natives tended his wounds and guided him back to Port Moresby.

Since their arrival in the defense of Port Moresby in late April, the 35th and 36th Squadrons were credited with downing 45 enemy aircraft for the loss of 26 Airacobras, but 13 of the pilots had been recovered. Later in the war this record would not be considered exceptional, but in early 1942, when inexperienced pilots were being fed into combat under the most difficult conditions, flying inferior aircraft, it was exceptional. The sheer courage and tenacity of these pilots had prevented the most important outpost and airdromes that the Allies possessed in New Guinea from being bombed into oblivion.

4 June 1942: Pursuit Designation Change

On 4 June 1942, the designations Pursuit Group and Pursuit Squadron were officially changed to Fighter Group and Fighter Squadron, even though several units had done so previously.

June 1942: 35th Fighter Group Arrives in New Guinea

The original 35FG was constituted as the 35th Pursuit Group (Interceptor) on 22 December 1939, and activated at Moffett Field, CA, on 1 February 1940 under Maj. O.R. Strickland. It consisted of the 18th, 20th, 21st, and 34th Pursuit Squadrons. The Group was moved piecemeal to the Philippines, with the 18th, 20th and 34th transferred there in November 1941. Headquarters and the newly joined 70th Squadron sailed for Manila on 5 December 1941, but returned to the US when war broke and it flew several patrols. Headquarters and 70PS were then sent to Australia on 12 January 1942, where the 70th was sent to Fiji at the end of January 1942. On 15 January the 18th, 20th and 34th Squadrons were relieved from the Group, as they were fighting in the Philippines. Meanwhile, three other squadrons still in the US were assigned to the 35PG from the 31PG: the skeleton 39th, 40th, and 41st Pursuit Squadrons, which were to be filled out by replacements. The 39th and 40th squadrons had been constituted on 22 December 1939 and activated on 1 February 1940, and were assigned to the 31st Pursuit Group under Lt.Col. Harold George and stationed at Selfridge Field, MI. The 41st was activated on 1 February 1940 and assigned to the 14th Air Base Squadron at Bolling Field, Washington, DC.

The 39th Pursuit Squadron was formed from members of the 94th Pursuit Squadron, the famed WWI Lafayette Escadrille, and its first CO was Capt. Allen Stringer. It was initially equipped with the P-36, but in spring 1942 transitioned to the Bell P-39 Airacobra. The 40PS under its first CO, Capt. John Eagan, was initially equipped with the P-35, which were later supplemented with P-40s in September 1940; by July 1942 the Squadron was fully equipped with P-39s. On 19 October 1940, the 41PS joined the 39FS and 40PS with the 31PG at Selfridge and came under the command of

Capt. Paul Wurtsmith, who would later lead the Fifth Fighter Command.

After maneuvers, the three squadrons arrived at Bear Field, Fort Wayne, IN, during early December 1941. At Pearl Harbor the three squadrons were alerted for overseas duty and left for Paine Field, Everett, WA, the next day. From 14 December 1941 to 21 January 1942, the Group underwent intensive preparations for overseas duty and flew daily patrols over the West Coast shipping lanes. The squadrons of the 31PS received separate orders for overseas deployment, and so all that remained of the 31PS was the HQ and HQ Squadron. The skeletal squadrons established an unnumbered Provisional Group HQ and left for San Francisco. It was anticipated that the squadrons could be built up to full operational strength there, but no replacements were available and the bare bones, paper squadrons sailed from San Francisco on 31 January 1942 aboard the USAT *Ancon*.

The Group arrived at Brisbane, Australia, on 25 February 1942, but was sent to Melbourne on 3 March, and traveled by train from there to Ballarat, where they were living with Australian families until they were sent to Mount Gambier on 16 March. In the interim, on 12 March Lt.Col. Richard Legg was named the CO of the 31FS in Australia and commanded about 30 pilots, 80 enlisted men, and 20 aircraft. The Japanese were rapidly advancing through the Southwest Pacific and placed Australia in impending danger of invasion. In case the Japanese captured northern Australia, the Allied strategy was to form a defensive line at Brisbane. This position would put the Japanese in bombing range of Sydney and Melbourne, so it was decided to move fighter units near these cities to protect them. Lt.Col. Legg received orders to move his squadrons from Mount Gambier to Sydney, and in late March he arrived at Mascot Airdrome, near Sydney, with his staff and procured three airfields in the area to begin training. By 5 April the Squadrons were in Sydney with approximately 90 enlisted men and 30 pilots who had never flown the P-400 version of the Bell P-39, which had been uncrated and assembled at Brisbane. During April and May the Group's ranks were filled by officers and enlisted men from the US. On 15 May the 31st Pursuit Group was redesignated as the 35th Pursuit Group, with Legg continuing as its CO.

On 8 April the 39th and 40th Pursuit Squadrons were ordered to immediately fly to Townsville, Queensland, to embark on an intensive regimen of flight and gunnery training. During the six week training period the 39th was based at Woodstock and the 40th at Antil Plains. In early June the 35th Pursuit Group was redesignated as the 35th Fighter Group, and all its Pursuit Squadrons became Fighter Squadrons.

After training, two 35FG Fighter Squadrons were sent to Port Moresby on 2 June, where they relieved two squadrons which had been in combat there. They were to operate as individual squadrons under the direct command of Lt.Col. Boyd "Buzz" Wagner, who was the "Director of Pursuit." The Group's two squadrons operated from different bases: the 39FS from Schimmer (14 Mile Drome) and the 40FS from Barry (12 Mile Drome).

Meanwhile, the 41FS and HQ Staff had been left behind in southern Australia and would not leave for Port Moresby until 20 July. Legg and the 41st arrived in New Guinea on 22 July to become the first complete AAF Group in New Guinea, but only for about a week, as the 39th and 40th would be relieved by the 41st and 80th Fighter Squadrons. The 41FS would operate from Jackson (7 Mile Drome), while the 35th Fighter Control Squadron operated from the 4th Fighter Sector and was located next to the HQ Squadron between Jackson and Schimmer Dromes.

4-6 June 1942: The Battle of Midway - SWPA Implications

On 4 June, thousands of miles to the northeast of New Guinea, off Midway Island, a crucial sea battle was about to begin which would be the turning point in the war in the Pacific, and would have a huge effect on future operations in the Southwest Pacific. The bulk of the Japanese fleet, under the command of Adm. Yamamoto, architect of the Pearl Harbor attack, was heading toward Midway Island. The Americans, using broken Japanese codes, rushed the carriers *Yorktown*, *Enterprise*, and *Hornet* from the Southwest Pacific to intercept a surprised Yamamoto. The main battle took place early on the morning of 4 June, when AAF, USN, and USMC bombers attacked units of the Japanese fleet. The operations of the land-based aircraft were unsuccessful, as neither the high altitude bombers nor the torpedo bombers were able to get any hits. Incoming Japanese planes bombed Midway and severely damaged installations there while their Zero escorts decimated the obsolete defending USMC F2A Brewster Buffalo fighters. However, after the disastrously unsuccessful attack by USN torpedo bombers from the USN carriers, USN dive bombers followed and destroyed the four Japanese carriers. The *Kaga* was sunk, and the *Soryu* was heavily damaged and later sunk by an American submarine. The *Hiryu* tried to escape, but was caught by dive bombers from the *Enterprise* and *Hornet* late in the afternoon and was damaged so badly that it sunk the next day. The fourth Japanese carrier, the *Akaga*, had retired from the battle, burning and so badly damaged that it sunk the next day. The carrier *Yorktown* was badly damaged by Japanese bombers and was left dead in the water, but was still afloat the next morning, so tow lines were attached and the ship was to be towed to Pearl Harbor. However, late that afternoon a Japanese submarine slipped through the USN destroyer escort screen and hit the carrier with a torpedo which further damaged the *Yorktown*, causing it to sink the next day. The Battle of Midway was a disaster for the Japanese, who lost four large fleet carriers, a heavy cruiser, nearly 300 aircraft, and 3,500 men. It was a crushing defeat from which the Japanese never recovered, and changed the course of the ware in every theater, including the SWPA.

3 June 1942: 8FG R&R

Some 8FG personnel began to rotate back to Townsville on 2 June, but many men feared that the Japanese would begin raiding Port Moresby before they could be relieved by the 39FS and 40FS, which were beginning to arrive when two 39FS aircraft flew in on 3 June. For the next months, and at intervals for the rest of the war, pilots and crews of the Fifth Air Force would spend rest and recovery leave generally in Australia.

5 June 1942: Former 17PS Java Veteran KIFA

1Lt. Dwight Muckley, who had survived the perilous days over Java, died in the crash of a B-26 in which he was a passenger near Amberley Field, Australia.

2Lt. Richard **Suehr** got his first of five victories. (AFAA)

9 June 1942: 35FG/39FS/40FS

Once the 35th Fighter Group and its 39th and 40th Squadrons moved to Port Moresby in June they did not seen much combat. 1Lt. Harvey Scandrett had scored the Group's first victory on 17 May when he downed a Zero over Seven Mile Airdrome. There was a flurry of action at 1040 on 9 June when P-400s of the 39th FS flew to defend a flight of B-26s that were returning from a mission over Lae when they encountered a group of Zeros over Morobe, New Guinea. 1Lts. Donald Green, Curran Jones, and John Price and 2Lts. Robert McMahon and Richard Suehr each claimed an enemy fighter. On the mission, 1Lt. Gene Wahl had been shot down while returning to Moresby. Wahl trekked six days through the dense jungles around Moresby before he was rescued and returned to base. After this day there were few encounters with the Japanese in the air for the 35FG.

16-18 June 1942: 35FG/39FS/40FS

On 16 June, 1Lt. Bernard Oliver of the 40FS and 1Lt. Francis Royal of the 39FS each shot down a Zero over Maima, and the next day 1Lt. Charles Sullivan (39FS) downed a bomber approaching Moresby. On the 18th, 1Lt. Donald Green got two Zeros over Rorona, near Port Moresby. It would not be until 4 July that another 35FG claim would be made.

July 1942: 80th Fighter Squadron Joins the 8FG

The 35th and 36th Fighter Squadrons had a relationship in the 8FG because they had been together almost from the time the Group was formed in the States, and then during combat from Port Moresby. However, the 80th was formed after Pearl Harbor, and had no combat experience when it arrived at the beginning of July 1942. It had been constituted as the 80th Pursuit Squadron (Interceptor) on 6 January 1942 and activated four days later at Mitchel Field, NY, under its first CO, 1Lt. Philip Greasley. It left Mitchel on 26 January and arrived at Brisbane, Australia, on 6 March, then transferred to Lowood for training on 28 March and then to Petrie on 10 May. It was redesignated as the 80th Fighter Squadron on 15 May 1942. During training in Australia the Squadron lost 2Lt. Tevis Ferguson (at Brisbane) and 1Lt. Joseph Cole (at Petrie) to flying accidents on 15 July. On 20 July it arrived at Port Moresby combat ready, with 17 additional pilots; among them would be the Squadron's leading aces: 2Lt. Edward Cragg and 2Lt. Marion F. Kirby. The 80th, arriving late and flying without the Group's other two squadrons, which were on R&R, considered itself part of the 8FG on paper only.

Clockwise from top left:

1Lt. Donald **Green** got the first of his two total victories. (AAF)

1Lt. William **Bennett's** victory was the last of two for him. (AAF)

2Lt. Robert **McMahon** scored his only victory in a P-400. (AAF)

Two photos of 1Lt. Curran **Jones** claimed his first of five victories. (AFAA)

1Lt. Clarence **Wilmarth** shot down his first of three victories. (AAF)

LEFT: 1Lt. Charles **Sullivan** also got his first of five victories. (AFAA)
RIGHT: 1Lt. Donald **Green** claimed victories #2 and #3 of three. (AAF)

4 July 1942: 35FG/39FS
1Lt. George Parker shot down a Zero near 30 Mile Airdrome.

11 July 1942: 35FG/40FS
The pilots of the 40th Squadron had sufficient warning, and by using diving tactics to best advantage, managed to bring down four bombers by 1Lts. Chester Trout, Clarence Wilmarth, Philip Schriver, and 2Lt. Garth Cottam, and a Zero by 1Lt. Robert Shick.

22 July 1942: 35FG/39FS
The 35th Fighter Group's last victory until December 1942 would be on 22 July, when 2Lt. Ralph Martin shot down a seaplane off Gona. During this time the primary mission of the P-400s were to bomb and strafe enemy installations up and down the Papuan Peninsula. Port Moresby continued to be bombed, but by smaller numbers and at a lesser intensity than it had been during earlier months. During June and July the Port Moresby area was active, with new airfields being built and other installations being rapidly improved.

3

Buna-Kokoda: 21 July to 21 August 1942

The Japanese landing at Buna was not a surprise to the Allied Command, as aerial reconnaissance spotted a convoy near Rabaul on 19 July and then nearing Buna, off Cape Ward Hunt, traveling south on the 21st. Thus, warned by reconnaissance, all Allied air reinforcements were put into the air to attack the beachhead. The 39FS and 40FS Squadrons of the 35FG were ready to return to Australia for rest, but they were pressed into service along with their replacements, the 41FS of the 35FG and the 80FS of the 8FG. All squadrons were based at Port Moresby and equipped with P-39s and P-400s. AAF bomber squadrons were brought up from Australia to stage through Port Moresby for their attacks on the Buna landings. Late in the afternoon of the landings, one B-17 and five B-26s succeeded in finding the Japanese force, and the B-26s dropped their 500 pound bombs from 6,000 to 7,000 feet and reported a direct hit on a transport.

21 July 1942: The Invasion of Buna

The Japanese chose to fight in the jungles of New Guinea, where it felt it had an advantage. But combat there favored the opponent with the ability to move supplies and build bases the fastest. So, although the Japanese initially had greater numbers of ground troops and equipment and trained air crews and aircraft, it was the Americans and Australians who had the logistical advantage. The short supply lines from Australia to Port Moresby allowed the ever-increasing amounts of men and materiel arriving from America to be delivered faster and more efficiently. The Japanese' first setback at the Battle of the Coral Sea, and later the debacle at Midway, unnerved the Japanese into desperate attempts to capture Port Moresby and then to isolate Australia. To do so, it became apparent to the Japanese that a new approach to Port Moresby was needed, since the route via the Louisiades was now blocked. Since their sea and air assaults had been unsuccessful, the Japanese decided on an overland attack across a passable sector of the Owen Stanleys Mountains from the Buna mission area. However, the Japanese did not realize how demanding in personnel and materiel this campaign would become, even without the upcoming American invasion of Guadalcanal in the critical Solomon Islands. Nonetheless, in early June the specter of Japanese invincibility lingered in the minds of the Allies.

On 21 July 1942, at 1440, a Japanese float plane strafed the mission station at Buna, and soon the Japanese convoy arrived off Gona and began disembarking troops. The convoy had eluded the Allied air forces, which were attacking another enemy convoy off Salamaua. The landing was unopposed, as most of the Australian troops were engaged either at Milne Bay or harassing the enemy's rear at Salamaua. After landing, the Japanese moved inland and began to prepare roads and supply lines for their Port Moresby invasion force. Buna was only a short 20 minute flying time across the Owen Stanleys to Port Moresby.

22 July 1942

Early during the morning of 22 July, the AAF and RAAF carried out a series of three heavy bomber, five medium bomber, and five fighter attacks on the convoy and landing barges, as well as on supplies and personnel already on the beaches. Aircraft from all four fighter squadrons took off from 7 Mile and 14 Mile Airdromes to provide cover for B-25s and B-26s on their bomb runs. The Japanese did not send up any fighters, but heavy Anti-Aircraft and machine gun fire kept the bombers at high altitudes, causing the ten B-17s, five B-25s, and six B-26s to be unsuccessful in their attacks on the convoy. Meanwhile, other medium bombers destroyed a number of the enemy barges and killed many troops, after which the fighters strafed the area. RAAF P-40s and AAF P-39s and P-400s dive bombed barges and supply concentrations and fired thousands of rounds of machine gun and light cannon ammunition into enemy positions.

By the afternoon of the 22nd, the Japanese landed between 4,000 and 5,000 troops and established a base protected by Anti-Aircraft, which had shot down one RAAF P-40 and an AAF P-400, in addition to damaging a heavy and medium bomber. The Japanese could now use Buna as a base for more powerful air attacks, and were in a position to begin the difficult overland drive through the Owen Stanley Mountain "Gap" to threaten Port Moresby. Fortunately, during this period the air raids on Port Moresby would decrease and enemy opposition in the air was limited, allowing P-400s to strafe the onrushing Japanese troops with their heavy cannon and machine gun armament and act as escorts to the C-47s that were supplying the ground forces.

20-22 July 1943: 8FG: The 80FS Arrives in New Guinea

On 20 July, the first contingent of the 80FS, led by Squadron CO Capt. Philip Greasley, arrived at 12 Mile Drome, Port Moresby, to relieve the

80FS P-400s. (AAF)

Capt. Philip **Greasley** was the 80FS' first overseas CO. (AAF)

39FS and supplement the fatigued 35FG in defending New Guinea. The 39th was exhausted from its combat over the last two months, and many of its personnel were sick with Malaria or Dengue Fever. The 80th was to be equipped with some of the 39th's war-weary P-400s to defend Port Moresby, fly ground support missions, and to fly cover for the few Allied A-24 and medium bombers. Just before sunset on 21 July Greasley led six 80FS Airacobras to 14 Mile Drome from 12 Mile to operate with the 39FS. The next morning he led the six P-400s on a strafing mission against the enemy landings at Gona. The members of his flight included Lieutenants William Greenfield, David Hunter, Cleveland Jones, Daniel Roberts, and Norbert Ruff. When they arrived over the beach they spotted five or six barges landed on shore and three motor torpedo boats floating nearby. Several "destroyers" were seen, but were actually misidentified transports. The Airacobras flew a low strafing pass with only their machine gun firing, as their cannons were not charged. The Japanese appeared to be surprised by the attack, as their troops either jumped overboard or ran for their guns to put up AA fire that was judged as medium but inaccurate. There were 12 to 14 barges moving from the transports toward shore. The barges were strafed, and at least one of the transports was badly hit and emitted heavy black smoke. During the attack, 1Lt. David Hunter was hit by 37mm AA fired from one of the barges, and when he jettisoned the door of the damaged Airacobra it almost hit Wingman Daniel Roberts' fighter. Before Hunter could bail out, his fighter splashed into the water about 100 yards from shore. Several members of the flight thought he may have swam to shore, but he was not found during searches. After the war Hunter's ring was found at Rabaul, where he had been transferred after capture and was executed.

22 July 1942: 35FG/39FS

On the 22nd 2Lt. Ralph Martin shot down a seaplane near Gona.

24 July 1942

Bad weather prevented attacks on the following day, and on 24 July the Japanese attacked, bombing the airfields at Port Moresby in poor weather. Before fighters could get to altitude to intercept the Japanese bombers had dropped their bombs and left.

26-28 July 1942: 8FG: Townsville

During the end of July, enemy flying boats, identified as H6K "Mavis" four-engine patrol bombers from Gasmata, bombed Townsville for three consecutive nights. On 26 July, despite a brightly moonlit night, three flying boats dropped their bombs into mud flats in the harbor. The next night four P-39s from each of the 8th Group squadrons that were stationed at Garbutt Field, located just outside the town, were sent up to intercept. However, friendly AA fire followed not only the enemy bombers but also the P-39s, who were forced to break off their attacks on the slow moving patrol planes that were silhouetted in clear skies and moonlight. The next night the AA batteries were instructed not to fire when the alert was sounded at midnight. Capt. John Mainwaring and 2Lt. Robert Harriger of the 36FS were scrambled and climbed to 21,000 feet, where they spotted a lone Mavis caught in the moonlight from above and in the searchlights below. Mainwaring fired a burst that killed the tail gunner and started a small fire. After he dove away, Harriger continued hitting the large Kawanishi until it turned north in a slow descent. The searchlights held their beams on the damaged enemy until it flew out of their range over the ocean. Harriger's P-39 ran out of ammunition and he had to turn away from the enemy bomber, which was dropping lower into the darkness, trailing flames. Both pilots were credited with a shared probable victory.

The 8FG's sojourn at Townsville was not at all safe and enjoyable R&R, as on the 27th 2Lt. Gilbert Oxley of the 35FS, detached from the 80FS, was ferrying a P-39 on a 20 minute flight from Woodstock to Wier Airstrip. He was the first to take off but lost power, crashing into the trees at the end of the runway and burning. On 10 September veteran Capt. James Bevlock of the 36FG was flying a Tiger Moth Trainer over Halifax Bay, near Townsville, giving S.Sgt. Weiss a pleasure ride when the port wings of the biplane crumpled and put the aircraft into a spin at 4,000 feet. Weiss was thrown out of the cockpit and his parachute momentarily caught on the tail but opened itself; however, all the chute's harness clips were opened by the jolt except for one leg strap. Weiss floated into the water hanging by one leg and was picked up by a boat. Bevlock's body was never recovered. On 28 September, Capt. Paul Brown of the 36FS took off from Garbutt Field headed for Milne Bay when he disappeared somewhere along the way. More pilots were lost in non-operational accidents during this period than in air combat over New Guinea.

New pilots came into the 35th and 36th Squadrons at the end of August: six pilots joined the 35FS, including Capt. Emmett Davis and Lieutenants Harold McClelland, Joseph McKeon, and Richard Sauve. The 36FS received several new pilots, including 1Lt. George Welch, who had downed four Val dive bombers during the Pearl Harbor attack while flying a P-40 with the 47FS.

28 July 1942

On 28 July, air reconnaissance spotted two medium transport vessels and two protecting warships heading south through St. Georges Channel, and the next day, another convoy consisting of at least two more transports and two destroyers was discovered. Despite the persistent attacks by RAAF Hudsons and PBYs and American B-17s and A-24s, only one or possibly two Japanese transports were hit, but the enemy succeeded landing their troops.

29 July 1942: 8FG/80FS

The 39FS had flown its last mission before being officially relieved by the 80FS on 24 July, and now the 80th would be largely responsible for attacking and stopping the Japanese landing force from advancing beyond Buna. On 29 July eight Airacobras were to escort seven A-24s (the AAF version of the Navy SBD dive bomber) to attack Barkembar, just north of Gona, on the expanding enemy beachhead around Buna. The poorly armed A-24 dive bombers were particularly vulnerable, and their pilots dreaded flying missions without fighter protection. However, the A-24 was so slow that the escorting fighters lacked sufficient fuel capacity to provide continuous protection even on the standard missions from Port Moresby to the New Guinea northeastern coast. Two flights of 41FS Airacobras provided top cover, while the seven fighters (one aborted early with engine trouble) of the 80th remained with the bombers flying at about 9,000 feet. Upon approaching the target area, three Zeros were spotted at 2,000 feet flying in different directions. The three daring Zeros attacked both the 80th's escorts and the A-24s. The untried American pilots managed to repel the enemy attacks in combats from 9,000 feet to 4,000 feet with no claims being made by either combatant. Two large ships traveling in line led by a smaller vessel flanked on both sides by the other ships were located in the target area. On their approach over the target, the American formation encountered a thick overcast at 9,000 feet. The Airacobras followed the dive bombers through the overcast, and the formation met Zeros climbing toward them. As the opposing fighters battled, the A-24s continued on course for their targets. The AAC version of the Navy's Douglas SBD Dauntless was regarded by most of its pilots as too slow, too short-ranged, and too lightly armed, and were without armor plate and self-sealing fuel tanks. The seven inexperienced A-24 dive bomber pilots made only one bomb hit, while the other six bombs missed. Even though the AA fire was recorded as "light and inaccurate," only one A-24 returned to base, with another returning the next day after an emergency landing at Fall River. Two had crashed on the beach, while another hit the water at Buna, and the remaining two disappeared, causing Kenney to relegate the A-24 for only non-combat missions; soon it was dropped from the status reports altogether.

30 July 1942: 39 and 40FS/35FG Leave New Guinea

Once new fighter squadrons reached New Guinea, the 39th and 40th Fighter Squadrons returned to Townsville and were replaced by the 41FS and 80FS. During the 35FG's campaign in New Guinea the 39FS had 10 pilots bail out, but all were saved. The 40FS had 32 pilots at the beginning of the campaign, but left with only 19 active pilots with six lost to combat.

A-24 was the AAF's version of the Navy's Douglas SBD Dauntless Dive Bomber. (AAF)

August 1942

30 July-26 August 1942: 8FG/80FS

The first month over New Guinea was uneventful for the 80FS. On 30 July the 80th escorted transports to Kagi, and on 2 August the Airacobras were unable to climb high enough to intercept a high flying enemy formation. On 3 August, 1Lts. William Brown and Noel Lundy flew a reconnaissance over Lae. From the afternoon of 3 August until the seventh, the Squadron escorted the 41st Bomb Squadron to bomb and strafe positions on the Kokoda Track, flew recon over Lae and Salamaua, and escorted transports to the Kagi area. On 13 August the 80th escorted B-26s to bomb Buna, but missed the landing of the convoy by two hours and it unloaded without interference. The Squadron returned to transport escort duty the next day. On 17 August, eight P-400s took off at 0910 to intercept 24 enemy bombers heading for 7 Mile Drome. The Squadron's pilots flew to the vector area and saw the bombers thousands of feet above in a giant V of Vs at 23,000 feet. The American pilots in their underpowered Airacobras could only watch as the Japanese bombed the base at will. On the 25th, the 80th was flying top cover again for the 41BS during a bombing mission on Buna Airfield, which was successful, as five aircraft were claimed as destroyed and 12 plus damaged on the ground. After this time the invasion of Guadalcanal was underway, and the Japanese air units on New Guinea were transferred to the Solomons Campaign, leaving only one Air Wing.

1 August 1942: 35FG/41FS

Capt. Albert Schinz shot down a "twin engine" photo recon while leading a flight escorting B-26s over Buna. Several hours later Maj. Jack Wilson shot down a Zero over Buna. After the victories of Wilson and Schinz, air action over Buna subsided until the end of August.

2 August 1942: 35FG/41FS

1Lts. Jesse Hague and Jesse Dore, 17PS veterans, were shot down when attacked by five Zeros over Cape Ward Hunt while flying bomber escort. Hague bailed out and was thought to be captured and later executed. Dore was listed as MIA.

3 August 1942: 35FG

The use of medium bombers for strikes against enemy supply lines and the necessity of maintaining fighters to defend strategic centers of supply, and on occasion as short range escorts, reduced the amount of direct fighter support which could be given to the infantry. Nevertheless, during the Buna-Kokoda phase of the campaign trials, often using new techniques of strafing and bombing against enemy positions, strikes were conducted in cooperation between air and ground forces which would be of significance later. On 3 August, four P-400s roared in at ten feet above the trees over Kokoda and nearby Oivi to thoroughly strafe ground positions. One of the Airacobras dropped a full belly tank and then returned to ignite it with incendiary bullets.

4 August 1942: 35FG/39FS - Command Changes

On 4 August, 39FS CO Maj. Jack Berry was flying a training practice bombing mission in a P-39 when his bomb exploded directly under his aircraft and flipped it into the sea for the only squadron Airacobra fatality. He was replaced by acting CO 1Lt. Stephen David, and then by 1Lt. Francis Royal on 17 August. Royal would be replaced by Maj. George Prentice on 18 September.

7 August 1942: 35FG

On 7 August, 32 P-400s from the Moresby-based 35th Fighter Group swept through the Gap in the Owen Stanleys on a mission aimed against enemy supply dumps in the Kokoda area. The 16 fighters, outfitted with bomb racks, dropped 500 pound bombs in dive bombing attacks and expended

25,000 rounds of ammunition, while several others remained overhead to provide top cover.

9 August 1942: Guadalcanal and 5AF

The American invasion of Guadalcanal and Tulagi on 7 August placed another burden on the limited resources of the Allied Air Forces. On 9 August, Gen. George Marshall urged MacArthur to concentrate his bombing operations on the neutralization of bases, such as Rabaul in New Britain and Kieta and Buka in the Solomons, which the Japanese could use to support their operations on Guadalcanal.

17 August 1942

In response to a new Japanese convoy attempting to land troops at Buna-Gona, attacks by B-17s and B-26s were ineffective due to both poor weather conditions and fighter protection, and four transports landed approximately 3,000 troops unscathed. The enemy did mount a heavy bombing raid on the Port Moresby area on the morning of 17 August, and three bombers and seven transports were destroyed on the ground at 7 Mile Airdrome. Some of the American fighters managed to get in the air, but they were too late to intercept the enemy bombers.

21 August 1942: 35FG/41FS

While Lt.Col. Richard Legg was leading the 41FS on a fighter sweep over the Owen Stanleys, 41FS CO Maj. Jack Wilson, leading one of the flights, became separated in the weather. Wilson came upon the Japanese strip at Buna and strafed it, destroying three Zeros. When he returned to base he reported his find and two more flights were dispatched to Buna. This second mission made six strafing passes, destroying aircraft and AA batteries. Four 41FS pilots were awarded the Silver Star for the mission.

Assessment of the First Air Operations in the Papuan Campaign

The contributions of the Allied Air Forces during the first months of the Papuan Campaign are difficult to assess. To begin with, any assessment should consider the probable situation if the enemy's air force had been completely unopposed. AAF Fighter Squadrons, aided by improved warning facilities, contributed to the declining number of damaging raids on Port Moresby and northern Australia. The heavy bombers, in turn, by their notably successful strikes on Rabaul, strengthened the Allies in the air over both New Guinea and the Solomons. Valuable experience in supply and troop transport was gained. Fighter aircraft were increasing the scope and scale of their strafing sweeps, and were learning the technique of escort for bomber missions. The effects of the attacks along the Kokoda Track were doubtful, despite the optimistic post mission reports. The jungle foliage made possible effective concealment of troop positions, and the bombing and strafing of villages did not necessarily result in large sale destruction of supplies, since it was doubtful that trained troops would have concentrated their supplies in such obvious targets. In spite of losses, the Japanese Navy was able to reinforce New Guinea almost at will. During the month, the inadequate resources available to the Allies' command was always a limiting factor. Since heavy bombers were mainly flying missions on distant targets, the burden of bombing attacks on Lae, Salamaua, Buna, and the Kokoda Track fell upon the B-26s of the 22BG and the B-25s of the 3BG, which never had more than 12 B-25s and 27 B-26s available.

In this phase of the war, heavy bombers on dangerous, long range missions were never protected by fighter escort. Maj. Felix Hardison, Commander of the 93BS of the 19BG, stated: "In my experience, since the war started, I haven't been escorted with my squadron, or in any squadron I have been in, once by pursuit." This deficiency caused war correspondents to criticize the high command for not providing fighters suitable for long range, high altitude missions, and against Brett for the incorrect employment of the fighters he did have. By July and August suitable fighters (e.g. P-38s) had not arrived for long range escort, but shorter missions, however, did have escort, and B-25s and B-26s, usually in formations of from three to twelve, frequently had a top cover of P-39s or P-400s.

The primary responsibility of the fighter units based at Port Moresby and Darwin was the defense of these supply bases. Throughout the period, Allied intelligence showed that the Japanese had deployed their air units in such a way as to maintain a constant threat to Allied positions, deploying a large force in New Britain and smaller forces on New Guinea and the Netherlands East Indies. During the Buna-Kokoda phase of the campaign there were only a few heavy Japanese air raids, but there were frequent small scale attacks, along with numerous nuisance raids directed against Horn Island, Darwin, and Port Moresby. Usually enemy bombers were protected by fighters which came in at 30,000 feet; too high for interception by P-40s, P-39s, and the P-400, which were the only fighters available in the SWPA, and their limitations seriously affected Allied operations. In July the P-39, though usually having a half hour's warning, only made contact with Japanese bombers four times during a series of nine bombing raids, and even then less than half of the fighters involved had reached a sufficient altitude for effective interception. In 16 contacts the P-39 never enjoyed an altitude advantage, and when combat with a Zero did begin at the same altitude, the enemy's superior climbing ability soon enabled it to outmaneuver its opponent. The P-40 also had its drawbacks. A July quarterly report described 12 occasions where the Warhawk failed to intercept the enemy, usually because of insufficient engine power at high altitudes. However, as pioneered by the Flying Tigers over China, these American fighters could out-dive the Zero and could break off combat almost at will.

The second responsibility of the air forces was to attack Japanese convoys, particularly during their voyages along the New Guinea coast, where the Japanese frequently reinforced their troops. MacArthur had inadequate naval forces, and had to rely on his air force to offer any opposition to these convoys. The 435th Bombardment Squadron worked relentlessly in spotting the movement of enemy shipping, but the Japanese took advantage of nighttime darkness and poor weather to mask their movements. Thus, during the month following the Japanese landing at Buna, the Allied Air Forces attacked Japanese bases and convoys, defended their own areas from Japanese air attack, and fought the Japanese for control of the air over New Guinea.

Nonetheless, the Japanese experienced almost complete success in New Guinea, as they kept the Allies on the defensive. They had firmly established themselves at Buna, and had advanced more than half the distance to Port Moresby, although they now faced the most difficult part of the Kokoda Track. Japanese successes in New Guinea overlapped with an increasing pace in the battle for Guadalcanal. The Allied Command was faced, therefore, with the question of whether the Japanese would persist in their invasion of New Guinea or concentrate their forces for a counter attack in the Solomons.

During the third week in August, the Allies would bring in a force of American and Australian engineers and infantry to construct airfields near Milne Bay, on the southeastern tip of New Guinea. This strategic area guarded the sea approaches from the Solomon Sea to New Guinea; the mistake of getting to Buna too late was not to be repeated. As quickly as an airstrip could be completed, two RAAF P-40 squadrons and a few Lockheed Hudson bombers were flown into the installation.

4

Milne Bay: 25 August to 10 September 1942

By mid-August 1942, Allied intelligence indicated that the Japanese were not going to abandon their Solomon Islands Campaign or their advance toward Port Moresby. Intelligence reports also showed that during the first three weeks in August they had flown some 300 aircraft of all types into the New Britain/New Guinea/Solomon Islands area, that they had completed an air strip at Buna, and were apparently preparing others at Dobodura, near Buna; at Buka, in the Solomons; and at Kavieng, in New Ireland. By 21 August, Allied intelligence determined that a major enemy effort would be directed against Port Moresby, with possible parachute landings there or near Milne Bay.

To date, the Japanese had advanced along the coast only slightly below Buna, but logically an attempt to occupy Milne Bay would be made by them to protect their left flank. The Allies also had good motives for securing Milne, as this strategic area guarded the sea approaches from the Solomon Sea to New Guinea, and would gain protection for shipping and a base for future advance along the coast. In July, the possession of Buna similarly played a part in Allied and Japanese plans. The Japanese reached Buna first, but the Allied mistake of getting to Buna too late was not to be repeated, as the Allies won their first notable victory of the Papuan Campaign when they captured Milne Bay.

MacArthur obviously recognized the importance of Milne as a strategic position, and had formulated his plans for the development of a base there. By August, American and Australian service units with some infantry and Anti-Aircraft support had moved into this area comprised of Malarial swamps and coconut plantations to immediately begin the construction of air strips. On 7 August, after a three day voyage from Townsville, the 8th Fighter Control Squadron arrived in Milne Bay to provide air warning facilities. Two weeks later, the Squadron had established itself near a newly-completed air strip at Fall River, located somewhat inland from the north shore of the Bay, and had sent detachments out to its sea flanks on Goodenough and Normanby Islands.

8th Fighter Control Squadron

The 8th Fighter Control Squadron was organized under 1Lt. Richard Fulcher at Mitchel Field to plot and coordinate operations against enemy aircraft. In the emergency of the new war Fulcher was forced to leave most of his men and some of his equipment behind at Mitchel, and was ordered to try to requisition new (and untrained) personnel in San Francisco. The resourceful Fulcher was able to sail to Australia with some of the new men he needed and reestablish the 8th Fighter Control Squadron. The squadron did not have the necessary radar equipment that was supposed to be its primary method of detecting enemy formations, and it had to decipher and process other information to direct their fighters. Upon arriving in Australia, "Fulcher's Cultured Vultures" were forced to beg, borrow, or steal to set up the air defense system for the Brisbane area. The Vultures set up spotter sites, radar sites, and communications to the Fighter Sector Control Center in Brisbane. In July, Fulcher was promoted to Captain and transferred to Headquarters to become Group Operations Officer; he was replaced by the squadron adjutant, 1Lt. Jose Berumen. On 7 August 1942 the 8FCS entered the real combat area when it transferred to Milne Bay.

11-24 August 1942: Milne Bay

By 11 August, as soon as the airstrip at Fall River was completed, the 75 and 76 RAAF P-40 Squadrons–some of whose pilots had taken part in the defense of Port Moresby in the spring–and a few RAAF Hudsons were based there. While the new airstrip was suitable for fighter operations, it was inadequate for use by heavy bombers. The adjacent coconut plantations were to be used for camouflaging parked aircraft, but heavy rains had further saturated the normally swampy terrain and made aircraft dispersal difficult. By 19 August, however, MacArthur was able to report a reasonably satisfactory situation: one strip would be ready for bombers by 25 August, and two others already under construction would be completed by 5 and 25 September, respectively. A brigade of the 7th Australian Division was expected to arrive the next day and would increase the garrison to 10,000.

The Japanese had increased their aerial activity, suggesting an impending push on Milne Bay. Port Moresby had endured its 78th raid on 17 August, when three bombers and seven transports were destroyed on the ground at 7 Mile Drome. Darwin experienced its 27th raid on 23 August. Meanwhile, the Japanese Air Forces increased their raids on Milne Bay, and for several days their fighters appeared over Fall River. On 24 August, experienced Australian pilots intercepted about a dozen Zeros, shooting down two and severely damaging others. On 24 August, 435BS air recon reported that an unknown number of Japanese landed near Tufi, on Cape Nelson, which was located some distance below Buna.

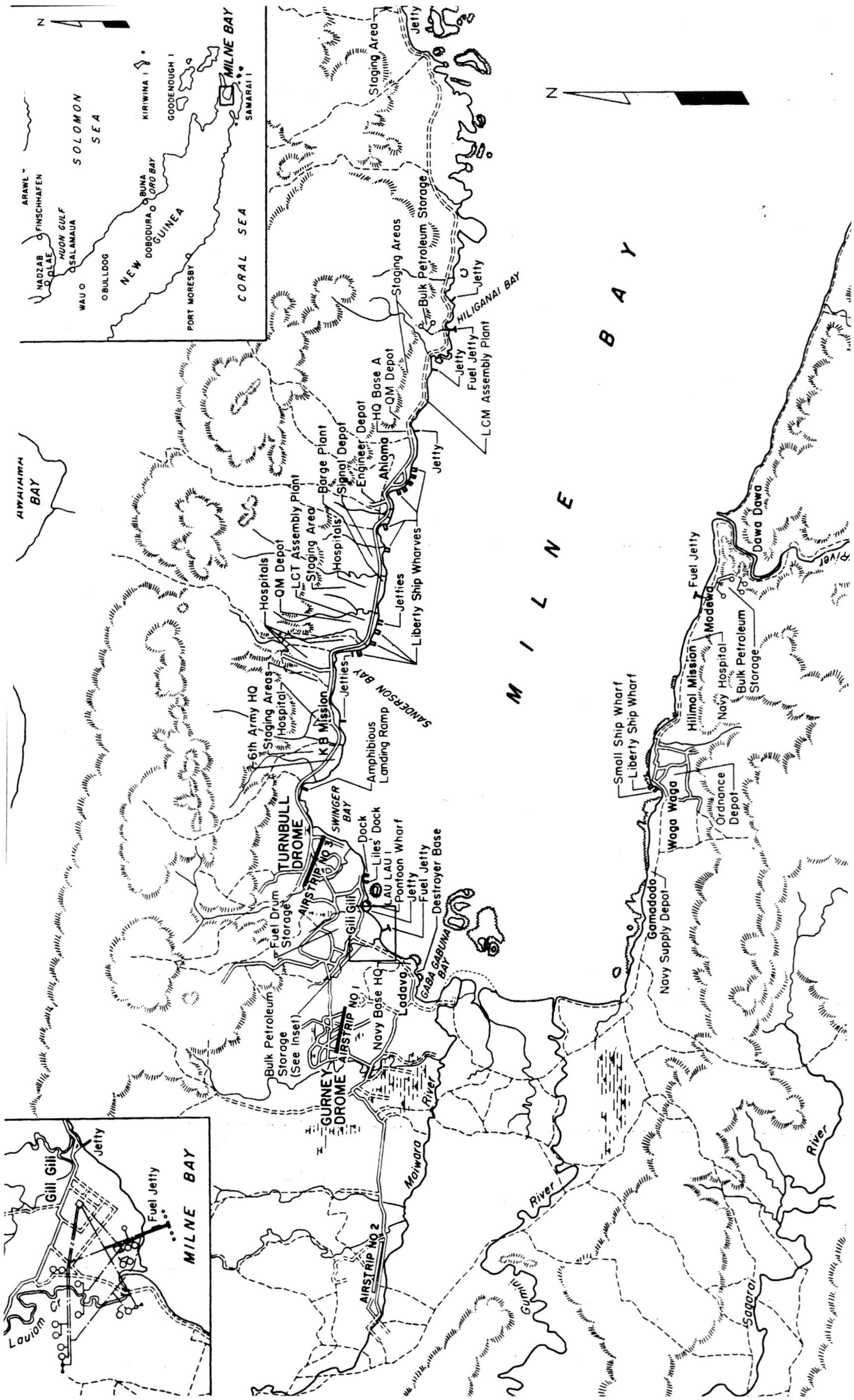

Milne Bay: 25 August to 10 September 1942

25-26 August 1942: Milne Bay

On 25 August, seven enemy barges were reported to have landed on Goodenough Island. On the same day, alert aerial reconnaissance shadowed a convoy of three cruisers (or probably destroyers), two transports, and an assortment of small craft until there seemed little doubt that its destination was Milne Bay. The approach of this convoy coincided with unseasonable weather, and for two weeks continual rains kept aircraft dispersal areas and landing fields under water and mud, and the low visibility concealed the approaching enemy force. On 25 August, a formation of nine 93BS B-17s failed to locate the convoy and returned to Port Moresby. Australian units from Fall River were no more successful. One Hudson was designated to lead 24 RAAF P-40s to the convoy and succeeded in spotting the rapidly moving ships 60 miles east of Milne Bay. Using six fighters for top cover, the remainder of the P-40s, each armed with a 300 pound demolition bomb, carried out dive bombing attacks. The destruction of one of the smaller, armed vessels was claimed at a cost of one P-40.

The Japanese had expected to use fighters based at the improved Buna air strip as cover for their landings, but the Allies were able to prevent them from doing so. As long as the Allies held the crest of the Owen Stanleys, the Japanese at Buna could not receive adequate warning of an approaching air attack until the Allied fighters reached Kokoda, which was only minutes from Buna. Allied air tactics took advantage of this fact. On 25 August, 17 P-400s of the 80FS left Moresby for Buna, but storms buffeted the light fighters as they tried to find their way through the perilous Owen Stanley Gap. Thirteen fighters turned back, but the remaining four pushed through and arrived at Buna, diving low over the airdrome and strafing many dispersed enemy aircraft. Shortly after, seven other P-400s zoomed through the mist and Anti-Aircraft fire in five separate strafing runs, leaving 10 Zeros burning on the ground.

By 25 August, the Allied garrison under Maj.Gen. C.B. Cloves was warned of an imminent attack somewhere along the swampy shoreline by an invasion force supported by cruisers (destroyers?). At about 0100 on 26 August, two Australian patrol boats moving through steaming rain and mist along the northern shore of the Bay located the Jap landing force. The enemy position was radioed to Australian ground force headquarters and troops were directed to them, just several miles from the airfield. Although the Japanese obviously knew Milne was being developed, despite extensive aerial reconnaissance they were apparently were surprised by the Allied strength, which had recently been reinforced. The small enemy force, estimated at 2,000 men, were jungle trained and well equipped. Attacking at night, they were supported by shell fire from destroyers and cruisers, and by wide-tracked light tanks that concealed themselves by day from Allied air attack.

During the day of the invasion, the opposing air forces tried to furnish support for their ground troops. Allied heavy and medium bombers patrolled Milne Bay in search of suitable targets, but generally they had little success. The next day, 19BG B-17s attacked the Japanese naval force from low altitude and thought they may have damaged a cruiser (destroyer). The RAAF No. 75 and 76 Squadrons based at Fall River began operations at dawn and strafed 15 beached landing barges and gasoline drums that were being floated to shore.

Although outnumbered, the Japanese initially advanced toward the airfield and hindered Australian counterattacks by leaving small groups of snipers in concealed positions in palm trees. The No.75 Squadron flew raids against these snipers, and 75 Squadron CO and veteran of the Libyan Desert Campaign, Peter Turnbull, caught his wing on the top of a coconut palm and crashed in flames. The Japanese advanced rapidly to the airfield, but well-trained, veteran Australian infantry and American engineers beat them back. The RAAF P-40s persistently attacked the tanks, many of which had became bogged down in mud, allowing the Diggers to advance.

Milne Bay Airfields

Milne Bay is located at the southeastern tip of Papua, New Guinea, between two rugged peninsulas formed by parallel mountain chains rising to elevations of 3,000 to 4,000 feet. The many reefs and small islands located along the eastern open end of the Bay make it a protected anchorage. The

Japanese tanks and infantry attacked the airstrip in the early morning but were driven back by Australian infantry and American engineers. (AAF)

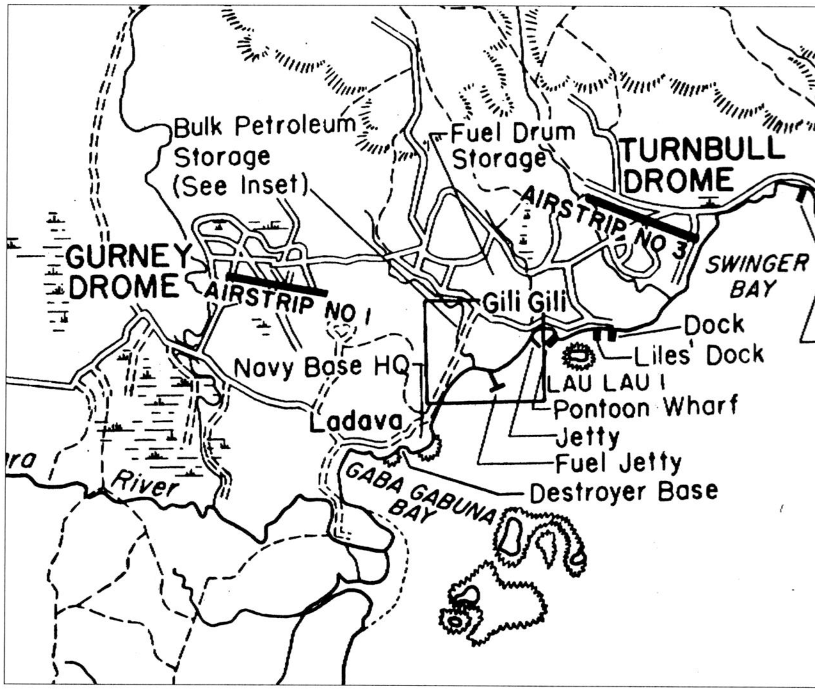

Map 2 Milne Bay Airfields. (AAF)

Bay, about 20 miles long and from five to 10 miles wide, has a deep channel (China Strait) flowing toward the southeast, and East Channel leading directly out toward the east. Deep water exists close to the shores of the Bay, and mountains abruptly rise behind narrow coastal plains, which receive an annual rainfall of about 200 inches. About 25% of this coastal area is situated at the head of the Bay and had been cleared for coconut plantations prior to World War II, while the remainder was Sago Swamps and dense tropical jungle. Only the plantation area was feasible for the construction of airfields and facilities when the engineers arrived in mid-1942. Milne was to provide flank protection for Port Moresby and permit Allied aircraft to strike at Rabaul and the northern Solomons without the necessity of crossing the Owen Stanley Range. Later, Milne Bay was to be a major supply base and the first important trans-shipment base for logistic support to future operations along the northeast coast of New Guinea. Initially, Milne Bay received shipping from Australian ports, but later direct shipments were also received from the United States, saving millions of ship-ton miles and eliminating the rehandling of cargo.

Airstrips 1, 2, and 3

"MacArthur's Engineer," Gen. Hugh Casey, and the Engineer Section, GHQ, SWPA made a reconnaissance of the area in June 1942 which disclosed the advantages of using both the Milne Bay and Buna areas as bases from which to launch offensives. However, when the Japanese moved into Buna in July, Milne Bay had to be prepared rapidly for defense against anticipated enemy landings there.

After the Japanese landings at Buna, the construction of facilities at Milne Bay for one fighter squadron became a priority. Native labor, under the 96th Engineer Regimen, began to clear high grass and undergrowth from the site of the proposed runway. On 12 June, the GHQ, SWPA, ordered the immediate construction of a fighter airstrip with two dispersal taxiways, 32 camouflaged hideouts, and camp facilities for 500 men; followed by the subsequent development of a bomber field. Preliminary construction at Airstrip No. 1 was begun by the 46th Engineers on 30 June, and the runway was sufficiently completed by 19 July to permit the landing of the veteran 75th RAAF P-40 Fighter Squadron only two days before the Japanese landings at Buna. Airstrip No. 1 was code named Fall River and later renamed Gurney Drome after RAAF S/L C.R. Gurney, a B-26 pilot and former Qantas pilot who was KIA as described earlier. By 6 August, only 4,950x80 feet of the planned 6,000x100 foot runway was covered with steel mat. This strip was in operational use by fighter aircraft at this time, and construction had started on Airstrip No. 2, located about three miles west of Airstrip No. 1. In order to clear the site for this second airstrip, it was necessary to remove about 5,000 coconut trees, after which the runway was partially graded. However, other sites were considered more favorable, and work on Airstrip No. 2 was discontinued. On 4 August work was immediately started on Airstrip No. 3, several miles east of Airstrip No. 1, and also on the expansion of facilities at Airstrip No. 1.

Meanwhile, the Japanese were firmly established at Buna and were moving south over the Kokoda Track, which caused the Allied command to put greater emphasis on the strategic importance of holding Milne Bay. By mid-August a US Fighter Control Squadron was established near the airstrips and posted detachments on Goodenough and Normanby Islands for additional protection. A second RAAF P-40 fighter squadron (the 76th), along with several Hudsons, was now operating out of Milne Bay. One bomber strip was projected to be operational before 1 September and another during that month. Allied Intelligence was concerned with enemy landing operations at Milne Bay, and on 25 August B-17 air recon sighted a Japanese naval convoy headed toward Milne Bay. Poor flying weather prohibited the bombers from taking off from Australia and Port Moresby to defend Milne Bay from the invasion, while 23 RAAF P-40s from Milne Bay dive bombed and strafed the convoy with little success. Before midnight on 25 August, the Japanese convoy arrived at Milne Bay and began landing troops within four miles of Airstrip No. 3. This strip had been cleared to 6,000x300 feet and grading had just begun. The engineer troops there were directed to continue their regular construction work until the Japanese attack was imminent, at which time they would come under tactical control of the Australian infantry brigade to defend the strip. The following day, many engineers were sent to man the defense line while construction by surplus engineers continued daily in the face of shelling from enemy gunboats and strafing and bombing from enemy aircraft. In the early morning of 31 August, the Japanese infantry finally made a maximum effort and charged the strip and the engineer service troops in the center of the line. These engineers, with no previous combat experience and only routine training, performed a key role in turning back the Japanese attack.

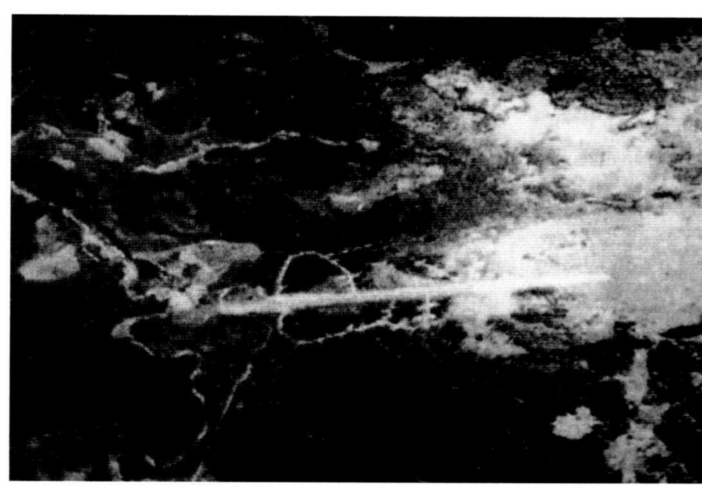

Gurney Airdrome. (Strip #1). (AAF)

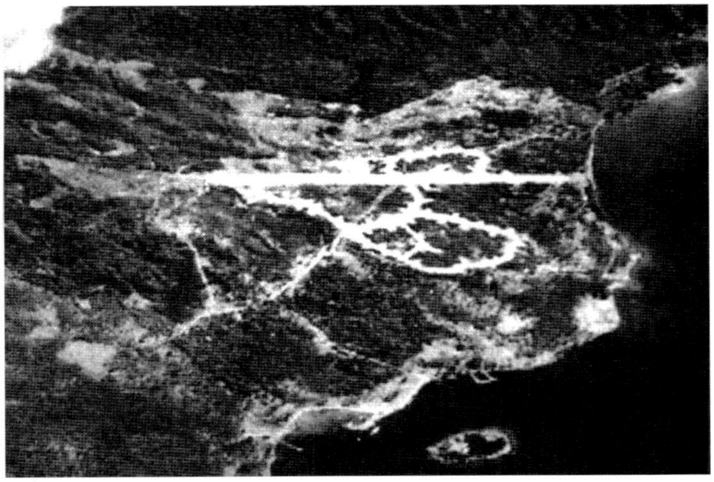

Turnbull Airdrome. (Strip #3). (AAF)

Airstrip No. 1 had been kept in continuous operation throughout the Japanese advance. Although the two RAAF fighter squadrons had been evacuated to Port Moresby, the tactical air support for the nearby ground forces had been possible only through use of this strip for necessary refueling en route for attacks against enemy tanks, supply dumps, vehicles, and landing barges, and for the strafing of treetops, where close by Japanese snipers had been concealed from ground observation. Subsequently, after emergency needs had been met through the construction of the PSP-surfaced No. 1 runway, it was possible to build a second and parallel runway with a bitumen-treated surface, 5,200x100 feet, to the north of the original runway. This second runway was constructed by the RAAF, and after its construction the original runway was used only for emergency landings or for taxiing.

During the Battle of Milne Bay, the Japanese were advancing from the east toward Airstrip No. 3, which was defended by the Australian 25th and 61st Battalions and US Army 43rd Engineers. Barbed wire was strung across the end of the runway and halftracks, guns, and mortars on the far side. The Japanese attacked the strip on 31 August 1942 between 0100-0500, but failed to capture the strip and pulled back. Construction on Airstrip No. 3 was temporarily suspended by the local command after the Japanese attack and was not resumed until 16 September. The strip was later named Turnbull Drome after RAAF S/L Peter Turnbull, who was killed on 27 August 1942 while landing on this strip. By the end of October the east to west site had been cleared, grading for a 6,000x100 foot runway was completed, and a gravel sub base was laid. A steel mat surface was then placed and the runway was declared operational. The construction of revetments, as requested by Allied Air Forces, would have been a large project at Turnbull Drome because, according to air operational plans, 67 planes were to be based there: 24 heavy bombers, 18 medium bombers, and 25 fighters. However, engineering personnel and equipment were not available for such a large scale revetment program, and by July 1943, under a revised program, hardstands without revetments were constructed for only 70 medium bombers.

Milne as a Port and Supply Base

By early 1943, the overall strategic plan of advancing up to the northern coast of New Guinea had been approved by the Joint Chiefs of Staff and Japanese forces had been pushed out of Buna. Milne Bay had been long advocated as the Theater's main overseas receiving and shipping port, and a location for bulk petroleum and covered supply storage. Milne Bay construction flourished and then declined as the battle front moved further away, until all construction was stopped in August 1944 and final evacuation was set for 31 July 1945.

5FC units based at Milne Bay included:

8FG; 36FS (P-39) from Townsville on 18 September 1942 to Mareeba on 22 February 1943

418NFS: (P-38 & P-70) from USA on 2 November 1943 to Dobodura on 22 November 1943

71TRG: 82TRS (P-39) from USA on 6 November 1943 to Dobodura on 23 November 1943

421NFS: (P-70) from USA on 4 January 1944 to Nadzab on 1 February 1944

26 August 1942: 8FG/80FS

To keep the Japanese Zeros from attacking the Australian fighter squadrons and infantry defenders at Milne Bay, the 80th and the 41st squadrons flew concerted attacks on the Japanese airfield at Buna on the morning of the 26th. At 0600, 10 Airacobras took off for a strafing mission to Buna, expecting to catch the Zeros based there on the ground. Soon two fighters would abort, including Squadron CO and Mission Leader Capt. Philip Greasley, whose P-400 developed electrical problems; 1Lt. William Brown took over the lead. To ensure surprise a circuitous route was to be flown, but after a while 2Lt. Daniel Roberts, flying on Brown's wing, noticed that the time to target seemed too long; being only a Second Lieutenant, Roberts maintained radio silence. As they continued three more Airacobras were forced to abort. 2Lt. Charles Able was on his way back home with engine problems when he encountered a lone Zero that had been on reconnaissance and fired a head on burst which only damaged the Zero. Finally, Roberts could no longer keep quiet and radioed Brown of the navigation problem, and Brown then headed across the Owen Stanleys. Just before 0730, six Zeros of the 2nd Wing were just preparing to take off for a patrol of Milne Bay when the six remaining 80th Airacobras came in flying low over the hills on their strafing run. Brown and Roberts were the first in and shot down two Zeros that crashed and burned just as they left the ground. 1Lt. George Helveston and Wingman 2Lt. Gerald Rogers followed closely and downed the next two Zeros taking off. After their strafing run Brown and Roberts zoomed up and away, and then turned back to take on two Zeros that got airborne in a head on pass and shot them down with cannon and machine gun fire. Roberts chased after another and damaged it. Helveston and Gerald Rogers were joined by 2Lts. Leonidas Mathers and Charles Able as they turned around and headed to engage the now airborne Zeros, and the two Second Lieutenants damaged one Zero each. After destroying a Zero, Rogers dived on another that had just landed, but the aircraft taxied into the revetment area before he could fire on it. Meanwhile, a Zero got on Rogers' tail and he attempted to escape by flying on the deck. The Zero

2Lt. Daniel **Roberts** shot down the first two of his 14 victims. (AAF)

hit Rogers' Airacobra, which caught fire and wounded him. Rogers cut his speed while gliding over the water and put his fighter down safely, but sustained additional deep gashes from the landing. Rogers managed to get out of his aircraft and swim to shore, where he soon was picked up by friendly natives and taken to a mission, where his wounds were treated. Several days later he was taken to an airstrip, where he was picked up by an Australian pilot and taken back to base on 13 September.

1Lt. William **Brown** scored his two victories of the war. (AAF)

27 August 1942: 35FG/41FS

On the 27th, 14 P-400s of the 41FS under Capt. Jack Wilson covered a B-26 escort to Buna. When they arrived at 0715, they were immediately engaged by 10 Zeros and shot down five. 2Lt. Francis Riggin and 1Lt. Albert Schinz both raced in to shoot a Zero off 1Lt. Albert Burr's tail, with Riggin claiming the kill for the Squadron's first victory. Other victories were scored by 1Lts. Edwin Jackson and William Turner (plus a damaged claim). 2Lt. Jean Jackson and 1Lt. George Callahan also chased a Zero, but Jackson got the fatal hits. Capt. Jack Wilson chased down a Zero as it was trying to land, but when the Zero pilot tried to pull up from his descent Wilson hit it and then followed as it flew on, exploded, and fell into the water to conclude the air battles over Buna. The 41st scored the first victories for the 35FG, claiming five victories, one probable and one damaged, and returned to base without a loss. The B-26 Marauders knocked out both Buna runways and damaged installations.

29 August 1942: 35FG/41FS

On 29 August, 17 P-400s of the 41FS escorted B-26s back to Buna, but met no air opposition. After the Marauders finished their bombing run the Bell fighters strafed the field and destroyed three Zeros and a Betty on the ground.

29 August 1942: The Victory at Milne Bay

By the 29th the Japanese were almost surrounded, and that night a large number were evacuated by destroyers. Both sides sustained heavy casualties; of the estimated 2,000 troops landed by the Japanese, from 700 to 1,000 were killed and most of the remainder were evacuated by sea. Of the 3,000 Australian veterans who fought in this no quarter given battle, more than 2,000 were lost. With the victory, the Allies severed the left prong of the pincers grasping for Port Moresby. Although the Japanese right flank along the Kokoda Track was still advancing, the Milne Bay victory removed at least a part of the threat. Allied air units, handicapped by the pre-rainy season storms, had not been able to prevent either the landing or the evacuation, but they did eliminate much of the Japanese fighter cover for the landings. Their constant attacks had probably hindered reinforcement and had destroyed supplies and aided the ground forces with low-level support.

5

Milne Bay: 25 August to 10 September 1942

September 1942: Disposition of the 5FC Fighter Groups

49th Fighter Group

After being refitted in Townsville, Australia, the first air echelon of the 7FS under Capt. William Hennon left on 11 September for 14 Mile Strip outside Port Moresby. The 8th Squadron, under Capt. Edward Sims, also flew their planes to Townsville for refit, but the Port Moresby airfields were still under construction, so their combat worthy P-40s were turned over to the 7FS. The 9FS was assigned to remain at Darwin as an operational training squadron under Capt. Ben Irvin, who replaced the popular Capt. James Selman. It would be months before the 9th would return to combat. Meanwhile, the remaining enlisted men at Batchelor and Strauss Fields had already crated their camp equipment for portage aboard the Java Sea battle survivor USAT *Seawitch* at Port Darwin.

Kenney had convinced the Chiefs of Staff in Washington to send the new Lockheed P-38 Lightning to the SWPA. In late September, Kenney notified 49th CO Lt.Col. Donald Hutchinson that, while new fighter aircraft were designated for the 49FG, not all the Group's squadrons would even receive replacement Warhawks in New Guinea. Col. Wurtsmith was similarly informed that the new Order of Battle for the 5th Fighter Command included a large number of "new generation" fighter aircraft due for October delivery to Townsville. Each Group Commander was to choose one of his squadrons to go to Townsville to take rigorous training in the new Lockheed fighter "at the earliest possible date." Wurtsmith and Hutchinson decided that Capt. Ben Irvin's veterans of the 9th Squadron, still in Australia, would be the best choice for the P-38 program.

However, this decision came when the 9th was in a manpower transition, as several of their most senior flight leaders were ready to rotate home. The senior pilots of similar rank who were not at the end of their tours were also in a dilemma, as there were very few high ranking positions in the other P-40 squadrons, and there was virtually no likelihood for promotions in rank. Also, not all of the senior pilots were eligible for the P-38 program at Townsville.

On 8 October, orders were issued for Irvin's air and ground echelons to move to Darwin instead of to P-38 transition. Irvin was very unhappy about not receiving the P-38s, and when his name appeared on the rotation home list on the 15th, he resigned in protest and joined Ops Exec John Randolph and veteran pilots Ben Brown, Jack Donalson, and Andrew Reynolds to ship home. Major Selman had transferred to 5th Air Force staff, and only senior Captain Jesse Peaslee was qualified to take over the 9th.

Lt.Col. Donald **Hutchinson,** 49th Group Commander. (AAF)

As of 15 October, the 49FG consisted of the 7th Squadron flying missions from 14 Mile Drome in New Guinea, the 8th Squadron flying shuttle service from Townsville, and the 9th air echelon arriving at Darwin from Townsville by truck and RAAF air transport, followed by the pilots flying the last P-40s added to the pool of fighters to be refit and held in reserve for 5th Fighter Command, while the remaining 9th Squadron pilots and crews were awaiting new P-38s at Townsville while their ground echelon set up camp at Rorona.

49th Group Commander Donald Hutchinson finally arrived in Port Moresby on the 15th with his group staff, and reported to his former Group Commander, Paul Wurtsmith, who introduced him to 5th Air Force Deputy Commander Gen. Ennis Whitehead. After formalities, Whitehead asked the 49er Commander if he knew what he required for his Group. Hutchinson relied, "General, just keep my boys out of the brig and we'll beat these damn Japanese."

35th Fighter Group

On 3 September 1942, the day that Maj.Gen. George Kenney became the Commander of the 5th Fighter Command and pending the organization of the 5FC, the 35FG was temporarily assigned to HQ 5AF at Moresby. On 11 November the entire 35FG would be assigned to the 5FC for operational control. On 16 September, the 35FG HQ and HQ Squadron had been disbanded, and its personnel were reassigned and transferred to Headquarters Squadron. By 21 September the 39th and 40th Fighter Squadrons began moving back to New Guinea to join the 41FS and HQ Squadron. The 35FG was completely deployed by 18 October in the Moresby area, and for the first time in its history was functioning in a combat zone with all four of its squadrons. Group HQ, the HQ Squadron, and the 35th Fighter Control Squadron were based at Jackson (7 Mile) and Schwimmer (14 Mile) Strips, while the 39FS operated from Schwimmer, the 40FS from Berry (12 Mile Drome), and the 41FS from Jackson. Maj. Jack Wilson was transferred to Group Staff and was succeeded as 41FS CO by Capt. Edwin Doss, who would later become 35FG CO.

8th Fighter Group/80FS

While the Japanese air forces had withdrawn from New Guinea combat, the 80FS was being worn down by dangerous ground support, routine transport escort, and seemingly ineffective bomber escort missions. On 5 September, the 80FS P-39s escorted A-20s to Buna, where they strafed AA guns before the bombers arrived, then shot up buildings on Buna Drome and then continued on over the harbor to sink two small boats before withdrawing toward Kokoda to strafe other targets along the way. The 80th flew a dive bombing mission the next day when it attacked enemy positions at Myola Lake on the Kokoda Track, south of Buna/Gona. Capt. Francis Potts' fighter was hit by AA fire and he was thought to have been captured and killed.

On 15 September, the 35th and 36th Squadrons and Australian troops were part of a five ship convoy with two escorting corvettes, and would arrive at Milne Bay four days later. Their new base at Gurney Field was miserable, with hot days and cold nights and continual rain. The mud was everywhere and oozed through the pierced steel runway matting, causing take off and landing accidents.

From mid-month the 8FG was joined by RAAF fighter bombers to strafe the Japanese on the Kokoda Track and Buna/Milne Bay. On 19 September the 80FS provided escort for a RAAF Beaufighter strafing mission to Buna. After the Australians left some of the Airacobras continued to strafe the Drome. On the 27th, the 8FG began to join in the mopping up operations around Milne Bay, with the 80FS credited with killing 250 Japanese troops while the 35FS 80FS got 140.

21 August to 2 November 1942: Situation: Kokoda-Iorabaiwa Ridge

While Allied air and ground forces in the SWPA were for the first time inflicting a severe defeat on the enemy at Milne Bay, the right flank of the Japanese Kokoda offensive was having greater success. On 31 August their troops, continuing a diversionary effort toward Wau, defeated the small Australian force in that remote area. Along the Kokoda Track, Japanese units were preparing to continue their drive toward their immediate goal, Port Moresby.

After being forced out of Kokoda, the Australians were reinforced by an additional battalion and established positions extending through the villages of Isurava and Deniki. Their objective was to maintain a defense in depth by holding positions designed to cover strategic areas, but their limited forces prevented the maintenance of adequate forces at any one point. By moving along the high ground, the Japanese consistently outflanked them or infiltrated through weak points. Communication presented almost insoluble difficulties, as control areas had to rely on a single telephone line supplemented by radio, which was undependable in the mountains and stormy weather.

On 29 August the Japanese launched a frontal attack, and while the Kokoda veterans held the line, the enemy achieved a major breakthrough over the militia troops, and the Australians retreated through the Gap, suffering heavy losses. By 15 September 1942 the enemy had made a remarkable advance to within 30 miles of Port Moresby. But on that day three fresh Australian battalions reached Iorabaiwa Ridge to reinforce the exhausted troops falling back from Kokoda, and the first members of the American 32nd Division were landed by air at 7 Mile Airdrome. Most importantly, Japanese supply lines were now dangerously extended, and now faced the same problem of supply that previously had seriously hampered the Allies. The Allied Air Forces were to maintain a continual attack on the Japanese supply lines.

12 September-3 October 1942: Ground Support

Although the Japanese were well trained in making full use of the terrain for concealment, it was not possible to camouflage some obvious targets, such as the new replacement Wairope Bridge, which crossed the Kumusi River, located slightly over half way between Buna and Kokoda. In the middle of September Intelligence reported the construction of this new bridge, and it became a tempting target for every kind of air attack by heavy, medium, and light bombers, and by fighter bombers. Between 21 September and 3 October there were 13 individual bombing attacks on the bridge, but on 25 September, after a dive bombing attack by P-40s carrying 500 pound bombs, the pilots reported the bridge to be completely destroyed. But on the 28th reconnaissance found the bridge to be intact, so on 30 September B-17s were sent out, but unsuccessfully bombed the bridge from 3,000 to 4,000 feet. They were followed the next day by attacks by B-17s and then P-400s. The Bell fighters dropped their belly tanks and then strafed the bridge, destroying 18 feet of the flooring, which was quickly repaired before the end of the day.

The first reported use of **parachute fragmentation bombs**, to be called parafrags, in the Southwest Pacific was during tests in a carefully coordinated attack on Buna on 12 September 1942.

The first reported use of parachute fragmentation bombs, to be called parafrags, in the Southwest Pacific was during tests in a carefully coordinated attack on Buna on 12 September 1942. First, seven B-17s swept in through rain squalls and heavy AA fire to drop 330 pound demolition bombs from 3,000 feet on the Buna airdrome. Five B-26s followed, dropping additional demolition bombs from 5,000 feet. Finally, covered by P-400s, A-20s zoomed in over the target area at 70 feet, emptying their .30 and .50 caliber machine guns on parked enemy aircraft and dropping over 300 23 pound fragmentation bombs attached to parachutes. The results of this preliminary test were extremely encouraging, but the parafrag supply was insufficient for immediate follow up attacks.

28 September-2 November 1942: Ground Support and End of the Battle for the Kokoda Track

A demanding stage of air operations occurred during direct air support provided to the troops along the Kokoda Track. The ground battles took place under a thick foliage canopy, which greatly increased the danger of mistaking Australian troops or friendly natives for the enemy, which was to be a difficulty persisting throughout the South Pacific Campaign and never was completely overcome. Air liaison officers were posted with the infantry, who were to identify targets by using smoke or panel signals to alert the attacking aircraft, usually American or RAAF A-20s covered by P-39s or P-400s. Sweeping low across mountain ridges and treetops, the A-20 crews watched for the signal and, having located ground forces, would strafe either indicated points or the length of the Track held by the enemy. After the A-20s had completed their attack and turned back for the 40 to 50 mile flight back to Port Moresby, the fighters would then drop down to treetop level and strafe with machine gun and cannon fire.

Finally, on 28 September 1942 the Australians launched a major attack, outflanking Japanese positions and forcing the beginning of the Japanese retreat back up the Track. The jungle and long supply lines had taken their toll, but the enemy continued to offer stubborn resistance during their retreat. Due to their lack of heavy artillery, the Australian infantry on the Kokoda Track paused at Eora Creek and held up MacArthur's offensive. Australian Commanders Herring and Blarney requested that Gen. Whitehead make Capt. William Hennon's 7th Squadron available to act as flying artillery. The P-40 pilots developed new tactics, and soon were dropping 500 pound bombs ahead of infantry patrols who directed the American fighter bombers against the Japanese fortified positions. The Screamin' Demons dispatched eight plane flights, three times a day, to glide bomb targets between Eora Creek and the Kumusi River. MacArthur also used the 7FS to cover his Pongani forces, dive bombing gun emplacements and flying high escort for 5th Bomber Command medium bombers that bombed and strafed the Buna forces. Fortunately, the Japanese Air Force did not counter these ground support sorties and their AA defenses were mostly meager and inaccurate.

The grueling combat schedule had taken its toll on both the men and their war weary model E Warhawks. Kenney had been promised new Warhawks, which were to arrive in the near future, and gave the 7th Squadron priority. Hennon's combat tour had come to an end as of 20 October, but there was no one immediately available of command rank who could replace Hennon. Maj. Morrissey was being treated for Malaria at Port Moresby, and Hutchinson was unwilling to hand over either of his competent Majors, George Powell or William Reddington, from his own staff. Capt. William Martin, a senior Captain from the 5th Fighter Command, was named CO of the 7FS.

On 28 October, the Japanese defense at Eora Creek was finally breeched by the 7th Australian Division, which now had the Japanese in full rout toward Kokoda Village. Japanese General Horii was drowned at Wairope while trying to evacuate his harried troops down the Kumusi River to the coast. Nonetheless, the major portion of his troops was able to withdraw from the Track for their final fierce defense of Buna. At last, on 2 November, only three months after they had captured Kokoda, the Australians recaptured the Village and moved on toward Buna.

Although the Japanese continued to reinforce and supply their troops by sea, Allied air power was reasonably successful in harassing their sea lanes by frequently strafing and destroying numerous barges and supplies on the beaches. Although the convoy of 5 October succeeded in reaching Buna, another convoy spotted off southern New Britain on 1 November was driven back by continued bombing and strafing assaults from virtually every type of aircraft in Kenney's air arsenal: B-17s, B-26s, B-25s, Beauforts, Beaufighters, A-20s, and dive bombing P-40s of the 49FG. The continued attacks on the airfields at Lae, Salamaua, and Buna, in conjunction with the air bombardment of Rabaul, served not only to support land campaigns in New Guinea and Guadalcanal, but also in eroding enemy air power. This policy Kenney himself had outlined in August shortly after he assumed command:

"Operating from advanced bases is a horrible handicap, but with the Japanese out-numbering us in the air about three to one and with a long range fighter for escorting their bombers I do not dare to base any bombardment in New Guinea until I weed Mr. Moto down to my size. That is what we're trying to do at the present time. . . . He built his whole strategy on fighter cover. If we take out his fighters, his bombers won't go. They are poorly defended and a P-40 or P-39 is good for about three or four of them before the ammunition gives out. If his fighters and his bombers don't go, his troops and boats don't go either, so I am going to continue working on the Jap air force as hard as I can."

With the end of the Battle of Iorabaiwa Ridge, purely defensive operations in the New Guinea Campaign ended. The prongs of the Japanese pincers aimed at Port Moresby had been broken, and Milne Bay and Iorabaiwa Ridge denoted the turning point in the campaign.

September-November 1942 Air Operations
35FG over the Kokoda Track

From the end of August through September 1942 the 35FG flew routine sorties, alternating patrols, escorts for medium bombers and transport, and strafing missions over the Kokoda Track. The Group's ground support missions and after escort strafing attacks damaged enemy positions, killed troops, and generally disrupted the Japanese movement along the Track. No enemy air opposition was encountered, but 2Lt. Cobb was lost on 30 August over Menga due to a fuel pressure problem. Generally this period was routine and even dull, as described by these excerpts from the Group History:

3 September: "saw nil activity other than routine, nil sights or flights."

5 September: "saw the 41st doing all the work. Flew twice to Myola (on the Track, author) and hit target area both times, then strafed with fires observed. Really supporting the fighting in the Pass."

16 September: "....41st escort Beaufighters to Buna. When didn't find any Nips to fight, dropped down with 4 planes and helped Beaufighters to strafe. Smacked some barges and a gasoline store, silenced machine gun posts."

21 September: "GALA DAY. 39th returned to New Guinea, this time flying the P-38."

25 September: "After spending a week trying to mess up the Wairope Bridge, Command took it easy on us; fished, etc., while routine patrols and training flights were the order of the day."

A singular difficult target for numerous Allied air attacks was the **Wairope** Bridge that spanned the Kumasi River. (AAF)

29-30 September: "Field Orders from ADVON noted that Nip air strength seems to be nil. Buna no activity. Working on Lae Strip. Some transient aircraft on Lae Strip. Nil at Salamaua and Finschhafen. Appears unused." ….. "We will continue to build up a striking force principally for use against invasion shipping, harassing Nips and to destroy communications."

1 October: A singular difficult target for numerous Allied air attacks was the Wairope Bridge that spanned the Kumasi River. It was a bottleneck of the Japanese supply line as it was the only crossing for many miles. After many efforts 18 feet of the bridge was finally destroyed by 1Lts. William Nolan and James Miller flying with HQ Squadron on 1 October. The still functioning Wairope Bridge was finally captured by Allied troops on 14 November.

19 September 1942: 49FG/7FS

By 17 September, P-40s of the 49th Group's 7th Squadron were transferred to Port Moresby as reinforcements when the Japanese approached Imita Range on the Track, which was only 20 miles from Port Moresby. This unit, which was combat tested at Darwin, saw their first action on 19 September, when eight of their aircraft escorted a flight of Australian Beaufighters on a strafing mission to Buna. Four of the P-40s set four Japanese barges and a gasoline dump on fire.

21-22 September 1942: 49FG/7FS

During the afternoon of 21 September, 10 7FS P-40s took off to fly their initial dive bombing mission against the Japanese in the Kokoda-Buna area. The target was the Wairope Bridge, an important river bridge that the enemy utilized in getting supplies to their troops at the front. Although no hits were made on the bridge with the 500 pound demolition bombs, there were strikes close enough to cause the bridge to sag and partially disconnected an end of it. The next day a dozen P-40s went back and hit the Wairope Bridge with 300 pound bombs, and further damage was done to the bridge supply warehouses, and buildings. The 7FS pilots strafed gun emplacements at Buna Airdrome and motor launches in the bay. Despite heavy ground fire, all of the P-40s returned safely to their base.

Late September 1942: Situation

During the end of September the Japanese sent a number of nuisance raids out against Port Moresby, but most of these were largely ineffectual and no interceptions were made by the American fighters. However, Allied bombers and fighters kept constant pressure on the Japanese troops on the Kokoda Track while infantry reinforcements were rushed to the front. Three new Australian battalions went into combat to face the Japanese in the ridges above Port Moresby, and units of the American 32nd Division were brought into 7 Mile Airdrome by AAF troop carrier C-47s.

A battalion of the American 32nd Infantry Division that had taken part in the fight at Kokoda pushed off into the jungle and over the mountains on a parallel course south of the Kokoda Track against the Japanese on 5 October, but the overall plan was to land the balance of the division by airlift in the vicinity of Wanigela, some 65 miles down the coast from Buna. From that point the American infantry would advance up the coast against Buna, while the Americans and Australians on the Kokoda front pushed the enemy back toward Buna from the west.

Throughout October 5FC fighters flew missions escorting the C-47s dropping supplies to the ground troops on the Kokoda front and strafing the enemy's supply lines to his rear. The frantic battle taking place on Guadalcanal had all but cleared the New Guinea skies of enemy air opposition, which were now fighting over the Solomons. So Allied bombers and fighters of the Fifth Air Force were able to relentlessly attack the Japanese in Papua.

Throughout October 5FC fighters flew missions escorting the C-47s dropping supplies to the ground troops on the Kokoda front and strafing the enemy's supply lines to his rear. (AAF)

October 1942: 35FS/8FG

On 1 October, Maj. George Greene relinquished command in the 35FS/8FG and moved up to Group HQ, and Capt. Norman Morris replaced him. Area air patrols continued throughout October over the Milne Bay sector but no enemy aircraft appeared.

5 October 1942: 36FS/8FG

On 5 October, 1Lt. John Barley of the 36th Squadron stalled just after take off during a routine transport escort flight and his fighter crashed into an Australian billet and killed three men there.

November 1942: Situation

By 3 November, the Australian ground forces had completely occupied Kokoda and its airstrip on the east side of the Owen Stanley Mountains. The immediate danger to the Allied bases at Port Moresby had now ended, and much of the credit must be given to the fighter pilots of the Fifth Fighter Command, who had escorted the bombers attacking the Japanese supply lines and who, through their own strafing attacks, had contributed greatly to the destruction of the enemy troops.

To protect the eastern flank in New Guinea, the 35th and 36th Squadrons of the 8th Fighter Group had been sent to Milne Bay in mid-September. They were joined by the 80th Squadron by early November 1942. By this time the 8FG was largely equipped with new P-39Ds, which were an improvement over the bedraggled P-400s. Also on the move were the 8th and 9th squadrons of the 49th Fighter Group. A wing of RAF and RAAF Spitfires moved into the Darwin area in October, and the men of the 8th and 9th Squadrons were given a short breather before moving on to the Port Moresby area late that month.

The contribution of the Allied Air Forces continued much as before, and despite poor food, Malaria and dysentery, and primitive living conditions, the pilots and ground crews of the American fighter squadrons performed superbly. Spare parts were non-existent, and often replacement parts were cannibalized from wrecks or borrowed from another aircraft until the next supplies arrived from Australia. As Japanese troops approached Moresby and had reached within 30 miles of the airfields, sentry duties and defensive preparations consumed even more of the airmen's time. Generally, experience and careful planning by the Squadron Commanders produced improvements in technique and results.

Medium and heavy bomber units attacked distant targets, harassed convoys, and bombed important supply points in New Guinea. Fighters provided top cover for bombers and transports when missions were within the limited range of P-40s, P-39s, and P-400s. Fighters and light bombers also conducted bombing and strafing patrols over the Track as continuously as the weather and the availability of aircraft allowed.

Rabaul and Buka continued to serve as key supply points and air bases for Japanese operations, both in New Guinea and the Solomons. After earlier attacks had concentrated on shipping and the important airfields, during September and October Kenney's heavy bombers carried out at least 12 missions against the airdrome at Buin, eight against Buka, and 15 against ground targets at Rabaul, including Rabaul town. The size and frequency of these attacks demonstrated the growing striking power of the Allied air power in the Southwest Pacific. However, these missions, crossing equatorial weather fronts and over targets heavily defended by AA and fighters, completely exhausted the aircrews.

In addition to distant bombing missions, the Allied Air Forces continued to patrol the New Guinea coast line in search of Japanese naval movement. During this period, the Japanese were sending supplies to Buna largely by small boat transportation, rather than by large convoys. They loaded supplies on any available seaworthy vessel: motor launches, canoes, luggers, and landing barges which, under cover of darkness or stormy weather, would sneak along the shoreline from Lae or Salamaua to Buna and Sanananda. Stopping these small craft was almost impossible, as they were much more elusive targets than the larger vessels making up the July and August convoys. The barges and other vessels beached in the Buna-Sanananda area offered targets that were continually bombed and strafed.

A few large convoys were seen off the New Guinea Coast during September and October, with the Japanese attempting one sizeable landing at Buna. Reconnaissance early on 5 October 1942 warned of the approach of a light cruiser, a destroyer (or two), and one 10,000 ton transport escorted by Zeros, which drove off bombing attempts by B-25s and B-17s. The troops and supplies that the Japanese landed either by convoy or small boat in the vicinity of Buna had to travel over the Track almost 100 miles to the front at Iorabaiwa Ridge; over the same mountains and gorges that had so disheartened the Australians earlier. Intelligence Officers also suspected that enemy submarines were transporting supplies to the garrisons of Lae and Salamaua, and were then to be carried over the Owen Stanleys. The knowledge of the vulnerability of this supply line encouraged the Allies to carry out continual air attacks that could possibly cut off the enemy troops at Iorabaiwa. Kenney, therefore, unleashed all available aircraft against supply points along the Kokoda Track. Fighters based at Port Moresby and medium and heavy bombers based in northern Australia, using Port Moresby as a refueling stop, were joined in September by modified A-20 light bombers, which soon would monopolize low level attack missions. These air attacks wreaked proverbial havoc on the Japanese Track supply lines and left their troops on the far end without food or ammunition.

6

Reorganization of the Fifth Air Force: August-December 1942

The Protagonists

Douglas MacArthur (26 January 1880-5 April 1964)

Douglas MacArthur was born on 26 January 1880 at Arsenal Barracks, Little Rock, AR, as the youngest son of US Army officer Arthur MacArthur. He was raised as a "military brat" on a succession of posts in the American Old West. He attended the West Texas Military Academy, where he was valedictorian, and after two rejections he attended West Point, where he was First Captain and graduated top of the class of 1903. During the 1914 United States occupation of Vera Cruz he conducted a reconnaissance mission for which he was nominated for the Medal of Honor. In 1917, he was promoted from Major to Colonel and became Chief of Staff of the 42nd (Rainbow) Division. In the fighting on the Western Front during World War I he rose to the rank of Brigadier General, and was again nominated for a Medal of Honor. He was twice awarded the Distinguished Service Cross, as well as the Silver Star seven times, which led to the accusation that MacArthur was a "glory hound."

From 1919 to 1922 MacArthur served as Superintendent of West Point, where he attempted a series of reforms. At this time MacArthur became romantically involved with socialite Louise Cromwell Brooks, and married her on 14 February 1922 at her family's villa in Palm Beach, Florida (she would divorce the absent and busy MacArthur in 1927). In October 1922, MacArthur left West Point to assume command of the Military District of Manila. His next assignment was in the Philippines, where in 1924 he was instrumental in quelling the Philippine Scout Mutiny. In 1925, he returned to the US and became the Army's youngest Major General at 45. He served on the court martial of Brig. Gen. Billy Mitchell and was president of the United States Olympic Committee during the 1928 summer Olympics in Amsterdam. In 1930 he became Chief of Staff of the United States Army. As such, he was involved with the controversial expulsion of the Bonus Army protesters from Washington, DC, in 1932, and the establishment and organization of the Civilian Conservation Corps (CCC). In 1934 MacArthur sued journalists Drew Pearson and Robert S. Allen for defamation after they described his treatment of the Bonus marchers as "unwarranted, unnecessary, insubordinate, harsh and brutal." In turn, they threatened to call Isobel Rosario Cooper as a witness. MacArthur had met the Eurasian Cooper while in the Philippines, where she had become his mistress. MacArthur was forced to settle out of court, secretly paying Pearson $15,000.

Douglas MacArthur. (AAF)

When the Commonwealth of the Philippines achieved semi-independent status in 1935, Manuel Quezon, President of the Philippines, asked MacArthur to supervise the creation of a Philippine Army. Quezon and MacArthur had been personal friends since MacArthur's father had been Governor-General of the Philippines 35 years earlier. With President Roosevelt's approval MacArthur accepted the assignment, and it was agreed that MacArthur would receive a salary and allowances and the rank of Field Marshal from the Commonwealth, in addition to his Major General's salary as Military Advisor to the Commonwealth Government of the Philippines. MacArthur sailed from San Francisco in October 1935 on his fifth tour in the Far East and brought his long time aide de camp, Capt. Thomas Davis, as well as Majors Dwight Eisenhower and James Ord, a friend of Eisenhower's, as his assistants. Also accompanying MacArthur to the Philippines was Jean Marie Faircloth, an unmarried 37 year old socialite, and over the next two years the two were frequently seen together; they would marry in April 1937.

MacArthur retired from the US Army in 1937 to become Military Advisor to the Commonwealth Government of the Philippines, and named Lt.Col. Richard Sutherland as his Chief of Staff and Richard Marshall his Deputy Chief of Staff. President Quezon officially conferred the title of Field Marshal on MacArthur in a ceremony at the Presidential Palace on 24 August 1936, where he was presented with a gold baton and a distinctive and unique uniform. MacArthur and Eisenhower were to establish the Philippine Army from universal conscription with a goal to train 40,000 men per year at 128 camps. For the next several years the 40,000 trainee goal was not nearly met, and mostly obsolete cast off American equipment and weapons were received to equip them.

On 26 July 1941 Roosevelt federalized the Philippine Army, recalled MacArthur to active duty in the US Army as a Major General, and named him Commander of US Army Forces in the Far East (USAFFE). MacArthur was promoted to Lieutenant (three star) General the following day, and then to General on 20 December. At the same time Sutherland was promoted to Major General, while Marshall, Spencer Akin, and Hugh Casey were all promoted to Brigadier General. On 31 July 1941 the Philippine Department had 22,000 troops assigned, 12,000 of whom were Philippine Scouts, and between July and December 1941 the Department received 8,500 reinforcements. Prewar defense plans assumed the Japanese could not be prevented from landing on Luzon, and called for US and Filipino forces to abandon Manila and retreat with their supplies to the Bataan Peninsula. MacArthur attempted to slow the Japanese advance with an initial defense against the Japanese landings, but the Filipino troops could not contain the Japanese landing force. MacArthur subsequently ordered a retreat to Bataan and Manila was declared an open city. On 25 December MacArthur moved his headquarters to the island fortress of Corregidor, in Manila Bay, but a series of air raids forced most of the headquarters to move to Bataan, leaving only the nucleus with MacArthur on Corregidor. The beleaguered troops on Bataan called him "Dugout Doug." On 1 January 1942 MacArthur was offered and accepted a gigantic secret (until 1979) payment of $500,000 (about $8 million today) from President Quezon of the Philippines as payment for his prewar service. MacArthur's staff also received payments: $75,000 for Sutherland, $45,000 for Marshall, and $20,000 for Huff. Eisenhower, after being appointed Supreme Commander Allied Expeditionary Force, was also offered money by Quezon, but declined.

In February 1942, as the Japanese forces were about take the Philippines, MacArthur was ordered by Roosevelt to evacuate to Australia. Legend has it that MacArthur considered resigning his commission and fighting on as a private soldier in the Philippine resistance, but that Sutherland persuaded him otherwise. During the night of 12 March 1942, MacArthur and a select group (that included his wife Jean and son Arthur, as well as Sutherland, Akin, Casey, Marshall, Willoughby, Diller, and George) left Corregidor in four PT boats. MacArthur and his party reached Del Monte Airfield, on the island of Mindanao, two days later and were flown by USN B-17s to Australia.

MacArthur arrived on 17 March at Batchelor Airfield and made his famous "I came out of Bataan and I shall return" speech on the way to Adelaide by train at Terowie, a small railway township in South Australia, on 20 March. Upon his arrival in Adelaide, MacArthur abbreviated this proclamation to the now famous, "I came through and I shall return" that made the headlines. Officials in Washington asked MacArthur to amend his promise to "We shall return," but he ignored the request. For his leadership in the defense of the Philippines, General Marshall decided to award MacArthur the Medal of Honor, the decoration for which he had twice previously been nominated. It was admitted that MacArthur had not actually performed acts of valor in battle on Bataan, but the 1927 award to Charles Lindbergh set a precedent. MacArthur chose to accept the Medal on the basis that "this award was intended not so much for me personally as it is a recognition of the indomitable courage of the gallant army which it was my honor to command." Arthur MacArthur, Jr., and Douglas MacArthur thus became the first father and son to be awarded the Medal of Honor.

On 18 April 1942, MacArthur was appointed Supreme Commander of Allied Forces in the SWPA, while Lt.Gen. George Brett became Commander, Allied Air Forces, and V.Adm. Herbert Leary became Commander, Allied Naval Forces (neither of these men were MacArthur's choice). Since the majority of land forces in the theater were Australian, General Marshall insisted an Australian be appointed as Commander, Allied Land Forces, and the job went to General Sir Thomas Blamey. Although predominantly Australian and American, MacArthur's command also included small numbers of personnel from the Netherlands East Indies, the United Kingdom, and other countries. MacArthur established a close relationship with the Prime Minister of Australia, John Curtin, although many Australians resented MacArthur as a foreign general who had been imposed upon them. The staff of MacArthur's General Headquarters (GHQ) was built around the nucleus of officers who had escaped from the Philippines with him and would become known as the "Bataan Gang." Though Roosevelt and General Marshall pressed for Dutch and Australian officers to be assigned to GHQ, the heads of all the staff divisions were American, and such officers of other nationalities as were assigned served under them. MacArthur's GHQ was initially located in Melbourne, but was moved to Brisbane in July because Brisbane was the northernmost city in Australia with the necessary communications facilities. After MacArthur lost confidence in Brett the stage was set for the formation of the Fifth Air Force.

Richard Kerens Sutherland (27 November 1893-25 June 1966)

Richard Sutherland. (AAF)

Sutherland was born in Hancock, MD, on 27 November 1893, the only son of Howard Sutherland, who later became a US Senator from West Virginia. He graduated from Yale University in 1916 and, while at Yale, joined the Reserve Officer Training Corps. In 1916 he enlisted as a Private in the Connecticut National Guard, and later that year the National Guard was federalized. He served on the Mexican border during the Pancho Villa Expedition and accepted a National Guard commission as a Second Lieutenant in the field artillery. Soon after, he transferred to the Regular Army with a commission in the infantry and was promoted to Captain in 1917, serving with the 2nd Division on the Western Front during World War I.

After returning to the United States, Sutherland was an instructor at the United States Army Infantry School from 1920 to 1923 and professor of military science and tactics at the Shattuck School from 1923 to 1928. He graduated from the Command and General Staff College in 1928. Fluent in French, he attended the École Supérieure de Guerre in 1930. From 1932 to 1933 he attended the US Army War College, and then served with the Operations and Training Division of the War Department General Staff. In 1937 he went to Tientsin, China, in command of a battalion of the 15th Infantry; however, after 21 years he was finally promoted to Major in March 1938, when he was assigned to the Office of the Military Advisor to the Commonwealth Government (Philippines), Manila, under Gen. Douglas MacArthur. Though he had never commanded troops in the field at any rank higher than Captain in World War 1, MacArthur's patronage allowed him to hold the "local rank" of Lieutenant Colonel in 1938, and he was then promoted to that official rank. Sutherland served under MacArthur's Chief of Staff, Lt.Col. Dwight Eisenhower, but the ambitious Sutherland soon maneuvered his superior out of his position, and the pandering Sutherland would remain MacArthur's Chief of Staff throughout the war. Sutherland became a Brigadier General in July 1941 and Major General in late 1941. Following the fall of Manila, MacArthur's Headquarters moved to the island fortress of Corregidor, where it was the target of numerous Japanese air raids. During his stay he became friendly with Philippines President Manuel Quezon and was given a very large (for the time) cash payment of $75,000 for his prewar service to the Philippines. In March 1942 MacArthur was ordered by Roosevelt to "relocate" to Australia, and Sutherland was one of a selected group of advisors and subordinate military commanders that would accompany MacArthur in evacuating the Philippines in four PT boats.

Sutherland was thought of as MacArthur's lackey and one of the so-called "Bataan Gang." He was disliked and distrusted by many subordinate American and Australian officers, who considered him to be high handed and overprotective of MacArthur. Sutherland was often given the role of "hatchet man" by MacArthur, and "bad news" invariably came through Sutherland, rather than from MacArthur himself. A fellow officer described Sutherland as a "hard man who was more feared than liked." It was Sutherland who represented MacArthur before the Joint Chiefs of Staff, and on many occasions Sutherland opened, read, and frequently answered communications to MacArthur, including those addressed to him personally or "Eyes Only." Some decisions often attributed to MacArthur were actually made by Sutherland. For instance, Gen. Lewis Brereton alleged that Sutherland's protectiveness prevented vital information from reaching MacArthur during the first day of the war. Later, the decision to bypass Mindanao and move on directly to Leyte was made by Sutherland on MacArthur's behalf, while MacArthur was traveling under radio silence.

In 1943 Sutherland and Kenney took part in an effort to promote General MacArthur's candidacy for the Presidency. They worked with Senator Arthur Vandenberg of Michigan to have the War Department rescind the order that prevented MacArthur from seeking or accepting political office, but to no avail.

While stationed at MacArthur's GHQ SWPA in Melbourne, Sutherland became involved in a personal scandal when he met socialite Elaine Clarke, whose husband, a British Army officer, was a POW in Singapore. When GHQ moved to Brisbane in July 1942 Clarke moved with it, as did two other civilian women who worked as secretaries for Generals George Kenney and Richard Marshall. Sutherland set up Clarke as the receptionist at MacArthur's GHQ, but when GHQ began planning to move to New Guinea, Sutherland was informed that there was an agreement between MacArthur and the Australian Prime Minister, John Curtin, that Australian civilians could not be sent outside Australia. To circumvent his separation from Clarke, Sutherland requested personnel from the Women's Army Corps (WAC) to replace civilian employees of GHQ, and Sutherland asked for direct WAC officer commissions for Clarke and Kenney's and Marshall's secretaries. This exploited a loophole whereby enlistments in the WACs were restricted to American citizens but officer commissions were not. Maj. Gen. Miller White, the US Army Deputy Chief of Staff for Personnel, and Col. Oveta Culp Hobby, the Commanding Officer of the Women's Army Corps, were strongly opposed to Sutherland's ploy. But they were overruled by Deputy Chief of Staff Joseph McNarney when he was informed that the commissions were personally desired by General MacArthur as essential to the operation of his headquarters and the prosecution of the war. Clarke was commissioned as a Captain (as was Gen. Eisenhower's driver, Kay Summersby). Although Clarke's rank was more a reflection of Sutherland's status rather than her own, she became an assistant to the Headquarters Commandant, with duties corresponding with her rank, and moved with Advance GHQ at Hollandia. However, her presence there in contravention of his agreement with Curtin ultimately brought about MacArthur's disapproval and he ordered her to be returned to Australia, first from Hollandia, and after Sutherland defied him, MacArthur finally had to evict her from the Philippines. Although Sutherland remained as MacArthur's Chief of Stall throughout the war, the Clarke situation caused a rift between the two and Sutherland lost much of his annoying power over subordinates.

George Howard Brett (7 February 1886-2 December 1963)

George Brett. (AAF)

George Howard Brett was born in Cleveland, OH, on 7 February 1886, the second of five children of William and Alice Brett. George's older brother Morgan graduated with the West Point class of 1906, but the family was unable to obtain a second West Point appointment, so George graduated from the Virginia Military Institute in 1909. He was commissioned as a Second Lieutenant in the Philippine Scouts in March 1910 and transferred to the 2nd US Cavalry in August 1911. He returned to the US in May 1912 and was first stationed at Fort Bliss. In December 1913 he moved to Fort Ethan Allen, where he became friends with a fellow Lieutenant Frank Andrews, who was engaged to the daughter of Brig.Gen. James Allen. While a groomsman at Andrew's wedding he met bridesmaid Mary Devol, who was the daughter of another Army officer, Maj.Gen. Carroll Devol. He married Mary in March 1916 and, influenced by Allen and Andrews, Brett transferred to the Aviation Section of the US Signal Corps on 2 September 1916. He attended aviation school, and on graduation in 1916 was assigned to the office of the Chief Signal Officer in Washington, DC, where he was promoted to First Lieutenant on 1 July 1916 and to Captain on 15 May 1917.

Capt. Brett arrived on the Western Front in November 1917, but suffered an appendicitis which caused him to lose his flight status. After making a partial recovery, he served in France as Senior Materiel Officer under Brig.Gen. William "Billy" Mitchell, attaining the temporary rank of Major on 7 June 1918. After briefly returniong to the US to serve in Office of the Director of Military Aeronautics in Washington, DC, from 1 August to 23 September 1918, Brett was sent to England to command the United States Army Air Service Camp at Codford.

After the war Brett was posted to Kelly Field, TX, in December 1918, where he commanded the Aviation General Supply Depot until February 1919, when he became the maintenance and supply officer at the Air Service Flying School. He commanded the Air Service Depot in Morrison, VA, for a month in October 1919 before being assigned to the office of the Director of the Air Service in Washington, DC, where his rank of Major became permanent in 1920. That year he took command of Crissy Field. His first son, the future USAF Lt. Gen. Devol "Rock" Brett, was born in 1923. From 1924 to 1927 Brett was stationed at the intermediate depot at Fairfield, OH, where he was the officer in charge of the Field Service Section. Beginning in June 1927, he attended the Air Corps Tactical School at Langley Field, VA, after which he was selected to attend the two year Command and General Staff School at Fort Leavenworth, KS. He commanded Selfridge Field, MI, before he returned to Fort Leavenworth as an Air Corps instructor from 1933 to 1935. After 16 years as a Major he was finally promoted to Lieutenant Colonel, and was selected to attend the Army War College. On graduation, he was given the temporary rank of Brigadier

General and became the Commander of the 19th Wing, based in the Panama Canal Zone. While he was stationed there, his oldest daughter Dora married his aide, the future General Bernard Schriever. On his return from Panama Brett reverted to his permanent rank of Lieutenant Colonel. He was then briefly stationed in Menlo Park, CA, before moving to Langley, VA, where he became Chief of Staff to his old friend Frank Andrews, now the Commander of GHQ Air Force. In February 1939 Brett moved to Wright Field as Assistant to the Chief of the USAAC, also serving as the Commandant of the Air Corps Engineering School and the Chief of the Materiel Division. He was promoted to the permanent rank of Brigadier General and then was promoted to Major General on 1 October 1940.

When his immediate superior. Maj. Gen. Henry H. "Hap" Arnold, was temporarily transferred to the Army General Staff in November 1939, Brett became the acting Chief of the Air Corps. In May 1941, he formally became Chief of the Air Corps for a four year term, but the June 1941 reorganization that appointed Arnold the Chief of US Army Air Forces made the position of Chief of the Air Corps redundant but active. Brett was then sent to the United Kingdom to determine how the AAF could aid RAF Lend Lease requirements. His recommendation that American labor and facilities be established in the UK to conduct the repair, assembly, and equipping of American Lend Lease aircraft was controversial, and was ultimately rejected by Arnold because the personnel and equipment were not available. Brett next visited the Middle East, where his outspoken criticism of preparations there irritated his British hosts to such a degree that the British Ambassador to Egypt, Sir Miles Lampson, complained about him to the Foreign Secretary, Sir Anthony Eden. Air Marshal Sir Arthur Tedder noted that "the charms of General Brett's company were beginning to pall. After a talk with him on the afternoon of 25 September I wondered in my journal how he and all the American visitors could lay down the law about things of which they knew next to nothing." Arnold ordered Brett to return to the United States in December.

After the Japanese attacked Pearl Harbor Brett was ordered to Rangoon to meet Sir Archibald Wavell, the British Commander-in-Chief in India. The two then flew to Chungking, where they met with Generalissimo Chiang Kai-shek, who promised Chinese troops to assist in the defense of Burma. He arrived in Darwin on 28 December 1941 and was appointed Deputy Supreme Commander of the American-British-Dutch-Australian Command (ABDA), under Wavell, on 1 January 1942. After he was promoted to Lieutenant General on 7 January 1942 he joined Wavell at his headquarters at Lembang, in West Java. Soon, the rapid Japanese advance through South East Asia divided the Allied held area. Brett left Java for Melbourne on 23 February 1942, where he continued his command of US Army Forces in Australia when the ABDA was formally dissolved on 25 February.

Brett received a notice from the Chief of Staff, Gen. George Marshall, that MacArthur was going to request that he send a flight of long range bombers to Mindanao to bring him and his staff back to Australia. The only aircraft that were available were B-17s of the 19th Bombardment Group, which had seen relentless service in the Philippines and the Dutch East Indies Campaigns. Brett asked V.Adm. Herbert Leary, the Commander of Naval forces in the ANZAC area, to lend him some of the newly arrived B-17s in his area, but Leary turned him down. Only the B-17 piloted by 1Lt. Harl Pease arrived at Mindanao; two turned back with engine trouble, while a fourth ditched safely in the sea. MacArthur was infuriated with Leary and sent a message to Marshall, who "persuaded" Leary to release four new B-17s to Brett. These bombers reached Mindanao on 16 March 1942 and evacuated MacArthur and his staff to Australia. This incident was to initiate an intense dislike between the two Generals. After MacArthur arrived Brett expected to command American forces in Australia, but Australian Prime Minister John Curtin was persuaded to recommend that MacArthur be named Supreme Commander South West Pacific Area. The April 1942 reorganization that established the Southwest Pacific Area under MacArthur downgraded the US Army Forces in Australia to a supply and administrative organization that would soon be renamed the Services of Supply. Brett became the Commander of Allied Air Forces, Southwest Pacific Area, with his headquarters in Melbourne. One of MacArthur's first orders to Brett was for a bombing mission to the Philippines, an order which was delivered personally by MacArthur's Chief of Staff, Maj.Gen. Richard Sutherland. Brett objected, stating that his men were exhausted and his aircraft were worn out, and that the Philippines were a lost cause. Sutherland told Brett that MacArthur insisted that the mission be carried out despite the possibility of high losses. Brett's protest irritated MacArthur, who wrote a personal reprimand to Brett. Thereafter, communications with Sutherland would be conducted through Air Vice Marshal William Bostock, Brett's Chief of Staff. Further disagreements between MacArthur and Brett followed. On 6 July 1942 Marshall radioed MacArthur that Maj.Gen. George Kenney had been selected to be Brett's replacement. The day after MacArthur awarded Brett the Silver Star "for gallantry in action in air reconnaissance in the combat zone....during the months of May, June and July, 1942" Brett was sent to the US on 4 August 1942.

Brett languished for a time without a command before being appointed as Commander of the US Caribbean Defense Command and the US Army's Panama Canal Department in November 1942. He remained in this backwater position until 1945, when the Inspector General investigated allegations against Brett concerning the misuse of Army funds and property. The Inspector General's report to Marshall mostly exonerated Brett and no action was recommended. Brett's four year tenure as Chief of the Air Corps was concluding at the end of May 1945, and Brett requested voluntary retirement. He retired on 30 April 1945 with the rank of Major General, only to be immediately recalled to active duty the next day as a temporary Lieutenant General and as Commanding General of the Caribbean Defense Command and Panama Canal Department, which he held until 10 October 1945. After being hospitalized he reverted to retired status on 10 May 1946, but was later advanced to the grade of Lieutenant General on the USAF retired list on 29 June 1948. After the war Brett served on several committees and Air Force boards and lived in Winter Park, FL, until his death at age 77 from cancer on 2 December 1963.

Lewis Hyde Brereton (21 June 1890-20 July 1967)

Lewis Brereton was born in Pittsburgh, PA, in 1890. He attended St. John's College, Annapolis, MD, and then entered the US Naval Academy in 1907, where he graduated in June 1911 as an Ensign. He resigned from the USN and was appointed as a Second Lieutenant in the Coast Artillery Corps of the Regular Army on 17 August 1911. After a year there he joined the Aviation Section of the Signal Corps in September 1912. He received flying training at the Signal Corps Aviation School at San Diego, qualifying as a military aviator on 27 March 1913. In July 1916, he was transferred to the 2nd Field Artillery in the Philippines, but was re-assigned to the Signal Corps with the 2nd Aero Squadron in January 1917. He returned to the States in March

Lewis Brereton. (AAF)

1917 and was assigned to the Office of the Aviation Section as Chief Signal Officer in Washington, DC.

He was sent overseas in October 1917, and the following March was named the Commander of the 12th Aero Squadron, which was one of the first American flying units on the front. Brereton was involved in extensive operations, and on 5 July became Chief of Aviation of the First Army Corps. He took command of the Corps Observation Wing immediately preceding the St. Mihiel operations, and in October 1918 became Operations Officer on the Staff of the Chief of Air Service of the American Expeditionary Forces. After the Armistice he was appointed Chief of Staff, Headquarters Air Service of the Third Army.

Upon his return to the US in February 1919, he spent the next six years mainly in training positions until June 1925, when he became Commanding Officer of the Second Bombardment Group at Langley Field, VA. In August 1927 he entered the Command and General Staff School at Fort Leavenworth, KS, and after graduating the following June he was appointed as the Commanding Officer of the 88th Observation Squadron at Post Field, Fort Sill, OK. In August 1931, he became commanding officer of France Field, Panama; and then successively CO of the 6th Composite Group; CO of the Panama Air Depot; and Air Officer of the Panama Canal Department. In July 1935 he became an instructor at the Command and General Staff School at Fort Leavenworth, where he served until June 1939. From July 1939 to October 1940 he was Base Commander at Barksdale Field, LA, and then was assigned to command the 17th Bombardment Wing, GHQAF at Savannah, GA. On 29 July 1941 he was assigned to command the Third Air Force at Tampa, FL.

In October 1941 he was named as the Commander of the Fifth Air Force, taking over for Brig. Gen. Henry Clagett. At the beginning of World War II, he commanded the Far East Air Force (FEAF) in the Philippines and urged immediate air attacks. He failed to disperse his parked aircraft and the FEAF was consequently mostly destroyed on the ground. Although he received no discipline for this failure, MacArthur never again had confidence in him. In January 1942, in addition to his duties as Commander of the Fifth Air Force, he was designated Air Commander-in-Chief of the Allied Air Forces on the staff of General Wavell, stationed in Java. After the defeat in Java Brett was sent to organize and command the Tenth Air Force in India in March 1942.

Brereton was considered slapdash and hedonistic, and was unsuccessful in every wartime command he was assigned. Yet whenever he failed at one command, he was able to be transferred to an important position elsewhere. One of his greatest gaffes was ordering the disastrous August 1943 low-level attack on the Axis oil complex at Ploesti. True to expert intelligence expectations, nearly half of the 164 B-24s that made the attack were lost without affecting Ploesti's productivity. However, this blunder had no effect on Brereton's career, as he played an important role in the Allied defeat at Arnhem in September 1944. He then returned to the US for assignment to Air Force headquarters at Washington, and in July 1945 was assigned to command the Third Air Force at Tampa, FL.

George Churchill Kenney (6 August 1889-9 August 1977)

Kenney was born in Yarmouth, Nova Scotia, Canada, but grew up in Brookline, MA. He attended the Massachusetts Institute of Technology for three years, but left to take a job as a railroad instrument technician. In June 1917 he enlisted as a Private in the US Signal Corps, but was soon accepted as a Flying Cadet in the Aviation Section, where he received flight training from noted aviator Bert Acosta. He was commissioned a First Lieutenant in December 1917 and was immediately sent to Advanced Flying Training School in France. In February 1918 he was assigned to the 91st Aero Squadron, where he flew 75 combat missions and shot down two German aircraft (one of the German pilots he shot down was future Luftwaffe leader Hermann Goring). During the war he was shot down and was awarded the Distinguished Service Cross and Silver Star. After the war, Kenney remained for a time

George Kenney. (AAF)

with the Allied occupation forces in Germany. He was promoted to Captain in 1919 and was appointed Commander of the 91st Aero Squadron. He remained with the occupation forces in Germany after cessation of hostilities until June 1919, when he was sent to the United States and reassigned to the 8th Aero Squadron at McAllen, Texas.

Finally, Kenney would receive assignments where his talents would finally be utilized and recognized. The contacts he made during this period would help advance his future career. In 1926, he was sent to the Air Corps Tactical School at Langley Field, VA, and next attended the Command and General Staff College at Fort Leavenworth, KS. Kenney then served in a variety of assignments. He was an instructor at the Tactical School at Langley Field; and he made a survey of possible airdrome locations in Puerto Rico and the Virgin Islands, selecting sites which are in use today. He attended the Army War College in Washington, DC, graduating in 1933. In March 1935, Kenney was promoted to Lieutenant Colonel, bypassing the grade of Major, and his first promotion in 17 years. Kenney was active in aeronautical research and development during this period, and pioneered the use of machine guns mounted in the wings of Air Corps pursuit planes.

When Brig.Gen. Frank Andrews was appointed to command the General Headquarters Air Force in March 1935, he appointed Kenney to be his Assistant Chief of Staff for Operations and Training. Andrews knew Kenney well from the Air Corps Tactical School, where from 1927 to 1928 Kenney was an instructor and Andrews a student. In this important position on the GHQ Air Force staff Kenney was responsible for combat flying training. At the Tactical School, Andrews had been impressed with Kenney's talent to explain and solve technical problems. While at GHQ Air Force Kenney developed doctrine and revised the basic attack aviation primer; emphasized training in instrument and night flying; compiled tables of organization; planned maneuvers; and traveled extensively to other bases.

Also while at GHQ Andrews and Kenney advocated the new B-17 long range bomber and autonomy for the Air Corps, but Maj.Gen. Oscar Westover, Chief of the Air Corps, and the General Staff were unable to appreciate the concept of such a large bomber for the defense of America and preferred the status quo of the Air Corps, which had been hard pressed during the Depression. The often curt and abrasive manner of the temporary Lieutenant Colonel and a permanent Captain Kenney irritated Westover and the other Generals around him, and he was exiled to Ft. Benning, GA, where he taught tactics at the Infantry School from 1936-38.

When Westover was killed in an air crash in 1938, Brig.Gen. Hap Arnold became Chief of the Air Corps, and one of his first actions was to send Kenney to Wright Field, OH, to head the troubled Production Engineering Section of the Air Corps Materiel Division. In March 1940, he was promoted to Colonel and sent to France as Assistant Attaché for Air in France to observe combat tactics and technical developments of the combatants in Europe. As a result of his observations and recommendations, improvements were made in American military aircraft during the year before Pearl Harbor. Kenney was seen to be a rising star in the Air Corps and was promoted to Brigadier General in January 1941, and the following month to Major General.

After the Japanese attacked Pearl Harbor Kenney was assigned to the West Coast as Commanding General of the 4th Air Force in March 1942. As the United States began its preliminary planning and organization of its forces in the Pacific, Arnold's first requirement was to assign an energetic and aggressive officer to replace Lt.Gen. George Brett, the Air Commander who had fallen out of favor with MacArthur in the Southwest Pacific Theater. Arnold wanted to send Lt.Gen. Frank Andrews, who was then commanding Caribbean Defense Command. However, Andrews vehemently refused to work for MacArthur, with whom he served in the 1930s and whom he loathed. Brig.Gen. Laurence Kuter, Deputy Chief of the Air Staff, suggested that Arnold send Kenney to MacArthur, but Arnold thought that the demanding and pompous MacArthur would soon send the candid Kenney packing. But Kenney possessed the requirements for the job: he was an experienced and effective leader and organizer and could tolerate MacArthur and would win his favor.

Ennis Clement Whitehead (3 September 1895-12 October 1964)

Ennis Clement Whitehead was the eldest of three children born to J.E. and Celia Whitehead on a farm near Westphalia, KS, on 3 September 1895. In 1914, he entered the University of Kansas to study Law, but upon America's entry into World War I joined the Army in April 1917. He was posted to Officers' Training Camp at Fort Riley, where he volunteered for the Aviation Section, US Signal Corps. After training at the University of Illinois at Urbana-Champaign and Chanute Field he qualified as a military aviator on 19 October 1917. He arrived in France on 14 November 1917 and was posted to the 3rd Aviation Instruction Center at Issoudun for more training, and attended gunnery school at Bordeaux. He became a test pilot and spent the remainder of the war in that capacity.

Ennis Whitehead. (AAF)

Whitehead was discharged from the Army in 1919 and returned to the University of Kansas, where he graduated with an Engineering degree in 1920. He became a reporter in Wichita to earn enough money for law school, but before long his love of flying led him to apply to the US Army Air Service, where he was commissioned as a First Lieutenant on 11 September 1920. Whitehead was initially posted to March Field, where he served as a flying instructor. In 1921 he was transferred to Kelly Field, where he assumed command of the 94th Pursuit Squadron of the 1st Pursuit Group. On 20 July 1921, he participated in General Billy Mitchell's controversial aerial bombing attacks on the ex-German Battleship *Ostfriesland*. The 1st Pursuit Group transferred to Selfridge Field, MI, in July 1922. In 1925, Whitehead was involved in a mid-air collision and had to bail out, but suffered only a sprained ankle; however, the other pilot was killed. On 25 September 1925 he married Mary Nicholson. In 1926, Whitehead attended the Air Service Engineering School at McCook Field, graduating first in his class. He then attended the Air Corps Tactical School at Langley Field in 1930 and was promoted to Captain. He returned to the 1st Pursuit Group and was assigned command of the 36th Pursuit Squadron at Selfridge Field. He did tours in Panama with the 16th Pursuit Group (1932-34), at Barksdale Field with the 20th Pursuit Group 1934-35), and as Inspector of the General Headquarters (GHQ) Air Force at Langley Field (1935-37). He was promoted to Major and attended the Command and General Staff School at Fort Leavenworth in 1938. On graduation from the Command and General Staff School Whitehead was posted to the G-2 (Intelligence) Division of the War Department, where he was promoted to Lieutenant Colonel on 3 December 1940. In February 1941, he was transferred to become the CO of the new training base at Luke Field, AZ, where he was promoted to Colonel on 5 January 1942.

In May 1942 Lt.Gen. George Brett, the Allied Air Forces Commander in the South West Pacific Area (SWPA), requested that Lt.Gen. Arnold, the Commanding General of the USAAF, promote Whitehead to Brigadier General as a replacement for Brig.Gen. Harold George, who had been killed in an air crash near Darwin on 29 April 1942. Whitehead was promoted on 16 June 1942 and ordered to the SWPA with bomber specialist Brig.Gen. Kenneth Walker. When Whitehead arrived in Australia on 11 July 1942 he found his new command disorganized and lacking aircraft. The Japanese had land and air superiority, and were threatening Australia. Gen. Arnold decided to replace Brett with Maj.Gen. George Kenney, who arrived in the theater on 28 July. Unable to supply more aircraft and crews, Arnold hoped that Kenney, Whitehead, and Walker would be able to make the best use of what was available. Kenney assumed command of the Allied Air Forces on 4 August, and three days later he instituted a sweeping reorganization of the Allied Air Forces. The Australian components were assigned to RAAF Command under Air Vice Marshal William Bostock, while the American components were consolidated into the reformed Fifth Air Force under Kenney's personal command. On paper the organization followed the orthodox pattern, consisting of 5th Fighter Command under Brig.Gen. Paul Wurtsmith, 5th Bomber Command under Walker, and an Air Services Command under Maj.Gen. Rush Lincoln. Kenney realized that he would have to maintain his headquarters near MacArthur's GHQ, which moved to Brisbane on 20 July while the fighting was thousands of miles away in New Guinea, with the Fifth Air Force's principal forward bases around Port Moresby. Moreover, Walker's headquarters was in Townsville, as heavy and medium bombers were based there and only staged through Port Moresby. Accordingly, Kenney appointed Whitehead as Deputy Fifth Air Force Commander and Commander of the Advanced Echelon (ADVON) in Port Moresby. On arriving in New Guinea, Whitehead concentrated on strengthening infrastructure, thereby bringing in additional engineer units and construction equipment. New airfields were developed, along with roads, housing, taxiways and revetments to protect his aircraft from the frequent Japanese air raids. He also attempted to build up the morale and leadership of his units. At this time the Japanese were advancing along the Kokoda Track, and despite the best efforts of the ground troops and his airmen, the Japanese advanced steadily on Port Moresby. Ultimately, the Japanese were turned back short of Port Moresby due to a lack of supplies caused by the air attacks on their extended supply lines. For his part in the Papuan Campaign, Whitehead was awarded the Distinguished Service Cross and the Australian government made him an honorary Commander of the Order of the British Empire. Whitehead encouraged and utilized ingenuity, improvisation, and innovation in building up Allied air power. Whitehead's influence was instrumental in the great Allied air victory during the Battle of the Bismarck Sea in March 1943, and he was promoted to Major General on 15 March 1943. As the Allied offensive began its rapid advance, Whitehead was able to move his air units and bomb line forward to support further advances. The arrival of the P-38 Lightning in the theater in late 1942 gave Whitehead a fighter that could match the Japanese fighters and the range to keep up with the leap-frogging land advances. Whitehead assumed command of the Fifth Air Force in June 1944, although he remained subordinate to Kenney. Initially, MacArthur's advance during the Philippines Campaign was beyond the range of land-based aircraft, and later developed into a long battle of attrition on the ground and in the air, but Whitehead finally gained the upper hand and was promoted to Lieutenant General on 5 June 1945. Whitehead was an able air leader during the war. MacArthur praised Whitehead for his "masterful generalship ... brilliant judgment and inexhaustible energy." Lt.Gen. Sir Iven Mackay, commander of New Guinea Force, reported that "I have found Brigadier General Whitehead of the USAAF extremely cooperative. In fact there is no question of asking for help; he takes the initiative."

Whitehead continued in command of the Fifth Air Force during the Occupation of Japan and succeeded Kenney as Commander of the Far East Air Forces in December 1945; he remained in command until March 1949. He returned to the United States to command the Continental Air Command, and was influential in dividing this organization into the Tactical Air Command and Air Defense Command, commanding the latter from January 1951. When Hoyt Vandenberg rather than Kenney was named as Chief of Staff of the USAF in 1948 he relieved Kenney as Commander of Strategic Air Command in October 1948, and Whitehead lost his mentor. Later, he was seen by some in the US Air Force hierarchy as "too closely attached to Kenney and MacArthur, too political, too outspoken, and too tactically focused" to be named as the Vice Chief of Staff of the USAF. Whitehead was passed up in receiving his fourth star and then had health reversals, so he retired on 31 July 1951. In retirement, Whitehead pleaded for the quick creation of an atomic strike force ready to conduct retaliatory attacks within a few hours after an attack on the United States, and at least 30 wings of all-weather jet fighters to intercept enemy bombers. He died of emphysema in Newton, KS, on 12 October 1964 and was buried in Arlington Cemetery. His son, Ennis Whitehead, Jr., later became a Major General and, in March 2003, his grandson Ennis Whitehead III was promoted to Brigadier General to become the third Whitehead generation of Air Force generals.

Paul Bernard Wurtsmith (9 August 1906-13 September 1946)

Paul Bernard Wurtsmith was born in Detroit, MI, on 9 August 1906, the eldest of three sons of Fred and Ella Wurtsmith. He attended the University of Detroit, where he earned an aeronautical engineering degree, and then enlisted in the Army Air Corps as a flying cadet on 4 August 1927. After earning his wings through the successful completion of flight training at Kelly Field, San Antonio, TX, he was commissioned as a Second Lieutenant in the Air Reserve on 23 June 1928. On 2 February 1929 he received a regular commission in the US Army Air Corps, after which he married Irene Gillespie (the pair had no children). Wurtsmith joined the 94th Pursuit Squadron, the famed World War I "Hat in the Ring" Squadron, at Selfridge Field, MI. Over the next 13 years he served in numerous instructor and command positions, with a highlight being the winning of the Mitchell Trophy Air Race in 1930. On 1 October 1934, he was finally promoted to First Lieutenant and to temporary Captain from 7 August 1935 to 16 June 1936, before being promoted substantively on 2 February 1939. He graduated from the Air Corps Tactical School in 1939.

Capt. Wurtsmith commanded the 17th Pursuit Squadron at Selfridge Field from September 1939 to July 1940, then the 41st Pursuit Squadron until January 1941; continuing there, he served with the 50th Pursuit Group until December 1941, when he assumed command of the 49th Pursuit Group at Key Field, MS. The 49th Pursuit Group was soon sent to the South West Pacific, arriving in Australia in February 1942. Because of the 102 pilots in the group 89 pilots had no pursuit time at all, so additional training was undertaken. By March there were three USAAC Pursuit Groups in Australia (the 8th, 35th, and 49th), but only Maj. Wurtsmith's 49th was combat ready. The 49th moved to the Darwin area in March and April 1942. Darwin had been bombed a number of times, and the Group's P-40s became its principal defense. At Darwin, the Americans met primitive conditions and lacked adequate logistical support, replacement aircraft, and spare parts, and were heavily dependent on Australia. By using tactics that would exploit the strengths of the P-40 and minimize its weaknesses, as well as the efforts of the ground crews and service troops to keep as many fighters serviceable as possible, between March 1942 and January 1943 his fighters claimed to have downed 78 enemy aircraft over New Guinea. Wurtsmith was promoted to Colonel on 6 July 1942. In August 1942, Maj.Gen. George Kenney assumed command of the Allied Air Forces in the SWPA, becoming the Senior Allied air officer under the Theater Commander, Gen. Douglas MacArthur. Kenney split the Allied Air Forces into their Australian and American components, with the American part becoming the reformed Fifth Air Force in September 1942. Kenney concurrently commanded the Fifth Air Force, with Brig.Gen. Ennis Whitehead as his Deputy. The major commands of the Fifth Air Force were the V Service Command under Maj.Gen. Rush Lincoln, 5th Bomber Command under Brig.Gen. Kenneth Walker, and the V Fighter Command. The 5FC was activated at Fort George Wright in April 1942 as the V Interceptor Command, and was redesignated as the 5th Fighter Command in August. Col. Wurtsmith assumed command on 11 November, with his Headquarters at Port Moresby. Kenney informed Wurtsmith that if he "made good, he would be promoted to Brigadier General. If not, he would be sent him home on a slow boat." By early 1943 Wurtsmith had "made good," and on 8 February 1943 Wurtsmith received his promotion. When Kenney submitted the papers recommending Wurtsmith's promotion to Brigadier General, one of Macarthur's staff jibed that he hoped Wurtsmith was over 21, as MacArthur had been promoted to the rank of Brigadier General at age 37 (Wurtsmith was actually 36). Kenney icily replied that "We promote them out here for efficiency, not age." Wurtsmith also became one of few American officers to be decorated by the Australian government, being awarded the Commander of the Order of the British Empire for "excellence of training and direction of fighter operations in New Guinea" (presented by General Sir Thomas Blamey on Leyte in March 1945).

By September 1943 Wurtsmith's five fighter groups had almost 600 fighters, but one third were antiquated P-39s, P-400s, and P-40s; half of which were in service depots. Although two thirds of the 5FC fighter missions in New Guinea were to escort bombers and transports, it also participated in the Allied offensive that pushed the Japanese back along the Buna trail, took part in the Battle of the Bismarck Sea in March 1943, fought for control of the approaches to Huon Gulf, and supported ground forces during the campaign in which the Allies eventually recaptured New Guinea. In late November 1943 Wurtsmith left for home on leave and 348FG CO Neel Kearby took temporary command of the 5FC. He returned on 13 January, just as the 5FC moved its HQ from Port Moresby to Nadzab. The 5FC then covered landings on Noemfoor and had a part in the conquest of Biak. After having used P-38, P-40, and P-47 fighters, in September 1944 it was completely equipped with P-38s, which were used to fly long range escort and attack missions to Mindanao, Halmahera, Ceram, and Borneo. In October 1944 the 5FC arrived in the Philippines, shortly after the assault landings on Leyte. They engaged enemy fighters, attacked shipping in Ormoc Bay, supported ground forces, and covered the Allied invasion of Luzon.

On 30 January 1945, Wurtsmith replaced Maj. Gen. St. Clair Streett as Commander of the Thirteenth Air Force and was promoted to the rank of Major

Paul Wurtsmith. (AAF)

General on 19 March 1945. Wurtsmith's 13AF supported the US Eighth Army to clear the Southern Philippines, and also supported the Australian I Corps against Japanese forces in Borneo. Wurtsmith relinquished command of the 13AF in July 1946 and returned to the United States, where he was assigned to the Headquarters of the Strategic Air Command (SAC), which was then commanded by Gen. George Kenney. In September 1946 Wurtsmith was appointed Commander of the Eighth Air Force. On 12 September 1946 he took off from MacDill Field, FL, in a B-25 and, after visiting his family for the first time in three years, he flew back to MacDill at the controls of the B-25 in bad weather. He was flying at a low altitude and crashed into Cold Mountain, NC, and all on board were killed. He was buried in Arlington National Cemetery, and in February 1953 the Air Force named Wurtsmith AFB in Oscoda, MI, in his honor.

The Reorganization of the Allied Air Forces

The Allied Air Forces were being completely reorganized during autumn 1942. There was a criticism that American units were too controlled by the Australians, and now with competent American headquarters personnel available, it was felt that a separate American Air Force could be established. When Maj.Gen. George Kenney was selected to succeed Brett, his appointment promised an effective reorganization and vigorous implementation of air operations in the Southwest Pacific that summer.

MacArthur requested authorization from the War Department for the formation of a typically American organization of AAF units, and suggested the designation of Fifth Air Force in honor of his former air command in the Philippines. Authorization was received on 9 August, and the Fifth Air Force was officially constituted on 3 September, but several months passed before the reorganization was fully complete. Kenney immediately assumed command, but also retained his command of the Allied Air Forces. The Fifth Air Force was to include the 5th Fighter Command, the 5th Bomber Command, and the 5th Air Base Command. But the Headquarters and Headquarters Squadrons of the 5th Air Force and the 5th Bomber and 5th Air Base Commands were not officially transferred from the Philippines to Australia until 2 November. Only the 5th Fighter Command was transferred directly from the United States, and although many of its personnel were already in the Southwest Pacific, the Headquarters and Headquarters Squadron did not officially arrive until 24 November.

During the formative period of the new organization, between August and December 1942, staffs were being chosen and operational methods discussed and tested. By September, Kenney had established an advanced echelon at Port Moresby under his Deputy Commander, Maj.Gen. Whitehead, and had selected Brig.Gen. Walker, who had already distinguished himself by accompanying numerous bombing missions, to obtain firsthand information for the 5th Bomber Command. Whitehead also temporarily filled in as Fighter Commander until succeeded on 11 November by Col. Paul Wurtsmith, who had so ably led the 49th Fighter Group in the defense of Darwin during the spring and summer.

Kenney Takes Over as Commanding General of the Allied Air Forces

As Commanding General of the Allied Air Forces, Kenney held operational control over both the Fifth Air Force and the RAAF, with the latter retaining its administrative autonomy. Moreover, it was decided to establish a reasonably clear line of demarcation between the operational responsibilities of the RAAF and the Fifth Air Force. Except for the Northeastern Area, the RAAF assumed the responsibility for defense of the Australian continent, and in addition, full responsibility for the Northwestern Area, from which reconnaissance and bomber operations against the Netherlands East Indies were usually flown. The Fifth Air Force was entrusted with the Northeastern Area, from which the planned offensive was to be launched. The arrangement was by no means inflexible. RAAF squadrons were attached to the Fifth Air Force and repeatedly participated in its operations, while the Fifth frequently furnished units to its ally on request. American heavies, for example, were often based near Darwin as insurance against a possible Japanese offensive thrust from the East Indies.

Kenney Wins Over MacArthur

When Kenney assumed command from Brett, his main concern and greatest challenge was to win the support and confidence of MacArthur. Before arriving in the Pacific, Kenney knew of the problems between Brett and MacArthur and understood that he needed to get along with MacArthur if he was to succeed. But MacArthur had an extremely close and loyal staff that controlled both access and information to their Commander. These officers evacuated the Philippines with MacArthur, and on their arrival in Australia earned the nickname "the Bataan Gang." Kenney also had to deal with the acrimony between air and ground officers over the role of air power that had been building up since World War I. Ground officers maintained that air power was an adjunct to and should be controlled by the infantry. Airmen contended that air power could be best utilized strategically and tactically as a united force under the control of a single air commander.

Brett told Kenney of his constant problems with Sutherland and MacArthur, explaining that Sutherland was a bully and overly protective of MacArthur. Brett had not seen MacArthur personally for weeks, and he

When **Kenney**. (R) assumed command from Brett, his main concern and greatest challenge was to win the support and confidence of **MacArthur**. (L). (AAF)

had only talked to Sutherland on the telephone and concluded that "They just didn't get along." He said that neither MacArthur nor his staff had an understanding of air operations and, nonetheless, MacArthur, after conferring only with Sutherland and his immediate staff, made all decisions, and often Sutherland had taken it upon himself to write air operations orders.

Kenney scheduled a meeting with Sutherland, whom he had known when they were classmates at the Army War College in Washington. Kenney considered Sutherland a "brilliant, hardworking officer, who had always rubbed people the wrong way. He was egotistic, like most people, but an unfortunate bit of arrogance combined with his egotism had made him almost universally disliked. However, he was smart, capable of a lot of work, and from my contacts with him I had found he knew so many of the answers that I could understand why General MacArthur had picked him for his Chief of Staff." Kenney had gotten along with him at the Army War College, "and I decided that I'd get along with him here, too, although I might have to remind him once in a while that I was the one that had the answers on questions dealing with the Air Force. Sometimes, it seemed to me, Sutherland was inclined to overemphasize his smattering of knowledge of aviation." In a later meeting Kenney became so frustrated with Sutherland that Kenney drew a dot on a plain piece of paper and said "the dot represents what you know about air operations, the entire rest of the paper what I know."

During the meeting, Sutherland began his tirade against the Air Force by stating that Brereton and all the senior air officers were to blame for the loss of the Philippines. After designating the blame for losing the Philippines, Sutherland finally got to present conditions by saying "Brett certainly was in wrong. Nothing that he did was right." According to Sutherland, "none of Brett's staff or senior commanders was any good, the pilots didn't know much about flying; the bombers couldn't hit anything and knew nothing about proper maintenance of their equipment or how to handle their supplies." He also thought "there was some question about the kids having much stomach for fighting." He thought the Australians were "undisciplined, untrained, over advertised, and generally useless as the Air Force." He said the one good point about the USAAF was, "It seemed that up on Bataan, after all their airplanes were gone and they had been given some infantry training, they made good ground troops...." Kenney writes, "This was going to be fun. Already it began to look like a real Number One trouble-shooting job."

Immediately after his meeting with Sutherland Kenney introduced himself to MacArthur, and for the next half hour MacArthur listed the shortcomings of the Air Force that became more and more serious, until finally, as Kenney relates:

> "There was MacArthur in Australia nothing left but an inefficient rabble of boulevard shock troops whose contribution to the war effort was practically nil. He thought that, properly handled, they could do something but that so far they had accomplished so little that there was nothing to justify all the boasting the Air Force had been indulging in for years. He had no use for anyone in the whole organization from Brett down to and including the rank of Colonel. There had been a lot of promotions made which were not only undeserved but which had been made by Washington on Brett's recommendations. If they had come to him, he would have disapproved the lot. In fact, he believed that his own staff could take over and run the Air Force out here better than it had been run so far. Finally he expressed the opinion that the air personnel had gone beyond just being antagonistic to his headquarters, to the point of disloyalty. He would not stand for disloyalty. He demanded loyalty from me and everyone in the Air Force or he would get rid of them."

At this point Kenney stated his case:

> "(I) decided it was time for me to lay my cards on the table. I didn't know General MacArthur any too well as I had just met him a few times when he was Chief of Staff of the Army six years before, but if he was as big a man as I thought he was, he would listen to me and give me a chance to sell my stuff. If not, this was a good time to find out about it even if I took the next plane back to the United States. I got up and started talking. I told him that as long as he had had enough confidence in me to ask for me to be sent out here to run his air show for him, I intended to do that very thing. I knew how to run an air force as well or better than anyone else and, while there were undoubtedly a lot of things wrong with his show, I intended to correct them and do a real job. I realized that so far the Air Force had not accomplished much but said that, from now on, they would produce results.... If at any time this could not be maintained, I would come and tell him so and at that time I would be packed up and ready for the orders sending me back home.
>
> The General listened without a change of expression on his face. The eyes, however, had lost the angry look that they had had while he was talking. They had become shrewd, calculating, analyzing, appraising. He walked toward me and put his arm around my shoulder. 'George,' he said, 'I think we are going to get along together all right.' I knew then that we would. I had been talking with a big man and I have never known a truly big man that I couldn't get along with."
>
> He wanted to know what my recommendations were for the use of the Air Force. I told him that I didn't have any, as I didn't know what there was to work with, but I intended to fly to New Guinea that night, look the show over there, and visit the airdromes in the Townsville area on the way back to Brisbane about the end of August. I said we would do everything possible to help him carry out his commitments; but that I would prefer to tell him what that possible was when I got back. General MacArthur agreed and said, 'As soon as you get back, come in and see me and we'll have another talk.' We shook hands and I left."

Kenney then went back to meet Brett again, and was introduced to all his top heavy staff. Kenney decided that there were too many personnel in his complicated Headquarters "directorate system," which had about a dozen men issuing orders in his name. Kenney decided that they could be better utilized at the combat squadron level. At the time only an advanced American echelon of Brett's air organization was stationed in Brisbane while the rear echelon remained at Melbourne, 800 miles away, under Maj. Gen. Rush Lincoln. Kenney described this situation as: "It was just as if the headquarters were trying to function at Chicago with its rear echelon in New Orleans, except that we would have had much better telephone service." To facilitate creating a truly Allied air organization, Brett had integrated Americans and the Australians, not only on the staff level, but also mixing aircrew. AVM William Bostock of the RAAF was Brett's Chief of Staff of the Allied Air Forces, while Group Captain Allan Walters of the RAAF was Director of Operations and Air Commodore Joe Hewitt, also RAAF, was Director of Intelligence; all had several American officers as assistants.

Kenney had inherited antiquated aircraft that were often grounded due to bureaucracy, general disorganization, and the lack of spare parts. But he concluded that, "Luckily, I would have two good Brigadier Generals to work with me as Ennis Whitehead and Ken Walker....I had known both of them for over 20 years. They had brains, leadership, loyalty, and liked to work. If Brett had had them about three months earlier, his luck might have been a lot better."

By the end of 1942, Kenney finally won over MacArthur, "It's a lot of fun to talk to General MacArthur. He thinks clearly, does not have preconceived ideas, weighs every factor, and plays the winning game for all it's worth. As soon as air power could show him anything, he bought it."

Kenney's Air Strategy

Once Kenney outmaneuvered Sutherland to get MacArthur's ear, his aggressive but sociable personality, together with his expert knowledge, allowed the two to embark on a close personal and professional relationship, which allowed Kenney to prevail over MacArthur's blockading staff (Sutherland) and the traditional dogma that separated airmen and ground officers. He made a point of establishing his Headquarters close to MacArthur, which allowed him to speak with MacArthur regularly during the day and then while socializing in the evening. Despite the growing personal chemistry between the two, Kenney would have to continually prove his ability as a commander, drawing on his long experience and knowledge about air warfare.

Europe First

Kenney was continually frustrated by Washington's Europe first strategy and Arnold's depiction of the SWPA as a "defensive" theater. Kenney persisted in asking Arnold for aircraft and personnel to conduct offensive operations. But Arnold made it clear that he could not "maintain every theater at offensive strength," as this "dispersed effort would invite disaster." Arnold's intention was to keep Kenney's forces at adequate strength to enable them to support themselves defensively, and also to carry out a limited offensive against the Japanese. During his several trips to Washington, Kenney was caught between the proverbial "rock and a hard place," as he needed to balance his loyalty to MacArthur, as Theater Commander, with his loyalty to Arnold, the AAF Chief. On one trip Kenney "made the rounds," meeting with Undersecretary of War Robert Patterson and Assistant Secretary of War for Air Robert Lovett, and then met with President Roosevelt and the Joint Chiefs of Staff. Kenney emphasized the need to replace his losses in order to maintain air superiority in the theater. Roosevelt told Kenney to "be reasonable about it," but would look into the matter, even if he had "to argue with the whole British Empire about it."

Kenney. (R) was continually frustrated by Washington's Europe first strategy and **Arnold's**. (L) depiction of the SWPA as a "defensive" theater. Kenney persisted in asking Arnold for aircraft and personnel to conduct offensive operations. (AAF)

Air Superiority

For Kenney, gaining "control of the air situation before you try anything else" was the basis of successful air warfare. Establishing air superiority was essential to other air, ground, or sea operations, and "an absolutely vital first step in modern warfare." Since the Japanese aircraft factories and other industrial targets were well beyond the range of Allied bombers in the SWPA, Kenney achieved air superiority by destroying Japanese aircraft on the ground and in the air, which was simple in premise but "actually a long and difficult job." Kenney would continue his pledge to gain air superiority through every campaign in the war.

Interdiction

The reorganization of the air forces did not profoundly change the operational routine which had been established during the opening months of the campaign. However, the success of the MacArthur plan for the destruction of the Japanese Army depended to some extent upon the increased effectiveness of Kenney's air units. It was becoming obvious that MacArthur's proposed annihilation would not take place unless the transport of enemy reinforcements and supplies could be stopped en route on the sea, and then on their movement inland. The air force operations against enemy convoys, therefore, gained an increasingly significant magnitude. Such operations included strikes against shipping along the New Guinea coast and long range bombing missions against supply points which served as bases for enemy forces both in the Solomons and in New Guinea. To carry out heavy bomber raids against such objectives in October and November, Kenney had two bomber groups equipped with B-17s, the veteran 19th Group and the 43rd. This strength was insufficient to conduct a general air offensive in the Southwest Pacific, and Kenney constantly pressed his needs for reinforcements to Gen. Arnold. On 6 December, Arnold replied to Kenney that he planned to keep the Fifth Air Force strong enough to defend the area "and to carry out a limited offensive. . . .," as "Hitler is the more powerful opponent, both presently and potentially, and it would be far more dangerous to maintain a defense in his case until such time as he could gather his forces for a combined effort." In July 1942, Washington planned to replace all B-17s in the Pacific areas with B-24s. This change in heavy bomber type led to considerable controversy as to the relative merits of the B-17 and the B-24. But it was Kenney's ability to establish new low altitude tactics using new munitions carried by medium bombers that was the most effective against the enemy on the land and sea. Also, Kenney took advantage of the Allied intelligence on Japanese movements to restrict the combat areas of New Guinea during the last half of 1942.

Close Support

While Kenney realized the importance of using air power to support ground combat, he argued fervently for flying interdiction missions and against close air support, which dedicated aircraft to bombing enemy positions at the front lines. Nevertheless, at times during the fighting in New Guinea Kenney sent aircraft on close air support missions, though with less than ideal results. Pilots had difficulty locating and attacking targets on the ground through the thick jungle, and often could not locate their own forces, occasionally bombing friendly troops.

Airlift Operations

Opposing the Japanese in head on jungle confrontations had proved to be costly, and Kenney offered to airlift ground troops to outflank the Japanese advance. Although certain members of MacArthur's staff believed that Kenney's proposal was unfeasible, MacArthur promptly understood the benefits of Kenney's plan and eagerly accepted the offer. Soon transport aircraft were flying troops, food, and ammunition to the front lines and evacuating the sick and wounded.

The **P-39** would find its niche as a ground support aircraft but not without initial problems. (AAF)

Kenney Wins Over MacArthur

Kenney's attitude and ability, and continuing success, increased his status with MacArthur, allowing him to become a close advisor and even a friend to the aloof MacArthur. Meanwhile, MacArthur would prove to be a willing student of air power, and he and Kenney would spend much time discussing future operations. Kenney convinced MacArthur of advantages of air power while MacArthur's support of Kenney provided him with the opportunity to implement his ideas.

Throughout the war, MacArthur and Kenny maintained a close professional and personal relationship, and Kenney played an important role in shaping the general conduct of MacArthur's operations in the SWPA. But, in spite of this relationship, it is apparent that MacArthur accepted Kenney's advice only when it corresponded with his goals. For instance, MacArthur gladly followed Kenney's suggestions for accelerating an advance, but when Kenney attempted to discourage MacArthur and suggested a strategy that threatened to slow the pace of the war his concerns were ignored. Kenney's influence on the actual conduct of the war varied to the extent that it was in agreement with MacArthur's objectives.

Gen. Arnold summarized the importance of the rapport between the two when he told Kenney, "I don't believe the units could possibly perform the missions in the manner that they are doing without the most sympathetic support from General MacArthur. It requires complete understanding between General MacArthur and you."

However, Kenney's problem of dual loyalty to the Army officer MacArthur and the Air Force officer Arnold was never entirely resolved, as its importance oscillated during the course of the war. During more critical times Kenney set aside his loyalty to the Air Force and sided with MacArthur, the Theater Commander. But by the end of the war his loyalty to the Air Force would take on a greater role due to the looming post war conflict between the American Armed Services.

7

October to Mid-November 1942: 35th and 49th Fighter Group Operations

49FG Receives the P-40K

Finally, on 24 October Kenney's pledge to supply new fighters to the 49ers was fulfilled when ferry pilots delivered eight new P-40K-5s from Townsville to 14 Mile Drome. The K-model P-40 was basically an upgraded E-model, and was to be the heaviest P-40 production version. The main difference in the K was a supercharged Allison V-1710-73 engine rated at 1,325 hp for take off and 1,150 hp at 11,800 feet engine (the K-5 added rotary valve cooling). To compensate for the increased torque of the added horsepower, a fillet was added to the leading edge of the tail in addition to a slightly broader and rounded rudder, which was the K's only characteristic that distinguished it from the E. These P-40Ks, like the 49ers' earlier Es, were appropriated from part of British Lend-Lease production blocks; so several were painted with the sand-and-olive drab desert camouflage, while most were the standard AAF olive drab and gray. However, despite the increased horsepower these new K-models still were considered as only adequate high altitude interceptors. The increased power at lower altitudes significantly increased their ordnance carrying capacity for their tactical role. Curtiss/AAF specifications directed that operational limits of maximum loads be a single belly-mounted 500 pound bomb or a pair of wing mounted 300 pound bombs with a belly fuel tank, or another 300 pound bomb, which nearly doubled the tactical bomb capacity.

49FG Finally Receives the P-38

Before the 49ers received their P-38s Maj. George Prentice, former 7FS Commander, returned to 14 Mile Drome, but now as the CO of the 39FS/35FG and with 12 new Lightnings. The 39th was assigned at the opposite end of the field, making ground control difficult, as the 7FS Warhawks would take off from the south and the 39FS Lightnings from the north.

The P-38s promised by Kenney arrived at Townsville, and would cause uproar all the way up to Wurtsmith's Fighter Command HQ. The 16 new P-38s arrived under the pretext of being of the 17th Fighter Squadron (Provisional), which riled the veterans of the former Java 17PS now at Townsville awaiting their next combat assignment. Worse, the new P-38s arrived with permanent pilots who were attached to the 9FS. With these additional pilots the 9th's flight roster was at nearly 60 pilots, which left most of Capt. Jesse Peaslee's pilots without aircraft. Peaslee immediately requested that Wurtsmith find combat assignments for his senior officers in any available position in the 5th FC. So, during October the 9th Squadron remained in Townsville, unsure if they would return to combat or in what fighter they would fly.

After their initial inspection at the Townsville Maintenance Center, the P-38s were found not to be combat ready and would have to go through a complete workup. The major modification was the installation of rubber self sealing tanks in the leading edges of the wings, along with additional alterations to be made, with the radio equipment and the gun camera systems mounted in the fuselage nose, which were vulnerable to corrosion. By the end of October Townsville became so crowded that five Lightnings were flown to Rogers (30 Mile) for installation of the self sealing tanks and modifications. At Rogers, each plane required four men and at least three days to complete, and the P-38 modification program would not be ready for another six weeks, causing more defections by the disgruntled 9FS pilots to the other units in New Guinea.

2 October 1942: 35FG/30FS

Eight P-38s of the 39FS flew top cover for B-17s that were transporting Gen. MacArthur to 7 Mile Drome.

2 October 1942: 8FG

Capt. Norman Morris took over as 80FS CO from George Greene, who became its CO in January 1942.

Late October 1942: 49FG/8FS

Capt. Edward Sims was ordered to move his 8th Squadron to Port Moresby by the end of October to augment the intensified air offensive. However, Sims was due to be rotated home, but requested that Hutchinson extend his tour. Sims was by far the oldest 49er flying officer, but his experience and leadership was greatly needed, and 49er CO Lt.Col. Donald Hutchinson allowed Sims to take his unit to Port Moresby's 3 Mile Strip if he would stop flying combat missions. So, the 8th Squadron's weary P-40Es were overhauled once more, and the Squadron was reinforced with the war-weary P-40E castoffs of the 7th Squadron once they received their P-40Ks. The 3rd Attack Group also operated from 3 Mile Drome and required a dispersal

Maj. George **Prentice**, former 7FS Commander, returned to 14 Mile Drome but now as the CO of the 39FS/35FG and with 12 new Lightnings. (AAF)

area for their larger twin-engine A-20 Havocs, so the 8FS' Warhawks were parked along the inland side of the runway that ran parallel to the coastline and was surrounded by rolling hills and dense brush.

25-31 October 1942: 49FG/8FS Begins Combat Over New Guinea
After beginning to patrol above the Moresby area on 25 October, the Eightballers flew their first escort mission on 29 October. The mission was high cover for the 7FS Screamin' Demons and the medium bomber missions for Whitehead's air offensive against the three airstrips surrounding Lae village. On 31 October, eight Eightballs flew cover above 14 3AG A-20s and the 49th was opposed in air combat for the first time over New Guinea with no combat claims.

Late October 1942: 49FG Command Changes
In late October replacement pilots arrived at 14 Mile Drome, many of whom had trained in the US since the beginning of the war, accumulating many hours of P-40 flight time. There was also a small group from Hawaii called the "Pineapple Boys," which included a few that had seen combat during the Pearl Harbor attack. As the squadron rosters increased the Command structure also changed. Capt. William Chapman became 7FS Ops Exec. and appointed 1Lt. Frank Nichols as Deputy Ops Exec. Capt. George Manning became Ops Exec. when Chapman rotated home in early November.

November 1942
Japanese Air Situation
The intense 5AF offensive, supporting MacArthur and Blamey's combined land offensive against Japanese forces pinned down at Buna, was devastating. While the Japanese High Command at Rabaul was frantically trying to reinforce their beleaguered forces at Buna and further east at Guadalcanal, the Aussies captured Kokoda Village at the end of the Track on 1 November. The Imperial Navy air groups at Lakunai Airdrome, on Rabaul, were hopelessly committed to supporting both campaigns. The renowned Tainan Kokutai Air Group, which had scored numerous victories over the Philippines and Netherlands East Indies, had experienced irreplaceable losses of veteran pilots during the long range escort missions against either Port Moresby or the Solomon Islands during the Port Moresby offensive. Along with combat losses, the Group's pilots and ground personnel in New Britain and New Guinea were suffering with Malaria, scurvy, or Dengue Fever. Taking advantage of the weakened state of the enemy air force, Whitehead dispatched missions against the Lae airfield complex in an effort to establish Allied air supremacy over New Guinea in the beginning of November.

1 November 1942: 35FG/39FS
Eight pilots of the 39FS flew P-38s to Guadalcanal to supplement the 13AF and were attached to the 339FS out of New Caledonia under the

Lae Drome. (AAF)

command of Maj. Dale Brandon, and under the operational control of the USMC. While there these pilots did not engage in combat, but flew patrols and were on alert. Seven of the eight would return to Moresby on the 22nd.

1 November 1942: 49FG/8FS

At sunrise, Flight Leaders 1Lts. Richard Dennis and Bruce Harris each led four P-40s from 3 Mile Drome and rendezvoused with 14 A-20 Havocs of the 3BG over Moresby Harbor, then flew north for the hour long, 200 mile overland flight to Lae for a bombing and strafing attack. The formation broke out of the clouds over the Huon Gulf, just south of Salamaua, and looked for the river delta of the Markham Valley as a landmark for the main runway of Lae Airdrome, which ran north to south on the east bank of the river delta. The Havocs had been modified with forward firing machine guns for low level strafing attacks and descended to strafe the Lae runway. Dennis dispersed the eight fighters to provide the largest possible air cover over the A-20s, and he and Harris flew a wide sweep over the area until the last Havoc signaled its withdrawal from Lae airfield.

The two flights had separated in the clouds, and at 0745, as the Havocs withdrew, Dennis called for Harris to regroup. Dennis' flight, consisting of Wingman William Day, Element Leader Ross Baker, and his Wingman, rookie Glenn Wohlford, was bounced by eight to 10 Zeros about 10 miles from Lae. The P-40s dropped their tanks, and Dennis and Day dove to gain speed and then climb to attack the Zeros. But Baker and Wohlford were forced to continue to dive, and Wohlford was hit immediately and was last seen diving with white smoke trailing from his aircraft with two Zeros on his tail. Dennis fired at several Zeros and finally was able to pull up to get a good head on burst directly into the engine of one, sending it into a fatal dive into the ground. Day fired a head-on burst to send another of the Zeros down in flames.

1Lt. William **Day** claimed his first of five victories. (AAF)

8FS P-40s at Kila. (3 Mile Drome). (AAF)

2 November 1942: 35G and 49FG

35FG/39FS and 49FG/7FS

On the 2nd, a mission was sent out against Japanese supply ships at Buna and the airdrome at Lae. The mission was unsuccessful, as eight Lightnings of the 39FS and 11 7FS P-40s in escort of nine RAAF Beaufighters hunted for the alleged convoy but were unable to find them, so the Allied formation strafed the Buna garrison instead.

49FS/8FS

That afternoon, 10 B-26 Marauders escorted by 16 Eightballs were intercepted by 10 Zeros south of Lae in a brief combat, during which no claims were made by either side. Shots were exchanged but no 49ers claimed any hits. On his return to 3 Mile Drome, 2Lt. Bryant Wesley's P-40 had its engine seize up in the landing pattern and he crash landed in the shallows of Bootless Bay and swam ashore.

3-5 November 1942: 35FG/41FS

The 41FS flew a transport escort mission to Pongani, and 2Lt. J.R. Miller, flying with HQ Squadron, was listed as MIA due to the weather. Capt. Jack Wilson led a search flight and first spotted an abandoned P-39 crashed on a beach, but as they flew on the searchers recognized a P-40 which appeared to be intact near a village with a white man and natives nearby. Miller had bailed out over Kappel Point and landed in the jungle, then hacked his way out to the shore. Here he met an Australian civilian and stayed the night, and was taken by boat to a native village the next morning. He was then taken to an intact P-40 located near the village where he had been seen by the search flight. The next day another search flight led by Lt.Col. Richard Legg dropped a message to Miller at 1120, telling him that a Tiger Moth would pick him up. However, at 1445 a P-40 approached 7 Mile Drome and made a perfect landing with Miller at the controls. To the onlookers' surprise Miller was followed out of the cockpit by a small native. Miller explained that since he had no parachute to sit on he could not see out of the cockpit, and enlisted the native's lap to give him enough height to see.

6 November 1942: 35FG/39FS

The 39FS was redesignated as the 39th Fighter Squadron (Twin Engine) and was officially reorganized and equipped with the Lockheed P-38.

7 November 1942: 35FG

The 35FG received the following telegrams commending it for its contributions to the New Guinea Campaign:

> Please express to all ranks of the Air Corps concerned my admiration for the magnificent part you have played in the campaign which has resulted in the capture of Kokoda.
>
> Signed: MacArthur
>
> The splendid work by all ranks is a tremendous source of pride to me, and I desire to congratulate and thank all for their whole-hearted effort in consummating a job which merits the commendation of the Commander-in-Chief.
>
> Signed: Ennis C. Whitehead
>
> I desire to add my commendation to those of General MacArthur and General Whitehead for the excellent work done by the fighter units and for the splendid cooperation with other branches of our forces which has resulted in the accomplishment of this mission.
>
> I wish also to particularly commend those of the ground echelon for their untiring efforts in the maintenance of aircraft.
>
> Signed: Paul D. Wurtsmith

8 November 1942: 49FG/8FS

Rookie 2Lt. Nelson Brownnell's P-40E was heavily hit by AA over Buna. Brownell realized that his damaged fighter would be unable to climb over the Owen Stanley's to return to base and tried to reach the newly built Australian 3,000 foot runway on the forested hillside at Kokoda Village. This strip was built to accommodate smaller liaison aircraft, and as he approached his engine quit east of Kokoda and he crashed and was killed.

9 November 1942: 49FG/8FS

During a morning mission, 8FS newcomer 2Lt. Robert Howard's war-weary P-40 failed to get enough power to climb over the Owen Stanley's and he attempted an emergency belly landing on the small supply strip built on a slope near Myola. The struggling P-40 slid off the wet runway and crashed into the jungle, but Howard emerged from the wreckage with only minor injuries and was returned to Moresby by an Australian patrol.

10 November 1942: 8FG/80FS

A number of new pilots joined the 80FS during October and November 1942. Lieutenants John Jones, Edward Robertson, and Jay T. Robbins came up to Port Moresby early in October, and Robert Siebenthal, Cornelius "Corky" Smith, Albon Hailey, and Alexander Woodall arrived about the time the Squadron moved to Milne Bay. Smith and Jones would become aces in the group, while Robbins would become the 8th Fighter Group's top ace with 22 victories. On 10 November the 80th Squadron moved to Turnbull Field, Milne Bay, the ground echelon arriving on the motorship *Karsik*, and by the next day the Squadron was operating on patrol and air transport escort once again.

16 November 1942:49FG/9FS

While the Screamin' Demons and Eightballs were in combat over New Guinea, Flying Knights of the 9th Squadron transferred the last of their old P-40s to Rogers (30 Mile) and also increased the number of their P-38s to ten. The quasi 17th Provisional Squadron was officially disbanded and its pilots were permanently assigned to the 9FS, even though they would fly in the 39FS mission schedule.

17 November 1942: 49FG

49FG CO Lt.Col. Donald Hutchinson finally had all three of his squadrons flying combat over New Guinea. The 9th flew its first mission in New Guinea escorting C-47 transports to a newly built advanced strip just north of Pongani. Although the Squadron flew the mission without a problem, 1Lts. Floyd Finberg and William Haning encountered a heavy overcast and over-flew the Moresby airbase complex; the two pilots crash landed on the coast near Point Hood but were uninjured.

The 9FS flew its first mission without enemy contact but rookie 1Lts. William **Haning**. (shown) and Floyd Finberg got lost in heavy overcast and crashlanded safely. (AAF)

The 7th and 8th Squadrons also flew escort over Lae on that day. On the early morning mission, the 7FS sent up 16 P-40s and 7FS Flight Leader 1Lt. Raymond Melikian, flying a new P-40K, damaged one of eight attacking Zeros that broke off combat and fled into the heavy cloud cover south of Lae airfield. Senior pilots commandeered the new K-models as soon as they arrived and relegated their well-worn Es to the rookie pilots.

18 November 1942: 49FG/8FS

The 8th Squadron flew two uneventful missions: mid-day and late afternoon. The second was an interception over Buna in which eight P-40s flew through heavy overcast to the north coast, but the Japanese aircraft were gone. On the return flight, two worn P-40Es were lost due to mechanical failure. 2Lt. Bernard Makowski's engine overheated and seized as he tried to climb over the Owen Stanley Mountains, and he attempted a landing at the same small Kokoda strip where Nelson Brownnell was killed ten days earlier. Makowski made an emergency landing and escaped with non-life threatening injuries. Meanwhile, 2Lt. William McConnell's engine also overheated and seized during his descent to 3 Mile Drome, so he tried to land at 4 Mile Field, which was under construction, but crashed into the trees and was badly injured. Both pilots returned to combat, and 8th CO Sims was forced to ask 49th Group Ops Exec. Reddington for replacement P-40s, which he appropriated from the hard-pressed 9th Squadron.

Late November 1942: Eddie Rickenbacker Visits

Top American World War I ace Eddie Rickenbacker arrived in Port Moresby in late November on a special inspection tour for the Secretary of War. He met with MacArthur, Sutherland, and Kenney, where he was briefed on the situation in New Guinea and of the Southwest Pacific Area. The next day Rickenbacker and Kenney toured airdromes around Port Moresby and met the young fighter pilots. Rickenbacker was a hero to the fighter pilots, and after a discussion about combat tactics at one of the Dromes a pilot asked Rickenbacker how many victories he had in the last war. Rickenbacker told him 26. At the time several pilots had only two or three victories, while Buzz Wagner had eight to lead the list but had shipped home. The consensus was that the record 26 was going to stand for a long while. Kenney announced that he would give a case of Scotch to the first pilot to beat Rickenbacker's record, and Rickenbacker immediately replied to put him down for another case. The next day the story made the rounds at the 5FC Dromes around Moresby.

8

Buna-Gona Campaign: Mid-November-December 1942

The Buna phase of the New Guinea Campaign marked a change from a defensive to offensive action for the Allied Air Forces. In the preceding months, of necessity, Allied strategy had only been to fend off the Japanese along the Kokoda Track and to forestall enemy occupation of Port Moresby and other New Guinea bases. MacArthur's ultimate intention for New Guinea, however, was much more than a purely defensive one, as he planned to eradicate the enemy forces and capture bases on the northeastern coast as a prelude for further offensives. He would accomplish this by an enveloping movement in which fresh American troops would move around the Japanese left flank by a northeasterly route across the Owen Stanleys to cut off the enemy in the neighborhood of Wairope. Cargo planes were to supply the troops moving overland by dropping rations and equipment at specified points until they had reached a point near enough to the coast to be supplied by small boats from Milne Bay. Chief among the ground forces available for the operation were the American 32nd Division, which had been receiving combat training in Australia, and the Australian 7th Division, most of which was already engaged in the Kokoda fighting.

The Australian 7th Division, advancing on the central Kokoda Track, had closed within 35 miles of the coast, while MacArthur's forces to the south had advanced even closer from Pongani. By 15 November the Australian brigades, aided by 7FS and 8FS close air support, had crossed the Kumusi River, but would be halted for two weeks by the final line of Japanese defenses laying 15 miles from the coast. Finally, the Australians beat the tenacious Japanese back to the coastal village of Gona, just north of Buna, where the Japanese made a desperate last stand and stopped the Allied advance. For the next month the Australians assaulted Buna, losing over 1,400 casualties before taking the town and ending Japan's dream of taking New Guinea.

Buna, New Airfields, and the *Tulsa Plan*

By mid-1942 airfield construction in the forward areas had been accelerated, and by early July, the airfields in the York Peninsula-Horn Island area of Australia were well advanced, and air units were occupying them as rapidly as they became ready for use. At Port Moresby seven fields were projected, and work was moving ahead on four. At Milne Bay, three Allied airfields were under construction and one strip was expected to be in full operation by the end of the month.

These burdensome construction commitments made it necessary to send more US engineer troops to New Guinea to assist the American and Australian engineers already in the area. The 808th Engineer Aviation Battalion, then at Darwin, was ordered to Port Moresby on 21 July. The 2nd Battalion of the 43rd US Engineers (less Company E, which was at Port Moresby) was ordered to Milne Bay the same day to join with the 46th Engineers, which were already building the critically needed airfields there.

The Theater plan of operations, code named the *Tulsa Plan*, was the "Joint Basic Plan for the Occupation of the Area New Britain-New Ireland-Admiralty Islands." The Plan was revised in response to the new 2 July directive to exploit the war-changing victory at Midway. Previously the Plan indicated the need of a major airfield in the Buna area if Lae and Salamaua were attacked. As now revised, the Plan provided for the immediate establishment of an airfield in that area with the intention that it might be available for support of operations against Lae and Salamaua as set by *Elkton* Task Two, the seizure and occupation of the remainder of the Solomon Islands, Lae, Salamaua, and the northeast coast of New Guinea.

To build this new major strip a survey of the region would be necessary, and on 9 July GHQ ordered a reconnaissance of the Buna area. There was a small abandoned emergency strip just southeast of Buna about which little was known, except that it appeared to be too wet and too low lying to be of value for military use. The object of the reconnaissance was to determine whether the existing strip had any military value and, if not, to find an all-weather site elsewhere in the area which could be constructed for military use.

The reconnaissance was made on 10 and 11 July by a party of six officers who were flown from Port Moresby to the area in a RAAF PBY Catalina. The party was led by Lt.Col. Bernard Robinson, a senior US Army engineer officer, and included three Australian officers who had personal knowledge of the area, Lt.Col. Boyd Wagner, US Fighter Group Commander at Port Moresby, and Col. Yoder. After thoroughly examining the terrain of the entire area, Robinson's team determined that, while the existing strip was practically useless for military purposes, the grass plains area at Dobodura, 15 miles south of Buna, was an excellent site that would be suitable for large scale air operations, even in the rainy season, which was then only a few months away.

In his special report to MacArthur's Chief Engineer, Gen. Hugh Casey, Col. Robinson recommended that the existing strip not be developed, except possibly as an emergency landing field for fighter aircraft. In contrast, the Dobodura site was considered almost ideal for large scale military use, as the drainage was good; stone, gravel, and timber in adequate amounts were found in the area; and abundant local native labor was available for the construction of the field. The site would provide ample area for suitable aircraft dispersal, and with only slight clearing and grading would provide an excellent landing field, 7,000 feet long and more than 300 feet wide, lying in the direction of the prevailing wind.

The Battle for Buna-Gona

As the Allies converged on the Buna area, the ground forces were organized as follows: General Blamey, with headquarters at Port Moresby, was in command of the New Guinea Force, which had administrative control over all Allied land forces in New Guinea. The Allied troops north of the Owen-Stanley's, known as the Advanced New Guinea Force, were under Lt.Gen. E. F. Herring, but the responsibility for operations rested directly upon the division commanders, Maj.Gen. Edwin Harding of the 32nd US Division and Maj.Gen. C.A. Vasey of the 7th Australian. These leaders could look optimistically at the victorious Australians moving along the Kokoda Track and the growing effectiveness of the Fifth Air Force.

After the Japanese had withdrawn from the outskirts of Port Moresby and had lost Guadalcanal on 16 November 1942, Australian and US Forces attacked the main Japanese beachheads at Buna, Sananda, and Gona. The terrain in the Buna-Gona area was mainly a tidal swamp set in 95 degree temperatures and 85% humidity. The bush, swamp, forest, rivers and beach made it virtually impossible to flank the Japanese positions. Along the edge of the sea was a strip of dry, sandy soil where the Japanese had built numerous well-camouflaged, reinforced bunkers in mutually supporting positions that blocked all available approaches on the north coast. The Japanese defenses were concentrated in three strongholds: Gona, Sananda, and the third and largest in the Buna area. Allied Intelligence greatly underestimated the number of enemy troops at 1,500 to 2,000 and the quality of the Japanese defenses. Sutherland referred to the Japanese fortifications as "hasty field entrenchments." Combined with the forces who had returned from the Kokoda Track, the Japanese initially had nearly 5,500 troops in the Buna-Gona area, which were reinforced to 6,500 later. Both opponents lacked the even most basic supplies, especially food, medicine, and ammunition. The Japanese were at first resupplied by destroyers that sneaked in from Rabaul, and later by submarines that arrived by night, until the Allies' increasingly effective air and naval forces interrupted further supply.

When the Allies attacked the three Japanese strongholds beginning on 16 November, they were immediately thwarted by the Japanese defensive positions and suffered heavy casualties without making any gains on the ground. They had only a few artillery pieces and mortars and limited ammunition, and they received only partially effective air support. Kenney was confident that his planes would supplant the role of traditional artillery:

> "Tanks and heavy artillery can be reserved for the battlefields of Europe and Africa. They have no place in jungle warfare. The artillery in this theater flies, the light mortar and machine guns, the rifle, the tommygun, the grenade and knife are the weapons carried by men who fly to war, jump in parachutes, are carried by gliders and who land from air transports on grounds which air engineers have prepared."

MacArthur constantly expressed disappointment with the US 32nd Infantry Division's lack of progress and heavy casualties. On 29 November, he ordered Lt.Gen. Eichelberger, Commander of the US Eighth Army, to relieve Maj.Gen. Edwin Harding and most of his regimental and battalion commanders. Harding was replaced first by his former artillery commander, Albert Waldron, then by Eichelberger's Chief of Staff, Brig.Gen. Clovis Byers, and finally by Eichelberger himself. Once in command Eichelberger fully understood the difficulties his processors faced.

Eichelberger had been appointed Commanding General of US I Corps and left for Australia in 1942; in October 1942 he was promoted to Lieutenant General. At the time the 32nd Infantry Division was a poorly trained and ill-equipped National Guard unit that had been ineffective in the Allied offensive against Buna and Gona, and MacArthur assigned Eichelberger to command the Division, admonishing him:

> "Bob, I'm putting you in command at Buna. Relieve Harding ... I want you to remove all officers who won't fight. Relieve regimental and battalion commanders; if necessary, put sergeants in charge of battalions and corporals in charge of companies ... Bob, I want you to take Buna, or not come back alive ... And that goes for your chief of staff, too."

Some of the 32nd Division's officers privately denounced Eichelberger as a "ruthless Prussian" when he removed ineffective commanders. But he also rewarded effective officers with increased command responsibilities. Eichelberger would lead the combined Australian-US Advanced New Guinea Force to victory over the Japanese at Buna in early 1943, and then in 1944 he also would have notable victories at Hollandia and Biak, in Dutch New Guinea. As Commanding General of the newly formed Eighth Army he led the invasion of the Philippines, conquering the islands of Mindoro, Negros, Cebu, and Mindanao.

The Allied ground forces only made significant progress when tanks and artillery arrived. On 2 January they captured Buna, and finally on 22 January 1943, after protracted brutal fighting in extremely difficult conditions, the Allied forces killed or captured almost the entire defending Japanese, with only a few hundred escaping to the north. Casualties on both sides were extremely high, as the percentage of casualties, KIA or WIA, at Buna exceeded the better known battle for Guadalcanal by a three to one ratio. After almost three months of fighting the Japanese lost 1,500 men, the Australians 2,700, and the Americans 798. Of the 9,825 men who entered combat with the 32nd Division, 7,125 were casualties due to illness, 586 were killed in action, 1,954 were wounded, and 100 more were dead from other causes.

Fifth Air Force's Role at Buna-Gona

The Allied forces were to be maintained by sea from Milne Bay and Port Moresby. Supply dumps would be established at Wanigela or Porlock Harbor, and from there small boats would run a shuttle service to points nearer the forward area. In these plans air transport held a secondary position, in that advance and Headquarters did not demand air transport if the movement could be made by sea.

However, small boat transport was particularly vulnerable to enemy air attack, and it was hoped that the 5FC could provide protection against marauding enemy bombers and fighters. Although Gen. Whitehead recognized the danger, he insisted that fighter cover over the entire coastal area was impracticable. He believed that ships could move from Wanigela around Cape Nelson to Porlock Harbor in comparative safety, but recommended that ships take cover during daylight, particularly if they were engaged in the shuttle between Porlock Harbor and Pongani, which was recognized as being especially open to enemy attack.

On 16 November 1942, three small boats and a landing barge carrying Maj.Gen. Edwin Harding, 32nd Division Commander, and Brig.Gen. A.W. Waldron, and loaded with supplies and ammunition moved up the coast toward Cape Budest with no air protection. In the early evening Zeros and dive bombers attacked the flotilla, burning all four boats, but the two Generals and other personnel reached shore. The following day another bombing sank two more cargo craft and severely damaged a third. The destruction of these small boats necessitated increased dependence upon air transport for supply. The air transports faced many hazards, including poor weather, high mountains, rough landing fields, and enemy fighters. They were slow and unarmed, and without fighter escort were easy victims for enemy fighters, making fighter escort necessary. Before the end of the Papuan Campaign, transports on flights of over 200 miles were provided with continuous fighter escort from a rendezvous point 20 to 50 miles from take off. Since the air distance to Buna was less than 120 miles, it was considered more efficient to provide area cover rather than continuous protection. Consequently, when the transports, sometimes as many as 30, headed for the combat zones, they would hope to find fighter protection over Buna. Toward the end of the campaign, the plan was for full squadrons of fighters to replace one another over the area in short shifts. The importance of air transport in the Buna operation was revealed in MacArthur's telegram of 1 December:

> My campaign in northern Papua is being supported and supplied entirely by air." Two weeks later Kenney asserted that "since the movement of United States troops to northeastern New Guinea, their sole source of supply for all food, ordnance, and other materiel has been Fifth Air Force transport aircraft.

To be able to provide more effective top cover for bomber and transport missions, Allied fighter squadrons were being moved to forward bases. By the beginning of November the 35th and 36th Squadrons of the 8FG were flying their P-39s and P-400s from Jackson and Gurney air strips at Milne Bay. Within two weeks the 80th Squadron of the same group had joined them. During November and December the 49th Group continued to base all its P-40s at Port Moresby, along with two squadrons of the 35th Group. Of all AAF fighter squadrons, only the 40th Squadron of the 35th Group was based in Australia by 1 November. The Fighter Command received welcome reinforcement during the fall of 1942, when the 39th Squadron of the 35th Group replaced its worn out P-400s with P-38s. These much needed fighters had been first allocated to the SWPA in summer 1942, when Gen. Brett was informed that he would receive 25 P-38s per month from July through October and 10 a month thereafter. By 1 September 21 P-38s had arrived, and a month later the number had tripled.

Kenney intended to have a P-38 squadron operational by mid-September, but maintenance problems prevented meeting this schedule. On 23 October nine P-38s were grounded for lack of replacement inverters. Leaking internal fuel tanks caused continual grounding of many aircraft during the fall, as the tanks manufactured by B.F. Goodrich were found to be unsatisfactory and the Firestone tanks only minimally acceptable for the time being. The improved Goodrich tank was tested, but again was found to be unacceptable, as it leaked after only 25 hours. By default the Firestone tanks were chosen as replacements, and on 5 November, the Air service Command shipped 40 sets of Firestone tanks by emergency water shipment. On 22 November, two of four Lightnings on a patrol mission over Buna returned to base because of oxygen failure, while the other two had their 20mm cannon jam in combat. On 3 December Kenney reported that faulty superchargers, intercoolers, inverters, and armament were keeping the P-38s out of operations, because mechanics completely unfamiliar with the P-38 had improperly assembled them in Australia; fuel leaks in the riveted joints in the wings could be attributed to Lockheed. To try to remedy the problems the P-38s were being disassembled and rebuilt.

During November and December, in addition to its efforts in the Solomons, the Japanese Navy continued to bring relief to the increasingly hard-pressed Buna defenders. Allied attempts to attack these convoys had varied success, as weather and visibility was often poor and anti-aircraft and fighters protected the convoys, so the Japanese continued to

Milne Bay aerial view. (AAF)

Personnel facilities at **Milne Bay**. (AAF)

80FS taking off from **Gurney Field**, Milne Bay. (AAF)

attempt to reinforce these exhausted garrisons. Finally, during the last days of the campaign no large convoys approached the Buna area, as the Japanese had decided on a withdrawal from the area, or at least to supply the remaining troops only by small boat. Nevertheless, the enemy had definitely not decided to relinquish their hold upon New Guinea, and convoys continued to head to Lae and Salamaua. One of the most decisive Allied air attacks of the campaign, for example, occurred between 6 and 10 January 1943 against a convoy approaching Lae, and will be discussed in chronological order. AAF Headquarters at Port Moresby considered these anti-shipping attacks so important that no aircraft were spared for direct support missions.

In conjunction with their primary mission against convoys, heavy bombers from the Southwest Pacific continued to make the long flight to Rabaul. On 25 December, however, the Thirteenth Air Force joined them in their attacks on this stronghold, thus removing a part of the Fifth Air Force's bombing responsibilities. Shipping in the harbor, the twin airdromes, and Rabaul town itself were favorite targets of this two-way attack. The increasing success of the heavy bombers not only prevented large scale reinforcement, but in so doing lowered Japanese morale. Although their troops continued to resist fanatically, captured diaries indicate that by the middle of December many Japanese had given up hope of victory.

Wanigela Strips

The need for landing strips, first to ferry troops and provide supplies and then for use for fighter offensive and defensive operations, had been imperative. At Wanigela Mission, on the northwestern shore of Collingwood Bay, Australian officers, assisted by native laborers, burnt the kunai grass and hacked off the remaining tussocks for the prospective landing fields. A small detachment of Australian engineers then carved out a runway using machetes, cane knives, and picks and shovels to give the Allies an air strip within 65 air miles of Buna, which was connected by an overland track.

Other strips were soon projected. Cecil Abele, a local resident, with native laborers, braved Malarial swamps to press inland from Wanigela. They were soon joined by a band of American engineers under Col. L.J. Sverdrup, who cleared a series of strips, first in the upper valley of the Musa River near Sepia, and then moved down toward the coast, finally completing a more important strip at Pongani, on Dyke Auckland Bay, on 4 November.

The tropical rains prevented the use of the Wanigela strip and the connecting overland tracks from 16 October until 8 November. After the assault troops landed by parachute and by glider, engineers also landed with airborne bulldozers, jeeps, and light tools, with the entire operation preceded and accompanied by fighters. By the last of December attacking medium bombers, air transport crews, and ground troops could depend upon an increasingly effective fighter patrol to protect them against the occasional attacks of Japanese aircraft. P-40s usually patrolled in formations of 16 aircraft, separated into two to four flights that covered the area at different altitudes from 5,000 to 20,000 feet. Later the patrol was greatly strengthened by the addition of P-38s.

Dobodura and Oro Bay Airfields

In mid-1942, MacArthur wanted to establish an airdrome at Buna to conduct the Allied counteroffensive and to attack Lae and Salamaua, and had issued orders for occupation of Buna and to begin local airdrome construction. As of July 1942, Theater plan *Tulsa* called for an airfield to be established for military aircraft at Buna Airfield. On 9 July 1942, the reconnaissance led by Lt. Cols. Bernard Robinson, Boyd Wagner, Colonel Yoder, and three Australian officers examined the terrain of the entire area and determined that the kunai plains area at Dobodura be developed as an airfield instead of Buna Drome used by the Japanese.

But on 22 July 1942, the Japanese had occupied the area in preparation for what would become their unsuccessful attack on Port Moresby. By November 1942 Australian forces had succeeded in driving the Japanese back from Moresby and across the Owen Stanley Range back to the Buna-Gona area. MacArthur then ordered the capture of this strategic area, and once captured, airdrome construction was to be started immediately for use in continued operations. Progress was slowed by the desperate defense by veteran enemy infantry, but finally, after brutal fighting, the enemy was defeated and the Buna area secured. Allied forces then started their slow forward movement along the northern coast of New Guinea.

Until more P-38s arrived, 5FC missions had to be flown by the Moresby-based P-40s, whose operations were hindered by the 13,000 foot Owen Stanley Range and the ensuing descent to remote Lae. All 5AF fighter sorties would stage to Wurtsmith's HQ at 17 Mile Field on the preceding day of a given mission. Similarly, the 7FS at 14 Mile, the 8FS at 3 Mile, and the 9FS temporarily at 4 Mile would each keep two flights of fighters on alert for Port Moresby's defense. To release the Port Moresby air strips for bombers and to make the P-40s more effective tactically, the Warhawks had to be based much closer to Lae, so the previously recommended large flatlands at Dobodura were the solution to the problem.

In the early morning of 16 November 5 FC CO Wurtsmith and 49FG CO Hutchinson left Fighter Command HQ at the recently completed 17 Mile Field in a C-47 transport loaded with a Jeep and landed on the kunai stubble of the Dobodura landing strip. After their gear and jeep were unloaded, the two Colonels drove over the broad grassy plain to scout out a new landing field, which would be staked out as an inverted T. Within a few days the Corps of Engineers would arrive and begin construction, soon cutting and dragging two basic landing strips. The main 5,500 foot runway (to be known as Horanda Strip) ran northeast to southwest, and the other 4,500 foot perpendicular strip ran southeast to northwest (to be known as Kalamazoo). Soon the 78th Squadron Signal Corps instituted air traffic control for the increased transport supply landings and the other Allied aircraft that staged there in the continuing offensive against Lae. At the height of the Battle of Buna and Gona cargo was flown in, unloaded, and was immediately put into battle. After the battle it was developed into

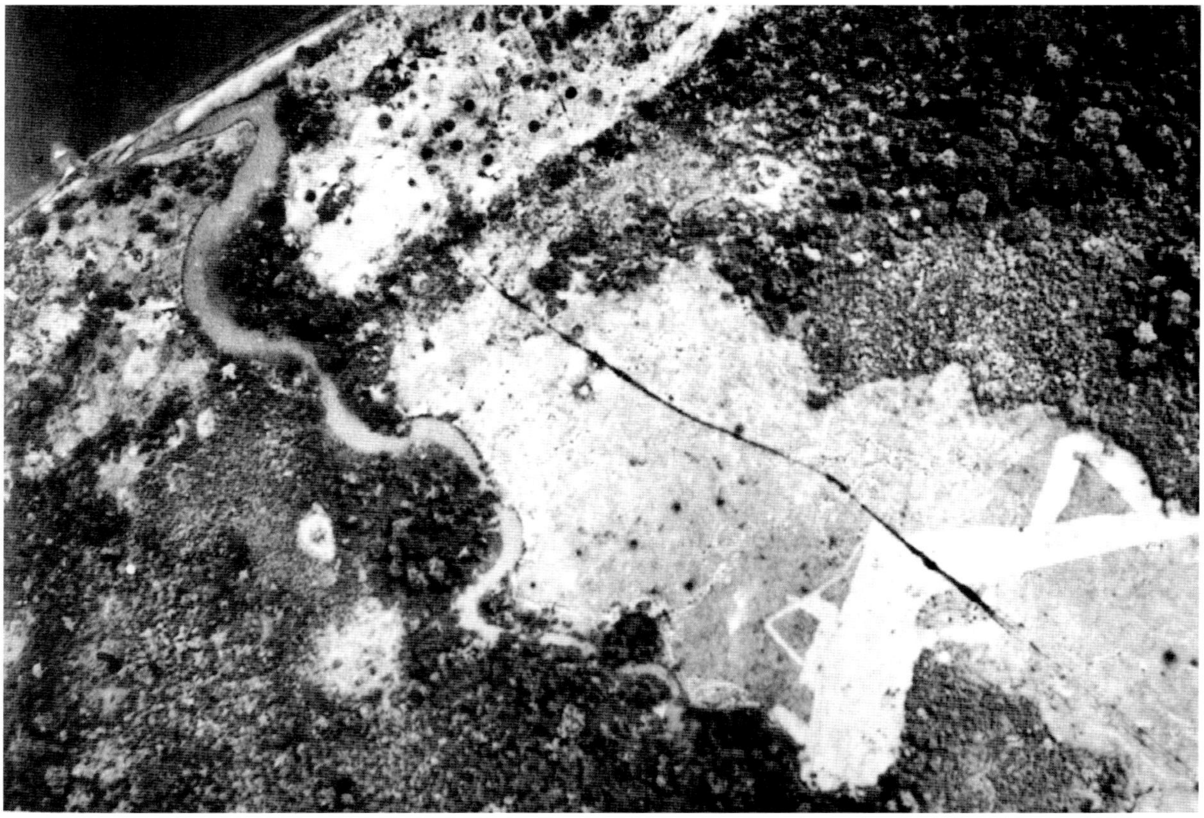

Buna Drome. (AAF)

Oro Bay Base B. (AAF)

a major airbase, with storage and repair facilities, and interconnecting taxiways to adjacent airfields.

Oro Bay (Base B)

Oro Bay, located on the east coast of Papua, is approximately 160 air miles from Milne Bay. Base B was a triangular-shaped area with Oro Bay and Buna, about 20 miles north, forming the base and Dobodura the apex. Oro Bay, formed by two spurs jutting out from a neighboring mountain, is the only deepwater harbor in the vicinity, and is well sheltered except from storms from the east. Oro Bay was chosen over Buna because there is no harbor at Buna, and there also are numerous coral heads near the shore which extend many miles from land to create a hazard to shipping. On the land side, Buna is cut off by swamps and creeks and can be approached only along four narrow corridors. The place names for locations like Gona, Buna, Soputa, Dobodura, Embogo, or Embi did not signify the existence of towns in even the broadest sense, but were simply named locations on a map with possibly four or five native huts or, at Buna Mission, several mission buildings.

Airdromes

Buna had not yet been secured when, on 18 November 1942, elements of the 114th Engineer Combat Battalion arrived at Dobodura after a two day march from Embogo. Dobodura, located less than eight air miles from Buna in the interior jungle, could only be reached over convoluted trails. The Dobodura-Embogo-Buna-Gona area lays in the large delta of the Samboga and Girua River systems. This flat land is intersected by many streams, sloughs, and swamps, and has subsoil consisting principally of gravel of varying sizes from large stones to fine sand. This subsoil is overlain by from six inches to 10 feet of vegetable muck and silt which forms an almost watertight seal, and water accumulates and remains on the surface until it evaporates.

On 20 November, these engineers began construction on Strip No. 1 by clearing grass and scrub trees over a 4,000x120 foot area. The engineers, equipped with only four brush hooks, two axes, one machete, and bayonets, completed the grass airstrip on 21 November. The following day, after the airstrip had been widened to 240 feet, a 600x45-foot taxiway had been constructed before this platoon moved from Dobodura. On 25 November, elements of the 43rd Engineer Regiment were flown into Dobodura from Port Moresby. They cleared three 3,000x200 foot grass airstrips using only hand sickles and machetes. Soon engineering equipment, which had been cut apart with a torch or dismantled to fit into transport aircraft, was flown in. The equipment included two D-2 and two D-4 bulldozers, two graders, two carryalls, three tractors, and three mowing machines, which were all reassembled and immediately used to prepare three airstrips for transport use. By the end of 1942, 15 airstrips had been prepared in this area to meet the demands for tactical air support and air supply essential to the success of ground forces moving through the jungle on Buna from several directions.

These airstrips served not only as transport landing strips, for which they had been planned, but also as emergency operational fields. For instance, when the weather over the inland mountains closed down on New Year's Day 1943, a number of aircraft, including 15 fighters, four medium bombers, and five transports landed at Strip No. 4. The next morning, after a heavy rain during the night, these various aircraft were able to take off without trouble.

Meanwhile, on 20 December more engineer units and their equipment were shipped by water from Milne Bay and landed at Oro Bay; they were then were to be moved overland to Dobodura. However, the heavy equipment could not be driven to Dobodura from Oro Bay and was loaded onto barges which were towed up the coast to Hariko, where it was off loaded over improvised ramps. It was then driven or dragged across the beach and up the Buna-Dobodura native track to the construction site.

Once the Buna area was secured in January there was a consolidation and improvement of early tactical air facilities in the general area. On 2 January 1943 GHQ, SWPA, issued new instructions on airdrome construction in the Dobodura area. In order to prepare an advanced 5AF base there, three construction priorities were established:

1) preparation of two fighter airstrips;
2) preparation of dispersal and revetment facilities for two fighter squadrons; and
3) conversion of one of the two fighter airstrips into a heavy bomber airstrip with dispersal facilities and revetments.

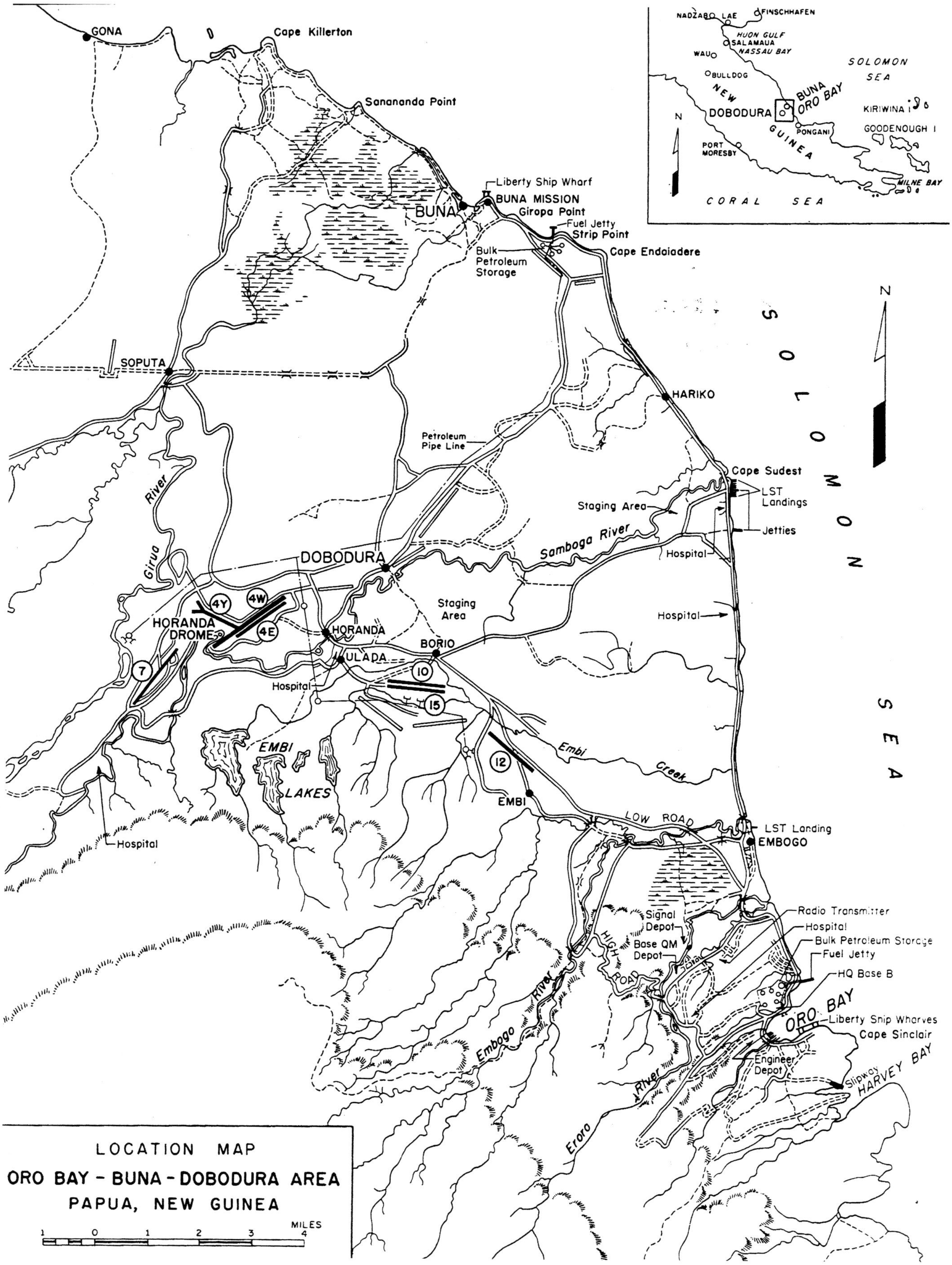
LOCATION MAP
ORO BAY - BUNA - DOBODURA AREA
PAPUA, NEW GUINEA
MILES
GONA
Cape Killerton
Sananonda Point
Liberty Ship Wharf
BUNA MISSION
BUNA
Giropa Point
Fuel Jetty
Strip Point
Cape Endaiadere
Bulk Petroleum Storage
SOPUTA
HARIKO
SOLOMON SEA
Petroleum Pipe Line
Cape Sudest
LST Landings
Staging Area
Jetties
Samboga River
Hospital
DOBODURA
Girua River
Staging Area
HORANDA DROME
HORANDA
BORIO
ULADA
Hospital
EMBI LAKES
Embi Creek
EMBI
LOW ROAD
LST Landing
EMBOGO
Signal Depot
Base QM Depot
HIGH ROAD
Radio Transmitter
Hospital
Bulk Petroleum Storage
Fuel Jetty
HQ Base B
ORO BAY
Liberty Ship Wharves
Cape Sinclair
Engineer Depot
Slipway
HARVEY BAY
Embogo River
Eroro River
NADZAB LAE
FINSCHHAFEN
HUON GULF
SALAMAUA
NASSAU BAY
WAU
BULLDOG
NEW GUINEA
DOBODURA
BUNA
ORO BAY
PONGANI
PORT MORESBY
SOLOMON SEA
KIRIWINA I
GOODENOUGH I
MILNE BAY
CORAL SEA

The responsibility for all airdrome construction was assigned to US Army Service of Supply (USASOS), while exact locations and specifications were to be supplied by Allied Air Forces. From these and other instructions, seven strips of the 15 that were initially mowed and leveled for transport landings during the period of combat operations were further improved.

Dobodura Dromes
The Dobodura Dromes were located west of Dobodura and Horanda Villages and north of the Samboga River.

Raways Strip (Dobodura #1)
Raways was a US built single runway to the east of Dobodura and was used by liaison aircraft.

P-38 of the 475FG landing on Horanda. (AAF)

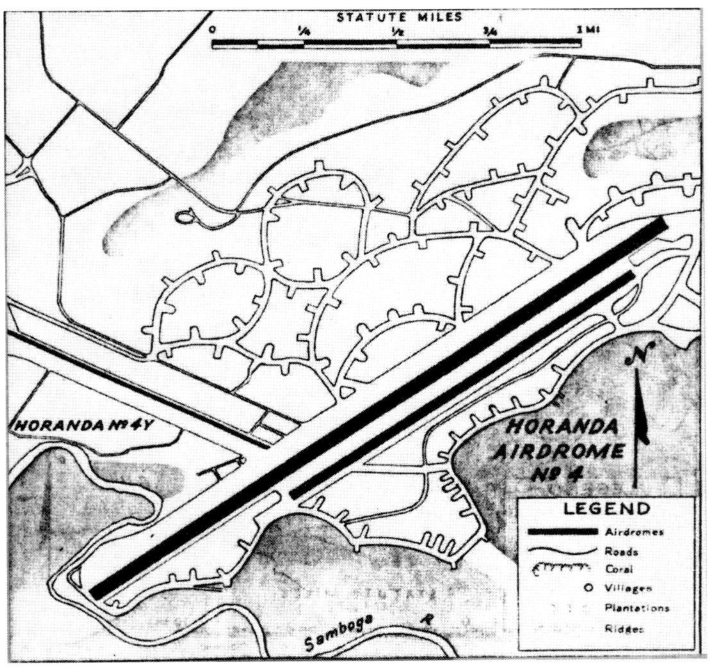

Horanda Drome #4

8FS P-40s on **Kalamazoo**. (AAF)

Horanda #4 with dispersal areas and Strips #4E and #4W. (center) intersecting Strip #4Y. (right center). (AAF)

Horanda #4 Revetments. (AAF)

Horanda area campsite. (AAF)

#4 Main Horanda Strip

The first airstrip to be developed to operational standards was Strip #4, near Dobodura. This airstrip, together with a 4,000 foot steel mat fighter runway (Strip #4Y/"Kalamazoo"), which met it at an angle, was developed in accordance with the operations instructions and became part of Horanda Drome. By the end of February a P-38 fighter squadron was stationed at Horanda, and from then until the fighter runway was completed they flew from Strip #4, although at that time it had been only graveled and treated with an oil mixture to keep the dust down. Strip #4 was subsequently extended to 9,000 feet and covered with steel mat, and another 6,000 foot runway, east of and parallel to it, was surfaced with bitumen. Eventually Horanda Drome consisted of four runways: Strips #4 East, #4 West, #4Y, and #7. Strip #7, located to the southwest of the other runways, was 7,000 feet long and surfaced with bitumen. Many miles of taxiways, dispersed hardstands, and revetments were also constructed. The revetments were located around the south and north of the runways, with the taxiways connected to the dispersal areas. The air transport of supplies for the Buna operation increased as the construction of air facilities had progressed. During the running battle of the Bismarck Sea in early March the facilities at Horanda Drome were essential for the immediate launching of fighter aircraft to support the operation. A detachment of 43rd Engineers was flown in from Moresby to lay additional steel mat at Horanda for the battle. Horanda became the main airfield in the Dobodura complex and was fully developed by mid-1943, when Nadzab was developed. By July 1945, only Horanda West #4 and East #4 were operational.

Girua Airfield (Dobodura #7/West 7/Kenney)

Girua was located near Dobodura to the northeast of Embi Lakes, northeast of Inonda, and south of Mt. Lamington. It was also called "Kenney strip" after the 5FC CO.

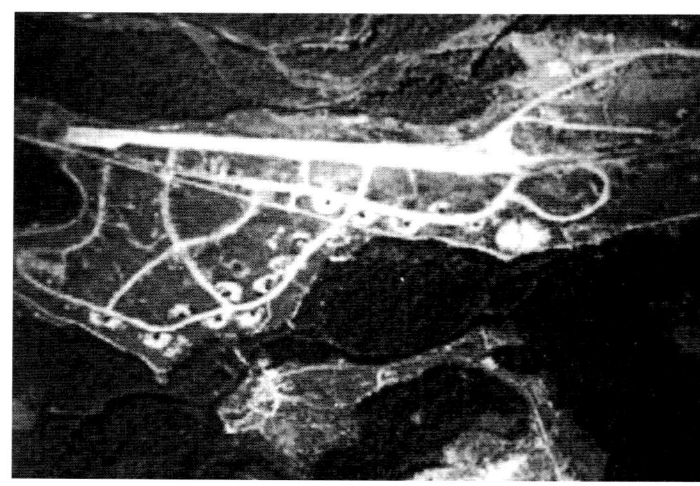

Girua Airfield. (Dobodura #7/West 7/Kenney). (AAF)

49FG encampment **Girua**. (AAF)

5FC units based on Girua:
58FG: HQ from Brisbane on 28 December 1943 to Saidor on 2 April 1943
58FG: 310FS (P-47) from Brisbane on 28 December 1943 to Saidor on 2 April 1943
58FG: 69FS (P-47) from Brisbane on 29 December 1943 to Saidor on 2 April 1943
49FG: HQ, 7FS, 8FS (P-40), & 9FS (P-47) March to 20 November 1943
418NFS: (P-61) 22 November 1943 to 28 March 1943

North Embi Drome (Dobodura #12)
Of the initial 15 airstrips hastily prepared for tactical purposes during the Buna operation, the site located near the native village of Embi, approximately six miles southeast of Horanda, was thought to be "exceptionally favorable" for a second airdrome. Construction was started by the 808th Engineer Aviation Battalion immediately after its arrival at Oro Bay on 8 July 1943. This site was on the level Embi plain, but due to the high water table and geological conditions, the one foot thick layer of black loam was usually saturated with water. The 808th solved the problem by digging a four foot deep longitudinal ditch on a line 150 feet to the right of the center line of the runway. By removing 60,000 cubic yards of rain soaked loam the water table was lowered one foot. This sealed fighter runway, 150x6,000 feet (Strip #12), was in operation by early October 1943. The 808th also began the preparatory clearing for a 7,000 foot concrete bomber runway to be located parallel to the first, however, this second runway (#13) was never constructed. During 1944 Strip No. 12 was abandoned, and the area was subsequently used for ammunition storage.

North Embi. (Dobodura #12). (AAF)

5FC units based on North Embi: 475FG's 431FS (P-38) to 26 March 1944 Nadzab

431FS P-38 being fueled at **North Embi.** (AAF)

Borio Drome (Dobodura #11)
At Borio, located about half way between Horanda and Embi, Borio Drome (Dobodura #11) was the first of the Borio strips built. It was located south of Borio Village, and later North Borio Airstrip was constructed to the southeast of Dobodura and Horanda. Its taxiways connected directly with the North Borio Strip (Dobodura #15) and the North Embi Airstrip (Dobodura #12).

5FC units based on Borio: 475FG/433FS (P-38) from 14 August.

North Borio. (Dobodura #11). (AAF)

North Borio Airstrip (Dobodura #15)
North Borio was located near Horanda Villages, south of Borio Village, and to the southeast of Dobodura and Horanda. Its taxiways spanned the single runway and connected to North Borio Strip and the North Embi Airstrip (Dobodura #12).

5FC units based on North Borio:
475FG/432FS (P-38) Amberley 14 August 1943 to ?
475FG/433FS (P-38) Amberley 14 August 1943 to ?
8FG/80FS (P-38) 1943

The Oro Bay-Buna-Dobodura area was a critically important and active base during the opening Allied offensive drives, and the Dobodura airstrips played a vital role in the victory at Buna. Subsequent development of these air facilities during the spring and early summer 1943 promoted the increased efficiency in the employment of the aircraft available. By refueling at Dobodura, heavy bombers from Port Moresby could more effectively patrol the Bismarck Sea and attack Rabaul in force. Heavy bomber missions, accompanied by medium bombers, were frequently dispatched to Gasmata and Cape Gloucester. Japanese shipping at anchor in Kavieng Harbor, New Ireland, were attacked by bombers staging from these newly developed forward areas. Troop carrier aircraft continued to fly large numbers of men and materials onto the airstrips at Dobodura. The port at Oro Bay provided troops and supplies for the Allies in New Guinea. Base B became a major staging area for many subsequent major offensive operations. The 1st Marine Division was staged there prior to the invasion of Cape Gloucester; the 1st Cavalry Division prior to the attack

432FS P-38 on **North Borio** dispersal. (AAF)

on the Admiralty Islands; and the 31st, 38th, and 11th Airborne Divisions prior to their movement to combat areas. However, by late 1944 combat operations had shifted to the Philippines, and all Allied units and supplies were moved to areas too far forward for further dependence on Base B's support; it had served its purpose. All usable engineer materiel at Base B was salvaged to meet needs in advance areas. The aviation gasoline fuel line and tanks were dismantled, and steel landing mat was taken up, passed through straightening machines, and bundled for forward shipment.

USAAF Units based at the Dobodura Airfield Complex:
3BG/8BS (A-20s) from Port Moresby 10 April 1943 to ?
3BG/89BS (A-20s) from Port Moresby 9 May 1943 to ?
3BG/HQ from Port Moresby 20 May 1943 to ?
3BG/90BS (B-25s) from Port Moresby 21 May 1943 to ?
3BG/13BS (B-25s) from Port Moresby 23 May 1943 to ?
22BG/19BS (B-26s, B-25s) from Woodstock 11 July 1943 to ?
22BG/2BS (B-26, B-25) Ried River 0 October-19 December 1943 to Nadzab
22 BG/HQ/33BS (B-25) from Australia 15 October 1943 to ?
22BG/408/BS (B-25) from Australia 15 October 1943 to ?
43BG/63BS (B-24s) from Port Moresby 29 October 1943 to ?
49FG/7FS, (P-40s) Port Moresby 15 April-16 November 1943 to Gusap
49FG,/8FS (P-40s) Port Moresby 15 April-30 August 1943 to Tsili-Tsili
49FG/HQ from Port Moresby 6 March-20 November 1943 to Gusap
49FG/9FS (P-47s) from Port Moresby- 16 December 1943 to Gusap
17TRG/17TRS (B-25s, P-39s) from Milne Bay 22 November 1943 to ?
17TRG/82TRS (B-25s, P-39s) from Milne Bay 22 November 1943 to ?
5FC/418NFS from Milne Bay 22 November 1943 to ?
90BG/319BS/320BS (B-24s) from Port Moresby 1 December 1943 to ?
90BG/321BS/400BS (B-24s) from Port Moresby 1 December 1943 to ?
43BG/HQ/64BS (B-24s) from Port Moresby 10 December 1943 to ?
43BG/HQ/65BS (B-24s) from Port Moresby 11 December 1943 to ?
8FG/80FS (P-38s) from Port Moresby 11 December 1943 to ?
43BG/HQ/403BS (B-24s) from Port Moresby Dec 13, 1943 to ?
375TCG/HQ from Port Moresby 19 August 1943 to 19 December 1943 to Port Moresby
345BG/501BS from Port Moresby 23 December 1943 to ?
58FG/HQ/310FS/311FS (P-47s) from Brisbane 28 December 1943 to ?
58FG HQ/69FS (P-47s) from Brisbane 28 December 1943 to ?
345B/500BS (B-25s) from Port Moresby 1 January 1944 to ?

9

November 1942 - January 1943: Air Operations

22 November 1942: 35FG
41FS
The 41FS "finally got some combat after a long dry spell" at 1105 when 12 of its P-400 Airacobras intercepted three Vs of 15 Val dive bombers escorted by eight Zeros over Buna at 14,000 feet. The Vals turned away, while the Zeros bore in to attack in a climbing turn that resulted in a frontal attack. In the fight 1Lts. Arthur Burger, George Callahan (in three passes), and Capt. Furlo Wagner each shot down a Zero, while two other Zeros were claimed as probables by Callahan and 1Lt. Herbert Hill. Lt. Roy Lawhorn's P-400 suffered damage to the wing and stabilizer but he landed safely.

39FS
The 39FS flew over Buna Drome in their Lightnings and encountered 20 Zeros at 1115. The squadron made no claims, but one P-38 was slightly damaged.

22 November 1942: 49FG/7FS
By late afternoon the weather cleared, and the Japanese sent up 18 Zeros to intercept Beaufighters and A-20 Havocs that were on a bombing mission to the Japanese airfield at Lae. At 1710 the 7FS, led by Capt. William Martin, was searching for the returning Allied bombers at 15,000 feet in heavy clouds over Cape Ward Hunt when eight Zeros dove through the clouds. The Zeros headed in line toward the 7th Squadron at the same altitude, and Martin's flight circled to the right to attack from the rear while another flight led by 1Lt. Paul Slocum met them head on after dropping their belly tanks. After the initial pass the fighters separated to engage in a massive twisting and turning dogfight. Slocum, now without any wingmen, circled and pulled up to fire at a Zero that rolled and started to spin, but he lost sight of it. He climbed above and away from the fight and then headed back and started after a Zero, but broke off to pursue another which was on the tail of a P-40. He pulled up and got on the Zero's tail and fired from about 200 feet. His bullets hit the wing and fuselage just behind the cockpit, immediately setting the flammable Zero on fire. At the same time 1Lt. Frank Nichol's Flight arrived and was followed by the circling attack by Capt. Martin's Flight. Martin and Element Leader 2Lt. Carl Aubrey chased and hit two Zeros, but lost them in the clouds and claimed them as probables. A two plane flight led by 1Lt. Donald Dittler and 2Lt. Kenneth Johns was cut off by the Zeros, and Johns was able to escape, but last saw Dittler under heavy attack. Flight Leader Slocum and 1Lt. Irving Voorhees each shot down a Zero during head on passes before Martin called off the combat in order to return to Moresby before sunset. For the claims of five Zeros and three other probables, two of the P-40s failed to return to base. 2Lt. Lucius Lacroix crashed on landing without being injured, but 2Lts. Dittler and Donald Sutliff did not return. Sutliff bailed out of his damaged P-40 and wandered through the bush for 21 days before being rescued.

1Lt. Paul **Slocum** scored his first of two victories. (AAF)

1Lt. William **Harris** scored his first of three victories. (AAF)

2Lt. Warren **Blakely** scored his first of two victories. (AAF)

25 November 1942: 35FG/39FS
Capt. Robert Faurot was leading the 39FS on a dive bombing attack on Lae Drome and saw a Zero taking off as he arrived. He chased it down and his volley put it into the sea.

26 November 1942: 49FG/8FS
The 8FS claimed three Zeros and two probables at 1010 over the Embi Lakes, near Buna. A C-47 transport was bounced by eight Zeros and the top cover P-40s, led by 1Lts. William Harris and Earl Kingsley, dove into the attack on the Zeros. Harris set a Zero on fire during a head on pass but found himself under attack from the rear. 2Lt. Warren Blakely, who had just downed a Zero, spotted Harris' dilemma and closed from the rear, damaging the pursuing Zero and causing it to break off its attack. Harris, unaware of the Zero behind him, was firing on another Zero that was on Kingsley's tail for his second victory of the day. The dogfight developed into a large Lufbery circle heading toward Lae as the fighters turned around and around trying to gain the advantage on each other. The Eightballs continued the chase until they reached Lae Drome, where they broke off, not wanting to fly near the Japanese AA batteries there.

2Lt. Arland **Stanton** scored his first of eight victories. (AAF)

29 November 1942: 8FG/35FS
The 35FS of the 8FG was assigned to the 35FG for operations and would return to the 8FG on 10 December.

29 November 1942: Lt.Col. Boyd Wagner KIFA
After returning to the US, Lt.Col. Wagner left Eglin AFB in Florida on a flight to Maxwell AFB, AL, but he never arrived in the stormy weather. His aircraft was found six weeks later, only 25 miles from Eglin. At 26 years old Wagner was the youngest Lt. Colonel in the AAF, and his funeral in January 1942 drew over 12,000 mourners. In 2008 an excavation at his crash site unearthed more remains which were verified by a DNA sample from Wagner's nephew and last surviving relative. These remains were interred with the original at his Johnstown, PA, gravesite in 2008, and a special memorial ceremony was held for America's first hero and air ace in October 2010.

1Lt. Frank **Nichols** scored his first of five victories. (AAF)

30 November 1942: 49FG/7FS/8FS
7FS
Shortly before noon, 16 P-40s of the 7FS were dive bombing Japanese positions covered by a dozen 8th Squadron P-40s when a dozen Zeros dove

2Lt. Howard **Nelson** scored his only victory. (AAF)

2Lt. Lucius **Lacroix** (center) (with his ground crew) got his only victory. (AAF)

on them from out of the clouds. 7FS Green Flight Leader 1Lt. Carl Aubrey and Wingman 1Lt. Irving Voorhees, Element Leader 1Lt. Donald Lee, and Wingman 2Lt. John Johnson were patrolling at 8,000 feet when the two elements became separated. Both elements were attacked from behind by a flight of diving Zeros. Lee turned and got on the tail of an enemy fighter, which immediately pulled up in a stall turn and made a head on pass at him. Lee was able to fire off one quick burst when he saw two Zeros on Voorhees' tail, but was unable to get to the enemy before his Wingman was shot down. Wingman Johnson was also shot down south of Buna, and surviving Element Leaders Aubrey and Lee would have suffered a similar fate if 1Lt. Frank Nichols' Red Flight had not arrived. Nichols, Wingman 2Lt. Lucius Lacroix, Element Leader 2Lt. Sheldon Brinson, and his rookie Wingman, 2Lt. Arland Stanton, were joined by Green Flight survivor Donald Lee, and the quintet attacked the Zeros. After three passes in a twisting dogfight, Nichols and his four wingmen each claimed a Zero. Brinson attacked two Zeros at once and shot one down, but then made the near-fatal mistake of watching his victim go down, allowing the second Zero to get on his tail and forcing Brinson to dive for cloud cover. A third flight of Screamin' Demons arrived late in the combat, and 2Lt. Howard Nelson claimed victory during a chase into the clouds.

8FS

While the 7FS fought off the Zeros overhead, the Eightball dive bombers dropped twenty 300 pound antipersonnel bombs on enemy installations before they were attacked by 10 Zeros. In a brief encounter they met the Zeros in a turning fight under the overcast. Rookie Flight Leader 1Lt. Ernest Harris and rookie Wingman 2Lt. Robert Moose, along with Flight Leader and Darwin veteran 1Lt. Bruce Harris and rookie Wingman 2Lt. Bryant Wesley, maneuvered to catch the Zeros, but only Moose was successful. Moose saw a Zero being pursued by two P-40s and decided to join in the chase. When the Zero tried to climb and then dive it exposed its underside to Moose, who fired three long bursts into the wing root, almost tearing off the wing, and the Zero went down in flames. Wesley was shot down by a Japanese veteran pilot and bailed out over Big Embi Lake, south of Dobodura. After bailing out safely Wesley swam and waded for two days through the great swamps surrounding Embi Lake before being rescued. Just before the fight ended 8FS Darwin veteran 1Lt. Harold Learned met a diving Zero head on and set the Jap on fire before the enemy pilot could fire a return shot. The Eightballs broke for home, climbing to clear the mountains to the west.

1 December 1942: 8FG

On 1 December Philip Greasley, who had taken over the command of the 80FS on 10 January 1942, moved up to 5FC HQ and was succeeded by Capt. I.C. Conner.

3 December 1942: 35FG/40FS/41FS

The 40Fs was flying top cover for the 41FS, which was dive bombing and strafing barges at Sanananda Point. The mission was successful, in that the P-39s thoroughly strafed the landing barges and bridge at the end of the new Buna Strip, as well as enemy positions on Cape Endaiadere, but the 41st lost two pilots.

December 1942: The Attack on Buna

Strategically, in the face of their loss of Guadalcanal and at Milne Bay and Kokoda in New Guinea, the Japanese were committed to defending the north coast of New Guinea. If Gen. Kenney, the new Allied Air Commander, were to establish airfields around Buna, those bases would menace Lae and ultimately imperil the Japanese SWPA Imperial HQ at Rabaul. To strengthen his resolve to defend Buna and to reverse Japanese fortunes in New Guinea, Lt.Gen. Hitoshi Imamura was to attempt another reinforcement of Buna to halt the critical Allied assault there. Lae would also be reinforced to provide for another assault on Port Moresby after the rainy season.

On the ground there was an influx of Allied troops, equipment, and supplies in Northern Australia and southern New Guinea. In early November, Allied Supreme Commander MacArthur moved his Southwest Pacific HQ from Brisbane to Port Moresby, where he could be more personally involved in commanding operations. For a month the Japanese at Buna had driven off Allied attacks, and MacArthur sacked both American Maj.Gen. Edwin Harding and Australian Maj. Gen. C.A. Vasey as field commanders, replacing them with Lt.Gen. Robert Eichelberger. As Eichelberger increased the tempo of his attack on Buna, the Japanese dispatched a troop ship convoy from Rabaul in the last week of November. However, the convoy was unable to approach the besieged stronghold, which was patrolled by massed Allied fighters and bombers. The convoy withdrew 15 miles north to the mouth of the Kumusi River, but was brutally harassed for four straight days by the 5AF.

After two months of combat, often flying three sorties per day against high odds, the Fifth Fighter Command finally achieved air superiority, causing the Japanese Navy Air Forces high losses. The odds were reversed with the arrival of AAF personnel and aircraft, including the superior P-38. In late November the 35th and 36th Squadrons of the 8FG were transferred to 14 Mile Airdrome at Port Moresby from their bases at Milne Bay to support in the air cover over Buna. AAF bombers and fighters constantly flew missions in the Buna area in early December 1942 to prevent enemy troop and supply buildups, and to intercept Japanese attempts to reinforce their forces from the sea.

Lt.Gen. Robert **Eichelberger**. (US Army)

Maj.Gen. C.A. **Vasey**. (AFHRC)

Maj.Gen. Edwin **Harding**. (US Army)

A Gen. Hitoshi **Imamura**. (US Army)

7 December 1942: 8FG/35FS/36FS

On 7 December Imamura sent a flight of Betty bombers escorted by Zeros from Rabaul to interdict Allied forces near Buna. By late morning, the enemy formation reached the Papuan coast north of Cape Ward Hunt, then turned to attack the Allied forces closing in on surrounded Japanese troops at Buna. The 5th Fighter Command would meet them just as they reached their objective. Sixteen P-39s of the 35FS and 36FS took off from Laloki at 1100 with two Airacobras soon turning back. When the Group reached Buna at 1130 they entered combat when a loose formation of seven Vals and two Zeros was spotted.

35FS

1Lt. John Casey entered combat when he dove from 8,000 feet to make a frontal attack on a Val flying at 3,000 feet and hit the forward fuselage of the dive bomber, causing it to roll over trailing black smoke and head for the sea. 1Lt. Edwin Connell also made a head on pass at a Zero but missed, and the Japanese fighter escaped. Connell then fired a deflection shot at a Val, but a Zero got on his tail and Connell put his Airacobra into a sudden skid to elude the Zero, which then put him dead astern of the original Val. He fired a volley that killed the Val gunner and then another volley that put the Val into a steep dive to crash into the water. 1Lt. William Feiler fired at

2Lt. Howard **Peterson** scored his only victory of the war. (AAF)

1Lt. William **Feiler** scored his only victory of the war. (AAF)

1Lt. George **Welch** scored three victories to become and ace with seven. (AAF)

1Lt. Joseph **McKeon**. (35FS) scored his first of 5 victories. (McKeon)

2Lt. George **Welch**. (L) after scoring 4 victories with the 47FS over Pearl Harbor. Also shown are 2Lts. Kenneth Taylor. (2v.) and Harry Brown. (1v.). Brown would later score 5 more victories in the SWPA. (AFAA)

A **Val** Navy Aichi D3A Type 99 two place carrier borne dive bomber. (AFHRC)

four of the Vals. His first attack caused smoke to pour back from one but it dove away; he then fired at another with no observed results, and then at yet another, which also escaped. Feiler finally fired an accurate burst at the wingroot of a fourth Val, and the wing twisted over and the Val fell in flames. 1Lt. Joseph McKeon attacked a Zero covering two other Vals, and as the bombers scurried off in different directions McKeon fired on the Zero, which burst into flames into the water off Buna. 2Lt. James Watson claimed a damaged Val for the 35FS.

36FS
A flight of four 36FS P-39s, led by 1Lt. Lieutenant George Welch, was patrolling at 13,000 feet when they encountered nine Zeros at 5,000 feet covering nine Val dive bombers flying at 3,000 feet, all of which were attacking Allied ground positions near Buna. As a Zero was pulling up from a strafing pass Welch dove on it from 4,000 feet, but failed to score any hits. After coming out of his dive he followed the Zero toward Kokoda, but the enemy fighter changed course for Buna. Welch tried to get within firing range, and after 10 miles he finally got off a long five second burst that hit the Zero in its engine and cockpit, causing it to burst into flames and fall into the sea in a steep glide. Only moments later, Welch and Wingman 2Lt. Howard Peterson saw Vals at 5,000 feet and attacked from the rear. Welch's first burst struck the dive bomber between the pilot and the gunner, causing it to explode and crash into the sea. Before returning to base Welch went after a second Val and closed to within 100 feet before he opened fire. A three second burst hit the Val at the wing roots and center section of the fuselage and it crashed into the sea. This victory gave Welch three victories for the day for the first triple victory in a day score for an 8FG pilot (not including the three Zeros claimed by Wagner on 30 April), making him an ace exactly a year from the day that he had scored four victories over Pearl Harbor. Peterson shot down another. The 8FG had scored nine victories for the day with the only damage being a bullet hole in Watson's P-39.

7 December 1942: 35FG/40FS
At 1120, eight P-39s flying in two flights led by Capt. Malcolm Moore was patrolling the Buna area at 7,000, but didn't see four well camouflaged Zeros 1,000 feet below them until they were a half mile away flying toward them, head on. The Japanese went into a defensive Lufbery Circle to gain an altitude advantage, and each 40FS flight broke off and separated to attack. The Japanese scattered as the Americans turned into them, and in the combat Capt. Moore destroyed a Zero in a stern attack; 1Lt. Clarence Wilmarth shot down a Zero making a tight climbing turn; and 2Lt. Charles Klein shot down another Zero in a head on attack. All three were seen to crash in the Gona area. 1Lt. John Babel and 2Lt. James Herbert got good hits for probables.

7 December 1942: 49FG/8FS/9FS
8FS
After being airborne for 20 minutes, 1Lt. Frank Nichols' 8FS Red Flight had begun their high cover assignment at 14,000 feet for Squadron dive bombers north of Buna. The Dobodura Air Controller passed on a report of a large enemy formation approaching from Lae. Nichols and his Wingman, Lucius Lacroix, and Element Leader 1Lt. John Hood and Wingman 1Lt. Arland Stanton, were ordered to fly northward nearer to the coast. Nichols led Red Flight in a climb to 3,000 feet and spotted the enemy formation flying a parallel course in two line abreast waves of nine aircraft each. The Screamin' Demon Flight continued south until they were slightly ahead of the G4M Bettys in scattered clouds. Nichols ordered the Flight to jettison their belly tanks and break for the attack as the enemy bombers approached the coast near Gona. At 1320, the four P-40s went into a turning dive concealed by clouds toward the enemy bomber lead V elements on the right flank. The Zero escorts were surprised, as the Americans closed into point blank range on the bombers as they remained 1,000 feet above the bombers. Nichols fired at 300 yards and hit the starboard engine and wing of the lead Betty, which began to descend. Red Flight Element Leader Hood and Wingman Stanton immediately followed, and Hood set fire to the bomber to the right of Nichol's victim. On Hood's attack he fired from out of range, and when he saw his tracers falling short he raised his sights

1Lt. Robert **Vaught** scored his 2nd and 3rd of five victories. (AAF)

1Lt. Frank **Nichols** scored his second victory. (AFAA)

and fired very long bursts, raking the bomber from engine to cockpit. After their pass Red Flight regrouped over the foothills for another pass, but the enemy had dropped their bombs between Gona and Buna and quickly retreated into the eastern haze. After they had escaped the Demons they flew directly into a patrol of eight P-40s of the 9FS Flying Knights.

9FS

The 9th, led by 1Lt. Robert Vaught, had been vectored north toward the approaching enemy formation by the Controller. They climbed to 18,000 and finally overtook the enemy bombers flying in close formation as they were descending east of Buna. Using the proven interception technique he used at Darwin, Vaught peeled off into a high speed dive against the trailing bomber V elements. He raced down through the bomber's inaccurate defensive fire and then snapped upward in a climbing attack on the vulnerable bellies of the G4Ms. He fired at two bombers, scoring good hits on one, and then closed in on a wounded straggler and set it on fire, as the now alerted Zeros caused him to break off the attack with two victories. Veteran Element Leader 1Lt. William Levitan and newcomer 2Lt. Duncan Myers followed Vaught's lead and attacked the G4Ms from below; each scored a victory each before the escorts interfered. Both pilots escaped, but Levitan exceeded his Warhawk's maximum velocity in his escape dive into the clouds and flipped into a violent spin; after a frightening descent he was able to regain control after descending thousands of feet.

1Lt. John **Hood**. (R). (with Harry Brown) scored his first of three victories. (AAF)

9 December 1942 to New Years: 8FG

After 9 December 8FG operational plans changed, as the 35th and 80th Squadrons divided training and special missions from Milne Bay, while the 36th operated out of Port Moresby until the end of the year. Besides practicing bombing or gunnery, the 35FS and 80FS patrolled Milne and Oro Bays and flew uneventful reconnaissance and escort missions.

10 December 1942: 35FG

The 36FS of the 8FG replaced the 35FS, which had joined the 35FG on 29 November. On the same day Lt.Col. Richard Legg, Group CO, was promoted to full Colonel.

10 December-2 January 1943: The End at Gona/Buna

On 10 December the Australians finally overran Gona, and on the 14th, Gen. Imamura evacuated Buna Village garrison and retreated north up the coast to link up with the reinforcements landed at the Kumusi River, but that night the 800 survivors there had re-embarked their barges and escaped to land still further north at Mambare Bay. Imamura's rear guard defended the shores between Sananda and Gona and fought to the last man in true Bushido tradition. It would not be until 2 January 1943 that Eichelberger's 32nd Division secured the Buna coastline.

15 December 1942

On 15 December the Japanese landed their last reinforcements into Buna when a convoy was spotted by recon during the afternoon, but bad weather prevented effective air attacks on the vessels, which landed troops that night. However, all through the next day Allied aircraft flew missions against supply dumps and troops on shore. All available fighters were put into the air, escorting bombers in addition to bombing. As American and Australian troops pushed toward Buna enemy resistance became more and more fierce. The Japanese were well dug in, and many missions were flown against their installations. A-20s, B-25s, and B-26s dropped tons of bombs on the enemy targets as the fighters flew continuous patrols overhead to prevent enemy fighters from getting through to the bombers.

18 December 1942

Despite the daily routine of ground support and standing patrols, the 49FG did not meet Japanese air opposition for ten consecutive days following the success on 7 December. On 18 December the AAF and RAAF again combined forces for another mission to draw up the veteran Japanese Navy pilots at Lae Airdrome on 18 December. Beaufighters and A-20s bombed and strafed the Lae Airdrome, while 12 Eightballers flew in high cover over the target. The bombers withdrew as a tropical storm front closed in over the Markham River Delta, shrouding the approach of defending Zeros. The enemy fighters swept out of the clouds for one firing pass that separated the P-40s, which escaped in flights of ones and twos. Mission Leader veteran 1Lt. Richard Dennis was killed in the quick attack.

26 December 1942: 49FG/9FS

Due to the monsoon rains that limited missions over the entire New Guinea north coast, there was no enemy contact after 18 December. Once the weather permitted 5AF HQ ordered more coastal patrols over Buna and escorts to Lae, which decreased dive bombing sorties. These missions were to be met by the JAAF 11th Sentai, which had moved onto the Malahang Airstrip, located northeast of Lae Village. The Sentai had flown a small number of reconnaissance flights before the weather had improved during mid-morning on 26 December. Meanwhile, between the intermittent rain showers, 9FS patrols took off from their Port Moresby fields and climbed over the Owen Stanley Mountains to orbit over Buna. 1Lt. John Landers led a dozen Warhawks, leaving White Flight in top cover at 14,000 feet, 1Lt. James Watkins' Blue Flight at 10,000, and his Red Flight at 8,000. As they arrived the Dobodura Air Controller urgently called for fighter cover, as "Zekes" were strafing the landing area and attacking a flight of RAAF Hudson transports, one of which carried Gen. Blamey, head of the Allied Army in New Guinea.

Landers' Flights dropped their auxiliary tanks and raced off to intercept the "Zekes," which actually were Lae Army Oscars that were attacking the Hudsons at low altitude. Landers' Red and Blue Flights attacked the enemy out of the hazy overcast over Dobodura airfield, and a ferocious dogfight began that would rage from 5,000 feet down to the deck. Watkins' Blue Flight entered the fight first, as he and Wingman 2Lt. Arthur Wenige made two coordinated passes on the Oscars, with each claiming a kill and a probable. Blue Leader 1Lt. William Levitan and Wingman 1Lt. William Sells separated during the first tight turn, with Sells downing an Oscar when he attacked two enemy fighters flying under the hazy overcast. Levitan also shot down an Oscar. Low on ammo and fuel, Blue Flight was forced to break off combat.

During Red Flight's diving attack through the broken overcast, Landers' elements became separated and remained so during the remainder of the mission. In his first combat engagement, Landers' Wingman, 2Lt. Robert McDaris, claimed a "Zeke" destroyed and another heavily damaged, but was unable to rejoin Landers and returned to Moresby. 2Lt. John Bagdasarian chased an Oscar off the tail of Blue Flight's Watkins, but Warhawk's engine blew and he made a safe emergency landing at Dobodura.

Landers dove into the center of six Oscars that were reforming, and had no choice but to attack all of them at once. Lander's attack surprised the Japanese pilots, and he was able to shoot down two of them before they

1Lt. William **Levitan** scored his second and last victory. (AAF)

Oscar Army Nakajima Ki-43 Type 2 one place SE fighter. (AFHRC)

could react. Landers dove away from the other four, but one enemy pilot got on his tail and hit Landers' P-40 with a long, accurate burst. Landers broke down and away south toward the Owen Stanley foothills, but the Japanese pilot followed and fired again, scoring more hits. Landers dropped behind the crest of a hill at 1,000 feet and pulled his canopy back, stepped out on the wing, and was swept off in the slipstream. Landers landed safely in the dense forest due east of Pongani, on the coast. After three days of wading through swamps and hacking his way through heavy forest he came upon a native village. He was taken to Pongani Village and transported to Port Moresby the next day. The two victories gave him six in the Pacific to make him an ace. He would later score 8.5 more victories (with 20 strafing kills) in the ETO to make him one of America's two aces to score five of more victories in the Pacific and Europe. Maj. James Howard was credited with six victories with the Flying Tigers and then six victories in the ETO. The seven victories claimed on 26 December brought the Group to 100 victories, which made it the top scoring Fighter Group in the USAAF.

1Lt. John **Landers** scored his last two victories in the Pacific to become an ace with six. (shown being decorated by Wurtsmith). (AAF)

Landers posing with P-40 "Skeeter." (AFAR)

Col. John **Landers** also scored 8.5 victories in the ETO. (plus 20 ground victories) to become one of two pilots. (James Howard) to become aces in both the Pacific and Europe. (AFAA)

27 December 1942: 35FG/39FS

The Japanese attacked Buna again on the 27th, as the Japanese Staff at Rabaul decided that they would shift their attention to New Guinea, since the Solomon Islands missions were temporarily reduced due to seasonal storms. In the first combined JAAF/JNAF mission in the Southern Area, 20 Zeros and Oscars and seven Vals flew toward Dobodura at 14,000 feet. At 1130 the Controller at Dobodura, coded *Wewoka*, plotted enemy aircraft approaching the Buna area, and at 1155 Dobodura reported two Zeros were strafing the #2 strip and that 27 enemy aircraft had been counted.

At 1210, 12 P-38s in three flights of four of the 39th Squadron took off on their first major combat of the war. Three flights made a diving attack on a Japanese formation of more than 20 fighters and seven Val dive bombers in the vicinity of Cape Endaiadere. At 1215 the Vals had attacked the Allied garrison that had just captured Buna. The standing patrol of four P-38s of the 39FS was orbiting above Buna at 25,000 feet. Flight Leader Capt. Thomas Lynch, Wingman 2Lt. Richard Bong, Element Leader 2Lt. Kenneth Sparks, and Wingman 2Lt. John Mangas simultaneously jettisoned their belly tanks and dove towards the Vals dive bombing Buna. Midway in their dive enemy escorts crossed the P-38s' path. Capt. Lynch quickly aimed and disintegrated a Zero, then continued his dive toward the Vals. The Lightnings were soon followed in their dive by a flight of Hamps, and Bong side slipped his P-38 "*Thumper*" to fire at a Hamp who was on Lynch's tail The Hamp was hit and spun away, but as Bong looked back he saw three others circling behind, so he increased his descent angle and dodged his pursuers. He finally pulled his P-38 out of its 400 knot plus descent only "two inches above the shortest tree in Buna." Suddenly, a Val that had just pulled out of its bombing run appeared just in front of Bong at point blank range. Before the rear gunner could swing his guns the concentrated firepower of Bong's P-38 struck the inflammable dive bomber, which exploded into a fireball for America's future Ace-of-Aces first victories of a total of 40. It was only after the mission that Bong's casual mention of the shots he fired at the Hamp gave him a second confirmed kill. Bong's account of the combat was:

> "Took off 1130/L, direct to Buna. Arrived 1250/L, at 21,000 feet. Wewoka called 27 aircraft. Saw 7 to 8 Vals (dive bombers), 7 to 8 Zekes. Vals were low, Zekes above 3,000 feet. Vals at 4,000 feet over old Buna Strip area released bombs and went down on the water to the northeast. Flight dived on a Zeke. I dropped belly tank, took a pass at Zero without firing, dived away from four Zekes which jumped my tail, taking shot a one Zeke on the way down without observed result. Reversed direction in dive and took shot at one Val near Buna, missed, turned left, and went out to sea at 500 feet. Saw Val and fired long burst at range of 350 yards. Val blew up as a result of direct hit from cannon and crashed into water. Zeke on my tail, as I headed out to sea. Three Vals ahead of me. Right Val pulled off to right. Zekes still behind me, so took short burst at center Val without observed result, so made shallow turn to right, found one lone Val, took pass without firing and went home. Out of ammo. Combat lasted 1210 to 1218L. Landed 1250L."

Capt. Thomas Lynch became the first ace of the squadron when he destroyed two Oscar fighters. Lynch's description of the battle was even more succinct:

> "I fired at the last Oscar, firing from 300 yards until I went over him. Observed side of fuselage blow away. Followed another Oscar. Fired a long burst from 200 yards. Observed him dive in the water, (Two Oscars down)"

2Lt. Kenneth Sparks saw a Zero at 2 o'clock low and dove on it as its pilot went into a vertical dive off his port wing. Sparks fired and saw it crash into the ocean, then chased a Val and got fatal hits on its wings, starting a fire. When Sparks landed back at Dobodura #4 he nosed over because his wheel door had received damage in the battle. Sparks' Wingman, 2Lt. John Mangas, made a circling starboard dive on Oscars but did not fire on his first pass. The Oscars turned into the attack and Mangas fired five short bursts from 300 yards. The enemy dove into the sea and exploded while Mangas evaded another Oscar diving on him.

In the battle, 1Lt. Hoyt Eason was credited with two Zekes and a probable. Eason saw three Zekes below and dove, closing on a Zero that turned right, but Eason put two bursts at 300 yards into it, which hit the cockpit and it dove into the water. Eason's second kill was chasing a P-40 when he shot it down.

2Lt. Harris Denton fired at the leading Zero that attacked his flight but missed, then took a second full deflection shot at 150 yards and a third full deflection shot at 100 yards that exploded in the enemy cockpit. 2Lt. Ralph Bills was flying with Denton at 1,000 feet and shot a diving Zero off the tail of a P-38 in his flight with a deflection shot.

1Lt. Charles Gallup shot down a Zero that overshot its attack on his tail and shot a long burst at it at 100 yards as it passed. Gallup had to pull up sharply when the enemy bust into flames in front of him. Gallups' Wingman, 2Lt. Carl Planck of the 9FS on TDY to the 39th, shot a Zero off his tail. Planck pulled up directly behind the Zero and fired two short bursts and a long burst that hit the bottom of the fuselage, and it crashed near Watutu Point.

2Lt. Stanley Andrews saw three Zeros at 5,000 feet and dove on them. The Zeros rolled to the left and Andrews followed the left plane in a turning dive, firing a long continuous burst from 500 to 50 yards. As the Zero pulled up its damaged tail assembly sheared off and it spun into the water a half mile offshore.

After scoring 12 previous victories over New Guinea, the 39th Squadron matched its entire output for the war with 10 fighters and two dive bombers in this action. The day's success inspired Gen. Whitehead to write "We have the Jap air force whipped."

Capt. Thomas **Lynch** scored two victories to make him an ace with five. (AAF)

2Lt. Richard **Bong** scored his first of 40 victories on his way to becoming America's Ace-of-Aces. (AFAA)

1Lt. Charles **Gallup** was credited with his first victory of six. (AAF)

2Lt. Ralph **Bills** claimed his first of two victories. (AAF)

2Lt. Stanley **Andrews** scored his first of six victories. (AFAA)

27 December 1942: 49FG/7FS/9FS

At the same time as Lynch's P-38s began their attack, 7FS and 9FS P-40s and another flight of 39FS Lightnings came on the scene. More than 50 fighters were in a churning dogfight in the haze at 6,000 feet. The inexperienced Lightning pilots were unable to differentiate between the Warhawks, Oscars, and Zeros in the haze and confusion, and fired at any single engine aircraft that crossed their path. The P-40 pilots shouted out their identity over the radio to the "trigger-happy" P-38 pilots and broke off combat before they could engage their real enemy. In the battle 1Lt. William Haning and 2Lt. Birge Neuman of the 9FS each claimed a Zero probable for their last P-40 claims before the 9FS transitioned to the Lightning.

After 7FS Ops Exec 1Lt. George Manning landed at 17 Mile Drome, he became livid when he found bullet holes in his fighter. 2Lt. Birge Neuman's P-40 was hit the worst, with bullet holes in the cowling, propellers, and rear canopy. Manning and Neuman, accompanied by Harry Dillworth, William Haning, and Clay Tice, drove to confront the 39th at 14 Mile Drome. When the furious Manning confronted the 39FS fighter pilots an intense shouting match took place, and Manning went for his Colt .45 and had to be restrained and escorted away. 9FS CO Peaselee and 7FS CO Martin both wanted to bring charges against the 39FS, but 49er Group Deputy Maj. Morrissey demanded that the issue be ended, which it was.

Before long the 49th would get P-38s of its own, and by New Year's Day all of the Group's P-40Es were assigned to the 8FS, and the senior pilots of the 9FS were initiated into P-38 school, while the junior pilots were reassigned to the two other squadrons.

2Lt. Carl **Planck** of the 9FS TDY to the 39FS scored his first. (AAF)

28 December 1942-4 January 1943: 8FG/36FS

During the last week of the year several pilots from the 36FS were back at Milne Bay. On 28 December 1Lt. Verl Jett was on a patrol near Goodenough Island as part of a 36FS flight when a twin-engine Japanese aircraft (Sonia or Dinah?) was sighted at 1010, and he shot it down for the 8FG's last victory of 1942.

31 December 1942: 35FG/39FS

The score of the 39th Squadron increased steadily over the next few days when 11 P-38s flew escort for 18 B-25, B-26, and A-20 bombers that were attacking Japanese targets at Lae and Gasmata. The Squadron saw 11 or 12 Zeros in loose formation in a dive on them and turned into the attack. The top scorer for the day was 1Lt. Hoyt Eason, with three victories to make him an ace. In his ICR Eason only stated that he got his three Zeros by "Diving at a small angle of deflection from the rear." Double victories were credited to Capt. Thomas Lynch and 2Lt. Kenneth Sparks. Single victories were scored by 2Lt. Ralph Bills, who had to escape a diving Zero before shooting down another Zero. 2Lt. Normand Hyland dove on a Zero that turned into him head

2Lt. Kenneth **Sparks** scored his first two victories of 11. (AFAA)

1Lt. Verl **Jett** scored his first of seven victories. (AFAA)

2Lt. Normand **Hyland** claimed the first of four victories. (AAF)

2Lt. Ralph **Bills** scored his last of two victories but Bills would also be awarded with five probables during his career. (AAF)

2Lt. Kenneth **Sparks** claimed victories over two Zeros to give him four. (AFAA)

1Lt. Hoyt **Eason** downed three Zeros to become and ace. (AAF)

Top pilots of the 39FS: Front Row. (L-R) Charles **Sullivan**, Thomas **Lynch**, Kenneth **Sparks** Back Row. (L-R) Richard **Suehr**, John **Lane**, Stanley **Andrews**
On 31 December **Lynch** and **Sparks** would claim two victories each and **Lane** one. (AAF)

on and Hyland had to dive away to safety. He then climbed back and shot down a Zero that went into a stall and fell off into the ocean. 2Lt. John Lane dove on a Zero that turned into him, but Lane persevered and then destroyed the Zero. 2Lt. Richard Bong of the 9FS on TDY "shot at six Zekes in succession, all head on attacks…." On the sixth pass Bong hit the Zero's engine, but it escaped and he settled for a probable claim.

Nine Zeros were destroyed, while two P-38s suffered minor damage in the battle. In the Special Comments section of their CFs, "The (enemy) aircraft and pilots were very much superior to those on contacted over Buna on 27 December 1942." (2Lt. Carl Planck) "High grade Jap pilots, aggressive and made head on attacks." (2Lt. R.L. Bong)

Late December 1942: 5FC Command Changes

In late December, Gen. Wurtsmith asked Gen. Whitehead to transfer the capable 49er CO, Lt.Col. Donald Hutchinson, to the 5FC as his Chief of Staff. Maj. Robert Morrissey had recovered from Malaria and replaced Group Adjutant George Powell, who had rotated to the States before Christmas. Morrissey was the next in line to take command of the Group and moved the 49FG HQ to 17 Mile Drome to operate closer to Wurtsmith at 14 Mile Drome.

The 49th Fighter Group Disposition: End of 1942

As 1942 closed, the 49th Fighter Group continued to find its three Squadrons dispersed. When the P-38s of the 39FS/35FG were assigned to 14 Mile Drome, the Screamin' Demons transferred to 17 Mile Drome, home of 49er CO Hutchinson's HQ. The Eightballs continued at 3 Mile Drome, attempting to keep their old Warhawks in service while initiating new pilots into Squadron ranks. The Flying Knight Squadrons were based at three different locations. The 9FS P-40s were attached to 7th Squadron operations at 4 Mile and 14 Mile Dromes. The 9th Squadron P-38 pilots were on attached duty with the 370th Materiel Squadron based in northern Australia, where the remaining P-38s were finally being prepared for combat. Finally, 9th Squadron CO Capt. Jesse Peaselee persuaded HQ to move Squadron HQ from the wretched conditions at Rogers (30 Mile) Field. On 24 December Peaselee united his two P-40 units at 4 Mile Drome, while his P-38 units were to move to the new Dobodura strip once it was completed. By the end of December, the majority of the 9FS were based at Port Moresby and could function as an integral unit.

10

Strategy and Planning for 1943

The role of air power in Southwest Pacific operations had been established before the end of the Papuan Campaign as essentially that of a tactical air force, although in contrast to the later tactical air force, the Fifth Air Force contained heavy bombardment units. Kenney considered the defeat of the Japanese Air Force as his first priority, with 5FC fighters designated to destroy enemy aircraft attempting to attack Allied bases and his bombers attacking and neutralizing Japanese air bases. Kenney's second priority was the destruction of Japanese communications and supplies. Strategic objectives, with the possible exception of Rabaul and Balikpapan, were out of the range of Allied bombers based in the Southwest Pacific, but worthwhile alternate targets were available along the shipping lanes to Japan's advanced garrisons. Kenney's third priority was to use his air force in the destruction of selected objectives in the battle area.

In a theater as large as the SWPA, it would have been particularly easy for MacArthur to dissipate his limited air power in numerous small attacks on widely separated targets. In fact, such attacks had been necessary before July 1942, when he was desperately trying to defend Australia. But even before this wholly defensive period ended he was considering a plan which would utilize both his air and ground forces in a coordinated offensive to recapture Japan's vital base at Rabaul, on New Britain Island.

By August 1942, the Combined and Joint Chiefs of Staff had established that the Pacific Theater was to be subordinated to the European, and soon afterward the Joint Chiefs of Staff listed 10 general objectives of overall Allied strategy. It was not until the No. 6 position on JCS' agenda that a Pacific concern appeared: "the general objective of securing Australia, New Zealand, Hawaii, and Alaska." In the No. 7 position was that of carrying out limited offensive operations with amphibious forces in the Pacific. To fill this No. 7 Slot MacArthur suggested that Rabaul should be the object of an offensive. Initially, the Navy did not support this suggestion because it thought an attack on Rabaul would be too uncertain unless Tulagi, in the Solomons, was captured first. In a radio communication of 24 June 1942 MacArthur agreed it would be unrealistic to attempt a direct attack on Rabaul with the limited land-based air power that was then available, and that the capture of Rabaul was not the immediate, but the ultimate goal of the proposed offensive. His plan would first require "a progressive movement involving primary action against the Solomons and the north coast of New Guinea in order to protect naval surface forces and to secure airfields which essentially would be the plan that was finally agreed upon." The operation was to consist of three phases:

1) The occupation of the Solomons,
2) The occupation of British New Guinea (Papua), and then
3) The occupation of the Bismarck Archipelago, including Rabaul.

The first phase of the plan was to be carried out by Adm. Robert Ghormley, the Commander of the South Pacific Area, while MacArthur was to direct the second and third phases. Initially the dates of these operations were left as indefinite, pending the arrival of sufficient American forces, but Japanese advances, including the occupation of Tulagi in April and of Guadalcanal early in July, together with their landing in Papua late that same month, accelerated Allied counter operations. The first phase landings in the Solomons were, therefore, scheduled for 3 August 1942, or as soon as possible afterward, with the intention of preventing further enemy advances in the South Pacific. Simultaneously, MacArthur was confronted with the obligation of defending the Papuan Peninsula, an area from which he had anticipated to launch his original attacks.

While these developments did not change the basic Pacific strategy, they did generate discussions on aircraft allocations. Dispatches from both the South and Southwest Pacific Theaters to the War Department urged a reconsideration of earlier aircraft allocation decisions by the Joint Chiefs of Staff. On 31 August MacArthur radioed that he understood a strategy which assigned "present missions as holding ones to enable concentrations to be made elsewhere," but that "holding areas must have sufficient forces actually to hold," and that "the strength of holding forces can be determined only by a constantly changing accurate appraisal of the enemy's power." The Navy also supported the reassessment of the needs of the Pacific areas. Adm. Nimitz believed that he had insufficient carrier strength available to support two important operations at the same time. The Guadalcanal operation was already under way, and amphibious operations would also be necessary for the recapture of eastern New Guinea. These operations would require the cooperation of aircraft flown from carriers, but Nimitz feared that enemy submarines and land-based aircraft made the employment of

LEFT: Gen. H.H. **Arnold**, Chief of the AAF and Gen. George **Kenney**, CO 5AF. (AAF) RIGHT: Admiral Ernest **King**, the Chief of Naval Operations. (USN)

the few remaining American carriers far too dangerous. Therefore, Nimitz recommended that more land-based aircraft be sent to MacArthur.

In early July the decision to abandon the proposal for an invasion of Continental Europe in 1942 led to suggestions that aircraft could be diverted from *Bolero*, which was the movement to England of air combat groups beginning in May 1942 with the shipment by fast troopships (usually former ocean liners) of their ground echelons. The movement of the aircraft began in June after the decision was made that the most efficient and rapid buildup could be made by having the air groups themselves ferry their planes overseas. Fighters, having only a single crewman and not equipped with proper navigational and communications equipment for trans-oceanic flights, were to be divided into flights of four and escorted by single bombers navigating the route for them. On 21 July, these suggestions received some official sanction in a decision that "over and above the US forces required from *Bolero* for operations in North and Northwest Africa, a readjustment of present US commitments to *Bolero* will be made for the purpose of furthering offensive operations in the Pacific." This readjustment envisaged the transfer of 15 Air groups to the South and Southwest Pacific, with the majority being sent to the latter theater.

Although there was some agreement on the deployment of these aircraft among the Joint Planners, Army and Navy members disagreed as to the order of priority of the various theaters. The Army listed the priorities thus: *Torch* (North Africa), Middle East, United Kingdom, and the Pacific; whereas the Navy placed the Pacific before the United Kingdom. The arguments advanced by Admiral King, the Chief of Naval Operations, and General Arnold, Chief of the AAF, verified these opposing points of view. King stated that the air power in the Pacific was inadequate, and although he understood the high priority of *Torch* and the Middle East, he did not agree to the placement of the Pacific Theater last in priority, which was not in agreement with the requirement there, and that an appropriate authorization for diversion of aircraft to the Pacific existed in an earlier decision. Arnold, who had just returned from a brief visit to the Pacific, disagreed with King's view. He insisted that the earlier decision "to conduct the strategic offensive with maximum forces in the Atlantic/Western European Theater at the earliest possible date and to maintain the strategic defensive in other areas" was still valid. Furthermore, he argued that the invasion of North Africa required not only air cooperation for the operation itself, but an intensive air assault from the UK as well. To back his point Arnold quoted Gen. Marshall as having stated that the transfer of the 15 groups from *Bolero* "had been recorded only as an agreement for transfer of planes from one jurisdiction to another, and that priority of allocation, once commitments to the special operation and possibly the Middle East had been fulfilled, should be made in accordance with strategic necessity as the planes should become available."

As the King/Arnold debate drew to its climax in mid-October 1942, the tactical situation in the Pacific had changed significantly. While the Japanese were retreating in New Guinea, where the 5AF had won air superiority, the Marines on Guadalcanal were being hard pressed to maintain an uncertain foothold in the face of relentless enemy counterattacks by land, sea, and air. It was obvious that the immediate threat to the Pacific strategy was at Guadalcanal, rather than in Australia/New Guinea.

The Joint Planners felt that adequate aircraft were available in the Southwest Pacific to defend the area and to conduct a limited offensive. This had been Arnold's opinion prior to his trip to the Pacific, and he maintained the same views after his return, repeating them in a letter to Kenney on 6 December 1942. But Kenney contended that his Air Force was under strength, and that previous aircraft commitments had not been met, and the Joint Planners had sent Joint Chiefs of Staffs statistics supporting Kenney's assertion. The statistics compared aircraft previously committed and those on hand on 28 February 1943. While there was a +16 surplus of heavy bombers (110 committed to 116 on hand), there was a -33 deficiency in medium bombers (132/99) and -56 in light bombers (87/31). However, there was only a -6 deficiency in fighters (338/332). The Japanese were estimated to have 332 fighters (vs. 332 US) and 343 bombers (vs. 245 US) available in the SWPA and Pacific, but could probably withdraw 400 additional aircraft from other theaters, along with approximately 600 carrier-based aircraft. Despite these apparently overwhelming figures, the Joint Planners concluded that, although the aircraft available did not meet Kenney's requirements, there was a sufficient number to continue the limited offensive operations contemplated in the Southwest Pacific.

During the Papuan Campaign MacArthur continued to consider the objectives of the offensive he had planned in the summer of 1942. In early January 1943 he outlined his concept of the execution of that plan. His tactics were to be mainly based upon two principles which, with some modification, were to lead to a continuous succession of victories in the Southwest Pacific. His experiences in the first year of the war had confirmed the value of air power. One major tactical principle, therefore, was that air echelons should move forward progressively in order to provide fighter and bomber cover for "all surface elements." A second key principle was that, in the course of these progressive movements, the objective should be isolated prior to the final assault. Again, air power was to be the principal factor for this process of isolation in a theater where great distances and difficult jungle country made rapid movement of land and sea forces difficult.

Admiral King's suggestion that the Admiralty Islands would be a logical objective for initial action caused MacArthur to oppose this suggestion, because it would have advanced surface operations beyond the range of land-based aircraft. He envisaged the campaign as a series of steps, each of which would be protected by aircraft flying from newly captured bases. He did not believe that success could be achieved if the elimination of any preliminary step would result in a movement into Japanese held areas where air advantage was entirely the enemy's. In the South Pacific MacArthur pressed for the capture of Guadalcanal and to establish air bases there, followed by a movement against other enemy bases, including Munda, Buin, and Buka. Once these objectives were captured land-based aircraft could provide protection for surface elements, and it would be possible for "the fleet to operate offensively with the destruction of the enemy's fleet as its primary mission."

While the Joint Chiefs of Staff were in agreement with the necessity for a limited offensive in the Pacific, within the Combined Chiefs of Staff there was some disagreement. Though the Pacific was an area of American strategic responsibility, the British were concerned over the future extent of the American plans for the Pacific campaign. They worried that the decision to make Europe the war's main strategic effort could be forgotten, and that

American resources in Europe might be drawn off into the Pacific. The British realized that pressure had to be maintained upon Japan, and that their operations in Burma were important, but advocated that Allied operations toward Truk after the Rabaul Campaign was postponed.

The Americans also realized that if a debacle had occurred in the Pacific, a huge diversion of effort to the Pacific would have been necessary. So America was forced to go on the offensive in New Guinea to prevent the capture of Port Moresby, and had to utilize every method for reinforcing the Allied troops in New Guinea. Heavy bombers allocated to Europe had been diverted to the South Pacific, and at a time when *Torch*, the invasion of North Africa, was ongoing, assurance was needed that other previously assured allocations to the Pacific would not be withdrawn. King was against the setting of definite limits to Pacific operations, and maintained that after the Allies captured Rabaul, the same forces could be used to continue the offensive in the Marshalls.

The decision, which was incorporated in a report to FDR and Churchill before the end of January, permitted a continuation of plans for a limited offensive in the Pacific. Generally, offensive plans for the Pacific in 1943 consisted of the capture of Rabaul, destroying enemy merchant and warships, interdiction of enemy lines of communication and supply, and to persistently attack enemy land, sea, and air power. Any advance from the Rabaul area toward the Guam-Truk line was to be delayed until adequate forces were available. Limited advances were considered toward the Samoa-Jaliut line and the Malay Barrier, possibly Timor. Defensively, the Allies were to maintain the "Midway/Hawaii Line," maintain communication and supply lines to Australia and New Zealand, and to block enemy approaches to Australia.

Elkton Plan

The Joint and Combined Chiefs of Staff continued to make Rabaul their chief objective in the Pacific, and on 28 February 1943 MacArthur formulated his strategic plan for Rabaul, known as the *Elkton Plan*. MacArthur formulated this strategic Plan to capture Rabaul from bases in Australia and New Guinea. Adm. Ernest King proposed a plan with similar elements but under Navy command. Army Chief of Staff George C. Marshall, whose main goal was for the United States to concentrate its efforts against Nazi Germany in Europe and not against the Japanese in the Pacific, proposed a compromise plan in which the task would be divided into three stages: the first under Navy command and the second two under MacArthur's direction and the control of the Army. This strategic plan, which was similar to MacArthur's 24 June 1942 proposal, was never formally adopted by the US Joint Chiefs of Staff, but was ultimately implemented. The *Elkton Plan* called for:

1) Capture of Tulagi (later Guadalcanal) and the Santa Cruz Islands (*Operation Watchtower*)
2) Capture of the northeast coast of New Guinea and the central Solomons
3) Reduction of Rabaul and related bases

The "scheme of maneuver" for *Elkton* was based on seizure of the Huon Peninsula followed by converging attacks through New Britain and through the Solomon Islands to Kavieng. both culminating in a combined assault on Rabaul. The attack along the New Guinea coast was to capture operating airdromes in the Huon Peninsula and to precede the attack through the Solomons; then both attacks were to proceed toward the objective, Rabaul, as a converging mutually supporting operation. These operations were to be preceded by strong land-based air action and covered by the Allied Fleet to prevent a major Japanese naval "interruption." The forces along the "western axis" (New Guinea) were to operate against successive objectives to capture air operating bases in western New Britain by airborne and small craft operations, and thence by amphibious operations to the capture of Rabaul. The forces along the "eastern axis" (Solomons) were to progress northwestward by amphibious operations through successive objectives to a meeting with western forces in a combined attack on Rabaul. Throughout these operations, the employment of aviation by both forces was to be coordinated by MacArthur in support of either force requiring the maximum assistance at the moment. The Allied Fleet was to "seek decisive combat with hostile naval forces." To insure the security of the Southwest Pacific Line of Communications, the defense of the Torres Strait area was to be undertaken along the line Darwin to Merauke by the action of ground, air, and naval units. Merauke was to be occupied and used as an air operating base. The schedule to secure successive objectives was to be considered separately, and was to exploit favorable conditions and take advantage of the momentum achieved by either advance.

MacArthur's explanation of his strategy was:

> "My strategic conception for the Pacific Theater, which I outlined after the Papuan Campaign and have since consistently advocated, contemplates massive strokes against only main strategic objectives, utilizing surprise and air-ground striking power supported and assisted by the fleet. This is the very opposite of what is termed 'island hopping' which is the gradual pushing back of the enemy by direct frontal pressure with the consequent heavy casualties which will certainly be involved. Key points must of course be taken but a wise choice of such will obviate the need for storming the mass of islands now in enemy possession. 'Island hopping' with extravagant losses and slow progress...is not my idea of how to end the war as soon and as cheaply as possible. New conditions require for solution and new weapons require for maximum application new and imaginative methods. Wars are never won in the past."

Although Lt.Gen. Walter Krueger's Sixth Army headquarters arrived in SWPA in early 1943, MacArthur had only three American divisions, and they were tired and depleted from the fighting at Buna and Guadalcanal. As a result, it became obvious that any military offensive in the SWPA in 1943 would have to be carried out mainly by the Australian Army.

Allied Air Forces in *Elkton*

The 5AF, RAAF, and air elements of the Southwest Pacific Force not required for defense of installations, facilities, or shipping in the SWPA were to destroy "hostile aviation in general supporting areas of the Northern Solomons, New Ireland, eastern New Britain, and the north coast of New Guinea." They were to destroy naval forces and shipping; support the operations of the Southwest Pacific Task Forces; support the defense of Allied forward bases and the Torres Strait; provide transport aviation support for operations; and be prepared to provide air support for operations of the South Pacific Area and the Naval Striking Force.

Air bases were to be seized and/or developed along two general directions of advance: to the west through New Guinea to New Britain and on the east through the Solomons. The initial operations to the west were to seize airdromes on the Huon Peninsula of New Guinea. Following this, points on New Georgia to the east would be similarly occupied. In the final stages of the operations, airdromes in New Britain in the west and on Bougainville in the east would provide convenient bases for the isolation of Kavieng and Rabaul. The eastern flank of these operations was thought to be fairly secure, since the sea and land areas south of a line from Buna to Guadalcanal were under Allied control. On the other hand, the enemy forces positioned in the Netherlands East Indies were a constant threat to the western flank. MacArthur believed, however, that Moroke, in southwestern New Guinea, could

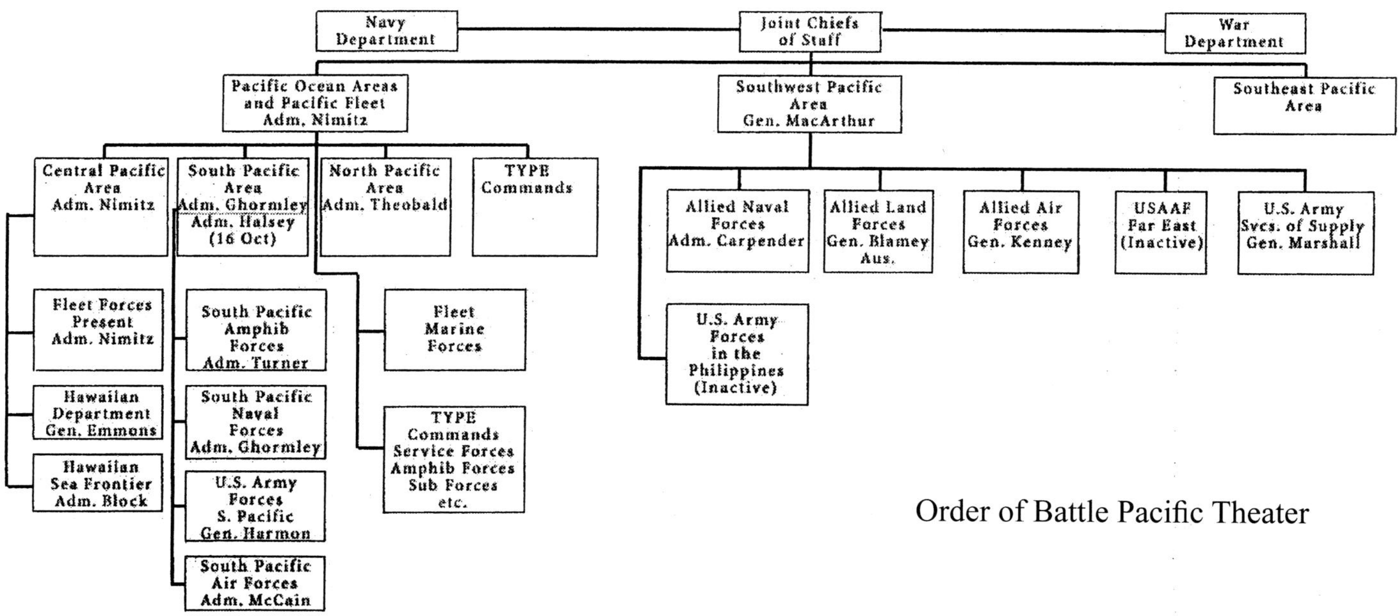

Order of Battle Pacific Theater

be occupied as an air base, and that a holding force could be concentrated along a line from there across the Torres Strait to Darwin.

MacArthur as *Elkton* Supreme Commander

As the Commander in Chief of the SWPA, MacArthur assumed the Supreme Command of the general offensive. In its earlier phases, he would serve in actual command of the western axis and as coordinator of the operations of the South Pacific Forces. His command would include the following elements:

In this command setup, each force was assigned certain general tasks. The Naval Striking Force was to cover operations and to seek out decisive action with the enemy fleet. The Allied Air Forces were to destroy enemy aircraft throughout operational areas, to attack any enemy naval forces and shipping, to support operations of Allied Task Forces, to defend forward bases and the Torres Strait, and to provide air transport. The Allied Naval Forces, composed of two task forces together with PT boat squadrons and escort vessels, were to give naval support, to defend forward bases and the Torres Strait, and to protect lines of communication. The West Force, a self-contained task force equipped for ground and shore-to-shore operations, was to capture Lae and Madang and secure the Huon Peninsula-Markham River Valley areas in order to acquire air bases. The Center Force, organized primarily for airborne and over water operations, was to consolidate airfields behind a general line Gasmata-Talasea in New Britain and to capture Rabaul. The capture of Rabaul would be carried out in conjunction with the South Pacific Forces after they captured New Georgia, Bougainville, and possibly Kavieng. These operations were to be supported by the transport ships and landing craft of the Southwest Pacific Amphibious Force, and by logistical support from an intermediate base located in the Milne Bay area.

Elkton Plan Objectives

The first objective in the *Elkton Plan* was the capture of Lae, on the Huon Gulf in northeast New Guinea, by a combined American and Australian force. An advance east through the Markham Valley was to be carried out by an airborne force, while small craft supported by light naval vessels were to carry out a series of "shore-to-shore over water" moves, bypassing Salamaua and landing near Lae. Once new bases were acquired in the Markham Valley, new airborne and shore-to-shore operations could be carried out to converge on Madang, 180 miles across the Huon Peninsula on Astrolabe Bay, overrunning intermediate objectives, such as Finschhafen, along the way.

MacArthur left the detailed planning of the South Pacific phase of the operation to that Command so that he could assume control of actual operations to acquire several advanced bases to provide air support for amphibious operations. MacArthur believed that the line of Japanese airdromes at Kavieng, Rabaul, Buka, and Buin should be neutralized by use of bases in the Vitiaz Strait area of New Guinea prior to an American invasion of the New Georgia group. Specifically, MacArthur recommended the acquisition of bases on the Huon Peninsula before a landing by the South Pacific Forces in New Georgia.

The next operation was to consist of simultaneous landings by both South and Southwest Pacific Forces with the purpose again to acquire new airdromes in western New Britain and southern Bougainville. Preceded by heavy air attacks on Rabaul and Kavieng, the Southwest Pacific Forces were to seize Cape Gloucester and Arawe, followed by Gasmata and probably Talasea. At the same time, South Pacific forces would land on Bougainville.

The final objectives of the *Elkton Plan* were the capture of Kavieng by the South Pacific Command and a main landing against Rabaul to be made by the Southwest Pacific Forces landing southeast of the town. South Pacific troops, meanwhile, were to make a secondary landing at Atalikikun or Talili Bay. *Elkton* indicated that MacArthur would decide whether Rabaul or Kavieng should be captured first. MacArthur believed that the execution of this rather elaborate plan required additional air units. The Fifth Air Force had the equivalent of two heavy bombardment, two medium bombardment, three fighter, and two troop carrier groups, together with two light bombardment and one photo reconnaissance squadrons. In addition, the RAAF could probably release from its mainland defense forces five medium bombardment, four light bombardment, and six fighter squadrons equipped with relatively modern aircraft.

Although MacArthur did not suggest an increase of RAAF strength at this time, he did estimate that he would need the following additional American units for the Huon Peninsula Campaign: two heavy, two medium, and two and a half light bombardment groups, together with three fighter, one observation, and two troop carrier groups. In addition to these units, he considered the following essential for the New Britain operation: one medium and two heavy bomb groups, one fighter, and three troop carrier groups.

Navy Objections to MacArthur as Supreme Commander

There were several problems introduced by the *Elkton Plan* which required action by the Joint Chiefs of Staff. Perhaps of most importance was the necessity to confirm or reject MacArthur's suggestions as to command of the operations. On 27 March Gen. Marshall submitted a directive for consideration which would establish command responsibilities for certain future operations, including the establishment of airfields on Kiriwina and Woodlark islands, the seizure of the Lae-Salamaua-Finschhafen-Madang area and western New Britain, and the occupation of Bougainville. He recommended that these operations should be conducted under the Supreme Commander, Southwest Pacific Area (MacArthur); that the operations in the Solomons should be under the direct control of the Commander, South Pacific Area (COMSOPAC) (Nimitz) operating under the general directives of the Supreme Commander, Southwest Pacific; and that "naval units of the Pacific Fleet assigned as task forces engaged in these operations remain under the control of the Commander in Chief, Pacific."

The principal objections to Marshall's proposed directive came from Adm. King, whose official memorandum commenting on that directive stated that, while he recognized the importance of a unified command, he felt that it would be impossible to separate operations carried out by forces of the Pacific Ocean Areas in the Solomon Islands from the remainder of the Pacific Ocean Areas. He, therefore, recommended that when such forces were to act in conjunction with forces of the Southwest Pacific, they should do so under the command of the Commander in Chief, Pacific Ocean Areas. MacArthur would control the operations in his theater, while those in the Solomons would be under the direct command of COMSOPAC, subject to the general directives of MacArthur. Adm. King also urged that something should be stated in the directive regarding the timing of the operations. He objected to MacArthur's proposal, which delayed the renewal of operations in the South Pacific until after the completion of the earlier phases of those in the Southwest Pacific.

Differences on this subject were soon resolved. Marshall declared that the wording of the directive avoided the subject of unity of command. He wanted to avoid a situation where a large naval force would be controlled by an Army officer (MacArthur) but believed, however, that operations should be coordinated by a single commander. From the beginning King had tried to prevent a situation where differences of opinion between MacArthur and Nimitz might arise. At that time, however, there was uncertainty as to where the Japanese planned to strike next, so King believed that it was necessary to maintain flexible control of the fleet in order to meet any enemy advance. Therefore, he suggested a rewording of one paragraph of the directive to meet this requirement, but basically the directive as originally proposed by Marshall was accepted. The operations were to be conducted under the Supreme Commander, Southwest Pacific Area, but the essential paragraph, changed in accordance with the Navy's desires, was made to read, "Units of the Pacific Ocean Areas, other than those assigned by the Joint Chiefs of Staff to task forces engaged in these operations, will remain under the control of the Commander in Chief, Pacific Ocean, Areas."

Aircraft Allocations under the *Elkton Plan*

Almost as important as the subject of the command for the proposed operations was the question of additional allocations required under the *Elkton Plan*. The general policy of the Joint Chiefs of Staff was to honor the requests of a theater commander as much as possible. On the other hand, they were faced with the recurrent problem of an inadequate number of aircraft to fill the requirements of all commanders. Under these circumstances shortages had to be divided among the theaters. It was impossible at this time for the Joint Chiefs of Staff to give MacArthur any assurances that they could meet his final estimate. They did expect, however, to meet his needs for the Huon Peninsula phase of the campaign before the end of 1943. Of some significance, for example, was the Joint Planners' decision in late 1942 to equip a Dutch squadron with 26 B-25s by April 1943 and a reaffirmation in January of a JCS decision to equip 45 RAAF squadrons before the end of the year.

However, the Joint Planners had not made the most important decisions concerning new units for reinforcing the Allied Air Forces. In a memorandum of 18 March 1943, the Joint Planners carefully considered two schedules for air reinforcement. In their recommendations they abandoned the more ambitious schedule of sending additional aircraft to the Pacific, as it would delay the implementation of the now overdue bomber offensive from the United Kingdom. They held that the Eighth Air Force should be brought to a minimum strength of 1,200 heavy day bombers, together with supporting aircraft, as soon as possible. Maj.Gen. Ira Eaker, worried over the slowness with which his 8AF heavy bomber strength was being built up, wrote in a letter to Arnold, stating: "I hope that you will not let that fellow George Kenney or that other fellow Toohey Spaatz, steal any of our heavy bombers." Nonetheless, Eaker was soon informed by Gen. George Stratemeyer that "as a result of a lot of brass hats that are here from the South and Southwest Pacific, you are going to lose another heavy bomber group." Apparently the Joint Chiefs of Staff felt that the Southwest Pacific warranted more reinforcements than the Joint Planners had recommended. Therefore, they selected a second and more ambitious schedule which allocated the following units to the Fifth Air Force, two of which, a medium and a heavy group, had been previously allocated to Eaker:

Planned Initial Shipment Strength

Units	9 March 1943*		30 June 1943		30 Sept. 1943		31 Dec. 1943	
	Units	A/C	Units	A/C	Units	A/C	Units	A/C
BG (H)	2	103	2	96	3	144	3	144
BG (M)	1.5	80	2	114	3	171	3	171
FG	3	253	3	225	5	375	6	450
FG (N)	—	—	2	24	2	24	2	24

*Present or enroute

With the promise of these additional aircraft came that of additional infantry units, which prompted the Commanders of the SWPA and Central Pacific to rethink their future strategy for 1943. They informed the JCS that they would be able to push along the New Guinea coast to capture strategic points, including Madang, and would be able to land on the southeast portion of Bougainville Island, on Cape Gloucester, and on Kiriwina and Woodlark Islands.

While these allocations fulfilled the requirements for new units, Kenney's immediate concern was to maintain the units already in the theater at authorized strength. In November he had received 34 combat aircraft and lost 55; December the figures were 37 received and 48 lost; and during the first three weeks of January he received 16 fighters and lost 20.

The War Department's policy on the allocation of replacements was not entirely clear. Gen. Arnold, in commenting to Gen. Stratemeyer on Kenney's dilemma, stated that "in some instances it is quite apparent that Kenney is calling 'Wolf, Wolf,'" but added that in other instances he had a "justifiable kick." Arnold pointed out that according to his records "the highest loss Kenney had in fighters in any one month was 43%, and the lowest, 11%, an average of around 21%. The highest loss in bombers in any one month was 25% and the lowest about 15%." Arnold emphasized that a solution to the problem was essential, and that he did not "want this matter to go so far that we will be in as deep as we were in North Africa."

The Joint Chiefs of Staff incorporated a decision on this matter in the same memorandum which assigned additional units to the Southwest Pacific. Their plan was to maintain a 25% depot reserve in the theater, a flow of 20% of the initial equipment per month as attrition aircraft for

The **A-36 Apache** was the dive bomber version of the Allison-engined P-51 Mustang. (AAF)

The **A-25 Shrike** was the Army's version of the Navy's Curtiss SB2C Helldiver dive bomber. (USN)

combat units, and an actual plane-for-plane replacement of transport losses. Arnold qualified this to some extent, however, in a personal letter of 30 March, which informed Kenney that the 25% reserve for all units was to be furnished as soon as availability of airplanes would permit, and that the attrition rate "you'd be 20% if losses justify."

To the extent that it went Arnold's decision was clear enough, but did not solve the problem as to what type of aircraft the replacements would be. A definite policy had been established late in 1942 for heavy and medium bombers. After none of the coveted B-26s or B-17s had arrived in the SWPA since November, Kenney was informed that only B-24s and B-25s were to be allocated to the Pacific areas. No policy, however, had been established as to the type of light bombardment to be furnished to the Fifth Air Force. Kenney wanted A-20Gs, but the situation was rather confused as to the number of this type which would be available from production early in 1943. Furthermore, the Twelfth Air Force was being given the priority in A-20s, and a project to convert A-20s into P-70 night fighters was taking others. Consequently, there was some thought of sending the Fifth Air Force either A-36 (P-51 Mustang) or A-25 Shrike (Curtiss SB2C Helldiver) dive bombers as light bomber replacements. In January Kenney radioed that he preferred the A-25 if it could be made immediately available, or if not he requested more B-25s. On 5 May the Joint Planners issued a final statement regarding A-20Gs, saying that any which were not needed by the 12AF would be allocated to Kenney.

The fighter allocation policy was no more apparent than that of light bombers. The fighter requirement for the SWPA was a high altitude, maneuverable fighter capable of out-fighting the Zero and with ample range to provide cover for transports and bombers. P-40s and P-39s had scored a notable number of victories in the SWPA while defending their bases and on short range escort missions. From 14 November 1942 until 20 March 1943, in 81 P-39 sorties, 22 enemy fighters and nine Japanese bombers were destroyed with only one P-39 lost. During the same period six P-40s were lost on 99 sorties, in which 54 Japanese fighters and five bombers were shot down.

Nevertheless, by March 1943 a base defense interceptor was no longer required, and the short range medium altitude P-39s and P-40s did not have the qualities necessary for future fighter operations in the theater. The Curtiss-Wright factory representative in Australia also realized that, while the P-40 had done a good job, a new and improved Warhawk model was needed. The Bell Aircraft representative also reported adverse comments on the P-39. After flying a P-39K1 for the first time, Col. Richard Legg, CO of the 35th Fighter Group, stated that "after a year of combat I find, for a Christmas present the Army has purchased a plane and sent it over to us in combat area which is at least 20mph slower than the original aircraft we have been fighting the war with. If this called progress, I would like to know what Bell Aircraft has been doing."

Kenney wanted P-38s, but the production schedule and requirements of other theaters caused the War Department to allocate them judiciously. In January Kenney was told that his monthly fighter group allocation would be one P-39, one P-40, and one P-38 Group, and his replacements would be 15 P-38s per month beginning in January, 15 P-39s in March, nine in April, and 15 per month thereafter; no replacement P-40s were allocated until April, when 30 P-40Ks were to be sent, followed by 15 in May and June and 30 in July. By the end of February the schedule had changed, as the situation in North Africa had become critical, and all P-38s were sent there. After receiving eight P-38s in January, Kenney was informed that he would receive no more until June or July. The P-40 schedule was also changed, and the first 40 P-40s would not arrive until June, after which only enough would be sent to maintain authorized strength.

As more P-38s were scheduled to arrive at Townsville, Morrissey requested them to replace the war-weary P-40s of the 8FS. Unfortunately Kenney and his deputy, Ennis Whitehead, had already allocated these Lightnings elsewhere. Fifth Fighter Command CO Wurtsmith appealed the P-38 allocation on the behalf of his old friend but was told the decision was non-negotiable, as the 80 FS, now on R&R at Townsville, would be the next P-38 unit.

By the end of March the attrition rate and situation in the SWPA were considered satisfactory, and a new, more liberal replacement schedule was approved. A flexible command structure was authorized, and a plan for future operations had been proposed, discussed, and generally accepted. Arnold wrote to Kenney that "an analysis of your requirements and the enemy opposition . . . compared with the additional forces you are now scheduled to receive, make it appear that you are no longer the forgotten man."

On 26 April 1943 the Joint Chiefs of Staff presented a new directive for offensive operations in the Pacific with MacArthur as Supreme Commander of *Elkton III/Cartwheel*, which will be discussed later.

Air Strategy for the Beginning of 1943

Allied

Once Buna and Gona were secured, MacArthur was positioned to advance up the north New Guinea coast toward Salamaua. This small village was located 20 miles south of Lae on an isthmus that gave it a port accessible to transport vessels. Nearby was an inland landing strip that could accommodate transport and fighter aircraft. MacArthur intended to use Salamaua as a springboard for the invasion of Lae, which was tentatively planned for early April 1943. In the meantime, MacArthur would utilize the 5AF as his main strategic weapon to maintain pressure on the retreating Japanese. Over the next two years in the Allied offensive along the northern New Guinea coast, MacArthur's strategy was to capture airfields and harbors. As airfields were captured or built when necessary, the 5FC would transfer its groups to these forward bases to gain air superiority over the advancing

Allied infantry.

More 5th Bomber Command units arrived at Port Moresby, while the 5th Fighter Command moved forward to the new airdrome at Dobodura, which was only 175 miles from the large Japanese garrison at Lae. The 5th Fighter Command was to provide the decisive air superiority over the rapidly developing Allied North New Guinea Coast air base complex centered at Dobodura. It was also to escort 5BC medium and heavy bombers on their continued effort to reduce the Lae Airdrome and to interdict the Solomon Sea supply routes.

There were two main facilities that supplied MacArthur in his Papuan offensive. First was Dobodura, which processed the supplies brought in by air transport, while the second was Oro Bay, about ten miles southeast of Dobodura, where Navy and merchant supply vessels unloaded; their cargoes would travel to Dobodura once the old road was rebuilt. Without enemy air interdiction the Allies had the upper hand in the theater, leaving the Japanese no choice but to ram through reinforcements and supplies via a convoy to Lae.

Japanese

In late 1942, with the deteriorating situation in the Solomons and SWPA, the naval and land factions in the Japanese High Command were forced to reach an involved agreement in which Adm. Yamamoto was to assume the overall command in the South Pacific, while the JAAF would provide supplementary convoy air cover assisting the JNAF. In return Yamamoto was to supply naval units to evacuate Japanese troops from the lost cause at Guadalcanal. Without adequate air transport and with his army at Buna destroyed and another trapped at Guadalcanal, the dishonored Lt.Gen. Imamura, the 8th Area Army Commander, was forced to plead for support from the Imperial Navy.

By late October 1942, the Imperial Navy Staff understood that its fighter force had been depleted in the air battles over the last months and needed to be reinforced. However, there were no local units readily available in the South Pacific, so several carrier-based units were reorganized for land-based operations and sent to New Britain as reinforcements. These units, with their valuable veteran pilots and crews, were thrown into the battle, flying the long distances between both Guadalcanal and New Guinea and incurring staggering losses; by late December, many of the units were diminished to as few as 10 Zeros and pilots per squadron. With this new Order of Battle in the Southeastern Area, the Imperial Staff needed to transfer JAAF air units from China and Malaya to support the defense of Lae, and to fly convoy cover for reinforcements from Rabaul.

In late December, Japanese Army Air Force (JAAF) fighters and bombers ferried through Indochina and the Philippines or through the Truk Atoll bastion to eventually be stationed at the developing airfield complex surrounding Rabaul. For now, the JAAF command was based at the headquarters garrison of Vunakanau Field. The first JAAF fighter unit to arrive in New Britain was the celebrated 11th Sentai (Group), which had gained distinction in the early China campaigns and during the Japanese conquest of Burma and Sumatra. The capable Sentai was chosen to be one of the first JAAF units to fly the new generation Nakajima Ki-43 Oscar. Although not as heavily armed as the Zero, the Oscar was arguably the most maneuverable fighter in the world. Once the 11th Sentai was established on Rabaul it joined the Zero units there in the escort of bombers and ship convoys that ventured out against the Allies in the Solomon Islands and New Guinea. By the end of December the Sentai was stationed as a resident squadron at Lae.

Lae Drome. (AAF)

11

January 1943: Lae Convoy

On 30 December, enemy shipping concentrations were the largest ever sighted at Rabaul, numbering 91 vessels, including 21 warships and some 300,000 tons of merchant ships. Although a portion of this shipping was routine traffic to and from this important base, Intelligence determined that it was obvious that an extraordinary operation was being planned. Furthermore, floatplanes had been sighted in the vicinity of Lae, an indication usually interpreted to mean antisubmarine patrol in advance of ship movement. Also there was renewed air activity on nearby landing fields. The first of the Lae reinforcements were selected from the 12,000 bedraggled evacuees from Guadalcanal, who were assigned to Gen. Hatazo Adachi's 18th Army at Rabaul. Adachi had taken command of the Rabaul garrison on 9 November 1942 after leading the Japanese North China Area Army during its ruthless scorched earth campaign during 1941-2. On 5 January, 6,000 of these troops embarked on five merchant ships from Rabaul's Simpson Harbor for the 600 mile voyage to Lae.

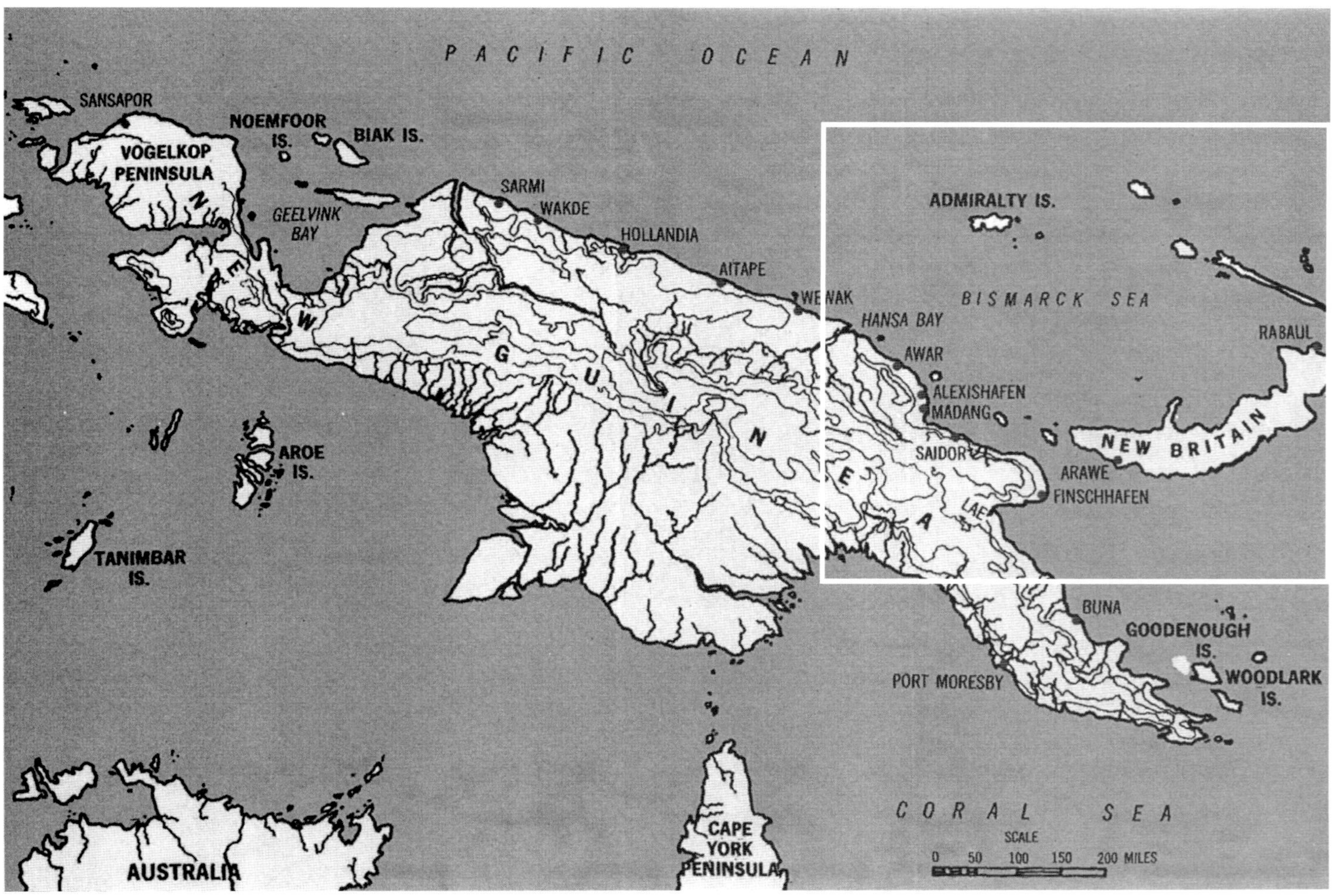

LEFT: 1Lt. Charles **Sullivan** scored his second victory. (AFAA) MIDDLE: Capt. Curran **Jones** scored his 2nd and 3rd victories. (AFAA) RIGHT: 2Lt. Richard **Smith** scored his first of seven total. (AFAA)

4 January 1943: 35FG

During early 1943 the 35FG would be supporting the final stages of the Buna air campaign, sending its fighters from Port Moresby over the Owen Stanley Mountains and conducting a nonstop cycle of fighter sweeps and harassing attacks. They flew protective cover for C-47 transports and flew local patrol for Moresby, which was still experiencing frequent attacks from enemy bombers. But during the first week of the new year the Group would attack the Japanese convoy heading for Lae. On 4 January, 2Lt. George Goolsby of the 35th Squadron shot down a "Type 1 bomber" flying recon near Goodenough Island at 1030 in a preliminary to the attacks on the Lae Convoy.

6 January 1943: 35FG/39FS

During the morning, Coast Watchers located on New Britain's south shore reported the enemy convoy as it navigated west. In a mid-day search and destroy mission against the convoy, Port Moresby-based medium bombers were escorted by 16 P-38s of the 39th Squadron led by Capt. Curran Jones. The P-38s were to fly high cover, but half were armed with 500 pound bombs for dive bombing. The enemy ships were discovered off the southern New Britain coast near Gasamata, and the Oscar fighter escorts engaged the Lightnings in a furious air battle. Nine Oscars were destroyed, with three probables and two damaged also claimed. Capt. Jones was credited with two victories, and single victories were scored by 1Lts. Richard Suehr and Charles Sullivan and 2Lts. Stanley Andrews, Walter Markey (on TDY from the 9FS), Harvey Clymer, John Mangas, and Richard Smith. Although the 39FS had excelled in the air combat, the dive bombing attacks weren't particularly successful. Post mission analysis concluded that the speed of the P-38 was too great for high angle bombing; the bomb release was dangerous; and the pilot had poor visibility in aiming, requiring too much estimation in the bombing run. That evening, Kenney ordered a maximum effort by all available flight crews for a morning strike against the Lae bound convoy.

7 January 1943: 49FG: The Morning Attack on the Convoy

Newly promoted to Major, William Martin, 7FS CO, chose his senior pilot, Ops Exec Capt. George Manning, to lead the Squadron's mission on the convoy. The newer P-40Ks were chosen as fighter bombers because of their heavier ordnance carrying ability to mount two 300 pound HE bombs attached to underwing shackles. The older Es were to fly cover for the Ks. The two flights of four P-40Ks consisted of Capt. Manning's White Flight and Capt. Frank Nichols' Red Flight. The P-40K dive bombers were to attack the convoy once it was confined in Lae harbor. 1Lt. Ray Melikian's Green Flight would fly close escort at 10,000 feet, followed by 1Lt. John Yancey's Yellow Flight at 11,000 feet and 1Lt. Oliver Vodrey's Black Flight on high cover at 12,000 feet. Morning rains delayed the mission until 1300, when the five Demon Flights took off from 17 Mile Drome to intercept the convoy, which had been diverted to Salamaua, an hour away.

As the 49FG Flights crossed the Owen Stanleys, Vodrey's Black Flight and Yancey's Yellow Flight remained in their high cover positions while Manning's dive bombers flew on toward the nine enemy ships. Manning's two dive bomber flights circled over Salamaua twice at 9,000 feet, expecting to find the ships in the harbor, which was empty. Manning chose to attack the ships sailing in the open sea 50 miles from the northern shore. When Manning directed the flights to drop their belly tanks his tank did not release, and Manning, knowing that his P-40 would hinder the attack, reluctantly conceded the mission lead to the Red Flight Leader, Frank Nichols. While Nichols led the six P-40s towards the convoy, Manning dropped his pair of 300 pound bombs on Salamaua.

Black Leader Vodrey led 2Lts. Carl Houseworth, Joseph King, and 9FS transfer Birge Neuman through the clouds to join Yancey's Yellow Flight at their lower altitude. The Flights had lost visual contact with Manning's dive bombers and turned back toward the harbor to search for them. King and Neuman, in Black Flight's rear element, had just finished circling the harbor at 13,000 feet when they spotted three unidentified aircraft approaching head on to their right and 1,000 feet above. Both pilots were hesitant to call out the approaching fighters, as they could be friendlies, but just as the three passed overhead the lead fighter snapped into a port wingover, and the Americans saw the red meatballs on the wings of the Oscars. Neuman shouted a warning and Black Flight instantly dispersed.

Yellow Flight Leader Yancey looked to the rear and above to verify Vodrey's warning and saw the Oscars diving on Black Flight's rear element. Yancey and wingmen 2Lt. Irving Bagdasarian, and the rookie element of 2Lts. Sheldon Brinson and John Griffith, turned to close on the Oscars. Yancey's Warhawk stalled in the climb and he decided to fall away briefly to pick up speed. Yancey then re-entered the combat, rolling into firing position, but was unable to maintain his advantage over the maneuverable Oscar. Second Element Leader Brinson followed Yancey, and after several high speed turns his P-40 stalled and dropped away from the combat. Yellow Flight had become utterly separated from one another. Bagdasarian was unable to regain altitude after the initial attack and returned to base. Griffith chased an Oscar north toward Lae and was joined by Yancey, but the Oscar eluded both Americans, who then turned back toward the enemy convoy. Yancey flew offshore to orbit the convoy once, then rejoined Griffith and 2Lt. David Allen, a Red Flight dive bomber pilot, to return to 17 Mile Drome. While the flight was returning, Allen radioed Yancey to ask him why he was still carrying his drop tank, which Yancey had forgotten to jettison in the confusion.

Oblivious that the top cover Flights were in combat with Oscars above, Melikian's Green Flight escorted Nichols' two dive bombing Flights to the convoy. As the dive bombers peeled off to attack the first ship in the convoy, Melikian spotted four Zeros below diving on Manning's Warhawks. Green Flight released their belly tanks and rolled down to the starboard, and the entire Green Flight became separated. Melikian immediately cut off one of the Zeros but was outrun. His Wingman, 2Lt. Duncan Myers, fired a long burst at another Zeke, but his port wing guns jammed. Green Flight's Element Leader, 2Lt. Robert McDaris, also fired at a lone Zeke, but flew too close to the convoy and had to break off the chase, as accurate enemy AA fire exploded close to his fighter. Rookie Wingman 2Lt. Albert Smith had to leave the combat when his engine malfunctioned due to water contaminated fuel and he had to land at Dobodura, as the Alison engine could not gain enough altitude to climb over the Owen Stanleys. Melikian saw a P-40 being chased by a Zeke and fired a burst at long range, missing, but causing the enemy to dive away from the attack and ending the combat. While not scoring a victory, Melikian's Green Flight succeeded in keeping the Japanese from distracting Nichols' dive bombers.

While Green Flight was engaging the Japanese above, Flight Leader 1Lt. Frank Nichols led two flights of four P-40s each on the five ship convoy, which were sailing in tandem and were flanked by two destroyer escorts that were maneuvering in "S" turns. Nichols led Red Flight in the first attack from 8,000 feet on the 5,500 ton lead transport. Nichols dropped his bombs at 1,000 feet, which exploded just to the starboard of the vessel's stern. Wingman 1Lt. David Allen followed Nichols' attack on the transport, but his bombs exploded 100 feet wide to the right. As he raced away at only 50 feet above the waves Nichols saw no other Warhawks and turned for the long flight back to Port Moresby and 17 Mile Drome. As he passed over Buna, Allen was joined by Griffith and Yancey of Yellow Flight. Red Flight's third attacker was Darwin veteran 1Lt. C.T. Johnson, who dive bombed the second transport in the convoy. Midway in his dive he was suddenly sidetracked by a Zeke that passed under his fighter at 5,000 feet. Johnson tried to fire at the Zeke and drop his bombs simultaneously, but was unsuccessful in both activities, as the bombs exploded to starboard over 100 yards away and the enemy pilot got on Johnson's tail. The veteran Warhawk pilot lost his attacker and returned to strafe the transport through heavy AA fire before he turned toward 17 Mile Drome. 1Lt. Arland Stanton was the last Red Flight attacker, but his bombs missed the transport and he remained in the area to view the attacks of the three P-40s in White Flight.

The three White Flight dive bombers were flown by Darwin veterans Flight Leader 2Lt. A.T. House, 2Lt. Claude Burnotte, and rookie 2Lt. Lawrence Succop. House led the White Flight down over the right flank of the convoy to bomb the last 5,800 ton transport. At 8,000 feet, House dove on the transport in the face of heavy machine gun fire, which he returned in his dive. After he dropped his bombs and missed, House broke away in the opposite direction to escape under the barrage of AA fire from the destroyers on the left flank. Burnotte dove next and targeted the next to the last 4,100 ton transport; he also encountered heavy but inaccurate machine gun fire. Burnotte scored a direct hit amidships with one of the 300 pound bombs and then followed House. Burnotte's bomb tore through the base of the funnel and exploded in the engine room, heavily damaging the transport's engine. However, the vessel was able to struggle into Lae Harbor and debark her troops onto barges later that evening, after which she was beached and abandoned. Succop also attacked another transport but missed, and luckily escaped through the heavy volley of AA fire to join Johnson for the flight back to 17 Mile Drome.

7 January 1943: 35FG/39FS: Early Afternoon Attack on the Convoy

Meanwhile, and unknown to the P-40 Squadrons, the high escort of Lightnings from the 39FS Squadron had scrambled from 14 Mile Drome and headed directly across the mountains toward the convoy. Since the dive bombers were vectored first to Salamaua, the P-38s encountered the JAAF fighters escorting the convoy much sooner at 65 miles over Huon Gulf. 1Lt. Charles Gallup and 2Lt. Richard Bong shot down Oscars about 70 miles off Cape Ward Hunt and returned to quickly refuel and rearm at Dobodura for a second sortie.

7 January 1943: 35FG/39FS: Late Afternoon Attack on the Convoy

On their second sortie of the day, two flights of 39FS Lightnings under Capt. Thomas Lynch were hunting for the convoy at 18,000 feet when they came upon 16 JAAF Oscars that had just refueled at Lae airdrome. Despite the odds, the seven P-38s dove on the Oscars over Huon and five were shot down; there were also claims for three probables and six damaged in a raging dogfight, where keeping track of claims was nearly impossible. The second element team of 2Lts. Richard Bong and Carl Planck both damaged a Ki-43 in their first pass, and then Bong claimed his fourth kill and a probable on his second pass. Single victories were also claimed by Capt. Thomas Lynch for his eighth victory; 2Lt. Kenneth Sparks, who became an ace; 1Lt. Charles Gallup, who claimed his second kill of the day; and 1Lt. George Bartlett. When the Oscars broke off the battle into the clouds below near the Markham River outlet, they ran into the 8FS and a large dogfight at the lower altitude.

1Lt. Charles **Gallup** scored two victories. (AFAA)

2Lt. Kenneth **Sparks** damaged an Oscar and shot one down to become an ace. (AFAA)

7 January 1943: 49FG/8FS: Late Afternoon Attack on the Convoy

After the 7FS pilot debriefings and US and Royal Australian Navy reports were evaluated by the Port Moresby Command, it was established that the enemy convoy had turned north toward Lae, and they ordered a second strike to be launched. 8FS CO Maj. Edward Sims assigned his Ops Exec., Capt. Ellis Wright, to lead four flights of 16 Warhawks off Kila Drome at 1600 on a strafing mission on the convoy. Wright's White Flight would attack from 4,000 feet, to be followed by 1Lt. Ernest Harris' Yellow Flight at 6,000 feet. 1Lt. Lawrence Kirsch's Green Flight and 1Lt. Rufus Jordan's Blue Flight would remain at 8,000 feet providing top cover. The 16 plane 8FS formation flew north for over an hour, but when it approached the mountains, Flight Leader Wright found his old P-40E was unable to climb over them and he turned back to base with his Wingman. Wright put Yellow Flight Leader Harris in command and 1Lt. Lowell Lutton and Wingman 2 Lt. Bob Moose joined up as the third element.

White and Yellow Flight Strafers

Harris led his eight strafers to the mouth of the Markham River. As the Warhawks approached the river delta, the silhouettes of enemy ships were seen offshore from Lae Village. Harris mistakenly called out one of the destroyers as a heavy cruiser and observed three transports and two smaller burning vessels. Harris ordered tanks to be jettisoned at 7,000, and then led five Warhawks of White and Yellow Flight down toward the ships. The diving Warhawks were immediately met by Zeros that had just reformed after their previous battle minutes before. The Zeros were successful in breaking up the Warhawk attack, and only Harris was able to strafe one of the troopships, knocking off pieces of the deck. Harris pulled out of his attack and climbed through the thin overcast at 6,000 feet, closing to shoot down a Zero that was on the tail of another P-40. He pulled up and fired three long bursts at a second Zero which rolled over out of control, shedding pieces, and disappeared into clouds. Harris immediately pulled up and pressed his attack to very close range and fired two long bursts that hit near the cockpit. Harris followed the smoking enemy through the clouds and identified three crash sites on the sea below to confirm his first three of 10 career victories. Harris met several Zeros, but he was unable to do any damage in three passes. Harris called for his scattered Flights to regroup and headed south to 3 Mile Drome.

Meanwhile, Yellow Element strafers battled against the Oscars of the 11th Sentai that had broken up their strafing attack. Despite the maneuverable Oscar's advantage at low speeds and low altitudes, Yellow second Element Leader 2Lt. Warren Blakely shot down an Oscar and damaged another, but as he dropped into the overcast his rookie Wingman, 2Lt. Eugene Dickey, was unable to follow and was quickly shot down. Dickey was last seen ditching his damaged Warhawk in the shallow river delta near the Lae Strip and wading ashore.

Blue and Green Flight Top Cover

While Yellow Flight elements were battling the Oscars above the overcast, the high cover Blue Flight simultaneously spotted 10 Oscars at 2,000 feet above, with more Hamps circling below close to the transports. Blue Flight Leader 1Lt. Rufus Jordan directed his wingmen, 1Lt. William Day and 2Lts. Joseph Littleton and Robert White, to quickly climb to gain altitude on the Oscars, which flew into the glare of the sun.

Blue Flight Leader Jordan and Littleton remained together for a complete circle with the first pair of Oscars. Jordan's newer P-40 was faster and he became separated from Littleton. As Littleton broke out of formation he came head on with a Zero and fired a quick burst that exploded the enemy. Jordan met the Zeros at 6,000 feet and got on the tail of two which separated, and he and Littleton chased it toward the Bay; Jordan fired first and more effectively for the victory. Jordan was then attacked by a Zero that dove from the hazy cloud cover, forcing Jordan to dive away to safety. As Jordan climbed back to 5,000 feet, a Hamp turned headlong into him and fired as the gap between the two fighters closed. As they passed one another, both the pilots zoomed their fighters upward, then stalled out and dropped away to confront one another again. After a second and third pass, the Japanese pilot made the first and last error when he snapped out of his fourth climb and streaked across Jordan's line of flight. Jordan fired as his Warhawk came within only 30 feet of the enemy fighter, which was hit by a deadly .50 caliber barrage. Jordan and Wingman Littleton separated after their first combined attack. While pulling up through the overcast Littleton met a Zero head on and fired a quick burst that exploded the Zero directly in front of him. As Littleton returned to the battle he saw another Zero climbing in front and parallel and fired. The Zero rolled over, apparently out of control, and Littleton had to settle for a probable. Jordan's second Blue Element Leader, 1Lt. William Day, and Wingman 2Lt. Robert White also held formation (1,000 feet higher than the Blue Flight Leader), and went after the second Zero that broke away from Jordan. Day got on its tail and fired a good burst, hitting the cockpit and engine, and it was seen going down in flames. White also fired on Day's Zero, getting hits, but it was Day's victory. When he pulled up he saw another Zero below and to starboard. White turned down into it and fired. He then used his diving speed, pulled up, and made another pass on the Zero, which was smoking in a flat spin as he fired again. It continued to go down and burst into flames. White joined Day, and they saw P-40s chasing several Zeros. One of the Zeros made a sharp climbing turn directly in front of Day, who "cut loose" on it and tore its wing off at the fuselage; Day had to quickly dip his wing to avoid the wing. As White continued on a Zero got on his tail, and by later count put 27 holes in his fighter. But the Zero pilot overran directly in front of White, who fired a short burst that exploded the Zero. Day and White headed to Kila with two victories each.

Green Flight, which had lagged behind the rest of the Eightball Flights, broke out of the scattered clouds at 7,000 feet and was approaching the Bay when Flight Leader 1Lt. Lawrence Kirsch called out Zekes approaching from below and Oscars peeling off from above. Kirsch wanted to cut off the diving Oscars, but as they passed through the sun's dazzle Kirsch lost visual contact. Wingman 2Lt. Cyrus Lynd and Element Leader 1Lt. Kenneth Johns each engaged an Oscar, but Wingman 2Lt. Robert Howard became separated and had joined Jordan.

As Kirsch led Green Flight at 7,000 feet and they were fired on by the enemy convoy's destroyers, they saw two Zeros 3,000 feet overhead, circling to get on their tails. The Zeros got into the sun and dove, and Green dove but separated. Kirsch dove into a cloud and climbed. When he came out of the

1Lt. William **Day** scored two victories. (AAF)

2Lt. Robert **White** scored his first two victories of 9 total. (AFAA)

1Lt. Ernest **Harris** scored his first three victories of 10 total. (AFAA)

2Lt. Robert **Howard** scored his first victory of 6 total. (AFAA)

LEFT: 2Lt. A.T. **House** damaged an enemy fighter, and 50 years later the claim would be verified to make him an ace. (AFAA)
RIGHT: 2Lt. Andrew **Kish** scored his first victory. (AAF)

cloud he looked down and saw four or five Zeros in a Lufbery over the convoy at 4,000 feet. One peeled out of the Lufbery and Kirsch used his altitude advantage to close to within 100 yards almost dead astern and fired low, but adjusted his aim and hit the base of the right wing and cockpit; the Zero was going down in flames as Kirsch broke away to shake another Zero on his tail. Meanwhile, Lynd attempted to rejoin his Leader and was attacked by an Oscar that destroyed his starboard wing guns, but he was able to escape into the clouds. Lynd rejoined Kirsch, and they saw two Zekes in a shallow turning dive. Lynd fired with only three guns from the rear quarter, getting hits for a damaged claim before he had to dive away from a Zero on his tail. He hid in the clouds for as long as possible before returning to base. Because he knew there was the possibility that his damaged Warhawk would not climb over the Owen Stanleys he headed for Dobodura. He landed safely on a flat tire with no brakes and 23 bullet holes in the wings, fuselage, and tail surfaces. Johns saw a Zero flying directly in front of him, and when it turned into him Johns saw another 30 degrees to starboard and about 1,000 feet above. Johns had no choice but to attack the Zero coming head on at him and fired from slightly out of range, but then held his fire until he closed. The Zero pilot pulled up sharply and Johns fired at its exposed belly, but had to break quickly away when tracers whizzed by from the neglected Zero. Johns dove into the clouds to escape and Wingman Howard confirmed the victory.

Meanwhile, while flying at 7,000 feet, 2Lt. Robert Howard saw a Zero about 1,000 feet below in a slow right turn and made a 90 degree deflection shot and saw no results as it turned away. He then saw a Zero on a P-40's tail 1,500 feet below and used his diving speed to get on the Zero's tail. He opened fire at 150 yards down to 50 yards, and it started smoking badly as it spiraled down. Howard gave him an "extra" burst before it fell into the Bay. Howard climbed to 5,000 feet when he saw a Zero coming at him from 9 o'clock, 1,000 yards away and 500-1,000 feet above. Howard climbed left to meet the Zero head on and fired, and saw "splashes" where his bullets hit the engine that "looked like "white hot sparks...the size of a dime." The wounded Zero passed Howard within 15 feet and passed under him (for a probable). Instead of following it down Howard saw three Zeros and fired a "very unsatisfactory burst at one." As he went after another and was firing a cannon shell exploded on his port wing near the fuselage and bullets hit the outer port wing. All Howard's guns ceased firing at once and he headed for the nearest cloud. He then headed toward Kila, running low on fuel, and landed at 30 Mile Strip. He landed safely, despite having no left brake and severed hydraulics which left him with no flaps and having to pump his landing gear down manually. The Service Squadron crew rigged a brake line and Howard flew, wheels down, back to Kila the next day.

During the successful mission of the 7th the Eightballers scored 13 victories, with the high score honors going to 1Lt. Ernest Harris, who was credited with his first three victories. The 49ers were collectively given credit for sinking the *Myoko Maru*. For the next two days, Fifth Fighter Command squadrons returned to attack the Lae area and Harbor, but the strikes were limited by marginal weather. On the afternoon of 9 January, 7FS 2Lt. A.T. House reported engaging and getting good hits on a single Oscar over Salamaua Harbor, but the crash of House's victim, which was witnessed by another unit in the area, was never correlated to his combat report. House's claim, which would have made him an ace, would finally be confirmed by an Air Force board and the American Fighter Ace's Association nearly 50 years later.

8 January 1943: 35FG/39FS: Early Morning Mission (0810)

On 8 January 1943, P-38s of the 39FS flew to Lae Harbor in three missions to attack shipping. The early morning mission consisted of 15 P-38s flying in two ship elements, each flying at 10,000 feet on B-26 bomber cover over Lae Harbor. The Squadron spotted 12 to 15 Oscars at 9 o'clock low attacking the Marauders. The Americans dove and the Oscars tried to turn into their attack. During the mission four Oscars were shot down: one each by mission leader Capt. Robert Faurot and 2Lts. John Lane, Andrew Kish, and Kenneth Sparks. Since the pilot's reports were on RAAF Form C.F. there was no detailed description of the battle. Faurot "pulled up" and the enemy "Split-S'd" while Lane made a "diving attack, head on" into an enemy that "turned into us and went below us." Lane's fighter was "shot up a wee bit." Sparks was somewhat more descriptive: "On our first pass I knocked a Zero off Lt. Kish's tail. He went down and out. I saw about a yard of orange flame shoot out from behind his cockpit."

8 January 1943: 35FG/39FS

Mid-Afternoon Mission (1435)

During the mid-afternoon attack 10 P-38s in flights of six and four went to cover B-25s, B-26s, and Beaufighters on a bombing and strafing to Lae Harbor and Salamaua. Nine Oscars in twos and threes were sighted at 9 o'clock and 2,000 feet below at 10,000 feet. The P-38s dove but the aggressive Oscars climbed into them, passed through P-38s, and then dove back into the Americans. Five Oscars were destroyed, two probably destroyed, and four were damaged.

1Lt. Charles Gallup, who became an ace with two victories, described in his RAAF Action Report simply as: "Type of Attack Delivered on Enemy: 90 degrees----90 degrees head on." Actually Gallup had shot the wing off his Oscar. 2Lts.

1Lt. Charles **Gallup** became an ace with two victories. (AFAA)

LEFT:
2Lt. Stanley **Andrews** claimed his third victory. (AAF)

RIGHT:
2Lt. John **Lane** scored two victories. (AAF)

Stanley Andrews, Harvey Clymer, and John Lane all claimed one victory each. Andrews described his victory: "Out of a 3 ship formation I shot one Oscar. It was one of two that turned up to the right. I came in on it firing up to 75 yards on the quartering attack. His course never changed as though the pilot was shot. It was still going down smoking when I Last saw it. Capt. Faurot and Lt. Lane saw it go down….I saw Lane's plane (the one he was shooting at) begin to smoke, I then started to dive toward the water. I was flying on his (Lane's) wing and this and the above (description) happened on the first pass. Lane's combat was described as: "Diving attack, head on."

Late Afternoon Mission (1800)
The last 35FG mission flew in bad weather to arrive over Lae at 1800 and was attacked by a mixed formation of Oscars and Zekes, which would lose three Oscars and four Zekes. The 39FS sent out seven P-38s in two flights flying at 15,000 feet when they spotted "12 to 18 or more….Zero and Oscar types….in bright green camouflage." The first Lightning flight attacked from the right, while the second came from the left; both dove from an altitude advantage. The Japanese saw the attack and all rolled to face their attackers.

2Lt. Richard Bong became an ace with a victory over an Oscar. His Form C.F. states: "Diving from the front, the front head on from 30 degrees deflection. Two passes the say (typo: same) way. Second time he started spinning down out of control into Huon Gulf about 5 miles off the coast." Action taken by the enemy: "Vertical turns toward me but not directly into me. They made no attempt to shoot at me head on."

1Lt. Hoyt Eason also became an ace when he attacked one of the Zeros that rolled out too late at 10,000 feet. Eason fired an "unusually long burst while the Zero suspended from 2,000 to 100 feet." The Zero crashed just offshore near Lae. Knowing he was out of ammunition, Eason dove on three to five Zeros attacking B-17s and diverted them until they "ganged on me" during his last pass.

After claiming an Oscar victory and probable during the early morning mission, 2Lt. Kenneth Sparks flew in the late mission and claimed another Oscar. Sparks describes the battle: "On the first pass I was forced out of position but scared two Zeros off Lt. Bong's tail without ever firing on them, I was out away from my formation when I saw another formation of which Lt. Thompson (2Lt. Thomas) was a member, attacking Zeros just off the cost (typo: coast) at Lae Airdrome. I saw Lt. Thompson knock one into the sea, I was trying to climb to join my own formation and they passed over my head going 180 degrees to my course. I was attacked by a Zero and cut off into the cloud. When I came out on the other side a Zero made a level head on attack on me, I fired 5 to 8 seconds, raking him and as I broke away I saw smoke and flame coming from his motor. He never tried to turn but went out of control into a cloud. I climbed to 20,000 feet with my engine running rough. I looked around and saw Lt. Suehr (1Lt. Richard) make a pass and it fell burning. I counted ten Zeros and was planning my next attack when my left engine cut out. I feathered my prop and came home."

LEFT:
1Lt. Hoyt **Eason** also became an ace with a victory over a Zero. (AAF)

RIGHT:
2Lt. Richard **Bong** became an ace with a victory over an Oscar. (AAF) be changed to a victory and House would become an ace. (AFAA)

Two Zekes were shot down by 1Lt. Richard Suehr, whose RAAF C.F. states: "About 16 (enemy fighters), 4 to 6 in usual maneuvering tactics, sticking in two ship (formations)….Saw Lt. Bong take one off my nose and it went over sharply out of control….Two sure, two possible. No damage to own aircraft." 2Lts. Thomas Thompson and James Walters contributed one each. Three probable and one damaged enemy aircraft were also claimed to total 16 victories, six probables, and six damaged for the three missions.

9 January 1943: 49FG/7FS
2Lt. A.T. House damaged an enemy fighter over Salamaua Harbor for the last claims against the Japanese defense of their convoy.

Lae Convoy Attack Results
Only two convoy transports were lost, and the Japanese attempt to relieve the Lae garrison was a success, as the majority of the troops on the transports survived to disembark at Lae. There were 5,000 enemy infantry reinforcements in position to contest the advance of Australian forces near Salamaua. The Zeros and Oscars of the JAAF and JNAF had protected the Lae convoy, but their losses greatly reduced their effectiveness for the next three weeks. In the combat, the P-38 had shown its superiority over the veteran 11th Sentai, which had seven pilots killed, three badly wounded, and 17 Oscars lost in aerial combat, or that were written off after heavy landings due to extensive combat damage. The 11th Sentai was withdrawn from Lae back to Rabaul to refit for more convoy escort duty by the end of the month.

January 1943: Air Attacks on Rabaul Resume
Gen. Ennis Whitehead had thrown all available bombers and fighters against the Lae convoy, necessarily limiting operations against Rabaul, which remained the principal supply point for the Japanese forces in Northeast New Guinea. Although the amount of shipping in the harbor declined somewhat during January, nevertheless, worthwhile shipping targets remained to be attacked. The enemy was also expanding Rabaul's air facilities by improving the two important airdromes Vunakanau and Lakunai, and by rushing a third, known as Rapopo, to completion. The Fifth Air Force, in spite of the limited quantity of heavy bombers available, carried out a number of harass-

ing missions against the shipping, airfields, and the town. About 10 days after the first sighting of the Lae convoy intensive attacks were begun, again at relatively regular intervals. Exclusive of the raids by lone bombers on armed reconnaissance missions, B-17s and B-24s attacked the Rabaul area on 13 nights in January. The formations on these missions never consisted of more than 12 bombers, and the total number of bombers on the 13 missions amounted to more than 100 B-17s and approximately 12 B-24s. The weather was generally poor, with perilous equatorial fronts encountered on these 1,400 mile flights. The searchlight and anti-aircraft could be hazardous over Rabaul, but only two B-17s failed to return to base.

Because these missions were carried out at night, darkness or the glare from searchlights prevented the results from being observed, but the bombs usually hit in the target area and caused large fires. Perhaps the most destructive mission of the month was carried out on 5 January by two squadrons of heavy bombers. Forty 500 pound demolition bombs and 24x1,000 pound bombs were dropped from 8,500 feet. The official retort read: "nine vessels estimated over fifty thousand tons including one thousand pound bomb hit on destroyer tender with destroyer along side destroyed or left burning." Anti-Aircraft fire was heavy, and fighter attacks by rather inexperienced pilots were continuous. Two B-17s were shot down and the crew of one was lost, including Brig.Gen. Kenneth Walker, V Bomber Commander.

Sally Army Mitsubishi Ki-21 Type 97 5 place TE bomber. (AFHRC)

The heavy bombers usually dropped their bombs from a medium altitude of 5,000 to 9,000 feet. All bombardment squadrons had some training in skip bombing. The 63BG, whose former commander, Maj. William Penn, had pioneered the low level attack, was adept at it. In the early morning of 21 January three bombers of the Group, led by Maj. Edward Scott, swept over Rabaul Harbor at 250 feet. Scott skipped three 500 pound bombs with a five second delayed action fuse against a 6,000 ton transport, and it was observed lifting out of the water and rocking violently. He missed a second ship with two other bombs and finally dropped three more on an airfield from 1,600 feet. Meanwhile, Lt. James Murphy released his first two bombs from a skip-bombing altitude without results, circled over land at the same altitude, and came back over water to drop a string of six 500 pound demolition bombs against a 2,000 ton merchant vessel. The ship was at least severely damaged.

Attacks against convoys and harbor, the airfields, and the town of Rabaul were among the principal responsibilities of the Fifth Air Force. Not always so rewarding were attacks carried out to relieve pressure on ground forces. Nevertheless, this type of air cooperation, used with some success in the Papuan Campaign, continued to be a definite responsibility of light and medium bombers, and of fighters. In January and February their attention was concentrated on the Morobe District of Northeast New Guinea. They bombed the buildings and airfields of Lae and Salamaua; patrolled the native supply tracks which ran from the coast to Komiatum and Mubo, and the "Black Cat" Track, or the "Crystal Creek" route to Wau; strafed everything that moved in specified areas; dropped frags and parafrags along the tracks; and bombed points of resistance as requested by the Australians.

January 14-30 1943: Japanese Attacks on Port Moresby and Milne Bay

The eight Japanese attacks on Port Moresby during the last two weeks of January 1943 were particularly ineffective, as only one B-17 and another aircraft were destroyed on the ground. These attacks were usually carried out by no more than three or four bombers, and Allied fighters and anti-aircraft had sufficient early warning to force most of the enemy raiders to turn back. At the same time, Milne Bay was subjected to frequent Japanese air attacks, with the most devastating occurring shortly after noon on 17 January, when warning was received of the approach of enemy aircraft. Four P-39s of the 80th Fighter Squadron were scrambled directly over the field at maximum altitude, and 15 minutes later all remaining aircraft on the field were ordered into the air to save them. But before they could take off, more than 20 bombers escorted by Zeros were overhead and the Airacobras were unable to intercept. The enemy bombers dropped about 150 fragmentation bombs, destroying two B-17s, one B-24, two P-39s, and one RAAF Hudson, as well as six vehicles and six fuel dumps. Although destructive raids were the exception rather than the rule, the fear of attacks on this relatively exposed base, particularly at night, persuaded the Fighter Command to send a P-38 from Port Moresby as a night fighter.

17 January 1943: 8FG/80FS

After the flurry of activity on 7-8 January, it would not be until 17 January that the 5FC would score again. The Japanese sent 23 Sally bombers over Turnbull Drome, Milne Bay, at about 25,000 feet just before noon. The formation was undetected, and an alarm was only sounded as the enemy bombers were about to drop their bombs. Immediately after the bombers left, 16 Airacobras of the 35th and 36th Squadron took off, but they had no chance of reaching the bombers' altitude even if they did had enough warning. A flight of P-39s seems to have been in the air, as 8FG records note that 1Lt. Gerald Rogers and 1Lt. Jay Robbins each hit the same Sally bomber near Ferguson Island at 1310, but the 5AF board gave the victory to Rogers. Robbins was credited with two damaged Sallys and 1Lt. Leonidas Mathers damaged another. However, this combat was an isolated event, and the Japanese would concentrate their air efforts over Guadalcanal until the first week in February.

27 January 1943: 35FG/39FS

During the late night of 27 January, Capt. Robert Faurot of the 39FS took a P-38 up on a night interception from Moresby. Faurot took off at 0230 using only navigation lights, and at first he had trouble focusing his eyes, but by concentrating on the ground his eyes adjusted within five minutes. He climbed to 22,000 in 25 minutes and circled outside the searchlight's orbiting beam. There was a haze at that height, but the searchlight beam allowed Faurot to hold level flight without banking steeply to locate the light on the ground. Faurot was not wearing flying clothing or gloves, and the intense cold became very uncomfortable. At 0320, after 15 minutes of orbiting the searchlights picked up three Betty bombers flying in a V at 3 o'clock and five miles away at 22,000 feet. Faurot did not reach the Bettys until they left the searchlight radius and continued to circle, waiting for them to return. At 0330 the searchlights picked up the enemy flying at 12 o'clock and four miles at the same altitude. He made a head on pass on the #2 bomber and passed over it without getting observable hits. As Faurot passed through the searchlight beam he looked down at his cockpit floor to maintain his night vision. He made a 180 degree turn, closed on the rear quarter of the #2 bomber, and fired at 50 yards, hitting the bomber's right wing and fuselage. Faurot lost his chance to fire at the other two Bettys because he had closed too fast. He pulled up and made a circle, and although it was out of the searchlight beam he found the #2 Betty by its blue navigation light and then dove on it from astern, but did not observe any hits. On his third stern pass the Betty's rear and side gunners fired at him, but were silenced after he fired again. The #2 Betty began to slowly lose altitude and was abandoned by the other two. Faurot saw the other two escaping above him and climbed and circled, but lost them when they turned out their navigation lights and returned to base.

12

23 January 1943: End of the Papuan Campaign

General Summary and Results

The Papuan Campaign was officially considered at an end on 23 January 1943, as Allied air units and Australian infantry, taking advantage of the enemy's overextended supply lines, had driven back a Japanese force which by late summer 1942 had pushed over the Owen Stanley Mountains to within 30 miles of Port Moresby. With the aid of elements of the American 32nd Division, which Fifth Air Force transports had flown across the Owen Stanleys, the Japanese had been compressed into the Buna-Gona area, where they were virtually annihilated in December. Only scattered remnants had crept along the swampy coastline to join well-established enemy garrisons in the Salamaua area and at Lae, 150 miles to the northwest.

During the remainder of January, MacArthur used the lull in land and air combat to reinforce his Australian troops, who had moved further north up the coast nearer Salamaua. The enemy reinforcements that had reached the Lae garrison would next confront the advancing Australian forces that had taken a flanking route inland to occupy the old German mining town at Wau. The town had a small dirt airstrip which put it only 25 miles southwest of Salamaua. During this time the 49FG Squadrons flew unopposed armed recon missions along the coast from Buna to Salamaua, looking for barges, troop landing areas, and coastal supply dumps. The Group's P-38s and P-40s flew escort for C-47 transports supplying the isolated Australian garrison at Wau.

Air Power Results of the Papuan Campaign

On 24 January 1943, after the Horii Army had been annihilated, MacArthur announced that the destruction of the remnants of the enemy forces in the Sananada area had concluded the Papuan Campaign. An exact evaluation of the role of air power in this victory is, of course, impossible. What can be affirmed, however, is that without the cooperation of the 5AF and the RAAF, the fighting would have continued through many more days of savage combat. On 1 January 1943, Kenney put the air combat during the Papuan Campaign in proper perspective when he stated that "we learned a lot and the next one will be better." Air operations in 1942 were largely experimental to meet unexpected conditions and situations with limited resources; new weapons and new techniques had to be developed.

Air Supremacy

Kenney's air units gained their greatest victory over Papua by establishing Allied control of the air. Bombers contributed to the victory by destroying Japanese aircraft on the ground and some in air combat. Fighters did their part in turning back and destroying aircraft during raids on Allied bases and providing successful cover for transport and bomber operations. The Papuan Campaign had given the Fifth Air Force fighter pilots the experience and confidence to take and never give up the offensive. The P-40s and P-39s had done yeoman duty as bomber escorts, dive bombers, and strafers; however, the introduction of the P-38 into combat over New Guinea was the panacea in gaining air superiority. A Japanese diary entry on 3 December 1942 significantly comments, "they fly above our position as if they owned the skies," while Allied G-2 Intelligence reports refer to the almost total lack of enemy air support. The enemy air raids on Darwin and Port Moresby decreased in effectiveness even while Allied recon continually reported large numbers of enemy aircraft based within bombing range. The Japanese attacked Port Moresby five times during September with a total of approximately 60 bombers, but from October through January only 40 enemy bombers were counted over Moresby. Nevertheless, the Allied fighter patrols were unable to continually cover the entire Buna area when the Japanese sent sporadic raids to that area. November Japanese attacks on the Allied small boat supply line had been costly, and their frequent attempts to bomb Allied artillery positions at night were also effective. On 7 December, three Japanese Navy planes bombed the clearly marked Second Field Hospital and three direct hits caused heavy and inexcusable casualties, including several deaths. On 24 December the Japanese sent six waves of bombers over Allied positions in full moonlight, dropping at least 110 bombs, but this attack was the last large raid of the Papuan Campaign.

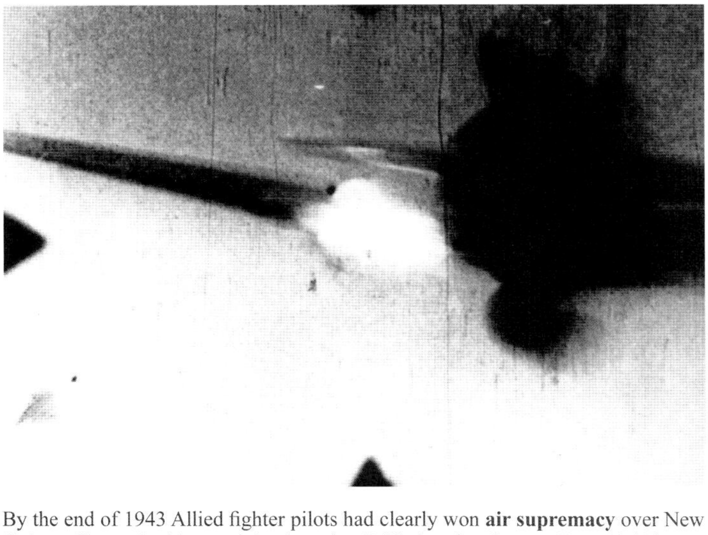

By the end of 1943 Allied fighter pilots had clearly won **air supremacy** over New Guinea. Shown in this gunsight photo is a P-38 shooting down a Zero. (AAF)

Air Transport

The role played by overworked troop carrier planes and crews was of paramount importance during the Papuan Campaign. Col. Frederick Smith, 5AF Deputy Chief of Staff, stated:

> "In view of the bad weather and bad terrain, the handling of ground units was the key to the final outcome. It was in the transport of such units and their supplies that our air power was most useful. Certainly the ferrying of the majority of the 32nd Division over the Owen Stanleys and the evacuation of thousands of sick and wounded stands out in a campaign where the terrain features conspired against rapid movement."

The 32nd Division was not sufficiently prepared for the fighting in New Guinea, and the combination of the enemy and the jungle had virtually decimated it. Casualties, including the sick, ran to over 10,000. That only 7% of this figure was deaths can be credited in part at least to the ability of the medical corps, and also to the speed with which the 5AF transports evacuated the sick and wounded.

Anti-shipping

Allied air power was successful in threatening Japanese control of the Bismarck Sea. From the beginning of the campaign, anti-convoy attacks and long range missions against shipping and supply concentrations had received high priority. Early efforts proved unsuccessful, as the Japanese landed troops almost at will. But as Allied airmen became more experienced and utilized new techniques, such as mast-height bombing attacks on shipping, they met with growing success, which was climaxed during the January attacks on the Lae convoy, when Japanese control of the sea was successfully challenged.

Air transport played a significant role in not only supplying supplies and troops but also in evacuating the wounded. (AAF)

Ground Support

The learning curve was particularly true of the use of air power in support of ground troops. From 26 August 1942 until the end of the Papuan Campaign, the infantry made 110 requests for direct and other support. Of these, the air controllers refused 15 because the targets were unsuitable, 12 because of the lack of aircraft, and 11 because of unfavorable weather. The 72 completed missions deployed 568 aircraft, which dropped 474,000 pounds of bombs and expended over 400,000 rounds of ammunition. During these 72 missions only 121 carried out direct support missions, dropping 30,000 pounds of bombs and firing 97,000 rounds. The support missions employing medium bomber strafer/bombers using the newly developed parachute fragmentation bomb against area targets were highly successful.

Anti-shipping strikes were successful the Japanese control of the Bismarck Sea. (AAF)

Part Five
The New Guinea Campaign

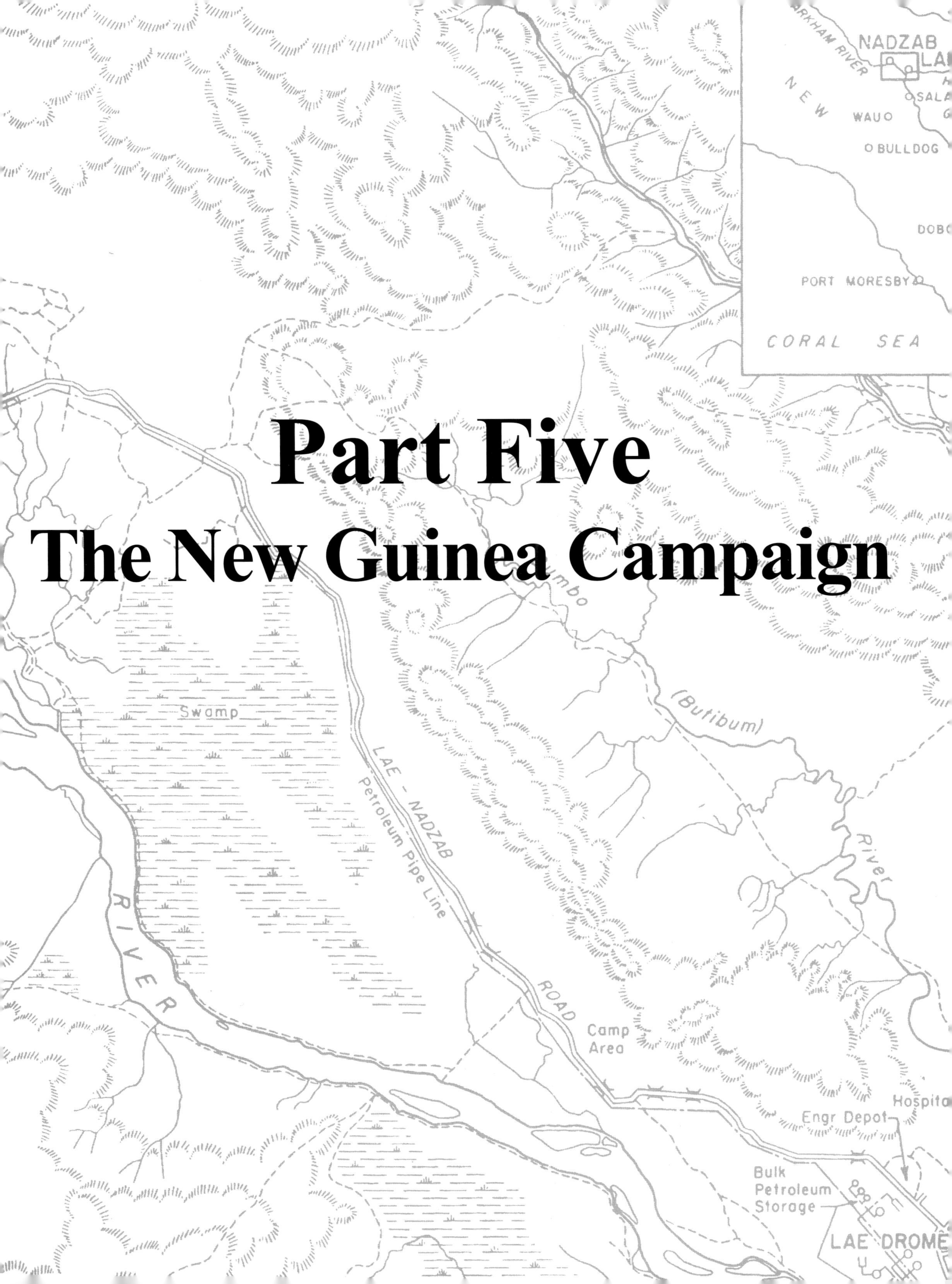

1

January 1943

Situation in the SWPA

By 23 January 1943, the Allies had driven the well-entrenched Japanese from Papua in a brutal three month struggle. The Australian 7th and US 32nd Infantry Divisions were decimated and the Australian 5th and US 41st Infantry Divisions were depleted. The American infantry would need six months to reconstitute, but the Australian Divisions, despite heavier losses, would continue as the front line of defense against the Japanese.

In January 1943, regardless of their defeat at Buna and continuing heavy losses in their struggle for Guadalcanal, Japan remained dominant in air, naval, and ground strength in the SWPA, and maintained the strategic initiative in New Guinea. With these advantages they planned to capture Port Moresby again. The Japanese built the prewar airfield and harbor at Lae, in northeast New Guinea, into a major air base and anchorage on the Huon Gulf. Using air cover from Lae, the Japanese attacked and seized the isolated and weakly defended Australian airstrip at Wau to be used as a forward air base. Wau was located in the Bulolo Valley, about 150 miles west-northwest of Buna. Standing in the way of the Japanese plans was the Allied Dobodura airstrips and staging base at Buna, on the north coast.

Although the victory in the Papuan Campaign was the result of an offensive operation, it was fundamentally a defensive operation forced on the Allies by Japanese initiative. Once the Japanese were driven from Papua, the Allies were situated to commence a full scale offensive for the recapture of New Guinea, which was to be used as a springboard for MacArthur's return to the Philippines. The initial phase of this offensive was the recapture of Wau at the end of January 1943, and then a grueling campaign continuing from the Australian attack on Mubo on 22 April 1943 and ending in the capture of Lae and Salamaua, on the Huon Gulf, by mid-September 1943. In an extremely challenging overland action, Australian infantry battled their way across high mountains and through steaming swamps to Wau, about 30 miles inland from Salamaua. Other American and Australian ground units captured their objectives through a succession of amphibious landings along the coast of Northeast New Guinea.

Without the continuous support of the Allied Air Forces, the Papuan Campaign could not have been a success. American and Australian airmen, employing tactics learned the hard way in earlier Pacific fighting, preserved the aerial superiority over New Guinea gained in the Papuan Campaign. Engineers built advanced airdromes, providing fighters and even bombers with new bases from which to attack the enemy's lines of communication throughout the Bismarck Sea. Unarmed transport planes, usually protected by fighters, faced tropical storms and enemy fighters to supply otherwise isolated positions. Meanwhile, service units and ground crews continued the unappreciated task of organizing supplies and maintaining aircraft.

During the New Guinea Campaign, Allied forces would be challenged with possibly even more difficult terrain than in the earlier Papuan fighting, and by similarly poor weather conditions and fanatical enemy opposition. Though this was to be a small-scale campaign when considering the forces in direct contact with the enemy, it was to be among the most complicated operations in World War II. The long distances, dreadful weather, and uncharted sea and land areas, as well as prickly and continual command problems made it difficult for the air, land, and naval forces of Australia and the US to function efficiently together.

Importantly, an uncertainty existed as to the geographical and command limits of the SWPA and South Pacific Command's responsibility. The March 1942 choice of MacArthur as Commanding General of the Southwest Pacific Area was one that placed a General wholly capable of administering the wide-ranging strategic problems of a theater which included not only Australia, New Guinea, the Solomons, and most of the Netherlands East Indies, but significantly the Philippines as well. In May 1942 the original description of the Pacific areas had given the Solomons to the SWPA, but preceding the American landing on Guadalcanal in August, the eastern boundary of MacArthur's command was shifted to follow the 159th meridian south from the equator. Thus, the South Pacific forces, primarily a naval command, were given definite authority over Guadalcanal and Tulagi, while MacArthur maintained control over the upper Solomons.

Although this was not a problem during 1942, it was obvious that the future operations of air and naval forces of the South Pacific and SWPA would begin to coincide and cause difficulties. Consequently, in September 1942 the Operations Division of the War Department General Staff sent a paper to the Joint Staff Planners which attempted to institute a more satisfactory delineation of responsibilities between the two theaters. This paper remained on the JSP's agenda until March 1943, when a subcommittee was selected to evaluate the proposal but was unable to agree on the report. There was a "definite feeling on the part of some of the planners that for coordination in planning and operations, it is essential that there be unity of command in the Solomon Island-British New Guinea-Bismarck Islands Theater of Operations." It was difficult, however, for them to come to an agreement as to how such a unified command could be established and in the end the arrangement remained unchanged and the boundary between the South and Southwest Pacific remained the 159th Meridian."

Decisions concerning overall command and general strategy probably had little effect upon the local problems facing the land and air forces whose mission was to drive the enemy from British New Guinea. More important was the organization within the theater itself. The Papuan Campaign had shown that MacArthur had devised a flexible strategy for jungle warfare which, with some modifications, was to be used during the New Guinea Campaign. MacArthur's headquarters was located in Brisbane, but he frequently commanded from ad-

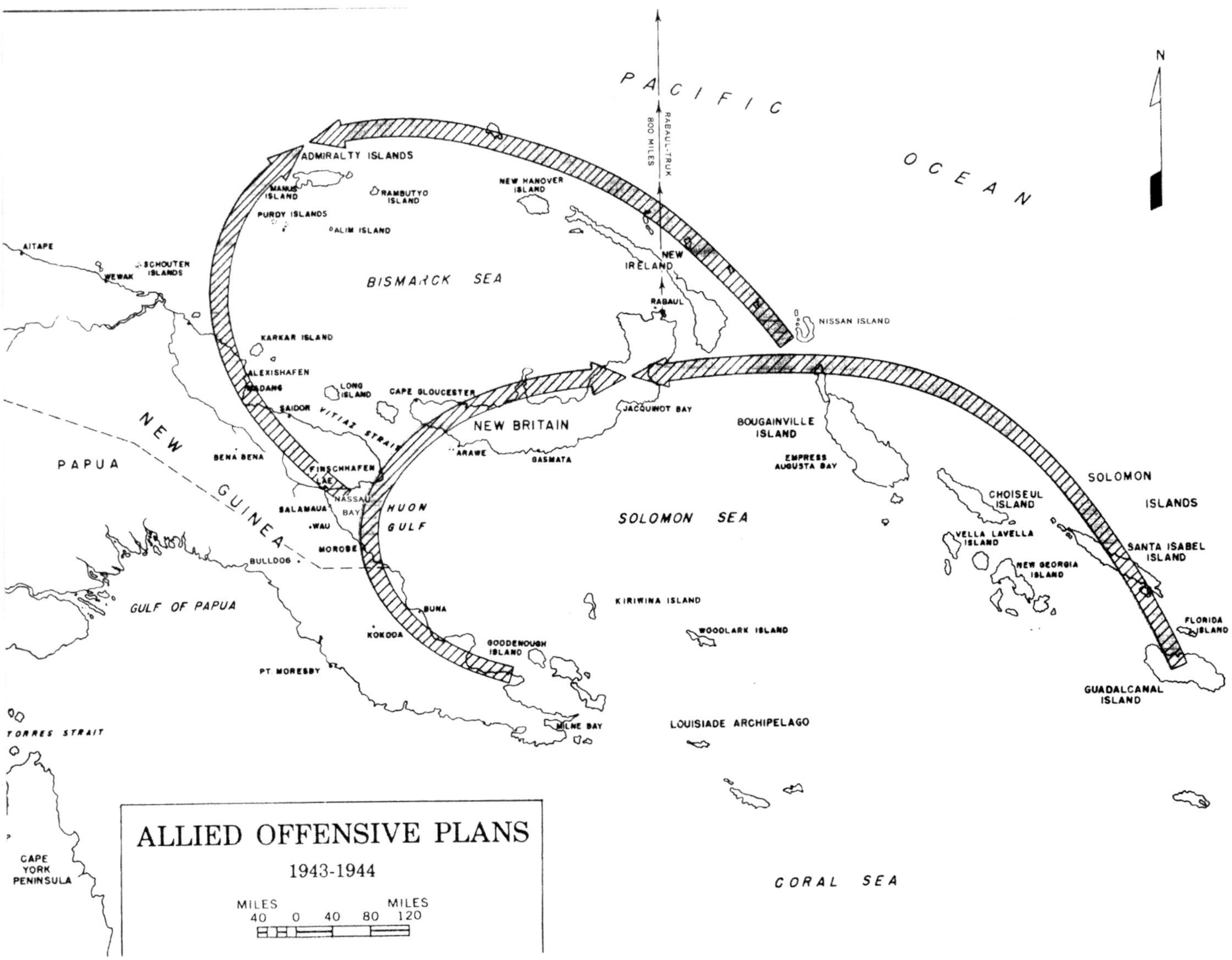

vanced headquarters in Port Moresby or, occasionally, even from forward bases. The Allied Land Forces continued under the command of Australian Gen. Sir Thomas Blamey, under whom Lt.Gen. E.F. Herring, another Australian, commanded the New Guinea Force in January 1943.

At the conclusion of the Papuan Campaign, MacArthur felt that his ground forces were not prepared to immediately continue their offensive. There were only two US Army, one US Marine, and three Australian divisions available for combat. Of these, the US 32nd Division had been depleted during the fighting and was transferred to Australia for rehabilitation; it was replaced by the 41st division. The First Marine Division after being withdrawn from the brutal combat at Guadalcanal had been sent to Australia and would require six months to become combat ready. The Australian 6th and 7th Divisions were so badly decimated that they needed to be reconstituted, while the 9th Australian Division, which was returning from fighting with the British in the Middle East, would have to be completely re-equipped.

Allied Air Force Command

In January 1943, the Allied Land Forces in New Guinea were mostly under the control of Australian Commanders; however, the Commanders of the Allied Air Forces were principally American, but were staffed by both Australian and American officers. Of the two components of the Allied Air Forces (the Royal Australian Air Force and the American Fifth Air Force), only the 5AF was sufficiently equipped for offensive action. The RAAF was gradually building up a substantial force, and several of its squadrons equipped with Beaufighters, Beauforts, P-40s, A-20s, and PBYs had already contributed greatly during the Papuan Campaign while attached to the Fifth Air Force. Lt.Gen. Kenney, Commander of both the Allied Air Forces and the Fifth Air Force, was chiefly concerned with the interests of the 5AF, which he deemed the "Best Damn Air Force in this or any other army." While Kenney regularly overstated the potential of air power, he possessed a combination of limitless energy, a dislike of bureaucracy, and a readiness to experiment which, linked with his indisputable understanding of both engineering and flying problems, inspired confidence in his command from MacArthur down to the squadron level. Kenney established his permanent headquarters at Brisbane, where he could be in close communication with MacArthur's Brisbane HQ. Kenney's 5AF command was located at Port Moresby and consisted of Brig.Gen. Ennis Whitehead, Commander of the Fifth Air Force Advanced Echelon who, in turn, commanded Brig.Gen. Paul Wurtsmith, CO of the 5th Fighter Command and 5th Bomber Command under Brig.Gen. Howard Ramey, who had succeeded Brig.Gen. Kenneth Walker (MIA over Rabaul early in January). The only other command level organization, the Air Service Command under Brig.Gen. Carl Connell, was located at Brisbane with an advanced echelon at Townsville. (Note: At this time there was no Troop Carrier Command.)

After the activation of the Fifth Air Force in September 1942, the organization of the Air Force in the SWPA was still in its formative stage, and even though the organization was new, most of its component units were veterans in the theater, with several leaving the US within two months after Pearl Harbor. However, these units had become so depleted during the Papuan Campaign that both MacArthur and Kenney believed the air forces, like the ground forces, were not prepared to join in a protracted offensive.

At the conclusion of the Papuan Campaign, the 5th Bomber Command consisted of two heavy bomber groups, two medium bomber groups, and one light bomber group. The 43rd Bombardment Group had been in such intense combat for six months that it had only 14 B-17s available for daily bombing missions. As the last Bomb Group to arrive in the theater, the B-24-equipped 90BG was ready to assume a major share of heavy bomber operations in January 1943, but maintenance problems with the Liberators were more difficult than with the B-17s, and of its 60 B-24s no more than 15 were available for daily bombing missions.

By the beginning of 1943 Gen. George **Kenney** had established himself as a superlative innovator and organizer. (AAF)

Because of the threat of enemy air attacks during 1942, AAF heavy bombers were based in Australia and used Port Moresby as an intermediary refueling base. But by 1 February the Allies had gained air superiority, so that five heavy bomber squadrons could be safely based at the Port Moresby airfields. The medium bombardment groups consisted of the B-25 equipped 38th and the B-26 equipped 22nd. However, both of these medium bombardment units were under strength after the fighting in Papua subsided. The only Light Bombardment group was the 3BG, which began flying the ill-fated A-24 dive bombers and then flew A-20s, but had to be reequipped with B-25s due to heavy losses.

Three fighter groups (the 8th, 35th, and 49th) had arrived in the SWPA in January and February 1942, and a year later their nine veteran squadrons were based in New Guinea with 330 aircraft available. However, of these 330, 74 were well-worn P-39/400s and only 80 were P-38s, which were suitable for the long range, high altitude missions that would be required in the next phase of the air campaign. The fighter pilots of the 8FG had been based in the swampy Milne Bay area for three months and were suffering from Malaria and exhaustion, and were sent to Australia to recuperate.

Six of the seven airfields operating within 38 miles of Port Moresby were regularly used and consisted of extensive runways, taxiways, and dispersal areas. The Milne Bay bases, while not nearly as developed as the Moresby airfields, had made great progress, and two of the three were in daily use despite chronically rough and muddy landing strips.

Without air transport of reinforcements, supplies, and equipment, the early operations in New Guinea would have probably failed. The major transport bases were located at Dobodura, just east of Buna, and at Wau, 30 miles south of Salamaua; both were virtually inaccessible by other transport means. Transport pilots not only faced the perils of tropical weather and high mountains but also enemy fighters. Although the Fifth Fighter Command had gained air superiority, it could not completely prevent Japanese air attacks from Rabaul and occasionally from Lae. Due to the improved air warning system these attacks were generally ineffective. During summer 1942 Port Moresby's air warning system consisted of Australian coast watchers and spotters in the mountains who were equipped with binoculars and a radio, and were referred to as "Poor man's radar." In September the 565th Signal Air Warning Battalion arrived at Port Moresby, and within two months the area was well-protected by four radar installations. Soon Milne Bay was equally well-protected by three radar installations at Tufi Point (125 miles northwest) and at Normanby and Goodenough Islands. Despite these new radar warning installations, the coast watchers continued their important function from their stations along the New Guinea coast and from islands far to the northeast.

Kenney in January 1943

Kenney viewed the Papuan Campaign, which ended in January 1943, as a "template to future operations in the Southwest Pacific." While the Japanese held large areas of the Southwest Pacific in early 1943, in reality, their defensive perimeter was controlled by relatively small forces deployed in a chain of strong points along the New Guinea coast and on island outposts. The Japanese were limited to these areas by the terrain and geography of the region, which allowed the Allies to isolate and then defeat them, or merely bypass them. To achieve this operational plan Kenney would employ his maxim of gaining advanced air superiority while simultaneously isolating the Japanese ground forces from receiving reinforcements and supplies. When the enemy garrisons were weakened and unprotected by their air forces, Kenney would concentrate his air units on bombing the enemy positions near the Allied amphibious landing area both prior to and during an invasion. At times, Allied ground forces were transported by air into an area and then resupplied by aircraft, eliminating the need for amphibious landings. Once the ground troops drove the enemy forces from the area, engineers arrived to construct an airfield from which the next advance could be based, and then the routine was repeated. Except for details specific to the operation, MacArthur's methods in the Southwest Pacific remained the same: leapfrogging the most strongly held Japanese positions and defeating the remaining outposts.

Kenney the Innovator

Although inflexible in his thinking about the correct progression of air operations, Kenney exhibited great flexibility in the implementation of the missions. The hallmark of Kenney's command was his intelligence and willingness to undertake innovations. To gain air superiority, Kenney needed to engage and defeat Japanese fighters. It was not before long that Kenney realized that the 5th Fighter Command required the development of long range fighters, and he ardently looked for methods to increase the range of his fighters so that they could escort bombers to their targets. Possibly the most significant change Kenney made from the prewar dogma involved the shift from high altitude bombing of enemy shipping to low level attacks. Although Kenney would take credit for conceiving this tactic, he had adopted it, and the low level bombing of enemy shipping became routine and successful in the SWPA. The success of low

Kenney referred to Maj.Gen. Ennis **Whitehead** as "my strong right arm all through the war.". (AAF)

During January 1943 enemy attacks resumed on the Milne Dromes with 11 attacks or recon missions. (AAF)

level shipping attacks would be demonstrated by the enormous success of the Battle of the Bismarck Sea in March 1943, which signaled the Japanese High Command that they could no longer send large reinforcements to New Guinea and effectively sealing the fate of enemy garrisons there.

Kenney the Organizer

While Kenney launched many technical and tactical adaptations, he also introduced a number of organizational changes. On his arrival in Australia he found that the command scheme there was incompatible with the demands of the theater. Maj.Gen. George Brett, Kenney's predecessor, had, mostly out of necessity, combined American and Australian air units into one command, going as far as combining nationalities in the same aircraft. Brett's policy distressed MacArthur, who opposed the idea of American forces being under the command of officers from another nation. Kenney quickly separated Australian and American air units into distinct organizations, a division he found helpful for improving both combat effectiveness and his rapport with MacArthur.

The long distance and poor communications between Kenney's (and MacArthur's) Headquarters in Brisbane and the forward airfields in New Guinea forced Kenney to delegate much of the responsibility for daily operations to a commander near these airfields. For this crucial position Kenney appointed Maj.Gen. Ennis Whitehead to command the 5AF Advanced Echelon (ADVON) at Port Moresby, who was responsible for overseeing daily missions. Whitehead was a good choice, as he and Kenney were of the same military "generation." They entered the service at the same time and shared the same "air power viewpoint," and would seldom disagree on a strategy. Frequently, Kenney's planning for an operation had been anticipated and planned at ADVON headquarters. Kenney referred to Whitehead as "my strong right arm all through the war." With Whitehead in command of offensive operations from Port Moresby, Kenney appointed Air Vice Marshal William Bostock to command the now separate Royal Australian Air Force (RAAF) Command based in Australia, which was committed to the air and sea defense of their country.

Milne Bay and Port Moresby Attacks

Milne Bay

Japanese air raids on Milne Bay Dromes were always a continual threat, starting on 4 August 1942 with six more before ending five weeks later. During January the enemy attacks resumed, and the area suffered through 11 attacks or recon intrusions. The largest and most effective attack occurred on 17 January, when two B-17s, one B-24, one P-39, and two Lockheed Hudsons were destroyed, along with over 10,000 gallons of gas and numerous gas trucks and command cars. 1Lt. Norbert Ruff of the 80FS, stationed at Milne, wrote ammunition was "exploding like mad" from the ammo dumps. He continued to describe the raid in his book *Ruff Stuff*:

> "On January 17, 1943, we had our biggest air raid to date. They hit us with 24 bombers and (20) Zeros. There was a mix up on the orders as to whether only the anti-aircraft guns were to be used or if our fighter planes would be scrambled. I counted only two bursts being fired. When the Japs saw no other firing and no enemy interception, the planes dropped so low that I remember standing dumbfounded, and I could see the bomb bay doors opening and the bombs falling out. When they started hitting the ground, it sounded like some giant's footsteps coming at me. All hell broke loose. As there was no opposition, the Jap planes kept coming in at us time and time again. The raid lasted over two hours or so. It was almost the last of me I thought, but I remember hitting a slit trench near me and fell on top of some other guys. I guess I was so fascinated about the whole event that I kept fuel dump burning in background as I stood there like a fool and watching the bombs falling."

Port Moresby

The air raids on Port Moresby had begun with a recon over the city by two Mavis flying boats on 28 January. During February the Japanese sent two ineffective nighttime flying boat raids on the 3rd and 5th that were followed by daytime Betty bomber raids on the 24th and 28th, the former dropping 130 bombs that wounded 10. However, the enemy attacks stepped up markedly in March, with 26 attacks occurring on 20 of 31 days. The heaviest raids occurred on 23 and 24 March, when 19 and 18 Betty bombers, respectively, escorted by Zeros bombed the city, but little damage was done except for a direct hit on a well-marked hospital.

Creature Comforts

Food

While units located near the cities and towns of Australia generally received adequate rations, a severe problem was the lack of a balanced diet in isolated areas of Australia and in New Guinea. In New Guinea all food had to be shipped from Australia, and the inadequacy of waterborne shipping facilities, air transport, and refrigeration limited the quantity and variety of the foods; consequently, canned or dehydrated food was shipped in quantity. While the canned food usually satisfied minimum nutritional requirements, they were almost invariably of Australian manufacture to Australian tastes. It was bantered that the Australian Army regularly supplied its mess with bully beef and rice, except on Christmas Day, when they had rice and bully beef. The 8FS/49FG history reported that the food was "bad and without variety," while the 35th Fighter Control Squadron reported that "the food problem more serious than air raids."

"Bully Beef" was a finely ground corned beef in a "small" amount of gelatin and was shipped in distinctive oblong tin cans, much like the later infamous Spam. Most Americans detested the Australian meat, and a standing joke was if any pilot would actually stop a Zero from shooting down any transport carrying it.

Health

With the prevalence of tropical diseases, the medical organization in Australia that had been established on 6 March 1942 was significantly expanded by 1943. Once the Fifth Air Force had been activated, Col. Bascom Wilson was designated as Air Force Surgeon and other medical officers were assigned to the Advanced Headquarters at Port Moresby and to other subordinate commands. These officers directed the activities of the medical detachments of Groups and component Squadrons. Air Force medical officers were dependent upon the Army Services of Supply (SOS) to some extent, since both hospitals and medical depots were under SOS control. Fortunately, cooperation between the two branches of the service was good.

Until June 1942 there were no American hospitals in New Guinea, but within six months three had been established in Port Moresby with a total of more than 2,000 beds, and two more at Milne Bay with 350 beds. Evacuation from the forward combat areas to hospitals in New Guinea or Australia was difficult, and would have been virtually impossible had it not been for the growing reliance upon air transport. After airfields had been made available for transport aircraft at Wau and Dobodura, it became possible to evacuate patients from forward areas to Port Moresby; usually in less than an hour. Between 25 November and 31 December 1942, 7,631 sick and wounded were flown from the Dobodura area to Port Moresby. By January 1943 there was an increasing incidence of illnesses, such as Malaria, Dengue, and dysentery. The health problems of personnel continued, as troops based in New Guinea might expect to lose from 15 to 20 pounds due to a poor diet and the abnormal conditions of the tropical climate, which also contributed greatly to a general lowering of resistance to illness.

Medical officers were assigned to inspect the living quarters of officers and enlisted men in their camp areas. In well-established bivouac areas, such as many of those at Port Moresby, both officers and enlisted men lived three or four in screened-in tents. Tents with gravel floors were the rule for living quarters, however, although officers occasionally enjoyed wooden flooring. The mess halls, latrines, and the incinerators for garbage disposal were often similar to those bivouacs in the United States. Mess halls were normally constructed of wood with screens, and occasionally with concrete floors; however, it was customary for officers to have a separate mess. Water supply was continually a problem, since there was no central supply system, so each unit had to lay its own pipes and maintain its own tanks, and all drinking water had to be chlorinated. Some units developed improvised showers and used halved 50 gallon drums for sinks. In areas where dysentery was prevalent, greater efforts than usual were taken to improve sanitation facilities. The washing of cooking pots and mess kits was carefully done with boiling water. Liquid food wastes were placed in soakage pits and periodically burned out, while solid waste was burned in incinerators. Latrines were built to the usual Quartermaster specifications; usually of eight holes with hinged lids and fly-proofed pits.

Although there was little Malaria incidence in Australia, the occurrence in New Guinea was high. Col. Bascom Wilson, Surgeon of the 5AF, concluded that all natives were infected and provided a constant pool of the infection. At Milne Bay the Malaria problem was especially severe, and it was an almost a foregone conclusion that everyone would sooner or later be afflicted. During December, for example, there were 100 new cases in the 9th Fighter Group alone, and 150 more were reported during January. The troops at Port Moresby, on the other hand, had a much smaller percentage of Malaria, but were beleaguered by dysentery, which seemed to be endemic there. However, the individual soldier was partially responsible for the high incidence of tropical diseases, as while in areas prone to Malaria he was supposed to wear pants and long sleeved shirts, sleep under mosquito nets, and use mosquito repellents.

Trenches were dug to drain stagnant and rain water from billet areas to eliminate mosquito breeding areas and improve sanitation. (AAF)

Leave

By the first of February 1943 the Malaria-ridden 8FG was withdrawn from Milne Bay and sent to Australia for R&R. While in Australia, pilots and ground officers received regular leaves to Sydney, and enlisted men were granted furloughs to Brisbane and passes to nearby towns. There was beer in the camp during the evening, but little liquor of any kind could be found in the towns, and that which was available was at exorbitant prices. Some men felt that it was better to stay in camp, where the PX was well stocked with beer and soft drinks, or to go to the occasional dances arranged by the Red Cross.

Replacements

One of the most urgent problems was the question of replacements. Many pilots had been in continual combat for as many as 10 months, while ground crews and service and depot personnel were being worn down by 12 to 18 hours of daily hard labor. Flight Surgeons reported that 45 to 60% of the pilots in some units were suffering from combat fatigue owing to combat operations with irregularly spaced missions, the existence of poor living conditions without suitable recreational facilities, and the lack of promotions. The signs of combat fatigue were irritability, short temper and general apathy. Fifteen pilots of the 8FS of the 49FG had served for a year in the combat zone and the squadron combat status report stated that their "ability, aggressiveness and morale were becoming very low." The absence of a definite policy of rotation gave these war-weary veterans little hope of relief.

So, even though the need of a personnel rotation policy was recognized, it was difficult to establish a satisfactory balance between the demands of the theater for replacements and the realities in quantity and quality of the training program supplying replacements. It was a question of whether it was more prudent to keep exhausted veterans in the theater or to replace them with untrained newcomers. In October and November 1942, after its extended operations in the Philippines, the NEI, and Australia, the 19th Bombardment Group (H) was the only combat group in the SWPA to be replaced as a unit since the beginning of the war. The return of the 19BG to the United States and the initial arrival of some replacements did give hope to those veterans who had been in combat for lengthy periods that they would be rotated home. In reality, it was impossible to depend on regular trained replacements in large enough numbers.

The arrival of replacements created a new problem, as frequently high-ranking officers and enlisted men, arriving directly from the States, had no combat experience and required extensive instruction from veterans of lesser rank. These veterans had not been promoted during their long months in combat, while their "students" had received undeserved stateside promotions, and the veterans found this to be an intolerable situation. Kenney championed the cause of his veterans by constantly urging that no high ranking officers should be sent to his theater unless specifically requested, and that he should be authorized to promote his deserving men regardless of the table of organization. When a Major and 10 First Lieutenants arrived from Hawaii Kenney sent them back, urging that only Second Lieutenants be sent in the future. Kenney was allowed to fill 200 vacancies for First Lieutenants above the T/O of the Fifth Air Force, and was promised that consideration would be given to a similar provision for the promotion of First Lieutenants and Captains. Nonetheless, the promotion and rotation problems remained unsolved in early January 1943.

2

February 1943

The Japanese were building a 4,200 foot landing strip on **Wakde Island** and a 3,900 foot strip inland from Hollandia Bay, as well as roads at Madang and Alexishafen. (AAF)

With Allied air supremacy, the Japanese could no longer rely on convoys and large vessels but turned to barges, luggers, and submarines for resupply and reinforcement. The barges shown here could move only at night or suffer the fate of these barges. (AAF)

Situation in the SWPA

While the capture of Guadalcanal was of great overall strategic importance, it had small immediate effect on the operations of the Fifth Air Force. The *Elkton Plan* called for continued coordination of tactical operations between the South and Southwest Pacific Theaters of the type that had been successful during the Guadalcanal Campaign. Previously Fifth Air Force heavy bombers had repeatedly cooperated with South Pacific Army and Navy forces by attacking enemy bases at Buka, Buin, Faisi, and Rabaul. Their heaviest raids were on Rabaul, which was the largest base from which enemy aircraft and ships could move equally either toward the Solomons or New Guinea. The Japanese defeat at Guadalcanal increased the importance of these Japanese air, sea, and supply bases to the west, as there were indications during February that some of the forces and supplies which the Japanese had previously directed through these bases to the Solomons were now to be directed to New Guinea. Allied air recon revealed the increasing activity of Japanese engineers on Buka, located in extreme northwestern New Guinea, to points as far east as Lae. They were building a 4,200 foot landing strip on Wakde Island and a 3,900 foot strip inland from Hollandia Bay, as well as roads at Madang and Alexishafen.

The Japanese used submarines, small boats, barges, and air transport as their main means of supplying these widely dispersed bases in New

Guinea. It was obvious that if the Japanese planned to save face after their disaster in the Solomons, either to control New Guinea or to launch any significant offensive from it, a very large scale venture would be necessary to provide the necessary troops, equipment, and supplies. Therefore, during February the 5th Bomber Command continued to focus on isolating New Guinea, particularly the northeastern portion, from the enemy controlled islands to the north.

5th BC medium and light bombers focused primarily on the supply lines in the Lae area, attacking targets in the forward areas around Mubo, where the Japanese had retreated after their defeat at Wau; bombing and strafing airfields at Lae and at the nearby Malahang Airfield; and sweeping the coast from Finschhafen to Madang. During February RAAF and 5AF bombers harassed the area daily, except when a tropical cyclone interfered. A-20s carried out at least 105 low level sorties; B-25s, 84; and RAAF Beaufighters, 43. B-17 and B-24 heavy bombers and RAAF PBY patrol bombers, meanwhile, were reconnoitering the Vitiaz Strait, St. Georges Channel, and Buka Passage in the Solomons, and conducting occasional strikes against Rabaul. The B-17s of the 43rd Group carried out most of the harassing attacks on the New Britain area during February. B-17s were over Rabaul on an average of every other night, at times singly, but usually in flights of six. The air attacks carried out by the Bomber Command during February were important in maintaining pressure upon the Japanese both in New Guinea and in New Britain. However, these missions were not really effective, as there were not enough aircraft in the Southwest Pacific both to completely neutralize important bases or to maintain an aerial blockade of the New Guinea coasts. Only by careful conservation of available aircraft and by the impressive efforts of ground crews and service units could the Fifth Air Force maintain an average of 75 bombers and 140 fighters in service. The general procedure was to rotate squadrons so that approximately one third was occupied in training and maintenance, one third flying on combat missions, and the remainder held constantly on alert. In this way at least two thirds of the available air units could be mustered in case of an emergency.

During late January and February 1943, the training program of the Allied Air Forces was dedicated mainly to increasing the effectiveness of the bomber attack forces. The results of medium and high altitude bombing against shipping had been less than satisfactory, with a high number of misses. Experiments at Eglin proved the superiority of low level attack against shipping, but heavy bombers flying at 200 feet were vulnerable to anti-aircraft fire, so newly modified B-25s supported by their own forward fire power had been designed. After extensive experimentation and training effective masthead level bombing techniques were developed. During this period of intensive training the Bomber Command had little opportunity to demonstrate the effectiveness of these new techniques, but March would give them the chance.

The 39FS of the 8FG received the chance to introduce the P-38 into combat in the Fifth Air Force by a coin toss. In January 1943 the 9th Fighter Squadron joined the 39th as the second Fifth Air Force P-38 squadron. An 8th Fighter Group squadron was to be the third 5th Fighter Command squadron to receive the P-38; again, the lucky squadron would be selected by a coin flip, and the 35th Squadron won. Before long some of the 35FS' P-39s were being transferred to the 80th, and on 23 January the 35th was ready to move to Mareeba, Australia, to transition to the Lightning. Soon Gen. Ennis Whitehead issued a change of orders and the 80FS was to become a Lightning Squadron. Col. William Wise had taken command of the 8FG when Col. Frederick Smith moved to Gen. Whitehead's 5FC HQ Staff. Wise asked Smith to intervene on behalf of the 35FS, but Smith found that Whitehead had made his decision on the basis of serviceability. The 35th had a good record in battle, high morale, and was combat ready, while the 80th was beset with Malaria and Dengue Fever. Whitehead did not want to remove the seasoned battle ready 35th Squadron from combat to transition to a new fighter, so he decided that the 80th could use the transition time to recuperate.

On 19 February, the 8th Fighter Group's 35FS, 36FS, and 80FS, as well as Group Headquarters, boarded the Liberty Ship *Robert McCreary* for the R&R trip to Cairns, on the temperate central eastern Australian coast. The Group disembarked on 22 February and boarded a train for the short trip to Mareeba. The 35FS were happy to leave combat at Milne Bay, but were still perturbed at losing the P-38s. At Mareeba the men found good facilities, food, and climate, and their general health improved almost immediately with a lowering of the Malaria rate.

Wau Campaign Background

With the close of the Papuan Campaign on 23 January 1943, the Allied forces were prepared for large scale offensive operations and to start the Huon Campaign, which was to include the blockade of Lae and the air and sea reduction of Rabaul. The Joint Chiefs of Staff had not yet had an opportunity to consider the *Elkton Plan* and the decisions for future allocations for the Southwest Pacific had not been made. At least two of Kenney's combat groups, the 8th Fighter and the 22nd Medium Bomber, were out of action, and many of the bomber squadrons, particularly those equipped with B-25s, were devoting much of their time to training in low level bombing techniques. Other Allied air units, however, kept the pressure on the enemy, fulfilling their primary responsibility of interdicting the sea lanes, mapping future combat areas, bombing Rabaul and other centers of enemy supply, and otherwise harassing the Japanese wherever they could be found.

When the last organized Japanese resistance in Papua ended, Allied ground forces were facing the enemy in only one small sector of the Southwest Pacific. This was in an almost inaccessible area of Northeast New Guinea between Wau and Mubo, inland from Salamaua. Here a small Australian force, based at Wau, had been fighting a miniature land campaign with the Japanese for nearly a year, during which time they had been supplied almost entirely by air.

Since the discovery of an important gold deposit near Wau in 1926, no road had been constructed from the coast inland to the area mines, and the economic development of the area had been almost entirely dependent upon the use of commercial and private aircraft. A runway was constructed in 1937, and by mid-1942 the Japanese had improved the field to a 4,500x300 foot grass surfaced field running uphill at five to 10 degrees and heading directly toward 9,000 foot Kainde Mountain. Wau could be reached by a few inadequate native tracks which meandered through a labyrinth of mountains and jungle and over razorback ridges and swamps; all infested with insects and disease. The town of Wau was approximately the size of Port Moresby, and had been built with materials all flown in by air freight. As soon as the Japanese captured Lae in March 1942 they advanced inland toward this rich area. Wau was an attractive military objective, not because of the gold, but because of its well developed airfield, which was located just 150 miles north of Port Moresby; it could be used by transports, fighters, and even by bombers in an emergency. In late spring 1942, to defend this area the Allies could rely on only a "raggle-taggle army of miners, foresters, and civil servants called to the colors on the day of Pearl Harbor" called the "New Guinea Volunteer Rifles." They were joined early in July by a specially trained 55 man commando group which had moved overland, an extremely rigorous trip which caused 47 of the 55 men to be hospitalized upon their arrival. Of the 800 white men available in the area only 300 were healthy enough to fight. The sea and overland supply service was inadequate, while air supply was also inadequate due to the other demands of the theater. Nonetheless, the Australians, by "superb jungle craft denied control of the area to the numerically superior enemy forces, and maintained for the benefit of Port Moresby an effective observance of Japanese plane movements from enemy held fields in the Markham Valley." While this uneven contest continued throughout the months, the Allied air forces gave all possible aid. By January transport pilots were becoming accustomed to Wau's tricky uphill approach. The pilots, some of them Sergeants, had learned to maneuver the clumsy C-47s like fighter planes while flying under clouds through dangerous passes, dodging a peak here and a cloud there, and landing at unbelievably high speeds.

By late December, the purpose of the majority of Allied air strikes was to isolate enemy troops in the Mubo-Lae-Salamaua area. At this time the Japanese were having increasing difficulty sending convoys to Buna and Gona, and were changing their focus from Papua to Northeast New Guinea. The Japanese were regularly transporting supplies to Lae by submarines, and although the Allies maintained an air alert, the Japanese sporadically tried to sneak small convoys through to Lae.

After three months of insipid frontal attacks, the Americans and Australians had finally beaten the well-entrenched Japanese, and by January 1943 had driven the enemy from Papua, securing an airstrip and staging base at Buna on the north coast. Despite their greater casualties, the Australian infantry would continue be the front line of defense against the Japanese who, to block the Allied counteroffensives on New Guinea and in the Solomons, sent thousands of reinforcements to Rabaul for deployment to the Solomons and New Guinea. In January 1943, despite their defeat at Buna and the heavy losses in the continuing battle for Guadalcanal, the Japanese continued to maintain their air, naval, and ground advantage in the SWPA and maintained the strategic initiative in New Guinea. In January 1943, the Japanese Eighth Area Army ordered reinforcements to Lae with the intention of attacking Port Moresby once more. American Intelligence was able to decrypt Japanese naval communications which gave forewarning of a forthcoming reinforcement convoy.

In early January, despite the air attacks on their convoy as described earlier, the Japanese landed additional troops at Lae which advanced toward Mubo, and were congregating there for another assault upon Wau. On 29 January, the 200 Australian defenders at Wau held off a sharp patrol attack, but a few hours later an enemy regiment began to infiltrate toward the airfield. Transport aircraft at Port Moresby were ready to transfer Australian reinforcements to Wau, but heavy thunder storms over the mountains closed the passes the transports were to fly through to reach Wau. The Australians feared that they would have to abandon the struggling Wau garrison, but the weather cleared and reinforcements, food, equipment, ammunition, and some artillery were loaded on the C-47s escorted by P-39s, P-400s, P-40s, and P-38s of the 35th and 49th Groups. During 29 and 30 January, over 2,000 troops were flown in just as the Japanese had closed in on the airfield and were firing mortar shells onto the runway. Upon landing, the Australian reinforcements immediately rushed to defend the end of the runway, and occasionally the transports circled the field until the Japanese were driven back so they could land safely. By noon on 30 January, the reinforcements drove the enemy into the jungle, leaving 250 dead behind during this last serious attempt to capture the Wau airdrome. During this action the Japanese did not attempt to intercept the Allied transports or to provide air support for their ground troops, even though Allied Intelligence estimated over 50 bombers and from 50 to 150 fighters were regularly based in the New Britain-New Ireland area. There may have been two reasons for this: perhaps the Japanese were surprised at the rate the Allies could fly in troop reinforcements from Port Moresby; or possibly their air forces had been exhausted by Allied air attacks on their airdromes and on the Lae convoy.

Japanese Air Counterattack

After their losses on 7-8 January, the Imperial Naval and Army Air Forces focused once more on the Solomons to provide air cover for the evacuation of the last Japanese troops from Guadalcanal, who were transported to Rabaul to be refitted as the next reinforcements for Lae. Their only air operations in the SWPA were small bomber formation night attacks against the Allied buildup for their next land offensive. These attacks caused only minimal damage to the Port Moresby complex, the Australians at Wau, to Dobodura Airfield, and to Allied shipping at Oro Bay. To prevent any major Allied ground operation from advancing from Wau down the mountain trail into Salamaua, the Japanese sent JNAF medium bombers on their first major daylight air operation against the Australians at Wau. During the first week of February the JNAF 45th Sentai, veterans of the China campaign, staged into Lae Airdrome from Rabaul. The unit was equipped with the twin-engined Kawasaki Ki-48 Type 99 bombers, code name Lily. The Lilys were to bomb the Australian Wau dirt airstrip and bivouac area to prevent resupply, and the JAAF 11th Sentai Oscars were to provide close escort. 6 February 1943 was to be a crucial clash between the 11th Sentai and the 49th Fighter Group during the next stage of the New Guinea campaign. The 11th Sentai would lose 22 fighters, and had three others written off and two damaged in the battle, but also would lose its Commander and many veteran pilots. The battle would devastate the Sentai and force it to stand down, giving JAAF Command no choice but to import a fresh new fighter unit.

6 February 1943: The Air Battle over Wau
35FG/40FS/41FS

Wau airstrip provided the Japanese with a "compact target," as it was situated at an altitude of 3,500 feet in a deep canyon located between heavily forested 9,000 foot mountains. A north to south 4,000 foot dirt runway was cut that was just long enough to accommodate the heavily loaded and heavily escorted C-47 Dakotas that flew nonstop supply flights to Gen. Blamey's Australian troops. Finally, the Japanese sent air support to the Wau area, but it did not arrive until six days after their defeat near Wau airfield on 30 January. Meanwhile, Allied transports continued to carry troops and supplies to Wau. On 6 February the Japanese sent out a large fleet of Sally and Lily bombers escorted by fighters to attack Wau.

40FS

Eight P-39s of the 40th Fighter Squadron took off from Berry Drome at 0915 and were patrolling at 12,000 feet over Wau, waiting for a flight of five C-47 transports to take off for a routine cargo mission. Shortly before 1045 the P-39s sighted 18 Zekes at their altitude, but then suddenly discovered that six others were approaching from another direction on their tails. Capt. Thomas Winburn and Wingman 1Lt. Henry Campbell, followed by Element Leader 2Lt. Eugene Deboer and Wingman 2Lt. Lewis Raines, led the P-39s in a steep dive into the larger formation, which broke formation when the Americans approached. Winburn fired a long burst at one which burst into flames and crashed into a mountain side. As he pulled away he shot at a second Zero but missed. He attacked another Zero that caught fire after a long burst. Winburn's prop malfunctioned and he broke off combat and returned to base.

Winburn's second Element Leader, Deboer, and Wingman Raines did not fire on the first pass and lost Winburn. As Deboer circled the mountains north of Wau he saw a Zero peel off and shot it down in a sheet of flames. When DeBoer and Raines returned to altitude Deboer saw another Zero below to port. DeBoer made a 90 degree firing pass and the Zero flew into it, but he did not see it crash for a probable. DeBoer climbed to 15,000 feet and saw two Zeros over Wau at the same altitude. As he closed he saw 1Lt. Robert Schick ahead to port shooting down a Zero. DeBoer chased the other two Zeros, but one peeled off and the other outmaneuvered him and got on his tail. The P-39's engine stopped as DeBoer dove, but he got it restarted; he had one more scare as a P-40 chased him half way back to Moresby before his pursuer realized he was a P-39. Meanwhile, Raines had left the formation when a Zero was approaching from head on and below. Raines began firing when the Zero pulled up in front of him in a wingover and Raines followed him up, firing, and the Zero spun out. Raines dove out of the fight, and then climbed up and made two more passes at Zeros but saw no results. When he looked back he saw four Zeros on his tail and dove away, and then joined Schick and Campbell and returned to base.

Lt. Edwin **Schneider** claimed the first three of four total victories. (AAF)

2Lt. Lee **Taylor** scored his only victory of the war. (AAF)

2Lt. Lewis **Raines** got his only victory. (AAF)

1Lt. Robert **Shick** got a probable and the last two of three victories. (AAF)

2Lt. Eugene **Deboer** got his only claims of the war a victory and probable. (AAF)

Capt. Thomas **Winburn** claimed his only two victories. (AAF)

40FS pilots on 2 January:(L-R) 2Lt. Eugene **Deboer**. (1 victory/1 damaged), 2Lt. **Reiner**. (no claim), Capt. Thomas **Winburn**. (2 victories), and 1Lt. Henry **Campbell**. (1 damaged). (AAF)

1Lt. William **McDonough** scored his first two victories and a probable. (AAF)

1Lt. William McDonough led his wingman, 2Lt. Edwin Schneider, and Second Element 1Lt. Robert Schick and 2Lt. Lee Taylor in a dive. McDonough fired at the Zeros but made no observable hits. He made a left climbing turn and took a long range shot from astern at 30 degrees deflection which hit the cockpit. At this time all members of his flight separated into a confused dogfight. McDonough fired a good burst from the front beam and saw his tracers hit the wing and engine of a Zero just as hit the Zero behind it. McDonough continued closing for a head on attack when the Zero turned off. McDonough did not follow and had to dive to shake off a Zero firing on his tail. When McDonough climbed back up into the fight he saw Schick trying to shake a Zero firing on his tail. McDonough was above them and rolled, and as the Zero pulled up McDonough got a long burst into its cockpit and it spiraled into the ground. McDonough climbed almost to Salamaua, where he saw three Zeros at 8,000 feet and two at 6,500 feet. He dove on the last two, but they turned into him before he got into range. He fired a quick burst before he sped away for Wau, scoring for a probable, but still had the Zeros on his tail. After about half a minute the enemy pilots gave up and McDonough returned to Wau, where he found that he was alone, and he returned to base with his first claims of the war.

. When the three Zeros pulled up and turned toward the flight Schick and Taylor turned to port and lost McDonough's element, then turned back into the Zeros. Schick closed on the right Zero and fired from 100 yards, tearing pieces off its wings. The Japanese pilot went into some confused left-right-partial chandelle maneuvers before Schick fired into the cockpit at 50 feet. The Zero caught fire, and as it fell off to the right it almost collided with the Airacobra. Schick turned sharply to the right and saw Taylor shoot down a Zero which was turning left, and it spiraled into the ground in flames. Schick then saw another Zero turning onto his tail and firing from the left. Schick writes that he was "more or less saved" by McDonough, who was on its tail and shot it off. Schick was in a dive when he saw two Zeros just 500 feet above him. Schick used his diving speed to zoom onto the tail of the right Zero and fired into its fuselage and wings. It started smoking badly, but he was unable to observe the results, as four Zeros were seen circling overhead. Schick dove to 7,000 feet, where he was rejoined by Wingman Taylor and climbed toward the end of the Wau Valley, where they saw a Zero 2,000 feet above at 5 o'clock. The Zero turned to attack and the two P-39s turned into its attack. The Zero pilot then climbed back up, turned into the American attacks, and continued this maneuver five times as the dogfight climbed to 11,000 feet. The two Americans finally gave up their fruitless attacks on the skilful enemy pilot and chandelled away into the sun. They then circled back to the Valley looking for the C-47 transports and circled, picking up Raines and Campbell before returning home.

Schneider followed McDonough into the attack. They both fired during the first pass, but both missed and pulled up to port. McDonough shot down one Zero whose Wingman pulled away but then turned into Schneider, who dove away. In his dive Schneider saw a Zero crossing in front of his sights and shot it down in flames. Schneider descended several thousand feet and leveled off, and as he turned he saw that he was on the tails of a number of Zeros. He fired at one and missed as it half rolled. Another Zero turned into Schneider and he went into a shallow dive; as he escaped he saw more Zeros heading toward Lae. As he closed Schneider saw a fighter escorting a twin engine bomber that he thought was an RAAF Beaufighter. But as he got closer he saw that it was a Sally and fired, causing fires in both engines. Schneider broke off when a Zero approached, but the enemy pilot did not follow. Schneider pulled up to 15,000 feet toward a number of fighters, and once he was above them, leveled off and approached a flight of three Zeros. He fired a long burst at one that started smoking and spun straight in. Schneider broke off when the other two Zeros turned into him. He dove until he thought he was safe and then climbed to 12,000 feet and saw four Zeros below. He dove and fired on one, but only one of his .50s fired and he dove through the enemy formation to escape. One Zero tried to follow, so Schneider then decided to dive away with three victories. The 40FS Airacobras had destroyed 11 Zekes and one Sally and claimed five other probable kills with no losses to themselves.

The same combat was described in more florid language in a *Chicago Daily News* dispatch by Pulitzer Prize winning reporter George Weller, "from somewhere in New Guinea":

Lieut. Lewis Raines of Louisville, GA, 40th Fighter Squadron, who is 23, said:

> "By the time we dropped the belly tanks, the Japanese were already coming in. A Zero came a me head on, raked me, then came up in front. I got him with a full raking shot from fuselage to tail. (2Lt. Lee) Taylor watched me and saw him spin into the mountain afterward. I dived then, came up and found myself in a fight with Zeros passing in front of me. I got two short bursts at the rear quarter. They kept swarming around me, so I dived again."

McDonough (Lieut. William McDonough of Temple City, CA) said:

> "When (1Lt. Robert) Schick reported them in, I said, 'Let's get in there,' and called 'Bandits' over the phone three times. Then I saw five Zeros with round wing tips ahead. I fired at the yellowish green lead ship in an overhead pass and missed. I came up and found three more, took the outside ship and peppered the cockpit with cannon shells and gunfire. I saw shells explode. I turned over in time to see (2Lt. Edwin) Schneider shoot down a Jap with one long burst/ In the general combat, I got in a long shot slightly in front and from below. I pulled up and saw a Zero on Schick's tail. I fired but the Jap evidently saw the tracers and pulled up."

My tracers went right into the dashboard, that is, right into the Jap's lap. I noticed a little fire in there with him. I gave him another burst and the Jap turned into a left hand spin. The fire took hold of the whole front and the plane was burning as it fell and when it lit the ground it made a big black patch because it exploded. Then saw three or four planes fluttering around Lae like a dog fight. I went over but it was more Japanese forming up. Only my light machine guns were working but I got in a couple of good shot before two went for me and I finally was able to tack onto one of our own formations."

Lieut. Edwin Schneider, 40th Squadron, flying on McDonough's wing, said:

> "I saw Japanese at 12 (o'clock) and another group of specks at 1 (o'clock) on the horizon. When Mac (McDonough) missed the first his buddy went for me. I veered away to the left and met another. Seeing his own exposure he started to dive but I led him and gave him a very long burst for three of four seconds with everything. I kept diving and at about 4,000 feet above the valley saw a bomber. When he saw me coming he started to skid to try to miss my pass. I gave his tail end Charlie a long, long burst. His left wing went right into flames, then his right, then flames engulfed the engine. The whole thing was covered by flame. I figured that more bombers were ahead. This looked like duck soup. I thought I wound knock off a long ling. But a Zero came in on my tail and spoiled the fun. So I climbed to 15,000 feet and jumped into what looked like a fight between two Zeros and one P-39 but it was three Zeros."

Seeing the three Zeros, I took the Leader and kept with him till he spouted black smoke and went spiraling down. It was this one which Taylor reported seeing fall in flames and smoke. I went back to 12,000 and picked another. The Jap did that Split-S trick they always do-fall over on his back and spinning-but I gave him a four second burst as he fell. Then one of his friends started on me. I dived outside the fight, then saw another bunch of Zeros and started for them, indication 300 miles per hour. But when I saw only one gun had ammo left, I decided to call the thing off."

41FS
The 41FS sent out eight Airacobras (five P-400s and three P-39s) in two flights in a midday interception over Wau. At 1240 six Zeros were seen attempting to reform at 10 o'clock low at 13,000 feet. The 41st dove undetected head on and to full deflection four miles northeast of Wau.

For Red Flight, Capt. Fred Thompson, Flight Leader, "got four good shots on four different Zeros," but got a victory credit for the one that was seen smoking. 2Lt. Robert Boucher was credited with a Zero, while 2Lt. John Weber damaged a Zero and 1Lt. Tony Prince did not score.

For White Flight, its Leader, 1Lt. Francis Dubisher, made two initial unsuccessful diving beam attacks from under and head on in which the Zeros turned inside and his tracers went behind. His third attack was on a Zero approaching from above and head on. The Zero rolled over as if to dive away and Dubisher hit it; the Zero went into a spin and crashed out of control into the sea. 1Lt. Dugan Woodring fired a long burst, downing a Zero, while 2Lts. Carey Wooley and Lucian Johnson did not score.

Meanwhile, Whitehead's headquarters had been informed of the large enemy raid on Wau and scrambled three more fighter squadrons. Fifteen minutes later, 1Lt. David Harbor of the 9th Squadron, which had only recently been equipped with P-38s, destroyed a Zero. At approximately the same tine P-39s and P-400s of the 41st Squadron surprised six Zekes by diving out of the sun and shot down four of them. Flight Leader Capt. Fred Thompson, 1Lts. Francis Dubisher and Dugan Woodring, and 2Lt. Robert Boucher each shot down a Zeke.

49FG/7FS
Morning
Frank Nichols, who was newly promoted to Captain, was to lead a routine mission to escort six C-47s to Wau. Nichols was surprised to find that Group Commander Lt.Col. Robert Morrissey was on the mission roster as the second Element Leader of Blue Flight. Morrissey had just recovered from Malaria and was approved for flight duty, and he was eager to be "a group leader by example."

At 0945 Nichols led eight P-40s of Red and Blue Flight from 17 Mile Drome toward a rendezvous with the C-47 transports that were flying in from Townsville for their daily morning supply run to Wau. The rendezvous took place as scheduled over the Owen Stanleys, and after an uneventful 30 minute flight the Dakotas landed while the Warhawks went into a routine

2Lt. Robert **Boucher** scored his only victory of the war. (AAF)
1Lt. Dugan **Woodring** claimed his first of two victories. (AAF)

orbit of the Wau area. Nichols led Red Flight elements Wingman 1Lt. David Allen and second Element Leader 2Lt. Donald Sutliff and Wingman 2Lt. Arland Stanton at 10,000 feet. Two thousand feet overhead were 1Lt. John Hood's Blue Flight elements of 2Lt. Robert Greene, Lt.Col. Morrissey, and 2Lt. Lawrence Succop, who trailed a few minutes behind. At the same time another flight of Dakotas escorted by 40FS Airacobras were also descending into the Wau area, creating momentary confusion.

At that particular time, a large enemy formation consisting of nine Lilys of the 45th Sentai escorted by 28 Oscars of the 11th Sentai flew out of the clouds at 9,000 feet just west of Wau. As the enemy bombers descended on their bombing run, Nichols' Red Flight sighted these green twin-engined aircraft and assumed they were RAAF Beaufighters, because of red and blue markings on the fuselage. They soon discovered, however, that three of these "Beauforts" were bombing the Allied airfield.

When the Lilys dropped their bombs east of the strip, Nichols finally saw their identifying red wing roundels and called for the break. After dropping their belly tanks Red Flight broke away from 10,000 feet and chased after the enemy bombers, which then hurried off toward Salamaua. Soon Nichols closed on the Lilys and fired a damaging burst into the enemy Wingman on the right flank of the lead V, then broke hard to starboard and climbed at full throttle for another diving pass on the bombers. As he climbed Nichols saw the P-39s come under attack by the Oscars and decided to engage the enemy fighters instead.

LEFT TO RIGHT:
Capt. Frank **Nichols** scored his third and fourth victories. (AFAA)

1Lt. David **Allen**. (L). (with 2Lt. Arthur Wenige) scored his first two victories toward becoming an eighth victory ace. (AAF)

2Lt. Arland **Stanton** scored a victory and a damaged. (AAF)

Lily Army Kawasaki Ki-48 four place TE light bomber. (AFHRC)

As he approached an Oscar it turned into Nichols' attack, forcing him to dive away to safety. Nichols then used his diving speed to climb again to 11,000 feet, where he spotted another Airacobra below with an Oscar on its tail. Nichols descended into a high speed dive and fired a broadside deflection shot that caused the Oscar to instantly burst into flames, roll over slowly, and glide into a scorching explosion on a hillside north of Wau Airfield. As he watched his victim descend another Oscar appeared overhead, and Nichols dove off to the west to gain more speed to make a third pass. Nichols engaged the agile Oscars and maneuvered with them until one stalled out within firing range. The Warhawk's .50 caliber bullets hit home, and the mortally wounded Oscar fell away in a flat spin toward the jungle. Nichols was low on fuel and ammo, and prudently dove away and headed for 17 Mile Drome.

Nichol's Wingman, David Allen, remained in position for the attack on the bomber formation and damaged a Lily on the left flank. As Nichols maneuvered with the Oscars, Allen was able to elude them and, partially hidden by the clouds, approached the Lilys from beneath for his second attack. Allen closed in on two Ki-48s and fired fatal bursts on both before the escorts appeared and drove him off. The enemy followed and Allen dove at 400 knots back toward Wau, hoping to escape flying through the friendly AA corridor at only 500 feet above the runway. Allen hoped that the Aussie AA gunners would hold their fire on him and then open up on the Oscar. The AA gunners complied and the Oscar broke off. Afterward Allen went into a steep climb but was intercepted by another Oscar; he had to use the AA corridor to escape for a second time. Allen then headed south and landed safely at 17 Mile Drome.

The second Red Flight elements of Sutliff and Stanton reached the bombers moments after Nichols' attack. While approaching the Lilys, Sutliff and Stanton were attacked by a pair of Oscars that hit Stanton's fuselage, forcing him to break and dive to safety. Stanton's wounded P-40 had problems reaching 10,000 feet, but after four attempts the persistent American finally reached the swirling dogfights and hit an Oscar in a head on pass northwest of the strip. Finally, an attack by an Oscar forced Stanton to break off and return alone to 17 Mile Drome. Element Leader Sutliff engaged the Lilys, but found he had not charged his guns and had to retreat to a considerable distance to rearm his guns before re-engaging. Now separated from Wingman Stanton, Sutliff flew northeast toward Salamaua, hoping to cut off the escape of the Lily formation. At 12,000 feet he saw three enemy fighters in a spread formation, 2,000 feet below and cruising toward the coast. Sutliff chose the trailing Oscar on the left and went into a diving attack from the rear and flamed the enemy, which dove into a hillside in a brilliant orange explosion near the north end of the Wau strip. As Sutliff broke down and away for Wau he made a quick head on firing pass at another escaping Oscar without result. He then zoomed over the field, only to find the combat was over, and joined Nichols and Blue Flight's Bob Greene for the flight back to Moresby.

When 1Lt. John Hood's Blue Flight flew through the cloud cover and arrived at Wau Airstrip they encountered AA bursts, exploding bombs on the east side of the runway, and a raging dogfight between Warhawks, Airacobras, and Oscars. Hood led his Flight against the second wave of Lilys and Hood, Morrissey, and Succop each claimed a Lily as a probable before the Oscars arrived and they were forced to break off and scatter. Morrissey headed toward a distant cloud before he could escape and turn back for the Wau battle. Hood dove under the Lily formation and was ready to make another firing pass from the rear, but was forced to dive away when another Oscar dove on him. Hood rolled into to a high speed dive and zoomed back up to 16,000 feet, where he met Morrissey and Succop, and the trio turned south for Moresby. Robert Greene, Hood's Wingman, was able to make contact on his second pass and made a diving attack on the left flank of the Lily formation without making a hit. He climbed back up to 11,000 feet and cut off an Oscar that was turning with a P-39, shooting it down just northwest of the field. Greene climbed back to 12,000 feet, but only found Red Flight's Sutliff to accompany him back to base.

49FG/9FS

Meanwhile, Whitehead's headquarters had been informed of the large enemy raid on Wau and scrambled three more fighter squadrons, including the 9th Squadron led by Capt. Sid Woods, which had only recently been equipped with P-38s. 2Lt. David Harbour was able to overtake an Oscar in a dive that began at 18,000 feet and shot it down for the first official confirmed victory by a 9FS P-38 pilot.

6 February 1943: 35FG/39FS/41FS

39FS

Thirteen P-38s of the 39th Fighter Squadron took off from Schwimmer Airdrome at 1110 and intercepted 12 Oscars over Wau between 10,000 to 18,000 feet. 1Lt. Walter Beane shot down one and damaged two others, and George Weller's *Chicago Daily News* article went on to describe this noontime combat of the 39th Fighter Squadron:

"From another quarter of the sky five Lightnings (of the 39FS-author), led by 23 year old Lieut. Walter Beane, Jr. came banging into the fray. Beane who is nicknamed 'Skeleton,' is a former Navy inspector of aeronautical equipment, who a few months ago bailed out at a level too low for his parachute to open fully but had the canopy open barely above the ground by a puff of air caused by the exploding aircraft, Skinny Beane had the following Lieutenants with him...John (Shady) Lane, a former railroad man....John Rogers, a former student at Wheaton College....Robert Bake, a former student at the University of Texas....and John Dunbar, a former student at the University of Pittsburgh. Beane said:

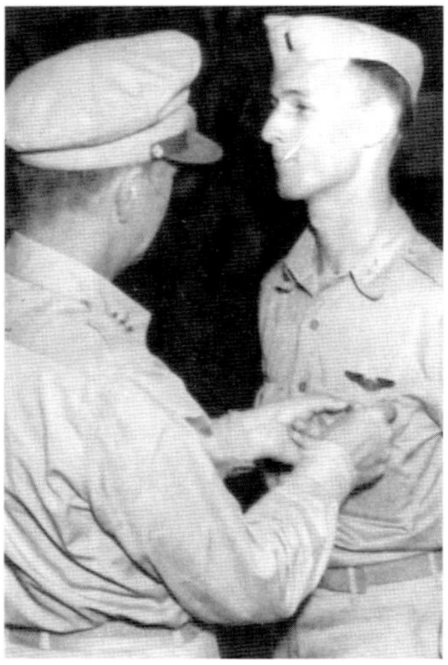

A 1Lt. Walter **Beane** got his only claims of the war; a victory and two damaged. (AAF)

We got over enemy territory after 11 and I heard Maj. George Prentice....order us: 'Continue on mission.' Then I saw 11 Zeros 1,000 feet below and five miles away. When I dived again from 17,000 feet the Japanese started climbing. We out climbed then and made a half tail rear quarter attack. All of us had a pass at Tail-End Charlie and all missed.

We next tangled with four Zeros which were doing a Lufbery Circle for mutual protection. My machine gun bit into one's cockpit. Guess I must have forgotten to turn on the cannon. Anyhow, he fell like dead, doing snap rolls all the way and I followed him to 9,000. Then I went back up and saw three left. They did not want to fight but just to protect themselves.

I picked one of these three and got him from underneath. The minute that the bullets began ripping into him he began shaking all over, vibrating like a leaf. Then he turned over and began spinning down all chopped up. The other two went for me so I scrammed. The funniest thing I saw all day was a single Zero with five Lightnings on his tail. They must have been from some other gang."

41FS

The last 35FG combat of the day occurred at 1240, when the 41st Fighter Squadron got four single Zero victory claims over Wau: Capt. Fred Thompson, 1Lts. Francis Dubisher and Dugan Woodring, and by 2Lt. Robert Boucher. The Squadron of five P-400s and three P-39s was flying at 13,500 feet about four miles northeast of Wau when they spotted six unaware Zeros in string formation about 5,000 feet below at 9 o'clock. Thompson led the attack on the Zeros, which saw the Airacobras as they closed and turned into the American attack. Thompson took shots at three Zeros before getting fatal hits on the fourth. Dubisher made a diving beam attack on his two Zeros, but each turned inside him and his tracers went behind the targets. His third attack was on a Zero approaching head on and above. As the two fighters headed toward each other the enemy pilot rolled into a dive; Dubisher fired and the Zero went into an uncontrolled spin into the water.

6 February 1943: Results of the Air Combat

Thus, in this attempt to support their ground forces, the Japanese lost 22 fighters and three bombers without doing much damage to the Wau airfield and without destroying a single American aircraft. This aerial reverse over New Guinea coincided with the Japanese acknowledgment of a much more serious defeat on Guadalcanal. During the last week in January it had seemed to Allied Intelligence that the Japanese were going to defend the Solomon Islands to the end. However, several days later the Japanese officially announced that it had been "abandoned," but did not indicate the true enormity of the defeat. Their announcement emphasized that Guadalcanal had only developed as a diversion while they built bases in the rear, and therefore their departure was not forced by the Allies but was planned. However, the Japanese retreat from the lower Solomons unquestionably changed the Allied strategic position in the South and Southwest Pacific. The Japanese were no longer a threat to the line of communications running from the Fiji Islands to the New Hebrides and New Caledonia, and the central and northern Solomons could now be considered primarily as "outer perimeter defenses" for Rabaul.

7-28 February 1943: 49FG Uneventful Escort Missions

After the dogfights over Wau the 49FG's three squadrons continued to fly tactical strikes near Lae, but by-and-large this was a time of relative calm, with new pilots and aircraft arriving daily. During the last weeks of February uneventful escort missions for 5BC heavy and medium bombers probed farther up the New Guinea coast, far beyond Lae and over western New Britain.

February 1943: 5FC Command Changes

Group Changes

Lt.Col. Donald Hutchinson was promoted to Colonel and transferred to the 5FC HQ as the new Chief of Staff. Under CO Hutchinson the 49ers were credited with 124 aerial victories by late January, and of 11 Fifth Fighter Command aces, seven had been with the 49FG at one time. The 49ers would be awarded two Distinguished Unit Citations for their role in the Papuan Campaign.

Hutchison's successor as 49er CO was Maj. Robert Morrissey, who was responsible for the transfer of the Group to the north shore of New Guinea at Dobodura. At the end of the month veteran Maj. James Selman would rejoin the 49ers as Group Deputy, while 7FS CO Maj. William Martin was transferred to 49er Group operations, and command of the Screamin' Demons' would go to Capt. George Manning.

Squadron Changes

Darwin veteran Capt. Jesse Peaslee of the 9FS was considered to be a first rate administrator, but was not regarded as a very good combat pilot by the more aggressive officers in the 5th Fighter Command, particularly by his Group Commander, Lt.Col. Robert Morrissey. Morrissey was an officer who played 5th Fighter Command politics, but also firmly believed in leading by example, and often flew sorties with either the 7th or 8th Squadrons. Morrissey believed that his promotion to 49th Group Commander confirmed his views of command, and he insisted that his Squadron Commanders also comply with them. Peaslee was a reflective and somewhat reticent officer who, from his arrival in the 49FG, did not fit into Morrissey's command concept. In late February, when Peaslee contracted jungle fever, Morrissey temporarily replaced him with 9FS Ops Exec Capt. Sidney Woods, and two months later Peaslee would transfer to the United States and never fly fighters again. Capt. Woods, another Darwin veteran, was a vigorous leader and an excellent pilot. In December 1942, 1Lt. Woods survived a crash in his P-40 at Rogers (30 Mile) Strip but refused to leave the theater, instead asking for P-38 qualification training in the Lockheed School at Townsville. After transition to the P-38 he was soon promoted to Captain, and had shown himself to be a proficient pilot and a capable flight leader. Ultimately he was selected as the 9th Squadron Assistant CO. His interim command of the 9th in March was a popular choice, and his subsequent

At the end of January, Maj. Edward **Sims** had completed his tour as CO of the 8FS and would be replaced by Capt. James Porter. (AAF)

assignment as permanent 9FS CO would make the Squadron the leading scorers in the SWPA.

By the end of January Maj. Edward Sims had completed his tour as CO of the 8FS, and Capt. Ellis Wright was slated to succeed Sims. However, the petulant and arrogant Wright was not liked by squadron personnel, and in mid-March was forced to reluctantly accept a promotion to Wurtsmith's Fighter Command Staff as Assistant Ops Director. Morrissey named the competent Capt. James Porter to take over for Sims, as he had specifically transferred Porter from the 9FS in January for that post. By mid-February he had moved the Squadron's P-40s to their new base at Dobodura.

Most of the replacements arriving for the 49FG were P-40 pilots, and were fittingly assigned to the 7FS and 8FS. By late January, 24 Lightnings had been completely refurbished for permanent combat assignment to Capt. Jesse Peaslee's 9FS Flying Knights and were moved up to 14 Mile Drome. In the first week of February, the Knights were able to stage three full P-38 flights in rotation to Horanda Strip (Dobodura) for patrols and escorts. The 12 fighters normally would return to 14 Mile Drome in the evening, until the entire air echelon could move to the Horanda camp.

February-June 1943: Situation

From February to June 1943 the battleground in eastern New Guinea lapsed into a stalemate, as the opponents reinforced and replaced earlier losses. Shipping shortages created logistics and transportation bottlenecks for both combatants. The Imperial Navy could not make good its heavy losses in naval aircraft and pilots, so the Japanese Army Air Force was gradually taking control of air bases and operations in New Guinea. For the Allies, the Europe first priority for long-range heavy bombers and fighters was imposed when the North African Campaign ran into problems. Kenney found himself trying to justify to Washington the shipment of additional warplanes to New Guinea that were in limited supply. Carrier-based aircraft in the Pacific and the greater part of the Pacific Fleet remained firmly under US Navy control. The Navy limited MacArthur to cruisers, destroyers, and submarines, and he lacked transports, cargo vessels, and landing craft, as well as the specialized crews to man them. In early 1943 neither side had the resources to force a decisive victory, and the New Guinea Campaign seemed likely to continue as a war of attrition.

3

March 1943

March 1943: The Lae Convoy and the Battle of the Bismarck Sea

The Lae Convoy and Allied Intelligence

Allied Intelligence had intercepted Japanese radio messages which specified that a convoy would shortly attempt to run the air blockade, probably either to Lae or to Madang. Accordingly, the 5th Bomber Command prepared three different operational plans. The first assumed that the convoy would head for Lae, in which case it would come within range of nearly all aircraft in the Allied Air Forces. If the convoy should separate north of the Dampier Strait area, however, a second plan directed the heavy bombers to concentrate on the segment of the convoy heading toward Madang, while light and medium bombers were to intercept the remainder of the ships if they came within range. The third plan was drafted if the entire convoy proceeded toward Madang, which was out of range of all but the heavy bomber units.

The Japanese Plan for the Lae Convoy

By March 1943 the Japanese had reached a turning point in their Pacific campaign, as they had lost Buna, Guadalcanal was evacuated, and the frontline in the Solomons was falling back toward Rabaul, placing their position at Lae at risk. The Japanese were determined to reinforce the Lae area at all costs. Gen. Hatazo Adachi's plan, code named "*Operation 81-Go*," was not a unanimous choice among all the Japanese Staff, as some wanted to land further north up the New Guinea coast and then advance down the coast to Lae. Also, some of Adachi's staff were apprehensive that he had underestimated the strength of MacArthur's forces. Nonetheless, the Lae garrison could not wait to be annihilated, and on 1 March Adachi implemented his order of battle. The reinforcements were to consist mainly of the 6,900 troops of the 51st Infantry Division together with supporting units, equipment, and supplies, along with a 250 man army air echelon contingent. It was planned that a convoy, originally consisting of eight merchant vessels and eight destroyers (one destroyer was assigned as a rescue ship for aircraft shot down), should be loaded in the Rabaul area beginning on 23 February. The loading was to be completed on 27 February, and the convoy was to leave the following night at 2300. Detailed plans were prepared as to speed, formation, and evasive tactics. The convoy was to reach Lae on 3 March, and after being unloaded was to depart on 5 March for Rabaul, where it was scheduled to arrive approximately three days later.

Gen. Hatazo **Adachi's** plan for the Lae Convoy was code named "Operation 81-Go". (AFHRC)

Japanese air cover for the convoy was to be provided for a half day each by 60 JAAF fighters (starting on 1 March providing all day, and then 0500-1200 cover except 4 and 6 March, when their coverage was to be from 1200-1800) and 40 JNAF fighters (starting on 2 March 1200-1800 cover, except on 4 and 6 March, then their coverage was from 0500-1200, with all day cover on 7 March). Additionally, to divert Allied fighters the JNAF was to fly attacks on Port Moresby and Milne Bay while the JAAF was to attack Wau and Buna during 1 to 7 March.

27 February-1 March 1943: The Lae Convoy Enroute

At the outset it seemed that the weather favored the Japanese plan. On 27 February southeastern New Guinea and the adjacent islands were covered in low clouds, and there was stormy weather over New Britain. On the following day flying conditions were considered fair to good, but on 1 March storms were prevalent in both the New Britain and New Guinea areas, hindering the B-24s of the 320th and 321st Squadrons that maintained a continual search over the sea lanes. During the morning of 1 March two B-24s of the 321st Squadron patrolled the routes along the north and south coasts of New Britain and reported that the weather had cleared, but otherwise reported nothing of importance. At 1130 a third B-24 was sent on a similar mission, and at approximately 1500 its crew sighted 14 ships escorted by Zeros on a westerly course 40 miles northwest of Ubili. At Port Moresby Kenney was informed of the enemy convoy sighted sailing westbound along the northern coast of New Britain. Kenney was determined to prevent enemy troops from reaching Lae as they had in January and sent heavy bombers with P-38 escorts to stop the convoy, but the poor weather thwarted the mission. Kenney advised Col. Wurtsmith at 5FC HQ to restrict his current tactical operations and to go "on a high state of readiness."

Two hours later another B-24 was sent out to shadow the convoy in rapidly decreasing visibility. At about the same time seven B-17s of the 63rd Squadron, followed a few hours later by a single B-17 of the 65th Squadron, tried unsuccessfully to locate and attack the convoy. By this time the Advanced Echelon (ADVON) was fully alerted and prepared to send its aircraft into combat. Since only a few missions had been flown during the preceding two days a maximum number of aircraft were available. Of the units assigned to ADVON and prepared to participate in the convoy attack, the following aircraft were available: 43 P-40s and 18 P-38s of the 49th Fighter Group; 17 P-38s of the 35th Fighter Group; 17 P-40s of the RAAF 75 Squadron; six B-25Cs and Ds of the 13th Squadron, 11 B-25Cs of the 90th Squadron, and 15 A-20s of the 89th Squadron (all of the 3rd Bombard-

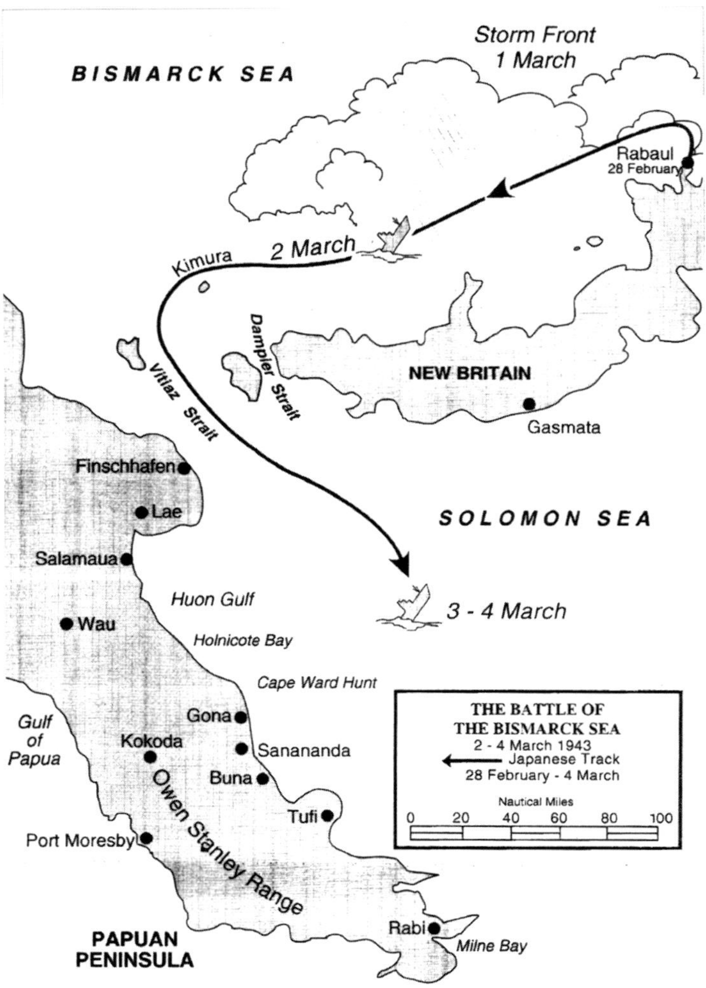

ment Group); 11 B-25Cs and Ds of the 38th Group; 28 B-17s of the 43rd Group; nine B-24s of the 90th Group; and six Bostons, 13 Beaufighters, and 13 Beauforts of the RAAF Operational Group. Thus, on 1 March the Allied Air Forces had a total of 154 fighters, 34 light bombers, 41 medium bombers, and 39 heavy bombers available for the mission.

2 March 1943: The First Attacks on the Lae Convoy

On 2 March the convoy remained too distant for coordinated strikes by all types of aircraft, and consequently the burden of the attack rested upon the heavy bombers protected by long range P-38 fighters. However, the first mission was designed to hamper Japanese fighter opposition by neutralizing the Lae airfield. Six RAAF A-20s took off from Port Moresby before dawn, bombed the field from both medium and treetop altitudes, and heavily strafed the runway and dispersal areas. Meanwhile, a 320th Squadron B-24 searched the Bismarck Sea for the convoy, but despite poor visibility the convoy had been located by mid-morning and a series of attacks was initiated by Bomber Command.

The first major strike was assigned to eight B-17s of the 63rd Squadron, which were to be escorted by 12 P-38s of the 9th Squadron. The fighters failed to reach the rendezvous point on time and the bombers were relegated to deal with enemy fighter attacks without protection. Shortly before 1000 they carried out their attack from 6,500 feet against a convoy which they reported as containing one light cruiser, five destroyers, and eight merchant vessels. The B-17s dropped 1,000 pound demolition bombs, and Maj. Scott and. Lt. Murphy were each credited with sinking a merchant vessel.

An hour after this attack, 18 B-17s of the 64th and 65th Squadrons that had taken off at 0740 were over the target. According to the plan, these bombers were to have been escorted to the target by 16 P-38s of the 39th Squadron. Again there was confusion, and these Lightnings escorted the earlier 63rd Squadron part way on their bombing mission, and thus this attack also was carried out without top cover. The weather was undoubtedly partly accountable for this rendezvous error, as low broken clouds and heavy intermittent thunder showers forced the attacking squadrons to break formation in order to search for their targets. The convoy, taking advantage of the weather, was scattering so that individual ships could take cover in rain squalls. The 64th Squadron reported three destroyers, two light cruisers, one 750 ton gunboat, and eight or nine cargo vessels of various sizes in the convoy. Of these, it reported that one 6,000 to 7,000 ton cargo vessel was "seen to burn and explode," and that another slightly smaller vessel was "in a sinking condition," while another report stated that a large cargo vessel was "smoking and burning amidships." This damage must have been caused largely by the earlier attack of the 63rd Squadron, however, since of the 69 x 1,000 pound bombs dropped, the 64th and 65th Squadrons claimed only two direct hits and four near misses.

35FG/39FS Morning Mission

The 39th sent out eight P-38s in two flights under Capt. Thomas Lynch. At about 0900 they arrived 50 miles WNW of Arawe at 15,000 feet, where they spotted five Oscars flying at 14,000 feet. Lynch led the diving attack but missed his target. The second element of Capt. Charles King and 1Lt. Wilmot Marlatt followed Lynch and dove to the attack. King's target went into a steep dive; when it pulled out King fired and hit the fuselage, and the enemy fell out of control for his first victory on the way to becoming an ace. Marlatt's Oscar did not evade, and he closed from above and the side and got solid hits between the enemy's engine and wing. Capt. Curran Jones claimed a probable just as the squadron was leaving the area.

Capt. Charles **King** scored his first victory toward becoming an ace. (AAF)

Afternoon Attacks

During the afternoon of 2 March, the convoy was still out of range of any aircraft except heavy bombers. A shadowing 63rd Squadron B-17 reported that "two possible CLs (cruisers)" left convoy at 1730, and that two unidentified ships had been added between 1530 and 1600. Reconnaissance counted 16 vessels, two of which were on fire. Approximately three hours later the final attack of the day was made by 11 B-17s off Rooke Island, at the entrance to Vitiaz Strait, the wider of two sea lanes between New Britain and Papua's Huon Peninsula. Enemy fighters, though not particularly persistent, were numerous, and one was shot down. They caused little damage to the bombers, but a heavy burst of antiaircraft struck the bomb bay of a B-17, which was saved after the fire was put out. Meanwhile 43 x 1,000 pound bombs were dropped, which according to the report scored two direct hits amidships of a 5,000 to 6,000 ton cargo vessel that "was left sinking." A RAAF PBY maintained contact with the convoy during the night, and the next morning at 0545 another B-17 relocated it off the Huon Peninsula; it was now within reach of medium and light bombers.

3 March 1943: Air Battle over Huon Gulf

The first attack of 3 March was carried out by the RAAF 100 Squadron Beaufort torpedo bombers based at Milne Bay. A weather front off Cape Nelson and the failure of flares to illuminate the ships frustrated the mission, however, and only one torpedo was released. But the threat of torpedoes was very real to the Japanese, and when, a short time later, RAAF Beaufighters carried out their attacks, the enemy, mistaking them for the similar Beaufort, maneuvered their ships to decrease the possibility of torpedo hits.

Capt. Clay **Tice** led a 9FS flight but was forced to return to base. (AAF)

Maj. Edward **Larner** led 90BS B-25s into the attack. (AAF)

Morning Missions

The RAAF 30 Squadron Beaufighters took off at 0700, and were to assemble over Cape Ward Hunt and follow tactics tested against the Moresby wreck only three days earlier. This involved low level attacks coordinated with those of B-17s, B-25s, and A-20s bombing and strafing from low and medium altitudes under protection of 39FS P-38 top cover.

At 0930 all aircraft had reached the assembly point, and 30 minutes later began the attack about 70 miles east of Lae. Thirteen Beaufighters in flights in line astern attacked the convoy, and by the time they were within AA range of the destroyers they had dropped to 500 feet. They then lost altitude more rapidly and, using rated power, attacked in line abreast at a speed of 220 knots on the now scattered convoy. The attack was superbly timed; just as the Beaufighters began their sweep on the convoy, 13 B-17s of the 64th, 65th, and 403rd Squadrons began to drop their bombs from 7,000 to 9,000 feet. After the RAAF finished its attack, Maj. Edward Larner led 90BS B-25s into the attack and used their forward-firing guns to keep the Japanese AA gunners from firing back at them. The Mitchells swooped in at wave-top level under a cloud deck of only 200 feet and attacked the convoy. As the B-25s pulled away the A-20s of the 89BS were next to attack, and within a few minutes the convoy was virtually destroyed. Every transport was on fire and most were sinking. Several of the destroyers had also been damaged. A second attack later in the day finished off the survivors. The only transport that was not sunk was dispatched later that evening by a PT boat. After the ships had been put out of action, the B-25s and A-20s callously went to work strafing the Japanese survivors. General MacArthur did not want a single Japanese soldier to reach shore where he could join the fight against the US and Australian troops fighting their way northward.

B-25 attacking a destroyer. (AAF)

35FG/39FS and 49FG/9FS

39th Squadron Leader Maj. George Prentice led 14 Lightnings, including six Flying Knights led by 1Lt. Edgar Ball, in a sweep to engage the large number of enemy fighters that had not stopped the slaughter of their convoy. Meanwhile, Warhawks and Beaufighters kept a constant patrol over the Lae airdrome complex.

49FG/9FS

Long range P-38s engaged in the majority of fighter combat over the Lae convoy. After a brief delay in the dispersal area at 14 Mile Field, Capt. Sidney Woods led three flights of 12 9FS Flying Knights P-38s. Once airborne, the last Flight, led by Capt. Clay Tice, was forced to reform when Tice returned to base with a problem and 1Lt. Edgar Ball took the Lead. Tice found that a fuel tank cap had come loose and was banging against the wing in the slipstream. He returned to base to retighten the cap and took off to catch up to his flight. He was unable to find them and joined eight B-17s bound for the convoy as a lone escort. Tice orbited the B-17s as they dropped their bombs on the enemy transports. Tice was then vectored

A-20 bombing and strafing a troop transport. (AAF)

2Lt. Richard **Bong** scored his first victory in two months after becoming an ace on 8 January. (AAF)

1Lt. William **Haney** scored his first victory. (AAF)

A Japanese destroyer seeping oil after a bomb hit. (AAF)

1Lt. Edgar **Ball** scored his only two victories of the war. (AAF)

elsewhere by the Air Controllers, but when he tried to jettison his tanks, the drop switch failed and he had to return to Dobodura. The port tank broke free during a high speed descent, and after landing the ground crew at Horanda Strip freed the starboard drop tank. After refueling Tice took off for the third time, and as he arrived over the Bay at 22,000 feet, he saw a burning warship surrounded by six rescue barges. As Tice went into a shallow descent to record the shipping with his gun camera he spotted an Oscar directly ahead at 4,000 feet below and immediately commenced an attack. The Oscar tried to evade the diving P-38 and broke hard to the left, but Tice fired a deflection shot of 200 rounds of .50 caliber and 30 rounds of high explosive 20mm cannon fire. The Oscar shuttered from the heavy concentration of fire and spiraled onto its back, plunging into the overcast above the sea. Still alone, Tice decided to return to 14 Mile Drome with his second and last victory.

Meanwhile, Tice's original 9FS Flight, now led by Edgar Ball accompanied by wingmen 1Lt. Leroy Donnell and 2Lt. Clay Barnes, was orbiting the convoy area at 12,000 feet, while another Flight of three under Flight Leader 1Lt. William Haney and wingmen 2Lts. Richard Bong and William Gersch was directly below at 11,000 feet. At this altitude the Flights were out of range of the convoy's AA batteries. Bong called out a mixed bag of enemy escorts above the ships and peeled off to his left, and the other five Lightning pilots followed Bong far out over the Gulf. The

Capt. Clay **Tice** scored his second and last victory in a Pacific career that would stretch into August 1945. (AAF)

P-38s made several passes, with Ball, Donnell, Barnes, and Bong each destroying an Oscar and damaging three others. Haney and Wingman Gersch each downed a Zero before running low on fuel and returning to 14 Mile Drome. In the battle Haney had been hit in his right rear fuselage and Gersch had received slight damage to his starboard engine, but all the Flying Knights landed safely.

35FG/39FS Morning Mission

The 39FS sent out 16 P-38s under Maj. George Prentice to escort bombers during the morning of the 3rd. At 1000, 75 miles east of Lae they saw "approximately 25" Zeros and Oscars four miles away, 1,000 above at 16,000 feet. The descriptions of the battle in the ICRs are very sparse, as they were still being done on the RAAF Forms, but the 39th had a great day, shooting down five of the seven Zeros (plus one probable) and five of the seven Oscars. 1Lt. Paul Stanch was the high scorer with two Zeros, while single Zeros were shot down by Capt. Curran Jones, 1Lt. Charles Sullivan, 2Lt. Henry Turick, and a probable by Capt. Charles King. Oscars were shot down by Maj. Prentice, Capt. Thomas Lynch (his 9th victory), and 2Lts. John Lane, Stanley Andrews, and Richard Smith. Jones' assessment of the enemy pilots was "Pretty good Nip pilots." The Squadron lost three P-38s, but the pilots are unnamed in records.

2Lt. John **Lane** admires his fourth victory AFAA)

1Lt. Paul **Stanch** was a high scorer with two Zeros for the day and would get another the next day. (AFAA)

Hands on leader, Maj. George **Prentice**, shot down second and last enemy aircraft. (AAF)

Capt. Curran **Jones** would be credited with his last two victories to become an ace. (AFAA)

39FS pilots: Standing. (L-R): Charles **Sullivan**, Thomas **Lynch**, Kenneth **Sparks** Kneeling. (L-R): Richard **Suehr**, John **Lane**, Stanley **Andrews.** Lynch would score his 9th victory. (AAF)

1Lt. Charles **Sullivan** claimed his third victory. (AFAA)

Descriptions from the RAAF ICRs for the combat included:

Capt. Curran Jones ICR simply stated, "Head on, beam, quartering, and stern." This would be Jones' fifth and last victory of the war. He would transfer out of the unit in April and return to the US in June. He would not return to combat and was promoted to Lt. Colonel in May 1945. After the war he remained in the Army and then retired from the Air Force in 1961.

Maj. George Prentice fired on an Oscar from 300 yards in a shallow diving astern attack. His Lightning was hit by two 20mm shells on the leading edge of his starboard wing.

Capt. Thomas Lynch got a "good quartering shot at one enemy aircraft (an Oscar) which went into a steep spiral, smoking badly. Then spun straight down."

2Lt. John Lane made a "75 yard astern attack on an unaware Zero that immediately started smoking and crashed into the sea."

2Lt. Richard Smith's ICR went into a little more detail, "I went into a diving starboard turn when I saw an Oscar on my left and below me. I immediately turned toward him, leveled off my dive, and fired a short burst into him. My shots whet directly into his cockpit. I saw the canopy shatter into pieces and several large holes appear in the right side of the fuselage next to the cockpit. He rolled to the left then dove straight downward and crashed into the ocean."

2Lt. Stanley Andrews dove from 3,000 feet, approached to 100 yards and opened fire, and hit the Oscar, which went out of control into a sweeping dive into the water.

1Lt. Paul Stanch was the high scorer of the day with two victories. He was flying as Wingman for Maj. Prentice. He followed Prentice in a climb from 15,000 feet, but his engine cut out at 20,000 feet and he fell behind Prentice as the Zeros closed. "I found myself in an apparent helpless situation. I turned into the Zeros (at least 25)." He fired a short burst head on and immediately dove away, but was followed by "at least" five Zeros, which fortunately only chased him for a short time. Stanch's P-38 began to operate "properly" and he turned back into the fight and rejoined Prentice. As he was about 3,000 feet behind Prentice he saw the Major open fire on one of two Zeros, one of which turned and got on his tail. Stanch raced to the rescue and opened fire from out of range on the Zero on Prentice' tail. That Zero turned away to port, and Stanch turned inside it and fired from 200 yards level. The Zero began a climbing turn and Stanch fired another burst from 100 yards, getting hits in the cockpit. The Zero fell off to port, and Stanch followed and fired another short burst from 200 yards, then watched it crash into the water. Stanch then climbed to 3,000 feet and circled over the convoy when he was attacked by three more Zeros, but escaped after firing a short burst with unobserved results. He then saw three B-17s heading toward the convoy with four Zeros heading toward the Flying Forts head on and high. Two Zeros peeled off to attack the American bombers, and Stanch got on the tail of the second while the first broke away. Stanch closed on the second pilot, who was apparently unaware, as he continued his shallow dive and never tried to evade. Stanch emptied his guns, firing two bursts from 200 feet, and watched the flaming Zero crash into the water.

Results of the Morning Combat

Any accurate appraisal of individual aircraft totals was difficult, as within 15 minutes the skies over the convoy had filled with rapidly maneuvering aircraft. Bombing was good, and five direct hits were reported to have resulted in the sinking of one 4,000 ton cargo vessel and the probable sinking of another slightly larger one. Closely following the B-17s, but just after the Beaufighters' first run, were seven B-25s of the 71st Squadron and six more from the 13th also attacking from medium altitude. Their bombing, however, was considered "a mixed success." The 71st Squadron reported that their attack "Badly hit. Believe sunk one destroyer." But the 13th could claim no more than near misses on a transport and a cargo vessel. The Beaufighters were over the convoy for 20 minutes, concentrating their heavy fire power on the decks, setting fire to cargo and, importantly, putting Japanese gun crews out of action or driven to take cover.

The 90th Squadron's 12 modified B-25s in their first combat attack roared down to 500 feet, then broke formation, with each pilot seeking his individual target. Although this occasionally caused some confusion, the results could be devastating, particularly when two pilots attacked the same target. The six to eight forward firing .50 caliber machine guns overwhelmed Japanese AA fire, and 500 pound bombs struck ship after ship. Of 37 x 500 pound bombs dropped 17 direct hits were claimed. According to the ADVON report after the 20 minute attack, of the 11 vessels in the convoy, an 8,000 ton transport was "badly damaged"; a destroyer "rolled on its side and sank"; a 4,000 to 5,000 ton cargo vessel "burst into flames and sank"; a 9,000 ton transport was left "burning violently"; a 4,000 to 5,000 ton cargo vessel stopped and "began to settle"; a 5,000 ton cargo vessel "appeared to be sinking"; a 6,000 to 8,000 ton transport was "sinking"; a destroyer and a 3,000 ton cargo vessel were "left smoking" after three direct hits; and a 5,000 to 8,000 ton cargo vessel was "left burning" after another direct hit. At the same time, six B-25s of the 405th Squadron and A-20s of the 89th were also having similar success. Two flights of six A-20s each came in at mast height, dropped 20 x 500 pound bombs, and claimed 11 direct hits. The 405th B-25s then dropped 35 x 500pound bombs from less than 200 feet and claimed four direct hits.

Only four Allied aircraft were shot down during these relentless morning attacks. The only bomber lost was from a four plane formation of the 63rd Squadron which arrived over the target after most of the medium bombers had completed their attacks. As they dropped their 16 bombs without result they were aggressively intercepted from all sides by 15 Hamps. Although at least five were shot down by P-38 top cover, one evaded the P-38 cover and badly damaged a B-17, forcing seven crewmen to bail out before plummeting into the ocean. The parachuting crew was strafed as they floated toward the sea 6,000 to 7,000 feet below. These men and the pilots of three P-38s were lost, but the 28 P-38s providing cover shot down at least 15 enemy fighters.

Afternoon Missions

After the morning strikes, the remaining Japanese ships in the convoy were attacked shortly after 1500 in another series of carefully coordinated missions. Allied units received their orders shortly after noon and almost immediately took off from the Moresby airdromes heading toward Lae. In the attack plan all available RAAF A-20 Bostons were to carry out a coordinated attack on the widely scattered convoy's last reported position. The aircraft were to rendezvous at Cape Ward Hunt at 4,000 feet and remain in visual contact during their approach. The primary targets were the transports, with the warships as the first alternative and Lae airdrome the other. Order of assembly and approach to target was one squadron of B-17s at 9,000 feet, one squadron of B-25s at 8,000 feet, one squadron of B-25s at 7,000 feet, one squadron of Beaufighters at 6,000 feet, one squadron of B-25Cs at 5,500 feet, one squadron of B-25s at 5,000 feet, one squadron of A-20s at 4,500 feet, and one squadron of Bostons at 4,000 feet. The order of attack was to strafe the convoy at masthead level first by the Beaufighters, then strafing and bombing by B-25s, then B-25Cs, followed by A-20 Bostons all carrying 500 and 250 pound bombs with five second delay fuses. Then the B-17s were to bomb from 7,000 feet to 10,000 feet with 1,000 pound demolition bombs with instantaneous fusing, followed by one squadron of B-25s bombing from 3,000 to 6,000 feet with 500 pound demolition bombs and instantaneous fuses. In case the enemy convoy was escorted by fighters, Allied fighter cover was to be called in by bomber Flight Leaders who were to identify and locate themselves relative to the convoy.

Initially, the afternoon bombing attacks did not proceed according to plan, as the weather over the Owen Stanleys was poor and none of the Beaufighters crossed the mountains, while 11 A-20s of the 89th Squadron could not climb above or find a hole through the weather, and of the 29 B-25s which took off, six failed to reach the target. But when the remainder of the bomber force arrived they relentlessly attacked the last floating vessels and strafed the Japanese survivors struggling in the water or trying to escape in small boats. For approximately half an hour the remorseless attack continued, and again the Japanese were overwhelmed.

The first of the afternoon attacks of 3 March occurred at 1512. B-17s of the 63rd Squadron reported five vessels in flames and claimed two direct hits on a large destroyer which "stopped and burned." Then the B-25s struck, and within five minutes, the 90th Squadron's eight B-25Cs had left a large destroyer "definitely sinking" after four direct hits from mast height, another probably sinking after four more hits, and two merchant vessels badly damaged (one of which was claimed as sank). At 1517, nine more B-25s from the 405th and 71st Squadrons dropped part of their bombs from medium altitude and the remainder from 200 feet. Six of their 500 pound bombs hit their target, leaving a destroyer burning and exploding and another "ship disintegrated." Five minutes later six B-25s of the 13th Squadron dropped 25 x 500 pound bombs from 5,500 feet. Four of them crashed into a "light cruiser" which was "left in a sinking condition." Almost simultaneously 15 B-17s began their attack. Generally bombing runs were made in flights of three, with each bombardier releasing a bomb every 75 feet. This bombing was also successful, as a direct hit was scored on a merchant vessel which was left "sinking" and other hits were claimed on two destroyers. Before the B-17s had finished their bomb run, five RAAF Bostons circled a hapless destroyer and flew numerous strikes in quick succession, claiming at least two direct hits which, with numerous near misses, were considered sufficient to have caused another sinking.

49FG/7PS/8FS

After the morning attacks some surviving JAAF and JNAF fighters headed back toward Lae airdrome, while others headed for Malahang and were ambushed by diving Eightball Warhawks led by Capt. Ellis Wright, newly promoted to 5FC Assistant Ops Exec., which was supposedly a non-flying position. Wright led his White Flight of four Warhawks beneath the dissipating overcast and orbited the shoreline east of Lae at 8,000 feet. The P-40s dove on the Zekes, which tried to escape, but Wright swept in behind four of them and cut off their approach to Malahang. Wright shot down two Zekes at 400 feet above the waves and just offshore, while Wingman 2Lt. Robert White shot down a Zeke that exploded in the jungle off the south end of the strip. Minutes later, Wright raced up the Bulu River toward Malahang and closed in, unseen, behind another Zeke flight of four and blew up the trailing fighter at point blank range for his third victory of the day. The Second Element of White Flight consisted of Leader 1Lt. Ernest Harris with wingmen 2Lts. Robert Moose and Warren Blakely. Harris and Moose made the first pass, with the victory going to Harris. Blakely shot down another Zeke before a lone Zeke chased him from the area. Red Flight, led by 1Lt. Charles Galatka and flying top cover at 11,000 feet for the 7th Squadron dive bombers, did not encounter any enemy fighters at their altitude. They followed the Demon dive bombing attack on Lae's main runway. Red Flight strafed the runway and a landing barge on the Markham River Delta, which was sunk. Galatka then led his Flight back to 3 Mile Drome in the mid-afternoon.

The 7FS P-40K dive bombers of Blue Flight had just arrived in the 5FC and were not yet permanently assigned, so they were on attached squadron duty for the attack on the convoy. Capt. Robert McHale, Blue Flight Leader, led the four dive bombers from Dobodura to the Lae area, where he had hoped to bomb the convoy at anchor in the harbor. However, by the time his dive bombers reached the Bay in the early afternoon the convoy had already been heavily damaged and its survivors dispersed. McHale then sent his dive bombers up the Markham River Delta to bomb Lae's main runway. In a stacked inline formation, McHale began his bombing attack from 9,000 feet toward the north end of the Lae strip, followed closely by Wingman 1Lt. John Benner. The two released their 500 pound bombs at 1,200 feet before the enemy AA batteries could accurately target their speeding Warhawks. Seconds later, the other Blue Flight element of Flight Leader 1Lt. A.T. House and Wingman Maj. James Martin, who had tagged along on the mission, arrived. Both were forced to pull out of their initial descent after the now alerted Japanese AA gunners quickly adjusted their aim. The duo leveled off briefly at 6,000 feet as heavy caliber flak burst around them, then rolled over into a near vertical dive and dropped

LEFT:: 1Lt. A.T. **House** claimed victories #3 and #4. (AAF)

RIGHT: 1Lt. Robert **White** (L) and Crew Chief after his third and fourth victories. (AAF)

their bombs near the north end of the strip, then strafed down the east flank of the landing area. All four Blue Flight pilots had broken off to the right over the Delta trailed by scattered, inaccurate flak. McHale spotted a lone barge, which the Flight strafed and sank, and then strafed a lugger chugging toward the western shoreline and killed all on board during a number of strafing passes. In his third pass over the smoking barge, House pulled up over the shoreline just above the trees and saw 11 enemy fighters approaching from the east, 3,000 feet overhead. McHale and Benner had both expended all their ammunition while strafing the barge and immediately retreated at full throttle on the wave tops. House and Martin still had ammo, so they turned north over the mainland to engage the approaching Zekes, which had begun to separate into paired elements for their attack. After climbing in a port turn to 2,000 feet over the river delta House had planned to cut off a lone Zeke, but quickly changed his plans when an enemy Wingman headed directly toward the two Americans. House pushed the throttle forward and set up for a head on pass against the onrushing Zeke pilot, who began to fire. The enemy's tracers fell short and House returned a long burst which hit the Zeke's engine. House went into a hard climbing port turn above the Zeke, which had disintegrated in flames. While House climbed, Martin broke to his right and briefly engaged two of the pursuing Zekes that had stalled out in the abrupt maneuver. As House reengaged, one of the Zeke pilots made a fatal mistake and pulled out in front of him. House closed into the enemy's rear quarter, sending the Zeke in flames into the surf near Lae Airfield. Now outnumbered and low on ammo, the Americans fled over the water for a 350 mph escape toward the inland cloud cover. House and Martin searched at 3,000 feet in the broken clouds for the rest of Demon Blue Flight, but both were low on fuel and climbed out of Markham Valley for Moresby. On their approach to the north coast weather forced them to cross the Owen Stanleys far north of Port Moresby, and they redirected and landed safely at Rogers (30 Mile) Field.

35FG/39FS

At 1500, the 39FS went out on its second mission of the day with 18 P-38s and intercepted the last of the Japanese Zekes over Huon Gulf. At 1545 they saw seven Zeros and seven Oscars. The seven Zekes were scattered over their convoy at 5,000 to 7,000 feet, while the seven Oscars were bunched at 17,000 feet. When the 39th attacked the Oscars did not engage and tried to head back toward New Britain, as they probably were low on fuel and were being relieved by the seven Zekes. Capt. Curran Jones added another Zeke to the one he claimed in the morning to become an ace. Three other 39FS pilots (1Lts. Kenneth Sparks and Edward Randall and 2Lt. Harris Denton) claimed damaged Zeros.

Thus ended the last coordinated series of missions against the Lae convoy. In one of the classic victories of air power over sea power, an entire convoy had been destroyed for the loss of a single B-17 and three P-38s. Gen. Kenney's reaction was typical of him: "Tell the whole gang that I am so proud of them I am about to blow a fuse." Meanwhile, reconnaissance aircraft were out searching the battle area, making certain that none of the burning hulks were able to escape during the night. One destroyer was still afloat, and numerous survivors were in the water or trying to escape in barges and launches. For days thereafter mopping up continued. During the following morning at least one other badly damaged destroyer was sunk by B-17s and B-25s. Beaufighters, A-20s, and B-25s searched the seas and strafed survivors headed for New Guinea and other islands as far away as Goodenough and Kiriwina to the east.

4 March 1943: Air Battle over Lae

After debriefing the elated but exhausted pilots of the 5th Air Force collapsed in their tents while the ground crews worked late into the night to repair and rearm the fighters and bombers. Meanwhile, the Operations Staff discussed targets and planned new sorties. Kenney was determined to destroy the remainder of the Japanese Air Forces at Lae on the ground and in the air.

49FG/7FS/8FS

The 7th and 8th Fighter Squadrons were sent out on morning missions and strafed several enemy aircraft on the airstrip unopposed, as the Japanese sent up no interceptors. Later missions were aborted due to heavy rain.

35FG/39FS

As the Beaufighters and Havocs pulverized the airfield at noon, the 39th Squadron tangled momentarily with the enemy Lae Wing. The Lightnings were at 17,000 feet when Zeros and Oscars were spotted at 3 o'clock low. 1Lt. Kenneth Sparks shot down a Zero and Oscar; one on a front quarter attack and the other on a 90 degree attack, and both from 100 yards range for his 8th and 9th victories. 1Lt. Benjamin Widmann shot down a Zero. As the Beaufighters withdrew back to Port Moresby, the Lightning pilots continued east in a sweep of the Huon shoreline. At 1230, 1Lt. Harry Brown called out a dozen patrolling Oscars 40 miles east of Lae and dove into the attack. Brown and Wingman 2Lt. John O'Neill raced through the enemy fighters in three looping passes, and each pilot claimed an Oscar destroyed before the

1Lt. Harry **Brown** claimed his victory since getting a Val over Pearl Harbor. (AAF)

Left: 2Lt. Harry **Brown**. (L) with the 46FS being decorated at Pearl Harbor. (with L-R 2Lts. Philip Rasmussen, Lewis Sanders, Kenneth Taylor, and John Wheeler; all of whom were promoted to 1Lt. that day). (AAF) Right: 2Lt. Kenneth **Sparks** shot down a Zero and Oscar for his 8th and 9th victories. (AAF)

enemy escaped into the clouds. It was Brown's first victory since he shot down a Val over Pearl Harbor while flying a P-40 for the 47FS.

1Lt. Paul Stanch shot down a Zero from astern firing a three second burst from 100 to 50 feet, shattering the canopy and destroying the vertical fin. The Squadron also claimed four probables: one Zero each by 2Lts. Ralph Bills and John Lane and 1Lt. Harry Brown; an Oscar by 1Lt. Charles Sullivan; and four other Oscars damaged by 2Lts. John Dunbar (2), James Walters, and Maj. George Prentice. Stanch was last seen heading down the coast with his port engine trailing smoke from a 20mm shell into his intercooler but returned to base safely.

5 March 1943: Air Battle over Lae

49FG/7FS/9FS

7FS

The next day 12 Eightballs and 16 Demons escorted the RAAF Beaufighters taking off from 17 Mile Drome at sunrise. Green Leader Capt. Raymond Melikian crossed the island in close formation with the Beaufighters under a hazy cloud ceiling at 6,000 feet heading for their attack on Malahang airstrip. Green Flight's fourth man, 2Lt. Duncan Myers, aborted the mission early when his landing gear failed to retract. At 0830 the Australian Beaufighter strafers flew north over the water and then turned to descend for their strafing approach when Oscars were called out to the east, just off shore. The 7FS Green Flight made contact with the 1st Sentai Oscars in a brief but fierce clash over the Markham River Valley, northeast of Lae village. Melikian saw two enemy fighters about a 1,000 ft below and signaled his wingmen to attack, so the two dropped their belly tanks and rolled into an inline pursuit. Melikian, Element Leader 1Lt. Donald Lee, and Wingman 2Lt. David Baker sped inland over the Malahang runway at 4,000 feet, but the Oscars looped up through the cloud ceiling. As the Beaufighters broke off and escaped to the west, Melikian circled his Green Flight 180 degrees to the east, back toward the shoreline, and crossed the Malahang landing pattern. Melikian and Lee each intercepted an Oscar and chased them upward in looping maneuvers. The enemy pilots tried to reach the safety of the clouds but were shot down in flames and crashed into the hills northeast of Lae.

Baker also cut off one of the Oscars, but this Sentai pilot was able to reach the safety of the clouds. Baker followed it and climbed through the haze. He broke out above the overcast to see his Oscar engaged by a flight of Lightnings. Greatly outnumbered and outgunned, the Oscar quickly dove away from the P-38s in a twisting Split-S. Baker dove after him in a 400 mph dive through the haze, but the enemy pilot repeated the looping escape maneuver and the determined Baker again followed. Once the two were above the clouds Baker came within firing range, but the Oscar quickly rolled over and away into the clouds. Baker followed down through the clouds and spotted the Oscar 1,000 feet below, exposed in a large clearing in the overcast. With the altitude advantage, Baker dove and hit the enemy aircraft with a long accurate burst from dead astern and flamed the Ki-43, which dove to a fiery explosion against a hillside north of Lae village. These three 7 FS victories would be the last aerial victories for the Screamin' Demons in the March air battles.

9FS

Shortly after the 7FS left for Moresby, eight P-38s of the 9FS, led by Capt. Robert Vaught, came into the Lae area as part of the high cover for the mid-morning strike. In a short combat, the Flying Knight pilots would engage a scattered enemy fighter formation within the heavy clouds high above the Lae target. Vaught made the only Flying Knight claims on the mission, downing two Zekes in dead astern firing runs and making him an ace. Vaught was forced to withdraw when his Lightning's port engine malfunctioned. As the Squadron left for Dobodura Vaught's other engine began to run rough, just east of Wau village. Vaught's choices were to gamble on the rough-running single engine running all the way to Dobodura, risk a bailing out and possible capture, or finding an alternate landing strip. He decided to try to land at the short dirt strip at Wau. Vaught descended into the Wau pattern, sure that he could stop the big Lightning on the 4,000 foot strip if he landed uphill on the sloping valley floor. He lowered his landing gear and turned into the southern approach above the rows of coffee trees that surrounded Wau Village and the narrow dirt strip. Landing on one engine meant that Vaught had to land with more air speed than usual, so he dropped full flaps to aid in slowing the approach. Suddenly, at 100 feet, his fighter's right engine shut down short of the runway and Vaught had no time to react as the Lightning sank without warning at 120 knots. Without power the fighter pounded into the end of the dirt runway in a large cloud of mud and debris; sliding off the edge of the strip and plowing through the coffee trees, finally coming to a stop as a twisted wreck. The remaining fuel did not ignite, and the rescuers immediately arrived and carefully removed Vaught's lifeless body from the wreckage, which was taken to the small Australian dispensary where a medic pronounced him dead. Vaught's body was wrapped in canvas and put aboard a C-47 for transport back to Moresby. Before the C-47 took off the loadmaster instructed the crew to secure the corpse. When the shrouded body was moved it let out a deep moan and was quickly flown to the hospital at Port Moresby. The tough veteran recovered from his injuries and returned to the States; he would later fly another combat tour in Europe and retire from the Air Force as a Lt. Colonel in 1959.

35FG/39FS

On 5 March, eight P-38s of the 39FS were flying top cover at 11,000 feet for Beaufighters and A-20s. At 0930 two (four?) Oscars were spotted at 6 o'clock low over Lae and Capt. Charles King damaged one.

LEFT: Capt. Ray **Melikian** finished the day with his third and last victory. (AAF)

RIGHT: Capt. Robert **Vaught** scored two victories to become an ace. (AFAA)

Results of the Attack on the Lae Convoy and Lae Airdrome

Kenney's air campaign against the Lae Convoy had been a huge success, and is now referred to as the Battle of the Bismarck Sea. Of the more than 7,000 troops in Gen. Imamura's 18th Army, nearly half had been lost, including the entire 18th Army HQ staff. Fourteen merchant ships and eight warships had been sunk; however, the five Imperial Fleet destroyers which had escaped were able to rescue 2,700 survivors from the Gulf and were then returned safely to Rabaul. Only 900 men from the convoy would ever join the Lae garrison, while thousands of tons of crucial war supplies were lost. The 5FC claims were 27 enemy aircraft destroyed, 12 probably destroyed and nine damaged, while the 5BC bombers shot down 32, probably destroyed 12, and damaged none. The fighter claims were much more accurate than the bomber gunner claims. The bombers expended 233,847 rounds of 20mm, 30 caliber, and 50 caliber ammunition, mainly during strafing attacks, and dropped 514 bombs. The 253 1,000 pound bombs scored 19 hits and 42 near misses, and the 261 500 pound bombs scored 59 hits and 39 near misses. Of 137 500 pound bombs dropped at mast top level 48 scored hits, while only 11 hits were made by the remaining 124 500 pound bombs dropped from 4,000 to 8,000 feet.

The Bismarck Sea victory was due to the successful employment of new tactics and coordination made possible by careful preparation and an accurate evaluation of intelligence. MacArthur emphasized these points in a cable sent on 11 March, saying that the success of the Bismarck Sea action was provided by two main factors: "complete anticipatory diagnosis" of enemy plans and intentions and "careful preparation for and exact execution of coordinated medium and low altitude bombing." These carefully rehearsed tactics, however, would not have been possible without the remarkable technical developments accomplished in the theater: the A-20 attack bomber, the powerful B-25C, and the modified M106 fuse, which had been further customized in New Guinea only 24 hours before the attack. Nevertheless, it is doubtful if the low flying B-25s, A-20s, and Beaufighters could have bombed so destructively had it not been for the careful coordination of a wide variety of attacks: B-17s and B-25s confused the defenders with the accuracy of their bombing from medium altitudes, and the P-38s provided top cover that occupied many defending enemy fighters and prevented them from attacking Allied bombers.

Kenney's 5AF had successfully redeemed itself for its poor showing against the January convoy and canceled the last real opportunity of a Japanese offensive to be based from Lae. The loss of the convoy so discouraged the Japanese that they did not attempt to run further convoys into Lae, which was of great significance. Throughout the Papuan Campaign Kenney's airmen were unable to block off incoming enemy shipping, but in the past three days this was accomplished. From now on enemy troops in the Lae-Salamaua-Mube areas were to be dependent on supplies and reinforcements transported by submarines, air transport, or barges which either crossed Vitiaz Strait from Cape Gloucester or moved down the coast from Madang or Wewak. From then on, initiative in New Guinea would be the Allies', and MacArthur and Kenney immediately went on the offensive to first capture Lae and then expand the campaigns in New Guinea and New Britain.

The Bismarck Sea victory was won by concentrating virtually all available air power against the enemy, and it would have been difficult to repeat this victory if the Japanese immediately sent out other reinforcement convoys. Despite the great victory, the Allies could not assume that their situation in New Guinea was secure, and MacArthur and Kenney needed to fight the overconfidence produced following the victory. MacArthur stated that "We are waging a holding war in this area. Nothing more. We have hardly enough even to do that. The Japanese at Lae are punch drunk but we don't have sufficient troops or equipment to deal the knock out blow." Kenney further stated that if "he were in the Jap's place he could take out the entire 5th Air Force. The Japanese would have to pay plenty for it but it could be done."

Dobodura in Early 1943

For the first time in the New Guinea Campaign, the Dobodura airbase complex, located on the large savannah plain, afforded Kenney the extravagance of having a base with an extensive dispersal area that could accommodate the majority of his Fifth Fighter Command, along with medium bombers, transports, and reconnaissance squadrons.

One of the most critical problems facing planners of immediate and future operations in the SWPA was the arrival of reinforcements and the development of new bases after the conclusion of the Papuan Campaign and after the development of Port Moresby and Milne Bay as advanced bases. Dobodura, a base which had played a crucial part in the winning of the Papuan Campaign, needed to be enlarged and improved. Its airstrips had been cleared and improved by the combined efforts of natives, infantry men, and detachments of the 114th Engineer Battalion and the 43rd Engineer Regiment, and had received transport aircraft by the end of November 1942. But its further development was handicapped not only by the presence of Japanese forces in the area, but by difficulties encountered in moving supplies from the coast to the base. It was planned to build a road from Oro Bay to Dobodura by the middle of January, but work did not actually begun on this project until the first of February, and would not progress far enough to be considered open for traffic until 13 May.

Long before this date, however, the base had been considerably improved. Wharves were constructed in Oro Bay, combat personnel unloaded the small boats that moved along the coast from Milne Bay, and equipment and supplies were carried by jeep or native carriers over improved native tracks to Dobodura. Meanwhile, the troop carriers continued to fly men and materiel onto the base. With each transport plane carrying 5,000 pounds, the average air lift during a period of six weeks in March and April was 300 tons per day. By March a number of service units had arrived to organize the routine of an established air base. A detachment of the 205th Quartermaster Company had been flown to Dobodura shortly after the fall of Buna and Gona in December, and for a time it was the only Quartermaster unit based there. The Company was equipped with only four jeeps and quarter ton trailers with which to fulfill its responsibility for supplying all units in the area, equal to approximately 6,000 men. On 1 January 1943, a C-47 brought a detachment of two officers and 45 men of the 480th Service Squadron from Wards Drome to repair, service, and salvage aircraft in the area. Communications were improved after a platoon of the 440th Signal Battalion arrived in February. Aircraft warning facilities also became far more reliable when the first radar in the Buna area, an Australian set, arrived by air transport in December, and then in February units of the 565th Signal Aircraft Warning Battalion arrived at Oro Bay. By the first of March, radar platoons were located at Oro Bay itself, Tufi, McLaren Harbor, and at Ionanda. Two weeks later these initial service and signal units were joined by the 46th Service Group.

Except for occasional emergency use by fighters from the end of 1942, only transports regularly used Dobodura until, in February, it was decided to post flights of the 49th Fighter Group on alert at Dobodura during the day. Accordingly, in February a small detachment of ground personnel was stationed there and aircraft would fly to Dobodura each morning and return to their Moresby base in the evening. In this way not only was the area north of the Owen Stanleys given greater air protection against enemy aircraft, but the area in which fighters could provide cover for bombers and transports was considerably extended. In fact, the existence of the Dobodura strips, with servicing and refueling facilities, had been a vital factor in maintaining fighter cover for the bombers in the Bismarck Sea victory.

Meanwhile, preparations were being made for the transfer of the entire 49th Group to this advanced base. On 26 February Lt.Col. Robert Morrissey, Group Commander, arrived to scout sites for his headquarters and squadrons. In the middle of March the Headquarters Staff and Squadron, together with the 8th and 9th Squadrons flying P-40s and P-38s, arrived at

Dobodura, leaving only the 7th Squadron to follow about a month later from Moresby. This movement into a forward area met the inherent difficulties in such a change, with aircraft servicing being particularly affected. Fueling facilities were slow and awkward, and high pressure, portable units were needed. Supply and ordnance stores were inaccessible mainly due to a lack of transport equipment. As always, the stock of spare parts was insufficient and the 9th Squadron stripped an out of commission P-38 to keep the remaining 16 serviceable. The incidence of Malaria and Dengue Fever was high, and from 15 to 20% of base personnel were regularly incapacitated; it would not be until late June that improved sanitation measures began to take effect. Once the bivouac site with the usual tents, mess halls, latrines, and garbage disposal facilities had been established, living conditions at Dobodura were probably no worse than in Port Moresby. The Special Service Section set up a post office and regular cable service and arranged for a canteen, movies, a baseball league, a library, and even a band. USO shows occasionally visited Dobodura, with the popular Joe E. Brown visiting during early April.

One of the main operational disadvantages at Dobodura was the lack of reliable communications with ADVON at Port Moresby. Radio was the principal method of communicating, but the central mountains separating Port Moresby and Dobodura, along with the tropical weather conditions frequently interrupted reception. Despite the deep gorges and razorback ridges a telephone line was laid, with units starting at Kokoda on one end and Port Moresby on the other. The impossible task of stringing 150 miles of wire by 230 natives and 100 American and 100 Australian Signal Corps troops supplied by air drops was completed on 24 June, in just over a month. However, the line required constant maintenance due to jungle humidity, which corroded the wire and rotted the poles, and the frequent tropical storms severed the wire.

Maj. Jesse Peaslee's 9FS P-38 operations were located on the south side of Horanda runway in the forest that grew between the landing field and the Safflboga River. The Lightnings would taxi directly onto the main strip to take off to the northeast, often in flights of four abreast on the 500 foot wide dirt runway. Transports landed or took off parallel to the P-38s' operations. The north end of the shorter Kalamazoo runway was known as "Warhawk Row," as the P-40s of Capt. Manning's Demons and Capt. Porter's Eightballs were dispersed in the trees there. They usually took off in pairs to the southeast over the dispersal area of the Flying Knights. This northern dispersal area was also used by the B-26 Marauders of the 22BG, as well as being a staging area for Moresby-based Airacobras in escort to the C-47 transports. The short range Warhawks returned to their tactical missions, or patrolled over Dobodura and Oro Bay, while the 9FS engaged in missions of even greater distances to find the enemy during March. 9FS pilots would challenge the high scoring 39FS P-38 pilots and outscore all other P-38 units over Papua and the Solomon Sea. Thus, during the next seven months, Dobodura would be the hub for Col. Paul Wurtsmith's 5th Fighter Command air offensive against the Japanese, who were based 175 miles to the northwest at Lae and 400 miles to the northeast at Rabaul, on New Britain. The American buildup at Dobodura and Oro Bay threatened the Japanese, and they immediately initiated a counter offensive that would last throughout 1943.

March 1943: Air Situation

In the months following the Bismarck Sea victory over the Lae convoy, there were some indications that the Japanese were actually planning, in Kenney's statement, to "take out the entire 5th Air Force," It was obvious that the enemy did not intend to abandon either the Upper Solomons or New Guinea. Actually, in New Guinea their strength was, if anything, greater than at any time since the Allied victory at Iorabaiwe Ridge, which stopped the Japanese only 30 miles from Port Moresby in September 1942. The enemy's development of Hollandia, Wewak, Hansa Bay, and Madang was not interrupted by the disaster in the Bismarck Sea. Shipping of all kinds, safe from any air assault except heavy bomber attacks, continued to reach those areas, and it was clear to Allied Intelligence that the Japanese thought northwestern New Guinea was destined to assume almost as important a place as New Britain and New Ireland. At the time these latter areas were steadily reinforced.

Aerial photographs and other intelligence sources showed a gradual increase in the number of enemy aircraft based on fields at Rabaul, Kavieng, and in the Solomons. The estimated enemy order of battle for 12 March 1943 reported 159 aircraft on New Britain, 60 on New Ireland, and 145 in the Solomons, but the numbers for 18 March showed that the three Rabaul airdromes alone (Lakunai, Vunakanau, and Rapopo) based 80 medium bombers, 52 light bombers, and 101 fighters.

Allied Southwest Pacific bases were threatened, as enemy aircraft from Rabaul could hit points either in New Guinea or in the Solomons with equal ease. The Japanese had previously shown a facility in deploying their air units and in replacing lost aircraft by transferring others from Yap, Truk, the Palaus, and other bases to the north. The Allies, meanwhile, had received few if any air reinforcements. In March, as had been the case for the previous five months, the total number of aircraft lost outnumbered those received. The March monthly status report showed that the following aircraft reached Australia during that month: 13 B-25s, eight B-24s, one C-47, eight P-38s, and four F-5As (P-38G photo-recon). At the same time four P-38s, two B-17s, one B-25, one P-400, and one A-20 were either lost or reported missing after enemy action; three P-38s were destroyed on the ground; and 11 fighters, seven bombers, nine transports, and one F-4 (P-38E photo-recon) were destroyed in accidents.

This situation was eased to some extent by improved training facilities in the theater and by the return of one Fighter Squadron to combat. In February, the first steps had been taken to establish a replacement center at Charters Towers, Australia. Actually this was a school rather than a replacement center, as its purpose was the acceleration of the assignment of newly arrived personnel to the fighter and bomber commands. This involved a considerable amount of specialized training which had previously been accomplished by tactical units in addition to their combat duties. In April, the 35th Service Group officially assumed the responsibility of the school. The school consisted of two camp areas with mess halls, administration buildings, tents with concrete floors, class rooms, a Link Trainer building, two skeet ranges, and a bombing range. While the school was important for the preparation for future operations, of more significance for the immediate combat problem was the return of the 80FS of the 8FG to duty. Since the middle of February, when it had been evacuated to the mainland from Milne Bay, this unit had been recuperating from its almost total incidence of Malaria, while at the same time training in its newly acquired P-38s. On 21 March an advanced echelon with nine Lightning fighters landed at Kila Airdrome, near Port Moresby, and began to carry out escort missions and stand its share of alerts. The arrival of these new aircraft was welcome at a time when many of the other fighters, particularly the P-40s, were nearly worn out. By the end of March, for example, of the 25 P-40s assigned to the 8th Fighter Squadron, five had flown 400 or more hours, seven had 300 or more, and the remainder had 200 or more. Fighter units, therefore, were slightly better equipped, except in experience, than they had been in the fall of 1942. The same was true of the bombardment units. Consequently, the official tabulation of two heavy, two medium, one light bombardment group, three fighter groups, and two troop carrier groups did not give a true picture of the strength of the Fifth Air Force. Actually, during this period (March through May) there were seven heavy bomber squadrons ready for combat, and of these one was based in Darwin. There were three B-25 medium bomber squadrons and an A-20 squadron available. There were seven fighter squadrons available, but at least five were equipped with obsolete P-39 and P-40 fighters.

By the middle of March, MacArthur and Kenney were informed of the recent JCS decision to reinforce the Fifth Air Force, but only the first of the promised allocations was to arrive within the next two months. On 28 March Kenney was authorized to activate two medium bombardment squadrons, but the personnel and aircraft could not be prepared for operations before the end of June at the earliest. By that time, the 345BG(M) and the 380BG(H) were diverted from the UK and were being ferried to Australia by the end of April.

The outlook for an increase of fighters by the end of June was less promising. The OPD had decided by the end of March that the 345th Fighter Group, equipped with P-47s, would be diverted to the Fifth Air Force from the United Kingdom. The flight and ground echelons were ready to depart by the middle of May, but the aircraft were not, since the P-47D-1s had operational bugs which had to be removed before being committed to combat.

March 1943: First Air Task Force Formed

Under the circumstances, it was obvious that if authorization was required from Port Moresby or Brisbane for every mission based on the north side of the Owen Stanleys these operations would be seriously delayed. The organization in place at the end of the Papuan Campaign was not able to function in this situation. Kenney's Fifth Air Force Headquarters was located in Brisbane, but had to coordinate with MacArthur's GHQ, the Allied Air Forces HQ, and various Australian HQs. ADVON, at Port Moresby, continued to have administrative responsibilities too complicated to permit its movement. A new headquarters was considered necessary to exercise operational control over units based at Dobodura.

Kenney's answer to this problem was the creation of the First Air Task Force in March 1943. This new organization, initially known as the Buna Air Task Force, consisted of fighter, bomber, and troop carrier units which could be attached for an indefinite period or for a particular operation only. When a fighter unit was attached to the task force the Fighter Command retained administrative control, but operational control was assumed by the Task Force. The same applied to bomber units in their relationship with Bomber Command. Theoretically Gen. Whitehead, as Commander of ADVON, retained authority for direction of the operations of combat units in northeast New Guinea. Actually, however, the Commander of the Task Force could assume, when necessary, the responsibility of the posting of his own units on operational missions, including fighter sorties in defense of the area, missions requested by Allied ground troops, and attacks on urgent targets, such as convoys.

There was some difficulty in implementing the organization of the Task Force because of the opinion in Washington that the Fifth Air Force was requesting too many headquarters personnel in higher grades. Kenney insisted that three headquarters for the Fifth Air Force were necessary and wrote that "G-3 has no idea of the details of the problem out here and has no conception of the number of officers required to run a show in three echelons." The Task Force, however, never was officially authorized by the War Department, and personnel had to be taken from other organizations for Task Force Headquarters. Col. Frederick Smith, who continued to be listed on official rosters as Deputy Chief of Staff of the Fifth Air Force, was named to the important position of Task Force Commander. This administrative hocus pocus had to be used to fill all of Smith's staff positions.

Initially, the only combat unit attached to the Task Force was the 49th Fighter Group, but by the end of June the First Air Task Force was a balanced organization. In addition to service units, it consisted of the following squadrons: one P-38, two P-40s, one Beaufighter, one A-20, one B-25C, and one unmodified B-25.

Although the primary purpose of the First Air Task Force was to maintain control of the sea approaches to the Huon Gulf, a secondary role was to provide aircraft for ground cooperation missions. In this the Task Force concept replaced that of an Air Support Command, which had been suggested by AAF Headquarters in Washington. In January, 10 officers trained in air support tactics had arrived in Australia and had become a part of the A-3 section of the Fifth Air Force, with an advanced echelon at Port Moresby. By 1 February Kenney had decided that the theory of an Air Support Command did not suit the SWPA Theater. The functions of the Air Support Command, therefore, were merged with those of the various operations sections: at Port Moresby if the missions in question were the responsibility of ADVON, or at Dobodura if that of the First Air Task Force.

The creation of the First Air Task Force and the merging of air support officers into A-3 sections were generally successful in increasing the flexibility of combat units in the forward areas. Of immediate importance was another new organization which was being planned for troop carrier units to provide a headquarters on the same echelon as the commands for fighter and bomber groups. During the campaigns in the SWPA air transport was to play a vital role in carrying troops, supplies, and equipment.

Air Operations March 1943

8 March 1943: 49FG/9FS

At 1315, 16 P-38s were scrambled to Oro Bay and intercepted a formation of nine Betty bombers 30 miles from Oro Bay headed toward Gasmata at 13,000 feet. At 1345, the Squadron was about 4,000 feet above and slightly ahead of the Bettys when they made their first pass, coming up under the right side of the formation and crossing over toward the left. The first three passes were without effect. Capt. Richard Taylor was warned of three Zeros on his tail by his Wingman, and when he looked around Taylor also saw "about five more half-rolling on me from above, so I dove away steeply." Taylor went into a cloud layer and turned sharply to port; when he emerged from the cloud he saw that he had lost all his pursuers. Taylor turned back toward the bombers, and after several minutes crept up on two Zeros. He fired on the rearmost enemy fighter and both Zeros chandelled up, with one bursting into flame at its wing roots at the top of its chandelle. The other Zero disappeared into the clouds and Taylor continued after the Bettys. He caught them at 6,000 feet in a slight dive and fired a "good burst" at the #2 bomber of the right element from underneath, getting hits on its engines and nose. The Betty left the formation and crashed in a vertical dive into the water. Taylor made several other passes on the Bettys and claimed two more damaged. These were Taylor's only claims of the war, but later he would be credited with only one damaged Betty.

Capt. Richard **Taylor**. (receiving a decoration from Gen. Kenney) had his only two victory claims of the war. (AAF)

11 March 1943: 49FG/8FS/9FS

In mid-morning the Japanese sent a large formation over the Solomon Sea from Lae that was detected by a USN patrol vessel due east of the Allied port at Oro Bay. The 49FG Controllers at Oro Bay, code named *Cator*, immediately alerted the four P-38s of Green Flight patrolling at 15,000 feet over Buna Village to climb and rendezvous with the 8th Squadron. Veteran flight leader 1Lt. Thomas Fowler and his Wingman, 2Lt. Carl Planck, as well as Element Leader 1Lt. William Haning and his Wingman, 2Lt. Keith Oveson, went into a climbing turn to the south, through clouds at 18,000 feet.

Meanwhile, Capt. Lawrence Kirsch led eight old P-40Es of the 8FS from Kalamazoo Strip at Dobodura and labored to climb to 10,000 feet, where they were notified by *Cator* that the Japanese had turned toward Dobodura. Kirsch turned his flights around, and at 1020 the Eightball pilots saw bombs exploding on their base. The raiders turned out toward the sea in the clouds at 19,000 feet with Kirsch' Curtiss fighters in pursuit.

On Horanda strip, 9FS CO Capt. Sidney Woods' standby Red Flight took off just as the string of bombs exploded behind them. Red Flight consisted of Capt. Woods, Wingman 1Lt. Jack Mankin, and Element Leader 1Lt. Richard Bong and his Wingman, 2Lt. Theron Price, but Price's P-38 had engine problems and he aborted the mission.

Meanwhile, Fowler's Green Flight climbed to 26,000 feet when *Cator* informed them that the Japanese formation had now descended to 15,000 feet. Green Flight dropped their belly tanks and went into a deliberate descent, and shortly Fowler spotted a formation of 24 Bettys with an escort of about 25 Zeros that trailed the bombers. Fowler led his flight over the enemy formation to position themselves at 23,000 feet and up sun from the enemy's right flank. The Flight peeled off to port, diving on the bombers, but as the four Lightnings dove three Zeros turned into them, causing the Americans to divert their attack from the bombers. The Zeros and Lightnings fired on each other in a high speed head on pass. Fowler hit his target with a sustained burst and immediately broke to starboard when he saw he was being followed by a Zero. Wingman Planck simultaneously broke to port to protect his Flight Leader from a turning Zero and riddled the enemy from point blank range. Planck was forced to dive away when other Zeros appeared and then turned and climbed back to the combat. At 25,000 feet Planck saw a P-38 below in a shallow dive trailing smoke, but Planck was unable to go to the rescue, as he was attacked by more Zeros and was again forced to dive to safety.

The P-38 that Planck saw was that of Element Leader William Haning, who was left alone when he and his Wingman, 1Lt. Keith Oveson, engaged the Zeros. Oveson was forced to withdraw from the fight, leaving Haning to contend with three Zeros. After an initial high speed turn Haning shot down a Zero with a perfect 90 degree deflection shot. He then turned to dive on another Zero, but its veteran pilot turned into his attack and the two closed on each other and both fired. The closing speed was so great that Haning could not avoid a collision, and his starboard wingtip sheared through the enemy's cockpit; the enemy fighter flew away trailing smoke. Haning was able to quickly regain control and turned northwest, but his engines were shuddering and leaking Prestone coolant. Haning throttled back, he saw another Zero in the distance turn after him. Haning was able to remain ahead of the enemy pilot for 20 miles before the enemy entered into a shallow dive to catch the vulnerable Lightning over the coast. Haning nosed over into a diving turn for another head on firing pass. The two pilots closed and fired on each other in two passes, but Haning's fighter was too damaged and he was unable to maneuver away from the Zero, whose cannon fire destroyed Haning's cockpit and set his engines on fire. Haning climbed out of the cockpit and pulled the parachute ripcord just as his fighter exploded. Haning landed just off Oro Bay and was quickly rescued by an Australian tugboat.

Kirsch's Warhawks and Woods' Lightnings could see Green Flight in combat east of Oro Bay and turned to help. Woods' P-38s dropped their belly tanks and quickly passed Kirsch's old P-40s. Woods, with Mankin and Bong in close echelon formation to his left, overtook the Bettys flying in a formation of three V elements 30 miles offshore and positioned themselves for a slightly higher frontal assault. The three P-38s turned into a continuous firing pass against the right flank, then turned back for a second pass. The three Flying Knights were forced to break off the fight by a superior force of Zeros. Woods dived for the coast at 450 mph until the pursuing escorts turned away. Jack Mankin also lost his pursuers by taking refuge in the clouds and tried to locate the bombers again, but they had disappeared in the clouds. Soon he encountered a few of the trailing escorts and maneuvered with two of them; he hit one that stalled out in a climbing turn. In the combat Mankin lost his combat advantage against the Zero Wingman and was forced to dive away for the coast.

Bong, at the tail end of the Flight, had Zeros on his tail and escaped in an intense 475 mph vertical dive; he pulled out just above the waves and sped away. He realized he was headed due east and away from safety with one enemy fighter following at a distance behind. Bong reversed course and immediately had the approaching Zero in his gunsight. The Zero pilot was not expecting Bong's reversal of course, as he did not jettison his belly tank. Bong fired a long burst into the enemy fighter, then kicked left rudder and raced past as it erupted in flames. Bong was surprised by still another Zero carrying its tank coming at him head on. Bong quickly adjusted with left rudder and fired a short burst into the Zero's fuselage as seven more Zeros approached him head on. Bong laid on his right rudder and fired a long 20 degree deflection burst at the closest Zero, then reversed with left rudder as the Zero wingmen unsuccessfully tried to maneuver away, giving Bong his seventh and eighth victories. Bong tried to accelerate away from the pursuing Zeros, but one made a pass on him from the left rear quarter and hit his port engine with a short burst. Bong's faster Lightning allowed him to escape before the engine ran out of coolant. Bong feathered the engine and made a single engine landing at Horanda. Following are excerpts from Bong's ICR:

> "I took off just ahead of the falling bombs and climbed up to 24,000 feet. We intercepted the bombers on their way home. I made a 20-degree pass from ahead and above and put a good burst in the last bomber. There were no observed results. Nine fighters dove on me, and I had to dive to 475 mph indicated to get away. I tried to go back for another pass at the bombers but was intercepted by Zeros and chased down to water level.
>
> "We were headed toward Gasmata. I flew straight until I could see only one Zero behind me. I made a 180 degree turn

Capt. Sidney **Woods** scored the first of his two victories in the Pacific. (AAF)

1Lt. William **Haning** scored his only two victories of the war and was shot down but rescued. (AAF)

11 March **9FS** Victors:(L-R) 1Lt. Thomas **Fowler**. (1v), Capt. Sidney **Woods**. (1v), 1Lt. Jack **Mankin**. (1v), and 1Lt. Richard **Bong**. (2v). (AAF)

1Lt. William **Day** scored two victories to become an ace. (AFAA)

and put a long burst into the Zero head on. Instead of only one Zero, there were nine or more, and I turned 5 degrees left and put a short burst into another Zero head on. Both of these had their belly tanks on. Turned 10 degrees right and put a long burst into another Zero from 20 degrees deflection, then I turned 20 degrees left to observe the results.

"The first two Zeros were burning all around the cockpit, and the third one was trailing a long column of smoke. Three Zeros split-essed down on me and shot up my left engine and wing while I was running for home. I feathered the left engine and landed at home field safely."

After emptying their auxiliary fuel tanks, Kirsch's P-40s finally caught the Japanese 50 miles off shore. Kirsch was determined to attack the bombers after the Red Flight P-38s had failed. Kirsch's Flight was composed of his rookie Wingman, 2Lt. Leo Mayo, and veteran Ops Exec. 1Lt. Clyde Barnett and his Wingman, 2Lt. Benjamin Duke. As Red Flight retreated, Kirsch's Warhawks approached the Betty formation from 21,000 feet; unfortunately, the embattled Zeros were able to regroup and cut off Kirsch's flight before the Eightballs reached the bombers. The four Americans maneuvered through several turns with the Zeros until Mayo's P-40 was hit by a 20 mm shell which entered through the left rear of the canopy window and exploded in the cockpit. The shell wounded him in the hand and arm and destroyed many of his instruments, and the rookie pilot had enough and dove away from the battle. In the Flight only Barnett scored when he caught a Zero in a left turn, setting its engine on fire and then closing in at close range to finish it off before he returned to Kalamazoo.

The second 8FS Flight was led by veteran 1Lt. William Day, who had three rookies (1Lt. William Lown and 2Lts. Daniel Moore and Robert Hagerstrom) under his command. Their old Warhawks struggled to reach 22,500 feet and arrived just after the Kirsch Flight left to engage the enemy escorts below. With the altitude advantage Day's flight dove on the bombers, and as Lown and Hagerstrom closed behind the bombers they fired but, in their inexperience, misjudged the range at their high closing speed and missed. The two Americans were unable to make a second pass at the bombers, as their old Warhawks just did not have the power to catch the retreating bombers again. As Hagerstrom dove away from the bombers a Zero passed in front of him and he fired and claimed a victory that was not substantiated.

Day and Moore teamed up to fire on the same Betty in the right V element and both scored hits, but Day was credited with the victory (probably because he was the Flight Leader). The two then passed under the bomber formation and turned for another firing run, but Zero escorts approached at their altitude. Moore turned away, but the veteran Day went after the Zero who had briefly pursued Lown. Day closed inside the Zero's turn and fired, scoring hits on its fuselage before five of his six guns jammed during the high G turn. Day effectively used his lone .50 caliber to hit the enemy's cockpit and engine, but then his Warhawk stalled and a Zero got several rounds into Day's fuselage before he was able dive to safety in the clouds below. Day had Betty and Zero claims confirmed for his fourth and fifth victories, making him the first Warhawk ace over New Guinea. All of the Eightballs returned to Dobodura Kalamazoo to find that the Japanese had bombed their operations area and several of the ground crew were killed or wounded.

After the combat on 11 March the 8FS continued their patrols over Dobodura and Oro Bay, while the P-38s of the 9FS Flying Knights returned to their long range escort for the Fifth Bomber Command; neither would have any enemy contact for the next two weeks. Group CO Morrissey ordered the 7FS to move their ground and air echelons from Moresby to Dobodura by the end of March, where they would share Kalamazoo with Eightball P-40s.

LEFT: 1Lt. Jack **Mankin** shot down a Zero for his first victory of five. (AAF)
RIGHT: 2Lt. Carl **Planck** shot down a Zero for his last victory before being shot down and rescued after two months. (AAF)

1Lt. Richard **Bong** scored two victories: #s 7 and 8 and added two probables but had his vertical stabilizer and port engine damaged by enemy fire. (AAF)

14 March 1943

During a night raid on Oro Bay, 15 more Japanese bombers again damaged waterfront installations and set a small fuel dump on fire, then retreated without loss.

17 March 1943

Eighteen enemy bombers escorted by 32 fighters bombed Porlock Harbor at midday, causing some damage and again escaping without loss.

24 March 1943: 35FG/39FS: Lynch Named CO

Maj. Thomas Lynch was named CO of the 39FS when Maj. George Prentice was assigned to take over the newly formed 475FG, the first all P-38 Group in the Pacific. Prentice had ably served the 39th since 18 September 1942. Lynch, who had scored nine victories at the time, would lead the 39th with six more victories (15 total) until he went home in September, and would be replaced by Maj. Charles King. On his return to the theater Lynch would freelance with the 5FC HQ, scoring five more victories before he was killed nearly a year later.

25 March 1943: 49FG

As the Japanese prepared for their next air operations they sent high speed reconnaissance aircraft to scout the Allied Dobodura-Oro Bay facilities. Capt. William Haney led a patrol of five Lightnings over Buna at 20,000 feet when *Cator* Air Controller vectored them to a solo aircraft in their area. Haney proceeded north and spread his formation over a wider search area; they found a Betty cruising at 24,000 feet, headed due west. Haney was joined by veteran 1Lt. Edgar Ball, and as the Betty passed over Dobodura, Ball attacked first and killed the rear gunner while raking the fuselage. Haney then closed to point blank range and finished it off. Since Ball made the first devastating attack he was given credit for the victory (as per Olynyk).

7FS at an awards ceremony before their move to Dobodura. (AAF)

Capt. Kenneth **Johns** scored his second and last victory and two probables. (AAF)

1Lt. Harry **Lidstrom** shot down his only enemy aircraft of the war. (AAF)

2Lt. Martin **Alger** got his first of four career victories. (AAF)

1Lt. Floyd **Finberg** also claimed his only victory. (AAF)

28 March 1943: 49FG/8FS/9FS

During the previous three days the Japanese continued to dispatch small day and night raids against the Allies, as well as daily reconnaissance flights that were not intercepted. In mid-morning the JAAF and JNAF sent the largest formation thus far from New Britain to attack an Allied convoy of a dozen ships that had just arrived at Oro Bay. The Japanese heavy bombers would successfully avoid interception, but the Val dive bombers and their Zeke and Oscar escorts were intercepted after attacking Oro Bay.

At 1115 the Blue Flight patrol of five 9FS Lightnings led by the Darwin veteran 1Lt. Clyde Harvey was vectored from their air patrol east of Dobodura southward for Oro Bay, where *Cator* reported a large enemy formation approaching from the east at 16,000 feet. Blue Flight made a climbing turn to 27,000 feet over Oro Harbor, where Harvey soon spotted a formation of single engine aircraft that he estimated as a force "unable (to be) counted as they were too scattered, and I estimated 50 to 60 Zeros scattered all over." Smoke towered from two damaged vessels of the Allied convoy and from the fires raging on the docks. Four Bettys were also seen escaping in the distance, too far out of range to chase, but the even larger throng of Val dive bombers and fighter escorts were directly below, just turning away from their attacks on the harbor. Flight Leader Harvey immediately ordered his Flight to jettison their belly tanks for the attack, but 2Lt. Keith Oveson, the last man in the flight, was unable to drop his tanks and was sent to high position as a spotter for *Cator*. Harvey and 2Lts. Clay Peterson, Walter Markey, and John O'Neill dove after the retreating enemy formation in a broad "S" turn and separated to choose individual targets.

When the Blue Flight patrol answered *Cator*, two standing patrols of Eightball P-40s over Buna Village also answered the 1115 alert from *Cator*. The Red Flight was led by Mission Leader Capt. Kenneth Johns, with Wingman 2Lt. Robert Howard, Element Leader 1Lt. Cecil Dewees, and rookie Wingman F/O Merle Wolfe. 8FS Blue Flight was led by Darwin veteran 1Lt. Rufus Jordan, with Wingman 2Lt. Stanley Hunter, Element Leader 1Lt. Robert Moose, and Wingman 2Lt. Russell Francis. Johns led the Warhawks parallel to the coast, climbing to 24,000 feet over the burning shipping and docks at Oro Bay and above the escaping Vals just above the water. Blue Flight P-38s had just begun their diving attack, and Johns ordered his eight P-40s to drop their tanks and dive into the battle.

The 9FS Alert Flights at Dobodura scrambled on *Cator's* warning. At 1130 the Green Flight, led by Capt. William Haney, with wingmen 1Lt. Floyd Finberg and rookie 2Lt. Grover Fanning, left Horanda strip and were followed closely by three Lightnings of Yellow Flight led by Ops Exec 1Lt. Harry Lidstrom, with wingmen 2Lts. Arthur Beauhof and Martin Alger. These two Flights climbed to 24,000 feet, where Haney saw the approaching

Val dive bombers at Oro Bay and heard the 49ers in battle over the radio. Haney spread out the six P-38s in his flights and had them drop their fuel tanks and dive after the escaping enemy.

The following half hour of combat was a confusion of swirling American and Japanese fighters over the Solomon Sea. Capt. Johns' Red and Lt. Jordan's Blue P-40 Flights of the 8FS had initially been intercepted at 5,000 feet by the Oscars and Zeros from the close Val escort. Johns and Wingman Howard were able to penetrate the Oscar escorts to attack the Val dive bombers, and each claimed one destroyed and two probables. Johns and Howard broke off their attack to return to base and were joined just off shore by P-38s also fleeing Oscars. Captain Johns fired a wide deflection shot but missed, and he and Howard, running low on fuel, finally broke off for a safe landing at Kalamazoo.

Meanwhile, the initial 9FS Blue Flight attack was immediately attacked by the Japanese square-wing tipped Navy escorts. 2Lt. Walter Markey claimed a fighter in the first pass, and in the subsequent combat, Flight Leader 1Lt. Clyde Harvey and Wingman 2Lt. John O'Neill each claimed one, while 1Lt. Floyd Finberg downed a fourth and Ops Exec 1Lt. Harry Lidstrom then claimed a fifth enemy fighter.

8FS Red Flight's Element Leader Cecil Dewees and Wingman Merle Wolfe had separated from Red Leader Johns, due to Wolfe's slow climbing old Warhawk. After Dewees and Wolfe finally edged up to 22,000 feet, they saw Vals at 7,000 and dove on them together. Dewees fired at a Val flying in a V, but rookie Wolfe's P-40 struggled to hold his Wingman position as Dewees maneuvered for another pass. Wolfe did not notice that an Oscar had closed from behind to fire on Dewees, who was killed instantly by cannon shells that hit his cockpit. Soon cannon tracers whizzed past Wolfe's fighter and he dove for the coast. He pulled out at wave top level and raced in panic westward under the last of the fleeing enemy aircraft. When he crossed the coast just south of Buna he climbed to 6,000 feet to rejoin his Squadron, but was approached by a pair of Warhawks that dove through the hazy overcast and then just as suddenly disappeared. The completely exhausted Wolfe finally landed at Kalamazoo alone.

Meanwhile, the 8FS Blue Flight Leader Jordan and his wingmen had become widely separated after the first pass, but nonetheless fared well in the individual dogfights that followed: Jordan, Hunter, and Francis each claimed one Zero, while Moose claimed three destroyed. All four White Flight pilots returned safely to Kalamazoo.

Several minutes after the 9FS Knights' Blue Flight patrol's initial combat, Haney's combined Green-Yellow Flight of six P-38s dove on the rear defense flown by Haps. 1Lt. Martin Alger dove his Lightning to low altitude to aid a P-38 that was pursued by five Haps and closed on the last enemy fighter. After a long chase he fired and torched the Hap, which rolled over and plunged into the ocean. Alger immediately pulled up, but flew into cannon fire from a pair of trailing enemy wingmen and a 20 mm round exploded against his horizontal stabilizer. Alger immediately made a high speed turn into his opponents and fired, dispersing the Haps. Alger quickly climbed and made several head on passes against other Haps and scored a probable. Haney was credited with a probable in the battle.

29 March 1943: 49FG/9FS

Near mid-day, during a high altitude patrol north of Buna, a 9FS flight of four P-38s led by Darwin veteran 1Lt. Robert McComsey, with Wingman 1Lt. Leroy Donnell, Element Leader 2Lt. Clay Barnes, and Wingman 1Lt. Richard Bong, were vectored south to locate a lone enemy recon aircraft. The bogey evaded the Flying Knight patrol by flying in a large cloud formation that rose to 25,000 feet. McComsey spread his elements to broaden their search area and Barnes soon spotted a twin engine JNAF Dinah which had turned north back toward New Britain. After a 20 mile high speed chase down to 18,000 feet, Barnes and Bong closed and both fired at the evading enemy and missed, trying not to be hit by the return fire of the enemy rear gunner. On the fourth firing pass, Bong faced the return fire and fired from dead astern, hitting the Dinah's fuel tanks. The enemy disintegrated into a huge ball of fire, giving Bong his ninth victory to tie rival Capt. Thomas Lynch for top scorer in the SWPA.

30 March 1943: 8FG: First P-38 Mission

By the end of March the 80FS was considered ready for limited operations from Moresby's 5 Mile Drome. On 30 March four 80FS P-38s took off at 1140 to fly cover for A-20s, B-25s, and Australian Beaufighters to Finschhafen. The 80th Lightnings rendezvoused with ten P-38s of the 39FS over Cape Ward Hunt. At 1300 the Allied formation arrived over the target and the B-25s began their bombing and strafing run, followed by the A-20s, and finally by the Beaufighters. The attacks were very successful, with nine fires started and the landing strip rendered unserviceable. Since there was very little flak the Beaufighters remained over the target, but several of the P-38s flying top cover were running low on fuel before the Australians left the area at 1410. Clouds closed in over the mountains on the way back to base, and the 80th Lightnings landed at Dobodura almost out of fuel. They refueled and remained at Dobodura overnight, then left the next morning for 3 Mile.

P-38 Bootlegging Transports

Enterprising pilots of the 8FG found that the P-38 fighter could carry 58 fifths of liquor or beer in various parts of its airframe. Besides the obvious cockpit and luggage space, the radio and hydraulic spaces, and the storage space for operating manuals and technical orders were utilized. For a large alcohol run the space in the .50 caliber ammunition cans, the large area normally used for 20 mm cannon ammunition, and the 20 mm shell ejection space were put to use, hoping that the defenseless bootlegging Lightning would not be attacked. Enterprising Ground Crewmen cut an opening in the top of drop tanks which were then stuffed with wrap-protected beer or spirit bottles. There is a story of a pilot landing at a more civilized base with an ice making machine, filling the drop tank with ice and beer, and flying back to his base with a cargo of ready to drink cold beer.

4

April 1943

April 1943: Situation

In March 1943 the Wau garrison, called the Kanga Force, consisted of the Australian 17th Brigade, whose functions were to infiltrate the enemy positions in the Mubu area, to force the abandonment of these forward strong points, and to prevent the Japanese from landing troops in sufficient strength to oppose American invasions along the coast. The first of the amphibious moves was to be carried out under the general supervision of the Australian New Guinea Force. The principal American unit involved was the 41st Infantry Division, commanded by Maj.Gen. H.H. Fuller. Allied ground forces were advancing up the New Guinea coast, and on 31 March troops landed at the mouth of the Waria River and at Dona, which not only provided Allied aircraft with another emergency landing strip, but put American troops within 75 miles of Salamaua. On 3 April elements of the 162nd Combat Team of the 41st Infantry Division went ashore unopposed at Morobe Harbor. In five weeks the advance brought American forces to within 75 miles of Salamaua against weak enemy opposition, so air support was unnecessary.

Nevertheless, in spite of little ground opposition, the continuation of Japanese activity at other points was sufficient indication that the enemy still intended to maintain itself in New Guinea. Allied Intelligence reports during March, April, and May continually described the construction of airfields at Hollandia, Wadke, Wewak, and a number of other areas, and the construction of a road network around Madang, together with reports of a continual flow of shipping into Wewak. In addition, Japanese submarines made frequent attacks off the Australian coast, and the threat of Japanese air attacks was ever present. Under these circumstances, the functions of Gen. Whitehead's Advanced Air Echelon and Col. Smith's First Air Task Force were many and varied. They included photo and armed reconnaissance, antisubmarine patrol, convoy, troop carrier, and bomber escort, together with the conventional tactical functions of destroying the enemy air force, isolating the forward areas, and destroying selected objectives on the battlefield itself.

Following the 28 March raid on Oro Bay there was a pause in enemy air activity over New Guinea, as the Japanese concentrated to the east, where their aircraft were repeatedly attacking Allied bases in the Solomon-New Georgia area. Allied Intelligence forecast, however, that the Japanese would soon reassume their air offensive on New Guinea with the largest air forces they had ever assembled in the Southwest Pacific Area. On 5 January 1943 the Japanese had 145 aircraft on New Britain, and on 6 April this total had increased to 271 (93 fighters and 144 bombers), while on New Ireland these totals were no aircraft on 5 January and 97 (57 fighters and 36 bombers) on 6 April, and 74 aircraft in the Solomons on 5 January and 112 (54 fighters and 23 bombers) on 6 April. The question remained; would the Japanese deploy these air forces to Guadalcanal or against Allied bases on New Guinea? Previously the Japanese had shown great flexibility in their employment of their air forces, and on 7 April a large force of enemy bombers and fighters hit Guadalcanal. Four days later, on 11 April, a force of 15 enemy dive bombers heavily escorted by 30 Zeke and Oscar fighters was intercepted off Oro Bay by 50 P-40s and P-38s of the 49FG.

April 1943: Status of the 5th Fighter Command

During an attack on 28 March the final Eightball Flight led by 1Lt. Ernest Harris was scrambled from Kalamazoo, but their old P-40E models were again unable to reach combat altitude in time for contact. Even when airborne on patrol, the war-weary P-40Fs could scarcely climb to effective altitude in the same time it took the standby P-38s to scramble from Horanda to reach 20,000 feet. Eightball CO Capt. James Porter's 8FS had repeatedly proven themselves by continuing operations flying the oldest Warhawks in the AAF, but their assigned patrol area stretched from Cape Ward Hunt to Salamaua, which was beyond their operational limits. Porter was down to 18 serviceable P-40Es, and there was an acute shortage of spare parts, with engines, tires, and radio equipment in very limited stock. The 7FS Screamin' Demons flew the newer P-40Ks, but there weren't enough of them to cover the patrol area from Salamaua to Lae. In the face of future renewed enemy attacks, eight Warhawks from Capt. Manning's 7th Squadron were reassigned to relieve the Eightball patrol area. But those Warhawks would never be the equal of a flight of Lightnings. The superior Lightnings were even more in short supply. Capt. Sidney Woods' 9FS Flying Knights' Lightnings had become the most successful squadron over New Guinea, but they, too, were at their operational limit, with only 20 Lightnings serviceable most of the time.

While the old Warhawks clearly had to be replaced, the Airacobras had failed to make contact with enemy during all of March. Fifth Fighter

Command needed more modern fighter aircraft and additional combat units. Fortunately, the monsoon season had negated Lae as a current threat, thus obviating Dobodura's dangerously low fuel supply and the lack of pilots available for 48 hour rotation.

The 39FS Cobras at 14 Mile Drome had just completed reorganization under their new commander, leading 5AF ace Capt. Thomas Lynch, with nine victories. Former 39FS CO Maj. George Prentice was transferred to form the new 475FG all-P-38 group that was scheduled to begin operations by early May. Prentice had been given free rein to recruit the necessary pilots from the existing units, and several 49FG veterans left P-40 units to fly the superior P-38, which not only increased their survival chances, but being veterans in a new unit increased their chances for promotion and to fly as mission leaders. Experienced P-40 line crews were also commandeered by Prentice. As qualified pilots and crew chiefs transferred out of the 7th and 8th squadrons, Lt.Col. Morrissey and Group Ops Exec. Martin were able to temporarily induct staff officers from Fighter Command to fill the vacancies.

1 April 1943: 6NSF Arrives

MacArthur had first requested night fighters in October 1942 and repeated the request four months later. Delivery was delayed until an agreement was reached with the British in regard to night fighter protection in North Africa, "where the political situation and the possibility of concentrated night bombing made the matter one of paramount importance."

The 6th Night Fighter Squadron was stationed at Kipapa Airfield, HI, on 17 November 1942, from where a detachment was sent to Koli Airfield, Guadalcanal, on 28 February 1943, and another detachment was sent at MacArthur's request to Port Moresby, New Guinea. Newly trained night fighter teams arrived from Florida in late February to form the New Guinea Detachment, joining with the 6NFS at Kipapa Field for six weeks for additional training in the P-70 Night Hawk, the night fighter version of the A-20. Like the detachment on Guadalcanal, the New Guinea detachment was separated from the 6th Night Fighter Squadron and designated Detachment "A" Night Fighter Squadron.

On 19 March 1943 the 6th's second Detachment began its long journey across the Pacific under the command of Capt. Warren Hornaday. The flight consisted of six P-70s and two LB-30s carrying support personnel and equipment (one navigating and one trailing). Their route took them to Christmas Island, Canton Island, Wallis, Nandi, and New Caledonia, then to Brisbane, Australia, and finally Townsville. The flight left Townsville and arrived at 3 Mile (Kila) on 1 April, where they had their first jarring experience landing on pierced metal planking. As the P-70s' wheels hit the planking the great noise scared the heck out of the crews.

The Detachment's mission was to intercept enemy bombers sent over the installations around Port Moresby at night. However, these attacks were sporadic, making continual patrols unfeasible, so one plane was scrambled when ground radar picked up the enemy coming over the Owen Stanleys or down the coast. Each evening the Detachment would fly two or three planes from 3 Mile (Kila) to stand alert at 7 Mile airdrome (Jackson) and return to 3 Mile the next morning. Kila was not usable for night operations due to its short runway and the hills at each end of the runway, while 7 Mile was longer and had better approaches for night operations.

The P-70 Nighthawk proved unsatisfactory, as it took 20 to 25 minutes to climb to 20,000 feet at full power and another 15 minutes to reach 25,000 feet. It had hand fuel pumps, and "the pilot would be having a hell of a time pumping" at the same time he was trying to fly. When it finally reached altitude, "maneuverability was nil, and it was impossible to get up any overtaking speed." The Service Command experimented with improvements in Australia, and the 27th Depot Repair Squadron at Port Moresby added a number of other improvements. P-38 fuel boosters were installed behind engine-driven pumps to maintain constant fuel pressure at the highest altitudes; the B-17 paddle-type propellers replaced the original blades; a

The 6th **Night Fighter Squadron** arrived at Port Moresby flying the unsatisfactory **P-70 Nighthawk** night fighter version of the A-20. (AAF)

part of the air scoops were cut off to make room for the new propeller; all unnecessary weight was deleted by removing the bomb bay tank, the rear .30 caliber machine gun, and the .50-caliber flexible gun, as well as much of the armor plate; and two forward-firing .50-caliber guns were added. These modifications increased the combat ceiling about 5,000 feet and the speed almost 60 miles an hour.

Besides the P-70's poor performance, the New Guinea Detachment encountered the same problems that had plagued the Guadalcanal Detachment, mainly poor GCI coverage. The Owen Stanley Mountains behind Port Moresby created a constant ground echo. The P-70's radar equipment usually worked only intermittently, and often would fail entirely at altitudes over 20,000 feet. Bad weather would give false indications on the radar or cause the picture on the scope to fade out completely. The GCI operator's proficiency was quite good when the Detachment started their operations, but replacement personnel who arrived later proved to be unsatisfactory. The VHF radio equipment used in the aircraft at this time was at an early stage of development and did not function well, so the aircrews usually relied on their HF communication equipment. But the problem with using this equipment was that the Japanese could monitor the HF frequencies that the GCI/P-70 crews were using. The Japanese usually attacked in two plane raids, each plane spread 10 to 15 minutes apart, and would start taking evasive action as soon as they heard the GCI controller start vectoring the interceptor. The New Guinea Detachment suffered the same lack of cooperation with the searchlight/AA batteries as was experienced by the Guadalcanal Detachment. The old question was whether the AA should have a free field of fire or if it should be curtailed to give the night fighter a chance to make the kill. New Guinea AA had its way, and the P-70s were under orders not to enter the 12 mile radius of the AA zone of fire. New Guinea AA did not bring down a single enemy aircraft during the Detachment's stay. Soon the Detachment was sending three of their P-70s to the grass Horanda airstrip near Dobodura, on the north side of the island, to stand alert there also.

The first 6NSF fatality on New Guinea was that of CO Capt. Hornaday and his R/O, F/O Howard Krause, shortly after their arrival. Hornaday was flying under the hood in a practice flight, accompanied by a P-70 flown by John Florence. They entered a thin cloud layer, and when Florence exited he did not see Hornaday's P-70. Later an AA battery on the coast reported that Hornaday's plane had crashed into the sea. Capt. Robert McLeod became CO of the Detachment.

At both their 3 Mile and Dobodura bases on New Guinea, the 6th's responsibilities were to stand dawn to dusk alerts, with no patrols. The night fighters would be scrambled only when an unknown aircraft was detected on the GCI, usually about 30 miles out, and then the P-70 would be scrambled and vectored into position for the attack.

1-16 April 1943: *Operation I-Go*

While MacArthur continued to build up his forces in Papua, Adm. Isoroku Yamamoto and Jinichi Kusaka planned a major offensive, code-named *Operation I-GO*, for the Combined Mobile Fleet to finally annihilate the Allied air forces in the Solomon Islands and New Guinea with the most aggressive air attacks of the war. The goal of the operation was to halt the Allied offensives in New Guinea and the Solomons, and to give Japan time to prepare a new set of defenses in response to recent defeats to the Allies at Guadalcanal and in New Guinea at Buna-Gona, Wau, and the Bismarck Sea. Japanese fleet carriers flew off their Mobile Fleet air wings to the units at Truk Lagoon and at Rabaul, and by the beginning of the second week of April, almost 350 JNAF and JAAF combat aircraft congested the New Britain airfields. The operation consisted of several massed aerial attacks by Japanese bomber and fighter aircraft based at Rabaul, Bougainville, and the Shortland Islands against Allied targets on and around Guadalcanal and the Russell Islands in the Solomons and Port Moresby, Oro Bay, and Milne Bay in New Guinea.

Adm. Isoroku **Yamamoto**. (L) and Jinichi **Kusaka**. (C) planned Operation I-GO which planned for the Combined Mobile Fleet to finally annihilate the Allied air forces in the Solomon Islands and New Guinea. (AFHRC)

3 April 1943: 49FG/8FS

March ended, and early April brought a momentary lull in the air attacks on Papua. During the morning patrol eight 8FS Warhawks were patrolling off Cape Ward Hunt when 1Lt. Robert Moose and 2Lt. Stanley Hunter collided and both were lost.

11 April 1943: 49FG/7FS/8FS/9FS

9FS

At 1130 hours, Maj. Jesse Peaslee and 14 White Flight Flying Knights were over Dobodura at 24,000 feet when *Cator* vectored them due east to the coast to meet a large enemy formation approaching Oro Bay. At Horanda and Kalamazoo the standby units were scrambled toward their intercept areas. As Peaslee's White Flight neared Oro Bay *Cator* ordered the Flight to hold over Cape Sudest, at the mouth of the Samboga River. Peaslee did not understand the reason for *Cator's* vector, which would put him far out of combat range, and ordered his senior Flight Leader, 1Lt. Clyde Harvey, to lead 1Lts. Richard Bong, Harold Hoize, and Theron Price south toward Oro Harbor.

In their initial descent, Element Leader Richard Bong's P-38 experienced engine problems and he returned to Dobodura. Flight Leader Harvey, with Price and Hoize, continued down to 20,000 feet, and just north of Oro Bay spotted 12 Oscars of the 1st Sentai cruising above the thin overcast that covered the coastline at 15,000 feet. The three Lightnings dropped their belly tanks and dove into combat, but as they descended Price was forced to break away and turn into an Oscar that had suddenly come upon their rear quarter. Price fired a burst at the attacker that caused the pilot to roll away. The Knight trio then maneuvered into several high speed turns with the other Oscars, but these counter maneuvers split up the White Flight, and Hoize dove away at 400mph with three Oscars on his tail. Price and Harvey continued to dogfight against the odds and Price shot down one of the Ki-43s. A machine gun round shattered Price's canopy and he was hit with Plexiglas and shrapnel, and both Americans dove away. Harvey and Price soon found Hoize at 7,000 feet, where White Fight regrouped and climbed back up over Oro Bay. However, the Japanese had left and the trio returned to Horanda.

Flying Knight Green Flight scrambled from Horanda. Flight Leader 2Lt. William Gersch and Wingman 2Lt. Edward Howes took off first and were followed three minutes later by 1Lt. Leon Howk and 2Lt. Frank Nutter. Gersch and Howes were unable to find the Japanese in the mounting offshore cloud formation. Howk and Nutter overhauled the last enemy fighter elements north of the harbor at 25,000 feet and were attacked from above by Oscars. Howk was swarmed by Oscars and was only able to get ineffective short bursts off at several foes during his evasive maneuvering. Nutter fired and hit an escaping Ki-43 for a probable claim before the Green Flight duo dove for safety just south of Buna. When they climbed back to altitude the Japanese had left the area.

7FS

Capt. George Manning's 7FS pilots had spent the last month carrying out uneventful patrols and dive bombing sorties in the Salamaua area, and wanted to see some air combat after being relieved of that duty. At 1150 Manning led Red Flight's eight P-40Ks to 24,000 feet near Oro Bay, when they were vectored to meet an enemy formation approaching from the sea. However, Red Flight became separated from the Squadron as they flew through a cloud bank and were several miles out of range for the ensuing battle.

The 7FS White Flight P-40Ks would be more successful. After their Flight Leader aborted before take off White Element Leader 2Lt. Robert Greene led wingmen 2Lts. Joseph O'Connor and John Quinliven from Kalamazoo strip at 1150. This Flight also became separated in the clouds as they climbed to 24,000 feet, but would fortunately find 12 Vals in three V elements above the overcast at 17,000 feet preparing a dive bombing attack on the merchant ships outside Oro Harbor. The three White Flight pilots maneuvered to dive out of the sun on the right flank of the Vals. Greene set out after a dive bomber that had strayed from the main formation, and as the Val extended its dive flaps, Greene hit it with a long fatal burst from dead astern before the rear gunner could return fire. O'Connor and Quinliven remained together and covered Greene until he dove away to safety. The two then circled, looking for the Vals, and became separated. Quinliven joined fighters from the 8FS while O'Conner flew off alone to search for the Vals. O'Conner came upon the Vals and attacked a straggler, killing the rear gunner and setting the port wing on fire. O'Connor followed the wounded Nakajima bomber through the overcast, making more firing passes until the AA fire from the friendly vessels below caused him to return base.

8FS

At 1200 12 8FS Warhawks were vectored from Kalamazoo, and once more, the weary P-40Es would struggle to climb to 21,000 feet, where the three flights made contact. First to take off was Yellow Flight, led by 1Lt. Ernest Harris, followed by Wingman F/O Sammie Pierce, Element Leader Maj. William Martin of 49FG HQ, and his Wingman, 2Lt. Roger Grant. Next to leave were Green Flight veterans 1Lts. Bruce Harris and his Wingman, 2Lt. John Roth, followed by 5FC Ops Deputy Capt. Ellis Wright and rookie 2Lt. Richard Vodra. Last to take off was Red Flight, led by Capt. Lawrence Kirsch with his rookie Wingman, 2Lt. James Hagerstrom, and Element Leader 1Lt. Marlin Smith and his Wingman, 1Lt. Robert Aschenbrenner.

Harris' Yellow Flight stayed together in their initial pass against the escorts, with Harris and Pierce each destroying a Zeke. Afterward Harris and Pierce remained in loose formation as Harris downed a Val when they were attacked by the escorts. Then they turned into their attackers, and Harris shot down his second fighter of the battle to become the highest scoring Warhawk ace in New Guinea when his score rose to seven.

The Yellow Element of Maj. Martin and 2Lt. Roger Grant also attacked the escorts in the first pass. Grant's prop began to windmill and he left the area momentarily to allow his engine rpm to slow down. Meanwhile Martin was attacked and hit, and he dove away for safety. Martin then returned to 10,000 feet and made no contact, and returned alone to Kalamazoo. Once Grant recovered control of his prop he tried to join a flight of 80FS P-38s in pursuit of the Vals, but was unable to catch them and turned toward base. On his way back Grant saw several Zeros in the distance, and he carefully applied power to his rough running P-40. He closed the gap after a 20 mile chase to the coast and made one firing pass on two Zeros, scoring a probable on one, then sped away alone to safely land his overheated Warhawk at Kalamazoo.

Harris' Green Flight searched for the enemy, and Harris found a lone Oscar and fired, but lost it in the overcast at 15,000 feet. However, the independent minded 49er HQ man, Capt. Ellis Wright, left the Flight to search on his own. The wayward Wright found the dogfight and joined Ernest Harris' Yellow Element in attacking the escorts in the slight overcast at 16,000 feet, where Wright claimed three Zeros to become the first staff ace.

Capt. Kirsch's Red Flight dove into the midst of the battle being fought by other Eightball elements. The Flight did not stay together and Aschenbrenner, the last man in the Flight, was immediately cut off by the Zeros and dove for safety. Kirsch was also forced to dive away, but ran into a flight of Vals directly below and fired on a Val beyond effective gunnery range. Kirsch then saw 7FS White Flight rookie John Quinliven under attack by another Zero. Kirsch fired at the Zero pilot, who looped away, and Kirsch maneuvered so that the Zero crossed his path at point blank range. Kirsch's long burst sent the Zero into an inverted roll into the sea. Red flight Wingman 2Lt, James Hagerstrom had stayed with Kirsch through his initial pass, but during the second pass Hagerstrom spotted a Zero, and as he tried to fire nothing happened. In the excitement he had forgotten to flip his gun switch, and as he scrabbled with the switch, he almost collided with the Zero. The rattled Hagerstrom broke off his attack and joined two P-38s pursuing another Zero. Hagerstrom pulled inside the turn of the enemy pilot, who had unwisely banked gently to starboard, and Hagerstrom got off a long burst that riddled the length of the enemy's fuselage. The Zero's engine caught fire and the fighter stalled out and plunged through the overcast.

Green Flight Element Leader 1Lt. Marlin Smith also dove through the enemy escorts to attack the Vals. Smith hit one with a long burst, causing it to head for the sea, where the dive bomber somehow leveled out and turned head on into Smith, who sped away. As he turned to re-engage he saw the Val burst into flames and dive into the water.

LEFT: Capt. Ellis **Wright** was the day's co-high scorer with three victories to make him an ace with five victories. (AAF) RIGHT: Capt. Lawrence **Kirsch** got his second and last victory of the war. (AAF)

2Lt, James **Hagerstrom** got his first victory on the way to becoming an ace

F/O Sammie **Pierce** got his first of seven victories. (AFAA)

1Lt. Ernest **Harris** was the day's co-high scorer with three victories to make him an ace with seven victories. (AAF)

11 April 1943: 8FG/80FS

The alert that a large enemy formation was headed for Oro Bay came about noon, and 15 minutes later four 80FS P-38s were scrambled, led by Capt. Daniel Roberts with 2Lt. Dirck Hartmann as his Wingman, while 1Lt. Leonidas Mathers and 2Lt. Glenn Hope flew the second element in the flight. The flight was vectored toward the enemy, and 25 minutes later Roberts spotted 15 dive bombers covered by many fighters about 15 miles out to sea directly ahead at 19,000 feet. Glenn Hope became separated from the flight with radio problems when two Zeros flew out of the overcast at 21,000 feet in front of him but dove away. However, another Zero came out of the overcast even closer to him, and Hope rolled into a starboard bank to fire a deflection shot from 200 yards. Hope pulled the Lightning's wheel back hard and skidded in behind the Zero and fired more bursts. He saw his tracers hit the enemy fighter's fuselage, sending it into uncontrolled dive. Two more Zeros tried to get on Hope's tail, and he pulled away in a dive and headed back to base. Meanwhile Roberts, Hartmann, and Mathers headed toward the dive bombers, which went into a wide circle in a loose string formation bearing down on two cargo ships in the Bay. The 80th trio was about 1,000 feet above the bombers when Roberts descended on one of the bombers at 17,000 feet and immediately started firing, getting heavy cannon and machine gun hits that tore pieces off the dive bomber. Mathers was flying under Roberts in pursuit of another dive bomber, but two Zeros were on his tail. Roberts was about to roll over and go to the rescue when Mathers flamed his target and then accelerated toward land to lose the Zeros. Despite becoming disorganized by the interception, the Vals were able to bomb the Allied convoy and set at least one ship on fire. Roberts saw one group of Vals fly under him, and he rolled over to get into good position on the tail of one enemy plane and fired an accurate volley that tore off part of the target's starboard wing; the bomber rolled violently into the sea for his second victory of the day, his fourth in the war and first in the P-38.

Roberts described the combat:

> "My first burst at about 17,000 feet caught a bomber, which lost pieces as my Wingman and I passed very close on our way over. No. 3 man in the flight, Lieutenant Mathers, pulled out to the side and headed for one plane. The second half of the formation seemed to split wide open and they made no attack; however the first half had apparently scored a hit on one of the ships, as it was smoking badly. At this point three enemy planes flew under me and a sharp turn downward set me in a position for a good burst, which was fired at about 1,500 feet. A part of his right wing was lost and he immediately made a violent turn, apparently out of control, and headed for the sea, smoking as he went. The first plane was seen to strike the sea, and my No. 3 man passed under me with dive bombers in front of him and fighters on his tail. A dive toward the water to help him was in order but he had destroyed the plane in front of him. It burst into flame and hit the water burning, and he 'sold out for land, running from the enemy."

LEFT: Capt. Daniel **Roberts** was credited with two victories to draw him closer to acedom RIGHT: 2Lt. Glenn **Hope** got his only victory of the war. (AAF)

1Lt. Edward **Randall** claimed the 39FS' only victory of the day and his only victory of the war. (AAF)

11 April 1943: 35FG/39FS

1Lt. Edward Randall scored the only victory for the 39FS when he shot down a Zeke about 25 miles NW of Oro Bay. 1Lt. Robert Baker also claimed a probable for the 39FS. During the day's air battle the Japanese had lost 18 aircraft to all American squadrons; however, the enemy bombers scored two direct hits on a 2,000 ton Allied merchant vessel and other hits on a corvette and one small supply ship.

12 April 1943: *I-GO* Mission to Port Moresby

Ignoring their loss of 18 aircraft (and three probables and one damaged), the next day the Japanese attacked Port Moresby for the 106th time with an even larger force. Initially the Japanese sent a twin engine Dinah recon aircraft which was shot down. In the late morning the three 49er Squadrons at Horanda and Kalamazoo were awaiting vectors for the Oro Harbor area, but instead the 4th Fighter Sector plotted a formation of 45 Betty bombers escorted by 60 Zero and Oscar fighters flying at 30,000 feet that would fly past Dobodura for Port Moresby.

12 April 1943: 49FG/8FS/9FS

8FS

The air action began at 0730, when three 8FS Red Flight Warhawks led by 1Lt. George Davis, with wingmen 2Lt. Merle Wolfe and 1Lt. Joel Thorvalson, were escorting a flying boat to Oro Bay at 9,500 feet. The trio was alerted of a single unidentified aircraft approaching at above 29,000 feet. They turned inland over the fogged in shoreline toward the clear skies above Dobodura to search for the intruder, which was identified as a Dinah by Davis. Red Flight jettisoned their belly tanks and went into a steady climb due east on a parallel course to intercept the enemy recon plane. The

LEFT: 1Lt. Rufus **Jordan** claimed his third and last victory of the war. (AAF)
RIGHT: F/O Arthur **Talmadge** claimed his only victory of the war. (AAF)

Dinah pilot spotted the climbing Warhawks and climbed to 31,000 feet to get above the Warhawk's service ceiling. The Dinah flew off over the mountains with the three Eightballers following 2,000 feet below toward Port Moresby. At 0835, after following the Dinah from Dobodura to Port Moresby and back, the Dinah slowly descended and finally got within range as it passed over Cape Ward Hunt. Davis went into a high speed dive through scattered overcast 30 miles out to sea and closed to within 300 yards and flamed the enemy's port engine. Davis' guns jammed, so he recharged them, and fired until they jammed again. The stricken bomber flew on, but Davis had only one functioning gun as the bomber slipped down into the overcast trailing heavy black smoke. Davis followed, but his last gun malfunctioned and he immediately turned back for Kalamazoo, where he landed on empty fuel tanks.

As Davis' Red Flight followed the Dinah south, the Dobodura squadrons waited for *Cator* to issue the alert for the enemy bombers that generally followed the reconnaissance flight. The alert came at 0930, and three P-40s of Yellow Flight were scrambled from Kalamazoo. The hastily assembled Flight consisted of Flight Leader 1Lt. Rufus Jordan and wingmen 2Lt. Arthur Wenige and Capt. Ellis Wright of 5FC HQ, who soon turned back due to engine problems with his old E-model Warhawk. Green Flight followed immediately under the lead of 1Lt. William (Bruce) Harris, accompanied by 2Lts. Pleasent Barrett, Robert Howard, and F/O Arthur Talmadge. As the last Warhawks left Dobodura at 0945, 24 Lightnings of the 9FS were ready to leave Horanda to cross the Owen Stanleys and head for Moresby.

9FS

The 9FS flight of 1Lts. Ralph Wire, Grover Fanning, and Peter Alger climbed to 27,000 feet, and as they crossed the spine of the mountains Wire had a radio malfunction, so he passed the lead to Alger with hand signals. As the Lightnings flew south the elements split up to search for the bombers which had just been reported by Moresby's Fighter Controller, *Elsie*, as north of the harbor. Alger called out nine Vs of three Bettys each in a broad formation at 21,000 feet, followed closely above by as many escorts. As the P-38s dropped their tanks, Alger led them toward the left flank of the large enemy formation, which had just dropped their bombs on the Moresby docks. Alger and Fanning fired on the closest Bettys in the nearest V and then dove under the enemy echelon and zoomed across the Betty formation to fire on the elements on the right flank. Alger got one bomber, while Fanning destroyed one and badly damaged another for a probable. The Oscar escorts immediately dove on the Americans. Alger broke left, Fanning broke right. and Wire, flying cover for his wingmen, flew head on into the attackers. Fanning rolled away momentarily to the north, gaining speed and altitude, then re-engaged and fired again at a second bomber from point blank range. The Betty fell from the formation and was quickly joined by a single Oscar escort; the pair flew toward the safety of the clouds beyond the spine of mountains. Fanning eluded the other Oscars and sped toward the wounded bomber. He dove on the right rear quarter of the Mitsubishi, which fell away on its left wing in flames toward the jungle. The Oscar went into a climbing loop to counter Fanning's pass, but its pilot misjudged the Lightning's speed and missed his chance to fire. Using his high speed, Fanning easily climbed from beneath the Ki-43, turned hard about, and caught the enemy fighter at the top of its second loop. Fanning's cannon and .50s hit the enemy's forward fuselage, which erupted in flame, and it spun out of control toward the jungle. One of Fanning's three victories was the 49th Group's 200th victory of the war.

2Lt. Grover **Fanning** had a big day scoring his first three victories plus a probable and a damaged claim. (AAF)

The top scorer for the battle was 2Lt. Grover Fanning, who reported the combat as follows:

"I saw two formations of 18 bombers with lots of Oscars above the formations. We made our pass and came back from the other side for another one. This was a close pass, and I shot into the right engine of one Betty bomber and as it dove away in a left turn it was smoking. I peeled away to the right and Lieutenant Alger to the left because the fighters were coming down on us. After outrunning the fighters I turned back toward the bombers and saw one going down in flames. I came back at the bomber formation from the right. I made a quarter head on pass and attacked the front of one bomber formation. One bomber dove out of formation.

"Again I had to dive away from fighters. They were coming down mostly in threes. I came back at the bomber that had dived out of formation and made a diving pass as an Oscar was covering it. The bomber began to smoke. I believe I got the tail gunner because I passed right behind the tail and there was no fire this time. I chased the bomber back over the mountains, heading approximately 15 degrees. I caught up with the two after passing over the range. I had trouble getting in a position for a pass because of the Oscar. Finally he got close to the bomber, and I made a quarter tail pass. The Oscar moved to a position over the nose of the bomber. When I started firing, the bomber started a diving left turn. The Oscar went straight up, whipped over, and went straight down. I managed to avoid going under him.

"I fired a good burst into the bomber as it started to dive away again. The bomber burst into flames along the right side of the fuselage at the wing roots. The Oscar was ahead of the bomber and above. He went up again, and I caught him at the top of his stall. I fired, apparently right into the nose and cockpit of the plane. The Oscar fell off out of control and started smoking from both sides. It went into the low overcast, out of control, diving too low to the ground to pull out."

Meanwhile, Wire turned into the Oscars which climbed toward the Americans and hit one that flew off trailing heavy, black smoke. Unable to rejoin his flight, Wire rolled down and away from the combat and then climbed to 32,000 feet, looking for the Japanese formation that was disappearing in the clouds to the east. Low on fuel, Wire turned for Horanda and landed shortly after Fanning. Alger was caught by a diving Zero and plummeted in a twisting dive through 16,000 feet while the persistent Zero pilot knocked out his starboard engine and holed his right tail and right fuselage boom, and shattered his windscreen. Alger finally outran the Zero south of the harbor but realized he could not reach Horanda, so he turned for nearby 7 Mile Drome to safely land his fighter.

As the Lightnings exhausted their fuel and ammo they returned to Horanda, while the Warhawks patrolled over the enemy escape routes on the north shore. Jordan's Yellow Flight and Harris' Green Flight had orbited over Dobodura, waiting for the Japanese to return on their way back to base. The weather was quickly closing in on the northern coast, limiting the Eightballs' attack as they searched among the clouds over Oro Bay. Jordan sighted several enemy Bettys in scattered formation and led the Eightballs down from 16,000 feet into a rear quarter attack. Jordan made three unsuccessful passes and then climbed on a lone Zero which suddenly appeared on the scene and he quickly closed for the kill. Green Flight Leader Harris, Howard, and Talmadge each downed a Betty, and the six pilots landed at Kalamazoo.

Capt. Charles **Gallup** ended his scoring with six victories. (AAF)

12 April 1943: 35FG/39FS/40FS/41FS

39FS

Six P-38s of the 39FS met a large enemy formation estimated at "45 Betty bombers and 30 Zeke SSE fighters" about 40 miles east of Moresby at 20,000 feet and 20 miles away. At 0930 the P-38s closed and were attacked on all sides by the Zero escorts while the bombers continued on. 1Lt. Harvey Clymer made a diving rear quarter attack on four Bettys, but a Zero approached from the front quarter and below, giving Clymer a five second burst that exploded the Zero. 1Lt. Richard Smith and Capt. Charles Sullivan were at 20,000 feet when they saw Bettys and Zeros at 7,000 feet above at 12 o'clock and climbed to gain the altitude advantage. Smith and Sullivan closed on nine bombers to make diving attacks from the rear. On Smith's first attack he hit the left Wingman of a V of three and the Betty fell out of formation and dropped back. Capt. Sullivan also damaged his Betty, and it too dropped back with the other wounded bomber. Although Sullivan claimed a probable in his ICR, he was later credited with a victory

1Lt. Richard **Smith** claimed his third victory. (AAF)

Capt. Charles **Sullivan** claimed his fourth victory. (AFAA)

Veteran 1Lt. Richard **Suehr** with one P-39 victory got his fourth P-38 victory to become an ace. (AFAA)

for unknown reasons. Smith chased the two straggling damaged bombers for 20 miles, and north of Kokoda fired at one from 100 yards and hit its right fuselage; this started a fire in its right engine and it crashed into Mt. Victoria. 1Lt. Richard Suehr also attacked the Bettys, and when one turned into him he began a frontal attack, firing from out of range, holding the trigger down until he closed to 200-100 feet. The Betty's left engine exploded and pieces were ripped off the fuselage and cowling, and it finally crashed into the mountains. The victory was Suehr's fifth to make him an ace. At 1110, on returning to his Moresby base Capt. Charles Gallup ran into a returning Zero and hit the unaware enemy pilot with a 90 degree burst at 300 yards, then closed to 50 yards at 30 degrees, shredding the right elevator and stabilizer. The Zero went into an uncontrolled spin and crashed for Gallup's sixth and last victory.

40FS

At 0945, 16 Airacobras took off from Berry (12 Mile) to intercept bombers north of Yule Island. Squadron Leader Capt. Thomas Winburn had to turn back with engine trouble, and Capt. William Davitt, leader of the second flight, took over. When the 40FS approached the area at 7,000 feet the bombers were sighted at 10 to 15,000 feet above them and due east of 30 Mile Drome. They were proceeding toward Moresby when 35 fighters were seen flying directly above them, and then groups of four or five fighters to each side and ahead of them. At this point interception was not possible, and Davitt headed his Airacobras toward Kokoda to attack them after the bombing run. About 1030 Davitt decided to intercept the enemy bombers around Lake Myola, and the Squadron began its attack. Davitt attacked into the fire from the enemy gunners in the formation and closed to 50 yards before firing on the extreme left bomber, which "resembled a B-26." He hit the port engine and wing, starting a fire, but as he broke away his windshield was spattered with oil. Davitt's #3 man, 1Lt. Houser Wilson, dove quickly and hit the left engine and wing of the lead bomber, which burst into flames and peeled out of the formation. Davitt was then bounced by six Haps and rolled violently to starboard and dove steeply to escape. He dove on a damaged Zero and fired a long burst at 500 yards and 45 degrees deflection, then fired again as he closed to 50 yards, shredding the Zero's cowling. Davitt continued down but the Zeros did not follow. As he climbed he saw Houser fire on a bomber and then was joined by his wingmen, and the flight was ordered to head home.

When Davitt attacked the #3 bomber Wilson attacked the lead bomber and shot it down. When the flight made its second pass Wilson was too far out of position and he dove away. He then saw another bomber with one of its engines smoking and with five or six Zeros hovering around it. Wilson dove and opened fire, and the bomber flew through the damaging stream of bullets. As he continued his dive Wilson saw Davitt following the bomber. Wilson broke away when a Zero fired on his tail until it ran out of ammunition but did no damage.

2Lt. Charles Klein was #4 in Davitt's flight, and when the flight made its initial pass he was unable to keep up and became a straggler. He was considerably behind the flight when he saw a Zero climbing to attack the other three Airacobras of his flight. Klein tried to radio a warning but got no answer. Klein rolled and dove on the Zero, getting enough hits for it to crash at the foot of Mt. Scratchley. He climbed and joined two other P-39s, which then spotted an unescorted flight of six enemy bombers below. Klein reported the bombers to the others but again received no reply; he dove after them, but hesitated as they flew into a cloud. As he was about to rejoin the improvised flight he saw a straggler which he identified as a dive bomber and made a diving turn, getting some hits as it entered a cloud (for a damaged claim).

The third flight, consisting of 1Lt. Martin Low and Wingman 2Lt. Anthell Kelly, with second Element Leader 1Lt. Eugene Heinz and his Wingman, 2Lt. John Davis, took off at 1000. They climbed to 23,000 feet over 30 Mile Drome, where they were attacked by "four to eight" Zeros and were forced to dive away. When Low climbed back up to 16,000 feet he was alone with a single enemy bomber. He closed in and got some possible hits on the bomber before he was attacked by four Zeros and turned into them before a Zero got on his tail and shot his elevator almost completely off. Low was able to disengage and return safely to base. Meanwhile, the remainder of the flight descended to 19,000 just west of Mt. Scratchley to find a lone formation of three enemy bombers returning from bombing Moresby, with another lone "twin engine, single tail bomber" flying to the left. Heinz and Davis attacked with Heinz, making the first pass from the right front quarter and getting some strikes. Davis followed closely and began firing from a long lead, but saw no results before he pulled up behind and over the bomber. When they circled to relocate the bomber it was gone, and an unseen Zero fired bullets into Davis' engine and wings. Davis dove to safety into the clouds surrounding the mountain, but another Zero found and attacked him. He evaded this Zero by dodging into a narrow, cloud filled valley. When he landed Davis found two holes in his prop, four in the wings, and bullets in the engine oil tank, magneto, and Prestone tank.

After Low's Flight was attacked over 30 Mile Drome by three (as per Heinz' ICR) Zeros, Low and Kelly turned into the right Zero, with Low then diving away and Kelly closing on the Zero, which turned into him head on. Kelly fired, but found that all his guns had malfunctioned, so he had to dive away to safety and return home. Meanwhile, Heinz and Davis pulled into the second Zero as the third Zero turned toward Davis and Heinz from the left. The Airacobras could not get within firing range and broke up and away while the Japanese broke down and away. After the two elements separated, Davis and Heinz joined three other P-39s and climbed for altitude to make another interception. Heinz saw a single bomber at 10,000 feet and four Zeros at 5,000 feet overhead. The two American pilots dove on the lone bomber with the Zeros chasing them. Heinz attacked the bomber from the front quarter and saw some puffs of smoke, but had to break off as the Zeros closed. Heinz then retuned to base, and on his approach to 17 Mile saw a parachute descending and circled until the pilot landed and waved.

1Lt. Louis Nagy was leading the fourth flight when his #4 man called out a large formation of enemy bombers and fighters. Nagy led his flight toward Port Moresby and gained altitude in a parallel course with the enemy. One of the bombers began losing altitude and dropped behind, so the flight attacked in echelon. The bomber's right engine started smoking. Nagy made two more passes, and the bomber started on fire and fell off. Nagy lost his flight during the attack and returned to base.

The first flight led by Winburn, and consisting of 1Lts. Francis Vetort and John Doordan and 2Lt. ? Dannacher, was unable to keep up with the high flights, but gained sufficient altitude to intercept a formation of three bombers that were trailing behind the larger formation. As they were about to attack the bombers Zeros came in and the P-39s were forced to dive away and never got into battle again.

41FS

Capt. Albert Schinz led 18 P-39s at 0945 on a mid-morning interception of enemy bombers incoming to attack Port Moresby. At 1000 the 41st, flying at 22,000 feet, spotted "40-50 Zeros" 10 miles away at 26,000 feet at 11 o'clock high. They did not see any bombers that had already bombed Moresby and were "running home, spread out between Moresby and Kokoda." The P-39s were observed by the enemy on their approach, and "we were in a very bad position, being underneath all the enemy fighters and behind the bombers. When the engagement started we were 3,000 feet below everything (Schinz)." The Japanese attacked the P-39s when they were at 3 o'clock to them. The Zeros attacked in pairs, mostly in clusters of six or eight, pulling up or turning into the P-39 attacks. Schinz considered the Japanese pilots "fairly good."

Schinz led the mission's lead flight after the bombers, but as he headed for Kokoda he realized there was no chance of catching them. Instead, he concentrated on gaining altitude, as the 40-50 escorts were scattered from Moresby to Kokoda waiting to pounce. Schinz turned into a Japanese attacker for a head on pass, firing continuously until it began a Split-S turn into him. Schinz dove away and pulled out at 400mph, and on his pull out was approached by another Zero. Schinz turned into it, and the two adversaries approached each other, firing at point blank range. The Zero passed Schinz so closely that his Wingman thought they would collide. The Zero was hit and went out of control, spinning into the clouds below. Schinz climbed to gain precious altitude, and as he went around a cloud he ran into a Zero. He fired, but saw no results and broke away. After he broke away he saw a straggling Betty, and as he prepared to make a pass he saw tracers whizzing by his cockpit and went into a high speed dive that lost his pursuers and returned to base.

1Lt. Dugan **Woodring** who had a previous P-400 victory got his last career victory flying a P-38. (AAF)

1Lt. Richard Culton, Schinz' Wingman, dove with Schinz on the first ineffective attack on the enemy escorts that dove for safety. After he and Schinz dove away, Culton pulled out and found a Zero on his tail and fired on his pursuer, making a quarter beam attack and shooting off the rudder or elevator, which almost hit Culton's fighter. The loss of the control surface caused the Zero to go into a half snap roll directly into the ground. As Culton was finishing his attack another Zero slipped up on him from 6 o'clock and hit and shut down his engine and shattered his canopy. Culton first checked his body for damage and found only some bleeding at the back of his neck. He then checked his instruments and found them to be OK, but radioed base to prepare for a crash landing. As he headed back, his engine began to run very rough and he bailed out to safely land in a lake. Culton's fighter crashed only 50 yards away, and he was soon approached by natives from Haima village, where he was given a cup of tea before being returned to his squadron later that afternoon by a search party. While Culton was tangling with the Zeros, 2Lt. Richard Kimball bailed out of his P-39 north of the airfield complex. Kimball's parachute became tangled in a tree and he remained swinging until natives climbed up and cut him down. After eight days the natives returned him to Moresby.

Flight Leader 1Lt. James Palmer chased the Bettys that were two miles ahead and level. Palmer closed in two plane elements on a straggling Betty in the nine bomber formation. They made a beam attack from 500 feet above and fired on the bomber. When Palmer looked around he saw that there was a P-38 and three other P-39s attacking the hapless Betty, which had an engine on fire. Palmer broke away and pursued the rest of the formation. He fired two rear quarter attacks on one bomber with no observable results. Other Zeros were closing in, and Palmer broke away toward Kokoda and was joined by another P-39 from the 40FS. They saw nine Bettys in a V of V formation escorted by nine Zeros. A plane zoomed past Palmer and he chased after it; when he caught it, he found it was another P-39. He was then fired on by another Zero at 1 o'clock that then passed under him. Palmer was unable to get a shot and turned after the Zero, and soon found it heading directly toward him. Palmer opened fire at 250-300 yards and continued firing until pieces flew off and it exploded. Palmer writes in his ICR, "The whole mess was lots of fun."

2Lts. Erick Kyro and Lloyd Rosser flew toward Kokoda and saw a Betty at 2,000 feet straggling from the rear of a formation of nine bombers and trailing a light plume of smoke. Both pilots made numerous passes while being fired at by the turret gunners. Kyro made four ineffective passes on one from the left, while Rosser made his first ineffective pass from the right. Rosser came around for a second pass that hit the cockpit and right engine, which started to smoke. Rosser made a third pass and saw that the top turret had stopped firing and there was a fire in the cockpit. He followed it down and saw it explode 500 feet above the ground.

1Lt. Roy Lawhorn chased a Nell that had an engine smoking. The enemy pilot turned sharply when approached, but Lawhorn followed and fired from 250 yards from slightly above and behind and shot it down. Other 41FS scorers for the day were 1Lt. Dugan Woodring, a Zero destroyed; 1Lt. Tony Prince, a Zero probable; and 2Lt. Roy Owens, a Betty probable. With these six victories, the Squadron would not score again until 15 August. The Squadron had acquitted itself well flying the inferior Airacobra by scoring 28 victories (18 Zeros and 10 bombers), seven probables, and two damaged.

12 April 1943: 8FG/80FS

The day after their large raid on Port Moresby, the Japanese sent 45 Betty bombers escorted by about the same number of Zero escorts, flying at between 30,000 and 33,000 feet. 1Lt. Donald McGee was leading a flight of three P-38s at 21,000 feet when he saw the Japanese above and ordered tanks to be dropped and began to climb. Second Element Leader 2Lt. Campbell Wilson's starboard engine had problems and he fell behind and descended to 17,000 in cloud cover. Several minutes later, while flying near Yule Island, a Zero dropped down behind Wilson and fired one burst that shattered his canopy and hit his good port engine. Luckily the Zero pilot did not press his attack, but climbed over Wilson's damaged P-38 and lingered there before making another attack. Wilson used the reprieve to roll to the left into a tight diving spiral and eluded another attack. Meanwhile, McGee and his Wingman, 2Lt. Robert Siebenthal, were trying to maintain contact and position themselves in the clouds at 30,000 feet for an attack. McGee lost the bombers during a turn, but then found them again on a course to Moresby. He made a front quarter attack on one bomber, then dove away and turned back to make another pass from below. As he was getting fatal hits on the Betty (which went down into the water near Mt. Nisbet), four Zeros came at him and the American broke off his attack. Siebenthal spotted four Zeros below in the distance and dove to 21,000 feet to initiate a 90 degree deflection shot. However, the Zeros saw him before he got into range and turned into the attack. As the Zeros closed, Siebenthal fired a brief burst at the leader without visible results, but his Lightning was hit by enemy fire that shattered his canopy, wounding his shoulder and piercing his eye. Siebenthal then outran the four enemy fighters once they had whizzed by and flew to 30 Mile Drome for a wheels up landing. With his impaired vision Siebenthal made a long approach, swerved off the runway, and badly his damaged P-38, but suffered no further injuries.

1Lt. Donald **McGee** shot down a Betty for his fourth victory. (AFAA)

Results of the 12 April Air Combat

The 5FC's outstanding total of 18 bombers and 10 fighters destroyed plus three probables and three damaged was at the cost of two American fighters. The Japanese bombs slightly damaged four A-20s; set a Beaufighter on fire; badly damaged one P-39; and set two B-25s on fire and damaged another beyond repair. Two B-25s and two C-47s were classified as badly damaged, and two B-25s and two C-47s were slightly damaged. The runways at Wards, Berry, and Schwimmer were cratered, and a fuel dump at Kila was destroyed. The heavy loss of aircraft on the ground was due to inadequate revetments, and post attack studies showed that damage would have been reduced by 60% if proper side protection for the parked aircraft had been available. Soon bases were provided with tractors and bulldozers for revetment construction.

The gun camera view of 1Lt. Richard **Bong's** victory over a Betty bomber to make him the first double ace in the Pacific with 10 victories. (AAF)

14 April 1943: 49FG *I-GO* Mission to Milne Bay

After two days of exhausting combat, weather closed air operations over the Solomon Sea on the 13th, and gave the pilots of the Fifth Fighter Command a brief break. The next day 27 Betty bombers accompanied by Val dive bombers with a large fighter escort arrived over Milne Bay harbor and airfield on the eastern tip of New Guinea. By 0830, the large formation turned due south out over the Solomon Sea and climbed over the cloud tops at 21,000 feet and flew three hours to their target.

Meanwhile, Air Controller *Cator* directed eight 49er P-38s to search for a large formation sighted over Goodenough Island, 130 miles southeast of Oro Bay. Mission Leader 1Lt. William Sells led the Knights in a climbing pursuit, due east toward the large cumulus cloud front on the far horizon. Soon the Sells' Flight began to deteriorate, as his Blue Flight had a Wingman lose an engine, while Green Flight Leader 1Lt. Richard Bong quickly lost half his Flight when 2Lt. Gilbert Milliff experienced engine failure, and then, only minutes later, 2Lt. Francis Nutter lost power and both returned to Horanda. Although 1Lt. Carl Planck's P-38 had a dead generator and was losing power, he closed in on Bong's wing and flew on. Sells' five remaining P-38s were the only fighters available for the interception. As they passed over Goodenough Island, Sells was unable to contact the Japanese and decided to extend the search. He led his Blue Flight wingmen, 2Lts. Ralph Hays and Edward Howes, down from 25,000 feet to search at a lower altitude within the scattered clouds. Bong and Planck of Green Flight were to maintain their high cover position. The Knights orbited south of Goodenough once, and when they found nothing, they headed for Milne Bay. Blue and Green Flights were now separated, but Sells and Bong maintained radio contact as they approached the mainland shore and met the widespread enemy formations.

Bong and Planck of Green Flight spotted Betty bombers and dropped their belly tanks, climbing 1,000 feet to get an altitude advantage over the Bettys, which had just released their bombs on Milne Bay Harbor at 27,000 feet. The Americans positioned themselves in the sun against the left flank of the trailing bomber V, and as Planck advanced his throttle, his starboard supercharger caught fire and he was forced to leave the battle. Bong was alone as he dove on the Betty Wingman on the left flank and fired and hit its cockpit and port engine. As the wounded Betty descended through the overcast, it was attacked by RAAF Warhawks which made several more firing passes before it crashed into Milne Bay. (Bong was credited with a probable.) Soon Bong was attacked by six diving Oscars, but used his Lightning's superior diving speed to escape and then turned after the escaping bombers. After a short chase to the north, Bong quickly overhauled the bomber's left flank as they passed over the mainland. He closed on the enemy bomber on the left and fired at point blank range from the left rear quarter. The tail gunner was only able to fire a few rounds before the port left side of the bomber's fuselage erupted in flames, and suddenly it began to descend steeply. Bong maneuvered for another firing pass on the Betty when two Oscars got on his tail. Bong broke off his attack and eluded the Oscars, then radioed for Sells to regroup. Bong's Betty claim at Milne Bay was his tenth victory, making him the first official double ace in the Pacific theater.

2Lt. Edward **Howes** got his first of four victories. ((AAF)

Meanwhile, Sells' Blue Flight was positioned over the Val and Zero flights that were in a stacked formation ranging from 16,000 through 20,000 feet. After dropping their tanks the Flight accelerated across the enemy flights to an up sun position against the enemy's left flank. Sells sent Howes to attack dive bombers while he and Hays would keep the Zeros away. The Zeros made a climbing turn into the P-38s, and Sells and Hays rolled into a 400 mph dive for the Zeros while Howes broke for the nine Vals flying in three tight Vs. Howes fired on the trailing echelon and nearly rammed one of them as the bomber elements veered to escape the attack. With the bombers now scattered, Howes pursued a lone Val, but rolled away as the Zeros came back. Howes then saw a P-38 surrounded by 12 Zeros and tried to regain altitude to reengage, but was unsuccessful in saving the hapless Lightning. Howes made a number of turns with the Zeros and scored fatal hits on one, but was too low on fuel and turned for base. Sells and Hays attacked the escorts, and in their initial pass they immediately became separated when Hays was forced to withdraw due to gun failure. Hays quickly recharged the errant guns and returned to the fight, where he scored probables on two Vals before he was overwhelmed by the other enemy fighters. Hays escaped with his superior speed and then followed the escaping enemy toward Goodenough Island, but prudently turned toward Dobodura.

The P-38 pilot that Howes tried to rescue was Sells, whose fighter had been shredded. The mission leader miraculously avoided being wounded and finally escaped into the clouds. Sells realized that he would be unable to make the return flight to base and attempted an emergency landing at the small dirt strip at the RAAF's Gurney Field, on the western shore of Milne Bay. As he entered into his landing approach his starboard engine seized, and he quickly responded with full flaps and left rudder just beyond the shore line. Suddenly a RAAF Warhawk came into the Gurney landing pattern in front of Sells, who desperately swerved out of a certain collision, but the damaged Lightning crashed into the jungle at the east end of the runway and exploded, killing Sells.

The *I-GO Operation*: An Assessment

Within a week the Japanese had carried out about 240 sorties against the principal Allied bases in New Guinea and the Solomons. Although the Japanese sank several Allied transports and warships, the attack failed to inflict serious damage on Allied forces. The Japanese lost over 60 aircraft (including those downed by AA fire), while the Imperial Combined Mobile Fleet claimed nearly 200 Allied aircraft either shot down or destroyed on the ground, which was a tenfold gross exaggeration. Based on these inflated reports from their aircrews Yamamoto and the Japanese Imperial Staff at Rabaul decided to end the *I-Go Operation* on 14 April as a victory that cost them large losses of aircraft and, worse, experienced pilots. The exhausted Japanese Naval air units stood down from missions during the last two weeks of April as battle worn aircraft were flown back to Truk, New Ireland, and Rabaul for overhaul. Meanwhile, Japanese Army air units transferred to the western airdrome Wewak in preparation for the next operations, which were scheduled for May. These were to be the last daylight attacks on Port Moresby by the Japanese until early May. For a month following the 14 April attack on Milne Bay, the Japanese flew only minor raids on New Guinea bases, despite AAF photo reconnaissance showing that on 16 April there were still 248 aircraft on the Rabaul airdromes (exclusive of medium bombers undoubtedly concealed in dispersal areas at Vunakanau). The *I-Go Operation*, however, did not significantly delay Allied preparations for further offensives in the South Pacific area. Yamamoto was killed shortly thereafter while traveling to congratulate units that had participated in the operation.

18 April 1943: Death of Yamamoto

Immediately following the *I-GO Operations*, Yamamoto dispatched a coded radio message of his plan to personally survey the forward airstrips of the Solomon Islands. Allied Intelligence accurately decoded the message, and on 18 April, a flight of Thirteenth AF Lightnings led by Col. John Mitchell were dispatched from Guadalcanal on a precision interception of Yamamoto's Betty transport near Bougainville. Yamamoto was assassinated, along with his entire staff, and the Americans had revenge on the architect of the Pearl Harbor attack.

5

May 1943

Situation and Planning

While the Joint Chief of Staff's dictum was the defeat of the Axis in Europe was to take priority over the campaign in the Pacific, the JCS nonetheless charged American, Australian, and British forces to continue unrelenting pressure on Japan. The pressure was to include preserving China as a base for operations against Japan, attacking Japanese lines of communication, preventing the consolidation of enemy military forces, and the securing of positions for later full scale operations. The Combined Chiefs of Staff authorized a specific number of operations projected for 1943 and 1944. In the Far Eastern (CBI) Theater there were to be air operations in and from China and a ground campaign in Burma. In the Pacific there were to be operations in the Solomons and Bismarck Archipelago in order to maintain the initiative, and to continue the defense of Australia; operations in New Guinea, not only to serve the same purposes as the Solomons and Bismarck campaigns, but to facilitate opening a line of communications to the Celebes Sea; a campaign into the Netherlands Indies to be limited to seizure of islands necessary for the capture of New Guinea; and operations in the Marshall Islands in order to shorten communications to the Southwest Pacific and to the Celebes Sea. These were pictured as limited offensives, carried out primarily by naval forces. Consequently, the US Navy in the Pacific was to be augmented to a maximum consistent with minimum requirements in the Atlantic. Air and ground forces provided were to facilitate joint action and to make possible optimal use of the US naval forces.

Specifically, the operations contemplated in May by the Combined Chiefs for the South and Southwest Pacific forces remained much the same as those outlined in the *Elkton Plan* as modified by a JCS directive of 28 March 1943. These were to establish airfields on Kiriwina and Woodlark Islands; to seize the line Salamaua-Finschhafen-Madang area; to occupy western New Britain; and to continue operations in the Solomons, with Bougainville as a chief objective. By the middle of May, MacArthur had fixed 15 June as the target date for starting the operations whose ultimate objective was the capture of Rabaul. The initial landings, however, were to be on Kiriwina and Woodlark Islands. The Joint Planners assumed that MacArthur, who directed the overall strategic direction of the campaign, would secure positions in western New Britain and southern Bougainville by 1 December 1943, after which at least another two months would be required before he would be able to launch his attack against the Rabaul area itself, which would not be completed until 1 April 1944 at the earliest.

The Joint Planners believed that sufficient forces would be on hand before the first phase of the scheduled campaigns. They estimated that 14 infantry divisions, adequate naval forces, and 2,106 aircraft would be available in the South and Southwest Pacific by 1 July 1943. MacArthur estimated that he would require seven infantry divisions, of which five were to be amphibious, for the invasion of Kavieng and Rabaul alone. The Joint Planners maintained that "with effective air neutralization" this number could be reduced to five divisions to be provided by 1 January 1944. Also, according to their estimate, the 2,577 combat aircraft allocated to the RAAF, RNZAF, and the Army and Navy in the South and the Southwest Pacific areas would be sufficient for the campaigns on the Bismarck Archipelago.

In addition to the campaigns to be implemented under the direction of MacArthur, decisions made at the Trident Conference in Washington during 12-27 May authorized operations in the Gilbert and Marshall Islands. By 15 June, the Joint Chiefs of Staff had concluded that naval strength in the Pacific made these operations possible. Their tentative plans involved the employment of the Second Marine Division and the main portion of the naval forces in the South Pacific, together with the First Marine Division from the Southwest Pacific. These units were to launch their attack in November from bases either at Pearl Harbor or in the South Pacific.

Five days after learning of these tentative plans, MacArthur contacted Gen. Marshall, clearly stating his dissatisfaction. He pointed out that the objective of both South and Southwest Pacific operations was the capture of Rabaul, and that preliminary operations were designed "to provide a base of departure for converging attack and adequate air support and flank protection" for obtaining this objective. He had previously scheduled the First Marine Division, his only amphibious unit, to make the attack on New Britain, and he alleged that if this unit were transferred, this attack would have to be cancelled. He admitted that a campaign in the Marshalls might be a sufficient diversion to assist the operation planned for his own forces, but he maintained that the troops for the diversionary effort should be brought from the US instead of being taken from the force available for the main attack.

Actually, MacArthur did not support the attack into the mandated islands, as he argued that "from broad strategic viewpoint" the best plan for an offensive in the Pacific was one based in Australia and intended for Mindanao, in the Philippines, via New Guinea. He preferred this option because of his conviction both that it would more quickly cut the enemy lines of communication with their conquered regions to the south, and that it would be the only action which could guarantee the support of land based air power. Conversely, MacArthur saw the advance through the Mandates as a succession of amphibious attacks supported by USN carrier-based aircraft against objectives defended by Japanese land-based aircraft. Such assaults, he emphasized, would be risky, and would result in the capture of no "strategic objective" until Mindanao was reached.

During this exchange, neither MacArthur nor the Operations Planning Division (OPD)* had broached the function of the Southwest Pacific air units in connection with the proposed offensive in the Marshall Islands. On 2 June, however, Assistant Chief of Air Staff, Plans informed MacArthur's Headquarters that the plan required the use of a heavy and medium bomber group in addition to available naval air forces. MacArthur was reminded of the effect that Central Pacific operations would have in diverting enemy air strength, and was requested to convey his outlook as to the effect on air operations in the South and Southwest Pacific if the two groups were withdrawn from either of these theaters. (*The OPD was charged with the responsibility under the Chief of Staff for the Army's part in the strategic planning and direction of operations in World War II.)

MacArthur's reply was clear and agreed to by Gen. Millard Harmon, Commanding General of the US Army forces in the South Pacific. They felt that the campaign against Rabaul should be the main effort, with the troops and equipment for operations under consideration in Washington being drawn from rear areas and the character of operations in the South and Southwest Pacific demanded more than "air superiority," but required total "air supremacy." While a heavy and medium bombardment group might not represent significant air strength in other theaters, in the SWPA it represented one-third of the heavy bombers and one-half of existing or one-third the projected strength in mediums. The withdrawal of these two groups would cause a collapse of MacArthur's projected offensives.

Previously, the offensive moves along the coast of New Guinea had been delayed by the lack of sufficient air strength to perform all the tasks allotted to the Fifth Air Force. By May an early improvement in the situation was expected, since two of the additional units allotted to the Southwest Pacific by the joint Chiefs of Staff, the 345th Bombardment Group (M) and the 380th Bombardment Group (H), were already on the way, and other units were scheduled for early deployment. Operations, Commitments, and Requirements (OC&R) recommended to OPD in April that two night fighter squadrons be shipped in August and October and one and one half troop carrier groups in June, plus another in the third quarter, and that three fighter groups be added in May, July, and October, the second of these to be activated in the theater. The JCS had also promised MacArthur two light bombardment groups, but these would not be available until 1944.

Kenney soon informed the OPD of the units upon which he based his future plans, and which generally conformed to those of the OC&R. The major differences concerned the fighter reinforcements. OC&R listed a P-47 group (the 348th) for May shipment, a P-40N Group to be activated in July, and a P-38 group to arrive in October. Kenney was planning on a group of P-47s to be shipped in May and another in June, and a P-38 group was to leave the US in August. He emphasized the need for P-38s, as their range and two engine operation were reassuring on the frequent long over-water flights in the Southwest Pacific. Kenney was not as enthralled with the P-47, which he stated "was probably a good fighter in spite of some of the adverse comments from England" and it did not have a "speedy enough rate of climb to intercept a Zero, with less than a half hour warning." For a time uncertainty continued as to the type of fighter aircraft to be provided with the first two reinforcing fighter groups. In early May Kenney was authorized to activate a fighter group by the third quarter to be equipped with the P-40N aircraft; however, Kenney had expected a P-47 group.

On 6 May Kenney emphasized that the Japanese had 250 fighters and 150 bombers within range of Port Moresby, and that, with less than 200 fighters in his command, his fighter situation was critical. He further stressed that the success of planned operations depended on the arrival of new and efficient fighter units. That same day Gen. Marshall informed Kenney that a P-47 group had been released following engine adjustments, but that there were still some operational problems, such as piston and ignition failures, potential fire hazards, and radio noise problems. The P-47s of the 348th Group were to be made completely operational and ready for shipment by 12 June. Flight and ground echelons were to depart as originally scheduled in early May. In addition, Kenney was authorized to activate the 475th Fighter Group (TE) in the theater and was assured that P-38s would be available for this group in June.

These assurances did not mean that the two fighter groups could be used in combat by the indicated dates. In late June Kenney wrote to Arnold that "the P-38s are expected to start arriving any minute now and I think I will meet the boat with a band to welcome them." By 3 July 79 P-38s and 59 P-47s had arrived, and a month later 36 additional P-38s and 56 more P-47s were delivered. The personnel of the 348th Group reached Australia on 14 June and waited in Brisbane a month for their aircraft. A month later the first P-47s landed on a Post Moresby field, and within 10 days three squadrons of the 348th, with 86 aircraft led by Group Commander Lt.Col. Neel Kearby, had made the 1,200 mile flight from Brisbane with only two damaged en route. When Kearby's P-47s arrived Kenney stated: "No matter what objections there are to the P-47, it has eight guns and is faster than the Zero at any altitude so I will use it and gladly take all I can get." For the time being, the 348th Group was to remain at Port Moresby, where aircraft warning units were giving an hour's notice of a Japanese attack to allow the Thunderbolts time to climb to intercept.

The 475th Group, the first all P-38 group to see action in the Southwest Pacific, was not ready for combat until mid-August. It had been activated by the 5AF on 14 May, but personnel and equipment problems caused delay. On 17 June, the first of a contingent from New Guinea arrived back in Australia, landing at Amberley Field as cadre personnel for the new 475th organization. The Group was to be commanded by Lt.Col. George Prentice, former 39th Squadron Commander. Within three weeks "filler" personnel arrived from America, as well as additional veterans from the forward areas. Problems arose in supplying construction materials for the Group's billets, which delayed the Group's move to Dobodura until the end of July. Meanwhile, P-38s were arriving from the Eagle Farm assembly line at Brisbane and ground crews were readying them for combat, a routine which was upset by the transfer of 33 of these fighters to the 5th Fighter Command HQ. Movement orders were confusing during the next few weeks. The ground echelon arrived at Dobodura by ship on 14 August, but the flying echelons of the 431st and 433rd Squadrons were held back at Port Moresby. A number of P-38s of the 433rd Squadron flew a combat mission from Dobodura on 15 August and were then transferred back to Moresby only three days later, to again join the First Air Task Force at Dobodura.

In May Kenney was notified to expect the P-38-equipped 55th Fighter Group scheduled to arrive in October, but as early as 29 June, however, he was informed that the P-47-equipped 58th Fighter Group was to be substituted. Upset over the switch, Kenney urgently requested the 55FG, stating "the P-38 is the only fighter capable of offensive action or useful for convoy of troop carrier or for bombardment operations in this theater." For the moment, however, his request was refused, as P-38s were being diverted for modification to the F-5 photo plane, which was in great demand. Kenney reiterated his request on 31 August, asking for twin engine fighters not only to equip the next group allocated to his air force, but to re-equip two squadrons of the 49th Group. Again his request was refused, this time because of difficulties and delays in P-38 production that would not permit any change in the planned delivery to his theater.

In spite of Kenney's inability to obtain the most desirable type of fighter for his theater, his fighter strength was to be more than doubled by the fall of 1943. By that time, too, bombardment strength was also substantially increased. The arrival of new fighter, bomber, and troop carrier units was to be the decisive factor in the scheduling of operations for the summer and fall of 1943. On 29 June Kenney wrote: "If any more delays occur in the arrivals of aircraft or personnel out here, we may as well start our planning, all over again, as timing will be all wrong and Jap reactions and movements in the meantime will completely change the picture." On paper the virtual doubling of the combat units in the Fifth Air Force "seemed to promise as much as could be expected." But even the actual arrival of units allocated by the Joint Chiefs of Staff did not resolve the continuously difficult problem of attrition and replacement in both personnel and crews.

In trying to satisfy Kenney's frequent requests for an allowance for the higher rates of attrition and personnel and a larger number of reserve aircraft, the War Department had the thankless job of trying to balance the needs of may different theaters. At the time, many air units in all combat areas were still operating at reduced Tactical Operating (T/O) strength in both aircraft and crews. The general policy as expressed on 6 June was to bring these units to full T/O strength only after aircraft and combat crews were available "in suitable numbers to man and sustain all units of the current Army Air Forces program at reduced T/O strength." For active theaters it was planned to provide replacement personnel up to 15% per month of reduced strength. This policy depended somewhat on priorities, and by August 1943 the UK held top priority, with the 5th and 12th Air Forces following in order.

On 7 June Kenney was informed by the OC&R (Office of Committments and Requirements) that the 5AF was to have the following schedule for combat aircraft delivery: two bombardment units to have a strength of 48 aircraft with a third unit to have a strength of 35 and all to have a 50% reserve; medium, light, and fighter bomber groups were to have a unit strength of 37 with a 50% reserve; fighter groups were to have a unit strength of 75 aircraft and a reserve of 50%; night fighter squadrons were to have a strength of 12 with a 59% reserve; and troop carrier units were to have 32 aircraft and 15% reserve.

Kenney had a particularly difficult time building up his heavy, medium, and light bomber groups to strength, but had better success with the 5th Fighter Command, as it was somewhat better equipped than the 5BC as far as numbers were concerned. Lt.Gen. Paul Wurtsmith, CO of the 5FC, had five groups in the theater with 565 aircraft at the end of July and 598 at the end of August, which on paper was the allocated strength plus a 50% reserve. However, these fighters included obsolete fighter types: approximately 70 P-39s, 30 P-400s, and 118 P-40s, and more than half of which were in depots for overhaul.

On 4 July John Gibson, a technical representative of Bell Aircraft, reported to Kenney that the P-39s and P-400s averaged approximately 300 hours of combat, and all needed a complete overhaul and replacement of accessories. The lack of spare parts made overhaul impractical, and Gibson suggested that new fighters replace them. Several days later Paul McNamara of Curtiss Wright came to a similar conclusion regarding the P-40s, which had 300 to 500 operational hours on them; this was considered to be equivalent to 2,000 hours of normal flying time. He suggested that the P-40s undergo a general depot overhaul and be "retired" to mainland Australia, where they could be used for training and emergency defense situations.

Allied and Japanese Land and Air Strategy

Allied land strategy for the summer of 1943 in the South and Southwest Pacific proposed several objectives. One objective was Rendova, in the Central Solomons, while in the New Guinea area the goals were Woodlark and Kiriwina Islands, which were located near the south coast of New Guinea, and the last goal was Nassau Bay, which was located 50 miles up the New Guinea coast from Morobe Harbor. Capturing these targets would put Allied forces in position for the invasion of Lae, as it had been decided that the enemy base at Salamaua would be bypassed.

The period from May through September 1943 witnessed not only the building of the Fifth Air Force in men and materiel, but also offensive operations on a larger scale than any yet undertaken by the Allied forces in either the South or the Southwest Pacific theaters. The reduction of Rabaul remained the ultimate goal of the Allied forces operating both from New Guinea and the Solomons. The immediate objective was to bring the Fifth and Thirteenth Air Forces into position for the culmination of the campaign against that enemy-held stronghold. And so, while the Allies in the South Pacific advanced from the lower Solomons through New Georgia toward Bougainville, those of the Southwest Pacific, using well-established bases at Port Moresby, Milne Bay, Goodenough Island, and Dobodura, had secured the Morobe area and were preparing to establish themselves on the Huon Peninsula, and were also carrying out the necessary preliminary moves against New Ireland and New Britain. Once the Allied offensive began during the summer of 1943 the Allied Air Forces struck with increasing frequency at targets along the northern New Guinea coast from Lae to Wewak, and along the southern New Britain coast from Gasmata, around Cape Gloucester, to Talasea.

During March, April, and May, while Allied fighters were intercepting Japanese air attacks in addition to running escort and patrol activities, Allied bombers were used in an assortment of missions. Their principal purpose was to attack enemy strategic bases, to isolate the battlefield by intercepting enemy convoys, and to cooperate with Allied ground forces in the forward areas. Nevertheless, other types of operations frequently took priority over these, such as reconnaissance, patrol, and convoy escort missions. In reality the 5th Bomber Command was relatively weak, but nonetheless effective in keeping the enemy off balance by concentrating its offensive power on a few vital enemy targets, particularly at Rabaul, Kavieng, and Wewak. Only a few of the attacks against Rabaul were directed against shipping in Simpson Harbor because the Japanese were making greater use of the more distant harbor at Kavieng. Allied air units had little success in intercepting Japanese convoys that were on the move, but they did maintain their blockade of the Huon Gulf area. Enemy shipping moving into Wewak Harbor and into Hansa Bay were out of range, however, of any but heavy bomber units. Only four convoys, two heading for Finschhafen, one in the Madang area, and the other off Arawe in New Britain, were located within range of light and medium units from March through May. The heavies did have some success, however, in attacks on enemy vessels which had already arrived at their destination. Being within range of the First Air Task Force based at Dobodura, the airfields and supply dumps at Cape Gloucester, Wewak, Madang, and Gasmata were important objectives. Wewak's airfields at Boram, Dagua, and But were hit by heavy bombers usually as an alternate when shipping targets could not be located. Medium bombers were able to reach Madang occasionally escorted by P-38s.

By the end May, the Japanese were feeling increased pressure from both Allied land and air forces. The Allied Air Forces were awaiting the arrival of additional aircraft before mounting a serious offensive. In the meantime, however, Allied fighters were fending off enemy air attacks; reconnaissance aircraft were constantly watchful for enemy attempts to strengthen their Lae garrison; and bomber units were continuing at least nominal attacks on important enemy supply points. The results of these Allied air attacks are somewhat difficult to evaluate, as the official reports frequently state that results were not observed. This was particularly true of attacks at night against distant bases and of bombing and strafing missions in cooperation with ground forces.

Also at this time, the Allied air forces were in a position to contribute more to offensive operations. Their potentialities had been increased by the development of Dobodura as a base ranking with Port Moresby and Milne Bay. The organization of the First Air Task Force gave promise of a flexibility of air action in northern New Guinea that was previously impossible. Moreover, aircraft were beginning to reach Australia in larger numbers. In April, the following aircraft arrived prior to the 24th: 25 B-24s, 13 B-25s, six P-70s, and six C-47s. During the same period two P-38s, two P-40s, and one P-400 were lost in combat; one A-20, one B-25, one B-17, and seven B-24s were missing; three B-25s were destroyed on the ground; and 21 fighters, 11 bombers, and two transports were lost in accidents. In May, the status report showed that 94 B-25s, 31 B-24s, 15 P-39C, and 17

0-47s arrived to offset the following losses: one B-25, five B-17s, and two B-24s missing in action; and 25 fighters, nine bombers, and three transports lost from accidents. Thus, although defensive fighter strength had received little or no increase since the first of the year, it was clear that the offensive power of Task Force and Bomber Command would be far greater in June than in previous months.

15 April-8 May 1943 Lull in Air Combat

After the mass Japanese bombing attacks of 11, 12, and 14 April, the Japanese, who still had superior aircraft numbers, conducted only harassing raids. With the exception of the large raid on 14 May in which the 49FG scored 22 victories, there was little in the way of defensive opportunities for the 5FC to score.

During the air combat lull, bomber and transport escort missions were flown over the northern New Guinea coast and routine combat air patrols were maintained. The 49FG was often down to four flights of 16 operational fighters per squadron, and assembling patrols of eight aircraft was unusual. The old P-40Es of the 8FS averaged more than 300 hours of combat per fighter and were often out of service. This reprieve gave pilots a chance to rest and overworked maintenance men the opportunity to repair and overhaul their well-worn P-38s, which were not going to be replaced for some time, since the European and the Mediterranean Theater especially had priority for procuring the P-38 over Kenney's beleaguered 5th Fighter Command in the SWPA.

During this respite the 49th Fighter Group at Dobodura improved living conditions. Camp life was frequently interrupted by tropical rain and wind storms which blew down tents and trees, soaked bedding, and rotted anything that could rot, causing more problems and discomfort than the bombing attacks of the Japanese. Platforms were built to keep the tents off the constantly damp and insect infested ground, and improvements in sanitary conditions were made to cut down the severe Malarial rate. To decrease the boredom at Dobodura, the 49BG introduced Bingo parties and set up a loudspeaker system to play music in the mess halls. Farewell parties were held for the first large group of men to be returned to the United States after a year of combat. Somehow 100 bags of Christmas cards and packages finally arrived six months late to cheer the men out of their lassitude. At Moresby, during this period of relative quiet, the 35FG celebrated "Over the Hump" week in honor of its first year of combat in New Guinea.

On 5 May, Allied Intelligence noted a decline in the number of enemy aircraft based in the Northeastern area from 611 on 7 April to 466 on 4 May, which they considered to indicate a continued reduced threat of aerial attacks in the theater. However, this peaceful interlude began to end as May arrived. On 2 May, 21 medium enemy bombers escorted by a large number of fighters flew an air raid on Darwin. The Japanese were intercepted by 32 RAAF Spitfires that shot down from three to five fighters and probably one bomber. While little damage was done to Allied installations on the ground, 13 valuable RAAF Spitfires were lost.

Situation: The Opposing Air Forces

The Japanese Air Forces

In May, to counter Australian troops who penetrated into the Markham Valley, the newly designated 4th Army Air Force, headquartered at Rabaul, was formed from the remnants of the 1st and 11th Sentais at Wewak and the veteran 24th and 59th Sentais from Indo-China. These Oscar units were to escort Lily light bombers of the 45th Sentai and Helen heavy bombers of the 61st Sentai. The 68th and 78th Sentais were based at Rabaul and equipped with the new Kawasaki Ki-61 Tony; they were to escort bombing raids and convoys between Rabaul and Wewak.

The Kawasaki Ki-61 Tony looked so different compared with the usual radial-engined Japanese fighters that at first the Allies believed it to be of German or Italian origin, possibly a license-built Messerschmitt Bf 109. In early reports, when it was thought to have been a German fighter, the Ki-61 had been code-named "Mike." The final and better known code name adopted was "Tony," because the Ki-61 looked like the Italian Macchi C.202 fighter. It was armed with a pair of synchronized 12.7 mm (.50 caliber) Ho-103 machine guns with a limited ammunition capacity of 250 rounds per gun. It was equipped with a self-sealing fuel tank (44 US gallon) located behind the pilot's seat, armored windshield, and a half inch armor plate behind the pilot. Almost all of the modern Japanese aircraft engines, especially the Ki-61's liquid-cooled engines, suffered a disastrous series of failures and ongoing problems. Both Sentais were based in a difficult theater, where jungles and adverse weather conditions, coupled with a lack of spares, quickly took their toll on both pilots and aircraft. Because the Ki-61 was so new, and had been rushed into service, it inevitably suffered from teething problems, all of which resulted in the obsolescent Ki-43 Oscar still forming the bulk of the JAAF's fighter capability.

The **Kawasaki Ki-61 Tony** looked so different compared with the usual radial-engined Japanese fighters that at first the Allies believed it to be of German or Italian origin. (AAF)

The American Air Forces

During May more veterans were rotated back home to the States, while others were transferred to training facilities in Australia or had applied for transfer and promotion to fly P-38s with Lt.Col. George Prentice's new 475th Fighter Group, "Satan's Angels," based at Dobodura.

Meanwhile, by May, there were ever decreasing numbers of war weary P-40Es available, and the Warhawk Squadrons eagerly waited for the promised arrival of new model Warhawk replacements from Townsville. The 7FS, under the newly promoted Maj. George Manning, continued tactical missions in support of the Australian troops near Salamaua. Capt. Franklin Nichols left for the 475FG, while Raymond Melikian took over as the Deputy CO and 1Lt. Arland Stanton assumed the Ops Exec position. The Demons continued to fly their old K model Warhawks, but neither of the Warhawk squadrons would encounter any airborne action for the next month.

With the departure of Jesse Peaslee, Capt. Sidney Woods was named CO of the 9th Squadron in late May, Capt. William Haney became Assistant CO, and Capt. Ross Blachly became the squadron Ops Exec. The Flying Knights extended their P-38 escort sorties and fighter sweeps beyond Lae and across the Huon Gulf to attack new enemy airstrips discovered at Cape Gloucester and Gasamata, on western New Britain.

At the start of May, advanced echelons of the 35th and 36th Squadrons of the 8FG were sent to Port Moresby, where they were assigned to 17 Mile Drome, renamed Durand Strip in honor of the first pilot of the 35FS to die in combat. The water echelon arrived on 16 May and occupied a camp aptly called "Mosquito Junction," located about a mile from the airstrip. The 8FG remained at 17 Mile until July, when the 341FS/348FG arrived and the 8FG moved to their new camp to Kila (3 Mile Drome), near Port Moresby. Compared to 3 Mile, 17 Mile was a paradise, with its hilltop location swept by gentle sea breezes and free of mosquitoes.

8 May 1943: 35FG

During an afternoon escort of 10 B-25s on an anti-shipping mission over Saidor, 14 P-38s led by Capt. Thomas Lynch intercepted four Zeros at 2,000 feet in a Lufbery over the enemy shipping in the harbor. Lynch made three passes at the Lufbery, and on the third head on attack he shot down one to become a double ace with 10 victories. Lynch credited the Japanese pilot with using "very good evasive tactics, never turning into the attacking ships until (they were) in firing range making it impossible to continue the diving attack without going into the water." Capt. Charles Sullivan damaged another Zero in the battle.

13 May 1943

A week after Allied Intelligence had declared the "diminished aerial threat" assessment in the Northeastern region of the theater, that assessment was proved overly optimistic. A new series of attacks began on 13 May with innocuous night raids, when five enemy bombers dropped their bombs on the 49FG at Dobodura but missed the field by the proverbial mile. Two Japanese bombers also dropped bombs on Port Moresby without effect.

14 May 1943: 49FG/7FS/8FS/9FS

During the second week of May, Japanese recon flights from Rabaul discovered the arrival of another large Allied merchant convoy in Oro Bay. Poor weather prevented the Japanese from mounting any attack until 14 May, when 18 Betty bombers of the 751st Kokutai, based at Kavieng, New Ireland, were sent to Oro Bay at sunrise. The Bettys flew 130 miles south to Rabaul, where they rendezvoused with 32 Zero escorts of the 251st Koukatai and arrived at the north coast of New Guinea at 1020. In the clear skies the Japanese formation had been detected well in advance, and all three 49er squadrons were ready for combat.

9FS

At 0800, 9FS Red Flight Leader 1Lt. Floyd Finberg led Wingman 1Lt. Grover Fanning and the second element of 1Lts. Martin Alger and Clay Petersen to investigate the first *Cator* alert. After 20 minutes Finberg had radio problems and transferred the lead to Alger. Immediately Red Flight encountered a fleeing Dinah, and Alger and Petersen closed at 350 mph on the bomber. Alger and Petersen both fired, and the damaged Dinah began to descend toward Cape Ward Hunt. Alger then approached to the enemy's left, fired, and flamed the port engine; he then dropped back to the right and set fire to the starboard engine. The powerless Dinah drifted into a slow roll, and Alger closed from dead astern and fired a long burst that exploded the fuel tanks, and the debris fell into the sea.

The Finberg/Fanning Red Flight Element quickly returned to Horanda, still fully armed, where their Lightnings were refueled. Finberg's Crew Chief rapidly corrected his malfunctioning radio, and the two attached themselves to Capt. William Haney's 11 ship Green Flight, which took off from Kalamazoo at 0930.

8FS

At the 1000 alert four flights of 16 old Warhawks from the 8th Squadron left Kalamazoo. They climbed to 20,000 feet and waited for the *Cator's* vector, but the *Cator* Controller garbled the plot of the enemy formation. Mission Leader Capt. Lawrence Kirsch led his Flight of F/O Arthur Tallmadge, Element Leader 1Lt. William Harris and rookie Wingman 2Lt. Elferd Elofson back to orbit above Dobodura. The mistake would take

Capt. Thomas **Lynch** became the Pacific's second double ace by shooting down a Zero. (AAF)

Kirsch's Flight out of the Eightball's most successful interception of the New Guinea Campaign.

8FS Red Flight Leader 1Lt. George Davis decided that *Cator's* garbled vector was to send them south to the coast line just below Oro Bay. After flying 30 minutes, Red Flight moved inland south of the harbor, where Davis saw the Betty bombers just to the east of the Harbor. Davis led 2Lts. Thomas Farley, Leo Mayo, and rookie Richard Vodra from 20,000 feet toward the enemy 2,500 feet below. Only seconds behind Red Flight were twelve more Warhawks of the 7FS.

7FS

The 7th Squadron was led by Deputy CO Capt. Frank Nichols, who had taken his eight P-40Ks up to 22,000 feet. Nichols and Yellow Flight Leader Capt. John Yancey saw the enemy bombers at the same time Davis of the 8FS had seen them. With their combined P-40 squadrons positioned in the sun ready to pounce on the enemy's left flank, the Nichols and Yancey Warhawks dove head on, in-line behind Davis' Eightball Red Flight.

Blue Flight Leader 1Lt. Warren Blakely, Wingman 2Lt. Merle Wolfe, Element Leader 1Lt. Robert White, and rookie Wingman 2Lt. Robert Aschenbrener saw Nichols' Flight peel off and follow 8FS Mission Leader Davis in the dive for the Bettys. Blakely accelerated forward and to his right so his Flight would target the center of the enemy formation.

2Lt. Richard **Vodra** claimed his only two victories of the war. (AAF)

2Lt. Lawrence **Succop** shot down his only enemy plane of the war. (AAF)

1Lt. Arland **Stanton** escaped an attack by several Zeros to score his fourth victory. (AAF)

1Lts. Martin **Alger** claimed his third of four victories. (AAF)

The Bettys began their bombing run, turning to the north, just as Davis and Element Leader Mayo chose their targets on the left flank of the enemy formation. The two leaders rolled in behind two bombers from the left rear quarter and both hit their targets with long fatal bursts. As the Eightballs sped past the other bombers toward the enemy's right flank, they immediately encountered the Zero escorts. Davis' flight engaged them in a dogfight down to 1,000 feet above the water, and Davis and Mayo each claimed victory over a Zero. Vodra also slashed a pair of Zeros in the battle.

Both Nichols' Red Flight and Yancey's Yellow Flight attacked the same enemy elements that Davis' Eightballs had only moments before. Nichols' Flight turned in behind the turning enemy formation, but Nichols and his two wingmen were forced out of the combat by approaching Zeros. Only Red Element Leader 1Lt. Arland Stanton was able to escape the Zeros when he followed the Betty formation out to sea, where he destroyed a straggler flying just above the waves.

As the first Warhawks were diving on the Betty formation, the first elements of the scrambled P-38s came on the scene at 24,000 feet south of Oro Bay. Only 8FS Yellow Flight Leader 1Lt. Ross Blachly, who was well out in front of his Flight, evaded early contact with the escorts, and he alone attacked the bombers while his wingmen, 1Lt. Donald Byars and 2Lt. Arthur Bauhoff, flew to the north beyond the harbor and back out to sea and engaged the fighters. Blachly made two head on passes on a straggler on the right flank, and during his third attempt to finish off the wounded bomber Blachly was forced to break off with a probable as he came into a swirling dogfight. Green Flight entered the battle led by Capt. William Haney, with Wingman 2Lt. Frank Wunder and newly joined wingmen 2Lts. Floyd Finberg and Grover Fanning in trail. The seven pilots jockeyed for position against the mostly inexperienced Zeros. However, a pair of Zero veterans singled out Bauhoff and bracketed his Lightning in a deadly crossfire. Byars tried to help Bauhoff, but was drawn into a fight with a Hap that led him down to 1,000 feet. Byars finally gained the advantage and splashed the Japanese pilot, but Bauhoff was gone before Byers could return to him. The two Zeros riddled Bauhoff's fighter, which nosed over into the sea, but a parachute was seen to open just above the crash site. Several pilots reported Bauhoff's position on the sea and circled his position for the rescue tug. When the rescue tug arrived the crew only found a school of sharks that probably savaged the bleeding pilot.

Capt. John Yancey's 7FS Yellow Flight, positioned at the end of the Scream'n Demon column, went into a high speed dive to pass the Bettys on their left flank and then turn into them from head on. Yancey fired on a Betty in the left wing position and it fell on fire into the ocean. Element Leader 2Lt. Lawrence Succop veered to the right to get behind the right flank of the Betty echelon. He closed on one and killed the tail gunner from dead astern, then hit the left engine, which exploded, covering his Warhawk's windshield with oil. With his vision severely limited Succop carefully turned for Kalamazoo.

1Lt. Warren Blakely's Eightball Blue Flight attacked the middle V elements of the G4M bomber formation. Blakely and 2Lts. Merle Wolfe, Robert White, and Robert Aschenbrener made numerous passes against the leading bombers, but only White succeeded in hitting a bomber. He hit and flamed the starboard engine of one that fell far below the formation, but before he could finish it off he was attacked by four Zeros. Although he was alone, White continued to fight and downed a Zero in a head on, nose-to-nose encounter. White raced for the safety of the coast, chased by another Zero, but was rescued by another P-38, and he left for Dobodura as an ace with his fifth victory.

In the interim, Maj. Peaslee and his five wingmen of Blue Flight were still confused by the original vector, and although close to the raging air battle, Peaslee declined to attack beyond his assigned area. Peaslee and rookie Wingman 2Lt. George Alber orbited back toward the coast, but Darwin veteran 1Lt. James Watkins could not resist and ignored the last *Cator* plot. He led 1Lt. Keith Oveson, 2Lt. Frank Nutter, and 1Lt. Leroy Donnell after the Betty formation, which had was headed east over the Solomon Sea. Their pursuit line took the Americans along the left flank of the bombers, and Watkins dashed forward to make a head on pass. However, the experienced Zero pilots tried to cut off the Lightnings before they reached the bombers, and only Oveson fired on a Betty that drifted from its left wing position; he shot out in its port engine before he was forced to turn into the Zeros. The three other Knights had separated when the Zeros arrived, and again only Oveson hit his target before Blue Flight made a 450mph dash toward home.

The succeeding flights from Kalamazoo also pursued the Bettys toward New Britain. 7FS Blue Flight Leader 1Lt. Raymond Hilliard led 2Lts. Harry Dilworth, Sheldon Brinson, and John Griffith 20 miles out to sea before they overtook the enemy. Hilliard suffered an oxygen equipment failure and stayed with Wingman Dilworth at 13,000 feet, waiting for a possible straggler. Blue Element Leader Brinson and Wingman Griffith came within sight of Nichols' Red Flight, but neither was able to make a successful pass on the bombers. Brinson was driven away by a veteran Zero pilot and dove away to join with other 49ers who circled Bauhoff's crash site. Griffith initially fired out of range on the bomber echelon's left flank and then turned to port, where he surprised a lone Zero and flamed its engine. Griffith was himself surprised when several rounds pierced his cowling, forcing him to dive away. Griffith turned to re-engage, but his damaged prop controls did not respond; he unwisely attempted to follow the Zero through a loop, only to have the enemy pilot slide in on the Lightning's starboard rear quarter and shoot out the hydraulics. Griffith rolled his perforated fighter into a dive and hurried back to Horanda with 15 7mm machine gun bullet holes in its fuselage and a 20mm cannon round that destroyed the left landing gear strut, which collapsed on landing. Griffith was unhurt, but his aircraft was written off.

7FS Green Flight, led by 1Lt. Donald Sutliff, was the last 7th Squadron element to overtake the descending enemy bombers. Sutliff's pilots were strung out in a loose formation, and only Sutliff and rookie Wingman 2Lt. Carl Houseworth reached the left flank of the retreating Japanese formation. They made one pass at the bombers at 17,000 feet, and Houseworth broke off in the opposite direction from Sutliff, who then dove away for safety at 3,000 feet. Sutliff, though alone, climbed back toward the enemy. Sutliff sighted a straggling Betty with three escorts at only 50 feet above the water. Diving at full throttle, he zoomed between the Zeros and made a concerted firing pass on the bomber's right flank and hit its starboard wingroot. Sutliff turned tail and raced for Dobodura. The Zeros turned to pursue, but they could not catch the Warhawk.

8FS

At 0940, 8FS White Flight Leader 1Lt. Ernest Harris, wingman 2Lt. Pleasent Barrett, and Element Leader 2Lt. Robert Howard and F/O Sammie Pierce were part of the last Flight to take off. Harris flew a direct northeast coarse to overtake the bombers. As they climbed to 22,000 feet, Barrett's fighter lost power and he turned back. Finally, after 60 miles the remaining trio overtook the Japanese, and Harris descended to the right flank of the ragged enemy formation without encountering the escorts. The three Warhawks pulled ahead of the Bettys and rolled to the left for a line abreast head on

1Lt. Ernest **Harris** shot down two Bettys for victories # 8 and 9. (AAF)

F/O Sammie **Pierce's** two victories gave him three so far. (AAF)

2Lt. Robert **Howard** became an ace by shooting down two Bettys. (AAF)

pass against the right wing elements. Harris attacked first, hitting the second bomber V on the right flank. Howard attacked the next bomber to the right and Pierce turned wider to the right to attack the bomber furthest in front of the formation. Harris' victim crashed in the ocean, while Howard flamed his target and Pierce's victim was also set on fire and began to lose altitude. White Flight then turned hard to port and sped back for the second pass.

They approached the rear of the ragged formation, where both Harris and Howard chose stragglers from the formation. Harris passed over Howard's first victim, which was trailing a long streamer of red flames that "looked like one of those movie newsreel films." The victory would make Howard an ace. Harris closed to point blank range on the second wounded bomber and emptied his guns on its fuselage from tail to nose. Howard pressed his attack through the Betty's return fire and fired to kill the gunners. Howard was so intent on finishing off the Betty that he almost rammed it. F/O Sammie Pierce lost his Wingman and was about to attack another bomber further down the echelon, but suddenly sighted a lone Zero which was about to attack the unsuspecting Howard. Pierce frantically turned and fired a long, desperate deflection shot from nearly 500 yards, and was surprised when he actually hit the Zero, forcing it to dive away. Pierce's old P-40E had just been overhauled, and he dove 6,000 feet at 450mph and shot down the escaping Zero. Pierce wrestled the stick back and rocketed back up to 5,000 feet toward the bombers. Pierce approached a trailing Betty with a burning port engine and made a long firing pass with the last of his ammunition. The wounded bomber headed inside a cloud bank and Pierce circled, waiting for the Betty to reappear, but it never did. Pierce turned toward Dobodura and passed over the wreckage of Harris' first victim, with its stranded crew hanging on to the wings of the floating wreck, but he was out of ammunition to strafe them. Minutes later, he met a Zero which turned nose on into his line of flight. With empty guns Pierce feigned a head on attack and the Zero snapped into a loop and rolled for Pierce's rear quarter. Pierce shoved his throttle forward and dashed to safety at 450mph. Meanwhile, Harris and Howard had formed up at 8,000 feet and reconnoitered the area one last time, passing over two oil slicks and three plumes of smoke rising from the water. At noon Harris and Howard turned south and were the last fighters to land at Horanda.

The score for the day was, of the 18 Bettys that reached their target, 11 failed to return, and there were also 10 escort victory claims. The 251st Koukatai, which had refitted during the previous month, was composed of experienced veterans who claimed 13 AAF fighters destroyed and five more as probables, but actually the only 49er fighters lost were Griffith's P-40K and Bauhoff's P-38. Some of the rookie officers from the three separate flights of the 49FG, which attacked over 45 minutes, probably duplicated some of the claims. Some elements on the Betty's left flank had been hit numerous times by the long procession of P-40s in the first attack. These bombers were also attacked head on by the first P-38s. It was also possible that the 8FS' attack on the center elements while over the harbor was duplicated in the final attack by Harris' White Flight farther out to sea. Nonetheless, official records credit the 49ers with 11 Betty and 10 escort victories, two Betty probables, and one Betty damaged (as per Olynyk).

15 May 1943: 49FG

On the day after their rout of the Japanese attackers, the 49ers returned to their patrols and alerts in anticipation of a follow up mission, but unlike the raids in April, there was very little contact. The Japanese sent a heavily escorted search flight of Bettys to find their missing crews, but were met by six Mitchell bombers which shot down three Zeros in a short battle with the B-25 gunners. No American fighters were involved.

15 May 1943: 6NSF: Only Confirmed Victory over New Guinea

During May the Japanese flew several small night raids, but their only effect was to interrupt a stage show being put on by men of the 41st Infantry Division. On the 15th, the Japanese sent a Sally bomber over Jackson Field near Port Moresby, which was intercepted and shot down by a 6NFS P-70 piloted by 2Lt. Burrell Adams with radar operator F/O Paul DiLabbio for the one and only confirmed air victory of the New Guinea Detachment. DiLabbio describes the combat:

> "Nips were reported coming over in elements of two. We weren't high enough to intercept when they made their first run. The controller, Captain Ball, vectored us to the other side of the anti-aircraft ring from which we were flying - a good guess - Nips came out at about 19,000 feet heading northeast, and we were given about three or four vectors, which then placed us behind and above. This gave me a contact about 18,000 feet on the scope, about 4,000 feet below us and 40 feet to starboard. I then said 'contact' to Lt. Adams and gave him the general route. When I told him to 'steady' we were about 5,000 feet and in a general dive, going 350 mph, IAS, and just about the same level. I started to give Adams degree correction to the left, but Adams reported back Tallyho, which placed us about 1,000-1,500 feet behind, with the Nip a little to our left. The tail gunner of the Nip evidently saw us at the same time for he opened fire, but the bullets went over my head. By this time Adams had turned into the Nip and fired a burst which silenced the gunner and evidently wounded the pilot because the Nip turned into a general dive to the right. Adams then followed, fired another burst which hit the gas tanks, the fuselage and the wings. By now the craft was ablaze. He (Adams) fired another burst, and the Nip plane blew up. We were now about 15,000 feet - we watched enemy aircraft go to 3,000 feet - another explosion. While Adams was firing and trailing this Nip the other enemy aircraft in the element had made a general climbing turn to the left. He was about 5,000 feet away, about 20 degrees above us and about 30 degrees to our left. But try as I did, I couldn't reach Adams on the interphone, so I gave up and watched him get the other."

Shortly after Adams' victory, the Japanese discontinued sending their raiders over at 18,000 feet and climbed to between 24,000 and 29,000 feet for their attack; altitudes at the top end of the P-70's maximum effective performance and radar ceiling.

While changes and modifications to the P-70 were helpful and did improve the aircraft's performance, the P-70 never did meet the requirements of an acceptable night fighter aircraft and, unfortunately, Adams' kill was the exception rather than the rule. Adams and fellow pilot Samuel Blair both transferred out of the unit because of their frustration over the P-70's performance. Adams would attain six more victories as a day fighter pilot, and Blair would be credited with seven. MacArthur and 5th Fighter Command still wanted a better night fighter, but until another was available, the six Detachment "A" P-70s were the only night air defense for Port Moresby.

15 May 1943: 8FG/80FS

On what promised to be the most productive mission in a month, the 80FS flew an escort of B-17s and B-25s to search for a Japanese convoy near Gasmata, but there was no contact.

16 May 1943

During the morning a small enemy formation made a surprise attack on Dobodura, and like the day before there was no interception by the 5FC. These hit-and-run raids continued for the next week, but damage was negligible. During the last week of May, the Japanese Navy was absorbed with the new Allied offensives in Alaska and the Solomon Islands and the JNAF raids against the Allies New Guinea diminished.

Vivigani Strip was located at the northeastern corner of Goodenough Island lying in the Solomon Sea. (AAF)

Vivigani Airdrome Goodenough Island

17 May 1943: Vivigani Strip/Goodenough Island in Use

Vivigani Strip was located at the northeastern corner of Goodenough Island, lying in the Solomon Sea. It is the westernmost of the three large islands of the D'Entrecasteaux Islands in Milne Bay Province of Papua New Guinea. A small prewar mission airstrip existed at this location and was used by the Japanese during their brief occupation of the island. The Australian 2/12 Battalion reached Vivigani on 27 October 1942 accompanied by an American airfield engineer, and a strip was built and first used on 17 May 1943. The field eventually consisted of two runways, each 6,600x150 feet. It was used as an important staging point for operations in the SWPA as a part of *Operation Cartwheel* by both the 5th Air Force and RAAF.

17 May 1943

Meanwhile, enemy formations attacked Wau four times during the week using new tactics. Sallys and Bettys, unescorted by Zekes or Hamps, swept in over the mountains at such low altitudes that Allied signal units had little opportunity to give warning. At the same time Japanese pilots disrupted the efforts of Allied controllers by maintaining constant chatter on fighter radio frequencies. The heaviest raid occurred on 17 May, when 25 or more Bettys destroyed the headquarters, signal office, and operations office of the 17th Australian Brigade. However no real damage was done, as only two hours before the raid the Australians had moved out of Wau. The Japanese returned the following day and caused little damage.

These attacks on Wau were no longer merely isolated raids, but had become almost daily occurrences, and when considered together with other attacks against Morobe, Mambare, Douglas Harbor, and the Wau-Bulolo areas, it seemed clear that the Japanese were beginning to give some direct support to their infantry. Also, the enemy had developed fully operational bases in northern New Guinea, particularly in the Wewak area. The Japanese continued to send supplies from New Britain and other northern islands into Hollandia, Hansa Bay, and Wewak, where roads and airfields were being constructed; and Sallys, Bettys, and Lilys were using these fields for their increasingly frequent attacks on Allied bases and on troops in the forward areas.

21 May 1943: 8FG/80FS

First Flight

Another bombing raid on 21 May not only caused no damage, but cost the Japanese dearly. At 0815, 12 P-38s of the Moresby-based 80th Fighter Squadron led by Capt. Edward Cragg had taken off on a "Bully Beef" C-47 transport escort to Wau. They rendezvoused with transports at 0850 under overcast at about 23,000 feet, but the Fighter Controller quickly switched their mission to a scramble over Salamaua. After one P-38 aborted the mission, the remaining 11 were flying below a broken overcast at 23,000 feet when 15 to 20 Haps, Zekes, and Oscars were sighted slightly above and to the left of the formation. The Japanese fighters were in no distinct formation, but in groups of three at various altitudes, enabling the P-38s to maintain formation so that attacks could be made by elements. Once the enemy fighters were identified the transports were recalled back to base and the 80th went into combat.

At 0910 Cragg ordered belly tanks dropped and chased after the enemy fighters before they could escape into the clouds inland. Cragg and a Hamp closed head on and both fired, but Cragg's heavier armament tore off half the Hamp's wing and it went into an uncontrollable spin and disappeared under Cragg's wing. As it passed by Cragg came around for another attack, but he was attacked from slightly above at 1 o'clock. Bullets hit Cragg's fighter's nose, wing, and left engine, which lost power. Cragg fired, and his burst hit the enemy's cockpit. As Cragg looked around, another enemy fighter attacked him from the rear and he had to dive toward Wau to escape. Fortunately, the enemy pilot chandelled away and Cragg then feathered the prop and made a safe landing at 7 Mile Airdrome. Cragg's rookie Wingman, 2Lt. John Jones, had stayed behind Cragg, but noticed tracers zipping by his canopy and went into a fast turning dive; he then discovered that his Lightning had a hung up drop tank. Jones maneuvered wildly but was unable to lose the pursuer on his tail, until finally he reached the safety of the clouds below. Once Jones broke out of the protective clouds he saw a Hamp flying leisurely below and to port. The rookie was anxious over his first chance to fire at a Japanese aircraft and fired a long burst from maximum effective range (300-400 yards), but fortunately flames began to pour back from the heavily damaged fighter as it dove back into the clouds. Another Japanese fighter got onto Jones' tail, forcing him to dive back into the clouds, and when he emerged the sky was empty and he returned to base.

When the enemy attacked, 2Lt. Howard Peterson, Cragg's second Element Leader, saw three Zeros and three P-38s dogfighting to the north, while below he saw a Zero closing on the tail of another P-38. Peterson chose to leave the flight to rescue the single imperiled Lightning. Before Peterson could close on the Zero he was attacked from above and to the left. In desperation Peterson fired a long range burst at the original Zero, which broke off his attack, although it appeared not to be damaged. He escaped his attacker but was now alone, with the action going on above him. Soon Peterson was attacked by three Zeros in a V above at 2 o'clock but easily eluded them and left for home.

2Lt. Zack Dean was flying Wingman to Peterson, and when Cragg ordered the tanks to be dropped a light on Dean's panel indicated that one did not drop. He left the flight and tried to jettison the hung up tank when two or three Zeros started firing on him. Dean began evasive maneuvers, but Peterson came in and cleared his tail. Dean made a slow climb when another Zero suddenly made a head on pass. Dean did not fire until the two were only 300 yards apart; the Zero broke off out of control. Dean looked down and saw three Zeros chasing a P-38 and immediately dove and fired on the lead Zero without observing a result. Dean then returned to base.

Second Flight

1Lt. James Ince, the second Flight Leader, was patrolling at 24,000 feet when six Zeros attacked the flight from head on and slightly above. As the two opponents headed toward each other, Ince's port engine prop cut out and he dove out of the action. He was able to adjust his prop manually and got back into the battle. Ince saw three Haps 2,000 feet below and ahead. One went into a loop and the other two chandelled steeply. Ince chased the one that chandelled to the left and fired a two second burst when his prop went out again, flipping Ince's fighter on its wing. Ince chopped his throttles and dove for Lae. As he looked back Ince saw two Haps firing at him from either side of his tail. He went into a steeper dive and the two Haps broke off. Ince circled Lae at 18,000 feet and resolved his prop problem, then returned to action, only to find two Haps coming at him from port ahead. He turned into them and fired a short burst before his prop went out again. The Haps turned away, and Ince readjusted his props and climbed toward Salamaua at full throttle. Once over Salamaua, at 22,000 feet he joined two other P-38s in a Lufbery to the left. He spotted three Haps in a loose formation below in the middle of the Lufbery and dove on them. Other P-38s also dove through the Hap formation and two went into steep turns, the other into an Immelmann in front of Ince, who fired a short burst which went behind it. Ince pulled a tighter turn and fired a longer burst and the Hap went straight down in a Split-S. Ince's prop went out again, and at his high speed flipped him over on his back; he went into a partial spin and recovered. Once he recovered he adjusted his prop and returned to base.

Capt. Edward **Cragg** claimed his first of 15 victories and added a probable. (AAF)

2Lt. Robert **Adams** claimed his first of five victories. (AAF)

2Lt. John **Jones** claimed his first of eight victories. (AFAA)

1Lt. James **Ince** claimed his first of six victories. (AAF)

Ince's Wingman, 2Lt. Robert Adams, made three unsuccessful passes after the initial Japanese attack. After pulling up from his third pass Adams saw a P-38 (2Lt. Earl Smith/third flight #4) with a Zero about to make a quarter beam attack on it. By holding his position Adams would be head on with the Zero when it passed the P-38. So when the Zero passed under the P-38, the two pilots fired, with Adams getting hits and the Japanese bullets going over Adams' P-38. Adams had to dump his nose to avoid colliding with the enemy, which passed just over him. As he followed his victim Adams saw another Zero directly ahead and gave chase, firing a short burst before its pilot made a violent turn to escape.

1Lt. Marion Kirby was flying as Ince's #3, but had his Wingman abort. When the Japanese attacked his flight he left it to attack three Zeros above and behind. He missed the first but got a good shot on the #2 man, and it began to smoke. Kirby claimed it as a probable, as he did not "know if the damage was sufficient to down the plane." The #1 enemy fighter got on Kirby's tail and he quickly climbed away. He sighted another enemy fighter but did not get a good shot.

Third Flight

Capt. Franklin Tompkins, leading the third flight with Wingman 2Lt. Cyril Homer, was searching for the enemy under an off shore cloud bank between Lae and Salamaua at 23,000 feet. As they were making their turn inland, approximately 15 to 20 enemy fighters dove on them through the clouds inside their turn. The two Lightnings dropped their belly tanks and turned into four of the enemy that passed under them. Tompkins made a pass on two enemy fighters to his right and below, firing his .50s and 20mms. He saw pieces fly off the second Zero, and as he passed he saw that the fuselage had disintegrated and the entire tail section was missing. Tompkins made a pass at four Zeros, but had to break off when other Zeros got on his tail. Homer had remained with him throughout the combat, and intercepted the Zeros chasing Tompkins and diverted them to himself. All three fired at Homer head on, and he fired on the middle man, who fired first and hit Homers' right prop and left rudder stabilizer. Homer hit the enemy's engine, and the pilot seemed determined to crash into Homer, who had to dive quickly and evaded only by feet. After claiming that Zero as a probable, Homer began a gentle climb to rejoin Tompkins when he saw a Zero at the top of a loop coming at him and then looked around to see another Zero on his tail. Homer throttled away from his pursuers, but as he returned to rejoin Tompkins he saw four Zeros about to bounce his leader. Homer had to turn to slow down and get behind them, but Tompkins was able to pull away as Homer made a quarter stern attack, which caused the Zeros to dive away. Homer rejoined Tompkins, and the two circled the area at 7,000 feet south of Salamaua for half an hour providing top cover for two flights of P-39s before they left for Kila.

1Lt. Noel Lundy, Tompkins' second Element Leader, climbed into the initial attack at 23,000 feet, but a diving Hap cut off his climb. Lundy raced after four enemy fighters chasing a P-38 and fired and missed, while another enemy got on his tail, causing him to dive again. As he dove, a Hap chasing a P-38 crossed his path and Lundy fired, getting hits on the Hap. The enemy went into a "sloppy" spin and fell in flames into the cloud cover. As Lundy was looking around he saw tracers streaking under his right wing from below and behind. Lundy rolled into a steep dive into a cloud and lost his pursuer, then headed back to base.

Third Flight #4 man, 2Lt. Earl Smith, was bounced by three enemy fighters in the initial attack and dove away to escape but lost his flight. When he pulled up he faced three or four more enemy fighters diving on him. Smith turned after one that pulled up and exposed its belly to him. Smith fired from 150 to 75 yards and raked it from right to left wing, and its mid-fuselage began to smoke and it rolled over out of control. Smith Split-S'd to clear his tail and climbed back into the action. He dove to attack three enemy fighters that separated; two got behind him, and the other exchanged fire with Smith from head on. Smith reported that he hit the closing enemy but made no claim.

Summer 1943: Strategy: *Elkton III/Cartwheel Plan*

On 26 April 1943, the Joint Chiefs of Staff presented a new directive for offensive operations in the Pacific, naming MacArthur Supreme Commander of *Elkton III* and the SWPA and Adm. William Halsey as direct commander of the Commander, SOPAC area, but operating under general directives from MacArthur. *Elkton III*, code-named *Cartwheel*, called for an attack by MacArthur against northeast New Guinea and western New Britain, and by Halsey against the central Solomons.

The Joint Chiefs of Staff directive of 28 March 1943 defined objectives in the SWPA as a line running across the straits between Finschhafen, New Guinea, and New Britain, and ordered MacArthur to establish air bases on Woodlark and Kiriwina Islands; to seize the Huon Peninsula and Madang; and to occupy western New Britain. Meanwhile, under the direction of Adm. William Halsey, C-in-C, South Pacific Area, the Navy, along with Army and Marine troops, were to seize the Solomons and southern Bougainville as preparatory for the eventual seizure of Rabaul.

The three Tasks of *Elkton III/Cartwheel* were:

1) Establish airfields on Kiriwina and Woodlark Islands.
2) Seize Lae-Salamaua-Finschhafen-Madang area and occupy Western New Britain.
3) Seize and occupy the Solomon Islands, including southern Bougainville

with the purpose to "inflict losses on Japanese Forces, to deny these areas to Japan, to contain Japanese Forces in the Pacific Theater by maintaining the initiative, and to prepare for ultimate seizure of Bismarck Archipelago."

The Rational and Objectives of *Elkton III/Cartwheel* were:

The sea and land areas south of the Wau-Russell Island line were generally under Allied control, with the enemy in control north of that line. Allied and enemy defenses were concentrated in and around airfields, with the remainder of the land areas generally unoccupied.

The objectives of Task 1 required the establishment of airfields on Kiriwina and Woodlark, neither of which was occupied by Allied or enemy forces. The objectives of Tasks 2 and 3 required two general lines of advance: on the West, along the northeast coast of New Guinea to seize the Huon Peninsula area as far as Madang, and then across the Vitiaz Strait to seize the western New Britain area; while on the East, northwestward through the Solomons to seize southeastern Bougainville. West and East objectives were preliminary to the seizure of Rabaul and the occupation of the Bismarck Archipelago.

The establishment of airfields on Woodlark Island was a prerequisite to the seizure of the southeastern Bougainville area in order to provide wider employment of air power and obtain closer support for operations against Buin-Faisi. The occupying forces for Woodlark Island were to be supplied by SOPAC, but the operation was to be undertaken by the SWPA, which was to establish their own air forces on Woodlark and control their operation. The establishment of airfields on Kiriwina Island was complementary to the occupation and consolidation of Woodlark, and was required for the control of the air over the Solomon Sea and to assist the Allied advance along the western axis. Early occupation and consolidation of both islands was "mandatory," but full scale consolidation was contingent on the provision of adequate fighter cover on Goodenough Island. In order to maintain the initiative and contain Japanese forces in the SWPA, continuous air activity and early infiltrating attacks along both axes were to begin immediately and be "prosecuted vigorously" while avoiding commitment of important forces.

Task 2 required the successive seizure of the Lae-Markham Valley area, the occupation of Huon Peninsula, and the seizure and occupation of western New Britain, with the objective of securing airdromes to cover further advances, as well as the seizure and occupation of Madang to protect the northern flank. Operations along the eastern axis required the seizure and consolidation, or neutralization, successively of New Georgia airfields, the seizure and consolidation of airfields in the Buin-Faisi area, the seizure of Kieta, and the neutralization of Buka.

On the whole, the success of the advance into the Buin-Faisi area along the eastern axis was considered doubtful, as it depended on the completion of land-based airfields on Woodlark Island to provide a wider deployment and closer support of that operation. The establishment of airfields on Kiriwina and in the Lae area was to neutralize supporting Japanese air bases at Buka, Rabaul, and Kavieng. Operations to seize and occupy the western portion of New Britain and Madang could not progress before the establishment of airfields in the Lae and/or Markham Valley area. The sequence of the advance along either axis alone, or one axis in relation to the other, could not be definitely preplanned, but had to remain flexible in order to take advantage of the situation, regardless of the chronology of Tasks 1, 2, and 3 in the directive.

The general scheme of maneuver for *Elkton III/Cartwheel* was:

> "to improve all presently occupied forward air bases; occupy and establish air bases that could be secured without committing large forces; employ air forces from these bases to soften up and to gain air superiority over the initial attack objectives along the two axes; neutralize with appropriate aviation supporting enemy air bases and destroy enemy naval forces and shipping within range; move land forces forward covered by air and naval forces to obtain first objectives (existing and potential hostile air bases) and consolidate same; displace aviation forward onto captured airdromes. This process was to be repeated on successive objectives, neutralizing by air action, or by air, land and sea action, intermediate hostile installations which are not objectives of immediate attack.
>
> "The entire movement was to be covered by air attack on Japanese air and sea bases along the general perimeter Buka, Rabaul, and Kavieng, and Wewak with the objective of interrupting and denying sea supply and/or support or reinforcement of objectives under attack.
>
> "In the initiation of the operations, SWPA forces by amphibious operations, first secretly infiltrate and later when air coverage was available from Goodenough Island, move in force to occupy and consolidate Woodlark and Kiriwina Islands. Diverting and covering air attacks on Japanese bases and infiltrating ground attacks northwestward through the Solomons and toward Salamaua and Lae were to support the operation.
>
> "Preceded by strong land-based air action, the forces along the western axis operate against successive objectives to capture by air-borne and shore-to-shore operations air operating bases in the Huon Peninsula-Markham Valley area, in western New Britain, and along the northeastern coast of New Guinea to include Madang; the forces along the eastern axis progress northwestward by amphibious operations, to secure airdromes in the Buin-Faisi area, neutralizing or capturing enemy airdromes of New Georgia, later occupying the Kieta area and neutralizing hostile airfields in the vicinity of Buka Passage.
>
> "The general sequence and timing of the operations along either axis, or along one axis in relationship to the other, was to "be governed by conditions at the time in order that the maximum benefit could be derived from the successes of our own forces or weaknesses of the enemy." Generally speaking for planning purposes, occupation of Woodlark and Kiriwina Islands was to be simultaneous. The advance northward along the New Guinea coast to secure airfields in the Huon Peninsula-Markham Valley area was to precede a major attack on the Buin-Faisi area and was to be covered by diverting air and ground infiltration attacks along the eastern axis. Following the displacement of SWPA Air Forces into Lae area, the seizure of southeastern Bougainville could progress covered by neutralizing attacks by SWPA Air Force on Buka, Rabaul, and Kavieng, The remainder of the operations along both axes were to be made simultaneously to the final objectives, the South Pacific Air Force assisting in the neutralization of the Rabaul area and thus partially freeing the SWPA Air Forces to neutralize hostile air action along the Northeastern New Guinea coast."

This plan required seven more infantry divisions than were already in the theater, raising objections from the British. The Joint Chiefs responded with a directive that approved the plan using forces already in the theater or en route to it, and delayed its implementation by sixty days, when *Elkton III/Cartwheel* was scheduled to begin on 30 June 1943.

By the middle of June plans had been virtually completed for a three-pronged advance toward the principal objective, Rabaul. These plans involved simultaneous landings by South Pacific Forces at Rendova, in the New Georgia group, and at other points in the upper Solomons, and by Southwest Pacific forces on Kiriwina and Woodlark Islands, as well as at Nassau Bay, 50 miles up the coast from Morobe Harbor in New Guinea. South Pacific naval forces, in addition to their part in the New Georgia operation, were to reconnoiter an area north of 1° north latitude in order to detect enemy forces coming south from Truk, and were to perform a similar function northeast of New Ireland and Buka Passage and east of 155° east longitude. The Southwest Pacific air and sea forces, meanwhile, were to provide defensive reconnaissance over the Solomons and Bismarck Sea areas west of the 155° longitude line and southwest of New Ireland and Buka Passage, and were to support a seizure of Woodlark and Kiriwina by attacks on such targets of opportunity as aircraft and ships.

On the New Guinea mainland, Allied land forces had formulated a master plan. Australian troops of the 15th Brigade were to seize Bobdubi Ridge, which dominated the Japanese supply line to Mubo; American troops, landing at Nassau Bay, were to push inland and along the coast, destroying the Japanese forces near Mubo in conjunction with the Australians and pushing those near Komiatum back to Salamaua. Meanwhile, outposts farther north and in the interior, notably at Bena Bena, 100 miles northwest of Lae, were to be built up as intelligence centers, and to attract the attention of the enemy away from activities at more vital Allied bases.

The Japanese, fully aware of potential Allied threats, were continuing to strengthen their forces in Northeast New Guinea. Shipping continued to flow into Wewak and Hansa Bay; barge traffic moved across the Vitiaz Strait from New Britain and along the New Guinea coast; and ground troops gradually moved into the Ramu River Valley, making contact with Allied patrols advancing out from the Bena Bena area inevitable. The Japanese also attacked Allied land forces from the air using their bases at Oro Bay, Dobodura, Wau, and Bena Bena. These air bases were hit a number of times in June, especially Bena Bena. Several of these air raids utilized relatively large forces; for example, the Bena Bena area was attacked by 27 medium bombers and 30 fighters on 15 June, by six bombers and six fighters the next day, and then by 18 bombers and 22 fighters on the following day. On 18 June Bena Bena was attacked by eight aircraft, and by an unknown number of aircraft which dropped 49 bombs on 19 June.

6

June 1943

For the three weeks from 21 May to 10 June 1943, 5FC fighters continued to fly uneventful escort for bombers and transports used for the build up of supplies and materiel for the upcoming attacks. By mid-June Japanese bombers had begun attacks on Allied bases and airfields.

7 June 1943: 49FS/7FS

On 7 June, Capt. Woods' 9FS Lightnings flew from Dobodura south to Port Moresby's 7 Mile Drome, now called Jackson Drome by the RAAF, to await the arrival of C-47 Dakotas from Australia. All aircraft were to refuel at Jackson for a 380 mile flight to the advanced base at Bena Bena Village, 175 miles northwest of Lae. These supply missions were flown for five days without confrontation.

June-July 1943: 8FG/80FS Personnel Changes

On 4 June, Capt. George Welch was transferred from the 36FS to become the Operations Officer of the 80FS. Welch was known to be self-centered and indifferent to those around him, especially enlisted men, a situation that would not be easily tolerated by the easy going 80FS. Other pilots that came into the 80th in July were Lieutenants Edward DeGraffenreid, Paul Murphey, Jennings Myers, and Louis Schriber, all of whom would become aces.

Meanwhile, the new 475th Fighter Group needed to have veteran pilots and ground crews to form its nucleus, and they were to come from every squadron in the 5th Fighter Command. For the 80FS, it meant that Ed Czarnecki, Noel Lundy, Daniel Roberts, Zach Dean, James Ince, Marion Kirby, and Campbell Wilson were transferred by the middle of July. The 35FS lost Warren Lewis, Joe McKeon, and Vivian Cloud, who would go on to become aces with the 475th.

June 1943 - Replacement Policy Continues to Demoralize

Kenney found the War Department's replacement policy was inadequate and demoralizing to his personnel. To Kenney, the problem of replacement personnel was of as great importance as that of replacement aircraft. Unlike the aloof MacArthur, Kenney was one of those old school officers who genuinely considered the men under his command as "my boys." During the middle of 1943 McArthur decided that all American airmen would stay in the combat zone until the end of the war. Kenney always followed orders explicitly and never openly criticized MacArthur, even after the war. But MacArthur's refusal to initiate a rotation policy caused Kenney to explain to McArthur that combat airmen and ground crews were highly trained personnel who after a time in combat became less and less effective.

Kenney wrote to General Arnold: "With the possible exception of Chennault (23FG P-40s in the CBI - author), I do not believe anyone else is flying stuff as old and worn out as these youngsters out here are. Every time I visit an outfit I have to listen to the same old question: 'How much longer do we have to push these old crocks around?'" Kenney added that he supposed he need not worry, since "the newspapers back home believe that Hitler….will throw in the sponge this year and that the Nips are out of boats and airplanes and will be a pushover." His personal opinions were expressed somewhat differently in his memoirs:

> "I have never read of any nation which was not hungry and still 300 divisions quitting cold but maybe the Germans are going to be different, maybe they will throw down their arms and allow the mobs of Czechs, Poles, Slavs, Belgians, Jews and so on massacre the whole nation. If I were a German I would figure myself better off at war until my opponents got tired enough to offer me acceptable terms. As for the Nip, I have quit arguing but insist that this fighting out here will keep us busy until 1948. In the meantime I would sure like enough people and planes to get the job done that soon."

Kenney felt that anyone who accumulated 300 hours should be rotated out, and calculated his monthly needs for the 5AF on this basis. Kenney calculated that of the 22 crews in his three heavy bomber groups, seven crews per month would be KIA or MIA; three would be out of action due to wounds, sickness, or battle fatigue before reaching 300 hours; and 12 crews would reach the 300 hour limit. For the four medium bomber groups he would need 20 crews; for three fighter groups 35 pilots were required, and 58 for five fighter groups. Kenney's replacement figures agreed almost exactly with the War Department's calculations based on 15% of assigned strength. But soon discrepancies arose between Kenney's replacement figures and those of the War Department.

On 14 June, all air forces were informed that Operational Training Unit (OUT) personnel planned for new units after July would be diverted to replacement crews only in order to bring crew strength to two and a half crews for each heavy and medium bomber and two crews for each light, fighter, and transport aircraft. AAF commanders were requested to immediately report their crew requirements necessary to reach this level. However, there were limits to the number of trained personnel available, along with special commitments to certain air forces. Arnold stated that if this proposal were carried out, no additional combat units could be available between 15 August 1943 and January1944. To effect this change in policy, Arnold asked the commanders of each of his Air Forces to submit "carefully considered recommendations that you must have on hand for each type of combat aircraft."

Kenney submitted his estimates on 9 July, and they were not acceptable to War Department planners. His general requirements were two crews per aircraft in all tactical units, including troop carrier, with a minimum of 15% per month replacement. The War Department, after considering the requests of the different theaters and the established commitments and priorities, notified Kenney that for the next year he would receive a replacement flow of no more than 15% per month for all units except troop carrier, which would receive 7.5%. Also, any increase of combat crews to more than one crew per aircraft would have to be accomplished by using these authorized replacements, as no others could be supplied.

In character, Kenney did not accept this decision as final, as he did not believe that he could conduct the imminent offensive without more replacements and insinuated that the War Department did not understand his problem. Kenney had been satisfied with the quality of replacements, as "the 345th Medium Group and the 475th Fighter Group were the best he had seen." But he stated that if the replacement program as set up by the Air Staff was carried out, "I am sunk." Kenney forcefully argued his position to Arnold, who was persuaded that "certain exceptions could be made in the general War Department policy." On 17 August Brig.Gen. Malin Craig, AC/AS, OC&R, informed the Chief of Air Staff that "it now appears possible to furnish sufficient replacement crews in excess of 15% during the months of January and February 1944." The heavy, medium, and troop carrier units, but not fighter units, of the Fifth Air Force were to be supplied as Kenney requested.

10 June 1943: 35FG/39FS

On 10 June, Capt. Thomas Lynch and his Wingman, Capt. Charles Sullivan, were flying over the Japanese airbase at Bena Bena at 24,000 feet when they spotted a twin engine bomber at 2 o'clock about 1,000 feet above them. The two dropped their tanks and climbed. Lynch fired first at 150 yards astern but saw no observable results, as he broke away. Sullivan then attacked as the bomber headed toward Madang, but he, too, saw no damage, as the bomber continued on at high speed. As Lynch approached again the bomber's port engine was beginning to trail smoke. Lynch fired from astern and hit the port engine, which exploded, and the entire wing caught fire. After falling 3,000 feet the bomber exploded for his 11th victory.

12 June 1943: 49FG/9FS

During the early morning of 12 June, the 9FS again staged through Jackson to escort C-47s. However, the ground crews had problems with fueling and loading the 150 gallon belly tanks on the 12 Lightnings led by Squadron Leader Capt. Sidney Woods. At 0800 the Dakotas took off without fighter cover. It was not until 40 minutes after the Dakotas left that 10 Lightnings flew north with the futile hope of catching the transports in the deteriorating weather. All 1Lt. James Watkins' Red Flight took off together, but Blue Flight Element Leader Capt. Gerald Johnson also stayed behind due to fueling problems, as did Wood's Wingman, 1Lt. Harry Lidstrom.

Woods led his Green Flight to 11,000 feet as top cover, but Mankin's oxygen system malfunctioned and he returned to Horanda, leaving Woods and 1Lt. Richard Bong to continue top cover above the Red Flight Elements of Flight Leader Watkins, 1Lt. George Albers, and 2Lts. John Howard and Frank Wunder, who were just ahead at 8,000. To Red Flight's starboard were the four P-38s of Blue Flight Leader 1Lt. Clayton Barnes, with wingmen 2Lts. John Stowe and Francis Nutter.

The nine Lightnings flew for more than an hour over the valleys of central New Guinea, which were covered by clouds. Watkins finally broke radio silence and told Woods that they certainly must have passed Bena Bena, and led his Red Flight down through the clouds to 7,000 feet while the rest of the formation circled through one complete turn. Watkins' Flight then climbed back to 10,000 feet and turned west in search of Bena Bena, just as Bong called out Oscars about to attack Blue Flight. To their right and above at 14,000 feet, eight Oscars of the 1st Sentai from Wewak dove into their attack and all of the Flying Knights immediately dropped their tanks.

Blue Flight dove a short distance to gain speed for a climb, but Nutter could not jettison his port tank, so he climbed to 10,000 feet with Barnes and Stowe. The three then turned starboard to face the descending Oscars, but only Barnes damaged an enemy fighter (a probable) on this pass. Another Oscar climbed in front of Barnes' guns and he fired a long burst on the climbing fighter until it stalled out and dropped off in a slow vertical spin, plunging into the jungle.

Woods and Bong turned hard right to cut off the eight overhead Ki-43s, but 9FS CO Woods, with the red diagonal command stripe across his tail, was selected by the lead Oscar, which was similarly marked with the broad red wing bands of a Sentai Commander. The Japanese Commander expertly gained a dead astern position behind Woods, who skillfully responded with a 400 mph roll away into the clouds. Bong continued on alone in a head on attack against five Oscars but did no damage before three Oscars turned in behind him. Bong escaped into the clouds and then climbed back to 12,000 feet to find seven Oscars only a mile ahead. Targeting the nearest, he closed, firing a long burst from 600 yards down to 50 yards without effect, and had to head for the clouds for a second time. He reengaged for a third time with a nose on pass on one of the Oscars that drifted to his port. Bong fired a perfect low degree deflection shot and two 20mm rounds exploded in the target's mid-fuselage; the enemy slowly rolled into a diving spin into the sea for Bong's 11th victory. Bong quickly fired on another Oscar, scoring some hits, but was forced to break off when his Lightning was hit.

1Lt. Richard **Bong**. (R) got his 11th victory two days after Capt. Thomas **Lynch**. (L) got his 11th. (AAF)

Capt. Thomas **Lynch** shot down a Betty for his 11th victory. (AAF)

Capt. Sidney **Woods**. (with Capt. Clay Tice) was an excellent and well-like and respected combat leader. (AAF)

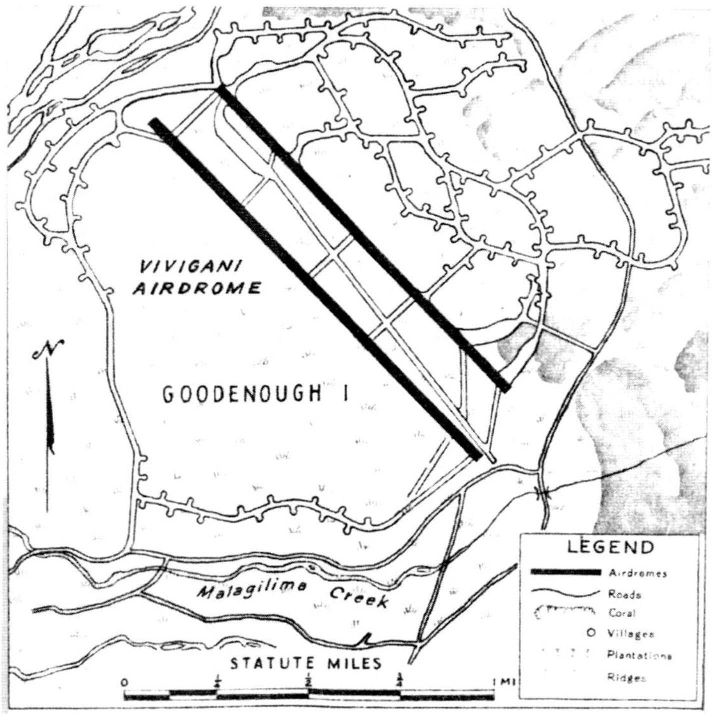

Vivigani Airdrome Goodenough Island

Red Flight had also turned into the Sentai, which quickly passed over them. Watkins was unable to get off a shot; Wingman Alber got off a wild shot, but he lost Watkins in the process; while Howard, hampered by a still attached fuel tank, made only a half-hearted firing pass before he broke off for Port Moresby. Wunder, in the tail end position, fired a quick, poorly aimed burst at an Oscar before rejoining Woods and Bong, and all 9FS P-38s arrived safely at Horanda, nearly out of gas. Bong landed with a flat tire, hydraulic lines severed, and numerous 7mm bullet holes in his right boom, as well as two additional holes in each wing.

Damage from these enemy air raids was negligible, but not because of Allied fighter interception. Fighters, which during June were concentrating upon the escort of bombers and transports, made contact with enemy planes no more than three times during the period 14 May to 10 June. Many of the raids on Bena Bena were not intercepted because no Allied fighters were based there, and attacks on other bases which did have fighter protection were usually small and carried out at night. Although these raids did little damage, they were a nuisance at times, as when a performance of the motion picture "Arsenic and Old Lace" was interrupted at Dobodura on 12 June. Meanwhile, on 16 June, 13AF fighters had the best day against the Japanese in the Pacific when they scored an astounding 43 victories; the 5FC would not engage the enemy until 21 June.

20 June 1943: 35FG/39FS

After serving as Squadron CO since 18 December 1943, Maj. Harris Denton stepped down and was replaced by Maj. Richard Cella, who had been with the squadron since the summer of 1942.

21 June 1943: 8FG/80FS

Thirteen P-38s and 100 enlisted men of the 80th Fighter Squadron had moved to Vivigani Strip, on Goodenough Island, to cover the invasion of Kiriwina and Woodlark. The 80 FS had not scored any victories since 21 May, and their escort of B-25s to Guadalgasal, a Japanese strongpoint between Lae and Salamaua to the southwest, did not seem promising for aerial action. At 0940 14 P-38s of the 80FS took off and joined the Mitchells at 15,000 feet. After the B-25s dropped their bombs and were headed for home the air combat began.

Lead Flight

The Lead Flight was led by 1Lt. Leonidas Mathers and Wingman 2Lt. Donald Hanover, with second Element Leader 2Lt. Campbell Wilson and Wingman 2Lt. Jess Gidley. At 1100 Mathers' flight encountered 15 or 20 well scattered enemy fighters at 15,000 feet. The enemies turned into the attack but were unsuccessful in reaching firing range, so Mathers and Wingman Hanover dove through the enemy without firing a shot and ducked into the clouds. Hanover's wing tanks did not release and he moved onto Gidley's wing. Mathers left the cloud and made a head on pass at a Zero from above, but did not see any results and went back into the clouds. As Mathers left the clouds again he passed through the enemy formation and got behind a Zero and fired as it turned away. The Zero caught on fire and fell through the clouds at 10,000 feet. Mathers pulled back into the clouds and dove out again to hit another Zero with a quick shot for a probable, then climbed back into the clouds as several Zeros tried to get on his tail. Mathers flew toward Lae, where he saw two P-38s engaging several Zeros. He dove on a Zero, getting several hits for another probable, and as he pulled up he saw another Zero. The Zero tried to turn away just as Mathers got into range, but he got a good burst into the enemy fighter, which caught fire and plunged through the clouds out of control. Mathers' ICR describes several more passes with possible hits; he claimed five damaged aircraft, but is officially credited with two victories and two probables. At the end of the combat Mathers had only one gun functioning while he was chased by a Zero that was unable to get within range as Mathers raced for home.

1Lt. Leonidas **Mathers** got his 2nd and 3rd victories of four and added two probables. (AAF)

Second Element Leader Wilson and Wingman Gidley met the initial enemy attack, and Wilson fired on the enemy Wingman with a long burst from the front quarter, but the two passed through into the same cloud layer as Mathers and Hanover. When Wilson and Gidley pulled out of the cloud they rejoined the flight and flew toward Huon Gulf, where they met three enemy fighters at 9 o'clock low. Wilson and Gidley dove steeply to port and made a stern attack, firing at a large deflection angle and hitting an enemy fighter for a probable. The other enemy fighters escaped by diving into cloud cover. During their attack three enemy fighters got on the two Americans' tails and they had to dive into the clouds before the enemy could get into firing range. Wilson flew on instruments for two minutes, and when he broke into the clear tracers whizzed by and forced him back into the clouds. He flew on instruments for a time, and when he broke into the clear he was alone and headed back to base.

When the flight pulled out of the clouds Gidley noticed that Hanover's tanks did not release, and there was a Zero on his tail. Gidley chased the Zero away and Hanover joined him as the two climbed into the clouds. When Gidley broke out of the clouds he was alone; he joined two other P-38s and flew at the tail end of the improvised flight. They spotted eight Oscars below, and the two P-38s took on the lead Oscars, while Gidley went after the tail end Oscar. Gidley fired a long burst on the Oscar, which seemed unaware of the attack until Gidley closed to within 200 yards; then the enemy pilot started to turn, but then slowly half rolled into the ground. Gidley then noticed several Oscars were diving on him and dove away in a high speed dive, reaching 450mph when he pulled out and climbed into a cloud. At 15,000 feet he joined two other P-38s as the tail end man. The three Lightnings circled for several minutes and saw eight Oscars below. Gidley and another P-38 closed, but the Oscars spotted them and separated, diving away as Gidley fired a short burst but missed. Gidley pulled up through the clouds and lost the other Lightning, but soon was joined by another P-38, and the two headed home. Gidley was on reserve fuel and landed at 30 Mile Drome to refuel, then headed home to Kila.

Second Flight

1Lt. James Ince led a flight consisting of Wingman 2Lt. Cornelius Smith and Element Leader 1Lt. Raymond Daly with Wingman 2Lt. Robert Adams. After Mathers' lead flight dove under the cloud layer Ince led his flight over the cloud layer at 18,000 toward Salamaua, then proceeded up the coast toward Lae. Halfway toward Lae, Ince saw eight bandits ahead and below and called the enemy fighters to second Element Leader Daly. Daly apparently didn't hear, as he and Adams turned out to sea. Ince then saw 10 more enemy fighters dead ahead and below at 14,000 feet and called them out. This time everyone in the flight saw them and dropped their tanks and dove. Ince made a quick firing pass, but saw no results as he passed through the enemy formation. He pulled up and made a quick tight turn and dove on three more Zeros. The two enemy pilots made quick tight turns to escape while the third Zero made a lazy turn and received a long burst from Ince's guns, getting hit just behind the cockpit. The fighter made two slow rolls and fell into a smoking spin. As Ince looked up he saw two fighters making an overhead pass on him and went into a violent barrel roll and dive. Ince continued the dive for about a minute and pulled out with nothing on his tail. He climbed to 15,000 feet and joined five other P-38s, then saw one peel off onto four Zeros below. Ince followed the P-38 as it shot down one of the four Zeros and went after the other three. All three turned into him and Ince took a quick shot without result, then pulled up and away. In his climb he met four more Zeros and took another quick shot at the one that turned into him. The two opponents closed so fast that Ince was unable to see any hits. Ince then climbed to 16,000 feet and searched the Salamaua area for more Zeros, then moved on up the coast with negative results. Ince joined several P-38s flying toward Lae where, they saw six Zeros over the entrance to the Markham Valley. He followed the first P-38 toward the Zeros and got behind one and gave it a long burst, setting it on fire. Ince had to claim a probable, as he had to dive into the clouds to get away from two or three Zeros directly on his tail. When he left the cloud he was alone and returned to base low on fuel.

80FS P-38 over the Markham Valley. (AAF)

After his initial attacks were unsuccessful, 2Lt. Cornelius "Corky" Smith finally pulled out and saw an enemy fighter firing on his tail. Smith went into a high speed dive, and when he had cleared his tail, he found himself in the middle of a dogfight. The eager Smith fired from too long a range and missed badly. 2Lt. Robert Adams dove in and fired a long burst that hit the Zero for a probable. Adams' radio, some instruments, and his guns all malfunctioned, so he motioned Smith to take the lead for an attack on several Oscars climbing toward them. Smith dove on one of the Oscars with the impotent Adams flying behind him to bluff the enemy into thinking Smith had a Wingman. Smith's first burst hit the Oscar's port left wing; the enemy aircraft lost pieces, inverted wildly, and spun toward the jungle. Immediately, Smith was attacked by another Oscar firing from behind. Adams made a bluffing pass at the Oscar, but the Japanese pilot turned into Adams instead. Adams flew frantically and was able to avoid this Oscar, as well as several other Japanese in the area. Adams finally escaped and tried to recharge his guns, but the solenoid seemed to be burned out. He had fired just one burst at the beginning of the combat and claimed a damaged Oscar. Adams' only option now was to return to base. After Adams left, Smith sighted several other Japanese fighters over the Lae area. These Japanese were flying a defensive Lufbery Circle while P-38s made occasional passes at them. Smith approached an Oscar flying in the circle and closed until he was within 300 yards before he opened fire and exploded its oxygen compartment mid-fuselage. Soon another Oscar broke out of the circle and looped up on its back to face Smith in a head on attack. Smith's cannon and machine guns tore the Oscar into pieces and it fell off into a spiral, trailing heavy smoke and flame. Smith then joined another flight of P-38s to patrol over Lae, but soon had to leave when his engines began to overheat and he was low on fuel.

2Lt. Cornelius "Corky" **Smith** began scoring in a big way by shooting down his first three Zeros and adding a probable. (AAF)

Third Flight

1Lt. Charles Taylor led a three plane flight that included 1Lt. Elwood Krisher and 2Lt. William Fotheringham. As Taylor was leading his flight out of a cloud bank at 17,000 feet toward Lae and 20 miles out he saw four fighters five miles ahead. At first Taylor thought they were P-39s, but as he closed he saw the Japanese markings and identified them as Oscars. Taylor made a 90 degree starboard turn and saw 10 more Oscars diving from 3 o'clock above. Taylor dove and was met by 10 to 15 more Oscars from 1 o'clock ahead. Taylor pulled up and fired a short burst from 350 to 200 yards and hit an Oscar for a probable. The harassed Taylor had to go into a vertical dive to escape his pursuers, then headed toward a small offshore island, where he saw seven or eight twin engine aircraft to starboard at 11,000 feet, two miles behind, heading in the same direction. Taylor thought they could be B-25s and circled around them, but then he saw that they were Japanese Sally bombers. When Taylor turned to get behind them another P-38 also made a pass on the bombers. Both P-38s were fired upon by the bombers' gunners, and the other Lightning was hit in one of its engines and dove away. Taylor made a head on pass from slightly above and fired two bursts, causing some damage, but before he could finish it off an Oscar came in from 5 o'clock and fired at 250 yards. Taylor dove away into some clouds with a damaged claim. When he emerged he climbed to 10,000 feet and saw the Sallys again in two three ship Vs. He made a quick firing pass, but broke off when he saw four Oscars escorting the bombers.

When the Zeros turned into the flight 1Lt. Elwood Krisher dropped his tanks and saw four more Zeros to starboard but some distance behind. These Zeros turned to follow, but Krisher was closer to the original 10 Zeros and decided to attack them. As he was diving into his attack Krisher looked back and saw the four Zeros closing from behind. He then saw 15 more Zeros coming toward him at 2 o'clock above, but still a long distance away. Krisher fired at a Zero from directly above, hitting behind the cockpit, and the fuselage began to break up. Seven or eight Zeros from the large formation were trying to cut Krisher off before he could turn into them, so he dove away from out to sea. When he was beginning to regain altitude Krisher saw six bombers flying south out to sea in two three ship Vs. Initially, Krisher thought they could be B-25s, but soon identified them as Sally bombers and made a beam attack on the rear three. He carried the attack to very close range and broke up their formation. As Krisher was turning to make a second attack another P-38 came in to make a front beam attack. When Krisher got into range to fire his port engine cut out and started on fire. He dove into the clouds, feathered his engine, and headed back to base.

During the initial attack, after he dropped his tanks and dove, 2Lt. William Fotheringham saw a Zero on Krisher's tail and turned into it and fired a five second 90 degree burst; the Zero Split-S'd away but Fotheringham saw no hits. He climbed and saw two Zeros on his tail and throttled away from them and came upon six Zeros. He made a diving pass and two turned into him while the others scattered. Fotheringham turned into one and fired and saw it smoke as he passed over it for a probable. He then saw three Zeros below and attacked, and when one turned into him he fired a short head on burst and saw some hits. Fotheringham continued in a diving right turn and ran into two Zeros coming out from behind a cloud. He fired a good front quarter burst on the lead fighter and then got a short burst on the second straggling Zero but made no claims. He then saw a P-38 below attacking several Zeros and dove on one, firing a long burst that sent it out of control through the clouds. Before heading for base Fotheringham took part in a combined attack on six Zeros but scored no observable hits. When he landed Fotheringham found a hole in one prop, a hole in the reserve fuel tank behind his cockpit, several holes in his port engine, and the trim tab was shot away.

Capt. George **Welch** scored his 8th and 9th victories. (AAF)

Fourth Flight

Capt. George Welch was leading his flight near Salamaua and saw five Zeros at 5,000 feet. He dove on one and started it smoking, but was unable to see the results, as his right engine cut out. The flight continued toward Lae, where he saw eight Zeros "doing aerobatics" (Lufbery) at 10,000 feet. Two Zeros broke out of the Lufbery and came head on in string toward Welch. He dove and set one on fire during a head on pass, and the Zero rolled over on his back and plunged into the sea. Meanwhile, 1Lt. Charles Cobb spotted a Zero closing on Welch's tail and gave it a burst and the enemy pilot dove away. Cobb followed and "shot six feet off its fuselage." Welch flew through a cloud and saw a Zero about 100 feet ahead flying at 90 degrees and fired, tearing off half a wing and pieces of fuselage. Cobb saw another Zero about to dive on Welch at 9,000 feet and dove on the unsuspecting enemy. He took a zero degrees deflection shot from directly behind and sent into a burning spin. Cobb climbed for altitude, and at 12,000 feet began another attack on three Zeros that met him head on in a ragged string formation. As they came into range they rolled over, fired, and dove straight down. Cobb attempted to follow but had to pull up, as his IAS was 550mph. The two victories gave Welch nine for the war. He had scored four victories during Pearl harbor flying P-40s for the 47FS, and then a year later, on 1 December 1942, he scored three more victories flying P-39s for the 36FS. Cobb's two victories were his only victories of the war. The Squadron's 13 victories, 10 probables, and two damaged established it as a major player in the 5FC.

2Lt. William **Fotheringham** claimed his only victory of the war. (AAF)

June 1943: 348FG Arrives in Australia

Beginning, Training, and Deployment

The 348th Fighter Group was constituted on 24 September 1942 at Mitchel Field, NY, and activated on 30 September 1942 at Bradley Field, Windsor Locks, CT. On 29 October 1942, the group moved to a newly built area just outside Westover Field, MA, which unlike their facilities at Bradley Field had indoor plumbing, central heating, and suitable mess facilities. Maj. Neel Kearby was named the first Commander of the 348FG in October after he had commanded the 14th Pursuit Squadron in Panama flying the low altitude P-39. The day Kearby arrived the Group received its 13,000 pound P-47 Thunderbolts, a P-47B, and a P-47C. The Thunderbolt had not yet been combat tested, but definitely promised to perform better than P-39s and P-40s, which were tenaciously trying to hold the line against the Germans and Japanese. Meanwhile, the Thunderbolt was intended for the ETO as a high altitude bomber escort, with the 348FG being one of the units scheduled to fly escort out of England. The P-47 was scheduled to be combat ready by May 1942, but was late in being deployed. By November the Group was assigned an Executive Officer, Capt. William Hovis, an Adjutant, 2Lt. William Parent, and an Intelligence Officer, 2Lt. Bernard Roth.

The 342nd Fighter Squadron was the first squadron to be assigned to the Group. It was organized at Bradley Field on 4 October 1942, with its cadre transferred from the 56th and 80th Fighter Groups, which were based nearby. Among these original pilots, George Burgess, George Dougherty,

David Eastham, and Randall Hilbig would become Squadron and Group Leaders, while Robert Gibb, Marvin Grant, Robert Knapp, Lawrence O'Neill, and Edward Popek would become aces. Capt. William Banks was appointed the Squadron Commander on 2 November 1942, but was Squadron Commander for only about three weeks, when the more senior Capt. Raymond Gallagher usurped the commanding role. By mid-November the 342nd received 25 P-47Bs and P-47Cs. On 28 October 1942, the 342nd moved to Westover Field, near Chicopee falls, MA, and at this time several more men who would shape the 348th appeared on the 342nd's roster. In December, 1Lt. Walter Benz arrived from the 326FG as a flight leader, and nearly three years later, just after Japan surrendered, he would be named Group Commander. Future ace and Commander of the 58FG, Capt. Edward Roddy, was named the Operations Officer for the 342nd.

Meanwhile, the other two squadrons (the 340FS and 341FS) were organized and began training. The 340FS was commanded in turn by 1Lt. LeRoy Sutler and 1Lt. Leighton Stevens before Capt. Frank Oksala took over on 6 November 1942. Future ace Capt. Meade Brown was named the Squadron's Operations Officer. When Oksala moved up to 348th Headquarters, Capt. Charles MacDonald became CO of the 340FS on 17 November. The very capable and popular MacDonald would lead the Squadron into its first combat in the Pacific, and after he left the Group a year later he would gain distinction with the celebrated 475th Fighter Group. Capt. David Campbell assumed command of the 341FS on 15 November, and was joined by future Squadron Commanders and aces Captains Samuel Blair and John Moore, and other prominent pilots of the original 341FS cadre: Lieutenants Arthur Weeks, Clarence Blend, Charles Cronk, Glenn Ferryman, and William Foulis. Meanwhile, Kearby was promoted to Lieutenant Colonel in November 1942.

During November the Group moved to Westover Field, where it met difficulties in training, as air traffic there was very congested over the base, and there also seemed to be a permanent haze that made navigation and observation hazardous for novice pilots learning to fly a high performance aircraft like the Thunderbolt. The first training casualty occurred on 1 December 1942, when 2Lt. Charles Hay of the 340FS was in the landing circuit over Westover in the overcast weather when he crashed and was killed. During training formation flying was stressed, as the pilots learned the basic grouping in twos, then threes, and finally in the standard four plane flight in which they would meet the enemy. Practice in navigation and instrument flying were completed before the pilots began high altitude training, which was to be the P-47's chief regimen as an escort fighter flying at its maximum efficiency at 20,000 to 40,000 feet. Once the pilots were proficient flyers they began gunnery training, and finally the aerobatics and mock dogfights. Soon the pilots began to appreciate the P-47, which could transform itself from the unwieldy "Jug" with a low rate of climb at lower altitudes to a high altitude fighter that could dive at very high speeds and then zoom up out of its dive using its dive inertia. Its heavy armament was comprised of eight .50 caliber machine guns in the wings, which could tear apart enemy fighters and bombers, and would also make it one of World War II's most effective strafers. Its ruggedness was legendary. In February 1943, Maj. Robert Rowland replaced William Hovis as Executive Officer, and Hovis moved up to Headquarters, New York Air Defense Wing.

The 348th moved to Bedford Airdrome from 13 January to 28 April 1943, where the training schedule was stepped up to meet the Luftwaffe over Europe. With this intensification in training accidents occurred; a pilot of the 342FS was killed on 1 March 1943, while on 12 April two P-47s of the 341st collided and the pilots were lost in the subsequent crashes. As training neared a close the 348th awaited orders for overseas shipment. Most groups that were equipped with P-47s were destined for Europe, and two (the 56th and 352nd Fighter Groups) would become renowned while fighting with the Eighth Air Force in England.

During this time Gen. George Kenney's undermanned and poorly equipped 5AF was desperately trying to defend Port Moresby and to thwart the Japanese from reinforcing their northern New Guinea garrisons. Kenney really wanted three P-38 groups, which had the proven speed, range, and altitude to combat the Japanese fighters and bombers, and even preferred the dated P-40 over the P-47, with its short range and slow climb, which was "probably a perfectly good fighter...in spite of some of the adverse comments from England." By the end of March the Operations Division, War Department Staff decided that the 348th would be diverted to the Fifth Air Force. But at the time the Group's P-47s were beset by difficulties, as engine adjustments were required to prevent piston and ignition failure, the radio had too much interference, and dangerous fire hazards had to be eliminated. Flight and ground personnel were scheduled to depart in early May, and their Thunderbolts would be ready by 12 June. The 342FS and Headquarters moved from Bedford back to Westover, while the 340th and 341st returned from Green Field, RI, on 26 April, where the two squadrons had conducted their winter training. Captains Hervey Carpenter and Max Wiecks, two pilots who had already seen combat in the Pacific flying the P-39, joined the 340FS during training. Carpenter would eventually take command of the squadron after MacDonald left, while Wiecks would score the Group's first confirmed air victory. By the end of March the 348th's pilots had averaged nearly 185 hours flying time in the P-47.

On 9 May 1943 the Group moved to Camp Shanks, NY, for its final stage of preparation for overseas shipment. The 348FG boarded the transport *Henry Gibbons* on 14 May and sailed the next day into the Atlantic; on 21 May it passed through the Panama Canal enroute to the Pacific. On 4 June the *Henry Gibbons* anchored off Bora, in the Society Islands, and then journeyed on to Brisbane on 14 June, where the 65 pilots and mechanics of the air echelon were disembarked while the ground echelon remained on the transport until it reached Townsville, on the northern Australia coast, on 23 June.

The air echelon proceeded to Eagle Farms, which was a major aircraft testing and assembly facility, to wait for the promised 100 P-47s. When the P-47s arrived their assembly took only minimal time, after which they were flown to Archer Field for 10 hours of check flight and boresighting for acceptance for squadron service. By the flip of a coin the 342FS Squadron received the first P-47s, followed by the 341FS and finally the 340FS.

Meanwhile, after only two days anchored off Australia, the remaining ground echelon left for Port Moresby, where they disembarked on the 23rd. The 342FS arrived at Moresby on 14 July, led by Maj. R.K. Gallagher, marking the first time an entire squadron flew from Brisbane to Moresby without losing an aircraft. The 341st, led by Maj. David Campbell, arrived in Moresby on the 20th, losing two aircraft during a taxiing accident in Australia. The 340FS, led by Maj. Charles McDonald, arrived on the 27th without incident. Lt.Col. Kearby and his new XO, Maj. Robert Rowland, were commended for having 86 of 88 fighters arrive safely.

June 1943: 348FG: P-47 is Tested and Improved

Soon after the P-47 arrived at Eagle Farms, rumors circulated in 5FC command ranks that the Thunderbolt was a poor substitute for the P-38 and even for the P-40. The first drawback was that it was "short-legged" due to lack of fuel capacity. The P-47 arrived at Eagle Farms to be assembled, but no drop tanks were supplied for them. Without the additional fuel carried in these tanks, the P-47 did not have enough range to fly into combat in the SWPA. Kenney complained that "engineers back home were developing planes with no more range than is needed to defend London or make a fighter sweep across a ditch (the Channel) that is no bigger than Chesapeake Bay." Earlier 210 gallon tanks had been tried by the Materiel Command in the US but were discarded, as they caused tail

Gen. Kenney set up a simulated combat between a P-47 flown by Col. Neel Kearby and a P-38 flown by Lt.Col. George Prentice. (AAF)

buffeting. In early July, the 27th Depot Repair Squadron at Port Moresby was assigned to develop a suitable tank with a reliable release mechanism. The first proposal was to modify the flat oval-shaped 110 gallon tank used by P-39s and P-40s. The Service Command at Patterson Field was to send 100 modification kits, but could only provide 10 kits per week due to production constraints and the demand from other theaters. As the 348FG was scheduled to go into combat in two months this was entirely unacceptable to Kenney. The 27th Depot Repair Squadron (DRS) worked 24 hour days and, using tools and materials on hand, were able to modify P-47 fuel tanks at a rate of seven per day and equipped over 100 fighters. The Depot Repair Squadron at Brisbane developed a 260 gallon tank which was superior to the 110 gallon tanks and would become the standard in the SWPA. Gen. Arnold commented on this fuel tank development: "There is no reason in God's world why General Kenney should have to develop his own belly tanks. If he can develop one over there in two months, we should certainly be able to develop one here in the United States in one month."

Besides its lack of fuel capacity and concomitant short range, the Thunderbolt required a very long take off run; it could not maneuver in a dogfight; it was difficult to pull out of a dive; its landing gear was weak; and its radial engine was undependable. Gen. Kenney met with 348FG Commander Col. Neel Kearby, whose group was to fly the P-47, and told him that he "expected him to sell the P-47 or go back home." Kenney "knew it didn't have enough gas but we would hang some more on somehow and prove it as a combat plane, especially as it was the only fighter that Arnold would give me in any quantities for some time." Kenney told Kearby that, "regardless of the fact that everyone in the theater was sold on the P-38, if the P-47 could demonstrate just once that it could perform comparably I believed that the 'Jug,' as the kids called it, would be looked upon with more favor." Lt.Col. George Prentice was scheduled to arrive that afternoon from New Guinea to take command of the new 475FG P-38 group to begin training at Amberley Field. Kenney told Kearby to fly over to Amberley in his P-47 and challenge Prentice to a mock dogfight. Kearby was an experienced pilot and had had several hundred hours in the P-47, and Prentice also was an excellent P-38 pilot. Kenney: "But for the sake of my sales argument I hoped George wouldn't be feeling in tiptop form when he accepted Neel's challenge but the combat came off as I had hoped." Prentice was surprised at the handling qualities of the P-47 against his P-38, and admitted that Kearby "shot him down in flames a half dozen times." Prentice still preferred his P-38, but began warning everyone "not to sell the P-47 short."

Late June 1943: Air Situation

During June, the principal function of 5th BC bombers was to soften up the enemy defenses in the Lae-Salamaua area. Wewak, with its four airdromes, was recognized as perhaps the most potentially dangerous base in New Guinea. These attacks on the airfields at Lae and Salamaua were preliminary to other missions designed to simplify the Allied landings now imminent on Nassau Bay on 26 June, Woodlark and Kiriwina Island for 30 June, and Munda, New Georgia, on 30 June. The number of heavy attacks upon airfields both in the Lae-Salamaua area and at Rabaul apparently had some effect. In early July, although the Japanese were able to mount substantial air strength against the American landings in the Upper Solomons and New Georgia, they did not have sufficient air strength to threaten both these landings there and the Allied operations at Nassau Bay on 26 June and Kiriwina and Woodlark on 30 June.

Except for the 21st, when the 80FS scored 13 victories, the last half of June saw escort missions to Bena Bena continue, as the 49ers tried to lure the Japanese fighters up over central New Guinea but were unopposed. During this time the 80FS Headhunters and 475FG Satan's Angels joined as escorts to Bena Bena to provide relief for Woods' 9FS pilots. Further help came when replacement pilots arrived from Australia.

Command Changes

A key command set back occurred on 17 June, as Maj. George Powell, 49er Group Exec, was returning from leave in Australia when his B-17 transport crashed at MacKay Air Drome in Queensland, killing 40 men on board. Over the months Lt.Col. Robert Morrissey had become a leading officer in the 5AF when his 49ers had continued to perform expertly under the harshest conditions and flying the oldest aircraft in the Fighter Command. The Demons, Eightballs, and Flying Knights had a victory tally of 231 aerial kills under his command. Deputy 5AF CO Gen. Whitehead had Morrissey transferred to his command, promoting him to full Colonel to become one of the main task force planners for future operations. Deputy 49th Fighter Group CO Capt. James Selman assumed command of the 49ers on 1 July with the promise that new Warhawks would soon arrive from northern Australia. Until then Selman was required to lead his Group's war-weary Warhawks in flying coastal patrols from Oro Bay to Lae and to cover the Salamaua landings.

On 26 June 35FG Deputy Commander Maj. Malcolm Moore was promoted to Lt. Colonel and named Group CO, succeeding Lt.Col. Richard Legg, who had commanded the Group since it left the US. Col. Legg would command the 82FG in the MTO in November 1944 until VE-Day.

Ace Capt. Thomas **Lynch**. (L) with Col. Richard **Legg** and Lt.Col. George **Prentice**. (AAF)

Capt. James **Selman** assumed command of the 49FG in July 1943. (AAF)

5FC Aircraft Modifications

One of Kenney's projects was the modification of the B-25 into a potent strafer by adding additional forward-firing machine guns and even a 75mm cannon. As these modifications on the Mitchell were under way, Service Units were erecting, repairing, modifying, and improving fighters that had been in the theater for many months and those that were just arriving. His worn out P-40s had new Allison V-1710-81 engines installed, and modifications were made on the inspection plates, main landing gear spindle, fuel lines, and fuel vent lines.

Kenney ordered 61 Bell P-39s and 50 P-400s on hand to be converted into the relatively modern P-39N by installing a new blower and propeller. Two .50 caliber machine guns in each wing replaced the two previous .30s, giving the fighter a punch of six .50s and either a 20mm or 37 mm cannon. A new self-sealing fuel tank added 15 to 19 gallons of fuel capacity. By mid-June Kenney was to receive 100 new P-39s, which was sufficient to partially equip five of his nine 5FC fighter squadrons. But on 19 June an unexpected order arrived directing several changes to be made on these new P-39s to conform to an AAC Technical Order dated 25 March 1943. Until these changes were made the Airacobra was restricted to "flying maneuvers that could be considered safe" (i.e. they could not be used in combat). Kenney was upset and wired Arnold, asking why these modifications were not made in America before they were sent overseas so that the fighters could go into combat immediately on their arrival in the theater. The directed modification orders were vague, and besides, there were no spare parts or instruction manuals available to carry out the modifications. The disgruntled Kenney asked Arnold to immediately replace all the P-39s with P-38s. The next day Arnold wired Kenney that a new technical order was being issued stating that the P-39s were acceptable to use in combat! Kenney then immediately received another wire from the Air Service Command at Dayton, OH, stating that as soon as the new part was installed the ASC would consider the P-39s to be combat ready! Fortunately one of the newly arrived Airacobras had the missing part already installed and Australian tool shops were employed to copy and manufacture the part; after a week's delay the P-39s were ready for combat.

Kenney and the Ground Echelon

When Kenney arrived in Australia he was confronted by a numerically superior enemy. By the astute use of air Intelligence he was able to concentrate aircraft for missions and make up part of this numerical discrepancy. However, by developing an efficient supply and maintenance organization Kenney was able to put an even larger proportion of aircraft into the air. Kenney moved supply depots nearer to the combat air bases and urged the personnel working in the rear echelons to increase the number of combat-ready aircraft. While his pilots received much of the media hype, Kenney realized the importance of hardworking mechanics and armorers, and tried to raise their morale by awarding decorations and improving their living conditions. While the number of aircraft increased slowly, the total number of sorties flown grew quickly through the backbreaking efforts made by ground crews to keep the same few aircraft flying more often. Kenney also benefited from the enormous productive capacity of the United States during the war. Kenney never had as many aircraft as he thought he needed, but America's great industrial capacity supplied him with increasing overall strength. By the time the war ended Kenney had 1,800 aircraft, a large supply of spare parts, and trained mechanics that had an 80% aircraft combat ready rate at any given time. This rate compares to the less than 50% rate of Japanese mechanic.

Meanwhile, the Japanese were handicapped by a lack of heavy equipment, trained engineers, and labor to build airfields. With fewer and lesser developed airfields they were unable to disperse their aircraft around the perimeter of the field and bunched their aircraft together, making them easy to destroy in large numbers at a time. The lack of heavy equipment also made it difficult to repair their runways quickly, which rendered the fields unusable for long periods.

Airdrome Construction and Supply

As the Allied counteroffensive in the SWPA gained impetus during the middle of 1943, airdrome construction followed directly behind the advance of the newly won enemy areas. The principal objective of Allied strategy had always been to advance airfields closer and closer to Japanese bases and troop concentrations so that Allied aircraft could effectively destroy the enemy's military potential in those areas. Before GHQ could issue operations instructions to engineer units, the initial construction requirements often had to be worked out in relation to the long distances over water and the completely undeveloped character of the interior terrain. These requirements were presented to Alamo Force (Sixth Army), which then issued field orders to correspond to the existing conditions in the operational area. Once the invading infantry became established on shore, engineer construction troops and equipment moved in and began the construction stage of the operation. These Task Force engineers were to instigate and complete those installations essential to the tactical phase of the operation before responsibility could be transferred to US Army Service of Supply (USASOS) forces for the ultimate expansion and operation in accord with GHQ instructions. Under these conditions, the Task Force engineers took on significant construction responsibilities which often had to be performed without the benefit of being immediately provided with additional equipment and supplies, and sometimes while enemy resistance continued nearby. The US Armies in the ETO and Mediterranean had the advantage of short overland lines of communications, which meant that the advanced sections of the USASOS followed with enormous quantities of supplies to quickly complete and/or expand the base.

As the advance in the SWPA continued, a series of airfields and bases were hacked out of the New Guinea jungles which made each succeeding advance possible. Without these "stepping stones" between the rear and advance areas no aerial or logistical support of forward operations would have been possible. Allied aircraft flying from the airstrip in the jungle around Tsili Tsili were able to minimize Japanese intervention from Wewak to the landings at Lae, where the future construction of a supply base facilitated the overland advance up the Markham River Valley and further amphibious landings along the New Guinea coast. The port at Lae received the seaborne supplies and equipment, which were then flown into Nadzab to make possible the construction of the main air base for future New Guinea operations. When the airdromes at Gusap were being developed, engineers and their equipment had to be flown in from Nadzab. Gusap was to fill a vital role in providing an air transport base to supply troops in the Ramu River Valley and placed Allied aircraft much closer to the Vitiaz Strait, where they could fly across to strike targets on the western tip of New Britain that were to be seized in the future. P-47s at Gusap were able to maintain the neutralization of Wewak, while shorter range P-40s and P-39s could attack Japanese concentrations at Madang and Alexishafen, which permitted the Fifth Fighter Command to withdraw its long range P-38s for increased attacks against Rabaul. Meanwhile Allied troops, staged through Lae, quickly made an amphibious landing at Finschhafen, just above the Huon Gulf, where construction of an airdrome would allow fighter cover for operations in New Britain. Finschhafen became a major base supporting not only air, but also ground and naval forces for ensuing landings on Arawe, Cape Gloucester, Saidor, and the larger operations which followed.

With the Huon Peninsula under control Allied aerial superiority had been achieved, and the effectiveness of joint air, ground, and naval operations was now becoming apparent. By late 1943 the forces of the SWPA and SOPAC were engaged in a two pronged counteroffensive which was beginning to reach its objective of neutralizing Rabaul. Attacks on Rabaul by SWPA based aircraft kept the Japanese off balance, while SOPAC forces advanced from recently liberated bases on New Georgia to Bougainville, which were the only obstacle between Rabaul and the Allied position in the South Pacific. SWPA forces that had established strategically located rear and advance bases were now enabled to attack across the Vitiaz Strait to Arawe and Cape Gloucester on New Britain. SOPAC based aircraft flew sustained attacks on Rabaul while SWPA forces swept into Arawe and Cape Gloucester. The seizure of the western tip of New Britain established Allied control of the Vitiaz Strait, through which subsequent naval convoys could sail covered by aircraft from both the New Guinea and New Britain sides of the Strait. To consolidate their gains on the Huon Peninsula another task force under Sixth Army moved up the coast and occupied Saidor, where the construction of airdrome facilities improved air coverage over Wewak. Wewak had been reinforced by the Japanese Fourth Air Army, which had been moved from Rabaul in August 1943 to assume responsibility for the New Guinea coast area east of longitude 140° E. With the seizure of bases along the coast of Northeast New Guinea and on the western tip of New Britain, the Allies (SWPA) were now going to capture the Admiralty Islands, which would expel the Japanese from the Bismarck Sea area. The Admiralties would provide a base from which Fifth Air Force aircraft could attack Kavieng, which was Rabaul's supporting base on New Ireland. Kavieng was a SWPA assignment, but was subsequently assigned to SOPAC for neutralization, and eventually was isolated like Rabaul.

Kenney and ULTRA

The Japanese never seriously believed that their radio codes had been compromised by ULTRA, which was of considerable benefit to Kenney in planning air operations and using the strengths of the 5AF to take advantage of the weaknesses of the Japanese. ULTRA permitted Kenney to concentrate his air forces, both offensively and defensively, when and where they would have the maximum effect on Japanese operations. Radio communications were essential to all facets of air operations, and the ability of ULTRA to intercept and decode even routine Japanese radio transmissions gave Kenney an exceptionally accurate interpretation of Japanese air strength. ULTRA allowed Kenney to concentrate on a particular area without unnecessary concern about air attacks or the size of the Japanese forces in other areas. ULTRA provided Kenney with worthwhile targets for concentrated raids, such as the bombing of the airfields at Wewak and Hollandia, after the Japanese reinforced the area with large numbers of aircraft. Without this secret information Kenney would have had to dispatch many more missions to airfields that could, or could not, contain enemy aircraft, resulting in a greater cost to Kenney's forces. ULTRA provided a decisive advantage in defending against enemy air attacks by giving an early warning of an imminent air raid, and gave Allied fighters enough time to gain altitude and be in a position to attack the Japanese formations before they reached their targets. Kenney also used ULTRA to great advantage in isolating Japanese garrisons and searching for and finding enemy ships that were sent to relieve or supply them. Because he knew the Japanese shipping schedules, Kenney did not need to send more aircraft out to scout for enemy ships, which left him with more aircraft available for other missions. The spectacular successes, such as the Battle of the Bismarck Sea in March 1943, would not have been possible without ULTRA.

26 June 1943: Landings at Nassau Bay

On 26 June the Allies made amphibious landings south of the Salamaua Isthmus at Nassau, and although Allied air cover was held up by bad weather for several days afterward, the Japanese also could not mount any air attacks. Despite the weather and no air cover, the Australian infantry was able to advance 15 miles inland to capture the higher ground at Mubo Village and its airstrip. By 30 June, the 5AF was able to send bombers and fighters out in marginal weather, and during their first three days of the operation the 49th Fighter Group flew under heavy overcast, as the northern coast of Papua was drenched by daily rain squalls. The Group flew fighter bomber sorties against coastal targets from Salamaua to Lae, as well as flying transport escort to the Mubo staging area. When weather allowed the 49ers sortied three times a day, but it would not be until D-Day+4 that the Warhawk pilots finally made contact with the Japanese. The first enemy attack on the Nassau Bay beachhead did not occur for a week after the invasion, when on 2 July 10 medium bombers made three bombing and five strafing runs over Allied positions. Although the American fighter command at Dobodura had ordered several sweeps over the area during the day, the fighters failed to intercept these enemy aircraft. The following day, however, the first fighter combat of the month occurred. Various squadrons of both Moresby and Dobodura based fighters had carried out periodic patrols over Lae and Salamaua.

30 June 1943: *Operation Chronicle*: Capture of Kiriwina and Woodlark

The victories at Buna by Southwest Pacific forces and on Guadalcanal by the South Pacific force had given the initiative to the Allies, and the two Theater commands were to collaborate under the *Elkton Plan*. The South Pacific Force was to advance through the Solomons, while the Southwest Pacific forces were to advance along the northeast coast of New Guinea with the objective of neutralizing or isolating the enemy bastion at Rabaul. The strong Japanese air defenses at Rabaul made it necessary to provide fighter cover for Allied bomber missions there. The long round trip distances between the airfields in New Guinea and the targets at Rabaul were not possible for fighters because of their limited fuel capacity. Two small islands, Kiriwina and Woodlark, located north and northeast respectively of Goodenough Island and about 150 miles off the north coast of Papua, would provide staging bases on the way to Rabaul. In addition, from these Islands Allied Air Forces could provide air support for Southwest Pacific ground forces in future attacks on the Salamaua-Lae-Finschhafen-Madang area of Northeast New Guinea and on western New Britain, as well as support for the South Pacific Force in subsequent operations on southern Bougainville. Aircraft warning stations had already been installed on both Kiriwina and Woodlark as part of the development of Goodenough Airdrome. *Operation Chronicle* was originally a part of *Cartwheel* codenamed *Operation Coronet*, with the landings there to take place in conjunction with the landing at Nassau Bay, Papua New Guinea, and the landing on Rendova, New Georgia.

During February 1943, an Army engineer reconnaissance team from the SWPA Force arrived in secrecy on both islands aboard a small naval vessel. On Kiriwina they chose a flat, well-drained area, about five miles in diameter and located northeast of Losuia, where an airdrome could

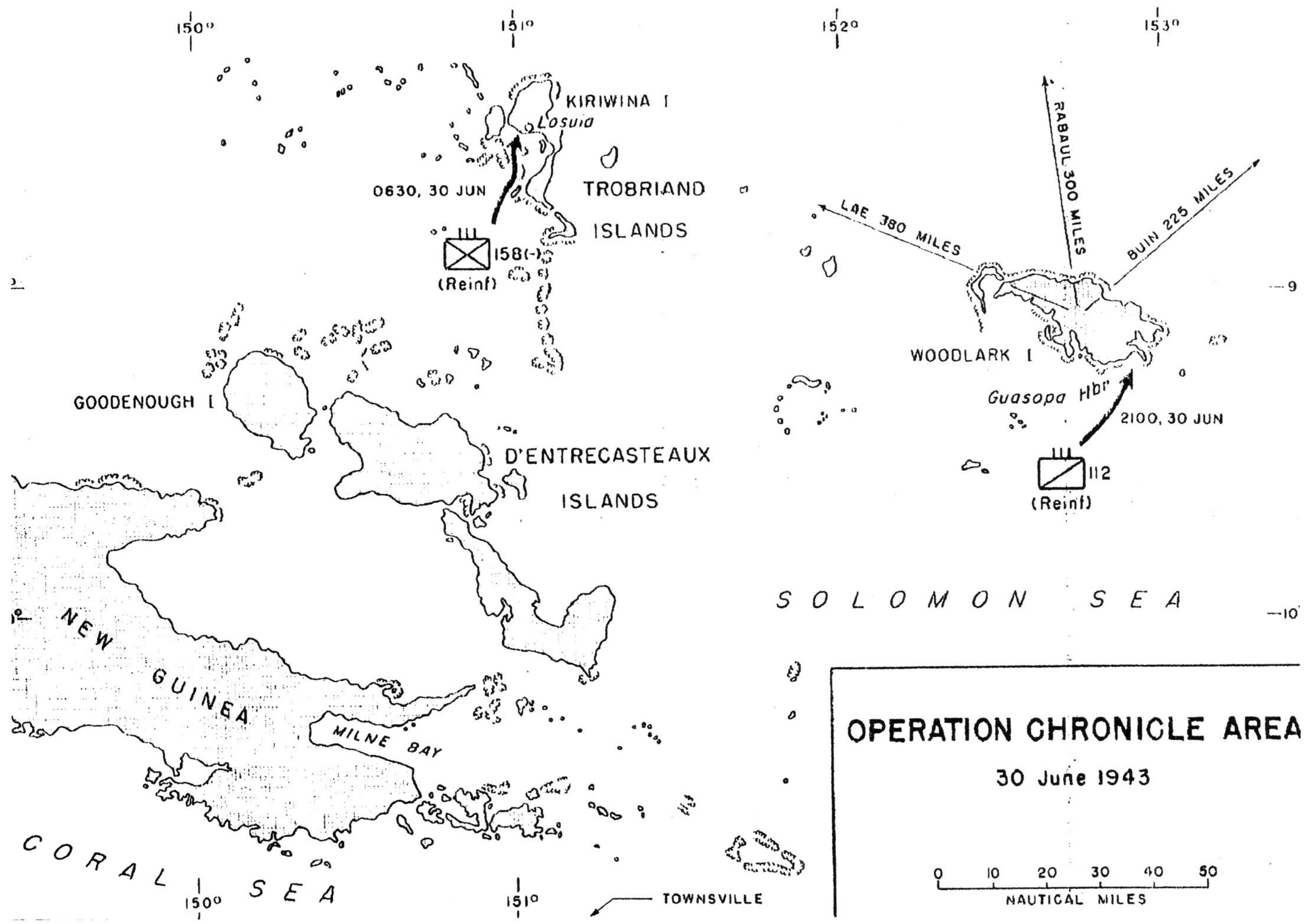

be built with minimum effort. They estimated that a fighter airstrip with dispersals could be constructed within three weeks, although revetments would require an additional two months. Just east of Boli Point the team found a fairly well protected harbor that could be connected with the airdrome site by an access road built on firm ground. On Woodlark, the engineer reconnaissance team found an excellent beach for landings and determined that the best site for the construction of an airdrome was at the southeastern tip of the island in the vicinity of Guasopa Harbor. Terrain in this location consisted of undulating coral ridges gradually rising from the shore line to heights of 50 feet or more. Except for a coconut plantation, the area was heavily wooded and covered by heavy root matting, which would make clearing and leveling a problem. The reconnaissance party had estimated that a fighter airstrip with dispersals could be constructed near the beach in approximately six weeks, and that revetments for 25 fighter aircraft would require an additional two months. Guasopa was an excellent harbor, and the construction of a jetty and access road would provide sufficient cargo unloading facilities. When comparing the islands, the reconnaissance team considered the airdrome site on Kiriwina the better of the two.

During early April 1943, the South Pacific Force sent a Navy reconnaissance team to obtain more information. They studied several possible airdrome locations and finally chose a definite site located near Guasopa Harbor on Woodlark Island. It was estimated that a fighter airstrip could be built there by a fully equipped naval Seabee construction battalion in four to five weeks, and that it could be extended in one to two additional weeks for bombers. On 6 May 1943 (D minus 55), the South Pacific Force issued construction requirements for the Woodlark Island Airstrip: a cleared width of 300 feet and a surface of an initial length of 4,500 feet to be extended later to 6,000 feet. If good coral suitable for surfacing were available nearby, landing mat would be omitted unless necessitated later by continuous operations of heavy aircraft. Because of the vulnerability of the airdrome to enemy attack dispersal of all facilities was necessary, and initially, dispersed hardstands for 25 fighter aircraft were required and dispersed hardstands for 35 bombers were to be added later. Building construction was to be kept to a minimum of operations buildings and shops with housing provided for air combat crews.

On 7 May 1943 (D minus 54), Alamo Force (Sixth Army) was assigned to organize the construction of the airdrome and air warning and radio navigational facilities on Kiriwina; for the construction of an airdrome and air warning facilities on Woodlark; and also for the construction of minimum port and base facilities on both Kiriwina and Woodlark Islands. Maximum use was to be made of local labor and materials. The Army's 46th and 59th Engineer Regiments were assigned for construction work at Kiriwina. The 20th and 60th Naval Construction Battalions were assigned to Woodlark. D-Day for the simultaneous landings on Kiriwina and Woodlark Islands was scheduled to be 30 June 1943. An advance party was landed on each island on D minus 6 to prepare landing points and dispersal areas for the main force, the arrival of which was expected to start retaliatory bombing by the Japanese.

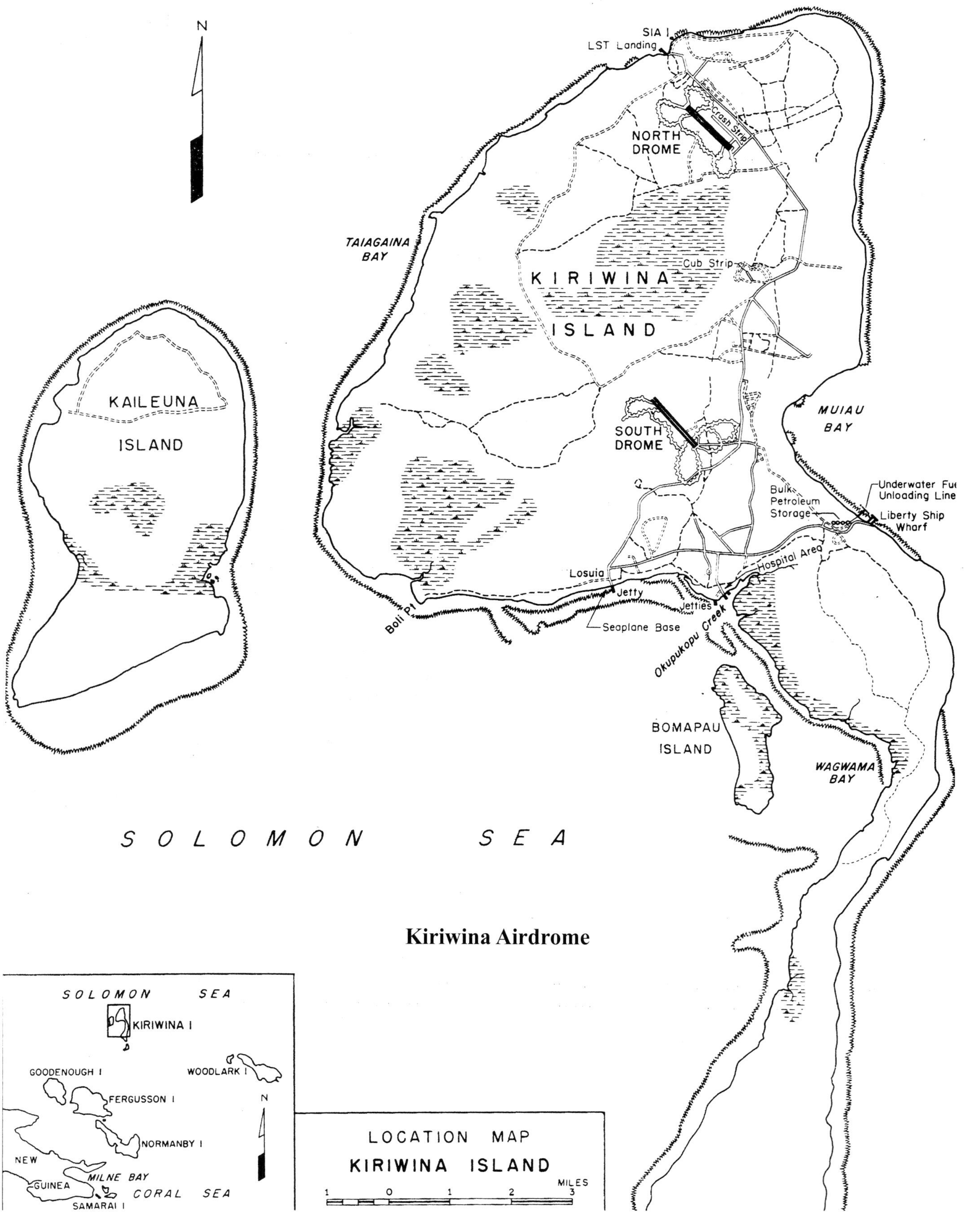

Kiriwina Airdrome

Kiriwina

The GHQ, SWPA, requirements for airdrome facilities to be constructed on Kiriwina were:

First-priority construction, to be completed by 15 July (D plus 15), was a runway suitable for troop carrier operations, including space at each end, off the runway, for loading and unloading.

Second priority of construction, and scheduled for completion by D plus 45, were two parallel runways, each 6,000 feet by 100 feet, with necessary alert areas and dispersal for one group of 75 fighter aircraft. The original troop carrier runway could be improved for use as one of these fighter runways.

Third priority was for a third fighter runway with parallel taxiway, to be ready by D plus 120. Simultaneously with completion of the third runway, dispersal was to be provided for three additional fighter squadrons, two medium bomber squadrons, and two heavy bomber squadrons.

Fourth priority was for construction of revetted dispersal for all aircraft based at the airdrome to be provided in the following order: 150 fighters, 36 medium bombers, and 24 heavy bombers, all to be finished by D plus 165.

On 30 June, Allied troops captured Kiriwina and Woodlark without enemy land or air opposition, except for reconnaissance flights and two small bombing attacks against Woodlark. The Japanese took no further action in relation to the occupation of the island. Soon engineers began airfield construction, and within a few days Army engineers and Seabees were converting the hard coral islands into air bases without having experienced either a land or air attack. By 5 July the Allied strength on Kiriwina was 5,200 men and on Woodlark 1,300.

On Kiriwina Island, the lack of adequate roads became the major problem during the first weeks of construction, as it was extremely difficult to move heavy equipment to the construction site. Then excessive round-the-clock wear and tear on equipment, shortages of spare parts, and the lack of supplies and material delayed construction. To expedite construction, engineers decided to first construct an airdrome at the site reconnoitered in February (South Drome), and afterward to construct a second airdrome to the north near Sia Island (North Drome). The topsoil of both airdrome sites was a fluffy loam that became fluid when wet, while the subsurface was coral which varied in hardness and texture, as some could be easily cut with graders while others required blasting. There were numerous large coral boulders that covered the entire area and needed to be removed. Many deep pockets of loam had to be excavated and filled with coral. A clean coral that was soft enough to be cut by a heavy grader was found to be ideal for surfacing material when overlaid on a coral base, compacted to a depth of eight to 10 inches.

By 21 July work was behind schedule, as the first runway at the South Drome was graded for 2,600 feet and surfaced for 500 feet, but grading was being completed at a rate of 500 feet per day. The second runway was

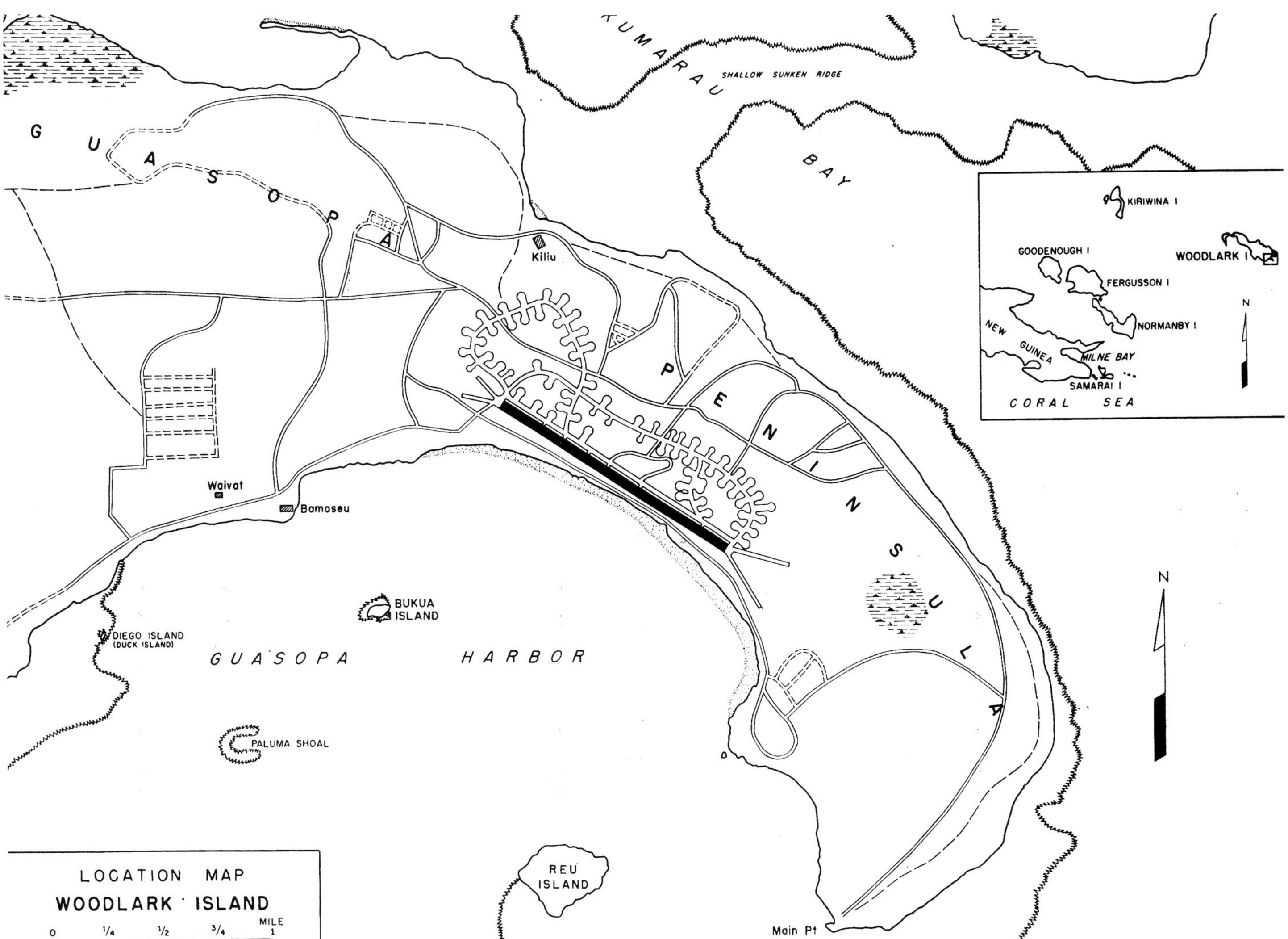

cleared for a length of 4,500 feet. By 18 August one runway and the taxiway at South Drome were usable when the first squadron of fighter aircraft was transferred from Goodenough. At that time the alert area could accommodate 50 fighters and 28 hardstands were complete. By 1 September this first runway was complete, and the second was scheduled for completion in six weeks. Meanwhile, planning for the North Drome had been completed and preliminary work on the first runway at that airdrome had commenced.

In late August 1943, GHQ, SWPA made plans to send Allied bombers from rear bases, escorted by fighter aircraft from Kiriwina, on daylight raids on Rabaul. The date for the launch of these retaliatory missions depended on the completion of the airdrome at Kiriwina, as the proposed missions required the staging there of approximately 200 fighter aircraft during bombing missions. The landing facilities there had to be capable of accommodating the almost simultaneous return of these fighters with critically limited fuel remaining from a mission over Rabaul. Upon landing, rapid refueling was essential so that fighters could land, refuel, and take off as quickly as possible to clear the area for other incoming fighters which would thus not become concentrated on the island, presenting a vulnerable target for an enemy attack. To expedite the implementation of their plans the GHQ, SWPA rescheduled previous target dates for construction on Kiriwina. A minimum of three runways and an emergency crash strip, together with the best possible facilities for refueling, were to be completed by 10 October, nearly seven weeks sooner than the previous construction schedule.

In order to provide these facilities on time, Alamo Force assigned the 856th Engineer Aviation Battalion to assist the No.6 Mobile Works Squadron in the construction of North Drome. Soon Alamo Force was authorized to transfer a detachment of the 20th Naval Construction Battalion from Woodlark. Even with these augmented construction forces all the planned work could not be completed on schedule, but North Drome was operational by 10 October for missions on Rabaul, which began two days later. To speed up completion of the airdromes and to reduce wear on the limited earth-moving equipment, the requirement for aircraft revetments at Kiriwina was canceled in October 1943. It was thought that by the time the revetments would be completed they would no longer be needed, and a large amount of engineer time and effort would be partially wasted. Upon the full completion in November, both the South Drome and North Drome consisted of two parallel runways, each 6,000x100 feet, with dispersal available for 198 aircraft. At North Drome a crash strip 3,000x150 feet paralleled the runways.

By March 1944 Japanese land forces were isolated and bypassed, while their naval and air forces had been driven from the area. The airdrome at Kiriwina was to continue operations until the airdrome at Cape Gloucester, New Britain, was in full service. All ground forces were withdrawn, and from March to September 1944 the RAAF operated transport and cargo aircraft from South Drome; by the end of 1944 the base was maintained for emergency use only.

Woodlark

While engineer units of the SWPA were working at Kiriwina, South Pacific Force naval construction battalions were occupied on Woodlark under SWPA direction and control. After arriving on Woodlark unopposed, the 60th Naval Construction Battalion battled torrential rainstorms when it began work. Nonetheless, the Battalion quickly and easily laid and leveled 18 inches of quarry gravel, and by the middle of July the strip was ready for transport planes.

On 14 July 1943, airdrome requirements for Woodlark were revised by GHQ, SWPA, to provide accommodations for the air elements of both the South Pacific and Southwest Pacific forces. By 23 July 1943, 5,000x150 feet of the runway had been surfaced with 18 inches of coral when the first squadrons of fighter aircraft began arriving, although dispersal areas had not yet been provided. By 14 August the runway had been extended to 6,000 feet and an alert area for 25 aircraft was completed; hardstands for 78 aircraft were available on 22 August. This airstrip was eventually widened to 300 feet, and a total of 118 revetted hardstands were provided.

After the South Pacific Force had captured an airdrome on New Georgia, Adm. William Halsey, the Commander of the newly formed Third Fleet (15 March 1943), advised GHQ, SWPA, that Woodlark Island was considered useful only as a temporary alternate base or staging area. GHQ, SWPA, then informed Allied Air Forces that the South Pacific Force would not station any personnel at Woodlark, and that it would be available for Fifth Air Force use. Subsequently, following the transfer of Fifth Air Force personnel from Woodlark to forward areas, the airdrome was operated by the RAAF for troop carrier and cargo transports. In October 1944 the island was completely evacuated except for the airdrome, which was maintained and operated as an emergency field only.

7

July 1943

3 July 1943: 49FG/7FS

Weather delayed the early afternoon Screamin' Demon transport escort to supply the Australian troops at Mubo Village. After take off, 7FS CO Maj. George Manning led 13 P-40Ks from Kalamazoo to position themselves over the long formation of C-47 Dakotas for the flight to Mubo. After a few minutes Manning's engine malfunctioned and his fighter began to lose altitude, and he was forced to transfer the mission lead to his Second Element Leader, 1Lt. Arland Stanton. Stanton led White Flight wingmen 1Lt. Clyde Knisely and 2Lt. Owen Swartz and the other Warhawks and Dakotas north through intermittent clusters of light clouds that formed under a heavy scud at 12,000 feet. Stanton's White Flight held the lead at 8,000 feet as the Americans continued north inland past Salamaua while the Dakotas dropped their supplies at Mubo. Flying 2,000 feet overhead was the top cover Green Flight under Flight Leader 1Lt. Carl Aubrey, with his elements of 1Lt. Sheldon Brinson and 2Lt. David Germain. Located on Aubrey's left flank was Yellow Flight led by 1Lt. Paul Slocum, with the rookie 2Lts. Elliot Dent, Element Leader 2Lt. Edward Peck, and Wingman 2Lt. George McMurry. On his right flank, a short distance away, 1Lt. Raymond Milliard led wingmen 1Lt. John Benner and 2Lt. Chester Phillips at 6,000 feet.

While the C-47s made their supply drops, Stanton's Warhawks orbited twice in formation west of Salamaua. Stanton joined the transports when they finished their drop, but as he passed Salamaua Bay he saw bombs exploding on the shore line. Slocum's Yellow Flight, nearest the coastline, spotted eight Lilys in line formation 3,000 feet below. These bombers were only a portion of the 20 from the 208th Sentai sent down from Wewak escorted by 16 Oscars of the 24th Sentai. These Lilys had also been limited over the past few days by the weather and had hoped to attack the main Allied force on the beach, but the landing ships had long since departed and the Australians had reached Mubo.

LEFT: 2Lt. Elliot **Dent** claimed his first victory of five. (AFAA) RIGHT: After scoring in November 1942 1Lt. Paul **Slocum** got his second and last victory of the war. (AAF)

After dropping their tanks, Slocum's Yellow Flight began a climbing turn to port toward the Lilys flying through intermittent cloud cover. Once they gained the altitude advantage four P-40s went into a diving left turn to attack a Lily with a pair of close escorts. But at 5,000 feet other veteran Oscar escorts climbed into the Warhawks' flight path. Slocum and Wingman Dent tightened their turn against the closest pair of enemy fighters, and both pilots rolled after a Ki-43s each as they sped under them. The Japanese pilots lost speed and tried to turn away for the clouds, but Dent closed in on his victim and hit it with a 90 degree deflection shot. The enemy pilot managed to bail out before his Oscar crashed into Salus Lake, south of Salamaua. Slocum had to maneuver after his turning Oscar before he hit it with a long burst that sent it down in flames.

Yellow Flight's second element of 2Lt. Edward Peck and Wingman 2Lt. George McMurry also gained the tactical advantage. Peck swept through a turn against his Oscar but did not fire, then broke off and climbed through the clouds to join Hilliard's top cover Red Flight. McMurry zoomed past the escorts and caught up with a straggling Lily just off the coast; he continued two firing passes, setting fire to the starboard engine as the bomber crashed 100 yards off shore.

Moments after McMurry downed his Lily, the three remaining Demon flights attacked the Oscars in a sweeping dogfight. Green Flight Leader Aubrey overhauled an Oscar off shore and shot it down, while Wingmen Germain and Swartz from White Flight chased another, with Germain claiming the victory. Green Flight's Brinson dropped an Oscar into the Salus Lake and then damaged another. In their first combat since their big day six weeks ago in May, the Demons claimed five fighters and a bomber and all landed safely at Kalamazoo.

4 July 1943: Nassau Bay Invasion

These enemy air attacks accomplished little more than to harass the American force that was establishing itself at Nassau Bay. Other problems, however, kept the Americans from immediately advancing to join the Australians in the Mubo area and from pushing farther toward the coast toward Salamaua. Initially, the High Command issued unsatisfactory and conflicting orders to American troops that were without combat experience. Intelligence was incorrect, and little was known of the enemy strength in the area. The major problem, however, was supply. The initial loss of landing craft which were later to supply the invasion forces was not anticipated, while once on shore supplies could not be delivered through the impenetrable jungle.

During the difficult ground fighting, the Allied Air Forces were working in cooperation with the infantry. Bombers and fighters, along with the all-important air transport missions, were accomplishing an extraordinary number of offensive and defensive sorties. The primary mission of the fighters was defensive, but defensive missions implied not only what the 67FS/347FG of the 13AF called "FAFSOAPing (Fifth Air Force Sitting On Ass Policy)"–otherwise known as ground alert–but also transport and bomber escort, together with routine scrambles or patrols. Most of these sorties proved uneventful, at least as far as making contact with the enemy was concerned, but there were many more interceptions in July than in the previous month. From the 3 July interception at Salamaua until the end of the month, there were 11 days on which Japanese aircraft made sorties over Allied positions, primarily in the Bena Bena and Salamaua areas. During this time Allied fighter squadrons shot down 58 Japanese fighters and four bombers for a loss of five P-38s, one P-40, and three pilots.

Despite these problems of supply and the Japanese soldiers' exceptional jungle fighting skills, the Allies gradually pushed forward toward Salamaua, and by 13 July the Australians and Americans had joined forces, cutting enemy communications. Meanwhile, American troops were forcing their way up the coast, and by 30 July had secured a beachhead on Tambu Bay, only five miles from Salamaua.

8 July 1943: The 9th and 35th Fighter Squadrons over Bena Bena

The Japanese continued their sorties against the Allies at Salamaua and returned to attack the growing Allied presence at Bena Bena. After a month of inactivity, the Flying Knights were laboring to maintain the demanding escort schedule. Then, at the start of the second week of July, newly promoted Maj. Sidney Woods and his 9th Squadron entered a number of air combats over central New Guinea against JAAF veterans from Wewak.

At 0830 Capt. William Haney led seven 9FS Flying Knights from their staging base at Port Moresby's Jackson Field in a routine morning escort of C-47 transports bound for Bena Bena. After climbing above broken 9,000 foot overcast, the Knights positioned themselves on the right flank of the transports while eight Lightnings of the 35FS Cobras protected the left.

However, after a few minutes Blue Flight Leader Capt. Lawrence Smith had to turn back with magneto failure, and taking his Wingman along for cover. 1Lt. Frederick Sibley assumed Smith's flight lead. Haney led his five wingmen in a loose formation stacked from 19,000 to 21,000 feet. After circling above the Bena Bena Valley, Haney spotted nine twin engine bombers below which he thought were friendly. They had approached from due east and now circled above the overcast just above Bena Bena, when abruptly four 35FG Lightnings peeled off in hot pursuit of the descending enemy bombers.

The Knights again circled north, searching for enemy fighters in closing clouds. After just ordering his Flight to begin a gradual climb to gain an altitude advantage, Mission Leader Haney called out six fighters approaching from the east, directly overhead at 21,000 feet. The Oscars dove on the rear right flank of Sibley's Blue Flight. The Knights dove to safety, but only the three Lightnings of Blue Flight continued contact.

Blue leader Sibley and 2Lt. wingmen Ralph Hays and Francis Love were together at 17,000 feet when they spotted the Ki-43s coming down on their starboard. Although Blue Flight separated and could not support each other, each pilot had gained the advantage. Love, the trailing Wingman in the mission, turned into the attacker that had first fired on Sibley and fired a front quarter deflection which damaged the Oscar's rear fuselage.

Salamaua Area with Nassau Bay at the top middle and Salamaua on the point on the lower left with the Francisco River running from the right center. (AAF)

Love's port engine rpm suddenly increased and he was forced to withdraw. Love's attack gave Sibley time to dive away and then climb to re-engage at 15,000 feet, where he made two passes against the retreating Sentai. He hit one from near dead astern and the Oscar attempted to loop out of the line of fire, but stalled in mid-climb and went into a flat spin through the overcast into a mountain. Sibley flew other passes and fired at long range at the last of the Oscars, which raced off for Wewak. Sibley's, Wingman Hays also flew several passes and also dispatched one of the Oscars into a flat spin through the cloud deck. Hays rejoined Sibley, and the two victors returned safely to Jackson with the squadron.

9 July 1943: Patrols over Salamaua-Lae

The day after the Bena Bena victories, Woods' 9FS Lightnings, based at Jackson Drome, were again patrolling over Lae but did not meet any air opposition.

10 July 1943: 49FG/9FS

Only two days after his Oscar victory over Bena Bena, Flight Leader 1Lt. Frederick Sibley was on a routine patrol over Lae when he radioed base of engine problems. He was thought to have crashed just north of Cape Ward Hunt but no wreckage was found.

11 July 1943: 49FG/9FS

During the morning the 9FS escorted transports to Salamaua, which also presented them with the chance to search for Sibley. As Mission Leader Woods led his seven wingmen in the routine orbit of the Mubo Village drop zone, four Oscars were seen circling in from below to attack the C-47s. Woods called out the enemy, but the Oscars turned into the Knights before they could open fire. Capt. Thomas Fowler, whose two wingmen had turned back earlier with engine trouble, attached himself to the 80FS. Fowler attacked independently from 16,000 feet and entered into the brief turning fight, where he first shot at an Oscar but then broke off to aid Woods, who was being pursued. Fowler and the Japanese pilot turned into each other, but Fowler chose to break off in a short dive to regain the advantage. Fowler saw another Oscar firing at rookie F/O Archie Davis and raced to the rescue, but was too late, as Davis' flaming P-38 dropped

Capt. Thomas **Fowler**. (9FS) scored his second of three victories while attaching himself to the 80FS after his wingmen turned back. (AAF)

1Lt. James **McLaughlin** scored his only victory of the war. (AAF)

into the haze. The victorious Oscar then turned into Fowler, and at the high closing speed they faced one another for only seconds; the American fired first from nearly head on. To prevent a collision he snapped his Lightning away in an aileron turn, watching his victim plummeting straight down into the overcast trailing smoke. The other Oscar pilots dove away through the haze, only to be caught by the P-39s of the 36 FS.

11 July 1943: 8FG/80FS

After patrolling for an hour and a half over the Wau/Bulolo area at 17,000 feet, the Air Controller called a number of bandits and then one for a lone bandit heading north from Target One, again at 17,000 feet. 2Lt. Earl Smith was heading toward the same area and spotted a lone fighter at 10,000 feet just above the cloud layer. Smith peeled over and got on its tail and slightly above. The Zero pilot did not see Smith and did not evade as Smith shot off large pieces of its right wing, rudder and elevator. The Zero went down into an uncontrolled spin as Smith climbed back to his formation. After the mission 1Lt. George Neater was buzzing low over Vivigani Strip at Goodenough Island and hit a truck, causing one engine to quit; he stalled trying to land and died in the crash.

11 July 1943: 8FG/36FS: The last big P-39 fight

Once the longer range P-38s came into the theater they pushed the Japanese air forces beyond the range of the P-39s of the 35th and 36th Fighter Squadrons, and combat opportunities were becoming scarce for these squadrons. Capt. Robert Smith led three flights consisting of seven P-39s and five P-400s on a B-25 escort to the Salamaua area. They took off at 0840 to rendezvous with 36 B-25s over Yule Island at 8,000 feet on a strafing escort mission to the Salamaua area. The B-25s flew at about 200 miles an hour, which forced the P-39s to use much of their limited fuel to stay with the Mitchells on long missions. Most of the 36th's pilots were veterans who knew how quickly the P-39 reached the end of its range. The B-25s flew over a pass through the Owen Stanleys at 10,000 feet with the P-39s about 2,000 feet higher. The B-25s then descended to the assigned 4,000 foot attack altitude while the P-39s circled the target area at 7,000 feet to take advantage of an almost solid overcast. The Airacobra pilots calculated that with the fuel they had already consumed they had about ten minutes to remain in the target area if they were going to be able to make it safely back to Port Moresby.

After rendezvousing with the B-25s they headed from Lake Wannan, and at 1045 they received a report of 10 bogies in the Salamaua area. When Capt. Smith and Wingman 2Lt. Orville Erdman arrived on the scene they saw five to seven enemy fighters attacking the B-25s. Smith attacked an Oscar from above and from the rear, and it started smoking and losing altitude. Erdman came and fired at it but missed. At the same time he was hit in the hip by a small caliber bullet, but continued to follow the Oscar and fired again, hitting its tail. He then watched as it hit the mountains. Smith and Erdman returned safely to base.

1Lt. James McLaughlin and his Wingman, 2Lt. Maryan Zaleski, saw a lone B-25 headed toward Salamaua at 6,000 feet under attack by two Oscars. McLaughlin attacked the one on the left and Zaleski the one on the right. McLaughlin fired a deflection shot from 300 yards as the Oscar was banking to the right. He saw hits on the Oscar's cockpit but saw no pieces coming off or smoke. McLaughlin lost both the Oscar and Zaleski, and then chased after some bogies that turned out to be P-39s. He then climbed to 6,000 feet, where he saw an Oscar with a P-39 on its tail, but soon the situation was reversed and McLaughlin dove to the rescue. The enemy pilot spotted McLaughlin and climbed and turned into a head on pass; the two closed on each other. McLaughlin continued firing until he had to pull up to avoid a collision. The Oscar smoked and then burst into flames behind the cockpit, which then spread onto its wings, and the stricken fighter rolled over and crashed west of Kila Point. Meanwhile, Zaleski fired and thought he hit the Oscar, but it passed over him, apparently undamaged. After looking around for other targets Zaleski returned to base and had to make a crash landing at 30 Mile Drome when he found that his gear was stuck half way down.

After the other two flights encountered the enemy fighters, 1Lt. Eugene Tuuri's Flight was at 12,000 feet, where they saw an enemy fighter climbing directly at them. Tuuri half rolled and tried to get his sights on the Oscar but stalled out. He recovered and climbed, then caught an Oscar coming out of a cloud and gave it several bursts that set it on fire. 1Lt. Eugene Zielinski, the Element Leader of the third flight, saw a straggling Oscar being chased by a P-39 that overran it. Zielinski then fired on it until it exploded into a river bank. He then saw another P-39 chasing a Zero and dove on it, giving it a short burst. The Zero pilot turned into Zielinski, who had to pull away when his guns stopped firing. Zielinski's Wingman, 2Lt. George Ghramm, dove on Zeros attacking the B-25s, and as he made his turn he saw a Zero ahead to his left with a P-39 making a pass from the other side. As soon as the other P-39 was clear Ghramm fired and hit the Zero's tail section. The Zero began to dive away, making small evasive turns, and Ghramm fired four or five short bursts, the last finally turning the Zero into a mass of flame.

1Lt. Warren Danson claimed "serious damage to one Oscar while the credit for the destruction of another Oscar goes to another member of our formation who apparently got bursts into the E/A before I was able to fire upon it." Danson's post mission report stated that the Japanese pilots were very inexperienced, seemingly having orders to focus on the bombers and ignore the fighters, which made them rather easy targets for the P-39s.

Smith's #4 man, 2Lt. Fred Burley, found that his guns malfunctioned as he closed to within 100 feet of a Zero, and soon his electrical system went out and his prop ran away. Burley left the fight and got his prop under control, then tried to reach Bulldog Base in case his engine quit. A short time later his engine did quit, and he descended for a wheels up landing on what looked like a smooth beach. He landed unharmed, despite demolishing his fighter. After destroying his IFF he was met by the natives of nearby Urika Village. They spent the next two days removing the guns from the P-39, but could not move the heavy fighter from the encroaching tides. He was taken by boat to Orokolo, where he stayed for several days, and then to Huiva, where he met a RAAF party that took him back to Moresby on 19 July after an overnight stay at Yule Island.

13 July 1943: 49FG

After the Flying Knights had recently lost Sibley, Davis, and Fowler, 1Lt. Francis Love left his formation due to failure of both engines on the return from the morning sortie. His P-38 was last seen gliding south parallel to the shoreline, entering the overcast just north of Cape Ward Hunt. Four days later Love was seen by scout aircraft, walking along the shore 20 miles north of the Cape. CO Woods was so intent on returning Love safely back to Horanda that he personally landed a Piper Cub on the beach to pick up Love, who was back on air patrol the next day.

14 July 1943: 49FG/7FS

Maj. George Manning's Screamin' Demons had joined in the close escort missions for the transports but had missed the combat actions fought by the Lightning Squadrons. It would not be until the morning of the 14th that the Demons met the enemy, and the action would see one of the most remarkable rescues of a downed pilot in the New Guinea campaign. Mission leader Capt. Raymond Melikian led four flights of 14 wingmen from Dobodura at 0730 to 21,000 feet over Cape Ward Hunt on the daily C-47 transport escort to the Mubo drop zone.

After an hour Melikian received a report from the Australians that the Japanese were bombing the beach landing area and he turned south to intercept. As he flew into an opening in the cloud cover at 10,000 feet, he saw two Val dive bombers escaping over the water beyond Salamaua. Melikian's Blue Flight jettisoned their tanks and dove to the left, with his Wingman, 2Lt. Logan Jarman, Element Leader 1Lt. Duncan Myers, and Wingman 2Lt. Robert DeHaven, while Orange Flight Leader 1Lt. Donald Lee followed with wingmen 2Lts. James Chandler, Element Leader 2Lt. Delman Moore, and 2Lt. David Germain.

The two flights dove 7,000 feet after the three enemy bombers, and at 10,000 feet Melikian fired a long range burst at the lead Val, which was about to enter the sea haze. The Val emitted a thin stream of dark smoke as it entered the cloud. Melikian, Jarman, and Myers pursued the damaged Val Flight Leader and one Wingman while the other Val Wingman turned away to the east. DeHaven turned after him and shot him down after a five mile chase.

Orange Flight Leader Lee also pursued Melikian's wounded Val heading for Lae through the cloud bank. Lee saw Blue Flight make their second attack on the north side of the cloud bank and his flight finally overtook the Val Wingman, whose fearless rear gunner continued to fire. Lee pressed into firing range and fired a long burst that riddled the Val, which plunged in flames into the sea. When Lee broke off, he noted that his temperature gauge was running hot and assumed the Allison had overheated during the long chase. After his Wingman Chandler finished his firing pass he saw that Melikian's fighter was trailing white vapor, which was caused by a holed radiator that was losing its glycol coolant. Lee descended to 800 feet above the Huon Gulf and bailed out, and as he fell away in the slip stream, his wounded fighter suddenly rolled and he smashed into the rudder. Despite being stunned Lee was able to pull the parachute ripcord and remain conscious as he hit the water. Chandler circled overhead to mark Lee's position. Melikian checked with his pilots for those who had adequate fuel and established an orbit over Lee until they were relieved. Black Flight, led by 1Lt. Robert McDaris, and Gold Flight, led by 1Lt. Lucius LaCroix, remained in high cover and would play a significant role in the rescue effort.

Melikian, Myers, DeHaven, and Chandler orbited at 4,000 feet while Moore circled on the deck. Melikian ordered McDaris to alert Navy patrol vessels off nearby Lasanga Island, and LaCroix's Flight orbited in a wide pattern north of Lee's position to intercept any enemy flights from the north and to communicate with other Allied aircraft in the area. The Demon pilots cut their rolled life rafts from their chute packs and tried to drop them to Lee, whose life raft would not inflate, as did only half of his Mae West. However, the rafts landed too far away from Lee, who had broken his left arm immediately below the shoulder. To add to the predicament, LaCroix spotted a school

Veteran 1Lt. Donald **Lee** scored the last of his four victories over a Val. (AAF)

2Lt. Robert **DeHaven** scored the first of his 14 wartime victories. (AFAA)

of sharks only a few yards from Lee and made several strafing passes on them until they swam away. Over Lasanga Island, McDaris' Flight was fired on by US Navy AA gun crews, and soon both LaCroix and McDaris had to return to base, as their flights were perilously low on fuel. Just in time a flight of 8FS escorts arrived and assumed the vigil, and one finally dropped a raft pack near Lee. Two A-20 Havocs soon arrived to relieve the Eightballs, and one dropped a large inflated raft and Lee climbed aboard the larger boat. There was no paddle, and Lee floated out to sea as sharks circled. After an hour Lee was rescued by a PT boat and taken to the Navy dispensary at Oro Bay. Lee transferred to the US; while his arm was healing he attended Command School, and the following year he commanded his own squadron.

18 July 1943: 35FG/39FS

On 18 July, six P-38s of the 39FS were escorting transports to Marilinan with 1Lt. Kenneth Sparks leading the first flight of three P-38s and 1Lt. John Lane the second. On the way back, at 1400 the Controller at Bulldog Base sent them to sweep the Lae-Salamaua area. Over Salamaua they saw seven enemy aircraft at 18,000 feet and engaged without result. Meanwhile, Lane looked down and saw 10 more bandits at 10 o'clock low. Lane's flight reassembled and made a pass, and he scored on a long deflection shot on a Zero. Lane made another unsuccessful pass and then began to have engine problems when a Zero got on his tail and fired. The attacker had too much speed and over-ran without hitting Lane's P-38. Lane's engine began to run smoothly again and he returned to the fight. A twin engine fighter turned into him and Lane fired at long range and got hits as the two fighters passed each other at high head on closing speeds. Lane then attacked another twin engine fighter head on but saw no hits. Two other twin engine fighters got on his tail, but Lane out-climbed them into the clouds. Lane returned to base with a probable and a victory, which made him an ace.

Just as 1Lt. Kenneth Sparks was about to climb into the attack, he saw four enemy fighters just ahead of him to the right still carrying their drop tanks. Sparks chandelled into them and fired at the first in line, then switched over to the second in line and got a good deflection shot for a probable before his guns ran away. Sparks headed for the clouds, where he turned off his gun switches and unsuccessfully tried to clear the trigger. Sparks left the cloud cover and saw an Oscar and got on its tail. He turned on his gun switches, but the guns started to run away again. Sparks cut inside the Oscar, letting his guns fire, and got good hits from 100 to 30 yards before Sparks' guns jammed. The Oscar crashed, spinning into the jungle. Sparks called for the two flights to reform over Wau and they engaged again. Sparks got his gun problem corrected and fired during a long frontal diving attack, damaging a Zero before his guns jammed again. Sparks was able to recharge his guns and make a few more passes before the guns jammed once more. He recharged them again, but the battle was over and he flew back to Lae to look for more enemy fighters; when he found none he flew back to Moresby with a probable, a damaged, and a victory, which made him a double ace with 10 victories. 1Lt. Lloyd Shipley and 2Lt. Walter Baker claimed a probable each, while 1Lt. Gene Duncan claimed a damaged. Both Lane and Duncan mentioned a fighter that "resembled a Me-109 which had an air scoop under the wing and in the middle of fuselage." This report caused initial speculation on the part of the pilots that Japan had imported Messerschmitt 109 fighters from Germany. Of course, this proved to be entirely false, as the sighting was the first appearance over New Guinea of the new inline engine Tony fighter.

1Lt. Kenneth **Sparks** scored his 10th to become a double ace. (AFAA)

1Lt. John **Lane** returned to base with a probable and a victory which made him an ace.

The Kawasaki Army Ki-61 **Tony** fighter which resembled the Luftwaffe's Me-109 made its first appearance in this combat. (AFHRC)

Mid-July 1943: Command and Aircraft Status

Command Changes

Soon after arriving at Port Moresby, Lt.Col. Neel Kearby was promoted to full Colonel and moved from 348th Group CO to Chief of Staff of the 5FC, while Robert Rowland, now a Lt. Colonel, became Group CO. Maj. Raymond Gallagher moved from 342FS CO to Group XO.

After veteran James Porter completed his tour as CO of the 8th Fighter Squadron he joined Group CO James Selman as the 49ers' new Operations Executive. The command of the 8FS would go to Capt. Ernest Harris, who was the first Eightball CO not to be a "Darwin Veteran," as he joined the Squadron from Hawaii and had become an ace.

In mid-July new **Curtiss P-40Ns** arrived at Dobodura to replace the war-weary Es in the 49FG. (AAF)

P-40

When the 348FG arrived at Port Moresby to stage into Dobodura, their gigantic fighters would park on the northeast side of the field, just east of 40FG's "Warhawk Row." The Thunderbolts would relieve James Selman's exhausted Warhawk Squadrons by flying both base patrols and support of the Salamaua operations. As part of their orientation, the 348th would take on the standing patrols of the Oro Bay area, allowing the Warhawks to concentrate on tactical missions over Salamaua and Lae.

In mid-July brand new Curtiss P-40 model Ns arrived at Dobodura to replace the oldest of the war-weary Es. The Ns were basically similar to the older fighters; the N model fuselage was longer by a foot and a half, was the same gross weight as the K model, and had an enlarged canopy area. However, its Allison engine provided more horsepower at higher altitude, a faster rate of climb, and increased speed by 25mph. Lighter weight struts and smaller wheels would cause some additional maintenance with the landing gear. The vacuum supplied instruments would eventually be replaced with salvaged electrical systems from the older planes. In the meantime, the last of the old E models would fly with the newer Ns until more replacements arrived.

In late July, more P-40Ns arrived at Dobodura and Manning's 7th Squadron was re-equipped with them to fly area patrols in conjunction with the newly arrived 348th Thunderbolts, as well as to provide the continuous escorts to the southern end of the Markham River Valley. However, Selman's two revamped Warhawk squadrons would not score an aerial victory for more than two months, as the P-38s of Maj. Wood's Flying Knights would engage the enemy.

As an official fighter identification aid, the 7FS and 8FS P-40 crews began to paint their tail sections and ailerons white, similar to the new Thunderbolts. RAAF fighters also began to appear with the white tails, which would eventually become the standard marking for all Allied single engine combat aircraft in the South Pacific.

20 July 1943: Marilinan Airstrip

While Allied land forces secured the areas near Mubo and Bena Bena in the north, Army engineers had secretly been positioned 80 miles north of Wau in the Watut Valley. These engineers had scraped out a 5,000 foot dirt runway from a small prewar airfield near the village of Marilinan, only 80 miles from the Japanese at Lae and northwest of Tsili Tsili Airdrome. As part of the Lae invasion planning Dakota transports had made many flights to the new airstrip escorted by Airacobras of the 35FG. But soon the Marilinan Strip had been discovered by the Japanese and the 49er Warhawks were needed for base defense.

During the evening of 19 July, 8FS CO Harris and Ops Exec Clyde Barnett informed all senior Flight Leaders to prepare to transfer to Marilinan the next morning. At sunrise Harris, Barnett, and ten wingmen took off and flew to Wau, then continued down the Watut Valley along the river until they could see the broad S turn in the stream which denoted the location of Marilinan's coarse red dirt runway. After dispersing their P-40s in the forested parking area at the southern end of the field, the pilots rode jeeps a short distance into the foothills to a primitive bivouac area where they set up quarters and stored their gear. Until more new Warhawk flights arrived, pilots were to rotate back to Dobodura on a weekly basis. The Eightball's Warhawks were to be maintained by the advanced flight crews, who serviced the Airacobras and Dakotas. By the end of the month, the Eightball's ground echelons would join their Squadron at Marilinan.

Late July 1943: Situation at Salamaua

As Australian troops closed in on the surrounded Japanese Salamaua garrison, Kenney increased the bombardment on enemy coastal targets in and around Lae. The 5FC fighters served as escorts and conducted sweeps to western New Britain. The Lightning Squadrons fought several intense actions against the new JAAF the Japanese had transferred to stop MacArthur. Meanwhile, American ground troops pushing in from the coast linked up with the Australians in the vicinity of Mubo by 13 July, and by 20 July American troops were within five miles of Salamaua.

21 July 1943: 8FG/80FS

Thirteen P-38s led by Maj. Edward Cragg of 80th Squadron took off at 0940 on a B-25 top cover mission to Bogadjim, with their friendly rivals of the 39th Squadron joining them on the mission. They arrived over the target at 14,000 feet at 1200 and saw dark green camouflaged Zeros "carrying two bombs, one on each wing." These bombs could have been drop tanks, and the layout of a drop tank under each wing distinguished the Oscar from the Zero, which usually carried a single tank under the fuselage for long range missions. Cragg fired, tearing pieces off the Zero/Oscar's fuselage, and it rolled over on its back and spun into a mountain side. He then climbed back up to 13,000 feet, where he saw two more Oscars flying ahead of him. He closed on one, but the enemy pilot made a quick starboard turn; Cragg was able to pull enough lead to hit the Oscar just behind the cockpit. The enemy fighter began to smoke and then exploded, going into a steep dive into the ground for Cragg's second victory of the day.

Element Leader 1Lt. John Jones and Wingman 2Lt. Donald Hanover joined Cragg's flight and spotted a pair of Oscars. Jones chased after the right hand Oscar, which began a right turn just as Jones was about to fire, but he was able to follow the nimble Japanese fighter long enough to fire a long burst into its engine and demolish the cockpit, killing the pilot. A Zero attacked Hanover, who turned into it and chased it off, but he lost Jones. As Jones dove

P-39 being refueled by a gasoline-powered pump at **Marilinan**. (AAF)

LEFT: Maj. Edward **Cragg** would score his second and third victories. (AFAA)
RIGHT: 1Lt. Jay **Robbins** claimed his first three victories and a probable on his way to a 22 victory career. (AFAA)

2Lt. Robert **Adams** got his second victory and a probable. (AAF)

1Lt. John **Jones** shot down two Zeros. (AAF)

away and started to pull up from this combat he found two Oscars were firing at him. Another P-38 shot one of the attackers off his tail and the other broke away. Jones climbed to gain altitude and saw three more Oscars in a string formation below. He then dove below them and then zoomed up into an attack from below. He exploded the last fighter and fired off a few quick shots in the following combat and claimed damage to an Oscar that was attacking another P-38. Meanwhile, Hanover made several unsuccessful passes before he saw a twin engine fighter and a Zero and closed and blew off three feet of the wing of the TE; it then went into an uncontrollable spin. The Zero didn't react until Hanover fired and then it Split-S'd away. Hanover joined some B-25s over Yule Island and returned to base with his first victory.

1Lt. Jay Robbins and his Wingman, 2Lt. Paul Murphey, were flying a two man flight in the very rear of the formation at 15,000 feet and were about to return to base when Robbins checked his rear toward Madang and saw enemy fighters descending from behind and to the right. However, neither Robbins nor Murphey could slow down enough to drop their tanks and waited for Cragg to turn and head them off. Robbins finally turned his fighter around and released his tanks but found an Oscar closing head on. Both pilots were in a gradual port turn and both fired, and their tracers passed each other. Robbins noticed that his tracers were passing slightly to the left of the Oscar, so he steepened the bank and fired a good burst into the enemy's engine; as the Oscar passed Robbins it burst into flames. At the same time Murphey also hit an Oscar and subsequently claimed it as probably destroyed. While he climbed to gain altitude, Robbins saw a Japanese fighter on the tail of another P-38. Robbins took a snap shot from long range and pieces broke off the attacker's wing and dissuaded the Zero from continuing his attack. Robbins claimed the Zero as a probable, as he had to break off his attack when two more Oscars attacked him and Murphey from the rear; both pilots dove from their pursuers. At the bottom of his dive Robbins turned left and saw another Oscar that was set up for a 30 degree deflection shot. He fired a long burst that tore off the entire starboard wing and the enemy plunged toward the ground. Robbins opened fired at another Oscar that was hit in the port wing and fuselage, but continued a half roll and plunged out of sight for his third victory of the day. After a few diving and climbing turns Robbins saw another P-38 being chased by an Oscar at very low altitude over the Valley. Robbins fired another burst at extreme range and the Zero broke off to the right, but Robbins was diving too fast to get another shot. Robbins and Murphey were too low on fuel to cover the distressed pilot and were forced to head for home, but they received an urgent radio call from 2Lt. Robert Adams that the Japanese were strafing a pilot descending in his parachute. When they arrived they saw the parachute in the distance at about 1,000 feet from the ground with four or five enemy fighters shooting at it until the pilot landed in the trees. The pilot in the parachute was 2Lt. Murthea McCarthy, who was on his first combat mission when he became separated and was shot down. Instead of waiting to open his chute until he descended to a lower altitude, the anxious McCarthy opened it immediately and then had to contend with a 10 minute descent from about 14,000 feet. The chivalry in the air of the First World War was rare on both sides over New Guinea, and the Japanese strafed the helpless McCarthy as he descended. Adams was alone when he first saw McCarthy being attacked by enemy fighters that lined up, taking turns at firing and then breaking off to get back in line. Adams was furious and radioed for help as he dove on the Oscars. Adams dove and turned two away, then closed on one and fired frantically until he saw it hit the side of a mountain. Adams hastily closed and fired on the other attacking Oscars, but there were too many. However, Robbins turned back in spite of low fuel and remained with Adams to cover the parachute, which landed in the treetops. McCarthy was undoubtedly killed as he drifted slowly toward the forest. Prior to his assistance to McCarthy Adams had made "seven or eight passes at the enemy, getting good shots each time but did not have time to observe results." On another pass Adams did observe pieces falling off a Zero's port wing and tracers bouncing off for a probable. The three victories were Robbins' first of 22 for the war.

At noon, 1Lt. Elwood Krisher was leading a four plane flight with Wingman 2Lt. Jess Gidley. The flight was the last in the formation, and as the lead flights were turning to return home Krisher saw a formation of four Zeros at 3 o'clock, flying parallel and at the same altitude of 17,000 feet. The P-38s dropped their tanks, and the Zeros dropped their tanks and broke away. Krisher fired without seeing any hits. Gidley fired a burst that missed, as he forgot to turn on his sights. As Krisher broke off he saw a twin engine fighter flying behind a Zero and directly ahead and above him. The twin engine fighter had bombs under each wing and dropped them on Krisher but missed. Krisher then pulled up for a quick pass at a Zero that pulled up and half rolled, and as Krisher was losing speed he had only time for a short burst and did not observe any results as the enemy passed under him. Krisher saw the Zero make a pass on his Wingman Gidley and called to tell him to dive. Krisher pulled around in a tight turn as the Zero turned toward him and he fired a short burst from a frontal beam pass, hitting the enemy's engine cowling. Krisher was unable to follow, as a Zero got on his tail, and he made a violent port turn while Gidley got on the Zero's tail and chased him away. But this Zero then rolled and half looped onto Gidley's tail. Gidley dove away to safety but lost Krisher. Krisher saw another Zero directly ahead and fired, and the Zero caught fire and plunged directly into the ground. As Krisher turned he saw another Zero and made a stern attack, but was unable to see results, as another Zero got on his tail and he had trouble shaking it; he had to dive steeply and then race over a long distance before losing his pursuer. He then headed home with his last two victories which gave him three total for his career. Meanwhile, after losing Krisher Gidley climbed, dove, and fired on a Zero which quickly rolled and looped onto his tail. To make matters worse, another Zero dove on him firing a 90 degree deflection shot, and Gidley dove steeply away to save his life. Gidley then joined Robbins and Murphey, who made a pass on a lone Zero that Split-S'd and headed back around toward Robbins and Murphey. Gidley dove on the Zero with a close shot from 45 degrees head on. He saw his tracers leading the Zero, but then a cannon shell exploded between the trailing edge of his wing and fuselage, and he claimed a probable.

1Lt. Howard Peterson and F/O Edwin DeGraffenreid made no claims for the day. The 11 victories and three probables was the best daily total since the 80FS claimed 13 destroyed and 10 probably destroyed on 21 June. This combat was to be a turning point, as the squadron inflicted heavy damage on a superior enemy force in an adverse situation. Over the next two months, not only the 80FS, but the entire 8FG, would distinguish themselves while going on the offensive in the SWPA.

1Lt. Harris **Denton** had a busy day with a victory, probable, and damaged claim. (AAF)

1Lt. Paul **Larson** got his only victory of the war. (AAF)

21 July 1943: 35FG/39FS

Capt. Charles King took off at 0930 with 13 P-38s of the 39FS on a noontime escort of a B-25 bombing and strafing mission to Bogadjim. As the Mitchells were leaving the target area the P-38s were attacked by a large formation of enemy fighters at 8,000 feet.

Capt. King was leading the first (Red) flight when he saw dogfights occurring between the Ramu Valley and the coastal range from 14,000 feet downward. The first attacker came at King from 2 o'clock and 3,000 feet above. King did not have enough airspeed to climb into them and flew on, radioing his two trailing flights to cover Red Flight. After the flight

LEFT:
1Lt. Gene **Duncan** scored his only victory of the war. (AAF)

RIGHT:
39FS. (L-R) 1Lt. Paul **Stanch**, 1Lt. Kenneth **Sparks**, 1Lt. Gordon **Prentice**, and 1Lt. John **Lane**. On this day **Sparks** would claim his 11th and last victory of the war while **Stanch** scored two victories to make him an ace. (AAF)

1Lt. Richard **Smith** scored two victories to become an ace. (AFAA)

Squadron Leader Capt. Charles **King** scored his second victory. (AAF)

1Lt. Stanley **Andrews** became an ace when he shot down a "Me-109"!. (AFAA)

had gained speed he made an unsuccessful deflection shot at an Oscar and proceeded to make a similar shot at another Oscar, this time getting hits on its wings and fuselage. King's Wingman, 1Lt. George Morgan, saw the pilot bail out and the Oscar crash. King continued to make another pass, getting enough hits to claim a damaged. He made another unsuccessful firing pass and headed to base.

1Lt. Kenneth Sparks' flight was at 7,000 feet and climbed to 15,000 to get into the fight. A fighter attacked him from starboard and Sparks fired a quick defensive burst with no observable results. Sparks' next pass was a right frontal attack on an Oscar, getting hits while firing for several seconds, but he broke off when another enemy fighter attacked him. While he was evading he saw the Oscar roll several times and fall out of control for his 11th and last victory of the war. 2Lt. Edward Maxwell, #2 man in King's second element, damaged two inline fighters despite having his guns run away.

1Lt. Stanley Andrews was leading the second (Blue) flight with Wingman 1Lt. Gordon Prentice and a three plane second element consisting of 1Lt. Gene Duncan and his wingmen, 2Lt. William Mettler and 1Lt. Paul Larson. Andrews was alerted to the attack when he saw King's drop tanks release. When Andrews looked around he saw a single inline engine fighter which "seems….to be a ME 109" diving on his flight from 3 o'clock high. He released his belly tanks and started into a climbing turn into point blank range when the new type enemy fighter broke away into a diving turn. Andrews followed, got on its tail, and fired at 300 yards, closing to 50 yards, when the Japanese pilot Split-S'd. Andrews followed in a dive and got on its tail once more, continuing to fire, but he was attacked by two other enemy fighters. He headed up the Ramu Valley without a claim and escaped by climbing up to 18,000 feet, where he met two Oscars flying in string. He closed and fired at full deflection at the last one, and only stopped firing at 75 yards, scoring hits on the fuselage near the cockpit. Andrews was forced to pull away when he was attacked again and had to claim the Oscar as a probable. Prentice, Andrew's Wingman, was switching to his main tanks to drop his external tanks when he saw the Zero that Larson had just missed suddenly climbing straight up directly in front of him. Prentice's guns and engine quit at the same time, and the Zero escaped as Prentice transferred fuel to his engine and recharged his guns. After firing unsuccessfully at another Zero he was attacked by two Zeros, but was able to outrun them. Prentice climbed back to 15,000 feet and started to fire at a Zero while it was out of range, but continued until it passed very close under him trailing smoke. Prentice was unable to see the enemy's fate, as he had to dive away from three Zeros that had latched on to his tail. 1Lt. Richard Smith later confirmed this "ME-109" victory.

The second element of Blue Flight Leader Duncan and his wingmen Mettler were climbing when Duncan saw two Zeros on his left and turned into the closest and fired. The Zero turned into Duncan and then turned slightly away. Duncan followed the enemy pilot's every turn, firing into its engine and fuselage until other enemy fighters appeared. The Zero was belching heavy dark smoke as Duncan broke away and headed home. After evading three Zeros Mettler claimed a damaged Zero as he followed his Leader in the battle. Larson dove to port and made a deflection shot on a SSE inline fighter and saw pieces come off. As Larson pulled over his victim he felt a backfire and explosion in his port engine and saw a piece of the cowling rip away; white acrid smoke filled the cockpit (Prestone?). He feathered the prop and, to prevent a fire, he shut down all electrical equipment, the booster pump, radio, transmitters, IFF, and gunsight. Larson turned toward cloud cover to return to base and crossed the Ramu River at 10,000 feet. Three inline fighters attacked and made six passes before Larson reached the clouds. One inline fighter continued to press attacks in the clear areas between the clouds. The ground undulated between 7,000 and 9,000 feet in this area, and Larson had to be careful when evading with diving pullouts with a dead engine. He was able to make turns into the dead engine and carefully skid as much as possible without causing adverse effects. He maintained a level airspeed of 190-200 mph on one engine while the inline fighter continued his pursuit for

20 minutes, then began diving attacks. Larson went into the steepest dives possible each time he saw the enemy roll over and dive. After 25 minutes and "about 18" enemy passes Larson entered a large cloud, made several sharp turns, and finally lost his attacker. He flew to Cape Possession, on the Gulf of Papua, at 2,000 feet and flew along the coast toward Yule Island, where his instruments began to fail. The good engine began to fail, and Larson tried to feather it and lower the flaps for a landing. He stalled the fighter in but hit the water with his right prop still windmilling, breaking the prop off. The P-38 spun around on the water's surface and settled safely near the beach.

1Lt. Paul Stanch, Leader of the third (White) Flight, led his flight down on the second batch of enemy fighters, and as he closed he saw two smoking Zeros that were hit by Blue Flight. Stanch closed to point blank range on an Oscar and fired shots into its engine and wing root; as the Oscar slid away its left wing tore off and it went into a violent spin. Stanch climbed to the right and saw a Zero chasing a P-38, so he dove into a 90 degree rescue. He fired without seeing any hits and then turned his attention to three more Zeros diving on a hapless P-38. Stanch dove on the three Zeros, and at 700 yards "raked" his fire from one Zero to another, then concentrated a three second burst on one Zero, starting a fire; smoke poured out of its engine and cockpit for his second victory of the day to make him an ace. Stanch made two more 45 degree deflection passes but missed and turned toward home, out of ammunition. He saw three Zeros making a stern approach on nine B-25s, and he bravely climbed behind them and closed, scaring them away from the Mitchells. 2Lt. Simpson Hollabaugh, Stanch's Wingman, saw two Zeros coming toward him very high and he turned up into them. One turned away out of range while the other continued in, but was too high for Hollabaugh to get it into his sights.

White Flight's second element, led by 1Lt. Harris Denton, was bounced by two or more enemy fighters from above at 5 o'clock, which broke up the flight. An inline enemy fighter dove on Denton at 12 o'clock, and Denton pulled up to meet it and fired from out of range. The enemy rolled and turned slightly right, giving Denton a short range shot that hit its right wing and fuselage, causing the enemy to smoke as it headed down in a tight spiral. Denton climbed and saw another inline fighter at his altitude and heading toward him. Both fighters fired; the Japanese fired a short burst but missed, while Denton continued firing until he almost rammed his opponent. Denton turned after the enemy pilot and made two more firing passes from above and at the same level, but could only submit a damaged claim. Another inline fighter then attacked Denton from 4 o'clock, and Denton pulled up and the enemy fighter passed under him. Denton made a sharp port turn and snapped off a 45 degree deflection shot from above, hitting the fuselage just behind the cockpit for a probable claim. Denton had to break away again when two more enemy fighters attacked from 2 o'clock; Denton passed under them and dove away to safety. Denton made a head on pass on another inline fighter without getting any hits before he returned to base.

1Lt. Richard Smith was flying as Denton's Wingman, and made his first attack on a "ME-109" with a 45 degree deflection shot from above and to the left. He had to keep his nose down to keep the turning enemy fighter in his sights, and at 150 yards he clobbered it so that it plunged straight down into the sea from 14,000 feet. His next pass on a "ME-109" was from head on at 20 degrees to the left and above, getting hits from the engine to the tail, and the enemy fighter rolled over on its back and plunged into the ocean to make Smith and ace.

This day would mark a milestone for the 39FS; its 11 victories put it over the century mark with 104 victories, the first 5FC squadron to accomplish this. The 9FS would surpass this mark on 26 July with 105 victories, and the 80FS would reach 100 on 26 September.

Capt. Kenneth Sparks scored his 11th and last victory. He would complete his tour and return to the US in early 1944, serving as an instructor. On 5 September 1944 he was killed in a flying accident piloting a P-38 near Muroc, CA.

Rookie 2Lt. Ralph **Wandrey**. (R) claimed his first victory of six. (AFAA)

23 July 1943: 49FG/9FS

Capt. Ross Blachly led 11 P-38s of the 9FS from Horanda to escort B-26 Marauders of the 22nd Bomb Group on a morning mission to Salamaua. Once airborne Blachly's radio malfunctioned, and 1Lt. Harry Lidstrom temporarily took the Yellow Flight lead as they ascended to 15,000 feet. 1Lt. Gerald Johnson held his Blue Flight off to the left at the same altitude, and 1Lt. William Bleecker's Green Flight quartet climbed to top cover at 22,000.

Lidstrom lost sight of the bombers in broken clouds and followed a C-47 transport flight that was also headed north. After leaving the transports west of Salamaua the Knights patrolled for nearly an hour and a half, and at 1000 the lower Yellow and Blue Flights spotted a large fighter formation arriving from the north. Initially, Blachly thought they possibly could be P-40s because of their profile, but he soon saw the red "meatballs" on the wings and fuselage of the 68th Sentai's new Tony fighters. Lidstrom hesitated and Blachly, still without a working radio, was uncertain of his Wingman's plan and became impatient, so he dove on the enemy fighters, rushing in head on at 15,000 feet. At the same time Gerald Johnson's seven P-38s of Blue Flight targeted the same enemy aircraft as Blachly. Simultaneously, eight Lightning pilots entered into their first dogfight against the new Tony Ki-61 in-line engine fighter.

The Yellow Flight remained in formation in its turn toward the enemy, but 2Lt. Frank Wunder, flying in the tail-end position, turned in the opposite direction and met a Tony head on and fired at point blank range, rolled, and saw the damaged Tony escape as a probable claim.

Blue Flight Leader 1Lt. Gerald Johnson also made a head on pass and missed, but immediately re-engaged and hit the Tony for a probable claim. Blue Element Leader 1Lt. Charles Ralph held formation for the first pass against the Tonys, but separated when he saw Oscars over the coast. Bleecker's Green Flight, on top cover, also spotted the Oscars and also dove on them at 17,000 feet. Ralph and Green Wingman 2Lt. Ralph Wandrey each claimed one Oscar destroyed. When rookie Wandrey tried to make a second pass on the Oscars a pair of Tonys arrived. One hit Wandrey's port wing but the explosive round did not detonate. 1Lt. Wilbert Arthur hit an Oscar and was credited with a probable.

23 July 1943: 35FG/39FS

The 14 P-38s of the 39FS took off at 0730 to escort C-47s to Wau and Bulolo. The formation was ordered to investigate a bandit near Lae, and on their arrival only saw six B-24s heading north 20 miles from Lae. At 0945, when they arrived over Lae at 18,000 feet, they saw a formation of 10 Zeros flying in the opposite direction 3,000 feet below. Soon two more large enemy formations of 10 each appeared below.

1Lt. Paul Stanch's flight patrolled over Wau for about an hour when they saw approximately 20 enemy fighters approaching Lae in a large

Lufbery Circle, with several "patches of three planes in no apparent formation outside the Circle." Stanch's first pass was through the formation with no observable hits. On his second pass he chose an Oscar and fired a three second quarter tail burst and hit the port fuselage and wing; it exploded about half way between Lae and Salamaua. Stanch's third pass was on a "ME-109." He saw hits on the cowling, but the fighter flew on and was claimed as damaged. On his final attack Stanch dove on two Zeros flying close together over Lae. He sprayed a four second burst back and forth over them but did not see any results, as his P-38 began buffeting so badly that he had trouble pulling out of the dive. He then returned to Wau and continued his patrol before returning to base. 1Lt. Robert Baker was flying in Stanch's flight, but was unable to maintain formation and made five unsuccessful large figure-8 passes at the Lufbery before climbing to 16,000 and returning to the flight heading toward Lae. Baker's next target was a "Mike-type" aircraft which Baker over-ran, and the Mike fired a short burst that missed Baker. Baker climbed back to 16,000 feet over the coast and dove on four enemy aircraft in loose echelon circling to the left. He made a 90 degree deflection astern attack and the enemy fighter rolled over into the overcast (Stanch later confirmed). Baker again climbed to 16,000 feet and orbited, finding an Oscar north of Salamaua. Baker fired as the enemy pilot rolled and his .50s entered both sides of the Oscar's fuselage. Prentice confirmed the victory. Once again, Baker climbed to 16,000 feet and saw a Hap near Bulolo and approached it at 45 degrees. The enemy fighter made a sharp turn in front of Baker and flew into his stream of bullets, but it flew off and Baker filed a damaged claim and headed home, low on fuel.

1Lts. Andrew Kish and Richard Smith were flying together when Kish dove on two enemy aircraft on his first pass but missed. He made his next pass from 15,000 feet in a diving turn, firing from the rear, and got hits on the engine and cockpit of a Tony that rolled over and crashed five miles off Lae. Meanwhile, Smith initiated a number of attacks but could not carry through, as there was always a Japanese fighter nearby ready to dive to attack him. His successful attack on an Oscar was from astern right at 60 degrees, and the Oscar went into a spin without burning and crashed two miles offshore and eight miles from Lae.

Capt. Charles King was leading one of the flights and made two ineffective firing passes. He dodged one attack by two Zeros, but was not so fortunate when two more Zeros attacked him. They chased after him as he went into a shallow dive inland, and after about two minutes they broke off. King looked over at his port engine, which was smoking heavily, and he was forced to feather it but returned safely to base.

The 39FS had claimed five victories, one probable (1Lt. Stanley Andrews), and four damaged (1Lt. William Anderson, 2Lt. Wayne Rothgreb, Stanch, and Baker).

Maj. Edward **Cragg** shot down a Zero and Tony to become an ace. (AFAA)

23 July 1943: 8FG/80FS

Maj. Edward Cragg led 14 Lightnings from Kila Airdrome at 0900 on an escort of a large formation of B-24s from the rendezvous at Marilinan to Bogadjim at 15,000 feet when five Tonys and 15 Oscars appeared over the target.

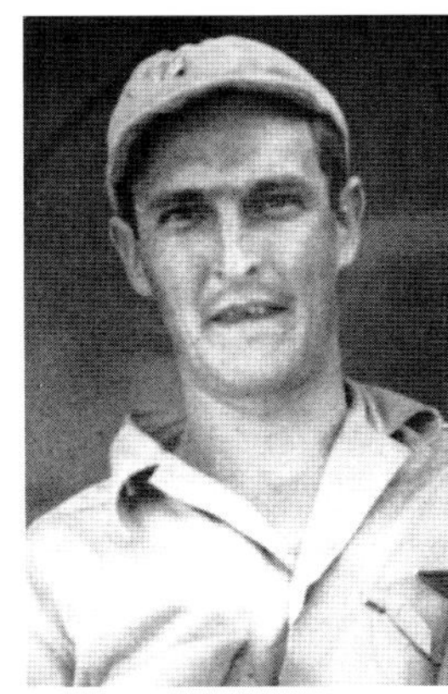

1Lt. John **Jones** shot down two Zeros to become an ace. (AFAA)

After flying the P-400 Capt. Norbert **Ruff** scored his first victory while flying a P-38. (AAF)

LEFT: 1Lt. Richard **Smith** got his sixth victory. (AAF) MIDDLE: 1Lt. Andrew **Kish**. (left) with 1Lt. Robert **Baker** scored his second victory. (AAF) RIGHT: 1Lt. Robert **Baker** shot down a "Mike-type" fighter for his second and last victory of the war. (AAF)

Cragg's Lead Flight

Cragg spotted one of the Tonys five miles away being pursued by a P-38 that was firing out of range. Cragg turned inside to quickly close on the Japanese fighter at near 500 mph, firing a burst into its fuselage and port wing; the damaged fighter caught fire as it passed by. Cragg climbed back to altitude and saw a Zero making a pass at a P-38. The Zero rolled over on its back as Cragg followed it down and started firing, and his burst hit the tail assembly as the two fighters neared the deck. The Zero exploded, and pieces hit Cragg's wings; he had to reef his Lightning violently to avoid hitting the trees. Cragg had scored his fifth victory to become an ace. Cragg was joined by 2Lt. Kenneth Ladd, and the two chased a Zero without result. Cragg's Wingman, 2Lt. Jennings Myers, did his job and followed Cragg throughout the combat, and after his Leader shot down his Zero Myers climbed back to 15,000 feet and returned to base.

2Lt. Kenneth Ladd, Cragg's second Element Leader, saw a lone Zero being chased by three P-38s. The enemy pilot broke away smoking and Ladd, with an altitude advantage, dove after it. At 4,000 feet he fired a long burst that caused more smoke, and then watched the Zero crash into the ground. As Ladd was climbing he saw another Zero and fired a 30 degree deflection shot, then made a tight turn to come around again when Cragg made a pass at the Zero, but neither man hit it. Ladd followed it down in a high speed dive and slowly gained on it, firing intermittent bursts that finally started it smoking, but then it disappeared into a cloud for a probable.

Ruff's Second Flight

At 1125, Capt. Norbert Ruff and his flight were performing steep turns over the target area when he saw a lone single seat fighter at 18,000 feet. Ruff was unable to drop his tanks, but he dove on the enemy anyway and fired, but could not close on it due to the drag of the tanks. Another P-38 dove in front of him and fired a short burst that sent the Zero down into the ground. Ruff was finally able to drop his tanks and tried to rejoin his flight when he saw two P-38s ahead and raced to catch them. Once he closed on them he turned back with them to the combat area. Ruff saw a lone Zero ahead and 3,000 feet below flying toward Madang, so he fired from very close range. His volley tore off its right wing about five feet from the cockpit, and it rolled over and crashed inland from Konstantin Harbor. Ruff saw another P-38 and they flew back to 30 Mile Drome.

2Lt. Robert Hanson was Ruff's Wingman, and he saw five enemy aircraft at 5 o'clock climbing, trying to get on the flight's tails. He then saw four more Zeros 1,000 feet above and closed on these four head on, shooting at the leader with no observed effect. He then turned 180° to get on the tail of another Zero, which crashed into a beach after being hit hard by Hanson's machine guns and cannon. He continued on and saw a Zero chasing a P-38 at 4,000 feet below and dove and fired, hitting it for a probable. Still in his dive, Hanson saw a Zero climbing and fired head on without seeing any hits in the rapid speed by. Hanson continued his dive, which was approaching 500 mph, and he needed his elevator trim to come out of the dive. Hanson climbed into clouds, and when he came out he saw five enemy fighters below heading for the Liberators, which were returning home. Hanson dove on the attackers, but they broke away into the clouds and he couldn't catch them. He then escorted the bombers on their way home.

1Lt. Donald McGee, Ruff's second Element Leader, and Wingman 2Lt. Robert Adams were doing steep turns with Ruff over the target. When Ruff and his Wingman went into their attack McGee tried to follow, but his port engine cut out momentarily. McGee saw an inline enemy fighter 2,000 feet ahead and above and turned into it, but could not climb fast enough because of the bad engine. He broke off the combat and returned to base on two bad engines.

2Lt. Robert Adams, Capt. Ruff's #4 man, was unable to drop one of his tanks and became separated from the flight. A Zero tried to get on his tail, but Adams was able to dive away after another P-38 intervened (1Lt. John Jones). He then saw another Zero far below and dove from 16,000 feet, and at 10,000 feet fired a volley that set its right wing on fire, and it plunged into the clouds below. Adams joined his Flight Leader Ruff and the two flew back to base.

Daly's Third Flight

1Lt. Raymond Daly was leading the third flight, and on his arrival over the target saw several Zeros. When he tried to release his tanks the right tank didn't release and he returned to base. 2Lt. Cornelius Smith was Daly's Wingman, and when Daly was unable to drop a tank he stayed with him on his return to base. 1Lt. Glen Hope was Daly's second Element Leader and was unable to drop either of his two tanks, so his Wingman, 2Lt. William Fotheringham, followed Hope, Daly, and Smith back to base.

Jones' Two Man Flight

1Lt. John Jones, Wingman to Flight Leader Capt. Cleve Jones, did not see the first enemy fighters, but did spot a P-38 (Adams) being pursued by a Zero and climbed toward it. Jones fired at long range, and the Zero dove away before Jones could get in range. Jones dove after the Zero and opened fire at closer range, seeing hits but no damage as he passed, but as he looked back he saw its starboard wing shear off. There were three barrage balloons in the area, and it appeared the Zero was trying to lure Jones into their cables but may have run into them, shearing its wing. Jones climbed back to the area where he thought the bombers would be located. When he got to 16,000 feet he saw a single engine fighter about a mile below. Jones dove and fired from long range at 90 degrees but missed behind. Jones continued to fire while reefing until he had a shot from directly behind. When he closed to 50 feet a sheet of smoke and flame erupted from its tail, and it went down in flames to make Jones an ace. This enemy fighter appeared to be a decoy, as four or five other Zeros were closing on him from slightly above, but Jones dove and the enemy was never able to get in range before Jones headed into a cloud. The two victories made Jones an ace. Flight Leader Cleve Jones was unable to drop one of his tanks when he went into combat. The tank was probably hit by enemy bullets and was set on fire. Jones elected to try to fly to the Nuru River to make a landing, but crashed and exploded about 10 miles short.

26 July 1943: 49FG/9FS

On the 26th, Capt. Lawrence Smith's three Flights of the 9FS were investigating a plot from the Air Controller and were sent up the Markham Valley for an interception. After the 1230 take off from Horanda Strip, two pilots aborted with engine problems and only 10 Flying Knights reached the Markham River Delta, but did not find the enemy. Smith and Wingman 2Lt. Ralph Hays, second Element Leader 1Lt. Normand Hyland, and Wingman James Harris searched due north further inland for 20 miles over the Markham River Valley at 14,000 feet. Mission Leader Smith turned them back toward the Markham Delta as clouds began to close in. Blue Flight Leader Watkins went into a shallow descent, trying to keep Smith in sight.

The area just beyond Lae airdrome was surrounded by thick clouds, but in a clear area the Knights met Oscars and "Type III" fighters (Tonys) flying down the Markham Valley at 12,000 feet. Smith ordered the Lightnings to drop their tanks, but Smith's and Hyland's tanks hung up and Smith led Red Flight through the nearest clouds, where Smith and Hyland were still unable to shake their tanks loose and orbited the area while Hays and Harris returned to the combat. Hays peeled off after an Oscar that flew through Hays' fire, and the Oscar "wavered and then continued his flight losing altitude"; Hayes did not follow as the enemy fighter flew under him for a probable. Hays was able to find Smith and the two returned to base. Meanwhile, Harris dove on a Type III enemy aircraft 2,000 feet below

1Lt. Richard **Bong** being decorated with the DSC by Gen. Wurtsmith for his four victory day which made him a triple ace with 15 victories. (AAF)

Veteran James **Watkins** was near the end his tour and had not scored a victory but shot down four Tonys in this combat. (AAF)

While scoring two victories 1Lt. Gerald **Johnson's** fighter suffered damage during the combat. (AAF)

climbing toward him, and Harris half rolled and fired a three second burst. Harris saw pieces coming off the enemy fighter, which fell off on its wing and passed under Harris. A Zero got on Harris' tail and the American climbed toward another P-38 and the Zero turned away. Harris claimed the Tony as destroyed on his ICR but was given official credit for a probable.

Trailing a short distance behind on the left flank was the Blue Flight, led by Deputy CO Capt. James Watkins, who was accompanied by Wingman 1Lt. Richard Bong with second Element Leader 2Lt. Robert Wood and Wingman 2Lt. John McLean at 16,000 feet. (Note: In his ICR Bong claims to be Blue Flight Leader, but it appears that Watkins, being the Deputy CO and a Captain, was Blue Leader, while Bong was the Element Leader and Wood was Watkin's Wingman.) Further off on the right flank was 1Lt. Gerald Johnson's Green Flight of Wingman 2Lt. Stanley Johnson and Element Leader Capt. Ross Blachly, who decided to tag along on the mission with Wingman 2Lt. Glade Hill. Since Smith was unable to drop his belly tank Watkins' Blue Flight became the Lead Flight.

Veteran James Watkins was near the end of his tour and had not scored a victory since his P-40 victory on 26 December 1942 over Dobodura; he was determined to score at least one more victory. Meanwhile, Watkins' Blue Flight was confronted by Tonys turning head on in front of them and approaching Blue Flight's rear quarter. Watkins turned into two Tonys coming down head on and hit the canopy of one, forcing its pilot to bail out. Watkins climbed into the overcast, and when he exited he saw five Tonys diving to get behind Gerald Johnson. A Tony turned into Watkins, who fired from 45 degrees head on above; its engine caught fire and it rolled over straight in from 9,000 feet. While Watkins was watching it go down two enemy fighters came at him from behind. Watkins turned and fired at the first one, which burst into flames as it passed under him. The second got on Watkins' tail, and Johnson pulled into it as the enemy pilot turned to the right and tried to get away. Johnson Split-S'd and fired until he flew past its tail, getting hits on its wings and engine; it was confirmed by 2Lt. Stanley Johnson, who was about to attack as it was diving away on fire. As he tried to break away Watkins saw a single fighter ahead and fired a burst from long range at 1,000 to 1,500 yards, "naturally" without result. Watkins climbed back to 10,000 feet into the middle of a dogfight and saw a Tony about 2,000 yards ahead. The enemy pilot turned left, and Watkins turned 180 degrees into him and fired from the rear and above. The Tony "whipped over" to the right and went into a spin without smoking; it was last seen still spinning when Watkins left. Watkins claimed four definitely destroyed, but soon "the standards of assessment will not allow the fourth aircraft to be classified as a definite destroyed (Lt.Col. Floyd Volk, A-2 5th FC)." But it seems this fourth victory continued to be credited and Watkins became an ace.

After Johnson shot down the Tony he tried to join two other P-38s when an Oscar passed in front of him and he and another Lightning began to fire. But it was Johnson who "rocked his ship's nose up and down" to maximize his long burst of fire that blew off its port wing and pieces of its engine cowling and cockpit. Johnson pulled up sharply just as the Oscar exploded violently, with pieces hitting his aircraft. When he looked around to assess any damage Johnson saw that his port vertical stabilizer was blown off from the boom and headed to Horanda with his first two victories of 22 of the war.

Pictured as a young cadet 1Lt. Gerald **Johnson** scored his first two of 22 victories as one of the 5FC's most illustrious fighter pilots. (AFAA)

Meanwhile, in Green Flight, Element Leader Capt. Ross Blachly and Wingman 2Lt. Glade Hill became separated from Green Flight Leader Johnson and had to climb out of the combat; they joined the 80FS top cover. After Johnson's Wingman, 2Lt. Stanley Johnson, dropped his tanks and accelerated he blew out his starboard supercharger. He was able to stay with Johnson through his first pass on the Oscars but could not re-engage.

1Lt. Richard Bong fired a quick burst at a Tony, missed, dove out to regain speed, and came upon a Zeke head on. Bong fired quickly and the enemy burst into flames. Bong then positioned himself above and behind a Tony and gave him a quick burst that knocked pieces off the fuselage. Coming around in a port turn from the rear quarter, Bong saw another Tony and his long burst set it on fire. Immediately, a Zeke came head on and Bong fired a long burst which knocked off the Zeke's canopy and struck its engine. The four victories for the day made Bong a triple ace with 15 victories. Bong issued his usual brief report on the combat:

> "I was leader of Blue Flight (?-author) when we were scrambled to the Salamaua-Dropping Area at 1230. We went up there and made a circle over Lae, came down to Salamaua and then went down to the Markham Valley just back of Lae at 16,000 feet.
>
> On our way there I called in airplanes at 12 o'clock and we were intercepted at 1350 over the Markham Valley. There were about 20 fighters; 10 inline engine fighters and 10 Zeros. I dropped my tanks and shot at an inline job and missed.
>
> I dove out and shot at a Zeke head on and he burst into flames. I shot at an inline job 45 degrees from behind and above and knocked pieces off his fuselage. I shot at another inline job and he burst into flames. I shot at another Zero head on and knocked pieces out of his canopy and engine cowling or engine. I shot at one more inline job and missed left the area at 1410 and returned to base and landed."

The squadron historian added the following comment on Bong's modestly brief report on his destruction of four enemy fighters: "He would describe a major engagement in the same amount of space another man would take to tell of drinking three beers."

Bong's Wingman, Blue #4 2Lt. John McLean, dove too fast and had to use his trim tabs to bring his fighter out of its dive, then found three Zeros on his tail and had to dive away. Once free he was alone and returned to base.

26 July 1943: 35FG/39FS

The 39FS sent out 15 P-38s to escort B-24s to Komiatum led by Maj. Thomas Lynch. Capt. Charles Sullivan was leading one of four flights when he saw seven or eight Oscars 12 miles away at 12 o'clock. The flight dropped their tanks and climbed, and Sullivan closed and dove sharply to port, firing two or three long bursts from astern. The Oscar rolled over on its back and went into a steep dive toward the ground. Sullivan climbed to gain altitude and saw a Zero below; he fired a deflection shot with some hits before it turned into him and sped past. In addition to Sullivan's victory, the Squadron claimed two probables (by 1Lt. Gordon Prentice and Lynch) and four damaged (by Sullivan, 1Lt. John Lane, and 2Lts. Wayne Rothgreb and Richard Tansing).

26 July 1943: 35FG Command Change

In late July Maj. Richard Doss was named CO of the 35FG, taking over for Lt.Col. Malcolm Moore. In June 1942 Doss had been appointed CO Commander of the 41PS, and by 1943 he was a Major. In November Doss would be promoted to Lieutenant Colonel, and under Doss' command the 35FG scored 397 victories, set a record for the longest fighter mission in the SWPA, and was the first fighter squadron to reach the Japanese mainland. Doss would be promoted to Colonel in 1945.

26 July 1943: 8FG/80FS

The 80FS Headhunters patrolled eastward but did not encounter the enemy.

Maj. Richard **Doss** was named CO of the 35FG taking over for Lt.Col. Malcolm Moore. (AAF)

Capt. Charles **Sullivan**. (changed his name to O'Sullivan after the war) became an ace with his fifth and last victory. (AFAA)

28 July 1943: 49FG/9FS

At 0630, two days after their very successful Markham Valley combat, Maj. Sidney Woods led 10 9FS Lightnings joined by 12 39FS Cobras. The fighters were to escort B-25s of the 3rd Air Group which were to attack enemy shipping in the Bay and strafe the airstrip at Cape Gloucester, on the western end of New Britain. Fifth Air Force mission planners, expecting resolute resistance over the new enemy complex, ordered 9FS Flights to remain in visual contact with the 3AG Mitchells at a lower altitude than normal. Red Flight Leader Sidney Woods and Wingman 2Lt. Robert Wood were in the lead position at 4,000 feet, followed closely behind by Green Flight's Capt. William Haney, Wingman 2Lt. Ralph Wandrey, Element Leader 2Lt. George Alber, and rookie Wingman F/O H.R. Prince at 6,000 feet. At 8,000 feet, trailing above them in high cover, was Capt. James Watkins and 1Lt. Richard Bong accompanied by 2Lt. Normand Hyland.

The American formation arrived at the target area without opposition, and the Mitchells hit several vessels off Cape Raoult, just east of the Gloucester complex. They also set fires near the airstrip while Maj. Woods' close escorts circled the target area. After 30 minutes over the target there was an alert calling enemy fighters approaching from the east. All three 9FS Flights dropped their belly tanks and climbed in a port turn out over the sea, where they met the large Oscar formation from Rabaul. Maj. Woods and Wingman Wood, with Green Flight's Haney and Wingman Wandrey, came into firing range against the oncoming enemy at 8,000 feet. Woods and Wandrey each destroyed an Oscar and damaged another during four hit-and-run passes in the turning fight, while Capt. Haney downed a third Oscar.

Blue Flight Wingman Hyland failed to hold position with Watkins and Bong, and he dove away with four Oscars closely behind. Hyland's great diving speed left the enemy fighters behind. Watkins first met an Oscar in a nose on pass and downed it. Bong joined Watkins on his second pass, and the two dove on a pair of Oscars. Watkins' burst exploded one, and his P-38 nearly collided with the debris. Bong and Watkins then separated, as the other Oscars outnumbered them. Bong dove for the safety of five wingmen in the distance, while Watkins dove to 4,000 feet and met another pair of Ki-43s head on. Both Oscars eluded Watkins' fire, but as the enemy Wingman dove away,

LEFT: Considered an excellent combat leader, Maj. Sidney **Woods**, scored his last of two victories in the Pacific. (AFAA) RIGHT: Maj. Sidney **Woods** as an ace in the ETO. (AFAA)

1Lt. Richard **Bong's** crew apply his 16th victory emblem. (AAF)

the Oscar Leader looped in front and stalled, hanging in the air by its prop and allowing Watkins to hit it hard with a stream of .50 caliber and 20mm explosive rounds, causing the enemy fighter to drop straight down into a huge explosion into the sea for his third victory of the day and seventh in three days.

Upon rejoining the Squadron Bong was attacked from behind and hit by machine gun fire. He quickly dove for safety and pulled out at 4,000 feet, where he saw two Oscars heading toward B-25s flying south on the deck. Bong went into a shallow diving turn and fired a 45 degree deflection shot on the trailing Oscar, which tried to turn into him and flew into the American's point blank head on volley. The Oscar slid away trailing heavy smoke and crashed into Rein Bay for Bong's 16th victory.

29 July 1943: 8FG/80FS

The 80FS took part in a B-25 and B-26 escort taking off from Dobodura to Cape Gloucester, New Britain. They arrived over the target at 1000 and circled as the medium bombers bombed and strafed an enemy destroyer. On their last circle of the area 1Lt. Jay Robbins and Wingman 2Lt. Kenneth Ladd saw a Dinah twin engine recon bomber. Ladd was in the best position to make the attack and "cut Robbins off and made a perfect tail shot" for his first of 12 victories.

Making up for lost time Capt. James **Watkins** again scored three victories to give him seven and make him a sure ace. (AAF)

2Lt. Kenneth **Ladd** scored the first of his 12 victories. (AFAA)

8

August 1943

Reno Plans

In the midst of *Elkton III/Cartwheel*, the Joint Chiefs met with President Roosevelt and Prime Minister Churchill at the *Quadrant Conference* in Quebec in August 1943. The foremost problems facing Roosevelt and Churchill were those connected with the war in Europe; particularly concerning that a final decision for the invasion of Continental Europe was due. But the war in the Pacific also required their consideration, as there still was no authorized long range plan to defeat Japan. However, in the summer of 1943 these long range decisions, while important, were not urgent, except when they affected plans for the immediate future. Thus, no long range Pacific plan was prepared, and while numerous valuable studies were completed, a long range Pacific plan would have to wait until the war in Europe became more settled and the future role of the Soviet Union and China in the war against Japan was more definite. So, although handicapped by the lack of a long range strategy into which to fit their plans for the immediate operational future, the Pacific planners proceeded as best they could to develop a plan of operations to be followed in the Pacific during the next 18 months, utilizing the studies already completed and tentatively approved as the basis for planning. Central Pacific strategy, at least through the seizure of the Marshalls, was established, but there was some doubt as to where Nimitz' forces would advance after that. *Elkton III/Cartwheel* also set a firm schedule for MacArthur and Halsey, but reservations had been recently expressed as to the necessity of the capture of Rabaul. To resolve these and other matters, the planners had to make a decision.

Quadrant's decisions gave priority to the Navy's drive across the Central Pacific, which was contrary to MacArthur's proposal for the capture of Rabaul. But Pacific planners made the decision to bypass and isolate Rabaul, rather than attempting to capture the base, and to attack Kavieng instead. Soon after the decision was made to bypass Kavieng as well. This all meant that MacArthur's *Elkton/Cartwheel Plan* had been achieved, and he was now to neutralize the Japanese on New Guinea as far west as Wewak. MacArthur would have to devise a new plan to accomplish this new directive.

MacArthur's answer came early in August in the form of his *Reno Plan*. After invading Saidor, the *Plan* outlined the steps extending through August 1944 by which he intended to return to the Philippines, which was to be an advance across the north coast of New Guinea to Mindanao. From February 1943 MacArthur's staff at SWPA General Headquarters had been planning *Reno*, which underwent five modifications in response to the amended operational and strategic requirements. *Reno I* was to leapfrog past Japanese strongholds in New Guinea and use paratroops to seize key bases en route to Mindanao, in the southern Philippines. The major obstacle to MacArthur's plan was the so called "Bismarck Barrier," namely New Britain, and its powerful naval and air bases at Rabaul, along with the Japanese air bases dispersed along the northern New Guinea coastline.

President Roosevelt and Prime Minister Churchill at the ***Quadrant Conference*** in Quebec in August 1943. (AFHRC)

Reno II was devised and divided into six phases, the first of which was identical with *Elkton III/Cartwheel*. According to *Reno II*, by March 1944 forces of the Southwest Pacific would have secured the objectives outlined in *Phase I*, the control of the Bismarck Archipelago, including the capture of Rabaul, and of eastern New Guinea. *Phase II*, which would begin in August, would carry the advance into the Hollandia area of Dutch New Guinea, bypassing Wewak. This move was to be accompanied by the invasion of the Kai, Aroe, and Tanimbar Islands in the Netherlands Indies off the southwest coast of New Guinea, a move designed to guard the left flank of the main drive up the northwest coast of New Guinea. The remainder of 1944 and the early months of 1945 would be devoted to *Reno III* operations in northwest New Guinea and would culminate in the capture of the Vogelkop Peninsula.

During *Reno IV* and *Reno V*, for which MacArthur set no dates, forces of the Southwest Pacific would continue their advance along the Netherlands Indies' axis to seize the islands between New Guinea and the Philippines, thereby gaining control of the Celebes Sea. At the same time the Palau group, in the western Carolines, was to be captured, either by MacArthur or Nimitz, to protect the right flank of the advance into Mindanao, *Phase III*, and the final phase of *Reno II*.

Reno II clearly reflected MacArthur's strategic and tactical concepts and his view of the importance of the Philippines in the war against Japan. It called for the capture of Rabaul as a necessary preliminary to control the Bismarck Archipelago, and for bypassing Wewak, whose capture General Marshall had suggested in July. Implicit in the plan was the view that the New Guinea route was superior to the Central Pacific, and that the step-by-step advance under cover of land-based aircraft was the safest course to follow. And it repeated his familiar arguments for the concentration of Pacific resources on the drive up the New Guinea coast as the most effective way to exploit the Allied advantages in that area and to increase the tempo of the war.

Though MacArthur's schedule of operations for 1943 and 1944 was generally acceptable in Washington, his views on broad Pacific strategy found little support. Not only had the Joint Chiefs of Staff and their planners become convinced of the desirability of the Central Pacific route, but they also seemed to have made a decision about Rabaul. Thus, the program drawn up by the planners for the remainder of 1943 and 1944 gave preference to the Central Pacific offensive and stipulated the neutralization, rather than the capture, of Rabaul. The reconciliation of the JCS' program with MacArthur's *Reno* proposal would be a difficult and contentious task.

In the opinion of the planners, Adm. Nimitz' forces, after they had completed the operations already scheduled in the Gilberts and Marshalls, would advance westward into the Carolines, first capturing Ponape, then Truk, "the key Japanese position in the Central Pacific," and finally Yap and the Palau Islands. From there, at some indefinite date, Central Pacific forces would move into the Philippines. Though no operations were scheduled for the Marianas, the planners indicated their intention of preparing an outline plan for the recapture of Guam in the near future.

The strategic objective of the program developed in Washington early in August was the line Palaus-Vogelkop Peninsula. This objective fit perfectly into MacArthur's *Reno Plan*, though the operations foreseen in Washington were not identical with those outlined by MacArthur. First Washington planners ruled out the capture of Rabaul as an unnecessary move and "an intolerable drain" on resources and manpower. For another, they included in their program the seizure of Wewak, despite MacArthur's contention that the operation "would involve hazards rendering success doubtful." Finally, they completely omitted the operations MacArthur had scheduled in the Netherlands East Indies to protect the left flank of his advance along the New Guinea coast.

However, the similarity of the Washington and *Reno* Plans was more obvious than the differences. In both, MacArthur's and Halsey's forces were to complete *Cartwheel*, and then they were to gain control of the Bismarck Archipelago. The seizure of the Bismarck Archipelago was to be accomplished under the Washington plan in three phases: first, seizure of the islands along the eastern border of the Archipelago (New Ireland, New Hanover, and St. Matthias); second, capture of the Admiralty Islands to the north and west; and finally, occupation of the New Guinea coastline as far west as Wewak. Once these tasks were completed, MacArthur was to continue along the northwest coast of New Guinea in a series of amphibious and airborne operations that would take him to the Vogelkop Peninsula by the end of 1944.

5AF Status

The increased activity of the 5th FC fighter units was more than matched by the 5th BC bombers, as the month of July had more sustained bombing effort against enemy ground positions in the battle area than any previous month in SWPA fighting. Attacks against shipping during this same period were limited almost entirely to interfering with enemy barge traffic. Barges continued to reach New Guinea from New Britain, and supplies still moved along the coast in the same manner. A-20s, B-26s, and B-25s carried out bombing and strafing sorties against these targets, sometimes with P-38 cover.

However, as the bombers of the Fifth Air Force were carrying out impressive missions against Japanese shipping, it plainly was not accomplishing its primary function of destroying the Japanese air forces. Although 5FC fighter pilots were destroying ten Japanese aircraft for every one of their own, the Japanese now seemed to be reluctant to make more than nominal interceptions of Allied bombing attacks in New Guinea, and thus were able to preserve their sizeable air force. From 1 June to 30 July, Allied air forces in the Solomons claimed 529 Japanese aircraft destroyed, while Kenney's fighter pilots claimed only 165 in the entire Southwest Pacific. If, as was likely, the Japanese were employing more aircraft in the defense of the Solomons than New Guinea, this would partially explain the difference in the victory totals. But from aerial photographs and air reconnaissance of the SWPA, Allied Intelligence determined that the Japanese had sufficient air strength but were conserving it for the future.

The Fifth Air Force had demonstrated that its medium and heavy bombers could carry out sustained attacks on an objective as distant as Madang. But the enemy's principal stronghold on the New Guinea mainland was Wewak, more than 200 miles farther along the coast. It was necessary to eliminate the Japanese fighter and bomber strength based at the Wewak airdromes in order to destroy the potential threat that these aircraft posed to Allied ground advances toward Lae and Salamaua. Before an air offensive against Wewak could be carried out, however, it was necessary to seize bases far enough advanced to permit fighters to accompany bombers over Wewak and extensive enough to base fighters and transports, as well as to provide refueling facilities for medium bombers if necessary. The 5AF had been considering the possibilities of acquiring such advanced bases for several months. In general, their plan was to determine the most suitable of the numerous airstrips which had been scattered throughout Northeast New Guinea prior to the war, and with the help of the Australian New Guinea Administrative Unit (ANGAU), Australian patrols, and native labor, to develop them into bases.

Marilinan and Tsili Tsili

Marilinan

Before the capture of Lae, the enemy's air units at airdromes in the vicinity of Wewak had to be neutralized. But first an advanced airdrome, forward of Wau, had to be developed to put Wewak within the range of escort fighters and to provide refueling facilities for medium bombers. To carry out this plan for the development of new airbases, Lt. Everette Frazier, XO of the 657th Engineer Aviation Battalion (Negro), had been transferred to the Fifth Air Force with orders "to locate one operational or staging fighter airdrome forward of Wau." Frazier had been a construction engineer with the Shell Oil Company prior to the war, and was thus well prepared to carry out such a mission. During a reconnaissance he reached Marilinan, on the Watut River, less than 50 miles from both Lae and Salamaua. The air approaches to this area from one end were blocked off by mountains, but the site of an old airdrome was considered adequate for transports, with a possibility that it could be improved for fighters. The local Australian officer recruited natives from a nearby village, who immediately began to clear and camouflage the prospective field. The natives were indispensable in the work of preparing the airdrome. The tall kunai grass was burned off, and in spite of the smoke the Japanese were not alerted, since the natives often started numerous fires. After the airdrome was completed Frazier returned to Moresby and informed Kenney that his base near Marilinan would be adequate for proposed operations until the heavy September rains began, after which it would have to be evacuated and abandoned. Kenney decided that he would select another more suitable forward area for an all-weather airdrome to be in Allied possession by September. Kenney and his advisers concluded that the offensive would have by then reached Nadzab, an area chosen by Australians familiar with New Guinea as an ideal site for a permanent base. Kenney and MacArthur determined that Nadzab could be captured, airstrips prepared, and all equipment transported there from the Marilinan area before rains made that move impossible. Shortly after the conference Gen. Wurtsmith, 5th Fighter Commander, and several officers flew to Marilinan in a B-24 and a P-40.

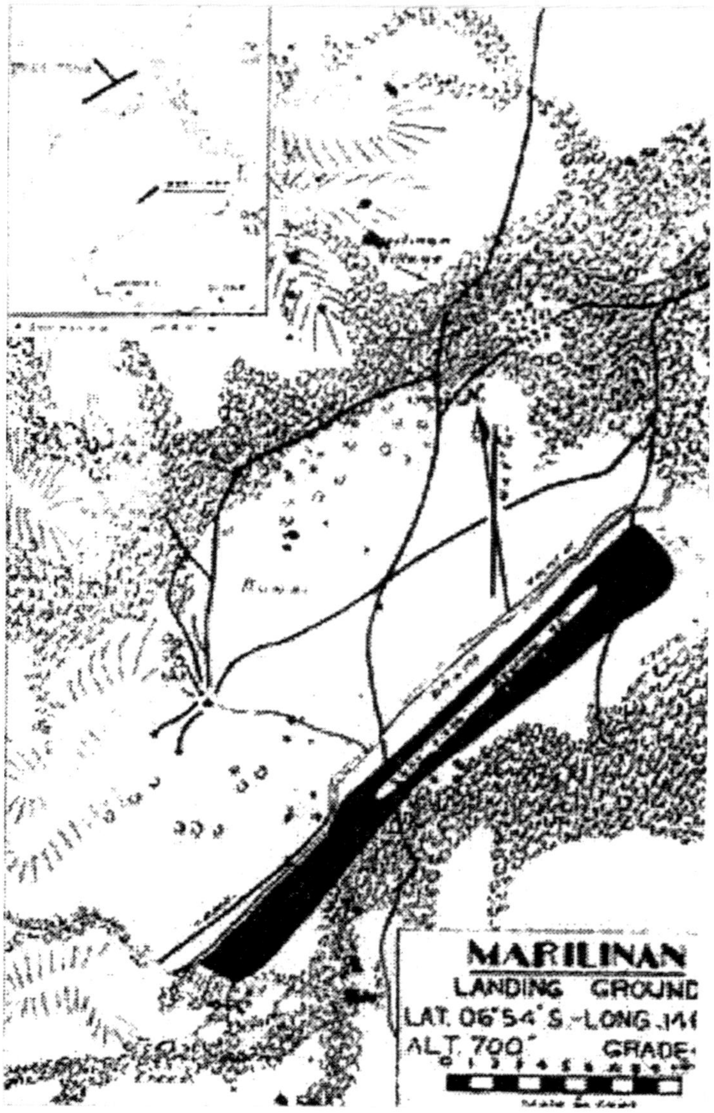

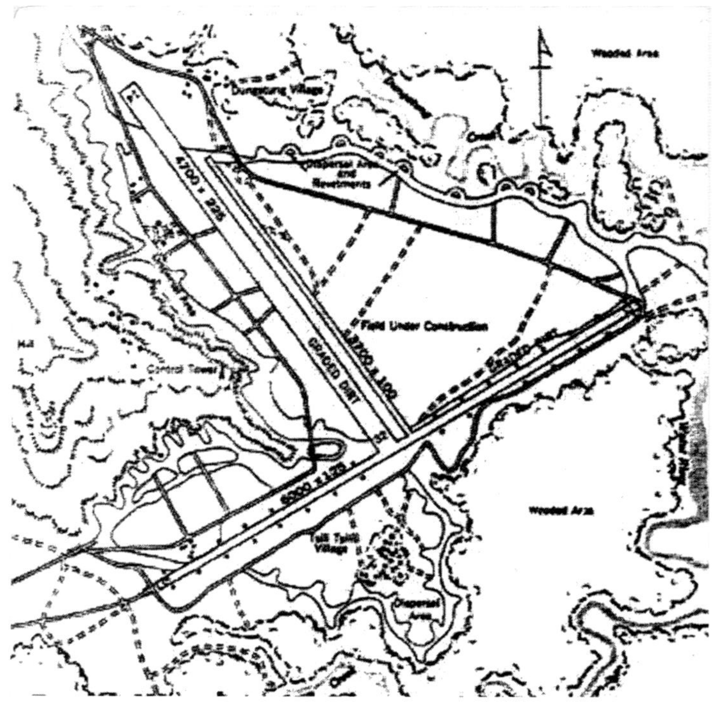

Tsili Tsili Airdrome

They conferred with Maj. Herman Cox of the 5th Bomber Command and Capt. Everett King of the 5th Fighter Command, who had reached Marilinan by foot before Frazier's departure. At this time it was decided that Tsili Tsili, five miles southwest of Marilinan, would better meet requirements for a temporary base until the heavy September rains began, at which time Tsili Tsili would have to be evacuated.

Tsili Tsili

Tsili Tsili (pronounced Silly Silly and sometimes spelled Tsile Tsile) was a name that Gen. Kenney opposed and wanted it to be renamed, as he thought the name was "demeaning" and could be used by the Japanese as such (the Japanese had called the area Fabua during their occupation of the region).

The construction at Tsili Tsili was under the direction of Col. Ward Abbott, Air Engineer for the Fifth Air Force, who was charged with the clearing of the new strips and the locating of dispersal areas, taxiways, and camp sites. Soon after the engineers arrived there was a 10 day weather delay. Nevertheless, by the time the weather cleared, this single company constructed a 4,200 foot grass strip which allowed the new base to handle as many as 150 C-47s daily. By July, C-47s were landing on the rudimentary airdrome, ferrying the 871st Airborne Engineers equipped with specially designed small bulldozers, graders, carryalls, and grass cutters. Meanwhile, for many weeks the existence of this field was successfully hidden from the enemy. By the end of July the additional engineer troops and equipment had been flown in and a second runway was constructed at an angle to the first, and 75 dispersed hardstands were completed. The runways measured 6,000x125 feet and 3,950x225 feet, respectively. By 1 August units of the Second Air Task Force, which was to operate out of Tsili Tsili, had begun to arrive. The 35th Fighter Group had received movement orders in late July, and on 1 August, the 35th Fighter Control Squadron and a platoon of the 565th Aircraft Warning Battalion arrived at Tsili Tsili. By the middle of August, a Fighter Control Sector and radar sets had been established, 40 miles of buried rubberized cable had been dug in for local communications, a message center and radio station were in operation, and an ordnance dump and quartermaster supply room were serving more than 3,000 troops already in the area. With the base well established, the next arrivals were to be the Headquarters and ground echelons of the 40th and 41st Fighter Squadrons of the 35FG. On 15 August, the headquarters of both squadrons set out from Port Moresby in two flights of C-47s escorted by P-39s of the 40th and 41st Squadrons. The campsite for the two squadrons was about two miles northeast of the main runway. It had been constructed on cleared jungle, and the ground would remain muddy for several days after even a moderate rain. The personnel were billeted in tents which were crowded together due to lack of space. Officers and enlisted men shared the same kitchen and mess hall, which were completely screened and centrally located. The importance of maintaining good sanitary conditions was recognized, and the Sanitary Detail paid strict attention to the Army requirements for water supply, garbage disposal, latrines, and proper eradication of insects. Water was obtained from a nearby creek and was chlorinated for drinking and cooking, while all laundry and bathing was done down stream.

Tsili Tsili provided a means for fighters from Dobodura and Port Moresby to form an escort of unprecedented size in the Southwest Pacific using all available elements of six squadrons. The pilots of the fighter escorts were reassured by the availability of adequate refueling and emergency landing facilities at Tsili Tsili. The missions were virtually uneventful, but the Japanese suffered a devastating reduction of their previously established air cover over Lae from Wewak.

Tsili Tsili Airdrome. (in center of photo on plain). (AAF)

Vetern Capt. Raymond **Melikian** took over as CO of the 7FS. (AAF)

5FC units based at Tsili Tsili:

35FG: HQ from Port Moresby on 16 August to ?
35FG: 40FS from Port Moresby on 14 August to Nadzab on October 1943
35FG: 41FS from Port Moresby on 14 August to Nadzab on 22 October 1943
49FG: 8FS (P-40) from Dobodura on 30 August 1943 to Gusap on 29 October 1943

August 1943: 49FG Command Changes

Many of Kenney's veteran Darwin pilots were eligible to be rotated home, and by the first week in August many were flown to Brisbane to embark on the USAT *Lurline* for San Francisco. 9th Fighter Squadron CO Maj. Sidney Woods was to be replaced by only a First Lieutenant. But this First Lieutenant, Gerald Johnson, was a veteran of the Alaska Campaign who was found to be the senior officer by date of commission and was promoted to Captain. Capt. Wallace Jordan became Squadron Duty Officer, and 1Lt. Harry Lidstrom was promoted to Captain and 9FS Ops Exec. The Flying Knights would find themselves short on senior Flight Leaders and their Lightnings were almost worn out. At the end of July, 7FS CO Maj. George Manning was relieved by his Deputy, Capt. Raymond Melikian. Unlike the depleted 9th Squadron, Melikian had many senior Flight Leaders and more new P-40Ns were arriving daily. Meanwhile, Capt. Ernest Harris' 8FS was flying patrol from the rain-soaked Marilinan airstrip. (Note: Lt.Col. Woods would later join the 4FG in the ETO flying P-51 Mustangs and become an ace and an "ace-in-a-day" when he downed five FW-190s on 22 March 1945. Woods was later shot down on a strafing attack and captured, then spent the last two months of the war as a POW.)

After scoring seven victories in a week, Capt. James **Watkins** continued his hot victory streak with three more to make him a double ace. (AFAA)

Newcomer to the 9FS, Capt. Wallace **Jordan,** claimed his first of six victories. (AAF)

2 August 1943: 49FG/9FS

At 1100, 38 B-25 strafers with an escort of 30 P-38s left Dobodura on a barge hunting mission to the Huon Gulf coast east of Lae. Capt. Lawrence Smith led 12 Flying Knight wingmen over the Gulf in close escort at 6,000 feet. After the bombers attacked targets just east of Markham Bay, Smith's Flights flew patrol over the Gulf, waiting for any enemy fighters out of Cape Gloucester.

The three Squadrons of the 9FS consisted of Smith's Green Flight of wingmen 2Lts. James Harris and Charles Ralph in the lead at 6,000 feet. On their left flank was 1Lt. Gerry Johnson's Red Flight of 2Lts. Stanley Johnson and John O'Neill. On the right flank was newcomer Capt. Wallace Jordan, who led Blue Flight wingmen 2Lts. Grover Fanning and Frank Wunder. Capt. James Watkins' Yellow Flight provided top cover with wingmen 2Lts. George Alber and Francis Nutter. The Oscars were headed toward the B-25 strafers when the Flying Knights dove on them.

2Lt. James **Harris** shot down an Oscar for his first of four victories. (AAF)

The Oscar pilots panicked and broke to escape to the north. Watkins dove at full throttle through a full circle for a head on attack on a lone Oscar that climbed from the formation. Watkins' first burst riddled the fuselage and destroyed the canopy, killing the pilot. Yellow Flight then turned to re-engage, but quickly separated, with Nutter and Alber in a wild pursuit of another lone Ki-43 desperately trying to escape just above the sea. Alber fired first and then broke away as Nutter closed to get the kill. The Yellow Flight wingmen climbed to find Watkins, who flamed a second victim after a short pursuit. Watkins then dove on his third target and fired on the desperately maneuvering enemy pilot just above the waves. As its turn tightened, the Oscar began to slide lower until its starboard wing hit a wave and it cartwheeled. Watkins' three victories would make him a double ace before he rotated home. Watkins would return to combat in the Pacific with the 49ers and score another victory in April 1945.

Blue Flight Leader Jordan also went into a circling dive to attack from port and head on. Jordan hit an Oscar, and its engine erupted into a fireball and it plunged directly into the sea. Wingmen Fanning and Wunder quickly followed, and each shot down an Oscar and then separated as Wunder sped after the fleeing enemy elements on the deck. Fanning had only dropped one belly tank before he engaged and his engine overheated, forcing him to join the high cover flight from the 80th Squadron Headhunters for the return to Horanda.

Red Flight Leader Johnson led a first pass moments after Yellow and Blue left, but Johnson's gun switch fuse had burned out while firing on his first target and his Wingman, Stanley Johnson, finished off the Oscar.

Meanwhile, Mission Leader Smith circled down with wingmen Ralph and Harris into a rear quarter attack on the scattering enemy fighters. Smith selected a smoking Oscar which had previously been damaged and finished it with a volley from dead astern. Then, as they sped down after the last of the fleeing Oscars, Harris turned off to the east in pursuit of a lone Oscar headed for Cape Gloucester. After several minutes at full throttle Harris fired from 500 yards, hitting the Ki-43, which rolled into the sea. Mission Leader Smith, Yellow Flight Nutter, Blue Flight Wunder, and Red Flight Stanley Johnson joined together in the pursuit of the last northbound Oscar. The veteran Sentai pilot outmaneuvered numerous American firing passes during his wild wave top escape into the haze beyond Finschhafen.

On this day Lt.Gen. Hatazo Adachi, Supreme Commander of the Japanese forces in New Guinea, was to fly to Lae to personally direct operations. After the weather cleared, a Ki-51 Sonia transported Adachi with a large Oscar escort toward Lae. Adachi's Sonia disappeared, but later that evening his plane landed back at Rabaul; the Oscar escort, however, had lost 11 fighters and their Commander.

3- 7 August 1943: 49FG

During the first week of August it rained for five straight days, and the 8FS bivouac became flooded and was moved closer to the airstrip. The Squadron struggled to get their Warhawks into the air. The Japanese at Wewak and Rabaul had similar problems with the rain and could only send lone raiders or reconnaissance aircraft toward Oro Bay, and there was rarely any contact.

August 1943: 35FG Begins to Move to Tsili Tsili

In late July the 35FG received orders to move the entire Group, less the 39FS from Moresby, over "the Hump" (the Owen Stanley Mountains) to Tsili Tsili. The Lightnings of the 39th were left behind, as everything the base required, including precious aviation fuel, had to be flown in, and their twin engine P-38s consumed twice as much as the single engine P-39s. The 35th Fighter Control Squadron left first on 1 August, and Headquarters Squadron followed two weeks later on the 15th.

The P-38 Comes on the Scene and the 475th Fighter Group is Formed

Background

After a mildly successful stint in the ETO and MTO, the Lockheed P-38 Lightning fighter was introduced into the Fifth Air Force during the last months of 1942. At the time American pilots in the Pacific felt that their Curtiss P-40 Warhawks, with some weight reduction and an improved high altitude engine with a supercharger, could more than hold their own against the fast and maneuverable Zero. The P-40 was already the most successful of the early American fighters. Although it was not as fast nor could turn as well as the Zero, it did have good diving speed and was ruggedly built, and its armament of six .50 caliber guns in P-40E and subsequent models could be devastating to the lighter and more delicately constructed Japanese fighters, which had no pilot armor or self-sealing fuel tanks. Meanwhile, American Warhawk pilots who had scored remarkable victories over the Japanese fighter by using the altitude advantage, which enabled them to either attack or escape in a dive, would have to continue that tactic.

Kenney, since assuming command of the newly formed Fifth Air Force in September 1942, was the P-38's greatest advocate, and used his influence to commandeer a large number from the ETO. When Kenney commanded

8FS at Marilinan. (L-R): 1Lt. James **Hagerstrom**, Capt. William **Drier**, 1Lt. James **Carter**, 1Lt. Nelson **Flack**, 2Lt. Harold **Sawyer**, and 1Lt. Arthur **Talmadge**. (AAF)

the Fourth Air Force in California during the spring and summer of 1942 he became convinced of the Lightning's worth, as its performance advantages over the P-39 and P-40 were apparent: the P-38 could fly higher, faster and, most importantly, farther than any American or enemy fighter then operational in the Pacific. But once the P-38 arrived, instead of being an improvement on the P-40, pilots were disappointed, as not only was the P-38 too heavy to turn with the Zero, it was more difficult to fly and land. Pilots were unable to just get into the P-38 and fly it, but had to transition to the twin engine fighter. The Lightning required more maintenance and fuel, and there were not enough trained mechanics to maintain it. Finally, by the end of 1942 Kenney had the P-38 operational over New Guinea. On 27 and 31 December 1942, P-38 pilots of the 39FS scored 11 and nine victories, respectively, for only two P-38s damaged. News of this success greatly improved the Lightning's status with 5FC pilots who would eventually transition to it.

The 9FS converted to P-38s during January and February, giving the 5FC two squadrons that began to turn the tide in New Guinea, as the Japanese were retreating from the Buna area and were confined to the coastal area of the northeast. The Lightning not only gained air superiority, but proved itself an adequate dive bomber, not only on local tactical sorties, but by devastating Japanese supply lines through Lae and making it easier for the Allies to reinforce their positions on eastern New Guinea. Soon P-40s and P-39s were assigned tactical missions so that the P-38 could concentrate on their intended role as an interceptor to establish air superiority.

In March, the decisive victory over the Bismarck Sea, which ravaged the Japanese reinforcement convoy from Lae to New Guinea, gave Kenney the rationale to convince Generals George Marshall and Hap Arnold to requisition more P-38s for the Pacific. The Generals presented Kenney with a compromise; he would be given enough P-38s to equip an entire group only if he could staff it with 5FC personnel; plus he would receive another group flying another type of fighter (348FG flying the P-47).

Meanwhile, Kenney met delays, and by the end of March 1943, the Fifth Air Force was promised one P-47 group in May, another in June, and a P-38 group to leave the United States in August 1943. Finally, on 6 May, Kenney informed Marshall that over 400 Japanese fighters and bombers were now within range of Port Moresby, and he was in dire need of a "suitable fighter aircraft." Marshall responded that P-47s were available by 12 June to equip the 348FG. At the same time Kenney was authorized to activate the 475th Fighter Group as a twin engine fighter group, and the P-38s that Hap Arnold had promised would be available for this unit in June.

Kenney still had to staff the Group from his own squadrons, and while half of the original cadre was supplied by the 11th Airbase Depot and other units outside the Fifth Air Force, the other half, consisting of the most experienced pilots and enlisted men, was drained from 5FC squadrons. Also, large numbers of replacement pilots were sent to the 475th for the first months of its existence. Throughout the war the 475th was known as "Kenney's pet" and more scornfully as the "glory-boy outfit."

Formation and Structure of the 475FG

Group HQ

The new fighter group was activated on 14 May 1943 and constituted the next day. Lt.Col. George Prentice officially took command of the newly formed group at Amberley, Australia, on 12 June. Prentice began his career with the 7FS/49FG in April 1941 and was sent overseas with that unit in January 1942. In August 1942 he became CO of the 39FS, and in late March 1943 he became the CO of the Fighter Training Station at Charters Towers, Australia. Maj. Albert Schinz of the 41FS (2 victories there) joined Group Headquarters as Executive Officer, while Capt. William Haning of the 49FG (2 victories there) took over as Operations Officer, to be later replaced by Capt. Meryl Smith. Capt. Claude Stubbs became Group S-4, and Capt. LeRoy Richardson was named Group Adjutant, while the Group Intelligence Officer was Capt. Bennett Oliver. About half of the new group's personnel came directly from other Fifth Air Force fighter squadrons while the remainder were new trainees.

431FS (Call Sign: *Hades*)

Maj. Franklin Nichols assumed command of the 431FS on 1 July 1943. Ace 1Lts. Edward Czarnecki (6 victories) and Marion Kirby (5 victories) transferred from the 80FS to the 431FS, but most of the personnel in the 431FS came from the 49FG, including new 431FS CO Nichols, who had four victories while flying P-40s before he left the 49FG. Also included were future aces Jack Mankin (4 with the 431FS and 1 with the 9FS), Harry Brown (4 with the 431FS, 1 with the 47FS, and 1 with the 9FS), Arthur Wenige (5 with the 431FS and 1 with the 9FS), and David Allen (6 with the 431FS and 2 with the 7FS). John Hood also came to the 431st from the 49FG and became a combat leader (with 2 victories with the 431FS and 1 with the 7FS). Seven victory ace (1 with the 36FS) Capt. Verl Jett also transferred from the 8FG to the 431st, where he would become Squadron CO after Nichols rotated home in November 1943. Jett had served with the 15FG in Hawaii at the start of the war, and with 1Lts. John Cohn, John Knox, and ace Paul Morriss (5 victories) was one of several pilots from the 15FG to join the 431st and the 475FG. Other pilots transferring from the 15FG to the 475FG were Capt. William Waldman and 1Lts. ace Billy Gresham (6 victories) and Howard Hedrick, who transferred to the 432FS, while 1Lts. Ralph Cleage and Robert Tomberg went to the 433rd.

432FS (Call Sign: *Clover*)

Maj. Frank Tomkins of the 80th (where he had one victory) assumed command of the 432FS on 1 July 1943. Although the 432FS received a few pilots from the 39FS/35FG, the majority of its original members came from the 8FG, particularly the 80FS, which had already been in combat with the P-38. From the 80FS, Tomkins brought future aces Zach Dean (6 victories), James Ince (6), Vivian Cloud (5), Grover Gholson (5), and John Loisel (11), who went on to command the 475th during the last days of the war.

Lt.Col. George **Prentice**. (L) assumed command of the 475FG. He is shown here meeting with Lt.Gen. Kenney. (back), Maj.Gen. Richard Sutherland, and Gen. MacArthur. (R) at Port Moresby. (AAF)

433FS (Call Sign: *Possum*)
Maj. Martin Low, formerly of the 40FS of the 35FG, was chosen as the first Commander of the new 433rd Fighter Squadron on 3 May 1943, but his poor executive qualities caused morale problems, as he was unable to fill administrative positions with qualified personnel. Enlisted men were irritated by his use of criticism as a means of negative incentive and his method of withholding promotions. Later in the war Low would transfer to the ETO, where he would very successfully command the 55FS of the 20FG and be awarded the Distinguished Flying Cross. Capt. Daniel Roberts would succeed Low as 433rd CO on 3 October 1943, and with this squadron he immediately established his reputation as an extraordinary leader. Six newly trained Lightning pilots came from the 39FS, including 1Lts. John Ehlinger, Charles Grice, William Jeakle, and John Parkansky.

The 475th in Australia
On 17 June Frank Nichols, 431FS CO, led the first contingent to Australia, and the remainder followed over the next three weeks. The new 475th crews had flown from hot, humid New Guinea to the winter cold of Amberley Field in civilized Australia, where they could finally have some R&R before getting their new P-38s ready. However, administrative snafus kept supplies from reaching the Group and threatened a delay in the move to Dobodura by the end of July. Meanwhile, P-38s began to arrive on 23 June 1943 when the first, a P-38G-5, was accepted by the 432FS. Two P-38H-ls were received on 28 June, three more the next day, and another on 30 June. By 16 July at least 12 pilots had been assigned to the 432nd and training flights had begun. New personnel were added to the Squadron and training continued throughout July. By 7 August preparations were being made for the Squadron to move north to its first operational base at Dobodura. On 9 July, 217 enlisted men were assigned to the 432FS: 63 new trainees and 154 veterans. Maj. George Prentice officially took command of the newly formed group at Amberley on 12 June, and he used his training experience at Charter Towers to give his pilots the essentials of flying the P-38 in combat. During the last days of July the accelerated combat training program was showing results, but Prentice was replaced by Capt. Franklin Tomkins as CO of the 432nd, with Capt. Danny Roberts as Ops Officer.

When Nichols was ready to take his 431st to New Guinea he named Capt. John Hood as Operations Officer and Captains Harry Brown and William Haning as Flight Commanders; all had been with the 9th Fighter Squadron, while the third Flight Commander was Capt. Verl Jett. 1Lts. Warren Lewis, Marion Kirby, Thomas McGuire, and Lowell Lutton were Flight Leaders.

As the time grew near for the move to Dobodura, some of the pilots were considered able to fly their P-38s directly to 12 Mile Drome and Jackson Strip near Port Moresby. One P-38 crashed on take off, but the pilot, Lt. John Cohn, escaped with only minor burns. Other group personnel arrived by C-47 transports or landed at Dobodura on the SS *Joseph Lane.*

11 August 1943
Except for two minor attacks on Tsili Tsili, Japanese air raids on Allied ground positions in August were limited to little more than a few bombs dropped on the new bases on Kiriwina and Woodlark Islands. Of these raids, probably the most serious occurred on 11 August against Woodlark, then protected by the 67th Fighter Squadron of the 13AF, a veteran unit from Guadalcanal. In this raid five enemy aircraft dropped 18 bombs, destroying one P-39 and damaging three others.

11 August 1943: 49FG/7FS
On 11 August, a 7FS patrol was vectored north to search for a suspected Japanese photo recon aircraft. One Warhawk flight made contact and pursued two unidentified aircraft into the clouds east of Lae. Later that afternoon, 9FS Lightnings were dispatched north to the Markham River Delta. While flying at 20,000 feet, they spotted about a dozen radial engine fighters far below, traveling west of Lae. The Lightnings dropped their tanks and went into a high speed dive, only to discover that the "enemy" was 348FG P-47 Thunderbolts that had scattered under the Lightnings' aborted attack.

7-14 August 1943: 475FG at Port Moresby
Capt. LeRoy Richardson led the ground echelon aboard the SS *Joseph Lane* on 5 August to Oro Bay, and then northwest to Dobodura on 14 August. On 7 August the air echelon had moved into the fields around Port Moresby formerly occupied by the 35th Fighter Control Squadron. In the next few days the air echelons regrouped, with the 431FS based at 12 Mile Strip, the 432nd at Ward's Drome (5 Mile Drome), and the 433rd at Jackson's Drome (7 Mile Drome).

12 August 1943: 475FG
Beginning 12 August, several patrol missions were flown directly from Port Moresby by the 475th, during which the pilots gained proficiency in learning basic combat tactics, particularly maintaining the integrity of the formation in combat. The 475th ground echelons quickly worked to prepare the Dobodura Strips and billets at Horanda. The area adjacent Dobodura was similar to Port Moresby, with dense forests surrounding the flat ground of the area and with dense marsh bordering the Giruo and Samboga Rivers that converged near the end of Horanda Strip West #4. The area was slightly moister than Port Moresby, and while there was somewhat more breeze, there was less dust. Generally, creature comforts were neglected until the strips and revetments were completed.

15 August 1943: 35FG
In preparation for the offensive against Lae and Salamaua a new airfield had been built at Tsili Tsili, and the first C-47s carrying the HQ Squadron into Tsili Tsili landed safely at 0910. But as the second flight transporting the ground echelon of the first fighter squadron to be based at Tsili Tsili approached for a landing, Sally bombers escorted by a mixed formation of enemy fighters swept in over the mountains to attack the strip. The Sallys had sneaked through the mountain passes flanked by mountains high enough to shield them from Allied aircraft warning units. The leading Dakota landed as the bombs fell on the runway; the pilot was killed, and the transport went out control and crashed and exploded. In the explosion the Group's Dental Officer incredibly was blown clear by the explosion with minor injuries. The following unarmed transports in the landing pattern raised their wheels, climbed over the tree tops, and headed back over the mountains, but one disappeared and was never found.

Mitsubishi Ki-21 **Sally** bombers attacked Tsili Tsili just a the C-47s carrying the 35FG ground echelon was about to land. (AAF)

40FS

At 0815, 15 P-39s of the 40FS took off from Berry. Yellow Flight Leader aborted the flight and second Element Leader 1Lt. Richard Schmalz and Wingman 1Lt. Robert Yaeger were joined by #2 man 1Lt. David Pardy. This flight never did join the rest of the squadron, but saw 12 unescorted transports heading for Marilinan and stayed with the transports until they landed. The three P-39s then joined a 41FS flight and encountered 12 bombers in the distance that looked "like B-26s" flying at 10,000 feet. The 41FS pilots investigated and Schmalz' Flight joined them. When the 41st dropped their tanks Schmalz' tank did not release, but Yeager's did, and he went on to attack the bombers, but made four ineffective passes. Schmalz lagged somewhat behind and made a pass at a rear bomber that was already smoking, getting some hits but seeing no obvious damage. Schmalz saw Yaeger fire at another bomber, setting it ablaze, and after Yaeger broke off Schmalz closed on this bomber, but before he could fire the bomber spiraled out of control and crashed south of the strip. Schmalz turned directly onto the tail of a third bomber which was diving toward the Markham Valley and opened fire at 400 yards; he held down the trigger until he almost collided with it. The bomber headed towards the mountains with its fuselage and both wing roots on fire. Schmalz thought he heard cannon fire and turned to see an Oscar behind him and several milling above. Schmalz was finally able to release his tank and pulled up. Yaeger looked down and saw the Oscar on Schmalz' tail, and as Schmalz pulled up Yeager made a diving head on pass on that Oscar; its engine caught fire and it crashed close to a river. Meanwhile, Yaeger had an Oscar on his tail, and as it passed over Schmalz' P-39 Schmalz tried to get a shot at it, but his windshield was covered with oil from the near collision with the bomber and he could not shoot. Schmalz immediately dove away from the three Oscars; two did not follow, but the third dove on him from above and slightly behind, but was unable to catch him during the 10 mile chase. Luckily it finally broke off, as Schmalz found that all his guns had jammed. Yaeger fired on another Oscar, but found that only his .30s were working, and then had to outrace another Oscar that was on his tail into a cloud. In the dogfight Pardy became separated and was attacked by two enemy fighters and dove away and returned home.

1Lt. Robert **Yaeger** claimed his second of five victories. (AAF)

41FS

At 0745, the 41FS sent 12 P-39Ns on a transport escort to Tsili Tsili in three flights: Blue Flight led by Capt. George Hilbert; White Flight by Capt. Francis Dubisher; and Yellow Flight by Capt. John Bailey. At 0905 they arrived and were making their first circle over the target when *Shadow* Controller called them to investigate a plot. Five minutes later they intercepted nine bombers to the west flying at 11,000 feet in three Vs of three stepped up.

Hilbert's flight attacked, and he fired on a bomber on the right side of the formation between the right engine and fuselage. When he pulled around to finish it off he saw that it was burning and shifted to another bomber. As he was about to fire his gunsight bulb went out, and he had to guess his range; after making five passes and seeing no results he broke off. By this time the Japanese attack had been foiled, with only two bombers reaching the target, and Hilbert decided to head home, as his fuel was getting low. As he crossed over the field he saw the transports and stayed aloft a while longer, as there were enemy fighters still lurking in the area. As he began to climb an Oscar crossed high and in front of him and Hilbert fired, but without a working gunsight. He was unable to judge the deflection, and the Oscar pilot Split-S'd onto his tail. Hilbert had lost speed in his climb and had to wing over, but couldn't shake the Oscar, which fired and shattered his canopy, then hit and stopped his engine. Hilbert bailed out, and as he descended the Oscar tried to strafe him, but was driven off by other P-39s. He landed in the jungle with a few minor scratches and was found by two Australians and returned to Tsili Tsili.

Blue Flight

2Lt. Robert Alder was Hilbert's Wingman in Blue Flight, and followed his Leader on the first attack on the bombers and chose the lead bomber in the right V. He closed from a little below and astern and fired from 250 yards; his 37mm cannon blew off the bomber's tail. The right bomber of the lead V was directly in line and Alder attacked it in the same manner, setting its right engine on fire and then setting the entire right wing on fire. The lead bomber of the first V was directly ahead with its right engine on fire and its rear gunner dead. He fired but didn't see any results, and then made two more passes from 8 and 4 o'clock before his 37mm and .50s malfunctioned. He cleared one .50 and returned to Tsili Tsili at 7,000 feet, observing an Oscar lolling along over the area. Alder closed and fired with his one .50, getting hits, but with little effect before the gun stopped firing after 10 rounds. The outgunned Alder dove away for home. Second element Blue Leader 1Lt. Carey Wooley and Wingman 2Lt. Albert Rothaar dove on the nine bombers and observed no hits, as three of the bomber's gunners returned fire. He pulled up sharply and made an overhead pass on another bomber, but again observed no hits. Wooley saw a bomber break away and fly directly over Tsili Tsili at 5,000 feet. He made two passes at right quarter astern and then pressed an attack from dead astern and set its engine on fire. The bomber continued to fly, and Wooley and Rothaar both made two passes. Finally the bomber crashed into a mountainside two miles north of Tsili Tsili. The two Airacobra pilots returned to Tsili Tsili and saw enemy fighters at 11 o'clock above, but could not pull up to fire. One Zero dove and made an overhead pass onto their tails and the American pilots dove away. The Zero closely pursued Wooley, who broke the throttle stop safety wire while speeding up the Watut Valley. After he escaped he climbed and returned to Tsili Tsili, and was again attacked by two Zeros, one from 10 o'clock and the other from 2 o'clock at the same altitude, so he again had to dive away to safety. He climbed over Tsili Tsili alone when *Shadow* called a plot. Wooley searched and found a lone enemy fighter at 8,000 feet and dove on it, opening fire at 100 yards; he closed to point blank range and flew through oil and debris as the fighter crashed into the Watut Valley.

White Flight

White Flight Leader Capt. Francis Dubisher and Wingman 2Lt. Kenneth Nuzum approached the three bomber Vs of Sallys from their left front side. After they dropped their tanks the Cobras got into position on the right side, about 500 feet above the bomber Vs. Dubisher attacked in a curving quarter astern pass at the top V. He closed very close and fired his 37mm cannon, which tore pieces off the fuselage and starboard engine, which began burning fiercely. Dubisher dove through the bomber formation, spraying it without any visual results and wishing he had saved the ammunition. He used his excess diving speed to climb to attack the left front of the Sally formation. He again used a curving astern attack to close and fire his cannon, setting its port engine on fire. As he broke away he saw bombs exploding on Tsili Tsili and expected to be bounced by the Sally's escorts. As he circled he saw two Sallys fleeing the area with a P-39 trailing the rear bomber and then shooting it down. Dubisher dove on the lead Sally and came so close that he almost rammed it as he fired. The Airacobra's guns and cannon again devastated the Sally for his third victory of the day. He climbed to reach the Oscars, but as he made a pass on one he found that only two of his .30s were firing. He broke off the combat, but the Oscar tried get behind Dubisher, who dove to save his life and headed back to base. 1Lt. Harold Nus, the second element White Leader, started to make a pass when the right hand bomber in the right V peeled out of the formation with its right engine on fire. Nus then shifted his attention to making a rear quarter attack on the next bomber in the V. Nus fired only a short burst when another P-39 made a pass from astern, and both fighters closed to point blank range before breaking off in opposite directions with neither American getting observable results. Nus swung around to make another attack, again without results. He then made a third pass from the right rear quarter on another bomber and set its right engine on fire just as it dropped its bombs. Nus saw two Sallys separate from the formation and head down the Watut Valley at 1,000 feet. Nus was joined by two other fighters (Wingman 2Lt. Richard Mikiska and an unknown pilot), and all three were firing when "someone" shot one down. Nus and Mikiska followed the other bomber and Nus scored hits; it went into a glide and leveled out, looking like it was going to crash land. As it landed it flipped over and caught fire. Mikiska and Nus rejoined and climbed back to Tsili Tsili at 7,000 feet, where a Zero crossed Nus' sights but pulled up steeply as he fired a burst at 5 o'clock with no visible results. Nus saw a bomber, and as he was about to make an attack on the bomber he was jumped by a Zero and went into a high speed dive into a cloud. He climbed back to 15,000 feet and circled for another 15 minutes before discovering a hole in the trailing edge of his port wing, so he headed along the coast in case he had to bail out or ditch.

Yellow Flight

Yellow Flight Leader Capt. John Bailey and Wingman 2Lt. John Bomar were at 12,000 feet; his flight would be the last 41FS flight to attack the Sallys. When Bailey closed from astern two bombers were already burning. He fired a long burst at the last bomber and hit both engines, and it crashed and exploded about four miles from Tsili Tsili. As Bailey looked around he saw Oscars on his tail and quickly dove and lost not only them, but also his flight. He flew toward Marilinan and saw two Oscars strafing the strip and then climbing steeply away from him. Bailey fire walled his fighter and caught up with them and fired. He couldn't see any results due to oil on his windshield, but did see the other Oscar turn into him, head on. Bailey and the Oscar pilot both fired. In his pass the enemy pilot had hit Bailey's wing and tire, but the Cobra was still airworthy; as the Oscar passed by it half rolled behind him and was seen to crash several miles from Tsili Tsili. As Bailey looked down he saw a P-39 being chased by two Oscars whose pilots decided Bailey was a better target and got on his tail. Bailey headed for the clouds covering the nearby mountains and lost them, then decided it was time to retreat back home. Capt. Tony Prince was the second Element Leader of Yellow Flight and led his Wingman from 18,000 feet to Sallys at 10,000 feet. On the way down enemy fighters were seen diving on them, and Prince turned into the Oscars and fired without effect and returned to his flight. Prince then made a quarter rear attack that ended as a rear attack on the lead bomber of the left V. He fired, and its right engine burst into flames. He shifted his fire to the next bomber and it also burst into flames. He then made passes on two more bombers with no observed results. He then saw an Oscar and Zero attacking a transport about to land and made head on and side attacks, and as he ran out of ammunition they turned on him. Prince headed up a canyon and was able to lose them and return to base. Although Prince's ICR combat description appears to have him destroy two Sallys, he only claimed one.

Left: Capt. Francis **Dubisher** shot down three Sallys to give him four total victories. (AAF) Right: Capt. Tony **Prince's** IRC had him shoot down two Tonys but he was only credited with his only victory of the war. (AAF)

Although four P-39s and one pilot did not return to base, the obsolete P-39s again proved themselves capable of more than holding their own when flown by veteran pilots by downing 11 Sally bombers and three Oscar escorts. On 18 August the ground echelons of the 40th and 41st Squadrons arrived at Tsili Tsili just ahead of their air echelons.

16 August 1943: 348FG: First Victory

Sixteen P-47s of the 340FS took off at 1320 to escort transports to Marilinan. After the transports landed at 1425 the 340FS' P-47s were circling the field from 10,000 to 13,000 feet, while P-38s were on top cover from 18,000 to 20,000 feet. *Shadow* Controller called out approaching enemy aircraft, and about five minutes later 11 or 12 Oscars were observed at about 15,000 feet.

340FS

"Oscar-type" fighters dove on the transports, and 2Lt. Thomas Barber, flying at 11,000 feet, spotted them coming in from above. One dove in front of Barber at 500 yards and 45 degrees, and he gave chase down to 6,000 feet and fired two bursts at a range of about 100 yards. The Oscar went into a half roll and Barber lost track of it when he dove away from an Oscar on his tail. Barber claimed a victory, which was confirmed by 2Lt. John Matson, who stated that the "Zero" was seen going down "into an unnatural diving position and from my point of view the Zero was a dead duck." Nonetheless Barber was officially credited with a probable.

1Lt. Charles Allen was jumped by the Oscars, and one got on his tail and he dove away after suffering several hits on his fighter. The Oscar went into an Immelmann and started to roll when Capt. Warren Lewis, flying a P-38 for the 431FS, got on its tail and drove him off. The Oscar zoomed up into the sights of a P-47 passing up in front of him at about 500 to 600 yards, and then going into a zooming Immelmann turn. When the enemy completed his turn he made a turn to port at the same altitude and Wiecks fired two short bursts at too long a range. Wiecks continued to close on it, and as the Oscar completed its turn its pilot approached head on. Wiecks then opened steady fire, dispensing about 700 rounds of .50s head on, and as the two fighters sped past each other at no more than 15 to 20 feet the Oscar fell off on one wing. Wiecks was prevented from observing his victory by Oscars that got on his tail. However, Allen and 2Lt. Myron Hnatio both confirmed the Group's first victory.

The 341FS also engaged the enemy while flying close cover for the transports over Marilinan at 16,000 feet when 2Lt. Wilburn Henderson spotted an Oscar chasing a P-38 3,000 feet below. Henderson dove out of the sun and leveled off on the Oscar's tail. His first burst was fired

Capt. Max **Wiecks** claimed the 348FG's and his first victory. (AAF)

from out of range, but he closed in and fired three long bursts that started a fire on the left side of its fuselage; the Oscar went down in a tight spiral and crashed five miles north of the Markham River. 2Lt. Leonard Leighton claimed an Oscar destroyed, but his fighter was hit and he was seen parachuting into the New Guinea jungle. His body was discovered by an Allied patrol some months later to become the first confirmed combat casualty of the 348FG. 2Lt. Merle Zeine was credited with a damaged Oscar for the 341st.

16 August 1943: 475FG/431FS

During the afternoon, the 475FS flew their seventh combat mission, with the 431FS escorting C-47 transports to Tsili Tsili, near Marilinan in the highlands west of the Huon Gulf. Capt. Harry Brown led 15 P-38s from Dobodura at 1230, and during the flight one P-38 aborted because of oxygen failure and another turned back due to a mechanical problem. The mission was promising, as over the same area the day before, the 35FG had scored 17 victories for the best day in their P-39s over New Guinea. At 1315, the 431st P-38s were flying high cover for the landing transports over Tsili Tsili at 18,000 feet through scattered clouds. Green Flight was the last of the high cover flights orbiting north of the landing transports, and at 1515 Flight Element Leader 1Lt. David Allen called out a lone single engine fighter flying to the west. Hearing Allen's call, the 431st flights ahead reversed course and headed west toward the sighted enemy and began to circle south towards the field. Five minutes later more enemy aircraft were spotted above and bounced Brown's Red Flight, which had to dive away to safety. Brown regained altitude by climbing into the sun and dove, making an unsuccessful snap shot. As he pulled up Brown saw a Zero dead ahead and slightly above and fired, exploding it for the Squadron's first victory. As Brown turned to starboard he and another P-38 fired at the same Zero, which immediately caught fire, and Brown was credited with the victory (due to his rank?). Brown and Wingman 2Lt. Edward Czarnecki made three or four unsuccessful passes before Brown caught a Zero pulling away from a pass on another P-38. The Zero flew directly into Brown's fire and was hit and exploded as its pilot tried to go into a stall. Brown became an ace with these three victories (after a Val victory at Pearl Harbor with the 47FS and an Oscar victory on 4 March 1943 with the 9FS).

Pearl Harbor veteran Capt. Harry **Brown** became an ace when downed three Zeros. (AFAA)

Soon Allen found himself in the midst of the combat, and he fired shots on two Zeros but missed. Allen then got on the tail of an Oscar that was turning to attack his Flight Leader, 1Lt. Lowell Lutton, and fired four .50 machine guns and the single 20mm cannon, which tore off the Oscar's right wing, and it spiraled into the jungle without burning. Allen quickly fired at another Oscar that was coming toward him with another P-38 firing on its tail. Allen thought he scored several hits, but the Oscar flew by so quickly that he was unable to see any results. Allen was alone at 14,000 feet and continued over Marilinan, where he encountered a Kate torpedo bomber that bravely turned into him. Allen had an ideal deflection shot and it went down in flames northwest of the airfield.

After his Element Leader Allen shot the Oscar off his tail, Flight Leader Lutton turned his flight into a climbing firing pass through the Japanese attackers and then dove away. When he came out of the dive Lutton had only his Wingman, 1Lt. Orville Blythe, with him, but continued on until two Oscars approached them in a head on pass at 15,000 feet. The first Oscar dove away before it was in range, but the second headed toward Lutton, firing while out of range. Lutton

1Lt. Warren **Lewis** scored his first victory on the way to becoming a seven victory ace. (AAF)

After a victory with the 9FS in December 1942, 1Lt. Arthur **Wenige** claimed two victories. (AFAA)

After a victory with the 9FS in March 1Lt. Jack **Mankin** claimed two victories with the 431FS. (AFAA)

held off firing until the Oscar was in his sights, and his fire tore away part of the engine and canopy; the Oscar went down directly over the Marilinan Airfield. As Lutton and Blythe dove away they made a pass on three Zeros, but one got behind Blythe and hit his coolant system and the starboard engine began to smoke. Blythe and Lutton dove away, but as he pulled out Lutton was unable to contact Blythe by radio. He did see that Blythe's propeller was feathered, and that his fighter was so badly damaged that it was unable to maintain altitude. Lutton remained with Blythe until he landed safely at Marilinan and then flew back to Port Moresby with two victories. Blythe returned to Moresby the next day by C-47 transport.

1Lt. Jack Mankin and his Wingman, 1Lt. Paul Smith, flying top cover, dove on Oscars that were attacking P-38s. Mankin closed to within 100 yards and set it on fire. The two then came upon another Oscar flying with a Kate, and when the two Japanese pulled up Smith fired at the Kate, which was making a tight turn, and it tumbled twice before crashing. Meanwhile Mankin devastated the Oscar, which fell into pieces, but his guns jammed and the two left for home.

During the initial Japanese attack 1Lt. Arthur Wenige dove out of danger, and when he reentered the fight a Zero turned into his sights. Wenige fired from close range and sent it down in flames. Wenige was then attacked by three Zeros from his right rear quarter and had to open full throttle to pull out of danger. He then saw a Zero pursuing a P-38 and raked the Zero as it crossed his path; it burst into flames and went out of control. A Zero had got behind Wenige and fired a few shots that missed before Wenige discovered that he was almost out of oxygen and headed home.

When White Flight Leader 1Lt. Warren Lewis saw Brown's lead flight being attacked, he ordered tanks to be dropped and led his flight into an attack that caused the enemy to break away. After Lewis turned north he shot an Oscar off the tail of a P-47 with a 60 degree deflection shot from 350 to 150 yards. The Oscar "started to roll as if hit" and was later confirmed by ground personnel at Tsili Tsili, as the Oscar crashed nearby. Brown rendezvoused with his fighters over Wau, with 12 Lightnings returning to Port Moresby and Blythe landing at Marilinan. The 431FS had scored its first 12 victories of 221 total with no losses in its first major combat of the war.

August 1943: Barge Busting

Meanwhile, during the first half of August the 5th Bomber Command and the First Air Task Force concentrated their bomber missions against barge movements and enemy ground positions not far from Lae and Salamaua. Between 24 July and 3 August, for example, at least 94 enemy barges were destroyed and 60 others damaged. A-2 calculated that the number of barges destroyed represented a means of transporting a division of men, or from 5,000 to 7,000 tons of supplies. Important as this destruction was, however, it represented only a fraction of the approximate total of 375 enemy barges in the SWPA.

16-20 August 1943: Attack on Wewak

By August 1943, the Japanese Fourth Air Army that had been formed in June for the New Guinea Campaign was sent to Wewak. During the US and Australian Lae campaign, the Japanese Fourth Air Army flew a large number of aircraft out of range of Allied fighters to a cluster of airfields near Wewak, about 400 miles west of the Huon Peninsula. On 30 July aerial reconnaissance had shown only 19 light bombers at the Wewak airfield at But. Four days later there were 18 light bombers and five fighters at But, 20 fighters and several light and medium bombers at Wewak, and a total of 56 aircraft at Dagua, including Army Ki-49 medium bombers code-named Helen, which was being used for the first time in the theater. This gradual build up continued, and on 13 August eight medium bombers, 31 light bombers, and 69 fighters were seen at Boram and Wewak, while 34 mediums, 34 light bombers, and 23 fighters were seen at But and Dagua, including state-of-the-art fighters like the formidable Ki-43 Oscar, the new in-line engined Ki-61 Tony, and the twin-engined Ki-45 Nick ground attack/night fighter. This was one third of its full complement of aircraft and embodied a low operational strength of 50% due to widespread illness among the aircrews and the lack of aircraft replacements.

The Fourth Air Army and the 6th and 7th Air Divisions had wanted to deploy their units more in depth, with a number of aircraft based on airfields further to the rear. But the Army High Command and the Eighth Area Army demanded that as many aircraft as possible be based on airfields as close to the front as possible to facilitate their use in operations. Actually, the Japanese did not have an adequate number of bases in the rear to make this feasible, so there were a large number of aircraft vulnerable in the Wewak area to the impending attacks.

At this time the Japanese were under unrelenting attack elsewhere by Allied air power that continued battering their installations at Salamaua and Lae, which was augmented by around the clock small scale B-24 heavy bomber attacks on Rabaul and Wewak. Allied medium bombers sortied further along the New Britain and New Guinea coasts, attacking shipping and installations. But on 12 August the Japanese Fourth Air Army began a succession of raids on the Allied air bases at Mount Hagen, Bena Bena, Wau, Salamaua, and elsewhere.

5FC escort fighters did not have the range to reach Wewak from existing Allied air bases, and the Allies considered a large scale, long range attack by unescorted bombers would be subjected to heavy losses. An attack on Wewak could not occur until medium bombers could join the heavy bombers in flying more than 1,000 mile missions and be es-

The Japanese utilized barge transport to carry men and supplies and although many were destroyed or damaged these were only a fraction of the barges available to the Japanese. (AAF)

The Army Ki-49 medium bomber code-named **Helen** first appeared in the Northeastern Area. (AAF)

corted by fighters. Kenney devised a plan for a major escorted air attack on Wewak by having Allied personnel begin to construct two dummy airfields relatively close to Japanese infantry positions on the Huon Peninsula, north of Lae, where the construction could be observed. These small construction crews created the impression that major construction was underway at these sites, and the Japanese responded by frequently bombing these "airfields," and were led to believe they were apparently preventing their use by Allied air units. Simultaneously at Tsili Tsili, 50 miles away, and the separate airfield at Marilinan, 40 miles from Lae, the Allies had constructed actual airfields and transferred fighter planes there. The new American bases were only minutes west of Lae, which was kept under a constant patrol of P-40s and P-39s to keep them secret from the Japanese.

During the time in which the Tsili Tsili airfield was being constructed, sufficiently developed, and stockpiled with fuel to provide a topping-off base for fighters and an emergency landing field for bombers, the rapidly developing Japanese airfield at Wewak, with its satellite bases at But, Dagua, and Boram, were mostly disregarded by AAF bombers. This would allow the Japanese to build up their air strength at these bases to make a full scale air offensive worthwhile.

The Japanese had also developed the Madang Airstrip, which was a prewar 1350-x60 foot coral strip. It was occupied in January 1943 by the Japanese Army to act as a forward operating base for aircraft from Wewak. On 19 April 1943 Gen. Adachi established his Headquarters at Madang. By mid-August it was expanded to a 3,350x240 with a single taxiway and 30 fighter revetments and one bomber revetment.

It was not until the middle of August that a productive target was available at Wewak, and Kenney would have both the aircraft and the bases necessary to make a series of heavy strikes against Wewak. Allied engineers had completed the extraordinary project, constructing the isolated mountain surrounded Tsili Tsili base and the base at Marilinan. The Fifth Air Force Service Command had completed modification projects on sufficient B-25s to equal five medium bomber squadrons and the troop carrier units in supplying these bases. Meanwhile, intelligence reports showed that more and more enemy aircraft were being brought into Boram, But, Dagua, and Wewak Airdromes. By mid-August the AAF bases at Marilinan and Tsili Tsili were able to support enough fighter aircraft to provide a large escort for the bombers to attack Wewak in strength.

Also, by the middle of August the new Fifth Fighter Command groups, the 475th with P-38s and the 348th equipped with P-47s, were in place for their first missions beginning 16 August. However, the 348th's P-47s were too short-ranged and flew transport escort missions, while the Lightnings of the 39th and 80th Squadrons were involved in strikes on New Britain and would not begin operations against Wewak until 20 August. Wewak was located about 300 miles from Port Moresby, over the highest peaks of the Owen Stanley Mountains, and the Lightnings flying escort had to fly for nearly two hours before they arrived over the target. If they encountered enemy fighters they had only 15 to 30 minutes of fuel remaining to run at full power before they had to break off for home, and that was with correct navigation. On 15 August, the two heavy bombardment groups in the Northeastern Area, the 42nd and the 90th, had 12 B-17s and 52 B-24s available. The 38BG(M) and the 3rd Attack Group had 58 B-25Cs and Ds available, which were able to make the 1,000 mile round trip. By this time the Tsili Tsili and Marilinan Dromes were sufficiently developed to permit fighters (and bombers in an emergency) to top off their fuel.

Madang Airstrip. (AAF)

Wewak Drome Gallery

Wewak area under attack with **Wewak Airdrome** in the center and **Boram Airdrome** on the right. (AAF)

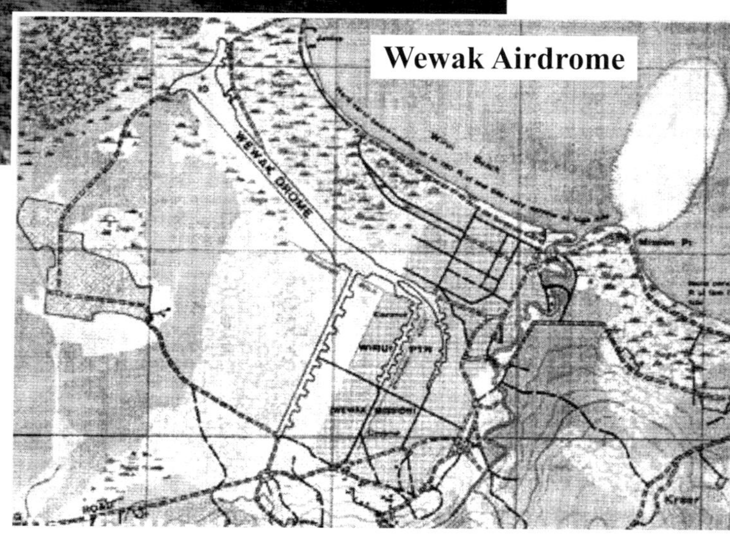

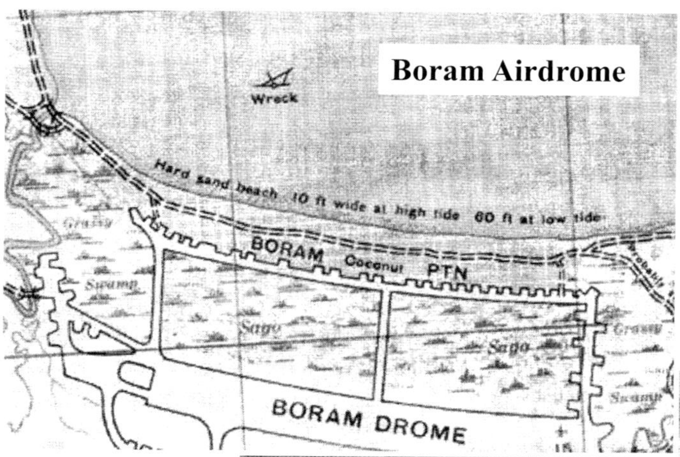

Wewak Airdrome on the coast with **Boram** runway directed vertically at the top of the photo. (AAF)

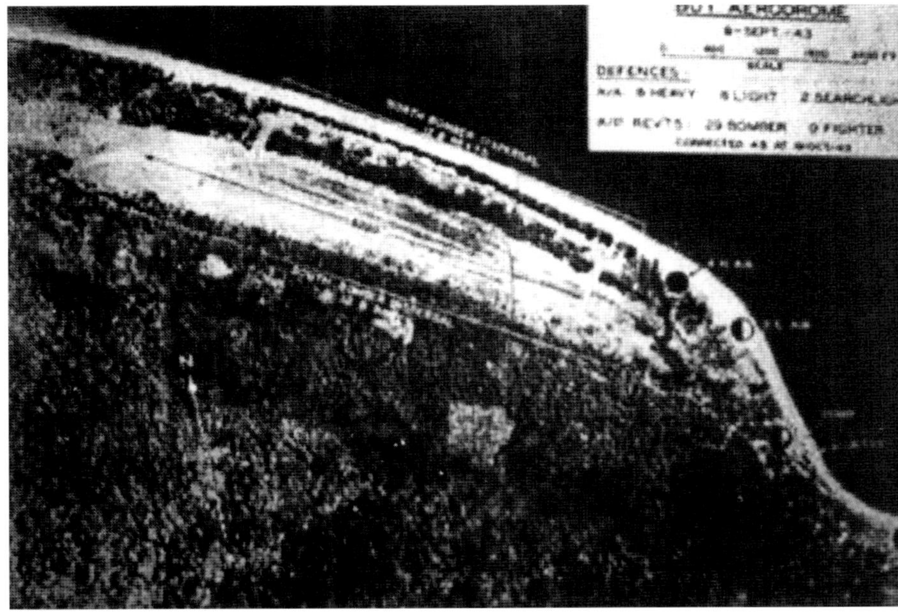

But Airdrome. (AAF)

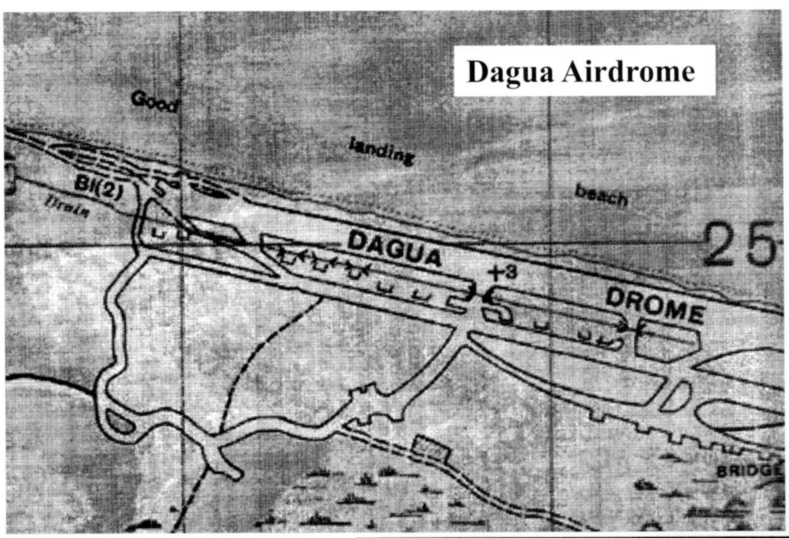

Dagua Airdrome. (AAF)

Wewak Attack Gallery: 16-20 November 1943.

Wewak under attack by **B-24s**. (AAF)

Wewak under low level strafing and bombing attack by **B-25s**. (AAF)

Dagua under attack. (AAF)

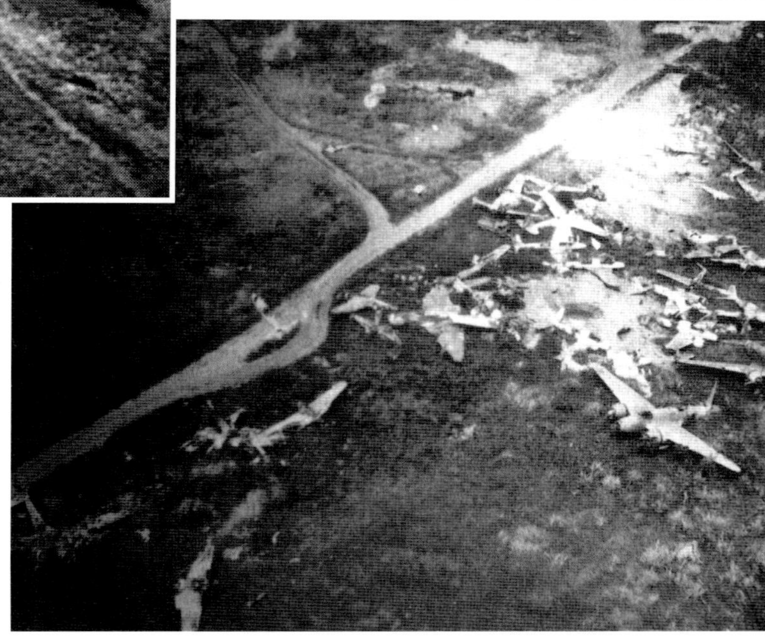

Recon Photo of the wreckage of aircraft destroyed on the ground at **Wewak**. (AAF)

The final plans for a coordinated offensive by heavy and medium bombers were made on the afternoon of 16 August. Eight squadrons of heavy bombers were to open the attack with night attacks on the four Wewak airdromes. After this preliminary softening, five squadrons of B-25 strafers, covered by a strong fighter escort, were to come in at minimum altitude to bomb and strafe every enemy plane remaining on the ground. Between 2100 and midnight of 16 August, 12 B-17s and 38 B-24s of the eight heavy bomber squadrons took off from Wards and Jackson Dromes near Port Moresby. The weather was generally good, although there were some clouds, and all aircraft reached the target except for two B-24s that turned back because of mechanical difficulties. Shortly after midnight the first heavy bombers crossed the target, and from then until after 0300 the attack continued, with the 63rd, 64th, and a part of the 65th Squadrons hitting Dagua; the reminder of the 65th and the 403rd hitting But; the 319th, 321st, and part of the 400th attacking Boram; and the 320th and the remainder of the 400th attacking Wewak Drome. According to the plan, the leading bombers were to drop incendiary bombs in order to illuminate the target for the remaining formations. But the lead attack was not conducted as planned, and incendiaries and parafrag clusters were haphazardly dropped on the fields. Searchlights were annoying, antiaircraft fire was intense, and several night fighters attempted interception, but only three aircraft were lost, and these apparently not from enemy action. Specific results from this mission could not be determined, but the attack was unexpected, as the Japanese had parked aircraft wingtip to wingtip on the runways. Photographs taken of Wewak, Boram, and Dagua prior to the next attack showed 204 aircraft, of which at least 18 were unserviceable.

The primary task of the heavy bomber night attack had been to keep the Jap aircraft grounded and subjected to the morning low level B-25 attacks. Between 0600 and 0630 the 8th, 13th, and 90th Squadrons took off from Dobodura and the 71st and 405th Squadrons from Durand Airdrome in Port Moresby. The Moresby-based B-25s met with a number of difficulties in making the 500 mile flight to Wewak, which was the deepest penetration of medium bombers into enemy-held territory to date. Of the 26 B-25s which took off from Moresby only three reached their targets. The 71st Squadron, with But as its target, failed to make a rendezvous with other Allied formations and turned back. Ten bombers of the 405th Squadron were also forced back, leaving only three to penetrate a bad weather front to reach Dagua. These three Mitchells, however, were extraordinarily successful, as they scattered 105 x 23 pound parafrags, destroying at least 17 aircraft on the ground, fired over 5,000 rounds of .50 caliber machine gun rounds, and shot down one of the 15 intercepting Oscars. Meanwhile, 29 of the 37 Dobodura B-25 strafers hit Boram and Wewak and dropped 786 23 pound parafrags, with the 90th claiming 15 aircraft destroyed or damaged at Wewak. The 13th Squadron claimed that they destroyed 15 aircraft and left at least 25 to 30 burning at Boram, while the 8th Squadron also attacked Boram at the same time and reported that all 70 to 80 aircraft there "were all believed destroyed or severely damaged." Except for one enemy fighter interception which the B-25s fought off, the Japanese resistance was limited to fairly heavy AA fire. The success of the heavy bombers played a large part in grounding the Japanese fighters, but the superiority of the 5FC fighter escorts probably played the largest part in keeping the Japanese from attacking the bombers. Every available P-38 was sent up to supply the most powerful escort thus far in the SWPA. The Lightning units included the veteran 9th, 80th, and 39th Squadrons and three squadrons of the new 475th. Shortly after 0600, 99 P-38s took off from Dobodura and Moresby to rendezvous with the bombers, but 14 were forced to turn back because of mechanical failure. Their mission report stated that the mission was "uneventful with nil interceptions."

On 17 August, 47 B-24 Liberators and B-17 Flying Fortresses made an unexpected pre-dawn attack on the main base at Wewak and the satellite airfields at Boram, Dagua, and But, where the Japanese continued to park aircraft wingtip to wingtip along the runways. At Boram, 60 Japanese planes were being warmed up by their crews, and some attempted to take off but were destroyed in the process. At 0900, more than 30 B-25 Mitchells, escorted by more than 80 P-38 Lightnings, made strafing attacks on Boram, Wewak, and Dagua. There were no enemy interceptors to engage the bombers.

During the morning of 18 August another attack on the airfields was sent off to strafe and bomb the fields from low altitude. The 3rd Attack Group was assigned to attack Wewak and Boram fields, while the 38th Bomb Group was sent further west to attack Dagua and But airdromes. Each of the 62 bombers was loaded with 12 clusters of three 23 pound parafrag bombs. B-24s of the 90th Bomb Group bombed Wewak from high altitude, while 53 B-25s attacked the airfields at Wewak again. Only three US aircraft were lost in the raids, but in one was B-25 pilot Maj. Ralph Cheli, who was awarded the Medal of Honor. The 475FG would claim 15 destroyed, three probables, and two damaged.

Two additional raids were conducted. On 20 August the 5FC claimed 13 destroyed, one probable, and two damaged, while the bombers added another seven enemy aircraft destroyed. On 21 August 475FG Lightnings claimed 35 destroyed, five probables, and seven damaged, while the bombers destroyed 35 more on the ground. The four raids over a five day period were a great success for the Allies, as the Japanese Fourth Air Army lost about 300 planes on the ground and in the air, reducing its operational strength to about 30 planes; more importantly, the P-38s decimated the ranks of the veteran Sentai pilots. Only 10 5AF aircraft were lost. These very successful escort missions by the 5FC Lightning pilots over Wewak will be described next.

The Japanese were completely unprepared for these attacks, as their New Guinea airbases were inadequate for the concealment of aircraft in revetments and hangars and they relied almost entirely on a visual warning system, which did not allow enough time for their fighters to take off to intercept. These problems were compounded by the poor quality of runways, a shortage of maintenance crews, and a lack of heavy equipment at forward bases. Col. Kazuo Tanikawa, an Eighth Area Army Staff Officer, stated:

> "At the time of the air attacks on Wewak on 17th and 18th August our defenses were not alert. We lost 100 planes including light bombers, fighters, and reconnaissance planes. It was a decisive Allied victory. We were planning to regain the balance of air power and were making plans to bomb Port Moresby and other areas. A few days before our projected plan was to materialize, we were bombed at Wewak and our air power was severely crippled. Consequently our air power was rapidly diminishing and was unable to aid our ground forces effectively which, in the end, constituted one of our chief reasons for losing the war."

After three days of attacks, the Japanese Fourth Air Army had been reduced to an operational strength of about 30 aircraft, which essentially caused an end to enemy air operations in New Guinea until replacements arrived. The Allies could now conduct air operations nearly uncontested as far away as Aitape, whereas previously Madang had been the extent of air operations. The Fourth Air Army recovered to an extent, but never again reached the strength it had in August 1943, and the last major air combat between Allied and Japanese aircraft took place on 3 June 1944, when the final aerial victories of the New Guinea campaign occurred.

18 August 1943: 475FG/431FS/432FS

The Japanese effort to save the Lae garrison had failed, and the area continued to be bombed night and day throughout August. On the 17th, Kenney sent B-24s on a high altitude late evening/early morning attack on the Wewak airdromes, followed by a devastating after dawn strafing attack by B-25 squadrons. The surprised and unprepared Japanese sent up no interceptors.

LEFT TO RIGHT: **1).** 2Lt. Robert **Cline** got the first of two career victories. (AAF) **2).** 1Lt. Thomas **McGuire** made an auspicious debut shooting down two Zekes and a Tony to begin a career that would make him America's second highest scoring ace with 38 victories. (AAF) **3).** 1Lt. Francis **Lent** got his first victory in an 11 victory career. (AFAA) **4).** After scoring two victories with the 41FS Maj. Albert **Schinz** from 475FG HQ shot down two enemy aircraft but would fall short of becoming an ace by one. (AAF)

On the 18th, heavy B-24 attacks were flown during the previous night to neutralize Wewak and its airfield complex. The next morning a large mission of B-25s attacking at low level and B-24s at a higher altitude was scheduled to be escorted by 74 Lightnings of the 431FS and 432FS led by Maj. Albert Schinz. Weather became a problem for the Liberators, and only 26 out of 49 heavy bombers which set out for this daylight attack reached the target. The Mitchells rendezvoused over Bena Bena, and upon reaching the target at 0930 they found an undercast that obscured the fields. However, the remaining B-24s bombed through it with satisfactory results and met little enemy opposition. Of the 62 Mitchells that took off 53 reached the target and attacked on the deck, simultaneously strafing and dropping their 23 pound parafrags with excellent results that either destroyed or damaged well over 100 enemy aircraft in the devastating attack. However, the Mitchell strafers destroyed an estimated (too high) 60 enemy aircraft on the ground, but ran into stiff opposition from Nicks from Boram and nine Zeros from But.

431FS

Maj. Albert Schinz from 475FG HQ led 15 P-38s from 12 Mile (Berry) at 0700 to fly low cover for two B-25 squadrons to Wewak. The 475th's P-38s had been airborne for nearly two hours before they reached the target area, which was 300 miles over the Owen Stanley Mountains from Port Moresby. If they were intercepted, the Lightning pilots could only run at full power for 15 to 30 minutes in combat before having to break off to return home, and navigation corrections could use another 20 to 30 minutes.

Schinz' Red Flight was on close cover, and was echeloned abut 3,000 feet above the lead two flights of strafers, which were descending to 1,000 feet. Just as the Mitchells were about to make their strafing run Zeros were sighted, and Schinz ordered tanks to be dropped. As the tanks dropped six Zeros attacked the P-38s from directly above and head on. Schinz turned into them and snapped off a shot at the lead Zero before the two planes passed at high speed. He then went after the second Zero, which headed for the clouds, and he followed him in and out of the clouds until he got on its tail and fired at close range; it crashed into the sea off Dagua Airstrip. While over the airstrip Schinz saw a strafing B-25 with a Zero closing on it, and he followed and chased it away without firing a shot. The B-25s left the target and were rendezvousing for the return home when Schinz saw six more Zeros about to attack his flight from above. He turned his flight into the attack and got a "perfect" shot at the third Zero for his fourth and last victory of the war. When the first wave of Zeros attacked, Schinz' second Element Leader, Capt. William Haning, saw a "cloud of tracers pass close under his tail" and followed the B-25s into a rainstorm, where he became lost. He passed over Wewak Airdrome alone at 7,000 feet and encountered heavy AA fire. When he saw a Zero across the strip he made a pass at it. The Zero pilot turned into Haning and got on his tail, but he was saved by three P-38s that shot down Haning's pursuer. Haning pulled up into a cloud, and when he emerged he was on top of a Zero and fired a long burst. As he climbed away he saw the Zero smoke for a probable claim.

Meanwhile, White Flight Leader Capt. Verl Jett and his Wingman, 2Lt. Robert Cline, chased Zeros that had just completed their attack on the B-25s. Jett's ICR is very succinct in describing his two victories: "On our first pass the wing came off the Zeke at which I was shooting. On out next pass on another Zeke, the Zeke burst into flames." Wingman Cline's ICR is as brief: "Then I shot a Zeke that was getting on Capt. Jett's tail. It burst into flames and when last see was falling." 2Lt. Edward Czarnecki was leading Jett's second White element and saw Jett and Cline drop their tanks, but waited to drop his until he saw enemy aircraft. A Zero popped up in front of him and he fired, getting "flashes" on its right wing before he dove away. Czarnecki pulled up to gain altitude and saw a P-38 being outmaneuvered by a Zero. He fired a burst into the Zero's cockpit and engine and it broke away, belching heavy smoke. As he was diving Czarnecki saw another Zero flying below and ahead of him and fired and exploded its right wing. He then closed on another Zero and nothing happened when he squeezed the trigger; he was either out of ammunition or his guns had jammed. He tried to recharge his guns but the charger was inoperative, and Czarnecki broke off to head home with his first two victories toward becoming an ace.

Blue Flight Leader 1Lt. Lowell Lutton led his wingmen, 1Lt. Donno Bellows and 2Lt. Kenneth Richardson (Lutton had his fourth flight member abort), down after Schinz and Jett led their flights in their firing passes. As the B-25s attacked the field Blue Flight was at 6,000 feet, where they were attacked by 10 Zeros. Lutton fired at a climbing Zero, and it continued to climb with a smoking engine as Lutton and Richardson dove away. This Zero continued to climb and then rolled over to follow them, but stalled and turned its belly toward Bellows, who fired a two second volley into its belly from 75 yards; it rolled over two or three times out of control. Lutton lost Richardson and quickly joined two P-38s of Green Flight flown by 1Lt. Thomas McGuire and 2Lt. Francis Lent of the last 431st flight, and flew in trail with them. Lutton saw an Oscar begin a head on pass at them, but its pilot changed his mind and turned to attack Lent's tail. As Lent pulled up Lutton got a good shot at the Oscar, hit its cockpit, and it went down in flames. At this point Lutton lost McGuire and Lent and joined two other

P-38s just as they were being attacked head on by another Oscar. The three Lightnings turned after the Oscar, which dove and turned toward the Drome. As the Oscar neared the Drome the other two P-38s broke off and Lutton followed it out to sea, firing with no apparent effect. As he pulled away and looked back Lutton saw the Oscar's wreckage on fire on the water.

In his first big air battle Green Flight Leader 1Lt. Thomas J. McGuire, Jr., made a propitious debut, shooting down two Zekes and a Tony to begin a career that would make him America's second highest scoring ace with 38 victories. McGuire describes the combat in his ICR:

> "As part of escort for B-25s, I was leading the last flight of our squadron over Wewak as close cover. Our flight consisted of three ships, one man having had to return to base. At 8,000 feet and at 0945 hours, Zeros started attacking us. One made a pass from 45 degrees at my flight, and I turned the flight into him. Then as he went by I turned again and fired two long bursts. I saw him burst into flames and head down. Lieutenant Sieber, my No. 3 man, saw him crash. Lieutenant Lent, my No. 2 man, called in there was a Zero on his tail. I turned to the left and got several shots at the Zero, chasing it toward Dagua Field. I saw hits around the cockpit; Lieutenant Lent saw him burning and crash. My No. 3 man had lost the formation at that time. We made a head on pass at a Zeke, which held a collision course. As I went under the Zeke, his left wing scraped my left wing. I had shot a couple of good bursts but observed no results. Lieutenant Lent and I closed up and chased a Zeke down to 1,000 feet above the water near Dagua Airdrome. After several shots I started back upstairs. Lieutenant Lent says he saw Lieutenant Lutton (who had joined us) shoot it down into the water in flames. Light and heavy flak was intense over most of the Wewak area. I saw another Zero going down in flames at the same time, chased by Lieutenant Czarnecki. We made a pass at a Zeke, which pulled up and Lieutenant Lent shot pieces off of it and it then exploded. We started for home escorting three B-25s. About 10 minutes out of Wewak a Tony attacked the bombers. In the start of his pass we headed him off, and I got to or three good bursts at him. The Tony started down smoking and the B-25s saw him crash. The Tony was camouflaged bright green, yellow, and brown. He appeared very fast."

McGuire's Wingman, 1Lt. Francis Lent, saw McGuire make a pass at a Zero at 5,000 feet and miss. This Zero "whipped around," did a half roll, and Split-S'd onto Lent's tail and fired. Lent radioed his plight and McGuire came in and shot the attacker off Lent's tail. Green Flight reformed and another Zero made a pass from 11 o'clock on McGuire's tail. The Zero passed in front of Lent, who fired a long burst that disintegrated its engine, canopy, and tail. Lent rejoined McGuire, and watched him and Lutton shoot down Zeros. McGuire's number four had aborted before reaching combat, and his Element Leader, 2Lt. Robert Sieber, became separated in the frantic combat. Sieber went on to claim a Zero probable near Wewak as he dove on the enemy aircraft that was on the tail of another P-38.

432FS

The 432FS, led by Capt. Daniel Roberts, was flying top cover for the 431st at 0930, but was forced down to 8,500 feet due to bad weather, which became increasingly worse after rendezvous and made it difficult to maintain visual contact with the 431st. The P-38s formed a circle over the area, and after the B-25s began their run four Zeros were seen from 3,000 to 9,000 feet.

Capt. William Waldman led the fourth 432FS flight and dropped his tanks when he spotted a lone Zero through a break in the overcast 2,000 feet above. Waldman realized that he would be unable to catch this Zero and began to fire immediately while climbing, continuing to fire almost until he stalled. The Zero looked as though it was about to dive on Waldman, but "sort of flopped over at a crazy angle," and Waldman's Wingman, 2Lt. Billy Gresham, confirmed the victory, the first for the 432FS. Waldman made a similar pass at a second Zero, taking a closer and longer shot, getting hits and "looking like he was out of control" when Waldman broke away (with a damaged claim).

Element Leader 1Lt. Vivian Cloud claimed a Zero probable when he saw a Zero being chased by two P-38s over Dagua. Cloud attacked from the rear and fired at 400 feet at the skidding Zero. He saw cannon shell bursts hitting its engine and belly. The Zero rolled over on its back and disappeared into the overcast below.

2Lt. Richard Ryrholm and his Element Leader were in the Lufbery Circle. They had left it two previous times to chase a Zero without result. On their third time a Zero attacked them head on and they turned into it. Ryrholm fired a long 15 degree deflection shot and the Zero fired back. Ryrholm got hits, and the enemy pilot missed and descended smoking as Ryrholm broke away for a damaged claim.

Fifteen enemy fighters were destroyed with an additional 3/2 probable/damaged claim by the 475th pilots. The Group's first operational casualty was 2Lt. Ralph Schmidt, who was last seen leaving his flight pursued by enemy fighters.

18 August 1943: 348FG/342FS

While the P-38s of the 475FG were over Wewak, the 342FS suffered its first combat casualties when Maj. Raymond Gallagher led the 16 P-47s through overcast weather between 6,000 and 12,000 feet on another transport escort to Wau, in the central highlands. When the fighters emerged from the overcast two were missing from the formation. F/O Wilfrid Desilets was never seen again. Lt. Cyril Andrews, flying on Gallagher's wing, became disoriented and his P-47 went out of control; he bailed out at about 1,000 feet and became entangled in the treetops, dangling 100 feet above the ground. Not wanting to be captured by the Japanese, Andrews quickly cut himself free and dropped through the branches to the ground, but fractured his right leg upon hitting the ground. Andrews was unable to move without severe pain, but was close enough to a stream to reach water and was able to cover himself with his parachute. All through the next day Andrews drifted in and out of sleep and ate the D ration bar in his jungle kit. Andrews decided to drag himself as far as he could, and spent three days and two nights of painful crawling before friendly natives found him and carried him to their village. A native patrol took him to Garaina Airstrip, where he was flown out to Port Moresby.

So after the first few days of operations, the 348FG lost three P-47s and two pilots for one definite Oscar claimed destroyed and perhaps three others listed as probably destroyed or damaged. During the same period the 475th Fighter Group had claimed more than 25 victories for the loss of two P-38s and one pilot. The 475FG was formed with many veteran pilots from combat-savvy squadrons, and this instant expert unit helped reinforce the opinion that the P-47 could not really compete with the P-38 in combat against the Japanese. But Kearby wanted to demonstrate his case that the P-47s, flown by suitably trained and motivated pilots, could be as successful as the Lightning.

Until September 1943, the 5FC was confined to local base defense, transport escort, or close bomber escort to Japanese bases, from which the enemy could intercept or not. Kearby and other fighter leaders lobbied for freedom of action, contending for free sweeps that would allow the fighter pilots to aggressively hunt down and attack the Japanese.

20 August 1943: 475FG/432FS

Another Wewak B-24 escort mission was flown on the 20th, and while the 80FS claimed 12 victories over Wewak, the 475FG, led by Lt.Col. George Prentice of HQ, was only able to chase after several reluctant enemy fighters. 1Lt. James Ince claimed a Zero "maybe damaged." Some P-38s of the 432FS landed at Marilinan to refuel, and 2Lt. Allan Camp from Capt.

Frank Tomkins' Flight was one of the last to leave. It appears Tomkins had gotten lost and tried to land at Karema, about 50 miles northwest of Port Moresby, where he overshot the runway and crashed into the Karema River, becoming the 432nd's first fatality.

20 August 1943: 35FG/39FS

The 39FS had not s,cored a victory since 26 July, but three weeks later Maj. Thomas Lynch who had scored his 11th victory on 10 June, led 16 P-38s on a B-24 cover mission to Wewak. As the Liberators were leaving Wewak they were attacked by a lone Zero that had climbed under their formation. Lynch dropped his tanks and made a diving attack without result. Lynch rejoined the bomber escort and saw a twin engine fighter approach from the right. He turned into it and then made a tight turn to get on its tail. He fired, scoring hits on its fuselage, then broke away and returned to get on its tail. He fired a devastating volley that shot out its right engine, and he jinked to hit the left engine so hard that the wheel dropped; he then blew the tail away, and the pilot bailed out, just missing Lynch's aircraft. Lynch rejoined the bombers, and 60 miles away from the target he saw a single twin engine bomber pulling up alongside the formation about two miles away. As Lynch closed the enemy turned into him, and he fired a quick burst, hitting the fuselage and starboard engine, which quit, and the enemy bomber rolled over on its back and went into the ground. 1Lt. Stanley Andrews claimed a Zero south of Boram Strip, but the claim was initially denied, as it was not witnessed. Later the claim would be verified for Andrews' sixth and last victory. After completing his tour Andrews returned to the US and served as a flight instructor. He returned to combat flying P-51s with the 39FS in 1945 but made no claims. In June 1945 he became CO of the 69FS/58FG, flying the P-47, also making no claims. He saw combat in Korea with the 27FW and retired from the Air Force in October 1963 as a Lt. Colonel.

39FS Aces. (L-R): 1Lt. Stanley **Andrews** got his sixth and last victory; Maj. Thomas **Lynch** shot down two to give his 13; while Capt. Charles **Sullivan** had became an ace days earlier with his fifth and last victory. (AAF)

1Lt. Stanley **Andrews** claimed a Zero but the claim was initially denied as it was not witnessed but later the claim would be verified for Andrews sixth and last victory. (AAF)

20 August 1943: 8FG/80FS

At 0830, 16 80th Squadron P-38s took off on a close cover escort of 24 B-24s to Wewak and rendezvoused with the bombers over Karkar Island at 1015 before heading toward the target. Maj. Edward Cragg led one formation of eight Headhunters to cover 17 bombers, while the other seven B-24s were covered by the other eight 80FS escorts led by Capt. George Welch.

Cragg: Copper White Flight

Cragg was flying at 16,000 feet approximately 20 miles southeast of the target when he spotted 15 to 20 "mixed-type" Japanese fighters flying randomly below. Cragg ordered his seven escorts to drop their tanks and they dove on the Japanese. Cragg fired on a Zero from astern until it began to smoke and then continued spiraling down in flames, followed by another P-38. Cragg followed a climbing Tony that was closing on a B-24 head on and shot pieces off the Tony, which rolled over and spun into the water. Cragg saw another P-38 (Taylor) being attacked by a Tony in a climb and intervened, but ran out of ammunition; the Japanese pilot broke off his attack, however. Cragg flew home with his sixth and seventh victories.

Cragg's Wingman, 1Lt. Charles Taylor, followed Cragg and was unsuccessful in his attack on a Zero that was firing on the bombers, but caused it to peel away. He attacked another Zero, but had to break off when another Zero got on his tail. Cragg came in on a 180° turn and chased it away. Taylor saw a twin engine fighter making an attack on a Lightning and fired a short burst just as the enemy pilot fired. The enemy fighter rolled over and disappeared, and Taylor followed Cragg back home.

Capt. Leonidas Mathers followed Cragg from his #3 position in the formation and fired on Cragg's Zero, also getting hits, but Cragg got the victory credit. He then made two passes on Tonys and got hits that damaged two. Mathers made a pass on a twin engine bomber from behind, starting a fire in its starboard engine for his fourth and last victory of the war (to go with two probable and four damaged). The veteran had been with the Headhunters for over a year and had damaged a Zero as early as 26 August 1942.

2Lt. Louis Schriber was flying as Mathers' Wingman. He also followed Mathers down in the first attack and fired on another Oscar. Pieces came off the enemy fighter, which slow rolled but disappeared for a probable. He then saw a Zero making a firing pass on a P-38 (Bateson, of Welch's Flight) and made a deflection shot that caused him to roll over smoking for a probable.

2Lt. Jennings Myers saw an Oscar pop out of the clouds below and make a firing pass at his Element Leader. Myers skidded in his descent to get in position to fire a deflection shot, which hit the Oscar's wingtip. He then fired a cannon burst into the cockpit and the Oscar rolled violently into the ground. Myers found another Oscar below him and dove to the attack, hitting the Oscar, which lost its rudder and elevator and went out of control and crashed. After his second victory Myers was at low altitude and looking to rejoin any friendly aircraft in the area; he found his Element Leader, who was heading home in a damaged P-38. Myers escorted his leader midway between Wewak and Port Moresby before he had to leave him to refuel at Tsili Tsili.

LEFT TO RIGHT:
After two previous probable claims 1Lt. Jess **Gidley** scored his first of three victories. (AAF)

2Lt. Jennings **Myers** shot down the first two enemy fighters of five. (AAF)

Maj. Edward **Cragg**. (L) scored two victories to give seven while Capt. George **Welch**. (R) got three to make him a double ace with 12. (AAF)

During the battle, 1Lt. Jess Gidley became separated from the Squadron and joined three P-38s of the 39FS in the B-24 escort. As the B-24s finished their bombing run and turned back home Gidley saw a twin engine fighter at 3 o'clock at the same altitude, and all four Lightnings dove steeply to the attack from different angles and all four missed. The enemy pilot Split-S'd, and Gidley and another 39FS pilot chased it. The 39th pilot dove at 45 degrees and missed. Gidley was high astern and dove slightly below, firing a long burst into its right engine, and it rolled over as Gidley continued his attack down to 75 yards, knocking off large pieces of its wing and engine. Gidley's fighter flew into the pieces, sustaining large dents in the leading edge of his port wing. The enemy's left engine was smoking and the right was on fire as it dove steeply into the clouds. The four P-38s rejoined and wove over the Liberators for the next half hour. They noticed a lone P-38 lurking near the bomber formation. They watched for about 10 minutes until it suddenly dove on the bomber formation. The flight turned to investigate, and they saw it was an enemy twin engine fighter whose pilot dove down and away. Capt. Thomas Lynch from the 39FS shot the enemy aircraft down, but the pilot was able to bail out. Gidley then returned to base.

Welch: Copper White Flight

Capt. George Welch led the second group of eight P-38s about a mile behind the bomber formation, which was flying through heavy AA fire. The flight met 15 to 20 bandits (Tonys) at 22,000 feet. Welch stayed with the bombers as they turned toward home. The Tonys then attacked individually, and one collided with a Liberator, which exploded. Welch made three 90 degree deflection shots and one 0 degree shot and scored three victories to become a double ace with 12 victories. After this combat a skilled Tony pilot dove on him, from above and behind, and Welch needed to lose him before he wouldn't have enough fuel to return to base. He tried to outrun the enemy pilot, but finally lost him in a high speed climb and headed home, landing with 60 gallons of fuel.

1Lt. Mark Kaspar was flying as Welch's Wingman. He dove with Welch and dutifully let him have the first shot at a Zero. Kaspar pulled up and saw a Zero closing on a B-24, then fired a short burst that caused the Japanese pilot to Split-S away into a cloud. Kaspar chased another Zero, but had to give up so as not to get too far away from the bombers.

1Lt. Charles Bateson, flying as Welch's Element Leader, saw four "Zero-type" fighters about 1,000 feet below. He followed Welch down and fired on one that Welch had bypassed. He fired from 400 yards in a vertical dive without observable results. Bateson climbed to 17,000 feet, where he saw a Zero to his left at the same altitude and 400 yards away traveling in the opposite direction. The enemy pilot turned in behind Bateson, who climbed away, and the Zero was hit by another P-38 (Schriber, of Cragg's Flight). He then saw another Zero low to starboard and dove on it. The enemy pilot turned and climbed into Bateson, who fired, and the enemy pilot turned away without observable results. Bateson climbed and saw a Zero crossing his line of flight and fired from 90 degrees deflection; the enemy pilot slow rolled away. Bateson saw a P-38 (Wingman Ladd) 2,000 feet below with a Zero only 300 yards from is tail. Bateson dove on the Zero and got to 300 yards behind and fired, but the Zero turned to get back under him. This maneuver made the Zero "a fine target," as Bateson fired a long burst and the Zero went down out of control.

2Lt. Kenneth Ladd was flying as Bateson's Wingman, and followed Welch and Bateson down and made a pass on a Zero, but did not see any hits. As Ladd came around he spotted another Zero below and dove steeply and fired again without seeing any results, despite getting hits before he lost sight of this Zero. A few seconds later a Zero came in from above and head on and fired. Ladd pulled up his nose and fired a short burst that missed, as did the Japanese pilot. Ladd looked around for other P-38s, but had a Zero get on his tail and dove away with full throttle; Bateson came in and shot the Zero down. Ladd left the battle without any claims.

1Lt. Raymond Daly, Welch's second Flight Leader, had problems dropping his tanks on the first pass, but dropped them after 10 minutes. He saw an enemy fighter (Zero or Oscar) making a pass on a bomber and went after it, but saw another enemy fighter coming in and attacked it and got hits, but no observable results. He then made several more passes at large deflection angles from 500 to 200 yards with no results.

2Lt. William Fotheringham was Daly's Wingman, and he too was unable to drop one of his tanks. After a few minutes of maneuvering he dropped the tank and saw two Zeros closing on the B-24s. He attacked a twin engine fighter without result, but then did see that it was shot down by other P-38s.

1Lt. Elwood Krisher was Daly's second Element Leader, and when both Daly's and Fotheringham's tanks did not release Krisher and his Wingman covered them until they dropped. He then dove on two Zeros that then turned into him. He was only able to fire a short burst at 90 degrees deflection. He then noticed that his nosewheel indicator showed the wheel to be halfway down and left the area. He left for home, pumping the wheel down by hand.

The 80Fs scored 10 victories, one probable, and two damaged without a loss. However, a day earlier 2Lt. Earl Smith crashed during a test hop when one of his engines cut out and his P-38 slow rolled into the water from 2,000 feet just off Paga Point.

21 August 1943: 475FG/431FS/432FS

432FS

On the 21st, the 432FS would see its first major combat of the war during a B-25 escort to But and Dagua Airdromes in the Wewak area. The Squadron's four flights were led by Captains Daniel Roberts (the Mission Leader) and William Waldman and 1Lts. Noel Lundy and Frederick Harris. The B-25s radioed that they had met Zeros near Wewak at 0945, and Roberts ordered the tanks to be jettisoned. He saw eight to ten enemy fighters at 6,500 feet attacking the B-25s. The 431FS continued the escort on to Wewak while Roberts dispatched his 432nd flights to attack the Japanese. Roberts and his Wingman, 2Lt. John Michener, intercepted the initial enemy fighters over Boram Airdrome. Roberts damaged a "Hap" (Oscar) that made a high frontal pass from a half roll from 11 o'clock. Michener then dove to starboard and fired a burst that "I thought connected," and it went down smoking from 3,000 feet for a probable victory. Soon Roberts and Michener found that they were alone at about 6,000 feet with 20 to 25 enemy fighters in the area. They saw six "Haps" (Oscars) chasing a single P-38, and Roberts took off to help the badly damaged Lightning, which was falling in flames (this Lightning was one of three 80FS P-38s lost on this day). Roberts chased the second Oscar and hit its engine with a short burst; the surprised Oscar pilot turned away from the attack and exposed his vulnerable belly to Roberts, who fired, and the enemy went down smoking near But Airdrome. Roberts then damaged another Oscar that attempted to climb away, and Roberts followed as it fell into the sea off Dagua Strip to make him an ace with six victories. As they left the area they were pursued by eight enemy fighters. They put their Lightnings into full throttle, and after two minutes the enemy gave up the chase. Running low on fuel and with worsening weather, they flew to 30 Mile Drome rather than Marilinan.

Mission Leader Capt. Daniel **Roberts** got victories #5 and #6 to become an ace. (AAF)

1Lt. Campbell **Wilson** shot down the first two of his four total victories. (AAF)

1Lt. John **Loisel** got two Tony victories, his first of 11 total. (AFAA)

2Lt. Billy **Gresham** got his first victory of six. (AFAA)

Roberts' second Element Leader, 1Lt. Campbell Wilson, and Wingman 2Lt. James Farris saw a lone Zero zoom up to port. Wilson turned into it but could not get into firing position, and he and Farris turned 180° to avoid a cloud bank and met a "twin engine fighter" that was climbing. As the enemy pilot began to turn Wilson followed him through its turn and fired a long burst, setting its starboard engine on fire, and it fell away with its entire front section ablaze. Farris broke away and fired a long burst on another T/E fighter that rolled over and began to descend for a probable. Wilson turned 360° and flew behind another Lightning that was attacking another T/E fighter. When the enemy pilot turned left Farris' P-38 could not match the enemy's tighter turn and broke off. However, Wilson was in position to open fire, and continued to fire as he held his diving turn until the enemy half rolled and disappeared under him. Wingman Farris confirmed the victory, as he saw flames enveloping the cockpit and both engines. As they circled the area three other P-38s joined Campbell's element, but two left beyond Bena Bena, with another joining them. A weather front developed and the four P-38s had to negotiate the Markham Valley to reach Marilinan. When they reached Marilinan it was socked in, and they landed safely on the strip at Bulolo.

White Flight Leader 1Lt. Frederick Harris and Wingman 2Lt. Elliott Summer became separated from the Squadron at the beginning of the combat. They were at 10,000 feet when they saw 15 or more mixed single and twin engine fighters 2,000 feet below. These fighters had just left combat with the lower P-38 cover, and despite being outnumbered, the Americans dropped their tanks and made "10 to 12 passes." After his second pass Harris hit an "inline" fighter (Tony) with a good burst that set it on fire. "About five passes later" Summer got a good shot on a "radial Zero" that lost several pieces and exploded. "Several passes later" Harris fired at a single engine inline fighter that Harris had seen damage the engine of another P-38. This enemy pilot was doing slow rolls and made himself an easy target and half rolled into the sea. "Out of several passes I (Harris) saw a total of four smoking and did not see them burst into flames nor go in. However, it is quite likely that they did not return home because my Wingman, Lt. Summer, got some good passed into them also. We had a very good flight." Harris was credited with two Tony victories and four damaged, while Summer shot down one Zero; both for their first victories towards becoming aces.

1Lt. John Loisel and Wingman 2Lt. Paul Lucas, the second element in Harris' Flight, dropped their tanks, and Loisel made four ineffective passes: one at a Tony, two at single engine fighters, and the last a twin engine fighter before he and Lucas were attacked by a Zero at 7 o'clock high. The two dove across the path of another P-38 element and lost the Zero. After he fired on a T/E fighter, a Zero banked slightly at 2 o'clock and Loisel hit it with a short burst, as did Lucas, who had time for a longer burst and saw the Zero go down in flames as it passed under his wing for a victory claim. Loisel then encountered a Tony that turned into him on a head on pass. Loisel flew directly at the Tony and fired from very close range, peeling off large pieces of the Tony's wing that hit Lucas' wing. Continuing over Boram, Loisel dove on a Tony that was coming out of an Immelmann and fired until he closed to 50 yards. The Tony began to burn and smoke as it plunged through a cloud layer at 1,500 feet. As they were leaving the area a "T/E job" made a long, high pass at them, but when they turned into them the enemy pilot turned away. The two landed at Tsili Tsili for refueling and returned to base. Loisel had scored his first two of 11 victories and Lucas the first of six victories.

1Lt. Thomas **McGuire** shot down two Zeros to make him an ace (AAF)

Capt. Verl **Jett** scored his fourth victory. (AFAA)

1Lt. David **Allen** shot down two Zeros and an Oscar to give him seven victories to become an ace. (AAF)

1Lt. John **Lent** got victories #2 and #3. (AFAA)

While flying at 9,000 feet, Flight Leader 1Lt. Noel Lundy saw two Tonys at 11 o'clock and 11,000 feet and called his flight to drop their tanks. Lundy turned into them but did not get a shot, then turned away when another P-38 flight approached. Lundy became separated from Wingman, 2Lt. Billy Gresham and went off and made passes at a Hap and a T/E fighter without result. Meanwhile, Gresham had pulled up into one of the two Tonys and fired a three second burst into its belly without result. He then saw three P-38s firing on a T/E fighter which was smoking. When the enemy fighter rolled and dove Gresham got on his tail, and as he followed Gresham saw the fire go out. Gresham fired at 100 yards and 15 degrees deflection until he ran out of ammunition. The enemy fighter continued to lose altitude and crashed into the ground, and Gresham claimed his first victory of six.

Lundy's Element Leader, 1Lt. Grover Gholson, and Wingman 2Lt. Thomas Sims saw five Tonys at 12 o'clock low and descended on them. Gholson fired a very long burst without result. Sims turned 90 degrees and fired without hits. Gholson closed on a twin engine fighter and fired, getting no observable hits. He then saw another T/E fighter chasing a P-38 and fired several long bursts, seeing large pieces flying off its fuselage, wings, and cockpit. The enemy fighter wobbled and went straight down, but Gholson had to break away, as two enemy fighters got on his tail. 2Lt. Thomas Sims confirmed the victory. Gholson would fire another long burst at a Tony that was climbing in front of him, again with no observable damage. Sims had remained on Gholson's wing and pulled up and fired a long burst into the Tony's belly behind the engine and into the cockpit between the wing roots. As Sims returned to Gholson's wing a Zero closed on him and got hits on Sim's wing, but did no mechanical damage. Sims dove away from the Zero and got away; only to have to outrun two more Zeros before returning to Bulolo for refueling. The gasoline at Bulolo was flown in by transport the day before in case of such emergencies.

431FS

Twenty minutes later, at 1000, the 431FS came on the scene and fell one victory short of equaling the 12 victories claimed by the 432nd for the day's combat. Capt. Franklin Nichols led 16 Hades P-38s from Berry (12 Mile Drome) at 0740, and over 30 Mile Strip were joined by the 432FS and the 80FS. The three Squadrons rendezvoused with two B-25 squadrons over Mt. Yonkie and arrived over the target at 1005.

Nichols' Squadron was assigned to fly top cover at 17-20,000 feet, and after uneventfully escorting the Mitchells over the target he led his P-38s back toward Wewak and Boram Dromes. At 1015 they spotted air activity over Boram, dropped their tanks, and dove into the attack. The flight lost sight of the bombers and low cover in the overcast and were not with the bombers when they made their run.

Capt. Franklin **Nichols** after his fifth and last victory. (AFAA)

They were a short distance from Dagua when low cover called for assistance and turned south and engaged the enemy at 1005. Nichols closed, followed by his Wingman, 2Lt. John Knox, and made his first pass on a Zero at 10,000 feet, causing no apparent damage. The Zero pulled up, and 1Lt. David Allen and his Wingman, 2Lt. Ronald Dunlap, fired at it; as they followed through, it rolled above them to the right without apparent damage. Nichols then saw an Oscar directly above and to port and turned and fired a long burst into it. The Oscar passed over Nichols, then descended smoking, and Nichols made another pass, but had to break off when he was attacked from above and lost sight of the Oscar. Nichols turned into the attacking Oscar, which broke away. Nichols climbed to 7,000 feet and then attacked another Zero off to his right when he saw three more Zeros coming down on him from the left. Nichols half rolled and shoved the throttle forward, but didn't have enough speed to get away. One Zero stayed on his tail until 1Lt. David Allen shot it down. Nichols saw an Oscar flying along the tree tops, apparently trying to hide, and dove and fired a 90 degree shot at it. As the speeding Nichols overran the Oscar he saw it pull straight up and half roll into the foothills. After four victories flying P-40s with the 7FS, this last victory made Nichols an ace. When Nichols landed he found seven bullet holes in his fighter. Allen and Dunlap continued down to 3,000 feet, where P-38s were attacking about a dozen scattered enemy fighters. Allen saw two P-38s trying to turn inside an Oscar, and as Allen dove the Lightnings broke away, giving Allen an "excellent" deflection shot from the rear quarter. He saw no damage, but Dunlap saw the Oscar go down in flames. Allen again saw P-38s chasing a Zero below and joined in. The Zero fled out over the water, and Allen continued his pursuit and fired enough rounds to start it smoking; 2Lt. Kenneth Richardson of Green Flight confirmed the victory. Allen climbed to gain altitude and saw Nichol's P-38 being chased by an Oscar, with others not far behind closing in on it. Allen turned left into them and fired at very close range, and the Oscar began to disintegrate as Allen had to pull up sharply to avoid more Oscars on his tail. These three victories and the two five days earlier made Allen an ace. Allen's Wingman Dunlap lost his leader and saw a Zero turning away from a P-38 directly in front of him. The enemy pilot went into a long gentle dive, and Dunlap closed to 200 yards and fired until his guns quit. The Zero rolled over and spiraled into the ground. Dunlap pulled up and his engine stopped, but he was able to restart it; it would no longer deliver full power and he headed back to Berry. Dunlap became lost in the overcast and was running low on fuel, so he started searching for Bena Bena or Marilinan. He finally spotted Bulolo Airstrip through a hole in the overcast and landed safely. Gasoline had to be flown by transport the next morning to refuel his fighter.

Capt. Verl Jett was again leading White Flight with 2Lt. Robert Cline as his Wingman, and again describes his victory succinctly: "We made a pass on a twin engine fighter which started to smoke and I thought that I saw some flame." Jett became an ace, as he had a Sonia victory flying a P-39 with the 36FS on 28 December 1942.

Maj. Merle Smith from 475FG/HQ was leading Green Flight with Wingman F/O Kenneth Richardson and second element 2Lt. Edward Czarnecki and his Wingman, F/O William Gronemeyer. Smith and Richardson basically remained as top cover, diving away from one attack from above and firing unsuccessfully at a "Me-109-type" (Tony) before heading to base after the bombers made their runs. Smith's second element saw more action. When Richardson called out two Zeros at 12 o'clock Czarnecki and Gronemeyer turned after them, until Czarnecki thought these Zeros might be bait for a trap and broke away. They saw a Zero that was being pursued by several P-38s and the two joined in; although Czarnecki fired, it was Lent that got credit for the victory. On his return to Berry Czarnecki saw a "wheels down aircraft (Nate)" and fired at it from dead astern until it started to smoke and burn. Czarnecki's guns jammed, but they were not needed, as the Nate went down. It seems peculiar that Czarnecki shot down a fixed landing gear Nate, which probably was a Zero with its gear extended.

1Lt. Thomas McGuire was leading Blue Flight, which again was the last flight; he was on top cover at 17,000 when the lower flights called for help. McGuire and Wingman 1Lt. John Lent dropped their tanks and dove to 5,000 feet, where McGuire made an unsuccessful pass on a Zero. As they circled they saw a Zero, and Lent made a pass and missed and McGuire came in and made a 45 degree deflection shot at close range and Lent confirmed the victory. Blue second element became separated at this point, but Lent and McGuire reformed and went after a twin engine fighter being chased by four P-38s. The two took some ineffectual shots at it before breaking away to chase two Zeros flying toward the Bay just over the deck. McGuire made a pass on the one on the left and missed, while Lent followed the one on the right and fired "burst after burst" at this Zero from directly astern before it finally crashed and burned in view of Czarnecki. Lent then rejoined McGuire, who was chasing a twin engine fighter, and as Lent pulled over to one side the Nick turned directly into him. Lent fired head on until his guns stopped, but the damage was done, as the Nick crashed and burned into a wooded area. The two climbed and McGuire got another pass at a Nick, getting hits on its cockpit and wing roots; this victory made McGuire the first pilot to become an ace by scoring all his victories with the 475FG.

Nichols critiqued the day's combat: "The tactics used today by the Zero pilots were inferior to those used in other engagements in which I have participated. They had no initiative and seemed afraid of the P-38s. Only when they found a single P-38 would they attack." This would be Nichol's fifth and last victory, and after helping to activate the 431FS/475FG he would serve as its CO from 1 July to 19 November 1943. Back in the US he was promoted to Lt. Colonel in July 1944 and remained in the Air Force as the CO of several Tactical Fighter Wings (TFW), retiring as a Brig. General in May 1970.

On its first three combats on the 16th, 18th, and 21st, the 475th claimed 50 victories and five new aces for the loss of one P-38 and pilot in combat (Scnmidt) and another in an operational accident (Camp).

21 August 1943: 8FG/80FS

After routing Japanese interceptors over Wewak the previous day, 16 P-38s led by Maj. Edward Cragg took off at 0730 on a close cover escort of B-25s to Wewak. By 1000 the bomber formation was at 8,000 feet just south of Dagua, a few miles east of Wewak. The Japanese were alerted and were circling Dagua with the altitude advantage, and they engaged the 80th in a swirling dogfight.

At 1000, near Boram, with the B-25s below and slightly behind, Maj. Edward Cragg ordered tanks to be dropped when Tonys were spotted below. Cragg dove and fired on a Tony without result, then continued the escort to Dagua, where he was chased by 10 Zeros that drew them away from the Mitchells about to make their bombing run. Cragg evaded these fighters and returned to the bombers and saw an Oscar close from the rear. Cragg turned into the enemy and made a head on firing pass that set its wing on fire; it would crash into the water near the Strip for his eighth victory.

1Lt. Seaborn Chiles followed Cragg in his attack and also took a shot at Cragg's first Tony; like his Flight Leader, he also missed. He became separated from Cragg and fired several ineffective shots at Zeros. He then saw another Zero headed toward him to starboard and turned into it, firing a long burst until they almost collided. As he turned he thought he saw the Zero crash near the Boram Strip, but despite this IRC he was given no official victory credit. 1Lt. Robert Bennett of Cragg's Flight fired on an enemy fighter but missed. Bennett's engine sputtered and he thought that his fighter had been hit, so he decided to dive away and retire from combat and head home.

1Lt. Donald McGee and Wingman 2Lt. Paul Murphey were in 1Lt. John Guttel's Flight, which had dropped their tanks before going down to strafe the But Airdrome. However, two Zeros were about to attack the B-25s at 3,000 feet and McGee peeled off with the Flight, but by the time they reached the area another P-38 flight was attacking the Zeros. McGee started a high speed climb just as a Tony began an overhead attack. McGee waited until the Tony pilot was committed to his dive and then turned into him, but did not fire, as a twin engine fighter tried to ram him. McGee ducked under the attacker and fired without seeing any hits. McGee then pursued the Tony and fired head on into its belly, but he lost the Tony for no claim. McGee climbed again and saw another twin engine fighter which turned into him. McGee turned with the enemy pilot and fired a long burst from 90 degrees to 30 degrees deflection, getting hits near the cockpit. The enemy pilot's turn forced McGee into a vertical dive with him, and when McGee pulled out the enemy continued its dive toward the ground, but McGee did not see the result and was given no credit, which would have made him an ace. Murphey, who was flying on McGee's wing, made a pass on a Tony, and as they pulled up a Hap closed and Murphey dropped his nose and fired, sending it down smoking and in flames, but was credited with a probable. Murphey lost McGee and joined 2Lt. Cyril Homer.

2Lts. Cyril Homer and Jess Gidley followed Flight Leader Guttel in a pass on two Zeros making an attack on the B-25 formation. The three man flight pulled up after the Zeros and Guttel fired at one and missed, while Homer and Gidley chased another Zero that Homer got a shot at but missed. Gidley followed it down, trying to get below it, but just as he started to fire the enemy pilot began a medium turn and steepened it. Fearing that he would lose the enemy Gidley dropped quarter flaps to take a good deflection shot that tore small pieces off its wings. Gidley lost it in the turn, and Homer broke to port and made a head on pass, firing beyond range. The Zero then turned away, giving Homer a 90 degree deflection shot that hit the cockpit area, where a fire started, and the Zero plunged out of control. A Zero dove on Homer from 6,000 feet above him, and Homer turned into him as the Zero pilot overshot. Homer fired and missed, but followed and caught him as he came out of a cloud at about 1,000 feet. Homer fired from about a 70° deflection and hit its wing and followed the Zero through a cloud, then saw it explode. McGee's Wingman Murphey then joined Homer, and the two climbed after a twin engine fighter as it dove on them. Both Americans fired, and it started to smoke from its right engine as it entered a cloud for a damaged claim for Homer. The duo climbed to about 6,000 feet, where they saw a Zero on the tail of the last of two P-38s. But before they could reach the area the P-38 was on fire and smoking badly. When Homer turned toward a Tony it turned into him and Homer fired a 90 degree shot that started it smoking; he followed it for another pass. The enemy pilot Split-S'd, and Homer fired again and hit the Tony again, starting a fatal fire. Homer had to break off because he had

2Lt. Cyril **Homer** got his first three victories on the way to becoming a trile ace with 15 total. (AFAA)

2Lt. Jess **Gidley** soon got his second victory. (AAF)

1Lt. John **Jones** got victories six and seven and would end his tour with eight. (AAF)

2Lt. Paul **Murphey** opened his six victory career by shooting down a Tony. (AFAA)

F/O Edwin **DeGraffenried's** first three victories put him half way to his six total. (AAF)

gained too much speed in his dive. New Wingman Murphey had stayed with Homer, and two enemy fighters dove on them. Homer fired and missed, but Murphey set it on fire and it exploded. The second Tony pulled up on Murphey's tail and Homer called him on the radio, but the Tony hit Murphey's starboard engine cooling system and that engine quit, so he feathered the prop. Homer looked back and saw the Tony following him and went into a steep 450 mph corkscrew; the two went into a cloud layer. When they emerged Homer saw the Tony below and behind. Homer chandelled and tried to turn, but was out-turned by the enemy pilot, and in desperation Homer turned into a cloud and lost his pursuer. Homer saw another Zero above and heading toward Wewak but did not engage, as he was running low on fuel. Homer then escorted Murphey to Marilinan, where he refueled. The three victories were Homer's first of 15 during the war.

After Gidley lost Guttel and Homer he saw an enemy twin engine fighter attacking a P-38, but as soon as the enemy pilot saw him it dove to port and Gidley followed, hoping to get below and behind without being seen. The enemy pilot didn't see Gidley slowly gaining, and the American fired a long burst at 150 to 100 yards, hitting the wing, then fired again at 40 yards until he ran out of ammunition, hitting the cockpit and starting a fire. Gidley just missed colliding with the enemy by ten feet, but as he passed by he saw the canopy open and the enemy pilot bailout. As Gidley looked up he saw seven Zeros 4,000 to 5,000 feet above when one of his engines began to miss and vibrate. One of the Zeros dove, but Gidley dove into some clouds and the enemy pilot broke off. Gidley saw five P-38s ahead and radioed them to wait, but they continued onward without him. Finally Gidley was able to join 2Lt. Hanover, and the two landed at Marilinan to refuel and then returned to base. 2Lt. Donald Hanover had seen Zeros in three flights at 10 o'clock directly over Wewak and made several ineffectual firing passes. A Zero then got on his tail and he lost it, then he joined Gidley on the way back to base.

1Lt. John Jones' first contact was with a Tony that was chasing some P-38s. He turned and dove, firing a long 60 degree burst from directly behind, but broke off when he saw tracers whizzing by. Jones pulled up and away and ran into a Tony at 90 degrees; he fired as it passed in front of him. Jones' guns jammed and he had to dive away to gain speed, but saw the Tony crash below. He managed to get some guns working when three Zeros or Oscars bounced him. He turned into them and fired a long range almost head on. One of the enemy fighters blew up, so his cannons must have started working again. Jones had experienced problems with his supercharger throughout the fight, and it finally failed. He tried to return to base but ran into batches of enemy fighters and fired snap shots and ran away. He then joined a P-38 flying on one engine and escorted it to Goroka. Jones was unable to find Marilinan and landed at 30 Mile with two victories.

F/O Edwin DeGraffenreid began his combat after circling Wewak when Zeros and twin engine fighters dove on the first flight. DeGraffenreid was able to get a short burst on the last Zero's tail, causing it to break away. He saw an enemy twin engine fighter to port being fired on by P-38s. When this fighter approached he took a shot, scoring hits for a probable. DeGraffenreid pulled up and more Zeros came down. One overshot, and DeGraffenreid fired from 100 yards and it started to burn. DeGraffenreid pulled up and made another pass on the tail of a Zero that was on the tail of the last Lightning of the first flight. This Zero broke off before he could fire, but he saw four P-38s chasing a twin engine fighter and joined in and fired one burst that sent it down in flames. A Zero turned in front of DeGraffenreid making a pass at two P-38s. The Zero straightened out when DeGraffenreid began to fire and then turned right and straightened out again, giving a non-deflection shot at 100 yards that started the Zero on fire. Two P-38s made a pass on a Zero that made a slight dive after they passed, and DeGraffenreid then closed to 150 yards and fired. The Zero did a roll and its wing snapped off close to the fuselage. When he pulled up to go home a Zero came in from behind and hit his P-38 in the starboard engine, tail, and the back of the canopy. DeGraffenreid dove for the clouds and outran the enemy. His engine quit twice on the way back, but he nursed the Lightning and was able to crash land in Moresby Harbor. He got out of his sinking fighter and was picked up within 10 minutes. The three victories were DeGraffenreid's first of six during the war.

The 80th daily score was 12 Japanese aircraft destroyed, two probable, and two damaged, but three pilots were lost: 1Lt. John Guttel, 2Lt. Robert Feehan, and 1Lt. Elwood Krisher.

21 August 1943: 35FG/39FS

Maj. Thomas Lynch led 16 Lightnings on a morning sweep from But to Wewak. At 1000 Lynch saw four enemy fighters offshore at Dagua Strip at 7,000 feet. Lynch dropped his tanks and made a head on pass from below on an Oscar, getting hits on the engine. Lynch followed as the Oscar headed for cloud cover inland. He fired a long burst just 200 yards from the cloud, and the Oscar started to smoke and burn for his 14th victory. Lynch then made four or five passes on two Zeros and saw hits on one and claimed a damaged.

Maj. Thomas **Lynch** scored his 14th victory over an Oscar. (AAF)

Mid to Late August 1944: Air Situation

During the remainder of the month, the air offensive against the Japanese at Wewak continued as B-24s carried out 102 more sorties and B-25s an additional 21. These targets were seriously damaged, and other heavy strikes were carried out against important enemy supply centers at Hansa Bay and Alexishafen. From the first Wewak raid on 17 August until the end of the month, American flyers ran up an impressive score: B-25 gunners shot down 22 enemy aircraft, while two Mitchells were lost in combat and three from other causes. B-24 gunners claimed "at least" 35 enemy aircraft downed, while three B-24s were destroyed in combat and one in an accident. On examination, the bomber gunners' claims proved to be much too high. American fighters shot down 69 enemy aircraft, while six P-38s were lost in combat and three P-38s and four P-47s from other causes. The aerial claims, moreover, were small compared to the Allied claims of Japanese planes destroyed on the ground at Wewak. Well over 200 aircraft were originally claimed to be destroyed on the ground, but this figure was revised to 175, which was still impressive, as the largest monthly total in previous months was six.

23 August 1943: 8FG/80FS

On two subsequent missions to Wewak after the 21 August mission the squadron did not score. However, 1Lt. Leonidas Mathers was returning from a mission from Wewak on the 23rd when both his engines quit about 10 miles from Kila Strip. He tried to glide into the runway, but one of his wingtips caught a wave, cartwheeling the Lightning and killing him.

24 August 1943: 35FG/39FS

Over the next several days Japanese aerial resistance greatly subsided, but on the 24th the 39FS sent 16 P-38s to escort B-24s over Wewak. 1Lt. Harris Denton saw two Zeros approaching the bombers and saw one peel off to make a pass. The Zero then climbed to make another pass and Denton chased after it. When Denton closed the enemy pilot Split-S'd and Denton followed, getting a good burst at close range while the Zero was on its back. Denton continued firing, raking the fighter from nose to tail. Denton had to break away, but a B-24 crew witnessed the victory. 1Lt. Gene Duncan claimed a Zero damaged on the mission.

24 August 1943: 475FG/433FS

2Lt. Stanley Northrup had to leave his formation before the rendezvous point with the bombers when his electrical system and starboard supercharger went out and he turned back toward Dobodura. After about an hour he was attacked by five Zeros, so he dropped his tanks, dove from 12,000 to 8,000 feet, and hid in the clouds. Northrup decided that he would go to Marilinan or Bena Bena to refuel, but could not find either field and crossed the island, hoping to find another field on the other side. Once he crossed over the island Northrup still could not find a field and followed a river and landed wheels up in the water near a native village. The plane settled in four feet of water, leaving its wings, tail, and cockpit out of water. A fighter aircraft landing in the river near the village scared the natives away from rescuing him, and he swam ashore and headed toward their village. A few native men approached Northrup, and he explained in pidgin English that he wanted to be taken to the White Man's camp; he was taken to a sawmill run by the Australian Army. The sawmill boat had to be loaded with lumber in several days and would take him to Moresby, so in the meantime he went back up river to collect equipment off his Lightning and returned to the sawmill. Once the boat was loaded, Northrup went with it to Moresby and then was flown back to Dobodura.

29 August 1943: 35FG/39FS

Sixteen P-38s of the 39FS again escorted B-24s over Wewak. 1Lt. Andrew Kish and his Wingman, 1Lt. Harold Round, saw two token Hap interceptors at 24,000 feet. Kish closed on the nearest one, which turned to the left, and Round took the farthest, which turned before he could get into range and the Flight scattered. After a time Round joined a lone P-38 which happened to be Kish, and they saw six or eight B-24s at 17-18,000 feet, with the straggling Liberator being attacked by the (same?) two Haps. Each Lightning pilot chose a Hap, which separated left and right. Kish went after the left one and got solid hits on its left wing root and canopy, and the Hap was seen to crash. Rounds closed to 100 yards on his Hap, but his guns malfunctioned and the Hap dove away. Rounds turned to recharge his guns and still hadn't recharged them when his Hap returned and began to head for Rounds, but the helpless Rounds turned into the Hap which, fortunately, broke off, not knowing he had missed an easy victory.

After the initial combats by other flights, 1Lt. John Lane's Flight, led by Maj. Thomas Lynch, did not participate, but continued to provide cover for the B-24s. After a while Lane looked down, and about 10 Zeros and Oscars were climbing to attack the bombers. The P-38s dove into the attack directly over Boram Airfield, and a swirling dogfight developed. Lane saw an Oscar pull up toward Lynch and cut it off with a direct tail attack, and his long burst exploded the Oscar. Oil spewed back from the Oscar and smeared Lanes' windshield, obscuring his vision. Lane joined Lynch, and an Oscar turned directly in front of him. Lane fired and got damaging hits on its wing. Lynch led Lane back to base, where he landed safely with his sixth and last victory of the war.

The two victories by Lane and Kish were supplemented by probables claimed by Kish and 1Lts. Benjamin Widman and Harris Denton, as well as damaged claims by Lane, Denton, and 1Lt. Leland Vining.

29 August 1943: 475FG/432FS/432FS

431FS

On the Group's last mission in August, 16 Lightnings took off from Berry (12 Mile) at 0830 led by Maj. Meryl Smith and flew at 17,000 feet on a medium altitude escort of B-24s back to Wewak. 1Lt. Thomas McGuire was leading a Blue Flight of three P-38s, as his Wingman aborted after take off, leaving him with 1Lt. Harold Holze and 2Lt. Edward Hedrick. The trio was flying at 17,000 feet at 1050 when they saw two Japanese single engine fighters attacking the Liberators at about 1,000 feet low. Blue Flight dropped their tanks, but the Zeros saw them and dove away. The lead Zero pulled up to expose itself long enough for McGuire to set it on fire. McGuire lost his wingmen but, nonetheless, chased after a Tony heading for the bombers, and the Tony turned to face McGuire head on, firing and missing. McGuire quickly turned around to get a good rear deflection burst that set the Japanese fighter spiraling down in flames for his second victory of the day. While climbing to gain more altitude, McGuire saw three Zeros and a Tony on his tail. McGuire put his P-38 into a screaming dive, but his fighter was hit in the port engine with an explosive shell that set it on fire. With the Tonys still behind, he shut down the burning engine and let the windmilling prop put out the fire at 9,000 feet. Two Tonys continued to follow, but the heavier Lightning reached the clouds at 4,000 feet first. McGuire made a single engine landing at Marilinan, but his fighter was written off and he returned to base

1Lt. Andrew **Kish**. (L) with 2Lt. Robert Baker scored his third and last victory. (AAF)

1Lt. Thomas **McGuire** shot down two Zeros to give him nine victories. (AAF)

aboard a transport the next day. After McGuire lost Holze and Hedrick they continued on. Hedrick called out an enemy aircraft at 10 o'clock, but the enemy pilot saw the P-38s and climbed into a thin cloud layer at 15,000 feet. Holze fired a few short bursts before the Zero went into a vertical dive with heavy smoke pouring from its engine, and it exploded as it entered low clouds. The two were then attacked by two Zeros and only lost them after a prolonged dive, after which they climbed to resume their escort of the bombers.

432FS

During the combat, the 432FS' Flights broke into a few enemy attacks and then quickly returned to their close bomber cover assignment. Capt. Daniel Roberts, Red Flight Leader, fired on a Tony without result.

29 August 1943: 8FG/80FS

On 29 August, 12 P-38s took off on a medium cover escort for B-24s, but returned 30 minutes later because of deteriorating weather. Meanwhile, 1Lt. Robert Adams and 2Lt. Albon Hailey took off late and continued on toward the target, unaware that the escort mission had been scrubbed. They continued on to Wewak and Boram to help to escort the bombers with fighters from other squadrons. At 1050 Adams and Hailey were flying with the bombers over Wewak at 18,000 feet when Hailey spotted Japanese fighters five to 10 miles out to sea. The two turned inland to cover the 11 B-24s about to make their bombing run. As the bombers were completing their run a lone Zero circled behind the bombers and was immediately chased by Hailey and Adams from 19,000 to 14,000 feet. Hailey fired a long burst from 300 yards and the enemy pilot slowly climbed to port, and Hailey fired again as the Japanese pilot veered to the right. Adams became separated from Hailey and fired at single and paired Zeros, but got observable hits on only one, which went into a flaming vertical dive. He then got behind a Nick whose rear gunner fired, but Adams' first burst silenced the rear gun position, and his next burst set the starboard engine on fire; the Nick plunged through the cloud layer to make Adams an ace. Hailey saw another enemy diving and pulling up sharply but had to break away, as a Zero had closed to 300 yards on his tail. When Adams and Hailey looked around they saw 10 to 15 more enemy aircraft approaching and wisely headed home.

31 August 1943: 475FG/432FS Moves to Dobodura

On 31 August, the first detachment of four flights of 19 432FS Lightnings flew from Port Moresby to Dobodura. Capt. Daniel Roberts led the first flight; 1Lt. Frederick Harris led the second flight; Capt. William Waldman the third; and 1Lt. John Loisel flew in with the last flight of three fighters.

431FG. (L-R):Harry **Brown**. (5v), John **Hood**. (3v), Frank **Nichols**. (5v), and William **Haning**. (2v). (AAF)

1Lt. Robert **Adams** scored his last victory to become an ace. (AAF)

9

September 1943

Air, Sea, and Ground Situation

By the end of August, therefore, Allied operations by air, land, and sea were approaching a zenith. Enemy aircraft that had not been destroyed on the ground had been shot down in the air, and the airfields in the Wewak area were nearly inoperable. Allied land forces were overcoming strong Japanese defenses and were ready for a final push into Salamaua. The Seventh Amphibious Force, commanded by V.Adm. Daniel Barbey, was prepared for action, and several of its destroyers had already sortied into the Huon Gulf to bombard a number of enemy shore positions there. The Allied Air Forces during July and August had increased their effort to such an extent that in the latter month they had more than tripled the number of sorties carried out in June, and in so doing had softened up enemy land positions and virtually eradicated the threat of Japanese air power from New Guinea. The Allies now had the upper hand, and Japanese-held Northern New Guinea lay open to attack.

Actually, the Allied offensive was not aimed at the initial capture of Salamaua, as the *Elkton Plan* originally envisaged an airborne force operating overland through the Markham River Valley in conjunction with a shore-to-shore over water movement leading to the capture of Lae. In this scheme of operations Salamaua was to be bypassed. As the slow campaign from Wau, Morobe, and Nassau Bay toward Salamaua developed, however, original plans were modified. By the middle of August, it had been decided that MacArthur's Seventh Amphibious Force should land the 9th Australian Division east of Lae, and that the major drive should then commence against Lae itself, with a subsidiary drive striking east toward Hopoi Mission and Finschhafen. Meanwhile, American paratroops were to land at Nadzab, a flat, grass-covered area suitable for transport landings on the Markham River 15 miles inland. When the paratroops had secured this area, troop carrier units were to ferry in the 7th Australian Division for a second drive on Lae.

Final tactical decisions were made at the Milne Bay Headquarters, some only shortly before the actual embarkation of the amphibious force. In general, the preliminary plans were satisfactory to all concerned, but there were a number of minor disagreements between representatives of the Navy and of the Fifth Air Force. For example, there were differences of opinion as to the method of providing air protection for the convoy and as to the need for pre-invasion strafing. Senior Officers of ADVON were at Milne Bay on several occasions to discuss these and other problems, but according to the official Navy report did not have sufficient authority and were slow in making definite decisions.

The final plan was not approved until shortly before D-Day. On the subject of air escort, ADVON initially favored convoy protection by fighters on ground alert, but was willing to compromise with the faction that preferred an "air umbrella." Ultimately it was decided to provide a cover of 32 fighters as continuously as possible by day, in addition to squadrons on constant ground alert. The solution to the difficult problem of whether or not to provide pre-invasion air and naval bombardment was also a compromise. The Army wanted to approach in darkness, with the actual landing taking place at 0515, approximately one hour before sunrise, with no air or naval bombardment. The Navy, on the other hand, insisted that because of inadequate means of beach identification H-hour would have to be after sunrise, and set it for 0620. Since this eliminated the possibility of tactical surprise, a naval bombardment and air strafing attacks on shore positions were considered desirable. However, strafers of the Fifth Air Force would be unable to reach the objective much before 0700, and so it was decided to use only bombardment by five destroyers and to forego the benefits of strafing.

Although decisions had been made on general tactical problems, several details for implementing them still remained. For example, the determination to provide a continuous air umbrella over the convoy did not specify how fighters maintained on ground alert would be coordinated with those participating in the escort. There were two fighter control sectors on the north coast of New Guinea, one at Dobodura and the other at Tsili Tsili. But the radar coverage of the waters through which the convoy was to proceed was incomplete. Ground radar sets were located in the Dobodura area and at Cape Ward Hunt, Morobe, Bulolo, Tsili Tsili, and Bena Bena. At this time, however, the set at Morobe was inoperative, and the high mountains limited the range of the others. The set at Cape Ward Hunt gave some sea coverage but did not reach Lae; consequently, Japanese aircraft from Wewak or Madang could fly behind the mountains toward Lae; others from New Britain could swing across Vitiaz Strait; and neither could be picked up until it was too late for the available radar to provide adequate warning.

A more effective means of providing warning and fighter control was necessary. A suggestion from an Australian Wing Commander furnished an innovative solution to the problem. He suggested that a destroyer, posted between Lae and Finschhafen, might serve as a floating radar station and provide far better coverage of the approaches to the beachheads than any available ground station. The destroyer *Reid*, which was serving part of the antisubmarine patrol from Buna to Lae, was ordered to proceed to a point approximately 45 miles southeast of Finschhafen for this purpose.

The fighter control network thus became a rather complicated one. On the destroyer were two controllers and two signal corps enlisted men equipped with radar and radio sets, two loudspeakers, two voice receivers, two voice transmitters, and two SCR-188 receivers. With this equipment the controllers were in position to monitor the normal radio channels of the fighter sectors, including the one which transmitted information to Port Moresby. In this way, they would be warned of the approach of aircraft picked up by radar sets in addition to those on the destroyer. Then, using grease pencils, they could record all suspicious plots on gridded maps covered with Plexiglas. In addition to the control party on the destroyer and the control squadrons at the various sectors, the 5th Tactical Air Communications Squadron furnished several parties to serve as air liaison units with the landing forces.

1 September 1943: 475FG/433FS Moves to Dobodura

The 433FS moved to Dobodura on 1 September, just after the 43rd Engineers completed their strip. HQ sent several 433FS flights on an escort to Cape Gloucester that same day. Eight P-38s led by Capt. Donald Byars of the 432FS escorted the so-called "Bully Beef Bombers."

2 September 1943: Lae/Nazab Invasion Preparations

The August annihilation of the Japanese air forces in the area gave the Allies air superiority, and by the end of August the airfields at Port Moresby, Milne Bay, and Dobodura based the largest aerial armada in the SWPA to date, as more than 300 aircraft were available to support the seaborne amphibious assault on Lae and for the airdrop at Nadzab. The Fifth Air Force struck enemy airdromes and coastal installations throughout the Huon Peninsula area on a daily basis, which left the Japanese guessing to where MacArthur's invasion force might land.

Fifth Air Force bombers and fighters continued to apply pressure on the Japanese air bases at Wewak, Madang, and Cape Gloucester, on the island of New Britain. Heavy bombers opened September with attacks on barges, fuel dumps, and other supply points along the southwestern coast of New Britain, as well as on fuel and ammunition dumps at Alexishafen and Madang. Low level B-25 strafers continued heavy attacks on the Wewak air and naval complex as they swept over shipping and airfields, attacking from 50 to 150 feet under a cover of P-38s. The Fighter Groups at Dobodura were on hand to escort the large number of transports that flew endless supply runs to support the invasion. So, as the amphibious force gathered off Buna, the fighters of the 5th Fighter Command continued to put pressure on the enemy in the air.

2 September 1943: 8FG/80FS

Twelve P-38s of the 80FS returned to Wewak at 1000 on a fighter sweep 10 minutes before a B-25 attack. As the 80th came in over the target they received a call from the P-38s of the 39th Squadron that they were in a battle with enemy fighters. Capt. George Welch led his 80FS Lightnings down to the attack and immediately made an unsuccessful pass on a Zeke. He then made a stern attack on two Zekes flying in close formation and "walked the rudder" on one and got hits on the other. The Zeke on his right half rolled off, and when the Zeke on the left also rolled in that direction, the two collided and went down together. Welch then made an expert 90 degree deflection shot that sent another Zeke burning into the Bay. On his way back to Moresby Welch spotted a Dinah twin engine bomber near Madang, but all his guns malfunctioned but one and the Dinah got away, despite Welch's several under-gunned attacks. Welch got two guns to work and, spotting another Dinah nearby, he put a long burst into the cockpit and watched it roll off and crash into the mountains north of Madang for his fourth victory of the day and his 16th and last of the war. Welch was the second ranking ace in the 5th Fighter Command, actually tying Dick Bong, who scored his 16th victory in July.

2Lt. Kenneth Ladd was flying on the wing of 1Lt. Mark Kaspar and was the tail end Charlie of the entire formation. During the mission Kaspar left the formation with engine trouble and Ladd followed him, but after 10 miles Kaspar corrected the problem and the two returned to the combat area. After circling the area twice they decided to return to base. About 20 miles from Madang they saw two P-38s (Welch and his Wingman) diving on an enemy aircraft and followed. The two Lightnings fired on the enemy, identified as a Dinah, but it flew on into a small cloud and Ladd followed it over the top of the cloud and fired on it as it emerged, setting it on fire into the mountains.

Five victory ace, 1Lt. Robert **Adams**. (left with John Jones and Jesse Gidley), was KIA. (AFAA)

With is 16th and last victory Capt. George **Welch** was the second ranking ace in the 5th Fighter Command, actually tying Dick Bong who had scored his 16th victory in July and none since. (AAF)

2Lt. Kenneth **Ladd** was given credit for destroying a **Dinah** for his second victory. (AAF)

F/O Edwin DeGraffenreid, 1Lt. Howard Peterson's Wingman in Welch's second element, dove with Welch and scored hits on a Zero and it exploded. A Zero then came in between Welch and DeGraffenreid, and the Flying Officer went into a steep turn and fired. The Japanese pilot half rolled and Split-S'd, while another pulled up and rolled onto Welch's tail. DeGraffenreid fired a burst, and the enemy pilot pulled up and over him and got away. On the way back to base he saw two Dinahs at 18,000 feet just west of Madang. Welch and DeGraffenreid made passes until Welch's guns jammed, and then closed in and scored hit after hit, but were unable to finish it off. DeGraffenreid pulled up and the Dinah went into a cloud, then Ladd finished it off.

After this mission 1Lt. Robert Adams, a five victory ace, left the bomber escort to attack a lone enemy aircraft, and his fellow pilots later heard a radio call that a pilot, probably Adams, was going to try a crash landing near the Fly River. Adams was never found.

After flying three combat tours, Welch's four victories were his last of 16 during the war, and he returned to the US in September 1943. In 1944 he was hired by North American Aviation as its Chief Test Pilot and flew the first P-82B Twin Mustang on 31 October 1945 and the E Model on 17 April 1947. Welch is probably best known for testing the F-86 Sabre, and flew its first flight on 1 October 1947. On 14 October Welch disregarded direct orders not to attempt to break the sound barrier before the expensive X-1 project and put the F-86 in a steep dive, and reportedly (and definitely, unofficially) broke the sound barrier only minutes before Chuck Yeager did so in the X-1. There was a sonic boom, but since the F-86 was not officially tracked Welch would not receive official recognition for his feat. During the Korean War, as Chief Test Pilot, engineer, and instructor for North American he reportedly downed several enemy MiG-15s while "supervising' his students. However, Welch's kills were in defiance of direct orders for him not to engage the enemy, so the credits for the kills were supposedly given to his students. After the war, Welch became the first man to break the sound barrier in level flight in the F-100A-1-NA Super Sabre on 25 May 1953. However, this aircraft had stability problems, and on 12 October 1954, Welch's Super Sabre disintegrated during a 7 G pullout at Mach 1.55. He is buried in Arlington National Cemetery.

2 September 1943: 475FG/433FS

Fifteen P-38s of the 433FS, led by Capt. Herbert Jordan, were assigned to rendezvous with the B-25s over Lae at 1010 and then fly toward the often attacked Wewak. The flight to Wewak was uneventful, but on their arrival they found the Wewak area partially hidden under low overcast, though the airstrip target was clear. The 433rd was flying high cover at about 10,000 feet, while the B-25 strafers were on deck attacking the Wewak Airstrip. The Squadron was alerted to Japanese fighters by B-25 radio calls that told of enemy fighters approaching from the sea.

Jordan ordered fuel tanks to be dropped and led his flight into combat. Former RCAF flyer 2Lt. Calvin "Bud" Wire was in the #4 position of Jordan's flight and saw a Zero at about 4,000 feet approaching Jordan's fighter from port. Wire turned quickly and snapped off a shot that caused the enemy pilot to break off his attack on Jordan. Soon four more Zeros dove on Wire, two under him and two behind him. The two Zeros were closing in on Wire's tail, and he tried to catch up with Jordan, who was several hundred yards ahead. Wire radioed Jordan to break to port with him, but apparently he did not hear him. Wire looked around and discovered that there were two more enemy fighters above him, and they rolled over in a Split-S dive on him. With the Zeros still firing on his tail, Wire frantically turned in and up into the Zeros before they could complete their Split-S roll. Wire shocked the Japanese pilots with this maneuver and he got a good shot at the lead Zero, which spiraled toward the Bay, trailing heavy smoke for a damaged claim. The other Zero broke off his attack on Wire and dove away. Wire now had three Zeros on his tail, but Jordan approached them and drove one off. Wire dove on one that was coming up from under and shot off large pieces for his first victory. While these enemy fighters headed toward the Bay two other Zeros then came after Wire. But one crossed too closely in front of him for an easy shot that hit the enemy's engine, but it disappeared behind him and he did not pursue for a probable claim. Wire climbed and rejoined as Jordan's wing, and the two headed toward an enemy transport ship in the harbor. When they ran into heavy AA fire they turned away to rejoin the Mitchells that had finished their attack and followed them home. 2Lt. Ralph Cleague claimed a Zero probable with a beam attack with no deflection that caused it to smoke as it got away. Cleague had a scare when he became separated from his flight and a Zero got on his tail. He dove to escape, but the enemy pilot continued to pursue for 15 minutes before turning around.

2Lt. John Smith was flying the #4 position in 1Lt. William Horton's Possum Blue Flight at 5,000 feet. He shot down a Zero and then claimed a Dinah probable. While covering the B-25s on their strafing runs about 25 enemy fighters approached from the sea and dove on the B-25s, so Blue Flight dove to attack. Smith made a quick head on pass at an Oscar that was attacking one of his flight's P-38s and then chased off a Zero that was on Capt. Joseph McKeon's tail. As the Zero pulled up over McKeon and turned to starboard Smith fired a 60 degree deflection shot that exploded the Zero. As the combat moved south of Wewak, Smith damaged the Dinah for a probable claim. With his ammunition almost gone he headed for home, but when he looked at his compass he found it was malfunctioning. He then found he had no maps of the area, but Bena Bena radioed him a fix on Dobodura. While over Lake Katabu Smith was able to contact Jordan, telling him that he was headed for Marilinan. Smith descended under the cloud cover to 3,000 feet and followed the coast. However, he was worried that he was headed toward Japanese held Finschhafen and made a 90 degree turn toward friendly territory, but after a while he became completely lost. Finally, as he was almost out of fuel, he radioed Bena Bena, describing the surrounding terrain below, and notified them that he intended to crash land. He flew back and forth, looking for the best place to land, and after firmly fastening his safety belts and cutting his switches he shielded his head with his arm and skidded to a safe stop. After destroying his radio and IFF sets, he unsuccessfully tried to remove the gun camera film to prove his Zero victory. He made a bag from his parachute to carry his gear and, not knowing whether he was in friendly or enemy territory, he headed off for two days until he reached a river, where he built a raft. During the first night, as he slept on shore, his raft and pouch were taken by the tide, and for the next seven days he walked along the river bank until he reached the Gulf of Papua. Finally, on the ninth day and in deteriorating physical condition he was found by a native who paddled him to an island, where he was given food and medical treatment. After a few days he was able to walk, and was paddled for 36 hours to Siabai Island, where

In this combat 2Lt. Calvin **Wire** had a mixed bag of claims; a damaged, a probable, and his first victory. (AAF)

two Australian radio operators were located. The Australians radioed for a PBY, which picked him up on 15 September and flew him to Port Moresby, and after six days in the hospital he was returned to Dobodura.

2 September 1943: 49FG/9FGS

On 2 September, Capt. Gerald Johnson led his first successful mission as 9FS CO. His 15 P-38s were part of the escort for the 22BG Marauders and 43BG Fortresses that were to bomb the enemy installations at Cape Gloucester. After taking off at sunrise from Horanda they rendezvoused with the bomber force, and at 0930 the American formation arrived over New Britain, where the B-26 attacked freighters off the Cape at a lower altitude, while the B-17s bombed the Gloucester airdrome from 8,000 feet, just above the scattered cloud deck.

Johnson positioned the Knights in a stacked formation from 7,000 through 15,000 feet to cover as wide an area as possible. Johnson's Blue Flight of wingmen, 1Lts. Grover Fanning and Theron Price, circled just over the shoreline at 7,000, while directly overhead was Yellow Flight, led by 1Lt. Peter Alger, flying top cover. For several minutes the Lightnings orbited directly over the Fortresses, who had encountered ineffective scattered flak reaching up to 10,000 feet. As their bombing run ended and the B-17s turned out to sea, they reported they were under attack by a twin engine fighter just north of the target area. Of all the elements in the vicinity, only Blue Leader Johnson and his two wingmen saw the intruder, which closed in on a B-17 that became separated. Johnson identified the enemy as a Dinah, but it was in fact the new Kawasaki Ki-45 twin radial engine Nick fighter. The Nick was somewhat smaller than a P-38 but was heavily armed, carrying a 20mm nose cannon, a forward firing 37mm ventral cannon, and a rear gunner with a hand held 7mm defensive machine gun.

Johnson rolled his Lightning into a 400mph dive and overtook the Nick as it maneuvered to the right and dove for the clouds. Johnson's accurate burst shattered the enemy's canopy and tore off pieces of its fuselage. Johnson pulled up sharply but lost the target as Price moved into firing position. Price, moving at a high speed, snapped a burst at the Ki-45, which continued to dive away to the right. Price turned hard about to attack again, only to cross directly behind a second Nick hunting for the American bombers. Immediately overhead, Yellow Flight Leader Peter Alger and Wingman 2Lt. Francis Love approached and would be the only high cover elements to see the same intruder. Price and Johnson put their P-38s through a tight turn for the second Nick, and Price fired first and set the port engine on fire. Price peeled out of the way as Capt. Johnson snapped off a short accurate burst and then quickly broke off as Yellow Flight attacked. Alger fired from above and behind, then Love made a run at a high degree of deflection, and then Alger fired again. Alger broke away just as Fanning approached from dead astern. Love turned toward the battered Nick from above for the last time, just as Grover Fanning closed in from below for the kill. Concentrating on their target, but not yet seeing each other, Love and Fanning simultaneously hit the twin engine interceptor until it fell into the Bay not far from the airdrome. Love turned away to regroup with Yellow Flight, while Fanning cut his speed and descended to observe his fifth victory. As new ace Fanning flew over his burning Nick a third Nick tried to sneak up on Fanning, but he saw the Nick and turned away. The Nick followed, and Fanning wheeled around and quickly closed and opened fire at point blank range. Fanning fired the last of his ammo until only one .50 caliber gun fired and saw the Nick on the end of the runway exploding into a fireball.

Meanwhile, Price and Johnson had descended for a final patrol over the shoreline, where they overtook their first damaged Nick, thinking it was a fourth interceptor. Price and Johnson each fired at it, and it glided into the overcast, lying against the inland foothills and vanishing, so Johnson confirmed it destroyed by Price. After one last survey of the target area Johnson recalled the Lightnings, and they regrouped out over the Gulf for a safe return to Horanda strip.

In the confused mission debriefing, the targets hit by Johnson, Love, and Price, regardless of redundancy, were judged to be three individual kills. Price was also awarded a probable, while Fanning was credited with his two kills and his ace status was confirmed. Despite how many enemy

Top Left:
1Lt. Grover **Fanning** was the 9FS day's high scorer with two victories which gave him six to become an ace. (AFAA)

Top Right:
Capt. Gerald **Johnson** shot down a Tony for his third victory. (AAF)

The newly arrived in the theater, **Ki-45 Nick** was heavily armed, carrying a 20mm nose cannon, a forward firing 37mm ventral cannon, and a rear gunner with a hand held 7mm defensive machine gun. (AAF)

fighters had actually been over the target that day, the 49ers would not see another Nick in the air until the Philippines campaign a full year later.

2 September 1943: 35FG/39FS

At 0950, 12 P-38s of the 39FS were on a fighter sweep to Wewak when they were attacked by at least 30 enemy fighters from every height and direction. Capt. Paul Stanch took a quick deflection shot on a "ME-109" without result and then left the battle, where he was outnumbered. About 10 minutes after he saw a twin engine fighter 300 yards to port and headed 180 degrees. Stanch made a 180 degree turn and chased it. The enemy pilot made three short dives and climbs, and each time the P-38 gained on it. The enemy pilot then started a shallow dive from 5,000 feet toward a cloud and Stanch fired from 300 yards until it entered the cloud. Stanch raced to the other side of the cloud to catch the enemy plane. When it came out of the bottom of the cloud Stanch was ready, but the plane was already so low that it crashed into the ground.

3 September 1943

While the largest Allied amphibious force yet assembled in the Southwest Pacific was congregating off Buna on 3 September, 5th BC heavy bombers continued their attacks on Gasmata, Bergen Bay, Lae, and Gape Gloucester. During the attacks on Rabaul the surrounding airfields were bombed with 500 and 1,000 pound demolition bombs and 20 pound parafrag in an attempt to keep enemy interceptors on the ground. The 5FC made no claims this day.

4 September 1943: Lae Invasion

In the early morning of 4 September the Allied amphibious force neared Lae. Shortly after 0500, the destroyer *Reid* moved off Finschhafen to take its position as an aircraft warning lookout. By 0550 the beaches–*Red Beach*, about 14 miles east of Lae near the Buso River, and *Yellow Beach*, three miles east of *Red Beach*–had been targeted. At 0615, five USN destroyers protected by heavy fighter cover began to fire hundreds of rounds into the small beach area. Thirty minutes before the first wave of landing craft had reached the shore, Allied aircraft took off from fields at Tsili Tsili, Dobodura, and Port Moresby to participate in the operation. By 0630 the first Australians reached the shore. A few minutes later the first fighter formations (16 P-39s from Tsili Tsili followed by 14 P-38s of the Dobodura-based 433rd Squadron) approached the landing area. At 0705, the air liaison party preparing to land the fifth wave identified what they thought were three Allied twin engine bombers as they dived out of a cloud. Suddenly the approaching bombers, now identified as Vals escorted by six Zeros, turned toward the landing craft and strafed and dropped bombs. After near misses on invasion shipping that killed three and wounded nine, the enemy attackers were driven off by the P-38s. At 0830, Lt.Col. George Prentice (475FG/HQ) shot down a Zeke for the only victory over the beaches.

Approximately an hour later, while landing craft shuttled from the transports to the beaches and back carrying men and supplies, another force of 5th Fighter Command aircraft escorted B-25 and B-26 medium bombers to attack the Japanese targets near the landing beaches; gun emplacements, buildings, and vehicles on the Lae airdrome; barge hideouts and airfields near southern New Britain; and the Gasmata airdrome and targets in the Cape Gloucester area.

Meanwhile, the landing continued according to plan, and by early afternoon the convoy was preparing to withdraw, as 7,800 men and sufficient vehicles, guns, and stores were landed to maintain the beachhead. Except for the early morning attack there had been little enemy air intrusion, although about 20 Japanese aircraft had dropped bombs sporadically around corvettes and destroyers along the coast.

Less than an hour after the convoy's departure, the Fighter Controller on the *Reid* began to monitor an ominous number of plots from New Britain, closing on the beachhead from a point southwest of Gasmata and about 100 miles away. However, at least three American Squadrons (the 341st equipped with P-47s, the 35th with P-40Ns, and the 39th with P-38s) had been patrolling the Lae-Finschhafen area for several hours. These fighters were scheduled for relief, but they had sufficient fuel remaining for possibly another hour of combat flying. The 9th and the 432nd relieving

The 5FC escorted B-25 and B-26 medium bombers to attack the Japanese targets near the landing beaches and on the Lae airdrome. (shown on right). (AAF)

squadrons had left their bases before noon for their scheduled patrol and would provide at least five fighter squadrons for interception.

At this time, the Fighter Controller on the destroyer *Reid* did not know the exact position of the American fighters in the area. He did know, however, that one squadron was escorting landing craft already returning to Buna, and that another was covering the land forces at Lae. Every fighter pilot carried a grid map of the area and was constantly tuned in to the radio frequency of his Fighter Controller. Thus, by sending the grid reference of the bogies over the fighter frequencies every minute to the fighter sectors at Dobodura and Tsili Tsili, the *Reid* could trace the course of the incoming enemy, and this information could be plotted by each fighter pilot. The *Reid* Fighter Controller continued to watch his radar scope and saw a large formation of aircraft until it appeared that the enemy aircraft would soon be close enough to observe visually. He then stepped out on the *Reid's* deck and saw about 60 enemy bombers. The destroyer was without fighter cover, and would have been an easy target, but for an unexplained reason the enemy formation turned and headed for Morobe. The radio operators on the *Reid*, meanwhile, were sending enemy radar plots to the fighter sectors. The Controller at Dobodura ordered the 433rd Squadron, still on ground alert, to join the 80th, which then was patrolling the Lae area. At the same time the 39th Squadron, which had moved from Schwimmer Airdrome to Tsili Tsili for the Lae operation, was scrambled, and the squadrons of the 348th Group took off from Wards Drone.

However, the American fighters could not prevent enemy bombers from causing substantial damage to the shipping off Lae. Four destroyers were damaged and two LSTs were hit, causing a high toll of killed and wounded. At the time of the raid troops and supplies were packed on the beach, and had Japanese bombs struck there, instead of the shipping, greater damage could have been caused. Three hours later, after the congestion on the beach had been somewhat alleviated, an attack by an indeterminate number of Japanese bombers hit an ammunition dump, killed two men, wounded 10 others, and damaged two beached LCIs. The destroyer's antiaircraft, meanwhile, shot down nine of 10 torpedo planes which had attacked at such a low altitude that the radar had failed to detect them. The Allied convoy escaped damage in this attack, and out of three P-38s shot down at least one pilot was saved.

4 September 1943: 475FG/432FS/433FS

432FS

At 0745, 16 P-38s took off to patrol Lae as medium cover for the landings. The Squadron arrived at 0830 and patrolled from 8,000 to 12,000 feet. Lt.Col. George Prentice was leading #4 Green Flight when he spotted a lone bogie flying low east of Hopoi. He flew to investigate and found it to be a Japanese Navy Zero, apparently on recon. Green Flight dropped its tanks and chased the enemy down to tree top level near the mountains. Prentice made three or four passes on the Japanese pilot, who expertly maneuvered his fighter before Prentice finally hit it sufficiently to bring it down. During the combat Prentice's Wingman, 2Lt. Richard Ryrholm, was seen descending with his right engine smoking, and he did not return from the mission and was listed as MIA. The reason for Ryrholm's death seems to be the collision of his fighter with Prentice's jettisoned drop tanks.

LEFT: At 0830 Lt.Col. George **Prentice**. (475FG/HQ) shot down a Zeke for the only victory over the beaches for his third and last victory. (AAF) RIGHT: Capt. Joseph **McKeon** got his second victory. (AFAA)

During the Lae landings 5FC fighters could not prevent enemy bombers from causing substantial damage to the shipping off Lae. Four destroyers were damaged and two LSTs were hit causing a high toll of killed and wounded. (AAF)

433FS
After an uneventful routine morning airbase patrol, that afternoon the 433FS, led by Capt. Herbert Jordan, was scrambled by the *Charter* Air Controller at 1330 to intercept enemy aircraft over Huon Gulf, approaching destroyers and landing barges near Lae. 1Lt. William Jeakle had to abort when his canopy blew off at take off, leaving 14 P-38s in three flights (Red, White, and Blue). At 1400 the Squadron was at 17,000 feet, when they spotted 12 Betty bombers and 25 single seat fighters 25 miles southeast of Salamaua at 9,000 feet. Red Flight Leader Jordon let down parallel to the enemy formation, and as he did the enemy fighters crossed and began to climb between the Americans and their bombers. Jordon thought that the bombers would make a level attack on three destroyers steaming in line astern heading south. As the bombers closed on the destroyers Jordan realized he wasn't closing fast enough and went into a steep 10 o'clock pass, with his Wingman, F/O Kenneth Kirshner, following, hoping the bombers would turn or break up. As Jordan closed on the bombers the lead Zero fired a 90 degree deflection shot on him but missed. Jordan and Kirshner missed on their first pass on the bombers and came in for their second pass. When two Zeros dove on them Kirshner chased them off. The enemy bombers turned to port and skidded in fairly tight formation, but were still short of their target when Jordan and Kirshner approached and made their second and third passes. Kirshner fired at one from dead astern and set its engine on fire, then turned to regain altitude. As he approached the Bettys again he saw the same Betty he had just hit and finished it off with a no deflection hit that exploded it. Jordan was unsuccessful in his passes, but the Betty formation loosened and was stringing out. Jordan followed through the bomber formation, firing as he closed to 50 yards on each bomber. As the bombers reached the Allied barges he fired on the lead bomber and then made a 180° turn to try to get on the tail of the last bombers. As he closed from above and astern, the top turret gunner hit Jordan's fighter but did no apparent damage. Jordan then came down and fired on it and saw it go down. As Jordan turned and took a 10 degree deflection shot on another bomber he noticed that his right engine was losing coolant, and as the engine's temperature rose he feathered it and turned for home.

Capt. Clarence Wilmarth was leading White Flight, and remained above Jordan's Red Flight as top cover when they went in to attack the bombers. Soon the escorts came in to attack Red Flight and Wilmarth led White into the attack. On the way down he lost his Wingman and was joined by Element Leader 1Lt. John Parkansky, who also lost his Wingman. Immediately two Oscars made a diving front quarter attack on them, crossing directly in front and then turning 90 degrees to their left. Parkansky pulled up and fired a two second burst at the enemy leader from 100 to 50 yards at less than 30 degrees and exploded its engine. As Parkansky caught up with Wilmarth they were attacked by two diving Oscars nearly head on. Parkansky aimed at the closest one, but his guns jammed as the enemy's tracers whizzed by, and he broke off and left the battle.

Blue Flight Leader Capt. Joseph McKeon was at 15,000 feet, 25 miles west of Salamaua and far behind Red and White Flights over Natter Bay, south of Lae. Looking down, McKeon saw Red and White Flights attacking the bombers and dove, and as he approached the area he saw a number of Japanese fighters below and led his wingmen, 2Lt. Walter Reinhardt, into the attack. McKeon made a head on pass on an Oscar which turned into him, but the Lightning's superior firepower immediately hit the Oscar hard, and it went into a steep burning dive into the water. Both McKeon and Reinhardt climbed and then dove back into the swirling battle. Both fired brief bursts at fleeting targets before they were forced to break away. The air battle continued for about 15 to 20 minutes until the Japanese broke off. McKeon's other Wingman, 2Lt. Dale Meyer, lost his Flight Leader and joined three other P-38s. He saw a Zero approach and fired a five second burst at 200 yards and 30 degrees, then saw it "sort of half roll" and head straight down, but when Meyer pulled up he lost sight of it for a probably destroyed.

Maj. Thomas **Lynch** scored two victories to make him a triple ace with 15 and his last victory with the 39FS. (AAF)

4 September 1943: 35FG/39FS
The 39FS scrambled 18 P-38s to the Huon Gulf area led by Maj. Thomas Lynch. At 1400, the Element Leader of Lynch's flight called out a single bandit heading northwest at 20,000 feet near Finschhafen. Lynch dove and closed to 150 yards and fired until the enemy plane (a dive bomber) exploded and plunged into the sea, with the pilot bailing out and landing near a destroyer below. Lynch then saw six to eight Zeros at 3 o'clock low and turned into a head on attack, getting hits, but Lynch saw tracers pass his cockpit coming from behind and "kicked rudder and took off." Later Lynch, with Wingman 1Lt. Hamilton Salmon, attacked Oscars. Lynch fired from astern and got some hits before the Oscar pilot pulled up in a loop and he lost him. Salmon followed his Leader but did not fire on the dive bomber. A few minutes later an enemy fighter dove toward the two P-38s and they turned into them. Salmon opened fire at 350 yards and held the trigger down until 75 yards. The Oscar's engine caught on fire and the wounded fighter passed directly over Salmon and exploded, but the pilot was able to bail out. Salmon was attacked from behind, but broke away safely and rejoined Lynch. Salmon made an attack on the Oscars with Lynch, but they missed on this attack. 1Lt. Harvey Clymer and 2Lt. Ralph Bills damaged a Zero and an Oscar, respectively. The victory was Lynch's 15th to make him a triple ace, and would be his last with the 39FS, as he shipped home on leave.

4 September 1943: 8FG/80FS
In September, during the Huon Gulf Campaign, the 80th Fighter Squadron would distinguish itself. Its first mission was on 4 September, when 16 P-38s of the 80FS took off at 1000 and climbed to about 16,000 feet to patrol over the invasion convoy, 25 miles east of Salamaua. The 80th formation was led by Red Flight Leader Maj. Edwin Cragg; Yellow Flight Leader 1Lt. Raymond Daly; White Flight Leader 1Lt. Charles Taylor; and Green Flight Leader Capt. James Wilson.

Cragg, with 2Lt. Cyril Homer flying on his wing and 1Lt. Jay Robbins leading the second element with 2Lt. Louis Schriber on his wing, was patrolling over the convoy at 8,000 feet. This "all star" quartet would eventually all be aces, with Cragg totaling 15 victories, Homer 15, Robbins 22, and Schriber 5. At 1320, Robbins noticed that Cragg had started climbing at high speed and followed Cragg and Homer, with Schriber as the tail end man. As the flight headed past Salamaua at 24,000 feet Cragg began a slow dive and Robbins tried to contact him, but his (Robbins) radio was malfunctioning. On the way down with Cragg and Homer (Schriber lost the flight during the climb), Robbins spotted a Zero to his starboard, cut his throttle, and made a quick turn and chased after the Zero, which made a slow starboard turn and gradual dive before Robbins got on its tail. Robbins cut his throttles to slow his dive and

LEFT: Maj. Edwin **Cragg** (R) shot down two Zeros to make him a double ace with 10 victories. (AAF) RIGHT 2Lt. Donald **Hanover**. (shown on left with Robert Adams' P-38 after Adams was KIA) after he scored victory #2 and #3 of four victories. (AAF)

New ace, 1Lt. Jay **Robbins**, after four victories. (and two probables) looks at the cowling scoreboard of his Lightning now showing seven victories. (AFAA)

fired, shooting off a large part of its starboard wing, but the pilot was able to bail out over Huon Gulf. Robbins saw half a dozen P-38s above and began to climb to join them when a Zero slow rolled ahead of these P-38s and they took off at full throttle after him, leaving Robbins behind. He then noticed about 20 other Japanese fighters coming in from behind and frantically called for the P-38s to turn around and help him, but his radio transmitter was useless. Soon the Zeros and Hamps surrounded him and were coming down in twos and threes, and even four ship flights to make passes at him. One Zero passed directly in front of Robbins, who turned after it and fired a quick deflection shot as it pulled up and hit it in the belly, exploding it. Robbins went into a quick starboard wingover that put him on the tail of another enemy fighter slightly below, and he fired a long accurate burst that tore off the starboard wingtip and into the cockpit of the doomed fighter, which spun into the water. A flight of four more Zeros came down and Robbins dove away, even further out to sea; all he could do was evade or turn into each attack as it came in. He got another perfect belly shot as he turned into these Zeros, taking off pieces of its port wing and rudder. He fired another very long burst to finish off this Zero for his fourth victory of the day to make him an ace with seven victories. Robbins was very low on fuel and started to slowly climb toward home when he was bounced by another bunch of fighters at about 6,000 feet and 70 miles northeast of Salamaua. Again, his only option was to turn into every attack and use more of his diminishing ammunition supply. During this escape run he used his last rounds to get good hits on two Zeros which were credited as probables. Without ammunition Robbins dove away, but when he looked back he saw two Tonys and a Zero diving after him and the enemy tracers were now hitting his tail and wings. Robbins had been running at full power for about 45 minutes (manufacturer specifications redlined the limit at 14 minutes) but pushed on, and when he finally leveled out at 200 feet, he looked around and found that he had outrun his pursuers and refastened the seat belts he had opened in case he had to bail out.

At the same time Cragg saw Robbins being chased out to sea, he spotted another Zero far below at 2,000 feet. Cragg dove and got within 100 feet before he fired a short burst that exploded the enemy fighter into burning wreckage that fell off into a spin and crashed into the water. The destroyer *Reid* was calling for fighter cover over the invasion convoy, and Cragg found one destroyer with about 15 Japanese fighters circling slowly in the area. He picked out one straggling Zero and fired a long deflection shot that flamed the Zero and sent it crashing into the sea. Maj. Thomas Lynch, who was flying with the 39FS, called out a Japanese pilot in a parachute. When Cragg arrived the parachute was floating in the water, but he did not strafe, as the downed Japanese pilot was submerged and obviously dead. However, a number of Zeros had now trapped Cragg, and he had to run at full speed toward the shore to save himself. Cy Homer dove with Cragg in the beginning of this skirmish and attacked a Zero that seemed immune to his gunfire on several passes; finally all Homer's guns jammed, and this lucky Zero pulled away, only to have another P-38 shoot it down. Homer was able to recharge two guns and shot down another Zero that hit the water and burned near one of the USN destroyers. Homer landed to refuel at Marilinan and came to Dobodura with Cragg.

2Lt. Donald Hanover was flying as the Wingman to 1Lt. Raymond Daly in Yellow Flight at 21,000 feet and spotted 15 to 20 Zeros and Vals below. They dove through the escorts and then into the Vals, making several firing passes without result, although they were sure that they had scored some hits. Hanover looked around and saw three Zeros on his tail. Hanover radioed Daly, who was ahead, and Daly ordered Hanover to outrun them while he started around. But a Zero put bullets through Hanover's canopy which grazed his arm, and he headed away to the south, where he saw two formations of P-38s engaging the enemy below. But looking ahead, he saw 10 to 15 Zeros and made a head on pass on one without result. This Zero did a wingover and Hanover took a 45 degree diving deflection shot and set the Zero on fire. He then dove on another Zero from 30 degrees and hit the canopy and it went down, smoking heavily, for his second victory of the day.

White Flight Leader 1Lt. Charles Taylor and Wingman 1Lt. Mark Kaspar were vectored to enemy aircraft at 25,000 feet and the flight immediately climbed, but was then told to circle at 18,000 feet over a group of USN invasion shipping that was firing on something. Taylor looked around to find what they were shooting at and saw several single engine aircraft below. 2Lt. William Fotheringham was flying on 1Lt. Albon Hailey's wing as the last man in White Flight when they saw two Zeros and dove on one but missed. Kaspar dove and also missed, then chandelled to gain altitude for another pass, but as he did his port prop went out. Kaspar put the prop in manual just as a Zero passed in front of him, and he got on its tail and fired two bursts that put it into a fatal spin. Kaspar then dove on two more Zeros and got on the tail of one and fired a short burst, but his engine overheated and its oil pressure went to zero and he broke off and returned to Marilinan. Meanwhile, Fotheringham turned around to look for his flight and saw four Zeros at 12,000 feet. He dove on the last Zero and fired a long burst, but could not determine if he shot it down, as another Zero was maneuvering to attack and Fotheringham dove away with a damaged claim. Initially Kaspar claimed a probable, but a pilot from the 8FS verified that a Zero had crashed in the area.

Green Flight Leader Capt. James Wilson and his Wingman, F/O Edwin DeGraffenreid, were patrolling over Huon Gulf when they saw four Zeros and five Vals. Wilson and DeGraffenreid were unable to drop one (Wilson) or both of their tanks. Wilson was restricted to one firing pass and hit a Zero, but did not see it smoke until he looked back. Wilson and DeGraffenreid then tried to release their tanks but returned to base, landing with their tanks still attached.

4 September 1943: 348FG/342FS

In the early afternoon, bogeys were expected in the Morobe, Salamaua, and Finschhafen areas as a response to the upcoming invasion. The 5AF interception was initially thought to be too early, and therefore somewhat indifferent and seemingly routine. The 342nd Squadron's Yellow Flight was scrambled first against the bogeys around Morobe at about 1400. Seven more P-47s of Blue and Green Flights followed a few minutes later, while Lt.Col. Neel Kearby led the last flight of 20 348th fighters from Dobodura. At about 1430, while flying at 25,000 feet, Kearby saw a flying boat just off the water flanked by two fighters flying 14 miles south of Hopoi Beach, east of Lae. Kearby did not wish to lose his altitude advantage when there were signs of an air battle developing in the Morobe area to the south, and several fires from downed aircraft were already in the water near Cape Ward Hunt several miles beyond. Nonetheless, Kearby decided to descend to identify the three aircraft below, and at 2,000 feet he identified a Betty bomber and Oscars off either wing, flying to the northeast. Kearby attacked from behind at an indicated airspeed of 400 mph and closed to about 300 yards, slightly above and to the left of the enemy bomber. Kearby, in his first bona fide air combat, set his sights on both the bomber and one of the fighters with a one half radii lead, hoping to shoot down both of them. His first tracers seemed to envelop the Oscar, and Kearby then concentrated on the Betty; his tracers converged on the surprised bomber and tore off pieces before the bomber burst into flames before it crashed into the sea. The Japanese escorts disappeared, but Kearby sighted one of the Oscars climbing away and Kearby turned back to attack. The Japanese fighter performed an adept climbing turn before Kearby could get in range and escaped. 1Lt. George Orr, Kearby's Wingman, reported later that the first Oscar had dived into the water after Kearby fired on it. The four P-47s continued to patrol until about 1515, when a P-47 of the second element was running low on fuel and returned to base. Kearby and Orr continued to orbit the area for about another hour until their fuel ran low. Although many of the 20 348th's P-47s saw action, only Kearby claimed two confirmed victories, while the P-38s had 18 victories. Despite the American intervention, the Bettys had hit at least three barges, a destroyer was damaged by a near miss, and four P-38s were damaged.

Lt.Col. Neel **Kearby** scored his first two of 22 victories in his illustrious career

5 September 1943: Nadzab Operation

Early in the morning, 79 C-47s of the 54th Troop Carrier Wing took off from Wards and Jackson airdromes to drop 1,600 paratroopers of the 503rd Paratroop Regiment and Australian supporting forces on the grassy kunai plains near Nadzab. When Kenney informed MacArthur that he planned to observe the operation from a B-17, MacArthur reminded Kenney of his orders to keep out of combat, orders that Brig.Gen. Kenneth Walker had disobeyed at the cost of his life. Kenney summed up the reasons why he thought he should go, and concluded that "they were my kids and I was going to see them do their stuff." Supposedly, MacArthur replied "You're right, George, we'll both go. They're my kids, too."

At 1007, 302 aircraft, transports, bombers, and fighters from eight different airfields in the Moresby and Dobodura areas made a rendezvous over Tsili Tsili. Forty-eight B-25s from the 38BG and 345BG were to lead the way to bomb and strafe, followed by A-20s of the 3BG(L) carrying smoke tanks to screen the battlefield. The C-47s were to follow and drop their paratroopers at 400-500 feet. Five B-17s followed the C-47s and were to para-drop supplies. The unarmed transports rendezvoused over 30 Mile Airdrome with part of their fighter cover, which was to consist of nearly 100 fighters: P-39s, P-47s, and P-38s. On each side along the column of transports and about 1,000 feet above them were the close cover fighters. Another group of fighters flew up in the sun at 7,000 feet, and staggered from 15,000 to 20,000 feet was another group of P-47s. From rendezvous the C-47s flew over New Guinea's central mountain ranges, and at 1022 nearly 1,600 paratroops made a successful drop on Nadzab. The Japanese made no attempt to interfere with the extensive Allied fighter cover that circled above the drop area. Although the transports would not be threatened, the 5AF contributed to the assault by strafing and dropping fragmentation bombs on the drop area just as the transports were taking off from their bases and just before the smoke screen laying aircraft arrived. After the drop all C-47s returned safely to base, and within 24 hours Nadzab had been secured. B-17s joined with the C-47 transports in dropping supplies to the troops on the ground, and by noon all of the transports were back safely at Port Moresby.

Soon the ground campaign against Lae and Salamaua was rapidly and unexpectedly reaching an end. The 7th Australian Division moved from Nadzab down the Markham Valley and, despite heavy enemy resistance, the Australians swiftly broke through and raced toward Lae. Meanwhile, the American and Australian forces outside of Salamaua were relentlessly pressing towards their goal, some advancing along the coast, and others down the Francisco River. By 11 September they had reached the Salamaua airfield, and within a few hours the area was under final attack. The successes on the ground during September were particularly decisive when compared with the slow advances of the previous months.

After long preparation, these advances on the ground were accomplished by the development of clever overall strategy climaxed by the overwhelming aerial successes of 4 and 5 September. During

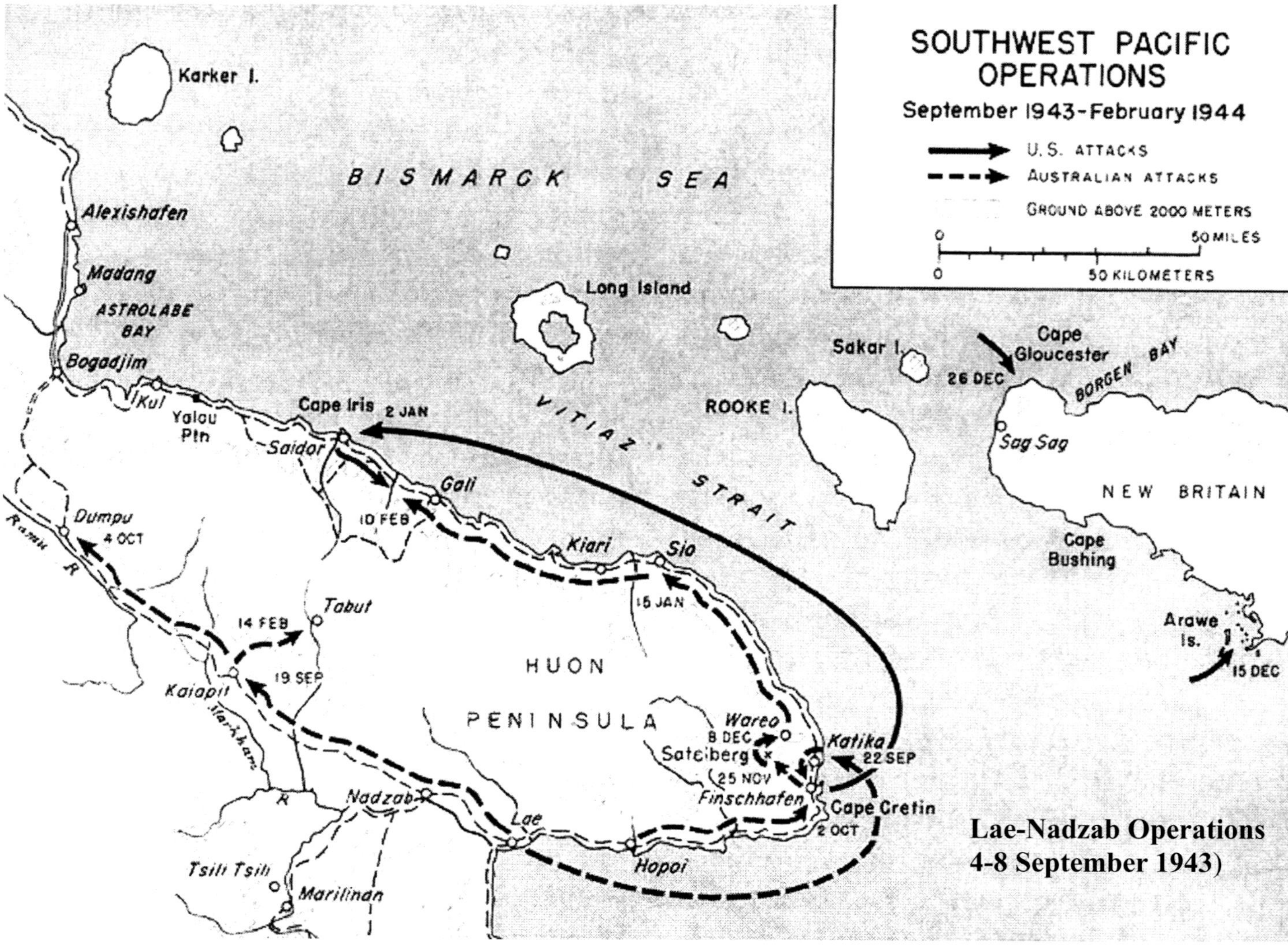

Lae-Nadzab Operations
4-8 September 1943)

Kenney and **MacArthur** confer on the tarmac at 30 Mile Drome as the C-47s carrying the paratroops prepare to take off. (AFHRC)

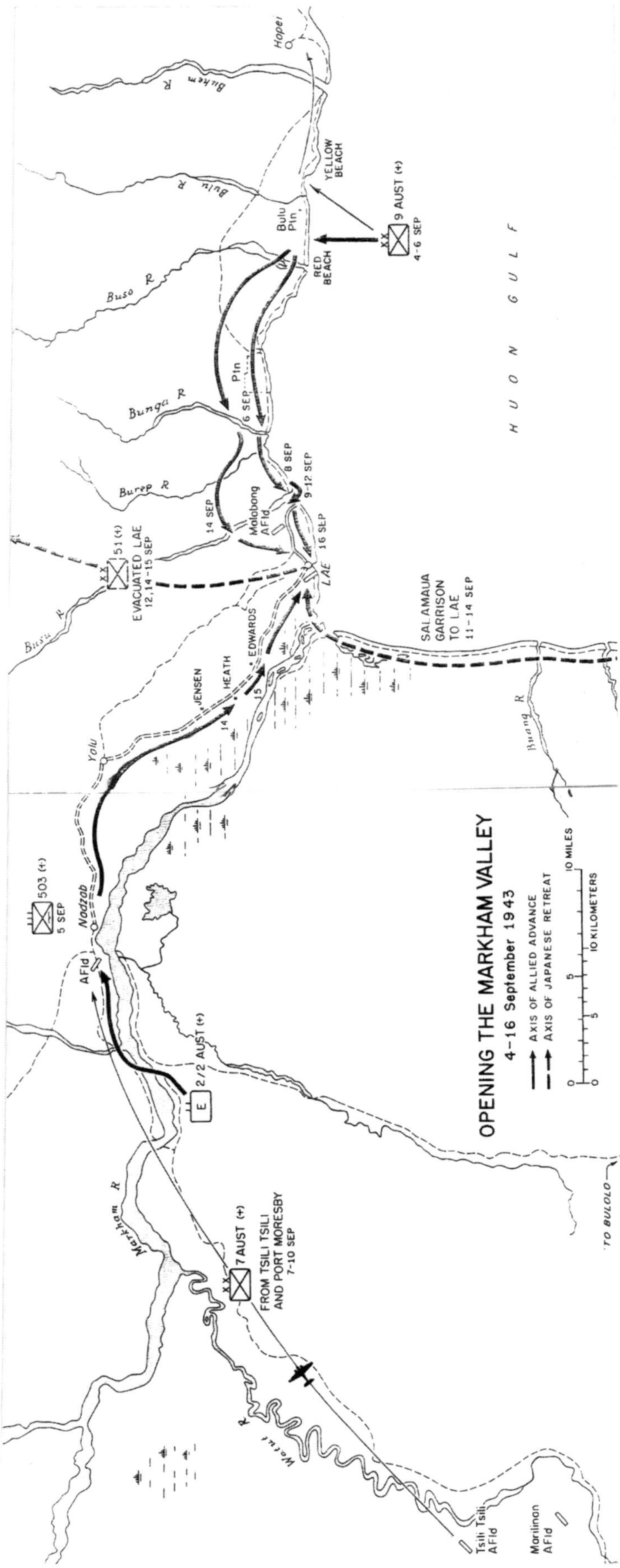

Under the cover of a smoke screen 1,600 paratroopers of the **503rd Paratroop Regiment** and Australian supporting forces descend on the grassy kunai plains near Nadzab. (AAF)

September, the Allied Air Forces contributed their share in the triumph over the Japanese. The spectacular airborne drop and the successful ferrying of the 7th Australian Division was only a part of their contribution. Fighters were constantly either on patrol, escort, interception missions, or ground alert. Bombers, in addition to heavy strikes against airfields and barge hideouts in New Britain, renewed their attack on the Wewak airdromes and carried out 421 sorties in support of the Lae ground operations.

To implement the escape of his Salamaua-Lae garrisons, Lt.Gen. Hatazo Adachi put up token resistance at the Huon beachhead. The Japanese retreat was to move to Madang through a narrow pass at the northern end of the Finistere Mountains. Once reaching Madang, the Japanese hoped that the approaching monsoon season would slow the Allied advance. However, the 5th Air Force and US Navy devastated Adachi's supply routes on the New Guinea mainland and throughout the Solomon Seas.

Their unexpected loss of Nazab caused the Japanese to completely go into a defensive/counter attack strategy in New Guinea. Despite the monsoons, their reinforced air forces at Wewak would attempt to eliminate the new Allied Nazab/Malahang complex before the entire Huon Peninsula was overrun. The Allies and Japanese would enter into another momentous air and land campaign for the control of northern New Guinea. The Australian infantry advanced east from the beachhead along the coast, pursuing the escaping Japanese headed for Finschhafen. The 4th JAAF at Wewak quickly assembled bombers to attack the large supply dump inland from the beachhead at Hopoi village.

5 September 1943: 475FG/433FS

During the morning, the 433FS escorted a bombing raid to Cape Gloucester and then flew a patrol covering ships and barges in the Morobe Bay-Hopoi area later in the afternoon, both without enemy contact.

6 September 1943: 49FG/8FS/9FS

8FS

Capt. Ernest Harris' Eightball pilots had flown transport escort sorties throughout the summer monsoons before being based at Marilinan. The Eightball Warhawks had not been in aerial combat for three and a half months. At 1330, an 8FS patrol that left Marilinan at 1305 was flying over Lae when their Controller, coded *Shadow*, alerted the Blue Flight Leader, 1Lt. Robert White, of a large formation coming in from the east. White, with Wingman 2Lt. William Drier, Element Leader 1Lt. Elfred Elofson, and rookie Wingman 2Lt. Robert Sherman flew beyond their patrol area while hunting for the enemy at 20,000 feet for 45 minutes. Trailing, Wingman

1Lt. Robert **White** shot down two Bettys and a Tony to give him a total of eight victories. (AFAA)

Sherman called a large enemy formation flying in two Vs of nine Bettys each at 4 o'clock low at 16,000 feet about 30 miles out to sea heading toward Hopoi Village and followed by the fighter escort. In his excitement and due to clouds, the rookie Sherman reported twice as many Bettys as he did in his estimate of enemy escorts. White informed *Shadow* and asked for help, as his Flight was the only one in the area.

Up sun and partially hidden by broken clouds, White led his Flight somewhat ahead of the second flight of Bettys and turned into them at about 60 degrees head on, still unseen by the escorts. A Betty pilot called out in English that his formation was friendly and flashed his lights, but to no avail, as White got a "very good burst" into the second bomber of the V, which fell out of formation and headed back toward New Britain; it was observed to crash near Tami Island by Wingman Drier. White and Sherman then dove to 9,000 feet and cut to the side of the bombers, which were apparently heading toward Salamaua. The two Americans then climbed toward the first Betty flight as it turned, and White and Sherman made a head on pass from slightly underneath. White fired a long burst into the cockpit of the second Betty in the right of the V. The Betty went out of control and just missed White on its way down. As White pulled up he encountered the trailing spin, and the bomber was seen to crash by Sherman six miles behind Malahang for his third victory of the day. As White was firing at the Tony, Sherman climbed under the lead Betty and raked the entire ventral fuselage. White verified that the Betty's tail section was almost separated from the fuselage.

Drier and Wingman Elofson also fired at the bombers from head on, but missed and broke away to return for a second pass; however, the escorts suddenly pulled in behind them and they quickly dove away. As Drier was planning to make another attack on the Bettys, four Lightnings arrived overhead and Drier tried to repeatedly ID himself over the radio and put his fighter into a bank to display his Stars & Bars insignia. The Lightnings went into a spread out Lufbery, and its leader then "started to fire with everything he had" and Drier dove away, fortunately unscathed. White and Sherman rejoined and headed off for Marilinan, leaving Drier to trail the escaping enemy and report their position to the next fighter unit to arrive. Drier remained hidden in the sun on the Japanese right flank as Mission Leader 1Lt. Ralph Wire's 15 9FS' "Flying Knights" Lightnings came into the area.

9FS

The 9FS took off from Horanda Strip at 1145, with 1Lt. Ralph Wire as the leader of four Flights of 14 P-38s on patrol, when the southern area Controller *Charter* sent them on a northern vector. They arrived over Morobe at 1205. Wire flew north and spread the four flights to increase the search area: mission Leader Wire's Red Flight was on the right flank; Capt. Richard Bong's Blue Flight was on the left flank; overhead in trailing high cover at 16,000 was Yellow Flight Leader 1Lt. Theron Price with a pair of wingmen, and to their right was 2Lt. Walter Markey's Green Flight.

At 1400 Wire and Red Element Leader 1Lt. Wilbert Arthur pounced on what they thought was a lone Tony flying escort over the right bomber flank, but it was actually Drier's shadowing Warhawk. Even though Drier rolled his fighter on its wingtip to display her Stars & Bars insignia and called out over the radio to the descending Lightnings he was not heard, as the 9FS was still on the *Charter* radio frequency. As Wire and Arthur's tracers zipped over Drier he dove at full throttle for Salamaua. Wire's Lightnings then attacked the Betty's right flank over the coast. Wire led his flights on and found the enemy bombers flying in two nine ship Vs at 15,000 feet covered by 11-15 fighter escorts flying behind and above the bombers. Wire climbed for altitude to attack the bombers when an "inline fighter" (Tony) made a rear attack on his #4, Alber. Wire met the Tony head on and got hits on its engine and cockpit, then watched as the enemy fighter went straight down smoking. Wire turned to make an attack on the second flight of Bettys and made a quarter head on firing pass, getting hits on its starboard engine and wing. As Wire closed on the Betty formation he was attacked by four Zeros and turned into them, shooting down one in flames. Wire again turned toward the bombers, which were 10 miles off, and as he approached to within three miles of the bombers, which were slightly descending at 6,000 feet, he was attacked by a Zero climbing from under his port wing. Wire climbed away and the Zero finally stalled and began to dive away. Wire went into a dive and fired into its cockpit, and it went out of control and exploded into the water for Wire's fourth claimed victory of the day. However, later Wire's last two claims and Arthur's claim were awarded as probables.

Green Flight Leader 1Lt. Walter Markey led his Flight on the bombers, but as he approached the Zero escort attacked Bong's Flight and Markey cut them off and fired. He then made several firing runs on the Bettys, but could claim no observable results on the Bettys or Zero. Second Element Leader 2Lt. Milby Marling also hit a Zero without observable results.

Yellow Flight Leader 1Lt. Theron Price led Wingman 2Lt. Charles Kamphausen, Element Leader 1Lt. Frank Wunder, and #4 man 2Lt. Francis Love. At the beginning of the mission Kamphausen's engine would not start and Price returned after take off with wheel well door problems, but both rectified their problems and took off together. Once they encountered the enemy Price made his first pass on the Bettys from the rear and saw his tracers enter the starboard side and tail of one; he knocked off small pieces of its tail and nose, and the bomber left its formation with its right engine smoking for a probable. Price followed another Betty and fired, with his tracers hitting from nose to tail, and the Betty went down with both its engines smoking and was seen to hit the water. Kamphausen saw hits on two Zeros but made no claims. Wunder had problems during the mission with prop control and returned to base, leaving Love to join Markey's Green Flight.

1Lt. Ralph **Wire** began his seven victory career with two victories and two probables. (AFAA)

Blue Flight Leader Bong and his Wingman, 2Lt. James Fagan, turned for the attack on the Bettys' left flank, while his Second Element Leader Hyland dove on a bomber that was straggling out of the formation and "definitely put the side and tail gunner out of action" with a 90 to 45 degree deflection pass; the bomber continued to fly "but appeared to be moving slower." Bong missed on his first two passes, and on his third zealous pass he pressed his attack on the lead enemy bomber, only to have his starboard engine hit by bomber gunners. Bong dove away to port and ducked into the clouds to check the damage, then shut the damaged engine down and feathered the prop for the long flight back to base. However, the weather to the south began to close in and Bong had to head for Marilinan. The airfield was clear and dry, despite the low hanging clouds over the surrounding hills, and Bong came in for a routine single engine landing. As his fighter settled on to the narrow strip its port engine seized, and without power and hydraulics the Lightning briefly slid sideways and then straightened in a fast rollout for the drainage ditch on the left side of the runway. Bong prepared himself as his damaged P-38 rolled toward the ditch. As the aircraft slowed its nose wheel sank in the soft ground at the edge of the runway, and as it continued to move the left gear followed. Finally, the soft ground gave way and the fighter gently slumped over, its left wingtip sticking down into the mud and its right wing and tail pointing into the sky. Bong's fighter had again been hit in combat, and he had lost Wingman 2Lt. James Fagan, who was flying his first combat. Once back at Dobodura, the visibly upset Bong met with 49er CO Johnson and Ops Exec Jordan and requested to fly future missions as an unattached pilot, as he could not stand losing another Wingman. Instead, Bong was given a two week furlough

6 September 1943: 35FG/41FS

The 41FS sent 16 P-39s on a mid-afternoon patrol of the Nadzab area when an enemy bomber and fighter formation was reported headed east from Lae at 12,000 feet. 1Lt. Keith Brown's flight caught the formation at 1400 at 50 miles east of Lae. As he was diving on a straggling Oscar another dove on him and fired from long range but missed. Brown went into a sharp right climbing turn which put his Airacobra into a spin. When he came out of the spin he saw the Oscar in a spin 200 feet below. Brown fired on the Oscar as it snapped a turn to the right as a cannon shell hit the fuselage behind the pilot. The enemy pilot began to turn inside Brown, who dove to port, but the Oscar pilot followed him down. As the Oscar fired Brown skidded sharply left and the Oscar over ran, with its tracers passing over the P-39's wing. Brown now was on the enemy's tail, and fired a long burst before the Oscar turned sharply right toward a cloud. Brown pulled up over this cloud and saw the Oscar emerge directly in front of him. Brown fired his third long burst of the combat at the Oscar, and it snapped over on its back and went into a spin and hit the water. Although 41FS' pilots had many targets, Brown's victory was their only one for the day.

7 September 1943: 49FG/7FS

On the 7th, the Japanese again raided the Hopoi beachhead between rain squalls. The 7FS Demons were able to get 17 Warhawks up over the Huon Peninsula and make their first interception since mid-July. 1Lt. David Harbour left late from Kalamazoo due to oxygen equipment problems and had to patrol at a lower altitude than normal; he continued into the Lae area through the poor weather. *Shadow* Control vectored Harbor to several interceptions, but he failed to contact any of them. Eventually, running low on fuel, he turned back for base and saw two radial engine fighters passing below through an opening in the overcast. Harbour dove in a firing pass on the trailing Oscar, whose pilot tried to evade with a port turn, but Harbour made a perfect rear quarter deflection shot and the Ki-43 crashed into the beach. Harbour turned back to re-engage the Oscar Wingman, who had fled to the north and escaped.

7 September 1943: 475FG/433FS/432FS

433FS

The 433FS was assigned close escort for B-25s that bombed and strafed along the Markham Valley. During the mission Possum pilots heard calls from Morobe Harbor that the Japanese were bombing there, but the squadron was committed to the B-25 escort.

432FS

However, the 432FS was able to respond to these calls with four P-38 flights: Capt. Donald Byars led the first Red flight; 1Lt. Noel Lundy led the second Green Flight; Capt. Daniel Roberts led the third Blue Flight; and 1Lt. John Loisel again led the rear White Flight. The Squadron was instructed by the Controller to take off at 1130 to patrol Morobe Harbor at 10,000 feet until *Nephew*, the Local Fighter Controller, instructed the 432nd to climb to 20,000 feet, where they spotted aircraft on the deck headed north. They descended and found these aircraft to be B-25s escorted by P-38s. *Nephew* then radioed that Arawe, New Britain, was being attacked but gave no coordinates. The Squadron's only clue was AA bursts seen over Morobe, so they headed there and saw aircraft in the distance retreating from the area. They chased these aircraft for 20 minutes and prepared to attack nine Betty bombers escorted by 15 to 20 fighters (Lundy counted 27 total).

Lundy's Green Flight was the first to sight the retreating Japanese formations and intercepted them at 15,000 feet about 60 miles south of Arawe after a 20 minute full throttle chase. Soon all four flights were engaged. Lundy saw a Zero make a pass at Blue #4 and pull up directly in front of him, and he fired an ineffective burst that alerted its pilot to chandelle sharply to port. Lundy followed but could not get the proper lead on it, as he fired his first burst from 350 yards and his second from 200 to 150 yards and then watched the enemy escape. Several Zeros attacked Lundy's flight but turned away on each approach. (Note: Researcher Frank Olynyk credits Lundy with a victory on this date, but Lundy's ICR makes no mention of a successful combat.)

Byars led his Red Flight into combat after Green Flight caught the Japanese, but soon his Wingman and second element aborted, leaving Byars alone with four Zeros making head on passes at him, so he dove out and returned to base.

Blue Flight, led by Capt. Daniel Roberts and Wingman 2Lt. Edwin Christian, was the most successful, with three victories for the day. Roberts followed Red Flight into the combat, where they saw Zeros protecting the Bettys. Before Roberts could lead his flight on the Bettys they had to get through the screen of protecting Zeros. Roberts immediately saw a Zero pursuing a P-38 and dove to the rescue, firing a long burst and closing to only 25 yards. The Zero was hit behind its cockpit, which exploded the fuel tank located there. Robert's second element (2Lts. Thomas Simms and Christopher Bartlett) also made several passes at the protecting Zeros, with Simms exploding one and Bartlett hitting another in its cowling, which exploded and burned vigorously. The closely knit flight then closed on the Bettys and began to fire at 350 yards and 300 yards above, even though there were 10 or 12 Zeros overhead. Three Zeros attacked Simms and Bartlett, and the two were forced to dive away; by the time the Blue Flight reformed the Bettys were a substantial distance away, and being outnumbered Roberts ordered the flight to return home.

1Lt. John Loisel's tail end White Flight were surrounded by Zero and Oscar escorts which made diving attacks on the P-38s, forcing them to dive away and try to return. Each attack and escape dive put White Flight further behind the bombers, and after a while they ran low on fuel and returned to base.

The next day 2Lt. Chester Philips of the 431FS was listed as missing during a routine flight 30 miles south of Wau in poor weather.

13 September 1943: 348FG/342FS

Since Kearby's pair of victories on the 4th, the 348th had flown uneventful routine missions, but on a transport cover mission to Tsili Tsili they broke back into the victory column. Eight 342FS Thunderbolts, one flight flying at 22,000 feet and the other at 19,000 feet, encountered 20 Tony and Oscar fighter escorts and 11 Betty bombers heading north at 20,000 feet about 50 miles from Marilinan. Capt. William Banks was leading the high flight at 22,000 feet and had to get through the escorts to get to the bombers. He dove on the rear Oscar escort and fired a long burst that hit its wing tanks. The Oscar rolled over on its back and went down. Banks lost his Wingman and tried to make one more pass, but was jumped by five Zeros and dove away back to Marilinan. 1Lt. Lawrence O'Neill was leading the low flight at 19,000 feet, and his flight dropped their tanks and climbed to about 500 feet above the enemy formation. As O'Neill went into a dive on the Bettys oil began to cover his windshield and canopy, but he pressed his attack on the middle bomber, and at 500 yards and 30 degrees began to fire a two second burst, but had to break away when he could no longer see out of his windshield. He opened his canopy and flew back to Tsili Tsili, where he landed safely and was informed by his Wingman that he had exploded the Betty.

LEFT: Capt. William **Banks** shot down an Oscar for the first of his nine victories. (AFAA) RIGHT: 1Lt. Lawrence **O'Neill** got his first of five victories. (AFAA)

13 September 1943: P-38s Over Wewak

As the 5FC flew sorties from Finschhafen to Lae for the next week, the Japanese avoided all contact until 13 September. By this time the Wewak airfields, with their few operational aircraft, were no longer a threat to Allied forces moving to the north, but the potential threat of a revived Wewak caused Allied Commanders to send occasional raids to the area. Although the decimated Japanese 78th Sentai could send up only a few Tonys, six 78th Tonys were sent to oppose the Allied landings near Lae. On 13 September, the 5BC sent B-24 Liberators to Wewak with the 431FS, 432FS, and 80FS to fly cover. The formation was attacked by the few Tonys and Oscars remaining at Wewak.

13 September 1943: 8FG/80FS

Maj. Edward Cragg led 16 P-38s on a fighter sweep previous to a B-24 attack on the Wewak airdromes of Dagua and But. At 1030 they arrived over Wewak, about five minutes before the bombers, and circled at 18,000 feet.

Capt. Norbert **Ruff** got victories #2 and #3 of four total. (AFAA)

Capt. Norman Ruff approached Wewak at 18,000 feet, where he saw one four plane enemy formation directly ahead; one flight at 4 o'clock; and another flight below diving on the bombers. Ruff dove on the enemy flight, menacing the bombers, and although no hits were seen, the P-38s turned them away from the Liberators. Ruff then saw 15 enemy fighters at 6,000 feet below and made three passes, getting no hits, but then fired on an Oscar and hit its canopy and the entire length of its fuselage. Ruff lost sight of it as it flew over him, but Wingman 2Lt. Cyril Homer had followed Ruff down during his attack and saw the enemy pilot bail out, stating "I (Homer) left him alone but could have strafed him." Ruff now had three Oscars on his tail and went into full throttle and out-climbed them. Ruff turned back into the battle and fired a long burst without seeing any hits. He then made lazy-8 passes through the enemy formation and had "no trouble out climbing those that turned to attack me." Ruff got on the tail of one Oscar that half rolled and "hung on its back," giving Ruff a good shot that sent it down in a roll and then a tight spiral into the overcast to crash into the mountains. Homer saw the enemy pilot bail out just before the crash. Ruff climbed back up through the overcast and fired at another Oscar at 90 degrees deflection, but again ended up with three Oscars on his tail. During the battle all the enemy pilots Split-S'd, causing Homer to pull up over Ruff, where he saw the Oscars get on his Leader's tail from above. Homer dove quickly to get close to the rear Oscar and fired. The Oscar rolled over and went down, and this pilot also bailed out. Ruff evaded the other Oscars, and soon he and Homer were down to about 5,000 feet, where Ruff shot down another Oscar. The two Americans climbed again and covered the B-24s for about 10 minutes before they turned toward Marilinan to refuel. 1Lt. Albon Hailey of Cragg's flight claimed an Oscar probable to end the day's scoring.

13 September 1943: 475FG/431FS/432FS

431FS

The 431FS sent out 14 P-38s led by Capt. John Hood at 0800, but three aborted before rendezvousing with the B-24s at 0940. The formation then proceeded to Wewak, arriving two minutes ahead of the bombers. At 1020, the P-38s were at 18,000 feet when they spotted about 15 Oscars and a lone Tony at 12,000 feet just south of Boram Strip. With a 6,000 foot altitude advantage the 431FS Lightnings dove on the Japanese, who began to weave to oppose the attack. Capt. Hood took the first shots of the combat when the lone Tony dove on him from 2 o'clock and he turned into it. Hood's guns weren't operating properly and his snap shot missed. Green Flight Leader Capt. Verl Jett and Wingman 2Lt. Francis Lent were unable to fire on the Tony as it quickly passed through the formation. Soon the 431FS flights became separated, chasing after the scattering Oscars. Jett saw six more Tonys 3,000 feet below, and he and Lent again dove into the attack, where two other P-38 flights were already making firing passes at the Tonys. Jett saw a twin engine Nick on the tail of one of the trailing P-38s and closed in and fired a few bursts. The Nick exploded into flames, and as it spun into the ground its rear gunner bailed out. 1Lt. Thomas McGuire and his Wingman, 2Lt. Vincent Elliott, comprised the second Green element. McGuire was unable to drop his tanks as the Tony dove through the formation and gave up after 10 minutes of trying, then headed back to Berry. Elliott continued on, looking for another flight to join or an enemy to attack. Soon he sighted three P-38s south of Boram Strip diving on four Oscars and joined the combat. Elliott fired two effective bursts from about 60 degrees deflection and the Oscar shed pieces and left a trail of smoke as it spun slowly into the ground. Elliott's victory was confirmed by Capt. Norbert Ruff of the 80FS.

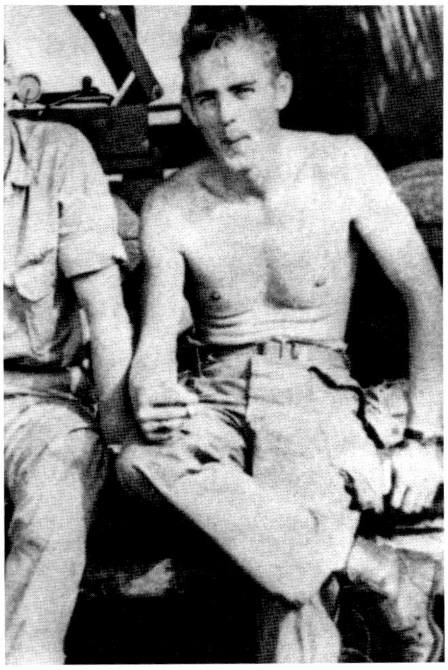

2Lt. Vincent **Elliott** scored his first of seven victories when he shot down a Zero. (AFAA)

Capt. William Haning's Blue Flight, with 1Lts. John Knox and Donno Bellows, became separated from the Squadron and were heading back to base when the Air Controller vectored them south of Madang and north of the Ramu River, where they saw four Tonys and six other single engine fighters circling the area in a Lufbery. There were three P-38s already making passes at the enemy Lufbery while the Tonys were scouting at the edges, trying to draw the Lightnings in. Haning immediately attacked a Tony which turned into him, but the enemy pilot got on Haning's tail. Haning went into a high speed dive and lost his attacker. Two Oscars and another Tony got on Bellows' and Knox's tails, but Capt. Ruff came in and shot down the two Oscars. During the chase Bellows had tried to evade with a few very tight turns and briefly blacked out. When he revived, he found that his fighter had been badly shot up and was on fire. He feathered his prop and slipped his fighter until the fire went out. About five minutes later Bellows smelled smoke and looked out to see flames in his right wheel well. The smoke entered the cockpit, and there was a fire in the radio compartment behind him. Bellows tried to get as close to base before he would be forced to crash land by the thick choking smoke. Finally, he cut the other engine and crash landed about a mile east of the Ramu River and escaped the burning fighter before the right fuel tank exploded. Meanwhile, Haning had escaped the pursuing Japanese and landed at Tsili Tsili, where he met Capt. John Hood, who was refueling his P-38. He told Hood that Bellows had gone down. Hood took off and searched for Bellows for two hours, finding him standing near his burning P-38. After circling for 20 minutes Hood dropped a note saying, "I'm sorry. Come back tomorrow." Natives arrived, and Bellows gave them cigarettes and chocolates from his jungle kit. The natives gave him bananas and stayed with him throughout the night. The next day a Piper L-l, escorted by two flights of P-39s, landed near the crash site and rescued Bellows, but Knox never returned to base.

432FS

Several minutes after the 431FS and bombers left the target and were heading home, Maj. Frank Tomkins led 16 Clover P-38s into the area, remaining on close cover with the B-24s over Boram Strip. The Liberators made a turn with half returning to base, while the other half continued on to bomb Wewak. Tomkins saw a pair of Zeros immediately below and he made a head on pass on the second, closing his attack and firing to within 20 feet until flames burst from the enemy's cowling.

1Lt. Noel Lundy was leading the Blue second flight, and he and his Wingman, 2Lt. John Weber, followed Tomkins into the attack. Soon Lundy saw a Tony Split-S from a cloud onto the tails of two P-38s. As these Lightnings passed Lundy and Weber they dove on the Tony's tail. Weber got a good lead and fired the first shots, but stopped firing when Lundy fired 20mm cannon shells into the Tony's canopy, forcing it into a tight turn and then into a sharp, flat spin into the sea. Lundy's second Element Leader, 2Lt. Paul Lucas, who was bringing up the rear, lost Lundy and Weber and joined with Tomkins to fly to Marilinan for refueling. Lundy and Weber were returning to Dobodura when three Tonys bounced them from below near the Ramu River at 10,000 feet. Weber warned Lundy of two Tonys coming toward him, but Lundy appeared to have not heard the warning, as the Tonys hit Lundy's P-38 hard. Meanwhile, the other Tony attacked Weber, who turned into it, but the Tony pilot raced away. Weber looked for Lundy, but only saw three Tonys diving away, and he dove after them. Two Tonys turned into Weber and he got a good shot at one, but the other got on his tail. Weber was able to out climb it to get to safety. Weber returned to the scene of the combat and made three circles looking for Lundy, but found no trace and returned to Marilinan. Lundy was credited with his third victory in his fatal combat, and his body was recovered in the jungle in January 1944 and was buried near Bena Bena.

The second element of the fourth flight, 1Lt. William Ivey from Group HQ and Wingman 2Lt. Clifford Mann, were over the mouth of the Markham River at 18,000 feet 50 miles south of Madang on their return to base when they spotted four Tonys. They radioed for help and circled to get into position, and soon a flight from the 431st arrived. Two Tonys got on the tail of one of their P-38s, and Ivey went after them as another Tony made a head on pass on him. The Tony pressed his attack to within 100 feet when Ivey fired and exploded the Tony's wing root. During the combat Ivey reported seeing two 431st Lightnings go down smoking (Bellows and Knox). The day's combat was costly, as three 475th P-38s were shot down and two pilots killed.

13 September 1943: 49FG/8FS

During the late morning Eightball ace 1Lt. Robert Howard led the standing patrol from Marilinan, and after orbiting the coast at 18,000 feet over Lae, Howard's 14 Warhawks were alerted of enemy bombers approaching the area. Just as Howard turned the patrol to the east they encountered 10 to 12 Bettys at 21,000 feet directly overhead through the broken clouds, with 20 to 30 "Hap and Tony" escorts trailing 200 to 300 yards behind in top cover formation. Howard signaled his flights to drop their tanks and to turn in a climbing parallel route toward the enemy. However, the war weary Warhawks were just able to remain in contact with the Betty formation, which was headed into Markham Valley. After several minutes of pursuit only Howard's Blue Flight and 1Lt. Bernard Makowski's Yellow Flight trio were still in visual contact, and the seven Eightballs slowly inched up to 500 feet above the enemy bombers' left flank. However, the Americans were too spread out and too low on fuel for a coordinated attack, and Howard ordered his pilots to mount individual attacks. Howard banked slowly starboard, attempting to sneak into the bombers' rear quarter. The Japanese escorts pounced just as the Warhawks turned on the bombers. The outnumbered and out of position Eightballs had no choice but to break off for home without a claim.

1Lt. Joel Thorvaldson's Warhawk was the seventh and last in the Eightball flight, which was strung out over their route. As Thorvaldson approached a bomber his prop malfunctioned and he put it into Manual and was cut off by the enemy escorts. He Split-S'd under them, but was unable to lose more than 2,000 feet altitude before he had to level off and turn toward an attacker. He fired, but his burst fell short, though he did make it turn away. As he pulled away his automatic prop control failed as a Zero was about to attack from 500 yards behind at 10,000 feet. Thorvaldson was flying at 300mph and pulled full left rudder and pushed the stick hard to port, turning the Warhawk completely around on the edge of a high speed stall. The Zero turned to port to avoid the American's fire, and Thorvaldson got on its tail and followed it at 300mph. As he fired his gunsight failed and his bullets drifted under the Zero; after he adjusted his aim he got hits on the tail surface, causing slight damage. The enemy pilot half rolled and skidded, and began to turn to port when Thorvaldson fired and missed high as the enemy pilot leveled off and began to turn to starboard. Thorvaldson fired again, with this volley going under the Zero. Thorvaldson adjusted his aim and raked the Zero from stem to stern, causing heavy smoke and flames to come from the engine. The Zero dropped off on one wing and headed into the ground. The victim's Wingman arrived and Thorvaldson rolled away into the clouds, breaking out above the Markham River Valley. Thorvaldson's prop windmilled at 4,000 rpm when the engine exploded and caught on fire. Thorvaldson prepared to bail out but the fire went out. He realized that he would never reach Marilinan and decided to belly land on a broad stretch of kunai grass near the junction of the Markham and Waffir Rivers. Thorvaldson fired off the last of his ammunition, lowered the flaps, put the Warhawk into a gentle glide and crash landed safely. Sitting unharmed in his cockpit, he turned off the switches, radioed his position over the emergency channel, and waited to be rescued. The next day, Thorvaldson waited until noon and then gathered his life raft and essential gear and floated down the river for Nadzab.

14 September 1943: 348FG/341FS

Lt.Col. Neel Kearby led eight P-47s of the 341FS White Flight to the Nadzab area at 0945 and orbited the target for about 45 minutes when a bogey plot was called to 8FS P-40s in the area. Kearby realized that his P-47s, flying at 20,000 feet, were higher than the P-40s and probably closer to the bogey. Kearby sighted the bogey even higher and off to the right, and the bogey was identified as a Dinah as it turned and dashed into the clouds. Kearby was aware of the unit's shortage of belly tanks and ordered his flights not to drop theirs while he jettisoned his to go after the bandit. But when he looked around he saw that six of his fighters had dropped their tanks anyway, and found later that the seventh P-47 pilot would have dropped his also if it hadn't hung up. Kearby climbed after the fast, twin engine Dinah reconnaissance bomber and closed on it from behind and slightly to the left. He opened fire at 300 yards for a single three second burst and the Dinah fell away in flames in a gentle dive for his third victory.

Lt.Col. Neel **Kearby** shot down a Dinah for his third victory. (AAF)

15 September 1943: 8FG/80FS

Sixteen P-38s led by Capt. James Wilson escorted B-24s at 20,000 feet to the area of the Sepik River, where they flew ahead for a fighter sweep prior to the attack on the Boram Airdrome, Wewak. Over Wewak Wilson spotted four enemy fighters breaking through the overcast and ordered tanks to be dropped and led his P-38s into combat. As they descended they saw 10 or 12 more enemy aircraft below. Wilson fired and missed a Zero coming in head on and pulled up and fired at several more without result. He then "feinted at one and pretended to pull off and then caught him loafing" and fired a long burst into its right wing root; the wing folded back and the Zero went down. Wilson made at least seven passes, but "the pilots showed so much skill in preventing my fire from reaching them." Wilson's Wingman, 2Lt. Allen Hill, saw a Zero coming in for a head on pass on them. When it came into range Wilson fired and missed as the enemy pilot slow rolled, intending to come in behind them, but the Japanese pilot came in too straight and level, flying just above Wilson. Hill was flying about 50 yards behind Wilson and had a head on shot. Hill pulled up slightly to be sure of getting the proper lead and fired, and the Zero flew into the stream of bullets went straight down in a spin into the overcast. 1Lt. Albon Hailey, Wilson's second Element Leader, and his Wingman, 1Lt. Cornelius Smith, both made "six to eight" firing passes without result. Hailey saw a Zero on Hill's tail and fired at close range. The Zero appeared to go out of control into the clouds at 8,000 feet for a probable. Another Zero got on Hailey's tail, and Smith dove on it and fired a long burst. The Zero went down, also seemingly out of control, but entered the clouds for another probable claim.

Capt. Norbert Ruff led a flight with 1Lt. Cyril Homer on his wing and saw two enemy fighters at about 10,000 feet, then another larger enemy formation at 5,000 feet below. They dropped their tanks and dove in a formation attack through the lower enemy formation. Ruff made firing passes on two Zeros at 300 yards but saw no hits and lost his flight members. As he climbed to join other P-38s, two Zeros made a frontal overhead pass from each side. The three traded shots and passed within only a few feet of each other without any damage. Ruff then saw a lone Hap 4,000 feet below and started down, but the enemy pilot climbed into him. Ruff leveled off and began shooting at 250 yards as the enemy pilot tried to go over him. Ruff climbed almost vertically and fired at 60 feet, exploding the Oscar, then dove away through its debris. Ruff pulled out of his dive at 3,000 feet and began to climb when he saw a Zero making a head on overhead pass on him, but the enemy pilot broke away when Ruff opened fire on him. Another Zero made a similar pass, and both pilots fired at 300 feet, but Ruff didn't see any results as the enemy passed under him. Ruff then

LEFT: 2Lt. Allen **Hill** scored the first of his nine victories. (AFAA)

RIGHT: Veteran Capt. Norbert **Ruff** fell short of becoming an ace when he got his fourth and last victory. (AAF)

saw a P-38 below with a Zero on its tail and made a very long range shot that drove off the pursuer. As Ruff tried to join that P-38 he saw a Tony behind him and dove away, but since he was at only 7,000 feet the enemy pilot stayed with him and began to fire. Ruff climbed toward a cloud, but a Zero came in and fired a 90 degree deflection shot and hit Ruff's right tail boom before he ducked into the safety of the cloud. As he came out of the cloud Ruff came upon a Zero and fired an ineffective burst. Ruff saw several Lightnings and climbed to join them when he saw a single enemy fighter heading for Wewak with its wheels down for a landing, but as Ruff approached the fighter retracted its gear and turned into him. Ruff fired from 100 yards, but the enemy passed under him and Ruff was unable to see the outcome of his attack.

The flight led by Capt. Clifton Troxell of 8th Fighter Command HQ was the most successful during the day's combat. The flight consisted of Troxell's Wingman, 1Lt. Jess Gidley, and second Element Leader 1Lt. James Griffin with 1Lt. Kenneth Ladd as his Wingman. At 1000 the flight was at 22,000 feet when two Zeros were spotted coming through the overcast, followed by more Zeros in two ship elements. Troxell led his flight in a dive on the two Zeros and fired a long range 80 degree burst without result. He then saw a fixed gear fighter, but had to break away when a Tony got on his tail. During his escape Troxell lost both the Tony and his Wingman. He encountered a Zero flying 90 degrees to his course and fired a 40 degree deflection shot at it, then followed this attack with a 30 degree head on shot at another Zero, but both attacks did not result in a claim. Troxell then saw a Zero chasing a P-38 and fired at it, causing the enemy pilot to turn away with his engine burning, He then saw two Zeros and dove on the Wingman, but closed too fast and switched his attack to the Leader and fired a short burst. Both enemy fighters turned away as Troxell pulled up in a fast climb. He saw another Zero and closed. The Zero pilot saw the P-38 and attempted to turn into Troxell, who rolled and fired a 30 degree deflection shot and saw pieces flying off its nose and tail assembly. Troxell was running low on fuel and there was heavy AA fire nearby, making him decide to return to base with two victories. Second element pilots Griffin and Ladd dove on the Zeros, but also missed their initial long deflection shots. On Griffin's third pass he got hits on a Zero that got away into the clouds for a damaged claim. On Ladd's third pass he got hits on the Zero's tail but it dove away. The two Lightning pilots made three or four more unsuccessful passes before a Zero got on Ladd's tail. Griffin came around and put a two second burst into the cockpit, and as the Zero went down in flames its pilot bailed out off shore of the Boram Strip. Four enemy fighters flew in to protect the parachuting pilot. As the Japanese circled, Ladd dove on the first fighter and Griffin on the second. Griffin closed to 50 yards and got hits, but did not see what happened as he lost sight of it. The two Americans made passes on other enemy fighters, whose evasive actions were effective and, running low on fuel, they returned to base.

By the time 1Lt. Donald McGee led his flight down on the initial batch of enemy fighters, the other three flights had dispersed them. McGee lost sight of the enemy, but kept his flight together at 17,000 feet until he sighted the enemy again. McGee made a diving attack on a Tony, closing on its rear from long range until 150 yards, where he fired a short burst. The Tony burst into flames, falling off on one wing and spinning into the ground. McGee and Wingman 2Lt. Howard Donaldson then saw 15 Zeros off Cape Boram and closed, but the Japanese did not seem eager to press their 15 to 2 advantage and Split-S'd away before the two Americans got within a half mile. The two then went into a high speed climb and were attacked by a Tony from the rear. McGee instructed Donaldson to split up so that one of them could get a shot at it. However, Donaldson did not go out far enough, and the two were losing the Tony when another P-38 came and drove it off. The two then circled the target area until the bombers finished and McGee and Donaldson returned to base.

The only loss for the day was the P-38 flown by 1Lt. Richard Strommen, whose P-38 went down near Bena Bena, about 90 miles northwest of Marilinan. Strommen returned to base after 11 days of walking through the New Guinea mountains.

1Lt. Donald McGee scored his fifth and last victory in the Pacific and returned to the US in November 1943, serving as a flight instructor. In late 1944 he was deployed to the ETO, serving as the CO of the 363FS and 364FS of the 357FG as a Captain. On 2 March 1945 McGee shot down a Me-109 near Magdeburg while flying a P-51 for the 363FS. He was also credited with two ground strafing victories in the ETO. He retired from the Air Force as a Lt. Colonel in October 1967.

15 September 1943: 475FG/431FS

Capt. John Hood led 16 P-38s from Berry at 0745 but five aborted, and the reminder of the Squadron rendezvoused with B-24s at 0905 over Mt. Yonkie at 16,000 feet. The Squadron escorted the last 11 B-24s as top cover at 20,000 feet and were attacked by a few Tonys, but made no claims, though they kept the B-24s safe.

LEFT: Capt. Clifton **Troxell** shot down two Zeros for four total victories. (AFAA) RIGHT: 1Lt. Donald **McGee** shot down a Tony for his fifth and last victory in the Pacific to become an ace. (AFAA)

Maj. Donald **McGee** (R) as the CO of the 363FS/357FG in January 1945. Pictured at left, is 13½ victory ace, Maj. Donald Bochkay, who succeeded him as 363FS CO. McGee claimed his sixth victory with this squadron. (AAF)

Actual gun camera film of **Lynch's** Dinah victory. (AAF)

16-19 September 1943: 475FG

Over the next four days there was a respite for the 475FG, as they flew uneventful patrols over Morobe, weather recon, routine intercept scrambles, and bomber escorts. The Japanese Air Forces were obliged to regroup, as the Allied invasion in the Huon Gulf steadily captured one airbase after another.

16 September 1943: 35FG/39FS

On the 16th Maj. Thomas Lynch led 16 P-38s in four flights of the 39FS on a B-24 escort and sweep to Wewak, but due to bad weather was unable to rendezvous with the bombers. The Squadron finally met the B-24s near Mt. Yonkie and escorted them to Hansa Bay, where Lynch saw a single Japanese bomber below. Lynch instructed the other three flights to remain with the bombers and led his flight on the hapless Dinah. Lynch had a long chase to catch the Dinah, which took no evasive action. He closed within 300 yards and opened fire, hitting the starboard engine, which caught fire and spread quickly. One of the crewmen bailed out before the bomber hit the water for victory #16, his last for almost five months (10 February 1944).

Maj. Thomas **Lynch's** 16th victory is registered on his P-38 and would be his last for almost five months. (10 February 1944). (AAF)

18 September 1943: 35FG/39FS

Capt. Charles Sullivan crash landed in the Ramu-Sepik area, and two weeks later he trekked out of dense jungle and was rescued. During the trek he had to shoot two unfriendly natives who seemed to want to turn him in to the Japanese for a reward. Despite their dangerous mission schedule, the 39th had suffered a very low loss rate since the Squadron began operations in May 1942. By the end of September 1943 the Squadron had lost only seven P-38s in combat as compared to their 113 victories.

Capt. Charles **Sullivan**, patch on head, after his trek out of the jungle after he crashlanded. (AFAA)

September 1943: 8FG: 35FS Equipped with New P-40s

The "Bully-Beef" supply transport escorts had been the main type of operation for the 35th and 36th Squadrons since May, and the squadrons were impatient to get back into real combat. By the end of September there were 24 new P-40N5s in the 35th, and those men familiar with earlier model Warhawks were impressed. Its longer fuselage made this new P-40 much more stable than earlier models while preserving its excellent turning performance. Maj. Emmett "Cyclone" Davis was to lead the 35FS back into an active combat and was known as a "fighting CO" rather than a desk jockey.

19 September 1943: JAAF at Wewak

During this time the Japanese 68th and 78th Sentais put up a determined battle, considering that they could muster no more than 12 Tonys over Wewak. By 19 September the 78th Sentai was briefly withdrawn until replacement fighters could be sent from the Philippines. Lightning pilots judged the Kawasaki Ki-61 Tony as the most dangerous Japanese fighter over New Guinea, since most of the P-38s lost in aerial combat were the victims of Tony fighters. However, the P-38 pilots felt that although the Tony was somewhat faster than other enemy fighters, it was still inferior and vulnerable.

20 September 1943: 475FG/432FS

The 432nd sent out 16 P-38s under Capt. Daniel Roberts on a B-24 escort to Wewak that was uneventful until the return leg. As they passed Marilinan at 19,000 feet the fighter controller called bandits in the area. When Clover Red, White, Blue, and Green Flights approached Bulolo they saw the bandits and turned back to meet them.

Green Flight, led by Capt. Campbell Wilson and consisting of Wingman 1Lt. Arthur Peregoy and second element 1Lt. James Ince and Wingman 2Lt. Billy Gresham, did not turn back, as they were completely surprised by six Tonys that appeared out of the clouds from above and behind and were first seen and called out by Ince. Ince and Gresham turned 180 degrees to rescue Wilson and Peregoy, who were about 1,000 yards ahead. As Ince saw Wilson and Peregoy turn into the enemy he saw a Tony fire on Peregoy, whose P-38 went down in a steep dive with its starboard engine smoking badly. As Ince and Gresham watched Peregoy, two Tonys attacked and began firing head on from 300 yards. Ince chose the closest as his target and waited until it was 100 yards away before he fired. When he squeezed the trigger nothing happened and the Tony passed under him. Ince dove away, trying to charge his guns, but was unsuccessful, and had accumulated three or four Tonys on his tail. Ince steepened his dive and headed home. Meanwhile, Gresham rolled away from the Tonys in a high speed dive that tore the rivets out of his Lightning's wing around the intercooler. Gresham

2Lt. Billy **Gresham** shot down two Tonys to total three victories. (AAF)

immediately climbed and sneaked behind two Tonys flying in a tight formation. Gresham waited and fired two or three two second bursts that spun one into the ground three miles from the Air Controller. Oil from the Tony had smeared Gresham's windshield, and to make matters worse, a Tony had gotten on Gresham's tail; it was evidently out of ammunition, as it closed well into range but did not fire. Gresham dove away and went after another Tony, firing long bursts into the length of its fuselage and tearing pieces off its tail. As Gresham overran the doomed Tony two more attacked him from above. One flew past while the other dove, making a shallow port turn and giving Gresham a 30 degree deflection shot from above into its left front quarter. The other Tony had gotten on Gresham's tail and, low on ammunition, fuel, and with both intercoolers out, he decided to break away toward the friendly base below and the enemy pilot also broke off.

Capt. Daniel Roberts led his Red Flight and the Blue and White Flights to make passes on Zeros at 17,000 down to 12,000 feet. The Lightning pilots mostly fired high degree deflection shots that were unsuccessful. Roberts and Wingman 2Lt. LeRoy Bryan followed a Hap that had Split-S'd, and the two Americans fired on it during their dive. When Bryan pulled out of his dive he was 3,000 feet lower than Roberts and at the same altitude as the Hap. Bryan fired "a pretty good burst," and the Hap went down smoking and disintegrated. Roberts' flight saw several more bogies near Marilinan, but the enemy pilots would not engage and fled. Red Flight was low on fuel and returned to base.

Capt. William Waldman, Blue Flight Leader, saw two Zeros slightly above him and led his flight into them, but soon they had four more Tonys on their tails and had to go into a weaving climb to safety. When he looked back, Waldman saw Zeros (later ID'd as Tonys) outnumbering the P-38s and went after them, but didn't hit anything on his first pass. When Waldman pulled up he saw two Tonys and dove after one that was in a slow turn. The fast moving Waldman almost overran it, but got good shots that tore off pieces of its right wing, but he broke away for a probable. The lead Tony pilot shot at Waldman and missed, and the American out climbed him. Waldman and his Wingman, who had stayed with him, made several more passes on enemy fighters without observable results. When the Air Controller informed them of enemy bombers bombing the American base Waldman checked the area and saw 16 enemy fighters 6,000 feet above and then checked his fuel, which was low, and wisely departed for home.

At the time Roberts called out the Zeros and ordered tanks dropped, White Flight Leader Capt. Frederick Harris followed, but saw "a bunch of Zeros" diving out of the sun on the tails of his flight. The Zeros "started pouring lead into us," and Second Element Leader 2Lt. Thomas Simms was hit. Harris' Wingman, 2Lt. Donald Garrison, saw Simms' Lightning start smoking and go into a half roll and followed him down. He saw Simms bail out, his chute open, and then head for an area between the Watut and Markham Rivers. Simms was never seen again.

21 September 1943: 49FG/8FS

At 1630, Eightball CO Capt. Ernest Harris led 15 Eightballers up for the last patrol of the day in four flights. It was scheduled to be a routine patrol in the Lae-Hopoi area, providing medium cover over a convoy in Huon Gulf. After they patrolled over the coast for an hour *Charter* signaled the approach of an enemy contact. The Flight spotted a twin engine Dinah recon bomber at 18,000 feet just east of Lae, but Harris' Red Flight could not overtake the speeding bomber. As the Flight flew back to the east, a flight of three Haps passed under them and Harris turned after the lead enemy fighter, which rolled for the nearby clouds. Harris' new N-model was able to catch the Japanese fighter after a 6,000 foot descent. Harris fired explosive rounds into the Oscar's canopy and mid-fuselage, and Harris' Wingman, 2Lt. Richard Polhamus, confirmed Harris' tenth victory, which made him the first Warhawk double ace in the Pacific. Harris then made five passes at a formation of three Bettys; although getting hits, these attacks were unsuccessful.

Red Element Leader 2Lt. Daniel David and his Wingman, 2Lt. Harold Sawyer, followed Harris, and David chased the other Zero encountered by Harris but it got away. After unsuccessfully chasing several more enemy fighters David fired on a "possible FW-190 which seemed to have a cross on both upper wing surfaces. Darkness made positive identification impossible." (Note: Davis' #3 man, 2Lt. Averette Lee, also ID'd it as a FW-190 in

Left to right: Eightball CO, Capt. Ernest **Harris** became the first P-40 double ace in the Pacific when he shot down a Zero for his last victory. (AAF)

2Lt. Daniel **David** claimed his second and last victory. (AAF)

2Lt. Harold **Sawyer** claimed his first of three victories. (AAF) his ICR.) The damaged enemy fighter smoked and Spilt-S'd, and Howard verified that the "Fred or Hap" crashed in flames into the ground. David and Sawyer started to climb back toward the bombers when they saw two Haps flying below. Since nightfall was quickly approaching David had to get quite close to ID it before firing. David fired on the right Hap but missed, then had to break off quickly, as another Hap got on his tail. David twisted and turned and dove into a valley, but these maneuvers only resulted in having a Hap now on each side and one on his tail. David found himself heading directly into the mountains, but luckily found a gap and flew through, just missing the trees. As he looked back David saw the following Hap catch a wingtip in the trees and tumble into the valley beyond. David's Wingman, 2Lt. Harold Sawyer, took on another Hap and fired a short burst that caused it to chandelle to port. Sawyer followed and fired a two to three second burst that started it smoking. He fired another burst from astern that caused it to burst into flames and head down. Sawyer pulled up and started back home when he saw a V of three Betty bombers high and to starboard. He climbed up from the 2 o'clock position and fired a long burst at the lead Betty, hitting its nose and right engine. The bomber started on fire and dropped off out of formation.

1Lt. Robert Howard was leading Blue Flight, consisting of Wingman 1Lt. Philip Kriechbaum, second Element Leader 1Lt. Harry McCullough, and Wingman 1Lt. Nelson Flack. Blue Flight approached the enemy formation in the approaching darkness and made a pass on Zeros and Tonys, but the two Eightball flights ahead had engaged them and Blue Flight had to remain on the edge of the battle. Each time they tried to chase an enemy fighter it already had a P-40 on its tail. The Flight bounced around 18,000 and 12,000 feet, waiting for its chance. The last time Howard climbed he found himself by chance behind a three Betty element and fired from out of the sun on the unsuspecting enemy. He fired two bursts at the wing bomber and hit it squarely, then transferred his fire from one bomber to another, depending upon the volume of fire he was receiving from their gunners. Finally, all his guns stopped firing and he had to break off to find the gun problem. He found that the circuit breaker had tripped, flipped it back ON, and climbed back toward the Bettys. He continued to fire on the Bettys; although their enemy escorts were only 2,000 feet above, they never interfered. One Betty had flames enveloping its fuselage, but as Howard closed to finish it off he squeezed the trigger and only about three rounds were expended before he ran out of ammunition. The left element bomber fell out of formation with a burning left engine and two other Bettys escaped trailing smoke. Howard would claim that victim as the sixth and final kill of his tour. Howard's Element Leader, McCullough, flew into the attack and could not immediately locate an enemy fighter in the rapidly approaching darkness. Suddenly, a Zero pulled up in front of McCullough from nowhere and he fired a very short burst that hit the starboard wing. The enemy fighter burst into flames with a large puff of black smoke and exploded as he passed over it. As McCullough was watching his victim two Zeros descended on him and he "pushed the stick to the corner and rolled as I went down" and lost his firing attackers.

While patrolling over the convoy, 1Lt. Roger Grant's White Flight went after a reported recon aircraft but were called back to the convoy after ten minutes when it radioed that it was under attack. As they headed toward the convoy's AA barrage they saw two Zeros that were engaged by Red and White Flights. Grant's Second element Wingman, 2Lt. John Hanson, spotted a Hap and dove after it, but was cut off by another P-40. The Hap pilot was in a shallow dive, turning left and right and doing half rolls. When the other P-40 made a pass at the Hap it would turn into it from the left, causing the American to pass under it. Hanson finally made a pass from the opposite direction and the Hap turned into him. The other P-40 was able to fire a short burst directly into the enemy's cockpit, probably killing the pilot, and it crashed into the mountains. Meanwhile, Grant had made a head on pass on the Oscars and shot one down, but White Flight had become separated in the clouds after the fight with the escorts. Hanson then formed on Grant, and they immediately spotted three bombers above to port in the far distance, headed toward Lae. Finally, in near darkness, Grant and Hanson caught the enemy bombers as they approached the Cromwell Mountains and separated. Hanson made beam attacks, from side to side, concentrating on the left bomber until it went down trailing smoke and flames. Hanson continued after the other two bombers, "making every kind of pass I could." Enemy return fire was weak, as Hanson believed that he had hit the tail gunners. Finally, the second Betty went down from an attack from 1 o'clock, and as he went after the third Betty Hanson found he was out of ammunition and filed a damaged claim. As Grant approached the left bomber Wingman he tentatively identified the bomber as a Lily that had no rear defensive armament. But as he approached, shells from the Betty's rear cannon hit his engine and Grant returned ineffective fire through a windscreen fouled with glycol coolant streaming from his damaged engine, which finally quit. After bailing out Grant found himself hanging in his chute 40 feet up in the trees covering the Cromwell Mountains. As darkness fell he "pendulumed" in his chute straps until he could grab the main tree trunk and cut his life raft and survival pack free; he then climbed down to the ground. The exhausted pilot fell asleep, and in the morning he began an epic trek though the dense forest, hauling his life raft and gear until the late afternoon. All that next day he struggled through the jungle until he came upon a large washed out chasm which plunged 2,000 feet to a river below. Grant spent the next day picking his way carefully down to the river. Once there Grant cautiously continued floating down the river until it became too shallow and rocky for his raft. Then he heard a Japanese patrol searching the river bank down stream. With his raft slung over his back Grant climbed back up the chasm. After 15 days Grant stumbled out of the forest and onto the coastal plain north of Hopoi village, where he was rescued and later returned to combat at Marilinan.

Capt. Ernest Harris scored his 10th and last victory and would add a Zero probable on 15 November as a new Major. He returned to the US in December 1943 and remained in the Air Force. While with the 36FG Harris was killed in a flying accident flying a P-80 on 24 August 1949 near Augsburg, Germany.

21 September 1943: 8FG/35FS

Complete security of the Huon Peninsula was gradually implemented throughout the later months of 1943. On 21 September, 18 P-40s of the 35FS were moved to Tsili Tsili in preparation for support of the Finschhafen landings. Tsili Tsili was only about 90 miles from the harbor and airfield at Finschhafen, and the P-40N could maintain a patrol there for about an hour.

22 September 1943: Finschhafen Invasion

The capture of Salamaua on 13 September and of Lae three days later, although decisive victories, did not end the threat of an enemy air counterattack in that area. Moreover, these objectives were only the first of a long succession which would carry MacArthur far along the New Guinea coast. Japanese forces were still located at points in the Markham River Valley and were to be reduced by the 7th Australian Division, supported and supplied by C-47 troop carriers. The Australians were to capture areas and build airfields to supply their advance. This process of gaining control of airfields in the Markham and Ramu River Valleys was a prelude to operations to be carried out against Madang and other locations to the west. The success of these operations would secure for the Allies the land approaches to the Huon Peninsula. Meanwhile, Lae and Salamaua had been captured much sooner than expected, which led to a change of plans so far as amphibious operations were concerned. The original schedule had included a landing near Finschhafen approximately four weeks after the fall of Lae. This objective was strategically located on the Huon Gulf and approximately 64 miles beyond Lae, and was to be developed as a staging area for future advances and as a forward base for aircraft and light vessels. However, in mid-September, Intelligence found that the Japanese forces in that area were vulnerable and considered the possible acceleration of the schedule. Three days later, MacArthur approved plans which scheduled the Finschhafen landing for 22 September. Less than five days had passed between the decision to execute the operation and the H-hour invasion. The Lae operation had provided the necessary experience for this invasion, and the troops, landing craft, and destroyers were available at Milne Bay. The Air Force also had benefited with its contribution in the capture of Lae. As the landing craft moved from Buna to Lae for the new amphibious operation, and as the troops and equipment were loaded there, the Fifth Air Force provided almost continuous fighter cover at two levels. The destroyer *Reid* again acted as a fighter control ship, but instead of cruising 60 to 70 miles away the *Reid* remained with the convoy to give more immediate contact with the large numbers of fighters escorting the convoy.

In preparation for the invasion, AAF B-24s and B-25s and the occasional P-39 unit attacked Japanese airfields, supply dumps, troops, and supply and reinforcement routes, such as bridges, trucks, and barges on the way to Finschhafen. During the night of 21-22 September, USN R.Adm. Daniel Barbey's Task Force 76 convoy, which had been loaded at Lae, moved east along the coast and rounded the tip of the Huon Peninsula. At 0445, without the benefit of pre-invasion naval bombardment or aerial strafing, Brigadier J.V. Windeyer's 20th Brigade landed at Scarlet Beach near the Song River, just north of Finschhafen. Simultaneously the 22nd Australian Militia approached from the coast. The Australians made rapid progress and quickly captured the key airstrip, while the American air attacks, despite cloudy conditions, continued with good results against installations in Finschhafen. Once it was obvious that the landings were completely successful the convoy headed back toward Buna shortly before noon.

Improving weather over northeastern New Guinea in the latter half of September prompted the Japanese 11th Air Fleet on New Britain to schedule air attacks on Allied shipping heading up the Huon Gulf. During the night of 21 September, the 751st Kokutai sent out four Bettys from Vunakanau, Rabaul, while five more Bettys of the 702nd Kokutai took off in the early morning hours of 22 September. Neither formation contacted the Finschhafen invasion force, nor was each required to bomb secondary targets. During the morning of 22 September, four 751st Betty bombers were returning from an attack on an airfield east of Nadzab when they observed an Allied invasion convoy moving north about 25 miles from Finschhafen. Once the Japanese Air Command was notified of the invasion convoy they sent out an order to arm every available Betty bomber with torpedoes. Eight 751st Kokutai Bettys armed with torpedoes and 23 Zeros of the 253rd Kokutai with approximately 15 others from the 201st and 204th Kokutais were hastily assembled. Meanwhile, the Australian 22nd Battalion made a flanking amphibious landing at Finschhafen to cut off the enemy's coastal escape route to Madang. Kenney's fighters flew above the Navy fleet and Australian troops that came ashore south of the town. At 0840, the Bettys took off in three waves and then headed down the length of New Britain toward the target with 20 Zeros in close escort above and behind the bombers. A number of 5FC fighter units were in the best position in the battle zone to intercept the Japanese: the P-40s of the 35FS and the P-38s of the 39FS and 432FS.

On 2 October, after a week of hard fighting, the Japanese had lost 1,500 defenders and the Australians had captured the town and nearby airfield. But the victory was incomplete, as 4,000 troops, the majority of the Japanese garrison, retreated to the 3,000 foot Sattelberg Peak that dominated Finschhafen and the surrounding area.

22 September 1943: 8FG/35FS

The 35FS sent up all of its 16 P-40s at 1030 from Tsili Tsili to meet a Yellow Alert sent by the convoy. Three P-40s aborted, including mission leader Maj. Emmett Davis, but the others began to patrol. When the Japanese arrived it was ill-timed for the Americans, as their patrols were just changing units.

Capt. Harold **McClelland** got his first of three victories. (AAF)

When Maj. Emmett Davis aborted he called Blue Flight Leader to take over, but was unable to contact him and appointed Yellow Flight Leader Capt. Harold McClelland to lead the mission. McClelland, with 2Lt. Olin Brewer on his wing, was patrolling at 18,000 feet when the Controller vectored them toward an enemy force heading toward the convoy. When the enemy arrived over the convoy P-38s also arrived and attacked. McClelland dove with his flight in string from

2Lt. Richard **West**. (standing beside his P-40's prop) began his 14 victory career with two Zero victories and a probable. (AFAA)

18,000 feet on the enemy aircraft that were flying from 1,000 feet to sea level. They saw two Zeros, but before they got to them four P-38s arrived first. McClelland then saw two Zeros and a Tony below, and Brewer went after the Tony, but his guns malfunctioned. McClelland's second Element Leader, 1Lt. Bennett McCoy, and Wingman 1Lt. John Brown both fired on the same Zero and Brown claimed the victory. Brown was low on fuel and headed back to base, but soon saw two P-38s chasing a Zero low on the water. The Zero pulled up to escape and Brown dove to the attack, but the Zero crashed into the sea as he closed to fire. McCoy then saw a Hap close to the water and fired on it, but at the same time a P-38 came on the scene and also fired. The Zero crashed into the sea, but McCoy did not claim this victory either. As he checked his rear McCoy saw a Zero 400 yards behind, but then saw a P-38 come in and shoot it down.

The Navy Fighter Controller *Duckbutt* called out and guided the 35th toward an enemy plot. 1Lt. Harold Souther was leading Blue Flight when the Controller guided him directly to the Betty bombers. Souther checked the Controller's warning of high cover for the bombers and then dove to attack the right side of the leading Betty formation while his second element attacked from the left. One Betty had already been hit by AA fire from the convoy and was in flames. The area around the convoy was filled with AA explosions, making it dangerous to come too close. Souther ordered his second element to close on a Betty head on from the left while he and his Wingman attacked from head on to the right. As Souther closed his windshield fogged up and he fired from too far, so his volley was wide. There were about a half dozen other fighters making passes in the area and Souther decided to break off until his windshield cleared. Once it cleared he found a Betty that was not under attack, but it disappeared into the clouds before he could fire. He flew over the cloud and found the bomber exiting on the other side and made two passes, but on his third pass a Zero approached and Souther fired and missed low and behind. The Zero and Betty continued on and Souther made a long approach on them. The Zero turned into Souther, who pulled up and evaded the Zero, which passed under him in a dive while the Betty flew beneath a cloud. The Zero pilot came out of his dive into a vertical roll, intending to get on Souther's tail. However, Souther pushed the throttle full forward and pulled the stick back into his lap, which gave him a slight lead, and he fired a short burst that caused the Zero to start smoking. The Zero headed for New Britain and Souther, who had lost his flight, decided to turn back toward the coast and was credited with a probable. Blue Flight second Element Leader 1Lt. Walter Posvistak and Wingman 2Lt. William Gardner broke off from Souther to attack another Betty formation. Posvistak made six passes on a Betty just off the water, and on the final pass from 90 degrees he fired and shot down the Betty for his only victory of the war. Just as Gardner was about to fire on the Bettys, a Tony escort appeared and was about to attack Posvistak. Gardner gave the Tony a short burst and its pilot pulled up into the clouds and lost Gardner, but he saw a Betty flying on the water. He made two passes, and on the second, the Betty turned into him and he fired a burst that hit its cockpit and port engine, setting the bomber on fire. Gardner climbed through the overcast, which was now only 500 feet off the water, and saw another Betty and fired without observing hits before he had to break off because of low fuel.

Capt. Richard Sauve was leading his flight in Lazy-8s over a plot and sighted two Zeros flying low over water. Sauve's Wingman, 2Lt. Glendi Holder, and #3 man 2Lt. Roy Klandrud went into a steep dive to make a pass at 30 degrees deflection starboard. Sauve and his Wingman pulled after the Zero to the right, while Klandrud made a sharp chandelle to the left, at the top of which was the Zero spiraling vertically. Klandrud fired and the enemy pilot leveled off. Klandrud fired a long burst at 300 yards that started it to smoke, and it set on fire and crashed into the sea.

2Lt. Richard West picked out a Betty and headed toward it, but broke off when a Hamp came in on his starboard side. With two P-40s protecting his rear, West closed on the Hamp and shot off pieces of its tail or wing and it went down. Suddenly, West saw tracers passing his cockpit, and when he looked around he discovered that instead of his P-40 Wingman there were enemy fighters following him. West dove away and was fortunate to find a cloud to duck into. When he emerged from the cloud another Hamp passed into range and West fired but missed. The Hamp turned into West's sights again and he fired, setting it on fire, and the Hamp crashed into the sea. He chased several more enemy fighters, but broke away when "more Hamps came uncomfortably close." When he returned to battle he saw three P-38s chasing another Hamp, but all three missed or overran. The Hamp pulled up and ahead of West, who fired from astern. The Hamp half rolled, caught fire, and crashed into the water. West turned for home low on fuel and ammunition with the first of his 14 career victories.

22 September 1943: 475FG/43FS/433FS

432FS

Just before 1300 *Duckbutt*, the destroyer *Reid* Controller, received a large number of plots coming from New Britain, less than 70 miles from the convoy. Three American fighter squadrons that were covering the convoy (the 341FS flying P-47s, the 35FS flying P-40s, and the 39FS with P-38s) were due for relief within a few minutes, but all had sufficient fuel to adequately engage the oncoming Japanese force.

Two relieving squadrons, the 9th and 432nd, were in the air and could be vectored toward the Japanese force. At 1200 Capt. Frederick Harris was leading the 432nd from Dobodura at 10,000 feet when *Duckbutt* picked up a plot on a large enemy formation 60 miles northeast, but were unable to determine its altitude, other than "it was very high." *Duckbutt* issued reports every five minutes until the enemy formation was spotted at 6,000 feet, a much lower altitude than expected. Harris soon identified six Bettys covered by 10 Zeros below, and also between 20 to 30 Zeros above in high cover doing "aerobatics." Harris decided to ignore the higher enemy force and ordered drop tanks to be jettisoned before diving to cut off the Bettys before they bombed the convoy. As Harris led the squadron in a fast dive, the Bettys, also in a fast dive, flew under a thin layer of clouds, disappearing from sight. The Hades Lightnings pulled up over the cloud layer, where they ran into the Zero close escort, but the Japanese high cover arrived from above and behind. The Zeros left their bombers unprotected, which left the last two flights of P-38s led by 1Lts. James Ince and John Loisel free to attack the bombers.

Red Flight leader Harris was attacked by a Zero of the high cover formation from behind, but Harris' Wingman, 2Lt. Zack Dean, shot it off his Leader's tail with a long, continuous burst that exploded it. Harris cleared his Flight from the escorts long enough to dive after three bombers which were separated from the others. Harris fired on the lead bomber, which he hit amidships, and it went into the sea with one crewman parachuting from the doomed bomber. Dean took the one on the left, which exploded violently, probably because it had not dropped its bombs. The two Americans then used their diving speed and peeled off. Harris fired at a Zero that was slightly below and ahead of him, and it went directly into the water. Harris and Dean climbed and looked for more Zeros and found some, but they were already capably engaged by P-47s and P-38s and saw four go down: three by the 39FS Lightnings and one by 348FG Thunderbolts. Harris spotted a lone Zero flying low, trying to sneak back home, and shot it down to become an ace with these three victories. Harris' second element, led by 1Lt. Vivian Cloud with 2Lt. Donald Garrison on his wing, became separated from Harris' lead element after the initial combat. The duo chased the Bettys as they approached the convoy and had come in range of the convoy's AA fire. Cloud's first burst killed the Betty's tail gunner and his second destroyed the dorsal gun position. Cloud closed on the now harmless Betty and hit its port engine and wing. As Cloud passed over his victim he immediately saw one of the escorting Zeros directly ahead making a slow roll that exposed it to Cloud's guns. Cloud closed in to fire when the Zero reached the top of its

LEFT: 2Lt. Zack **Dean** claimed his first two of seven victories. (AFAA)
RIGHT 1Lt. Vivian **Cloud** got his first two of five victories. (AAF)

1Lt. John **Loisel**. (smoking) scored his third of 11 victories. (AFAA)

1Lt. James **Ince's** two victories were his 3rd and 4th. (AFAA)

roll and tattooed the enemy fighter from the port side of the cockpit to the starboard wingtip, causing the Zero to fall off and dive straight into the water. As Cloud pulled away he saw a P-38 with an engine on fire being pursued by two Zeros, but as Cloud turned to help the Lightning four more Zeros dove from above and port to get on his tail. Cloud went into a steep dive, and when he lost his attackers his fighter's starboard engine burst into flames. As the fire neared his wing tanks he decided to bail out. He released his seat belt and canopy, but his fighter went into a dive, pushing Cloud back into his seat. Cloud leveled the fighter out, pushed himself up, and dropped towards the dead engine, and the slip stream sucked him out. As soon as he neared the water he unbuckled the chute and dropped into the water, but soon realized that his rubber raft was still attached to the parachute and had to swim back to retrieve it. He inflated his raft, and within 20 minutes a destroyer picked him up. Later Cloud learned that Wingman Garrison was missing; there is no record of the cause of Garrison's demise.

Capt. William Waldman's 432nd White Flight encountered the Zero top cover that was attacking Harris' lead flight. During the first combat Waldman and Wingman 2Lt. Howard Hedrick saw Cloud's P-38 being attacked and Cloud bail out. As Cloud descended the White First Element saw a lone enemy fighter make a half roll toward the parachuting American, but the enemy pilot turned away when he saw two P-38s turning into him. Waldman and Hedrick circled Cloud until he hit the water. The two then saw enemy bombers below and dove on them. On their way down they saw three Zeros that were diving in turn. Waldman took a snap shot on the lead enemy fighter and missed. Hedrick saw one bomber peel off to the right and closed behind it to 100 yards, firing a five second burst. The enemy pilot turned to port, and Hedrick followed and fired another burst, sending the fighter cartwheeling into the water. Waldman then made a 45 degree deflection shot from above on a Betty and got some hits on the rear fuselage before his guns jammed. Hedrick made a few more passes on the bombers before his gunsight malfunctioned. The impotent White Flight Lead Element pilots lingered in the area and saw several Japanese aircraft crash before retreating back to base. After this first combat White Flight Second Element, led by 1Lt. John Rundell with Wingman F/O Charles Ratajski, attacked two Bettys in succession without result, but then Rundell shot one of the Bettys down with a burst fired from directly astern, starting a fire on its entire port side, and saw it crash into the sea. As the Bettys left the area of the convoy Ratajski attacked them, and after his last pass at the bombers he lost his flight and climbed back toward land to about 3,000 feet. He saw a P-40 slowly closing on a Zero near the deck, and since he had the altitude advantage, Ratajski dove and beat the P-40 as well as Clover Green Flight to the Zero and fired a single burst into the Zero's canopy, killing the pilot.

1Lt. James Ince's Blue Flight was at 10,000 feet when Harris' Flight started to dive to the attack. Ince looked around to clear his flight before attacking enemy aircraft below, ordered the belly tanks to be dropped, and then led them into a fast dive. As they closed on the enemy Ince saw two P-38 flights intercept them and had to lead his flight away. While flying on they saw eight to 10 Betty bombers heading for the convoy at 100 feet. Ince led his flight in a fast dive at 30 degrees astern. At least three of the bombers jettisoned their bombs early, and Ince bypassed these to attack the five closing on the convoy. Ince fired a quick burst at the one closest to the convoy but saw no results. He then flew through the heavy AA fire of the convoy to get on the tail of a Betty making a right turn and fired from 150 to 50 yards, with cannon shells exploding into the middle of its fuselage. Ince closed and fired again, raking its nose, and the Betty crashed into the water. Ince's victim was followed by Bettys shot down by his Blue Flight. A Betty that crashed in a large explosion was shot down by 2Lt. Charles Willis and was followed by a Zero shot down by 2Lt. James Farris. Willis had seen his Betty 300 yards to starboard heading for the convoy and made a head on 30 degree deflection shot, then circled back to get on its tail to fire a long burst, getting numerous hits, but the Betty continued to fly on. Willis continued to follow, and just as he was about to fire again the Betty hit the water. Farris had been following Ince, but he had forgotten to switch fuel tanks and both engines quit; by the time he got them started he had fallen far behind. After the First Element made their second pass Farris finally caught up and made a pass at the third Zero. Farris continued to fire until he passed over it, and as he chandelled Farris saw his victim hit the water near Ince's and Willis' victims. Ince then led Blue Flight, searching for more Japanese, and they ran into five Zeros head on. Three continued directly toward them, while the other two peeled away. Ince fired at the lead Zero, and as he closed to 50 yards he saw the Zero roll over with smoke pouring from its engine cowling. As Ince turned sharply to port he saw another Zero and fired a short burst at it, but the enemy pilot turned too fast and Ince had to break off. This Zero was then chased by 2Lt. John Michener, who had cut inside Ince, and the Zero then flew directly into Michener's sights. He started firing from long range until close range and saw his tracers hit the Zero. Michener got in closer and jiggled his stick as he fired a long burst to spread out his bullets over the fuselage. Then either his guns jammed or he ran out of ammunition, and the Zero began to fly away. Michener tried to recharge his guns but was unsuccessful, and had to dive away with a probable claim when he was attacked by two Zeros. Farris then joined Ince and attacked a lone Zero circling over the convoy at 2,000 to 4,000 feet. They made three passes at it before Ince ran out of ammunition and then had to feather his engine when a USN AA fragment hit it.

1Lt. John Loisel kept Clover Green Flight on high cover at 10,000 feet until he was certain that there were no more enemy aircraft above him. Green Flight then dove on the Zeros dog fighting the other P-38s and continued making successive passes until they reached the water. Loisel caught a Zero that was climbing and knocked off large pieces with his cannon shells; its wing folded off just before it hit the water. Clover Green #3, F/O Henry Condon, was flying some distance behind the First Element when a Zero that had escaped their fire flew toward Condon, who fired from 300 to 50 yards and saw pieces come off its cowling. Condon's Lightning just missed colliding with his oncoming victim as it crash landed onto the water. While it was still floating Condon went down for another pass, but his guns malfunctioned and he turned for base. Meanwhile, Loisel and Wingman 2Lt. LeRoy Bryan chased after another Zero that was flying just off the water. When Loisel began to fire his ammunition ran out, so Bryan fired an initial long burst and closed more. He fired again and the Zero crashed into the water. Loisel and Bryan flew on and encountered another Zero; Bryan fired and the Zero disintegrated while Loisel went in and took a photo. Bryan's two victories were his last of three for the war.

Capt. Joseph **McKeon** destroyed hid third enemy aircraft. (AFAA)

433FS

Until then there had been very little air opposition, with the only action reported by the 433FS patrol at 1000 between Lae and Finschhafen by 16 P-38s. Capt. Joseph McKeon's Yellow Flight was flying at 27,000 feet south of Finschhafen and was vectored by *Duckbutt* Controller toward a lone bogie. McKeon led his flight down from high cover, and when the Lead Flight was unable to intercept the bogie McKeon happened to spot it 20 miles away and slightly above. McKeon approached in a dive from slightly port and above to be sure of its identity. The Tony made a zigzag starboard turn and then straightened out as McKeon throttled back and closed astern and fired. The Tony began to smoke and then exploded.

The 475th had their best day so far, with only two of the nine Bettys escaping from the 432FS, which also shot down 11 Zeros, plus McKeon's Tony for the 431FS.

22 September 1943: 348FG/341FS/342FS

On 22 September the 348FG was covering the Allied convoys off Finschhafen when eight Bettys covered by a number of Zeros attempted a low level torpedo attack. At 1000, 16 P-47s of the 341FS and 11 from the 342nd took off to fly for two hours to take their station at 20,000 feet just south of Finschhafen.

342FS

The 342nd Squadron patrolled monotonously for about two hours as its discouraged pilots listened to the battle over their radios. At 1130 the P-47s were patrolling at about 25,000 feet, but five early aborts had reduced their number to just 11. Capt. Walter Benz was leading one flight of four P-47s when he saw a single twin engine aircraft flying toward the south about 1,000 feet above him. Benz climbed after the bogey and cautiously approached the aircraft from behind and to port to about 50 yards, then fired a single burst into the apparently unaware Dinah. The enemy reconnaissance plane instantly burst into flame and fell away into the water; Benz had scored the first of his eight confirmed career kills.

Capt. Walter **Benz** got his first of eight victories when he shot down a Dinah. (AFAA)

1Lt. Charles **Cronk** got his only victories of the war when he shot down two Sally bombers. (AAF)

341FS

Just as the 341FS was about to leave their patrol, the Fighter Sector Controller reported the enemy about 60 miles away and the 341st turned to intercept. When their P-47s arrived the pilots saw about 50 enemy fighters and bombers below heading for Allied invasion shipping heading for the beach. At 1245, Capt. John Moore arrived over the Allied ships at 20,000 feet as the shipboard Air Controller reported the convoy was being attacked. Moore looked down and saw "bombs" (actually torpedoes) dropping in the water, and the bombers then making a sharp turn to port. As Moore dropped his belly tank and dove to get in position to make a pass at the bombers a Zero got on his tail, but his Wingman, 1Lt. James Nixon, made a pass at the Zero and drove it away; he was given a probable claim. Moore overshot the bombers due to his high diving speed, and when he turned to make another pass he saw another Zero on his tail and dove from 5,000 to 1,000 feet and pulled away from the Zero. He started climbing when he saw a P-38 dive on a Zero below to his right. The Zero escaped into a cloud and the P-38 climbed back up to the right. Moore saw the Zero through an opening in the clouds and dove from 4,000 to 1,000 feet before he got into range and started firing. The Zero began a gentle turn and climbed to the left, gradually increasing his turn and steepening his climb. Moore fired a long continuous 30 degree deflection shot, and as the enemy pilot tightened his turn almost at the top of his climb he flew through Moore's fire. The Zero stalled and dove straight down into the water. Moore was running low on fuel and returned to Dobodura. 1Lt. Charles Cronk, Moore's #3 man, made the initial diving attack but lost the formation. Near the end of his dive he spotted a lone Sally flying low on the water. Cronk made several steep turns to lower his diving speed and made a stern attack at 20 degrees deflection, opening fire from 400 to 250 yards and hitting the Sally, which dove and crashed into the sea. As Cronk pulled up to port he saw another lone low flying Sally. When the Sally pilot saw the Thunderbolt he went into sharp left to right evasive turns. Cronk closed into range from the rear and above with a slight deflection shot which also sent this Sally into the sea in flames. When Cronk pulled up to 1,500 feet he saw five Zeros 1,000 feet above and to the left. The Zeros immediately dove on Cronk; one fired from above and missed, and another attacked from head on and passed over without getting a hit. Cronk continued on course, and for some reason the Zero stopped their pursuit. He then saw four P-38s and a P-40 chasing a lone Zero, which was making steep evasive turns. Cronk closed on the pursuit and took a snap shot but missed, and then watched a P-38 shoot down the Zero.

22 September 1943: 49FG/9FS

In the raging battle, the 9FS was only to claim three stragglers as the combat abated. At 1130, during their midday patrol, Mission Leader Capt. Ralph Wire and his seven P-38s were at 28,000 feet when they encountered Oscars over the Finschhafen beachhead at 6,000 feet. Wire and his Wingman, 2Lt. Francis Love, dove through rain clouds and scattered the Oscars, with Wire heavily damaging one and Love damaging another.

Newly promoted Capt. Martin Alger was Yellow Flight Leader, and at 28,000 feet he saw five Oscars and three Vals flying far below at 6,000 feet. Alger led his flight in a dive and saw an Oscar in the distance and closed on it, firing several shots from astern. After his third or fourth pass he got hits that knocked chunks off its tail and saw its wheel drop. On his next pass he hit the pilot and the Ki-43 went directly into the water.

1Lt. James Harris was the Element Leader of Blue Flight, and while flying at 28,000 feet over Finschhafen at 1300 saw a lone Oscar 2,000 feet higher. Harris made a head on diving pass at the Oscar, which turned into Harris head on and began firing from out of range. Harris waited until the Oscar was at 50 yards and fired a short burst, and the Oscar rolled under the P-38 and fell in flames into the water.

Capt. Martin **Alger**. (R) and his CC admire his fourth. (but last) victory emblem. (AAF)

22 September 1943: 35FG/39FS

The 39FS (*Outcast*) was assigned a 1025 to 1230 patrol at 10,000-14,000 feet with 14 P-38s under Capt. Charles King. After patrolling over the convoy near Tami Island, off Finschhafen, the 39FS was about to be relieved by the Clover Squadron of the 475FG. However, *Duckbutt* Controller warned them of enemy aircraft approaching the convoy, 60 miles out to the southeast at 20,000 feet. Despite nearing the end of their patrol, the Lightnings still had enough

Capt. Paul **Stanch** shot down two Zeros for his 8th and 9th victories. (AFAA)

Capt. Charles **King** was leading 16 9FS P-38s when he shot down his third enemy fighter and added a probable. (AFAA)

1Lt. Richard **Smith** got his seventh and last victory of the war. (AFAA)

fuel to make the intercept. Twenty minutes later *Duckbutt* called out three enemy waves stacked from 18,000 feet to the deck over the convoy.

2Lt. Joseph **Forest** shot down a Zero but then collided with another Zero and crashed into the sea. (AAF)

Capt. King led the Squadron and his Red Flight to 24,000 feet, and descended to 20,000 when he heard that the convoy was being attacked. As he closed King saw AA fire and bombs exploding north of the convoy. King led the Squadron to 12,000 feet, where they saw a dogfight ahead between Zeros and P-47s at 8,000 feet, but also saw three twin engine bombers on the deck. As King descended he saw P-47s being chased by two Oscars. King dove to the rescue and took several long bursts from 45 degrees astern to directly astern on an Oscar that started to smoke and fell off to port. King made another pass on an Oscar from 10 degrees to dead astern, firing five bursts to within 50 feet and hitting the wings and fuselage, but the fighter was not seen to crash and each was claimed as a probable.

While King and his Wingman broke right to chase the Oscars and rescue the P-47s, 1Lt. William Anderson, #4 man in Red Flight, and his Element Leader, 1Lt. Edward Randall, went left to follow two Zeros. Randall made a short head on pass at an inline fighter with a scoop (Me-109/Tony) on its belly, but it got away as a probable. As Randall waited for Anderson to join him he saw another aircraft below to starboard, and as he closed the enemy turned away and Randall got a few hits (damaged claim), but had to dive away when other Japanese fighters approached. Meanwhile, Anderson had followed and got a long burst, and the Zero (Tony) rolled over and was observed to crash. As Anderson pulled up he saw a P-38 pursuing a Zero get too close and collide with it, severing the Zero's tail. The Zero headed for the water, while 1Lt. Joseph Forrest's fighter, minus four feet of its port wing, started to roll to the right with his supercharger smoking. He was last seen rolling two or three times out of control into the ocean. Anderson saw a Zero heading back to New Britain and chased it while expending all his ammunition, but had to give up and return to base.

Capt. Paul Stanch and Wingman 1Lt. Gordon Prentice made a diving astern attack at 8,000 feet and missed. The Zero chandelled to the left and made a vertical reverse to get on Stanch's tail, but also missed, as Stanch dove away. Stanch reversed and got on that Zero's tail again, firing a long burst from 200 to 100 yards that did not miss and sent it into the sea. Stanch climbed to 1,000 feet and saw a bomber about a mile away; as he approached a Zero dove on him and Stanch had to climb to safety. As Stanch turned back toward the bomber the Zero appeared again and Stanch quickly got on its tail and fired until he was out of ammunition to give Stanch his eighth and ninth victories.

1Lt. Richard Smith dove with the Squadron and made a front quarter pass at a Zero and damaged it as it passed to escape. Smith was down to 1,500 feet when he made another front quarter pass, and this Zero spun in for Smith's seventh and last victory of the war. 1Lt. George Morgan was also credited with a damaged Oscar.

2Lt. Raymond Kramme, 1Lt. Robert Baker's Wingman, released his tanks, but one would not drop, so he decided to return to base. As he made the turn it fell off, but by then he could not find his flight. He saw an Oscar down near the water and dove, making a 45 degree pass, but he was diving too fast and had to make a quick pull up to avoid hitting the water. Kramme then made a head on pass, but the enemy pilot turned away and Kramme throttled back to get behind the Oscar to make another pass. As he was about to fire another P-38 made a pass from the right rear and its tracers zipped between him and the Oscar. The enemy pilot pulled up and rolled away from the other P-38, which put it directly in front of Kramme, who fired, and the Oscar started on fire and Split-S'd into the water.

22 September 1943: 8FG/80FS

While the other 5FC Squadrons were having a good day against the Japanese, the 16 P-38s of the 80FS patrolling over shipping at Finschhafen made only one claim.

1Lt. Jess Gidley was flying as the #4 man on Capt. Norman Ruff's wing in Maj. Edward Cragg's lead flight. At 0945, while the flight was over Finschhafen at 6,000 feet, a bogey was reported to the north. The flight dove to about 500 feet and spotted a Val. Ruff made the first pass and Gidley followed with a snap shot, then turned to starboard and straightened as the Val turned into him. Gidley fired a 30 degree deflection shot, but led the Val too much and adjusted his sight and fired a long burst that sent the Val down in flames for his third and last victory.

1Lt. Jess **Gidley** got the 80FS only victory of the day which was his third and last victory. (AAF)

22 September 1943: Summary

In a little less than an hour, the combat air patrol had accounted for 13 bombers and 27 fighters; AA fire from the USN destroyers got another nine torpedo bombers. Three AAF fighters were lost, but two pilots were rescued.

24 September 1943: 475FG/433FS

On the 23rd, the main Allied landing force had captured one of the Finschhafen airstrips, but the enemy was well entrenched and held up the invading infantry during the first few days. Two days after their devastating loss of 49 aircraft, the Japanese sent out a few Haps over Finschhafen. The 433FS was flying cover for 12 B-25s hunting for Japanese barges from Sie to Alexishafen. While over Finschhafen, the four flights of 15 P-38s saw nine Betty bombers escorted by approximately 30 Haps ahead and above the bombers. At 1230, the three Possum Flights climbed toward the enemy formation. Capt. Joseph McKeon was leading Possum White Flight at 3,000 feet and following Jordan's Red Flight toward the enemy bombers. When the two flights were 1,000 yards away from the bombers the covering Japanese escorts dove and attacked. Red Flight broke away, but when McKeon looked around for his Wingman, 1Lt. Raymond Corrigan, he saw him descending with both engines smoking. McKeon was alone, and warded off the attack of two Haps, then joined Red Flight in string. Red Flight was now zigzagging around Corrigan, who was going into a dive. A Hap dove between McKeon and Red #3 and opened fire. McKeon turned and dove, closing to 150 yards and firing a short burst that hit the bottom of the Hap's fuselage. The Hap poured black smoke, flipped over on its back, and dove into the overcast. McKeon crossed over the circle that Red Flight was flying around Corrigan and made passes on several Haps that were making diving passes, putting holes in the wing of one. 2Lt. Ralph Cleage, Jordan's Red Second Element Leader, got a good hit on a Hap, which he badly damaged and was awarded a probable.

McKeon rejoined Red Flight, which was now circling an oil slick on the water made by Corrigan's downed P-38, and circled the area for 20 minutes after Red Flight left, but found no signs of Corrigan, who was the 433rd's first loss. Besides Corrigan's loss it was a bad day for the 433rd. F/O Kenneth Kirschner was missing, and after the war it was revealed that he survived the battle and was captured, but died in captivity at Rabaul. 1Lt. Donald Revenaugh, McKeon's #4 man, had his P-38's port engine hit and the prop run wild. After the engine was feathered 1Lt. William Jeakle escorted him safely back to base. Capt. Clarence Wilmarth's P-38 suffered several hits, but he also landed safely. Despite the 433rd's interception, the Betty bombers were able to reach their target and caused significant damage to the Allied advanced headquarters at Finschhafen.

Capt. Joseph **McKeon** sitting in his Lightning after getting his fourth victory. (AFAA)

F/O Edwin **DeGraffenreid** shot down a Tony to became an ace. (AAF)

26 September 1943: 8FG/80FS

On 26 September, a fighter sweep preceded an attack by B-24s that dropped approximately 35 tons of bombs on But and Dagua airdromes while being escorted by P-38s. The 80th Fighter Squadron sent 16 P-38s out ahead of the bombers and, finding no opposition, they orbited at 17,000 feet for rendezvous. As the P-38s approached the strip at Wewak, two or three enemy fighters were sighted very low over the water. However, immediately after this sighting 10 Tonys were then sighted at 15,000 feet. At 0950, the P-38s dropped their belly tanks and dove 1,000 feet into combat. Most of the enemy pilots were more inclined to break away from rather than engage in combat.

Capt. Carl Taylor from the 8FG HQ and his Wingman, 2Lt. Howard Donaldson, made a series of passes on eight Tonys. All except one turned into Taylor, but then half rolled and broke away. Taylor fired a long burst from astern on the one Tony that did not break away and it disintegrated. The two Americans then made a pass at another Tony at 8,000 feet that was flying directly in front of them. The Tony turned away, giving Donaldson a good 90 degree deflection shot from 100 yards, and it went down in flames. Donaldson then saw a Tony on Taylor's tail and dove on it, driving it off, and the two headed home.

F/O Edwin DeGraffenreid and Wingman 1Lt. Edward Robertson were members of the flight led by 1Lt. Jess Gidley and Wingman 2Lt. Norman Shea. The flight was at 20,000 feet when they saw six enemy fighters 5,000 feet below. They dropped their tanks, and all the Tonys broke away except one, which turned onto Shea's tail. Gidley fired on this Tony and it turned under him, giving DeGraffenreid a short burst at 60 degree deflection and 200 feet, hitting it from the engine back through the cockpit to make him an ace.

26 September 1943: 475FG/433FS

Maj. Martin Low led 17 P-38s as top cover on a bombing mission by four B-24 squadrons to But and Dagua Airfields. The Squadron took off at 0725 and rendezvoused with the Liberators at 0845 north of Point Yonkie. At 1010, while flying at 26,000 feet, *Copper* Controller vectored them away from the bombers to Wewak, where they saw 20 to 30 Zeros and Tonys between 10,000 and 14,000 feet. Low ordered tanks to be dropped, and in the battle Maj. Low, Capt. Clarence Wilmarth, and 1Lt. John Babel all hit Tonys that were badly damaged and descended into the overcast at 3,000 feet. Since the Tonys were not seen to crash they were credited as probables. Wilmarth also claimed a Hap as being destroyed, but on 6 October a review by 5FC/HQ downgraded this victory to a probable.

Capt. Clarence **Wilmarth** shot down a Zero for his third and last victory and also claimed a probable. (AAF)

2Lt. Calvin **Wire's** (Center) two victories were his 2nd and 3rd. (AFAA)

2Lt. Calvin Wire was flying on 1Lt. Ralph Cleage's wing in Maj. Low's Flight and lost the flight when Cleage was unable to drop his tanks and left without informing Wire, who then went off searching for him. Wire saw two P-38s below and dove to join them, but on his way down he saw a Hap dive on them. Wire turned into it, firing a two second burst that set it on fire, spiraling into the water. Wire climbed to join two other Lightnings chasing a Zero. As he was about to join the P-38s, Wire saw a Hap closing on their right and fired, tearing off about five feet of its wing tip. His ICR states: "but I do not know what happened to it from there." He had no witnesses, but his victory claim was, nonetheless, approved, whereas the three probable claims that day could have been claimed as victories just as easily, but were claimed by their pilots as probables.

26 September 1943: 35FG/41FS

Capt. Marion Wood led four P-39s at 0718 to escort two RAAF Boomerangs to Finschhafen and return. At 0820, while covering the Boomerangs at 7,000 feet over the target, bombs were seen exploding 10 miles up the coast at Long River. As they headed that way two Oscars below and three miles away saw them and fled toward Madang; one remained at 3,000 feet while the other climbed. The 41st Squadron chased and caught them 10 minutes later, 40 miles up the coast from Finschhafen. Wood and Wingman 2Lt. J.H. Farrar made quarter beam attacks on the lower Oscar that turned into the pair. Farrar fired and hit it as the two Americans dove away and became separated. Wood climbed to a position parallel and level with the top Oscar, which then started to turn and climb toward the American. Wood opened fire at 200 yards, but missed behind because he was flying too slowly to turn tightly enough. The Oscar pilot also opened fire and missed to the rear and then pulled up as if to do a wingover on Wood and escaped. The Airacobra pilot Split-S'd and continued on to Madang to look for his flight. As he was circling there at 5,000 feet Wood saw a Lily bomber flying toward Madang just over the ocean's surface. Wood dove and made a left quarter attack, opening fire at 500 yards to 75 yards. The bomber pilot made a 360 degree turn and chandelled toward Madang. Wood closed again from the right rear, and the Lily pilot made another steep right turn as Wood's gunfire hit the right engine. As he pulled up Wood saw the bomber's right wing catch the water and "scatter himself all over." Wingman Farrar was credited with an Oscar probable in this combat.

27 September 1943: 8FG/35FS

On this day 17 B-24s, followed an hour later by 90 to 100 B-25s, swept over the Wewak airfields and harbor installations, dropping more than 160 tons of bombs. Three B-25s were shot down by AA fire during the attack that, according to the official reports, left three tankers on fire and sinking; sank or probably destroyed four 1,000 to 5,000 ton merchant vessels; and destroyed or severely damaged nine luggers, five launches, and 10 to 14 barges. In addition, there was an estimated 50 aircraft destroyed on the ground. As an experiment on this mission, 16 P-40s of the 35th Fighter Squadron were sent to escort B-24s to Wewak. Because of the short range of the P-40s and the long distance to Wewak they refueled at Tsili Tsili and then staged through Bena Bena for the mission.

Mission Leader Maj. Emmett Davis saw the #4 man in his second flight being attacked by a single Tony and called a warning to the Flight Leader. Davis followed the diving Tony at 600 yards until the enemy pilot pulled out in a steep climb, giving Davis a chance to close. Davis fired a three second burst from 300 to 200 yards and the Tony began smoking from its port wing root. As the Tony pilot did a slow turn at the top of its climb Davis fired another burst from 75 yards and the Tony began to burn and was seen to explode.

Capt. Donald Thomas was 30 miles south of Wewak when he saw a single aircraft appear out of the overcast at 24,000 feet. The enemy pilot slow rolled, then half rolled on the B-24 formation at 15,000 feet. Thomas dropped his tanks and dove, closing rapidly and beginning to fire from 330 yards. The Tony went into a series of fast rolls in a dive, and Thomas fired three or four bursts that caused small explosions on the Tony and then started a fire. Thomas had to pull up to the right, as he was about to overrun the Tony, whose pilot pulled up to the left, and the two met head on. By then

Capt. Marion **Wood** scored his only victory. (AAF)

Cyclone's Flying Circus was the nickname the 35th Fighter Squadron gave itself honoring the CO, Maj. Emmett "Cyclone" Davis. (AAF)

Maj. Emmett **Davis**. (Right) posted his first of three victories when he shot down a Tony. (AAF)

the Tony had two other P-40s from Thomas' flight on its tail, but the enemy pilot fired on Thomas from extreme range. The Tony pilot tightened his turn, exposing his belly, and Thomas dropped on its tail and fired; a large stream of smoke gushed from the Tony as Thomas broke away.

27 September 1943: 49FG/9FS

On the 27th, Ops Exec Wallace Jordan requested that he be given his chance to lead the morning escort mission over Boram Airstrip, Wewak. Once over Boram, Jordan stacked his Lightnings from 10,000 down through 5,000 feet, but during their two hour orbit over the enemy airfield only one Tony appeared. At 1100, the Tony approached Boram from the west and Red Flight Leader Capt. Richard Bong, who had just returned from leave and was eager for combat, was the first to call out the Tony, which was 1,000 feet above the forest. Bong rolled from 5,000 feet, trailed closely by his three wingmen. The Ki-61 pilot saw the Lightnings approaching and accelerated and looped above the four diving Americans. All four Red Flight P-38s fired and missed as the Tony flashed over them. The Tony slowed at the top of its loop and flew directly into the firing line of Blue Flight Leader 1Lt. William Bleecker. The Japanese pilot turned hard starboard, but Bleecker chopped his throttle and pulled into point blank range from dead astern, and the Lightning's guns ripped the Tony until it burst into flames and the pilot bailed out.

28 September 1943: 475FG/431FS

On the 28th, 15 P-38s of the 431FS went back to Wewak as top forward cover for a formation of 40 B-24s which were to bomb the main ammunition and fuel dumps at Wewak and its airdromes. Capt. John Hood led the Squadron from Berry at 0905 and rendezvoused with the Liberators and 35FG P-38s from Dobodura over Bena Bena at 1030. When the 431st reached the Sepik River they flew ahead on a fighter sweep and circled the Boram-Wewak area at 24,000 feet. They headed toward But and Dagua Dromes, but found no opposition and headed back toward Wewak, as the bombers were beginning their runs. Hood led his Squadron to the left and followed the bombers across the target at 21,000 feet. Just after the Liberators came off their bomb run Hood spotted a Zero climbing under the bombers and called for the Squadron to drop their tanks and cover his flight as it dove on the Zero. Hood's Wingman, 2Lt. Robert Riegle, was unable to drop his tanks and Hood dove alone, firing a three second burst from 200 yards without seeing any hits. Hood's #4, 2Lt. Fredric Champlin, called that he had a Zero on his tail and Hood whipped around and fired a snap shot at it and the Zero broke away. Simultaneously, another Zero made a diving pass on Hood, and as he tried to turn into the Zero he stalled out. The Zero scored hits on Hood's rudders, ailerons, and trim tabs. A Tony was in a vertical bank, trying to turn into Hood, but the American pulled up into it and fired a long burst and disintegrated half its starboard wing; it flipped over and fell out of control. As Hood turned to go after the falling Tony a Zero pulled up directly in front of him at about 100 yards and Hood fired a three second burst; this victim burst into flame and fell away. Hood heard a call for help and dove 3,000 feet, chasing a Zero off the tail of a P-38. Hood received no credit for this attack, even though he was "sure that he (the Zero) was badly damaged." These two victories were Hood's second and third, and last of the war. After the flight reformed Hood and the second Element Leader O'Brien fired on a Zero, but the unaware Zero pilot turned directly head on into Champlin, who opened fire and hit it in its belly; it rolled over and descended from sight. Champlin lost contact with Red Flight, and as he was climbing a Tony climbed in front of him and Champlin fired but scored no hits. He dove away and immediately joined Hood, and after a few circles they returned to base.

1Lt. Warren Lewis led Blue Flight down from 17,000 feet after Hood attacked the lone Zero and encountered approximately 30 enemy fighters

LEFT TO RIGHT: **1).** Capt. John **Hood** shot down two enemy fighters over Wewak for his 2nd and 3rd and last victories. (AAF) **2).** 2Lt. Fredric **Champlin** got the first of his nine victories. (AFAA) **3)** 1Lt. Thomas **McGuire** shot down two Zeros to give him nine victories. (AAF) **4)** 1Lt. Warren **Lewis** claimed his second victory. (AAFA)

at 10,000 feet. Lewis made an unsuccessful pass on one of two Zeros, and as he was climbing he heard a radio call that a pilot had lost an engine and had a Zero on his tail. Lewis descended and chased the attacker away. Lewis then fired a 90 degree deflection shot at a Tony that half rolled away to escape. He then fired from astern of a Zero that rolled through his line of fire and a piece flew off its wing and tail as it went down.

1Lt. Thomas McGuire was leading Green Flight and had two men "snafu" and return to base. Then he had his #4 man, 2Lt. Edward Hedrick, move up as his Wingman. Meanwhile, White Flight Leader Capt. Verl Jett also had two men abort, and McGuire and Hedrick joined White Flight as its second element. McGuire made his first pass on the first lone Zero, but had to break away when two Zeros attacked him. Hedrick and the two became separated not only from each other, but also from White Flight. McGuire made a pass at a Zero but was unable to get a shot. He then saw a Zero on a P-38's tail and took a snap, unsuccessful 90 degree deflection shot as the Zero pilot turned down and out to port, but when he pulled up McGuire fired and it went down in flames. Climbing to return to his flight, McGuire fired at a Zero with no result, but saw a Zero making an attack on a flight of P-38s. When the Zero pilot saw McGuire he tried to rack around to get a head on pass but failed, which gave McGuire an easy deflection shot at very close range. The Zero started smoking and its prop windmilled, and the fighter began to burn as it went down. As McGuire started after two more Zeros, another Japanese fighter got on his tail and shot out his port engine as he tried to dive away. Fortunately, another P-38 came along and chased McGuire's pursuer away. McGuire feathered his prop and headed for the advance strip at Tsili Tsili with nine victories. He left his fighter at Tsili Tsili and returned to Berry in another P-38 that had been repaired. McGuire commented on the Japanese pilots as being Navy and "eager and experienced." They fought in pairs and "usually came to help each other out when in trouble."

28 September 1943: 35FG/39FS

At 1150, 16 P-38s of the 39FS were circling the last B-24s to leave the Wewak area after a bombing mission. While flying at 10,000 feet, 1Lt. Lloyd Shipley looked down and saw several Oscars at 7,000 feet and dove and flew inside the enemy, then made a climbing port turn. He fired a short burst followed by a large explosion (oxygen tanks?). 1Lt. Edward Randall added a Tony probable and another damaged.

1Lt. Lloyd **Shipley** scored his only victory of the war. (AAF)

30 September 1943: 475FG/432F/433FS

Eight P-38s of 432FS Red and White Flights took off at 0600 on a 0640 patrol over Finschhafen and were joined by two 433FS Possum Flights. At 0840 *Duckbutt* reported a "bogie low heading 80 degrees." Red Flight Leader Capt. Frederick Harris ordered tanks to be dropped and dove on the Betty flying at 5,000 feet without results. Harris' Wingman, F/O Theodore Fostakowski, followed and fired a burst that started a fire in its starboard engine. The Betty dipped slightly and then pulled up. F/O Henry Condon, Second Element Leader, started to fire from 300 yards down to 100 feet and scored the final 475th victory of September with hits on the Betty's fuselage and both wings. In less than two months of combat the 475FG had confirmed more than 90 aerial victories for 10 combat losses.

Late September 1943: Group and Squadron Command Changes

On 22 September, the 35th Fighter Control Squadron was reassigned from the 35FG and placed under the 5FC. On 26 September, the 35FG was placed under the operational control of the Second Air Task Force, which controlled all AAF units in the Tsili Tsili (*Mallet*) area. Lt.Col. Malcolm Moore, 35FG CO, was instrumental in establishing this Air Task Force, which was later commanded by Lt.Col. David Hutchinson. While operating from Tsili Tsili, the 7FS and 8FS of the 49FG were placed under the operational control of the 35FG. The 39FS, at Port Moresby, was directly under the operational control of the 5FC.

By late September 1943, the Allies had established the 18th Fighter Sub-sector along the line from Lae through Nadzab to Wau, and the Japanese were finally on the defensive. Their air efforts over the entire Huon Gulf coastline south of Finschhafen were nil, except for only a few ineffective night attacks. At this time there were more Japanese ground targets available, and the five Fighter Groups of 5FC were scheduled to more fighter sweeps, strafing, and ground attack missions, which were the missions to which the P-47 was most suited and would bring the Thunderbolt its greatest acclaim later in the war.

10

October 1943

2 October 1943: End of the Huon Campaign: Conclusions and Results
The Huon Campaign ended with the capture of Finschhafen on 2 October. Not only had it established Allied control of the Huon Gulf area, but it would also open the way for further victories which were to eventually lead to the reconquest of the Philippines. The offensive plan presented by MacArthur months before, in which land and naval forces were to capture successive sites to build advanced air bases, was demonstrated to be strategically and tactically viable. This plan required close coordination of land, sea, and air power, in which the role of land forces was to assist in advancing air units forward. Although the ground operations from Buna to Finschhafen had been mainly conducted by the Australians, the air operations, at least in the Northeastern Area, were predominately AAF, with the RAAF contributing one Beaufighter, one Beaufort, one A-20, and two or three P-40 Squadrons that were attached to the 5AF for operational purposes.

Throughout the Huon Peninsula Campaign, which was conducted from May to October 1943, the functions of the Fifth Air Force were chiefly those of a tactical air force to defeat the enemy air force, to isolate the battlefield, and to carry out sorties in direct cooperation with the ground forces, but from January through June 1943, the 5AF was barely able carry out these functions. Its combat units were only a little more numerous than they had been throughout the fall of 1942: two heavy, one and one half medium, and one light bombardment groups, three fighter groups, and two troop carrier groups. Moreover, many of these units were equipped with worn out aircraft and personnel. The flow of replacements, both in equipment and personnel, could not be relied upon, and even those units ready for combat frequently were used for other than combat (e.g. reconnaissance, anti-submarine patrols, convoy shipping, and even supply drops).

Kenney's competent Service Command Depots at Brisbane, Townsville, and later Port Moresby were efficient in erecting and maintaining aircraft that arrived at their Depots. Their ingenious modifications increased range and fire power, and produced new or more efficient weapons. By midsummer the situation had improved considerably, as replacement personnel to cover attrition (not rotation home) were arriving in the theater, as was the replacement of obsolete aircraft by new models with longer range and heavier and better armament. 5AF combat units had increased by three heavy, three medium, one light, five fighter, and four and a half troop carrier groups. The Service Command had five air depot groups, eight service groups of three squadrons each, and three additional service squadrons.

Thus, the Fifth Air Force was rapidly becoming strong enough to carry out its tactical functions and its highest priority, the defeat of the enemy air force. Both bombers and fighters contributed in establishing air superiority over Northeast New Guinea and New Britain. 5th Fighter Command fighters had an imposing 10 to 1 ratio of victories over losses while defending Allied bases and in escorting bombers and transports. Bombers were generally successful in defending themselves against Japanese fighters, and in August and September they were "officially" credited with destroying over 250 enemy aircraft on the ground, most of these on Wewak. The Japanese air forces in the area had been so completely beaten that, according to Allied Intelligence estimates, from January to September 1943 they carried out no more then an average of one sortie per bomber per month.

In isolating the battlefield, the Fifth Air Force met with mixed success. Following the enemy's disastrous naval (and air) defeat in the Bismarck Sea action in March, few if any Japanese convoys attempted to enter the Huon Gulf. For a time, however, all types of shipping poured into Hansa Bay, Wewak Harbor, Hollandia, and other areas in New Guinea further to the northwest. Heavy bombers carried out numerous strikes with some success against these concentrations, but it was not until August that medium bombers began to sweep over Hansa Bay and Wewak at masthead level, and thus threaten to establish a serious blockade of that portion of the coast. As it became increasingly difficult for their cargo vessels to reach New Guinea, the Japanese began to rely more and more upon barges, submarines, and destroyers, which could get in and out quickly. The Fifth Air Force, therefore, increased the number of sorties against rivers and lagoons where small vessels could take refuge, but enemy barges were numerous and elusive, and their passage was never entirely eliminated. With bombing efforts concentrated against objectives in New Guinea and in southern New Britain, other targets of importance, such as Rabaul, Kavieng, and Buka, received less attention from the Fifth Air Force in the summer than in previous months. During these attacks the results were often recorded as "unobserved." Definite results of sorties carried out in direct cooperation with ground troops were also difficult to determine, as the jungle terrain was not suited to such operations. Close ground support was found to be difficult, if not almost impossible, not only because of the difficulty in designating friendly front lines and in directing the pilots to the target, but also because most bombing attacks had to be carried out beyond the bomb line at a safe distance (more than 500 yards) from friendly troops. Bombing and strafing of rear areas and supply lines, however, was very successful, as was long range bombing against enemy bases and airfields. There is little doubt that the constant attacks on jungle tracks, supply points, and airfields in the Lae-Salamaua area contributed much to its speedy conquest when the offensive actually began in September.

The Fifth Air Force was generally successful in coordinating landings with the Seventh Amphibious Force. This was a new method of warfare, and required the testing of new techniques of fighter cover and of supplementary bombing and strafing attacks. The planning staffs of the two forces worked competently together, as the success of the Finschhafen operation, which was planned and carried out in little more than five days, confirmed. Additionally, the Navy recognized the difficulties of providing continuous fighter cover and commended the efforts of the Fifth Air Force, particularly those of the Fighter Controllers aboard the destroyer *Reid*. The Navy's main complaint against the 5AF in its participation in amphibious landings was the lack of aerial photographs to aid in the planning of the joint landing operations.

These and other minor complaints, however, were insignificant when compared with the Allied victories in Huon Gulf. These victories and the efforts of Australian scouts, infantry, and patrols, engineer troops, and native labor made possible MacArthur's main purpose of the creation of a series of advanced bases on New Guinea and nearby islands for land-based air power.

While ADVON continued to retain its headquarters at Port Moresby and Milne Bay, it was still an important staging base, but neither could be considered located in a forward area. From Mine Bay a series of Allied bases at Goodenough, Kiriwina, and Woodlark Islands extended into the Solomon Sea toward Japanese held New Britain. From Port Moresby, communications were forwarded to the headquarters of the First Air Task Force at Dobodura, but even that extensive and rapidly developed base, with its several airfields and seven runways, was far behind the line of advance. Tsili Tsili, headquarters of the Second Air Task Force and 150 miles to the northwest, had been hastily constructed for the specific purpose of contributing to operations necessary for the capture of Lae. It was a dry weather base and had to be evacuated before the rainy season, but fortunately the campaign progressed rapidly enough so that before the September rains began the units at Tsili Tsili could move forward, this time to Nadzab. By the beginning of October, engineers were improving runways and building taxiways and dispersal facilities to develop Nadzab as the new forward base for the Second Air Task Force. Meanwhile, units were moving up the Markham Valley, first to Kaiapit and then to Gusap, which was destined to become the base of units attached to still another Air Task Force.

Experience and ingenuity, together with the arrival of replacements and new equipment, had increased the effectiveness of the Fifth Air Force over the course of a few months, and by July these factors had begun to take effect. In June, the 5AF had carried out 3,703 sorties, dropped 753 tons of bombs, and destroyed one plane on the ground and 36 in the air. In September it carried out 10,277 sorties, dropped 2,298 tons of bombs, and destroyed 82 aircraft on the ground and 223 in the air. From January through September, 219 officers (combat crews) and 269 enlisted men were KIA; 160 officers and 192 enlisted men were MIA; and 24 officers and 52 enlisted men were WIA. Lae, Salamaua, and Finschhafen, which had been captured by the Japanese in March 1942, had been recaptured by the coordinated attacks of all Allied forces. But while these were only three of the many important bases held by the enemy in the SWPA, their capture did emphasize that, with the forward air bases built there, the cycle could be repeated in the future. General Arnold stated: "The sledge hammer blows of air power were impressive examples of how enemy bases can be pulverized and target areas reduced to a shambles cutting sharply the cost of victory in lives and time."

So, by mid-October 1943 the stage was set for the invasion of Bougainville. This island is the largest in the Solomons chain, and at that time possessed several Japanese airfields, harbor installations, and was manned by over 20,000 enemy troops. To enable US Marines to land on the island by the first of November it was necessary for Kenney to direct the operations of the Fifth Air Force bombers and fighters against the enemy bastion of Rabaul, on New Britain, while the planes of COMAIRSOLS (Commander, Air Forces Solomon Islands e.g. 13AF and USMC) sought to neutralize the Japanese air bases on Bougainville itself.

October 1943: Situation: Rabaul and the SWPA

Kenney's major shortcoming as a military leader was that he routinely overestimated his successes, and believed that Wewak had been neutralized as a military base by the end of August 1943. At least three times Kenney stated that Rabaul, on the northern end of New Britain, was also neutralized, but it continued to react forcefully when the 5AF and 13AF attacked. Since Rabaul dominated the Solomons to the east and New Guinea to the south it was necessary to annihilate the large naval and air base there. To accomplish this, the 5AF not only faced fierce AA barrages and veteran Japanese Army and Navy pilots, but also the unpredictable weather, which could create enormous fronts as high as 30,000 feet without warning. In addition to this was the long flying distances.

The capture of Finschhafen insured the complete control of the Huon Gulf, but while the Papuan Peninsula and its chief supply points Lae, Salamaua, Mubo, Kaiapit, and Finschhafen had been captured, none included a major air or sea base. The outer defense line of the new Japanese Empire had not been breached anywhere, and they could bring in reinforcements and supplies from three areas within their inner defense zones: from Burma-Malaya through the Netherlands East Indies; from the Philippines; or directly from the Caroline Islands. Rabaul, on New Britain, remained the largest and most important enemy stronghold in the SWPA. It was strategically located between the Solomons and New Guinea, and so could fly its aircraft to either and place Allied bases on the coast of New Guinea under constant attack. Supplies were transported to Rabaul's excellent Simpson Harbor via convoys escorted by warships, where they could be transshipped to the Solomons or New Guinea by submarines, barges, or luggers. The Allied advances and air base construction along the New Guinea coast put Rabaul under almost continual air attack, but did not significantly reduce the movement of shipping into Rabaul. On 1 October, air reconnaissance showed that there were 21 warships or auxiliaries and 25 merchant men totaling 138,000 tons. The Japanese considered Rabaul primarily a naval base, as most of its aircraft were from the IJNAF. By October there were five air bases in the Rabaul area: the much-used trio of Lakunai, Vunakanau, and Rapopo, and the newly completed base at Tobera and Keravat, which was being slowly constructed. On 1 October Allied Intelligence estimated that there were 116 fighters, 151 bombers, and 30 assorted miscellaneous aircraft on the Rabaul airdromes. In addition to the Rabaul bases, there were a number of bases scattered around the Bismarck Archipelago which were used for aircraft dispersal. There were many small strips on New Britain, such as those at Gasmata and Cape Gloucester; on New Ireland; Kavieng had an improved airdrome; and in the Admiralties', Los Negroes Island had a new airbase under construction at Momote Plantation. The Japanese could reinforce the Bismarck Archipelago by sending aircraft along a chain of bases that linked New Britain and the Solomons to the Philippines. On Halmahera, 500 miles from Davao and 250 miles from the Netherlands New Guinea, air reconnaissance had discovered four air bases under construction. Other new bases were discovered at Jefman and Takde in addition to the extensive base at Hollandia, which was 600 miles from the nearest Allied base.

In fall 1943, Allied air power had seldom attacked the Japanese in the Netherlands New Guinea, concentrating instead on nearby enemy installations; particularly Wewak, which was only 350 miles from Allied bases in the Markham and Ramu Valleys and ranked next to Rabaul. Within a 40 mile coastal area were the four large enemy airdromes at Wewak, Dagua, But, and Boram which, with harbor installations and supply dumps, received many of the Allies' heaviest air attacks. Other points to the southwest protected Wewak against attack by land and served as supply centers for garrisons and patrols in the area. There were several airdromes in the Alexishafen area which would assume considerable importance. On 1 October Allied air reconnaissance discovered only 91 fighters and 51 bombers at Wewak.

Generally, each air command retained control over the units assigned to it. However, this was a flexible principal, and when other designated commanders were given a military objective they were also given operational control to other air units selected for the task. All units were either assigned to the fighter or bomber commands. However, Kenney created three Air Task Forces which were designed to permit further flexibility of operations as the forward areas moved further away from their established bases.

The First Air Task Force (FATF), commanded by Brig.Gen. Frederick Smith and based at Dobodura, was established in March 1943, but the War Department had never authorized it, as it felt that the 5AF was becoming top-heavy with Headquarters personnel. The Second Air Task Force (SATF), commanded by Col. David "Photo" Hutchison (later under Col. Jarred Crabb), was presently being launched at Nadzab after spending two months at Tsili Tsili. Meanwhile, Gen. Whitehead announced the formation of the Third Air Task Force (TATF) at Port Moresby on 24 September 1943 and officially announced Col. Donald "Fighter" Hutchison as its commander. By the middle of October an advanced echelon had moved to Gusap to prepare that base, and a month later the remainder of the unit arrived. Kenney and MacArthur both insisted that each Task Force was necessary, and by November 1943 the War Department assured them that they would authorize three Bomb Wing and two Fighter Wing Headquarters. However, until February 1944, although the three Task Forces were very active, they remained unauthorized.

The new Third Air Task Force was to function much like the other two. Officers and non-commissioned officers were generally detached from ADVON or HQ, 5th Fighter Command. The Commanding Generals of ADVON and the Fighter and Bomber Commands were assigned Deputy Commanders to serve on their staffs. The Commanding Officer of the TATF was to exercise in his area of responsibility the same command functions as those of Gen. Whitehead in New Guinea, and was to be subject only to Whitehead in the chain of command. Normally decisions on strike missions would be made by Whitehead, but the Commander of the TATF could decide on offensive or defensive operations whenever he deemed an immediate decision was necessary "to do maximum damage to the enemy or to protect the safety of his command. The authority, responsibility, and decision as when to assume operational control of all or any Air Force units in his area were his alone." The administrative questions concerning matters such as personnel and aircraft strength and distribution which affected his Task Force were to be routed from the subordinate units involved through the TATF Commander. Otherwise, administration was to be direct between the subordinate unit and the command which ordinarily would have administrative control.

By October 1943 the 5AF had 5,388 Officers, 130 Warrant Officers, 207 Flight Officers, and 49,828 Enlisted Men, which made it approximately two-thirds larger than six months previously. It had three heavy bombardment groups: the 43rd, 90th, and 390th; three medium groups: the 22nd, 38th, and 345th; and the 3rd Bombardment Group (L). There was a great need for long range fighters in the theater, with the many widely scattered bases where the requirement for the escort for bomber and transport was almost continuous. On 9 October there were almost 600 fighters in inventory in the SWPA, but only 187 were the coveted P-38, while the remainder was 117 unsatisfactory P-39s, 143 P-40Ns, and 152 P-47s which needed extensive modifications before being considered suitable for SWPA operations. These 600 aircraft were allocated to five fighter groups, but as was the situation with the bomber groups, far fewer were in service than in inventory. On 9 October the 5th FC had 322 fighters on hand: the 8FG had 25 P-40Ns, 25 P-39s, and 13 P-38s; the 35FG had 15 P-38s and 47 P-39s; the 49FG had 39 P-40Ns and 10 P-38s; the 348FG had 82 P-47s; and the 475FG had 66 P-38Hs. In addition, the 67FS on detached duty from the 13AF had 16 P-39s and one P-40 on Woodlark Island; the 8PS had three F-4s, three F-5s, four P-38s, and one B-17; and Detachment A Night Fighter Squadron had three combat-ready P-70s.

Airbases

Theoretically, all New Guinea operations were directed from Port Moresby, as it was the HQ for the 5th Fighter and Bomber Commands and the 54th Troop Carrier Wing. Actually, the Air Task Forces had immediate control over the units in the forward areas. By October, while Port Moresby remained an extremely active area, there were no active AAF units based at Milne Bay, but it remained an important supply center. Goodenough and Woodlark Islands were no longer strategically important, but Kiriwina Island, captured in June, was improved and reinforced, and became a staging and emergency landing base. It was located about half the distance from Port Moresby to Rabaul, and thus reduced the route by almost 300 miles. So, by the beginning of October the stage was set for a Fifth Air Force assault on Rabaul that would include P-38 escorts for the first time. Kenney's optimism would lead to some over-confident operations that would result in tragedy for some crews. By 15 October it had two strips, four alert areas, and 107 hard stand dispersal areas.

However, Dobodura remained the principal base for operations against Rabaul, being located 120 miles across the Owen Stanley Mountains from Port Moresby and comprised of three airfields and seven runways that were generally well planned and comfortably laid out. By fall 1943 cargo ships were using the harbor facilities at Oro Bay to supply the bases at Dobodura, but living conditions continued to be plagued by mud in rainy weather and dust in dry weather. The air units at Dobodura were under the immediate control of the First Air Task Force, whose ultimate objective was the reduction of Rabaul. The unofficial organization in October consisted of the 22nd Bomb Group with medium-altitude B-25s and B-26s, the 3rd Attack Group with one squadron of A-20s and three squadrons of B-25 strafers, the 475FG with P-38s, and elements of the 49FG also with P-38s. Before the end of June 1943, MacArthur had authorized the future establishment of powerful bases on the Huon Peninsula.

Lae Drome

Lae was considered such a strategic location for a potential Allied base that MacArthur included it in an inspection tour by Maj.Gen. Lewis Brereton in mid-November 1941. Lae is located near where the Markham River links with the northwestern coast of the Huon Gulf, making it ideally situated for the establishment of a base to support both overland movements up the Markham River Valley and amphibious movements along the New Guinea coast. In fall 1941 the Allies initiated only rudimentary planning to establish a number of strategic bases in the enormous and primitive regions of the Southwest Pacific. However, long and detailed planning was required, and so on 7-8 March 1942, long before the necessary manpower and equipment were assembled to develop Lae into an Allied base, the Japanese overran Salamaua and captured Lae.

A year later, the Allies planned for an advance up the northeast coast of New Guinea, and again Lae was shown to be strategically positioned. Two airfields existed in the Lae-Markham River Valley area: the Lae Drome, with a runway 3,900 feet long; and the Nadzab Drome, 25 miles to the northwest, with an unimproved, but level, grass strip about 2,100 feet long. Both were easily adaptable for the development of 5,000 foot runways that could support fighter operations. Nadzab Drome, where weather conditions for flying were much better than those prevailing in the coastal regions near Lae, had several nearby adequate sites available for the construction of additional runways. A large and relatively open area was available for construction of a heavy bomber airdrome a few miles north of Lae. The road linking Lae and Nadzab would require extensive engineering effort before it could carry continuous heavy military traffic; it could, in the meantime, support jeeps and light vehicles over its entire length.

While ground operations of New Guinea Force were concentrating on Salamaua, final tactical preparations were made for the attack on Lae and Nadzab. A large combat force, consisting of the 7th and 9th Australian Infantry Divisions and the US 503rd Infantry (Parachute), was assembled

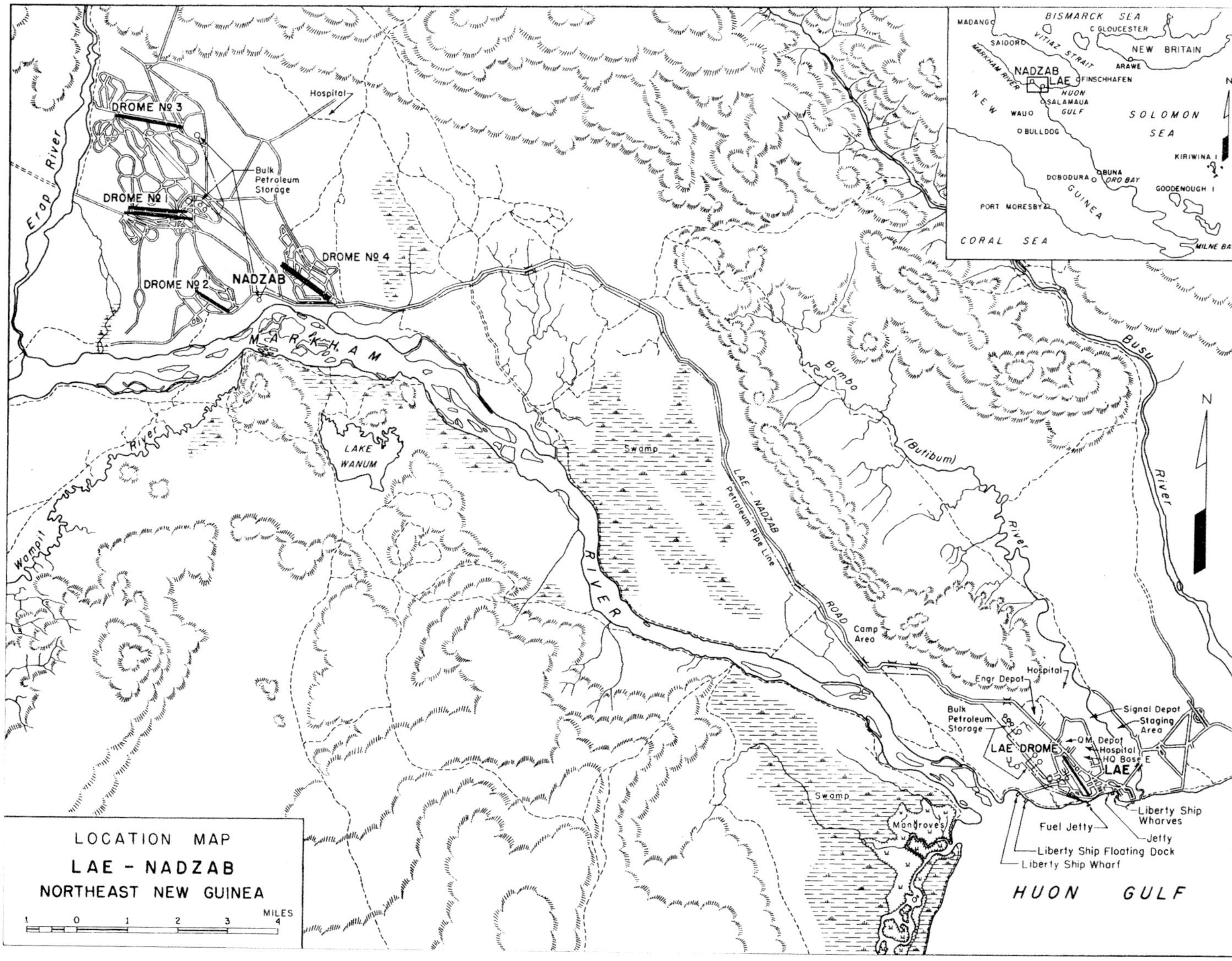

at Milne Bay and Port Moresby. On 4 September 1943 the 9th Australian Division, supported by Allied Air and Naval Forces, including elements of the 2nd Engineer Special Brigade, made a successful landing against light resistance on the beaches east of Lae.

So that base operations at Lae could begin as soon as possible after its occupation, the US Army Services of Supply (USASOS) was directed to organize an advance command at Lae. Initially under the operational control of New Guinea Force, the Advance Base Command was to provide logistic support, including construction, for both US Army ground units and Allied Air Forces elements in the area. Once the tactical situation was stabilized, the USASOS was to undertake total responsibility for the construction and operation of that part of the base required for support of US Army units, and to plan for and construct sufficient dock space to handle required supplies; to erect bulk petroleum storage tanks and pipe lines; and to provide adequate hospital facilities.

Lae Airfield was originally built in the 1930s on the north coast of New Guinea and faces the Huon Gulf. The airfield was the last field from which Amelia Earhart took off on her ill-fated around-the-world flight in her Model 10 Lockheed Electra on 2 July 1937. The Japanese captured the single 1,350x25 foot runway in February 1942 and subsequently developed it into a major base, which included the famous Japanese Tainan Kokutai featuring ace Saburo Sakai.

MacArthur's new base program was to include the construction of a port at Lae to accommodate Liberty ships at the rate of 3,000 tons per 24 hours and base facilities to service 20,000 American ground troops. The airfields at Lae, nearby Malahang, and Nadzab were to be improved, and eight new runways with revetted dispersal areas for 494 aircraft were to be constructed. By the time these areas were actually captured by the Allies the planned improvements were considerably expanded, with five additional all-weather runways with dispersal areas for 13 squadrons and staging facilities for 17 squadrons to be added, while a supply base and an airdrome of major proportions were scheduled for construction at Finschhafen.

By the second night after the capture of Lae Drome, the engineers had repaired, improved, and extended the existing enemy runway to a total length of 5,000 feet and a width of 200 feet. Installation of a drainage system, construction of access roads and hardstands, and maintenance of the gravel runway were assigned to an engineer aviation battalion also assigned with the construction of other supporting facilities. Lae Drome immediately became the scene of a tremendous airborne supply lift, which at its peak involved a landing or take off every 26 seconds. Gasoline drums shipped into Lae on LCTs and LSTs had to be rushed northward for essential aerial operations being conducted at the Nadzab Dromes. Unloaded as quickly as possible by the inadequate forces at Lae, these drums were trucked to the Lae airdrome, loaded into C-47 transports, and flown to Nadzab. This heavy air transport

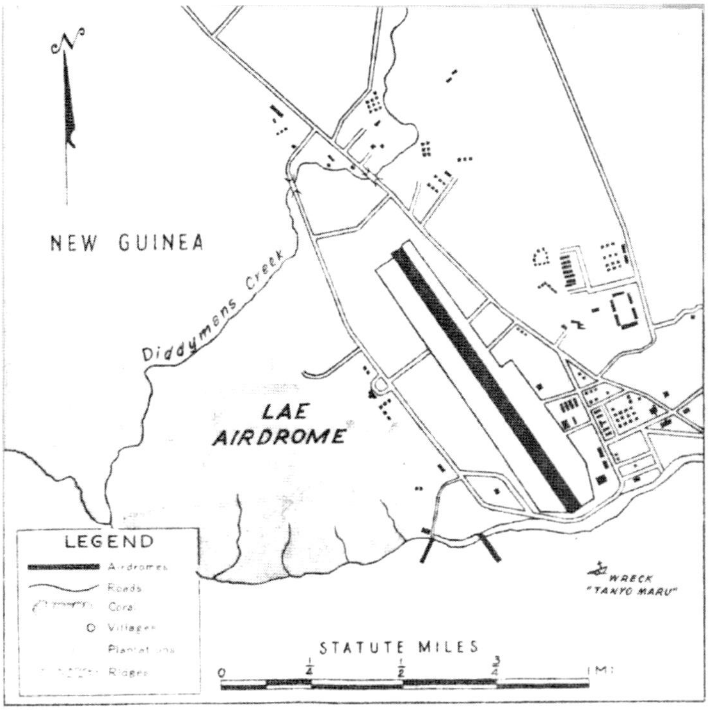

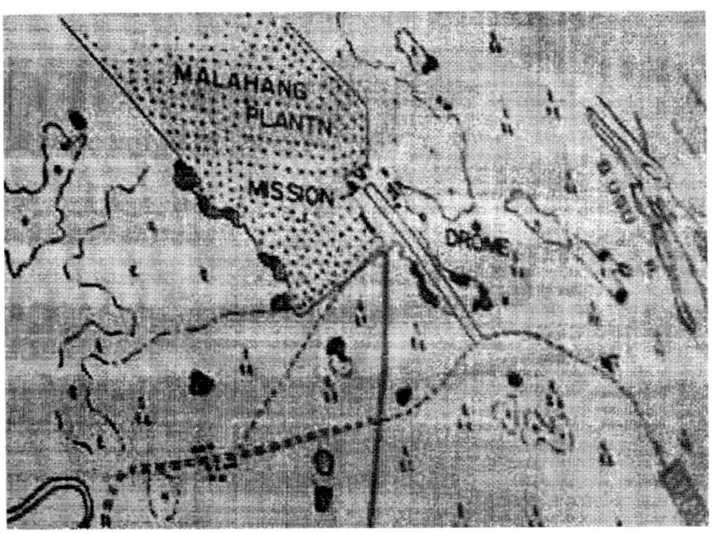

Malahang Airdrome

Lae Airdrome. (AAF)

traffic took a continuous toll on the runway, but the airlift could not be delayed; maintenance of the airstrip became a continuous operation.

This construction program was to be completed under extremely difficult conditions: the Huon Peninsula was over 200 miles from the nearest sizable Allied base; the water routes were continually threatened by Japanese attack; and the air route to Port Moresby, almost 250 miles away, crossed the dangerous Owen Stanley Mountains, which were prone to tropical weather fronts. Although there were a number of kunai areas suitable for airfields, they were surrounded by thick jungle and Malarial swamps, as well as cut by numerous ridges and streams fed by rainfall averaging close to 200 inches a year. Engineers estimated that with the few construction units assigned, the project could not be completed before February 1945.

Although air units were to benefit most from these new bases, their construction was the responsibility of the US Army Services of Supply (USASOS). The primary interest of the Air Force was recognized, however, by the appointment of Brig.Gen. Carl Connell as the Commander of the operation. Connell, previously Commander of the Fifth Air Force Service Command, was relieved from that duty on 29 August and assigned on detached service to the 23rd Port Headquarters, which was to be established at Lae. Connell was somewhat similar to Generals Kenney and Whitehead in his impatience with administrative detail, and contributed a drive and an engineering and mechanical know how which were decisive in bringing the operation to a rapid conclusion. He was constantly "building a fire" under the rear echelons of USLSOS, of the Air Force, and of GHQ 5AF as he requested more and better supplies and equipment. Connell's persistence in this was only a tad less than that of Kenney, who conducted a continuous fight with the War Department for more personnel and more aircraft.

By 1 April 1944 most of the construction program at Lae had been completed, and the few engineer units remaining in the area were mainly engaged in completing the airdrome facilities at Nadzab. By June 1944 the Allies had moved men and supplies toward advanced areas and engineer construction was concentrated in forward areas. Maintenance of existing facilities continued to be the primary engineer undertaking at Lae. In August 1944 the last engineer construction unit was replaced by a composite service company which became responsible for all maintenance. Lae Drome was transferred to RAAF control on 1 August 1945, and at the end of the war, Lae was one of the first bases closed. Final shipments from Lae took place in December 1945.

Nadzab Dromes

The day following the Lae landings, the 503rd Infantry parachuted on Nadzab to cut off the Japanese from their natural escape route and to give the Allies control of the Markham River Valley, which lies northwest of Lae. The operation included 302 bombers, fighters, and transports which left eight different airfields in the Port Moresby and Dobodura areas with MacArthur observing the operation from a B-17. The paratroopers landed successfully and seized the Nadzab Drome area as planned.

The day after the 503rd paratroops had secured the landing area, the engineers started work on the airstrip with hand tools, felling trees, filling craters and holes, and even putting up a windsock. Three light tractors, three mowers, a wheeled rake, and other engineering equipment were scheduled to be flown in from Dobodura by 14 gliders. Because there was no enemy opposition, no urgency, and some danger to the glider pilots, who had only minimal training, Gen. Blamey cancelled the drop, substituting instead the afternoon supply run by specially modified B-17s. Lacking mowers, the Kunai grass was cut by hand by the engineers, paratroops, and natives and then burned. By 1100 on 6 September the 1,500 foot strip, which had not been used for over a year, had been extended to 3,300 feet.

At 0940 on 6 September, a L-4 Piper Cub was the first plane to land, transporting Col. Murray Woodbury, the commander of the US Army's 871st Airborne Engineer Aviation Battalion. Three transports arrived in the morning, followed by another 40 aircraft in the afternoon, carrying American and Australian engineers.

By 7 September the first detachment of the 871st Airborne Engineer Aviation Battalion had been flown in to Nadzab with its small airborne bulldozers and graders. These engineers had immediately located an additional site for a transport airstrip (later called Drome No. 1) between the Erap River and the existing airstrip (Drome No. 2). The site proved to be excellent, being an old, dry riverbed with soil largely composed of gravel. A gravel base and steel plank were laid to accommodate the fighters now based at Tsili Tsili that were in danger of bogging down when the weather deteriorated. Construction started at once, and by 10 September a 3,000x100 foot segment had been cleared of kunai grass, the natural ground leveled as a runway, and the first C-47 landed. By the next day 333 transports had been shuttled in from Tsili Tsili and 87 more had flown up from airfields farther south. While work proceeded on the runway, the organization on the ground permitted 27 transport aircraft to land, unload, and take off every 45 minutes. Before the day's end this runway had been extended to 5,200 feet, and the 871st Engineers had started to lay down, compact, and seal four inches of gravel as a base for steel plank so that the runway could be used by fighter aircraft. As noted, it was rushed to completion even though it would have a short life, because the 35th Fighter Group's base at Tsili Tsili was in danger of closing during the rainy season.

Additional engineer units were arriving in the area. On 20 September the 842nd Engineer Aviation Battalion landed at Lae, and after some difficult construction on the Lae-Nadzab Road, it was ordered to Nadzab to relieve the 871st Engineers for planned construction at Gusap and Dumpu. Other engineer units arrived at Nadzab when they could get through the Lae-Nadzab Road with their heavy equipment to reinforce the construction endeavor on these tactically urgent Dromes.

Meanwhile, construction of a parallel runway and taxiways was also initiated; the existing Drome No. 2 was improved to a 5,000 foot dry weather runway; and by 20 September an additional 6,000 foot long dry weather runway (later named Drome No. 3) was cleared and leveled at a site north of Dromes Nos. 1 and 2. A few days previously, a site for the subsequently named Drome No. 4 had been laid out to the east of the other runways. By the end of September, an area of 6,000x100 feet had been cleared and leveled for a dry weather runway at this site, and before the end of the month two squadrons of P-39s were providing fighter defense. By the end of October there were four airstrips at Nadzab, one of which was 6,000 feet long and sealed with bitumen capable of handling 36 C-47s simultaneously. Nadzab developed into an immense airbase complex and was the home base to many air units during the war when it was a forward base of operations against Japanese positions and was vital afterwards as a staging area.

The actual construction, the problems of jungle terrain, and the almost continuous rain of October, November, and early December were the least of the tasks facing Maj.Gen. Connell's engineers working with the Second and Third Air Task Forces at Gusap and Nadzab. Transportation of construction material and heavy equipment was the major obstacle, as air transport would be insufficient for the job. Construction in the Nadzab area would have to wait until heavy construction equipment could be moved by road from Lae so that air transport could be used to construct the inaccessible Gusap base. The need to complete the Lae-Nadzab road by 1 December was imperative, and Connell had his engineers build the road from both ends, working day and night when weather permitted. It was an enormous project, as it rained 46 of the last 60 days, and work could only continue until a new deluge began. Finally, on 15 December 1943 the road from Lae to Nadzab was opened, but there was a lack of trucks to transport the equipment, which further delayed base construction until crated trucks were found and reassembled.

In January 1944, airdrome requirements for Nadzab were revised to Fifth Air Force specifications. Three dry weather runways at Dromes Nos. 1 and 3 were to be surfaced with steel mat to accommodate heavy bombers, and a

Lacking mowers, the Kunai grass was cut by hand by the engineers, paratroops and natives and burned. (AAF)

second parallel runway was to be constructed to all weather standards at Drome No. 4. By May 1944 all runway construction at Nadzab was completed, as the two airstrips at Drome No. 1 had been expanded and consisted of a 6,000x100 foot runway surfaced with steel mat and a 7,000x100 foot runway which was bitumen-sealed at the center and terminated with 1,000 feet of steel mat at each end. A portion of the runway at Drome No. 2, 4,000x100 feet, had been sealed with bitumen. The runway at Drome No. 3 had been expanded to 7,000x100 feet and its center section surfaced with bitumen, while 1,000 feet of steel mat had been placed at each end. Drome No. 4 finally consisted of two parallel bitumen-scaled runways, each 6,000x100 feet. In all, the taxiways provided at Nadzab approximated 50 miles of all weather construction.

Meanwhile, a number of combat organizations were preparing to move to Nadzab. On 5 October the HQ Squadron of the 35th Fighter Group made the short move from their temporary base at Tsili Tsili. Before the end of month, the P-39s of the 8th and 41st Fighter Squadrons were providing fighter defense for their new base, and by mid-November four airdromes were being used by combat and transport aircraft.

From its initial development, Nadzab was to be the main base for future New Guinea operations, and through necessity it was completely supplied by air until mid-December 1943, as its greatest drawback was the 27 miles of jungle which separated it from the ocean. Nonetheless, it was considered one of the best airfield sites in the world, as the area was an old, dry river bed with soil composed largely of well graded gravel and was called "an airport construction engineer's dream."

Nadzab Airfield No. 1 and 2 (East Base)

The area was occupied only by sporadic Japanese Army patrols and a rudimentary Japanese grass emergency airstrip was cut out at this site, but some sources do not agree on its existence. The area was captured by Allied paratrooper assault and, as previously described, the two parallel runways were built and surfaced with PSP. Running roughly east to west, No. 1 Strip was located to the north, while parallel and to the south was No. 2 Strip, closest to the Markham River.

Nadzab Airfield No. 3 (Fighter Strip or Strip No. 3 or Texter Field)

No. 3 was located due east of the Markham River north of Lae. This strip, furthest north of all the Nadzab area airstrips, was located to the north of Nadzab No. 5. By 31 January 1944 US Army Engineers had constructed a runway that ran approximately east to west and was operational as of April 1944. Taxiways connected it to No. 5 and the main Nadzab runways, and extensive revetments were located around the runway.

Nadzab No. 4 (Newton Field)

No. 4 was located outside of Lae, and was the closest to the village of Nadzab, just north of the Markham River. It was also known as Newton Field in honor of RAAF 22 Squadron pilot W.E. Newton, shot down by AA fire near Salamaua flying a DB-7B Boston and awarded the Victoria Cross. It was constructed by the RAAF and had extensive taxiways and revetments to the NE and SW of the strip.

Nadzab No. 5 Airfield (No 5 Strip)

No.5 was located between Nadzab No. 1 Strip (East Base) to the south and Nadzab No. 3 Strip to the north. The field ran north-west to south-east, and had two parallel runways. Taxiways connected the strip to Nadzab No. 1 Strip and Nadzab No. 3 Strip.

Markham Valley Airdromes: Kaiapit and Gusap

As soon as the Japanese had been ousted from Salamaua and the capture of Lae was pending, Allied ground operations were extended northwestward to block enemy penetration southward through the Ramu and Markham River Valleys. The New Guinea Force was directed to seize suitable sites in the Kaiapit and Dumpu areas by airborne operations to set up advance air bases to be used in the continued neutralization of Wewak. The Allied Air Forces were assigned the responsibility for the construction of an advance air base for the operation of a fighter group and two light bomber squadrons in the Kaiapit area, and for the creation of an advanced refueling airdrome with capacity to refuel approximately one fighter group and two

Nadzab at the end of 1943. (AAF)

Nadzab by mid-1944 as "one of the world's best airbases.". (AAF)

Nadzab Map Gallery

Nadzab Airstrip Area

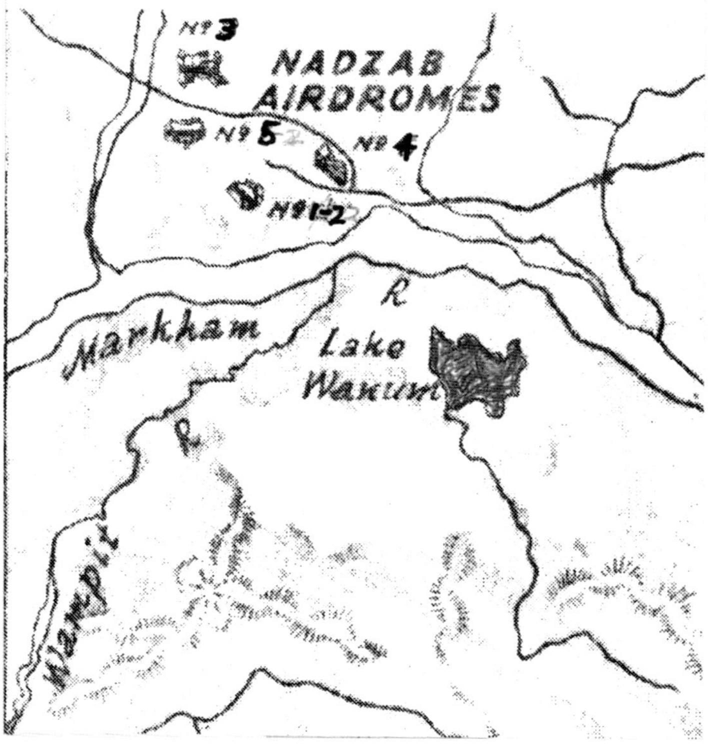

Nadzab Airstrip #1-2

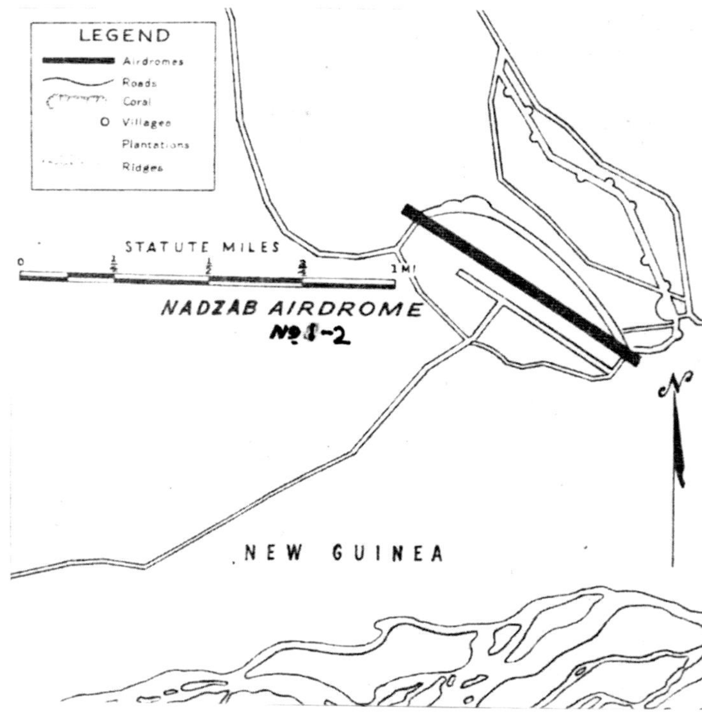

Nadzab Airstrip #3

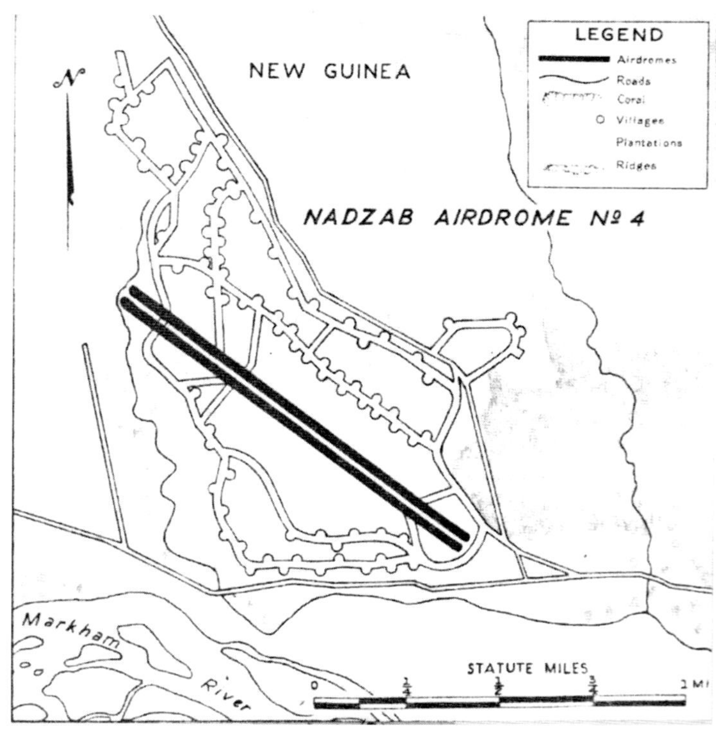

Nadzab Airstrip #4

Nadzab Photo Gallery

Nadzab Strips #1-2

Nadzab Strips #3

Nadzab Strips #4

Nadzab Strips #5

light bomber squadrons in the Dumpu area. Control of the 871st and 872nd Airborne Engineer Aviation Battalions was transferred from Advance Base Command at Lae to Allied Air Forces for this construction.

Kaiapit

On 17 September, 250 Australians of New Guinea Force were landed by troop carriers on a long, level, burned off area near the Leron River, a few miles from Japanese occupied Kaiapit. Three days later these troops drove the enemy from Kaiapit and began improving its old airstrip, which was soon sufficiently leveled for the landing of transports that brought in reinforcements, including engineers. While a few engineer units accompanied the Australians as they continued their advance through the Valley, others remained at Kaiapit for preliminary surveys of the field for the projected construction of a runway and dispersals. The engineers with the advancing force, meanwhile, moved forward to survey for strips where transport planes could land, since the ground troops were wholly dependent upon air support for rations and supplies in this area.

Gusap

As soon as the Japanese had been driven from Salamaua and the capture of Lae was imminent, Allied ground operations advanced northwestward to block enemy penetration southward through the Ramu and Markham River Valleys. In the plans for future operations in New Guinea, Nadzab was foreseen as a principal base. An essential part of the isolation of the Huon Peninsula was the advance of the 7th Australian Division through the Ramu Valley, called *Operation Cutthroat*. Part of this operation was to be airborne in cooperation with the Third Air Task Force based "at some suitable spot" in the valley. The New Guinea Force was directed to seize suitable sites in the Kaiapit and Dumpu areas by airborne operations for establishment of advance air bases to be used in the further neutralization of Wewak. Colonels Woodbury and Hutchison of the Third Air Task Force, accompanied by Gen. George Vasey of the 7th Australian Division, flew aerial reconnaissance of the area in a small Piper Cub and determined that the valley at the junction of the Gusap and Damu Rivers was such an ideal location for an advanced air base that it was decided to limit the establishment of the swampy, Malarial base at Kaiapit.

The Allied Air Forces were assigned the subsequent responsibility for construction of an advanced air base for the operation of a group of fighters and two squadrons of light bombers in the Kaiapit and Gusap areas. The establishment of an advanced refueling airdrome with capacity to refuel approximately one group of fighters and two squadrons of light bombers was assigned to the 871st and 872nd Airborne Engineer Aviation Battalions, which were to be transferred from Advance Base Command at Lae to Allied Air Forces for this construction.

On 17 September, 250 Australians of New Guinea Force were landed by troop carriers on a long, level, burned off area near the Leron River, a few miles from Japanese-held Kaiapit. Three days later these troops had dislodged the enemy from Kaiapit and begun improving the old airstrip there. The field was soon sufficiently leveled for the landing of transports, which brought in reinforcements, including engineers. While a few engineer teams accompanied the Australians as they continued their advance through the valley, others remained at Kaiapit to make preliminary surveys of the field for projected construction of a runway and dispersals. The engineers with the advancing force, meanwhile, moved forward for the purpose of surveying strips where transport aircraft could land, since the ground troops were completely dependent upon air support for rations and supplies in this area. By the time surveys were completed at Kaiapit, the advance had progressed as far as the junction of the Gusap and Ramu Rivers. The valley in this area seemed particularly good for airfield construction, and from engineer studies of both areas, it was obvious that Gusap possessed a number of advantages over Kaiapit for subsequent development of an advance air base, including unobstructed air approaches and good soil conditions. Plans were revised accordingly, and Allied Air Forces now directed construction of all-weather facilities at Gusap for two fighter groups and one medium bombardment group, together with servicing facilities capable of handling 200 transports daily. Since the area was all but inaccessible by overland transportation from Nadzab, arrangements were made to have engineer equipment brought in by air transport.

On 2 October 1943 an advance party of the 872nd Engineers, with some airborne engineer equipment, was flown in to Gusap and immediately started work to improve Airstrip #1. However, it was soon apparent that this site would not endure sustained air traffic and, as soon as a site for a second airstrip was located and mowed, Airstrip #1 was abandoned. The vicinity of Airstrip #2, which was situated about one mile north of Airstrip #1, also proved adaptable for the location of Airstrips #3 and #4. Working round-the-clock, the engineers prepared these runways for the use of

Gusap #2 Runway. (Fighter Strip #2). (AAF)

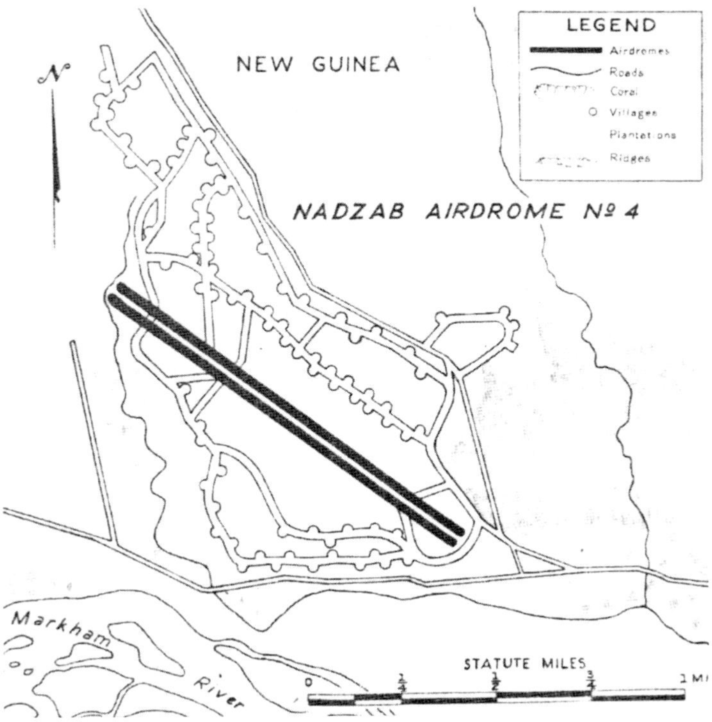

transport aircraft, while Airstrip #2 was developed for fighter aircraft. By late October sufficient facilities were available to accommodate the arrival of an air service squadron by troop carrier and a P-40 fighter squadron by the first of November. Sites for another transport runway (Airstrip #6) and three additional fighter runways (Airstrips #7, #8, and #10) were also selected and quickly brought into rough condition for operations. All of these were temporary grass and gravel runways that required little work other than mowing; some rocks were removed, a few holes filled, and slight bumps were leveled.

By analyzing the kunai grass, the engineers were able to determine the underlying soil conditions. About 10 October, a site for an all-weather runway had been selected (Airstrip #5). However, as soon as construction was begun it became evident that the large volume of excavation required at this site would wear out the light airborne equipment available to the 872nd Engineers. The 871st Engineers were moved from Nadzab in November to assist in operations at Gusap. With the exception of D-4 tractors, 3/2 yard carryalls, and 2/2 ton trucks, which were routed overland, all of this battalion's equipment was flown into Gusap via C-47 transport aircraft. But even with the personnel and equipment of two airborne engineer battalions combined, construction at Gusap lagged. A few pieces of heavy equipment no longer needed at Lae were disassembled and flown to Gusap. Eighty percent of the loam was stripped from the site as rapidly as possible, and the remainder mixed with the sandy gravel lying beneath it. After watering and compacting for stabilization, the surface was treated with bitumen and the runway was covered with PSP. By January 1944 an all-weather runway capable of sustaining fighter and dive bomber operations was complete.

At this time a third unit, the 875th Airborne Engineer Aviation Battalion, arrived at Gusap. From 1 January to 1 April 1944, the three battalions constructed taxiways, hardstands, roads, and camp facilities. However, the limited supply of construction material, which had to be transported by air, necessitated many makeshift practices to achieve end results. When the airdrome and its facilities were complete, all airborne engineer equipment used in their construction was worn out and had to be replaced. Nevertheless, a good all-weather airdrome had been made available at Gusap, "an airdrome which paid for itself many times over in the quantity of Japanese aircraft, equipment, and personnel destroyed by Allied attack missions projected from it." The necessity for airdrome construction at Wawin, Sawteeth Hills, Leron area, and Salamaua, as originally specified by AAF, was cancelled by subsequent changes in Allied tactical plans. Only modest work had been initiated at Kaiapit, Marawasa, and Dumpu when the AAF canceled airdrome construction requirements for all of these locations on 8 January 1944.

Gusap Runways

Gusap Runway
Sited to the SW of the complex, extending approximately NW to SE
Gusap #2 Runway (Fighter Strip #2)
Sited to the E side of the complex, parallel to #4, extending approximately N to S.
Gusap #3 Runway
Sited to the E side of the complex, connected to #2 extending approximately NW to SE.
Gusap #4 Runway (Transport Strip #4)
Sited to the E side of the complex, parallel to #2, extending approximately N to S
Gusap #5 Runway
Sited in the center of the complex, extending approximately NW-SE. This runway continues in use by light aircraft.
Gusap #6 Runway
Sited S of #5, extending approximately NE to SW
Gusap #7 Runway
Sited at the far W of the complex, extending approximately E to W
Gusap #8 Runway
Sited to the SE of #5, extending approximately NE to SW

USAAF units at Gusap

49FG, 8FS (P-47) from Tsili-Tsili 29 October 29 to 3 May 1944 to Hollandia
49FG, 7FS (P-40) Dobodura 16 November to 27 April 1944 to Finschhafen
49FG, 9FS (P-47) Dobodura 16 December to 16 May 1944 to Hollandia
49FG, HQ from Dobodura 20 November to 19 April 1944 to Finschhafen
41FS (P-47) from Nadzab 31 January to 9 June 1944 to Nadzab
312BG, 387BS (A-20) POM 25 December 1943 to 10 June 1944 to Hollandia
312BG, 386BS (A-20) POM 25 December 1943 to 12 June 1944 to Hollandia
312BG, HQ from USA 1 January 1944
312BG, 388BS (A-20) POM 3 January to 10 June 1944 to Hollandia
312BG, 389BS (P-40, A-20) POM 6 January 1944
71TRG, 110TRS (P-39) POM 7 February to 25 May 1944 Tadji
35FG, 39FS (P-47) from Nadzab 27 January to 9 June 1944 to Nadzab
35FG, HQ from Nadzab 7 February to 22 July 1944 to Owi
71TRG, 25TRS (L-5) det 16 February 1944 - ?
85FW HQ from USA 25 February to 24 July 1944 to Hollandia
310BW HQ activated 1 February to 1 May 1944 to Hollandia
5FC, 460FS ? to 23 July 1944 to Nadzab

By 1 November, a series of airdromes had been established running from Gusap through Nadzab, Lae, Dobodura, Kiriwina, Goodenough, Milne Bay and Port Moresby in the New Guinea area, and from Darwin in the northwest and Brisbane on the Australian east coast. However, the distances between the bases were very long: the distance from Brisbane to Port Moresby was 1,200 miles, and 1,100 miles from Darwin to Port Moresby. In New Guinea, the radius between bases was approximately 300 miles from Port Moresby. Even more of a problem than the air distances was the lack of overland transportation in New Guinea, and the movement of personnel, equipment, and supplies was entirely dependant on air and sea transport. The greater part of seaborne supplies shipped from America to Australia was transshipped to the New Guinea ports at Port Moresby, and then to Milne Bay and to Oro Bay and Lae as the advance continued.

However, sea transport was slow and initially hazardous, as the Japanese submarine and surface fleet threat was ever present. Thus, air transport was the principal means to move troops and supplies to forward areas where they were immediately required. Gusap during its existence and Nadzab for three months were completely supplied by air.

Elkton Updated to the *Montclair III Plan*

By October 1943, overall operations known as the *Elkton Plan* were being planned to complete the conquest of the Huon Peninsula and to begin the isolation and reduction of Rabaul, which was contained in Operation *Cartwheel*. The Japanese were as powerful as they were a year earlier, but the Allies had also greatly improved their situation. Their air, land, and sea forces were larger and more experienced. They had advanced their bomb line by capturing and constructing advanced bases much closer to the enemy's outer defense line. Through their resourceful combination of air and sea transport they were able to supply both their interior and island bases soon after they were captured.

As discussed previously at length, *Elkton* was originally drafted in February 1943 as a carefully coordinated offensive in the SWPA and South Pacific under the strategic control of MacArthur. But with the successful and early completion of the Wewak-Kavieng Campaign, the advance was now to proceed at a more rapid pace along the New Guinea coast using airborne and amphibious operations as far west as Vogelkop, and was to be completed by the end of 1943. *Elkton* and its successors will be further discussed in conjunction with the use of air power to meet their objectives. It was estimated that 1,379 aircraft of all types would be required to capture Hollandia; 1,051 for Wadke; 1,051 for the Japen-Schouten Islands; and 1,904 for Manokwari, on the Vogelkop Peninsula. Whether these aircraft requirements would be available would be dependent on the requirements in the ETO. In particular, heavy bomber requirements for the Pacific would not be fulfilled until Germany was defeated.

The August *Quadrant* decisions had necessitated the elimination of the *Elkton Plan* and the adoption of a new plan for "maintaining the unremitting pressure" against Japan by seizing points on the Bismarck Archipelago and on New Guinea as far west as Vogelkop. But on 2 October the War Department requested that MacArthur go beyond the *Quadrant* authorization, and after the capture of Vogelkop consider Mindanao as the next "logical objective," to be accomplished by a thrust from the Central Pacific through the Bonins. MacArthur was to prepare plans for his return to the Philippines based on two hypotheses: that the SWPA would continue to be built up in men and materiel, and that the main effort would be in that area.

By 20 October, MacArthur submitted the *Montclair III Plan* for operations in the SWPA and for the recapture of the southern Philippines. *Montclair III* was divided into two separate but coordinated operations: *Victor* for the southern Philippines and *Oboe* for the Netherlands Indies. The *Victor* operations were to be conducted entirely by American troops of the Eighth Army, while Australian troops were to assume responsibility for the seizure of Borneo, Java, and adjacent islands. Timing was dependent upon the progress of the fighting in Luzon, since the plan involved the commitment of available troops and resources as soon as requirements of the Luzon operation had been achieved. The use of guerrillas in the central and southern Philippines was expected to permit rapid progress without necessitating large naval or aerial support.

MacArthur's plan had the strategic objective of isolating Japan from the Malaya and Netherlands East Indies areas, with the principal offensive role played by land-based air power. The land-based bomb line was to move rapidly westward along the New Guinea coast toward the Philippines, bypassing and neutralizing by air action enemy forces "whenever practicable in order to avoid costly and time consuming operations." The Allied flank was to be protected "essentially by air operations and the necessary advanced naval bases were to be established under the protection of land-based aviation." Air attacks were to be used to destroy enemy air forces and gain air superiority over enemy bases threatening each advance; destroy enemy warships and supply ships; and send Allied ground forces forward by sea and air to capture and establish new air bases to continue the process. MacArthur maintained that the extent of each advance could be increased by employing carrier-based aircraft to provide close support for amphibious or airborne landing operations, and by extending the radius of bomber operations by advancing the "offensive fighter line" through inland airstrips constructed and maintained by air transport.

MacArthur's *Montclair III Plan* arrived in Washington just before the *Teheran* and *Cairo* Conferences, which was an opportune time, as one of the aims of these conferences was to discuss future strategy in the Pacific. Japan continued to be in a position of strength, as it controlled Burma, Malaya, the Netherlands East Indies, parts of China, and the Pacific islands. This kept the Allies a great distance from Japan, allowing it to maintain and even build economic and military strength. However, several weaknesses were becoming evident to the Joint Chiefs of Staff and Joint Planners. Japan's lines of communications were very long and becoming evermore overextended, with her shipping losses exceeding new construction. Her losses in aircraft and trained pilots and aircrew were also exceeding replacements.

Since Germany would not be defeated in 1944, and thus Russia would or could not enter the war against Japan, the Joint Planners shaped their Pacific strategy accordingly. They hoped to diminish Japanese military capabilities so that Honshu could be invaded by no later than spring 1946. The Joint Planners recommended that the advance along the New Guinea/Philippines axis continue concurrently with the capture of the Mandates in the Central Pacific; with the capture of the Marianas to establish bases for the strategic bombing of Japan; and with the intensification of aerial bombardment of the Netherlands East Indies and Rabaul.

During the discussions a basic conflict over allocations arose between MacArthur in the SWPA and Nimitz, backed by Adm. King, in the Central Pacific. The influential King argued that the Central Pacific Campaign offered greater rewards and should receive priority. Meanwhile, Arnold stated that strategic bombing by the massive B-29s of Japan's steel, aircraft, and other industries, as well as oil refineries and reserves, was to be a primary objective. The Navy maintained that since Japan's oil reserves were down to one to one and half years, an AAF air campaign by B-29s based in northern Australia against oil sources and refineries in the NEI, which supplied over 40% of Japan's needs, would be more productive in defeating Japan. Arnold agreed to the planning of the NEI oil campaign only, but not to its implementation, as he continued to maintain his desire for the Marianas-based bombing campaign of Japan. The Joint Chiefs and Joint Planners decided that US Navy forces were to be deployed to both the SWPA and Central Pacific to "support successive operations in both theaters with the transfer of forces and resources from one area to another." It was decided that "if conflicts in timing and allocation of means should develop, priority should be given to the Central Pacific," as operations there "promised.... a more rapid advance towards Japan and her lines of communication; the earlier acquisition of strategic air bases closer to the Homeland; and of greatest importance, the likelihood of precipitating a decisive engagement with the Japanese Fleet."

When he drafted *Montclair III*, MacArthur did so with the continued prospect of receiving limited resources to carry on to the Philippines and then the China coast. The most important of MacArthur's needs to launch a powerful offensive was aircraft. In October 1943 the 5AF consisted of one light, three medium, and three heavy bomber groups, five fighter groups, 4.5 troop carrier groups, one photo recon squadron, and one night fighter detachment. In September MacArthur was promised that within 60 days he would receive 33 more P-40Ns to join the 38 already in the theater; the 58FG was en route equipped with 31 P-47s and another 69 to be shipped; and the 418NFS was en route with 12 P-70s. A light bomber group and another night fighter squadron were also to arrive soon after. The lack of fighter aircraft was critical, as continued heavy attacks on Wewak and Rabaul were being planned. Kenney listed the requirements of a fighter for use in the SWPA in order: range, fire power, speed, rate of climb, and maneuverability. He continued to consider the P-38 as the only fighter to fulfill these requirements, since the P-47's great firepower was offset by its lack of range and single engine. Kenney noted that "there was a vast difference between the morale of fighter pilots flying twin engine fighters and those flying single engine fighters over long expanses of water."

October 1943: Aircraft Allocation, Real and Promised

Kenney had been authorized 226 P-38s for his six twin engine squadrons, and after reaching a high number of 212 in September his inventory would drop to 150 in February 1944, as he would lose 20 in August, 23 in September, and 27 in October, along with another 30 that were sent to depots but could not be "economically repaired." The arrival of new aircraft did not begin to compensate for these losses and would not do so for several months to come.

The War Department was aware of this fighter shortfall, but was bound by the "Europe First" priority. On 14 October the 8AF lost an inconceivable 64 bombers over Schweinfurt to over 500 Luftwaffe interceptors. Consequently, Gen. Arnold informed Kenney that the War Department had decided to send all P-38s and P-51s to the ETO during November and December, and that the P-47 was to be sent to the SWPA as a substitute. In addition to the 100 P-47s of the new 58th Fighter Group which were to arrive soon, an additional 270 in November and 100 in December were scheduled to be sent. With no choice, Kenney decided to replace the P-40s, P-39s, and P-400s in eight veteran fighter squadrons with these P-47s before equipping the 58FG. Each of these squadrons was to be equipped with 20 Thunderbolts until all eight squadrons were brought up to strength and sufficient P-47s were available to provide them with the authorized number.

The fighters were shipped deck-loaded or crated on cargo ships, deck-loaded on tankers, or crowded onto the decks of small aircraft carriers. The cargo ships and tankers could make their deliveries in about a month, while the carriers were able to cut the time to three weeks. The Navy was reluctant to divert any carriers from its operations to deliver Air Force aircraft, but did advance the departure date of one carrier already assigned to deliver fighters and allotted four fast tankers to deliver 50 P-47s. An additional 30 cargo ships and seven tankers, carrying 190 fighters, were scheduled to depart San Francisco between 20 November and 20 December. The actual number of fighters arriving in Australia from October and December were the 45 already promised P-38s and 207 P-47s.

In mid-December, when Kenney expressed his dissatisfaction with the slow arrival of fighters, the War Department informed him that his authorized 50% reserve was to include those aircraft under repair or erection, and that the monthly arrival of aircraft would not be at a set rate, but would be adjusted to actual losses. Kenney replied that this would not meet his requirements, as his allocated strength should only include aircraft that could fly or were under repair. The persuasive Kenney got P-38s scheduled for the South Pacific diverted to the SWPA. To placate Brig.Gen. Millard Harmon, CO of the South Pacific Theater, Gen. Arnold wrote him: "You were just a little bit fat....and Kenney was getting far behind." So 47 P-38s and 201 P-47s were scheduled for the SWPA between 23 December and 31 January 1944. Arnold also authorized a 70% fighter depot reserve instead of the 50%.

This flow of new aircraft did not significantly increase the number of front line aircraft in the theater. Only the 58th Fighter (P-47) Group added new aircraft, while the remainder of the arrivals went to replace obsolete and worn out aircraft. While not having the attributes of the P-38, the P-47s replaced the aging P-40s and P-39s to provide better defense for the advanced bases and to conduct more effective offensive sweeps and short range escort missions. Kenney was waiting for the P-38 Lightning to arrive.

Air Offensive Against Rabaul October-November 1943

After the Papuan Campaign ended in January 1943, the Allied Air Forces were so exhausted that they were unable to continue any sustained operations. But eight months later, after Lae, Salamaua, and Finschhafen had fallen, the situation was entirely different. The Allied Air Forces were not only able to support ground forces, but were prepared to begin a separate air offensive. Before beginning the air offensive they were to support the operations in New Guinea and the proposed operations of the New Britain Task Force and South Pacific Forces; support naval operations; engage enemy air, land, and sea forces; and establish advanced bases.

Gen. Whitehead, CO of ADVON, was to support the advance along the coast of New Guinea on as large a scale as possible without interfering with operations in the Markham-Lemu Valleys, with landings in New Britain, and with an air offensive against Rabaul. He was to conduct "intensive neutralization attacks against hostile air and surface forces in the Rabaul area," and be prepared to support Adm. Halsey's moves into the northern Solomons. He was to cooperate completely with the so-called "Escalator Force" in New Britain by preliminary bombardment, by missions in direct cooperation with ground forces, by providing fighter cover and aircraft warning, and by insuring air supply end evacuation. Finally, he was assigned reconnaissance missions over the Bismarck Sea, the approaches to Truk, the "assembly of enemy air end naval forces" in Rabaul, Kavieng, Wewak, and bases farther west, the approaches to the Torres Strait, and the Solomon Sea west of 155 degrees west longitude and south of the line Buka-New Ireland and the approaches to the Bismarck Sea.

1-12 October 1943: Fighter Operations over New Guinea

On 2 October, only 10 days after landing, veteran Australian troops fought their way into the town of Finschhafen. Although this placed Allied troops on the north side of Huon Gulf, it still wasn't the end of the campaign. The enemy retreated into the jungle and prepared itself for the Allies' next step. The Japanese airfields at Wewak had been neutralized for the landings, but the enemy still had pilots and aircraft to feed into the battle. The air supremacy that the Fifth Air Force had won was beginning to pay dividends, as many of the skilled veteran pilots of the Japanese Army Air Force were being lost and the Japanese were beginning to have to pull veteran units from other theaters of operation into the Battle of New Guinea. The AAF established airbases at Lae, Nadzab, Finschhafen, and a new site to the north known as Gusap. As soon as the fighter units could be moved to these airbases, the sooner operations could begin to eliminate Wewak and neutralize the enemy bastion of Rabaul, on New Britain. Before the fighters and bombers of the Fifth Air Force could concentrate against Rabaul, it was mandatory to continue attacks to neutralize the Japanese in the Wewak area.

The 5th Fighter Command and fighter units of the Air Task Forces had varied missions: the escort of bombers and transports and ground alert; regular patrol missions; and to convoy shipping. In carrying out these numerous tasks, AAF fighter pilots actually engaged Japanese fighters a surprisingly few times, as there were few large scale enemy air raids on Allied bases. Between 1 and 12 October, although enemy aircraft attacked Finschhafen seven times, Dobodura three times, and Lae once, the raids were usually carried out at night by no more than two or three aircraft, and generally were ineffective; of these 11 raids, only one was intercepted.

October 1943: 6NSF

By October 1943, the 6NFS was so disheartened by the poor performance of the P-70 as a night fighter and their lack of success that they began converting a P-38 into a night fighter. A P-38G was furnished, and 1Lt. Melvin Richardson and the squadron's Engineering Officer removed a SCR-540 AI radar set from one of the P-70s and the HF and VHF radios, which were installed in a belly tank. A second seat was added behind the pilot, and the radio sets were wired to the pilot's and R/O's location, as well as a scope for the R/O. It was found that even with the additional weight, the P-38 could climb much faster to the same altitude as the P-70 and was also capable of greater altitudes than the P-70. A second P-38G Lightning was also modified, but the Detachment was disbanded before they could be used.

2 October 1943: 49FG/9FS

After the grueling air battles of September, both the 5FC and the Japanese were inactive over New Guinea and New Britain during the first 11 days of October The Japanese sent Dinah recon bombers on patrol, and the 5AF sent up patrols to intercept any enemy attacks. Air combat was infrequent during this period, and the 9FS sent 14 P-38s to Cape Hoskins and the new airdrome at Gasmata, on the south shore of New Britain. The Japanese did not send up any interceptors, but Capt. Richard Bong, leading Green Flight at 15,000 feet, saw a lone, seemingly oblivious Dinah flying north at the same altitude. At 0925 Bong made a gentle turn to the right which put him directly behind the Dinah. Bong fired four bursts and it started smoking and fell into the water in a vertical flaming dive for his 17th victory.

3 October 1943: 475FG/433FS

Capt. Daniel Roberts took over the 433FS from Maj. Martin Low, who though unpopular did a commendable job of fashioning a combat worthy Squadron before he finished his tour. Roberts was able to get the best from his men by being indulgent but authoritarian, and when needed led them through example.

5 October 1943:49FG/8FS

During a late afternoon patrol north of Finschhafen by eight 8FS Warhawks at 9,000 feet, a Dinah was spotted as it tried to escape to the north. All Eightballs dropped their tanks and tried to catch the speedy Dinah in a climbing pursuit to 18,000 feet, where it leveled off. White Flight Leader 1Lt. James Hagerstrom tried to keep the twin engine bomber in sight, but heavy clouds and the fading daylight made contact difficult; he finally closed to 2,000 yards behind it. Hagerstrom held his throttle in "emergency war power" for 12 minutes and followed the Ki-46 up the coast, from Finschhafen to Astrolabe Bay, nearly reaching Madang. Finally, he crept up to within 250 yards and fired from dead astern. The enemy's port engine exploded and spewed oil that enveloped the Warhawk. Hagerstrom's eyes began to burn from the fumes, but he continued to follow the maneuvering Dinah and fire several more bursts that set its fuselage on fire for the 100th Eightball aerial victory.

1Lt. James **Hagerstrom** shot down a Dinah for his second the 8FS' 100th victory. (AFAA)

An armorer checks the 20mm cannon ammo drums after Capt. Richard **Bong** (above) scored his 17th victory, his first since 28 July. (AAF)

Early October 1943: 35FG Tsili Tsili Moves to Nadzab

The 35FG had moved to Tsili Tsili in August, primarily to cover the US Sixth Army and Australian Units during their successful operations in northeastern New Guinea: Nadzab on 5 September; Salamaua on 12 September; Lae on 16 September; Kaiapit on 18 September; and the Finschhafen Campaign on 21 September to 2 October.

During early October the Group was preparing to move to Nadzab, where new fighter strips were being constructed. Advance echelons of the 35th were flown into Nadzab on 8 October to establish billets for the 40th and 41st. The site was located in a dense jungle that required extensive clearing. Also the Malarial mosquito was prevalent, and intensive anti-mosquito measures were required. The HQ Squadron arrived at Nadzab and was followed shortly by the 40FS and 41FS.

Meanwhile the 39FS, still at Moresby, was involved in the air campaign to reduce Rabaul, providing cover for the 5BC bombers that destroyed the shipping and installations there. Shortly after the Rabaul missions, the 39FS transitioned from their beloved Lightnings to the ponderous Republic P-47 Thunderbolt and transferred from Moresby to a prepared site adjacent to the other two squadrons. By the end of the year all three squadrons were together.

10 October 1943: 49FG

A small Japanese formation escaped detection and bombed Dobodura, but did only minor damage, and no claims were made by any of the standing 49FG patrols.

Mosquito control spraying standing water with DDT at Nadzab. (AAF)

10 October 1943: 348FG/341FS/342FS

When the Allies established the 23rd Fighter Sector over Finschhafen, targets became available not only in the northern New Guinea area, but also included the New Britain bases at Cape Gloucester and Rabaul. The Japanese only had three remaining bases that could threaten the Allies in northern New Guinea: Wewak, Hollandia, and Rabaul. In October these targets were opened to the 348th's Thunderbolts. On 10 October 1943, four P-47s of the 341FS and 342FS swept Borgen Bay, Cape Gloucester, and strafed 12 barges, claiming three destroyed and several others damaged. However, a sweep to Wewak was turned back by overcast up to 23,000 feet over the target.

11 October 1943: Kearby CMH Mission

The 341FS flew several uneventful transport escort missions to Nadzab beginning at 0800. A flight of four Thunderbolts flown by the 348th's ranking officers flew a mission to Wewak. Col. Kearby led the mission with Capt. John Moore, the 341FS' Operations Officer, as his Wingman, while Maj. Raymond Gallagher, the 342FS' CO, led the second element with Capt. William Dunham as his Wingman. The mission took off from Wards Drome at 0730 and landed at Tsili Tsili for refueling at 0900. At 0930 the mission took off and headed 200 miles northwest along the coast to Wewak. They climbed to 26,000 feet in clear weather and encountered only scattered clouds between 2,000 and 8,000 feet on their approach to the target area. When the four P-47s were just about 50 miles from Wewak Japanese radar detected them. Japanese Lt.Col. Tamiya Teranishi, CO of the Japanese Army Air Forces' 14th Fighter Bomber Group, happened to be at Wewak at the time and decided to personally lead his fighters in an ambush against the incoming Americans, leading about 20-25 Oscars and Tonys to intercept.

As Kearby's flight orbited at this very high altitude from 1035 and 1100 over the Boram Strip, on the southeast corner of Wewak, they saw aircraft below, with one taxiing. There were two large ships just off the coast, about a dozen barges in Hansa Bay, and four others in the Sepik River heading toward a larger vessel several miles upstream. At about 1100 the fuel in the flight's belly tanks was nearly depleted, and Kearby ordered them dropped to increase speed and to conserve internal fuel, but within the next few minutes Kearby would be committed to go into action or return to base, as they had reached the halfway home point in their fuel supply. Dunham radioed that he was having engine trouble and was returning to base and Gallagher joined him, splitting the flight.

At 1115, Kearby's decision was made when he sighted an Oscar below and to his left at about 20,000 feet. (Kearby had misidentified the enemy as a Zero in the bright sun.) Kearby put his fighter into a high speed steep dive toward the left rear of the Japanese fighter and opened fire at 7 o'clock when the range closed to about 500 yards. The Japanese pilot apparently was surprised, as he took no evasive action before Kearby's gunfire torched his fighter, which rolled over and crashed into the sea.

Instead of heading back home, Dunham surprised Gallagher by rolling into a dive following Kearby. Gallagher also followed and saw a lone enemy fighter about five miles out to sea, but it ducked into a large cloud. Gallagher realized that he had pursued the enemy far out to sea and headed back toward land and circled, trying to find the other three P-47s, but by then the battle would be over.

Meanwhile, Kearby and the other two P-47s began climbing back to 26,000 feet, where Dunham sighted an enemy fighter below at 18,000 feet (the same one that Gallagher had chased into the cloud, now returning to Wewak?). Just as Dunham was preparing to attack, a large enemy formation of 36 fighters at about 10,000 to 15,000 feet was called out by John Moore, who identified them as "many Tonys with a few Oscars and Zekes" (Teranishi's interceptors from Wewak.) There were also about a dozen bombers coming into the area at 5,000 feet, and both the fighters and bombers were approaching from the sea about four miles from the coast and approximately 12 miles from Borum.

The three Thunderbolts (minus Gallagher) maneuvered around to the rear of the Japanese formation and above it at about 8,000 feet. Kearby, followed by his two wingmen, led the way down, rolling over to attack the Japanese fighters. The fighters gained an IAS of 425 mph and Kearby

Col. Neel **Kearby** become an ace-in-a-day when he shot down six enemy fighters. Kearby and his wife. (L) are pictured here with their pre-war friends, the William Leverettes. Leverette was also an ace-in-a-day with seven Ju-87 Stuka victories in the MTO, only two days earlier. (AAF)

Kearby receiving the first AAF Medal of Honor in the Pacific from Gen. MacArthur in early January 1944. (AAF)

closed; again, the Japanese pilot made no effort to evade when he opened fire from 300 yards from 7 o'clock behind the lead Oscar (which Kearby again misidentified as a Zero in his report). The enemy fighter burst into flames and spun into the water. Kearby turned slightly to starboard and opened fire at 500 yards from 8 o'clock on another Oscar (which he identified as a clipped wing Zero/Hamp), which burst into flames for his fifth career victory to make him an ace. So far none of his three victims had made an attempt to evade. As Kearby finished off his third Oscar a Tony quickly closed from Kearby's rear, but his Wingman, Dunham, protecting his leader's tail, fired two bursts which struck the Tony in the cockpit area and left wing, sending it down in flames. Kearby saw another Oscar turning slightly to the left and closed to about 500 yards behind the enemy and opened fire, setting it on fire for his fourth victory of the fight.

After exchanging fire with several Japanese aircraft, Moore noticed that his fuel was nearing the critical point and he had lost Kearby and Dunham. He had heard both Gallagher and Dunham report that they were low on fuel and heading back to Ward's Drome. He gradually climbed to 16,000 feet on a heading that took him along the coast toward the Allied airfields in the southeast. After flying for about 20 miles on this course he saw a lone P-47 with six circling Tonys at about 4,000 feel below. Moore knew it was Kearby in trouble and dove to help him out. As he closed on the battle Moore saw Kearby hit a Tony, sending it down trailing heavy smoke for his fifth victory of the day to make him an "ace-in-a-day." Moore closed on a flight of three Tonys and went after the last Tony in the formation, taking a 35 degree deflection shot that started the Tony smoking; a second burst caused the Tony to erupt into flame and fall off to port into an uncontrolled spin. While Moore was dispatching their companion, the first two Tonys had pulled up steeply to starboard and racked their fighters around to get behind Moore, who put his fighter into a full power dive to escape. But as he was about to pull out he saw that, although he had gained some distance, the first Japanese pilot was still behind him, followed by the other by at about a 1,000 yards.

After he finished off his fifth victim, Kearby observed Moore's problem and turned back to help him. Kearby went after the last Tony in another 400 mph dive and opened fire at about 700 yards, tearing off pieces that caused the Tony to fall off trailing smoke for his sixth and final victory, which was confirmed by Moore. Kearby's and Moore's combat reports differ on Kearby's last two victories. Moore's report states that the first of Kearby's victims was shot down before Moore entered the area, while Kearby reported that both of the Tonys he shot down were on Moore's tail. It appears that the Tony nearest to Moore either broke off combat when his Wingman was shot down or he was shot down himself. Kearby made one more pass at a Tony from the 10 o'clock position, but his deflection was incorrect and the enemy escaped. Another Tony closed on Kearby's tail and he headed his Thunderbolt into a nearby cloud at about 7,000 feet. When he came out of the cloud he was alone, so he climbed to 15,000 feet and called for the rest of the flight to check in. By this time the P-47s were very low on fuel, and Kearby led his flight to the emergency refueling base at Lae, where they landed at 1245 with less than 75 gallons in their tanks. Two and a half hours later they returned to Port Moresby.

After the war, using Japanese and American sources, Japanese researchers who examined the Wewak action of 11 October 1943 concluded that one of Kearby's victories was over Japanese Col. Teranishi. Their research found that the pertinent time of the action was about 1125, which was the same time that the debriefed returning Japanese pilots reported losing contact with Teranishi. Kearby had become an ace, an ace-in-a-day, shot down an enemy air leader, and was awarded the AAF's first Medal of Honor. Most important to Kearby was that he had proved the P-47 in the SWPA. A telegram to Kenney from the 342FS Intelligence Officer lavishly stated the newly won status of the Thunderbolt:

> 342ND FIGHTER SQUADRON
> OFFICE OF THE INTELLIGENCE OFFICER
> A.P.O. 929
> 12 OCTOBER 1943 SUBJECT: NARRATIVE OF AIR COMBAT
> TO: COMMANDING GENERAL, FIFTH AIR FORCE,
>
> .....THE HISTORY-MAKING ASPECT OF THIS FLIGHT IS UNQUESTIONABLE. THE RESULTS OBTAINED-COL. KEARBY'S SIX VICTORIES (2 ZEKES, 2 HAPS, 2 TONYS), CAPT. MOORE'S 2 TONYS, CAPT. DUNHAM'S 1 TONY-A TOTAL OF 9 FIGHTERS DESTROYED WITHOUT A SCRATCH ON A SINGLE THUNDERBOLT DEMONSTRATES THAT THIS TYPE OF PLANE HAS COME INTO ITS OWN IN THIS THEATER, AND THAT ITS TERRIFIC SPEED BOTH IN THE DIVE AND STRAIGHTAWAY, ITS FLASHING AILERON ROLL AND MURDEROUS FIREPOWER WILL HENCEFORTH STRIKE TERROR INTO THE HEARTS OF THE LITTLE YELLOW AIRMEN.
>
> IN CONCLUSION, IT SHOULD BE NOTED THAT THIS PLANE FLEW WELL OVER 300 MILES, FOUGHT FOR ONE HOUR, AND RETURNED, THE WHOLE MISSION CONSUMING ABOUT THREE HOURS AND ONE HALF. ABOUT 3,500 RDS. OF AMMUNITION WERE EXPENDED AND OVER 100 FEET OF FILM TAKEN.
>
> BERNHARD A. ROTH
> 1ST LIEUT. AIR CORPS
> INTELLIGENCE OFFICER

Gen. Kenney thought that Kearby would have been granted credit for a seventh victory if his gun camera had not run out of film at the wrong time, and demanded that a second camera be installed on Kearby's P-47 *Fiery Ginger*, named after his wife. Kearby describes the battle in his ICR:

"I was leading a flight of four P-47s over Wewak. We took off from Tsili Tsili at 0915 and arrived over Wewak at 1030 at 28,000 feet. The weather was excellent, with a few scattered clouds between 2,000 and 8,000 feet. We saw a number of aircraft parked on Boram strip, and 1 aircraft taxiing on the runway. He did not take off. The fuel in our belly tanks had been consumed, so we dropped them to increase our speed and conserve fuel. At 1115 1 Zeke was sighted at 9 o'clock below at 20,000 feet. I came in on him from 7 o'clock above and opened fire at 1,500 feet. He took no evasive action, caught fire, and dived into the sea.

"We climbed back to 26,000 feet and at about 1125 saw about 36 fighters, Tonys, Hamps, and Zekes, and 12 bombers approaching from the southeast along the coast. The fighters were at about 10,000 to 15,000 feet and the bombers at about 5,000 feet. We came in from above. I opened fire on a Zeke at 1,500 feet and closed as he burst into flames. No evasive action was taken.

"I turned slightly and opened fire at 1,500 feet from 7 o'clock on a Hamp, which burst into flames taking no evasive action. I looked up and another Hamp was turning slightly to the left. I closed to 1,500 feet and opened fire from slightly above and from about 1 o'clock. He burst into flames after he had passed beyond my sights in the turn. I was indicating over 400 miles per hour during this period.

"By this time the Japanese realized we were there so I pulled up sharply to about 20,000 feet and saw Captain William Dunham. I joined him and we started home. Immediately at 2 o'clock below at about 10,000 feet I saw Captain John Moore in a P-47 with one Tony about 3,000 feet to the rear and another Tony about 3,000 feet behind the first one. Captain Moore was headed for home. I turned and came in at 400 miles per hour on the tail of the rear Tony opening fire at 1,500 feet. He took no evasive action and burst into flames. I closed for the other Tony, which was on Captain Moore's tail, but he must have seen me as he turned and dove down in front of me. I opened fire from about 2,000 feet closing in and saw tracers going into him and pieces of his wing and fuselage flying off. I did not see him catch fire nor did I see him crash, as I did not have time to watch him. Captain Moore saw this Tony burst into flames and crash into the sea.

"He then turned back toward Wewak, and I turned with him. Tonys were all over the sky. I made another pass at a Tony from about 10 o'clock, but deflection was wrong. I looked behind and saw a Tony closing on my tail, so I dived for the nearby clouds. We were now at about 7,000 feet. When coming out of the clouds I could no longer see the Tony. I climbed to 15,000 feet and called the flight. They all checked in, and we proceeded to Lae and landed there at 1240. Captain Moore destroyed 2 enemy fighters and Captain Dunham 1. Major Gallagher had chased a Zeke into the clouds and was unable to find another enemy aircraft when he came out. We refueled at Lae and returned to Port Moresby. Claim two Zekes, two Hamps, and two Tonys."

Kearby's CMH Citation reads:
"For conspicuous gallantry and intrepidity above and beyond the call of duty in action with the enemy near Wewak, New Guinea, on 11 October 194 Colonel Kearby volunteered to lead a flight of 4 fighters to reconnoiter the strongly defended enemy base at Wewak Having observed enemy installations and reinforcements at 4 airfields, and secured important tactical information, he saw an enemy fighter below him, made a diving attack and shot it down in flames. The small formation then sighted approximately 12 enemy bombers accompanied by 36 fighters. Although his mission had been completed, his fuel was running low and the numerical odds were 12 to 1, he gave the signal to attack. Diving into the midst of the enemy airplanes he shot down 3 in quick succession. Observing one of his comrades with enemy fighters in pursuit he destroyed both enemy aircraft. The enemy broke off in large numbers to make multiple attacks on his airplane but despite his peril he made one more pass before seeking cloud protection. Coming into the clear he called his flight together and led them to a friendly base. Colonel Kearby brought down 6 enemy aircraft in this action, undertaken with superb daring after his mission was completed."

Preparation for the Rabaul Offensive

Allied Air Background

The varied missions of the 5FC and fighter units of the Air Task Forces, together with the building up of air bases in the Ramu and Markham River Valleys, were in agreement with the Allied plans for September and October 1943. But these plans also gave priority to operations for the isolation and neutralization of Rabaul. First in a carefully integrated timetable was an air offensive against Rabaul by Southwest Pacific air units to cover South Pacific landings on Treasury, Choiseul, and Bougainville Islands. Kenney's air units were then to assume the major burden of the Rabaul Campaign, while MacArthur's forces captured Cape Gloucester and the remainder of the Huon Peninsula. By the middle of August the Allied Air Forces had prepared detailed plans for a preliminary softening of Rabaul. This was to consist of a week's maximum effort carried out by all types of bombardment aircraft, except A-20s and A-26s, and protected by all available P-38 units. At that time Kenney was considering October as a possible date for the beginning of the air offensive, but hesitated to make any definite commitment because of a lack of a suitable staging point for fighter escorts. Dobodura, over 400 miles from Rabaul, was too distant for fighters to make the round trip if they were forced into combat over the target. Finschhafen was 75 miles nearer, but no field that was satisfactory to station a major force had yet been established there. The only answer seemed to be Kiriwina Island, which was approximately 350 miles from Rabaul and was occupied on 30 June for the specific object of constructing a staging base for escort fighters.

A potential problem was that the escort of 100 or more P-38s low on fuel might arrive over Kiriwina at about the same time on their return from the target, and this large number of aircraft could be difficult to service simultaneously, and while concentrated on the ground would be vulnerable to an enemy air attack. Extensive construction to handle this large number of aircraft and the permanent RAAF air garrison was begun under the direction of GHQ shortly after the occupation of Kiriwina. By the middle of August, Chief Engineer Gen. Hugh Casey had indicated that three strips would be completed by 5 October, hard stands for 213 medium bombers by 10 October, and hard stands for 100 fighters five days later. If this schedule was met, the air planners were convinced that the opening of the Rabaul offensive could begin on 15 October. The planners worried, and urged that MacArthur's Headquarters to make "every effort" to complete the Kiriwina project. Kenney's Chief of Staff, Brig.Gen. Donald Wilson, stated, "Facilities for the landings of aircraft, their maintenance, and refueling must be considered as a special tactical project and are not to be associated, with the phlegmatic progress of normal bases."

Meanwhile, the Fifth Air Force had stopped even the comparatively small raids against Rabaul that had been carried out with periodic frequency in 1942 and early 1943. During August and September, aircraft from the SWPA had attacked that Japanese base only once, and this mission was in early September by a dozen RAAF Catalinas. By 1 October, however, the 8th Photo Squadron was sending its F-5s and P-38s over Rabaul's airdromes and harbors, and heavy bomber squadrons, particularly the 63rd, were tracking the weather over the entire New Britain area. On 1 October, photos discovered one heavy cruiser, one light cruiser, 10 destroyers, five submarines, and 25 merchant vessels in the harbor; and 87 medium bombers, 37 light bombers, and 59 fighters on the four main Rabaul airdromes. Ten days later shipping had slightly decreased, but the numbers of medium and light bombers showed little change, and fighters had also decreased from 183 to 145.

Japanese Background

The Eighth Area Army's counterpart of Admiral Kusaka's air fleet, the 6th Air Division, was almost totally committed to the support of operations on New Guinea by the end of 1942. During the brutal fighting in Papua Japanese air support had been infrequent and insignificant, which Gen. Imamura needed to rectify in his air defense of Rabaul. Rapopo Airfield, which became operational in April 1943, was constructed by the Army to accommodate a growing number of aircraft, and work was begun on a Navy field at Keravat to operate even more. At about this time, the strength of the 6th Air Division topped out at 300 aircraft of all types, many of which were ordered to New Guinea on 12 April.

On eastern New Guinea, as in the Solomons, the airfields closer to the battle front than those at Rabaul were needed to provide effective air support to Japanese troops. Consequently, two major airbases were developed at Wewak and Madang on the coast northwest of the Huon Peninsula. Despite the heavy use of these fields, the operating efficiency of Army air units declined steadily in the first part of 1943. The rate at which 6th Air Division planes were destroyed by Allied fighter pilots and bomber gunners was so large that the average monthly 50 aircraft replacement rate was not able to make up these losses. In July, the 7th Air Division was sent from the Netherlands East Indies to Eighth Area Army, and the Fourth Air Army was assigned to direct and coordinate air operations. By the time the Air Army's Headquarters arrived at Rabaul on 6 August, a move of all Army combat aircraft from the Bismarcks was well in progress.

Considering the Eighteenth Army on New Guinea was in critical need of air support, the Imperial General Headquarters had urged Gen. Imamura to relinquish the air defense of Rabaul entirely to the Navy and concentrate all his air strength in the Eighteenth's sector. After discussing this proposed change with Adm. Kusaka, who would gain singular responsibility for directing air operations at Rabaul, Imamura ordered the transfer. By the end of August, Fourth Air Army's headquarters was established at Wewak and all Army aircraft, except a few reconnaissance and liaison types, were based on New Guinea.

During this time Japanese naval air groups were rotated in and out of Rabaul to be organized and disbanded there. Two administrative headquarters, the 25th and 26th Air Flotillas, operated under Eleventh Air Fleet to control the air groups; for tactical purposes, the flight echelons of the flotillas were organized as the 5th and 6th Air Attack Forces.

In September 1943, at the beginning of the Allied air offensive against Rabaul, the Eleventh Air Fleet had gathered about 300 planes and 10,000 men, including about 1,500 flying personnel. Three fighter groups (the 201st, the 204th, and the 253rd Air Groups), each with a nominal strength of 50 aircraft and 75 pilots, were the nucleus of the Japanese air defense. The 705th Air Group was the only medium bomber unit, along with elements of at least two more groups, but heavy losses had reduced all these units to only a fraction of a bomber group's normal strength of 48 planes and 300 crewmen. The dive bomber-torpedo bomber 582nd Air Group had a strength of 36 attack aircraft and 150 crewmen. The 938th and 958th Reconnaissance Groups each had 28 float planes and about 100 flying personnel. A few flying boats and transports were assigned to each air group, and headquarters and liaison aircraft were also at hand.

To maintain operational strength, 50 replacement aircraft were sent to Rabaul each month. Approximately one third of these planes were lost in transit, but the remainder (80% fighters) reached their destination after a long over water flight staged through Truk and Kavieng. Many land-based naval air units stationed in non-combat areas of the Pacific were sent as replacements for lost aircraft and pilots, and sometimes to relieve battle-fatigued veterans from Rabaul. The drain of Japanese naval aircraft and personnel from the Netherlands Indies became so acute toward the end of 1943 that the Army's 7th Air Division had to be returned to the area to bring the NEI back to operational strength.

The Allied attack on Rabaul was inevitable and impending, and the Japanese tried to prepare for it. Air operations from the most exposed forward airstrips in the Solomons were significantly reduced to preserve aircraft and crews. At all Rabaul airfields, the Japanese constructed more revetments and expanded dispersal areas. Antiaircraft guns were sited in depth to cover approaches to airfields and the anchorages. Tobera airfield was rushed to completion to lessen the concentration of aircraft at Vunakanau and Lakunai, and to provide space for aircraft reinforcements from the Combined Fleet. Two carrier air groups with about 300 aircraft were positioned at Truk under Adm. Kusaka, and were to be committed if the situation demanded. Although the Japanese did assign some of their newest fighter types to Rabaul's air defense as they became available, the great majority of the fighters deployed to meet the Allied attacks would be the venerable Zero.

Rabaul, New Britain

Rabaul, on the island of New Britain, along with Port Moresby, was one of two major ports in the Australian Territory of New Guinea. It was the main Japanese naval base for the Solomon Islands Campaign and Papuan and New Guinea Campaigns. Simpson Harbor was captured from Australian forces in February 1942 and was known as "the Pearl Harbor of the South Pacific." Rabaul Town was located on the shore of Simpson Harbor, one of the best natural harbors in the Southwest Pacific. Simpson Harbor, the innermost part of Blanche Bay, is circled by hills that are actually the walls of the crater of a gigantic volcano measuring six miles long and two and a half miles wide, with the only opening in its rim being an entryway from the sea and St. George's Channel. In the Harbor there is anchorage for at least 20 10,000-15,000 ton vessels, plus numerous smaller vessels. Separated from this principal anchorage is Matupi Harbor, and just inside the headlands at the entrance to Blanche Bay are two further protected harbors. The remainder of the Gazelle Peninsula is mountainous, covered by inhospitable heavy jungle broken frequently by swamps and rivers.

Rabaul Airfields

The beginning of 1943 had found the Japanese on the defensive everywhere in the Solomons, New Britain, and New Guinea, but they were still able to mount a significant air response and AA fire, especially over the Rabaul area. Rabaul needed to be neutralized if the offensive on New Guinea was to succeed in defeating the Japanese troops there, and to provide a base for the invasion of the Philippines. The key targets for the 13AF and 5AF were the five all-weather airfields near Rabaul, all strategically sited around Simpson Harbor and Keravia Bay. All five fields were close enough together to be mutually supporting and to allow the exchange of aircrews and aircraft, but separated enough so that all could not be neutralized at once.

Vunakanau

After the Japanese captured Rabaul there were two small airfields (Vunakanau and Lakunai) maintained by the Royal Australian Air Force which they enlarged from single unpaved strips into major airdromes. The largest airdrome near Rabaul was Vunakanau (also called Rabaul Upper Airfield and West Airfield), and was located on a 1,000 foot plateau inland from Keravia Bay, 10 miles south of Rabaul. Except for two coconut plantations, the plateau was covered by scrub growth and kunai grass. The ground was quite irregular and laced with deep gullies, and the improved 5,100x750-foot runway and the new parallel 4,100x140 foot concrete runway were the practical limit of expansion for Vunakanau. The field had 81 fighter and 64 bomber revetments connected by six and a half miles of taxiways on both sides. It had one large ex-RAAF hangar and barracks for 2,500 personnel. Vunakanau became the largest Japanese airdrome at Rabaul, and its sprawling network of dispersal lanes and revetments spread over almost two square miles. The field was well defended by AA guns, as by November 1943 there were 15 heavy, 14 medium, and 12 light guns supplemented by three searchlights. It did not benefit from the supporting AA fire from Rabaul Town installations as did Lakunai. Bombers of the 5AF and 13AF would neutralize the field by mid-February 1944, when the Japanese evacuated their remaining flyable aircraft to Truk, but their AA defenses were active until the end of the war.

Lakunai (Rabaul Lower)

Lakunai was located on the east side of Simpson Harbor, and only about a mile south of Rabaul Town on the coastal flats of Crater Peninsula. Before the war the RAAF built a single 4,700 foot runway surfaced in sand and volcanic ash. On 23 January 1942 the Japanese occupied Rabaul, and the Japanese Navy had improved the field to 4,750x525 feet, with two and a half miles of taxiways with some steel matting and with 90 fighter and

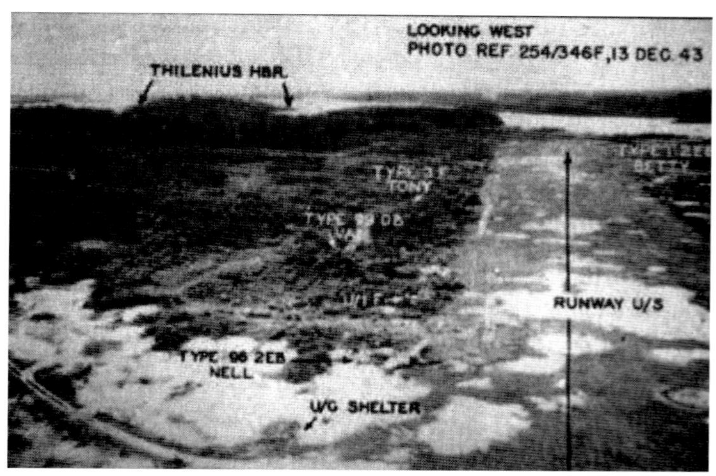

Aerial view of **Simpson Harbor** with Rabaul Town and Lakunai Airdrome in upper center of photo. (AAF)

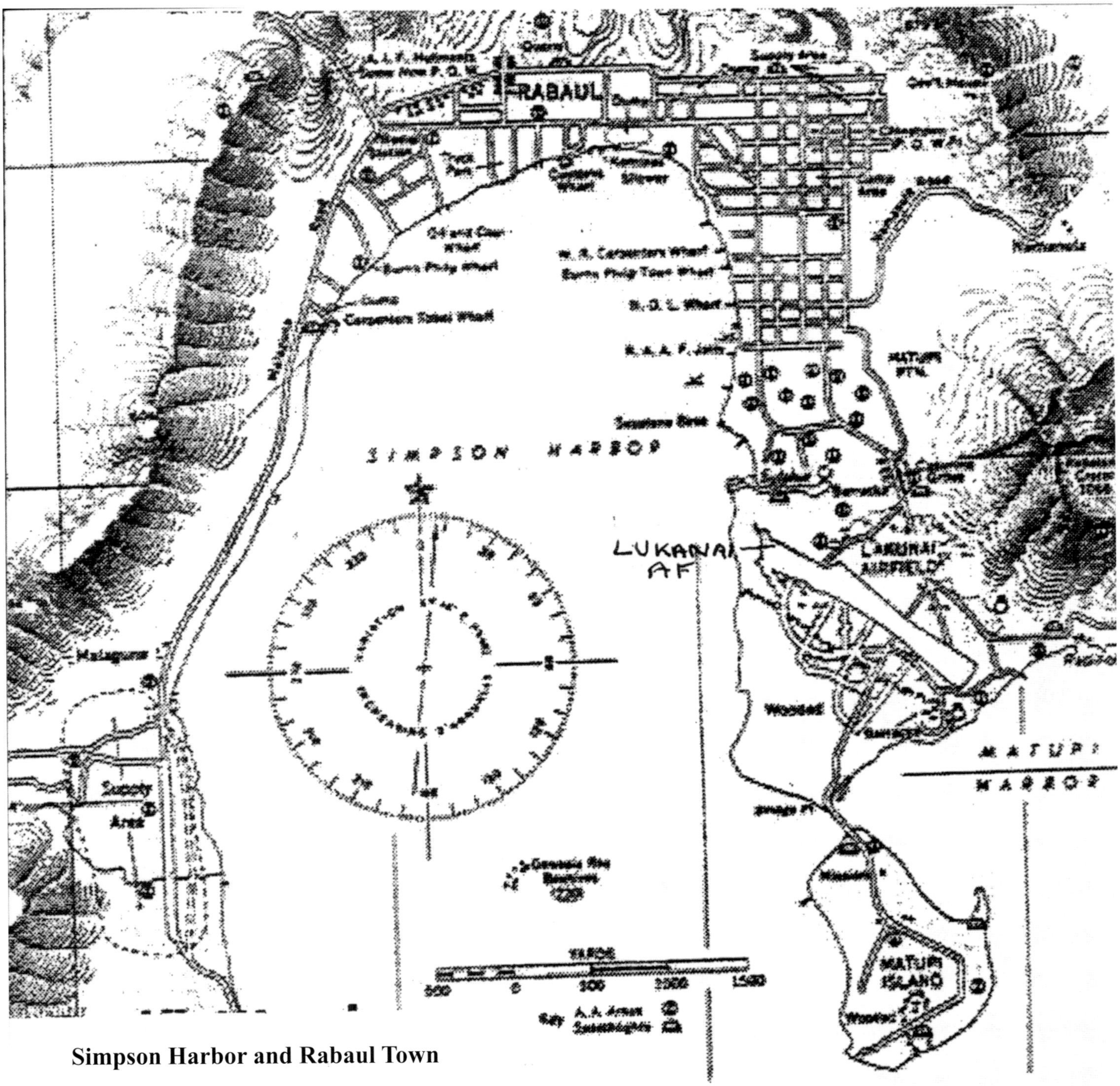

Simpson Harbor and Rabaul Town

10 bomber revetments to the north and south of the field. There were two small wooden and steel hangars and 20 barracks for 800 personnel. Lakunai Airfield and its hardstands and revetments occupied all the available ground on a small peninsula. The distinctive, sharply rising slopes of Rabalankaia Crater blocked any extension of the field to the northeast and a small creek was a barrier on the northwest.. The base was defended by AA guns around the base and from nearby Rabaul Town, Matupi Island to the south, and Sulphur Creek to the north, and was the heaviest defended of the Rabaul bases. The first aircraft arrived by the end of January and were mainly used by the Japanese Navy, although several Army units were based there in early 1943 until most were transferred to Lae or Wewak. The airfield was bombed into neutralization and abandoned.

Rapopo

In the summer 1942 the Japanese began construction on two new fields. The first was Rapopo, located at Lesson Point, at the site of the former Ropopo Coconut Plantation that gave it its name. It was on the coast about 14 miles southeast of Rabaul on the northeast corner of Gazelle Peninsula. When completed in December 1942 as a bomber field, Rapopo had the longest Rabaul runway, measuring north-south 6,900 feet from the sea to a river that effectively barred further extension. Although it was constructed of concrete, it suffered from severe drainage problems and was replaced in October 1943 by a coral-surfaced runway extending 4,600x135 feet from a low, coastal bluff and occupied the full width of the cleared space. It

Rabaul Airfield Map/Photo Gallery

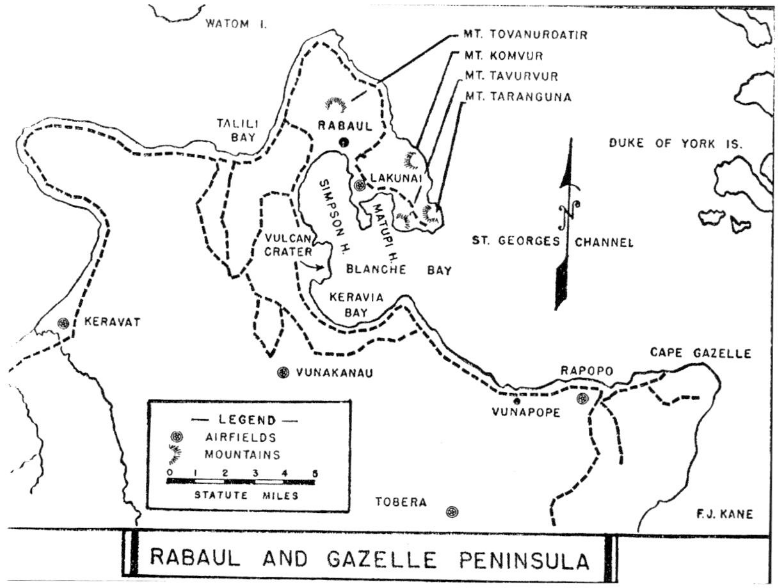

Rabaul Area Airfields

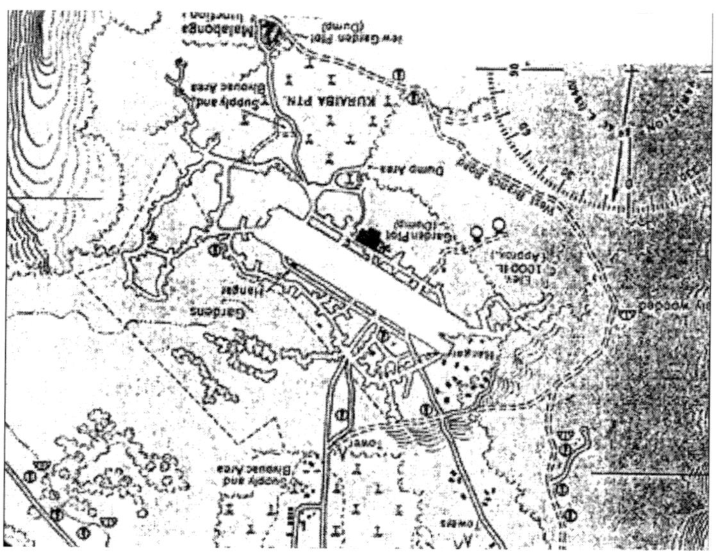

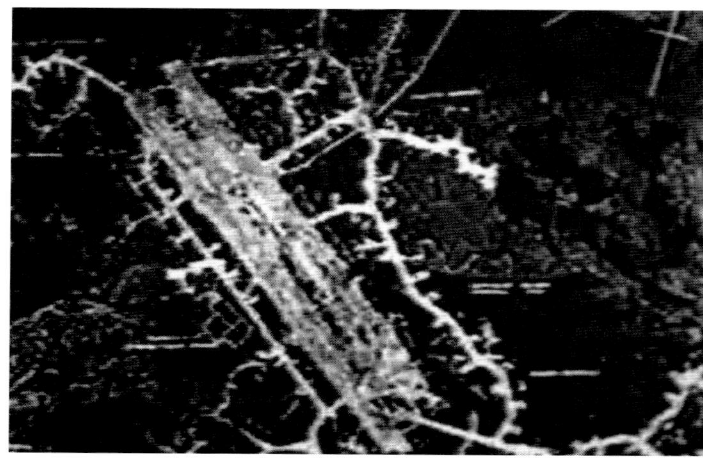

Vunakanau

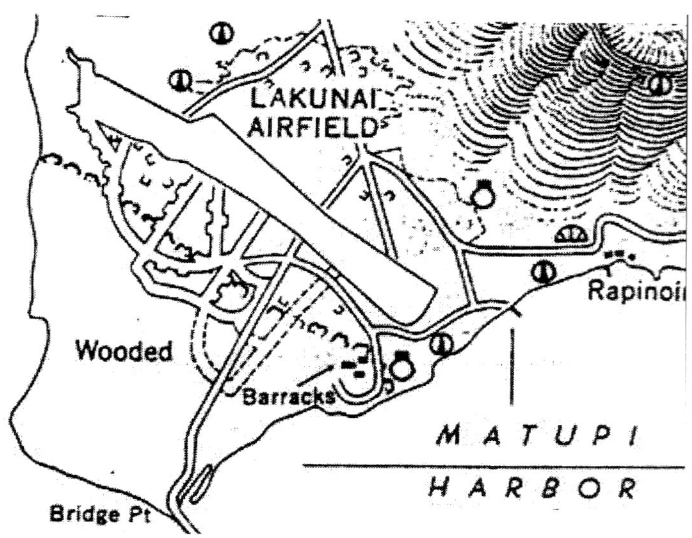

Lakuna

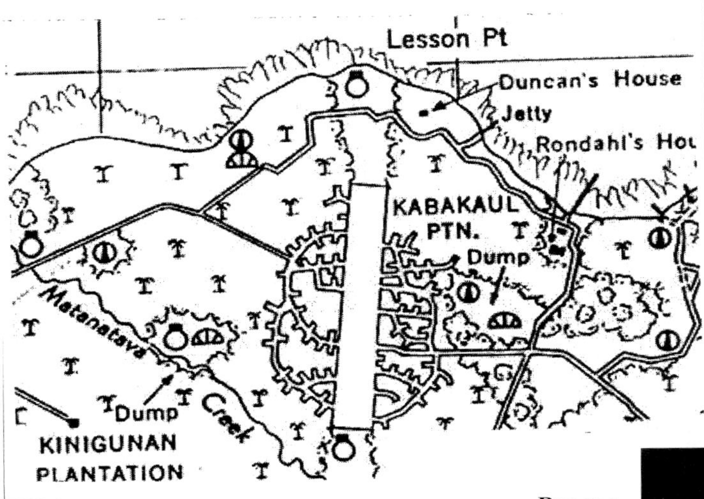

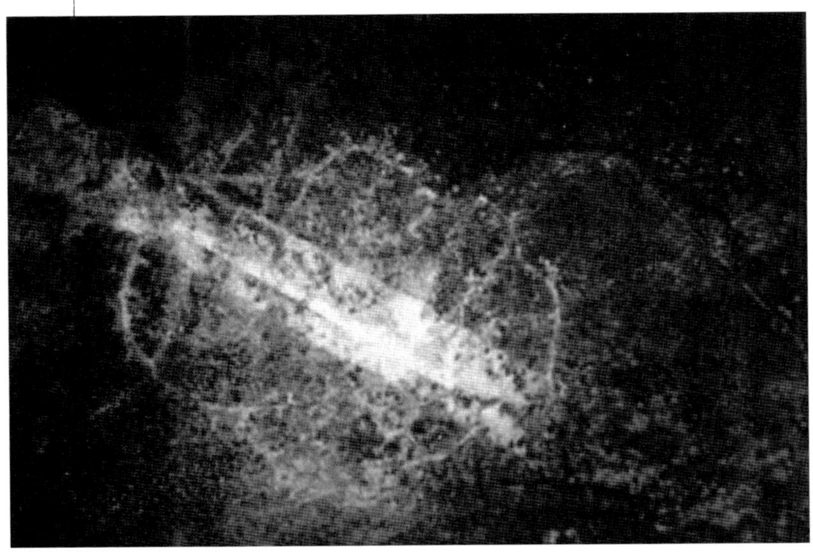

Ropopo

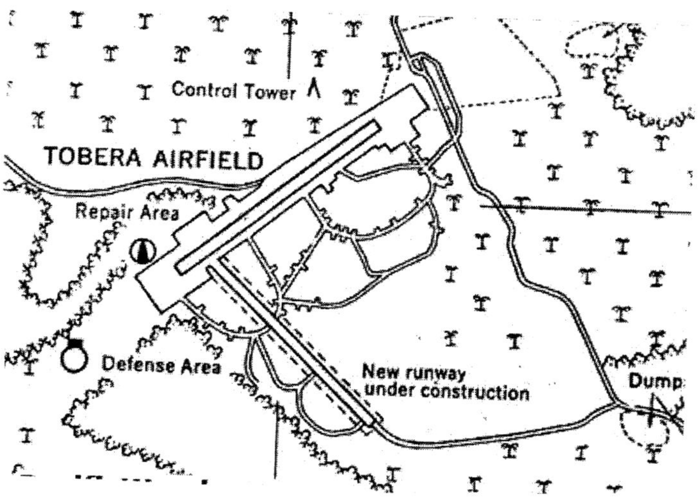

Tobera

too suffered from drainage problems and was constantly muddy for long periods after rains. The fields had three miles of taxiways that connected 94 bomber and 10 fighter revetments. Rapopo was heavily defended by 29 heavy, 21 medium, and 13 light AA guns supported by 5 searchlights. The field was pounded and neutralized by mid-June 1944.

Tobera (South Field)
In the early summer of 1943, the Japanese began construction on a fourth field well inland from the other airfields: 15 miles southeast of Vunakanau, eight miles southwest of Rapopo, and about 13 miles southwest of Rabaul. It was built on the Tobera Coconut Plantation, occupying a gently sloping plateau that divided the streams which flowed north to the sea from those which ran south to the Warangoi River. It had a 5,300x700 foot runway with a 3,600x100 foot concrete central runway and had two miles of taxiways for 75 fighters and two bombers; it was completed in August 1943. Because Tobera was constructed on a plantation area, its dispersal areas and field installations were scattered amidst the coconut trees. It was neutralized by Allied attacks by late February 1944.

Keravat
The fifth airfield at Rabaul was located on Ataliklikun Bay, just north of the Keravat River and 13 miles southwest of Rabaul on Kabaira Bay. This Army airfield was plagued by drainage problems, and of all the Rabaul airfields had perhaps the poorest location and the greatest engineering problems. The drainage problems halted initial construction, but the Navy resumed construction. By the end of November 1943, the Japanese had been able to grade and surface a 4,800 x 400 foot runway, but Keravat never was surfaced nor became fully operational and saw very limited use as an emergency landing ground.

Anti-Aircraft Defenses
The Japanese anti-aircraft defenses were well coordinated by army and naval units. The Army operated 192 of the 367 antiaircraft guns and the Navy 175. The naval guns guarded Simpson Harbor and its shipping, as well as the three airfields Tobera, Lakunai, and Vunakanau. The Army units defended Rapopo airfield, army supply dumps and installations, and assisted the navy in defending Simpson Harbor. An effective early warning radar system provided 90 mile coverage from Rabaul and extended coverage with additional radars on New Britain, New Ireland, and at Buka. These sets provided 30 to 60 minutes early warning of an attack.

Other New Britain Area Japanese Airstrips
There were also several other airstrips on New Britain. Gasmata was on the south central coast of New Britain and was redeveloped from an existing Australian runway captured in February 1942. Once Allied air attacks began Gasmata became non-operational, as its dispersal areas were poorly placed. Cape Hoskins airdrome, located opposite Gasmata on the north central coast of New Britain, was completed in September 1943. Cape Gloucester, on the far western end of New Britain, had two airstrips that threatened Allied bases on eastern New Guinea. There were four additional operational airfields near New Britain. Kavieng and nearby Panapai were located off the northern tip of New Ireland Island, WNW of Rabaul. After Rabaul, Kavieng was the largest Japanese airbase complex in the Bismarcks. Kavieng was completed in August 1942, and a satellite field at Panapai was completed in April 1943. Namatami and Borpop were 50 miles northeast of Rabaul, on New Ireland's eastern shore. The Admiralty Islands far to the WNW had two airfields, but neither was used to any degree. In August 1943 the 60 fighters and 40 bombers of the Fourth Air Army were withdrawn from Rabaul to defend Wewak from the 5AF. During the Munda Campaign, the 11th Air Fleet took heavy losses that forced the 2nd Carrier Division to transfer to Rabaul from Truk, and further losses forced the transfer of the 1st Carrier Division to Rabaul. The Fourth Air Army was decimated over New Guinea by the 5AF, and further weakened

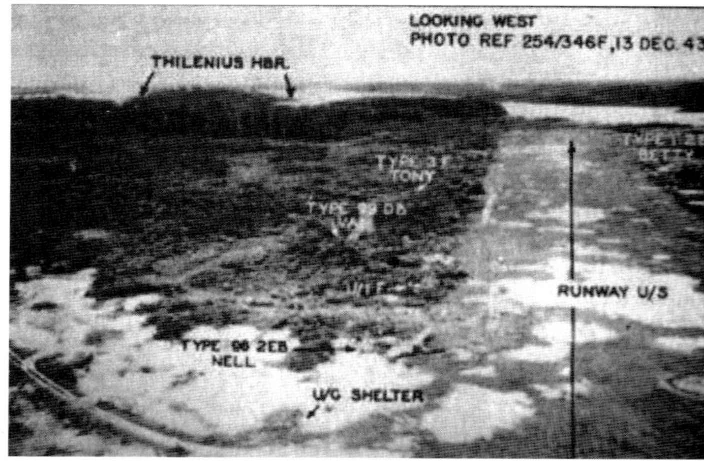

Gasmata. (AAF)

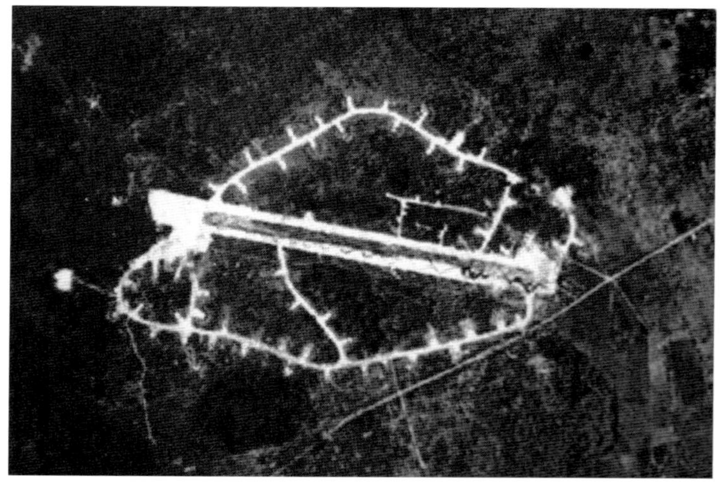

Kavieng. (AAF)

when it was forced to transfer its 7th Air Division to the Celebes in November 1943 to replace naval aircraft that had been sent to Rabaul.

There was also an auxiliary airfield that was started and never finished on Duke of York Island. The Island is the largest of a group of 13 islets located in St. George's Channel midway between New Britain and New Ireland. The urgent need for additional airstrips on which to locate and later disperse and protect Rabaul's air garrison was met instead by fields on New Ireland.

The Japanese Air Defense of Rabaul
The Japanese usually sent up all available fighters to intercept Allied air attacks, ranging from 50 to as many as 200 aircraft. After take off the Japanese fighters formed up over Lakunai or Tobera Airfields, then flew out over Cape St. George to wait at different altitudes to meet the incoming Allied formations. Early in the air campaign the Japanese fighter aircraft maintained disciplined fighting formations, but after they lost a large number of fighters and their experienced pilots and Allied air strength increased they resorted to individual attacks. Japanese fighters were reported to have frequently dropped small aerial bombs on bomber formations before their firing runs, but these attacks were ineffective, achieving few casualties and failing to break up the bomber formations. The favored Japanese gunnery tactic was to approach bombers from the front and fighters from the rear. However, the Japanese found that their fighters were unable to catch the fast American F6Fs, F4Us, and P-38s, and had to resort to frontal attacks on them also. The American fighters scissored over their bombers during their escort, and this tactic was particularly effective against frontal attacks. The American fighter pilots

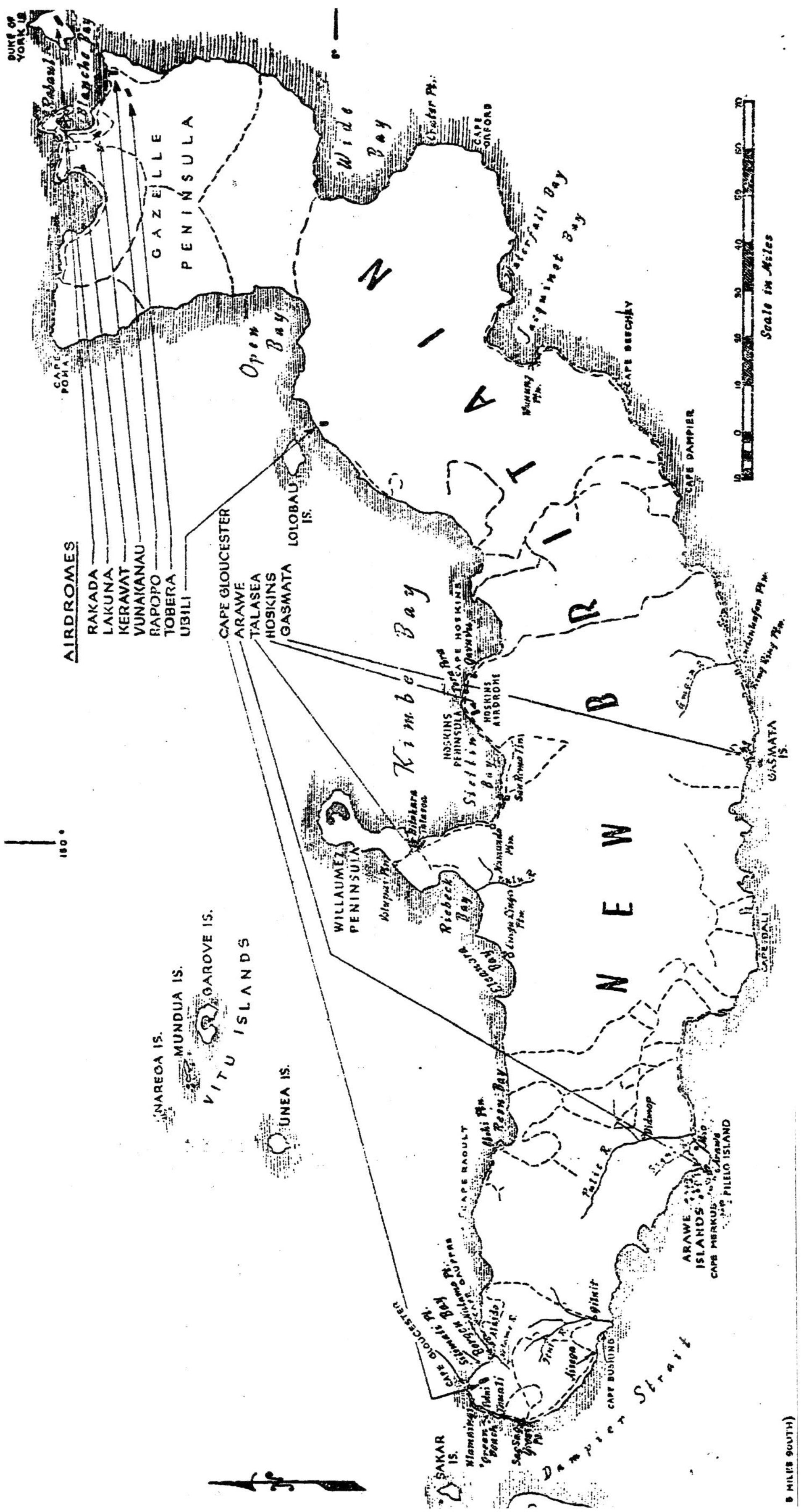

were disciplined, and were not easily drawn off by Japanese decoy attacks. The post-war USSBS interrogations of Japanese pilots revealed that they considered P-39s, then P-40s, and then P-38s easier prey than the F6F, but considered the F4U the best Allied fighter. Allied bomber and fighter pilots feared Rabaul's concentrated AA defenses, which were augmented by that of Japanese shipping while it was anchored in Rabaul's harbors. Until July 1944 the Japanese were able to expend large amounts of AA shells on Allied air attacks.

12 October: Attack on Rabaul

With a favorable long range weather forecast, the B-25 strafers were ready to make their largest attack since those on Wewak in August. Two squadrons of the 38BG and the entire 345th Bomb Group had joined the veteran 3rd Attack Group at Dobodura on the previous day. At 0731 Lt.Col. Clinton True, 345th Bomb Group Commander, led 113 B-25s off the Dobodura Dromes. The three Squadrons of the 36th Bomb Group assembled and were met by 21 P-38s of the 9th Fighter Squadron and a number of others organized for the mission as the "1st Provisional Squadron." Three squadrons of the 475th Fighter Group joined the bomber formations over Oro Bay. Within an hour after take off, the attack force descended to 1,000 feet across the Solomon Sea toward Kiriwina Island in order to avoid alerting enemy spotters and radar. At the mouth of the Warangoi River on the New Britain coast, the formation turned sharply inland. The 3rd Group headed for Rapopo Airdrome, and the other six squadrons, keeping below a range of hills, turned off toward Vunakanau.

The five B-25 squadrons dropped parafrags and strafed runways and dispersal areas. With the exception of one downed B-25, Japanese fighters were relatively ineffective, probably because of both the element of surprise and the dominant fighter escort. The escort fighters met little opposition, with the 9th Squadron and the 1st Provisional encountering no enemy aircraft over Rapopo and the 475th Group encountering only a few at 2,000 to 3,000 feet. The 432FS claimed a Betty bomber over Rapopo, and the Lead Flight of the 432FS intercepted four Oscars over Vunakanau and destroyed one. Within 10 minutes, and with no further losses, the attacking bombers had completed their mission and were headed toward New Guinea. The fighters and one or two damaged bombers landed at Kiriwina for refueling and repair, while the remainder of the B-25s landed at Dobodura shortly after 1300.

Less than two hours after the low level B-25 attack on the two Japanese airdromes, seven heavy bomber squadrons made coordinated attacks on shipping in the Rabaul harbors. After take off they rendezvoused over Kiriwina with two P-38 squadrons of the 80th and the 39th, which were to provide top cover. This escort did not appear to be adequate when compared with the 140 or more Japanese fighters based on Rabaul.

Each bomber squadron had been thoroughly briefed on the location of specific ships and had been assigned a target, and they claimed a number of sunk and badly damaged enemy ships. The pilots of the 28 P-38s which reached Rabaul encountered very few enemy planes. The 39FS made no contacts, but a flight of the 80FS spotted a number of enemy fighters and shot one down.

On the mission, 120 P-38s escorted 115 B-25s, 100 B-24s, and 13 Beaufighters that had taken off at 1040. Of the bombers leaving their bases for Rabaul, 31 bombers and 19 P-38s returned to base due to mechanical problems. Despite the inadequate P-38 escort that was clearly unable to provide total protection for the bombers, only one B-25 and four B-24s were lost to AA fire or the 40+ enemy fighters that continued running attacks on the 5BC bombers. The surprise attack had done much damage to docks and warehouses, with approximately 1,000 drums of fuel set afire and four ships sunk. Two enemy fighters and nine medium bombers were set on fire on the ground and 36 medium bombers damaged.

12 October 1943: 475FG

433FS

This was the first mission that Capt. Daniel Roberts would lead as the new 433FS CO. Roberts' 19 P-38s rendezvoused with 35 B-25s over Oro Bay and proceeded to the target (Rapopo), but when they arrived the Airdrome had been "plastered," so they went on to Vunakanau, where the B-25s strafed and dropped their fragmentation bombs on about 30 twin engine aircraft. At 1040, the 433rd crossed the field at 4,000 feet and engaged four single seat aircraft. Roberts fired at one which banked away, and Robert's Second Element Leader, 1Lt. Ralph Cleage, fired a 30 degree deflection shot from 200 to 75 yards, and the Oscar immediately started smoking and headed in flames for the trees.

432FS

At 1050, five miles south of Rabaul, 2Lt. John Fogarty followed Squadron Leader Maj. Merle Smith in his unsuccessful pass on a Betty bomber. On his pass he also fired seemingly without effect, and was fired on by the Betty's tail gunner. 1Lt. Thomas McGuire made the third pass, but broke off when he saw the Betty in flames from Fogarty's attack.

431FS

Maj. Merle Smith led 15 P-38s from Berry at 0745 on a B-25 escort to Rapopo. At 1040, while flying over the mouth of the Warangoi River at 2,000 feet, they saw one Betty flying at 3,000 feet and then saw three Bettys taking off from Rapopo. Smith did not want to leave the Mitchells during their attack and remained with them, but on the return they looked for the Bettys. Five minutes later a Betty was spotted flying just over the trees and Smith made a pass at it and made some hits, but 2Lt. John Fogarty of the 432nd made a pass, as did Smith's Element Leader, 1Lt. Thomas McGuire. McGuire's ICR states that the Betty was in flames when he made his pass (in which his guns did not fire). Fogarty was given the victory credit.

12 October 1943: 8FG/80FS

The 80FS sent 17 P-38s on a B-24 escort mission against enemy shipping in Simpson Harbor with a refueling stop at Kiriwina. Capt. James Wilson led a flight of six fighters, but was unable to catch the lead 5BC bombers until they reached the New Britain coast. Wilson took his flight over Simpson Harbor, where he saw two Tonys make a pass on the bombers, and when he tried to release his tanks one stuck, so Wilson ordered the rest of his flight to attack. Wilson climbed to 25,000 feet to work on releasing his tanks but failed, so he joined some bombers leaving the target. Wilson saw a Zero below and dove on it, "tank and all to save face in front of the bombers." Wilson found himself with an enemy fighter firing at him from extreme range and another on his tail. The one in the rear stopped chasing him and the other "went asleep," and Wilson continued his attack on this Zero. He closed to 800 yards on a 40 degree deflection run and managed to stay inside it, even though his supercharger was running wild. Wilson opened fire at 400 yards with no results. "Being in an irritable mood," he held down the "button," and as Wilson closed he saw some smoke, but by the time he was within 100 yards the Zero was burning furiously for the only 8FG victory for the day.

12 October 1943: 49FG/9FS

The day's mission was to be a morning escort for strike cover on the enemy headquarters at Rabaul. For the mission Ops Exec Harry Lidstrom selected mission pilots from senior pilots, and the 9FS Knights staged 16 Lightnings to Kiriwina Island in the pre-dawn hours to top off their tanks. They then climbed to rendezvous in mid-morning with other Lightnings to assume their station over the B-24 Liberators heading due north for New Britain. Halfway across the Solomon Sea the weather began to deteriorate. By the time the bombers reached their objective, only a small number of 432nd and 80th Squadron Lightnings were able to hold their position and engage the Rabaul defenders. 9FS Flying Knight CO Gerald Johnson orbited south of Simpson Harbor as high cover for B-24 target egress, but the Knights never saw the bombers and turned back for Dobodura when the B-24s radioed they were on their way back. On their way back Johnson's Lightnings separated in their attempt to penetrate the great cloud bank that covered the Solomon Sea. Individual fighters arrived over Dobodura through the overcast, but by nightfall senior Lieutenants Ralph Hays, Theron Price, and Frank Wunder had not appeared, and no sign of them was found during the search the next day.

12 October 1943: Results at Rabaul

Although the 5FC claimed only three aerial victories, the 12 October mission on Rabaul has often been referred to as "Japan's Pearl Harbor." This attack was the 122nd on Rabaul, which had previously dropped a total of about 1,000 tons of bombs that included the 60 tons dropped on 10 October 1942 and the 54 tons on 24 March 1943, both being the most dropped previously on a mission. During this attack the 5th Bomber Command dropped 300 tons of bombs and expended 250,000 rounds of ammunition while strafing. They reported that their bombs caused the loss of six JAAF aircraft and eight others damaged, while the JNAF had nine destroyed and three damaged. Four (to seven) transport ships were claimed to have been sunk and two to three were damaged (or sank later), while two destroyers and three submarines were also damaged. Post-mission photo recon showed additional damage to 25 ships, five "factories" burned, and the main motor pool transport depot and a large shipping depot were set on fire.

A post mission propaganda press release by the Allied GHQ Public Relations Office proclaimed that the three Rabaul Airdromes had suffered the loss of 100 aircraft destroyed and 51 damaged on the ground, and the Japanese sent up 40 aircraft to defend, of which 26 were shot down, and that the total of 177 aircraft that the Japanese lost represented about 60% of the enemy's air strength. The shipping losses, however, were claimed to be only two merchant ships sunk, but 43 were claimed as severely damaged, as were 70 harbor craft. The release concluded: "This operation .... gives us definite mastery of the air over the Solomons Sea and adjacent waters and thereby threatens the enemy's whole perimeter of defense."

12 October 1943: 348FG Attacks on Wewak

12 October marked the first day of P-38 escorted bombing missions to Rabaul, but the short-range P-47s of the 348FG would be assigned on a fighter sweep over Nubia-Wewak. Lt.Col. Robert Rowland's Flight of four left Port Moresby at 0715 and landed at Tsili Tsili at 0830 for refueling. After taking a detour to avoid enemy aircraft spotters at Bogadjim and Madang, they arrived at Nubia at 1230 and began patrolling along the coastline at

Although the 5FC claimed only three aerial victories the 12 October mission on Rabaul has often been referred to as "Japan's Pearl Harbor". (AAF)

Lt.Col. Robert **Rowland** scored his first of eight victories. (AFAA)

30,000 feet toward Wewak. Rowland spotted a twin-engine Ki-46 Dinah reconnaissance aircraft flying at 5,000 feet just off the coast opposite the Wewak strip. After Kearby's six victories the day before, Rowland was suspicious that the Japanese were setting a trap using this easy target as a decoy. But it appeared that the Dinah was alone and unaware, as it was losing altitude as if preparing to land at Wewak. Rowland needed to destroy the Dinah before it landed and pushed his P-47 into a wingover and an almost vertical dive to level out behind the enemy at 3,000 feet and almost 500 miles per hour. The Dinah made no attempt to evade as Rowland opened fire from dead astern at approximately 250 yards, getting hits on both wing roots. Just as Rowland was about to pull up to avoid a collision the Dinah exploded and crashed, then burned on the water for Rowland's first of eight victories. The flight reformed at 24,000 feet and headed to Tsili Tsili for refueling, then returned to Moresby at 1830.

13 October: Attack on Rabaul

The day's operation called for a saturation bombing of Rabaul Township shortly after an initial attack against airdromes and shipping. It was to be a coordinated strike protected by as many P-38s as the maintenance units at Kiriwina could service overnight. By morning, however, weather reports were unfavorable and the medium bombers were grounded, but at approximately 0800 70 heavy bombers left Port Moresby. At Kiriwina, industrious service units prepared more than 100 P-38s for the rendezvous with the heavy bombers. The weather rapidly deteriorated, and about 150 miles from Rabaul the bombers flew into a turbulent front extending from 5,000 to 30,000 feet, with icing conditions above 15,000 feet. The fighter escort was forced to turn back, but meanwhile, the bombers were flying on instruments in the increasingly impenetrable storm and individually they turned back, with none reaching their primary objective.

13 October 1943: 8FG/80FS

During the morning of 13 October, 17 P-38s of the 80FS took off to refuel at Kiriwina at 1010 and then rendezvous with B-24s to escort them to Rabaul. About 50 miles north of Kiriwina the American formation ran into a weather front that towered over 30,000 feet high. The Liberator navigators plunged through, but the fighters were unable to get around or over the front and called the B-24 Commander to let him know that they were turning back. The mission had been canceled by the time the fighters returned Port Moresby at 1315.

15 October 1943: Large Japanese Attack on Oro Bay

Bad weather continued to impede the Allied air offensive on Rabaul, and for a few days almost completely closed the enemy bastion down as a target. Therefore, medium bomber units escorted by P-47s and P-38s were sent to other targets on New Britain and to New Guinea. These attacks on enemy held areas in New Guinea were not simply diversionary raids necessitated by a weathered-in Rabaul, but rather were a part of an Allied attempt to stem Japanese ambitions in the New Britain/New Guinea Theater.

The Navy D3A **Val** (below) two place dive bomber and the Army Ki-48 **Lily** (above) four place light bomber suffered increasingly heavy losses as the war progressed. (Both AFHRC)

Allied Intelligence believed that the Japanese plans to recapture Lae and Salamaua had been abandoned, and were replaced by a decision to hold a line extending from Rabaul, along the south coast of New Britain, to Arawe, across the Vitiaz Strait to Sio, and up the New Guinea coast to Wewak. This speculation was supported by constant Japanese counterattacks near Sattelberg, barge movements along the coast, a few ships moving into Madang, and indications of the Japanese Army Air Force being augmented by withdrawing aircraft from the Northwestern Area.

The Japanese Commanders at Rabaul and Wewak knew they could not afford any further losses than those that they had incurred in the last ten weeks. Their garrisons at Wewak, Rabaul, and Cape Gloucester were not only enduring continuous round-the-clock Allied air raids, but were also suffering from disease and starvation. Now these large attacks on Rabaul made the Japanese anxious, and they assumed that an invasion of New Britain was imminent. Japanese intelligence was making an estimate of the situation on the basis of the Allied scale of effort. Considering the heavy Allied attacks conducted despite the poor weather that was normally expected in October and November, the Japanese undoubtedly expected a major amphibious attack at some area on New Britain. It was logical, and therefore not unexpected, that the enemy should strike at the Allied bases most likely to be key points in such an invasion attempt. One of these was Oro Bay, an anchorage where there were probably a large number of Liberty ships and many small naval vessels and supplies, and troops, including a Marine Division that was staging there. During the night of 13 October and morning of 14 October, Allied photo reconnaissance aircraft discovered the ominous arrival of bombers and fighters on the airdrome complex surrounding Rabaul. The JAAF and JNAF would again combine their air units for operations, but would now be met by an Allied fighter force nearly tripled in size. So on 15 October, shortly before 0600, USN radar picked up a number of unidentified plots close to Oro Bay. Soon the first large formation of 15 Val dive bombers of the 582nd Kokutai and 39 Zeros of the 204th Kokutai from Rabaul appeared over Oro Bay. They hoped that the crowded shipping in the Bay could be surprised and demolished before Allied defenses could react and then be finished off by the next formations from Rabaul and Wewak.

15 October 1943: 49FG/7FS/8FS/9FS

Just after sunrise, *Charter* Controller detected significant air activity over northern New Britain. 49FG Group Exec James Porter hurriedly consulted with Squadron Ops Executives Capt. Carl Aubrey of the 7FS and 1Lt. Harry Lidstrom of the 9FS to coordinate the Group's Warhawks and Lightnings. After all early morning missions were canceled, an alert was given at 0800 and more than 100 fighters left Dobodura for Oro Bay. Aubrey led seven 7FS Warhawks from Kalamazoo Strip, and minutes later Johnson led his seven 9FS Lightnings from Horanda Strip. They were soon followed by 60 P-38s of the 475FG.

7FS

After climbing south for 30 minutes, 5FC pilots made the first contacts with the large enemy formation of JNAF dive bombers escorted by fighters approaching Oro Bay. Lightnings and Warhawks dove into the enemy formation from a dozen different directions over the next 30 minutes. Aubrey's Blue Flight climbed to 15,000 feet to start their search through the clouds over the coast. Almost immediately, three Vs of Val dive bombers heading back out of the sea were seen, and Aubrey and Wingman 1Lt. John Roberts, Element Leader 1Lt. Roger Farrell, and Wingman 1Lt. John Miller dove on the enemy bombers flying a 1,000 feet above the waves. In that first attack Aubrey and Farrell overtook a maneuvering Val, and after three passes Farrell claimed the Val and the Squadron tried to regroup.

1Lt. Duncan Myers' Yellow Flight had dropped their tanks and sped after four Zeros and six Hamps flying 2,000 feet overhead. The four Yellow Flight Warhawks turned and climbed into the sun, but the veteran enemy pilots quickly countered the attack, and only Yellow Element Leader 1Lt. Robert Harrison was able to engage; he claimed a Hamp probable, as the Hamp dove away trailing smoke. Harrison and Wingman 2Lt. Edward Peck turned to try to reengage the dive bombers. Soon frenzied voices were heard over the radio trying to identify themselves to the P-38s that were firing on them. Myers' port ammo bay exploded, but fortunately a Lightning Wingman identified their opponents as Warhawks.

Simultaneously, Capt. Gerald Johnson had arrived at Oro Bay with eight fighters and immediately engaged 18 Vals that had just begun their attack on Allied shipping in the harbor. Johnson and his Red Flight rookie Wingman, 2Lt. Raymond Swift, attacked the Val lead element at 15,000 feet, and each Knight claimed one. Red Element Leader 1Lt. Grover Fanning and Wingman 2Lt. Robert Wood fought their way through the escorts, and after four passes Fanning and Wood each shot down an Oscar from dead astern. Johnson and Swift turned through the bomber formation, and just as Johnson was about to fire on a second dive bomber the escorts appeared. Johnson chased an Oscar down through the haze and fired

1Lt. Robert **Wood** scored his only victory of the war. (AAF)

Capt. Gerald **Johnson** had the best day of his career shooting down two Vals and an Oscar to make him an ace with six victories. (AAF)

until the fighter rolled over and crashed just beyond the harbor for his fifth victory to make him an ace. Johnson turned after the Vals, which had dropped down to sea level to escape under the cloud cover. The relentless Johnson closed on his third victim, killing the rear gunner and shooting away the bomber's port wing, and it exploded in a ball of fire for his sixth victory. The 5AF Intelligence eventually accredited Johnson's first kill on the 15 October mission as the Knights' 129th victory and the 49ers' 300th aerial victory overall.

Blue Flight's 1Lt. LeRoy Donnell (lead) and Wingman 2Lt. John McLean each shot down a Val from the first Val formation in their initial attack. Blue Element Leader 2Lt. Milby Marling and Wingman 2Lt. Charles Kamphausen attacked the escorts. Marling fired on what he thought were three enemy escorts trailing the Vals, which were actually the 7FS' Blue Flight P-40 elements. Aubrey and Farrell escaped, but wingmen Roberts' and Miller's P-40s were badly damaged from Marling's attack. Miller had turned into the P-38's fire and scarcely escaped when a .50 caliber round exploded in the nose of his fighter. Roberts was not as fortunate, as .50 caliber rounds tore huge holes in his left aileron, right stabilizer, and rear fuselage. Meanwhile, Kamphausen had left Marling when his port engine briefly cut out and then engaged the escorts, following his first combat victim to its fiery crash in the sea. Kamphausen then joined a pair of Satin's Angels, and the three searched 100 miles out to sea from Buna, where they overtook a pair of Zeros, and Kamphausen scored his second victory of the day with a hard turn to port down to 500 feet above water for a perfect 90 degree deflection shot. Soon a JNAF Wingman zoomed up behind him and put three 7 mm rounds into his right radiator, but he was saved by the two 80FS Lightnings who chased the enemy off.

When the 49er flights returned to Dobodura, both Capt. Aubrey and Element Leader Farrell were incensed over the attack by friendly P-38s. Demon CO Melikian met with Flying Knights CO Johnson, and Johnson decided the appropriate punishment. After giving the two a "sounding out" heard throughout the base, he warned the rookie Kamphausen that if he ever separated from his Flight Leader again, it would be the last time he ever flew with the Squadron, and Marling was fined a case of scotch whiskey which he personally had to deliver to the Demons' officers club.

8FS

The White Flight had already flown three missions and was about to frequent the Officer's Club when Operations ordered Capt. Joseph Littleton to escort a pair of RAAF Boomerang fighter bombers which were to be target spotters for the Australian artillery north of Finschhafen. Littleton objected, saying that "the Aussie fighters could probably take care of themselves." Wingman 2Lt. William Runey asked one of the Australian pilots about how the Boomerangs did against the Zeros, and he was told, "We don't know, Yank. No one's made it back to tell us." So at 1600 Capt. Joseph Littleton's exhausted pilots Wingman Runey, Element Leader 1Lt. William Elliott, and Wingman 1Lt. James Carter took off for the Finschhafen beachhead and orbited the Boomerangs as they began their spotting assignment. As the mission was nearly completed, Littleton saw nine aircraft approaching and the four Warhawks dropped their tanks and climbed until they were behind Lily bombers from Wewak that were making the last bomb run of the day. Littleton began an inline attack against the three bombers in the left V and destroyed the right Wingman. The other three pilots attacked the V, and tail-end P-40 pilot Carter dropped another Lily from the V. Littleton then turned abruptly port and his Flight spread out as they went into the second pass. Littleton fired a long burst to destroy his second Lily. After Carter fired, Runey saw that the Lily was annihilated and flew on toward the V leader. In the fading daylight he had trouble judging the distance to the target and was met by return fire from the bomber's turret gunner. Once at point blank range he fired a short, fatal burst and then rolled up to the left as his victim drifted toward hills and exploded. As Littleton maneuvered for his third pass, Element Leader Elliott called out Oscars overhead and the two chased after them. Littleton damaged one, but Elliott's guns jammed and he broke off. Runey and Carter chased after the last of the stragglers. Runey climbed through a thin cloud layer, and in a diving turn he re-engaged a Lily that had been hit in the second pass. Runey again closed in to point blank range, shut down the enemy gunner, and set the Lily on fire. Carter determinedly pursued a Lily beneath the overcast and finally overtook the Ki-48 15 miles north of Finschhafen Village, then followed it down through a port turn while shooting out both its engines.

9FS

As the main 9FS Lightning force was engaged over Oro Bay, a reserve flight led by 1Lt. John O'Neill was vectored 300 miles further east to Woodlark Island in search of a downed transport. O'Neill and Wingmen 1Lts. George Alber, Francis Love, and Frank Nutter searched for over an hour until they had to set down on Woodlark Island's crude staging strip to refuel. They were airborne again at 1000, and O'Neill decided to search north of the island on the return flight to Dobodura. As the four P-38s avoided a growing squall line at 1,500 feet just outside of Oro Bay they passed directly under two

Left to right: Capt. Joseph **Littleton** shot down two Lily bombers for his third and last victories of the war. (AAF)

2Lt. William **Runey** shot two Lilys for his first two of three career victories

1Lt. James **Carter** scored his only victory of the war. (AAF)

Zeros headed back to New Britain. O'Neill and Alber dropped their tanks and closed in a climbing turn onto the unsuspecting enemy's rear. O'Neill's burst instantly knocked down the trailing fighter, and Alber set the leader on fire when he turned slightly to port to check on his Wingman. As the storm front rolled in the four P-38s regrouped and headed for Horanda.

15 October 1943: 475FG/431FS/432FS/433FS

431FS

At 0805, veteran and former 80FS pilot 1Lt. Marion Kirby led 16 Lightnings of the 431FS as they scrambled with the other squadrons. As they were climbing the Air Controller first vectored them to Porlock Harbor, but then the Flight was turned around to fly 10 miles northeast of Oro Bay, where they climbed to 19,500 feet and patrolled. Kirby, leading White Flight, saw the Vals below making their bombing runs and immediately dove to the attack, pulling out at 700 feet and putting him on the tail of a Val. Kirby started firing when the enemy dive bomber came into range, continuing until he overran it. As Kirby pulled up for another pass he saw the Val burst into flames and hit the water. Kirby's Wingman, 2Lt. Vincent Elliott, followed Kirby down on his attack on the Vals and saw a Val being chased by three or four Lightnings; he raced to cut it off before the other P-38s got to it. Elliott fired from 45 degrees deflection, and the Val caught fire and banked sharply into the water. Elliott's ICR states: "I tried to intercept other Zeros but they were always shot down before I could get to them." 2Lt. Francis Lent was leading Kirby's second element with Wingman 2Lt. Edward Hedrick, and watched Kirby shoot down a Val and then broke away after a Val heading out to sea. He fired five bursts at 150-200 yards from directly astern and was met by return fire from the Val's rear gunner, who was silenced when the Val burst into flames and headed into the sea. Lent then saw two Zeros being chased by three P-38s and tried to catch them, but before he could get into range they both had been shot down. Lent went after a Val about 1,000 feet off the water, and as he attacked it three more P-38s arrived, so Lent took a quick 90 degree deflection shot but missed and the other P-38s claimed it. Lent headed out to sea to hunt for retreating Japanese aircraft and spotted a lone Zero heading home on the deck. The enemy pilot did not see Lent, as he got very close astern without the Zero taking any evasive action and fired shots that set it on fire. Lent saw three P-38s chasing two Zeros and joined in the chase. One of the Zeros went into a loop and half roll, giving Lent a good deflection shot to make him an ace with six victories.

Blue Flight Leader 1Lt. Carl Houseworth had his Wingman and second Element Leader abort, and he and #4 man, 2Lt. Franklin Monk, dove after Kirby's White flight. After the Vals scattered the two Americans climbed to attack Zeros coming in from above. Houseworth became separated from Monk and joined other P-38s, then made several unsuccessful passes

2Lt. Francis **Lent** shot down a Val and two Zeros to give him six victories. (AFAA)

2Lt. Vincent **Elliott** got his second victory. (AAF)

LEFT TO RIGHT:
1Lt. Thomas **McGuire** shot down a Val. (and claimed two Zero probables) to become a double ace. (AAF)

2Lt. William **Sieber** shot down a Val for his only career victory. (AAF)

F/O William **Gronemeyer** shot down his first of four victories. (AAF) during the heated competition between the American pilots to score victories. Monk's right engine cut in and out, and he was unable to stay with Houseworth and dove out and away. He then saw a Zero below him. Monk fired a 45 degree burst to start it smoking, but was unable to see it crash, as another Zero got on his tail. However, 2Lt. James Malloy of the 433FS would later confirm this victory. Monk managed to escape his pursuer, but his engine continued to run rough and he headed home.

Green Flight Leader 1Lt. Edward Czarnecki, Wingman F/O William Gronemeyer, and second element 1Lt. Paul Morriss and Wingman 2Lt. Robert Riegle entered the battle by encountering a four ship enemy Lufbery. Czarnecki and Gronemeyer sparred with the Lufbery, waiting for a good opportunity to attack. Czarnecki led Gronemeyer into the Lufbery, and Czarnecki fired at the end Zero from its rear quarter. The lead Zero rolled over on its back and came down, and Czarnecki had to push his stick forward and roll away to escape. Another Zero came out of the Lufbery and fired, then half rolled away, and Gronemeyer got on its tail and fired until it burst into flames and crashed. Gronemeyer and Czarnecki became separated, and Gronemeyer joined with other P-38s in the free for all to score and made a few unsuccessful passes before returning home. Meanwhile, Czarnecki missed on his next pass. He then saw a Zero Split-S down to 1,000 feet and Czarnecki dove after it. When the Zero rolled out Czarnecki took a rear quarter shot, and it burst into flames and Czarnecki had to pull up quickly, missing a collision by 25 feet. As he was pulling up, a Zero fired on him from the rear and above. Czarnecki rolled and climbed to starboard, ending up on his back, went into a partial Split-S, and got on the Zero's tail. Czarnecki fired on it until he ran out of ammunition; he saw it start to smoke as it flew away, losing altitude, for a probable claim. Green Flight second element 1Lt. Paul Morriss and Wingman 2Lt. Robert Riegle had dropped their tanks and started down after the scattered Vals, but saw 20 Zeros above to port and climbed after them, but Morriss lost Riegle. Morriss then flew toward Houseworth and Monk, but before he could join them a Zero made a beam attack on him but overshot. As the Zero flew past, Morriss took a few short deflection shots and the Zero rolled over and Monk saw it explode. Morriss' engine began to vibrate "fiercely," and he had to throttle back to diminish the vibration to get back to base. The reason Riegle became separated from Morriss was that on their dive Riegle's aircraft was hit by the cannon shells of a diving Zero. Riegle went into a fast dive and escaped, and when he pulled out he assessed the damage to his fighter and found his radio was out, his starboard engine was streaming coolant, and his starboard aileron was almost entirely shot away. Morriss was bleeding from wounds to his left arm, right shoulder, and back. When he neared his base Morriss decided to crash land instead of bail out. He dropped his wheels and lowered his flaps and made a safe landing.

Red Flight, the last flight in the Squadron, was led by 1Lt. Thomas McGuire and Wingman 2Lt. Robert Hunt, with a second element of 2Lt. Robert Cline and Wingman 2Lt. William Sieber. At 0840 McGuire spotted a pair of Vals 1,500 feet over the water and got on the tail of one and shot it down. In the dive McGuire lost his second element, and during the attack Wingman Hunt's guns jammed and he pulled away and became separated from his leader. McGuire started after a second Val and fired several times through a fogged windshield; he saw the Val go down smoking slightly through his side window as it passed under him for a no claim. Once his windshield partially cleared he saw a Zero on the tail of a P-40 and intervened, firing as it turned down to starboard. McGuire saw it smoking badly, but another Zero came down on McGuire and he turned into it, losing sight of his possible victim for another probable claim. He then saw a Zero on the tail of a P-38 and fired several deflection shots; it was smoking as it passed under McGuire and out of sight for another probable. McGuire took a few more shots at a Val flying on the water, but another P-38 came in and finished it off. Hunt rejoined McGuire, and the two were about 50 miles out to sea when they saw three Zeros climbing at 4,000 feet and finally caught them at 100 miles out at 9,000 feet. McGuire closed to 100 feet behind the tail end Zero and found he was out of ammunition. A Zero then turned on Hunt and started firing almost out of range at 500 yards, but Hunt waited and fired, getting hits that caused the Zero pilot to break away into the clouds smoking for a probable. The two returned to base with McGuire now a double ace with 10 victories.

On the initial Red Flight attack Sieber lost not only McGuire and Hunt, but also his second Element Leader, 1Lt. Robert Cline, who "saw quite a few Vals being shot down but had no good shots myself" during the rest of the battle. After the first three Red Flight pilots made their passes Sieber "had my turn" and fired, getting hits that started a fire, but passed over the smoking Val and could not make a valid claim on it. Sieber joined another unknown P-38 and followed it out to sea after another Val on the deck. The lead Lightning made a pass and missed, and Sieber closed from astern and exploded it. Immediately, Sieber's right engine was hit by cannon and machine gun fire and heavy smoke entered the cockpit. Sieber decided to bail out, so he released the emergency hatch and pulled up in a climbing turn to 1,000 feet, released his safety belt, rolled the plane over and dropped out. A Zero strafed him on his way down, and although the enemy pilot did not hit the helpless American, he tore a hole in the chute with his propeller. Sieber landed hard in the water and quickly removed

Left to right:
1Lt. Paul **Morriss** also scored his first victory on the way to becoming a five victory ace. (AAF)

2Lt. Franklin **Monk** scored his first of five victories. (AFAA)

1Lt. Marion **Kirby** was another future five victory ace who shot down his first aircraft this day. (AFAA)

LEFT: Maj. Frank **Tomkins** claimed his last two of four victories to fall short on becoming an ace. (AAF)
MIDDLE: Capt. John **Loisel** shot down two Zeros to total five victories to become an ace. (AFAA)

Maj. Charles **MacDonald** shot down two Vals for the first two of his 27 victories. (AFAA)

his chute, as four enemy fighters hovered overhead but soon left. Sieber only suffered minor wounds on his hands and was able to inflate his life raft. He floated for four days and three nights. Finally, the HMAS *Benalla* picked up Sieber halfway between Oro Bay and Lae. Sieber was suffering from exposure and was badly sunburned, with ulcerated wounds from the salt water. He remained in the hospital for four days, and on 24 October Sieber returned to his squadron via Nadzab and Moresby.

432FS

Air Control ordered the first scramble at 0810, and the 432FS scrambled in three waves between 0810 and 0825. Maj. Tompkins led Red and White Flights, which included 1Lt. Leo Mayo and 2Lt. Christopher Bartlett at 0810. At 0815 Capt. John Loisel led off Blue and Green Flights, with Capt. Frederick Harris and 1Lt. Vivian Cloud the last two off at 0825, as they were delayed because they had to taxi their P-38s out of their revetments and then taxi out to the runways.

Capt. John Loisel's Blue and Green flights climbed to 22,000 feet when he spotted bombs exploding nowhere near the shipping, five miles out to sea. Loisel and Wingman 2Lt. James Farris quickly dove to 3,000 feet and found "15 to 20 Vals escorted by the same number of Zeros." Loisel passed over the Vals to attack the more dangerous Zeros and closed behind one and set it on fire with a short burst. Farris remained close on Loisel's wing and fired at the second Zero, which rolled inside Loisel. Farris fired a short burst and the Zero caught fire and half rolled onto its back. Loisel had to bank hard to avoid it before it crashed into the sea. Loisel cleared his tail, and he and Farris headed toward New Britain, looking for stragglers; they saw one just off the water and chased after it. Loisel fired at 300 yards and the Zero exploded, sending pieces flying back toward Loisel. Soon 10 to 15 Zeros dove from the clouds on Loisel and Farris, who accelerated and used evasive maneuvers, and after about three minutes the Zeros broke off their pursuit and the two headed home, with Loisel becoming an ace.

2Lts. Zach Dean and Wingman Billy Gresham were flying at 24,000 feet as the last element in Loisel's two flights. They were informed by *Nephew* Controller that Vals were at 8,000 feet. They dropped their tanks and descended to about 3,000 feet, where they spotted the Vals. Dean pulled behind a Val and fired a long burst, but the Val Split-S'd, which was impossible for Dean to follow, and this Val got away. Gresham was far enough behind that Val so when it came out of its Split-S the Lightning pilot got on his tail. Because of his high diving speed Gresham was only able to fire a short but effective burst, and Dean witnessed the Val's wing hit the water and cartwheel and sink. Dean soon came upon another Val flying at 300 feet and closed dead astern and fired. The frantic Val pilot tried to Split-S away, but was too close to the water and dove straight in.

1Lt. Elliott Summer, Blue Flight Element Leader, and Wingman 2Lt. Stuart Lawhead dove and saw 10 to 15 bandits in the air and about 10 others flaming in the sea. As they closed Summer saw a Zero pull up, and he fired an accurate shot and the Zero flamed and rolled inverted into the water. Summer lost Lawhead, and the rest of the Squadron and returned home.

Maj. Frank Tomkins' Red and White Flights were vectored over Oro Bay, and about 20 minutes after they scrambled they had climbed to 24,000 feet when six Zeros were sighted to the east. Tomkins "sailed in and drew a bead" on the tail end Zero but missed. Tomkins then saw five Zeros peeling off toward Oro Bay and again "latched onto" the tail end Zero and fired a long burst. As he was diving at "about 550mph" he saw it burst into flames as he sped past. Continuing to 12 miles off Oro Bay, Tomkins saw four other P-38s making a pass at a Val. After all missed the Val flew into Tomkins' line of fire and exploded. 1Lt. Leo Mayo of Tomkins' flight became separated and joined three Lightnings of 1Lt. John Smith's 433FS that were diving on the Zeros. Smith and Mayo dove on and each shot an "Oscar-type" fighter that tried to chandelle away. Mayo fired two short bursts at 80 degree deflection to finish off his victim.

Just as the alert was called, Maj. Charles MacDonald had flown into Group Operations from 5FC HQ. He and Capt. William Ivey searched the field to find available P-38s to fly to join in on the fight. There were none on the 432nd flight line, but some were ready for take off on the 433rd line. As 475th Group Executive Officer, MacDonald commandeered Calvin Wire's Lightning and quickly took off with Ivey. As soon as they were off the ground they encountered Vals. MacDonald chose his first Val from a formation of seven and pressed a head on attack until he passed overhead and turned into a stern attack and exploded the enemy bomber. MacDonald fired on another Val that began to smoke and was then shot down by Ivey. MacDonald made another head on pass on another Val and got hits on the bomber's engine, but it continued flying away just over the water's surface and disappeared from view to give MacDonald a damaged claim. The next Val MacDonald attacked tried to escape in a steep turn, but took good hits around the cockpit before it exploded. MacDonald had flown 50 miles out to sea alone after an escaping Val. When it was finally in range he made three passes, but was only able to damage the tough dive bomber. He had to break off his attack when a Zero arrived and shot out MacDonald's port engine, electrical and hydraulic systems, and perforated his fuel tanks. Luckily, several P-38s came to MacDonald's rescue and he limped back and crash landed at Dobodura with the first two of his eventual 27 victories. MacDonald's Lightning was so badly damaged that it was written off. Capt. Frederick Harris and 1Lt. Vivian Cloud of Tomkins' 432FS White Flight filled out the MacDonald/Ivey flight and climbed to 6,000 feet, where they saw an enemy plane below. At first Harris had trouble releasing his auxiliary tanks, but dropped them in time to catch his flight and close on the tail of a Val that he started smoking from his gunfire. As he was about to make a second pass he saw it crash into the sea. Harris climbed again and saw both MacDonald's and Ivey's Vals crash. Harris hit another Val that tried a steep turn to escape but lost control and crashed directly into the sea without smoking. Harris reports in his ICR that he saw "8 to 10 Vals go down burning." Cloud shot down a Val in his first attack, but then was unsuccessful on six or seven subsequent "good" passes and saw pieces fly off one. Cloud complains in his ICR that "two or three other P-38s would come in and polish off his victim."

433FS

Seventeen P-38s took off to intercept enemy aircraft attacking Allied shipping in Oro Bay. When they arrived at 0815 there were 30 to 40 Vals, Oscars, and Haps headed back to base after making their attack. The Squadron dropped their tanks on sighting the enemy and the battle broke out into individual dogfights at minimum altitudes. There were Lightnings, Vals, Zeros, and even some P-40s from the 7FS everywhere. 7FS pilots complained that "the P-38s attacked them as keenly as they did the Japanese." One 7FS P-40 was reported to be so badly damaged by a P-38 that it had to be taken out of combat to be repaired.

1Lt. Richard Kimball's flight consisted of his Wingman, 2Lt. Donald King, and Second Element Leader 2Lt. Virgil Hagan and his Wingman 2Lt. James Malloy. Kimball entered combat by firing on a Val from dead astern at 50 feet off the water and it burst into flames and crashed into the sea (Hagan claims in his ICR that he also fired on this Val simultaneously). Kimball and King then dove on a Val, but another P-38 got there first and shot it down. The Flight turned to the right and saw a Val climbing and skidding from the deck to about 1,000 feet, where Kimball and King fired simultaneously. King scored the better hits with a five second burst and got credit for the victory. They chased several more Vals out to sea and saw a P-38 of the 9FS shoot one down. Kimball's starboard engine lost power and he had to break off his pursuit. Hagan lost Kimball after their simultaneous attack and became King's Wingman after Kimball turned back. Hagan saw an Oscar in the distance and set off alone after it. After a lengthy chase he caught it with a long burst and it exploded into three pieces. Hagan joined a P-38 from the 432FS, and the two flew into 15 Oscars. One Split-S'd from directly above and Hagan turned into it, but could not turn tightly enough to fire. This Oscar did not hit Hagan's fighter, but another did, and his P-38 went out of control temporarily with a hit to the aileron. Hagan dove away, but three Oscars came in and got more hits on the Lightning; Hagan managed to skid away. Hagan made it back to base worrying about a low fuel supply and possible coolant leaks. On the flight's first pass Malloy got in a short burst on a Val which Kimball shot down. Malloy then made a pass at another Val that had pulled up to escape other attacking P-38s. Malloy fired from 150 yards, and this Val trailed smoke as Malloy lost sight of it as he tried to catch up with his flight for a probable. While flying at 1,000 feet Malloy saw a Val coming directly toward him at about 500 feet above. He pulled up and the Val passed through his gunsights and burst into flames as it passed above him and continued in a right hand dive into the water. Malloy then joined Hagan, who had joined a 432FS Lightning, and as they turned for home the three were attacked by the Oscars. Malloy's starboard engine failed, but he escaped and returned to Dobodura on one engine.

Capt. Joseph **McKeon** shot down a Val to get his fifth and last victory to become an ace. (AFAA)

Flight Leader Capt. Joseph McKeon and Wingman 1Lt. Donald Revenaugh came upon the dogfight, and McKeon chose one from the pack of scurrying Vals and Lightnings. McKeon opened fire at 200 yards with a single two second burst, hitting the wing root and setting it on fire to crash 10 miles offshore. He and Revenaugh then chased three Vals and two Zeros out to sea at 1,000 feet, and McKeon fired on a Val and saw a flash of flame but no further results as it turned inside and escaped. The two Americans pursued a Zero 50 miles out to sea and made a stern attack. McKeon found only one of his machine guns would fire, and the Zero turned away into some clouds above him. McKeon then found himself in position to fire on a Val at 9 o'clock low, but his last gun jammed and Revenaugh closed to 50 yards astern and fired continuously; the Val broke out into flames from cockpit to tail. McKeon's Element Leader, 1Lt. William Jeakle, attacked a Val which was alongside McKeon's first Val. He overshot on his first pass and "foolishly" passed over it, giving its tail gunner a target, but Jeakle skidded in time to avoid being hit. He then turned back on the Val and set it on fire. The Val continued to fly and Jeakle made another pass, but overshot it again. As he was about to make a third pass the Val broke into two and flamed into the water.

2Lts. John Smith and Clarence Rieman of the third flight entered the battle and saw a flight of P-38s chasing an Oscar below them. Smith correctly thought that the Japanese would try to escape by climbing and turning. Smith waited, and the Japanese pilot went into a steep climbing Immelmann and then turned right 180° in a shallow dive, giving Smith a 30 degree deflection shot from 300 to 50 yards. The first volley fell short, but the second went into the fighter's fuel tanks and cockpit and it burst into flames. Before he left the combat area Smith was joined by 1Lt. Leo Mayo of the 432FS, who shot down another Oscar.

Fourth Flight Leader 1Lt. John Babel found that his flight arrived too late and could only pursue some stragglers. They did not catch any and returned to base.

Summary for 15 October 1943

The day was another disaster for the Japanese, as they lost 54 aircraft, eight probables, and two damaged. In all, 27 Vals, five Lily bombers, 14 Zekes, and eight Oscar fighters were lost.

After this combat, McGuire's squadronmates reported that his personality drastically changed from reticent into brazen swagger, which led to unpopularity with not only his squadron, but over much of the Fifth Air Force. Whether it be toward peers or subordinates, McGuire's unyielding character irritated all, and when he acquired rank he used it to irritate even more of those around him. He named his P-38 "*PUDGY*," a nickname for his wife that she detested. Despite being considered only competent in training, he did excel as a fighter pilot, and though McGuire had his defenders, his critics were legion.

Including his Zero victory in a P-39 with the 35FS on 7 December 1942, McKeon became an ace, but this was to be his last victory. McKeon continued in combat until his tour ended in January 1944, when he returned to the US. In July 1944 he transferred to the 77FS/20FG, flying P-51s, where, on 16 August 1944, he shot down a Me-109 and damaged a FW-190 near Mulhausen. After a mid-air collision on 7 October 1944 he was captured and held as a POW until the end of the war. He retired from the Air Force Reserves as a Lt. Colonel in October 1963. He earned his PhD in 1969.

16 October 1943: Air Combat Over New Guinea

On 16 October, 32 B-25s escorted by two squadrons of P-38s were sent out to attack shipping reported between Cape Gloucester and Madang, but were unable to locate them. Four other B-25 squadrons escorted by two P-38 squadrons left to attack Alexishafen, but due to bad weather, failure to rendezvous with the fighters, and poor target coordination part of the formation attacked the secondary target near Sio. Only the B-25G squadrons mounting 75mm cannon bombed and strafed Alexishafen and were intercepted by a strong enemy fighter force. The P-47 escort shot down 13 Zekes, Hamps, and Tonys.

The most successful attack of the day was by the B-25s of the 345BG, which took off from Port Moresby early that morning and meeting three P-38 squadrons near Bena Bena. The formation proceeded to Wewak via the Remu Valley, and after three hours attacked the Boram and Wewak Airdromes. Japanese interceptors were engaged by the P-38s, which shot down five.

These air attacks in New Guinea were not considered a separate New Guinea offensive, but rather were an attempt to maintain the status quo in New Guinea while the major attack was to concentrate on Rabaul. So, these attacks served to hold the New Guinea flank, which in the future would be the scene of a determined drive up the New Guinea coast. During this time the Japanese attempted to rebuild its devastated airpower at Wewak and sent out occasional air strikes to break through that flank.

16 October 1943: 8FG/80FS

The Japanese air forces became more active in the Wewak area, and MacArthur ordered Kenney to resume strikes against the airfield complex there. On the 16th, 16 Headhunter P-38s took off at 0840 to escort B-25s to Boram, which was located a few miles southeast of Wewak. One of the P-38s aborted with a leaking fuel tank. The Squadron flew to the target at 1,000 to 1,500 feet and pulled up to 6,000 feet on its approach. While covering the Mitchells over Boram at 1100, four or five Japanese fighters were sighted at about 15,000 feet, but made no move until the bombers completed their attack run and headed for home over the water.

Capt. Carl Taylor, who was with Group HQ, was leading the first flight, and 1Lt. Cornelius Smith was leading the second flight. Taylor arrived on the scene at 1050 at 4,500 feet, just after the Mitchells had completed their attack, and saw six to eight enemy fighters making a pass on the B-25 formation. Taylor made three passes at three Tonys from 100 feet above the water but without result. He then fired at another Tony from very close range, whose pilot seemed to be unaware, as he made no evasive maneuvers as it crashed.

1Lt. Harrison Freeman with Wingman 2Lt. Allen Hill was flying as the Element Leader of the Lead Flight under Capt. Carl Taylor when they spotted a lone single seat fighter. All four flight members attacked and fired, but the enemy pilot continued on. Freeman joined two Lightnings that were chasing a lone Tony, and Freeman was able to turn inside it 120 degrees and got a long burst from short range, starting a fire and shooting off the tale section, which caused it to spin out of control into the ground.

Smith and Wingman 2Lt. Jennings Myers climbed to 6,000 feet while the bombers were on their low level attack run and saw three enemy fighters attack the rear of the bomber formation just off the water. The lead flight dove first, followed by Smith's flight, and Smith watched Taylor's victory. Smith continued on and fired at a few Tonys without getting any visual hits, but was informed by Wingman Myers on landing back at base that one of the Tonys burst into flames and crashed. After Myers followed Smith down, an "Oscar-type" fighter approached Myers from starboard at about 1,000 feet, and Myers fired a long burst that caused the wing to fold back and the enemy fighter (a Zero) dived into the woods. As Myers turned to join Smith a Tony dove on the B-25s. Jennings got on its tail and fired two short bursts, and it crashed into the water and skidded up onto the beach. Smith and Myers then joined up and headed back for home, since the Japanese interceptions were apparently over. The 80th claimed five victories for the day.

16 October 1943: 348FG/340FS/342FS

The 340FS and 342FS took off just before 0900 and rendezvoused with two B-25 flights over the target (Alexishafen) at about 1100. Almost immediately about 15 to 20 Japanese fighters were sighted about 1,000 feet above the American medium bomber formations at 9,000 feet and readying to attack.

340FS

First Flight

Col. Neel Kearby assembled another special flight made up of high ranking officers consisting of his Wingman, Capt. Frank Oksala, and a second element led by 340FS CO Maj. Hervey Carpenter with Wingman Capt. Meade Brown. This flight was to sweep ahead of Capt. Max Wiecks' second flight

LEFT: Smith's wingman, 2Lt. Jennings **Myers**, scored two victories to give him four. (AAF) RIGHT: 1Lt. Cornelius **Smith** came closer to becoming an ace with is fourth victory. (AFAA)

Col. Neel **Kearby** assembled another special flight made up high ranking 348FG officers and during the mission became a double ace. (AAF)

and took off at 0750. They landed for 40 minutes to refuel at Tsili Tsili and then took off to sweep the Wewak area. Kearby patrolled the area at 23,000 feet without encountering the enemy when, at about 1100, he heard Wiecks' P-47 pilots on the radio saying they had engaged the Japanese. Kearby saw a lone Japanese aircraft flying along the deck, but decided not to give up his altitude advantage. Kearby's flight continued their patrol around Boram for about 25 minutes when Kearby saw an Oscar at 18,000 feet off to his right at about 2 o'clock. Kearby immediately led his flight in a fast dive that gave the enemy little opportunity to react. The Oscar tried a climbing turn to the right, but Kearby had closed to 500 yards and opened fire, starting a fire in the enemy's cowling. Kearby watched the Japanese Army pilot get out of the cockpit and parachute while his plane fell into the sea for Kearby's 10th victory to become a double ace.

Capt. William **Dunham** is shown sitting in his P-47 after getting a Pete for his fourth victory

Second Flight

Capt. Max **Wiecks** shot down two enemy fighters for his 2nd and 3rd victories

Capt. Max Wiecks was leading 15 P-47s of the 340FS on a B-25 escort to Alexishafen when they were attacked from 1,000 feet above by 15 to 20 Oscars and Tonys at 7,000 feet over Madang. Wiecks passed through the Japanese formation and was initially forced to dive away with two other P-47s, but climbed back through a cloud layer to a position above the battle. He dove on the first of three Haps and fired without observable results before he was forced to dive away by the other two and met a Zero. He fired at about a 45 degree deflection and saw a hit directly in the cockpit; the Zero burst into flames as he passed over. After this attack Wiecks pulled up and then heard 1Lt. Andrew Lytle radio that Zeros were on his tail. Wiecks looked down to see three Hamps chasing Lytle and dived and shot at the first of the three closest to him. Wiecks turned into the other two Hamps, but was unable to turn with them to get a shot. He was running low on fuel and ordered his flight to return to base. After Lytle had flown through the Japanese formation and escaped his pursuers he turned to find a Tony a mile below him at 4,000 feet. He dove on the Japanese fighter and caught it with a long burst as it turned left and exploded. Lytle flew on to Madang, where he met two enemy fighters to starboard and below. Lytle rolled over and got behind the Haps and shot off the wing of one. 1Lt. Thomas Barber was flying as Lytle's Wingman, and the two became separated while Wiecks was rescuing Lytle. Barber dove from 7,000 feet to tear off a large piece of a Zero's fuselage that just missed Barber's canopy as it flew by. Lytle joined 1Lt. Jesse Ivey, and the two of them were returning to base when they spotted two more Japanese fighters. The two Thunderbolts immediately rolled over and attacked from the rear, and Lytle fired from close range until the Japanese fighter's port wing crumpled and tore off. 1Lt. Guy Johnston made several ineffective long range, high deflection passes on Tonys and Zeros before he flamed a Tony from 200 yards. 1Lt. Jerome Fischer and 2Lt. Marion Burt claimed a Tony and Zeke probable, respectively, to complete the 340th's scoring for the day.

342FS

The 342FS, led by Capt. William Dunham, was patrolling at 15,000 feet inland from Alexishafen, about three miles from Madang, when 2Lt. Willis Cooley called out Bogies at 9 o'clock low. Cooley and his Element Leader, 1Lt. James Pratt, dove on three Haps, with Cooley attacking a straggler from point blank range that exploded; Cooley just managed to evade the debris. Cooley then climbed to 10,000 feet and made a pass at another Hap, getting hits on the port wing and starting a fire that caused this Hap to spiral into the water. Cooley went after yet another Hap, but a Tony got on his tail and he had to head for the safety of a cloud bank as the Tony fired at him. Pratt started firing at his Hap, which turned steeply to port. His Thunderbolt could not turn tightly enough to get sufficient lead and he missed with a three second burst. Pratt then engaged a Hap at 300 yards with a 45 degree deflection shot, getting hits near the canopy. The Hap emitted some flames that went out as it dived toward the sea, when suddenly the Hap zoomed up to get into the battle again. Capt. Dunham and his Wingman, 2Lt. William Upton, were patrolling above the battling second element and watched Pratt almost score his first victory, then make another head on pass at another Hap. Dunham saw another enemy fighter maneuvering onto Pratt's tail and dove quickly to dead astern of Pratt's attacker. Dunham fired a short burst from 200 yards and saw the Hap plunge into the sea with its engine flaming. Meanwhile, Pratt's head on pass set the Hap on fire, and it passed under him into the water. Pratt then took quick passing shots at several Haps, and on an 80 degree deflection shot, while steeply banking to port, he scored hits at the enemy's wing roots, setting the fighter on fire and plunging into the ocean. The remaining Hap was seen flying at 1,000 feet, fleeing towards Madang with Dunham racing after it. Dunham overtook the Hap 200 yards offshore and shot it down with a long 30 degree deflection shot; the enemy pilot bailed out and landed 100 yards off shore. The 348FG had its best day, claiming 13 Japanese fighters confirmed and three others were probably shot down for no P-47 or B-25 losses.

16 October 1943: 49FG/8FS/9FS

8FS

After the Eightballs had flown sorties throughout the day they were again called upon by the Australians to intercept a bogie near Finschhafen, 140 miles away. With four refueled planes, 1Lt. James Hagerstrom, 2Lt. Robert Sherman, 2Lt. Douglas Lenore, and 2Lt. Sammie Pierce took off in the late afternoon at full throttle for the coast. As they reached the beachhead they were informed that the bogie was after a wayward C-47 transport which had been lost in a storm front now over Finschhafen. The P-40s had burned copious fuel in their approach and were unable to return to Marilinan, so they would have to attempt a hazardous landing on a nearby rain-soaked Aussie airstrip. Hagerstrom landed first, but his Lightning crashed on the muddy runway and blocked it for the others. Sherman, Lenore, and Pierce could not land, and were trapped by the approaching storm. The three decided their only choice was to bail out as near the Australian base as possible. In the rainy black overcast the three Eightballs bailed out, but only Sherman landed on the beach near the village, while Pierce and Lenore had the wind carry them over the coastal hills into the forest. Lenore landed two miles from the shore, near Australian Commandos who rescued him. Pierce landed eight miles inland. He immediately took off his chute and buried it, then escaped into the forest and waited until dark to set off down a stream bed in a narrow valley. The next day Pierce rested until he heard Japanese voices and decided to leave the stream bed and avoid paths or clearings. For the next three days he slowly moved through the dense undergrowth and eventually to the shore, where he headed south. During the morning of the fifth day he crossed Australian lines.

9FS

After the debriefing of the morning missions over Wewak, 16 Flying Knights were assigned to a B-25 escort to Madang at 1130. Capt. Wallace Jordan's Red Flight, flying at 5,000 feet, spotted a single Zero flying at 7,000 feet and dropped their tanks and climbed to the attack. Red Flight #4 man, 2Lt. George Haniotis, opened fire at a head on attack and passed by without seeing any evidence of damage. Haniotis followed the Zero as it descended low over the water and fired three bursts from about 200 yards, hitting the canopy and right wing. The Zero began to smoke, then slipped off on one wing and exploded into the water. Haniotis' Element Leader, 1Lt. Douglas Barrett, had a close call when a bullet passed through his canopy only inches from his head.

As the Knights were returning to Horanda, Ops Exec Harry Lidstrom reported engine problems and landed at the emergency strip at Lae. After some engine adjustments Lidstrom decided to head to Dobodura before dark. But Lidstrom soon told the Dobodura flight controllers that he was just north of Cape Ward Hunt and had lost power. A scout plane was immediately sent out, but no trace of Lidstrom was found. There was, however, the hope that he would walk out of the jungle, but four months later a native tribesman found Lidstrom's remains.

16 October 1943: 8FG: Rabaul

An armed reconnaissance flown by four brand new 80FS P-38J models headed to Rabaul during the morning, but after they refueled at Kiriwina they ran into an impassable weather system and returned to base.

October 1943: Origin of the "Booze Map"

1Lt. Ralph Wandrey was on a check out flight with an overhauled Lightning and midway down Horanda strip when both Allison engines seized without warning at only 20 feet. The fuel-heavy fighter smacked down on its landing gear at 120mph and headed straight for a parked B-26 Marauder. Wandrey steered away from the bomber, but his out of control fighter jumped over a drainage ditch that sheared off its landing gear, then bounced off a culvert, hurdled back into the air, and came to rest 200 yards beyond the dispersal area. Astonishingly, Wandrey was unhurt and jumped out of the wreck as it caught fire. Wandrey walked back to the service road and hitched a ride back to the Flying Knights' bivouac. As he entered his tent he found his fellow pilots all drinking to his demise and they had already begun to distribute his belongings. Tent mate Dick Bong was wearing his leather jacket and his good friend Paul Yeager had his fleece-lined Aussie flight boots in hand. During the following good-natured celebration someone asked him where he hid his booze, and from then on, each Flying Knight made a map of the location of his liquor stash and left the map with trusted CO Gerry Johnson. If a man went down, his booze would be consumed in his honor.

Mid-October 1943: The Eightballs Become the Black Sheep

The pilots of the 8th Fighter Squadron had become disenchanted with the name "Eightballs." 1Lt. Richard Vodra had drawn a crude cartoon of a black lamb wearing a leather pilot's helmet and sent it to a friend who worked as an illustrator for Walt Disney Studios. Soon the squadron received the Disney depiction of Vodra's "Black Sheep" decked out with flight goggles in the shape of the figure eight. 8FS CO Harris enthusiastically approved, and soon the squadron and Air Force adopted their new Black Sheep mascot and name.

17 October 1943

On 17 October, the First Air Task Force was preparing a ground support mission on Sattelberg; its fighter squadrons were on normal escort and patrol duties; and several Moresby-based medium bomber units were being moved to Dobodura in preparation for a major strike on Rabaul scheduled for the next day. Shortly after 1000 several of these medium squadrons arrived over Dobodura and were ready to land when they received a Red Warning. Soon an enemy formation of Zekes and Tonys were coming in low over Oro Bay. As the B-25s were turning away from landing, fighters called from ground alert and patrol missions began to arrive on the scene.

17 October 1943: 475FG/431FS/432FS/433FS

432FS

Twelve P-38s of the 432FS were returning to Nadzab from a patrol over Dobodura when *Nephew* Controller vectored them 40 miles out over Oro Bay, toward bogies heading southeast and very high. When the three flights arrived at 26,000 feet they saw what looked like a dogfight at 10,000 feet and dropped their tanks. When they entered the combat area they found no enemy aircraft among the P-38s and P-40s. Low on fuel and oxygen, the Squadron headed back to base. Only Squadron Leader Capt. Frederick Harris came close to making a victory claim. As Harris was about to open fire at an Oscar, a P-40 interloper from the 49FG who had joined the Squadron swooped in and shot down the Oscar.

431FS

Three flights of 13 P-38s of the 431FS, led by 1Lt. Marion Kirby, were scrambled at 0945 from Strip #12 and were vectored over Oro Bay. The 431st climbed toward Tufi Point at 11,000 feet and were circling there when they were ordered back to a position northeast of Buna Point 15 to 20 miles out to sea. Kirby's Red Flight was the lowest and 1Lt. Thomas McGuire's White Flight in the middle, while 1Lt. Carl Houseworth's Blue Flight was on top cover. At 1015 the Squadron was patrolling there at 23,000 feet when they saw 20 Zeros at 25,000 feet. Kirby circled his flights in a climb and got behind the Zeros. Kirby's Red Flight attacked the lead Zeros first, and Kirby made a pass on the lead enemy pilot and missed. 2Lt. Vincent Elliott, Wingman to Red second Element Leader

2Lt. Vincent **Elliott** scored his third of seven victories. (AFAA)

1Lt. Edward **Czarnecki**. (L). (shown with 2Lt. Robert Cline) shot down two Zeros to give him six victories. (AAF)

1Lt. Edward Czarnecki, selected the last Zero, which made a sharp turn into Elliott head on. Elliott opened fire from 300 yards and hit its engine and canopy, and it went down in flames. Kirby's Wingman, 2Lt. Charles Samms, had problems dropping his tanks and then his port engine quit and he did not follow. Samms had a Zero firing on him at 6 o'clock and called Kirby for help but was not heard. Samms put his Lightning into a steep dive, losing the Zero. When he pulled out at 6,000 feet he restarted the engine and climbed back into the fight, but returned to base after a minor skirmish. Meanwhile, Kirby made a pass at a Zero being engaged by three other P-38s, one of which was Kirby's second Element Leader, 1Lt. Edward Czarnecki. In the initial attack Czarnecki dove but was unable to get off a shot, and the Zero then got on his tail and he dove down to 10,000 feet to escape and confirmed Elliott's victory. Czarnecki then joined the P-38s that Kirby saw and shot down the Zero that they were chasing. He was briefly joined by Richardson of White Flight, who confirmed his victory before returning to base after his guns jammed. Czarnecki climbed and took a 45 degree deflection shot at a Zero but saw no results. As he reached 17,000 feet he made a rear quarter attack on another Zero that went down in flames. Czarnecki continued to climb toward Zeros milling at 23,000 feet, but was forced to break off when he was attacked by diving Zeros. Czarnecki persisted, but was driven off each time, and when he finally was able to get off a 45 degree deflection shot from astern, his guns stopped firing. Czarnecki's final two victories of the war made him an ace with six victories.

McGuire ordered White Fight to drop their tanks and followed Red Flight directly into the battle. McGuire's Flight consisted of Wingman 2Lt. Robert Hunt and a second element of 2Lt. Edward Hedrick and his Wingman, 2Lt. Kenneth Richardson. McGuire attacked a Zero on the right side of the formation and opened fire; it began smoking and rolled away to starboard, with McGuire following it down to 18,000 feet firing when he could, but he did not see the Zero crash for a probable. McGuire's Wingman, 2Lt. Robert Hunt, was unable to release his drop tanks, but continued to follow with his leader but couldn't pull out of the dive until he reached 4,000 feet and lost McGuire. After Hunt leveled off a Zero crossed his path and he claimed it as probably destroyed. McGuire had climbed back alone to 21,000 feet just as two Zeros attacked Kirby's Red Flight from above and behind. After he fired a few bursts to drive these Zeros away, four more Zeros attacked McGuire from dead astern and he was forced to dive 7,000 feet before losing them. McGuire then climbed and fired at another Zero, but other Zeros forced him to dive away again with enemy bullets piercing his cockpit. As McGuire climbed to regain altitude, he saw a P-38 being pursued by seven Zeros. When one was just nearing McGuire's firing range he fired an effective 90 degree deflection shot that hit the Japanese fighter, which burst into flames. The overconfident McGuire pushed his advantage and attacked the other six Zeros, shooting a second down for his 12th victory. But one of the other five closed behind *Pudgy* and began firing before McGuire saw it, and he had to dive away to safety again. When he pulled out McGuire assessed the damage and found that cannon shells had started the starboard engine on fire and bullets had raked the fuselage. One cannon shell exploded directly behind him in the radio set, but the back armor plate warded off most of the shrapnel; some pieces of metal had penetrated the seat and lodged in his buttocks and right arm. A 7.7 bullet punctured his wrist and hit the instrument panel. The shocked McGuire looked at the perfect hole in his wrist but felt no pain. As he had tried to pull the Lightning out of its high speed dive he found that his control column was also damaged, and he decided to release his canopy and stood up in the rush of the slipstream to bail out. As he tried to move his pant's legs were caught in the cockpit wreckage, and he was blinded by the oxygen mask that had wrapped itself around his eyes. He ripped away the mask, tore at his pants, and finally extricated himself from the cockpit and jumped. When he landed in the water he found that his life vest would only partially inflate and that his life raft was punctured by shrapnel and did not inflate. As he looked around he saw that the nearest land was about 20 to 25 miles away, but he had to wait only about a half hour before PT-152 rescued him and dropped him off on the PT tender USS *Hilo*.

Hunt had followed McGuire down from 23,000 feet in his attack and fired at the same Zero that McGuire fired at it in a head on pass from 150 yards. It went down in a spin, but neither pilot saw it crash, and it was claimed a probable by each pilot. As Hunt tried to pull out of his steep dive he experienced severe buffeting due to his unreleased belly tanks and was unable to recover from the dive. He tried to use the trim and release the tanks, but the buffeting became even worse. Finally the tanks released and the buffeting stopped, and Hunt pulled out at 4,000 feet. Hunt joined three P-38s of the 432FS and patrolled for a while before returning to base. On 8 November 5FC Intelligence Officer 1Lt. Dennis Cooper issued an amendment to Hunt's and McGuire's ICRs, taking away Hunt's probable claim and upgrading McGuire's probable to a victory. "Inasmuch as Lt. McGuire recently found witnesses (enlisted members of the Marine Corps) who confirmed as definitely destroyed (by Lt. McGuire) the Zero previously claimed as probably destroyed by Lt. Hunt, the latter withdraws his claim." McGuire now had 13 victories. While aboard the PT Boat McGuire found a witness to his second and third victories, while two Marines were found that had seen the first "probable" go down while viewing the air battle through field glasses on the beach.

After separating from McGuire, his second element of Hedrick and Richardson made a pass on several Zeros that passed in front of them, but broke off when they saw three more Zeros at 7 o'clock high turning on their tails. The two pilots dove away, and Richardson's ICR reports that he never saw Hedrick again, as it appears that Hedrick was shot down at this time and he never returned to base. Richardson returned to the fight, saw a lone Zero, and closed, and his fire knocked off pieces of its cockpit when his guns stopped firing. Richardson followed, unsuccessfully trying to recharge his guns and having to settle for a probable claim. He then joined Czarnecki and confirmed his victory.

1Lt. Carl Houseworth's Blue Flight was composed of Wingman 2Lt. Franklin Monk and a second element of 1Lt. Paul Morriss and his Wingman, 2Lt. Roger Pare, with Capt. Verl Jett tacking on as a spare. As Kirby's Red and McGuire's White Flight made their initial attack, Houseworth saw nine to 12 enemy aircraft 2-3,000 feet above to the right. Houseworth decided to circle and climb away from these newly spotted enemy aircraft to draw them away from attacking Red and White Flights from the rear, and in the meantime gain an altitude advantage on them for an attack. However, Pare was unable to drop his tanks and Monk had lost power in his port engine, which left Houseworth and Morriss to continue on. They turned 180° and made a head on pass at the enemy formation. Houseworth fired, but saw only thin smoke coming from the Zero. Pare later confirmed the victory, as he saw the Zero descend past him in flames as he began his return to base. Houseworth and Morriss rejoined, and Morriss saw an enemy fighter and pulled up to fire just before the enemy pilot went into a loop. Houseworth anticipated the Japanese pilot's intention and cut his throttles a few seconds before Morriss' pass, then fire walled his fighter and caught the Zero at the top of its loop, where it stalled. Houseworth fired and the Zero burst into flames. Houseworth lost Morriss at this point and joined other P-38s, then made passes at several more enemy fighters. On one pass on another Zero that went into a loop, Houseworth again caught it at the top of its loop and shot it down as it too stalled, but he did not see it crash for a probable. These two victories were Houseworth's only claims of the war. Pare and Monk flew back toward their base, but the Controller told them to circle, as there were Zeros over the field. Pare became dizzy while landing and collapsed his nose wheel and crash landed, with his Lightning skidding 150 feet along the runway.

433FS

Capt. Daniel Roberts was leading 19 Possum P-38s (one abort) on a mission to cover shipping in Morobe Harbor when the Tenth Fighter Controller Sector detected enemy aircraft 50 miles east of Cape Ward Hunt at 18,000 feet. The scramble order was issued at 1030, and Roberts climbed the squadron quickly to 20,000 feet, where they dropped their tanks and spotted 12 Zeros approaching from the southwest and separated into flights to attack the enemy formation. Roberts and his Wingman, 2Lt. John Smith, were the first flight down, but the Zeros saw them and turned away to dive toward New Britain. Roberts and Smith dove at top speed, and after 10 minutes Roberts closed dead astern of a Zero at low altitude and fired. The Zero started to smoke and then a small fire broke out; the enemy pilot tried to bail out, but was thrown from his fighter just as it crashed. Two Zeros tried to escape but were caught by the Lightning's superior speed, and Roberts chased the next Zero down to 150 feet above the Bay. The enemy pilot tried unsuccessfully to skid and yaw, but Roberts' three accurate bursts set it on fire and it crashed into the sea for his eighth victory. In view of the enemy's evasive maneuvers described by Roberts and other pilots, for some reason Robert's ICR states: "The enemy pilots realized they were outclassed and made no attempt to fight back. They dove from 20,000 feet straight to the water." Smith had followed about a mile behind and was unable to catch Roberts, so he joined another P-38 that was chasing a Zero. This Zero pulled up into Smith's range, did a skidding 180, and Smith closed to 150 yards and fired a two second burst, and it crashed into the sea in flames. Smith then joined 2Lt. Robert Tomberg and the two chased a Zero. Tomberg closed and shot it down. The duo then chased another Zero that maneuvered wildly side to side and then pulled up into a steep climb. Smith gradually climbed after it and closed. The frantic Zero pilot started to turn, which gave Smith a good shot from 50 yards into the Zero's wing tank and it exploded.

2Lt. Jack Fisk was flying on 1Lt. William Horton's wing when he dove after a Zero that was being chased by several other P-38s. Fisk outraced Horton to the scene as the Japanese pilot pulled up in front of Fisk, who fired a 45 degree deflection shot from head on that entered the cockpit and the Zero caught fire, rolled over, and spun into the Bay. Horton and Fisk chased after another Zero, and Horton took a long shot from out of range. Fisk closed from under Horton's wing and fired a short burst at the Zero that made no evasive maneuvers to escape and presented an easy target and exploded.

Capt. Daniel **Roberts** got his 8th and 9th victories. (AAF)

1Lt. Charles Grice and Wingman 2Lt. Dale Meyer pursued another Zero that went into a series of aerobatics to evade. Grice tried to fire at it in a Split-S and it then dove in a loop. Grice decided not to attempt to follow the more agile Zero, but waited until it leveled out and headed for Gasmata. After several minutes Grice's faster Lightning caught up with the fleeing Zero and shot off the starboard wing with cannon fire, and the Zero tumbled into the sea. Meyer followed a Zero and took a shot as it pulled up and half rolled. Meyer half rolled as the acrobatic enemy pilot Split-S'd and Meyer rolled back into a dive, but blacked out when he pulled out. Meyer saw a Zero on the water being chased by 1Lt. John Ehlinger, who fired three ineffective bursts from 300 yards and then turned away. Meyer closed to 50 yards astern and fired a two second burst into its cockpit as it dove into the sea.

1Lt. John Babel's third flight was in the thick of the battle, and Babel's Wingman, 2Lt. Virgil Hagan, was lost in the action just two days after his first victory.

As the other P-38s were landing, an informal flight of five P-38s under Maj. John Smith were scrambled at 1020 by the Controller toward enemy fighters over Oro Bay. Upon their arrival at 8,000 feet they circled for 20 minutes and then climbed to 11,000 feet, where they sighted enemy aircraft in the distance but were recalled by the Controller.

Capt. Daniel **Roberts** got his 8th and 9th victories. (AAF)

2Lt. Jack **Fisk** claimed his first of two victories. (AAF)

17 October 1943: 49FG/7FS/9FS

7 FS

The Japanese at Wewak sent out a formation of Lilys protected by Zeros that was met by Flying Knights and the Screamin' Demons patrolling over the coast. The 7FS Demons had answered the 1000 alert with only three Warhawks: Flight Leader 1Lt. Lawrence Succop and Wingmen 1Lt. David Germain and 1Lt. Robert DeHaven, who took off several minutes afterward but failed to catch up to the Flight. Succop and Germain climbed to 15,000 feet to try to join the Satin's Angels, but their new N-model P-40s were unable to catch the rapidly climbing Lightnings. As the two Demon pilots flew through the clouds just off shore from Buna, they were attacked from behind by a flight of Zeros and three got on Succop's tail. Germain turned on the third Zero on Succop's tail but spun out and had to dive away. Germain escaped and found safety with the Angel's P-38s, but Succop was lost. Germain lost the 80FS Lightnings, and when an enemy bullet knocked out his prop control he headed for Kalamazoo. Meanwhile, DeHaven had descended to 17,000 feet and saw 10 to 12 P-38s chasing two enemy planes and joined their flight. Soon this flight was engaged by about 15 Zeros. DeHaven was only a half mile away when he saw an Oscar stall out in its turn, followed by a lone Lightning piloted by Capt. Frederick Harris of the 433FS. The Oscar flew through the haze directly into DeHaven's path and he fired and got hits at point blank range and the pilot bailed out. Mission Leader Succop did not return to base; CO Melikian sent out a search party, but nothing was found.

LEFT: Veteran 1Lt. Grover **Fanning** shot down a Zero and Tony to give him a final total of nine victories. (AFAA)
RIGHT: 1Lt. James **Harris** and his CC apply Harris' fourth victory decal. (AFAA)

9FS

Meanwhile, 12 9th Squadron P-38s in three flights under Mission Leader 1Lt. George Alber were deployed. Alber flew ahead with Blue Flight, but he and one of his elements turned back early due to mechanical failures. The Flights reorganized en route, and Green Flight Leader 1Lt. Grover Fanning assumed the lead. Soon 1Lt. John Stowe aborted with a runaway prop and the Knights reorganized again. After reaching the Oro Bay coast, Charter Fighter Control reported the enemy was inbound from the north and Fanning took his Flight through a wide port climbing turn up to 25,000 feet over Buna, where they met a formation of over 30 enemy fighters. Fanning called for the break, but Robert Wood could not jettison his port belly tank and left the flight. The remaining eight Knights went into a steep dive to intercept the Oscars and Tonys 2,000 feet below.

The Green Flight of Fanning, rookie Wingman 2Lt. Charles McElroy, Element Leader 1Lt. James Harris, and Wingman 1Lt. Delman Moore attacked the lead elements of four Tonys. McElroy's port engine was hit, forcing him to leave the fight. The remaining three Green Flight Lightnings turned in ideal close formation to catch the Oscars in their turns. As Fanning was about to fire at a Tony that tried to cut off Element Leader Harris he made a full throttle turn to get behind the surprised Tony, which he disintegrated. Meanwhile, Harris turned with the Oscars until one stalled out in a high angle wing over and his machine guns blew off the Ki-43's port stabilizer and it fell away in a spin. Harris then got behind another Oscar and fired, starting an engine fire, and it rolled into the overcast 4,000 feet below. Wingman Moore heavily damaged an Oscar and the enemy fighters dove for the safety of the clouds far below, where they were cut off by Fanning, who downed one with a fatal burst from head on.

Red Flight Leader John O'Neill was followed only by 1Lt. Ralph Wandrey, and they made their attack moments after Green Flight. Wandrey made a pass on the #2 man, firing cannon shells into the lower front of the canopy and sending it down smoking and flaming from its engine. Wandrey made a head on pass on a Zero flying directly below and saw pieces come off its canopy for a probable. O'Neill attacked his first Zero simultaneously with Wandrey. The Zero flew through O'Neill's 45 degree deflection burst and he saw large pieces fly off from behind its canopy and wing root.

17 October 1943: 35FG/41FS

At 1012, four P-39s took off to escort two RAAF Boomerangs to Finschhafen, and when they reached the target area at 6,000 feet they saw six Lily bombers at 7,000 feet and 10 or 12 Haps and Oscars at 12,000 feet. The enemy bombers spotted the Americans and dove and headed away. Flight Leader 1Lt. Carey Wooley and Wingman 2Lt. King Brooker closed on a formation of three bombers, with Wooley taking the leader and Brooker the bomber on the left. Wooley's Lily was set on fire as he fired from out of range down to point blank, and it crashed into the sea. Wooley began a second pass, but snap rolled away when he was attacked by two Oscars. On pulling out he saw five Oscars headed back to Rabaul while four others milled around. Wooley had an altitude advantage and opened fire from 300 to 100 yards, observing some hits (probable) before it dove away. Brooker's Lily was hit in the wings, fuselage, and engines and crashed. Brooker closed on the second Lily formation and shot down the left bomber, but his cannon and one .50 caliber jammed. He fired enough to send it down on fire into a hill near the beach. Brooker fired on a third Lily and scored a number of hits, but did not see it crash and claimed a probable.

Meanwhile, second Element Leader 1Lt. Carl Bohman and his Wingman, F/O Jamie Wallace, were closing on the bombers when a Tony closed on Bohman and Wallace turned into it and chased it off. The two continued toward the bombers, and Bohman set both engines on fire from 150 yards and then peeled away for another attack on another bomber, but it was already under attack by a P-39 that left it with its right engine smoking. Bohman then attacked this damaged Lily, getting a few hits before breaking off. Bohman then saw another Lily directly in front and below him and fired, seeing no hits, as he had to break off sharply to avoid colliding with its wing. As he pulled up Bohman saw an Oscar that had just dove on a P-39 pull up directly in front of him and he fired a 45 degree burst from the rear quarter. The Oscar pilot whipped back to port as Bohman closed to 50 yards and devastated the Oscar. Meanwhile, Wallace separated from Bohman and closed and fired on the left bomber of the V, closing to 100 yards, and fired a three second burst. The cannon shells exploded the bomber. After Wooley set the center bomber on fire Wallace joined Brooker and watched him send his Lily into a hill. Wallace then chased a Lily out to sea as it was trying to escape into a rain squall, but managed to close enough to start a fire in its wing before it disappeared into the squall (this

Lily was later shot down). In his attack Wallace had expended his ammunition and returned home. After his Oscar victory Bohman saw an inline fighter approach and thought it was Wallace's P-39. However, it was a Tony, which hit Bohman's fighter's tail and wings with small caliber 7.7 caliber machine gun bullets. He gave hard right rudder and left stick and lost the enemy. Bohman saw a bomber and fired at extreme range without hope of result, then turned back to Finschhafen. A Zero came on Bohman's tail and the American skidded. The Zero missed and flew off to the rear, and Bohman returned toward Lae. After 25 miles his engine started to smoke and it filled his cockpit, forcing Bohman to bail out. He landed safely in low brush and started off toward a river in the rain. Bohman had carried his parachute and rubber raft with him and used the raft to cross the river, where he came upon a native village that had recently been deserted by the Japanese. He returned to the river shore and spread his chute out on a sand bar, and an hour later he saw P-39s approach and fired his pistol, which contained tracers. He was seen, and the P-39s directed some USN barges traveling just off shore to pick him up. Bohman was taken to Finschhafen and returned to his base in the early evening.

Army Ki-10 **Pete** two place observation float biplane. (AAF)

18 October: Rabaul Missions

These Japanese air raids did little more than delay the arrival of the Port Moresby B-25s at Dobodura, and plans for the next Rabaul mission continued. Eight squadrons of heavy bombers and two B-25 strafer squadrons were to attack Vunakanau, Lakunai, and Tobera. It was expected that these landing fields would be so badly damaged by the bombing that airborne enemy fighters would be forced to land at Rapopo, where they would be destroyed by a later low level strafing attack. Although the previous day's Japanese attack did not prevent the AAF attack, the weather interfered, as 77 B-24s set out as planned shortly after 0700 and flew in good weather until they reached Kiriwina three hours later, where three P-38 squadrons joined them. Simultaneously six attack squadrons took off from Dobodura, rendezvoused over Oro Bay, and proceeded toward Kiriwina, where they were joined by an escort of three more P-38 squadrons. Meanwhile, the B-24s were encountering heavy weather at 25,000 feet before reaching New Britain. After about an hour and a half, all of the 55 P-38 escorts returned to Kiriwina, while the B-24s continued to fight the weather front and finally bombed targets. The B-25s encountered the same weather front about an hour later, and their fighter cover was also forced to turn back. The B-25s flew at minimum altitude under the weather front to successfully attack their targets despite heavy attacks by fighters over the target.

At 0650, 19 Lightnings of the 80FS left Port Moresby and landed at Kiriwina at 0825, but after taking off and flying 30 miles north they hit an unbroken weather front extending from sea level to 30,000 feet. All 80FS turned back and landed safely and, although the B-24s didn't get through, the B-25s attacked Tobera and Ropopo. Meanwhile, the 36FS conducted a routine strafing mission. When 1Lt. Robert Rosenbloom returned to Ward's Drome he buzzed the base, lost power at the end of the strip and crashed and was killed.

Col. Neel **Kearby** shot down two Pete float planes to give him a dozen victories. (AAF)

It was becoming obvious that the weather situation would not permit the total execution of the plan for an early reduction of Rabaul. The loss of three B-24s on 18 October because of the weather, together with the failure of the entire force to reach its objective, had convinced Gen. Whitehead that the use of heavy bombers should be limited. He contended that any plan which would send B-24s at night against targets in the Solomon Sea, such as Kavieng, Buka, and Rabaul would result in losses of 15 to 30%. His suggestion was to attack Kavieng at night with PBYs and B-24s by day with coordinated fighter sweeps to Rabaul designed to keep the enemy fighters there.

19 October 1943: 348FG

With his 10th victory on 16 October Col. Neel Kearby was the only 348th ace, and was followed by Captains John Moore of the 341FS and William Dunham of the 342FS, each having three victories. By the middle of October Dick Bong was the leading ace of the Theater with 17 victories, closely followed by Thomas Lynch and George Welch with 16 and Thomas McGuire with 13. With Lynch and Welch back home on rotation, Kearby had a chance to gain ground over the next few weeks.

On 19 October 1943, Kearby led three other P-47s on a high altitude patrol over the besieged Japanese airbase at Wewak. 1Lt. Theodore Wood was on Kearby's wing, while Capt. William Dunham led the second element with 1Lt. Frank Love as his Wingman. The flight took off from Port Moresby at 0800 and landed at Tsili Tsili to refuel at 0845. They were off again at 0915 and arrived over the Wewak area at 1100 at 28,000 feet. After patrolling for 15 minutes Kearby saw four single engine fighters flying on the deck near Wewak and led a dive but lost them in the clouds.

When the P-47s turned back to their patrol they sighted six Pete floatplanes taking off from the waters near Kairiru Island. The Americans were at 8,000 feet when the Petes cleared the water, and they were helpless under the fire from .50 caliber machine guns; each of the four Thunderbolt pilots scored a victory on their first passes. The first element of Kearby and Wood attacked first, and Wood describes his initial pass: "We dove in and I picked my Pete and opened fire at 300 to 350 yards closing to 100 feet. The Pete nosed over to the left....I looked back....and saw him burning on the water." After his easy first astern victory Kearby then turned and hit another Pete with a 90 degree deflection shot to start it smoking. Kearby wheeled around and finished the Pete off with another 90 degree deflection shot.

Dunham witnessed Kearby's and Wood's victories, then saw a Pete making a violent turn directly toward him. Dunham opened fire at 400 down to 200 yards before the Pete crashed into the sea. Love described his victories: "After making a large figure 8 over the Strait at 300 feet altitude. I saw one Pete flying straight ahead of me at about 1,000 yards. Dead Head. Another Zeke crossed my line of flight at 30 to 45 degrees. I gave him a long burst and he veered off in flames." Love continued after the first Pete he saw and fired a long burst at 90 degrees, knocking off one pontoon and causing it to fly into a hill.

After his flight shot down all six Petes, Kearby looked up and saw 12 Japanese aircraft far above at 20,000 feet. Kearby did not violate his basic combat premise of always having the altitude and speed advantage before attacking and led the flight under the clouds at 2,000 feet. On the way back to Tsili Tsili to refuel Kearby and Wood strafed an enemy held village. When they landed at Tsili Tsili one of the P-47s blew a tire on the hot runway and the flight was delayed for an hour before returning to Moresby.

1Lts. Edward **Popek** was awarded his first of seven victories. (AFAA)

Capt. Walter **Benz** claimed his third victory. (AFAA)

20 October 1943: 8FG/36FS

1Lt. Gordon Gates of the 36FS was checking out a new P-47 at Ward's Drome when his Warhawk lost power. He crashed into a revetment and was killed.

19-22 October: Operations in New Guinea

Any interference with the major scheduled operations complicated the entire operational routine of the Air Force. "The beating down of Rabaul" was the primary mission of the First Air Task Force, and Gen. Whitehead had to save heavy bombers, two attack bomber groups, and the six P-38 squadrons for any possible opportunity to achieve that objective. However, severe limitations were placed on the fighter force available for escort and patrol missions. Now LCMs and other small craft carrying rations and supplies to the Australians in the Finschhafen area would have to move at night and take cover by day. The most fighter escort Gen. Whitehead could promise the Navy to cover a convoy was two flights of P-40s from sunrise until 0900, two to four flights of P-47s and two flights of P-40s between 0900 and 1500, and two flights of P-40s from then until sunset. This would leave no more than one squadron of P-47s and two of P-40s on ground alert to cover the shipping in Oro Bay. Whitehead predicted that the Navy would "squawk to high heaven" at any reduction in fighter patrols, but added that he could not use his P-38 force to cover shipping and troop carriers and also accomplish his primary mission of eliminating the enemy air force at Buka, Kavieng, and Rabaul.

Following the 18 October mission, the weather forecasters issued increasingly dismal predictions for continued bad weather, which would not permit a renewal of the Rabaul offensive until at least 23 October. Thus, the Fifth Air Force was again forced to attack to the west. Although there had been a number of minor strikes against the stubborn Japanese in the Sattelberg area, Gen. Whitehead was unable to plan a major attack there because of a continued lack of specific information from Australia as to the target. The pause in the Rabaul/New Britain operations offered an opportunity for a large coordinated mission planned for 21 October that would come at an opportune time, as the enemy was threatening to recapture lost ground. Sattelberg Village was leveled when 56 B-24s dropped over 200 tons of bombs on it. A few hours later 10 B-25s bombed and strafed Japanese supply routes and positions in the same area from minimum altitude. However, on that day, a failure to provide for the fighter escort prevented the execution of a scheduled mission on Wewak. The plan was to use B-25s escorted by P-47s from Port Moresby, which would require refueling on the way both to and from the target. Mission planners did not take into consideration that this would so delay the B-25s that they would be unable to climb over the regular afternoon build up of high cumulus clouds over the mountain tops on the return to base, so the attack was postponed until the entire air echelon of the 348th Fighter Group could move temporarily to Tsili Tsili. The attack took place on 22 October, when two squadrons of B-25 strafers escorted by almost 50 P-47s attacked But and Dagua Airdromes, while another B-25G strafer squadron attacked shipping off the nearby coast. The bombers destroyed 13 aircraft on the ground, silenced AA positions, and sunk two small luggers. Antiaircraft fire was slight and inaccurate, and the P-47s provided protection from intercepting fighters.

22 October 1943: 348FG/341FS/342FS

On 22 October, the 341st and 342nd Squadrons flew a B-25 escort mission to Wewak. Eight P-47s of the 342nd led by Capt. Walter Benz took off at 0800 from Tsili Tsili, followed 30 minutes later by nine more from the 341st.

At 1020, the 342nd was flying over Wewak when seven Tonys bounced them from the rear at 2,000 feet about five miles off Dagua. The P-47s separated and tried to gain the offensive. Benz saw a P-47 being chased by a Tony and dove, causing the Tony to break off. He then saw another Tony at 2,000 feet closing on the B-25s. Benz closed from astern and shot and hit the Tony, which crashed in flames into the water. Meanwhile, 1Lts. Edward Popek and Robert Martin were flying at 7,000 feet west of Kairiru Island when Martin went after a Tony at 10 o'clock and 5,000 feet and missed. The two rejoined just as two Tonys were coming into the area, and one dove onto the tail of a P-47 from another formation. Popek quickly dove and shot at the Tony with a 45 degree deflection into the cockpit and it spun in flames into the water. 2Lt. Wynans Frankfort, flying on Benz' wing, saw a Hamp slightly above and climbing after a P-47. Frankfort fired a short burst and the Hamp broke off into a steep dive; Frankfort followed, firing, but was unable to get enough lead. Frankfurt straightened out past the Hamp, which climbed and then did a wingover, giving Frankfort the opportunity to fire a 90 degree deflection at about 1,000 feet; he emptied his guns on it, causing it to fall off into the water. In the battle Frankfort's fighter ran out of fuel, and he was forced to bail out over the Fly River, where he was rescued by natives and returned to base on 31 October.

Meanwhile, the 341FS approached Wewak at 5,000 feet from over the sea when its rear flight was jumped by five Tonys from the rear coming from the cover of a rain cloud. The P-47s were at an extreme height and altitude disadvantage and lost Lt. Harold Jacoby. 2Lt. Ernest Ness, flying on Element Leader 1Lt. Charles Whistler's wing, was also MIA for the 341st.

23 October: Rabaul: 49FG/475FG/35FG/8FG

Weather recon B-24s reported more favorable weather over the Solomon Sea and New Britain. Intelligence reports stated that the Japanese were replacing air losses in New Britain as quickly as they occurred, as recon photos of 19 October showed 211 aircraft on the four Rabaul airdromes. This alarming development resulted in a plan to renew the air offensive on 23 October.

The schedule called for heavy bomber attacks on Lakunai (90BG) and Vunakanau (43BG), and a fighter sweep by three P-38 squadrons prior to the bombing attack. A fighter squadron was to escort each bomber group, while six fighter squadrons were to provide overall top cover. The mission began according to plan, with 57 B-24s meeting their escort of 100 P-38s over Kiriwina. When this large formation reached the Rabaul area, it found that its two targets were completely covered by cloud layers reaching up to 20,000 feet. Although there were no provisions for a secondary target, the Group Leader decided on Rapopo. The change led to confusion, and the bomb hits were scattered and ineffective, while other B-24s did not drop their bombs at all. Enemy fighter interception was "not particularly effective," but made bomb damage observation difficult. The official bomber report claimed 20 medium bombers and fighters destroyed on the ground in addition to four Zekes in combat. The P-38s provided excellent cover and claimed 13 additional enemy fighters.

49FG/9FS

The escort of the bombers had taken its toll on 49FS Lightnings, as Capt. Gerald Johnson's 9FS had only 16 P-38s in service despite the 24/7 effort by ground crews. On the 23rd, Johnson was assigned high cover for bombers returning to Rabaul. After a dawn take off Johnson's 16 Lightnings staged to Kiriwina Island, and then were to rendezvous with the bombers off the southern New Britain coast at 1100. Johnson was down to 14 escorts after two pilots aborted. At the rendezvous they flew in high cover on the right bomber flank at 26,000 feet until they approached the Rabaul area at noon. Looking down, they saw Rapopo Airdrome on the northern shore and Tobera Airdrome about ten miles inland, southwest of Cape Gazelle. Allied intelligence had identified these bases as the quarters of the regrouped 253rd Kokutai, which defended the eastern and southern approaches to Simpson Harbor.

Capt. Gerald **Johnson** after shooting down a Zero for his seventh victory. (he also included a victory claim in the Aleutians that was denied). (AAF)

While the 80FS Satin's Angels were engaging the enemy directly over the harbor, the Liberators made their turn from the harbor and headed toward the Knights when Johnson spotted 10 enemy fighters closing in from the north at 1,000 feet below. Johnson's Red Flight included his Wingman, 2Lt. Raymond Swift, Element Leader Capt. William Haney, and Wingman 2Lt. Stanley Johnson. CO Johnson and Swift immediately engaged a solo Zero which had just completed a firing pass at the B-24 formation. Johnson dove, cut his throttle, and fired a dead astern volley into the enemy, which caught on fire and rolled into a fatal dive. Swift's burst sent a smoking Zero scurrying away for a probable. 1Lt. Francis Nutter of Green Flight and 1Lt. Francis Love of Yellow Flight both pursued Zeros to below 10,000 feet, but their orders were to cover the Liberators and they returned to do so.

475FG/431FS/432FS/433FS

Poor weather had prevented fighters from escorting bombers to Rabaul, but on the 23rd, P-38s of all three 475th Squadrons were to sweep ahead of a major B-24 effort and try to catch the Japanese fighters before they reached altitude. The three squadrons rendezvoused over the *Gona* wreck, although Capt. Daniel Roberts' 433FS took off last; they still got above and a little ahead of the other two Squadrons before arriving over the target. P-38s of the 433FS were at about 28,000 feet, while the other two squadrons were between 25,000 (432FS) and 27,000 (431FS) feet. The 431st and 432nd went into battle first, intercepting a large formation of mixed enemy fighters flying far below, while the 433FS remained on top cover duty.

431FS

Capt. Verl Jett led 15 P-38s from Dobodura at 1010 and climbed to 27,000 feet. The 431st would join the 432nd and easily rendezvoused in clear skies over the water at about the same altitude, arriving over the target at 1215. Red Flight Leader Jett, his Wingman, 1Lt. David Allen, and the second element of 1Lt. Edward Czarnecki and Wingman 1Lt. William O'Brien saw enemy fighters climbing toward them from 15,000 feet. Red Flight descended and made only a few passes, then climbed back to altitude. Upon clearing the target area at 1250 they made passes on two enemy fighters. As they left they found that Czarnecki was not with them; it was thought that his fighter had been hit by AA fire and landed in the water about 30 miles south of Wide Bay. A pilot from the 432FS reported seeing a yellow life raft being paddled toward the coast of New Britain, but Czarnecki was never seen again.

Kirby's wingman, 2Lt. Vincent **Elliott**, shot down two Zeros to become an ace. (AFAA)

1Lt. Marion **Kirby** claimed his third victory. (AAF)

1Lt. Marion Kirby led the second White Flight, with his Wingman 2Lt. Charles Samms and Element Leader 1Lt. Harold Holze and 2Lt. Vincent Elliott on his wing. Mission replacement pilot 2Lt. John Smith from the 433FS replaced Holze when he aborted, and then flew as the Wingman to new second Element Leader Elliott. The flight started patrolling the area when enemy fighters began to climb, but 1Lt. Lowell Lutton's Blue Flight engaged them.

Lutton's Flight was at a disadvantage from the start, as the #4 man had aborted. As Lutton led his flight to higher altitudes his engine misfired, but smoothed out once he dropped back down to 22,000 feet to join Clover Squadron as their third flight. When the enemy fighters climbed to intercept, the P-38s formed in a string of 10 fighters, with Blue Flight following Maj. Charles MacDonald's flights as they made passes on the enemy. Meanwhile, three Zeros tried to attack Lutton's tail end of the string. Wingman 2Lt. Robert Herman chased a Zero off Lutton's tail, while Element Leader 1Lt. Arthur Wenige chased one off Herman's tail. In the round robin Lutton saw one on Wenige's tail, but another P-38 got to it first. Lutton and Herman became separated from their second element and joined another four plane flight. Lutton saw a lone Zero and peeled after it and fired, missing as it half rolled away. A Zero got a shot on Herman's fighter and hit his canopy and intercooler, and Herman could no longer keep up with his Leader. After Lutton lost Herman he joined other P-38s which always seemed to be above, keeping the enemy fighters below. Lutton kept making diving passes and then returned to join the P-38s above. Finally, Lutton dove on a Zero from behind and above, and his short burst hit the cockpit and wings. As the Zero half rolled Lutton took another shot that hit its starboard wing and sent it into a spin; it was seen to crash by Smith. Lutton made several more ineffective passes before returning to Kiriwina. Once at Kiriwina, Lutton had to remain overnight to have his oil cooler flap repaired.

Lutton's Element Leader, 1Lt. Arthur Wenige, was alone, since his Wingman turned back due to mechanical problems, but he was able to shoot a Zero off Lutton's Wingman's (Herman) tail. A lone Zero passed in front of Blue Flight, but out of range of Lutton and Herman, who did not fire. Wenige was able to intercept it, but although it was hit it continued flying and was claimed as a probable. AA fire hit Wenige's port engine and severed its coolant lines. A P-38 from the 432FS shot a Zero off Wenige's tail, but his engine began to burn. He feathered it and slipped the fighter, blowing out the fire. Elliott and another 432FS P-38 escorted Wenige back to Kiriwina, and the next day he was flown by B-24 to Moresby and then by transport to Dobodura.

Meanwhile, Kirby's White Flight continued to patrol until they saw P-38s in trouble below and dropped their tanks, but pulled back up when another P-38 flight interceded. Kirby saw two Zeros slightly above, and as Kirby climbed toward them, one pulled up and was immediately engaged by other Lightnings. Kirby attacked the other from directly behind and fired, scoring "quite a few hits," and it rolled over, seemingly out of control, but was not smoking. Later Elliott confirmed that he saw the Zero crash. During Kirby's attack Samms saw another Zero and made an attack which was interrupted when a bullet struck Samms' windshield and pieces of glass hit him in the eyes. Kirby escorted him back to base. The White Second Element of Smith and Elliott dropped their belly tanks and started down after Kirby. They saw two Zeros closing on Kirby and Samms. Elliott closed with a head on pass and fired at close range. The Zero's port wing exploded, and the Zero half rolled and went into a tight spin. Smith attacked the first Zero, which got away without being hit. After missing his target, Smith went into a shallow dive and met an Oscar head on and fired at close range, knocking pieces off the enemy's engine cowling. Smith pulled up sharply to avoid being hit, but a piece dented his P-38's wing leading edge but did not affect its flight. Elliott and Smith climbed away from their attack, but were then bounced by least eight enemy fighters. After a several minute chase the Lightnings outraced their pursuers into cloud cover. Elliott saw a lone Hamp and hit it with a 45 degree deflection shot that sent it down smoking and losing pieces as it crashed into the water, giving Elliott five victories to become an ace. Elliott then came upon Wenige's crippled P-38 and escorted it back to base.

432FS

The 432FS took off with the 431FS and headed toward Keravia Bay with Maj. Charles MacDonald at the head of Red Flight along with 2Lt. Howard Hedrick as his Wingman. Maj. Frank Tomkins was the Leader of Clover Blue Flight, while 1Lt. Campbell Wilson led Clover White and Capt. William Waldman led Clover Green in the rear.

The 432FS was the last squadron over the target area at 1220 and didn't see any enemy aircraft when they arrived, but encountered heavy and medium caliber AA fire that was of light to medium intensity. Soon MacDonald sighted about a dozen enemy fighters heading northeast over Glanges Strait, but realized that this group was a decoy for an even larger group climbing southwest of Rabaul. When the larger enemy fighter group arrived he ordered auxiliary tanks to be jettisoned and attacked the larger group, consisting mostly of Oscars. Wingman Hedrick followed MacDonald down, and the two made several ineffective passes before MacDonald reefed into an Oscar that was about to pass below him and set it on fire. He then continued on to fire on an incoming Tony (?) when suddenly, during this firing pass, only one of MacDonald's guns was firing. Hedrick pulled up, closed in, and shot down the enemy aircraft, whose pilot bailed out as his fighter disintegrated. Despite having only one gun firing, MacDonald and Hedrick made four or five more mostly head on passes before being forced to retreat when two Oscars got on their tails approaching from below and to port. MacDonald's second Element Leader, 1Lt. John Weber, followed his leader in the attack against the larger groups of Oscars, also without result. After MacDonald made an unsuccessful pass on an Oscar it passed under Weber, who got a good burst that started it on fire, but Weber was unable to see its fate. Weber fired three more head on shots with nil results before returning to Kiriwina. On 10 November Capt. Ronald Mollack, AAF Intelligence Office, amended Weber's Oscar to a probable. Weber's Wingman, 2Lt. Edward Dickey, found that his port engine was malfunctioning and fell behind. After Dickey fired on an Oscar that made a head on pass he fired at 60 degrees deflection at another Oscar that descended smoking. Before Dickey could follow another Oscar dove on him from above and Dickey was forced to escape, claiming a probable.

Fortunately for MacDonald's flight, 1Lt. Campbell Wilson's Clover Blue Flight arrived and the enemy pilots quickly broke off. Another Oscar closed directly behind MacDonald, but changed course and fled when Campbell' flight climbed on its tail. When Wilson looked behind to clear his tail he saw a P-38 to his starboard with heavy smoke pouring from its port engine and with a Zero closing from the rear. Wilson turned quickly into the enemy fighter, causing it to break off its attack before Wilson could open fire. Wilson wove behind the wounded P-38. Two more Oscars closed on the crippled Lightning at 8 o'clock, but turned away from Wilson's fire. As Wilson was chasing these Oscars away another approached the crippled P-38 from underneath, but Wilson turned at high speed and got a 200 to 100 yard deflection shot at the unaware pilot, whose fighter received hits in its fuselage and port wing that put it into a sudden stall turn to port; it fell in flames toward Blanche Bay for a probable. Wilson then escorted the crippled P-38 safely to Kiriwina, where he found the grateful pilot to be Arthur Wenige of the 432FS, who reciprocated by confirming Wilson's third victory in Mollack's report on 10 November.

MacDonald's assessment of the Japanese pilots was: "The Nip pilots didn't appear to be too eager and most of them half rolled at the first sign of attack."

433FS

Despite arriving over the target area first, the 18 Possum Lightnings remained on top cover and entered the combat at its height. While circling, Roberts saw over 25 Japanese fighters being successfully combated by

Capt. Daniel **Roberts** shot down two Zeros to make him a double ace with 11 victories. (AAF)

the other 475th squadrons, but when 35 more enemy fighters appeared, Roberts ordered his flights to drop their tanks and follow him as he dove a mile from 25,000 feet. However, only White Flight heard the radio call and followed Robert's Red Flight down into battle, while the other two remained at altitude. Eight Zeros were attacking a flight of four 431FS P-38s when Roberts closed in from behind and tore up the wing of one and set it on fire. Roberts quickly turned into another Zero on a quarter head on pass, firing a long burst that immediately set it on fire; it then rolled over. The pilot dropped out of the cockpit, but no parachute opened as the Zero fell into the sea from 19,000 feet. The two victories made Roberts a double ace with 11 victories. On the initial pass on the 35 enemy planes 2Lt. Dale Meyer was in White Flight, which followed Roberts down. Meyer missed a Zero on his first pass, but as he was returning to his flight he saw a P-38 chasing a Zero, but it had a Zero on its tail. Meyer dove to help, but as he closed on the Zero another fired on him, putting a hole in his fighter's tail, and he had to break off his attack and climb away. As he leveled off Meyer saw another Zero ahead and slightly below and closed to 150 yards, firing a long fatal burst into its cockpit and fuselage for his second and last victory of the war. During the battle Roberts' Wingman, 1Lt. Chase Brenizer, had his intercooler damaged and he had to return to base on one engine.

By late afternoon the 475FG Lightnings had refueled at Kiriwina and were back at Dobodura by 1700. There were 13 American fighter claims for the day over Rabaul: 11 for the 475FS and one each for the 9FS and 39FS. No B-24s were reported lost, but one P-38 was missing, flown by the veteran 1Lt. Ed Czarnecki.

35FG/39FS

Twenty P-38s of the 39FS were sent on a B-24 escort to Rabaul. At 1300 a three plane flight led by Capt. Paul Stanch, with wingmen 1Lts. Howard Round and Gordon Prentice, encountered 10 to 12 Zeros flying at 2,000 to 3,000 feet overhead in the AA fire over Rabaul. The Zeros started to dive on the Liberators. Stanch turned his flight into them, but his right engine began to stream Prestone and overheat. But Stanch continued on, pulling under the Zeros, which chandelled down away from the bombers and toward him. Since his P-38 had lost power

Capt. Paul **Stanch** became a double ace with his 10th and last victory. (AFAA)

he could not pull away from the Zeros, but they would still have problems catching him. A Zero came in on him at 12 o'clock and Stanch started to climb into it as it did several vertical rolls to get away. Meanwhile the other Zeros were gaining, so Stanch leveled out to maintain the standoff. Another Zero came ahead in at 1 o'clock level, and Stanch met its pass and fired from 500 to 50 yards, getting hits from the rear of the cockpit to the tail. The Zero was seen exploding in the water by a B-24 gunner. Wingmen Round and Prentice each damaged a Zero. The victory was Stanch's 10th and last of the war. He remained in the post war Air Force, retiring as a Colonel in August 1966.

8FG/80FS

On the 23rd, at 1040 18 Lightnings of the 80FS took off from Kiriwina and arrived over the target by noon to sweep in ahead of the main raid. Although other squadrons engaged and shot down enemy fighters, the 80th met no enemy interceptors. The bombers did bomb Rabaul for the loss of only one B-24 that went down into St. George Channel, probably due to the flak.

23 October 1943: New Guinea
348FG/341FS

Capt. Samuel Blair was leading four flights of 14 P-47s of the 341FS, taking off at 0810 for a patrol of the Finschhafen area at 20,000 feet. When they reached an area about 15 miles northeast of Finschhafen at 1040, two formations of eight Oscars and Tonys each approached from the direction of Saidor about a 1,000 feet higher than the P-47s. The enemy seemed to be unaware of the Americans as they dropped their belly fuel tanks and climbed above and behind the Japanese formation. Blair chose an enemy fighter that made a sudden, sharp turn to port, and Blair quickly switched his aim for the next Oscar in line. He opened fire out of range and the enemy fighter went into a steep dive and began a left turn. Blair fired another burst from closer range and a much tighter lead, and his bullets and tracers began to converge on its fuselage until his guns jammed. The Oscar rolled over in flames and plunged straight into the water. Once attacked the Japanese broke up into four, four plane flights.

1Lt. James Rowe, Element Leader in the Second Flight, claimed a Zero with a deflection shot. 2Lt. Samuel Galik, Rowe's Wingman, shot down a Zero, but was lucky to use his Thunderbolt's superior dive speed to dive 15,000 feet to safety when a Zero got on his tail. 1Lt. James Rea, a Flight Leader in the Second Flight, claimed two Zero probables. Element Leader 2Lt. Eugene Spencer shot down a Zero when he hit its cockpit after taking two quick shots at passing Zeros. Capt. Kenneth Briggs shot down a Zero that was on the tail of two P-47s. Initially, Briggs over ran and lost

Lt. Samuel **Galik** scored his only victory of the war. (AAF) **ADD**

the Zero under his wing. He then climbed and spotted a lone Zero about five miles away, and Briggs closed on the unaware enemy pilot and fired a long burst that emptied his guns. Briggs broke away to safety when he was attacked by two Zeros. It was the 341st's best day of the war so far, with five victories and two probables without a loss.

8FG/35FS

During a convoy patrol over Finschhafen, eight P-40s were patrolling at 4,000 feet. Flight Leader 1Lt. Harold Souther spotted a lone Tony at sea level and dropped his tanks. His Flight followed as Souther dove on the Tony's tail and then pulled up to port and waited for the rest of his flight to make their passes. Souther then made a 90 degree deflection shot as two P-40s were about to make a second firing pass from the rear. He closed very close and fired a long burst that flamed and then exploded the Tony.

Lt.Col. Malcolm Moore was relieved as Group CO by Maj. Edwin Doss, the former Group Deputy CO and 41FS CO before that.

1Lt. John **O'Neill** shot down two Zeros to become an ace with six victories. (AFAA)

24 October: Rabaul 49FG/8FG/35FG/475FG

The air offensive on Rabaul continued on 24 October. The First Air Task Force was to send a low level attack on three Rabaul airdromes: Vunakanau, Rapopo, and Tobera. At 0800, two hours before these low level attacks, another attack by the 3BG was planned to confuse the enemy fighter defenses. Unfortunately, take off was delayed for over an hour, and then the 3BG became separated over the Solomon Sea and lost more valuable time by reassembling over New Britain. By the time the leading bombers crossed the coast line, more than 20 Zekes, Hamps, and Oscars were waiting and attacked the leading bombers. Although six fighter squadrons were providing escort for the mission, none were in the immediate vicinity of the 3BG, and by the time P-38s of the 80FS could reach the bombers one B-25 had been shot down. Upon their arrival the P-38 pilots engaged in "the hottest battle yet encountered." However, the remainder of the B-25 units was well protected by their fighter escort and experienced "no persistent interception." The attack was a success, as at least 21 aircraft were destroyed on the ground at Rapopo and 27 more at Vunakanau. In addition, the B-25s were credited with shooting down eight enemy fighters, while the P-38 escort claimed 37 more. The 80FS was the highest scoring P-38 unit of the day with 12 confirmed victories. Two B-25s were lost and two P-38s crash landed at Kiriwina, but the pilots escaped. Only one P-38 was lost (from the 475FG). The high altitude B-24 bombing attacks caused only moderate damage, but the low level B-25 bombing and strafing attacks were the most successful and feared type of attack by the Japanese on Rabaul. The B-24 escort mission was not particularly dangerous for the P-38s, as the Japanese interceptors paid more attention to the American low level bombers and combat on the deck was confused and dangerous. The predominance of Zekes and Hamps in the Rabaul area was due to these aircraft being Japanese Navy fighter types, while Tonys and Oscars were Army fighter types and the Japanese Army air units had all been consigned to New Guinea by this time.

49FG/9FS

9FS mission leader Capt. Richard Bong led 11 Lightnings to stage at Kiriwina again. They waited there until 0830 to join other P-38 units in escorting the Mitchells over the Solomon Sea to Rabaul. The Knights descended in close escort position on the right flank of the 3rd Attack Group, and an hour later reached the New Britain coast and passed over the mouth of the Warangoi River, which was the final check point for their turn into the target just minutes ahead. Bong led Red Flight rookie Wingman 2Lt. Woodson Woodward, Element Leader 1Lt. Normand Hyland, and Wingman 2Lt. Gilbert Milliff inland at 2,000 feet, while 1Lt. William Bleecker's Blue Flight of 1Lts. John Stowe, James Harris, and Milby Marling followed closely to starboard. Flying overhead in trail at 6,000 feet were 1Lt. John O'Neill's Green Flight of 2Lt. John McLean, 1Lt. Ralph Wandrey, and 1Lt. Delman Moore. As the 3AG Mitchells skimmed the tree tops toward Tobera Airdrome, the 39FS high cover flights warned of several contacts with enemy fighters along the northern shore of Cape Gazelle. Soon three radial engine fighters were seen zooming in from the north, and Bong's Flight dropped their tanks and climbed toward the incoming enemy fighters. Bong fired at all three but missed, and the other Red Flight elements separated without firing a shot. Only Bong and Milliff reformed to return to the 3AG Mitchells, while Hyland flew toward a fight going on near Tobera and the rookie Woodward disappeared.

When Hyland arrived he found Blue Flight climbing to engage 10 Zeros, but the Blue Flight elements became separated and had to break off. Blue Flight Leader Bleecker and Hyland joined forces just north of Tobera airdrome. Hyland fatally hit a turning Zero with a high angle deflection, while Bleecker got on the tail of a Zero who had dropped into a shallow dive, attempting to out run the Lightning. Bleecker easily followed and fired on the Zero until it crashed into a hillside. Bleecker and Hyland then turned due east to join with the Satin's Angels at the designated rendezvous point near the coast.

O'Neill's Green Flight, flying at a higher altitude, had also seen the same 10 Zeros and dove into a rear quarter attack. O'Neill maneuvered through several passes with the enemy pilots in and out of the clouds until one slowed at the top of a wing over and O'Neill ripped off the Zeke's tail to become an ace. O' Neill chased another Zeke trying to escape into the clouds, caught it, and fired a fatal burst from dead astern.

Green Element Leader 1Lt. Ralph Wandrey and Wingman 1Lt. Delman Moore got into a swirling dogfight in the clouds above Tobera and fired at several Zeros, but neither pilot could make a claim, as their targets disappeared into the clouds. Soon a pair of Zeros turned head on into the two, and Wandrey hit the lead Hamp hard on the inside of his turn while Moore downed the Wingman.

Mission Leader Bong was perturbed by the disappearance of his Wingman Woodward and the scattering of the Flying Knights, so he recalled his flights, which were scattered in the clouds along Cape Gazelle's eastern shore. While Bong and Milliff waited for the squadron they came across three small luggers staying close to the safety of the shoreline. The duo made a low level firing run, leaving one burning before they turned for home. When Bong returned to Horanda he learned that Woodward's badly damaged fighter was last reported descending toward the sea east of Buna. Woodward was the fourth Bong Wingman to be lost.

8FG/80FS

On 24 October, Maj. Edward Cragg led 16 80th Fighter Squadron P-38s as they escorted B-25s to Rapopo Airdrome. The Squadron left Dobodura between 0830 and 0900, but after four aborts 12 Lightnings arrived over the Rabaul coast, where they dropped their tanks at 2,500 feet 10 minutes from the target. At 1120, 40 to 50 Hamps and Zekes were sighted scattered in pairs from 11,000 feet to sea level. The enemy fighters quickly shot down a Mitchell before the Lightnings could intercept, and then they evaded into the safety of the clouds and down at water level over the harbor.

Cragg led the first flight into the combat and managed to get several undetermined hits on one of the Zeros before it went into the clouds. Cragg then attacked several Hamps without success before he saw a climbing Hamp. Cragg fired a long deflection shot at 30 degrees, and the enemy trailed some smoke as it crash landed on Rapopo Strip. Cragg followed it down, debating whether to strafe it, when he saw another Hamp heading for the clouds and climbed and fired without result before it entered the clouds. Cragg turned and made an attack on a Hamp that was in a shallow dive. He fired a long burst that tore pieces off the enemy fighter's port wing. The enemy pilot bailed out just as Cragg was attacked from behind by a Zero. Cragg's fighter was hit in its starboard boom, Prestone cooler, and elevator, as well as through his window, putting glass shards and metal pieces into his arm. Cragg outdistanced his pursuer and then had to feather his right prop due to coolant loss. The Japanese pilot caught up to Cragg and chased him for the next 15 minutes, but Cragg was able to evade seven passes before the Zero peeled away. Cragg joined B-25s that covered him on the way back home, where he celebrated a dozen total victories. F/O Willis Evers was flying as Cragg's Wingman and followed Cragg during his attacks, finally firing a long burst on a Hamp and sending it down in flames. As Evers was protecting Cragg's rear he was attacked from the rear and dove into a cloud to escape, but as he emerged from the cloud he was attacked by another Hamp and had to duck into the cloud again. As Evers emerged from hiding, tracers flew by his fighter and he escaped into the clouds again. When he emerged Evers saw that his rear was clear and joined a lone P-38 flying three miles away. The two made several ineffective passes, but Evers lost his new partner and then joined several other P-38s and proceeded to Kiriwina to refuel. 1Lt. Harrison Freeman was Cragg's second Element Leader, with 2Lt. Vernon Jenner as his Wingman. The two followed Cragg and Evers through the initial passes before they became separated. Freeman saw a Zero get on Evers' tail about 1,000 feet below and dove and fired a long burst that sent it exploding into the ground. Freeman and Evers then lost the lead element and ran into a lone Zero. Freeman maneuvered into a

1Lt. Jay T. **Robbins** after getting four victories and two probable to make him a double ace with 11 victories. (AAF)

1Lt. Harrison **Freeman** scored the last two of four victories. (AAF)

1Lt. Cornelius **Smith** shot down a Zero to become an ace. (AFAA)

Maj. Edward **Cragg's** P-38 "Porky" before scoring his 11th and 12th victories. (AAF)

LEFT: After hitting a Zero for a probable, 1Lt. Paul **Larson's** fighter was hit and he nursed it back safely to Kiriwina. (AAF) MIDDLE: 1Lt. Ralph **Bills** damaged three Zeros and ended his career with two victories, two probables and five damaged. (AAF) RIGHT: 1Lt. James **Walters** shot down his second and last enemy aircraft of the war. (AAF)

good tail shot, but as he fired the Zero made a turn and Freeman followed, firing a 90 degree deflection shot. Jenner also fired at the Zero, but had to stop when Freeman flew into his sights. Freeman fired again and tore off large pieces of the enemy's tail and wings. Freeman and Jenner broke off the combat as they were greatly outnumbered and headed home.

1Lt. Jay T. Robbins was leading the third flight, but moved up as second flight leader after the four aborts. 2Lt. William Caldwell was Robbins' Wingman, and ex-night fighter pilot 1Lt. Burnell Adams and his Wingman 2Lt. Jess Corallo completed this flight. As they arrived near Kabanga Bay they saw Hamps shoot down a B-25 before they could intercept. Robbins and Corallo got on the tail of a Hamp, and Robbins scored some hits and chased the wounded enemy fighter through a cloud and lost the Hamp (a probable). Robbins rejoined Corallo and Adams just as another Hamp was seen flying only 300 feet above the water. Robbins fired first and flamed the Hamp, which went down into the Bay. Robbins got his second definite victory during a head on pass at a Hamp that looked as if it was going to ram him. Robbins fired a quick accurate burst that sent it rolling over in flames toward the water. Robbins made another deflection firing pass and got hits but saw no results. He then shot down a third Hamp on a 30 degree deflection shot from the rear that tore its entire wing off and started it on fire. Robbins, Adams, and Corallo pursued another Hamp, and all three fired at once. At the debriefing the other two pilots did not claim the Hamp, and Robbins was credited with the victory to give him eight in his last two missions (on 9 September) and 11 total. Adams and Corallo made several firing passes but missed, and Adams became separated from Corallo and Robbins. A Hamp got on Adams' tail, which he lost by evading into the clouds. When he emerged from the cloud Adams came upon Wingman Corallo, and the two went after another Hamp. Adams looked behind to clear his tail and saw a fighter which he took to be his Wingman and fired a deflection shot that set the Hamp on fire. But then gunfire from behind–from a Hamp, not Corallo–shattered the rear of his canopy and shut down his port engine. Adams dove into a convenient cloud, but the skilled enemy pilot followed and continued to hit Adam's Lightning in the cloud. Adams flew in the cloud for as long as possible, and when he exited the cloud Adams had lost his pursuer and feathered his port engine. Then he found that his radio was inoperable, and his coolant and oil systems were damaged, but fortunately, other P-38s arrived to escort his badly damaged fighter back to base. When Adams tried to operate the flaps or landing gear he found the hydraulics were out, and once he arrived at Kiriwina he had to fly around the island for half an hour to use up fuel before attempting a crash landing. He finally made a successful wheels up landing on the strip.

Meanwhile, 1Lt. Cornelius Smith and his Wingman, 2Lt. Paul Murphey, followed Robbins down to cover him and missed one Hamp that went into a cloud. When it emerged Murphey fired a short burst and did not see any results until he looked back and saw it explode before entering another cloud. After they had been in combat for about a half hour Murphey radioed Smith that he was running low on fuel, and they escorted a crippled 39FS Lightning and several B-25s from the battle. When Smith landed he learned that mission debriefing determined that one of the Zeros he had attacked was seen to crash to make him an ace.

35FG/39FS

Capt. Charles King led 16 P-38s on their cover for a B-25 low level mission over Rabaul. Just as the Mitchells crossed the New Britain shore King spotted four or five Zeros flying very low in front of the bombers. As King started to dive P-38s from another squadron interfered, and King led his squadron around some clouds in front of the bombers, where he saw a lone Oscar at about 1,500 feet. King closed from 300 yards to 75 yards when the Zero turned sharply left, and Wingman 1Lt. Gordon Prentice now got a three second, 60+ degree deflection shot. The Zero was set on fire and its pilot bailed out.

When his drop tanks failed to release, Flight Leader 1Lt. Harvey Dunbar had to turn back with his Wingman, leaving second Element Leader 1Lt. Howard Round and his Wingman, 1Lt. James Walters, to fend for themselves. They tagged onto Capt. Ralph Bills' flight over Rapopo Airstrip, where a number of Zeros were seen at 3,000 feet overhead. Round saw a lone Oscar closing from 12 o'clock high on a P-38 and fired ahead of it from out of range and the Oscar turned away. Round fired a deflection shot from 150 yards and the enemy pilot turned sharply and passed under the P-38. As Round turned after it he saw flames and a long plume of smoke trailing behind. Round caught up with Walters, and the two were attacked by six enemy fighters diving from 6 o'clock high. The two Americans dove and skidded, but Round's wing was hit and he dove hard right and lost three of his pursuers. As Round rejoined Walters, the other three Oscars dove from 5 o'clock high, followed by two more enemy elements that Split-S'd. Round dove to 900 feet above St. George's Channel and saw 30 enemy fighters milling above. Although his port engine intercooler was shot out, he was able to outrun the last Oscars. Round was alone, and looked for friendly fighters to escort him back to base. He saw a four plane Lufbery that looked like P-38s, but as he approached he saw they were Japanese and turned without being followed. Soon his right intercooler light came on and he had to feather his right engine and fly on the damaged left engine. He joined some B-25s and landed safely at Kiriwina with his first and only victory of the war. After Round's fighter was damaged Walters became separated and joined three P-38s that were covering B-25s. They saw a lone Zero at 3 o'clock, slightly below and just past Cape Gazelle. The Flight Leader dove first and used all his ammunition and left. The second P-38 dove but missed and turned away. Walters then closed and fired into the cockpit, and after several small explosions the pilot bailed out.

1Lt. Harvey Widmann and Wingman 1Lt. Paul Larson encountered five enemy fighters, and in the following dogfight Widmann fired at one and smoke was seen from the top of the engine for a damaged claim, while Larson got hits on a Hamp for a probable. Larson called that there was a Zero firing on his tail and Widmann fired a hurried burst that scared the enemy away. Larson's port engine and boom were hit, but after feathering the damaged engine he nursed his fighter safely back to Kiriwina. In the meantime, Widmann looked back and saw three fighters on his tail and dove and lost his pursuers over Rapopo. While climbing back over Rapopo, Widmann saw a lone Zero being chased by three Lightnings and he "horned in." As Widmann started his pass the Zero turned away and exposed its belly. Widmann fired and hit the Zero's belly and engine, and it burst into flames. Widmann had to avert a collision with the other disgruntled P-38s with a quick turn. Widmann climbed and joined a P-38 from the 80FS, and the two made five or six passes over Rapopo at Zero pilots who "seemed experienced in evasive tactics…." During one of his passes he got a short full deflection shot that damaged the cockpit area.

The 39FS also had three probables (Larson, Dunbar, and 1Lt. William Anderson) and five damaged (two by Widmann and three by 1Lt. Ralph Bills) in the battle.

475FG/431FS/432FS/433FS

At 0830, 18 P-38s of the 433FS led by Capt. Daniel Roberts and 19 of the 432FS led by Maj. Frank Tomkins took off, but before they reached the target area three 432FS P-38s and another from the 433FS aborted with mechanical problems. The 431FS, led by Capt. Harry Brown, took off at the same time with 10 P-38s, and one of those turned back with generator difficulties. Another bad omen occurred when a B-25 landed in the water near Buna. As the bombers closed on the New Britain coast near the southern end of the Gazelle peninsula, enemy AA gunners opened fire but were unable to hit any of the fast, low flying Mitchells or Lightnings. However, the element of low level surprise was now lost as they continued toward the eastern end of Blanche Bay on their approach to Rabaul. Once over the target the three 475th Squadrons deployed themselves, with the 432nd and 433rd on each flank of the bomber formation and the 431st as top cover. The bombers were in close contact with the three squadrons and made a large circle around Wide Bay to avoid enemy spotter stations, then approached from due north from the Warangoi River. In order to avoid enemy radar, the entire approach was made at less than 4,000 feet. Approximately 25 mixed enemy fighters were scattered from 6,000 to 14,000 feet as the bombers and P-38s approached the target.

431FS

Capt. Harry Brown led 10 P-38s that took off from Dobodura #12 at 0830 and rendezvoused with two B-25 squadrons over Oro Bay at 0915. They proceeded to drop their tanks over the Warangoi River and rapidly climbed to 8,000 feet in anticipation of enemy interception. At 1110, while nine (one aborted) 432FS P-38s were climbing still higher, about 25 to 30 Zeros, Oscars, and a few Tonys scattered at over 20,000 feet were sighted flying above on the approach to the target. A Zero rapidly crossed in front of Brown, who took a quick but ineffective burst at it. Another Zero was an easy target for Brown, who set it on fire, and the Zero rolled over slowly and exploded just before it plunged through the cloud layer below. Brown's Wingman, 2Lt. John Cohn, confirmed the victory. The victory was Brown's sixth and last of the war. He had scored two P-40 victories over Pearl Harbor with the 47FS; one P-38 victory with the 9FS; and three P-38 victories with the 431FS. Although Brown, Cohn, and the Red second element of 1Lt. Paul Morriss and Wingman 2Lt. Kenneth Richardson all saw the 25 enemy fighters above, these fighters "made no attempt to come down on us and we left them alone."

As White Flight Leader 1Lt. William O'Brien ordered tanks to be dropped his second Element Leader radioed that he was unable to drop his tank and left the flight with his Wingman. O'Brien and his Wingman, 2Lt. Fredric Champlin, made a few ineffective passes before the two joined Brown's Red Flight without seeing any more combat.

Blue Flight, led by Capt. Warren Lewis, leveled off over Red and White Flights at 15,000 feet, but were called down to help out. As Lewis descended he got on the tail of a Zero and followed it down as its pilot Split-S'd, firing "five good bursts" that caused it to smoke and one of its wheels to drop for a probable claim. Lewis' Wingman, 1Lt. John Lent, followed Lewis down in his attack and found two Zeros on his tail that were being chased by another Lightning element, which itself was being chased by three Zeros. Lewis and Lent went into a steep dive and shook off the pursuing Zeros at 12,000 feet. As they climbed for altitude Lewis fired on another Zero, seeing no results. Lent's engine began to run roughly, and he radioed Lewis that he was leaving for Dobodura. As Lent turned for home he was attacked by a Zero that flew slow rolls on Lent's tail and fired some bursts that missed. Soon Lent encountered a Tony that flew directly in front of him, and he fired two short bursts from 60 to 90 degrees; pieces flew off its tail section, and it trailed a small wisp of smoke from its engine. Lent could not follow it due to his right rough engine, but a B-25 pilot from the 501st Bomb Squadron confirmed the victory. Lent's two victories made him an ace with six.

433FS

The escorting 432nd (leading the bombers) and 433rd (protecting the rear) met the brunt of the enemy interception. Eighteen of Roberts' P-38s were over Tobera Airfield at 5,000 to 6,000 feet when they were intercepted by an estimated 40 to 50 Oscars, Tonys, and Zekes. Roberts led his well disciplined Squadron down to 3,000 feet, where they peeled off in flights and elements to attack the enemy fighters that were now scattered or had been driven down from above between Vunakanau and Rapopo airfields. Roberts fired a long burst on the tail of a diving Zero that began to burn and then crashed and exploded about midway between Vunakanau and Tobera. Roberts' 12th victory put him only one victory behind the hospitalized Tom McGuire, who was top ace of the 475FG with 13 victories. After Element Leader 2Lt. Clarence Rieman turned back with fuel problems, 2Lt. Stanley Northrup, the third pilot in the lead flight, took over the element lead. Robert's #4 man, 2Lt. Herbert Cochrane, followed as Roberts chased a Zero, and when it turned sharply to port, Cochrane got inside the turn and got off a short one second burst at 100 yards and 70 degrees deflection. The Zero burst into flames, went into a steep dive, and crashed into the ground. A Zero came head on into the flight, passing under Roberts, and 2Lt. James Malloy began firing from 300 to 50 yards. "Pieces started flying off from nose to tail, practically stripping the underside of the Zero." The P-38s had problems maintaining enough speed to "do good work" against the enemy fighters that were constantly overhead. The Squadron stayed together and retreated back toward the Harbor, where they reengaged the enemy at 10,000 feet. Malloy made three unsuccessful passes and turned into a fourth Zero with a head on 90 degree deflection shot that caused heavy smoke and pieces to break off,but Malloy did not see any final results and was credited with a probable.

Clockwise from Upper Left:

Capt. Daniel **Roberts** led the 433FS and shot down a Zero to give his a dozen victories. (AAF)

2Lt. Donald **King** after shooting down two fighters for the middle two of his four victories. (AAF)

2Lt. Herbert **Cochrane** claimed his first of two victories. (AAF)

2Lt. Calvin **Wire** shot down two Zeros to become an ace. (AFAA)

2Lt. Jack **Fisk**. (L), with 2Lt. Clarence Rieman, shot down the third of seven victories. (AAF)

In the initial engagement, 2Lt. Donald King and Wingman 2Lt. Calvin Wire saw a Zero coming in on their left and broke off in a dive after it. King was unable to get the Zero in his sights and Wire closed to 200 yards. As it pulled up he fired a two second burst from about 80 degrees, hitting its right wing and causing pieces to fall off, then it crashed into the ground. Wire then saw King chasing a Zero, but King also had another Zero on his tail. Wire went after King's pursuer, and it rolled away to port to escape. Wire fired a long burst and the enemy plane exploded, shearing off a wing to make Wire an ace. As King pulled up to starboard a Zero began firing at him from far out of range. King waited and fired at 300 yards, and smoke began to pour out of the enemy's engine. The Zero rolled so close to King's fighter that he thought that it "brushed" him and spattered his windshield with oil. After King rejoined his flight and began to climb toward the Harbor, an Oscar came in from the side and King turned into it. The enemy pilot half rolled away and King Split-S'd and closed directly behind it and fired a two second burst that hit its cockpit and shattered its canopy. The Oscar plunged straight into the ground and exploded. When King pulled up and was about to enter a cloud he saw a Zero directly behind him. When they exited the cloud the Zero was in front of King, who fired two rounds before his guns quit and he had to return home.

1Lt. John Babel and Wingman 2Lt. Jack Fisk met an Oscar head on, and it rolled over on its back and fired, with its tracers passing just over Babel's wing. Babel fired but undershot, and Fisk pulled above Babel and closed to 25 yards, firing shots that hit its engine. The stricken Oscar half rolled between Babel and Fisk and burst into flames, then dove into the ground. The two made an unsuccessful pass at a Zero that climbed away at 3 o'clock high and then turned hard to port. Babel followed and fired a long burst at 50 degrees deflection, and he saw his tracers hit the Zero's port wing and fuselage at the cockpit. The Zero immediately began to smoke, caught fire, and dove into the sea from 1,500 feet. As he returned to his flight

Babel chased two Zeros off the tails of two P-38s and started one smoking, but it did not catch fire and Babel listed it as a probable.

1Lt. Charles Grice was flying on Flight Leader 1Lt. William Horton's wing in a Lufbery Circle and made three passes on Zeros without result. On his fourth pass, Grice came into range on a Zero that slow rolled and pulled up when tracers appeared over Grice's starboard wing from 2Lt. Walter Reinhardt's guns. Reinhardt's ICR states that his tracers hit the Zero, but that "Grice beat me to it," because as the Zero pulled up, Grice fired three cannon shells into its cockpit which exploded, but the enemy pilot somehow managed to bail out. Grice made a pass at the descending Japanese pilot but decided not to shoot.

432FS

Sixteen 432FS P-38s led by Maj. Frank Tomkins crossed Wide Bay at 3,000 feet and headed for Rapopo Airfield, on the northwestern end of the Gazelle Peninsula. Fifty Japanese interceptors were alerted and had the advantage of altitude and cloud cover as the 432FS approached. At 1140 Maj. Tomkins ordered tanks dropped, but his own wouldn't release, and he and his Wingman left the flight. His second element, 1Lt. Elliott Summer and 2Lt. Raymond Krantz, joined Capt. Frederick Harris' Clover White Flight.

While Summer was climbing at 8,000 feet behind Clover White Flight, he spotted a slowly rolling Oscar at about 2,000 feet below. Summer Split-S'd on top of the Oscar and fired a three second burst that tore off the enemy's port wing, sending it into a violent spin. During the pullout Summer blacked out with his fingers squeezing the triggers, exhausting his ammunition before he recovered, and continued his escort of the Mitchells for the rest of the mission.

The 6/10 cloud cover made it very difficult for the P-38s to keep the Mitchells in sight. To protect the B-25s, Harris had decided to climb quickly in close formation to intercept the enemy fighters above them before they attacked the bombers. As Harris' Lightnings climbed the Japanese Split-S'd on the P-38s above them, and when Harris reached 10,000 feet the Japanese began to attack his flight. Harris engaged and made several good firing passes before he dove on the tail of a Zero and sent it down for his eighth and last victory of the war. On his next pass Harris fired a long 30 degree deflection shot that hit the Zero's cockpit and wings, but it disappeared into the clouds for a probable claim. Wingman 2Lt. Zach Dean stayed close to Harris, and just after Harris got his victory Dean saw a Zero diving and pulled up, firing a long burst and hitting its engine with fatal shots. Another Zero then tried to ram Dean, but 2Lt. Donald Willis warned Dean, who evaded. The Zero then turned around for another attempt to ram. This time Dean was ready and raked the charging Zero, which spun into the ground to make Dean an ace. Dean's port engine began to misfire and he feathered it, and as he did he joined 2Lt. James Farris, whose port engine was out; the two left for Kiriwina. On the way back to base Capt. Harris came upon a P-38 of the 39FS with an engine feathered and escorted it safely back to Kiriwina.

2Lt. Billy **Gresham** shot down a Zero to become an ace. (AFAA)

2Lts. Billy Gresham and James Farris climbed and joined the 431FS as top cover. Soon they dove into an attack, but as they did six enemy fighters dove out of the clouds and got on their tails. Farris made a steep starboard dive that caused Gresham on his right to pull up steeply to avoid Farris. The Japanese split up, and three went after Farris and three after Gresham. Gresham saw Farris' engine begin to smoke and last saw him dive away, thinking he had been shot down. Gresham escaped the Zeros and made a few unsuccessful passes before he approached a Zero that was on the tail of a P-38, and as Gresham closed the Zero broke off and dove through a cloud. The Zero pilot exited the cloud, thinking he had lost Gresham, who was only 50 yards behind. The enemy pilot tried to gain altitude in a roll and steep climb as Gresham fired a few short bursts to get a lead. The Zero eventually stalled out, and Gresham fired a three second cannon burst that shattered the cowling and pieces flew off the tail assembly. The Zero rolled and went into a vertical dive from which it did not recover. Three more Zeros dove on Gresham, who used maximum power to escape. Gresham got one more good tail shot on a Zero and saw white vapor trail behind it, but made no claim and returned to Kiriwina as an ace.

1Lt. Grover Gholson, leading Clover Blue Flight, made an initial 90 degree deflection shot at an Oscar without seeing any hits, as he "was busy keeping Zeros off his tail." Gholson's Element Leader took a deflection shot at an Oscar that then pulled up into Gholson's sights. He fired at the Oscar, which smoked and crashed in the woods southwest of Tobera.

2Lt. Clifford Mann lost his Element Leader, but latched onto another lone P-38 and they flew as an element. Mann made several unsuccessful passes before taking a good shot at a Zero that began to smoke badly, but Mann lost sight of it when it flew into a cloud for a probable.

475FG Totals

The 475th was credited with 17 of the day's 40 victories over Rabaul, with the 433FS scoring 10 victories, the 432FS six, and the 431FS only one. The only casualty was 2Lt. Eugene McGuire of the 432nd, who safely crash landed his damaged P-38 at Kiriwina.

24 October 1943: New Guinea: 49FG/7FS

While the 9FS was over Rabaul, the 7FS attacked enemy positions on the Huon Peninsula. While strafing barges south of Madang, 1Lt. Daniel David was hit by ground fire. David attempted a belly landing on a sandbar on the Waffir River, but his fighter crashed and the injured pilot crawled from the wreck and was rescued by a L-5. He was hospitalized at Oro Bay and returned to the States. For David, who had downed two Haps on 21 September, the trauma changed his life, as he never flew again. After the war he changed his name to Rowan and later became famous as the Dan Rowan of Rowan and Martin of the hit TV program "Laugh-In".

25 October 1943: Rabaul 8FG/475FG

The large Japanese fighter base at Lakunai had not yet been attacked, as on two previous occasions heavy bombers were forced to abort their missions due to weather. A successful attack on that airdrome would decrease enemy fighter numbers and make future attacks on other productive targets around Rabaul, especially the shipping in Simpson Harbor, less dangerous. So following the missions of 23 and 24 October, Gen. Whitehead scheduled first a heavy bomber attack against Lakunai and a second coordinated attack on shipping on 25 October.

Although the weather forecasters predicted poor weather, two heavy bomber groups comprised of 61 B-24s took off for Lakunai, to be joined over Kiriwina by 81 P-38s of four fighter squadrons. The mission was preceded by a fighter sweep by two other P-38 squadrons. After the escort rendezvous the weather grew worse, until after 45 minutes the Fighter Commander informed the bombers on the command frequency that the escort was turning back. At that time 11 bombers and 73 P-38s turned back, but apparently the message was not received by the other bombers, as they continued on with eight P-38s led by Maj. Charles MacDonald of the 432FS, who was determined to give the bombers at least some fighter support. The Japanese cruisers and destroyers in the harbor and land-based batteries sent up a heavy AA barrage over the harbor and airdrome. Just as the B-24s reached Lakunai they were intercepted by more than 60 Oscars, Hamps, and Tonys, which began a series of harassing attacks. Only one B-24 was lost over Lakunai, while the Japanese lost 39 fighters in combat to bomber gunners (much too optimistic) and their ground installations had been heavily damaged. Post-attack photos showed that another 21 aircraft were lost on the ground.

8FG/80FS

The 80FS was sent ahead of a B-24 mission to sweep the area south of New Ireland. However, the weather was bad near the target area and the 80th turned back before completing the mission.

475FG/432FS

The 5BC sent out another large attack on the 25th, but the 475FG contributed only a small force of escorts because of the large number of P-38s remaining at Kiriwina or in maintenance. Maj. Charles MacDonald came down from Group HQ to fly with 432nd Clover Squadron. At the 0645 take off he led 14 Lightnings with new ace Zach Dean as his Wingman and 1Lt. Paul Lucas leading the second element of his Clover Red Flight, while 2Lt. Howard Hedrick flew the number four position. Soon after take off, one flight of four P-38s did not rendezvous and one P-38 aborted, leaving McDonald with nine fighters to cover the 43rd and 90th Bomb Groups heading for Lakunai. After 45 minutes the lead P-38 squadron reported that the weather was bad and it was turning back. By this time two more of MacDonald's P-38s had turned back, leaving him with seven Lightnings to escort the B-24s. The weather to the east was bad, and MacDonald climbed to 27,500 feet over the weather. McDonald's P-38s crossed back and forth over the bombers to give them the best possible coverage that his small force could offer. MacDonald had attached his P-38s to the leading bomb squadron, hoping that "the Nips seeing us would be discouraged and perhaps figure that there were lots more of us." The lead bomb group was intercepted off Cape Gazelle by Zeros and Tonys, but MacDonald led his fighters down and scattered the halfhearted enemy interceptors. But soon the bombers called that Zeros were attacking, and the P-38s maneuvered over and around the bombers and again scattered the reluctant enemy fighters before they could press home their attacks on the B-24s. The 432nd stayed over Rabaul for 45 minutes despite heavy flak from ground batteries and warships. Finally, McDonald fired a deflection shot at a Zero that burst into flame and exploded for his fourth victory. All the 432FS' P-38s landed safely at Kiriwina by 1330.

MacDonald describes his action and those of his squadron that certainly saved many B-24s from enemy fighters that day:

"The weather to the east of the target was bad. Rather than let the bombers go on alone I took my seven men very high and covered the lead bomb squadron of the 90th Group, so that the enemy seeing us would be discouraged and perhaps figure there were lots more of us. We figured to be mostly moral support.

"Off Cape Gazelle the lead bombers were intercepted. We made a dive and scared them off. Then all the squadrons began talking at once that they were being hit. We helped them out mostly through scaring the enemy, who weren't too eager. Over Vunakanau I shot a Zeke who burst into flames-witnessed by all the flight and some bomb crews. Flak was terrific over the harbor. We stayed over the target 45 minutes. The flight was attacked on at least two occasions, but we kept weaving and covering the rear men so that none of the attacks were pressed home."

27 October 1943: New Guinea: 49FG/35FG

49FG/7FS

On 27 October, the 7FS at Dobodura was assigned fighter cover over the Huon Peninsula's southern shore, temporarily taking over the 8FS' patrol area while they transferred to Gusap. The Squadron hoped it would see some action after flying routine patrols over southern harbors and airfields. In the late afternoon Capt. Ray Melikian dispatched a scramble from Kalamazoo led by newly promoted Capt. John Benner, who directed seven Wingmen north to rendezvous with 40FS Marilinan P-39s to cover a supply ship convoy approaching Finschhafen. At 1745, Benner led Red Flight Wingman 2Lt. Allen Osborne, Element Leader 1Lt. William Ferris, and Wingman 2Lt. Robert Croft over Finschhafen Village at 10,000 feet. Capt. Arland Stanton led Green Flight Wingman 1Lt. David Germain, Element Leader 1Lt. Duncan Myers, and Wingman 1Lt. Robert DeHaven on a parallel course ten miles off shore. The two Demon flights passed just beyond the beachhead, where Benner climbed another 3,000 feet with his Red Flight to take advantage of the remaining daylight, while Stanton searched a 1,000 feet lower to the west, where he would rejoin with mission leader Benner. After a few minutes nine Lily bombers escorted by 16 Oscars came into view overhead to the north. The 7FS Warhawks and 40FS Airacobras dropped their tanks and climbed, with the faster Warhawks arriving first.

Benner's Red Flight closed on the bombers just as they turned to the west, where they began to drop hundreds of small parachutes, and soon the Americans realized that the parachutes were not bombs, but supplies dropped to the surrounded Japanese troops at Sattelberg. Benner and Wingman Osborne climbed, and both made two passes at Oscars attempting to escape into distant clouds. Benner quickly demolished one from dead astern, while Osborne got a probable after cutting off another Airacobra in the chase. Once the Lilys departed Benner withdrew to reform his flight.

During the initial attack, Ferris and Croft of Red Element also made firing passes at the Oscars. Ferris heavily damaged one, and as he was about to finish off his victim he was attacked by a Tony. The two entered a turning dogfight, but every time Ferris got into firing position the veteran enemy pilot repeatedly avoided each of his firing bursts. At this time DeHaven ran into Red Flight's Ferris, who was having problems with the veteran pilot. After Ferris had completed another head on pass, DeHaven approached in a shallow dive and the enemy pilot tried to escape to the north. DeHaven had the altitude and speed advantage and fired a burst that immediately set the Oscar on fire and its pilot bailed out. Meanwhile, Croft was attacked by an Oscar which was chased off by another P-39.

As Stanton's Green Flight crossed the beach they saw the Lily supply drop and fought their way through the escorts in an attempt to reach them. The ensuing dogfight extended 30 miles inland, with Element Leader Myers and Wingman DeHaven each claiming a Hamp, while Germain heavily damaged another. Germain then joined Stanton in a head on attack against a straggling Lily, and Germain attacked from under and behind, riddling the bomber. Germain made a second climbing pass from rear right quarter and set it on fire, sliding into a shallow port turn and drifting down into an impressive explosion in the forest. Green Flight then reformed and headed south.

Melikian's 7FS continued to fly missions over the southern Huon Peninsula, but by the first week in November the Japanese had abandoned the area. As the air war moved to the northwest into the Ramu River Valley, the Screamin' Demons continued to fly their tedious defensive patrols over the southern half of the Markham Valley without meeting any enemy attacks against the new 5AF HQ at Nadzab. Melikian's pilots could only look forward to the time that their new base would be ready somewhere to the north.

35FG/40FS

Eight P-39s of the 40FS took off in two flights (Blue and White) from Tsili Tsili on a late afternoon local area patrol and barge cover over Finschhafen. Blue Flight consisted of Flight Leader 1Lt. John Clapper and Wingman 2Lt. Nathan Smith, and second Element Leader 1Lt. John Young and Wingman 1Lt. Robert Allison. White Flight consisted of Flight Leader 1Lt. Edwin Schneider and second Element Leader 1Lt. Carl Nelson and Wingman 1Lt. Philip Wolf.

At 1730, *Rex* Controller called in 12 enemy bombers escorted by 16 fighters at 15,000 feet from the northwest. Clapper's Blue Flights were patrolling over Langemac Bay, one flight at 9,500 feet and the other at 11,000 feet, and were joined by eight P-40s ("Pinkys") of the 7FS/49FG. Clapper led his P-39s to the vector and saw nine bombers at 8,000 feet almost to Sattelberg. Once there they dropped 100-150 supply parachutes, after which they made a sharp 180 degree turn in a shallow dive to gain speed. At this time 10 Zeros appeared at 9,000 feet in loose formation. Clapper called out the bombers covered by fighters at 11 o'clock, while Schneider's White Flight called them out at 2 o'clock but without fighter escort. At the time this was confusing, until it was later determined that there were two flights of bombers. Blue Flight would attack the nine bomber flight, while White Flight would attack the 10 bomber flight.

At 1730, Clapper led Blue Flight in a steep dive from 9,000 feet and caught the nine bombers near Zankoa approaching to port and slightly above at 6,000 feet in three, three ship shallow Vs with about 20 fighters lurking at 13,000 feet. Clapper initiated his attack on the bomber's left element at 350mph at 7 to 8 o'clock and fired at the first two, getting hits. He then fired a concentrated burst at the third bomber from the left and hit the fuel tanks in its left wing and it dropped away in flames. As Clapper broke, Wingman Smith made a long range pass from 7 o'clock at the bomber on the left end of the formation and then raked the second and third bombers, which Clapper had fired on. Smith then concentrated his fire on the fourth bomber, which caught fire. As these two 7FS pilots completed their passes on the bombers the enemy fighters closed on the Airacobras. During his attack Smith's starboard wing was hit and his aileron controls were destroyed, and he spiraled out of the fight. Clapper then saw a Tony firing at him from 5 o'clock, but was not hit, as the enemy pilot misjudged his lead on the fast flying Airacobra. After he finally eluded the Tony, Clapper climbed back into the battle above and saw that Smith had regained control of his damaged fighter and escorted him out of the battle.

Meanwhile, Young and Allison had followed Clapper and Smith during their pass on the bombers, but were attacked by the enemy fighters before they could fire on the bombers. Young and Allison turned into the enemy fighters, and Young chased one that was closing on Clapper and Smith. He fired a several second burst at one from very close range but was unable to observe the results (damaged claim), as he had to escape two Zeros on his tail. Young dove steeply to escape and the Zeros did not pursue, so Young climbed back to 10,000 feet. Young saw 12 enemy fighters below flying between him and the bombers below them. Young made several attempts to break through to the bombers or pick off a Zero, but each time was rebuffed when several Zeros got on his tail. Young was getting low on fuel, so he joined a P-40 and returned to base. Allison had fired a long burst at the leading Zero and continued firing through his turn at the second Zero, but observed no damage to either. As he continued his right climbing turn toward the enemy fighters an Oscar came in at right angles to his flight line and Allison fired at point blank range for a victory claim. When Allison looked behind he saw two Zeros firing on him with two more behind them. Allison full throttled straight down, and when he pulled out at 7,000 feet the Zeros were gone. Allison climbed toward a swarm of enemy fighters at 12,000 feet and joined some P-40s that were about to attack a lone Lily bomber. Allison came in first from 10 o'clock and well above and fired a long burst that killed the Lily's gunner. Two P-40s came in and finished off the bomber, which was in flames from the cockpit back. Allison reported in his ICR: "Whether the fire started from my passes or the P-40s. I could not say," but he was given credit for a probable. As Allison turned toward home he saw a Tony zoom by on his right and began to turn into it, but had second thoughts and dove toward some clouds, "offering a little prayer, snuggling behind the armor plate, and gave it full throttle." As he looked back he saw the Tony firing from 150 yards astern and thought "this was it." The clouds had mountain tops poking through them, but Allison was "resigned….that it would be better to splatter myself all over the mountain than to let him shoot me. Fortunately, the clouds weren't stuffed and when I popped out of them 10 miles later, the Jap was gone."

1Lt. Edwin Schneider's White Flight was following above Blue Flight at 11,000 feet when *Rex* called, sending him climbing to 15,000 feet. They spotted the (second) enemy bomber formation 7,000 feet below and 20 miles ahead at about 2 o'clock without fighter cover. White Flight had a difficult time, but finally caught up with the nine Lilys flying in three ship elements almost line abreast in a shallow dive with a lone Betty straggling behind. The bombers were difficult to see against the trees below and in the haze and bad light. Schneider started a rear quarter pass that ended as a tail pass due to the P-39's slow rate of closure on the fast Lilys. Schneider fired a very long seven second burst into the middle Lily and blew off its left engine, setting its left wing on fire. Schneider then moved over to the right Lily and fired a four second burst that caused hits, but the bomber did not burn for a damaged claim. He broke away to the right and pulled up on three Lilys from the rear and somewhat above. He fired a long burst on the center Lily and it flew away smoking heavily but did not burn for a probable. As he broke away his engine began to vibrate, and he thought his prop had been hit by the Lily's rear turret gunners, who had fired at the White flight on most of their passes. As Schneider pulled up he saw Wolf behind him make several tail passes at a straggling Lily at 2,000 feet and send it crashing near a reef, 100 feet offshore. Wolf was low on ammunition (he had made several unsuccessful firing passes previous to this Lily victory), and returned toward base with his antenna shot off. At this time Nelson, who made a successful 400 yard firing pass at an initial Lily that caused hits but was not confirmed, moved onto the straggling Betty. He made two four second front quarter shots and put it down into the water, then headed from the battle out of ammunition. Schneider made another pass at two Lilys and put a five second burst into one of them, but it too did not smoke for another damaged claim. As Schneider pulled up he saw Wolf climb on the tail of his Lily victory. The White Flight was widely separated after the combat and returned to base individually. The P-39s of the 40th had again more than held their own with a total of six enemy aircraft destroyed, five probables, and three damaged for no losses.

29 October: Rabaul 35FG/49FG/475FG/8FG

After the Lakunai attack, Gen. Whitehead had planned to have the First Air Task Force carry out a low level anti-shipping mission on Rabaul, but again the weather proved to be an intervening factor. On 26 October, 82 B-25s took off, but a weather front over Kiriwina prevented the fighter cover from taking off, and all the B-25s returned to base. For the next three days no large daylight attacks were sent to New Britain, but Gen. Whitehead's proposal to send night attacks on New Ireland was being put into effect, as the RAAF had already been carrying out numerous missions from Kiriwina.

The interruption of the Rabaul offensive had given the Japanese an opportunity to repair most of the previous damage to their airfields and reorganize their AA defenses. Japanese documents record that 75 interceptors were sent up that day. Whitehead decided to strike the airdromes again with heavy bombers, rather than to risk the B-25 strafers on low level attacks on shipping. It was not until 29 October that the First Air Task Force was able to renew the Rabaul offensive, and even then the weather report was not very good. Nonetheless, the attack on Vunakanau Airdrome proved to be routine and quite successful, as the 46 B-24s destroyed runways and revetments and 18 aircraft on the ground. However, there was confusion on the part of the escorts, as the 39FS never made contact with the bombers over Kiriwina and the 431FS was assigned top cover, and on rendezvous found other P-38s flying above it. The bomber gunners and fighter escort pilots found that enemy interceptors were numerous but not especially effective. It seemed obvious that less experienced Japanese pilots were being sent in as replacements, and that "the eager pilots were not experienced and the experienced not eager." B-24 gunners destroyed seven enemy fighters, while fighter pilots shot down 18 more, though one P-38 and its pilot (2Lt. Christopher Bartlett/475FG) failed to return.

35FG/39FS

Squadron CO Maj. Charles King led 14 39FS Lightnings on a fighter sweep to arrive five minutes before the bombers began their run. As they crossed Tobera Island and headed over Vunakanau at 23,000 feet they saw 20+ single seat fighters to the east at the same altitude. King closed on the last four or five fighters and went after one that turned out of the formation. He fired several bursts in a dive from 15 to 20 degrees and then followed in a shallow climb and fired at 30 yards into its wing root, opening a large hole, and the Zero spun into the ground. King climbed back up into the battle and made a few unsuccessful passes. On "about" his fifth pass an Oscar made a snap roll directly in front of King and the American followed to 100 yards and fired when the enemy pilot went into a barrel roll and burst into flames. King made a final pass at an enemy fighter, but his guns ran out of ammunition after firing only 10 rounds. With his engine beginning to run rough, he joined his Wingman to return to base. The two victories were King's last of the war, but made him an ace. King's Wingman, 1Lt. Gordon Prentice, followed King out of his first pass when they were chased by enemy fighters. On King's second pass his quarry made a quick right turn, giving Prentice an open shot, but despite having only a cannon and one .50 caliber working he exploded the Oscar. The rest of the squadron added three Zeke probables (1Lt. Lloyd Shipley and 2Lts. Lewis Lockhart and Leland Vining) and a damaged (2Lt. George Morgan).

49FG/9FS

Although Capt. Gerald Johnson's Squadron had flown every day in the mission rotation, they had not seen aerial combat since the low level raid on Tobera on the 23rd. For this mission the Knights' role was changed from close escort over Cape Gazelle to their first sortie to Rabaul proper. Capt. William Haney was the Mission Leader as the Knights staged through Kiriwina to join the B-24 strike force and continued on schedule over Cape Gazelle, turning to the west-northwest to their bomb line for the shipping in Simpson Harbor. Haney's three flights were stacked between 20,000 to 22,000 feet in a clear sky when they were attacked by "hordes of fighters." All P-38s except Blue Element Wingman 2Lt. Glade Hill dropped their tanks and dove en masse into the enemy fighters.

Without Hill, Haney led Blue Flight with Element Leader 1Lt. John O'Neill and Wingman 2Lt. John McLean toward the enemy fighters. Hill finally rocked his tanks free, only to find his starboard supercharger did not run at full power; nonetheless, he joined the flight, following several seconds to the rear. The four Blue elements dove on the JNAF fighters from 18,000 feet and made two firing passes during their 400mph descent to the deck. Ace John O'Neill shot down two Zeros for his seventh and eighth victories and the last victories of his tour.

Capt. Richard Bong's Red Flight, missing an aborted Wingman, chased their targets down to the hilltops to the west of Simpson Harbor, where Bong battered a Zero in a shallow diving head on firing pass. Bong Wingman 2Lt. George Haniotis damaged another Zero as he frantically tried to stay with Bong, who raced after the escaping enemy. As he pursued north to Open Bay, the top ace in the Pacific shot down his 19th enemy plane in flames into the Bay.

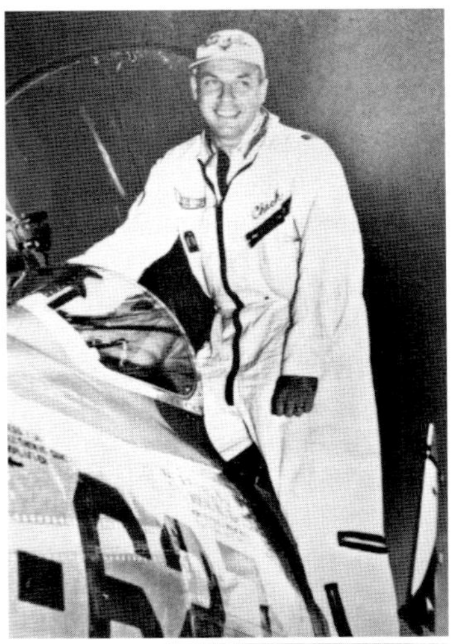

King flying F-86s with the 4th Interceptor Wing during the Korean War. (AFAA)

Maj. Charles **King** shot down a Zero and Oscar to become an ace. (AFAA)

1Lt. John **O'Neill** shot down two Zeros to give him eight victories total. (AFAA)

Capt. Richard **Bong** after becoming a quadruple ace AAF)

2Lt. Herbert **Cochrane** ended the war with two victories. (AAF)

Capt. Daniel **Roberts** scored his 13th victory. (AAF)

From their high trailing position at 22,000 feet, Yellow Flight was the last Knight Flight to enter into the dogfight. Flight Leader 1Lt. Charles Ralph dove with Wingman 2Lt. Raymond Swift, Element Leader 1Lt. George Alber, and Wingman 1Lt. John Stowe. Ralph and Swift each downed a Zero, while Alber and Stowe were briefly diverted by flak over the harbor's western shore; the two regrouped and flew south to find the rest of the Knights. Soon a solo Zero suddenly appeared from the haze over the mountains and hit trailing Yellow Wingman Stowe's P-38 with 20mm cannon and 7mm machine gun rounds that exploded in his starboard nacelle. Stowe was not wounded and flew his damaged fighter into the clouds along the south coast. When Stowe safely landed at Kiriwina his Lightning was written off, and the Flying Knights had only 12 war weary fighters operational.

475FG/431FS/432FS/433FS
At 0700, during the morning the weather was foggy at Dobodura when 44 Lightnings of the 475FG took off to escort B-24s to Rabaul.

431FS
At 1215, the 431FS was the first to arrive over the target with 13 P-38s, and was first into action in deflecting several enemy attacks on the bombers. While they were successful in keeping the enemy away from the bombers, they did not shoot any down and suffered two casualties. 2Lt. Paul Smith was bounced by a Tony that dove out of a Lufbery and hit Smith's Lightning. Smith dove his smoking fighter to safety and then surveyed the damage. He found that his port engine and radio were not functioning, and his canopy and gas tank were holed, and he had suffered numerous cuts about his head and neck. He tried to leave the combat, but found two Tonys and three Zeros on his tail and headed for the nearest clouds. He had just entered them when his starboard supercharger cut out and started on fire. By slipping back and forth he was able to put out the fire. As he tried to retreat toward home he was chased back into the clouds twice by enemy fighters, but when he finally sneaked out of the clouds he had missed Kiriwina and found his way to Goodenough Island, where he landed with about five gallons of fuel remaining. 2Lt. Robert Cline returned to Dobodura with 30 holes in his fighter but was uninjured. Capt. Harry Brown's starboard engine failed, and he limped back to base on one engine. 1Lt. William O'Brien's fuel pump went out and he had to return to base early.

433FS
Capt. Daniel Roberts led four flights of 15 P-38s on a mid-day escort of three B-24 Squadrons to Vunakanau. As the Liberators began their run over the target area at 1225, Roberts' Squadron provided top cover for them at 25,000 to 28,000 feet. Just as the B-24s were withdrawing an estimated 30 to 40 Zeros, Oscars, and Tonys were at 18,000 feet, engaging P-38s of the 39th and 80th Fighter Squadrons. Roberts and his Wingman, 2Lt. Herbert Cochran, dove on the Zeros, which turned away and took refuge in clouds that ranged from between 12,000 and down to 3,000 feet; they then left the clouds to make individual attacks on the bombers. Roberts waited, and when one of the Zeros left the clouds he closed to within 50 yards and fired a 20 degree deflection shot from astern that sent the enemy fighter plunging in flames. Roberts fired at another Zero and started a fire, and as it dove away, Roberts' Wingman Cochran made a frontal attack on it, firing from 60 degrees, and it burst into flames that immediately died out. Cochran followed it down to 4,000 feet and saw it smoking heavily with two large pieces coming off before it crashed into the ground. 2Lt. John Smith got his sixth and last victory while leading Roberts' Second Element. Roberts and Cochran overran a Zero and could not get a shot, but Smith, flying in the rear, was able to cut it off and be in a better position to take a shot. Smith fired a long burst while closing and the Zero smoked, caught fire, and then spun out of control into the ground. Smith made several more passes, but his guns jammed and his port engine began to malfunction, so he decided to retreat to the safety of the clouds before he headed back to base. Smith's Wingman, 2Lt. Louis Longman, dutifully followed his leader and did not fire a shot in the combat.

Second Fight Leader 1Lt. Charles Grice followed Roberts' Flight, and in his dive he fired and missed a Zero going into a steep turn to the right. Grice's Wingman, 1Lt. Chase Brenizer, followed Grice's escaping Zero, while Grice went after another Zero that was on the tail of a P-38. Brenizer continued after the escaping Zero pilot as the enemy went into a port turn, rolled, and then chopped his throttle. Brenizer fired and missed as the enemy pilot righted his fighter from its roll, but then the Zero rolled again. Brenizer rolled with it and fired a two second burst from 100 yards or less, getting hits on the port wing root and cockpit, and it crashed into a mountain southwest of Rabaul. Brenizer then joined a Lightning from the 431FS, and the two chased after a Zero that had just attacked two P-38s. Meanwhile, Grice's guns were not firing properly and he recharged them. Grice saw a Zero on the tail of a P-38 about a mile away and dove and fired at long range, and the Zero pilot broke off the attack, pulling up and away to starboard. Grice followed the Zero as it attacked another P-38. Grice fired and the Zero pilot peeled away, slow rolled to starboard, leveled out, and then chandelled left. Grice fired while closing from 250 to 50 yards, shattering its canopy, and he watched as it started to smoke and then spun and crashed into a hill.

Flight Leader 1Lt. John Babel and Wingman 2Lt. Donald King were attacked by a Zero from 8 o'clock high to port on the first attack. King turned steeply up into the Zero and the two collided, with the Zero taking off a piece of King's starboard wingtip. The Zero continued its dive, smoking heavily, and Babel followed it down and fired, hitting its port wing, but as King states in his ICR: "it made very little difference as the Zero was in its death dive and crashed into the ground." Back at base King was given credit for his fourth and last victory.

The Japanese pilots were judged to be "better than usual....wary but fearless once they began an attack...." (Grice). "Aggressive and hesitated leaving a P-38's tail...." (Roberts). "More aggressive than usual...." (Smith).

432FS

Capt. Frederick Harris led 16 P-38s from Kiriwina at 1030 and arrived over Vunakanau Airdrome at 1235 at 27,000 feet, where they saw fires on the field and three ships burning in the harbor. The Liberators were returning home when Harris saw a dogfight at 18,000 feet. The 432FS engaged enemy fighters for 15 to 20 minutes without result.

The only 475th loss for the mission was 2Lt. Christopher Bartlett, who was flying as 1Lt. Arthur Peregoy's Wingman on a diving attack through a formation of Zeros at 10,000 feet. As they pulled out of the high speed dive Peregoy saw Bartlett over Wide Bay, New Britain, and in no apparent trouble. But when he leveled out over the northern edge of the Bay Peregoy lost Bartlett and circled over the area, but could not locate his Wingman. After the Wide Bay area had been captured by the Allies, infantryman Capt. Floyd Bartlett, Christopher Bartlett's brother, went to the area to search for him. After exploring a few miles inland in a large swamp, Capt. Bartlett found his brother's fighter, identified through its serial number and a large #140, with its port engine badly damaged by gunfire. The Captain went to a nearby native village, where he was told that his brother escaped from the wreckage unharmed and that he lived with them for about two months. However, a German missionary who lived in the village informed the Japanese of Bartlett and a patrol captured him. No further trace of him was ever found, but as conditions for the Japanese on Rabaul grew progressively worse, many prisoners there were either executed or died in captivity.

2Lt. Allen **Hill** shot down his second Japanese aircraft of the war. (AFAA)

8FG/80FS

Fourteen P-38s of the 80FG were assigned a fighter sweep to come in only a few minutes ahead of the B-24s of the 43BG and 90BG heading for Vunakanau. At 1230, the formation arrived over the target at 19,000 feet and the attack seemed to be a surprise, as the Japanese shipping in the Harbor was just under way and aircraft could be seen just taking off from Lakunai Airfield. Maj. Edward Cragg led the Squadron into combat when he saw six enemy fighters, flying line abreast, preparing to make a coordinated attack on the bombers at 15,000 feet. Cragg dove 1,500 feet and fired at a Zero that immediately caught fire and rolled over, then plunged into the Harbor for his 13th victory. Cragg fired at another Hamp, getting hits, and he had to pull up sharply to avoid colliding with it as it escaped into cloud cover for a probable. 2Lt. Allen Hill pulled up to 75 feet and fired a burst that shattered its tail, and it went out of control for the Squadron's only other victory of the day.

29 October 1943: New Guinea
348FG

During October 1943 the 348FG had scored about 50 victories for a ten to one kill ratio, and also maintained pressure on ground targets on northern New Guinea and the west coast of New Britain at the end of the month. On 29 October 1943, the 341FS strafed villages and huts at Cape Bushing and destroyed three barges off the Talasea Peninsula of New Britain the next day.

8FG/36FS

Meanwhile, over New Guinea a flight of 36FS P-39s led by 1Lt. John Pickens was returning from a routine patrol when it ran into severe weather near Bull Dog Base at 1600. All three members of Pickens' flight were lost: 1Lt. Francis Pitonyak and 2Lts. George Fenn and William Melville.

31 October 1943: 475FG/432FS

Bad weather would prevent further missions on Rabaul until 2 November, but on 31 October eight victory ace Capt. Frederick Harris of the 432FS was testing a P-38 that had experienced excessive vibration thought to be due to loose drop tanks. After the braces were tightened Harris took off to test them, and a searchlight company reported that his fighter went into a dive at 500 feet and crashed into the water, killing him.

11

November 1943

Conclusion of the Rabaul Offensive: 2-11 November 1943
During October the Japanese air force suffered a devastating defeat, as Intelligence estimated that 5AF air units in the SWPA had destroyed 648 aircraft, with 215 probably destroyed and 138 damaged. While its aircraft numbers were diminished, Japan's air force remained formidable, as there were ample aircraft reserves to draw from, and these reinforcements were sent to the SWPA to maintain a substantial force. The Japanese Order of Battle on 12 October was estimated to be 163 fighters and 174 bombers, and on 12 November, despite these heavy losses, there were 210 fighters and 165 bombers. Despite the relatively large number of bombers available, their monthly offensive productivity remained meager at only 1.33 sorties per bomber per monthly period, compared to 1.09 for the previous monthly period. It was the Japanese fighter force that suffered most from the Rabaul Offensive, as the average number of offensive sorties per fighter declined from 2.17 to 1.53 sorties per month. Obviously, the Japanese bomber force was unable to mount any effect attacks on Allied bases while their fighters were forced to defend their bases. Of the 5,409 Japanese sorties flown from their bases in the SWPA and South Pacific, only 902 were against Allied bases or air bases. The Japanese Army Air Force at Wewak and elsewhere on New Guinea, as well as the Japanese Naval Air Force in the Bismarcks and Solomons were unable to venture far or often from their bases in the face of Allied air power.

2 November: Rabaul Simpson Harbor, Bloody Tuesday Attack
Again, an impenetrable weather front settled over the Solomon Sea and prevented a follow up mission on Rabaul, which was to be a low level strafing attack on Simpson Harbor. There were a number of reasons to attack shipping, as attacks on Rabaul's airfields were becoming less and less profitable. The Japanese bomber force had been reduced to 40 aircraft, and the fighter force, consisting of some 100 planes, was usually able to avoid being caught on the ground. Thus, it seemed that an attack on Simpson Harbor shipping offered the best target opportunity and would support the offensive operations then in progress in the South Pacific. Allied forces had invaded the Treasury Islands on 27 October as a preliminary for the major landing at Empress Augusta Bay on 1 November. Since Rabaul was the principal source for the reinforcement of the entire area between the Solomons and New Britain, an Allied strike on shipping in Simpson Harbor would contribute directly to the success of Adm. Halsey's forces on Bougainville.

A low level attack on Simpson Harbor was hazardous, as the Japanese not only would send up every available fighter to defend their valuable shipping there, but they had established an intense AA belt around the

FIFTH AIR FORCE UNITS
RABAUL RAIDS OF OCTOBER-NOVEMBER 1943

3rd Attack Group
Dobodura
8BS B-25s
13BS B-25s
90BS B-25s
(89BS A-20s)

38th Bomb Group
Dobodura
69BS B-25s
70BS B-25s
71BS B-25s
405BS B-25s

90th Bomb Group
Moresby
319BS B-24s
320BS B-24s
321BS B-24s
400BS B-24s

43rd Bomb Group
Moresby
63BS B-24s
64BSB-24s
65BS B-24s
403BS B-24s

345th Bomb Group
Dobodura
498BS B-25s
499BS B-25s
500BS B-25s
501BS B-25s

8th Fighter Group
Moresby
80FS P-38s
(35FS P-40s)
(36FS P-40s)

35th Fighter Group
Moresby
39 FS P-38s
(40FS P-40s)
(41FS P-40s)

49th Fighter Group
Moresby
9th FS P-38s
(7FS P-40s)
(8FS P-40s)

475th Fighter Group
Moresby
431FS P-38s
432FS P-38s
433FS P-38s

Total Units On Hand
11 B-25 squadrons
8 B-24 squadrons
6 P-38 squadrons
(6 P-40 squadrons did not have the range for missions against Rabaul)

To cover Japanese land defenses with smoke prior to the strike on shipping **white phosphorous bombs** armed with instantaneous impact fuses produced the ideal effect. (AAF)

Despite the suppression of the AA defenses with phosphorous bombs the mission became known in the 5AF as **"Bloody Tuesday"** as Japanese AA accounted for eight B-25s and enemy fighters for another. Nine P-38s did not return while another was totaled in a crash landing. (AAF)

P-38s of the 475FG, 49FG, 35FG and the 8FG escort 60 B-25s to Rabaul. (AAF)

A B-25. (center arrow) flying through enemy AA fire over the twin volcanoes near Lakunai Airdrome and Rabaul Town. (AAF)

bathtub-shaped harbor. Simpson Harbor was rimmed by high ground that was ideal for the placement of heavy and automatic AA batteries, and these batteries along the shore and those on the warships in the Harbor provided a ferocious barrage against low level attacks. So the primary objective in the plan of attack on Simpson Harbor was the neutralization of these AA defenses. While enemy fighter interception could be partially eliminated by a fighter sweep preceding the arrival of the strafers, the antiaircraft defenses were the problem. Whitehead's solution was to cover the land defenses with smoke prior to the strike on shipping. Experiments by tactical units in cooperation with chemical warfare and ordnance experts had shown white phosphorous bombs armed with instantaneous impact fuses produced the ideal effect. There were some hazards in dropping the chemical from a low altitude, but it was found that cutting the powder charge in the burster by 50% permitted the safe release of the bombs at altitudes above 100 feet.

On four successive days medium bomber and fighter units were alerted and were on final readiness for the mission. But on each day the First Air Task Force called the mission off at the last minute because of the poor weather. The mission was carefully planned. Two fighter squadrons, the 9th and 80th, were to fly a fighter sweep over Lakunai and Simpson Harbor three minutes before the bombers came in from the northeast in order to take advantage of protecting hills and the flow of the ocean tide, which caused ships to lie broadside to this approach. Four B-25 squadrons from the 345BG, covered by the 431st and 432nd Squadrons, were then to neutralize the shore antiaircraft batteries using smoke, strafing, and bombs. The 13th and 90th Bomb Attack Squadrons, closely covered by P-38s of the 9FS, were to fly through a hole in the smoke screen to attack shipping in the Harbor. Four minutes later the 8th, 71st, and 405th Medium Bomber Squadrons, protected by the 433FS, were to conclude the attack. The 8th Photo Squadron had flown recon missions over Simpson Harbor and found seven destroyers, one tender, and 20 merchant ships in the Harbor and 171 fighters and 37 medium and 20 light bombers on the airfields.

By 1100 on 2 November, nine bomber and six fighter squadrons consisting of about 60 B-25s and the same number of P-38s of the 475FG, the 49FG, the 35FG, and the 8FG were on their way towards Simpson Harbor to begin their fighter sweep of Lakunai and the Harbor. By this time the first two neutralizing B-25 squadrons of the 345BG were over the shoreline of Simpson Harbor and the nearby hills that concealed Japanese AA positions, and they had dropped white phosphorous bombs. More B-25s followed, dropping parafrags through the clouds of smoke on the AA positions. The mission became known in the Fifth Air Force as "Bloody Tuesday," as Japanese antiaircraft and interceptors had accounted for eight B-25s and for another nine P-38s, while another was totaled in a crash landing.

1Lt. John **Jones** shot a Zero for his eighth and last victory. (AFAA)

1Lt. Donald **Hanover** claimed his fourth and last victory. (AFAA)

2Lt. Allen **Hill** claimed two victories and a probable to give him four victories. (AFAA)

8FG/80FS

The 80FS was assigned a preliminary fighter sweep for B-25s over Rabaul at 8,000 feet a few minutes before the bombers arrived. As the 16 Lightnings led by Maj. Edward Cragg arrived at 1315 they were met by an unexpectedly large number of enemy fighters composed of Zeros, Hamps, Tonys, and even Val dive bombers from the supposedly beaten enemy air forces. Cragg led the Headhunters down over Simpson Harbor to 4,000 feet to intercept 10 to 12 Zeros that were taking off from Rapopo Airfield. Cragg's gunfire hit a "Val-type," tearing off pieces of its port wing, but the enemy disappeared into the clouds for a probable. Cragg was alone after losing 2Lt. Louis Schriber and his Wingman, F/O Willis Evers. Cragg then joined a large dogfight over St. George's Channel and saw four P-38s chasing a Zero that Split-S'd and was flying close to the water, heading inland. Cragg dove 3,000 feet and fired a direct astern shot from 100 yards. Cragg claimed that it crashed onto a beach, but he was officially credited with a probable.

Schriber and Evers followed Cragg down to meet the climbing Zeros. Schriber's first shot missed a Zero, but Evers set fire to his target, which spiraled to crash in the Harbor. Schriber dove and fired at another Zero that began smoking but disappeared. Schriber became separated from Evers and flew southeast over the St. Georges Channel, where he joined other P-38s engaging in a large dogfight. Another Zero came into range and Schriber scored heavy hits on its tail assembly, reporting that it was spinning toward the water when he last saw it. Schriber continued his dive and saw a Zero attacking the B-25s at 1,000 feet. Schriber chased it down to wave top level, but before he fired his guns the Zero's wingtip hit the water and the enemy plane cartwheeled 500 to 600 yards along the water. Schriber climbed to 4,000 feet when he spotted more Zeros below him. He circled in lazy-8s and dove on one with a deflection shot that sent it smoking into the Channel. After the battle an examination of Schriber's gun camera film was determined inconclusive, and these three claims, to Schriber's chagrin, were all credited as probables.

Third Flight Leader 1Lt. Albon Hailey and Wingman 2Lt. Edwin DeGraffenreid dove on several Zeros taking off from Ropopo Airfield and engaged them at 1,000 feet. Hailey and DeGraffenreid dove from 8,000 feet to tree top level to get at the Zeros that were attacking the B-25s completing their bombing run over Simpson Harbor. Hailey made three long range passes without success, and finally dove on three Zeros and closed in on the Leader, who chandelled. Hailey fired at 800 yards and continued to close head on until the Zero pilot had to turn to avoid a collision and then bailed out. DeGraffenreid fired from 600 yards on a Zero that was approaching Hailey's tail, but his dive angle was too steep and the Zero broke away. Another Zero came in from the right on Hailey's tail, and again DeGraffenreid fired a short burst that drove it off. This Zero then turned into DeGraffenreid but broke off, and the American fired a short burst, getting hits in its fuselage from 300 yards for a probable. Hailey tried to turn into a Zero that was coming in at 60 degrees, but the enemy pilot turned into DeGraffenreid head on at 500 yards and the American started firing at 450 yards, getting hits on its engine and wings. The two fighters kept closing on each other, and at the last instant the Japanese pilot pushed over and missed a collision "by five feet," but exploded soon after for DeGraffenreid's sixth and last victory of the war.

As 2Lt. Allen Hill arrived over the cloud deck over Wide Bay at about 10,000 feet he was unable to free his tanks for several minutes. He was then joined by 1Lt. Hamilton Salmon of the 39FS, and as they descended under the clouds they quickly ran into "40 to 50 Zeros" chasing a flight of six B-25s. Hill closed from 5,000 feet on two Zeros and took a 90 degree deflection shot from 300 to 400 yards that put a Zero into the water. Hill and Salmon were flying at 1,500 feet and 400 mph when they attacked two more Zeros. Hill fired two bursts on the right one that set it on fire, while Salmon attacked the left Zero and set it flaming and out of control. Hill opened fire on another Zero and fired at 150 yards, then again at 75 yards, and claimed his second victory of the day. Continuing down to 900 feet, he saw 15 to 20 Zeros diving and then peeling away from the B-25s. Hill caught one peeling up and fired a long burst from 60 degrees deflection and blew it to pieces. As Hill pulled up his fighter was hit in the starboard wing and engine, and after he feathered his engine he was accompanied to base by Schriber and Hanover. After the mission one of Hill's three victories was downgraded to a probable.

1Lt. John Jones was leading a flight at 10,000 feet over Rabaul Town and made several passes, but lost his second element when his right engine developed manifold problems. Once Jones got his Lightning trimmed he saw enemy fighters above and made a pass at the last one and it burst into flames. Jones went on to claim a probable, as he did not see the badly damaged Zero crash. 1Lt. Edward Robertson added a Zero probable to give the 80th a daily total of eight victories and an improbable 10 probables. It seems as though the claims officers were very tough on awarding victory claims on this day compared to other days. The victory was Jones' eighth and last of the war. He would claim a Tony probable on 13 December 1943 before returning to the US in February 1944, where he served as a flight instructor before leaving the service in July 1945.

1Lt. Donald Hanover was leading the second element of Jones' flight when the flight ran into black and brown painted Zeros that were "damn hard to see." Jones and his wingman did not see the Zeros, and lost Hanover and his wingman as they dove after the enemy. Hanover fired too early and the Zeros Split-S'd away. However, one enemy pilot decided to turn around and press an unfortunate head on attack, during which Hanover first hit the Zero's spinner and then exploded its port wing tank. The enemy pilot half-rolled and missed Hanover by only 10 to 20 yards. Meanwhile, Hanover's Wingman, 2Lt. Norman Shea, was attacked from astern. Hanover made a quick 180° but was too late, as Shea's right engine began to stream Prestone and he headed straight down. Hanover was "boxed in" by two Zeros and had to dive away. At the end of his dive he saw Capt. Hill flying on one engine and being chased by several Zeros, which broke away upon Hanover's approach.

For the 80FS, F/O Willis Evers and 2Lt. Norman Shea were both believed to be shot down by enemy fighters over Simpson Harbor.

475FG/432FS/433FS/431FS

432FS

The 432FS, led by veteran 1Lt. Grover Gholson, would be the first squadron into action when it arrived over the entrance of Simpson Harbor at 1330 while escorting B-25s at 4,000 feet, as 20 Japanese fighters came in from 2,000 feet above. He led his flight into a climb to get an altitude advantage, but once there he made several unsuccessful deflection passes until a climbing Oscar passed directly in front of him. Gholson's first burst set the Oscar on fire momentarily, but his second burst exploded it to make him an ace. Gholson then got on the tail of a Zero and followed it into a turn, getting in some long bursts that sent it flaming into the sea. Gholson's Wingman, 2Lt. Theodore Fostakowski, also had made an unsuccessful initial pass on an Oscar, but as Gholson shot down his Oscar Fostakowski saw an Oscar approach and then make a starboard turn. The American pilot fired a 90 degree deflection shot and followed it into a 30 deflection shot, then watched the Oscar burst into flames. Fostakowski claimed the Oscar as a definite, but it was later downgraded to a probable.

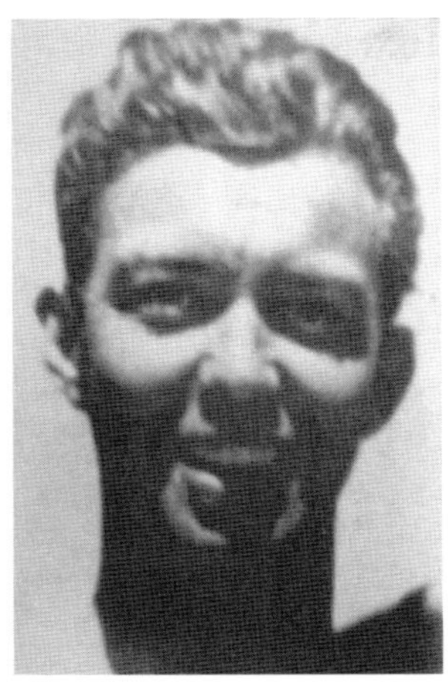

1Lt. Grover **Gholson** shot down two Zeros to become an ace. (AFAA)

Blue Flight, led by 1Lt. Arthur Peregoy, was attacked by five Zeros from 8 o'clock and turned into them. Peregoy went into a steep, tight diving turn that put him into a head on pass, but the Zero pulled up, giving Peregoy a belly shot. Peregoy passed under the Zero without seeing any results, but the victory was confirmed by Gholson. Peregoy lost his Wingman, 2Lt. William Ritter, and his second element, and then had his starboard engine cut out as he was making another pass. As Peregoy was leaving the fight he was attacked by several Tonys and dove away under reduced manifold pressure. Blue Flight Second Element Leader 1Lt. John Weber and Wingman 2Lt. Ferdinand Hanson separated from Peregoy and Ritter over Simpson Harbor, and soon met four Oscars. Weber pressed his trigger button and nothing happened. Hanson made a head on pass, firing a long seven second burst, and saw some smoke coming from its wing root for a probable claim. The two then headed back to Kiriwina.

Clover White Flight Leader 1Lt. Leo Mayo, his Wingman, 2Lt. John Fogarty, and the second element of 1Lt. John Rundell and Wingman 2Lt. Howard Hedrick attacked several of the lone Japanese fighters that had filtered down from the "approximately 75" fighters above. The Flight made unsuccessful passes at several enemy fighters and two tried to ram Rundell and Hedrick. An Oscar was pulling up in a steep climb and stalled directly in front of Hedrick, who fired, causing it to smoke and then go down in flames (observed by Gholson). Red and White Flights became separated. Hedrick continued on and took a quick shot, damaging a Zeke that seemed to try to ram him. White Flight fighters were running low on fuel, and Mayo took them over Wide Bay, heading toward Dobodura. When they reached Kabanga, south of the Gazelle Peninsula, Mayo spotted a Tony below and dove at high speed to get on its tail. Mayo began firing at 200 yards from dead astern and the Tony began burning. Mayo pressed his attack until the Tony exploded directly in front of him, shedding large pieces that tore off a large section of Mayo's right wing, sending him immediately into a violent spiral. The very fortunate Mayo managed to bail out of the wildly spinning wreck and landed just a few yards off the beach. Rundell went down to cover Mayo while Fogarty and Hedrick remained at higher altitude and had to fend off another diving Zero. There were four or five other Japanese fighters above Hedrick, and he tried to break away to catch the other Clover Lightnings as they headed for base. The Zeros caught Hedrick and shot out his port engine, so he had to feather it. The enemy fighters continued to fire on him for about six or seven minutes, and he skillfully evaded by skidding, and when one Zero would become particularly menacing he would kick hard left rudder and almost snap roll. After a while one enemy pilot carelessly flew ahead of him and Hedrick hit this fighter, causing thick blue smoke to come from its belly and it fell away for a probable claim. The enemy pilots made several passes, but soon were running low on fuel and gave up the chase, so Hedrick turned for Kiriwina to catch the rest of his flight and landed safely at Kiriwina. Mayo was never found, despite searches over the next few days.

During the fight the squadron met heavy AA fire from the Japanese warships in Simpson Harbor. "Umbrella AA" was observed in "considerable quantity," which made "a large white blossom which left streamers shooting out from under it." Nonetheless, the squadron suffered no AA hits. Two pilots (Hedrick and Rundell) reported that two enemy pilots seemed to attempt ramming attacks. Ritter reported that "over the target enemy fighters seemed to be dropping something on us from above. At first it seemed to be belly tanks but they were too small for that. They proved to be aerial bombs that exploded at our altitude and lower altitudes."

433FS

Capt. Daniel Roberts led 12 P-38s on an escort of two B-25 Squadrons to Rabaul. As Roberts started his take off roll for the Squadron's stopover flight to Kiriwina on the first leg of the Rabaul mission, he saw that the port main fuel cell cover was not tightened and had opened, and highly flammable aviation gasoline was running over the wing.

Roberts and his Wingman, 2Lt. Lewis Yarbrough, continued to climb and made a wide port turn while the Squadron climbed to join them. Roberts turned the fuel tank selector valve to the cross feed position and fed both engines off the port tank, and soon the fuel in this tank was used and a possible fatal fire prevented. When Roberts reached the target area he had to drop to tree top altitude to escort the B-25s under the cloud layer over Lakunai Strip. Roberts then "shot everything I had" during a 30 degree frontal attack on a Zero making a pass on a B-25. Roberts' ICR claims a victory for the day, but it was listed as a probable in official records; a victory that would have given Roberts 14 victories to make him the 475th's leading ace. 1Lt. Donald Revenaugh also claimed shooting down a Zero that was making a pass on a flaming B-25, but his claim is also listed in the official records as a probable. Revenaugh's fighter was badly shot up. He returned to base with cannon holes in both wings, the aileron trim and port aileron control shot away, a machine gun hole in his canopy, and numerous AA holes in his booms.

Although Roberts' Possum Squadron saw action that day, and although 433FS records show a confirmed Zero kill for Roberts and one for 1Lt. Donald Revenaugh near the Lakunai airfield area, official records credit the two pilots with probables. Possum pilot 1Lt. Donald King was lost as he tried to shoot Zeros off the tails of his Flight Leader Horton and his Wingman, Neely.

431FS

At 1100, 1Lt. Marion Kirby was supposed to lead 12 P-38s off Dobodura #12 on a low cover escort for a B-25 strafing mission to Rabaul, but had problems with his airspeed indicator and 1Lt. Arthur Wenige took over as Squadron Leader. Kirby took off late and joined the Squadron over Oro Bay, rejoining Red Flight and his original Wingman, 2Lt. Kenneth Richardson. Blue Flight Leader 1Lt. Lowell Lutton, who had lost three men to aborts, joined White Flight as its fifth man. The Squadron was reformed into two flights. White Flight (now the lead flight) consisted of Leader Wenige and Wingman 2Lt. Franklin Monk, a second element of 1Lt. Fredric Champlin and Wingman 2Lt. Owen Giertsen, and Lutton, while Red Flight consisted of its original members: Kirby and Richardson, and 1Lt. Francis Lent and Wingman 2Lt. Robert Hunt.

The nine remaining P-38s escorted the B-25s heading for Simpson Harbor, where several Japanese destroyers had just arrived from the recent naval battle at Empress Augusta Bay. As the medium bomber formation arrived over the mouth of the Warangoi River they accidentally flew over the enemy warships at mast top altitude and the anti-aircraft gunners opened fire. The B-25s had been surprised by the unexpected heavy fire, and their formations separated when the Japanese gunners claimed several American aircraft. At 1325, White Flight Leader Wenige saw the AA fire in the distance, which he thought was coming from ground batteries on the

Clockwise from far left:
1Lt. Marion **Kirby** shot down two Zeros to become an ace with his last victories of the war. (AFAA)

1Lt. Arthur **Wenige** shot down two Zeros to become an ace and would shoot down a Tony five days later for his last victory of the war. (AFAA)

2Lt. Franklin **Monk** claimed his second victory. (AFAA)

1Lt. Lowell **Lutton** scored his fifth and last victory to become an ace. (AFAA)

1Lt. Fredric **Champlin** was another multiple scorer for the day with two Zero victories to give him three. (AFAA)

route to Simpson Harbor, and ordered his flight to drop its belly tanks off Cape St. George. White Flight started over the target string formation 15 minutes later at 3,000 feet and was followed by Red Flight. The bombers then turned southeast, and had crossed Cape Gazelle's east coast when Wenige estimated that "60 to 70 Japanese fighters" were approaching. The P-38s met heavy AA fire as they crossed the Harbor, and while White Flight remained together, two elements of Red Flight had separated in the face of the large enemy attack. The ensuing air combat became a free for all whose sequence is difficult to establish from the ICRs.

As they crossed the Harbor, Kirby and Richardson dove toward Lakunai Airdrome. Kirby saw a Tony being shot down in flames by a P-38, but the enemy pilot remained in enough control that he tried to get on Kirby's tail before crashing. Kirby started down the coast toward Rapopo Airdrome and encountered heavy AA fire; he also saw a B-25 lose its right engine to the flak. Three Zeros closed to finish off the Mitchell, and Kirby dove and shot one down, which was confirmed by Lent for Kirby's fifth victory to become an ace. Kirby then attacked another Zero and got many hits, but had to break away, as a Zero got on his tail and he claimed a probable. Champlin came in and shot the Zero off Kirby's tail. Red Second Element Lent and Hunt saw Champlin shoot the Zero off Kirby's tail, and while they were circling over the bombers a Zero came down on Hunt's tail. Lent fired a few bursts at it and "damaged it considerably" for a probable. During this pass Lent lost both his flight and Wingman Hunt, and headed down the coast of New Ireland to get into the overcast there to evade the "60 to 70" enemy aircraft in the area. At this time Richardson left his flight and joined Lent, and as the two proceeded toward New Ireland they saw six to eight Zeros making passes at six B-25s. The two dove to their rescue and chased the Zeros away, with Lent firing on one from head on, which was later confirmed by Monk to have crashed for Lent's eighth victory. About five minutes later the Zeros came in to attack the Mitchells and Lent and Richardson again turned to the rescue. Two or three Zeros got on each pilot's tail, and while Lent succeeded in losing his pursuers, Richardson's P-38 was seen in flames about three miles offshore Rabaul. Meanwhile, Hunt's P-38 lost manifold pressure and was unable to keep up with Lent, so he flew on behind Lent. Hunt encountered no enemy aircraft until he approached Vunakanau Airdrome, where he saw a B-25 go down and acquired a Zero on his tail. Lent turned and chased the Zero away but then separated from Hunt. As Hunt flew along the coast he saw a B-25 go down without any survivors and another being chased by Zeros. Hunt saw yet another Zero on a Mitchell's tail and closed to 500 yards. The enemy pilot went into a gentle climb and stalled at 350 yards. Hunt fired a long burst and the Zero went down and exploded in the ocean. At this point Hunt was attacked in three directions: one on his tail and by two on each side firing from 30 degrees deflection. Hunt half rolled away to escape and came upon a Zero on the tail of a P-38. Hunt fired an initial deflection shot and then got directly on its tail, and as it climbed Hunt fired a long burst into it and it fell off onto one wing; after falling 300 feet its entire port side became enveloped in flames. Hunt was low on fuel and his prop governor was malfunctioning, so he decided to head toward Kiriwina after scoring his only two victories of the war. Hunt stayed overnight while his fighter was repaired.

Wenige led White Flight across Simpson Harbor, weaving through the intense AA fire and trying to take advantage of the cloud cover in the area. Wenige heard a call for help and assumed it was from someone in his flight, so he weaved back and forth looking for the caller and lost Lent's Red Flight. As Wenige continued he then followed his new #5 Lutton down over Tobera, but lost his second element of Champlin and Giertsen. As Wenige passed over Tobera Drome he made a high speed strafing run on the revetments. As the Mitchells completed their run and crossed the east end of Cape Gazelle they were attacked by 50 to 60 enemy aircraft from above, and the P-38s intervened and diverted the enemy attack on the bombers. Lutton fired a 90 degree deflection shot and a Zero went down in flames for his fifth victory to become an ace. Wenige followed by shooting another Zero off Lutton's tail with several short bursts that put the enemy fighter into a spin into the water for his fifth victory. The two made unsuccessful passes on Zeros attacking the bombers, and two Zeros then made a head on pass on Lutton and then broke off to go after Wenige. Wenige fired a short burst but saw no results, but his Wingman Monk saw it explode. Another Zero attacked and Wenige climbed and fired, only to find that he was out of ammunition. Wenige's Wingman Monk, who had followed his leader in the strafing run on Tobera, watched as Lent, Lutton, and Wenige each shot down enemy fighters. When Lutton was attacked by two Zeros Monk and Wenige pursued the two attackers. While Wenige downed one, Monk fired a long burst at the other, but it broke away before he could see any results. During the next enemy attack on Lutton, Wenige again shot down one while Monk's target again escaped. Another Zero attacked Monk and Wenige from 1 o'clock and momentarily escaped by flying under Wenige, but Monk got a good shot that sent it down in flames. Wenige saw two more Zeros on the beleaguered Lutton's tail, and although out of ammunition made a "dry run" and drove them off. Five more Zeros arrived, and one made a 90 degree deflection shot at Lutton. Wenige again climbed to the rescue toward the Zero, which broke off in a half roll. Lutton joined the end of Wenige's flight, and when contacted said he was more than ready to return to base. As they were returning to Kiriwina, Wenige looked back and did not see Lutton, who had disappeared. Lutton either ran out of fuel, or his fighter had been so damaged from the numerous attacks that it went down.

After Champlin and Giertsen became separated from White Flight in the clouds they were attacked by Zeros from above and behind. Giertsen broke down and left, while Champlin broke level and right and got behind a Zero that got on Giertsen's tail. The Zero made a break to the left which put the turning Zero into Champlin's gunsight. Champlin fired a quick shot that struck the Zero and set it on fire. Giertsen also escaped a tailing Zero, but was hit by enemy AA fire and bailed out near the area that Czarnecki had gone down in on 23 October. Soon Zeros were swarming everywhere, and Champlin evaded by heading into a cloud and then attached himself to five other Lightnings. He saw a Lightning below with engine trouble and about to be attacked by two Zeros. Champlin dove, expecting the other P-38s to follow, but was able to shoot one off the P-38's tail while the other broke away. Champlin was again attacked by Zeros and evaded by ducking into a cloud, then headed for Kiriwina.

The Squadron's 10 victories could not be compensated by the loss of Lutton, Giertsen, and Richardson.

433FS

1Lts. John Babel and William Grady of the 433FS took off at noon to escort the photo recon aircraft that were to document the results of the mission. They spent 20 minutes circling above Simpson Harbor, where AA batteries continued to fire up flak, and returned to base with photos but no enemy contact.

475FG After Action Report:

The after action report of the 475th Fighter Group describes the groups' mission for media distribution:

> "At last, at 11 o'clock in the morning of the second, 37 of our pilots set out for Rabaul. Their assignment was to protect B-25s during a low level strafing and bombing attack on the enemy shipping in Simpson Harbor. The weather was bad. Almost all the way the ceiling was well below 4,000 feet altitude. Bombers and fighters roared low across the sea. Enroute the escort was weakened when two fighter pilots snafued and went home with one escort. In St. George's Channel, a Japanese battleship and cruiser blazed away at the striking force. The element of surprise

had been lost. The enemy would be warned and ready. Fighters and bombers continued on nevertheless, circled to the north of the target, and then came in. Danny Roberts with 12 planes of the 433rd Squadron provided close cover. Leading his flights, he flew beneath a 2,000 foot overcast at treetop level, slipped over the mountaintops, and then roared down over the harbor into a blizzard of ack-ack.

"Just before reaching the harbor, nine planes of Hades Squadron (431st) ascended to 7,000 feet, then made a long, slanting dive across the target. Thirteen planes of the 432nd Squadron climbed to a scant 4,000 feet altitude to meet Japanese fighter attacks. The time was 1335.

"Ack-ack almost blotted out the harbor as the entire fleet and shore batteries hammered at the Mitchells and Lightnings. Over head more than 100 enemy fighters circled, dropped aerial burst bombs, then peeled down through rifts in the overcast to attack the raiders. Deliberately Danny Roberts kept his flight low, warding off fighter attacks, weaving through ack-ack, staying with the bombers to help them although he sacrificed to the enemy fighters the tremendous advantage of superior altitude.

"The nine planes of Hades Squadron dived again and again to the rescue of the bombers, scorning the scores of Japanese that sought to kill them from behind. When Marion Kirby saw three enemy fighters working over a crippled B-25, he went after the enemy alone. The first foe fell to his gunnery, then he tackled the others. As he sent the second Zeke spinning to destruction, the third swung in behind him and opened fire. But even as the enemy moved, Fred Champlin was turning to his teammate's aid. He had the skill to do it. Before the enemy could make his kill, Champlin had shot him down.

"A swarm of Japanese were diving on a group of B-25s and the bombers called for assistance. Single-handedly, Lowell Lutton engaged the foe. He set one Zeke ablaze but two others came at him from astern. Ed Wenige and his lean, tall Wingman, Franklin Monk, went after the two Japanese, Wenige knocking down the first and Monk forcing the other to break away. The three Lightnings weaved back and forth above the bombers firing and blocking enemy attacks. The enemy then turned on the Lightnings. Two Zekes dived on Lutton from 1 o'clock high. Again Wenige and Monk met them, with the same results. A third Zeke followed the first pair in, but as Wenige opened fire, his guns ran out of ammo. Unable to fight, he ducked under the attack while Monk met the enemy and shot him down. Lutton was still in the thick of the fight and heavily outnumbered. With his useless guns Wenige dived at the enemy while Monk teamed with him to break up attacks. Five more Japanese boxed them in but failed to bring them down.

"Meanwhile, scissoring in and out of the clouds, the 432nd Squadron fought to break up the diving attacks from above. Enemy Navy fighters circled overhead waiting to pick off any plane which became separated in the overcast. The 4 planes of White flight lost their squadron, moved to the edge of the combat, and began to engage enemy fighters as they came into the clear. One fanatic failed in a desperate attempt to ram Howard Hedrick and John Rundell. As they dodged the enemy, Leo Mayo flashed down on a Zeke at terrific speed. Closing rapidly, he opened fire. The enemy plane exploded as Mayo's flight came up behind him. To their horror, a flying mass of wreckage sheared off the wing of his plane. As it hurtled down, he jumped and his parachute flared out. Fogarty and Rundell circled their friend as he dropped toward the sea, blocking the Japanese who sought to strafe him. Hedrick, alone, stayed up to cover them. Four Japanese dived down upon him, shot out one engine, then tried desperately for the kill. Slipping, skidding, and turning, Hedrick dodged their fire. One of the enemy passed in front of him, and Hedrick shot him down. Finally the rest gave up the chase and left him. Giertsen of the 431st was shot down but escaped into the jungle. Two other P-38s were lost. For 40 minutes the Lightnings held off the Japanese and sent 19 to destruction. At last, 54 miles south of Rabaul some 60 enemy fighters gave up the chase and turned home.

"Somewhere, more than 200 miles to the south, lay the tiny island of Kiriwina, the closest landing field for the men of the 475th. The weather had grown worse. To the east a towering front paralleled their course. The ceiling ahead had lowered to 2,000 feet, and a thickening haze dimmed their vision. North of Kiriwina another front forced them to consume precious gas in a detour. From 3 to 4 o'clock that afternoon the P-38s straggled in to Kiriwina. When they landed some had only 10 gallons of fuel left.

"Lieutenant Lutton never arrived. In his gallant fight over Simpson Harbor he had used the gas he needed for the long flight home. The rest of the planes refueled and flew back to Dobodura. Mayo, too, was lost forever, despite all the efforts to get him down safely. The over-all claims for the day by the Fifth Air Force were 40 enemy fighters downed by the Lightnings and 26 by the B-25 crewmen. Eight B-25s and nine P-38s had been lost in the fierce air fighting." (Note: Leo Mayo was seen to bail out and was seen to go ashore near Cape Mope and was thought to have been captured but was never heard from again.)

Capt. Daniel Roberts sums up the day's combat in his ICR: "....they outnumbered us 3 to 1, were all above us, and were quite eager." He noted that there was intense AA fire, particularly over Rabaul Township and Lakunai Strip. "The Ack Ack was heavy, intense, and accurate to our altitude...." (2Lt. Austin Neeley)

49FG/9FS

Capt. Gerald Johnson led his dozen serviceable P-38s in close escort to the 345BG Mitchells that were to attack the docks and ships around Simpson Harbor. En route to the southern New Britain coast, Green Flight Leader Wallace Jordan reported mechanical problems and relinquished his Flight to Element Leader 1Lt. Carl Planck and returned to Kiriwina. The remaining 11 Knights flew on in stacked formation position from 1,000 up through 3,000 feet on the Mitchells' starboard flank.

At 1345, the B-25s and P-38s turned hard to port to begin the second wave of the low level attacks into the flak from hundreds of anti-aircraft guns that ringed the target, plus the firepower of the Japanese warships at anchor. The first wave of strafers had set fires on the docks and on two merchant ships, along with attacks on Lakunai airfield. The second wave Mitchell crews attacked at tree top level to strafe the docks through the heavy flak, while Johnson's three flights dropped their tanks and flew directly over the village to protect the Mitchells' flank from the enemy fighters that were approaching from every direction.

Johnson's Red Flight was over the docks within range of the AA from the anchored warships, while Planck's Green Flight and Hyland's Blue Flight were to the left over the heavy AA guns sited in the hills above the town. Just as the Lightnings passed over the town, Blue Flight Leader 1Lt. Normand Hyland was suddenly met head on by a Zero and instinctively pressed the trigger on his control wheel, destroying the enemy fighter, but as Hyland looked back to check on his elements, he saw Love's P-38 in flames and crashing into the jungle. The Mitchells completed their low level strafing run and turned back to the east, followed by the Knights, but they were met by 50 Zeros near a large volcanic cone called Crater Mountain, located on the west bank of the Harbor. The remaining 10 Flying Knights turned into the overwhelming enemy force and a massive dogfight began. Blue Wingman 1Lt. Delman Moore climbed to 3,000 feet to fire on a Zero which rolled straight down into the bay. Blue Wingman 1Lt. Douglas Barrett riddled a Zero at point blank range just above the water, causing it to cartwheel into the water. Barrett damaged another Zero while he and the other Blue Flight pilots battled their way out of danger beyond Cape Gazelle.

Planck's three plane Green Flight flew through the thick smoke over the western shoreline and saw a mass of enemy fighters approaching them. They turned with the Mitchells and then climbed to meet the Zeros. Planck and an onrushing Zero exchanged fire, but it was the enemy that received the fatal burst and exploded. Planck then fired at a second Zero from head on, and the enemy fighter plunged straight into Planck's port engine and sheered off the prop, then slid under the Lightning and tore into the port tail assembly. Without rudder control, Planck managed to glide downward through a full turn to port and headed off to the southeast.

Meanwhile, Green wingmen 2Lts. Alfred Lewelling and Robert Wood had also fired at the oncoming mass of fighters. Lewelling shot down an Oscar whose pilot bailed out, but as he looked to his right he saw Planck in a mid-air collision. Lewelling and Wood veered instinctively away, but neither saw what happened next to their Flight Leader, as the two surviving Green wingmen headed for Kiriwina.

Squadron Leader Johnson's Red Flight of Wingman 1Lt. Stanley Johnson, Element Leader Capt. William Haney, and Wingman 2Lt. Glade Hill all fired at the first wave of Zeros that attacked them north of Rabaul Town. Johnson's first victim crashed just west of the town, and when the Flight turned east he destroyed his second victim, while Wingman Stanley Johnson shot down another Zero that crashed near Vunakanau Strip. Red Flight climbed and found themselves in a mammoth dogfight just east of the anchored enemy ships.

Red Element Leader Haney and Wingman Hill turned through four violent firing passes, in which Haney hit four fighters, but neither pilot could confirm the result of the Captain's shooting, and he was awarded two probables and two damaged. As the two withdrew, Haney chased off a Zero which had attacked a smoking Lightning, but he was then sidetracked by another enemy fighter. After looking for the damaged P-38 Haney left for home.

During mission debriefing it was determined that Francis Love's fighter had exploded in the jungle, but there was the question of the burning P-38 that Haney had covered during the withdrawal which was determined to be Planck's. Planck had survived cannon rounds and a midair collision to nurse his shattered fighter to the Japanese-occupied east coast of New Britain, then ditched in Wide Bay, badly cutting his head. He was able to swim to shore before sunset and stumbled into the jungle for cover, collapsing from exhaustion. The next morning he trekked into the high country looking for friendly natives. He subsisted on coconut meat and rain water, and after six days finally found a friendly tribe. After regaining some strength, for the next two weeks he was ushered deeper into the interior highlands and finally taken by another tribe to Australian coast watchers. After two months Planck and three other survivors were finally rescued by a USN submarine. After a brief reunion with his squadron Planck could tell very little of his ordeal, as he was under strict orders to protect the secrecy of the other survivors still in New Britain, and left for home and never flew again.

35FG/39FS

The 39FS was assigned to a fighter sweep prior to the B-25s' arrival. At 1400, just as the P-38s reached the target area, several enemy fighters were seen. 1Lt. Hamilton Salmon was unable to drop his tanks and began to leave the area, but after five miles he dropped his tanks and joined with 1Lt. Allen Hill of the 80FS, and they returned to the combat area. On his first attack, Salmon made a stern attack that damaged a Zero and followed it with a successful tail attack on another Zero over Cape Gazelle. At 1400, Capt. Ralph Bills of another 39FS flight damaged an Oscar. Salmon's victory would be the 39th's last until a year later, when the 39th shot down three Oscars over Cebu in P-47s on 6 November 1944.

Bloody Tuesday Totals

The weather on the way back to base between Rabaul and Kiriwina was appalling, and may have caused some damaged P-38s and B-25s to crash on the way back. Nonetheless, nine P-38s and eight B-25s did not return from the mission, which was one of the 5AF's most costly of the war up to that date. The overall claims for the day by the Fifth Air Force were 40 enemy fighters downed by the Lightnings and (an improbable - author) 26 by the B-25 crewmen. Actually, the final total of Japanese losses was 31 destroyed with 21 probables and three damaged, plus 10 flying boats and float planes destroyed in the harbor.

5 November 1943: Rabaul
The US Navy Comes on the Scene

When Bougainville was invaded on 1 November, Rabaul also became threatened by the US Navy. During a too hurried attempt to drive Allied forces from Bougainville, the Japanese Navy had been defeated in the Battle of Empress Augusta Bay. Adm. Mineichi Koga, who replaced Yamamoto as the Japanese

LEFT:
1Lt. Normand **Hyland** claimed his third and last victory. (AAF)

RIGHT:
Capt. Gerald **Johnson** with news correspondents after getting his 7th and 8th victories. (AFAA)

Navy Combined Fleet C-in-C, then planned to reinforce Rabaul and overwhelm the limited Allied forces in the Bougainville area while most of the US Navy was involved in preparations for the invasion of Tarawa, in the Gilberts.

R.Adm. Frederick Sherman planned to preempt this threat with a carrier raid by Task Force 38. The carriers *Saratoga* and *Princeton* steamed for New Britain under cover of a weather front and launched 97 aircraft against Rabaul on 5 November. While the USN sunk no ships, six cruisers were damaged (four heavily), and three destroyers were also lightly damaged. Most of the Japanese warships returned to Truk the next day for repairs and to escape further Allied attacks.

49FG/9FS

On 5 November, aircraft from USN carriers of Task Force 38 struck Rabaul, and the Fifth Air Force cooperated with them by dispatching a group of 27 B-24s escorted by 58 P-38s from the 8th, 49th, and 475th Fighter Groups to attack the wharf area. A number of enemy aircraft were seen in the vicinity of the target, but Capt. Richard Bong of the 9FS/49FG was the only Lightning pilot to score that day.

After losing two Lightnings on the 2nd, ground crews labored to add two overhauled war-weary P-38s to the 9FS' flight line. On the 5th, Capt. Bong led 11 Flying Knight P-38s to Rabaul as high cover for B-24 Liberators, but the decimated Japanese fighter command was only able to offer token resistance. At 1215, Bong's Flights flew high over Vunakanau Airdrome, where widely scattered enemy fighters were 3,000 feet below. Blue Element Leader 1Lt. Francis Nutter led his flight into a dive and fired, but completely missed his target. Green Flight Leader William Bleecker fired at two enemy fighters, one of which rolled away trailing debris, but there was no confirmation of a crash and Bleecker had to settle for a probable claim. Bong exploded his first victim from 100 yards dead astern to make him a quadruple ace with 20 victories. Moments later he fired a long burst the plane Split-S'd and disintegrated as his 21st victim in a fireball 5,000 feet above Vunakanau.

As the Knights left the target area, Bong's Wingman, 1Lt. George Haniotis, radioed his position to the standby rescue flights at Kiriwina and bailed out several hundred yards off shore east of Arawe. Search flights never found a body, but the life raft assigned to Haniotis was found later.

When Bong returned to base he found Gen. Kenney waiting for the first pilot in the Pacific to score 20 victories, and who was approaching the 26 victories set by American Ace-of-Aces, Capt. Eddie Rickenbacker, in WWI. Kenney was eager to have Bong gain six more victories for promotional purposes with the War Department. During his 21 victories Bong had flown 158 missions in 12 months, in which his fighter had been damaged by enemy fire seven times, and three times seriously. He had been awarded a DFC, a DSC, and a number of Flying Crosses. America's third ranking ace after the Marine Corps' Joseph Foss and Gregory "Pappy" Boyington was scheduled to go home on leave.

35FG/39FS

Capt. Charles King led 14 P-38s of the Squadron on a sweep over Rabaul prior to the arrival of the B-25s. As they approached Vunakanau at 24,000 feet they saw several single seat fighters at 5,000 feet below, but these were chased by other P-38s. West of Vunakanau King fired a long deflection on a SSF with no visible results, and then encountered three to the west. King and Wingman 1Lt. Gordon Prentice attacked and King got hits, damaging a Zero. King made a 40 degree deflection shot as the enemy pilot went into a stall, getting explosions behind the cockpit. The Zero went into a spin toward the ground, but just as it was about to crash the pilot pulled out and King reported: "due to the size of the explosion probably did not get back." King closed on two Zeros getting to within 50 feet of the Leader for a few damaging hits. These would be King's last claims of the war, giving him five victories, three probables, and four damaged.

5 November 1943: 348FG/341FS
New Guinea

On 5 November, four P-47s from the 341FS left Port Moresby at 0730, landed at Lae to refuel at 0830, and left an hour later on the way to their fighter sweep over Wewak at 1100. The 341st, led by Lt.Col. Robert Rowland, was patrolling at 27,000 feet when they spotted 12 Tonys at 16,000 feet, eight Hamps at 12,000 feet, and about 15 "unidentified single seat aircraft" just taking off from Wewak. The 341st made their attack on the Tony formation from astern at 6 o'clock high out of the sun in a high speed 400mph dive.

Rowland attacked the number four Tony in the first flight in his high speed dive, firing from 200 yards and then evading so as not to collide with his flaming victim. As Rowland approached the Tony Flight Leader, he was too close to attack, as his speed was too high, and had to pull up and over him. He turned left and fired on the number two man of the first element from 150 to 50 yards and sent it flaming into the sea. Capt. Franklin Oksala was flying as Rowland's Wingman and picked out the number three man of the first Tony flight just as he pulled down to starboard. Oksala opened fire from 250 yards and closed to 50 yards, and the Tony burst into flames.

Capt. Samuel Blair, leading the second flight, had problems releasing his belly tank, but closed on the Tony and began firing at 500 yards to point blank range and watched it plunge into the sea. Capt. Edward Roddy (342FS), Blair's Wingman, dove and opened fire on the number four man of the third enemy flight and did not fire until he closed to 50 yards and exploded the Tony. As he continued his dive, Roddy saw the Hamp formation below and chose one, opening fire at 300 yards and closing to 50 yards. He exploded his second victim of the day and his first two of eight during the war.

LEFT: Capt. Richard **Bong** shot down two Zeros to make him a quadruple ace with 21 victories. Going on leave he would not score again until 15 February 1944. (AAF)

RIGHT: Lt.Col. Robert **Rowland** shot down two Tonys to give him three victories. (AFAA)

7 November 1943: Rabaul
8FG/80FS

Meanwhile, after the prevailing poor weather between New Guinea and Rabaul had canceled missions on 6 November, the next day B-24s and escorts were ordered to Rapopo Airdrome. Weather fronts impeded the mission, and seven of the original formation of the 80th Squadron's 16 P-38s had turned back before the target was reached. 80FS CO Maj. Edward Cragg decided to fly a fighter sweep over the area in an attempt to keep the enemy below the level of the bombers, leaving the 431FS/475FG to escort the bombers. The 80th flew in at 25,000 feet, and Cragg sighted at least 60 to 70 Japanese fighters at 15,000 feet in the area. Cragg let down slowly, and the Zekes and Hamps climbed into the battle. The P-38s took violent evasive maneuvers during five to six passes on the enemy. 1Lt. Allen Hill fired on every pass, and on one of his passes hit a Zero on a head on from 250 yards and started a fire in its wings and cockpit, sending it down in flames for his fifth victory to make him an ace. Flight Leader 1Lt. Cy Homer dove through a formation of approximately 30 fighters on his first pass and fired at and missed two Zeros, then fired on a third. His tracers hit the cockpit of the enemy, which pulled up gradually and fell off to the right. It was claimed as a probable, as Homer did not see it crash because he was then attacked by six Zeros. Homer was forced to dive violently, and after recovering from this dive, he climbed back to altitude but lost his flight. He then saw two Zeros chasing a P-38 and dove to the rescue, causing them to break off their attack. Homer continued to attack, but was unable to get any good shots, as he was constantly forced to evade after being attacked during six passes. He saw a lone Zero at 19,000 feet and got a good deflection shot that blew off its aileron, then followed it down as it went out of control. Although none of the other 80FS pilots scored, all made passes at the enemy and kept at least 50 of them occupied and away from the bombers; all of the B-24s returned to base safely. On this day F/O Robert Gentile was flying on the wing of 1Lt. Leland Blair when the two ran into the weather front and Gentile did not return. Also two Squadron P-38s returned on a single engine.

1Lt. Allen **Hill**. (L) became an ace with two Zero victories. (AFAA)

475FG/431FS

At 1007, 1Lt. Marion Kirby led 12 P-38s on right flank low cover for 90BG B-24s attacking Rabaul with his White Flight Wingman, 2Lt. Frederick Champlin, and second Element Leader 1Lt. Paul Morriss with Maj. Merle Smith. Soon Red Flight Leader Capt. Frank Nichols and his Wingman, 1Lt. George Viet, aborted, and Red Second Element 1Lt. Arthur Wenige and his Wingman, 2Lt. Robert Herman, joined Blue third flight, consisting of 1Lt. Jack Mankin and his Wingman, 2Lt. Roger Pare, and the second element of 1Lt. Harold Holze and his Wingman, 1Lt. William Gronemeyer. The Squadron stayed on the Liberator's right flank until they were about to make their run, when Kirby saw two unidentified aircraft above and to the rear of the last bomber in the formation. By the time these aircraft were identified as P-38s the Squadron had fallen far behind the bombers and tried to catch up. They passed near thick clouds at 23,000 feet over the Duke of York Islands. Twenty Oscars and Tonys bounced the Squadron from above and the rear.

Kirby and Wingman Champlin tried to turn into the enemy but were attacked, and the two dove away with the rest of the formation. After Kirby and Champlin escaped both missed passes on the same fighter and returned to the bombers and escorted them home. Kirby's second element (Morriss and Smith) followed Kirby down, and Morriss chased an enemy fighter off Kirby's tail. The two made a few passes before joining Kirby and Champlin in their escort of the bombers.

Mankin led his expanded Blue Flight (six in a string) into the attackers, and on his first pass Mankin set a Tony on fire that was flying at 90 degrees below and in front of him. Mankin had to dive away to evade the other enemy fighters. After he got away his engine began to misfire and he had to throttle back as he met some Oscars coming in from Wide Bay, over Cape Gazelle. The Oscars attacked, and Mankin and Wingman Pare both fired at them and missed, but then Mankin "made a pass at one Oscar and he also burned." Mankin's two victories made him an ace. After Mankin downed his Tony, second Element Leader Holze fired at very close range at an attacking Zero and he saw hits on its nose, but it continued to fly and was listed as a probable. While flying over the Warangoi River Holze saw a Tony attack Pare, who was flying ahead of him, and moved in and fired into its engine and cockpit. The Tony exploded, half rolled, and went into a vertical dive toward the ground. While Holze was making his attack his Wingman, Gronemeyer, did his job and scared an enemy fighter off Holze' tail. Over Alder Bay Wenige, from Mankin's add on element, saw the eight to ten enemy fighters returning from their attacks on the bombers. A Tony made a pass on Wenige's Wingman Herman, who turned slightly and fired, and the Tony burst into flames as it passed by. Herman then made a near head on pass at a Zero which began to smoke and then burst into flames. Wenige's victory was his sixth and last of the war, while Herman's was his only victory. The 431st would not have another claim until 16 December.

1Lt. Jack **Mankin** shot down a Tony and Oscar to give him five victories. (AFAA)

49FG/9FS

Also that day, newly promoted Capt. John O'Neill led seven 9FS Lightnings on another high altitude sweep of Rabaul and Simpson Harbor. O'Neill's Flight encountered a small Zero formation and hit several, but none were confirmed.

7 November 1943: New Guinea
35FG/40FS/39FS

The 35FS remained at Dobodura throughout the greater part of the October-November Rabaul operations, and did not participate in anything more than routine convoy patrol. By 3 November the squadron was back at Port Moresby for a few more days, and then it was off again on another special mission to operate with the 2nd Task Force at Nadzab. Soon after their arrival at Nadzab, the 35th Fighter Group underwent the first major Japanese air raid on their new base on 6 November. During the morning a formation of 10 enemy bombers escorted by 10 fighters surprised the base and dropped a large number of fragmentation bombs. The 41FS suffered two killed and 16 wounded and two P-39s destroyed and 23 slightly damaged. There were no local air patrols and no fighters were sent up.

40FS

After suffering losses in personnel and aircraft on the ground the day before without sending up any opposition, at 0700 eight P-39s of the 40FS took off for a patrol over Nadzab. Red Flight consisted of Leader Capt. Joseph Lamphere and his Wingman, 1Lt. Walter Thayer, as well as 2Lt. William Strand (the second Element Leader had aborted). White Flight consisted of Flight Leader 1Lt. Benjamin Ewers, his Wingman, 2Lt. Henry Wilkes, and second Element Leader 1Lt. John Doorden and Wingman 1Lt. Carl Nelson.

The two flights were to rendezvous over Kaiapit at 0735 at 15,000 feet. But before the rendezvous Red Flight was called to check a plot 20 miles away, which turned out to be friendly. Another plot was called 20 miles north of Saidor Airfield, and Red Flight investigated again. At 0755 Red Flight was at 18,000 feet when they spotted nine bombers at 20,000 feet and an unknown number of Oscars at 25,000 feet. Since the flight was at an altitude disadvantage Lamphere called the coordinates and attempted to gain altitude, but the Oscars prevented this by diving on the P-39 flight, which had to dive away to escape. Finally, the Oscars returned to their bombers and Lamphere climbed to 25,000 feet, keeping in visual contact with the bombers. The bombers turned east to make their bombing run and then turned north to return to base. Lamphere chased after them and caught them over the mountains, but had to hold up, as a flight of P-47s (36FS) arrived from the east and attacked the left side of the bomber formation; when they broke away they left a bomber on fire and another fell out of the formation. The bombers were in a slight dive to maintain their speed on the way home, but Red Flight stayed with them by turning into them and not diving, thus giving up valuable altitude. At 10,000 feet near Saidor Lamphere lost both the bombers and his flight, but got an overhead shot at an Oscar for a probable. Thayer waited for the P-47s to finish their attack on the bombers and attacked the third bomber from the rear, setting the right engine on fire, and the Sally fell away in flames. As he climbed to regain altitude Thayer was attacked by two Oscars and dove away, and with no hope of catching up with the bombers again he headed back to base. When the Oscars made their passes 2Lt. Strand saw an Oscar close on Lamphere and Wilkes, and Strand fired a head on pass at it; the enemy fighter staggered and trailed smoke, but was not seen to crash by him (probable). Lamphere climbed to 21,000 feet, where he chased three Zeros heading north and overtook them and fired on the Leader, and his cannon shells tore into his wing and he was given a probable.

1Lt. Walter **Thayer** scored his only victory of the war. (AAF)

As White Flight prepared to make their attack on the Sallys, two Oscars dove on them from the left and above. White Flight Leader 1Lt. Benjamin Ewers made his first pass from dead astern immediately after the P-47s left and saw no hits or fire. He then pulled up on an Oscar that was only trailing 50 yards behind a P-47 and fired a deflection shot that hit it, but there was no smoke (for a probable). Ewers returned to the bomber formation and fired from dead astern on a Sally that flew away trailing smoke (for a probable). Ewers broke away to the right level and turned back to attack another Sally. He fired a close in long burst that started the bomber's starboard engine on fire, and it peeled down and the wing tore off; it crashed into a mountain. Ewers rejoined his Wingman, 2Lt. John Wilkes, and followed him back to base. Wilkes made no claims for the day, but was almost a claim himself by a "friendly" P-47. While standing by as the P-47s attacked the Japanese, Wilkes saw a pair of Thunderbolts turn toward him and called "P-47s, this is a P-39 don't shoot." Wilkes flew straight ahead, tipping his wings to flash the Stars and Bars. The P-47s continued toward him, and Wilkes continued to shout his warning over his radio. When tracers passed under his wings Wilkes went into two vertical rolls straight down, and after several hits on his tail, wings, and prop he heard to his relief, "P-39, we're sorry." 1Lt. John Doordan, White Flight second Element Leader, followed Ewers and his Wingman to attack the rear of the Sally formation, firing a long burst, and the right side of the bomber started on fire and it plunged down, but he was only credited with a probable, as there was no confirmation. Doordan continued to close from down and left on another Sally, firing with both his cannon and machine guns, and the bomber exploded directly in front of him. He was lucky that no pieces hit his fighter. As Doordan broke away he was being chased by enemy escorts, but was rescued by P-47s. Doordan was unable to find his flight and joined several P-40s of the 8FS and returned to base. Doordan's Wingman, 1Lt. Carl Nelson, turned on an Oscar that turned away, and he then found himself to be the last of his flight to attack the Sallys' left flank. He closed on the left Sally Wingman from dead astern with a 20 degree deflection shot that hit the port engine and the bomber trailed smoke. He then shifted his fire to the right Wingman in the face of fire from the dorsal turrets of the bomber flight and broke off without observing any hits.

For the day, the 40th had shot down four Sallys plus two probables and an Oscar plus three probables. The Squadron lost two pilots in combat, while the Group had four men wounded on the ground and lost two more P-39s on the ground with 12 more slightly damaged.

39FS

The 39FS was flying a sweep to Rabaul and waited at 28,000 feet for the Zeros to come up after them. They arrived at 24,000 feet and the Squadron dove on them. 1Lt. Gordon Prentice made several passes but was not able to get within range, and then became separated from his flight. He made a head on pass on a Zero but his guns quit at very close range, and it went into a stall and fell off out of control but was scored as a probable. This would be the 39th's last claim until 8 January 1944.

8FG/36FS

The 36FS had not scored a victory since 11 July, when it had its last hurrah in its P-39s, scoring five victories. The Squadron was now equipped with their new P-47s and was eager to find out what they could do in combat. The Squadron sent out a Special Flight of four patrolling Thunderbolts consisting of Flight Leader 1Lt. James McLaughlin and his Wingman, 1Lt. William Giroux; and Element Leader 1Lt. Joel Clements and his Wingman, 1Lt. Edward Milner. The flight took off from Wards Drome at 0710 and landed at Nadzab

1Lt. Edward **Milner** got his only victory of the war. (AAF)

after patrolling from Nadzab to Gusap during the take off and landing of the bombers. As they neared Bulolo, the flight was alerted to enemy aircraft approaching from the northwest. After they climbed to 21,000 feet between Lae and Nadzab they spotted nine to ten bombers of the "Sally or Helen type" five miles ahead at 10 o'clock and 1,000 feet making their bombing run, escorted by about a dozen fighter escorts. After completing their bombing run the enemy bomber formation turned north, which set them up for a firing run by the Americans. McLaughlin ordered tanks to be dropped, but Clements was unable to jettison his tanks and Giroux forgot to switch tanks and his engines quit until they were switched to MAIN; both fell behind during the initial attack. McLaughlin and Milner continued a 45 degree frontal attack and fired on one bomber but saw no hits, then made another attack on two more bombers, getting hits on both but without seeing any damage. He then climbed for another attack, but oil covered his windshield, and at the top of his climb McLaughlin heard machine gun fire and saw a fighter closing from behind. McLaughlin skidded to port and the enemy fighter passed by on the starboard and made a climbing turn in front of McLaughlin, who pulled up to get a stall shot but was unable to see the results through his oil-spattered windshield. Clements saw pieces come off for a damaged claim. An Oscar came on the scene and Milner shot it down.

After Giroux got his engines restated he flew to the left side of the bombers and found that his guns would not fire, discovering that the switch would not stay in the ON position. Giroux went into another attack but his gun switch failed again. He kept on flicking the switch while holding down the trigger and the guns began to fire. Giroux fired a short burst to establish range and a longer burst from the rear and got good hits before breaking away to attack another Sally, firing another long burst from the rear. This Sally left the formation after suffering hits. Giroux then chased another Sally and got more hits. Giroux's ICR describes three Sallys as crashing or on fire which may or may not have been his victims, and he was officially credited with a frustrating three probables for his first claims of the war. However, the 36FS Historian gave him two victories and a probable for the day.

Clements was unable to release his tanks and dropped behind and stayed out of range, as he could not make a deflection shot without exposing his belly tank to enemy fire. He then pulled up 1,500 feet with the intention of Split-S'ing directly on the lead bomber. But as he was about to roll over on the lead bomber an enemy fighter dove from 3,000 feet and hit his Thunderbolt from its tail through its left fuselage and wing. Clements kicked right rudder and dove away, which put him over the lead bomber of the last three ship element of the formation. He rolled down and out at 60 degrees and fired a three second burst that exploded the bomber. As he pulled away Clements fired on the Wing bomber, seeing hits on its right wing and engine for a probable claim.

The Squadron's ICRs described that when the Sallys lost a bomber from their formation they closed quickly. The Sally gunners put out a large volume of ineffective fire that was often fired from out of range.

348FG/341FS

On 7 November, Lt.Col. Robert Rowland led a flight of four P-47s from Moresby at 0710 on a fighter sweep to Wewak consisting of his Wingman, Capt. Frank Oksala, and the second element led by Capt. Samuel Blair and his Wingman, Capt. Edward Roddy. When they were over Wau *Crossroads* Controller vectored them to an enemy plot near Nadzab. The flight climbed to 18,000 feet over the Markham Valley when *Crossroads* told them that the enemy fighters were at 25,000 feet and the bombers at 18,000 feet. The flight began to climb for the altitude advantage to get their backs to the sun. *Crossroads* then directed them northward toward Saidor at 26,000 feet, where Roddy spotted five Hamps and one Tony at 22,000 feet. Roddy, with Oksala as his Wingman, dove toward the Tony, but found that it was a P-39 being chased by the five Hamps. Oksala slowed his dive and saw a Hamp get on his tail, which gave Oksala a point blank shot at the Hamp, which caught on fire and crashed into the ocean.

Lt.Col. Robert **Rowland** shot down two Zeros to become an ace. (AAF)

Meanwhile, two Hamps ahead and below pulled up into a loop, and Rowland closed and shot down the enemy Wingman from 6 o'clock just as he pulled up even with him in his loop. The Hamp caught on fire and crashed about 20 yards from the Saidor shore. The Element Leader then completed his loop and got on Rowland's tail. Rowland went into a quick rolling starboard turn and escaped. As he climbed back to altitude he saw a diving Hamp heading in front of him and to his right. Rowland turned and got off a 15 degree deflection shot that hit the cockpit and engine, and this Hamp crashed just inshore. Blair dove with Rowland and got on the tail of a Hamp and began firing at 150 yards to 50 yards, until the enemy's prop wash flipped him on his back. The Hamp burst into flames and crashed into a mountain. Blair saw another Hamp and went into a dive, but lost him and rejoined the flight at 32,000 feet, where the four P-47s continued to fly patrol over Nadzab until they ran out of oxygen.

49FG/8FS

Australian Commander Gen. George Vasey's 7th Division had forced the Japanese to retreat into the Finistere Mountains, on the eastern flank of the Ramu Valley, but a tenacious enemy rear guard in the Shaggy Ridge highlands stalled the Australian advance. Capt. Ernest Harris' 8FS Black Sheep had recently moved to a dirt strip designated as Gusap #3 during the last week of October. The strip was only five minutes by air from Vasey's beleaguered troops, and the Warhawks delivered their 500 pound bombs on enemy positions entrenched on the 5,000 foot promontory known as the "Pimple." By the end of October the 7th Division resumed their offensive, forcing the Japanese into the coastal valley, and began the final attack to capture the enemy airdromes at Bogadjim, Madang, and Alexishafen, which were located only 30 miles beyond the Finistere Range. Until the other Allied Gusap airstrips were completed, base defense and dive bombing sorties to the Highlands were the responsibility of the Black Sheep. The Japanese usually sent air raids from Wewak, Madang, and Bogadjim each morning that interrupted work on the strip and forced the men into rain-filled trenches.

8FS Morning Flight

Black Sheep Ops Exec Capt. Clyde Barnett, the last of the Darwin veterans to be on combat duty with the 5th Fighter Command, decided to do something about these annoying raids, and the 49er CO gave him permission to attack Bogadjim. During the morning mission Barnett, Wingman F/O Walter Linder, Element Leader 1Lt. James Carter,and Wingman 1Lt. Nelson Flack took off at 0700 and climbed due north through the thin haze over the Finistere Range. The four Black Sheep reached the coast in only 10 minutes, and then flew 10 miles north at 10,000 feet over the sea past Bogadjim to attack out of the sun. A few minutes later they neared Alexishafen and saw a large enemy formation of nine bombers and about 25 radial engine fighters heading toward New Britain. As the enemy formation was too far out of range, the 49ers headed back toward Alexishafen. Over Alexishafen, Barnett saw 25-30 enemy fighters below at 10,000 feet and ordered belly tanks to be dropped. The Flight attacked directly out of the sun and completely surprised the enemy.

Barnett began firing at the leader of the highest three ship element from 300 yards and continued to fire to 100 feet, observing numerous hits along the entire fuselage, and the enemy pilot went down in flames. F/O Walter Lindner followed slightly behind and below Barnett and fired on the right fighter in the V missing with a short burst that passed under its tail. Lindner raised his nose and moved level and slightly astern, then fired another burst that hit its tail. Lindner held the trigger, and the tracers continued hitting from the tail to the cockpit and hitting the engine and propeller. Flack fired a burst from 200 yards that exploded the wing roots, and it went into a spin trailing flames. After firing at another enemy fighter without result, Flack started climbing when he saw an Oscar and four Zeros circling in a Lufbery below climbing toward him. Flack out-climbed and out-turned them during five 360 degree turns and got on the tail of the last Zero in the string. Flack fired and the Zero flew through the stream of bullets, climbing momentarily before going straight down "as if the pilot were dead." Flack followed his smoking victim down and watched it crash, but was unaware of the Zeros on his tail. Flack quickly became aware when a 20mm shell hit his fuselage fuel tank, which self-sealed as Flack climbed away.

1Lt. Nelson **Flack** claimed his first victory and a probable on his way to becoming a five victory ace. (AFAA)

Capt. Clyde **Barnett** fell short of becoming an ace getting his fourth and last victory. (AAF)

1Lt. Robert **White**. (being decorated by Gen, Wurtsmith) claimed his ninth and last victory of the war. (AFAA)

8FS Afternoon Flights

The 8FS sent two more flights to Alexishafen that day, but the Japanese did not respond until the last 8FS sweep was flown early in the afternoon to Bogadjim. Capt. Ernest Harris with Wingman 1Lt. John Hanson, Element Leader 1Lt. Charles Petersen, and Wingman 1Lt. Philip Hurst led the Red Flight, while 1Lt. Robert White headed the Blue Flight of 1Lts. Joel Thorvaldson, Element Leader Elferd Elofson, and Wingman 2Lt. Merle Wolfe. This quartet climbed to 12,000 feet over the coast, where they sighted enemy aircraft to the north beyond Alexishafen. Before they could close, the enemy fighters disappeared into the overcast when the Gusap Controller reported a radar contact approaching from the southwest back over their home base. The Black Sheep turned 180 degrees and headed south back inland, where they made enemy contact directly over Bogadjim Village.

A northbound line astern formation of six Zeros was approaching below at 5,000 feet, heading toward the Ramu Valley. Harris' Red Flight immediately attacked from head on. The enemy fighters responded by climbing into the Black Sheep attack, and Harris followed the enemy leader, who began to climb. Harris followed him into a loop and fired a long burst at the top of the loop, but Harris stalled out and was unable to see the results of his attack. Red Element Leader Petersen had held his position throughout Harris' initial maneuvering while keeping watch on the other Zeros. When the Zeros went into a loop to get on Harris' tail Peterson went after the first two, which then chandelled to the right. He fired a one to two second burst at the second Zero without observable results. The third Zero began a Split-S at 1,000 feet slightly to the left and Peterson followed, getting two good bursts at 200-300 yards into its right wing and cockpit. As Peterson did not see the final results he claimed a probable. Red #4, 1Lt. Philip Hurst, had a Zero pull up in front of him to the right, and Hurst fired into its cockpit and it rolled over and began to disintegrate before crashing into the trees below.

Blue Flight got into action when they encountered Zeros at 5,000 feet over Bogadjim. Blue Leader 1Lt. Robert White caught a climbing Zero with a good burst into its port wing ammunition container, which exploded and set the wing on fire. Both Elofson and Thorvaldson made passes on White's target, but when its port wing fell off White got his ninth and last victory of the war. Blue #2 (Thorvaldson) made a pass on White's Zero when it dropped off on one wing toward him and had to maneuver quickly to avoid a midair collision. As he pulled up he saw a Zero on the tail of a P-40. The Zero turned toward Thorvaldson, who fired head on until he was forced to break away. The Zero rolled on its back at 1,500 feet and crashed inverted for Thorvaldson's only victory of the war.

Harris radioed for the two flights to regroup and they returned to Gusap, where Hanson's prop control failed on his final approach leg, causing him to over run the dirt strip. The Warhawk pancaked, but Hanson walked away uninjured. The score for the Black Sheep mission was six kills, two probables, and no losses, for which Harris was summarily promoted to Major.

8 November 1943: Bong Loses Wingmen

On his last mission of his first overseas tour, Capt. Richard Bong, with 21 victories, was frustrated when he missed several good opportunities to increase his score. Bong and his Wingman, 1Lt. Stanley Johnson, went after about 10 Zeros that were chasing a lone P-38, and when he pulled out of the unsuccessful attack Johnson was no longer behind him. Bong was low on fuel and could not search for him, so he headed toward Dobodura, but did chase Zeros off the tail of 1Lt. Delman Moore, who was flying on one engine. Two days earlier Bong's Wingman, 1Lt. George Haniotis, went down and was not rescued. The loss of Johnson and Haniotis in two days has been the basis for the claim that Bong had a tendency to lose wingmen by various researchers. However, on 6 September he also lost Wingman 2Lt. James Fagan, who was flying his first mission. Bong was said to be so distraught over the loss of Fagan that he refused to fly another mission with a Wingman, but was put on a two week furlough instead. By and large members of Bong's flights have defended him, but also pointed out that Bong was quick to jump into combat, and being a much more experienced and natural pilot than his wingmen, they were unable to stay with him, and in concentrating on staying with him they became vulnerable. After the loss of Haniotis, the #4 man in Bong's flight, 1Lt. Charles McElroy wrote; "I can not imagine Bong being at fault for the loss of this Wingman. There was some gossip about his loss of wingmen but I did not know of any bitter feelings. Possibly his superior ability as a pilot made it difficult for some to stay with him."

9 November 1943: 475FG/431FS/432FS/433FS

While the P-38s of the 5th Fighter Command had been allocating most of their attention to Rabaul shortly after the Bougainville invasion, it was still necessary to hit the enemy airfields at Wewak, Madang, and Alexishafen in New Guinea to prevent buildups of enemy aircraft in the theater.

431FS

The 431st was assigned to fly top cover for B-25s attacking Alexishafen. Ten P-38s took off at 0815, but due to snafus only five rendezvoused with the bombers over the *Gona* wreck. The Squadron was met by several enemy fighters, and although they made no claims, they succeeded in protecting the B-25s. The day before 1Lt. Paul Smith was lost during a local flight.

432FS

Maj. Charles MacDonald flew up from Group Headquarters to fly with the 432FS, and led 12 P-38s from Dobodura at 0815 to fly escort for B-25s to Alexishafen. MacDonald led Red Flight, with 1Lt. John Runnell on his wing and 1Lt. Eugene McGuire as his second Element Leader, who had 2Lt. Henry Condon on his wing. 1Lt. John Loisel led White Flight with Wingman 2Lt. Ferdinand Hanson and 2Lt. Joseph Forster as #3 after the Second Element Leader dropped out. 1Lt. James Ince led Blue Flight with 2Lt. Perry Dahl on his wing and 1Lt. Charles Willis as the second Element Leader with 2Lt. Howard Hedrick on his wing.

At 1020, after the B-25s finished their bombing and strafing attack, 10 to 15 fighters closed on the Lightnings. MacDonald led his P-38s to 8,000 feet, where he closed on these aircraft and ID'd them as enemy. He over flew the first enemy fighter, but Wingman Runnell shot it down. MacDonald then closed on another Zero and fired a long burst at slight deflection, and it spun out of control and crashed into the sea. The other enemy fighters abandoned their attack on the B-25s to deal with MacDonald's flight. MacDonald "mixed it up with three more Zeros," and they shot holes in his Lightning's boom, wing, and stabilizers. Wingman Runnell came in and attacked, hitting a Zero turning in his direction. The Zero pilot steepened his turn, but his damaged fighter took him straight into the water. MacDonald chased another of his attackers that was diving for the safety of the Alexishafen Airstrip. Despite the damage to his fighter, MacDonald closed on the enemy to minimum range and fired a long burst that tore it into fiery pieces on the airstrip below to make him an ace. As MacDonald pulled up over the Alexishafen strip he observed a burning P-38 about to crash near the shore (probably that of ace 1Lt. John Smith of the 433FS). Another Zero approached Runnell and pulled up steeply, and the American fired but saw no results. Runnell flew on and fired on another Zero from close range, directly astern. Pieces flew off the Zero, and it went into a spin and crashed. Second Element Leader (Eugene) McGuire fired at two to three enemy fighters, but did not see any results. Condon, in the #4 position, fired a long burst from 300 yards directly behind a Zero and saw red flashes near the cockpit, but the enemy pilot Split-S'd away and Condon lost sight of it for a probable. Condon made two more unsuccessful passes and then joined Runnell and watched him shoot down his Zero. Runnell made a violent maneuver and separated from Condon, who took a deflection shot at a Zero whose engine quit, and he watched as the enemy pilot glided toward a crash. While Condon watched three P-38s swooped in and finished off his stricken Zero. Condon tried to catch up with his flight with a quick turn and blacked out. When he regained consciousness he joined MacDonald, and the two flew down the Markham Valley and climbed toward a dogfight over Nadzab. They attacked an Oscar, and MacDonald made a head on pass, but it dove away and was hit by a P-39, whose cannon shells tore off the Oscar's tail. Condon returned to base low on fuel, while MacDonald made a head on pass on another Oscar and fired a long burst into its cockpit and

Maj. Charles **MacDonald** finally became an ace with two Zero victories. (AFAA)

2Lt. Perry **Dahl** was awarded the first of his nine victories. (AFAA)

engine. MacDonald almost collided with the Oscar, coming so close that his port wing was thrown up by the enemy's air stream. It was impossible for MacDonald to see the Oscar crash because of the clouds below and he was credited with a probable, but the two victories made him an ace with six enemy fighters downed.

1Lt. James Ince led Blue Flight from 16,000 feet to 10,000 feet, where he saw two Zeros below and ordered belly tanks to be dropped. Ince dove and fired a long shot at one that rolled away and then sharply climbed after the second Zero that Split-S'd in front of him. Ince fired a quick burst but did not see any results. He then dove on another Zero, taking a quick shot as it was in a tight turn, getting behind Willis and Hedrick. Ince's Second Element Leader Willis fired a short burst before a Zero got on his tail. Willis made a turn to port to escape, but lead the enemy pilot toward Ince. Ince pulled a very tight turn and got behind Willis' pursuer, firing a short burst before it rolled away. As Ince straightened out another Zero made a head on pass, but Ince held his fire until the enemy closed to 100 yards, and the Zero went into a slow roll and started to smoke when 2Lt. Perry Dahl came in from behind and fired to receive credit for his first victory. Ince then led his flight from the enemy strip toward the hills, where a lone Zero approached in a diving turn. Ince pulled around and fired a 30 degree deflection shot from head on, and the Zero rolled under Ince, who lost sight of it as it passed under him. However, Hedrick confirmed the victory, which made Ince an ace. Meanwhile, Willis has lost Ince. He climbed to 7,000 feet and got an unsuccessful shot at an Oscar before he saw three blue nosed P-38s chasing a Zero. The enemy pilot Split-S'd toward Willis 30 degrees head on. Willis fired a long range cannon burst that hit the Zero in its wing and tail. As Willis completed his firing pass he banked to the right and saw the Zero explode as it hit the water south of the airstrip. Willis joined a fight between four Lightnings and five Oscars, where he took a shot at an Oscar that Split-S'd out of the fight. When the Oscar leveled out he was shot down by another P-38. Willis was almost out of fuel and had to land at Lae to refuel before returning to Dobodura.

433FS

At 0830, Capt. Daniel Roberts led 12 P-38s to the usual rendezvous over a grounded ship near Gona. Possum Squadron was assigned to provide low cover between 6,000 to 8,000 feet for four B-25 Squadrons of the 38BG. Roberts' lead Red Flight consisted of Wingman 2Lt. Dale Meyer, followed by 2Lts. William Jeakle and William Grady in the Second Element. The Mitchells were able to leave the area with the 432FS protecting them from above and the 433FS from below. After the bombers completed their run the flight encountered 15 to 20 Oscars and Tonys head on at 2,000 to 6,000 feet over Sek Harbor, between Alexishafen and Madang. The Flight made a number of passes, mainly on Hamps. Grady followed one down to about 50 feet above the water and fired a long burst from 100 yards. The Hamp pilot turned sharply and crashed into the water. Jeakle fired at "about 10 E/A," and finally met a Hamp head on just above the water. When it turned away in a chandelle Jeakle followed through and fired a long burst that sent it directly into the water. Roberts attacked a Hamp that burst into flames directly above the water. Roberts and Meyer chased another Oscar toward the airstrip, but the Oscar turned sharply to the starboard and both P-38s tried to turn with it. Unfortunately, Roberts cut the corner much tighter than Meyer, and Roberts and his Wingman died in a horrendous crash east of the airstrip.

Flight Leader 1Lt. John Babel and Wingman 2Lt. Jack Fisk, with Second Element Leader and ace 1Lt. John Smith, dropped their tanks and went after three Hamps but lost them. They saw a dogfight offshore and approached a number of Zeros. Babel reports that he saw Smith diving on a Zero on the Flight's first pass but never saw him again. Babel and Fisk continued on and made passes that missed when the enemy pilots Split-S'd away. A Hamp came at them at 1 o'clock, and Fisk turned up into it and fired a two second burst at 200 yards, hitting the engine and fuselage; it passed under Fisk and crashed into the water. Babel then caught a Zero at 2,000 feet, 12 o'clock low and turning to port, with a deflection shot and fired a long burst, closing down to 75 yards. The Zero caught on fire and crashed into the trees south of Alexishafen Airdrome.

Capt. Warren Lewis led White Flight, and had followed Roberts down on a pass on a lone Zero, but was unable to follow it and broke off after a short time. Lewis turned sharply toward shore and saw a Tony heading inland and chased after it. He closed to 200 yards and fired a long burst that started it smoking, and it crashed just offshore. Lewis then made four passes on a Hamp that resulted in only a damaged wing. As he was leaving for home he saw a lone Hamp and closed to 75 yards. He fired his machine guns and cannon into its cockpit and watched it crash into the water. Lewis' #4 man, 2Lt. Herbert Cochran, was unable to drop his tanks and left the flight. He was followed by a Hamp that made a number of passes on him. Cochran led the Hamp in front of the lethal forward fire power of the B-25 that shot it down. He was finally able to drop his tanks and rejoined White Flight. Cochrane made a pass on a Hamp from astern just above the water and fired a long burst that sent the enemy fighter into the water. Although the 433rd claimed eight victories, Lewis' two victories and those of Cochran and Jeakle were downgraded officially to probables.

Although 475FG pilots downed nine Japanese fighters and three others probably destroyed to give them 225 aerial victories, they lost three fighters and pilots. Roberts' victory gave him 14 for his illustrious career. Roberts' and Smith's bodies were eventually found and buried in the American Cemetery and Memorial at Manila. Dale Meyer was never found.

9 November 1943: 8FG/35FS/36FS

35FS

The 35FS sent up eight P-40s on a patrol over Nadzab, and at 1115 the Controller called enemy aircraft over the field. The Squadron was nearby and saw eight to ten aircraft milling around. 1Lt. Harold Souther was leading Blue Flight with 2Lt.Carl Weaver on his wing. Weaver spotted two Zeros

Capt. Daniel **Roberts** and his P-38 marked with his 14th and last victory. (AAF)

500 feet under their flight, and Souther ordered the tanks to be dropped and dove in a long half roll but lost the Zeros. They climbed back to altitude and saw a Tony straggler. Souther and Weaver dove on it and Souther fired, but the Tony pilot rolled and Split-S'd away trailing smoke for a probable. Souther and Weaver climbed to 16,000 feet, where they sighted two Zeros below them. Souther half rolled on one while Weaver did an aileron roll down and got on the other Zero's tail. This Zero was trying to do a tight turn to get on Souther's tail. Weaver's first shot was short, and he tightened his turn and fired a long burst "which seemed to disappear into the Zero." The Zero rolled, its starboard wing broke off near the root, and a fire erupted from the stump. As Weaver pulled up he saw a fighter approaching, but it was a P-39, and Weaver tagged along for a while before running low on fuel and returning to base.

36FS Last Successful P-39 Mission

By 3 November the 36FS had 18 P-47s in inventory, and two days later the strength of the squadron included 12 more P-39s. The Squadron flew several missions using both types, but by 27 November all the Airacobras were transferred out of the 36th, and the P-39 was no longer on front line fighter duty with the 5AF. The last successful combat fought by the P-39 in the SWPA occurred on 9 November when a flight of P-39s consisting of Flight leader 1Lt. Jack Ericsson and Wingman 2Lt. William Turner, along with Second Element Leader 1Lt. Thomas Huff and his Wingman, 1Lt. James Drymon, left Ward's Drome to patrol the Nadzab area at 21,000 feet. When they arrived at 1050 there already was a dogfight going on over the Markham River between the Huon Gulf and Lake Wanum in the direction of Nadzab between eight Oscars and another flight of P-39s and two P-38s. Ericsson and Turner dropped their tanks and dove first, with Ericsson chasing an Oscar that was in a port turn. The Oscar pilot went into a vertical reverse and climbed in front of Ericsson, who fired a 30 to 0 degree deflection shot, knocking pieces off its wing. The enemy pilot rolled over and dove away, and Ericsson filed a damaged claim (however, in his IRC Wingman Turner thought he saw the Oscar disintegrate and its pilot bail out, but this was Huff's victory, not Ericsson's). Ericsson and Turner climbed to 19,000 feet, and then circled to the right and dove on another Oscar. Ericsson fired as he pulled up but without apparent result. Turner closed in quickly and established a lead and fired, also without result, and lost Ericsson as he went into a high speed stall and lost considerable altitude. As he pulled up he joined two P-39s from another Squadron and was joined by Drymon; they returned to base after patrolling for another 20 minutes above Nadzab before running low on fuel. Meanwhile, Ericsson circled again and two Oscars dove on him, and he had to dive 8,000 feet to escape and return to base.

Second Element Leader Huff and his Wingman Drymon followed Ericsson and Turner. An Oscar made a 45 degree turn in front of Huff, who fired long burst at about 45 to 0 degrees deflection, and as the Oscar eased his turn Huff came in behind him but had to break away to avoid a collision. Drymon reported that he saw Huff's Oscar's tail break off and its pilot bail out. Drymon turned to port and got a two second burst, causing a few hits. The two climbed back up to 17,000 feet, and Huff made an ineffective pass on an Oscar flying 2,000 feet below that was in a long diving turn. Drymon made a 30 degree deflection shot and closed to 0 degrees, hitting the Oscar in its wing roots; its flying pieces dented Drymon's wing. The Oscar rolled over on its back and dove into the ground. The two then climbed back to 19,000 feet, and Drymon made an 80-90 degree shot on an Oscar in a steep port turn that hit it in the tail. He lost it as it passed under him. Huff separated from Drymon and circled for another 10 minutes before retuning to Nadzab. Drymon lost Huff when two Oscars dove on him from 7 o'clock above and Drymon went into a 400mph dive to escape. Drymon climbed to 20,000 feet, where he joined Turner.

9 November 1943: 35FG/40FS

1Lt. John Clapper, the Mission Leader and Blue Flight Leader, took off at 1055 with White Flight under Capt. Jack Grimm on a local patrol with eight P-39s. At 1105, Blue Flight had reached 7,000 feet when a transport called that it was being attacked. The Squadron climbed to 20,000 feet toward Lae, where they saw about a dozen enemy fighters at 12 o'clock and slightly below. Clapper fired at an Oscar, setting it on fire, and passed on to another Oscar, getting good hits on its fuselage at the wing root back to the tail (victory confirmed later). Clapper went into a high speed stall and then a half turn spin straight down, pulling out at 10,000 feet. He climbed to 15,000 to look for a reported bomber in the area when an Oscar attacked out of the sun. His P-39's nose and engine were hit, sending oil over the windshield while bullets hit his tail, putting his radio out of commission. Clapper turned down and over, and as he went into a Split-S he saw another Airacobra (2Lt. Nathan Smith) firing a long shot from 1,000 yards at the tail of the threatening Oscar, which suspended his attack.

Capt. Grimm and Red Flight were flying between base and Lae at 18,000 feet when he saw an Oscar 2,000 feet below and dove on it. He stayed on its tail and fired until its wing fell off. 1Lt. John Davis was the Red second Element Leader, and saw two Oscars below engaged by P-47s. Davis dove but his Wingman did not. Davis: "There was an Oscar chasing my Oscar but the enemy was slow rolling and the P-47 was missing him." Davis maneuvered ahead and above the Oscar and fired as the enemy pilot began a slow port turn and fired three bursts. The first missed, but the next two hit the hit the tail and fuselage and then the canopy. The Oscar banked steeply to the left and Davis had to increase his lead, but the left wing blew at the wing root.

11 November 1943: 35FG/41FS

Four 41FS Flights were assigned to strafe the #2 Strip at Alexishafen Airdrome. Two flights remained at top cover while Blue Flight and Red Flight, led by Maj. Fred Thompson, strafed the Drome. Thompson spotted a lone Val flying at about 500 feet about two miles from the field, and while the rest of his Flight strafed the field Thompson closed on the enemy dive bomber. He fired a short burst that exploded the enemy's wing for his second and last victory.

Maj. Fred **Thompson** claimed his second of two WW-2 victories. (AAF)

11 November 1943: 49FG/9FS

On the 11th, the last six serviceable aircraft in the 9FS sortied with the Lightning wing to Rabaul. Realizing that Bong had been affected by his loss of several wingmen, 1Lt. Ralph Wandrey reassured Bong that he would stay on his wing during Bong's determined hunt for the six victories keeping him from Rickenbacker's American record of 26. Once over Rabaul's Simpson Harbor the P-38s found no action, and Bong decided to search over Rabaul Town to lure Japanese fighters up to combat. The two Lightnings raced down the main street of Rabaul Town at tree top level and escaped through bursting flak, but no enemy fighters challenged. On their return, the Flying Knights were stood down from the mission schedule after 169 aerial victories and the Squadron's third Distinguished Unit Citation; this DUC awarded for the Knight's role in the Rabaul raids. The concerted air campaign resulted in Lightnings that were too worn out to continue and were sent to the maintenance squadron at Dobodura. Most of the senior officers, including Bong, were given the option to return to the States or transition to the Republic P-47 Thunderbolt, which would become the Flying Knights' new ride.

Dobodura had been greatly improved since it had been established during the Buna campaign of 1942. But the Japanese had long since retreated to the north or had been killed at Salamaua and Lae, and the situation at Dobodura had changed significantly for Lt.Col. James Selman's 49'ers. With the loss of the 9FS Flying Knights' P-38s, Melikian's 7FS Screamin' Demons were the last 49er unit on flight status at the expanding airdrome, as more bomber units were being based at Horanda and air traffic had become a problem.

So with the battle front far beyond the range of their P-40s and P-47s, it was time for the 49ers to move forward, and the Demons were ordered to move to their new base at Gusap, in the Ramu River Valley. While the 49ers at Dobodura prepared for their November move, the Japanese also attempted to reinforce their weakening hold on the northern New Guinea coast. More soldiers and pilots were marshaled to aid their besieged forces at Wewak, but the Empire was desperately short of supplies and fresh troops. There would be no enemy forces strong enough to stop MacArthur on the land and Kenney in the air.

11 November 1943: 49FG/7FS

On 11 November, 1Lt. Paul Kell led the first echelon of the 7FS into their new bivouac 20 miles southwest of Gusap Village and five miles below the junction of the Ramu River and smaller Gusap River. The strip, designated Gusap #7, was a rough 5,000 foot long dirt runway laying east-west and ended close to the east bank of the Ramu. Within the week, Lt.Col. James Selman moved his 49ers Group HQ into their new bivouac just a few miles southeast of Gusap #7. Operations then began, as the Demons flew daily patrols to familiarize themselves with their new setting. A squadron of 3rd Attack A-20 Havocs also began to fly from a longer strip called Gusap #10, just north of the Demon base on the north side of the Gusap River. All of the Gusap runways were in the open, with no forest to provide a secure dispersal area, so low earth revetments were constructed by graders that merely pushed dirt up into low walls in a U shape. At Gusap #7, the Demons dispersed their P-40s on the north side of the runway via a dirt track that wound through the earth revetments.

11 November 1943: 5AF Rabaul Missions End

The Fifth Fighter and Bomber Commands had been assigned to the Rabaul air campaign from 12 October until its last mission on 11 November. The campaign to reduce Rabaul would be the low point for Kenney as the Commander of the 5AF. He had neither the forces nor the strategic position to support his overly optimistic expectations to finally neutralize Rabaul, which caused him to lose some standing with MacArthur. After the 11th the 13th Air Force, along with Navy and Marine air attacks, finally would force the Japanese to evacuate their air forces from Rabaul during March 1944. The cost of the Rabaul air campaign to the 5th Fighter Command was high, with 22 P-38s lost and many others written off due to combat damage, while others were simply worn out by the prolonged stress of combat on engines and airframes. During the 2 November mission alone nine P-38s were lost over New Britain, and at least five others received major damage. During November 1943 Gen. Kenney was forced to reequip the 9FS and 39FS with P-47s, not P-38s, just to keep the 475FG and the 80FS of the 8FG equipped with P-38s. During the next several months there were not enough Lightnings available in the 5FC when it was to be committed to new air battles over western New Guinea.

On 7 November Adm. William Halsey had carrier Task Group 50.3 of the US Fifth Fleet available, containing the carriers *Bunker Hill*, *Essex* and *Independence* commanded by R.Adm. Alfred Montgomery. Halsey ordered Montgomery and Task Force 38 to execute a double carrier strike against Rabaul on 11 November. Sherman's Task Force 38 launched a strike which attacked in bad weather about 0830 from near Bougainville. After its aircraft returned, Task Force 38 retired to the south without being detected. Meanwhile, Montgomery launched from 160 miles southeast of Rabaul. Only the cruiser *Agano* remained at Rabaul and was torpedoed and heavily damaged. The Japanese launched a series of counterattacks involving 120 aircraft against the US carriers, but were intercepted and lost 35 planes without inflicting damage on Montgomery' ships.

It has been argued that the Rabaul raids revealed the dangers of the divided American SWPA and South Pacific offensives. Halsey had no heavy warships and few carriers because most of these ships were preparing for the Gilberts campaign. Conversely, the heavy losses sustained by the land-based Japanese carrier air groups at Rabaul meant that the Japanese were unable to mount a serious naval defense of the Gilberts.

Results of the Rabaul Campaign

Beginning with the 2 November mission, the nine day Fifth Air Force Rabaul offensive from the Southwest Pacific had not accomplished the results anticipated by both Kenney and Whitehead, as the weather had prevented any type of sustained operations required to destroy a large base such as Rabaul.

The damage inflicted during these attacks has never been determined, first by post-mission photo recon and then by post-war analysis. Exact totals of Japanese aircraft losses were muddled by the large influx of replacement aircraft, and the fact that damaged aircraft could escape on their bases below to safety and repair. Also, the sustained Allied attack was interrupted by bad weather, which gave the Japanese some respite.

An accurate estimate of shipping damage was practically impossible. After the 19 October attack on Rabaul the Imperial Navy withdrew its warships to Truk. The official communiqué claimed that three destroyers, eight large merchant vessels with an aggregate tonnage of 50,000 tons, and four small coastal vessels had been sunk. A later report of the Fifth Air Force listed one destroyer, five merchant vessels totaling approximately 13,000 tons, and 22 other vessels damaged, but even these figures do not entirely agree with the reports of the participating squadrons.

So, although the contribution of the 5AF in the Rabaul Offensive was substantial, as it destroyed supplies and buildings in the Town and on the docks and sunk or damaged tons of shipping, their major contribution was the losses they inflicted on the Japanese air force. Kenney stated: "Our first target has been and will be the destruction of the Japanese Air Force….Even when attacks are directed on enemy shipping; our primary objective is still the destruction of Jap fighters enticed into the air to protect that shipping."

Parafrags were the bombs of choice for low level attack by B-25s and A-20s **phosphorous bombs** were also used. (AAF)

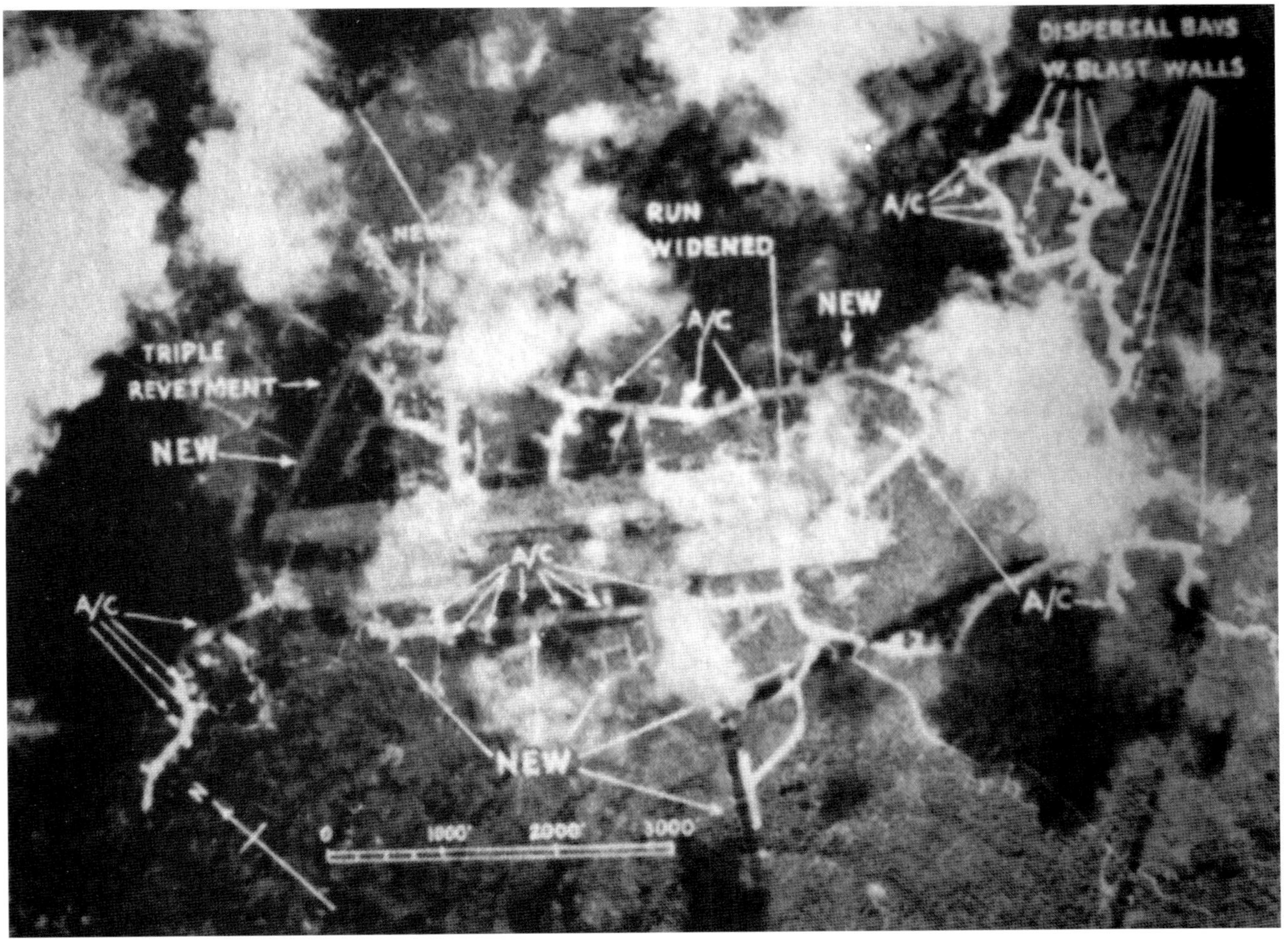

Vunakanau under high altitude bombing attack by B-24s. (AAF)

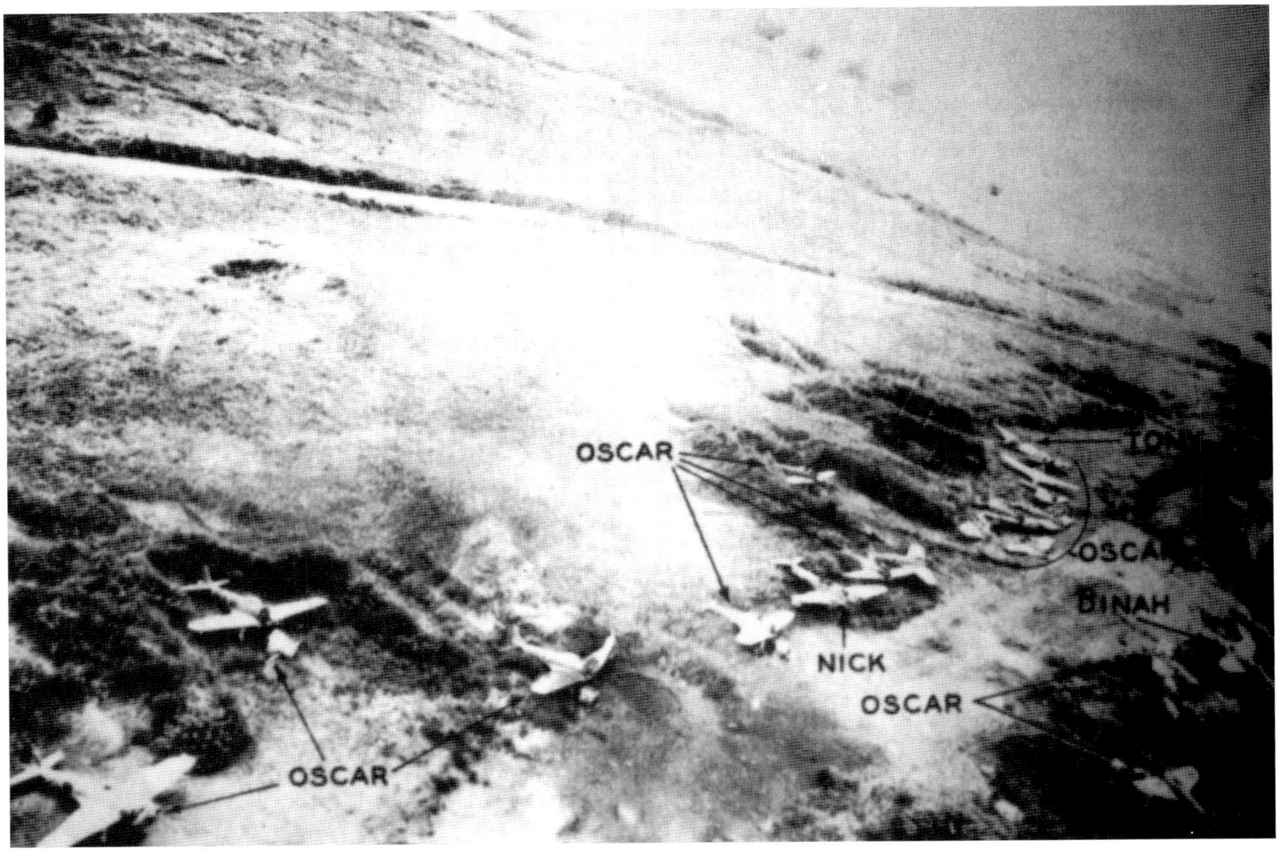

Post mission recon photos of the damage done to aircraft on **Vunakanau**. (AAF)

Although enemy aircraft were the primary objective of the attacks on Rabaul merchant shipping also suffered losses. (AAF)

FIFTH FIGHTER COMMAND CLAIMS OVER RABAUL

Unit	Oct. 12	Oct. 23	Oct. 24	Oct. 25	Oct. 29	Nov. 2	Nov. 5	Nov. 7	Nov. 11	TOTALS
9FS	--	1	6	--	7	6	2	--	--	22
39FS	--	1	4	--	3	1	--	--	--	9
80FS	1	--	12	--	2	8	--	1	--	24
431FS	--	4	2	--	--	9	--	5	--	20
432FS	1	2	6	--	--	5	--	--	--	14
433FS	1	4	10	--	6	--	--	--	--	21
475FG	--	1	--	1	--	--	--	--	--	2
Totals	**3**	**13**	**40**	**1**	**18**	**29**	**2**	**6**	**0**	**112**

FIFTH FIGHTER COMMAND LOSSES OVER RABAUL

Unit	Oct. 12	Oct. 23	Oct. 24	Oct. 25	Oct. 29	Nov. 2	Nov. 5	Nov. 7	Nov. 11	TOTALS
9FS	--	--	--	--	3	2	1	1	--	7
39FS	--	--	1	--	--	--	--	2	--	3
80FS	--	--	1	--	--	2	--	1	--	4
431FS	--	1	--	--	--	3	--	--	--	4
432FS	--	--	--	--	--	1	--	1	1	3
433FS	--	--	--	--	--	1	--	--	--	1
Totals	**0**	**1**	**2**	**0**	**3**	**9**	**1**	**5**	**1**	**22**

All victory credits derived from Frank Olynyk

Losses include all causes: enemy action, weather and operational accidents.

(Note: No fighters arrived over Rabaul on the October 18 mission)

Profiles

[1.] **Curtiss P-40N-5 WARHAWK** s.n. 42-104957 A/C **'white 13'** of Lt. Bob DeHaven, **7 FS / 49 FG** based at Gusap, N.G., late '43 - DeHaven gained his first aerial victory in a Model-K in July, followed with three more kills made in October with the Model-N seen here. The move to Gusap nearly ended his career when on 10 December, he had just shot down his 'ace-maker' fifth victim when **'white 13'** was in turn riddled by a very capable TONY marksman. Resilient DeHaven survived the crash landing back at Gusap and in time collected five more P-40 kills plus four P-38 victories to retire as the highest scoring *'Screamin' Demon'* in the war.

[2.] **Lockheed P-38 G-1-LO LIGHTNING** s.n. 42-12705 A/C **'yellow aVa '** a.k.a. **'Cotton Duster'** of the 80 FS *'Headhunters'* / 8 FG at Dobodura, N.G., mid-'43. As 5 FC's second Lightning unit to join the P-38 wing, the *'Headhunters'* were quickly inspired by Lt. Cyril *'Cy'* Homer's hunting skills aboard the **'Cotton Duster'** which got him two of his first five confirmed aerial kills as of early November. In the following year, 'silent Cy' tripled his score as his 80th Sqn wingmen momentarily wrested the individual squadron scoring lead from the rival 9 FS 'Flying Knights.'

[3.] **Aichi Type 99 D3A-2** A/C (AI-I-) **'red 228'** a.k.a. **'VAL'** aboard the Imperial Mobile Fleet carrier *Zuikaku* for Vunakanau Field, Rabaul, New Britain in late '43. After their staggering losses in the naval battles of the Coral Sea, Midway and Guadalcanal, the Mobile Fleet air wings were forced to adopt land based operations at their principle strongholds of Lae, Rabaul and the expanding 4th Air Army airdromes at Wewak. It was to no avail as the obsolete **Type 99** became a hapless victim to the new generation of 5 FC fighters raging over the coastal airdromes of New Britain and New Guinea.

[4.] **Lockheed P-38 G-5-LO LIGHTNING** s.n. unknown for A/C **'white 73'** of the **9 FS / 49 FG** at Dobodura, N.G., mid '43. In October '42, there was a tumultuous induction of P-38 ferry pilots competing with the cadre 9 FS *'Flying Knights'* waiting in Queensland, Australia for the coveted Lockheeds. Co Capt. Jesse Peaslee in time assigned qualified flyers for attached duty with the 39th Sqn 'Cobras' as of December. Newcomer Lt. R.I. 'Dick' Bong excelled in the venture to reach ace status in just ten days. By the end of July '43, he tripled his score flying venerable **'white 73'** handed down by the 'Cobras' with its "eye" remnant of an unfinished 'shark' face. (see Profile 13)

[5.] **Seversky P-35A** s.n. unknown of A/C '**black 17**' in the **34th Pursuit Sqn** / 5 AF, a.k.a. the Far East Air Force, based at Clark Field, Luzon, P.I., attributed to 2Lt. Ben S. Brown in late '41. '**Black 17**' represents one of the forty-some obsolete Seversky types swept aside by the Imperial Mobile Fleet in the first week of the doomed Philippines defense. Brown may well have scored the only confirmed aerial kill for a P-35 pilot and is purported to have accounted for the last two aerial kills in a P-40 over Cavite, Luzon, on 12 March '42.

[6.] **Curtiss P-40-E-1 WARHAWK** s.n. unknown of A/C '**white 13**' a.k.a. '**P.I. or Bust**' attributed to 1Lt. Nathanial "Cy" Blanton of the **17th Pursuit Sqn (Prov)** in the ABDACOM defense of Java, Indonesia, in the February-March '42 era. Senior flight leader Blanton and his refugee wingmen pledged to liberate the Philippines airfields chalked on the nose of his WARHAWK '**white 13,**' but reality overtook them in their rear action retreat through Indonesia. By mid-year at Darwin, Australia, mission-weary 'Cy' with his four confirmed aerial victories opted out of his 7th Sqn Deputy CO stint for a flight instructor's job back in the States. No one questioned his choice.

[7.] **Curtiss P-40E-1 WARHAWK** s.n. 41-24818 A/C '**white 10**' of CO Capt. Bob Morrissey, **7th PS 49th Pursuit Grp**, Batchelor Field / Darwin, North West Territory, Australia. Morrissey's aerial victory at Horn Island on 14 March, '42, was the first of the "49ers" 600-plus aerial victories claimed at war's end. In the operations at Batchelor Field, the CO's "**white 10**" displays the improved tactical markings of blue "command stripes" and large graphic "flight numbers" which did nothing to remedy the aggravation of the WARHAWK's crucial need of drop-tank belly shackles.

[8.] **Mitsubishi A6M2 Model 21 ZERO-SEN** s.n. unknown of A/C '**black X-172**' in the red tactical trim of the **3rd Kokutai** (Group) based at Takao, Formosa (Taiwan). The **3rd Ku,** a.k.a. "**Takao Ku**" was an all-fighter unit roughly akin to a U.S. Marines fighter wing. They were led by China-veteran Capt. Takeo Shibata who advocated for the **Takao** to immediately advance to captured airfields rather than rely upon the Mobile Fleet carriers. By late summer, the **Takao Ku** was joined by the equally lethal **Tainan Ku** to occupy Lae, New Guinea, and dominate the entire SW Pacific front. The long ranging ZERO-Sen duelists of the Lae Wing seemed virtually invincible to the fledgling 5 FC.

[9.] **Bell P-39D AIRACOBRA** s.n. 41-6941 A/C '**yellow Q**' of 2Lt. Don McGee, **35 PS / 8 PG** a.k.a. '***Nip's Nemisis***' at 7-Mile Field, Pt. Moresby, New Guinea. McGee used the ***Nemisis*** on 1 May,'42 to shoot down a ZERO near 7-Mile Strip before he in turn bail out due to battle damage. Archival photos suggest early AIRACOBRAs bore this serial number style and that the yellow 'squadron color' on the spinner and tail-tip are only speculative. Future ace McGee would soldier on in the replacement '*Nemisis II*' P-39 until his transfer to the P-38 quipped 80th Sqn at year's end.

[10.] **Curtiss P-40E-1 WARHAWK** s.n. 41-25167 A/C **'white 92'** of Second Lt. Clyde Harvey Jr., **9 FS (Flying Knights) 49 FG** based at Livingstone Field, Darwin. Harvey sortied in the first 'Flying Knights' Pursuit interception over Darwin on 28 March '42 where one of his two VAL bomber claims was confirmed. On 30 July, his flew his '*shark*' to gun down a 'twin-engine' Imperial raider and riddle a ZERO escort just west of Darwin town. Slated for an upgrade of belly tank gear, the '*shark*' would 'prang' a September landing and be salvaged by the local RAAF blokes, teeth and all. Exactly one year from his first air battle, Flt Ldr 1Lt. Harvey would score his single P-38 kill over Dobodura, New Guinea.

[11.] **Bell P-400 AIRACOBRA** s.n. unknown, RAF s.n. AH736 a.k.a. **'yellow K'** of Lt. Nobert Ruff, **80 FS / 8 FG** (previously 'white 19' of the 35 FG) U.S. Navy successes in the Coral Sea and at Midway Island was followed by a perceived threat to Milne Bay, New Guinea. In August '42, the well traveled P-400 'shark-**yellow K**' was adopted by pilot Ruff who endured the 80 FS Milne Bay venture and moved on to the squadron's P-38 era at year's end. Promoted Capt. Ruff would account for four confirmed enemy fighters by mid-September '43.

[12.] **CURTISS P-40E-1 WARHAWK** s.n. unknown for A/C **'yellow 43'** a.k.a. '***snake eyes'*** of the **8 FS / 49 FG** at 3-Mile Strip, Kila, N.G., attributed to cadre pilot Lt. Dick Dennis. The able flight leader had two enemy bomber kills confirmed over Darwin in April and had knocked down a ZERO over Buna, N.G. in November. The 8th Sqn's inventory of faded 'stager' P-40s was depleted once more on 18 December '42, when mission leader Dennis in old '*snake eyes'* was MIA after an airborne ambush by ZEROs just south of the 'Lae Wing' airdrome.

[13.] **Lockheed P-38 F-5-LO LIGHTNING** s.n.42-12654 of 1Lt. Paul Stanch, **39 FS 'Cobras' / 35 FG** A/C **'white 30'** a.k.a. **'*Regina I*'** arrayed in the jungle green camouflage typical of the early F-5-LO and G-5-LO production-block Lightnings deployed to the SW Pacific theater. Group CO Col. Legg literally won a coin toss that made the 39th Sqn of CO Capt. Prentice's **'Cobras'** the pioneer Lightning outfit of Pacific air war. Thirteen of Prentice's P-38 drivers in the 1942-43 operations would become aces. Stanch scored his first two kills in '***Regina I***' and used four other P-38s to become a double-ace.

[14.] **Nakajima Ki-43-Ia HAYABUSA** (Peregrine) s.n. and pilot unknown, **1st Chutai** (squadron) **11th Sentai** (group). The JAAF 4th Air Army brought their highly touted 11th Sentai veterans of the pre-war China campaigns to shore up their struggle in New Guinea as of December '42. Arguably the most maneuverable fighter of its era, the lightly armed *Hayabusa*, designated "**OSCAR**" by Allied intelligence, was fundamentally vulnerable to the rugged WARHAWK, let alone the long range LIGHTNING or the equally foreboding THUNDERBOLT. The doomed **OSCAR** pilots were shot down in droves and their airdromes bombed into oblivion, from New Guinea to be finally annihilated in Philippines.

[15.] **Bell P-39K AIRACOBRA** s.n. 41-24349 A/C **'white 9 (yellow I)** of Capt.Tom Winburn, **40 FS / 35 FG** based at Port Moresby, N.G. - On 6 February 43 in the Allied buildup against Lae, a flight of 40th Sqn AIRACOBRAs led by Capt. Winburn joined P-40s of the '49ers' in the rout of enemy aircraft attacking the advanced Allied camp at Wau village. Winburn accounted for a pair of 'ZEKE' (ZERO) fighters out of a dozen confirmed for the 40th Sqn alone. JAAF twin-engine bombers were likewise claimed in the shoot-out which suggests the opposing fighters may very well have been Ki-43 OSCARs.

[16.] **Curtiss P-40 K-1 WARHAWK** s.n. 42-45966 A/C **'white 24** – *the shark'* of Ops Exec Lt. F.A. "Nick" Nichols, **7 FS / 49 FG** based at 14 Mile Strip, Port Moresby, N.G. - An issue of Model-K type WARHAWKS in a variety of camouflage schemes arrived in late '42 solely for the 7th Sqn *'Screamin' Demons*.' The conspicuous *'shark'* with red spinner, fuselage stripe and a pair of victory flags was the mount of the bold Ops Exec as of mid December. Two more kills came on 6 February fostering the sobriquet *"Nick Nichols' Nip Nippers"* inscribed on the four P-40s in his flight. Maddening to some but respected by all, promoted Capt. Nichols claimed his fifth and final victory in his P-38 on 21 August '43 as CO of the 431 FG.

[17.] **Bell P-39D AIRACOBRA** s.n. 41-38366 A/C **'white K'** of 1Lt. Ralph Tuuri, **36 FS / 8 FG** based at Pt. Moresby, N.G. – On 11 July '43, a 36 FS escort to a B-25 bomber strike on Salamau, N.G., resulted in the last aerial contest for the aging AIRACOBRAs. Tuuri flew A/C 'white K' and claimed one of five OSCAR victims claimed in the brief but furious exchange. Promoted to captain in the new year, he led a P-38 sweep over Wewak, N.G., on 15 March, scored another OSCAR for his second and last aerial victory.

[18.] **Curtiss P-40N-5 WARHAWK** s.n. 42-104957 A/C **'yellow 55-*MiaMi MisHap'*** of Capt. Clyde "Smiley" Barnett, **8 FS / 49 FG** based at Marilinan, N.G., just 20 minutes air time from Lae. Cadre "Darwin defender" Barnett was now 8th Sqn 'Blacksheep' Ops Exec and flying the the '*MiaMi MisHap*' in homage to his hometown. It wore the full white tactical markings ordered for all Allied single-engine A/C. The '*MisHap*' got him his fourth and final kill on 7 November '43, in the aerial ambush he led against the enemy airstrip at Alexishafen.

[19.] **Kawasaki Ki-61-Kai HIEN** (*swallow*) a.k.a. **'TONY'** of the **1st Chutai / 78th Sentai** based at Rabaul, New Britain, mid-'43. The JAAF 4th Air Army hoped the 78th and the 68th Sentais equipped with the inline-engine **TONY** would put an end to the hated B-24 and B-25 air raids, but the Ki-61 did not meet the task. A "bomber killer" variant with paired wing-mounted 20 mm Orlikon canon did not reach the 'southern front' in sufficient numbers. Despite a clutch of pilots who made deadly use of the sleek fighters, they were swept from the New Guinea skies while the 4th Air Army landing fields were completely razed by heavy bombardment. By mid-'44, all vestiges of the 78th Sentai vanished in the New Guinea jungle.

[20.] **Curtiss P-40N-5 WARHAWK** s.n. 42-105476 A/C **'yellow Q'** of the **35 FS / 8 FG** based at Nadzab, N.G., late '43. On 16 January '44, Lt. W.A. Gardner flew **'yellow Q'** in the last P-40 dogfight for the 35 FS. Covering the Allied landings at Saidor, N.G., he adding three HAMP victims to the 5 FC mission record of 19 kills confirmed that day. Four more kills in P-38s that summer put him on the ace roster, but he truly underscored his combat career as the first Fighter Command flyer to land his flak torn Lightning on embattled Tacloban Airfield at the height of the Leyte landings in the Philippines invasion.

[21.] **Lockheed P-38 H-1-LO LIGHTNING** s.n. 42-66550 A/C **'white 134'** of **431 FS / 475 FG** based at Dobodura, N.G., in late '43. Second Lt. Francis Lent in the all-Lightning '*Satin's Angels*' Group flew to every major target from August '43 to March '44. His first eight confirmed kills came in a three-month tour aboard **'white 134'** culminating in the epic 2 November '43 air raid on Rabaul. He last two victims were shot down over Hollandia, N.G., on 31 March, for a career victory total of eleven. He served on staff and was up for furlough to the States only to be lost in a test flight off Lae on 1 December '44.

[22.] **Republic P-47D-4-RA THUNDERBOLT** s.n. 42-22623 A/C **'yellow 37'** of **341 FS / 348 FG** based at Finschafen, N.G. After six months of missing out in the sweeps over New Guinea's orth shore, Lt. Frank Morrison finally got the chance to apply the "Kearby concept" of a 400 Mph descent against a hapless OSCAR and a pair of VALs. Ten days later over the south coast of New Britain, Morrison drove his **'yellow 37'** down on another OSCAR as his final contribution to the Group's Distinguished Unit Citation for their lethal December fighter sweeps.

[23.] **Lockheed P-38 F-5 or G-5LO LIGHTNING** uncertain for A/C **'white 51'** of **418 (Det. A) NFS** based at Dobodura / Finschafen, N.G. in December '43 to mid '44. Six radar equipped P-70 (A-20 HAVOC) night fighters were joined by a similar number of field-modified P-38s with their standard five–gun mounts reset forward to accommodate the temperamental radar gear. The Lightnings faired little better than the HAVOCs as CO Maj. Carrol Smith had the single confirmed airborne kill with a P-38 in that "developmental" six-month tour. Their greater effect was the interdiction of enemy airfields at dusk or dawn, plus the tactical sweeps of coastal shipping.

[24.] **Mitsubishi G4M-1 '*RIKKO*'** a.k.a. **'BETTY'** s.n. unknown of A/C **'white** (51-)**346'** of the **751 Kokutai** at Vunakanau Field, Rabaul, N.B., in the strategic operations of 1943 over the Empire's crumbling 'southern front.' Veteran JNAF air crews and increased defensive weaponry could not negate the **BETTY**'s fateful lack of self sealing fuel tanks. The high performance LIGHTNING and THUNDERBOLT erased her high altitude sanctuary making her all the more vulnerable to incendiary gunfire. Torching a **BETTY** was a crowning achievement for many a 5 FC hunter.

Other Books by William Wolf

Death Rattlers: Marine Squadron VMF-323 over Okinawa

Victory Roll: The American Fighter Pilot and Aircraft in World War II

American Fighter-Bombers in World War II: USAAF Jabos in the MTO and ETO

13th Fighter Command in World War II: Air Combat over Guadalcanal and the Solomons

Boeing B-29 Superfortress: The Ultimate Look: From Drawing Board to VJ-Day

Consolidated B-32 Dominator: The Ultimate Look: from Drawing Board to Scrapyard.

Douglas B-18 Bolo: The Ultimate Look: from Drawing Board to U-Boat Hunter

North American B-25 Mitchell: The Ultimate Look: from Drawing Board to Flying Arsenal

U.S. Aerial Armament in World War II The Ultimate Look:
Vol.1: Guns, Ammunition, and Turrets

U.S. Aerial Armament in World War II The Ultimate Look:
Vol.2: Bombs, Bombsights, and Bombing

U.S. Aerial Armament in World War II The Ultimate Look:
Vol.3: Air-Launched Rockets, Guided Missles and Secret Weapons